# ESSENTIALS OF CROSS-BATTERY ASSESSMENT AND X-BASS



Fourth Edition

# Essentials of Psychological Assessment Series

Series Editors, Alan S. Kaufman and Nadeen L. Kaufman

Essentials of CAS2 Assessment
*by Jack A. Naglieri and Tulio M. Otero*

Essentials of Child and Adolescent Psychopathology, Second Edition
*by Linda Wilmshurst*

Essentials of Cognitive Assessment with KAIT and Other Kaufman Measures
*by Elizabeth O. Lichtenberger, Debra Y. Broadbooks, and Alan S. Kaufman*

Essentials of Conners Behavior Assessments™
*by Elizabeth P. Sparrow*

Essentials of Creativity Assessment
*by James C. Kaufman, Jonathan A. Plucker, and John Baer*

Essentials of Cross-Battery Assessment, Third Edition
*by Dawn P. Flanagan, Samuel O. Ortiz, and Vincent C. Alfonso*

Essentials of DAS-II® Assessment
*by Ron Dumont, John O. Willis, and Colin D. Elliott*

Essentials of Dyslexia Assessment and Intervention
*by Nancy Mather and Barbara J. Wendling*

Essentials of Evidence-Based Academic Interventions
*by Barbara J. Wendling and Nancy Mather*

Essentials of Executive Functions Assessment
*by George McCloskey and Lisa A. Perkins*

Essentials of Forensic Psychological Assessment, Second Edition
*by Marc J. Ackerman*

Essentials of Gifted Assessment
*by Steven I. Pfeiffer*

Essentials of IDEA for Assessment Professionals
*by Guy McBride, Ron Dumont, and John O. Willis*

Essentials of Individual Achievement Assessment
*by Douglas K. Smith*

Essentials of Intellectual Disability Assessment and Identification
*by Alan W. Brue and Linda Wilmshurst*

Essentials of KABC-II Assessment
*by Alan S. Kaufman, Elizabeth O. Lichtenberger, Elaine Fletcher-Janzen, and Nadeen L. Kaufman*

Essentials of KTEA™-3 and WIAT®-III Assessment
*by Kristina C. Breaux and Elizabeth O. Lichtenberger*

Essentials of MCMI®-IV Assessment
*by Seth D. Grossman and Blaise Amendolace*

Essentials of Millon™ Inventories Assessment, Third Edition
*by Stephen Strack*

Essentials of MMPI-A™ Assessment
*by Robert P. Archer and Radhika Krishnamurthy*

Essentials of MMPI-2® Assessment, Second Edition
*by David S. Nichols*

Essentials of Myers-Briggs Type Indicator® Assessment, Second Edition
*by Naomi L. Quenk*

Essentials of NEPSY®-II Assessment
*by Sally L. Kemp and Marit Korkman*

Essentials of Neuropsychological Assessment, Second Edition
*by Nancy Hebben and William Milberg*

Essentials of Nonverbal Assessment
*by Steve McCallum, Bruce Bracken, and John Wasserman*

Essentials of PAI® Assessment
*by Leslie C. Morey*

Essentials of Planning, Selecting, and Tailoring Interventions for Unique Learners
*by Jennifer T. Mascolo, Vincent C. Alfonso, and Dawn P. Flanagan*

Essentials of Processing Assessment, Second Edition
*by Milton J. Dehn*

Essentials of Psychological Assessment Supervision
*by A. Jordan Wright*

Essentials of Psychological Testing, Second Edition
*by Susana Urbina*

Essentials of Response to Intervention
*by Amanda M. VanDerHeyden and Matthew K. Burns*

Essentials of Rorschach® Assessment
*by Tara Rose, Michael P. Maloney, and Nancy Kaser-Boyd*

Essentials of Rorschach Assessment: Comprehensive System and R-PAS
*by Jessica R. Gurley*

Essentials of School Neuropsychological Assessment, Third Edition
*by Daniel C. Miller and Denise E. Maricle*

Essentials of Specific Learning Disability Identification, Second Edition
*by Vincent C. Alfonso and Dawn P. Flanagan*

Essentials of Stanford-Binet Intelligence Scales (SB5) Assessment
*by Gale H. Roid and R. Andrew Barram*

Essentials of TAT and Other Storytelling Assessments, Second Edition
*by Hedwig Teglasi*

Essentials of Temperament Assessment
*by Diana Joyce*

Essentials of Trauma-Informed Assessment and Interventions in School and Community Settings
*by Kirby L. Wycoff and Bettina Franzese*

Essentials of Treatment Planning, Second Edition
*by Mark E. Maruish*

Essentials of WAIS®-IV Assessment, Second Edition
*by Elizabeth O. Lichtenberger and Alan S. Kaufman*

Essentials of WISC®-IV Assessment, Second Edition
*by Dawn P. Flanagan and Alan S. Kaufman*

Essentials of WISC-V® Assessment
*by Dawn P. Flanagan and Vincent C. Alfonso*

Essentials of WISC-V Integrated Assessment
*by Susan Engi Raiford*

Essentials of WJ IV® Cognitive Abilities Assessment
*by Fredrick A. Schrank, Scott L. Decker, and John M. Garruto*

Essentials of the Tests of Dyslexia
*by Nancy Mather, R. Steve McCallum, Barbara J. Wendling and Sherry M. Bell*

Essentials of WJ IV® Tests of Achievement
*by Nancy Mather and Barbara J. Wendling*

Essentials of WMS®-IV Assessment
*by Lisa Whipple Drozdick, James A. Holdnack, and Robin C. Hilsabeck*

Essentials of WNV™ Assessment
*by Kimberly A. Brunnert, Jack A. Naglieri, and Steven T. Hardy-Braz*

Essentials of Working Memory Assessment and Intervention
*by Milton J. Dehn*

Essentials of WPPSI™-IV Assessment
*by Susan Engi Raiford and Diane L. Coalson*

Essentials of WRAML2 and TOMAL-2 Assessment
*by Wayne Adams and Cecil R. Reynolds*

Essentials of WRAML3 and EMS Assessment
*by Wayne V. Adams, David V. Sheslow, and Trevor A. Hall*

Essentials of Evaluating Bias in Intelligence Testing
*by Craig L. Frisby*

Essentials of WJ V™ Assessment
*by Erica M. Laforte, Nancy Mather, and W. Joel Schneider*

NIH Toolbox Version 3 Cognition Tests
*by Julie N. Hook, Amy Kovacs Giella and Erica M. LaForte*

Essentials of Cross-Battery Assessment and X-BASS, Fourth Edition
*by Dawn P. Flanagan, Samuel O. Ortiz and Vincent C. Alfonso*

# Essentials

## of Cross-Battery Assessment and X-BASS

Fourth Edition

Dawn P. Flanagan

Samuel O. Ortiz

Vincent C. Alfonso

WILEY

Published by John Wiley & Sons, Inc., Hoboken, New Jersey.



*Library of Congress Cataloging-in-Publication Data applied for:*

Print ISBN: 9781394230822

ePDF ISBN: 9781394230846

ePUB ISBN: 9781394230839

Cover Design: Wiley
Cover Image: Robert/stock.adobe.com

Set in 10/12pt Adobe GaramondPro by Straive, Pondicherry, India

SKY10165737_081826

# CONTENTS

# LIST OF FIGURES

# LIST OF TABLES

# FOREWORD

## Kevin S. McGrew

*The world needs dreamers and the world needs doers. But above all, what the world needs most are dreamers that do.*

(Sarah Ban Breathnach, 1995)

This foreword departs from the traditional format typically found in scholarly books; it functions more like an introductory chapter. The fourth edition of *Essentials of Cross-Battery Assessment and X-BASS (XBA-4E)* is a comprehensive and seminal work, supported by an integrated software system that brings its principles to life. My perspective is somewhat unique. I was directly involved in and a witness to the two pivotal developments that ignited the paradigm-shifting Cattell–Horn–Carroll (CHC) movement in cognitive ability assessment. When invited to contribute this foreword, I asked the authors for the freedom to offer a critical yet personal reflection on the more than 25-year evolution of Cross-Battery Assessment (XBA).

My commentary centers on the three principal components of XBA-4E: the XBA method; the CHC-based Pattern of Strengths and Weaknesses Dual Discrepancy/Consistency (DD/C) framework for identifying specific learning disabilities (SLD); and the Culture–Language Interpretive Matrix (C-LIM). Each of these components could easily warrant its own dedicated volume. What distinguishes XBA-4E is the cohesive integration of these elements into the overarching Cross-Battery Assessment Software System (X-BASS 3.0; Flanagan et al., 2025).[1]

My decision to focus primarily on the XBA method is grounded in three considerations. First, I am mindful of the boundaries of my expertise and do not claim the depth of knowledge necessary to comment authoritatively on the DD/C or C-LIM research literatures. Second, my scholarly work over the past four decades has centered on the development of CHC theory and the measurement of CHC abilities, particularly through the Woodcock–Johnson family of individually administered IQ[2] and achievement batteries (WJ through WJ V), as well as my collaboration with Dr. Dawn Flanagan on the original XBA method. Third, and most importantly, the XBA computational engine, perhaps best described as the *g*-factor of X-BASS, directly feeds XBA composites, and composites from ability batteries, into the DD/C SLD and C-LIM modules. I remain deeply impressed by the computational sophistication and foundational principles underlying the XBA method.

### THE CHC COGNITIVE ABILITY REVOLUTION: A PERSONAL PERSPECTIVE

Although Flanagan and colleagues provide an excellent overview of the evolution of XBA and CHC theory in Chapter 1 (see Figures 1.1 and 1.4), I offer additional context and nuance not covered in XBA-4E. My vantage point is that of someone who was present in the rooms where these developments unfolded—someone who can name names and recount the inside stories (see McGrew, 2005, 2023b).

The emergence of CHC-based IQ test design, assessment, and interpretation in the mid-to-late 1990s (Kaufman, 2009) marked a genuine paradigm shift in cognitive assessment. CHC theory is now the dominant framework in the field. This transformation was catalyzed by the development of the first two comprehensive, nationally normed CHC-based cognitive and achievement batteries: the WJ-R (1989) and WJ III (2001). These instruments were created by Dr. Richard Woodcock and colleagues, who, beginning in 1986, collaborated closely with Drs. John Horn and Jack Carroll (McGrew, 2005). Their work laid the foundation for what would become the CHC revolution.

Shortly thereafter, the CHC-based assessment and interpretation framework known as Cross-Battery Assessment (XBA) emerged. The earliest iteration of XBA (Flanagan, 2000; Flanagan & McGrew, 1995a, 1995b, 1997; Flanagan et al., 2000; McGrew & Flanagan, 1998) began as a valuable clinical framework, but was acknowledged to have psychometric limitations. Over time, XBA matured into a sophisticated, empirically grounded, and psychometrically sound method, as fully documented in XBA-4E.

[1] Given limitations of space and my own limited direct experience with the various versions of X-BASS, I refrain from commenting on this part of XBA. This includes refraining from discussion of X-BASS figures featured in the chapters. My primary focus is on the XBA component of X-BASS.

[2] The abbreviation "IQ" is used in the interest of brevity. Although I am aware of the multiple meanings and potential misconceptions associated with this term, it is more concise than repeatedly referring to "intelligence test(s)" or "tests of cognitive abilities."

My professional journey has been closely intertwined with these parallel developments in CHC-based assessment. The evolution of CHC theory, the emergence of CHC-aligned test batteries, and the development of XBA were not isolated events; they were interconnected movements that shaped, and continue to shape, the landscape of cognitive assessment.

## A Satisficing Foreword

In preparing this foreword, I found myself returning to Nobel laureate Herb Simon's foundational behavioral economics concept of *satisficing* (Simon, 1956)—the idea that, although we may aspire to optimal solutions, real-world constraints often require us to settle on what is both *satisfactory* and *sufficient* (hence, the portmanteau term *satisficing*). That principle guided my approach here. Within the bounds of my expertise and the expansive scope of XBA-4E, my aim has been to craft a foreword that is concise yet appropriately comprehensive—a satisficing balance between depth and practicality.

## A Tribute to the Authors and Contributors

This foreword is, above all, a tribute to Flanagan, Ortiz, and Alfonso. Their collective expertise spans intelligence theory, psychometrics, specific learning disabilities, and cultural and linguistic influences on test performance. Their work is strengthened by the contributions of key consultants, including Drs. Daniel Hajovsky, Christopher Niileksela, Joel Schneider, and Peng, whose technical insights helped shape XBA-4E. Readers will notice that the XBA-4E authors have placed extensive technical material in the appendices, alongside other supplemental XBA resources. XBA-4E is organized much like the manuals of a traditional stand-alone ability battery: the chapters function as examiner's manuals, while many of the appendices serve as the technical manual. This structure is both elegant and practical, reflecting the authors' deep understanding of how practitioners actually use assessment tools.

## CHC and XBA: Theory Highlights

XBA-4E is a remarkable book. It represents more than three decades of research and innovation, led principally by Dawn Flanagan and, later, in collaboration with Samuel Ortiz, Vincent Alfonso, and Jennifer Mascolo (see Figure 1.1 in Chapter 1). XBA is one of the two major applied assessment initiatives that helped establish CHC theory as the most empirically supported psychometric framework for cognitive test design and interpretation (McGrew, 2005, 2009, 2023a, 2023b). The CHC framework has played a central role in narrowing the gap between theory and practice in cognitive assessment.

The progression from a single *g*-factor model to CHC theory is clearly and accurately depicted in Figure 1.4 and the accompanying text in Chapter 1. This opening chapter serves as an accessible synthesis of contemporary CHC literature—so much so that it could stand alone as a *Cliff Notes*®-style summary of recommended CHC readings. The authors' domain-specific expertise is evident throughout. Chapter 1 is an effective introduction, inviting readers to engage deeply with the subsequent chapters and appendices. It is the appetizer that whets the appetite for the main course.

## Beyond g: A Broader Context for Cognitive Assessment

I was particularly pleased to see the overview chapter's discussion of research outside the traditional boundaries of school psychology (see Rapid Reference 1.5, "Fields Outside of School Psychology Weigh in on *g*"). This broader context is essential. Too often, certain corners of school psychology remain anchored in a parochial, factor-analytic, *g*-centric perspective. The XBA-4E authors challenge the view, still held by some researchers, that IQ tests primarily reflect psychometric *g* and that broad CHC abilities are trivial or unimportant for interpretation[3]. Their critique echoes Wasserman (2019), who concluded, "My hope is that some of our 'psychometric iconoclasts'—researchers who conduct the same types of critical statistical analyses on every new edition of every new test—will turn their attention to improving CHC theory or building better tests and theories of their own. Ultimately, there is much more satisfaction in creating something new than tearing something down" (p. 263). The XBA-4E authors' stance aligns with this call for constructive scholarship and theoretical innovation.

Chapter 1 also highlights the emergence of alternative, non-*g* theories of intelligence, most notably the Process Overlap Theory (POT; Conway et al., 2020) and the Parietal–Frontal Integration Theory (P-FIT; Haeir & Jung). These frameworks, grounded in psychometric network analysis and neurocognitive research, challenge the assumption that the *g*-factor represents a singular psychological or biological entity. Instead, they conceptualize *g* as a *statistical emergent property*, a position strongly advocated by Horn. As Burgoyne et al. (2022) observed, "by itself, the *g*-factor is merely a statistical description [a necessary algebraic consequence] of the positive manifold [among

[3] See further discussion in Flanagan et al. (2025) regarding a particular research group that "demonstrates bias through heavy self-citation, while disregarding contrary evidence from groups such as the Keith-Reynolds researchers, who endorse multifactorial intelligence theories (e.g., Caemmerer at al., 2020; Keith & Reynolds, 2028, Reynolds et al., 2013). This one-sided citation approach allows them to advocate for a *g*-only interpretation without sufficient empirical support (McGrew et al., 2023)" (p. 814).

subtests]—not a psychological explanation" (p. 101629). Similarly, the architects of POT argue that *research should prioritize understanding broad cognitive abilities rather than focusing solely on general intelligence or psychometric g.*

Despite more than a century of factor-analytic research consistently revealing a robust psychometric *g*-factor, there remains no compelling evidence linking *g* to a specific molecular, biological, or neurocognitive mechanism. As I have written elsewhere, much of academic school psychology has been "stuck on *g*," a construct recently described as a "black hole" (Bruton, 2021) or the "Loch Ness Monster of psychology" (McGrew, 2021, p. 126). Drawing on the image of Winnie-the-Pooh wedged in Rabbit's doorway after overindulging in honey, some researchers remain stuck on *g* because their intellectual diet is saturated with a narrow set of statistical tools and lacks broader theoretical or substantive context. There is a pressing need for parts of the field to become "unstuck" from psychometric *g* by incorporating insights from cognitive psychology and neuroscience and by applying a broader array of structural analytical methods (LaForte et al., 2025; McGrew, 2023a). Contemporary non-*g* theories and methodologies *support the interpretation of broad CHC abilities in IQ tests and within the XBA framework.*

## CHC AND INNOVATION: THE XBA BACKSTORY

### Revolutionary and Evolutionary Change

Innovation in technology and assessment can be understood as a progression of successive hills and cycles—much like the repetitive rise and fall of sinusoidal waves or the continual crashing of waves upon a shoreline (Norman & Verganti, 2014). *Revolutionary* innovation represents a paradigm shift: a leap across the gap separating two adjacent innovation peaks or a dynamic surge (a "dyno" in mountaineering) that propels progress toward the summit of an existing innovation hill. Such change is inherently disruptive, challenging entrenched norms and the "inertia-of-tradition"—for example, the longstanding dominance of the Wechsler series in intellectual assessment. Revolutionary change compels adaptation to an emerging paradigm, such as CHC theory, or risks obsolescence. The CHC revolution, led by the WJ-R, forced practitioners and test publishers alike to reconsider and update their methodologies.

In contrast, *evolutionary* progress consists of incremental refinements that improve existing systems. Ascending the metaphorical innovation hill, such as the evolution of IQ assessment, occurs through a series of small, cumulative enhancements, a process known as *hill-climbing* (Norman & Verganti, 2014). Examples include the transition from the WJ-R to the WJ III's broad CHC ability cluster scores, the incremental changes from the WAIS-III to the WAIS-IV, and the ongoing refinements to CHC definitions from XBA-3E to XBA-4E (see Appendix A). Importantly, evolutionary and revolutionary changes are not mutually exclusive. They often intersect, creating dynamic, mutually reinforcing cycles. The development of XBA-4E exemplifies this interplay—an integration of revolutionary conceptual advances with evolutionary refinements that together have shaped contemporary CHC-based assessment.

### The WJ-R as a Revolutionary Turning Point

The catalyst for modern CHC-based assessment practices was Richard Woodcock's transformative revision of the Woodcock–Johnson (WJ) from its original 1977 edition to the WJ-R in 1989. This was followed by evolutionary updates—WJ III (2001), WJ IV (2014), and the digital WJ V (2025)—but the leap from the WJ to the WJ-R was the true revolutionary moment. As Kaufman (2009) noted, "Woodcock revised his original test so thoroughly that the WJ was barely recognizable in its rebirth as the WJ-R" (p. 93). My involvement with the WJ-R—calculating norms, conducting validity analyses, authoring the technical manual, and later presenting and writing extensively on the instrument and emerging CHC theory (McGrew, 1994)—provided a unique vantage point on the broad spectrum of reactions to this major advancement.

The publication of the WJ-R Tests of Cognitive Abilities marked the moment when Gf–Gc theory (now CHC theory) moved from the realm of intelligence scholarship into practical application, particularly within educational contexts (McGrew, 2005). With the benefit of hindsight, the 1989 WJ-R stands as a revolutionary lightning-bolt tipping point, embedding what would become CHC-based test development and interpretation into both the intellectual assessment literature and the broader intelligence theory landscape. The introduction of the Gf–Gc (CHC)-based WJ-R disrupted the long-standing Wechsler trilogy, creating a kind of Piagetian cognitive disequilibrium among practitioners and test publishers. Restoring cognitive homeostasis required adaptation or assimilation of the new model.

The WJ-R's arrival signaled a decisive shift. It led to the widespread adoption of "Gf–Gc [CHC] as a second language" in educational and school psychology training programs, academic publications, and professional discourse (McGrew, 2005, p. 145). In 2009, I published "CHC theory and the human cognitive abilities project: Standing on the shoulders of the giants of psychometric intelligence research" in *Intelligence* (McGrew, 2009), which helped introduce the term *CHC theory* into the scholarly intelligence-theoretical literature. Kaufman (2009) captured the irony of this evolution: "talk about the tail wagging the dog! What had begun back in the late 1970s and early 1980s as a search for the best theories on which to build an IQ test had come full circle: Two decades later, the needs of test publishers and test authors forged the theory that underlies almost all current-day IQ tests" (p. 99).

By 2010, Keith and Reynolds concluded that "most new and revised individually administered tests of intelligence are either based on CHC theory or pay allegiance to the theory. Even the latest versions of the traditional, and traditionally atheoretical, Wechsler scales reference CHC theory in their manuals" (Keith & Reynolds, 2010, p. 635).

A survey of school psychology graduate coursework by Lockwood and Farmer (2020) confirmed this shift. Compared to surveys from 1986 and 2000, they found that "the most salient change for the training and practice of cognitive assessment in the past two decades has been the merger of two dominant theories of cognitive ability (Extended Gf–Gc theory [Horn & Blankson, 2012] and Three-Stratum Theory [Carroll, 1996]) into the Cattell–Horn–Carroll [CHC] theory of intelligence (Schneider & McGrew, 2018)" (pp. 266–267). Approximately 93% of instructors taught CHC theory, and 61% taught the CHC XBA method. After the WISC-V (Wechsler, 2014)—taught by 95% of instructors—the WJ-IV was required by 71%. The latest Wechsler Adult Intelligence Scale—Fifth Edition (WAIS-5; Wechsler, 2024) now features a five-factor model (*Gc, Gv, Gf, Gwm*, and *Gs*) aligned with CHC theory.

The CHC revolution in school psychology is, for all practical purposes, complete. Incremental enhancements will continue as other IQ batteries revise their structures, but the paradigm shift has already occurred. In retrospect, the 1989 WJ-R, grounded in an early form of CHC theory, was the field's "Sputnik moment," catalyzing the development of XBA and accelerating the broader integration of CHC theory into cognitive assessment[4].

## Woodcock's CHC-Based Joint CFA Study: The Catalyst for XBA

As shown in Figure 1.1 of Chapter 1, the authors trace the genesis of XBA to Woodcock's (1990) seminal paper, which presents a series of CHC-based joint confirmatory factor analyses (CFAs) involving the WJ and WJ-R alongside four other major IQ batteries. These analyses revealed a pattern that would become foundational: some batteries measured certain broad Gf–Gc abilities adequately, while others contained significant gaps. Woodcock proposed that practitioners seeking to approximate the Horn–Cattell Gf–Gc (now CHC) model should "cross batteries" to fill these gaps. The 1989 WJ-R publication, Woodcock's 1990 CFA research, the 1986 Horn–Carroll–Woodcock WJ-R planning meeting, Carroll's *Human Cognitive Abilities* (1993), and Flanagan et al.'s *Contemporary Intellectual Assessment* (CIA; 1997) book together represent the pivotal events of the CHC revolution (McGrew, 2005). Importantly, the CIA volume deserves explicit recognition as a key catalyst in this paradigm shift[5].

## The 1994 Vermont Meeting: A Serendipitous Turning Point

In 1994, after presenting on the WJ-R and the Horn–Cattell Gf–Gc (CHC) theory in Vermont, I met Flanagan for the first time. She shared an outline and preliminary draft of a proposed edited volume, "Contemporary Intellectual Assessment: Theories, Tests, and Issues" (CAI). At that time, Carroll's (1993) Three-Stratum theory had not yet entered applied IQ assessment literature. Recognizing its importance, I recommended that she include a chapter by Jack Carroll. Flanagan also encouraged me to contribute a chapter on a topic yet to be determined, and I agreed.

Shortly thereafter, we collaborated on a CHC-based CFA of Alan Kaufman's KAIT (1993) with the WJ-R. Although our focus was on broad CHC factors, we both recognized a critical gap: existing CHC CFA studies lacked Carroll's "three-stratum vision." We needed to move beyond broad-ability (Stratum II) classifications to include narrow abilities (Stratum I). That realization sparked the idea for my contribution to the original CIA volume (McGrew, 1997): an integration of the Horn–Cattell and Carroll models to enable comprehensive classification of IQ subtests by both broad and narrow CHC abilities.

The broad and narrow CHC classifications presented in that chapter were derived from a small group of assessment experts through an informal, semistructured consensus process. During this period, the first official set of broad and narrow CHC definitions was also developed. I drafted the initial definitions by abstracting from Carroll's (1993) book and sent them to him for review. Carroll graciously provided comments and edits. We exchanged several iterations until he was satisfied with the working definitions. As a result, the original definitions published in 1997 carried the informal stamp of approval from Carroll, but not from Horn. If one were to issue an official CHC definition birth certificate, the parents would be Carroll and McGrew. These definitions, later revised and now regarded as the gold standard, were essential for completing the subtest classification process. Their origins are described in detail on my *IQ's Corner* blog, commemorating their 20th anniversary in 2017 (see Appendices A and B for the most current set of classifications for subtests new to X-BASS).

---

[4] A "Sputnik moment" is a metaphor or idiom for a sudden realization that a nation or organization has fallen behind a rival in a critical area, such as technology, science, or education. It typically results in the triggering of an urgent effort to catch up. The term originates from October 4, 1957, when the Soviet Union launched Sputnik 1, the world's first space satellite. The launch stunned the United States which had assumed it held technological superiority.

[5] The original 1997 *Contemporary Intellectual Assessment* book (aka, the CIA book) has gone through three more revisions (2005, 2012, 2018) with Flanagan being the primary editor of each edition. It includes the most comprehensive CHC theory updates in each edition (McGrew, 1997, 2005; Schneider and McGrew, 2012, 2018). Not only was the original 1997 CIA book central to the CHC revolution in intelligence testing, but it, together with two other books of Flanagan et al.'s (Kaufman and Kaufman-directed Wiley "essentials" series of assessment books), resulted in Flanagan being one of the two authors with the most frequently used books in school psychology graduate courses on intelligence testing. In a formal survey of cognitive assessment course syllabi (Miller et al., 2020), Dawn Flanagan and Jerome Sattler were identified as the two leading authors of the most often used textbooks. Flanagan's 3rd- and 4th-edition CIA books were second only to Jerome Sattler's classic *Assessment of Children: Cognitive Foundations* (5th and 6th eds.).

Serendipity played a central role in these developments. My 1997 chapter is now credited as the first to integrate the Horn and Carroll models (see Figure 1.4 in Chapter 1 of XBA-4E), forming the foundation of what is now known as CHC theory. This advancement was made possible by that chance 1994 meeting with Flanagan—an embodiment of Louis Pasteur's (December 7, 1854) famous observation that "chance favors the prepared mind[s]."

## The First Generation of Cross-Battery Assessment (XBA)

Following these developments, Flanagan and I turned our attention to operationalizing Woodcock's (1990) recommendation that practitioners "cross batteries" when working with non-CHC-organized IQ tests. Drawing on Woodcock's findings and other joint Gf–Gc (CHC) CFA studies, I developed tables for my WJ-R clinical interpretation book (McGrew, 1994) to supplement the WJ-R broad cognitive ability clusters with measures from other established IQ tests. For example, in Table 4.9 in Chapter 4 of my book, I identified "Measures of Processing Speed (*Gs*) in Major Intelligence Batteries," listing the WISC-R, WISC-III, and WAIS-R Coding, Digit Symbol, and Symbol Search subtests as strong supplemental indicators for the WJ-R Processing Speed (*Gs*) cluster. In total, seven tables (Tables 4.7 through 4.13) provided supplemental subtests for WJ-R Gf–Gc clusters, including *Glr*, *Gsm*, *Gs*, *Ga*, *Gv*, *Gc*, and *Gf*. Subtests from other batteries were classified as strong, moderate, or mixed indicators within their respective CHC broad ability domains.

While my initial focus was parochially centered on supplementing WJ-R clusters, Flanagan recognized the broader potential of the CHC CFA studies. She envisioned what would become the full XBA framework. Flanagan was the driving force behind expanding CHC XBA beyond the WJ-R, and she led the development and innovation of XBA over the next three decades.

## Expanding the Early XBA Framework

As our collaboration deepened, Flanagan and I developed CHC-aligned worksheets for all major IQ tests, enabling practitioners to translate non–WJ-R results into pseudo–WJ-R CHC frameworks. We were strategic in our approach. Recognizing the field's heavy reliance on the Wechsler batteries, we sought to increase practitioners' awareness of CHC theory by encouraging them to supplement their Wechsler assessments with WJ-R clusters (see Flanagan, 2000). This early method of introducing CHC cross-battery concepts quickly gained traction. As interest grew, we presented our evolving XBA method at state and national school psychology conferences and assessment workshops, and in local school districts. Throughout 1994 and 1995, we actively promoted CHC theory through what would become the XBA method.

The first publications documenting the CHC cross-battery approach appeared in 1995 in *The School Psychologist* (Flanagan & McGrew, 1995a) and the *NASP Communiqué* (Flanagan & McGrew, 1995b). Soon after, we recognized the need for a more formal articulation of the assumptions, foundations, and operational principles underlying Gf–Gc (CHC) XBA. This led to the first comprehensive chapter on the method (Flanagan & McGrew, 1997) in the 1997 CIA book. As I wrote at the time, "the cross-battery seed planted by Woodcock (1990) had given birth" (McGrew, 2005, p. 148).

## The 1997 CIA Volume as a Blueprint for the CHC Revolution

The significance of the 1997 CIA book has become increasingly clear. In addition to Woodcock's chapter on the WJ-R, the volume included separate contributions by Horn and Carroll, each outlining their respective intelligence theories that would later be unified under CHC. The book also presented my first integration of the Horn and Carroll models, including the broad and narrow CHC definitions and the classification of subtests in IQ batteries. Most importantly, it offered the first comprehensive account of the Flanagan and McGrew XBA method. Collectively, these contributions formed the blueprint for the CHC cognitive assessment revolution. Flanagan and colleagues' CIA book exposed, in one place, the essential elements that would shape the next three decades of CHC-based assessment.

## The Intelligence Test Desk Reference (ITDR) and a Transition to the Flanagan-Ortiz Era

During this period, following my 1994 WJ-R book, I proposed a new volume tentatively titled the *Intelligence Test Desk Reference* (ITDR)—a standardized conceptual comparison guide for IQ tests, inspired by the *Physicians' Desk Reference* (PDR). Work on the project began in earnest in 1994. Flanagan suggested integrating the ITDR with an expanded description of the XBA method, and the resulting publication, *Intelligence Test Desk Reference (ITDR): Gf–Gc [CHC] Cross-Battery Assessment* (McGrew & Flanagan, 1998), became the first comprehensive articulation of the Gf–Gc (CHC) XBA framework.

After completing the ITDR, Flanagan and I began developing a Wechsler-specific ITDR and CHC cross-battery text (*The Wechsler Intelligence Scales and Gf–Gc [CHC] Theory: A Contemporary Approach to Interpretation*; Flanagan et al., 2000). About three-quarters of the way through the project, my increasing professional commitments, particularly those related to co-authoring the WJ III battery, made it clear that I could not continue to fulfill my responsibilities as a co-author. Ortiz was the logical choice to join the author team. He contributed to both the completion of the Wechsler book and the advancement of Flanagan's pioneering cultural and linguistic test classification and interpretation system (see Chapter 8 of this book). As my direct involvement in XBA research and development gradually decreased, Ortiz assumed the role of Flanagan's collaborator in the continued evolution of the XBA method.

As depicted in Figure 1.1 of XBA-4E, my involvement concludes with the termination of the first row of green rectangles, while the 2000 purple rectangle marks the official transition to the Flanagan and Ortiz partnership. This collaboration culminated in the first edition of this XBA book (XBA-1E; Flanagan & Ortiz, 2001), marking the beginning of a new era in CHC-based assessment.

## XBA Evolution: Know Thy Instruments

Chapter 2 provides the substantive foundation following the introductory overview in Chapter 1. It offers a wealth of essential XBA principles and practices—so much so that its content could easily be expanded into a comprehensive volume dedicated to the sophisticated design and interpretation of "intelligent" (Kaufman, 2009) XBAs. Flanagan et al. address several key topics, including:

- how specific referral information influences test selection and organization
- how cognitive, achievement, and neuropsychological batteries can be used to measure broad and narrow CHC abilities and processes
- how to supplement any given battery with additional measures when the core battery does not assess all relevant abilities
- how to analyze and interpret XBA data using X-BASS

Chapter 2 stands as a pivotal chapter in XBA-4E, embodying the core philosophy of XBA. It is the heart and soul of clinical XBA design and interpretation. Given the comprehensive nature of the material and the extensive tables that offer critical guidance for assessment professionals, my review focuses on the elements most impactful for practitioners, particularly those that resonated with the latent school psychologist in me.

This chapter is a masterclass in selecting intelligence tests and constructing assessment batteries. A central message is the importance of individualized assessment, moving beyond routine reliance on standard batteries toward approaches that respond to each examinee's unique characteristics and needs. The chapter marks a substantial advancement in the structure and interpretation of XBAs. Table 2.1 ("CHC Broad and Narrow Ability Representation on Three Commonly Used Cognitive Batteries") provides a comparative summary of CHC subtest representation across the WJ V, WISC-V, and KABC-II NU, offering practitioners a succinct synthesis of current CHC assessment literature for these widely used instruments.

The next eight tables in Chapter 2 (Tables 2.2 through 2.9) provide in-depth analyses of task demands, subtest characteristics, and interpretive guidelines for the WJ V, WISC-V, and KABC-II NU. These resources are invaluable for practitioners selecting core batteries for specific referral questions, identifying appropriate supplemental measures, and interpreting score discrepancies across tests with similar CHC classifications. For example, the WJ V *Gl* cluster tests—Story Recall and Story Comprehension—are both classified as measures of meaningful memory (MM) and share the same presentation format (listening to short stories from an audio recording). Yet their correlation ($r = 0.63$ for ages 10–14; LaForte et al., 2025) demonstrates that, while related, the differing response modes (retelling a short story vs answering comprehension questions) tap distinct cognitive processes. Story Recall emphasizes narrative encoding and retrieval, whereas Story Comprehension focuses on integrating and applying meaning. The detailed tables in Chapter 2 illuminate these distinctions, preventing oversimplified interpretations based solely on CHC classifications.

Other examples include moderate correlations between WJ V tests with similar CHC classifications, such as Matrices and Concept Formation (*Gf-I*; $r = 0.50$), and Spatial Relations and Block Rotation (*Gv-Vz*; $r = 0.63$). These examples underscore the necessity for examiners to investigate unexpected score divergences rather than assume uniformity among similarly classified tests. As Flanagan et al. emphasize, "divergent scores should be investigated further, as it is unusual for them to differ significantly from cohesive scores" (p. 49). Cognitive assessment professionals must appreciate that *individual tests that move together statistically (i.e., are significantly correlated, load on the same broad CHC factor, and share the same narrow ability classification) are not necessarily similar or interchangeable.* The comprehensive tables in this chapter equip professionals with the tools to develop well-founded hypotheses when faced with such discrepancies, exemplifying the nuanced application of the XBA method.

The XBA-4E authors are masters at using tables to condense substantial amounts of information into accessible, digestible formats. Their liberal use of tables throughout the book enhances readability by reducing dense narrative text and providing efficient "look-up" reference tools for definitions, classifications, key principles, and brief summaries. One noteworthy consideration is the sheer volume and density of the tables. For practitioners, fully assimilating this information may feel overwhelming. These tables, however, serve as essential reference aids for both experienced and novice XBA users. Given their importance, it would be beneficial for the authors and publisher to consider offering key tables in additional accessible formats, such as a pocket guide, laminated reference sheets, graphically enhanced PDFs for printing, or a digital app. *The information is that important!* Such resources would support rapid access to essential content and assist both seasoned XBA professionals and those newer to the method.

Several additional tables in the chapter also serve as key sources of quick information for practitioners. Notable examples include:

- Rapid Reference 2.1: Key Considerations for Battery Selection Based on Examinee Characteristics
- Table 2.3: Recommendations for Battery Selection Based on CHC and Examinee Considerations
- Table 2.4: Examinee Characteristics That May Create Challenges for Digitally Administered Batteries
- Table 2.5: WJ V COG and WJ V VTL: Best Two Tests per Broad Ability + Cross-Battery Recommendations
- Table 2.6: WISC-V: Best Two Subtests per Broad Ability + Within- and Cross-Battery Recommendations
- Table 2.7: KABC-II NU: Best Two Subtests per Broad Ability + Within- and Cross-Battery Recommendations

In summary, Chapter 2 presents a systematic, multidimensional framework that functions as a Vygotsky-like form of external scaffolding for assessment professionals seeking to deepen their understanding of cognitive assessment instruments. The authors' expertise is evident throughout, offering invaluable guidance for both novice and experienced practitioners.

A central message of the chapter is that expert-level XBA design and interpretation require intimate familiarity with the tests in one's assessment library. The authors demonstrate a deep command of the available "gemstones"—batteries and subtests—and their ability to "romance the stones" reflects a sophisticated blend of art and science in test interpretation. I find myself wishing I had access to this information when I first learned cognitive assessment in graduate school and during my early years as a school psychologist.

This chapter is essential reading for all professionals involved in intelligence and cognitive ability assessment and interpretation, regardless of whether they use the XBA method. It reinforces the critical notion that the assessment professional is ultimately the most important instrument in the assessment process.

## CHC INNOVATION: ACHIEVEMENT TESTS IN XBA AND THE DUAL DISCREPANCY/CONSISTENCY (DD/C) SLD FRAMEWORK

The next major phase in XBA's evolution was the publication of the companion volume to the ITDR—*Achievement Test Desk Reference (ATDR): Comprehensive Assessment and Learning Disabilities* (Flanagan et al., 2002). The ATDR classified subtests from all major achievement batteries according to CHC theory and demonstrated how the XBA framework could be applied to organize and interpret achievement test results. Together, the ITDR and ATDR provided, for the first time, a unified psychometric and theoretical taxonomy, CHC, for all major individually administered cognitive and achievement tests. Flanagan, as the primary architect of the ATDR and coauthor of the ITDR, deserves explicit recognition for this pivotal unification of cognitive and achievement assessment.

As XBA continued to expand, collaboration with additional experts became essential. This led to the inclusion of Vincent Alfonso and Jennifer Mascolo in the core XBA team alongside Flanagan and Ortiz. Alfonso and Mascolo contributed to the development of updated, expert-consensus CHC classifications for both cognitive and achievement batteries. They also played key roles in conceptualizing and operationalizing an operational definition of SLD, which included a Pattern of Strengths and Weaknesses (PSW) component *before* an alternative research-based method (now synonymous with PSW) was sanctioned in the 2006 Federal Regulations[6].

PSW methods analyze an individual's cognitive and academic profile to detect meaningful inter- and intra-individual variability—specifically, average or higher general cognitive ability alongside relative weaknesses in cognitive processes empirically linked to deficits in academic domains such as reading, mathematics, or writing. Kavale and Forness's (2000) operational definition of learning disabilities provided Flanagan and colleagues with a foundation for developing their CHC-based operational definition of SLD (Flanagan et al., 2002; Kavale & Flanagan, 2007). The integrated ability analysis component of the operational definition, since its inception in 2002, has evolved into the *Dual Discrepancy/Consistency* (DD/C) PSW method (Flanagan et al., 2013, 2018) – same concepts, new name, and backed by psychometric rigor that is in all likelihood without peer. The method was first integrated into XBA-2E, accompanied by a CD (Flanagan et al., 2007) containing three separate software modules, all of which are now fully revised and integrated into X-BASS.

The ATDR also included the first major synthesis of the CHC cognitive–achievement relations literature, forming one of the empirical foundations for the DD/C method (i.e., consistency). Three tables in the ATDR presented comprehensive lists of research studies documenting associational (not causal) links between specific broad CHC abilities and achievement in reading, mathematics, and writing. This foundational research has since evolved further in XBA-4E (Appendix C, "The Evolution of Cognitive-Achievement Relations Research: Past, Present, and Future," authored by Hajovsky and Niileksela), representing a significant advancement in ability assessment and interpretation. Fast-forward 25 years, and the latest iteration of the DD/C SLD method is presented in Chapter 3 of XBA-4E.

### The Evolution of the DD/C SLD Method

It has been approximately 36 years since I last conducted SLD assessments as a school psychologist. As a result, I approached Chapter 3 of this book with a measure of trepidation. When I left my practitioner role in 1989—fresh Ph.D. in hand—for a faculty position at St. Cloud State University, Minnesota, I had fully embraced a regression-based Ability–Achievement Discrepancy (AAD) model for SLD identification. I worked under the AAD model for nearly a decade. By that time, we had retired our WISC-R kits (except for specialized follow-up assessments) and were relying exclusively on the original Woodcock–Johnson (WJ) and, later, the WJ-R Scholastic Aptitude–Achievement Discrepancy method and the Relative Proficiency Index (RPI) for SLD determinations.

Clinically, I harbored major reservations about the AAD method. I had become deeply interested in cluster-analytic research aimed at identifying SLD subtype profiles. But my transition to academia removed the need to remain fully immersed in the rapidly evolving SLD literature. Although I maintained surface-level awareness of developments in SLD research and the emergence of PSW methods, my engagement was limited. Still, the PSW approach resonated with my early interest in identifying "natural kinds" of SLD taxa—subtypes "carved at the joints of nature" (Campbell et al., 2011).

[6] The other two methods are ability-achievement discrepancy (AAD) and Response-to-Intervention (RtI).

Chapter 3 delighted me. It provides a much-needed synthesis of the evolving landscape of SLD identification, tracing its conceptual and methodological roots from early clinical observations to contemporary frameworks. It was precisely what I needed. The chapter's clear, well-written synthesis of the history and evolution of the SLD construct is exactly what many assessment practitioners need: a reminder of where the concept originated, how it has evolved, the various identification methods available, and where this complex and controversial field currently stands. The authors effectively highlight persistent challenges, including inconsistent criteria, competing identification methods, and the prevalence of cognitive diagnostic biases. Through a concise historical overview, the XBA-4E authors show how foundational theories, legislative mandates, and psychometric advances have continually shaped contemporary definitions and practices of SLD identification.

One of the strengths of Chapter 3 is its efficient organization of complex descriptive information through tables and rapid references rather than lengthy narrative exposition. Particularly helpful are the summaries of key historical contributions, the evolving definitions and identification criteria, the six conceptual features that distinguish the three major contemporary SLD identification methods (AAD, PSW, and RtI), and the commonly agreed-upon assumptions underlying the SLD construct. These summaries, often in tables and "rapid references," allow readers to grasp essential ideas quickly and return to them as needed during case analysis.

At the center of the chapter is a general overview of the PSW method, followed by a detailed explanation of the five essential elements of data collection required for the authors' operational definition of SLD and the DD/C method. The authors clarify common misconceptions and criticisms, some of which I address later in this foreword, and position DD/C as the method most closely aligned with the original conceptualizations of SLD and with the most widely accepted assumptions underlying the disability category.

Importantly, the current DD/C method has evolved substantially, both conceptually and psychometrically, since its initial introduction in the ATDR (2002). It reflects more than two decades of purposeful, research-driven development and innovation by the XBA-4E authors. As they noted, "the level of analysis required by the DD/C method is complex, but X-BASS fully automates it" (Chapter 3, p. 70), thereby eliminating the basis for this concern. The DD/C approach is also far more elaborate—and more firmly grounded in theory and research—than the AAD regression method I used during my years as a practicing school psychologist. To support the navigation of these multi-step procedures, readers are walked through the DD/C method step-by-step and provided multiple case studies. The reader is also shown how the X-BASS SLD module streamlines complex analyses while producing transparent, defensible, and well-documented decisions.

## The State of PSW in 2026

Chapter 3's "State of the Field: PSW in 2026" section provides an important synthesis of the current landscape of SLD identification. The authors conclude that PSW "remains one of the most widely used and most debated methods for identifying specific learning disabilities" (Chapter 3, p. 70). These debates persist because "there is no gold standard definition of SLD and no gold standard identification method. SLD is a latent construct...it is not a directly observable condition with a definitive diagnostic marker."

I concur with the XBA-4E authors that, although PSW methods are more complex than AAD or RtI alternatives, PSW represents the approach most closely aligned with the construct of SLD, one rooted in specific cognitive and linguistic processing weaknesses that give rise to unexpected academic underachievement. Moreover, X-BASS greatly simplifies the DD/C method, making it accessible to all practitioners, including those who might otherwise be overwhelmed by its analytic components.

Given my longstanding association with CHC theories and measurement tools, and my enduring belief that "real" SLD individuals exist (I saw such students during my years as a practicing school psychologist), I support the XBA-4E authors' approach to SLD identification and their continued efforts to refine and advance their CHC-grounded DD/C method. The theoretical and psychometric debates surrounding PSW are unlikely to dissipate soon. For assessment professionals or trainers seeking the most thorough, thoughtful, and passionate articulation and defense of SLD identification, this chapter is essential reading. The XBA-4E authors clearly stand as pioneers and innovators in PSW-based SLD identification.

## CHC XBA Innovation: Advancements in Psychometric Integrity

### *XBA ≠ DD/C*

Notably, readers and critics should avoid conflating the XBA and DD/C methods. The XBA computational engine, including its interpretation protocols, function independent of DD/C within X-BASS. The software generates XBA composites that serve as input for the DD/C analysis. Alternatively, norm-based scores from independent norm-referenced assessments (such as WISC-V or WJ V) may also be analyzed via the DD/C method. The XBA-4E authors, working with leading experts in measurement, statistics, and psychometrics, have introduced significant psychometric advancements in the XBA composite score engine and in the DD/C method.

## Enhanced Psychometric Integrity in XBA-4E

The earliest iterations of XBA were primarily systematic clinical frameworks with acknowledged psychometric limitations (McGrew & Flanagan, 1998; Flanagan et al., 2000). XBA-4E represents a major leap forward, both evolutionary and revolutionary, up the CHC assessment innovation hill. The authors' contributions are commendable. The classification of nearly 300 new subtests in XBA-4E was conducted with far greater rigor than in XBA-3E, resulting in improved accuracy and validity of CHC classifications. According to the *WJ V Technical Manual* (LaForte et al., 2025), Flanagan et al. received subtest descriptions of all WJ V tests for inclusion in the XBA-4E expert-consensus process. In return, the WJ V authors were permitted to use the preliminary XBA-4E consensus results as evidence of content validity in their technical manual.

## The WJ *V Technical Manual* describes the process as follows:

Flanagan and colleagues generated concise descriptions ("Test Descriptions") of all 283 subtests, relying on the actual test materials and other information provided by the publishers. The description of each test conveyed the task demands without explicitly stating what the test purports to measure. Flanagan and colleagues also created a CHC Manual that included the broad and narrow ability definitions proposed by Schneider and McGrew (2018). Four individuals with extensive knowledge of CHC theories were recruited to participate as reviewers. Each reviewer was assigned a dyad (Dyad A or Dyad B). Each reviewer received (1) the Test Descriptions file, (2) the CHC Manual, and (3) a list of five questions to consider when classifying each test. The order of the tests in the Test Descriptions file was randomized to control for order effects that may unintentionally influence the results. Using only these materials, the members of each dyad worked together to classify each individual test at the broad and narrow CHC ability levels. Then, percentages of CHC test classification agreement between Dyads A and B were determined using four levels of criteria at the broad CHC ability level and five levels of criteria at the narrow ability level. Subsequently, the two dyads worked together to resolve classification differences. Although three different levels of operational CHC test classification agreement were analyzed, the overall reported level of complete or partial agreement between the CHC experts' dyads was 97% and 93% for broad and narrow CHC abilities, respectively. Appendix B provides a comprehensive account of the expert-consensus process and its results.

## The Achilles Heel of Early XBA: Arithmetic Mean Composites

One of the longstanding psychometric vulnerabilities in early versions of XBA was the practice of combining standard scores from two or more subtests using simple arithmetic averages. This limitation was openly acknowledged by Flanagan et al. (2001), who cautioned that cluster averages should not be interpreted as actual normed cluster scores and should not be used for high-stakes ability–achievement discrepancy decisions. As Flanagan et al. (2000) wrote: "The Gf–Gc [CHC] cluster average standard scores...cannot be interpreted as if they represent actual cluster scores that were normed on a single norm group.... [They] should also not be interpreted as precise values that can be substituted or used as measures of aptitude or ability needed to make critical decisions about ability–achievement discrepancies...actual normed cluster scores do not always equal the average of the individual standard scores they comprise" (p. 277). This limitation has long been recognized in the measurement literature (Paik & Nebenzahl, 1987; Tellegen & Briggs, 1967). To generate psychometrically sound composite scores, one must account for each subtest's reliability and the intercorrelations among the subtests included in the composite. Schneider et al. (2026) provide a comprehensive explanation of best practices for combining standard scores in their article *Life-and-Death Psychometrics*.

## From Arithmetic Means to Psychometric Rigor

In XBA-2E, the authors initially defended the use of arithmetic averages for composite scores when the subtest scores were less than a standard deviation apart. Nevertheless, they acknowledged the need for improvement, stating that all XBA-derived composites would henceforth be calculated using subtest reliabilities and intercorrelations. As reported at a NASP 2023 poster session, XBA-3E subtest statistics were based on median values from approximately 50 batteries.

XBA-4E represents a decisive break from this earlier approach. With technical assistance from colleagues[7], the authors have grounded composite calculations in a rigorous psychometric framework. Meta-analytic average reliabilities and intercorrelations, derived from a large dataset of modern cognitive and achievement tests (Hajovsky et al., 2025), are now used to generate stable, defensible composite estimates. As stated in Appendix D, "The calculation of XBA composites in X-BASS 3.0 is grounded in a rigorous psychometric framework that balances accuracy, practicality, and consistency across batteries...These aggregated values allow X-BASS to generate stable, defensible composite estimates that reflect the best available evidence." This is a remarkable and innovative advance in the XBA method—a substantial leap up the CHC assessment innovation hill.

## The Scale of the X-BASS Composite Engine

The X-BASS composite engine now draws on:

- 568 correlation matrices
- 148 test batteries

[7] Dawn Flanagan and Vincent Alfonso joined forces with Daniel Hajovsky, Chris Niileksela, and Joel Schneider and together they created the largest database of ability batteries currently available. These are the data that were used to program many of the analyses conducted in X-BASS 3.0. More information about this database can be found in Hajovsky et al. (2025).

- 1,160 subtests (including revisions)
- 52,092 correlations
- 202,267 examinees

The number of source batteries for XBA-4E is several times more than those used in XBA-3E. Meta-analytic averages from this extensive dataset provide more stable and precise estimates for XBA composite calculations. Reliability coefficients derive from a database of:

- 89 unique batteries
- 789 subtests
- 170,595 individuals

Final intercorrelations and reliabilities are documented in Appendix D. These enhancements represent a major advancement in the psychometric integrity of XBA-4E and X-BASS.

### Validity Evidence for XBA Composites

Appendix E ("Convergent validity of X-BASS CHC Composites: A Large-Scale Comparison with Norm-Referenced Composites") presents a comprehensive comparison of norm-based and XBA-computed two- and three-subtest composites across ten widely used batteries. Of the 1,190 comparisons, 98.45% of XBA composites fell within the 68% confidence interval of the corresponding norm-based scores, with an average difference of 0.67 points and a maximum difference of 4.22 points. As Appendix E states, "By leveraging meta-analytic average reliabilities and intercorrelations derived from tens of thousands of data points, X-BASS ensures that composites are defensible and accessible...These composite estimates allow examiners to make informed, research-based interpretations that are consistent across batteries, age ranges, and subtest combinations." These findings provide strong validation of the XBA composite engine and its alignment with CHC theory.

### Enhanced Psychometric Integrity in the DD/C Method

Beyond improvements in XBA composites, the DD/C method has incorporated significant psychometric enhancements. Recent meta-SEM research on cognitive–achievement relations strengthens one of the core foundations of the DD/C method: *below-average aptitude–achievement consistency*. This critical component is now firmly grounded in CHC-organized meta-SEM research (Hajovsky et al., 2025; Niileksela et al., 2026; Niileksela & Hajovsky, 2024).

All PSW-based SLD identification models have faced substantial critique. In response, the XBA-4E authors—together with Joel Schneider—have provided thorough and well-supported rebuttals (e.g., Flanagan & Schneider, 2016; Schneider et al., 2024). Chapter 3 of XBA-4E includes a dedicated section, *Mischaracterized, Mis-modeled, and Ignored*, that directly addresses these issues. Several flaws in the critical narratives are evident. Critics often claim that PSW models demonstrate low reliability and diagnostic accuracy when strict threshold cut scores are applied. However, the XBA-4E authors clarify that rigid thresholds are *not* part of the DD/C method and Schneider et al. addressed the strict cut score problem and offered a sound solution, which has been incorporated into X-BASS. Simulation studies that impose strict cut scores misrepresent the intended procedure and therefore constitute "straw-man" critiques. It is well known that dichotomizing continuous variables reduces reliability. Studies that ignore measurement error around strict cut scores do not reflect best measurement practices. The DD/C method explicitly incorporates measurement error, confidence intervals, and consistency checks—features absent from many critiques.

### The Buffer Zone Simulation: Correcting the Core Misinterpretation of PSW Accuracy

Appendix F and Schneider et al. (2024) describe a simulation of 10 million cases using a simplified PSW method. By introducing a 5-point buffer zone around diagnostic cut scores, the authors demonstrate how the limitations of strict thresholds can be mitigated. As Schneider et al. explain, "The buffer zone [shows] how most diagnostic errors in previous simulation studies happen when observed scores and true scores are near a strict threshold and happen to fall on opposite sides of it. This means that most so-called diagnostic errors are unlikely to cause true errors of interpretation..." (p. 8).

The buffer zone—conceptually akin to the SEM around individual scores—acknowledges the measurement error inherent in strict cut-score decisions. The Schneider et al. (2024) study shows that the previously reported "inaccuracy" of PSW methods is misleadingly low because critical simulation studies (e.g., Stuebing et al., 2012) treated trivial score differences near thresholds as meaningful diagnostic errors. When measurement error is properly accounted for, PSW diagnostic decisions become increasingly reliable, especially as observed scores move away from the threshold.

There is an important distinction between making decisions about something that is truly dichotomous (e.g., Down syndrome) versus something that is truly continuous (e.g., cognitive ability). Dichotomous decision rules only make sense when the underlying construct is dichotomous. When a continuous variable is dichotomized, such as setting a cut score of 85, classification errors near the threshold are inevitable. If a student's observed score is 86 but their true score is 84, the "error" is not in the score; it is in the decision rule. This is why the DD/C and

X-BASS authors have always required practitioners to make decisions about strengths and weaknesses with special guidance for scores near cut points (Flanagan & Ortiz, 2001). Scores close to thresholds require additional scrutiny before being labeled as strengths or weaknesses.

Simulation studies that treat DD/C as a strict cut-point method fundamentally misrepresent the approach. Human cognitive abilities are complex, continuous, and should not be reduced to binary "above X/below X" decisions. Buffer zones provide a more precise, satisficing solution to the inherent problem of dichotomizing continuous variables. The Schneider et al. (2024) buffer-zone concept is an elegant correction to the most common misinterpretation of PSW diagnostic accuracy.

## A Troubling Omission in a Recent "Systematic Review"

Among the flaws in prior PSW diagnostic-accuracy critiques discussed in Chapter 3, I find the XBA-4E authors' response to Dombrowski et al.'s (2025) recent "systematic review" particularly illuminating—and troubling. The XBA-4E authors note that the Schneider et al. (2024) buffer-zone article is mentioned by Dombrowski et al. only in passing, with no discussion of its findings, implications, or relevance. I independently keyword-searched (and read) the full Dombrowski et al. article, looking for any substantive engagement with the buffer-zone concept. Although the authors cited the Schneider et al. article twice, indicating awareness, the only mention of the buffer-zone concept appears in the article's title in the reference list. This omission is puzzling. The buffer-zone findings directly contradict Dombrowski et al.'s central conclusion that "PSW procedures were about as accurate as flipping a coin" (p. 15). In my view, the Schneider et al. buffer-zone study provides the most statistically sound response to the most salient criticism of PSW methods.

## Integrating Buffer Zones into DD/C: A Necessary Evolution

Although the DD/C authors have always addressed the issue of cut points, the most current version of X-BASS integrates buffer zones and probabilistic statements about the likelihood that examinees' true scores fall within these zones. As Schneider explains in Appendix F, X-BASS 3.0 sets observed score criteria with an implicit 5-point buffer for both academic and cognitive criteria. Using the cumulative distribution function of the multivariate normal distribution, X-BASS estimates the probability that true scores fall within these buffer zones. This allows practitioners to distinguish cases that support confident interpretation from those requiring additional clinical review before reaching a diagnostic decision.

Chapter 3 and Appendix F provide detailed explanations of these statistical and psychometric innovations. Importantly, the XBA-4E DD/C method is currently the only PSW model that incorporates buffer zones, effectively raising the psychometric standards for all SLD identification methods, including RtI.

## CHC Innovation: The XBA C-LIM Backstory

The final chapter of the 1998 *Intelligence Test Desk Reference* (ITDR), authored primarily by Flanagan, was the first to classify subtests from major IQ and selected special-purpose batteries by their degree of cultural content and linguistic demand (see Table 14.4 in the ITDR). In a Wechsler cross-battery case study, Table 14.5 mapped all administered tests across these two dimensions. Flanagan presented her early culture–language classification framework at NASP in March 1997 as a tool for guiding assessment selection and interpretation for culturally and linguistically diverse students.

That presentation sparked a pivotal collaboration. Ortiz, who was in the audience, approached Flanagan afterward to discuss his interests. He provided valuable feedback on the ITDR chapter, refining the classifications and situating them within best practices in nondiscriminatory assessment. As a result, he was listed as a coauthor of the chapter in the ITDR table of contents. This collaboration marked the beginning of Ortiz's ongoing involvement in the evolution of XBA and the development of the Culture–Language Interpretive Matrix (C-LIM), which was formalized in XBA-2E (Flanagan et al., 2007, p. 149). The C-LIM guides practitioners in determining whether low test scores are more consistent with a learning disability or reflect a predictable pattern attributable to limited English proficiency or restricted exposure to mainstream cultural knowledge.

## C-LIM-ATE and the True Peer Estimator

XBA-4E introduces two Ortiz-inspired enhancements to the C-LIM framework:

- **C-LIM-ATE** (Culture–Language Interpretive Matrix–Achievement Test Extensions), which extends the C-LIM to achievement testing.
- **The True Peer Estimator (TPE)**, a semistructured rating scale informed by interviews and record reviews.

The TPE helps practitioners judge the degree to which an examinee's developmental experiences differ from those of the mainstream United States English-speaking population (e.g., slightly, moderately, or markedly). These data points are incorporated into the C-LIM and C-LIM-ATE models to support more nuanced interpretation. Together, the C-LIM, C-LIM-ATE, and TPE offer a systematic, clinically grounded approach for evaluating the influence of cultural and linguistic factors on test performance, complementing the psychometric components of X-BASS. I regard these tools as valuable structured guides that help reduce the complexity of interpreting test performance in culturally and linguistically diverse contexts. They support practitioners in organizing and evaluating assessment data when cultural and linguistic factors are relevant.

## CONCLUDING REFLECTIONS

In the film *Moneyball* (2011), Billy Beane (Brad Pitt) challenges entrenched baseball practices through data-driven sabermetrics. Despite intense criticism from traditional scouts, his approach transforms the Oakland Athletics. When Red Sox owner John Henry (Arliss Howard) offers Beane a position, he explains, "The first guy through the wall—he always gets bloody. Always." The line captures a universal truth about innovation: meaningful change is often driven by "dreamers that do," and such individuals inevitably encounter resistance. Innovative dreamers often get bloodied.

History is filled with innovators (disruptors of the status quo)—Galileo, Curie, Tesla, Jobs, Beane—who shared a common pattern: unwavering commitment to their ideas, persistence in the face of skepticism, and the ability to interpret resistance not as failure but as part of the journey toward progress. Breakthroughs occur because innovators persist long enough for evidence to accumulate and paradigms to shift. Richard Woodcock, whose work on the WJ series catalyzed the CHC cognitive assessment revolution (Kaufman, 2009; McGrew, 2005), was cut from the same cloth.

The authors of XBA-4E—Dawn Flanagan, Samuel Ortiz, and Vincent Alfonso—stand firmly in this tradition of principled disruption. For decades, they have challenged conventional cognitive assessment practices, often at personal and professional cost. Like Beane, they have endured sustained critique while continuing to revise, refine, defend, and advance their work.

Early criticism of XBA was forceful. In 2002, Watkins et al. questioned whether XBA met contemporary standards (i.e., American Educational Research Association, American Psychological Association, & National Council on Measurement in Education, 1999), concluding that more validity evidence was needed. Ortiz and Flanagan (2002a, 2002b) responded directly and comprehensively, arguing that the critics had mischaracterized the purpose and application of XBA while ignoring its benefits. As they wrote, "the comments offered by Watkins and colleagues misconstrue the very concept and purpose of CB [XBA] assessment...[and] ignore the benefits that may be gained by its use" (p. 32).

Revisiting this early debate now serves little purpose. The XBA method has evolved into a theoretically and psychometrically defensible practice.

More recent critiques of the DD/C method, often conflated with XBA, erroneously claim that it relies on strict cut points. It does not. Nevertheless, the latest iteration of DD/C addressed the claims of "poor diagnostic accuracy" by introducing psychometrically sound buffer zones and corresponding probability estimates (expressed as percentages) that a true score is below a threshold or cut point (Schneider et al., 2024). Over nearly 25 years, the XBA and DD/C methods have been subject to sustained scrutiny, yet the authors have consistently responded with data-driven refinements, not retreat. Chapter 3's section, *Mischaracterized, Mismodeled, and Ignored*, is essential reading for anyone seeking a clear, evidence-based understanding of DD/C.

Flanagan and colleagues are genuine innovators in applied cognitive assessment—*dreamers that do*. Their work has left an unmistakable imprint on the CHC cognitive assessment paradigm. Through my personal overview of 30+ years of XBA development and my familiarity with the history of CHC theory and assessment (McGrew, 1997, 2005, 2009, 2023b; Schneider & McGrew, 2012, 2018), I conclude that two primary forces infused CHC theory into applied practice:

- the publication of the 1989 WJ-R and Woodcock's 1990 joint CFA studies, and
- the development and evolution of XBA.

Although WJ V users may use XBA to supplement their CHC-designed batteries, XBA is especially vital for practitioners relying on other major instruments (e.g., the Wechsler trilogy, KABC-II NU). In this context, XBA serves as a critical bridge between theory and practice.

Through persistent scholarship, the XBA-4E authors have left an enduring imprint on the CHC IQ assessment paradigm. As of February 23, 2026, the authors collectively have over 3,900 citations to their XBA-related books and over 950 citations to 12 peer-reviewed journal articles specifically on XBA. In most fields, 100 citations is considered "highly impactful." Combined, the XBA-4E authors have approximately 4,850 citations—a remarkable scholarly footprint.

I began this foreword with the 1995 Breathnach quote, "The world needs dreamers and the world needs doers. But above all, what the world needs most are dreamers that do." The data speak clearly: the XBA-4E authors are dreamers that do. Among them, Dawn Flanagan has been the driving force behind approximately 90% of citations to XBA publications[8]. Her leadership, persistence, and intellectual courage have

[8] Flanagan, Ortiz, and Alfonso share many publications. The 90% figure is operationally defined as Flanagan appearing as the first author on publications with Ortiz and Alfonso (together as a team or separately with Flanagan). In publications where other non-XBA authors may have been the first author, the name of the XBA-4E author listed first, in a relative sense, was classified as the first XBA author. Ortiz's unique contributions to non-discriminatory and culturally sensitive assessment practices (e.g., C-LIM in X-BASS) are often published in outlets not associated directly with XBA and were not included in these calculations.

been central to the CHC theory-to-practice revolution. The architects of the CHC theoretical blueprint were Raymond Cattell, John Horn, and John "Jack" Carroll. In my view, alongside Richard Woodcock and me, Dawn Flanagan stands as one of the three key CHC theory-to-practice "bridgers" who helped transform CHC theory into applied IQ assessment practice.

XBA-4E has the character of a capstone achievement. What began in the late 1990s as a clinically driven framework with acknowledged psychometric limitations has matured into a sophisticated, defensible assessment system. Together, WJ V and XBA-4E represent tools that closely approximate the apex of the current CHC assessment innovation hill. Future advances, whether evolutionary or revolutionary, may include AI-driven expert-guided assessment systems that extend or replace X-BASS. Whatever form these innovations take, the legacy of XBA is secure. Through persistence, empirical rigor, clinical acumen, and intellectual courage, the XBA-4E authors have advanced the field of intellectual assessment by doing what true innovators do best, breaking through the *inertia-of-tradition* wall so others may pass through unscathed.

## REFERENCES


American Educational Research Association, American Psychological Association, & National Council on Measurement in Education (1999). *Standards for psychological and educational testing*. American Educational Research Association, Washington, DC.

Breathnach, S. B. (1995). *Simple abundance: A daybook of comfort and joy*. Warner Books, New York.

Bruton, O. J. (2021). Is there a "*g*-neuron"? Establishing a systematic link between general intelligence (*g*) and the von Economo neuron. *Intelligence, 86*, 101540.

Campbell, J. K., O'Rourke, M., & Slater, M. H. (Eds.). (2011). *Carving nature at its joints: Natural kinds in metaphysics and science*. MIT Press.

Carroll, J. B. (1993). *Human cognitive abilities: A survey of factor-analytic studies*. Cambridge University Press.

Conway, A. R., Kovacs, K., Hao, H., Goring, S. A., & Schmank, C. (2020). The struggle is real: Challenges and solutions in theory building. *Psychological Inquiry, 31*(4), 302–309.

Dombrowski, S. C., Benson, N. F., & Maki, K. E. (2025). A systematic review of the PSW diagnostic accuracy evidence for SLD identification: Is it time to abandon PSW? *School Psychology Review, 54*(3), 363–381.

Flanagan, D. P., Ortiz, S. O., Alfonso, V. C., & Mascolo, J. T. (2002). *The achievement test desk references (ATDR): A comprehensive framework for LD determination*. Allyn & Bacon, Boston, MA.

Flanagan, D. P., & McGrew, K. S. (1995a). A cross-battery approach to intelligence test interpretation. *NASP Communiqué, 24*(4).

Flanagan, D. P., & McGrew, K. S. (1995b). The field of intellectual assessment: A current perspective. *The School Psychologist, 49*(1).

Flanagan, D. P., Genshaft, J. L., & Harrison, P. L. (Eds.) (1997). *Contemporary intellectual assessment—theories, tests, and issues*. Guilford Press, New York.

Flanagan, D., & McGrew, K. (1997). A cross-battery approach to assessing and interpreting cognitive abilities. Narrowing the gap between practice and science. In D. P. Flanagan, J. L. Genshaft, & P. L. Harrison (Eds.), *Contemporary intellectual assessment. Theories, tests, and issues* (pp. 314–325). Guilford, New York.

Flanagan, D. P., & McGrew, K. S. (1998). Interpreting intelligence tests from contemporary *Gf-Gc* theory. Joint confirmatory factor analyses of the WJ-R and KAIT in a non-white sample. *Journal of School Psychology, 36*, 151–182.

Flanagan, D. P., McGrew, K. S., & Ortiz, S. O. (2000). *The Wechsler intelligence scales and Gf-Gc theory. A contemporary approach to interpretation*. Allyn & Bacon, Boston.

Flanagan, D. P., & Ortiz, S. O. (2001). *Essentials of cross-battery assessment*. John Wiley & Sons.

Flanagan, D. P., Ortiz, S. O., Alfonso, V. C., & Mascolo, J. T. (2002). *Achievement Test Desk Reference (ATDR): Comprehensive assessment and learning disabilities*. Allyn & Bacon.

Flanagan, D. P., Ortiz, S. O., & Alfonso, V. C. (2007). *Essentials of cross-battery assessment* (2nd ed.). John Wiley & Sons.

Flanagan, D. P., Sotelo-Dynega, M., & Alfonso, V. C. (2025). Overview of the Woodcock-Johnson V tests of cognitive abilities and virtual test library. *Journal of Psychoeducational Assessment, 43*(8), 802–844.

Hajovsky, D. B., Niileksela, C. R., Flanagan, D. P., Alfonso, V. C., Schneider, W. J., & Robbins, J. (2025). Toward a consensus model of cognitive–reading achievement relations using meta-structural equation modeling. *Journal of Intelligence, 13*(8), 104.

Horn, J. L., & Blankson, A. N. (2012). Foundations for better understanding of cognitive abilities. In D. P. Flanagan & P. L. Harrison (Eds.), *Contemporary intellectual assessment: Theories, tests, and issues* (3rd ed., pp. 41–68). Guilford Press.

Kaufman, A. S. (2009). *IQ testing 101*. Springer Publishing Company.

Kaufman, A. S., & Kaufman, N. L. (1993). *Kaufman adolescent and adult intelligence test (KAIT)*. American Guidance Service, Circle Pines, MN.

Kavale, K. A., & Flanagan, D. P. (2007). Ability–achievement discrepancy, response to intervention, and assessment of cognitive abilities: A critical analysis. In A. VanDerHeyden, S. L. Witt, & D. C. Gilbertson (Eds.), *Best practices in school psychology: Response to intervention* (pp. 147–182). National Association of School Psychologists.

Kavale, K. A., & Forness, S. R. (2000). What definitions of learning disability say and don't say: A critical analysis. *Journal of Learning Disabilities, 33*(3), 239–256.

Keith, T. Z., & Reynolds, M. R. (2010). Cattell–Horn–Carroll abilities and cognitive tests: What we've learned from 20 years of research. *Psychology in the Schools, 47*(7), 635–650.

LaForte, E. M., Dailey, D., & McGrew, K. S. (2025a). *Technical manual. Woodcock-Johnson V*, Riverside Assessments, LLC.

Lockwood, A. B., & Farmer, R. L. (2020). The cognitive assessment course: Two decades later. *Psychology in the Schools, 57*(2), 265–283.

McGrew, K. (1986). *Clinical interpretation of the Woodcock-Johnson tests of cognitive ability*. Allyn and Bacon, Boston.

McGrew, K. (1994). *Clinical interpretation of the Woodcock-Johnson tests of cognitive ability-revised*. Allyn and Bacon, Boston.

McGrew, K., & Flanagan, D. (1998). *The Intelligence Test Desk Reference (ITDR). Gf-Gc cross-battery assessment.* Allyn & Bacon, Boston.

McGrew, K. (1997). Analysis of the major intelligence batteries according to a proposed comprehensive *Gf-Gc* framework. In D. P. Flanagan, J. L. Genshaft, & P. L. Harrison (Eds.), *Contemporary intellectual assessment. Theories, tests, and issues* (pp. 151–180). Guilford, New York.

McGrew, K. S. (2005). The Cattell-Horn-Carroll (CHC) theory of cognitive abilities. Past, present and future. In D. Flanagan & Harrison (Eds.), *Contemporary intellectual assessment. Theories, tests, and issues* (pp. 136–202). Guilford Press, New York.

McGrew, K. (2009). CHC theory and the human cognitive abilities project: Standing on the shoulders of the giants of psychometric intelligence research. *Intelligence, 37,* 1–10.

McGrew, K. S. (2021). Is the intellectual functioning component of AAIDD's 12th manual satisficing? *Intellectual and Developmental Disabilities, 59*(5), 369–375.

McGrew, K. S. (2023b). Carroll's three-stratum (3S) cognitive ability theory at 30 years: Impact, 3S-CHC theory clarification, structural replication, and cognitive-achievement psychometric network analysis. *Journal of Intelligence, 11,* 32.

McGrew, K. S., Schneider, W. J., Decker, S. L., & Bulut, O. (2023a). A psychometric network analysis of CHC intelligence measures: Implications for research, theory, and interpretation of broad CHC scores "beyond *g*". *Journal of Intelligence, 11,* 19.

Norman, D. A., & Verganti, R. (2014). Incremental and radical innovation: Design research vs. technology and meaning change. *Design Issues, 30*(1), 78–96.

Ortiz, S. O., & Flanagan, D. P. (2002a). A response to Watkins et al.: Clarifying misconceptions about nondiscriminatory assessment. *Communiqué, 30*(5), 14–16.

Ortiz, S. O., & Flanagan, D. P. (2002b). Cross-battery assessment and the critique by Watkins et al.: A rebuttal. *Communiqué, 30*(6), 10–12.

Paik, M., & Nebenzahl, E. (1987). The overall percentile rank versus the individual percentile ranks. *The American Statistician, 41*(2), 136–138.

Schneider, W. J., Flanagan, D. P., Niileksela, C. R., & Engler, J. R. (2024). The effect of measurement error on the positive predictive value of PSW methods for SLD identification: How buffer zones dispel the illusion of inaccuracy. *Journal of School Psychology, 103,* 101280.

Schneider, W. J., & McGrew, K. (2012). The Cattell-Horn-Carroll model of intelligence. In D. Flanagan & P. Harrison (Eds.), *Contemporary intellectual assessment: Theories, tests, and issues* (3rd ed, pp. 99–144). Guilford, New York.

Schneider, W. J., & McGrew, K. S. (2018). The Cattell-Horn-Carroll theory of cognitive abilities. In D. P. Flanagan & E. M. McDonough (Eds.), *Contemporary intellectual assessment: Theories, tests and issues* (4th ed, pp. 73–163). Guilford Press, New York.

Schneider, W. J., Reynolds, C. R., McGrew, K. S., & Salekin, K. L. (in press). Life-and-death psychometrics: Generalizable best methods for combining scores in intellectual disability and other diagnostic assessments. *Journal of Pediatric Neuropsychology.*

Stuebing, K. K., Fletcher, J. M., Branum-Martin, L., & Francis, D. J. (2012). Evaluation of the technical adequacy of three methods for identifying specific learning disabilities: Severe discrepancy, regression discrepancy, and low achievement. *School Psychology Review, 41*(1), 3–22.

Simon, H. A. (1956). Rational choice and the structure of the environment. *Psychological Review, 63*(2), 129.

Tellegen, A., & Briggs, P. F. (1967). Old wine in new skins: grouping Wechsler subtests into new scales. *Journal of Consulting Psychology, 31*(5), 499.

Wasserman, J. D. (2019). Deconstructing CHC. *Applied Measurement in Education, 32*(3), 249–268.

Wechsler, D. (2014). *Wechsler Intelligence Scale for Children–Fifth Edition (WISC-V).* NCS Pearson.

Woodcock, R. W. (1990). Theoretical foundations of the WJ-R measures of cognitive ability. *Journal of Psychoeducational Assessment, 8*(3), 231–258.

# SERIES PREFACE

In the *Essentials of Psychological Assessment Series*, we have provided the reader with books that deliver key *practical* information in the most efficient and accessible manner. Typically, books fall into one of two categories. The first category features specific topics in a variety of domains, such as specific learning disabilities, social-emotional learning, neuropsychological assessment, cross-battery assessment, and adaptive behavior assessment. These books are intended for professionals in psychology and education—and for graduate students in these or related disciplines—who are committed to providing assessment and intervention services.

A second category of books in this series, such as *Essentials of Woodcock-Johnson V Assessment*, is devoted to a single test. These books offer a concise yet thorough review of an instrument, with special attention to the details of administration, scoring, interpretation, application, and tips for best practice use of the test. Students can rely on series books in both categories for a clear and concise overview of the important assessment tools and key topics informing skillful practice delivered efficiently, and ethically in their chosen fields. Experienced clinicians will feel equally at home with this series in their efforts to remain on the cutting edge of new research and new instruments as well as new editions of assessments in an array of diverse fields.

Wherever feasible, visual cues highlighting key points are used alongside systematic, step-by-step guidelines. Chapters are focused and succinct. Topics are organized for an easy understanding of the essential material related to a particular test or topic. Theory and research are continually woven into the fabric of each book, always to enhance the practical application of the material. With this series, we aim to challenge and assist readers interested in psychological and educational assessment to aspire to the highest level of competency by arming them with the resources they need for knowledgeable, informed practice. We have long been advocates of "intelligent" testing—the notion that numbers are meaningless unless they are brought to life by the clinical acumen and expertise of examiners. Assessment must be used to make a difference in the child's or the adult's life, or why bother testing? All books in the series—whether devoted to specific tests or general topics—are consistent with this credo. We want this series to help our readers, novice and veteran alike, to benefit from the intelligent assessment approaches of the authors of each book.

In *Essentials of Cross-Battery Assessment and X-BASS, 4e*, Flanagan, Ortiz, and Alfonso provide a clear and practical guide to implementing Cattell-Horn-Carroll (CHC)-aligned assessment in today's schools. This volume offers essential insights into the organization, interpretation, and application of Cross-Battery Assessment (XBA) and demonstrates how its corresponding software system, Cross-Battery Assessment Software System (X-BASS), streamlines data analysis, strengthens psychometric defensibility, and supports efficient, targeted evaluations. Designed for school psychologists, clinicians, learning disability specialists, and assessment practitioners, the book explains the rationale behind XBA; provides step-by-step guidance for selecting tests across batteries; and illustrates how X-BASS tools can be used to evaluate patterns of strengths and weaknesses, rule specific learning disability (SLD) in or out, and link assessment findings to meaningful interventions. Chapters address best practices in CHC-aligned assessment, interpretation of cognitive and academic profiles for multilingual learners, use of X-BASS decision rules, and the psychometric foundations that support defensible conclusions. Case studies and sample reports offer guided practice in applying the XBA method and X-BASS to real-world evaluations of suspected learning disabilities in reading, writing, and math. This book not only clarifies how to conduct efficient, accurate cross-battery assessments, but also deepens understanding of the cognitive and academic processes that underlie learning and inform high-quality educational decision-making for all students.

*Alan S. Kaufman, PhD, and Nadeen L. Kaufman, EdD, Series Editors*
*Neag School of Education, University of Connecticut*

# ACKNOWLEDGMENTS

The fourth edition of this volume would not be possible without the assistance of many individuals. We recognize all of them for their contributions and hope that they enjoy reading this volume as much as we have enjoyed preparing it. First, we want to recognize and express our deepest appreciation to Mr. Darren Lalonde, Executive Acquisitions Editor at John Wiley and Sons. We have been working with Darren for many years, and he has supported our scholarly publications no matter how delayed we were in producing them! Also, at Wiley is Mr. Nathanael Jude Mcgavin, Managing Editor, Psychology and Psychiatry, Social Sciences and Humanities. Mr. Mcgavin has been incredibly patient as we were preparing this volume and has always been respectful and encouraging. We are also grateful to Mrs. Mary Angelin Rose, a Content Refinement Specialist at Wiley, who assisted us with the copy edited and page proof stages of book production. Her prompt responses to our questions, kind nudges after we missed deadlines, and attention to detail were all greatly appreciated. She was a pleasure to work with!

We recognize and thank Dr. Shereen Allison for assisting with two important tasks. First, Shereen collaborated with us to write Chapter 4, "How to Use the PSW and SLD Evidence Tabs in X-BASS." Second, she assisted with gathering the research included in Chapter 3 and helped finalize our database of subtest descriptions used in our expert consensus research. This was a laborious task requiring many hours of editing. Thank you for reaching out to us years ago and collaborating with us on this volume!

Another valuable colleague, Dr. Gail Cheramie, prepared Chapter 7, "A Case of Conceptual/Reasoning Dyscalculia." Gail, who has been a staunch advocate of our work for more than two decades, used the Cross-Battery Assessment Software System (X-BASS) to evaluate the student's data and wrote a psychoeducational report that many readers shall find informative and helpful. Thank you, Gail!

Dr. Peng Peng collaborated with us on Chapter 9, "Linking Assessment Results to Intervention," and has been a strong supporter of our work for several years, having presented at our CAI PSYCHS conferences. Dr. Peng Peng is a prolific researcher on the relations between cognitive abilities and processes and academic success through evidence-based interventions. His research is impeccable and consonant with our most recent work.

Several appendices were written by colleagues who gave their time, energy, and expertise to augment this work. And they did not receive any compensation! We are grateful to the following individuals:

Drs. Chris "Croissant" Niileksela and Danny Hajovsky, who wrote Appendix C, "The Evolution of Cognitive-Achievement Relations Research: Past, Present, and Future," and Chris, who also assisted us with the analyses included in Appendix D, "Intercorrelations and Reliability Coefficients Used to Calculate XBA Composites in X-BASS" and Appendix M, "Calculation of the Facilitating cognitive Composite in the Dual Discrepancy/Consistency Pattern of Strengths and Weaknesses Method." These appendices were critical in informing many functions in X-BASS. We thank them and look forward to many more years of collaboration!

Dr. Craig Zinkiewicz collaborated with us in writing Appendix E, "Convergent Validity of X-BASS CHC Composites: A Large-Scale Comparison with Norm-Referenced Composites." We asked Craig to compute two- and three-subtest Cross-Battery Assessment (XBA) composites and compare the results to norm tables from many standardized, norm-referenced batteries. This was no easy task, and we thank Craig for helping us demonstrate clearly that XBA composites are nearly identical to published norms, with differences being attributable to measurement error.

Dr. Joel Schneider, who wrote Appendix F, "Continuous Variables and Categorical Decisions about SLD." In this appendix, Joel discusses what we affectionately call the "Schneiderian Probability Index," a version of which is found in X-BASS. This index addresses the inevitability of false positives and false negatives in clinical decision-making, especially in the context of the pattern of strengths and weaknesses (PSW) method of specific learning disability (SLD) identification. Joel has reviewed our work and pushed us to improve our operational definition, software, and thinking for many years. Thank you, Joel!

Dr. Benjamin "Ben" Lovett, who wrote Appendix G, "Exclusionary Criteria in the Diagnosis of SLD." Although many practitioners are aware of the exclusionary factor clause in the federal definition of SLD, they do not routinely and systematically consider these factors. Ben discusses each condition or situation that should be excluded as the determinant factor of academic deficits, lists the data relevant to collect as part of the exclusion process, and poses the key questions to ask and offers guidance on how to review those data. We appreciate Ben, who, over the years, has written chapters in our books, presented at our conferences, and supported our work.

Dr. Olivia Rogers contributed a much-needed study that is found in Appendix Q. It is an overview of her dissertation titled "Addressing Measurement Error to Improve SLD Identification Accuracy and School Psychologists' Confidence." This study was based on her dissertation and found that practitioners' accuracy and confidence in identifying SLD increased when additional information and "strength/weakness decision accuracy" (or the probability of making a correct decision) data were provided. This is the first study of its kind, and we are grateful to Dr. Rogers!

In addition to the authors of chapters and appendices, we are very appreciative of Drs. Kevin McGrew and Scott Decker, who contributed the foreword and afterword, respectively. Kevin was an original co-developer of the cross-battery method and has supported our work for decades! He is the consummate professional who not only pushes us to improve our thinking, our products, and the field, but who is a *true* quintessential senior scientist in our field. We have also known Scott for more than two decades, and over the years, he has presented his work at our conferences, written chapters in our books, and served as a valuable consultant, especially regarding neuropsychological processes involved in understanding academic performance. These scholars continue to be invaluable to us and the field in myriad ways, and for that, we are most grateful.

Finally, we offer a resounding thank you to Dr. Ridge Bynum, who has been assisting us with nearly every detail in preparing this volume, all while completing his dissertation! Ridge has edited, formatted, and organized nearly every chapter and appendix in this work. Moreover, he has completed the tasks meticulously and without ever complaining, delaying, or saying no to our requests. The completion of this book would not have been possible without him. Thank you, Ridge!

One

# OVERVIEW OF CROSS-BATTERY ASSESSMENT AND THE CROSS-BATTERY ASSESSMENT SOFTWARE SYSTEM (X-BASS)

The Cross-Battery Assessment method (hereafter called XBA) was introduced nearly 30 years ago by Flanagan and her colleagues (Flanagan & McGrew, 1997; Flanagan & Ortiz, 2001; Flanagan et al., 2000; McGrew, 1997; McGrew & Flanagan, 1998). It was introduced when practitioners had fewer intelligence, cognitive, and other ability batteries available to them and when test publishers and authors, in general, were not keeping pace with advancements in cognitive development, cognitive psychology, and theories of intelligence. XBA was presented as a defensible approach to narrowing the theory-practice gap and to designing assessments more responsive to referral concerns (Flanagan & McGrew, 1997). The development and history of XBA were described at length in the previous edition of this book and, therefore, will only be summarized here.

XBA was based primarily on the Cattell-Horn Fluid-Crystallized (*Gf-Gc*) model and later the Cattell-Horn-Carroll (CHC) model, and is now based on CHC and, to a lesser extent, neuropsychological theories. It provides practitioners with the means to make systematic, reliable, and theory-based interpretations of any ability battery and to augment that battery with cognitive, achievement, language, and neuropsychological subtests from other batteries to gain a more psychometrically defensible and complete understanding of an individual's strengths and weaknesses (Flanagan et al., 2017, 2018). Moving beyond the boundaries of a single cognitive, achievement, language, or neuropsychological battery by adopting the rigorous theoretical and psychometric XBA principles and procedures has been a significant improvement over single-battery assessment because it allows practitioners to focus on accurate and valid measures of the cognitive constructs and neurodevelopmental functions that are most germane to referral concerns (e.g., Caemmerer et al., 2020; Carroll, 1998; Decker, 2008; Flanagan et al., 2018; Kaufman, 2000; Reynolds et al., 2013).

> **DON'T FORGET**
>
> The XBA method is flexible, allowing practitioners to make systematic, reliable, and theory-based interpretations of composites composed of subtests from two or more batteries. XBA guides practitioners in supplementing any ability battery with subtests from other cognitive, achievement, language, and neuropsychological batteries, resulting in a comprehensive evaluation of an individual's strengths and weaknesses. This flexibility empowers practitioners to tailor their assessments to each individual's unique needs, fostering a more responsive, personalized approach.

Carroll (1997) noted that the CHC taxonomy of human cognitive abilities "appears to prescribe that individuals should be assessed with respect to the total range of abilities the theory specifies" (p. 129). However, he also recognized the challenges this would pose, stating that "[r]esearch is needed to spell out how the assessor can select what abilities need to be tested in particular cases" (p. 129). Flanagan and colleagues' XBA method provides this guidance, enabling practitioners to conduct assessments that cover a more comprehensive range of cognitive abilities and processes, academic skills, and linguistic and neuropsychological processes than what is possible with any single battery or collection of co-normed tests.

In an early review of the XBA method, Carroll (1998) stated that it "can be used to develop the most appropriate information about an individual in a given testing situation" (p. xi). In Kaufman's (2000) review of XBA, he said that the method is "based on sound assessment principles, adds theory to psychometrics, and improves the quality of the assessment and interpretation of cognitive abilities and processes" (p. xv). Decker (2008) stated that the XBA method "may improve school psychology assessment practice and facilitate the integration of neuropsychological methodology in school-based assessments [because it] shift[s] assessment practice from IQ composites to neurodevelopmental functions" (p. 804). A listserv thread of the *National Association of School Psychologists* focused on the potential weaknesses of XBA, Kevin McGrew, lead author of the Woodcock-Johnson V (WJ V), stated, "In the hands of 'intelligent' intelligence examiners the XBA system is safe and sound" (2011, March 30). In subsequent years, administering tests from multiple batteries became more commonplace in school and clinical settings. Perhaps the best example is Pearson's *Q-global* platform, where practitioners may select the batteries and the specific subtests from those batteries they want to administer, thus building their own cross-battery. Another example is the new WJ V, which includes a Virtual Test Library that may be used to supplement the WJ V COG and WJ V ACH batteries. However, neither *Q-global* nor the WJ V allows for the integration, analysis, and interpretation of data from batteries outside their respective platforms, such as those found in the *Cross-Battery Assessment Software System* (X-BASS 3.0; Flanagan et al., 2025). X-BASS 3.0 is referred to hereafter as X-BASS. Rapid Reference 1.1 provides a brief description of X-BASS.

## Rapid Reference 1.1

### What Is X-BASS?

- X-BASS is a software designed to assist practitioners in several aspects of assessment and interpretation, including:
  - The organization of evaluations specific to referrals that involve learning difficulties (see Chapters 2, 5, 6, and 7)
  - Organization of subtests into theoretically sound CHC broad and narrow ability composites (see Chapter 2)
  - Interpretation of XBA data (most chapters)
  - Recommendations for follow-up assessment (see Chapters 2 and 5)
  - Analysis of within-battery and cross-battery data according to the patterns of strengths and weaknesses (PSW) method of SLD identification, namely the Dual Discrepancy/Consistency method (see Chapters 3, 5, and 7)
  - PSW interpretation occurs within a broader operational definition of SLD (now integrated into X-BASS), providing guidance culminating in a defensible SLD decision (Chapter 3)
  - Analysis of within-battery and cross-battery data according to the degree of mainstream United States cultural influences and English language demands on test performance for multilingual learners (see Chapter 8)
  - Provision of interpretive statements and summary statements throughout to assist practitioners with report writing (most chapters)
- X-BASS is based on the most current research in the following areas:
  - The current CHC taxonomy (see Appendix A)
  - Expert consensus classifications of all new tests (see Appendix B)
  - The relations between cognitive abilities and academic skills based on large-scale data (see Appendix C)
  - Reliabilities and intercorrelations from the largest within-battery and cross-battery dataset currently available (see Appendix D)
- X-BASS 3.0 is more efficient than its predecessors in the following ways:
  - Easier to use; faster
  - Simplified and intuitive interface
  - More capabilities and features for multilingual learners
  - PSW analysis is embedded in an SLD operational definition and decision-making process designed to improve diagnostic accuracy
  - Expanded research base
  - Single data entry tab
  - Automatic features, such as graphs, score tables, and interpretation summaries, that are easily incorporated into reports

**CAUTION**

It is important to note that the XBA method does not simply mean using multiple batteries or parts of batteries in an evaluation. It is systematic and requires that specific procedures be followed. It also uses rules designed to reveal intraindividual strengths or weaknesses within ability domains that might otherwise have been obscured. If you are not following XBA principles and procedures, then it is more appropriate to use the term "flexible battery" rather than "cross-battery." If you use the XBA Analysis tab in X-BASS, then your data is analyzed following the XBA method.

Practitioners had "crossed" batteries before Woodcock (1990) recognized the need, before McGrew and Flanagan (1998) introduced the XBA method, and before Pearson and other test publishers made the option available online. Neuropsychologists have combined different standardized batteries to assess a wider array of brain functions than any single battery provides (Hale & Fiorello, 2004; Hale et al., 2011; Lezak, 1976, 1995; Lezak et al., 2004; Wilson, 1992). Nevertheless, many neuropsychologists' everyday test administration and interpretation practices lack the theoretical and psychometric rigor of the XBA method.

The introduction of *Gf-Gc* theory and the XBA method to school psychology dates back to the late 1980s and early 1990s (e.g., Carroll & Horn, 1981; Flanagan & McGrew, 1998; Horn, 1991; Keith, 1997). The Woodcock-Johnson Psycho-Educational Battery-Revised (WJ-R), published in 1989, was the first operationalization of *Gf-Gc* theory and measured eight broad cognitive abilities. Using data from the special validity studies from the 1977 Woodcock-Johnson Psycho-Educational Battery (WJ) and 1989 WJ-R, Woodcock (1990) completed a series of comprehensive *Gf-Gc*-driven joint factor analyses. Each analysis included the WJ-R cognitive tests and subtests from another intelligence battery (e.g., Kaufman Assessment Battery for Children [K-ABC], Stanford–Binet Intelligence Scale: Fourth Edition [SB:IV], Wechsler Intelligence Scale for Children–Revised [WISC-R]). Woodcock concluded that the WJ-R's eight-factor *Gf-Gc* model was supported based on these joint or cross-battery factor analyses. Equally important was his conclusion that other ability batteries have been underfactored, often resulting in misinterpretation of their factor structure. As such, Woodcock suggested that if practitioners are not using the WJ-R and would like to assess a broad range of abilities, they would need to "cross" batteries.

Several problems with "crossing" batteries (via flexible battery approaches) plagued assessment-related fields for years and most likely still do. Most of these problems have been circumvented by the XBA method (see Table 1.1 for examples). McGrew and Flanagan (1998) sought to create a set of principles and procedures that would allow practitioners to cross batteries psychometrically and theoretically defensibly. To achieve this goal, they used the results of Woodcock's (1990) joint-factor analyses, other similar studies, expert consensus, and an integrated version of *Gf-Gc* theory, drawn mainly from the work of John Horn and John Carroll as conceptualized by McGrew (1997), to classify all major intelligence batteries and a variety of special purpose tests according to the *Gf-Gc* broad and narrow abilities they measured.

Next, McGrew and Flanagan provided practitioners with guidelines for selecting and using the components of ability batteries either singularly or in combination to best address referral concerns. They described their assessment method as the "*Gf-Gc* cross-battery approach" in their

**Table 1.1 Parallel Needs in Cognitive Assessment-Related Fields Addressed by the XBA Method**

| Need Within Assessment-Related Fields | Need Addressed by XBA Method |
|---|---|
| School psychology, clinical psychology, and neuropsychology have lagged in developing conceptual models for assessing individuals. Contemporary models are needed. | The XBA method is grounded in CHC theories and the network of validity evidence that supports them (McGrew, 2023; Schneider & McGrew, 2018) for measuring and interpreting cognitive and academic abilities and neuropsychological processes. |
| Events external to a field of endeavor are needed to give impetus to new developments and fundamental advances in that field. | The CHC taxonomy and related research in cognitive psychology, cognitive neuroscience, and neuropsychology provided the impetus for and continued refinements to the XBA method, leading to better assessment instruments (e.g., WJ V) and interpretive procedures (e.g., X-BASS). |
| There is a need to utilize a conceptual framework to guide any assessment method. This would aid both in selecting instruments and methods and in interpreting test findings. | The XBA method is guided by the vast CHC literature, which includes substantive, structural, and academic outcomes research. Based on this research, selective, referral-relevant guidelines were developed and included in the XBA method to aid test selection (see Chapter 2) and interpretation (see Chapters 5 through 8). |
| The conceptual framework or model underlying assessment must incorporate various aspects of neuropsychological and cognitive ability function that can be described in terms of constructs recognized in the neuropsychological, cognitive psychology, and cognitive neuroscience literature. | The XBA method incorporates various aspects of neuropsychological and cognitive ability functions described in terms of constructs recognized in the literature. A consistent set of terms and definitions within the CHC literature (e.g., Schneider & McGrew, 2018) and the neuropsychology literature (e.g., Miller et al., 2022) underlie the XBA approach. |
| A conceptual framework is needed to measure the full range of behavioral functions the brain subserves. In neuropsychological assessment, no inclusive set of measures is standardized on a single normative population. | The XBA method allows for the measurement of a wide range of broad and narrow cognitive abilities specified in CHC theories and neuropsychological processes specified by neuropsychological theory and research. Although an XBA norm group does not exist, crossing batteries and interpreting assessment results are supported by large-scale within- and cross-battery data and based on sound psychometric principles and procedures. Other than XBA, the most extensive set of tests is within the WJ V assessment system, which consists of 60 co-normed tests. |
| Because psychological assessment lacks truly unidimensional measures, subtests from standardized instruments that appear to reflect the neurocognitive function of interest must be selected. In neuropsychological assessment, the aim is to select measures that, based on careful task analysis, primarily tap a given construct. | The XBA method is defined in part by a CHC classification system. Most subtests from the major cognitive and achievement batteries and selected neuropsychological instruments were empirically classified as measures of broad and narrow CHC constructs (via CHC within- or cross-battery factor analysis, expert consensus, or both) (Caemmerer et al., 2020; Reynolds et al., 2013; see Appendix B). Using evidence-based classifications allows practitioners to be reasonably confident that a given test taps a given construct (e.g., Flanagan et al., 2013). |
| An eclectic approach is needed when selecting measures, preferably subtests rather than omnibus IQs, to gain greater specificity in delineating patterns of function and dysfunction. | The XBA method ensures that two or more relatively pure, but qualitatively different indicators (i.e., measures, such as subtests) of each *broad* cognitive ability are represented in a comprehensive assessment. Two or more qualitatively similar indicators are necessary to infer specific or *narrow* CHC abilities. This process is eclectic in its selection of measures. |
| It is necessary to address potential problems that can arise from crossing normative groups and sets of measures with varying reliabilities. | In the XBA method, baseline data on cognitive functioning can typically be obtained across 8–10 CHC broad abilities using only two batteries standardized within a few years of each other, thereby reducing the effects of error due to norming differences. Additionally, since the interpretation of both broad and narrow CHC abilities is made at the cluster (rather than subtest) level, issues related to low reliability are uncommon in this approach. Finally, because cross-battery composites are generated from reliabilities and intercorrelations derived from a large-scale within- and cross-battery dataset, the composites produced by this method are psychometrically sound (see Appendices D and E). |

*Source:* Information obtained, in part, from Wilson (1992).

Woodcock-inspired *Intelligence Test Desk Reference* (ITDR; McGrew & Flanagan, 1998). They also devoted a chapter in the ITDR to "selective cross-battery assessment," which they defined as using cross-battery guidelines and principles to tailor a unique *Gf-Gc*-organized assessment battery to address specific referral concerns, mostly reading- and math-related difficulties. They presented a broad survey of the relations between individual cognitive and academic test performance to guide selective (referral-relevant) cross-battery assessment. Updates to this initial research on cognitive-achievement relations have been ongoing and continue to guide selective cross-battery assessment (e.g., Flanagan et al., 2013; Hajovsky et al., 2022, 2025; Niileksela & Hajovsky, 2024; Niileksela et al., 2016, 2026). The latest research on cognitive-achievement relations is described in Appendix C, and its applicability to identifying specific learning disabilities is discussed in Chapter 3.

Since the introduction and integration of *Gf-Gc* theory-based assessment into school psychology and other assessment-related fields, significant revisions, refinements, and expansions have been made to XBA, test development, assessment practices, and, most importantly, test interpretation (Alfonso et al., 2005; Flanagan, 2025; Flanagan et al., 2022; Keith & Reynolds, 2010; McGrew, 2023; Raiford, 2017; Schneider & McGrew, 2018). For example, McGrew's (1997) integration of the Cattell-Horn and Carroll models eventually became known as the Cattell-Horn-Carroll (CHC) theory—a union brokered by the diplomatic efforts of Richard Woodcock (cf., McGrew, 2005). CHC theory was operationalized by the Woodcock-Johnson III (WJ III) in 2001, WJ IV in 2014, and WJ V in 2025. The WJ V is the first battery to be based on the most recent CHC taxonomy (Schneider & McGrew, 2018) and will likely remain the best operationalization of CHC theories for many years to come.

Following Woodcock's lead, multiple authors and publishers explicitly used CHC theory and research to guide the revisions of their intelligence batteries (e.g., Differential Ability Scales–Second Edition [DAS-II], Kaufman Assessment Battery for Children–Second Edition [KABC-II], Stanford–Binet Intelligence Scales–Fifth Edition [SB5], and Wechsler Adult Intelligence Scale–Fifth Edition [WAIS-V]). Currently, over 120 batteries and 1,000+ subtests have been classified according to the *most recent CHC taxonomy*, using expert consensus and other data sources, and are included in X-BASS. The XBA method, automated by X-BASS, is grounded in rigorous, contemporary psychometric and theoretical research. For example, the most current research on cognitive-achievement relations was expanded to include 148 batteries, 1,160 subtests, 568 correlation matrices, over 50,000 intercorrelations, and over 200,000 individuals (e.g., Hajovskyet al., 2022, 2025; Niileksela et al., 2026), which provided a strong research foundation for the latest versions of the XBA method and X-BASS (see Appendix C for more details). Rapid Reference 1.2 provides a snapshot of the most salient research that guided current XBA procedures and the latest version of X-BASS. For those new to the method, the foundation and rationale for XBA are presented next, followed by a description of the XBA method. This chapter culminates with a section on "getting started" with X-BASS. In subsequent chapters, the reader is further instructed in using X-BASS for within-battery, cross-battery, and selective cross-battery assessments. Figure 1.1 provides a timeline for XBA's evolution. Figure 1.2 provides an overview of the information presented in this chapter.

**DON'T FORGET**

XBA is a method of assessing cognitive, academic, linguistic, and neuropsychological abilities and processes grounded in CHC theories (McGrew, 2023; Schneider & McGrew, 2018) and neuropsychological theory and research (e.g., Miller, 2024; Miller et al., 2022). The XBA method allows practitioners to reliably and validly measure a broader range (or a more in-depth but selective range) of abilities and processes than any given stand-alone assessment battery.

## *Rapid Reference 1.2*

**Selected Research that Guided Revisions and Refinements to XBA and X-BASS**

| Substantive (Content) Validity | Structural (Construct) Validity | Academic Outcomes (Predictive) Validity | Other Evidence |
|---|---|---|---|
| • CHC classifications for all new batteries in X-BASS 3.0 based on an extensive review of technical manuals, extant research, and an expert consensus study (described in Appendix B) | • Caemmerer and Reynolds (2020)<br>• LaForte et al. (2025)<br>• McGrew (2023)<br>• Reynolds et al. (2013)<br>• Schneider and McGrew (2018) | • Cognitive-achievement relations research based on data from 148 ability batteries, more than 500 correlation matrices, and over 52,000 correlations and 200,000 participants—provided guidance and support for consistency analysis in the PSW method (Hajovsky & Niileksela, 2024; Hajovsky et al., 2025) | • Psychometric network analysis (LaForte et al., 2025; McGrew et al., 2023)—*supports interpreting broad cognitive abilities* |

| Substantive (Content) Validity | Structural (Construct) Validity | Academic Outcomes (Predictive) Validity | Other Evidence |
|---|---|---|---|
| • A review of cross-battery factor analyses to verify existing classifications of all tests in X-BASS 3.0 | • *These studies guided and support the CHC structure upon which within-battery and cross-battery assessments are based* | • Cognitive-achievement relations research—from studies that include individuals with specific learning disabilities (summarized by McDonough et al., 2017)—*guided selective cross-battery assessments* | • Neurocognitive evidence (e.g., Kristanto et al., 2023) *supports broad ability interpretation.* Distinct broad abilities are associated with different combinations of brain subnetworks (Wang et al., 2021)<br>• Reliability and intercorrelation information, needed for analyses conducted in X-BASS, were derived from a large-scale dataset (described in Hajovsky et al., 2025)<br>• Schneider et al. (2024)—provided a psychometrically sound way to determine decision accuracy for PSW, which is in the SLD module of X-BASS |

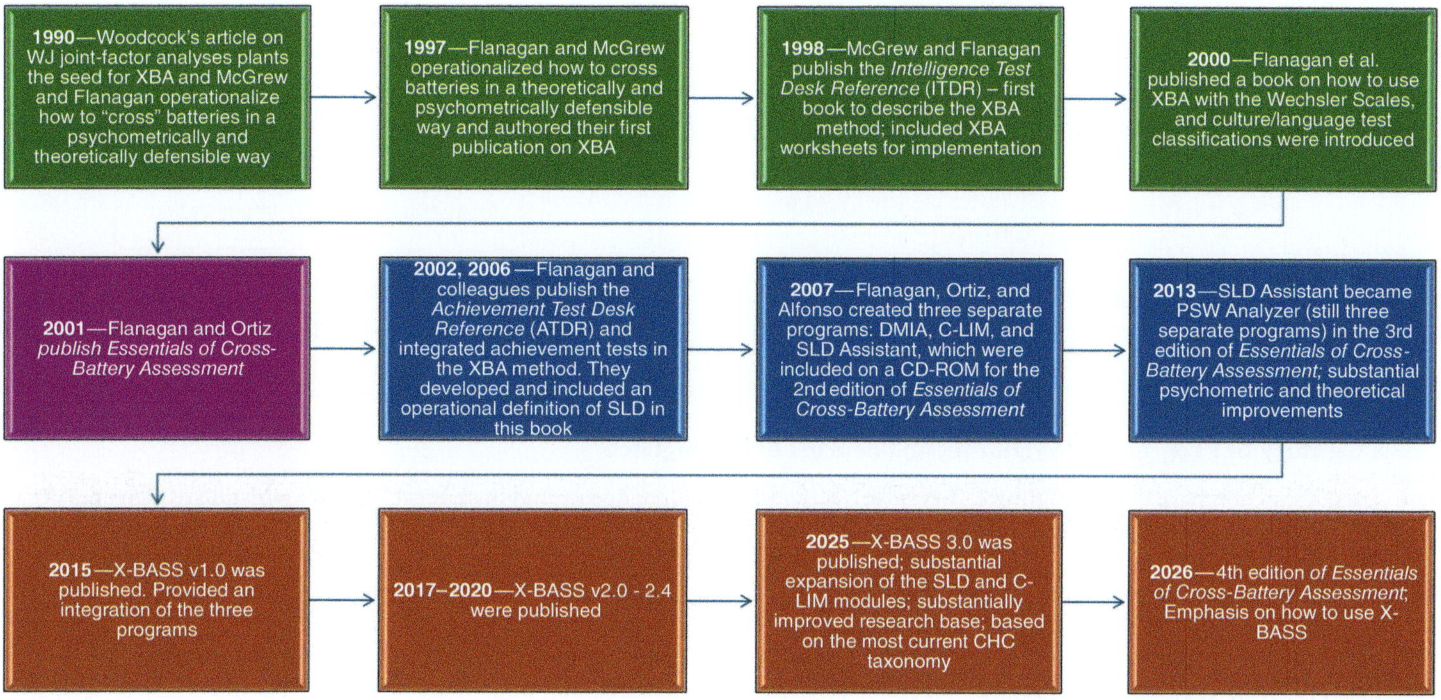


**FIGURE 1.1 The Evolution of the Cross-Battery Assessment (XBA) Method.** ***Note:*** **Green = The Original Developers of XBA, McGrew and Flanagan, Introduce the Method to the Field; Purple = Ortiz Joins and Assists in Expanding upon Flanagan's Culture/Language Test Classifications First Published in the ITDR; Blue = Alfonso and Mascolo Join, Contributing to Expanding XBA to Achievement Tests and Developing the SLD Operational Definition; Orange = Flanagan, Ortiz, and Alfonso Develop X-BASS and Continually Update, Revise, Refine, and Extend it to Meet the Needs of Practitioners**

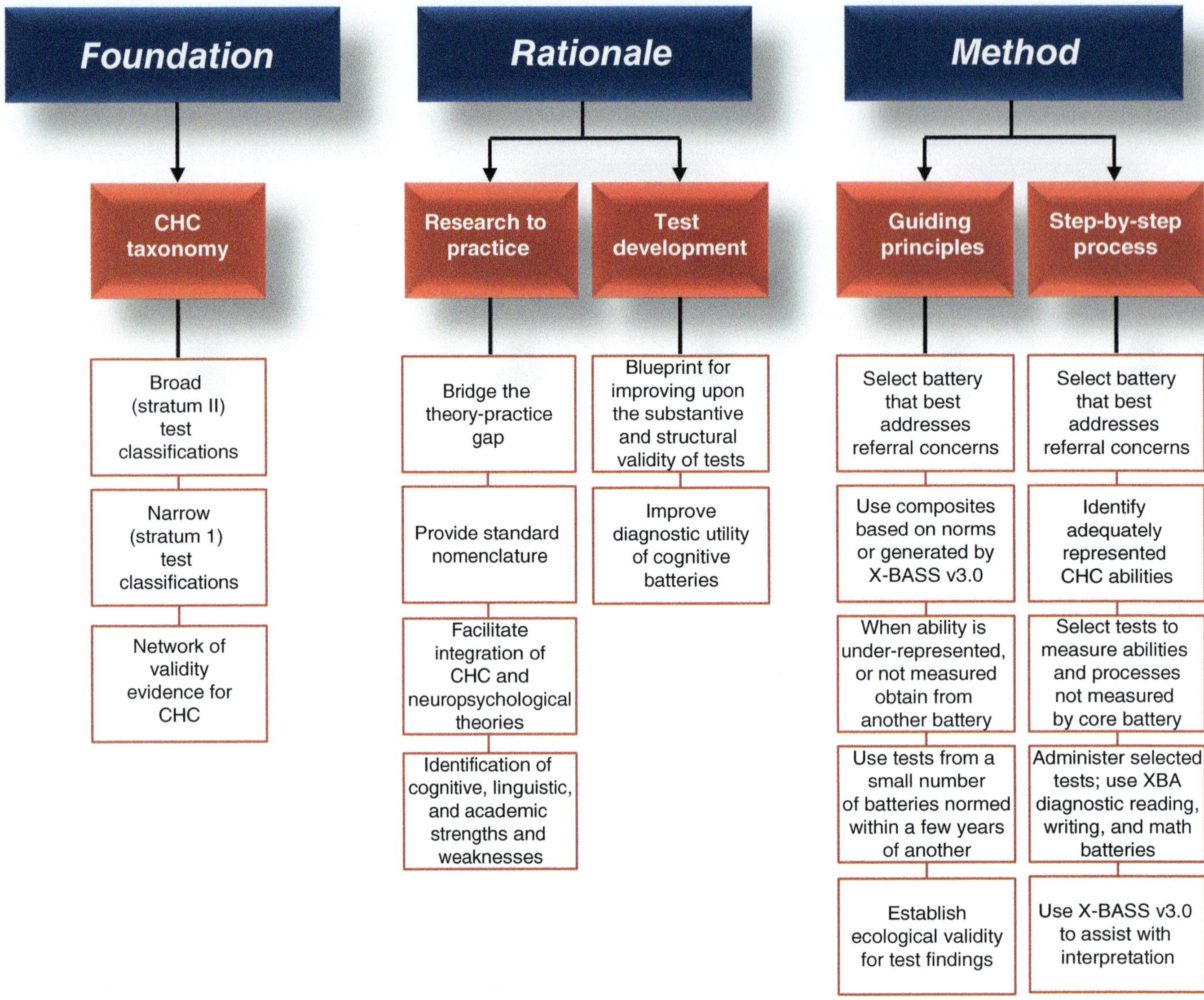


**FIGURE 1.2 Overview of XBA**

## FOUNDATIONS OF XBA

### Over a Century of Progress in Psychometric Theories of Intelligence

For decades, researchers have developed theories to explain the construct of intelligence and methods to evaluate individual differences in the abilities and processes that comprise these theories (e.g., Carroll, 1993; Cattell, 1941; Gustafsson & Undheim, 1996; Horn, 1991; Kaufman & Kaufman, 1983; McGrew, 1997; McGrew, 2023; McGrew et al., 2023; Schneider & McGrew, 2012, 2018; Taylor, 1994; Thorndike, 1997; Thurstone, 1938). Beginning with Spearman's *g* (Gottfredson, 2002; Spearman, 1904) and culminating in the most recent version of the CHC taxonomy (McGrew, 2023; Schneider & McGrew, 2018), as shown in Figure 1.3, progress in the psychometric or structural approach to understanding individual differences in intelligence and cognitive abilities has advanced considerably. Given space limitations, only the application of the CHC taxonomy to psychoeducational assessment and test interpretation is described here. See Figure 1.4 for a timeline of important developments in CHC theory and Rapid Reference 1.3 for salient revisions and refinements to the CHC taxonomy.

> **DON'T FORGET**
>
> The contemporary CHC taxonomy comprises 17 broad cognitive abilities and over 80 narrow abilities. Popular cognitive, achievement, language, and neuropsychological batteries, as well as special-purpose tests, measure a large subset of these abilities.

Note that Figure 1.2 omits a general ability (*g*) factor, primarily because the utility of the model (in assessment-related disciplines) is in understanding functioning in specific ability and processing domains, which are understood best through the operationalization of broad and narrow cognitive abilities and processes (e.g., Caemmerer et al., 2020; Compton et al., 2012; Evans et al., 2002; Flanagan et al., 2013, 2017; McCloskey et al., 2017; McGrew, 1997, 2009; Miller & Maricle, 2019; Reynolds et al., 2013;

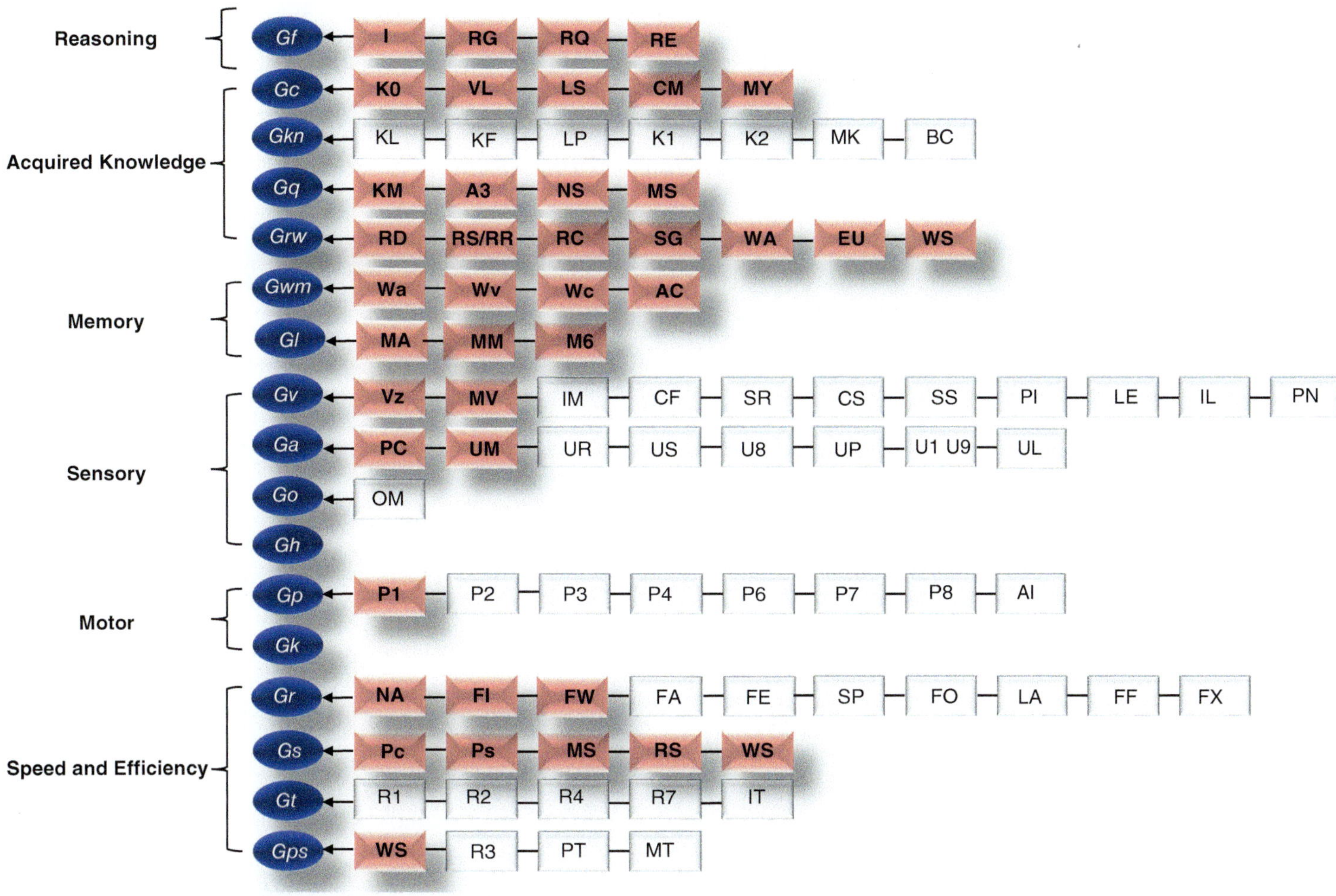


**FIGURE 1.3 The Current CHC Taxonomy of 17 Broad Abilities and Over 80 Narrow Abilities (Adapted from Schneider & McGrew, 2018).** ***Note:*** **Ovals Represent Broad Abilities, Rectangles Represent Narrow Abilities, and Left Braces Represent Groupings Consistent with Neuropsychological Domains. Narrow Abilities in Maroon-Shaded Rectangles Are Those More Commonly Measured Across Ability Batteries. Letter Codes and Corresponding Broad and Narrow Ability Definitions Are in Appendix A**

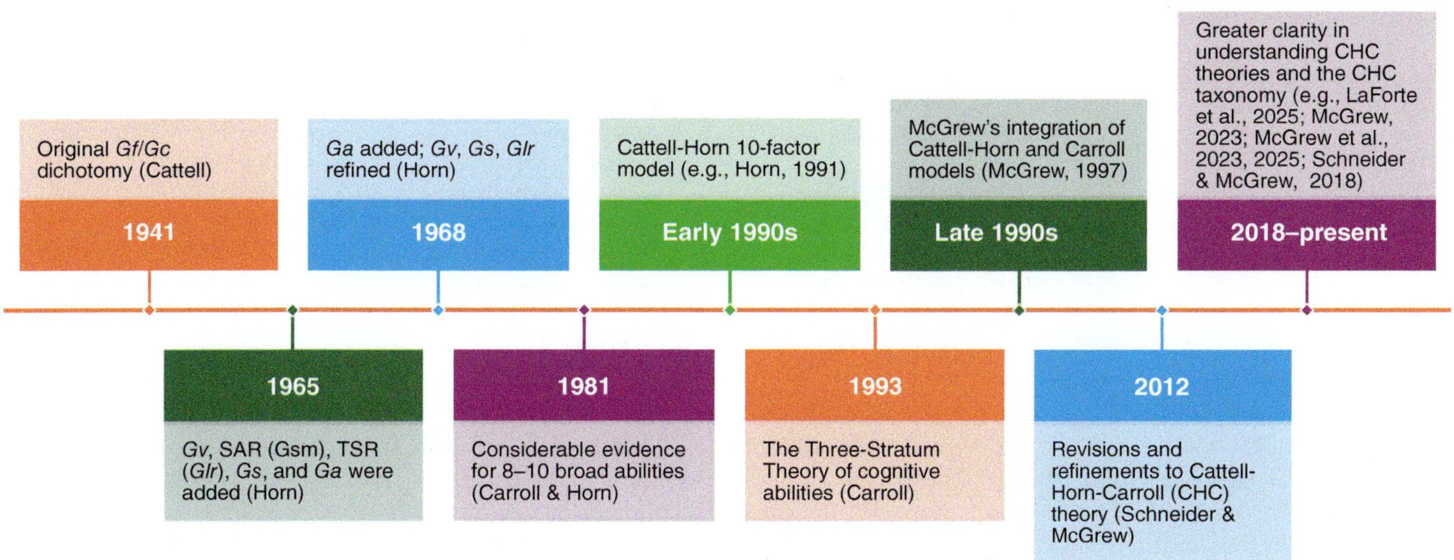


**FIGURE 1.4 Highlights in the Development of CHC Theories.** ***Note:*** **SAR = Short-Term Acquisition and Retrieval; TSR = Long-Term Storage and Retrieval. Critical Reviews of CHC Theories Have Been Published in Recent Years (e.g., Data from McGill & Dombrowski, 2019)**

## Rapid Reference 1.3

### Salient CHC Revisions and Refinements Reported in Schneider and McGrew (2018)

| Revision | Details | Comments |
|---|---|---|
| Long-term Storage and Retrieval (*Glr*) was dropped and replaced with Learning Efficiency (*Gl*) and Retrieval Fluency (*Gr*) | The *Gl* domain subsumes the narrow abilities of Associative Memory (MA), Meaningful Memory (MM), and Free Recall Memory (M6). The *Gr* domain subsumes narrow retrieval speed abilities, such as Naming Facility (NA), Ideational Fluency (FI), and Word Fluency (FW). | There are several implications of this change. For example, subtests measuring Glr needed to be reclassified as measuring either a narrow *Gl* ability (e.g., Meaningful Memory, Free Recall Memory) or a narrow *Gr* ability (e.g., Naming Facility, Ideational Fluency), which has implications for test interpretation. The Glr composite on the WJ IV is interpreted as *Gl* based on the new CHC taxonomy. Also, the composition of total test composites may differ in subsequent editions of batteries (e.g., the WJ V eight-subtest GIA includes a measure of *Gr* whereas the WJ IV seven-subtest GIA does not; LaForte et al., 2025). |
| Intermediate factors were added | Three intermediate factors were added, including Language Development (LD) in the *Gc* domain, Speed of Lexical Access (LA) in the *Gr* domain, and Perceptual Speed (P) in the *Gs* domain. | Carroll (1993) referred to LD as an intermediate category between the broad *Gc* ability and narrow *Gc* abilities (e.g., Lexical Knowledge, Listening Ability, Grammatical Sensitivity), which represented a combination of *Gc* narrow abilities working together simultaneously (Adapted from Schneider & McGrew, 2018). Fewer subtests were classified as LD than all narrow *Gc* abilities. No subtests were classified as LA, but many were classified as one of its two component narrow abilities, Naming Facility (NA) and, to a lesser extent, Word Fluency (FW). Any subtests that were classified as P included Pc (compare) and Ps (search) demands to a substantial degree. |
| Facets were added | In the *Gr* domain, narrow abilities are grouped into three facets: words, ideas, and figures. In the *Gs* domain, narrow abilities are grouped into two facets: cognitive and academic. | The *Gr words* facet consists of two narrow abilities—Naming Facility (NA) and Word Fluency (FW)—that are subsumed by the intermediate factor, Speed of Lexical Access (LA). Within the *Gr* domain, indicators of NA and FW are typically most sensitive to reading difficulties and dyslexia (Duke & Cartwright, 2021). The *Gs cognitive* facet includes the narrow abilities of Perceptual Speed-compare (Pc) and Perceptual Speed-search (Ps). The *Gs academic* facet includes narrow abilities that require quick and accurate performance with learned information and skills (e.g., Reading Speed [RS], Writing Speed [WS]). |
| New narrow abilities were added, and others were dropped | The narrow ability of Rate-of-Test-Taking (R9) in the *Gs* domain was dropped, and Perceptual Speed-compare (Pc) and Perceptual Speed-search (Ps) were added. Memory Span (MS) was dropped from the *Gwm* domain, and Auditory Short-term Storage (Wa) and Visual Spatial Short-term Storage (Wv) were added. Attentional Control (AC) was also added as a narrow ability in the *Gwm* domain. | In the *Gs* domain, all subtests previously classified as R9 were reclassified, mainly as Perceptual Speed-compare (Pc) or Perceptual Speed-search (Ps). In the *Gwm* domain, tests previously classified as Memory Span (MS) were reclassified as either Auditory Short-term Storage (Wa) or Visual Spatial Short-term Storage (Wv). The narrow ability code of AC is similar to the previously used Working Memory (WM) code. In other words, subtests previously classified as WM are now classified as AC (e.g., McGrew et al., 2025). Appendix B provides a more detailed explanation of how working memory subtests are classified in expert consensus studies and in X-BASS 3.0. |

Woodcock et al., 2017). Also, the CHC theory is compatible with network models, which renounce *g* and conceive of cognitive abilities as an interconnected network of cognitive processes that cognitive tests sample in various ways (Kan et al., 2019; Kovacs & Conway, 2016). Despite the ongoing debate regarding the existence of *g*, specifically in the field of school psychology, many researchers continue to accept *g* as a valid psychological construct and believe that a proxy for *g*, such as a Full Scale IQ, is the only score that can be interpreted from an intelligence or cognitive ability battery (e.g., Canivez & McGill, 2016; Dombrowski et al., 2015, 2017; Warne & Burnungham, 2019; Watkins & Beaujean, 2014). Research is abundant to the contrary. See Rapid Reference 1.4 for a commentary on test interpretation concerning *g*.

## Rapid Reference 1.4

### Fields Outside of School Psychology Weigh in on *g*

The studies that concluded that only total test scores from intelligence and cognitive ability batteries can be interpreted used bifactor and Schmid-Leiman (BF/SL) methods, which have been criticized for methodological confounds and for lacking a theoretical basis (see Decker, 2021; Decker et al., 2021, for a critical review of this research; see also Murray & Johnson, 2013; Schmank et al., 2021; see Dombrowski et al., 2021, for a rebuttal). Dombrowski et al. (2021) espouse g-theory and the importance of g-level interpretation over lower-order, broad-ability-level interpretations, based on their BF/SL research findings. However, the level of interpretation (g-level or broad ability-level) varies as a function of the methods and statistical procedures used (e.g., Burgoyne et al., 2022; Decker, 2021; Keith & Reynolds, 2018; McGrew et al., 2025; Murray & Johnson, 2013; Schmank et al., 2021; Schulze, 2005; see also Bornovalova et al., 2020, for similar issues in psychopathology). Also, these researchers rarely include or cite research that supports the interpretation of CHC broad abilities. For example, while Dombrowski et al. (2021) provided 19 references that included at least one member of their "g-centric" research group (or "Canivez et al. group"), they provided 0 references to any researchers who demonstrate a multi-factorial view of intelligence (i.e., the "Keith-Reynolds group," cf. McGrew et al., 2023, p. 2). Because the Canivez et al. group ignores the Keith-Reynolds group's research, it boldly promotes a g-centric view of intelligence test interpretation along with the de-implementation of test interpretation approaches that include CHC broad abilities (Dombrowski et al., 2021; Farmer et al., 2021a,b) *in the absence of sufficient empirical support to do so.*

"A statistical procedure is not an automatic, mechanical truth-generating machine. . ." (Meehl, 1992, p. 143) (see also Kell & Lang, 2017). Interpretations drawn from the Canivez et al. group's BF/SL models are limited because they are not based on theoretical models of intelligence and cognition (e.g., Decker, 2021; McGrew, 2023; McGrew et al., 2025; Murray & Johnson, 2013). Furthermore, the Canivez et al. group acknowledges that their bifactor models have estimation problems and, therefore, should not be trusted, but then use their untrustworthy models to promote g-only test interpretation and discourage CHC broad ability interpretation (see Wilson et al., 2023, for a discussion). Interpretations drawn from the Keith-Reynolds research group are less limited because they are supported by many sources of validity (e.g., Horn, 1991; Horn & Noll, 1997; McGrew, 2023; cf. Flanagan, 2025; see also LaForte et al., 2025).

Elusive g results from positive correlations among scores and is best conceived as positive manifold or *psychometric* g. Despite its predictive power and replicability (Jensen, 1998), it remains to be seen what g is. A general assumption in psychology is that an individual's intelligence or cognitive test scores are caused by g. However, there are other plausible explanations for g. For example, g may emerge *because* of the indicators, meaning that g is a formative latent variable (Conway et al., 2021; Kovacs & Conway, 2016). The latter explanation renders the strata below g (i.e., broad and narrow abilities) of primary importance (e.g., Colom et al., 2009; Haier et al., 2009; McGrew et al., 2023). There is a network of validity evidence for distinct CHC abilities beyond structural (i.e., factor analysis) evidence (e.g., Carroll, 1993; LaForte et al., 2025), including developmental (Schrank et al., 2014), achievement (e.g., Hajovsky et al., 2025; O'Connell, 2018), neurocognitive (e.g., Barbey, 2018; Kristanto et al., 2023), and heritability (e.g., Malanchini et al., 2020; Procopio et al., 2022) evidence (see also Daniel, 1997; Horn & Noll, 1997). Like broad abilities, an explanation of g requires stepping outside the domains of psychometrics and school psychology and into other fields, such as neurobiology and cognitive neuroscience (McGrew et al., 2023; cf. Flanagan, 2025).

The interested reader is directed to theories that explain g via overlapping brain networks (Conway et al., 2021; Decker et al., 2018; Haier & Jung, 2018; Jung & Haier, 2007; Kovacs & Conway, 2016; Schmank et al., 2021). For example, *Process Overlap Theory* (POT) postulates that domain-general executive processes, located primarily in the prefrontal cortex and partly in the parietal cortex, are the main reason for the emergence of positive manifold or g (Kovacs, 2019; Kovacs & Conway, 2016). The theory proposes that domain-general executive processes overlap with domain-specific cognitive processes more than the domain-specific cognitive processes overlap with one another and that any cognitive task requires several domain-general and domain-specific cognitive processes (e.g., Bailey et al., 2018; Klein & Knops, 2023). Central to the theory is that individual differences in executive processes can be a bottleneck for cognitive functioning. Theories like POT explain positive manifold or *psychometric* g, but dismiss *psychological* g.

Another brain network theory is the *Parietal Frontal Integration Theory* (P-FIT; Haier & Jung, 2018). P-FIT proposes that intelligence emerges from efficient integration across a distributed brain network, rather than from any single brain region, with individual differences in network connectivity creating the biological foundation for general intelligence. This distributed network model bridges psychometric models of intelligence structure and the underlying neurobiology, explaining how shared neural infrastructure produces positive manifold (Haier & Jung, 2018; Jung & Haier, 2007; Vakhtin et al., 2014). These theories provide a more plausible explanation of g than that found in the BF/SL research of the Canivez et al. group (e.g., Canivez & McGill, 2016; Dombrowski et al., 2018). Moreover, mounting neurocognitive evidence suggests that distinct broad cognitive abilities are associated with different combinations of brain subnetworks (Barbey, 2018; Decker et al., 2017; Kristanto et al., 2023; McGrew et al., 2023), thus providing additional support for the interpretation of broad cognitive abilities.

Theories such as POT and P-FIT will likely drive the future of intelligence and cognitive test development and interpretation, as well as research on intelligence and cognition (e.g., Kristanto et al., 2023; McGrew et al., 2023; Van Der Maas et al., 2017). Traditional psychometric intelligence testing may soon be replaced by portable neuroimaging technology that can provide a pathway to more precise, individualized educational approaches tailored to each student's cognitive strengths and weaknesses (Haier & Jung, 2018).

## CHC Broad (Stratum II) Classifications of Subtests on Ability Batteries

Based on the results of a series of cross-battery confirmatory factor analysis studies of the major cognitive and intelligence batteries (see Caemmerer et al., 2020; Keith & Reynolds, 2010, 2012; LaForte et al., 2025; Reynolds et al., 2013) and task analyses performed by cognitive test experts, Flanagan and colleagues classified over 2,000 subtests according to the CHC broad abilities they measure since the late 1990s. Because dozens of new batteries are published each year and many others are updated to new editions, the collection of batteries and subtests in X-BASS changes accordingly.

Classification of subtests at the broad ability level is necessary to improve the validity of cognitive assessment and interpretation. Specifically, broad ability classifications ensure that the CHC constructs underlying assessments are minimally affected by *construct-irrelevant variance* (Messick, 1989, 1995). In other words, knowing what tests measure what CHC broad abilities enables practitioners to organize tests into construct-relevant composites—composites containing only subtests *relevant to* the construct or ability of interest (e.g., Caemmerer et al., 2020; Laforte et al., 2025; McGrew & Flanagan, 1998; Reynolds et al., 2013).

Construct-*irrelevant variance* is present when an "assessment is too broad, containing excess reliable variance associated with other distinct constructs . . . that affects responses in a manner irrelevant to the interpreted constructs" (Messick, 1995, p. 742). Construct-*relevant variance* is important for test interpretation because it is often assumed that any given composite provides an estimate of a *single* construct. The narrow ability classifications of subtests help to verify this assumption. The ongoing cross-battery confirmatory factor analyses conducted by Keith, Reynolds, Caemmerer, and colleagues validate existing CHC classifications of subtests and improve how subtests are organized and interpreted within the context of XBA (e.g., Caemmerer et al., 2020; Reynolds et al., 2013).

Figure 1.5 illustrates construct-irrelevant variance using the WISC-V Expanded Fluid Index (EFI). The EFI comprises four subtests—Matrix Reasoning, Figure Weights, Picture Concepts, and Arithmetic—and is used when a more detailed assessment of fluid reasoning is needed (e.g., to determine giftedness). This figure shows that the Picture Concepts subtest also measures *Gc* substantially, most likely the narrow ability of Lexical Knowledge. Furthermore, the Arithmetic subtest has a long history of being factorially complex. In factor analyses, it has been found to load on *Gf*, *Gq*, and *Gwm* (see Flanagan et al., 2013, for a summary). Figure 1.5 shows the complexity of the Arithmetic subtest, sharing variance with *Gq* (i.e., the narrow ability of Math Achievement) and *Gwm* (the narrow ability of Attentional Control or Working Memory). Because the EFI contains construct-irrelevant variance, when Arithmetic is substantially higher or lower than other *Gf* subtests, the influences of *Gq* and *Gwm* should be considered as either facilitators or inhibitors, respectively.

Construct-irrelevant variance can also operate at the subtest level (rather than at the composite level). For example, the WJ IV contained a test called Phonological Processing (PP), intended to measure the broad Auditory Processing (*Ga*) ability. The PP test included three tasks, one measuring Word Fluency, a narrow ability in the broad Retrieval Fluency (*Gr*) domain, and, therefore, largely *irrelevant to* Ga. The construct-irrelevant variance in the PP test complicated interpretation, as it was unclear whether low performance was due to poor Phonetic

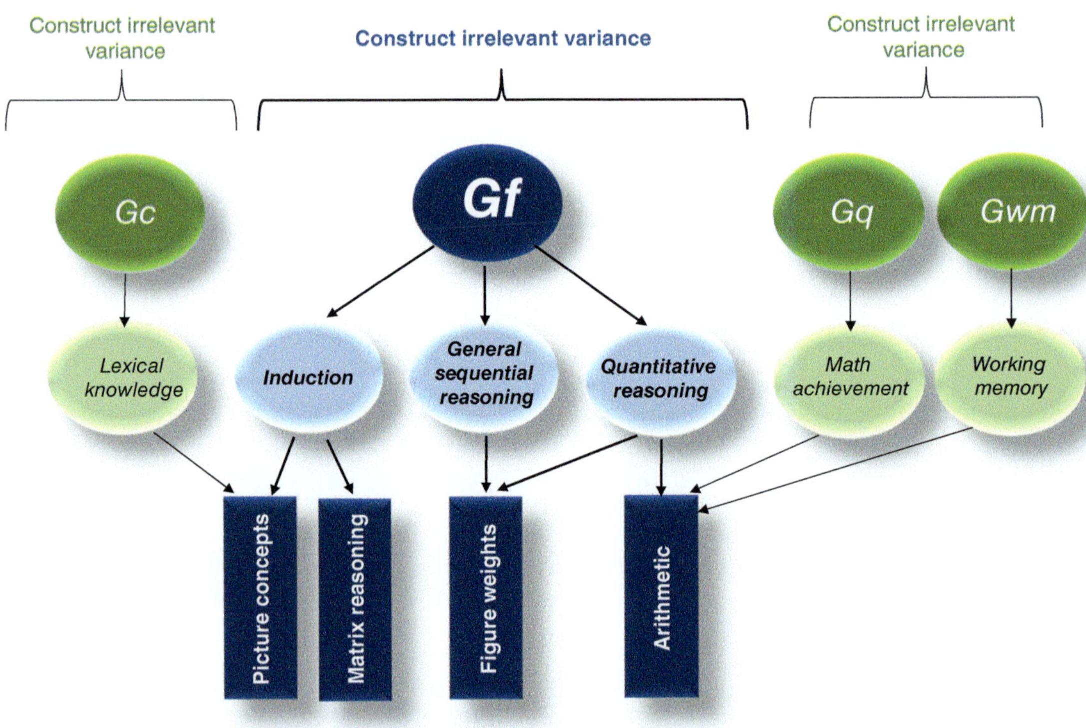


**FIGURE 1.5 The WISC-V Expanded Fluid Reasoning Index Includes Construct Irrelevant Variance**

Coding (a narrow *Ga* ability), poor Word Fluency (a narrow *Gr* ability), or both. Although new to the WJ IV, the PP test is not included in the WJ V, primarily because it is a mixed measure of abilities (LaForte et al., 2025). The WJ V Verbal Analogies test is another example of construct-irrelevant variance, as this test measures *Gf* and *Gc* to a substantial degree (LaForte et al.).

"Any test that measures more than one common factor to a substantial degree [e.g., the WJ IV Phonological Processing test] yields scores that are psychologically ambiguous and very difficult to interpret" (Guilford, 1954, p. 356; cf. Briggs & Cheek, 1986). Therefore, cross-battery assessments typically use only empirically strong or moderate (but not factorially complex or mixed) measures of CHC abilities. Most current cognitive and intelligence batteries contain at least a few factorially complex composites and subtests.

**CAUTION**

Construct-irrelevant variance occurs when a composite assesses two or more distinct constructs to a substantial degree. It can occur at the subtest or composite level, leading to scores that are psychologically ambiguous and confound interpretation.

## CHC Narrow (Stratum I) Classifications of Subtests

Narrow ability classifications were initially reported in McGrew (1997), then reported in McGrew and Flanagan (1998) and Flanagan et al. (2000) following minor modifications. Flanagan and her colleagues continued to gather content validity data on cognitive ability tests, expanding their analyses to include academic achievement and language batteries (Flanagan et al., 2002, 2006) and neuropsychological processes (e.g., Flanagan et al., 2010, 2011; see also Appendix B).

Classifications of ability subtests at the narrow (stratum I) ability level were necessary to improve the content validity of batteries and facilitate interpretation. Narrow ability classifications ensure that the CHC constructs underlying assessments are well represented (LaForte et al., 2025; McGrew & Flanagan, 1998). Construct underrepresentation is present when an "assessment is too narrow and fails to include important dimensions or facets of the construct" (Messick, 1995, p. 742).

**CAUTION**

Construct underrepresentation occurs when too few features (i.e., narrow abilities) are represented in the measurement of a construct (i.e., a broad ability) or when a composite intended to represent a broad ability includes two or more measures of the same narrow ability.

Interpreting the WJ V COG Matrices test as a measure of Fluid Reasoning (i.e., the broad *Gf* ability) is an example of construct underrepresentation because this test measures *one* narrow aspect of *Gf* (i.e., Induction). Figure 1.6 shows that at least one *additional Gf* measure, qualitatively different from Induction, must be included in an assessment to ensure adequate representation of the *Gf* construct (e.g., the Analysis Synthesis test measures General Sequential Reasoning). Two or more qualitatively different indicators are needed to adequately represent the construct (see Caemmerer et al., 2020; Comrey, 1988; Keith & Reynolds, 2012; McGrew & Flanagan, 1998; Messick, 1989, 1995). The composite of scores from the Matrices and Analysis-Synthesis tests provides an adequate estimate of the broad *Gf* ability because these tests are strong measures of *Gf* and represent qualitatively different aspects of this broad ability.

**DON'T FORGET**

Two or more qualitatively different indicators (e.g., subtests representing different narrow abilities) are needed to adequately represent a broad ability construct.

Most cognitive batteries yield construct-relevant composites, though some underrepresent the broad ability intended to be measured. This is because construct underrepresentation can occur when the composite consists of two or more measures of the *same* narrow (stratum I) ability. For example, the Number Recall and Word Order subtests of the Kaufman Assessment Battery for Children–Second Edition Normative Update (KABC-II NU; Kaufman & Kaufman, 2018) were intended to be interpreted as a representation of the broad *Gwm* ability. However, these subtests primarily measure Auditory Short-term Storage (Wa), a narrow *Gwm* ability. Thus, the *Gsm* (a code used in earlier CHC theories) Scale of the KABC-II NU is most appropriately interpreted as Wa (a narrow ability), not *Gwm*.

A scale or broad CHC ability composite will yield more information—hence, be a more valid measure of a construct—if it contains more differentiated or qualitatively different tests of the construct. XBA circumvents misinterpretations arising from underrepresented constructs by requiring the use of two or more qualitatively different indicators to represent a CHC broad ability when deemed necessary. To ensure that qualitatively different aspects of broad abilities are represented in assessment, classification of ability tests at the narrow (stratum I) ability level was necessary (see Appendix B).

In sum, the classifications of tests and subtests at the broad and narrow ability levels of CHC theory guard against two ubiquitous sources of invalidity in assessment: construct-irrelevant variance and construct underrepresentation. Together, CHC theories and the CHC classifications of tests that underlie the XBA method provide the necessary foundation for organizing assessments that are theoretically driven, psychometrically defensible, relevant to the referral concerns, and supported by current research.

Before discussing the applications of the XBA method, it is important to highlight how the method has evolved. Rapid References 1.5 and 1.6 list the major changes to the XBA method and to this edition of the book, respectively.

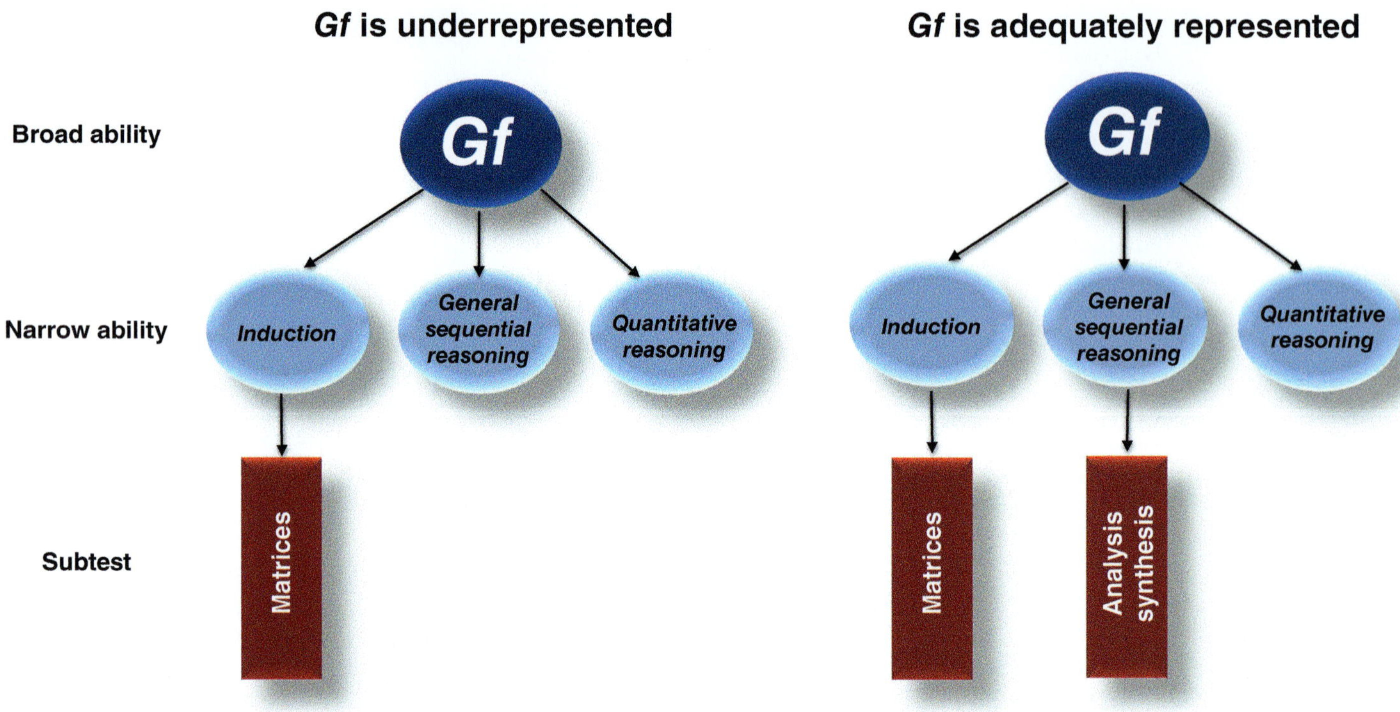


**FIGURE 1.6 Construct Representation. *Note:* At least two qualitatively different narrow ability indicators (subtests) are needed to draw inferences about the broad *Gf* ability**

## *Rapid Reference 1.5*

### XBA Revision Highlights

1. XBA is based primarily on current CHC theories (see McGrew, 2023) and the reclassification of all tests and subtests according to the most current CHC taxonomy (Schneider & McGrew, 2018).
2. All tests and subtests new to XBA were classified following a CHC expert consensus study (Appendix B).
3. XBA allows for the inclusion of neuropsychological constructs, such as attentional control, orthographic processing, psychomotor abilities, executive functions, sensory motor skills, and more.
4. The XBA method uses reliabilities and intercorrelations from the largest within-battery and cross-battery dataset currently available (Hajovsky et al., 2025; Appendices C and D) to create XBA composites.
5. Current research shows that the precision of XBA composites is similar to or the same as composites on norm-referenced tests (Appendix E).
6. While XBA principles remain the same, the procedure was substantially simplified because of improvements in automation via X-BASS 3.0.
7. XBA CHC composites can now be generated with up to six individual subtests (an increase from four).
8. All scores are entered into X-BASS on a single data entry tab, graphed, and organized into CHC domains, SLD areas (e.g., Basic Reading Skills, Math Calculation, Written Expression), and, if applicable, neuropsychological domains.
9. An XBA analysis is automatically conducted with one click of a button on the data entry tab.
10. Within-battery and cross-battery data are analyzed via a PSW analysis with one click of a button on the data entry tab.
11. Within-battery and cross-battery data are analyzed according to culture and language influences with one click of a button on the data entry tab.

## Rapid Reference 1.6

### What Is New to this Edition?

- Updated and simplified step-by-step guidance on conducting referral-relevant assessments (comprehensive and selective or diagnostic) to ensure evaluations are firmly grounded in current theory and research (e.g., Hajovsky et al., 2025; Schneider & McGrew, 2018) (Chapters 2 and 5).
- Step-by-step instructions in each chapter on how to use X-BASS.
- Updated CHC broad and narrow ability classifications of subtests based on a review of research, technical test manuals, and results of a CHC expert consensus study (see Appendix B).
- Current research on the relations between cognitive abilities and specific academic skills (see Appendix C) is used to inform decisions regarding specific learning disabilities.
- Discussion of the *True Peer Estimator* (TPE) for determining the degree of culture and language difference (Chapter 8).
- Improvements to the *Culture-Language Interpretive Matrix* (C-LIM) with new ways of viewing data and interpreting results (Chapter 8).
- Addition of the *Culture-Language Interpretive Matrix Achievement Test Extension* (C-LIM+ATE) (Chapter 8).
- Expansion of the *Dual Discrepancy/Consistency* (DD/C) method of SLD identification, including information on the probability that the user made accurate strength/weakness decisions and a summary of findings easily integrated into a report (Chapters 3 and 4, and Appendix F).
- Comprehensive guidance on how to proceed when the results of the PSW analysis are ambiguous (Chapter 4).
- Guidance on considering exclusionary factors in referrals for suspected learning disability (see Appendix G).
- Case studies demonstrating within-battery and cross-battery comprehensive and selective assessment, differential diagnosis, identification of SLD, and distinguishing learning differences from learning disabilities in individuals from diverse cultural and linguistic backgrounds. All case studies were completed using X-BASS (Chapters 5 through 8).
- Numerous examples of linking evaluation results to intervention (e.g., instructional strategies, remedial programs, compensatory strategies, and curricular and environmental modifications) (Chapter 9, and Appendices J, K, S, T, and U).

## RATIONALE FOR THE XBA METHOD

### Research to Practice

The XBA method has significant implications for research, practice, and test development. Regarding practice, the XBA method provided "a much-needed and updated bridge between current intellectual theory and research and practice" (Flanagan & McGrew, 1997, p. 322). The need for the XBA "bridge" was evident following Flanagan and colleagues' review of the results of several cross-battery factor analyses that were conducted prior to 2000 (Flanagan & Ortiz, 2001; Flanagan et al., 2002; McGrew & Flanagan, 1998). These results demonstrated that none of the cognitive and intelligence batteries in use at that time contained measures that sufficiently approximated the full range of broad abilities that defined the structure of cognitive abilities as specified in contemporary psychometric theory (e.g., Woodcock, 1990; see Table 1.2).

As may be seen in Table 1.2, of the major intelligence batteries in use before 2000, most failed to measure three or more broad CHC abilities (viz., *Ga*, *Glr*, *Gf*, *Gs*) that were (and are) considered important in understanding and predicting school achievement (see Chapter 2 for a summary). *Gf*, often considered to be the essence of intelligence, was either not measured or not measured adequately by most of the intelligence batteries used prior to 2000 (i.e., WISC-III, WAIS-R, WPPSI-R, K-ABC, and CAS) (Alfonso et al., 2005).

The finding that abilities not measured or underrepresented by cognitive and intelligence batteries are important for understanding students' learning difficulties provided much of the impetus for developing the XBA method (McGrew & Flanagan, 1998) and perhaps for engendering a movement away from sole or primary reliance on IQ in evaluating learning disabilities. The XBA method guided practitioners in selecting core and supplemental tests that provided sufficient measurement of abilities to explain plausible reasons for learning difficulties in the classroom.

Schneider and McGrew (2018) pointed out that "A pivotal foundation of CHC cross-battery assessment. . .which has contributed significantly to the extant construct validity evidence for the CHC model, has been CHC-organized XBA research" (p. 84), such as that conducted by Flanagan (2000), Reynolds et al. (2013), and more recently, Caemmerer et al. (2020). The CHC classification system that forms the foundation of the XBA method has improved communication among practitioners, led to improvements in research on the relations between cognitive and academic abilities (e.g., Hajovsky et al., 2025; Appendix C), and resulted in improvements in the measurement of cognitive constructs, as may be seen in the design and structure of current cognitive and intelligence batteries (e.g., WISC-V, WJ V). In summary, the XBA method has a strong research foundation. It addresses a long-standing need in assessment-related fields for a defensible assessment method for evaluating a broader range of abilities and processes. Comprehensive and selective XBA informs how students learn, how they are smart, and what may be impeding their ability to receive information from the environment and to store, process, and express that information.

## Test Development

Although there was substantial evidence of at least eight or nine CHC broad cognitive abilities by the late 1980s, the batteries of the time did not reflect this diversity in measurement. For example, Table 1.2 shows that the cognitive and intelligence batteries used at that time measured only two to three CHC broad abilities adequately. Table 1.2 shows that the WJ-R included measures of a wider range of broad cognitive abilities than other batteries. Nevertheless, many broad abilities were not measured adequately by the WJ-R (Alfonso et al., 2005; McGrew & Flanagan, 1998).

In general, Table 1.2 shows that *Gf*, *Gsm* (now *Gwm*), *Glr* (now *Gl* and *Gr*), *Ga*, and *Gs* were not measured adequately by most batteries published before 2000. It was clear that most test authors and publishers did not use contemporary psychometric theories of the structure of cognitive abilities to guide the development of their cognitive and intelligence batteries, resulting in a theory–practice gap, as demonstrated by Woodcock (1990) and others in the late 1990s through the mid-2000s (e.g., Alfonso et al., 2005; Flanagan & McGrew, 1997; Flanagan et al., 2000, 2013; Keith & Reynolds, 1997, 2005; McGrew, 2005, 2009; McGrew & Flanagan, 1998; Schneider & McGrew, 2012).

Table 1.3 parallels Table 1.2 but presents the most current cognitive and intelligence batteries. Several notable findings emerge when comparing Tables 1.2 and 1.3. First, coverage of *Gf* increased from 50% to 100%, meaning *Gf* is measured by all current batteries. Second, *Gc* continues to be adequately measured by most batteries. The CAS-2 is the only battery that does not measure *Gc*, but this was by design, as the CAS-2 operationalizes PASS theory rather than CHC theory. Third, while all batteries measured *Gv* adequately prior to 2000, it is now

**Table 1.2 Representation of Broad CHC Abilities on Eight Cognitive and Intelligence Batteries Published Prior to 2000**

| Battery | *Gf* | *Gc* | *Gv* | *Gsm** | *Glr** | *Ga* | *Gs* |
|---|---|---|---|---|---|---|---|
| WISC-III | × | √ | √ | • | × | × | √ |
| WAIS-R | × | √ | √ | • | × | × | • |
| WPPSI-R | × | √ | √ | • | × | × | • |
| K-ABC | • | × | √ | • | × | × | × |
| CAS | × | × | √ | • | × | × | √ |
| DAS | √ | √ | √ | • | • | × | • |
| WJ-R | √ | • | √ | • | • | • | • |
| SB:FE | √ | √ | √ | • | × | × | × |

*Note:* √ = Adequately measured; • = Underrepresented; × = Not measured.
* *Gsm* is now *Gwm* and *Glr* is now two broad abilities, *Gl* and *Gr*.
WISC-III = Wechsler Intelligence Scale for Children–Third Edition (Wechsler, 1991); WAIS-R = Wechsler Adult Intelligence Scale–Revised (Wechsler, 1981); WPPSI-R = Wechsler Preschool and Primary Scale of Intelligence–Revised (Wechsler, 1989); K-ABC = Kaufman Assessment Battery for Children (Kaufman & Kaufman, 1983); CAS = Cognitive Assessment System (Naglieri & Das, 1997); DAS = Differential Ability Scales (Elliott, 1990); WJ-R = Woodcock-Johnson Psycho-Educational Battery–Revised (Woodcock & Johnson, 1989); SB:FE = Stanford-Binet Intelligence Scale–Fourth Edition (Thorndike et al., 1986).

**Table 1.3 Representation of Broad CHC Abilities on Eight Current Cognitive and Intelligence Batteries**

| Battery | *Gf* | *Gc* | *Gv* | *Gwm* | *Gl* | *Gr* | *Ga* | *Gs* |
|---|---|---|---|---|---|---|---|---|
| WISC-V | √ | √ | • | √ | • | • | × | √ |
| WAIS-5 | √ | √ | • | √ | × | • | × | √ |
| WPPSI-IV | • | √ | √ | × | × | × | × | √ |
| K-ABC-II NU | √ | • | √ | • | • | × | × | × |
| DAS-II NU | √ | • | √ | √ | × | • | × | • |
| WJ V COG | √ | √ | • | √ | √ | √ | × | • |
| SB5 | √ | √ | • | • | × | × | × | × |
| CAS-2 | • | × | • | √ | × | • | × | √ |

*Note:* √ = Adequately measured; • = Underrepresented; × = Not measured.
WISC-V = Wechsler Intelligence Scale for Children-Fifth Edition (Wechsler, 2014); WAIS-5 = Wechsler Adult Intelligence Scale–Fifth Edition (Wechsler et al., 2024); WPPSI-IV = Wechsler Preschool and Primary Scale of Intelligence–Fourth Edition (Wechsler, 2012); K-ABC-II NU = Kaufman Assessment Battery for Children-Second Edition Normative Update (Kaufman & Kaufman, 2018); DAS-II NU = Differential Ability Scales-Second Edition Normative Update (Elliott, 2023); WJ V COG = Woodcock-Johnson V Tests of Cognitive Abilities (Laforte et al., 2025); SB5 = Stanford Binet Intelligence Scales-Fifth Edition (Roid, 2003); CAS-2 = Cognitive Assessment System-Second Edition (Naglieri et al., 2014).

underrepresented at 50%. This change is likely the result of research findings showing that Vz is the most well-supported of all *Gv* narrow abilities (see Schneider & McGrew, 2018, for further discussion). Also, the narrow ability of Visual Memory (MV) was cross-listed under *Gsm* and *Gv* in earlier versions of CHC theory, which may have led to seemingly better *Gv* construct representation on batteries used prior to 2000. Fourth, while *Gsm* was underrepresented on all batteries prior to 2000, over 50% of batteries now measure *Gwm* adequately. Fifth, only two subtests, one from the WJ-R and one from the DAS, measured *Glr*. Now, the WISC-V and WJ V are the only batteries that measure *Gl and Gr*, which are underrepresented in the former battery and adequately measured in the latter. Although measurement of these constructs has improved, they remain underrepresented or unmeasured in most current batteries. Sixth, prior to 2000, *Ga* was measured only by the WJ-R. To date, no cognitive or intelligence battery has added measures of *Ga*, and the WJ V COG no longer includes *Ga* tests. However, measures of *Ga* are included in the WJ V Virtual Test Library (VTL; Mather et al., 2025). It is likely that *Ga* is omitted from cognitive batteries deliberately because many achievement batteries and special-purpose tests measure the narrow ability of Phonetic Coding. Finally, the representation of *Gs* remains largely unchanged across current cognitive and intelligence batteries.

In summary, a wider range of CHC broad and narrow abilities is represented on current batteries than on their predecessors. Furthermore, greater attention was paid to adequate construct representation. Table 1.4 provides several salient examples of the impact of CHC theories on test development. Notwithstanding, to adequately represent all eight broad abilities listed in Table 1.3, the XBA method is necessary. One exception is the WJ V COG, which is co-normed with the VTL and measures Phonetic Coding (Ga:PC). Examples of adequate construct representation using some of the batteries listed in Table 1.3 are provided in Chapter 2.

## Guiding Principles of the XBA Method

To ensure that XBA procedures are theoretically and psychometrically sound, practitioners should adhere to a few guiding principles that have been refined over the years since the method was first introduced. These principles are described below.

1. *Select a comprehensive cognitive battery as your core battery in assessment*, ensuring that it (1) addresses referral concerns and (2) meets the examinee's unique needs. Standard core batteries include (but are not limited to) the Wechsler scales (e.g., WPPSI IV, WISC-V, WAIS-5), WJ V COG, DAS-II NU, KABC-II NU, and CAS-2.
2. *Use subtests and composites from a single battery or set of co-normed tests whenever possible to represent CHC broad and narrow abilities.* Norm-based composites are preferable to formula-generated composites that include subtests from different batteries. Notwithstanding, research shows that XBA composites are as precise as norm-based composites when generated with the same subtests (see Appendix E). Therefore, XBA composites may be used in the same way and for the same purposes as norm-based composites, *especially when there is ecological validity to support them*—a practice that should apply to norm-based composites as well (see Appendices H and P). Note that it is typically necessary to cross batteries for specific purposes, including (1) to broaden an evaluation, (2) to follow up on aberrant scores, and (3) to test hypotheses about unusual patterns in the data. The XBA method is the most psychometrically defensible way to meet these purposes. Chapter 2 details how cross-battery composites are organized, analyzed, and interpreted.
3. *When a broad ability is underrepresented or not measured by the core battery, supplement with subtests and corresponding composites from another battery*. For example, suppose an evaluator is interested in measuring Retrieval Fluency (*Gr*), and the core battery has only one or no *Gr* subtests, or two *Gr* subtests that measure the same narrow ability. In either case, the evaluator should select two qualitatively different indicators of *Gr* from another battery or a *Gr* composite from another battery to supplement the core battery. This practice ensures that actual norms are used to interpret broad-ability performance.

   Note that it is not always necessary to assess an ability broadly via two qualitatively different indicators. For example, the WAIS-5 has a Visual Spatial Index (VSI) that comprises two subtests—Block Design and Visual Puzzles—that measure the narrow Visualization (Vz) ability. As such, the VSI is better described as a measure of Vz, rather than the broad *Gv* ability. Based on the nature of the referral, however, a Vz composite may be sufficient. Moreover, Vz has the lion's share of research to support it compared to all other *Gv* narrow abilities. Unlike broad abilities, which are typically represented by two qualitatively distinct narrow-ability measures, narrow abilities are often underrepresented on cognitive batteries. This is because most batteries do not contain two or more measures of the *same* narrow ability. When batteries are crossed, X-BASS can be used to generate theoretically and psychometrically defensible narrow ability composites.
4. *Select subtests from the smallest number of batteries that were normed within 10–12 years of one another* to minimize the effect of spurious differences between test scores that may be attributable to differences in the characteristics of independent norm samples (McGrew, 1994). When tests and subtests are carefully selected and tailored to address well-defined referral concerns, it is typically not necessary to cross more than two or three batteries, depending on the evaluator's access to batteries (Shanock et al., 2022). Nearly all batteries included in X-BASS were normed within the past 12 years.
5. *Establish ecological validity for test performances that are suggestive of normative weaknesses or deficits.* The identification of a cognitive weakness or deficit is meaningless without evidence of its manifestation in activities of daily living, including academic performance in the classroom (Mascolo et al., 2014). The validity of test findings is bolstered when clear connections are made between the cognitive weakness and its educational impact. Furthermore, manifestations of weaknesses provide a focus for intervention (see Appendices H and P for a comprehensive list of manifestations of cognitive and academic weaknesses by grade level, respectively).

Once the practitioner has completed the evaluation, scores are entered into X-BASS for analysis and to determine whether a follow-up assessment is necessary. The next and final section of this chapter is a brief tutorial on how to begin using X-BASS. Data analysis is covered in detail in subsequent chapters.

**Table 1.4 Impact of CHC Theory and XBA CHC Classifications on Cognitive and Intelligence Test Development**

| Test (Year of Publication)<br>Impact | Revision (Year of Publication)<br>Impact |
|---|---|
| **WISC-IV (2003)**<br>Minor. Eliminated Verbal and Performance IQs; replaced the Freedom from Distractibility Index with the Working Memory Index; replaced the Perceptual Organization Index with the Perceptual Reasoning Index; included the measurement of fluid reasoning by adding the Matrix Reasoning and Picture Concepts subtests; enhanced measurement of Processing Speed with the Cancellation subtest. | **WISC-V (2014)**<br>Minor to moderate. CHC theory was one guiding factor in the development of this battery; the PRI was divided into the Fluid Reasoning Index (*Gf*) and Visual Spatial Index (*Gv*); a Glr factor was added that assessed associative memory and retrieval fluency; improvements were made in the measurement of working memory and fluid reasoning. |
| **WAIS-IV (2008)**<br>Minor to moderate. Eliminated Verbal and Performance IQs; replaced the Perceptual Organization Index with the Perceptual Reasoning Index; enhanced the measurement of fluid reasoning by adding the Figure Weights and Visual Puzzles subtests; enhanced the measurement of Processing Speed with the Cancellation subtest; enhanced the measurement of memory with the Working Memory Index. | **WAIS-5 (2025)**<br>Moderate to major. Includes many composites based on CHC theories; these include the Verbal-Expanded Crystallized Index, Expanded Fluid Index, and Expanded Working Memory Index; also included are more cognitively complex subtests such as Running Digits and Set Relations. |
| **WPPSI-III (2002)**<br>Minor. Incorporated measures of Processing Speed that yielded a Processing Speed Quotient based on recent research indicating the importance of processing speed for early academic success; enhanced the measurement of fluid reasoning by adding the Matrix Reasoning and Picture Concepts subtests. | **WPPSI-IV (2012)**<br>Minor. Eliminated Verbal and Performance IQs; enhanced measures of working memory, processing speed, and inhibitory control. |
| **K-ABC (1983)**<br>No obvious impact. | **KABC-II (2007)/KABC-II NU* (2018)**<br>Moderate to major. Provided a second global score that includes fluid and crystallized abilities; included several new subtests measuring reasoning; interpretation of test performance may be based on either CHC theory or Luria's theory; includes measures of five CHC broad abilities. |
| **WJ IV (2014)**<br>Major. Used expanded CHC theory (Schneider & McGrew, 2012) and introduced cognitive complexity in test development; changed Gsm to *Gwm*; added attentional control (AC) under *Gwm*; added speed of lexical access (LA) under Glr; added a *Gf-Gc* composite; brought back Scholastic Aptitude Clusters; added an Oral Language battery; provided adequate measurement of 10 broad CHC abilities across three co-normed batteries. | **WJ V (2025)**<br>Major. Used CHC theories as the blueprint for the battery; includes a Virtual Test Library (VTL) to supplement the primary batteries; includes many new or revised tests as well as new or revised clusters such as the Retrieval Fluency; covers the greatest breadth of CHC broad and narrow abilities across the two primary batteries and VTL than any other battery, as the WJ V COG, ACH, and VTL are co-normed. |
| **SB: IV (1986)**<br>Minor. Used a three-level hierarchical model of the structure of cognitive abilities to guide the construction of the test: The top level included a general reasoning factor or *g*; the middle level included three broad factors called Crystallized Abilities, Fluid-Analytic Abilities, and Short-Term Memory; the third level included more specific factors, including Verbal Reasoning, Quantitative Reasoning, and Abstract/Visual Reasoning. | **SB5 (2003)**<br>Minor to moderate. Used CHC theory to guide test development; increased the number of measures of fluid reasoning; included a Working Memory Factor based on research, indicating its importance for academic success. |
| **DAS (1990)**<br>No obvious impact. | **DAS-II (2007)/DAS-II NU* (2023)**<br>Moderate to major. Measures seven broad CHC abilities and also includes measures of certain narrow abilities not found on other major cognitive batteries (e.g., F6 or free recall memory). |

* The normative update (NU) did not change the content or structure of the battery.

## GETTING STARTED WITH X-BASS

X-BASS opens to a dashboard shown in Figure 1.7. The first time you open X-BASS, you will see "NOTIFICATIONS: ON" in the top right corner. This means that you will receive pop-up messages instructing you along the way. One of the initial pop-ups ask whether you would like to review the "GUIDE," which provides orientation to the program, system requirements, frequently asked questions, and more. You may return to the guide at any time by going to the dashboard and clicking the bottom-left button. Directly below the notifications option, there are two additional options labeled "HELP" and "NEXT." The help option describes where you are in the program (e.g., the purpose of the tab you are on), and the next option tells you what to do next. It is recommended that you enter at least one case into X-BASS before turning off notifications. When you do turn them off, each tab will display, in the exact location, "NOTIFICATIONS: OFF." You may click notifications on and off at any time while using the program.

The top blue-shaded area on the dashboard is where you enter the examinee's name, grade, and age, as well as the evaluator's name. If the examinee is a multilingual learner, be sure to check the box just below the space for the evaluator's name. By checking this box, the program will perform specific operations differently than for monolingual English-speaking peers, as described in Chapter 8. After entering the identifying information, click the "**CREATE RECORD**" button, which appears directly below "NO ACTIVE DATA RECORD" on the top right of your screen. When you create the record, the blue shading disappears, and the aforementioned text changes to "DATA RECORD IS ACTIVE" as shown in Figure 1.8.

Figure 1.8 also shows that the examinee's name appears in a drop-down menu containing all the records saved (the arrow on the left side of the figure points to this menu). Note that X-BASS can store over 100 cases, to which you can return at any time. The recommended next step is to click the "DATA ENTRY" button (see the arrow on the right side of the figure pointing to its location on the dashboard).

Figure 1.9 shows the data entry tab. When you start data entry on the data entry tab, you can move your data to other tabs for analysis. If you start data entry on another tab (e.g., XBA tab, C-LIM tab), your scores cannot be transferred from that tab to the data entry tab. At the top left of Figure 1.9, you will see a place to select a test or battery. You can begin entering either the test or battery name or its acronym, and the full name will appear. At the same time, all composites and subtests will appear in the spaces below the battery name, in the same order they appear on the battery's record form. The data entry tab contains 124 tests and batteries and over 1,100 subtests. The tests and batteries included in X-BASS are listed in Appendix I.

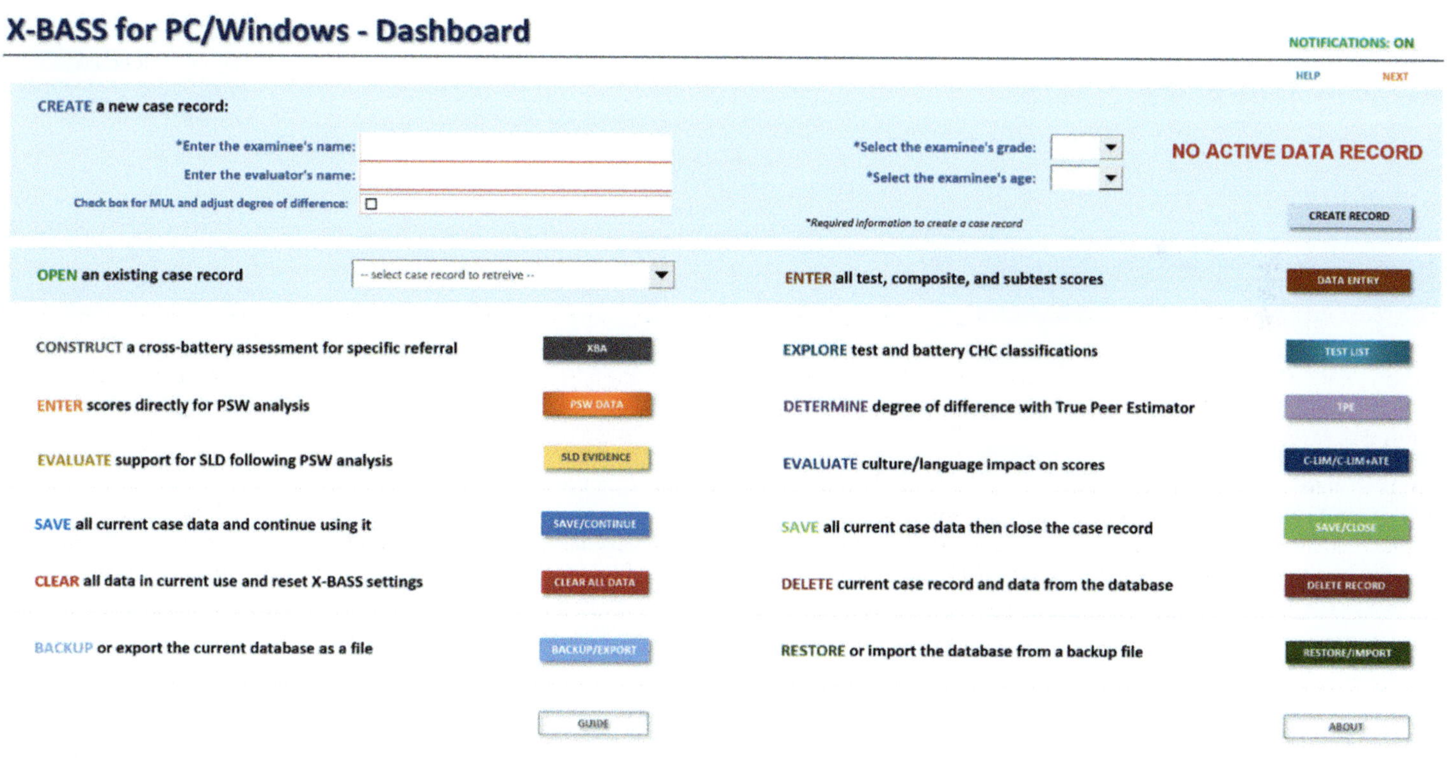


**FIGURE 1.7 X-BASS 3.0 Dashboard**

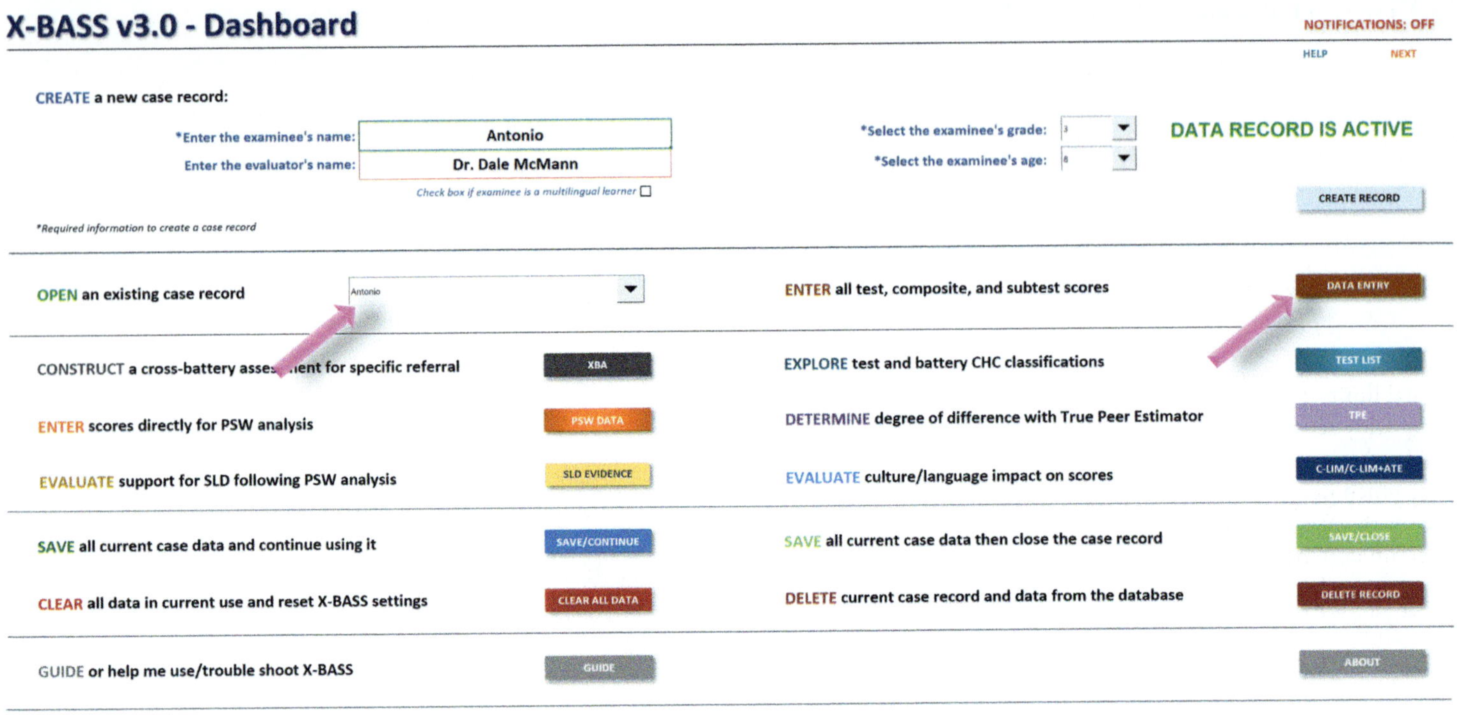


**FIGURE 1.8 Completing a Case Record**

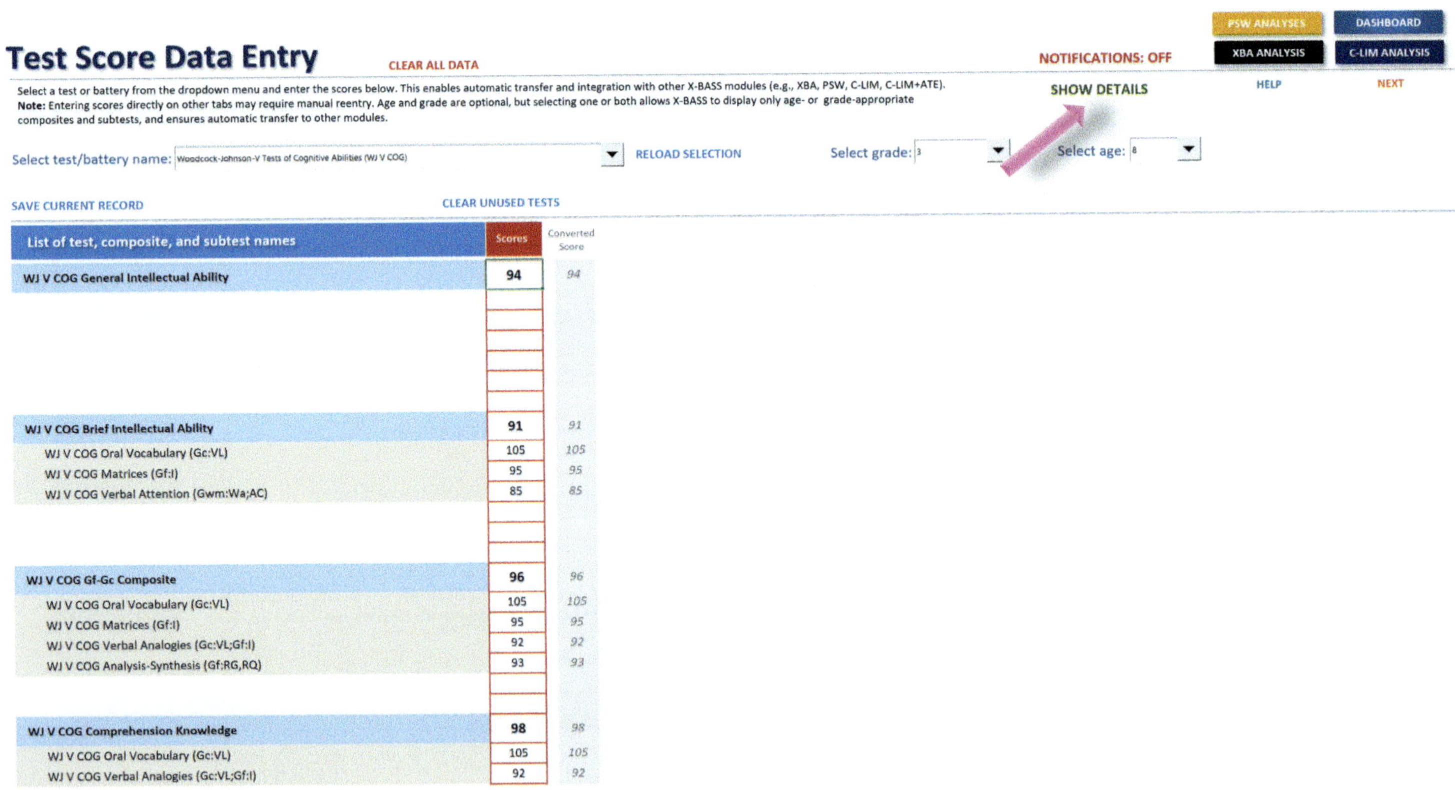


**FIGURE 1.9 Data Entry Tab**

Figure 1.9 shows ample white space to the right of the data entry column. The decision to leave this area blank was intentional, as one of the primary purposes of this version of X-BASS was to reduce the amount of visible information and details throughout the program. Details can be accessed by clicking "**SHOW DETAILS**" (see the arrow at the top right of the figure pointing to its location on the data entry tab). You can also "**HIDE DETAILS.**"

> **DON'T FORGET**
>
> Always enter your data on the DATA ENTRY tab. If you choose to begin data entry on another tab (e.g., the XBA tab), you will not be able to transfer your scores to the data entry tab.

By clicking "**SHOW DETAILS,**" you can view either a score graph (top left arrow) or a domain summary (top right arrow), or both, as shown in Figure 1.10. The score graph shows where scores fall within a normal distribution of standard scores from 40 to 160. The light shading on the score graph shows the Average range of ability (i.e., standard scores of 90–110). The darker shading on the left and right sides of Average extends the shading to encompass standard scores from 85 to 115, generally referred to as "within normal limits" (WNL) or "within typical limits" (WTL). As you scroll down this tab, you can quickly see where test scores fall for the examinee.

> **DON'T FORGET**
>
> If you do not see a composite you believe should have been graphed in a CHC or SLD domain, on the DATA ENTRY tab, scroll down to "MX – Mixed Composites," where it is most likely graphed.

The domain summary shows scores organized according to the current CHC taxonomy, which may differ from how the test developer and publisher group scores. For example, on the WJ IV, the *Gf* composite included Number Series and Concept Formation. Based on current research, the Number Series test is best interpreted as a measure of math achievement (see Laforte et al., 2025; Schneider, 2016), which falls under *Gq* (Quantitative Knowledge) rather than *Gf*. Therefore, the score graph shows these two subtest scores directly beneath the *Gf* composite, whereas the domain summary does not show the WJ IV *Gf* composite in the *Gf* domain graph. This may appear to be an error at first glance. However, the WJ IV *Gf* composite is now considered "mixed" (MX), comprising one *Gq* and one *Gf* test. Therefore, the WJ IV *Gf* composite is graphed at the bottom of the domain summary column under a domain called "**MX – Mixed Composites.**" Because batteries carried over from X-BASS v2.0 to X-BASS v3.0 were reclassified, you may encounter other examples like this one on other batteries.

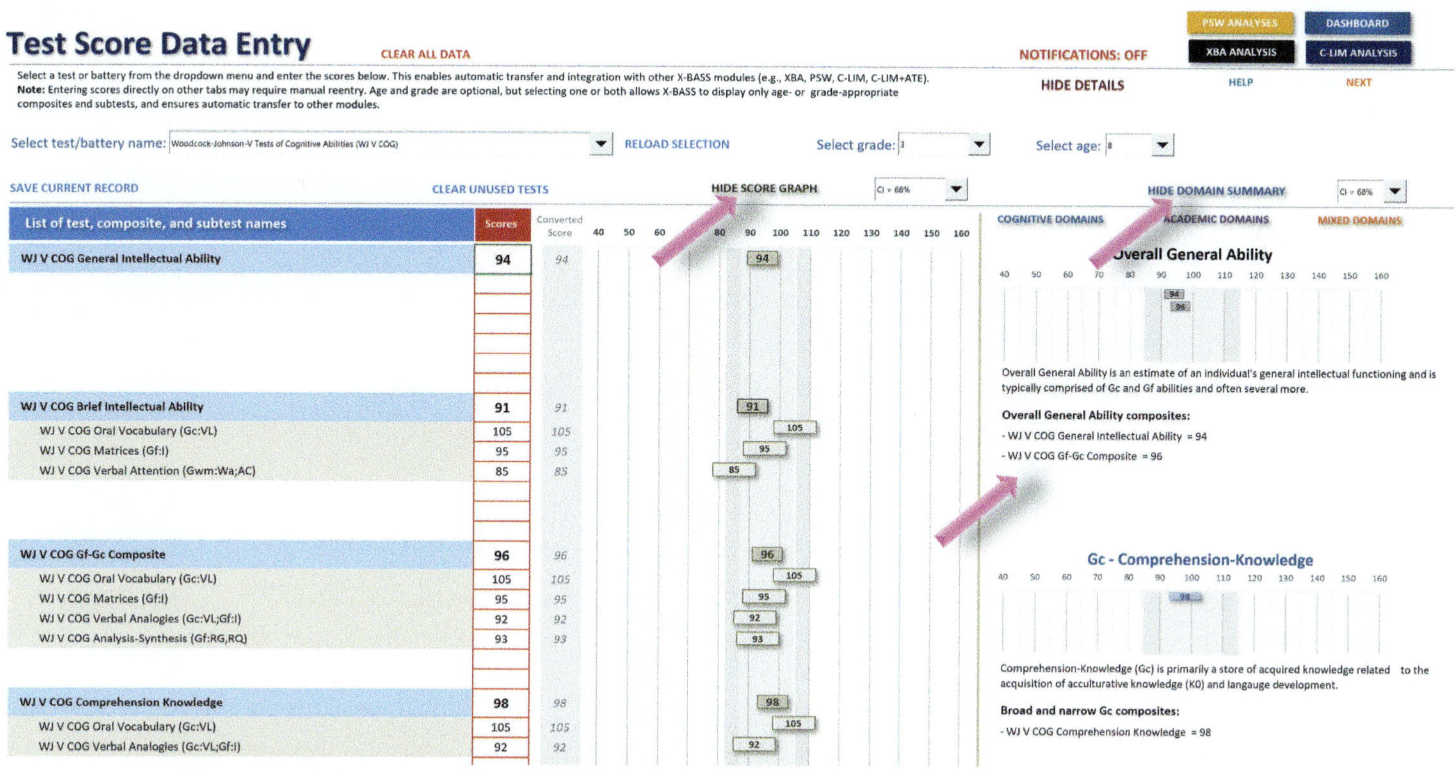


**FIGURE 1.10 Viewing Additional Details on the Data Entry Tab**

After entering scores for the WJ V COG, as shown in Figure 1.10, you may enter scores from another battery, such as the WJ V ACH. Begin typing the name or acronym for the WJ V ACH, and the name will automatically populate. At the same time, any WJ V COG test names for which no score was entered will disappear to ensure there is enough room for the next test or battery. In this example, the WJ V ACH composites and comprising tests will be displayed automatically directly below the last score entered for the WJ V COG, as shown in Figure 1.11. You may repeat this process until you have entered all scores from your evaluation. Note that the data entry tab can accommodate up to 40 composites and their subtests. Be sure to "SAVE CURRENT RECORD" after entering your scores. This option appears just below and to the left of the dropdown menu on the Data Entry tab. This option also appears on the Dashboard and at the bottom of all tabs. Rapid Reference 1.7 provides critical information on saving and storing your data within the program.

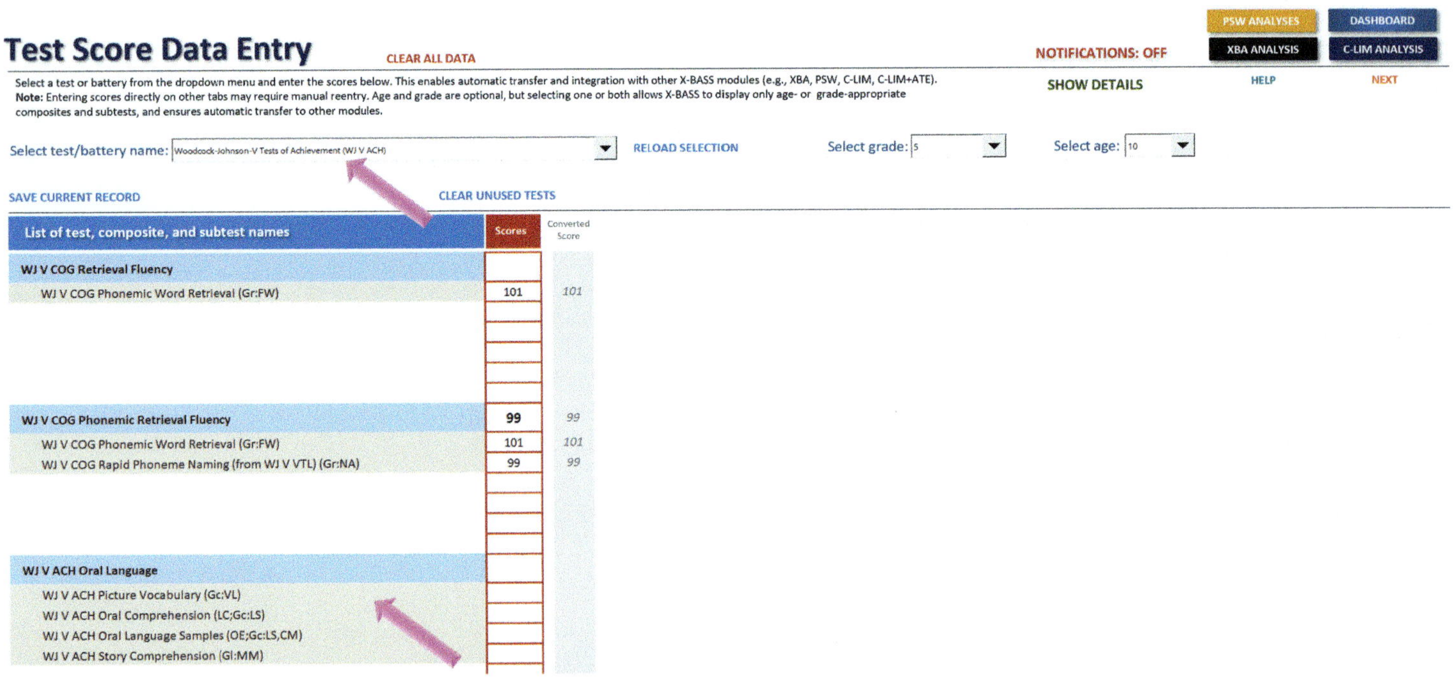


**FIGURE 1.11 Adding Additional Tests on the Data Entry Tab**

## Rapid Reference 1.7

### How to Save Data and a Case Record Within X-BASS

On the Dashboard, there are four buttons related to saving and deleting data, as shown below. The "SAVE/CONTINUE" button will save your data just as the "SAVE CURRENT RECORD" option.

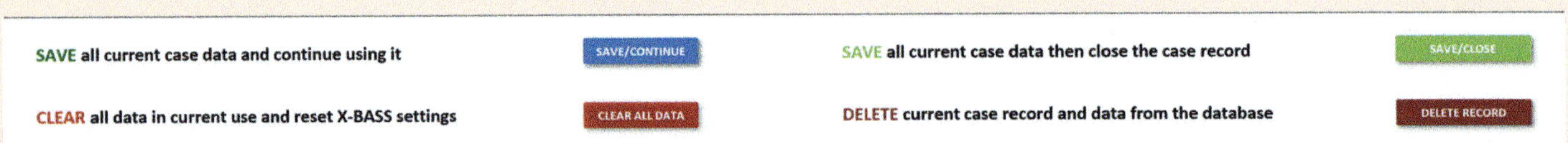


- The "CLEAR ALL DATA" button will delete all data on all tabs but will not delete any saved case records. This button resets X-BASS so that you can begin entering data for a new case. The only time you would use this button is if you do not want to keep the data you entered. If you want to keep the data, use the "SAVE/CLOSE" button.
- The "SAVE/CLOSE" button will save the current record and close it. This allows you to return to that record at any time in the future, as it is stored in the program and appears in the drop-down menu on the Dashboard.
- The "DELETE RECORD" button allows you to delete a case record that you previously saved so that it no longer appears in the drop-down menu on the Dashboard.

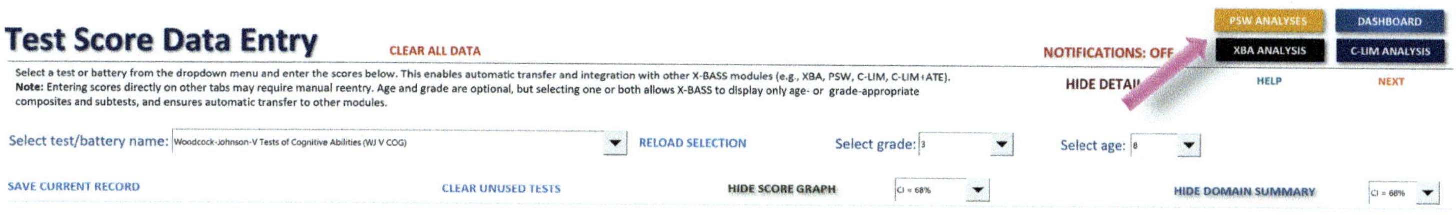


**FIGURE 1.12 Transferring Data from the Data Entry Tab**

After you have completed entering all scores, the next step is to analyze them. To do this, click on one of the buttons on the top right of the screen corresponding to the type of analysis you wish to conduct. The arrow in Figure 1.12 points to the location of these buttons on the Data Entry tab. There are four buttons. Three of them are for a type of analysis, and the fourth is a button that will take you back to the Dashboard. The three types of analyses you may conduct are: (1) an XBA analysis that will group all data according to CHC domain and SLD area and provide information related to composite cohesion and follow-up assessment, which is described in the next chapter; (2) a PSW analysis that will organize your scores and analyze them according to the DD/C method and guide you through the SLD decision-making process, as described in Chapters 3 and 4; and (3) a C-LIM analysis of test score validity for multilingual learners, as described in Chapter 8.

## CONCLUSIONS

The XBA method allows practitioners to augment or supplement any ability battery to ensure reliable and valid measurement of a broader range of abilities, in a manner consistent with contemporary theory and research. The foundation upon which the XBA method was built, along with its guiding principles and procedures, provides a systematic approach to construct a theoretically driven, comprehensive, and valid assessment of abilities that is responsive to referral concerns. X-BASS provides an efficient way to organize, analyze, and interpret data for different purposes, as described in Chapter 2.

### TEST YOURSELF

**1. The primary purpose of the XBA method is to:**

(a) increase Full Scale IQ interpretability.

(b) replace norm-referenced intelligence tests.

(c) narrow the theory–practice gap by aligning assessment with contemporary theory and psychometrics.

(d) maximize the number of subtests administered.

**2. According to the chapter, which of the following best distinguishes cross-battery assessment from a flexible battery approach?**

(a) use of multiple tests

(b) reliance on expert judgment

(c) adherence to systematic, theory- and psychometric-based rules

(d) emphasis on qualitative interpretation

**3. An example of construct underrepresentation is interpreting a single narrow ability measure as representative of a broad CHC ability. True or False?**

**4. When a broad ability is underrepresented on a core battery, XBA principles recommend:**

(a) interpreting the available composite cautiously without supplementing.

(b) supplementing with qualitatively different indicators from another battery.

(c) relying on a general ability score.

(d) postponing interpretation until additional normed data are available.

**5. Establishing ecological validity in XBA requires demonstrating that test-based weaknesses are meaningfully related to real-world functioning, including academic performance. True or False?**

**6. Which of the following statements best reflects the role of X-BASS?**

(a) X-BASS replaces professional judgment in assessment.

(b) X-BASS automates XBA procedures while preserving theoretical and psychometric rigor.

(c) X-BASS standardizes cross-battery norms.

(d) X-BASS limits assessments to within-battery analyses.

**7. Based on revisions to the CHC taxonomy, Long-Term Storage and Retrieval (Glr) was replaced by:**

(a) Learning Efficiency (*Gl*) and Retrieval Fluency (*Gr*).

(b) Attentional Control (AC) and Working Memory (WM).

(c) Perceptual Speed (*Gs*) and Processing Speed (*Gt*).

(d) It wasn't replaced.

**8. The XBA method is currently grounded primarily in:**

(a) *Gf–Gc* theory only.

(b) PASS theory and neuropsychological models.

(c) CHC theory, with selective integration of neuropsychological theory.

(d) Hierarchical g-theory.

**9. Fluid Reasoning (*Gf*), Comprehension Knowledge (*Gc*), and Processing Speed (*Gs*) are examples of:**

(a) general (stratum III) abilities.

(b) broad (stratum II) abilities.

(c) narrow (stratum I) abilities.

(d) intermediate factors.

**10. Narrow ability classifications were developed primarily to:**

(a) replace broad ability interpretation.

(b) improve the construct representation of composites.

(c) reduce administration time.

(d) support g-level interpretation.

*Answers:* 1. c; 2. c; 3. True; 4. b; 5. True; 6. b; 7. a; 8. c; 9. b; 10. b

## REFERENCES


Alfonso, V. C., Flanagan, D. P., & Radwan, S. (2005). The impact of the Cattell-Horn-Carroll theory on test development and interpretation of cognitive and academic abilities. In D. P. Flanagan & P. L. Harrison (Eds.), *Contemporary intellectual assessment: Theories, tests, and issues* (2nd ed, pp. 185–202). Guilford Press, New York, NY.

Bailey, D. H., Duncan, G. J., Watts, T., Clements, D. H., & Sarama, J. (2018). Risky business: Correlation and causation in longitudinal studies of skill development. *American Psychologist*, *73*(1), 81–94.

Barbey, A. K. (2018). Network neuroscience theory of human intelligence. *Trends in Cognitive Sciences*, *22*(1), 8–20.

Bornovalova, M. A., Choate, A. M., Fatimah, H., Petersen, K. J., & Wiernik, B. M. (2020). Appropriate use of bifactor analysis in psychopathology research: Appreciating benefits and limitations. *Biological Psychiatry*, *88*(1), 18–27.

Briggs, S. R., & Cheek, J. M. (1986). The role of factor analysis in the development and evaluation of personality scales. In special issue: Methodological developments in personality research. *Journal of Personality*, *54*(1), 106–148.

Burgoyne, A. P., Mashburn, C. A., Tsukahara, J. S., & Engle, R. W. (2022). Attention control and process overlap theory: Searching for cognitive processes underpinning the positive manifold. *Intelligence*, *91*, 101–629.

Caemmerer, J. M., & Reynolds, M. R. (2020). The relation between intelligence and academic achievement: A meta-analysis. *Intelligence*, *79*, 101449.

Caemmerer, J. M., Keith, T. Z., & Reynolds, M. R. (2020). Beyond individual intelligence tests: Application of Cattell-Horn-Carroll theory. *Intelligence*, *79*, 101433.

Canivez, G. L., & McGill, R. J. (2016). Factor structure of the differential ability scales–second edition: Exploratory and hierarchical factor analyses with the core subtests. *Psychological Assessment*, *28*(11), 1475–1488.

Carroll, J. B. (1997). The three-stratum theory of cognitive abilities. In D. P. Flanagan, J. L. Genshaft, & P. L. Harrison (Eds.), *Contemporary intellectual assessment: Theories, tests, and issues* (pp. 122–130). Guilford Press.

Carroll, J. B. (1998). Foreword. In K. S. McGrew & D. P. Flanagan (Eds.), *The intelligence test desk reference: Gf-Gc cross-battery assessment* (pp. xi–xii). Allyn & Bacon.

Carroll, J. B. (1993). *Human cognitive abilities: A survey of factor-analytic studies*. Cambridge University Press.

Carroll, J. B., & Horn, J. L. (1981). On the scientific basis of ability testing. *American Psychologist*, *36*(10), 1012–1020. https://doi.org/10.1037/0003-066X.36.10.1012.

Cattell, R. B. (1941). An objective test of character-temperament: I. *The Journal of General Psychology, 25*(1), 59–73.

Colom, R., Haier, R. J., Head, K., Álvarez-Linera, J., Quiroga, M. Á., Shih, P. C., & Jung, R. E. (2009). Gray matter correlates of fluid, crystallized, and spatial intelligence: Testing the P-FIT model. *Intelligence, 37*(2), 124–135.

Compton, D. L., Fuchs, L. S., Fuchs, D., Lambert, W., & Hamlett, C. (2012). The cognitive and academic profiles of reading and mathematics learning disabilities. *Journal of Learning Disabilities, 45*(1), 79–95.

Comrey, A. L. (1988). Factor-analytic methods of scale development in personality and clinical psychology. *Journal of Consulting and Clinical Psychology, 56*, 754–761.

Conway, A. R., Kovacs, K., Hao, H., Rosales, K. P., & Snijder, J. P. (2021). Individual differences in attention and intelligence: A united cognitive/psychometric approach. *Journal of Intelligence, 9*(3), 34.

Daniel, M. H. (1997). Intelligence testing: Status and trends. *American Psychologist, 52*(10), 1038–1045.

Decker, S., Fillmore, P. T., & Roberts, A. (2017). Coherence: The measurement and application of brain connectivity. *NeuroRegulation, 4*(1), 3–3.

Decker, S. L. (2008). School neuropsychology consultation in neurodevelopmental disorders. *Psychology in the Schools, 45*, 799–811.

Decker, S. L. (2021). Don't use a bifactor model unless you believe the true structure is bifactor. *Journal of Psychoeducational Assessment, 39*(1), 39–49.

Decker, S. L., Bridges, R. M., Luedke, J. C., & Eason, M. J. (2021). Dimensional evaluation of cognitive measures: Methodological confounds and theoretical concerns. *Journal of Psychoeducational Assessment, 39*(1), 3–27. https://doi.org/10.1177/0734282920940879.

Decker, S. L., Bridges, R. M., & Vetter, T. (2018). Cognitive neuroscientific contributions to theoretical understanding of SLD. In V. C. Alfonso & D. P. Flanagan (Eds.), *Essentials of specific learning disabilities identification* (2nd ed, pp. 285–306). Wiley.

Dombrowski, S. C., Canivez, G. L., & Watkins, M. W. (2018). Factor structure of the 10 WISC-V primary subtests across four standardization age groups. *Contemporary School Psychology, 22*(1), 90–104.

Dombrowski, S. C., Canivez, G. L., Watkins, M. W., & Beaujean, A. A. (2015). Exploratory bifactor analysis of the Wechsler intelligence scale for children—fifth edition with the 16 primary and secondary subtests. *Intelligence, 53*, 194–201.

Dombrowski, S. C., McGill, R. J., & Canivez, G. L. (2017). Exploratory and hierarchical factor analysis of the WJ-IV cognitive at school age. *Psychological Assessment, 29*(4), 394–407.

Dombrowski, S. C., McGill, R. J., Canivez, G. L., Watkins, M. W., & Beaujean, A. A. (2021). Factor analysis and variance partitioning in intelligence test research: Clarifying misconceptions. *Journal of Psychoeducational Assessment, 39*, 28–38.

Duke, N. K., & Cartwright, K. B. (2021). The science of reading progresses: Communicating advances beyond the simple view of reading. *Reading Research Quarterly, 56*(S1), S25–S44. https://doi.org/10.1002/rrq.411.

Elliott, C. D. (1990). *Differential ability scales*. The Psychological Corporation.

Elliott, C. D. (2023). *Differential ability scales* (2nd ed). Pearson. Normative update.

Evans, J. J., Floyd, R. G., McGrew, K. S., & Leforgee, M. H. (2002). The relations between measures of Cattell-Horn-Carroll (CHC) cognitive abilities and reading achievement during childhood and adolescence. *School Psychology Review, 31*(2), 246–262.

Farmer, R. L., McGill, R. J., Dombrowski, S. C., & Canivez, G. L. (2021a). Why questionable assessment practices remain popular in school psychology: Instructional materials as pedagogic vehicles. *Canadian Journal of School Psychology, 36*(2), 98–114.

Farmer, R. L., Zaheer, I., Duhon, G. J., & Ghazal, S. (2021b). Reducing low-value practices a functional-contextual consideration to aid in de-implementation efforts. *Canadian Journal of School Psychology, 36*(2), 153–165.

Flanagan, D. P. (2025). The Woodcock-Johnson V: Fifty years of excellence in ability assessment. *Journal of Psychoeducational Assessment, 43*(8), 799–801.

Flanagan, D. P., Alfonso, V. C., Mascolo, J. T., & Hale, J. B. (2011). The Wechsler intelligence scale for children–fourth edition in neuropsychological practice. In A. S. Davis (Ed.), *Handbook of pediatric neuropsychology* (pp. 397–414). Springer.

Flanagan, D. P., Alfonso, V. C., Ortiz, S. O., & Dynda, A. M. (2010). Integrating cognitive assessment in school neuropsychological evaluations. In D. C. Miller (Ed.), *Best practices in school neuropsychology: Guidelines for effective practice, assessment, and evidence-based intervention* (pp. 101–140). Wiley.

Flanagan, D. P., Alfonso, V. C., Zinkiewicz, C. J., Ortiz, S. O., & Dynda, A. M. (2022). An integrative theoretical framework for cognitive test interpretation in school neuropsychological evaluations. In D. C. Miller, D. E. Maricle, C. L. Bedford, & J. A. Gettman (Eds.), *Best practices in school neuropsychology: Guidelines for effective practice, assessment, and evidence-based intervention* (2nd ed, pp. 87–119). Wiley. https://doi.org/10.1002/9781119790563.ch6.

Flanagan, D. P., Costa, M., Palma, K., Leahy, M. A., Alfonso, V. C., & Ortiz, S. O. (2018). Cross-battery assessment, the cross-battery assessment software system, and the assessment–intervention connection. In D. P. Flanagan & E. M. McDonough (Eds.), *Contemporary intellectual assessment: Theories, tests, and issues* (4th ed, pp. 731–776). Guilford Press.

Flanagan, D. P., & McGrew, K. S. (1997). A cross-battery approach to assessing and interpreting cognitive abilities: Narrowing the gap between practice and cognitive science. In D. P. Flanagan, J. L. Genshaft, & P. L. Harrison (Eds.), *Contemporary intellectual assessment: Theories, tests, and issues* (pp. 314–325). Guilford Press.

Flanagan, D. P., & McGrew, K. S. (1998). Interpreting intelligence tests from modern *Gf-Gc* theory: Joint confirmatory factor analysis of the WJ-R and Kaufman adolescent and adult intelligence test (KAIT). *Journal of School Psychology, 36*, 151–182.

Flanagan, D. P., McGrew, K. S., & Ortiz, S. O. (2000). *The Wechsler intelligence scales and Gf-Gc theory: A contemporary approach to interpretation*. Allyn & Bacon.

Flanagan, D. P., & Ortiz, S. O. (2001). *Essentials of cross-battery assessment*. Wiley.

Flanagan, D. P., Ortiz, S. O., & Alfonso, V. C. (2013). *Essentials of cross-battery assessment* (3rd ed). Wiley.

Flanagan, D. P., Ortiz, S. O., & Alfonso, V. C. (2017). *Cross-battery assessment software system 2.0 (X-BASS 2.0)*. Wiley.

Flanagan, D. P., Ortiz, S. O., & Alfonso, V. C. (2025). *Cross-battery assessment software system 3.0 (X-BASS 3.0)*. Wiley.

Flanagan, D. P., Ortiz, S. O., Alfonso, V. C., & Mascolo, J. T. (2002). *The achievement test desk reference (ADTR): Comprehensive assessment and learning disabilities*. Allyn & Bacon.

Flanagan, D. P., Ortiz, S. O., Alfonso, V. C., & Mascolo, J. T. (2006). *The achievement test desk reference (ADTR): A guide to learning disability identification*. Allyn & Bacon.

Gottfredson, L. S. (2002). Where and why g matters: Not a mystery. *Human Performance, 15*(1–2), 25–46.

Guilford, J. P. (1954). *Psychometric methods* (2nd ed). McGraw-Hill.

Gustafsson, J.-E., & Undheim, J. O. (1996). Individual differences in cognitive functions. In D. C. Berliner & R. C. Calfee (Eds.), *Handbook of educational psychology* (pp. 186–242). Macmillan Library Reference USA: Prentice Hall International.

Haier, R. J., Colom, R., Schroeder, D. H., Condon, C. A., Tang, C., Eaves, E., & Head, K. (2009). Gray matter and intelligence factors: Is there a neuro-g? *Intelligence, 37*(2), 136–144.

Haier, R. J., & Jung, R. E. (2018). The parieto-frontal integration theory: Assessing intelligence from brain images. In *Contemporary intellectual assessment: Theories, tests, and issues* (4th ed, pp. 219–224). Guilford Press.

Hajovsky, D. B., Niileksela, C. R., Flanagan, D. P., Alfonso, V. C., Schneider, J., & Zinkiewicz, C. J. (2022, August 4–7). *A consensus model of cognitive-achievement relations using meta-SEM* [Poster Presentation]. American Psychological Association, Minneapolis, MN, United States.

Hajovsky, D. B., Niileksela, C. R., Flanagan, D. P., Alfonso, V. C., Schneider, W. J., & Robbins, J. (2025). Toward a consensus model of cognitive–reading achievement relations using meta-structural equation modeling. *Journal of Intelligence, 13*(8), 104.

Hale, J. B., & Fiorello, C. A. (2004). *School neuropsychology: A practitioner's handbook.* Guilford Press.

Hale, J. B., Wycoff, K. L., & Fiorello, C. A. (2011). RTI and cognitive hypothesis testing for specific learning disabilities identification and intervention: The best of both worlds. In D. P. Flanagan & V. C. Alfonso (Eds.), *Essentials of specific learning disability identification* (pp. 173–202). Wiley.

Horn, J. L. (1991). Measurement of intellectual capabilities: A review of theory. In K. S. McGrew, J. K. Werder, & R. W. Woodcock (Eds.), *Woodcock-Johnson technical manual* (pp. 197–232). Riverside.

Horn, J. L., & Noll, J. (1997). Human cognitive capabilities: *Gf-Gc* theory. In D. P. Flanagan, J. L. Genshaft, & P. L. Harrison (Eds.), *Contemporary intellectual assessment: Theories, tests and issues* (pp. 53–91). Guilford Press.

Jensen, A. R. (1998). *The factor.* Prager.

Jung, R. E., & Haier, R. J. (2007). The Parieto-frontal integration theory (P-FIT) of intelligence: Converging neuroimaging evidence. *The Behavioral and Brain Sciences, 30*(2), 135–154.

Kan, K. J., van der Maas, H. L., & Levine, S. Z. (2019). Extending psychometric network analysis: Empirical evidence against g in favor of mutualism? *Intelligence, 73*, 52–62.

Kaufman, A. S. (2000). Foreword. In D. P. Flanagan, K. S. McGrew, & S. O. Ortiz (Eds.), *The Wechsler intelligence scales and Gf-Gc theory: A contemporary approach to interpretation* (pp. xiii–xv). Allyn & Bacon.

Kaufman, A. S., & Kaufman, N. L. (1983). *Kaufman Assessment Battery for Children.* American Guidance Service.

Kaufman, A. S., & Kaufman, N. L. (1993). *Kaufman adolescent and adult intelligence test.* American Guidance Service, Circle Pines, MN.

Kaufman, A. S., & Kaufman, N. L. (2018). *Kaufman Assessment Battery for Children* (2nd ed). Pearson. Normative update.

Keith, T. Z. (1997). Comments on the relationship between intelligence, working memory capacity, and information processing speed and efficiency: A reply. *School Psychology Quarterly, 12*, 117–118.

Keith, T. Z., & Reynolds, M. R. (2010). CHC and cognitive abilities: What we've learned from 20 years of research. *Psychology in the Schools, 47*, 635–650.

Keith, T. Z., & Reynolds, M. R. (2012). Using confirmatory factor analysis to aid in understanding the constructs measured by intelligence tests. In D. F. Flanagan & P. H. Harrison (Eds.), *Contemporary intellectual assessment: Theories, tests, and issues* (3rd ed, pp. 758–799). Guilford Press.

Keith, T. Z., & Reynolds, M. R. (2018). Using confirmatory factor analysis to aid in understanding the constructs measured by intelligence tests. In D. F. Flanagan & E. M. McDonough (Eds.), *Contemporary intellectual assessment: Theories, tests, and issues* (4th ed, pp. 853–900). Guilford Press.

Kell, H. J., & Lang, J. W. (2017). Specific abilities in the workplace: More important than g? *Journal of Intelligence, 5*(2), 13.

Klein, E., & Knops, A. (2023). The two-network framework of number processing: A step towards a better understanding of the neural origins of developmental dyscalculia. *Journal of Neural Transmission, 130*(3), 253–268.

Kovacs, K. (2019). Process overlap theory: How the interplay between specific and general mental abilities accounts for the positive manifold in intelligence. In D. J. McFarland (Ed.), *General and specific mental abilities* (pp. 132–152). Cambridge Scholars Publishing.

Kovacs, K., & Conway, A. R. (2016). Process overlap theory: A unified account of the general factor of intelligence. *Psychological Inquiry, 27*(3), 151–177.

Kristanto, D., Hildebrandt, A., Sommer, W., & Zhou, C. (2023). Cognitive abilities are associated with specific conjunctions of structural and functional neural subnetworks. *NeuroImage, 279*, 120304.

LaForte, E. M., Dailey, D., & McGrew, K. S. (2025). *Technical manual. Woodcock-Johnson V.* Riverside Assessments, LLC.

Lezak, M. D. (1976). *Neuropsychological assessment.* Oxford University Press.

Lezak, M. D. (1995). *Neuropsychological assessment* (3rd ed). Oxford University Press.

Lezak, M. D., Howieson, D. B., & Loring, D. W. (2004). *Neuropsychological assessment* (4th ed). Oxford University Press.

Malanchini, M., Rimfeld, K., Allegrini, A. G., Ritchie, S. J., & Plomin, R. (2020). Cognitive ability and education: How behavioural genetic research has advanced our knowledge and understanding of their association. *Neuroscience & Biobehavioral Reviews, 111*, 229–245.

Mascolo, J. T., Alfonso, V. C., & Flanagan, D. P. (2014). *Essentials of planning, selecting, and tailoring interventions for unique learners.* Wiley.

Mather, N., McGrew, K. S., LaForte, E. M., & Wendling, B. J. (2025). *Woodcock-Johnson V virtual test library.* Riverside Assessments, LLC.

McCloskey, G., Slonim, J., Whitaker, R., Kaufman, S., & Nagoshi, N. (2017). A neuropsychological approach to interpretation of the WISC-V. In D. P. Flanagan & V. C. Alfonso (Eds.), *Essentials of WISC-V assessment* (pp. 287–333). Wiley.

McDonough, E. M., Flanagan, D. P., Sy, M., & Alfonso, V. C. (2017). Specific learning disorder. In *Handbook of DSM-5 disorders in children and adolescents* (pp. 77–104). Springer International Publishing, Cham.

McGill, R. J., & Dombrowski, S. C. (2019). Critically reflecting on the origins, evolution, and impact of the Cattell-Horn-Carroll (CHC) model. *Applied Measurement in Education, 32*(3), 216–231.

McGrew, K. S. (1994). *Clinical interpretation of the Woodcock-Johnson tests of cognitive ability-revised.* Allyn & Bacon.

McGrew, K. S. (1997). Analysis of the major intelligence batteries according to a proposed comprehensive CHC framework. In D. P. Flanagan, J. L. Genshaft, & P. L. Harrison (Eds.), *Contemporary intellectual assessment: Theories, tests, and issues* (pp. 151–180). Guilford Press.

McGrew, K. S. (2005). The Cattell-Horn-Carroll theory of cognitive abilities: Past, present, and future. In D. P. Flanagan, J. L. Genshaft, & P. L. Harrison (Eds.), *Contemporary intellectual assessment: Theories, tests, and issues* (pp. 136–182). Guilford Press.

McGrew, K. S. (2009). CHC theory and the human cognitive abilities project: Standing on the shoulders of the giants of psychometric intelligence research. *Intelligence*, *37*(1), 1–10.

McGrew, K. S. (2023). Carroll's three-stratum (3S) cognitive ability theory at 30 years: Impact, 3S-CHC theory clarification, structural replication, and cognitive–achievement psychometric network analysis extension. *Journal of Intelligence*, *11*(2), 32 https://doi.org/10.3390/jintelligence11020032.

McGrew, K. S., & Flanagan, D. P. (1998). *The intelligence test desk reference (ITDR): CHC cross-battery assessment.* Allyn & Bacon.

McGrew, K. S., Flanagan, D. P., Keith, T. Z., & Vanderwood, M. (1997). Beyond *g*: The impact of CHC specific cognitive abilities research on the future use and interpretation of intelligence tests in the schools. *School Psychology Review*, *26*, 189–210.

McGrew, K. S., Mather, N., LaForte, E. M., & Wendling, B. J. (2025). *Woodcock-Johnson V.* Riverside Assessments, LLC.

McGrew, K. S., Schneider, W. J., Decker, S. L., & Bulut, O. (2023). A psychometric network analysis of CHC intelligence measures: Implications for research, theory, and interpretation of broad CHC scores "Beyond g". *Journal of Intelligence*, *11*(1), 19 https://doi.org/10.3390/jintelligence11010019.

Meehl, P. E. (1992). Factors and taxa, traits and types, differences of degree and differences in kind. *Journal of Personality*, *60*(1), 117–174.

Messick, S. (1989). Validity. In R. Linn (Ed.), *Educational measurement* (3rd ed, pp. 104–131). American Council on Education.

Messick, S. (1995). Validity of psychological assessment: Validation of inferences from persons' responses and performances as scientific inquiry into score meaning. *American Psychologist*, *50*, 741–749.

Miller D. C. (2024, January 25–26). *Integration of CHC theory with neuropsychological theories* [Conference Presentation]. State of the Art of SLD Identification 2024: Innovations in Theory, Research, and Practice. Virtual.

Miller, D. C., & Maricle, D. E. (2019). *Essentials of school neuropsychological assessment* (3rd ed). Wiley.

Miller, D. C., Maricle, D. E., Bedford, C. L., & Gettman, J. A. (Eds.) (2022). *Best practices in school neuropsychology: Guidelines for effective practice, assessment, and evidence-based intervention.* John Wiley & Sons.

Murray, A. L., & Johnson, W. (2013). The limitations of model fit in comparing the bi-factor versus higher-order models of human cognitive ability structure. *Intelligence*, *41*(5), 407–422.

Naglieri, J. A., & Das, J. P. (1997). *Cognitive Assessment System.* Riverside Publishing.

Naglieri, J. A., Das, J. P., & Goldstein, S. (2014). *Cognitive Assessment System* (2nd ed). Pro-Ed.

Niileksela, C. R., & Hajovsky, D. B. (2024, January 25–26). *Consolidating evidence of cognitive-achievement relations: A preliminary meta-analysis of 496 data-sets* [Conference Presentation]. State of the Art of Specific Learning Disabilities Identification: Innovations in Theory, Research, and Practice, Virtual.

Niileksela, C. R., Hajovsky, D. B., Montenegro, F. P., Schneider, W. J., Flanagan, D. P., & Alfonso, V. C. (2026). Cognitive-mathematics relations: A meta-analysis of norm-referenced standardized test batteries. Manuscript submitted for publication.

Niileksela, C. R., Reynolds, M. R., Keith, T. Z., & McGrew, K. S. (2016). A special validity study of the Woodcock–Johnson IV: Acting on evidence for specific abilities. In D. P. Flanagan & V. C. Alfonso (Eds.), *WJ IV clinical use and interpretation: Scientist-practitioner perspectives* (pp. 65–106). Elsevier.

O'Connell, M. (2018). The power of cognitive ability in explaining educational test performance, relative to other ostensible contenders. *Intelligence*, *66*, 122–127.

Procopio, F., Zhou, Q., Wang, Z., Gidziela, A., Rimfeld, K., Malanchini, M., & Plomin, R. (2022). The genetics of specific cognitive abilities. *Intelligence*, *95*, 101689.

Raiford, S. E. (2017). *Essentials of WISC-V integrated assessment.* John Wiley & Sons.

Reynolds, M. R., Keith, T. Z., Flanagan, D. P., & Alfonso, V. C. (2013). A cross-battery, reference variable, confirmatory factor analytic investigation of the CHC taxonomy. *Journal of School Psychology*, *51*(4), 535–555.

Roid, G. H. (2003). *Stanford Binet intelligence scales* (5th ed). Riverside.

Schmank, C. J., Goring, S. A., Kovacs, K., & Conway, A. R. (2021). Investigating the structure of intelligence using latent variable and psychometric network modeling: A commentary and reanalysis. *Journal of Intelligence*, *9*(1), 8.

Schneider, W. J., Flanagan, D. P., Niileksela, C. R., & Engler, J. R. (2024). The effect of measurement error on the positive predictive value of PSW methods for SLD identification: How buffer zones dispel the illusion of inaccuracy. *Journal of School Psychology*, *103*, 101280.

Schneider, W. J. (2016). Strengths and weaknesses of the Woodcock-Johnson IV tests of cognitive abilities: Best practice from a scientist-practitioner perspective. In D. P. Flanagan & V. C. Alfonso (Eds.), *WJ IV clinical use and interpretation: Scientist-practitioner perspectives* (pp. 192–211). Academic Press.

Schneider, W. J., & McGrew, K. (2012). The Cattell-Horn-Carroll model of intelligence. In D. Flanagan & P. Harrison (Eds.), *Contemporary intellectual assessment: Theories, tests, and issues* (3rd ed, pp. 99–144). Guilford Press.

Schneider, W. J., & McGrew, K. S. (2018). The Cattell-Horn-Carroll theory of cognitive abilities. In D. P. Flanagan & E. M. McDonough (Eds.), *Contemporary intellectual assessment: Theories, tests, and issues* (4th ed, pp. 73–163). Guilford Press.

Schrank, F. A., Mather, N., & McGrew, K. S. (2014). *Woodcock-Johnson IV tests of achievement.* Riverside.

Schulze, R. (2005). Modeling structures of intelligence. In O. Wilhelm & R. W. Engle (Eds.), *Handbook of understanding and measuring intelligence* (pp. 241–263). Sage Publications, Inc.

Shanock, A., Flanagan, D. P., Alfonso, V. C., & McHale-Small, M. (2022). Helping school psychologists and districts estimate the cost of adopting the dual discrepancy/consistency PSW method for SLD identification. *Journal of Applied School Psychology*, *38*(4), 316–351.

Spearman, C. (1904). "General intelligence," objectively determined and measured. *The American Journal of Psychology*, *15*(2), 201–293. https://doi.org/10.2307/1412107.

Taylor, T. R. (1994). A review of three approaches to cognitive assessment, and a proposed integrated approach based on a unifying theoretical framework. *South Africa Journal of Psychology*, *24*(4), 184–193.

Thorndike, R. L., Hagen, E. P., & Sattler, J. M. (1986). *Standford-Binet intelligence scale* (4th ed). Riverside.

Thorndike, R. M. (1997). The early history of intelligence testing. In D. P. Flanagan, J. L. Genshaft, & P. L. Harrison (Eds.), *Contemporary intellectual assessment: Theories, tests, and issues* (pp. 3–16). Guilford Press.

Thurstone, L. L. (1938). *Primary mental abilities*. University of Chicago Press.

Vakhtin, A. A., Ryman, S. G., Flores, R. A., & Jung, R. E. (2014). Functional brain networks contributing to the Parieto-Frontal integration theory of intelligence. *NeuroImage, 103*, 349–354.

Van der Maas, H. L. J., Kan, K. Y. J., Marsman, M., & Stevenson, C. E. (2017). Network models for cognitive development and intelligence. *Journal of Intelligence, 5*, 16.

Wang, R., Liu, M., Cheng, X., Wu, Y., Hildebrandt, A., & Zhou, C. (2021). Segregation, integration, and balance of large-scale resting brain networks configure different cognitive abilities. *Proceedings of the National Academy of Sciences, 118*(23), e2022288118.

Warne, R. T., & Burnungham, C. (2019). Spearman's g found in 31 non-western nations: Strong evidence that g is a universal phenomenon. *Psychological Bulletin, 145*, 237–272.

Watkins, M. W., & Beaujean, A. A. (2014). Bifactor structure of the Wechsler preschool and primary scale of intelligence—fourth edition. *School Psychology Quarterly, 29*(1), 52–63.

Wechsler, D. (1981). *Wechsler adult intelligence scale–revised*. The Psychological Corporation.

Wechsler, D. (1989). *Wechsler preschool and primary scale of intelligence–revised*. The Psychological Corporation.

Wechsler, D. (1991). *Wechsler intelligence scale for children* (3rd ed). The Psychological Corporation.

Wechsler, D. (2012). *Wechsler preschool and primary scale of intelligence* (4th ed). Pearson.

Wechsler, D. (2014). *Wechsler intelligence scale for children* (5th ed). Pearson.

Wechsler, D., Raiford, S. E., & Presnell, K. (2024). *Wechsler adult intelligence scale* (5th ed). Pearson.

Wilson, B. C. (1992). The neuropsychological assessment of the preschool child: A branching model. In I. Rapin & S. I. Segalowitz (Eds.), *Handbook of neuropsychology: Vol. 6. Child neuropsychology* (pp. 377–394). Elsevier.

Wilson, C. J., Bowden, S. C., Byrne, L. K., Vannier, L. C., Hernandez, A., & Weiss, L. G. (2023). Cross-national generalizability of WISC-V and CHC broad ability constructs across France, Spain, and the US. *Journal of Intelligence, 11*(8), 159.

Woodcock, R. W. (1977). Woodcock-Johnson Psycho-Educational Battery. Technical Report.

Woodcock, R. W. (1990). Theoretical foundations of the WJ-R measures of cognitive ability. *Journal of Psychoeducational Assessment, 8*, 231–258.

Woodcock, R. W., & Johnson, M. B. (1989). *Woodcock-Johnson psycho-educational battery-revised*. DLM Teaching Resources.

Woodcock, R. W., Miller, D. C., Maricle, D. E., & McGill, R. J. (2017). *Evidence-based selective assessment for academic disorders*. School Neuropsych Press.

Two

# HOW TO ORGANIZE, ANALYZE, AND INTERPRET CROSS-BATTERY DATA USING X-BASS

*In the competitive marketplace, the major cognitive batteries are pitted against each other. Once they enter our possession, however, they are on the same side, a team of former rivals, united in purpose. There is a sense in which each could do the job of the other reasonably well. Used together, however, their complementary strengths and compensating virtues offer safeguards against the weaknesses and vulnerabilities that each of them would have if used alone.*

(Schneider, 2016, p. 191)

Dr. Joel Schneider insightfully articulated a challenge well-known to practitioners: the need to use ability batteries thoughtfully and efficiently, leveraging their strengths to the fullest. Traditionally, overall ability scores, such as IQ, have been the primary focus of most assessments, with intelligence batteries administered primarily to obtain this single metric. Although there are valid reasons to consider overall ability scores, such as their relationship to several life outcomes, they seldom provide the central insight needed to understand learning difficulties and exceptionalities beyond intellectual disability and giftedness. Instead, when assessing neurodevelopmental disorders, interpretation typically centers on broad and narrow ability domains. Lezak (1995) famously compared the routine reporting of IQ scores to "the tail wagging the dog," suggesting that if IQ scores were no longer reported, demand for them would diminish (p. 126). Similarly, Woodcock (2002) and McGrew and Flanagan (1998) urged practitioners to look beyond IQ to gain a richer understanding of the underlying issues.

Effective assessment requires careful, personalized planning instead of simply following a standard "one size fits all" procedure. For instance, a student exhibiting reading comprehension difficulties needs different assessments than a student with attention or social communication challenges. A well-articulated referral ensures that the assessment team understands the context and focus areas, guiding the selection of appropriate assessment tools and procedures. Usually, comprehensive assessments cover multiple areas, including cognitive abilities, academic skills, executive functioning, attention, memory, language, and adaptive behavior, depending on the specific concerns. The main goal of this chapter is to help practitioners balance thoroughness with efficiency to generate clear diagnostic information that guides intervention planning. Within the XBA framework, this chapter:

- Describes how specific referral information influences battery selection and organization;
- Demonstrates how cognitive, achievement, and neuropsychological batteries can be used to measure CHC broad and narrow abilities and processes;
- Provides examples of how to supplement any given battery with additional measures when the core battery does not assess all relevant abilities and processes;
- Demonstrates analysis and interpretation of XBA data using X-BASS; and
- Introduces selective, diagnostic cross-batteries for individuals suspected of having an SLD.

## ORGANIZING A CROSS-BATTERY ASSESSMENT

Referral information, including the purpose of the assessment, should inform decisions about battery selection and organization. Three scenarios best illustrate how such information affects decisions about test selection and organization within the XBA framework.

### Scenario 1: Consideration of Examinee Characteristics

The first scenario affecting battery selection and organization involves assessing individuals whose characteristics set them apart from the mainstream. For example, practitioners are often called on to assess the abilities of individuals with sensory or perceptual impairments (e.g., deafness, blindness), fine-motor impairments (e.g., cerebral palsy, tremors, seizure activity), or who come from culturally and linguistically diverse backgrounds. When assessing these individuals, test characteristics and demands must be carefully considered to ensure fairness, validity, and accessibility. Rapid Reference 2.1 provides key considerations in assessing these individuals.

## Rapid Reference 2.1

### Key Considerations for Battery Selection Based on Examinee Characteristics

**1. Sensory or Perceptual Impairments (e.g., Deafness, Blindness)**

- **Format and Accessibility**: Tests often rely on visual or auditory input. Simply converting a test to braille, large print, or audio does not guarantee validity. The appropriateness depends on how much the content relies on visual or auditory cues.
- **Assistive Technology Compatibility**: Computer-based tests must work with screen readers, magnification software, or other assistive devices. Students should be familiar with the platform before testing.
- **Item Adaptation**: Some items may be too visually or auditorily complex to adapt. These may need to be replaced with equivalent items or omitted with scoring adjustments.
- **Standardization Issues**: Students with sensory impairments are rarely included in norming samples, so adaptations can affect validity. Interpretation should rely on performance analysis rather than raw scores.
- **Specialized Tools**: Use assessments designed for these populations (e.g., Brigance Inventory in braille, Callier-Azusa Scales for deafblind students). [teachingvi...paired.com]

**2. Fine-Motor Impairments (e.g., Cerebral Palsy, Tremors, and Seizure Activity)**

- **Response Mode**: Tests requiring handwriting, drawing, or manual manipulation can disadvantage students with motor impairments. Alternatives include oral responses, scribing, or adaptive devices.
- **Timing and Fatigue**: Motor impairments often slow response speed and increase fatigue. Extended time and breaks are essential.
- **Technology Access**: Ensure compatibility with assistive devices (e.g., speech-to-text software, adapted keyboards).
- **Avoid Penalizing Motor Skills**: Scoring should reflect cognitive ability, not motor execution. For example, spelling tests should not penalize handwriting quality. [apa.org]—search "Top 20 Principles for Students with Disabilities."

**3. Multilingual Learners**

- **Language Demands**: Tests designed for native speakers may measure language proficiency rather than the intended construct.
- **Accommodations**: Provide bilingual dictionaries, translated instructions, or allow responses in the student's dominant language when appropriate.
- **Dynamic Assessment**: Use approaches that measure learning potential rather than static knowledge, reducing linguistic bias.
- **Cultural Relevance**: Ensure test content is culturally appropriate and does not assume background knowledge unfamiliar to the student.

**General Principles Across All Groups**

- **Universal Design for Learning (UDL)***: Incorporate flexible formats and accessibility features from the start.
- **Assessment Purpose**: Clarify whether the goal is diagnostic, formative, or summative, and select tools accordingly.
- **Validity and Fairness**: Adaptations must not alter the construct being measured. Interpret results cautiously, considering the impact of accommodations. [apa.org]—search "APA Guidelines for Psychological Assessment and Evaluation."

* *UDL is an educational framework grounded in learning science that guides the design of flexible learning environments and curricula to accommodate the diverse needs of all learners. It emphasizes providing multiple means of representation (how information is presented), expression (how learners demonstrate knowledge), and engagement (how learners are motivated and challenged). UDL aims to reduce barriers to learning by proactively creating accessible and inclusive instructional goals, methods, materials, and assessments, ensuring equitable opportunities for success for every student regardless of their abilities or backgrounds* (Bernacchio & Mullen, 2007).

## DON'T FORGET

Use this quick-reference guide when assessing students with sensory, motor, or language-related challenges:

**Sensory or Perceptual Impairments**

- ☐ Confirm test accessibility (braille, large print, audio, screen reader compatibility).
- ☐ Review item content for reliance on visual/auditory cues—adapt or replace as needed.
- ☐ Ensure assistive technology works seamlessly with the test platform.
- ☐ Interpret results cautiously—norming samples rarely include these populations.
- ☐ Consider specialized assessments designed for sensory impairments.

**Fine-Motor Impairments**

- ☐ Identify tasks requiring handwriting or manual manipulation—provide alternatives (oral response, scribe, adaptive devices).
- ☐ Allow extended time and breaks to reduce fatigue.

☐ Verify compatibility with assistive devices (speech-to-text, adapted keyboards).
☐ Ensure scoring reflects cognitive ability, not motor execution.

**Multilingual Learners**
☐ Evaluate language demands—does the test measure the intended construct or language skills?
☐ Provide accommodations (translated instructions, bilingual dictionaries, response in the dominant language).
☐ Use dynamic assessment to gauge learning potential.
☐ Check cultural relevance of test content.

**General Principles**
☐ Apply UDL principles.
☐ Confirm that accommodation does not alter the construct being measured.
☐ Document all adaptations and interpret results in context.

### Scenario 2: A Detailed and Thorough Assessment is Warranted

In educational settings, a comprehensive cognitive battery is typically administered when a detailed, thorough assessment of a student's cognitive strengths and weaknesses is needed to inform eligibility decisions. This approach is warranted when initial screening results or single-battery assessments are inconclusive or inconsistent, requiring a broader examination of multiple cognitive domains. A comprehensive assessment is also warranted when students present with complex learning difficulties that cannot be adequately understood through limited assessment. Comprehensive assessment often requires using the XBA method to capture the diverse cognitive processes aligned with theoretical models, such as the CHC model. Additionally, a comprehensive, theory-based assessment helps rule out exclusionary factors and provides rich data to guide individualized intervention planning. Ultimately, within a multi-source and multi-method assessment framework, administering a comprehensive cognitive battery supports legally defensible, accurate, and equitable eligibility determinations by ensuring that decisions are informed by a holistic understanding of the student's cognitive strengths and weaknesses. Rapid Reference 2.2 provides a summary of construct representation (discussed in Chapter 1) as a refresher.

## *Rapid Reference 2.2*

### A Recap of Construct Representation

**Adequate Construct Representation**

**Definition:** Adequate construct representation refers to the extent to which an assessment fully and appropriately samples the essential features, processes, and dimensions of the construct it is intended to measure, without omitting key components or introducing irrelevant ones.

In Messick's (1995) framework, it is the *positive* counterpart to the two major threats to validity: Construct underrepresentation (too little of the construct) and Construct-irrelevant variance (too much of what the construct is not)

**An assessment demonstrates adequate construct representation when:**

- The core theoretical components of the construct are included
- The breadth and depth of the construct are reflected in the tasks
- The test avoids contamination from irrelevant skills, knowledge, or processes
- The resulting scores meaningfully support the intended interpretations

**Cognitive Assessment Examples**

**1. Working Memory Capacity (*Gwm*)**

Adequate representation requires tasks that assess both:

- Maintenance (e.g., Digit Span Forward)
- Manipulation (e.g., Digit Span Backward, Letter-Number Sequencing)

A battery that includes both facets captures the construct more completely.

**2. Fluid Reasoning (*Gf*)**

A well-represented *Gf* construct includes tasks tapping:

- Inductive reasoning (pattern recognition, matrices)

- Deductive reasoning (logical rules, syllogisms)
- Quantitative reasoning (novel math reasoning)

This avoids narrowing *Gf* to a single modality.

**Construct Underrepresentation**
**Definition:** A validity threat that occurs when a test fails to capture essential components of the intended construct, resulting in an incomplete or too-narrow measurement.

**Cognitive-Assessment Examples**

**1. Measuring Working Memory Capacity with Only Digit Span Forward**

- **Problem:** Digit Span Forward primarily taps attention and rote repetition, not the manipulation component central to working memory.
- **Underrepresentation:** The construct of *working memory capacity* (*Gwm*) includes **maintenance and manipulation**, but the test captures only one facet.
- **Impact:** A student with intact attention but weak manipulation may appear to have "average working memory," masking an actual deficit.

**2. Assessing Fluid Reasoning Using Only Matrix Reasoning**

- **Problem:** Matrix reasoning measures inductive reasoning but not deductive reasoning, quantitative reasoning, or novel problem-solving breadth.
- **Underrepresentation:** The broader CHC construct *Gf* includes multiple reasoning processes.
- **Impact:** A student with strong visual-spatial induction, but weak quantitative reasoning may be misclassified as having "strong *Gf*."

**3. Construct-Irrelevant Variance**
**Definition:** A validity threat that occurs when test scores are influenced by factors unrelated to the intended construct, adding noise or contamination.

**Cognitive-Assessment Examples**

**1. Visual-Motor Demands Inflating or Depressing Processing Speed Scores**

- **Problem:** Tasks like Coding or Symbol Search require fine-motor speed and visual scanning.
- **Irrelevant variance:** Motor speed, visual acuity, or graphomotor fluency can influence scores even though the intended construct is cognitive processing speed (*Gs*).
- **Impact:** A child with motor coordination difficulties may appear to have a processing speed deficit when the issue is motoric, not cognitive.

**2. Language Load Contaminating Fluid Reasoning Scores**

- **Problem:** Some reasoning tasks require much verbal comprehension (e.g., verbal analogies).
- **Irrelevant variance:** Performance reflects language proficiency, not pure reasoning.
- **Impact:** English learners may score artificially low on *Gf* tasks due to linguistic complexity rather than a reasoning weakness.

*Source:* Messick, S. (1995). Validity of psychological assessment: Validation of inferences from persons' responses and performances as scientific inquiry into score meaning. *American Psychologist, 50*(9), 741–749.

## Using the XBA Guiding Principles to Select and Organize a Comprehensive Battery

Practitioners must review information on several aspects of available cognitive batteries to make informed decisions about final battery selection. When deciding to gather data from more than one battery, practitioners should review the XBA guiding principles presented in Chapter 1. Below are some simple steps to follow for battery selection and organization.

**Step 1.** Determine which batteries you have available and what broad and narrow abilities they measure. For example, suppose you have the WISC-V, WJ V, and KABC-II NU. Table 2.1 shows these three batteries side by side and lists their tests or subtests by CHC broad ability domain. The WISC-V column, for example, shows that this battery has four subtests that measure *Gc* (Similarities, Vocabulary, Information, and Comprehension). The cleanest estimate of the broad *Gc* ability on the WISC-V is the aggregate of Vocabulary and Information. These subtests measure two qualitatively distinct narrow *Gc* abilities: Lexical Knowledge (VL) and General Information (K0). Any other combination of subtests introduces construct-irrelevant variance (i.e., Induction—a narrow *Gf* ability). Therefore, Vocabulary and Information are printed in bold in Table 2.1 to indicate preferred subtests for measuring *Gc*.

**Table 2.1 CHC Broad and Narrow Ability Representation on Three Commonly Used Cognitive Batteries (Adapted from Benson et al., 2019)**

| CHC Broad Ability | WJ V COG & *WJ V VTL* | WISC-V | KABC-II NU |
|---|---|---|---|
| ***Gc***<br>Comprehension-Knowledge | **Oral Vocabulary (VL)**<br>Verbal Analogies (VL; *Gf*:I)<br>**General Information (K0)**<br>*Understanding Directions* (LS; *Gwm*:Wc) | Similarities (VL; *Gf*:I)<br>**Vocabulary (VL)**<br>**Information (K0)**<br>Comprehension (K0; *Gf*:I) | Expressive Vocabulary (VL)<br>Riddles (VL; *Gf*:RG)<br>Verbal Knowledge (VL)<br>Story Completion (K0 for ages 5–6 years) |
| ***Gf***<br>Fluid Reasoning | **Matrices (I)**<br>**Analysis-Synthesis (RG, RQ)**<br>Concept Formation (I)<br>Number Series (RQ) | **Matrix Reasoning (I)**<br>**Figure Weights (RG, RQ)**<br>Picture Concepts (I; *Gc*:K0) | **Story Completion (RG for ages 7–18 years)**<br>**Pattern Reasoning (I; *Gv*:Vz for ages 7–18 years)** |
| ***Gwm***<br>Working Memory Capacity | **Verbal Attention (Wa, AC)**<br>**Numbers Reversed (Wc)**<br>Visual Working Memory (Wc)<br>*Nonsense Word Repetition* (Wa; Ga:UM)<br>*Animal-Number Sequencing* (Wc)<br>*Memory for Words* (Wa)<br>*Sentence Repetition* (Wa)<br>*Sound Reversal* (Wc; *Ga*:PC) | **Digit Span (Wa, Wc)**<br>Picture Span (Wv)<br>**Letter-Number Sequencing (Wc)** | Number Recall (Wa)<br>Word Order (Wa for ages 4–18 years; Wc for ages 7–18 years)<br>Hand Movements (Wv) |
| ***Gv***<br>Visual Processing | Spatial Relations (Vz)<br>Block Rotation (Vz) | Block Design (Vz)<br>Visual Puzzles (Vz) | Conceptual Thinking (Vz; *Gf*:I)<br>**Face Recognition (MV)**<br>**Triangles (Vz)**<br>Pattern Reasoning (Vz: *Gf*:I for ages 5–6 years)<br>Rover (SS; *Gf*:RG)<br>Block Counting (Vz)<br>Gestalt Closures (CS) |
| ***Gs***<br>Processing Speed | Number-Pattern Matching (Pc, OP)<br>Letter-Pattern Matching (Pc, OP)<br>Symbol-Inhibition (Pc) | **Coding (Pc)**<br>**Symbol Search (Ps)**<br>Cancellation (Ps) | Not Represented |
| ***Gl***<br>Learning Efficiency | **Story Recall (MM)**<br>Story Comprehension (MM)<br>**Visual–Auditory Learning (MA)** | Immediate Symbol Translation (MA)<br>Delayed Symbol Translation (MA)<br>Recognition Symbol Translation (MA) | Atlantis (MA)<br>Atlantis Delayed (MA)<br>Rebus (MA)<br>Rebus Delayed (MA) |
| ***Gr***<br>Retrieval Fluency | **Semantic Word Retrieval (FI)**<br>**Phonemic Word Retrieval (FW)**<br>*Rapid Picture Naming* (NA)<br>*Rapid Letter Naming* (NA; OP)<br>*Rapid Phoneme Naming* (NA)<br>*Rapid Number Naming* (NA; OP) | Naming Speed Literacy (NA)<br>Naming Speed Quantity (NA; *Gq*:NS) | Not Represented |
| ***Ga***<br>Auditory Processing | *Sound Blending* (PC)<br>*Sound Deletion* (PC)<br>*Sound Substitution* (PC)<br>*Segmentation* (PC) | Not Represented | Not Represented |

*Note:* CHC narrow ability codes are listed in parentheses next to the name of the test/subtest. Green shading indicates CHC domains that are adequately represented; red shading indicates underrepresented domains; light gray shading indicates domains that are not measured; and subtests printed in bold are considered the best two qualitatively different indicators of the broad ability. Tests in italics are from the Woodcock-Johnson V Virtual Test Library (WJ V VTL). WJ V COG = Woodcock-Johnson V Tests of Cognitive Abilities; WISC-V = Wechsler Intelligence Scale for Children-Fifth Edition; K-ABC-II NU = Kaufman Assessment Battery for Children-Second Edition Normative Update. K0 = General Information; LS = Listening Ability; VL = Lexical Knowledge; I = Induction; RG = General Sequential Reasoning; RQ = Quantitative Reasoning; Wc = Working Memory Capacity; Wa = Auditory Short-Term Storage; Wv = Visual–Spatial Short-Term Storage; AC = Attentional Control; Vz = Visualization; MV = Visual Memory; CS = Closure Speed; SS = Spatial Scanning; Ps = Perceptual Speed-Search, Pc = Perceptual Speed-Compare; OP = Orthographic Processing; UM = Memory of Sound Patterns; PC = Phonetic Coding; MM = Meaningful Memory; MA = Associative Memory; FI = Ideational Fluency; FW = Word Fluency; NA = Naming Facility; NS = Number Sense.

**Table 2.2 Task Demands, Characteristics, and Interpretation of *Gc* Subtests Across WJ V, WISC-V, and KABC-II NU**

| Subtest (CHC Code) | Task Demands | Task Characteristics | Cognitive Interpretation | Conceptual Interpretation |
|---|---|---|---|---|
| **WJ V: Oral Vocabulary (VL)** | Define words; retrieve semantic knowledge | Open-ended; expressive language | Lexical knowledge; semantic precision | Depth and organization of semantic networks |
| **WJ V: Verbal Analogies (VL; *Gf*:I)** | Identify relationships between word pairs | Increasing abstraction; relational reasoning | Verbal reasoning; verbal induction | Ability to integrate meaning and reason with language |
| **WJ V: General Information (K0)** | Retrieve factual knowledge | Cultural and experiential exposure | Long-term semantic memory; general knowledge | Breadth of culturally mediated world knowledge |
| **WJ V: Understanding Directions (LS; *Gwm*:Wc)** | Follow multi-step oral instructions | Sequential processing; receptive language | Listening comprehension; working memory for language | Functional comprehension of spoken language in context |
| **WISC-V: Similarities (VL; *Gf*:I)** | Identify conceptual relationships | Abstract verbal reasoning | Concept formation; verbal induction | Ability to generalize and form higher-order verbal concepts |
| **WISC-V: Vocabulary (VL)** | Define words | Semantic retrieval; expressive language | Lexical depth; precision of semantic representation | Richness and clarity of semantic knowledge |
| **WISC-V: Information (K0)** | Answer factual questions | Cultural and experiential exposure | General knowledge; semantic retrieval | Accumulated experience and opportunity to learn |
| **WISC-V: Comprehension (K0; *Gf*:I)** | Explain social rules and practical situations | Applied reasoning; pragmatic language | Social judgment; applied verbal reasoning | Ability to use language to reason through real-world situations |
| **KABC-II NU: Expressive Vocabulary (VL)** | Name pictured objects | Expressive retrieval; confrontation naming | Lexical access; expressive vocabulary | Breadth of expressive semantic knowledge |
| **KABC-II NU: Riddles (VL; *Gf*:RG)** | Solve verbal riddles | Verbal reasoning; inferential thinking | Inductive verbal reasoning | Flexible verbal problem solving and meaning integration |
| **KABC-II NU: Verbal Knowledge (VL)** | Identify word meanings | Receptive vocabulary; recognition format | Semantic knowledge | Breadth of receptive vocabulary and conceptual understanding |
| **KABC-II NU: Story Completion (K0)** | Complete story logic using pictures | Social reasoning; narrative structure | Narrative comprehension; applied reasoning | Ability to infer, integrate, and apply verbal meaning in context |

*Note:* K0 = General Information; LS = Listening Ability; VL = Lexical Knowledge; I = Induction; RG = General Sequential Reasoning; Wc = Working Memory Capacity.

**Step 2.** Understand the task demands, task characteristics, and intended interpretation of the subtests to administer, as subtests with the same broad and narrow ability classifications can differ (e.g., in terms of input and output). To assist in understanding task demands and characteristics, Tables 2.2 to 2.9 compare the subtests from each of the three batteries listed in Table 2.1 by CHC domain. Specifically, these CHC domain tables provide a cross-battery comparison of how the WJ V, WISC V, and KABC-II NU assess each broad cognitive ability. For every domain, the tables outline the task demands, task characteristics, and interpretive meaning of the subtests within each battery, allowing readers to see the conceptual overlap and the unique contributions of each measure. By organizing the subtests in this way, the tables highlight how different batteries operationalize the same CHC constructs, where coverage is strong or limited, and how practitioners can integrate qualitatively different indicators to form defensible cross-battery composites.

## *Gc* Across Batteries

Across the three batteries, *Gc* subtests measure the richness, organization, and accessibility of verbal knowledge. The WISC-V emphasizes verbal reasoning (e.g., concept formation), expressive semantic depth, and pragmatic language through Similarities, Vocabulary, Information, and Comprehension. The WJ V provides a broad sampling of lexical knowledge, factual knowledge, and listening comprehension, making it comprehensive and strongly linked to academic achievement. The KABC-II NU emphasizes expressive vocabulary, receptive knowledge, and verbal reasoning through tasks such as Riddles, offering a developmentally sensitive approach for younger children or those with emerging language skills. Together, these batteries converge on the idea that *Gc* reflects accumulated verbal learning, semantic organization, and the ability to use language to reason.

**Table 2.3 Task Demands, Characteristics, and Interpretation of *Gf* Subtests Across WJ V, WISC-V, and KABC-II NU**

| Subtest (CHC Code) | Task Demands | Task Characteristics | Cognitive Interpretation | Conceptual Interpretation |
|---|---|---|---|---|
| **WJ V: Matrices (I)** | Identify visual patterns and relationships | Nonverbal reasoning; pattern completion | Induction | Abstract pattern recognition and rule discovery |
| **WJ V: Analysis–Synthesis (RG, RQ)** | Apply rules to solve logic puzzles | Sequential, rule-based reasoning | Deductive reasoning; relational reasoning | Cognitive flexibility in applying and integrating rules |
| **WJ V: Concept Formation (I)** | Identify rule-based categories | Inductive reasoning; concept discovery | Abstract categorization | Ability to infer, generalize, and form concepts |
| **WJ V: Number Series (RQ)** | Identify numerical patterns | Quantitative reasoning; sequential logic | Numerical induction | Ability to detect and extend numerical relationships |
| **WISC-V: Matrix Reasoning (I)** | Complete visual patterns | Nonverbal reasoning; pattern completion | Induction | Abstract visual reasoning and rule discovery |
| **WISC-V: Figure Weights (RG, RQ)** | Solve balance-scale logic problems | Quantitative and relational reasoning | Proportional reasoning | Understanding of quantitative relationships and equivalence |
| **WISC-V: Picture Concepts (I; *Gc*:K0)** | Identify conceptual relationships across pictures | Mixed verbal + nonverbal reasoning | Categorical reasoning | Integration of conceptual features across modalities |
| **KABC-II NU: Story Completion (RG)** | Complete logical picture sequences | Logical + social reasoning | General sequential reasoning | Applied reasoning in narrative and social contexts |
| **KABC-II NU: Pattern Reasoning (I; Vz)** | Identify and extend visual patterns | Nonverbal; visual-spatial reasoning | Induction | Visual-spatial pattern analysis and rule abstraction |

*Note:* I = Induction; RG = General Sequential Reasoning; RQ = Quantitative Reasoning; K0 = General Information; Vz = Visualization.

## *Gf* Across Batteries

Across the three batteries, *Gf* subtests converge on the ability to reason, solve novel problems, and identify underlying patterns. The WISC-V emphasizes visual–spatial and quantitative reasoning through tasks that require pattern completion, relational logic, and reasoning with proportions. The WJ V samples inductive, deductive, and quantitative reasoning tasks, providing a comprehensive view of general reasoning processes. The KABC-II NU includes developmentally sensitive reasoning tasks that blend visual, logical, and narrative reasoning, making it particularly appropriate for younger children or students who benefit from reduced verbal load. Across batteries, *Gf* reflects the capacity to approach unfamiliar problems, detect relationships, and apply logical principles to reach solutions.

**Table 2.4 Task Demands, Characteristics, and Interpretation of *Gwm* Subtests Across WJ V, WISC-V, and KABC-II NU**

| Subtest (CHC Code) | Task Demands | Task Characteristics | Cognitive Interpretation | Conceptual Interpretation |
|---|---|---|---|---|
| **WJ V: Verbal Attention (Wa, AC)** | Repeat sequences of words and digits | Auditory short-term storage; simple span | Attention, sequencing, verbal storage | Verbal holding capacity |
| **WJ V: Numbers Reversed (Wc)** | Reverse digit sequences | Manipulation; backward span | Executive working memory; mental manipulation | Mental reordering and cognitive control |
| **WJ V: Visual Working Memory (Wc)** | Recall visual sequences | Visual WM; simple span | Spatial storage; visual sequencing | Visual–spatial working memory |
| **WJ V: Nonsense Word Repetition (Wa)** | Repeat unfamiliar phonological strings | Phonological short-term storage; speech-sound retention | Phonological storage; phonological accuracy | Integrity of phonological representations |
| **WISC-V: Digit Span (Wa, Wc)** | Repeat, reverse, and sequence digits | Auditory WM; storage + manipulation | Verbal storage and executive working memory | Efficiency of verbal working memory |
| **WISC-V: Picture Span (Wv)** | Recall visual sequences of pictures | Visual short-term storage; sequential visual span | Visual storage; visual–spatial sequencing | Visual–spatial working memory |

*(continued)*

**Table 2.4 (Continued)**

| Subtest (CHC Code) | Task Demands | Task Characteristics | Cognitive Interpretation | Conceptual Interpretation |
|---|---|---|---|---|
| **WISC-V: Letter–Number Sequencing (Wc)** | Reorder mixed letters and numbers | Working memory capacity; sequencing + manipulation | Manipulation; cognitive flexibility | Executive control in reorganizing information |
| **KABC-II NU: Number Recall (Wa)** | Repeat numbers in order | Auditory short-term storage; simple span | Verbal storage | Basic verbal working memory |
| **KABC-II NU: Word Order (Wa/Wc)** | Sequence pictured words in order | Auditory short-term storage; sequencing | Verbal sequencing + manipulation | Verbal working memory with linguistic load |
| **KABC-II NU: Hand Movements (Wv)** | Sequence hand gestures | Visual short-term storage; visual–motor span | Visual–motor short-term storage | Embodied sequencing and motor working memory |

*Note:* WM = Working Memory; Wa = Auditory Short-Term Storage; Wc = Working Memory Capacity; Wv = Visual–Spatial Short-Term Storage; AC = Attentional Control.

## *Gwm* Across Batteries

Across batteries, *Gwm* reflects the capacity to hold, manipulate, and sequence information in short-term memory. The WISC-V emphasizes auditory and visual memory, providing strong measures of storage and working memory. The WJ V expands this coverage by including phonological short-term storage, which is particularly informative for individuals with reading, spelling, and language-based concerns. The KABC-II NU adds a motor-based memory span component (Hand Movements), which can be useful for younger children or for students whose verbal/auditory memory is difficult to assess due to language limitations. Together, these batteries converge on the idea that *Gwm* supports the temporary maintenance and transformation of information needed for learning and academic performance.

**Table 2.5 Task Demands, Characteristics, and Interpretation of *Gv* Subtests Across WJ V, WISC-V, and KABC-II NU**

| Subtest (CHC Code) | Task Demands | Task Characteristics | Cognitive Interpretation | Conceptual Interpretation |
|---|---|---|---|---|
| **WJ V: Spatial Relations (Vz)** | Identify how pieces form a whole | Visual–spatial analysis | Visual–spatial integration | Seeing part–whole relationships |
| **WJ V: Block Rotation (Vz)** | Mentally rotate shapes | Mental rotation | Spatial organization | Manipulating images in the mind |
| **WISC-V: Block Design (Vz)** | Recreate designs with blocks | Constructional; motor + visual integration | Visual–spatial construction | Construction of visual patterns via spatial analysis |
| **WISC-V: Visual Puzzles (Vz)** | Select pieces that form a shape | Mental assembly; no motor output | Visual–spatial analysis | Internal part–whole reasoning |
| **KABC-II NU: Conceptual Thinking (Vz; *Gf*:I)** | Identify conceptual visual relationships | Visual + reasoning | Visual categorization | Integrating visual features conceptually |
| **KABC-II NU: Face Recognition (MV)** | Recognize and match faces | Visual memory; configural processing | Holistic/configural processing | Socially relevant visual recognition |
| **KABC-II NU: Triangles (Vz)** | Recreate designs with triangles | Constructional; motor + visual integration | Visual–spatial construction | Construction of visual patterns via spatial analysis |
| **KABC-II NU: Pattern Reasoning (Vz; *Gf*:I)** | Identify visual patterns | Nonverbal reasoning | Induction + Vz | Pattern detection and rule discovery |
| **KABC-II NU: Rover (SS; *Gf*:RG)** | Plan routes on a map | Spatial planning; rule-based | Spatial reasoning; relational reasoning | Navigational problem solving |
| **KABC-II NU: Block Counting (Vz)** | Count blocks in 3D stacks | Spatial visualization | Depth perception; mental rotation | 3D spatial analysis |
| **KABC-II NU: Gestalt Closure (CS)** | Identify incomplete figures | Visual closure | Perceptual integration | Seeing wholes from incomplete parts |

*Note:* Vz = Visualization; MV = Visual Memory; CS = Closure Speed; I = Induction; RG = General Sequential Reasoning.

## *Gv* Across Batteries

Across batteries, *Gv* reflects the capacity to analyze, manipulate, and integrate visual–spatial information. The WISC-V emphasizes visual-spatial organization and part-whole relationships through Block Design and Visual Puzzles. The WJ V provides measures of visual–spatial integration and transformation. The KABC-II NU provides a broad range of visual–spatial tasks—including planning, closure, and pattern analysis—that capture reasoning and visualization. Together, these measures illustrate how efficiently an individual can process visual patterns, organize space, and mentally transform images.

**Table 2.6 Task Demands, Characteristics, and Interpretation of *Gs* Across WJ V and WISC-V**

| Subtest (CHC Code) | Task Demands | Task Characteristics | Cognitive Interpretation | Conceptual Interpretation |
|---|---|---|---|---|
| **WJ V: Number Pattern Matching (Pc, OP)** | Quickly match number patterns | Timed; simple visual scanning of overlearned symbols | Speed of visual–symbol processing; orthographic access | Efficiency with basic numerical symbols |
| **WJ V: Letter Pattern Matching (Pc, OP)** | Quickly match letter patterns | Timed; simple visual scanning of overlearned symbols | Speed of visual–symbol processing; orthographic access | Rapid discrimination of alphabetic symbols |
| **WJ V: Symbol Inhibition (Pc)** | Inhibit responses to certain symbols | Timed; inhibition + controlled attention | Executive processing speed; orthographic access | Controlled processing under time pressure |
| **WISC-V: Coding (Pc)** | Copy symbols paired with numbers | Timed; motor + visual integration | Visual–motor speed; associative learning | Efficiency of written symbol production |
| **WISC-V: Symbol Search (Ps)** | Scan and decide if target is present | Timed; visual scanning | Visual discrimination speed | Rapid decision-making with simple symbols |
| **WISC-V: Cancellation (Ps)** | Mark target pictures among distractors | Timed; visual search | Visual scanning + selective attention | Speeded selective attention in cluttered arrays |
| **KABC-II NU: Not represented** | — | — | — | — |

*Note:* Ps = Perceptual Speed-Search, Pc = Perceptual Speed-Compare; OP = Orthographic Processing.

## *Gs* Across Batteries

Processing speed tasks across the WJ V and WISC-V measure how quickly and accurately individuals can carry out simple, overlearned visual–symbol operations under time pressure. The WISC-V emphasizes visual–motor output and rapid visual scanning, while the WJ V adds an executive control component through Symbol Inhibition, capturing speeded performance that also requires inhibition and controlled attention. These measures are essential for understanding how time constraints may depress performance in reading fluency, written output, and math fact retrieval, even when underlying reasoning or knowledge is intact.

**Table 2.7 Task Demands, Characteristics, and Interpretation of *Gl* Subtests Across WJ V, WISC-V, and KABC-II NU**

| Subtest (CHC Code) | Task Demands | Task Characteristics | Cognitive Interpretation | Conceptual Interpretation |
|---|---|---|---|---|
| **WJ V: Story Recall (MM)** | Recall stories after hearing them | Meaningful verbal material | Verbal learning + memory | Encoding and retaining narrative information |
| **WJ V: Story Comprehension (MM)** | Answer questions about stories | Comprehension + memory | Verbal learning with understanding | Integrating, retaining, and applying story meaning |
| **WJ V: Visual–Auditory Learning (MA)** | Learn symbol–word associations | Immediate recall | Associative learning | Initial encoding efficiency |
| **WISC-V: Immediate Symbol Translation (MA)** | Learn symbol–word associations | Immediate recall | Associative learning | Initial encoding efficiency |
| **WISC-V: Delayed Symbol Translation (MA)** | Recall symbol–word pairs after delay | Delay interval | Retention over time | Consolidation of new associations |

(*continued*)

**Table 2.7 (Continued)**

| Subtest (CHC Code) | Task Demands | Task Characteristics | Cognitive Interpretation | Conceptual Interpretation |
|---|---|---|---|---|
| **WISC-V: Recognition Symbol Translation (MA)** | Recognize correct symbol–word pairs | Recognition format | Retrieval with cues | Strength and accessibility of associative traces |
| **KABC-II NU: Atlantis (MA)** | Learn nonsense names of fanciful pictures of fish, plants, and shells | Visual–verbal associations | Paired-associate learning | Novel word learning |
| **KABC-II NU: Atlantis Delayed (MA)** | Recall nonsense names after delay | Delayed recall | Retention | Durability of new learning |
| **KABC-II NU: Rebus (MA)** | Learn meanings of symbol combinations | Symbolic decoding | Associative + analytic learning | Learning a symbolic "code" |
| **KABC-II NU: Rebus Delayed (MA)** | Recall meanings of symbol combinations after delay | Delayed recall | Retention | Stability of symbolic learning |

*Note:* MM = Meaningful Memory; MA = Associative Memory.

## *Gl* Across Batteries

*Gl* tasks across batteries measure how efficiently individuals encode, store, and retrieve new information, particularly associative pairs and meaningful verbal material. The WJ V emphasizes narrative learning and paired-associate learning, capturing how well students encode and retain connected verbal information. The WISC-V focuses on symbol–word associative learning with immediate, delayed, and recognition components, offering a clear understanding of an individual's encoding, consolidation, and retrieval processes. The KABC-II NU uses novel, child-friendly associative tasks, such as Atlantis and Rebus, to provide developmentally sensitive measures of new learning. Together, these tasks illuminate how effectively individuals acquire, consolidate, and access newly learned information.

**Table 2.8 Task Demands, Characteristics, and Interpretation of *Gr* Subtests Across WJ V and WISC-V**

| Subtest (CHC Code) | Task Demands | Task Characteristics | Cognitive Interpretation | Conceptual Interpretation |
|---|---|---|---|---|
| **WJ V: Semantic Word Retrieval (FI)** | Name items within a semantic category | Timed; semantic fluency; generative | Speed and efficiency of lexical–semantic access | Efficiency of retrieving and organizing semantic networks |
| **WJ V: Phonemic Word Retrieval (FW)** | Generate words beginning with a target sound | Timed; phonemic fluency; generative | Strategic phonological retrieval; verbal flexibility | Ability to search, access, and manipulate phonological–lexical representations |
| **WJ V: Rapid Picture Naming (NA)** | Rapidly name pictured objects | Overlearned labels; timed; serial naming | Automaticity of lexical access | Efficiency of retrieving familiar verbal labels |
| **WJ V: Rapid Letter/ Number Naming (NA; OP)** | Rapidly name letters and numbers | Overlearned symbols; timed; serial naming | Orthographic access; symbol retrieval; automaticity | Automatic access to basic academic codes (letters, digits) |
| **WJ V: Rapid Phoneme Naming (NA)** | Rapidly retrieve and articulate phonemes | Timed; speech-sound retrieval; serial phoneme access | Phonological access; phonological retrieval; sequencing | Integration of phonological memory, retrieval speed, and articulatory coordination |
| **WISC-V: Naming Speed Literacy (NA)** | Rapidly name objects of various size and color, letters, and numbers | Timed; overlearned symbols; serial naming | Symbol–sound retrieval; orthographic–phonological integration | Automaticity of print-related codes supporting reading fluency |
| **WISC-V: Naming Speed Quantity (NA; *Gq*:NS)** | Rapidly name quantities (e.g., 1–5 dots) | Timed; quantity symbols; serial naming | Number–meaning retrieval; quantity mapping | Automaticity of basic numerical codes supporting math fluency |
| **KABC-II NU: Not represented** | — | — | — | — |

*Note:* FI = Ideational Fluency; FW = Word Fluency; NA = Naming Facility; OP = Orthographic Processing; NS = Number Sense.

## *Gr* Across Batteries

*Gr* tasks capture the speed and efficiency with which individuals can access and retrieve well-learned verbal labels, phonological codes, or academic symbols. The WJ V provides a broad sampling of naming processes, including semantic fluency, phonemic fluency, and rapid naming of pictures, letters, numbers, and phonemes. In contrast, the WISC-V concentrates on literacy- and quantity-based rapid naming tasks that reflect automatic access to print and numerical codes. *Gr* measures are essential for understanding reading fluency, math fact retrieval, and written-expression speed, particularly when reasoning skills are adequate but academic output is slow due to reduced automaticity in retrieval.

**Table 2.9 Task Demands, Characteristics, and Interpretation of *Ga* Subtests on the WJ V VTL**

| Subtest (CHC Code) | Task Demands | Task Characteristics | Cognitive Interpretation | Conceptual Interpretation |
|---|---|---|---|---|
| **WJ V VTL: Sound Blending (PC)** | Blend individual sounds into whole words | Phonological synthesis | Phonological awareness (blending) | Integrating phonemes into whole words |
| **WJ V VTL: Sound Deletion (PC)** | Remove a specified sound from a word and say the new word | Phoneme manipulation | Advanced phonological awareness (deletion) | Flexible manipulation of phoneme sequences |
| **WJ V VTL: Sound Substitution (PC)** | Substitute one phoneme for another and say the new word | Complex manipulation | Advanced phonological awareness (substitution) | Precision and stability of phoneme representations |
| **WJ V VTL: Segmentation (PC)** | Break words into individual sounds | Phoneme analysis | Phonological awareness (segmentation) | Awareness of internal sound structure |
| **WISC-V: Not represented** | — | — | — | — |
| **KABC-II NU: Not represented** | — | — | — | — |

*Note:* PC = Phonetic Coding.

## *Ga* Across Batteries

*Ga* is represented only on the WJ V VTL and directly targets phonological awareness and phonological manipulation. These tasks assess an individual's ability to analyze, blend, segment, delete, and substitute phonemes, all of which underpin decoding, spelling, and orthographic learning. Because phonological awareness underlies the development of accurate word reading and the internalization of spelling patterns, *Ga* measures provide essential diagnostic information for identifying reading and spelling weaknesses (see Appendices J and K for more information).

**DON'T FORGET**

**Tables 2.2–2.9 are particularly useful for determining:**

- why there may be a substantial difference between subtest scores within the same CHC domain
- why individuals may score differently on subtests that purport to measure the same underlying CHC narrow ability construct
- what subtests to use to test hypotheses, follow up on aberrant score performances, and better represent abilities, especially narrow abilities

**Step 3.** Consider CHC abilities measured by batteries and examinee characteristics when selecting a core battery. As noted earlier, battery selection must account for the individual's language background, behavioral presentation, motor skills, attention, anxiety, cultural and experiential factors, and developmental profile. Each battery has features that make it appropriate for different learners. Once the core battery is selected, consider the range of CHC abilities it measures, as the purpose here is a comprehensive assessment of a wide range of broad cognitive abilities.

Based on the information presented in Tables 2.2–2.9, the WJ V appears to be the best choice for a comprehensive assessment, as it provides the broadest CHC coverage and the most complete sampling of narrow abilities. However, it may not be the best choice for every examinee. Table 2.10 provides examples of CHC, examinee, and other considerations that might lead a practitioner to choose either the WJ V, WISC-V or KABC-II NU as their core battery.

**Table 2.10 Battery Selection Based on CHC and Examinee Considerations**

| CHC/Examinee Consideration | WJ V | WISC-V | KABC-II NU |
|---|---|---|---|
| **Breadth of CHC Coverage** | Broadest CHC sampling (*Ga, Gr, Gl, Gf, Gc, Gwm, Gv, Gs*) | Broad CHC sampling (*Gf, Gc, Gwm, Gv*, and *Gs* are best represented) | Strong "nonverbal" CHC coverage (*Gf, Gv, Gwm*) |
| **Expressive Language Limitations** | Language heavy | Language heavy | Low verbal demand |
| **Receptive Language Limitations** | Moderate to heavy language load | Moderate to heavy language load | Low language load |
| **Selective Mutism/ Minimal Speech** | High verbal demand | High verbal demand | Moderate to low verbal demand |
| **Attention Difficulties/ ADHD** | Longest battery; steady pace; moderate engagement | Moderate in length; variable pace; moderate speeded load | Short battery; consistent pacing; high engagement |
| **Low Frustration Tolerance** | Length and repetition may be difficult | Predictable structure is beneficial | Game-like tasks reduce frustration |
| **Fine-Motor Weakness** | Use of an iPad is required | Coding may be difficult | Minimal fine-motor motor demands |
| **High Test Anxiety** | Some tasks may feel "school-like," which can trigger anxiety | Multiple speeded tasks lead to pressure to "go faster" | Lowest performance pressure, fewest timed tasks, puzzle-based, playful |
| **Cultural/Linguistic Diversity** | Knowledge-based tasks may disadvantage | Knowledge-based tasks may disadvantage | Generally moderate to low culture and language load |
| **Hearing Difficulties/ Auditory Issues** | High auditory load | High auditory load | Moderate to low auditory load; strong visual emphasis |
| **Need for *Ga* (Auditory Processing)** | Only battery with Ga | Not represented | Not represented |
| **Need for Rapid Naming (*Gr*)** | Strongest Gr coverage | Good literacy-based naming, but underrepresented | Not represented |
| **Need for Learning Efficiency (*Gl*)** | Strong, meaningful memory coverage | Strong associative memory coverage | Highly engaging associative memory tasks |
| **Younger Students/ Developmental Concerns** | Moderate language; moderate complexity | Moderate to high language; moderate complexity | Low language; developmentally sensitive |

Note that a digital administration format introduces unique challenges for certain examinees. Table 2.11 shows that individuals with fine-motor or visual-motor weaknesses, limited experience with tablets, visual sensitivities, or attention regulation difficulties may struggle with the physical and sensory demands of touchscreen interaction. Likewise, learners with anxiety, sensory processing differences, hearing difficulties, or a strong need for tactile engagement may find the digital format less accessible or less reflective of their true abilities. For these individuals, a paper-and-pencil administration format may provide a more equitable and accurate assessment experience. Considering these examinee characteristics ensures that battery selection supports valid interpretation and prevents digital interface demands from obscuring cognitive strengths.

**Step 4.** Once a core battery is selected, the practitioner identifies what tests to administer from it and what supplemental tests may be needed. Keep in mind that the purpose of battery selection and organization here is to assess adequately a broad range of abilities to gain a comprehensive understanding of cognitive strengths and weaknesses. Therefore, practitioners should begin with two qualitatively different indicators of each broad ability. Rapid Reference 2.3 provides guidance on the best representation of each of eight broad abilities based on current research, as certain narrow abilities are more central to the broad ability than others (Schneider & McGrew, 2018). Table 2.12 shows the two best tests from the WJ V COG and WJ V VTL (which are treated as a single battery, since the tests comprising them are conormed) in terms of construct representation. Tables 2.13 and 2.14 provide the same information for the WISC-V and KABC-II NU.

**Table 2.11 Examinee Characteristics that May Create Challenges for Digitally Administered Batteries**

| Examinee Characteristic | Why This Creates Difficulty in Digital Format | Implications for Battery Selection |
|---|---|---|
| Fine-motor or visual-motor weaknesses | Requires tapping, dragging, and precise screen interactions | May underestimate reasoning abilities |
| Limited experience with tablets or touchscreens | Unfamiliarity with digital navigation slows responses | Performance may reflect technology exposure rather than ability |
| Visual sensitivity or visual fatigue | Screen brightness, contrast, and sustained visual focus can be taxing | May reduce attention or comfort; consider paper-and-pencil or tactile tasks |
| Attention regulation difficulties (ADHD, EF weaknesses) | Digital stimuli, animations, and transitions can be distracting | Increased impulsivity or inconsistent responding |
| Anxiety about technology or performance | Fear of "breaking" the device or making irreversible errors | Hesitation or slowed responding unrelated to cognitive ability |
| Sensory sensitivities or ASD-related needs | Screen-based tasks may be overstimulating or lack needed tactile input | Engagement may drop; KABC-II NU is often better tolerated |
| Hearing difficulties or auditory processing weaknesses | Digital audio cues or recorded instructions may be harder to process | Misunderstood instructions can attenuate scores |
| Need for manipulatives or hands-on materials | Digital format removes tactile tasks (e.g., blocks, cards) | May not capture true reasoning strengths; WISC-V (paper-and-pencil administration) or KABC-II NU preferable |
| Younger developmental level | Younger children may struggle with digital pacing or interface expectations | Engagement and accuracy may be higher with hands-on tasks |

## Rapid Reference 2.3

### Best Representation of CHC Broad Abilities

**Gc—General Information (K0) and Lexical Knowledge (VL).**
*Time permitting, a Listening Ability (LS) test is recommended. However, in most comprehensive assessments, LS is typically measured via achievement tests that include listening comprehension.*

**Gf—Induction (I) and General Sequential Reasoning. (RG).**
*Quantitative Reasoning (RQ) tests should be given only when math difficulties are part of the referral.*

**Gv—Two tests of Visualization (Gv:Vz).**
*Vz is the core ability of Gv. Of all the Gv narrow abilities, Vz has the highest predictive validity and the strongest loadings on a Gv factor in well-designed factor-analytic studies. The narrow abilities comprising Gv also have low correlations, leading to expected substantial variation if multiple narrow Gv abilities are measured. When measuring Gv, some practitioners include a Visual Memory (MV) test to provide better representation of Gv. However, tests of MV are not very useful for understanding most academic and learning difficulties or predicting educational success (Carroll, 1993).*

**Ga—Two tests of Phonetic Coding (Ga:PC)**
*Among all the Ga narrow abilities, most psychologists are interested in PC because of its relationship to reading. Some Ga narrow abilities are measured by audiologists, while others are important for understanding musical aptitude. PC is typically measured by achievement tests, diagnostic reading batteries, and special-purpose tests. If a referral involves reading difficulties, PC measures should be administered. Note that the WJ V VTL has four Ga tests that vary in their degree of complexity: Least complex (Sound Blending), moderately complex (Segmentation), higher complexity (Sound Deletion), and most complex (Sound Substitution). Paying attention to the degree of complexity in Ga tasks is essential because different phonological skills impose very different demands on learners. Simple tasks like blending reflect basic phonological access, while more complex tasks, such as deletion and substitution, require advanced manipulation, working-memory support, and precise phoneme representations. When evaluating for a potential reading disability, this progression helps determine whether a student struggles only with foundational skills or with higher-order phonological manipulation, which is far more predictive of decoding and word-reading difficulties.*

**Gwm—Auditory Short-term Storage (Wa) and Working Memory Capacity (Wc).**
*Wa tests should be of two kinds: one that minimizes the use of strategies, such as memory for digits, and one that has ecological validity, such as memory for sentences. Visual Short-term Storage (Wv) is not particularly helpful in understanding academic difficulties. Note that a battery that has two Gwm tests, one measuring Wa and one measuring Wv does not adequately represent the broad Gwm ability, despite meeting the "two qualitatively different indicators" criterion. This is because the Wa and Wv tasks measure memory span (i.e., how much information a person can hold in mind exactly as it was presented). They are storage-only tasks. Working memory (Wc) involves holding information while mentally manipulating it. Wc requires storage and manipulation, reflecting the mental workspace used for reasoning, comprehension, and problem-solving.*

**Gl—Associative Memory (MA) and Meaningful Memory (MM).**
*MM tests are most strongly related to academic learning because school tasks overwhelmingly involve remembering meaningful, organized content. MA tests are moderately related to academic performance. MA is important for initial learning of new associations and supports early reading (letter-sound associations), vocabulary learning, and math fact acquisition. Although Free Recall Memory (M6) is also part of Gl, it is the least related to academic performance, which is most likely why it is not commonly used in cognitive ability and intelligence tests. M6 tests are more commonly used in neuropsychological batteries because they are sensitive to executive functioning and attention. Because M6 tests are unstructured, performance may be affected by distractibility, inconsistent attention, poor self-monitoring, and weak organizational strategies (Carroll, 1993; McGrew, 2005, 2009).*

**Gr—Ideational Fluency (FI) and Naming Facility (NA).**
*NA is often referred to as the speed of lexical access, a form of verbal efficiency or automaticity of word retrieval. Although there are many narrow Gr abilities, FI and NA have the most predictive validity, particularly for reading.*

**Gs—Perceptual Speed-Search (Ps) and Perceptual Speed-Compare (Pc).**
*Given that Perceptual Speed (P) is now an intermediate factor and Ps and Pc are new narrow abilities that help to distinguish the nuances of the Gs construct and among Gs tests, it is important to understand the differences between them and how to interpret substantial Pc v. Ps score differences when they occur, as they represent qualitatively different cognitive demands. When Pc and Ps diverge, the pattern can reveal important information about visual attention, discrimination, efficiency, and cognitive control.*

**Table 2.12 WJ V COG and WJ V VTL: Best Two Tests per Broad Ability + Cross-Battery Recommendations**

| CHC Broad Ability | Best Two WJ V Subtests | Within-Battery and Cross-Battery Recommendation |
|---|---|---|
| ***Gc*—Comprehension-Knowledge** | Oral Vocabulary (VL)<br>General Information (K0) | Consider Understanding Directions (LS: *Gwm*:Wc) if a broader representation is desired. |
| ***Gf*—Fluid Reasoning** | Matrices (I)<br>Analysis-Synthesis (RG, RQ) | Consider *Number Series* (RQ) if a broader representation is desired. |
| ***Gwm*—Working Memory Capacity** | Verbal Attention (Wa)<br>Numbers Reversed (Wc) | Consider Sentence Repetition (Wa) in place of Verbal Attention to enhance ecological validity |
| ***Gv*—Visual Processing** | Spatial Relations (Vz) Block Rotation (Vz) | |
| ***Gs*—Processing Speed** | Number-Pattern Matching (Pc,OP) | **WISC-V**: Symbol Search (Ps) or other Ps subtest |
| ***Gl*—Learning Efficiency** | Story Recall (MM)<br>Visual-Auditory Learning (MA) | |
| ***Gr*—Retrieval Fluency** | Semantic Word Retrieval (FI)<br>Rapid Picture Naming (NA) | Consider including *Phonemic Word Retrieval* (FW) if a broader representation is desired or for reading referrals. Consider Rapid Letter Naming (*Gr*:NA, OP) for a reading referral |
| ***Ga*—Auditory Processing** | Sound Blending (PC)<br>Sound Deletion (PC) | Consider Nonsense Word Repetition (*Gwm*:Wa; *Ga*:UM) if a broader representation is desired |

*Note:* Tests printed in orange are from the WJ V VTL. Tests printed in italics are from the WJ V COG Extended Battery. On the WJ V COG+VTL battery, only Gs requires supplementing via XBA. K0 = General Information; LS = Listening Ability; VL = Lexical Knowledge; I = Induction; RG = General Sequential Reasoning; RQ = Quantitative Reasoning; Wc = Working Memory Capacity; Wa = Auditory Short-Term Storage; Vz = Visualization; Ps = Perceptual Speed-Search, Pc = Perceptual Speed-Compare; OP = Orthographic Processing; MM = Meaningful Memory; MA = Associative Memory; FI = Ideational Fluency; FW = Word Fluency; NA = Naming Facility; UM = Memory of Sound Patterns; PC = Phonetic Coding.

**Table 2.13 WISC-V: Best Two Subtests per Broad Ability + Within- and Cross-Battery Recommendations**

| CHC Broad Ability | Best Two WISC-V Subtests | Within-Battery and Cross-Battery Recommendation |
|---|---|---|
| *Gc*—**Comprehension-Knowledge** | Vocabulary (VL)<br>Information (K0) | Consider a test of Listening Ability (LS) if broader representation is desired. |
| *Gf*—**Fluid Reasoning** | Matrix Reasoning (I) Figure Weights (RG,RQ) | Consider a test of Quantitative Reasoning (RQ) for math referral |
| *Gwm*—**Working Memory Capacity** | Digit Span (Wa, Wc) Letter-Number Sequencing (Wc) | Consider a memory for sentences test (Wa) for its ecological validity (e.g., remembering directions in the classroom) |
| *Gv*—**Visual Processing** | Block Design (Vz)<br>Visual Puzzles (Vz) | |
| *Gs*—**Processing Speed** | Coding (Pc)—visual-motor speed; Symbol Search (Ps)—visual scanning | |
| *Gl*—**Learning Efficiency** | Immediate Symbol Translation (MA) | **WJ V:**<br>Story Recall (MM) |
| *Gr*—**Retrieval Fluency** | Naming Speed Literacy (NA) | **WJ V:**<br>Semantic Word Retrieval (FI) |
| *Ga*—**Auditory Processing** | | **WJ V VTL:**<br>Sound Blending (PC)<br>Sound Deletion (PC) |

*Note:* K0 = General Information; LS = Listening Ability; VL = Lexical Knowledge; I = Induction; RG = General Sequential Reasoning; RQ = Quantitative Reasoning; Wc = Working Memory Capacity; Wa = Auditory Short-Term Storage; Vz = Visualization; Ps = Perceptual Speed-Search, Pc = Perceptual Speed-Compare; MM = Meaningful Memory; MA = Associative Memory; FI = Ideational Fluency; NA = Naming Facility; PC = Phonetic Coding.

**Table 2.14 KABC-II NU: Best Two Subtests per Broad Ability + Within- and Cross-Battery Recommendations**

| CHC Broad Ability | Best Two KABC-II NU Subtests (Ages 7–18) | Within-Battery and Cross-Battery Recommendation |
|---|---|---|
| *Gc*—**Comprehension-Knowledge** | Verbal Knowledge (VL) | **WJ V COG:**<br>General Information (K0)<br>or<br>**WISC-V:** Information (K0) |
| *Gf*—**Fluid Reasoning** | Pattern Reasoning (I; Vz) Story Completion (RG) | |
| *Gwm*—**Working Memory Capacity** | Number Recall (Wa) | **WJV VTL (optional):**<br>Sentence Repetition (Wa)<br>and<br>**WISC-V:**<br>Letter-Number Sequencing (Wc) |
| *Gv*—**Visual Processing** | Triangles (Vz)<br>Block Counting (Vz) | |
| *Gs*—**Processing Speed** | | **WISC-V:**<br>Coding, (Pc)<br>Symbol Search (Ps) |
| *Gl*—**Learning Efficiency** | Rebus (MA) | **WJ V COG:**<br>Story Recall (MM) |
| *Gr*—**Retrieval Fluency** | | **WJ V COG:**<br>Semantic Word Retrieval (FI)<br>**WJ V VTL:**<br>Rapid Picture Naming (NA) |
| *Ga*—**Auditory Processing** | | **WJ V VTL:**<br>Sound Blending (PC)<br>Sound Deletion (PC) |

*Note:* K0 = General Information; VL = Lexical Knowledge; I = Induction; RG = General Sequential Reasoning; Wc = Working Memory Capacity; Wa = Auditory Short-Term Storage; Vz = Visualization; Ps = Perceptual Speed-Search, Pc = Perceptual Speed-Compare; MM = Meaningful Memory; MA = Associative Memory; FI = Ideational Fluency; NA = Naming Facility; PC = Phonetic Coding.

**Step 5. Use X-BASS to Analyze Cross-Battery Data**

Table 2.14 illustrated how to augment the KABC-II NU core battery with tests or subtests from other batteries to measure eight broad cognitive abilities. Recall that an XBA guiding principle (discussed in Chapter 1) is to use the smallest number of batteries possible in an XBA. Table 2.14 made it clear that either the WJ V or WISC-V would be a good choice. Table 2.15 shows the scores obtained from the administration of this KABC-II NU-based XBA using mostly the WJ V COG/VTL as the supplemental battery. The WISC-V was used to represent *Gs* only because it has measures of Pc and Ps, whereas *Gs* tests on the WJ V COG are measures of Pc and include only orthographic stimuli. A third *Gs*:Pc test, Symbol Inhibition, is included on the WJ V COG but does not contribute to the *Gs* composite.

Because we are interested only in a wide sampling of CHC broad abilities, which required us to use subtests from more than one battery, we will enter our data (from Table 2.15) directly on the XBA tab. To do this, create a case record on the X-BASS **DASHBOARD**, and then click on the XBA button, as shown in Figure 2.1. On the XBA tab, select the first battery for which you have scores to enter. After entering all relevant scores for the first battery, go back to the drop-down and enter the next battery name or acronym, and so on until all scores have been entered. At the top of the tab, click on "CLEAR UNUSED TESTS." The arrow in Figure 2.2 shows the location of this function on the XBA tab. This function deletes any subtest names that have no corresponding scores.

**DON'T FORGET**

When X-BASS determines that an XBA rule for calculating a composite has been met, the composite is calculated using a standard formula and meta-analytic average reliabilities and intercorrelations. This method provides a more stable and defensible foundation for composite estimation than age-specific coefficients from individual battery manuals (see Appendices D and E for details on the psychometric defensibility of XBA composites).

Figure 2.2 also shows the first two domains on the XBA tab, *Gc* and *Gf*. The figure shows that a composite is reported for *Gc* (SS = 103), but no composite was calculated and reported for *Gf*, even though this combination of test scores corresponds to a KABC-II NU Gf/Planning composite of 86. *Why didn't the XBA tab provide a two-subtest composite for Gf?* To answer this question, it is important to understand how, and under what conditions, the XBA tab calculates composites. The narrative at the bottom of each CHC domain on the XBA tab explains why a composite was calculated or not.

**Calculation of XBA composites on the XBA analysis tab of X-BASS.** One goal of the XBA method is to calculate reliable and valid CHC composites from scores drawn across different batteries. A second goal of the XBA method is to present score configurations within each CHC domain that are psychometrically defensible and clinically meaningful. X-BASS accomplishes this via explicit rules that determine when a composite should be calculated and when it should not. These rules center on the concept of **cohesion**—the degree to which scores within a CHC domain "hang together" and represent a unified underlying ability. When scores are cohesive,

**Table 2.15 Results of KABC-II NU-based XBA**

| Ability | KABC-II NU Subtests (7–18) | Score | Cross-Battery Recommendation | Score |
|---|---|---|---|---|
| *Gc* | Verbal Knowledge (VL) | 10 | WJ V COG: General Information (K0) | 105 |
| *Gf* | Pattern Reasoning (I; Vz) | 10 | | |
| | Story Completion (RG) | 5 | | |
| *Gwm* | Number Recall (Wa) | 11 | WJ V VTL: Sentence Repetition (Wa) | 101 |
| | | | WISC-V: Letter-Number Sequencing (Wc) | 79 |
| *Gv* | Triangles (Vz) | 12 | | |
| | Block Counting (Vz) | 11 | | |
| *Gs* | | | WISC-V: Coding (Pc) | 9 |
| | | | WISC-V: Symbol Search (Ps) | 6 |
| *Gl* | Rebus (MA) | 10 | WJ V COG: Story Recall (MM) | 84 |
| *Gr* | | | WJ V COG: Semantic Word Retrieval (FI) | 108 |
| | | | WJ V VTL: Rapid Picture Naming (NA) | 76 |
| *Ga* | | | WJ V VTL: Sound Blending (PC) | 99 |
| | | | WJ V VTL: Sound Deletion (PC) | 71 |

*Note:* Shading in this table is meant to clarify the subtests that comprise each broad ability. K0 = General Information; VL = Lexical Knowledge; I = Induction; RG = General Sequential Reasoning; Wc = Working Memory Capacity; Wa = Auditory Short-Term Storage; Vz = Visualization; Ps = Perceptual Speed-Search, Pc = Perceptual Speed-Compare; MM = Meaningful Memory; MA = Associative Memory; FI = Ideational Fluency; NA = Naming Facility; PC = Phonetic Coding.

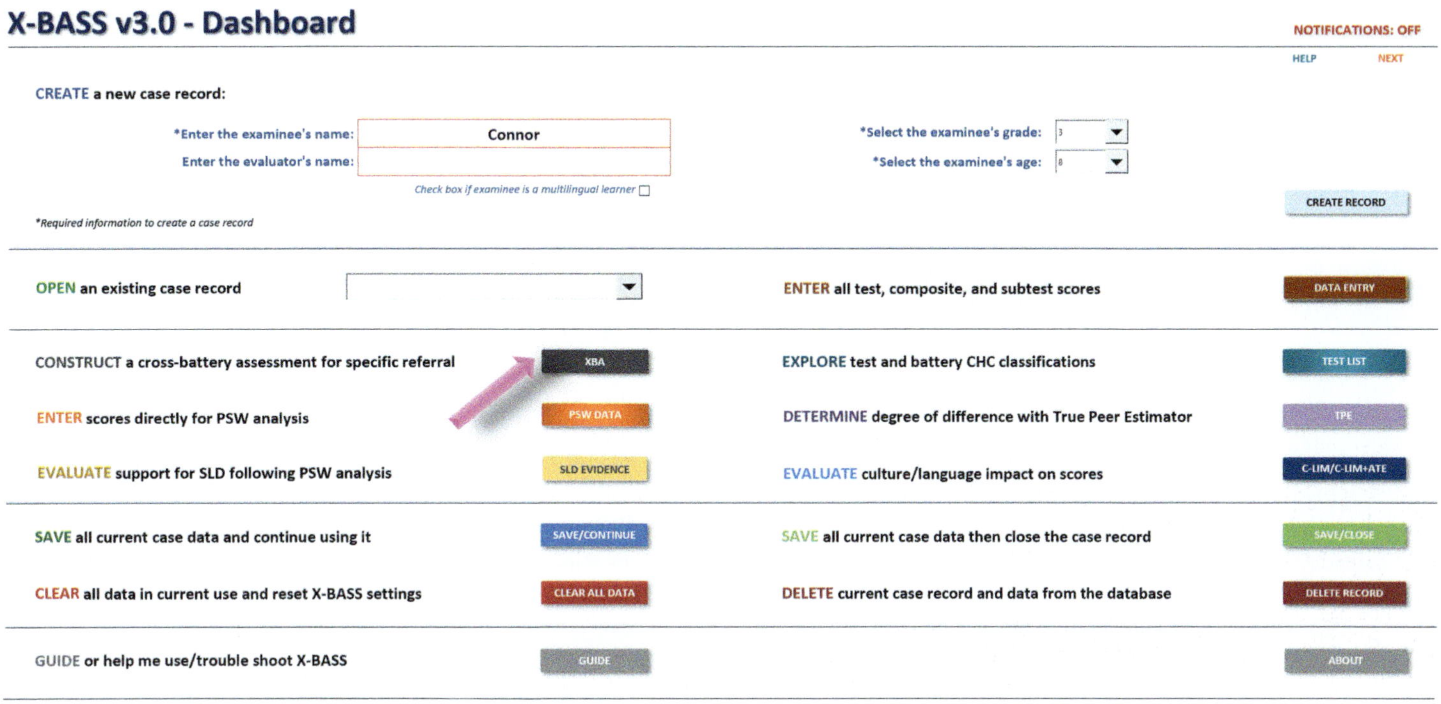


**FIGURE 2.1 Entering Data Directly on the XBA Tab**

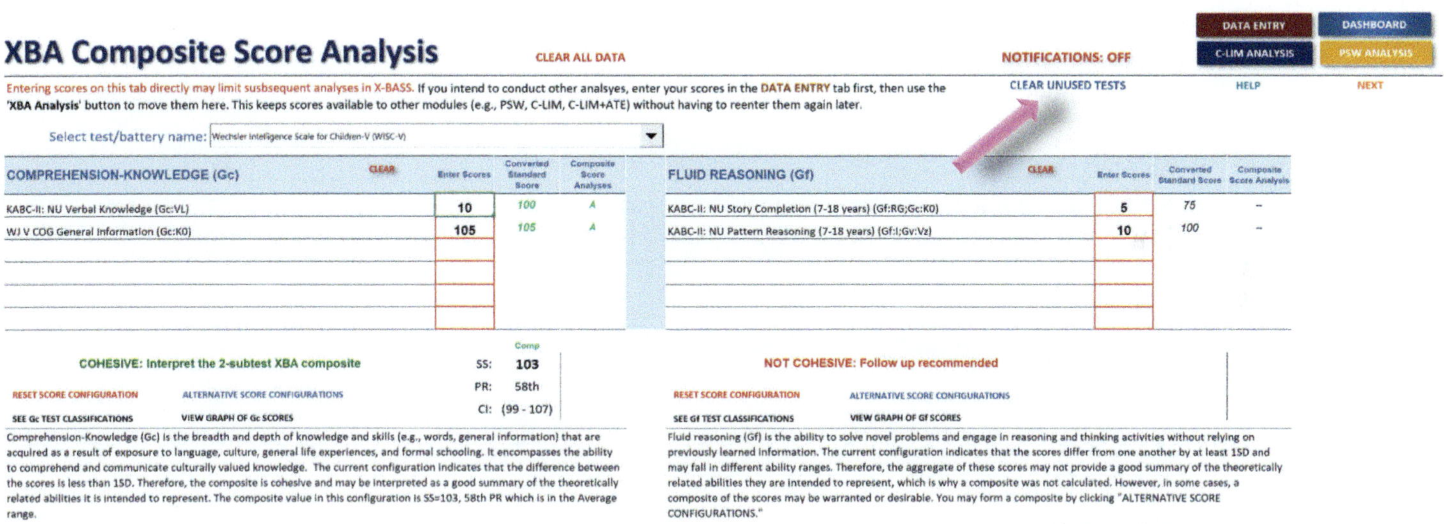


**FIGURE 2.2 Clearing Unused Tests from the XBA Analysis**

a composite provides a sound summary of the theoretically related abilities it is intended to represent. When scores are not cohesive, a composite may obscure important strengths and weaknesses; in such cases, the composite is calculated from a subset of scores or not calculated at all. Depending on how many scores are entered into a CHC domain on the XBA tab (up to six), different outcomes or score configurations are possible.

*Two-subtest composites*: When two scores are entered into a domain on the XBA tab, only two outcomes are possible:

A composite is calculated and reported, or
A composite is not calculated, and the scores are reported separately.

> **DON'T FORGET**
>
> Construct-validation research shows that when individuals perform well on one narrow ability within a CHC construct, they typically perform well across other narrow abilities within that same construct. When scores do not converge as expected, the discrepancy itself may be clinically meaningful and should be explored.

Returning to the *Gf* domain in Figure 2.2, Story Completion has a scaled score of 5, and Pattern Reasoning has a scaled score of 10. Because these scores differ more than expected, it is necessary to hypothesize why this occurred.

When hypothesizing about score differences, the first step is to understand, from a theoretical perspective, what each subtest measures. In this example, both subtests measure *Gf*. Story Completion measures General Sequential Reasoning (RG), and Pattern Reasoning measures Induction (I). These narrow abilities are moderately to strongly related, so performance is expected to be similar. Because it is not, it may suggest that sequential or contextual reasoning may be weaker than simultaneous pattern induction. Therefore, it will be helpful to measure RG using different stimuli and a different task format than that used in the Story Completion subtest. Another RG measure will help determine whether RG is intact or reflects a narrow ability weakness, as suggested by the Story Completion score.

> **CAUTION**
>
> The CTONI-2 has six Gf subtests. Each XBA domain can accommodate up to six subtests. Because the Gf domain already includes two KABC-II NU subtests, the CTONI-2 will populate the remaining four slots. If the subtest you need does not appear, delete one you do not need and select the desired subtest from the dropdown menu (Figure 2.5).

To locate an RG subtest that meets these specifications, go to the DASHBOARD and click the TEST LIST button. On the TEST LIST tab, select *Gf*. The program will display a list of subtests classified as RG (Figure 2.3). Depending on the available batteries, select and administer a follow-up measure. The first two subtests listed are from the CTONI-2 and provide RG information using different stimuli and formats. After administering one or both, select "CTONI-2" from the dropdown menu on the XBA tab. These subtests will appear below the KABC-II NU *Gf* tests (Figure 2.4).

Because one of the CTONI-2 subtests of interest did not appear in the *Gf* domain, delete a subtest you do not need and select the subtest of interest, which will then appear in its

| General Sequential Reasoning - Gf:RG | Age Range |
|---|---|
| CTONI-2 Pictorial Sequences (Gf:RG) | 6-89 |
| CTONI-2 Geometric Sequences (Gf:RG) | 6-89 |
| D-KEFS Proverb Test: Recognition (Gf:RG;Gc:K0) | 16-89 |
| D-KEFS Twenty Questions Test (Gf:RG) | 8-89 |
| D-KEFS Word Context Test (Gf:RG;Gc:K0) | 8-89 |
| DTLA-5 Geometric Sequences (Gf:RG) | 6-17 |
| KABC-II: NU Story Completion (7-18 years) (Gf:RG;Gc:K0) | 7-18 |
| KABC-II: NU Rover (Gv:SS;Gf:RG) | 5-18 |
| KABC-II: NU Riddles (Gc:VL;Gf:RG) | 3-18 |
| KABC-II: NU Story Completion (5-6 years) (Gc:K0;Gf:RG) | 5-6 |
| KBIT-2 R Riddles (Gc:VL;Gf:RG) | 4-90 |

**FIGURE 2.3 Snapshot of a Few General Sequential Reasoning Subtests from the Test List Tab of X-BASS**

| FLUID REASONING (Gf) CLEAR | Enter Scores | Converted Standard Score | Composite Score Analysis |
|---|---|---|---|
| KABC-II: NU Story Completion (7-18 years) (Gf:RG;Gc:K0) | 5 | 75 | divergent |
| KABC-II: NU Pattern Reasoning (7-18 years) (Gf:I;Gv:Vz) | 10 | 100 | A |
| CTONI-2 Geometric Sequences (Gf:RG) | 11 | 105 | A |
| CTONI-2 Pictorial Sequences (Gf:RG) | 10 | 100 | A |
| | | | |
| | | | |

**FIGURE 2.4 CTONI-2 Subtests Added to the XBA Analysis Tab**

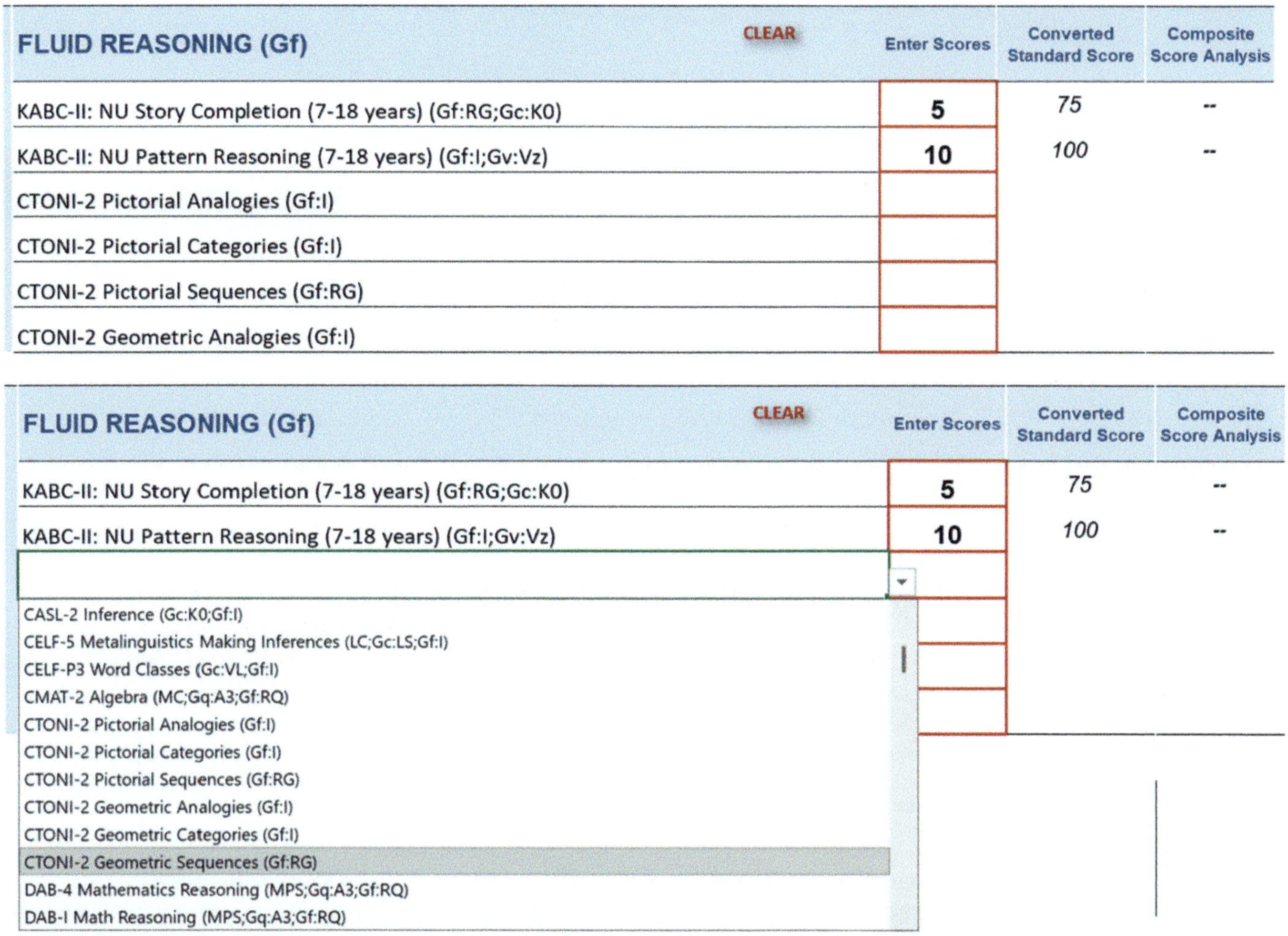


**FIGURE 2.5 Selecting the Desired CTONI-2 Subtests for XBA Analysis**

place. Figure 2.5 shows that Pictorial Analogies was deleted and the subtest of interest, Geometric Sequences, was selected. Figure 2.6 shows that the scores for the CTONI-2 subtests were entered, and a new score configuration emerged. Specifically, the two RG subtests from the CTONI-2 and Pattern Reasoning formed a cohesive composite (SS = 102), and Story Completion was marked as ***divergent***, meaning that it is substantially lower than the other scores. It can now be confirmed that measures of RG and I converge as expected. However, the reason for the divergent performance on the Story Completion subtest remains unclear. *Note that a single RG subtest from the CTONI-2 would have been sufficient. Two were administered in this example to demonstrate various features of X-BASS.*

A second consideration when hypothesizing about score differences is whether the subtests measure other CHC abilities to a substantial degree. Story Completion has *Gc* variance, and Pattern Reasoning has *Gv* variance. Because *Gc* and *Gv* are Average (Table 2.15), neither secondary ability explains the discrepancy. At this point, it is helpful to review the hypotheses in Table 2.16 for the Pattern Reasoning > Story Completion pattern.

The most plausible hypothesis based on the information in this table is that Story Completion imposes greater executive-functioning (EF) demands than Pattern Reasoning. Story Completion requires holding multiple story elements in mind, integrating them into a coherent whole, inhibiting irrelevant details, shifting flexibly between cues, anticipating what comes next, and using social-contextual reasoning. Therefore, a follow-up measure emphasizing similar EF demands is warranted. The best match is a test such as NEPSY-II Narrative Memory or WJ V COG Story Recall.

> **DON'T FORGET**
>
> When a constellation of scores contains one or more scores that would obscure important information if included in the composite, those scores are marked ***divergent***. Divergent scores should be investigated further, as it is unusual for them to differ substantially from cohesive scores. For example, if Story Completion were included in the Gf composite, the composite would drop from 102 to 94 (still Average). Although you can "force" a four-subtest composite using the **ALTERNATIVE SCORE CONFIGURATION** button, Story Completion is marked divergent to avoid missing potentially important information.

Narrative Memory and Story Recall require organizing and integrating multiple story elements. They involve working memory and monitoring; Narrative Memory also requires planning, while Story Recall emphasizes sequencing. Narrative Memory requires suppressing

| FLUID REASONING (Gf) CLEAR | Enter Scores | Converted Standard Score | Composite Score Analysis |
|---|---|---|---|
| KABC-II: NU Story Completion (7-18 years) (Gf:RG;Gc:K0) | 5 | 75 | divergent |
| KABC-II: NU Pattern Reasoning (7-18 years) (Gf:I;Gv:Vz) | 10 | 100 | A |
| CTONI-2 Geometric Sequences (Gf:RG) | 11 | 105 | A |
| CTONI-2 Pictorial Categories (Gf:I) | | | |
| CTONI-2 Pictorial Sequences (Gf:RG) | 10 | 100 | A |
| CTONI-2 Geometric Analogies (Gf:I) | | | |

NOT COHESIVE: Interpret the 3-subtest XBA composite

| | Comp |
|---|---|
| SS: | **102** |
| PR: | 55th |
| CI: | (99 - 105) |

RESET SCORE CONFIGURATION    ALTERNATIVE SCORE CONFIGURATIONS

SEE Gf TEST CLASSIFICATIONS    VIEW GRAPH OF Gf SCORES

Fluid reasoning (Gf) is the ability to solve novel problems and engage in reasoning and thinking activities without relying on previously learned information. The current configuration indicates that because the difference between the highest and lowest scores entered in this domain is greater than 1 and 1/3 SD, this set of scores is not considered cohesive, and a composite based on them may mask important information. Therefore, a composite based on the three highest scores was calculated. This composite is cohesive and may be interpreted as an adequate estimate of the theoretically related abilities it is intended to represent. The lowest score is considered divergent, requiring additional information for interpretation. The composite value in this configuration is SS=102, 55th PR which is in the Average range.

**FIGURE 2.6 New Score Configuration for Gf Composite in XBA Analysis**

**Table 2.16 Possible Explanations for a Substantial Difference Between Pattern Reasoning and Story Completion**

| Pattern A: Pattern Reasoning Average, Story Completion Substantially Lower | Pattern B: Story Completion Average, Pattern Reasoning Substantially Lower |
|---|---|
| **General Hypotheses to Consider** | **General Hypotheses to Consider** |
| • Language or narrative demands may depress Story Completion more than Pattern Reasoning | • Visual–spatial pattern induction may be weaker than contextual or narrative reasoning |
| • Social-pragmatic reasoning may be weaker than abstract visual reasoning | • Difficulty identifying relationships among abstract visual stimuli |
| • Sequential or contextual reasoning may be weaker than simultaneous pattern induction | • Weakness in simultaneous processing relative to sequential/contextual reasoning |
| • Background knowledge or life-experience differences may affect Story Completion | • Limited experience with visual puzzles or pattern-based tasks |
| • Executive function or working-memory load may be higher in Story Completion | • Executive function or working-memory load may be higher in Pattern Reasoning |
| • Attention, engagement, or task interest may vary across subtests | • Attention, engagement, or task interest may vary across subtests |
| • Cultural or contextual unfamiliarity may reduce Story Completion performance | • Visual–spatial unfamiliarity or low confidence may depress Pattern Reasoning performance |
| **Additional Interpretation** | **Additional Interpretation** |
| Story Completion is significantly weaker and is a normative weakness → may reflect non-*Gf* factors | Pattern Reasoning is significantly weaker and is a normative weakness → may reflect non-*Gf* factors |
| **Follow-Up Considerations** | **Follow-Up Considerations** |
| Evaluate *Gc*, EF | Evaluate *Gv*, EF, attention, or visual–spatial experience |

irrelevant details, and both require maintaining coherence. Importantly, Narrative Memory is sensitive to EF-based narrative weaknesses even when language is adequate, which is a useful feature here, as *Gc* is intact. Story Recall can also reveal EF-based weaknesses, though it is somewhat less EF-sensitive.

Because Story Recall was already administered (SS = 84), qualitative behaviors should have been examined. Individuals with EF weaknesses may show disorganized recall, omission of causal links, poor sequencing, irrelevant details, or difficulty maintaining the gist.

At this point, the practitioner may notice that the recommended follow-up tests are not measures of *Gf* but of Meaningful Memory (*Gl*:MM). EF is required for performance on all tasks to some degree, and within broad CHC domains, subtests with higher EF demands may be relatively weaker for individuals with EF weaknesses. This appears to be a viable hypothesis for the noncohesive *Gl* scores and may further explain the Pattern Reasoning > Story Completion pattern. To explore this hypothesis, Narrative Memory was administered. Figure 2.7 shows the selection of the Narrative Memory subtest from a drop down menu in the *Gl* section of the XBA tab.

After entering the Narrative Memory score (scaled score = 6), a new *Gl* configuration appears (Figure 2.8). Story Recall and Narrative Memory form a composite of 79, and Rebus is labeled ***divergent***, as it is substantially higher. Although this configuration supports the EF hypothesis, it is necessary to measure *Gl* more broadly to rule out a more pervasive weakness in *Gl*. The NEPSY-II List Memory/List Memory-Delayed subtest was selected because it measures Free Recall Memory (M6), a third narrow *Gl* ability.

After entering the List Memory score (scaled score = 9), a new configuration emerges (Figure 2.9). A four-subtest cohesive composite (SS = 87) is calculated. As more subtests are added to a composite, individual score differences are diluted, making the overall pattern appear more cohesive. This is a normal statistical effect of aggregating scores and does not necessarily reflect true cognitive uniformity. Although it has been argued empirically that the four-subtest composite is the most reliable and valid estimate of *Gl* (Schneider & Roman, 2018), it nonetheless obscures important information about the EF hypothesis and *Gl* performance more broadly.

The narrative in Figure 2.9 defines *Gl*, explains the composite rule, and characterizes the composite as Below Average. Yet the pattern tells a more nuanced story than the composite itself. The split between the scores influenced by EF and the Average scores reflecting different aspects of *Gl* (i.e., the narrow abilities of Associative Memory and Free Recall Memory) is clinically meaningful. This is when the **ALTERNATIVE SCORE CONFIGURATIONS** function is useful.

When the practitioner clicks this function, they will be asked a series of questions about the configuration they want to see (e.g., "Do you want to create a three-subtest

**CAUTION**

Alternative score configurations require *a priori* decisions. They are not meant to be exploratory. Making decisions a priori keeps the interpretation process disciplined and prevents unintentional bias. It ensures that judgments are guided by consistent, defensible interpretive guidelines.

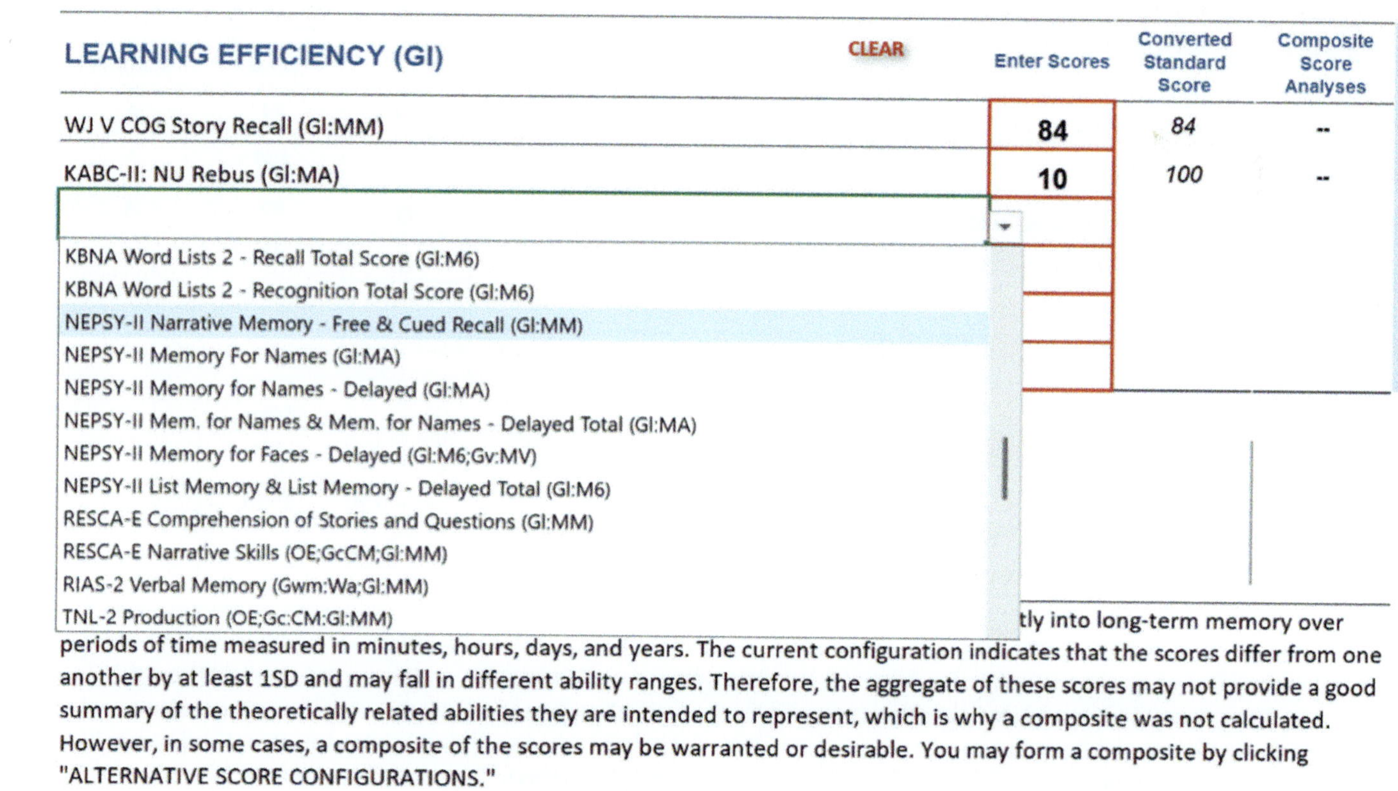


**FIGURE 2.7 Selecting Narrative Memory from the NEPSY-II**

| LEARNING EFFICIENCY (Gl) CLEAR | Enter Scores | Converted Standard Score | Composite Score Analyses |
|---|---|---|---|
| WJ V COG Story Recall (Gl:MM) | 84 | 84 | A |
| KABC-II: NU Rebus (Gl:MA) | 10 | 100 | divergent |
| NEPSY-II Narrative Memory - Free & Cued Recall (Gl:MM) | 6 | 80 | A |
| | | | |
| | | | |
| | | | |

NOT COHESIVE: Interpret the, 2-subtest XBA composite

| | Comp |
|---|---|
| SS: | 79 |
| PR: | 8th |
| CI: | (75 - 83) |

RESET SCORE ALTERNATIVE SCORE CONFIGURATIONS

SEE Gl TEST CLASSIFICATIONS VIEW GRAPH OF Gl SCORES

Learning Efficiency (Gl) is the ability to learn, store, and consolidate new information efficiently into long-term memory over periods of time measured in minutes, hours, days, and years. The current configuration indicates that because the difference between the highest and lowest scores entered in this domain is greater than or equal to 1SD, this set of scores is not cohesive, and a composite based on them may mask important information. Therefore, a composite based on the two lowest scores was calculated. This composite is cohesive and may be interpreted as an adequate estimate of the theoretically related abilities it is intended to represent. The highest score is considered divergent, but may be interpreted in the context of converging data sources. The composite value in this configuration is SS=79, 8th PR which is in the Well Below Average range.

**FIGURE 2.8 New *Gl* Composite After Entering the Score for Narrative Memory from the NEPSY-II**

| LEARNING EFFICIENCY (Gl) CLEAR | Enter Scores | Converted Standard Score | Composite Score Analyses |
|---|---|---|---|
| WJ V COG Story Recall (Gl:MM) | 84 | 84 | A |
| KABC-II: NU Rebus (Gl:MA) | 10 | 100 | A |
| NEPSY-II Narrative Memory - Free & Cued Recall (Gl:MM) | 6 | 80 | A |
| NEPSY-II List Memory & List Memory - Delayed Total (Gl:M6) | 9 | 95 | A |
| | | | |
| | | | |

COHESIVE: Interpret the 4-subtest XBA composite

| | Comp |
|---|---|
| SS: | 87 |
| PR: | 19th |
| CI: | (84 - 90) |

RESET SCORE ALTERNATIVE SCORE CONFIGURATIONS

SEE Gl TEST CLASSIFICATIONS VIEW GRAPH OF Gl SCORES

Learning Efficiency (Gl) is the ability to learn, store, and consolidate new information efficiently into long-term memory over periods of time measured in minutes, hours, days, and years. The current configuration indicates that the difference between the highest and lowest scores entered in this domain is less than or equal to 1 and 1/3 SD, and therefore, a composite was calculated. This composite is considered a good summary of the theoretically related scores it was intended to represent. However, in some cases, an alternative composite or composites may be warranted or desirable based on clinical judgment. You may form alternative composites by clicking "ALTERNATIVE SCORE CONFIGURATIONS." The composite value in this configuration is SS=87, 19th PR which is in the Below Average range.

**FIGURE 2.9 New *Gl* Composite Configuration After Administering Additional NEPSY-II Subtests**

| LEARNING EFFICIENCY (Gl) CLEAR | Enter Scores | Converted Standard Score | Composite Score Analyses |
|---|---|---|---|
| WJ V COG Story Recall (Gl:MM) | 84 | 84 | A |
| KABC-II: NU Rebus (Gl:MA) | 10 | 100 | B |
| NEPSY-II Narrative Memory - Free & Cued Recall (Gl:MM) | 6 | 80 | A |
| NEPSY-II List Memory & List Memory - Delayed Total (Gl:M6) | 9 | 95 | B |
| | | | |
| | | | |

Interpret the two 2-subtest alternative composites

| | Comp A | Comp B |
|---|---|---|
| SS: | 79 | 97 |
| PR: | 8th | 42nd |
| CI: | (75 - 83) | (93 - 101) |

RESET SCORE ALTERNATIVE SCORE CONFIGURATIONS

SEE Gl TEST CLASSIFICATIONS VIEW GRAPH OF Gl SCORES

Learning Efficiency (Gl) is the ability to learn, store, and consolidate new information efficiently into long-term memory over periods of time measured in minutes, hours, days, and years. The current configuration indicates that alternative composites based on the two lowest scores (Comp A) and the two highest scores (Comp B) were calculated. If any score comprising either composite is between 80-89 inclusive, additional supporting data may be needed to justify interpreting the composite as either a strength or a weakness. The first composite (Comp A) in this configuration is SS=79, 8th PR which is in the Well Below Average range and the other (Comp B) is SS=97, 42nd PR and in the Average range.

**FIGURE 2.10** ***Gl*** **Composite Alternative Score Configuration**

composite and call the highest score divergent?"). In keeping with the EF hypothesis, it is appropriate to select the option that creates *two two-subtest composites*. The program automatically determines which scores belong in each composite based on their relative values. Figure 2.10 shows the resulting composites: Story Recall + Narrative Memory (SS = 79) and Rebus + List Memory (SS = 97).

Based on this systematic approach to hypothesis generation and follow-up assessment, two main conclusions emerge:

1. Performance in *Gf* and *Gl* is Average, based on two qualitatively different indicators for each (RG and I for *Gf*; MA and M6 for *Gl*). These composites are 102 and 97, respectively.
2. Although Free Recall Memory and Associative Memory tasks require basic executive supports such as attention and monitoring, they do not require the higher-order executive processes involved in organizing and integrating multiple story elements. Therefore, when Free Recall Memory and Associative Memory are intact, but Story Completion, Story Recall, and Narrative Memory are weak, the pattern suggests that executive functioning, not memory capacity, is the primary limiting factor.

## DON'T FORGET

***Three-subtest composites.*** When three subtests are entered into a domain on the XBA tab, there are four possible outcomes: a three-subtest composite, a two-subtest composite with a divergent high score, a two-subtest composite with a divergent low score, no composite.

***Four-subtest composites.*** When four subtests are entered, there are eight possible outcomes: a four-subtest composite, two two-subtest composites, a two-subtest composite and two divergent scores (three different configurations of this pattern), a three-subtest composite and a divergent high score, a three-subtest composite and a divergent low score, and no composite.

***Five- and six-subtest composites.*** When five or six subtests are entered, a composite is calculated based on all available scores. The reasoning is straightforward. First, programming every possible score combination or outcome would be unnecessarily complex, and after three or four subtests are included, adding additional scores has only a minimal effect on the reliability of the composite. Second, when five or six subtests are entered, the amount of variability (i.e., highest minus lowest score difference) needed for the configuration to be considered statistically unusual is very large, typically a difference of about 2 SDs or more, making non-cohesive patterns rare in the general population (see Rapid Reference 2.4).

## *Rapid Reference 2.4*

### Rules of Thumb for Statistically Unusual Subtest Scatter in XBA Composites

When interpreting variability among subtests that contribute to a composite, it is often helpful to have a general sense of how large the highest–lowest difference must be before it becomes statistically unusual. Because subtests within a composite are positively correlated, some degree of variability is expected even in typical learners. The values provided here offer practical, rule-of-thumb thresholds for identifying when the score spread among subtests is large enough to occur in roughly 10% or fewer individuals.

| Number of Subtests in Composite | Difference Between Highest and Lowest SS Needed for Statistical Rarity at ≈ 10% | Difference Between Highest and Lowest ss Needed for Statistical Rarity at ≈ 10% |
|---|---|---|
| 3 | 32 | 6 |
| 4 | 36 | 7 |
| 5 | 39 | 8 |
| 6 | 41 | 8 |
| 7 | 43 | 9 |

*Note:* When the difference between the highest and lowest scores that comprise an XBA composite is equal to or higher than the values in this table, the difference is large enough to assume that it occurs in approximately 10% (or less) of the general population.

These values are intended only as rules of thumb because they rely on simplified psychometric assumptions, such as equal subtest variances, moderate intercorrelations (i.e., 0.50), and similar reliability levels that rarely hold perfectly in real batteries. Actual subtests differ in reliability, content demands, and measurement error, and true intercorrelations may be higher or lower than the estimated value used here. As a result, these thresholds should not be treated as strict cutoffs or diagnostic indicators. Instead, *they provide a general sense of when subtest scatter is larger than expected* and should be interpreted alongside qualitative task analysis, consistency with other data, and the learner's real-world functioning.

Interpreting score differences, such as those shown in Table 2.16, should be a routine part of test performance interpretation. When subtests within a broad ability domain show a non-cohesive pattern, it indicates that the tasks are likely not measuring a unified underlying ability for that individual. Even subtests classified within the same CHC domain—or even the same narrow ability—can place different cognitive, linguistic, or contextual demands on the learner. Examining the direction of the difference helps pinpoint the likely source of difficulty. Tables 2.17–2.19 parallel earlier tables but extend them to include possible reasons for score differences.

**Table 2.17 Comprehensive WISC-V-Based XBA with Representation of Eight Broad CHC Abilities and Potential Reasons for a Substantial Difference Between Scores Within Domains**

| CHC Domain<br>Best Two Subtests | Pattern A<br>Subtest 1 > Subtest 2 | Pattern B<br>Subtest 2 > Subtest 1 |
|---|---|---|
| *Gc*<br>**Vocabulary, Information** | **What it suggests:** Stronger expressive word knowledge and verbal concept formation than factual/conceptual knowledge tied to schooling and experience.<br>**Hypotheses:**<br>• **Background knowledge:** Limited exposure to factual content or academic topics may depress Information.<br>• **Schooling/experience:** Irregular schooling, cultural differences, or fewer opportunities to learn "common knowledge" may lower Information.<br>• **Test familiarity:** Less familiarity with test-like factual questions may affect Information more than Vocabulary.<br>• **Language load:** Student may do better defining words than answering open-ended factual questions.<br>• **Motivation/interest:** Less interest in factual questions than in word meaning tasks. | **What it suggests:** Stronger factual/conceptual knowledge than expressive vocabulary and verbal concept formation.<br>**Hypotheses:**<br>• **Word retrieval:** Expressive word finding or lexical access may be weaker than stored factual knowledge.<br>• **Language development:** History of language delay or weaker semantic networks may depress Vocabulary.<br>• **Instructional exposure:** Strong content teaching may boost Information despite weaker vocabulary depth.<br>• **Response style:** Student may give brief or vague definitions even when they know the words.<br>• **Cultural-linguistic factors:** Bilingualism or dialect may affect how Vocabulary responses are scored. |

**Table 2.17 (Continued)**

| CHC Domain<br>Best Two Subtests | Pattern A<br>Subtest 1 > Subtest 2 | Pattern B<br>Subtest 2 > Subtest 1 |
|---|---|---|
| ***Gf***<br>**Matrix Reasoning, Figure Weights** | **What it suggests:** Stronger nonverbal pattern induction than quantitative/proportional reasoning.<br>**Hypotheses:**<br>• **Quantitative reasoning:** Relative weakness in understanding numerical relationships or ratios.<br>• **Math exposure:** Limited experience with math concepts may depress Figure Weights.<br>• **Anxiety with numbers:** Math anxiety may selectively affect Figure Weights.<br>• **Visual vs. symbolic:** Student may reason better with purely visual patterns than with number-based analogies.<br>• **Working memory load:** Figure Weights may place higher simultaneous processing and EF demands than Matrix Reasoning. | **What it suggests:** Stronger quantitative/proportional reasoning than abstract visual pattern induction.<br>**Hypotheses:**<br>• **Visual patterning:** Difficulty detecting or integrating visual relationships in matrices.<br>• **Experience with puzzles:** Less experience with visual puzzles may depress Matrix Reasoning.<br>• **Instructional emphasis:** Strong math instruction may support Figure Weights performance.<br>• **Processing style:** Student may prefer structured, rule-based reasoning over open-ended pattern discovery.<br>• **Attention to detail:** May overlook subtle visual features in Matrix Reasoning items. |
| ***Gwm***<br>**Digit Span, Letter-Number Sequencing** | • **What it suggests:** Stronger rote sequential memory than complex manipulation and reordering.<br>**Hypotheses:**<br>• **Manipulation demands:** Difficulty mentally reordering information under time and accuracy pressure.<br>• **EF/WM load:** Higher central executive demands in LNS may exceed capacity.<br>• **Strategy use:** Student may rely on simple repetition strategies that work for Digit Span but not LNS.<br>• **Attention control:** Sustained attention may be harder to maintain during longer LNS sequences.<br>• **Anxiety/pressure:** Performance anxiety may increase as task complexity rises. | • **What it suggests:** Stronger complex manipulation and reordering than simple rote span.<br>**Hypotheses:**<br>• **Motivation:** Student may find simple repetition tasks boring and under-engage on Digit Span.<br>• **Chunking strategies:** May spontaneously use chunking or pattern strategies that benefit LNS more.<br>• • **Auditory encoding:** Basic encoding of digits may be inconsistent, but manipulation processes are relatively intact.<br>• **Practice effects:** Prior exposure to LNS-type tasks (e.g., games, training) may boost performance.<br>• **Testing behavior:** Student may "warm up" and perform better as tasks become more challenging. |
| ***Gv***<br>**Block Design, Visual Puzzles** | **What it suggests:** Stronger constructional/spatial organization than mental rotation and internal visualization.<br>**Hypotheses:**<br>• **Hands-on support:** Physical blocks provide concrete support that aids performance.<br>• **Mental rotation:** Internal manipulation of shapes may be more difficult than external construction.<br>• **Speed/pressure:** Visual Puzzles may feel more time-pressured and abstract.<br>• **Fine-motor comfort:** Student may be comfortable manipulating blocks.<br>• **Instructional exposure:** More experience with building/constructing than with mental puzzle tasks. | **What it suggests:** Stronger mental rotation and internal visualization than constructional tasks.<br>**Hypotheses:**<br>• **Motor demands:** Fine-motor or graphomotor issues may depress Block Design.<br>• **Perfectionism:** Student may overcorrect or slow down on Block Design.<br>• **Processing style:** Prefers internal visualization over physical manipulation.<br>• **Spatial efficiency:** May quickly see solutions mentally without needing concrete supports.<br>• **Test familiarity:** More experience with puzzle-like tasks than block construction. |

*(continued)*

**Table 2.17 (Continued)**

| CHC Domain Best Two Subtests | Pattern A Subtest 1 > Subtest 2 | Pattern B Subtest 2 > Subtest 1 |
|---|---|---|
| ***Gs*** **Coding, Symbol Search** | **What it suggests:** Stronger graphomotor speed and symbol copying than visual scanning and discrimination.<br>**Hypotheses:**<br>• **Visual search:** Difficulty rapidly scanning and comparing symbols may depress Symbol Search.<br>• **Decision speed:** Slower decision-making when judging matches/non-matches.<br>• **Task strategy:** Student may use efficient routines for Coding but not for Symbol Search.<br>• **Anxiety about errors:** May be overly cautious on Symbol Search.<br>• **Visual attention:** More vulnerable to distractibility in scanning tasks. | **What it suggests:** Stronger visual scanning and discrimination than graphomotor speed.<br>**Hypotheses:**<br>• **Fine-motor speed:** Motor or handwriting speed may limit Coding performance.<br>• **Motor fatigue:** Coding may be more physically tiring.<br>• **Practice effects:** Student may be more familiar with search-type tasks than coding-type tasks.<br>• **Perfectionism:** May slow down to avoid copying errors.<br>• **Visual strengths:** Rapid visual comparison may be a relative strength. |
| ***Gl*** **Immediate Symbol Translation, WJ V Story Recall** | **What it suggests:** Stronger associative/paired-associate learning than meaningful verbal memory.<br>**Hypotheses:**<br>• **Meaningful encoding:** Difficulty organizing and encoding stories into coherent structures.<br>• **Language comprehension:** Story Recall may be more affected by language and discourse skills.<br>• **Context use:** Student may rely less on context and more on direct associations.<br>• **Reading risk:** Weak meaningful memory is more closely tied to reading comprehension difficulties.<br>• **Attention:** Longer stories may tax sustained attention more than symbol pairs. | **What it suggests:** Stronger meaningful verbal memory than associative symbol learning.<br>**Hypotheses:**<br>• **Symbol learning:** Abstract symbol–meaning links may be harder to encode.<br>• **Contextual strength:** Student may benefit from narrative context and semantic structure.<br>• **Instructional alignment:** Classroom learning may emphasize stories and meaningful content.<br>• **Motivation:** Stories may be more engaging than arbitrary symbol pairs.<br>• **Visual-symbolic processing:** Symbol processing may be a relative weakness. |
| ***Gr*** **Naming Speed Literacy, WJ V Semantic Word Retrieval** | **What it suggests:** Stronger rapid naming of overlearned symbols than semantic category retrieval.<br>**Hypotheses:**<br>• **Semantic networks:** Category-based retrieval may be less efficient than automatic naming.<br>• **Vocabulary depth:** Limited semantic richness may depress Semantic Word Retrieval.<br>• **Reading risk:** Rapid naming strength with weaker semantic fluency may point to specific language vulnerabilities.<br>• **Task familiarity:** More practice with letter/word naming than category fluency tasks.<br>• **Executive control:** Category fluency requires more self-monitoring and strategy. | **What it suggests:** Stronger semantic category retrieval than rapid naming of symbols.<br>**Hypotheses:**<br>• **Rapid naming:** Slower access to phonological labels for letters/words.<br>• **Reading risk:** Weak naming speed is strongly associated with decoding/fluency difficulties.<br>• **Automaticity:** Overlearned symbol retrieval may be less automatized.<br>• **Practice:** Less exposure to timed naming tasks.<br>• **Attention/tempo:** Student may work more slowly and carefully on speeded tasks. |
| ***Ga*** **WJ V Sound Blending, WJ V Sound Deletion** | **What it suggests:** Stronger phonological synthesis than phoneme manipulation.<br>**Hypotheses:**<br>• **Phoneme manipulation:** Difficulty deleting sounds from words, especially medial/final phonemes.<br>• **Working memory:** Higher WM demands in deletion tasks.<br>• **Reading risk:** Deletion weaknesses are strongly tied to decoding/spelling difficulties.<br>• **Instructional history:** Limited explicit phonemic manipulation instruction.<br>• **Task complexity:** Student may manage simpler blending but struggle with more complex operations. | **What it suggests:** Stronger phoneme manipulation than blending.<br>**Hypotheses:**<br>• **Blending exposure:** Less practice with blending tasks specifically.<br>• **Task engagement:** Student may find deletion tasks more interesting or challenging.<br>• **Instructional focus:** Intervention may have emphasized manipulation skills.<br>• **Response style:** May guess or rush on blending items.<br>• **Ceiling/floor:** Blending may be too easy, leading to careless errors. |

**Table 2.18 Comprehensive KABC-II NU-Based XBA with Representation of Eight CHC Broad Abilities and Potential Reasons for a Substantial Difference Between Scores Within Domains**

| CHC Domain Best Two Subtests | Pattern A<br>Subtest 1 > Subtest 2 | Pattern B<br>Subtest 2 > Subtest 1 |
|---|---|---|
| ***Gc***<br>**Verbal Knowledge, WJ V General Information** | **What it suggests:** Stronger verbal concept knowledge (definitions, relationships) than broad factual knowledge.<br>**Hypotheses:**<br>• **Conceptual learning strength:** Student may learn and retain word meanings more easily than discrete facts.<br>• **Limited factual exposure:** Fewer opportunities to learn mainstream cultural or academic facts.<br>• **Cultural mismatch:** General Information items may be less culturally relevant than Verbal Knowledge items.<br>• **Instructional focus:** Emphasis on vocabulary and language arts over content-area knowledge.<br>• **Test engagement:** Student may find Verbal Knowledge more engaging than factual questions. | **What it suggests:** Stronger factual knowledge than verbal concept knowledge.<br>**Hypotheses:**<br>• **Semantic depth:** Vocabulary networks may be shallower than factual knowledge stores.<br>• **Language history:** Past language delays or reduced language stimulation may affect Verbal Knowledge.<br>• **Content-rich environment:** Home/school may emphasize facts, media, and information more than explicit vocabulary teaching.<br>• **Response style:** Student may under-explain or give partial responses on Verbal Knowledge.<br>• **Assessment language:** If bilingual, conceptual knowledge may be stronger in another language than the test language. |
| ***Gf***<br>**Pattern Reasoning, Story Completion** | **What it suggests:** Stronger nonverbal pattern induction than contextual/narrative reasoning.<br>**Hypotheses:**<br>• **Social-pragmatic reasoning:** Student may find social or narrative cues harder to interpret than abstract patterns.<br>• **Language/context load:** Story Completion may be more affected by language comprehension and background knowledge.<br>• **Processing style:** Preference for decontextualized, visual reasoning over contextual, story-based reasoning.<br>• **Life experience:** Limited exposure to social scenarios or story structures may depress Story Completion.<br>• **EF demands:** Integrating multiple story elements may place higher EF demands than Pattern Reasoning. | **What it suggests:** Stronger contextual/narrative reasoning than nonverbal pattern induction.<br>**Hypotheses:**<br>• **Visual patterning:** Difficulty detecting or integrating abstract visual relationships.<br>• **Strength in social cognition:** Student may use social understanding and narrative structure to reason effectively.<br>• **Language strengths:** Good comprehension of story language may support Story Completion.<br>• **Instructional exposure:** More experience with stories, reading, and narrative tasks than with visual puzzles.<br>• **Engagement:** Student may be more engaged by story-based tasks than abstract patterns. |
| ***Gwm*** **Number Recall, WJ V Sentence Repetition** | **What it suggests:** Stronger simple auditory span than complex sentence-level working memory.<br>**Hypotheses:**<br>• **Language complexity:** Sentence Repetition adds syntactic and semantic load beyond simple digits.<br>• **Verbal WM:** Holding and reproducing longer linguistic units may be more difficult than digits.<br>• **Language disorder risk:** Weakness may reflect expressive/receptive language vulnerabilities.<br>• **Attention to detail:** Student may miss small function words or morphology in sentences.<br>• **Processing speed:** Limited time to encode and rehearse full sentences. | **What it suggests:** Stronger sentence-level working memory than simple digit span.<br>**Hypotheses:**<br>• **Meaningful context:** Student may benefit from semantic context in sentences.<br>• **Digit encoding:** Digits may be less meaningful or harder to encode than language for this student.<br>• **Language strength:** Strong language skills may support Sentence Repetition performance.<br>• **Motivation:** Student may be more engaged by sentence tasks than digit lists.<br>• **Strategy use:** May use semantic or syntactic chunking strategies for sentences. |

*(continued)*

**Table 2.18 (Continued)**

| CHC Domain Best Two Subtests | Pattern A<br>Subtest 1 > Subtest 2 | Pattern B<br>Subtest 2 > Subtest 1 |
|---|---|---|
| *Gv*<br>**Triangles, Block Counting** | **What it suggests:** Stronger spatial construction and patterning than spatial sequencing/counting.<br>**Hypotheses:**<br>• **Sequential demands:** Counting blocks in complex arrays may overload sequencing and tracking.<br>• **Visual scanning:** Block Counting may require more systematic scanning and EF.<br>• **Working memory:** Holding partial counts while scanning may be difficult.<br>• **Task familiarity:** More experience with construction than with counting hidden units.<br>• **Attention control:** May lose track or double-count in Block Counting. | **What it suggests:** Stronger spatial sequencing/counting than construction.<br>**Hypotheses:**<br>• **Motor/coordination:** Fine-motor or visuomotor issues may depress Triangles.<br>• **Planning:** Student may struggle to plan efficient construction strategies.<br>• **Analytic style:** May excel at analytic counting and decomposition of shapes.<br>• **Instructional exposure:** Experience with math/ geometry may support Block Counting.<br>• **Perfectionism:** May overcorrect or hesitate on Triangles. |
| *Gs*<br>**WISC-V Coding, WISC-V Symbol Search** | **What it suggests:** Stronger graphomotor speed and symbol copying than visual scanning and discrimination.<br>**Hypotheses:**<br>• **Visual search:** Difficulty rapidly scanning and comparing symbols may depress Symbol Search.<br>• **Decision speed:** Slower decision-making when judging matches/non-matches.<br>• **Task strategy:** Student may use efficient routines for Coding but not for Symbol Search.<br>• **Anxiety about errors:** May be overly cautious on Symbol Search.<br>• **Visual attention:** More vulnerable to distractibility in scanning tasks. | **What it suggests:** Stronger visual scanning and discrimination than graphomotor speed.<br>**Hypotheses:**<br>• **Fine-motor speed:** Motor or handwriting speed may limit Coding performance.<br>• **Motor fatigue:** Coding may be more physically tiring.<br>• **Practice effects:** Student may be more familiar with search-type tasks than coding-type tasks.<br>• **Perfectionism:** May slow down to avoid copying errors.<br>• **Visual strengths:** Rapid visual comparison may be a relative strength. |
| *Gl*<br>**Rebus, WJ V Story Recall** | **What it suggests:** Stronger associative learning with pictorial/symbolic cues than meaningful story memory.<br>**Hypotheses:**<br>• **Visual support:** Student benefits from visual cues in Rebus tasks.<br>• **Narrative encoding:** Difficulty using story structure to support recall.<br>• **Language demands:** Story Recall may be more sensitive to language comprehension.<br>• **Reading implications:** Weak meaningful memory may relate to comprehension difficulties.<br>• **Attention:** Longer verbal tasks may be harder to sustain. | **What it suggests:** Stronger meaningful story memory than pictorial/symbolic associative learning.<br>**Hypotheses:**<br>• **Symbol abstraction:** Abstract rebus symbols may be harder to encode than stories.<br>• **Contextual strength:** Student may rely on narrative context and semantic links.<br>• **Instructional alignment:** Learning history may emphasize stories and meaningful content.<br>• **Visual-symbolic processing:** Visual symbol processing may be relatively weaker.<br>• **Engagement:** Student may be more engaged by story tasks. |

**Table 2.18 (Continued)**

| CHC Domain Best Two Subtests | Pattern A<br>Subtest 1 > Subtest 2 | Pattern B<br>Subtest 2 > Subtest 1 |
|---|---|---|
| ***Gr***<br>**WJ V Semantic Word Retrieval, WJ V Rapid Picture Naming** | **What it suggests:** Stronger semantic fluency than rapid naming of pictured objects.<br>**Hypotheses:**<br>• **Rapid access:** Slower speed in retrieving names for pictures.<br>• **Visual–lexical mapping:** Difficulty linking visual images to verbal labels quickly.<br>• **Reading risk:** Rapid naming weakness is a core risk factor for reading fluency problems.<br>• **Motor/verbal tempo:** Slower articulation may limit naming speed.<br>• **Anxiety:** Time pressure may increase hesitations. | **What it suggests:** Stronger rapid picture naming than semantic category fluency.<br>**Hypotheses:**<br>• **Semantic organization:** Category-based retrieval may be less organized or strategic.<br>• **Vocabulary depth:** Limited semantic networks may reduce fluency within categories.<br>• **Strategy use:** Student may not use clustering/switching strategies in semantic tasks.<br>• **Task familiarity:** More experience with naming pictures than generating category lists.<br>• **Executive control:** Semantic fluency places higher demands on self-monitoring. |
| ***Ga***<br>**WJ V Sound Blending, WJ V Sound Deletion** | **What it suggests:** Same as above—stronger synthesis than manipulation.<br>**Hypotheses:**<br>• **Phonological awareness profile:** Foundational blending is more intact than advanced manipulation.<br>• **Reading implications:** Risk for decoding/spelling difficulties if deletion is weak.<br>• **Instructional needs:** May benefit from explicit phoneme manipulation training.<br>• **EF/WM:** Deletion tasks place higher EF demands.<br>• **Attention:** More complex tasks may be more sensitive to inattention. | **What it suggests:** Stronger manipulation than blending.<br>**Hypotheses:**<br>• **Instructional history:** Prior intervention may have targeted deletion skills.<br>• **Task familiarity:** More exposure to deletion than blending tasks.<br>• **Response style:** May be more careful on "harder" tasks.<br>• **Measurement artifact:** Blending may show more variability or careless errors.<br>• **Overall Ga:** Both scores should still be considered within the broader Ga profile. |

**Table 2.19 Comprehensive WJ V COG-Based XBA with Representation of Eight CHC Broad Abilities and Potential Reasons for a Substantial Difference Between Scores Within Domains**

| CHC Domain Best Two Subtests | Pattern A<br>Subtest 1 > Subtest 2 | Pattern B<br>Subtest 2 > Subtest 1 |
|---|---|---|
| ***Gc***<br>**Oral Vocabulary, General Information** | • **What it suggests:** Stronger expressive vocabulary and verbal abstraction than factual knowledge.<br>**Hypotheses:**<br>• **Content exposure:** Limited exposure to mainstream factual content (history, science, culture) may depress General Information.<br>• **Cultural relevance:** Items may not align with the student's cultural or experiential background.<br>• **Instructional gaps:** Inconsistent instruction in content areas may reduce General Information.<br>• **Strength in language learning:** Student may acquire word meanings efficiently even with less factual exposure.<br>• **Test anxiety:** May be more anxious or uncertain when asked "knowledge" questions than definitional ones. | • **What it suggests:** Stronger factual knowledge than expressive vocabulary and verbal abstraction.<br>**Hypotheses:**<br>• **Lexical access:** Word retrieval or precision in definitions may lag behind conceptual understanding.<br>• **Oral expression:** Expressive language weaknesses may limit performance on Oral Vocabulary.<br>• **Reading vs. oral language:** Student may gain knowledge through reading or media despite weaker oral vocabulary.<br>• **Socio-educational context:** Strong emphasis on factual learning in school or home.<br>• **Shyness/communication style:** Student may respond minimally or cautiously on Oral Vocabulary. |

*(continued)*

**Table 2.19 (Continued)**

| CHC Domain<br>Best Two Subtests | Pattern A<br>Subtest 1 > Subtest 2 | Pattern B<br>Subtest 2 > Subtest 1 |
|---|---|---|
| ***Gf***<br>**Matrices,**<br>**Analysis-Synthesis** | • **What it suggests:** Stronger pattern recognition and analogical reasoning than complex, multi-step logical problem solving.<br>**Hypotheses:**<br>• **Sequential reasoning:** Difficulty following multi-step logic chains in Analysis-Synthesis.<br>• **Working memory:** Higher EF/WM demands in Analysis-Synthesis may tax resources.<br>• **Instructional exposure:** Less exposure to logic-type puzzles or "if–then" reasoning.<br>• **Language/mediation:** Internal verbal mediation may be weaker, affecting Analysis-Synthesis more.<br>• **Frustration tolerance:** Student may fatigue or disengage more quickly on longer, multi-step tasks. | • **What it suggests:** Stronger complex logical reasoning than basic pattern induction.<br>**Hypotheses:**<br>• **Visual abstraction:** Student may struggle with purely visual analogies in Matrices.<br>• **Learning history:** Experience with logic games or structured problem solving may boost Analysis-Synthesis.<br>• **Metacognitive strategies:** Student may use self-talk and stepwise strategies effectively on Analysis-Synthesis.<br>• **Attention to detail:** May miss key visual features in Matrices but track steps well in Analysis-Synthesis.<br>• **Motivation:** May find Analysis-Synthesis more interesting or meaningful than Matrices. |
| ***Gwm***<br>**Verbal Attention,**<br>**Numbers Reversed** | • **What it suggests:** Stronger simple auditory attention and span than backward manipulation.<br>**Hypotheses:**<br>• **Reversal demands:** Difficulty holding and reversing sequences under time pressure.<br>• **EF/WM:** Central executive control may be limited when manipulation is required.<br>• **Processing speed:** Slower internal processing may interfere with reversing sequences before recall.<br>• **Strategy limitations:** Student may not use effective rehearsal or chunking strategies.<br>• **Fatigue:** Numbers Reversed may occur later in testing, when fatigue is higher. | • **What it suggests:** Stronger backward manipulation than simple attention span.<br>**Hypotheses:**<br>• **Sustained attention:** Inconsistent focus may depress Verbal Attention more than Numbers Reversed.<br>• **Task engagement:** Student may be more engaged by the challenge of reversing sequences.<br>• **Self-monitoring:** May be more careful and deliberate on Numbers Reversed.<br>• **Practice/experience:** Prior experience with backward span tasks may support performance.<br>• **Auditory distractibility:** Verbal Attention may be more sensitive to environmental or internal distractions. |
| ***Gv***<br>**Spatial Relations,**<br>**Block Rotation** | • **What it suggests:** Stronger 2D spatial analysis than 3D mental rotation.<br>**Hypotheses:**<br>• **3D visualization:** Difficulty imagining objects rotated in space.<br>• **Complexity:** Block Rotation may place higher demands on mental transformation.<br>• **Instructional exposure:** Less experience with 3D puzzles or building tasks.<br>• **Processing speed:** May need more time to mentally rotate shapes.<br>• **Visual detail:** Student may focus on local details rather than global 3D structure. | • **What it suggests:** Stronger 3D mental rotation than 2D spatial analysis.<br>**Hypotheses:**<br>• **Global processing:** Student may excel at holistic 3D visualization.<br>• **Task engagement:** May find Block Rotation more interesting than Spatial Relations.<br>• **Instructional/experiential:** Experience with video games, building, or 3D tasks may support Block Rotation.<br>• **Attention to detail:** May overlook fine details in Spatial Relations items.<br>• **Response style:** May respond quickly and intuitively on Block Rotation. |

**Table 2.19 (Continued)**

| CHC Domain<br>Best Two Subtests | Pattern A<br>Subtest 1 > Subtest 2 | Pattern B<br>Subtest 2 > Subtest 1 |
|---|---|---|
| ***Gs***<br>**Number Pattern Matching, WISC-V Symbol Search** | • **What it suggests:** Stronger speed with numeric patterns than with symbol scanning.<br>**Hypotheses:**<br>• **Symbol familiarity:** Abstract symbols may be less familiar than numbers.<br>• **Task structure:** Number Pattern Matching may feel more straightforward or rule-based.<br>• **Visual search:** Symbol Search may place higher demands on rapid scanning.<br>• **Motivation:** Student may be more engaged by number tasks.<br>• **Attention:** Symbol Search may be more sensitive to lapses in focus. | • **What it suggests:** Stronger symbol scanning than numeric pattern matching.<br>**Hypotheses:**<br>• **Number processing:** Mild weaknesses in rapid number recognition or discrimination.<br>• **Math anxiety:** Negative feelings about numbers may slow performance.<br>• **Symbol familiarity:** Student may find symbols easier or more interesting than numbers.<br>• **Strategy use:** May use efficient scanning strategies on Symbol Search.<br>• **Instructional history:** Less practice with timed number tasks. |
| ***Gl***<br>**Story Recall, Visual-Auditory Learning** | • **What it suggests:** Stronger meaningful memory than associative learning.<br>**Hypotheses:**<br>• **Paired-associate learning:** Difficulty forming stable associations between visual symbols and words.<br>• **Symbol abstraction:** Abstract symbols may be less meaningful or harder to encode.<br>• **Reading implications:** Associative learning weaknesses may affect sight-word or symbol learning.<br>• **Strategy use:** Student may use story structure but not effective association strategies.<br>• **Attention to detail:** May miss specific symbol–word pairings. | • **What it suggests:** Stronger associative learning than meaningful story memory.<br>**Hypotheses:**<br>• **Narrative organization:** Difficulty organizing and retaining story details.<br>• **Language comprehension:** Story Recall may be more affected by language or discourse weaknesses.<br>• **Context vs. association:** Student may encode discrete pairs better than extended narratives.<br>• **Reading risk:** Weak meaningful memory may impact comprehension more than basic decoding.<br>• **Working memory:** Holding longer story units may overload WM. |
| ***Gr*** | • **What it suggests:** Stronger semantic fluency than rapid naming of pictured objects.<br>**Hypotheses:**<br>• **Rapid access:** Slower speed in retrieving names for pictures.<br>• **Visual–lexical mapping:** Difficulty linking visual images to verbal labels quickly.<br>• **Reading risk:** Rapid naming weakness is a core risk factor for reading fluency problems.<br>• **Motor/verbal tempo:** Slower articulation may limit naming speed.<br>• **Anxiety:** Time pressure may increase hesitations. | • **What it suggests:** Stronger rapid picture naming than semantic category fluency.<br>**Hypotheses:**<br>• **Semantic organization:** Category-based retrieval may be less organized or strategic.<br>• **Vocabulary depth:** Limited semantic networks may reduce fluency within categories.<br>• **Strategy use:** Student may not use clustering/switching strategies in semantic tasks.<br>• **Task familiarity:** More experience with naming pictures than generating category lists.<br>• **Executive control:** Semantic fluency places higher demands on self-monitoring. |
| ***Ga***<br>**Sound Blending, Sound Deletion** | • **What it suggests:** Stronger phonological synthesis than phoneme manipulation.<br>**Hypotheses:**<br>• **Phoneme manipulation:** Difficulty deleting sounds from words, especially medial/final phonemes.<br>• **Working memory:** Higher WM demands in deletion tasks.<br>• **Reading risk:** Deletion weaknesses are strongly tied to decoding/spelling difficulties.<br>• **Instructional history:** Limited explicit phonemic manipulation instruction.<br>• **Task complexity:** Student may manage simpler blending but struggle with more complex operations. | • **What it suggests:** Stronger phoneme manipulation than blending.<br>**Hypotheses:**<br>• **Blending exposure:** Less practice with blending tasks specifically.<br>• **Task engagement:** Student may find deletion tasks more interesting or challenging.<br>• **Instructional focus:** Intervention may have emphasized manipulation skills.<br>• **Response style:** May guess or rush on blending items.<br>• **Ceiling/floor:** Blending may be too easy, leading to careless errors. |

These tables illustrate how to interpret non-cohesive patterns across three core batteries (WISC-V, KABC-II NU, and WJ V COG) in comprehensive XBA evaluations. When two subtests within a domain diverge substantially, the pattern itself may be diagnostically informative. The higher score reflects relative strengths in the processes emphasized by that task, while the lower score highlights potential weaknesses, processing constraints, or non-CHC influences. Because each pair typically taps different facets of the same broad ability, analyzing the direction of the score difference helps practitioners generate hypotheses, avoid misleading composites, and select the most appropriate follow-up assessments.

## Scenario 3: Referral-Specific Diagnostic Evaluation

The third scenario concerns evaluating the relationship between an individual's manifest performance (e.g., academic skills) and cognitive abilities and processes. This is often the case in evaluations conducted under the Individuals with Disabilities Education Improvement Act (IDEA; 2004) to determine whether a disability exists, a determination that may be used to establish eligibility for special education programs and services. For example, if there are concerns about reading skills, practitioners should review current research that provides evidence for the links between specific cognitive abilities and processes and reading. Practitioners should then ensure that measures of these specific cognitive abilities and processes are included in the initial assessment.

Research on the relationships among cognitive abilities, neuropsychological processes, and specific academic skills has continued to expand, and contemporary work further validates earlier syntheses (e.g., Flanagan et al., 2006; Fletcher et al., 2007; Hajovsky et al., 2025; McGrew & Wendling, 2010). Recent analyses continue to interpret these relationships within the framework of CHC theories, which remain the most comprehensive and empirically supported model of cognitive abilities. CHC-aligned assessments and research increasingly examine how broad and narrow abilities contribute to academic outcomes, including updated investigations of reading achievement and its cognitive correlates (e.g., Hajovsky et al., 2025; Van Doren, 2018). Structural equation modeling remains central to determining the extent to which specific cognitive abilities explain variance in academic skills beyond general intelligence (*g*) (see Hajovsky et al., 2025; Appendix C), extending earlier findings (e.g., Floyd et al., 2008; Juarez, 2012; McGrew, 1997; Vanderwood et al., 2002). In addition, recent summaries continue to highlight the cognitive and neurobiological processes associated with specific academic skill deficits, integrating CHC-based interpretations with neuropsychological perspectives (e.g., Feifer & DeFina, 2005; Feifer & Della Toffalo, 2007; Flanagan et al., 2011; Fletcher et al., 2007; Fletcher-Janzen & Reynolds, 2008; Hale & Fiorello, 2004; Miller, 2010).

## Well-Documented Cognitive-Achievement Relationships

SLDs are characterized by persistent challenges in acquiring foundational academic skills. A substantial body of research indicates that these difficulties often stem from weaknesses in cognitive abilities and processing mechanisms (e.g., Chu et al., 2016; Fletcher et al., 1995; Hale & Fiorello, 2004; Keith et al., 2006; McGrew & Wendling, 2010; McGrew et al., 1997; Rohde & Thompson, 2007; Tikhomirova et al., 2020). Moreover, learning in domains such as reading and mathematics engages distinct cognitive networks and imposes different cognitive demands (Barbey, 2018).

Consequently, evaluations for suspected SLDs frequently incorporate measures of cognitive functioning. When such assessments are conducted, identified cognitive weaknesses must be empirically linked to the observed academic deficits. Research grounded in CHC theories consistently shows that broad and narrow cognitive abilities predict specific academic skills (e.g., Cormier et al., 2016, 2017) and account for significant variance in achievement beyond what is explained by general intelligence (*g*) alone (e.g., Caemmerer et al., 2018, 2023; Hajovsky et al., 2025; Appendix C).

Table 2.20 summarizes well-established relationships between CHC abilities and achievement in reading, mathematics, and writing. This line of research originated over two decades ago (e.g., McGrew & Flanagan, 1998) and continues to be refined through periodic updates (e.g., Flanagan, 2025; McDonough et al., 2017) and innovative methods, such as meta-analytic structural equation modeling (meta-SEM; Hajovsky et al., 2023, 2025; Niileksela et al., 2026). Meta-SEM examines cognitive-achievement relations by simultaneously analyzing correlation matrices from multiple batteries and samples (see Appendix C).

As illustrated in Table 2.20, abilities such as Fluid Reasoning (*Gf*), Comprehension–Knowledge (*Gc*), and Processing Speed (*Gs*) exhibit consistent associations with mathematics achievement across developmental stages. Similarly, reading achievement is most strongly linked to *Gc*, Auditory Processing (*Ga*), Working Memory (*Gwm*), Retrieval Fluency (*Gr*), and *Gs*, with additional contributions from Visualization (*Gv*) and Associative Memory (*Gl*) at select ages. Writing achievement shows a parallel pattern, with *Gc*, *Gwm*, *Gr*, and *Gs* emerging as the most consistent predictors, and *Ga* contributing primarily to spelling in the early grades.

These patterns have been replicated across multiple studies and analytic approaches—including structural equation modeling, factor analysis, regression, multidimensional scaling, and psychometric network analysis (e.g., Caemmerer et al., 2018; Hajovsky et al., 2020; Hajovsky, Niileksela et al., 2022; Holden & Hart, 2021; McDonough et al., 2017; McGrew et al., 2023; Meyer & Reynolds, 2022). McGrew and colleagues argue that findings from network analyses and *g*-plus-specific-abilities research "support the relevance of CHC broad ability scores [from intelligence and cognitive ability tests] for understanding school achievement" (p. 26). Furthermore, recent cross-national evidence

**Table 2.20 Summary of Consistent Findings on Relations Between CHC Abilities and Academic Achievement**

| CHC Ability | Reading | Math | Writing |
|---|---|---|---|
| *Gf* | Inductive reasoning (I) and general sequential reasoning (RG), particularly verbal reasoning, show small but meaningful effects on reading comprehension. | Inductive reasoning (I) and general sequential reasoning (RG) are consistently important for math performance at all ages. | Inductive reasoning (I) and general sequential reasoning (RG) relate to basic writing skills in elementary years (6–13) and to written expression across all ages. |
| *Gc* | Language development (LD), lexical knowledge (VL), and listening ability (LS) are important at all ages and become increasingly influential with age. | Language development (LD), lexical knowledge (VL), and listening ability (LS) are important at all ages and become increasingly influential with age. | Language development (LD), lexical knowledge (VL), and general information (K0) become increasingly important after age 7. |
| *Gwm* | Auditory short-term storage (Wa) supports basic reading skills (moderate effect), and working memory capacity (Wc) supports reading comprehension. | Visual short-term storage (Wv) supports basic math skills, and working memory capacity (Wc) supports higher-level math problem-solving. | Auditory short-term storage (Wa) supports spelling, and working memory capacity (Wc) supports more complex writing tasks (e.g., written expression). |
| *Gv* | Visualization (Vz) shows small but meaningful relations to early reading (e.g., letter orientation, symbol discrimination) and contributes modestly to comprehension in later years. | Visualization (Vz) relates to math calculation and problem-solving (moderate effect) and is strongly related to advanced mathematics (e.g., geometry, calculus). | Visualization (Vz) contributes to handwriting, spacing, and planning of written output, particularly in early and middle grades. |
| *Ga* | Phonetic coding (PC) and phonological awareness/processing are essential during the elementary years for developing basic reading skills; phonological memory (UM) also contributes. | — | Phonetic coding (PC) and phonological awareness/processing are important for spelling and written expression, primarily before age 11. |
| *Gr* | Naming Facility (NA; rapid automatic naming) and Word Fluency (FW) are important during the elementary years for developing basic reading skills (small–moderate effects). | Naming Facility (NA) relates to basic math skills, especially math fluency (moderate effect). | Naming Facility (NA) contributes to writing fluency (mostly small effects). |
| *Gl* | Associative Memory (MA) and Meaningful Memory (MM) contribute at select ages, particularly when learning new vocabulary or story structures. | Associative Memory (MA) supports storing math-related information (small effect). | Associative Memory (MA) contributes to learning and retaining new writing conventions (small effect). |
| *Gs* | Perceptual speed (P) is important across all school years, especially in elementary grades (e.g., decoding speed). | Perceptual speed (P) and math speed (MS) are important across all school years, especially in elementary grades. | Perceptual speed (P) and writing speed (WS) are important for basic writing and relate to written expression across all ages (mainly moderate effects). |

*Note:* For a more detailed explanation of cognitive-achievement relations, see Appendix C. The absence of comments for a CHC ability and achievement area (e.g., *Ga* and mathematics) indicates that the reviewed research either showed mostly negligible effects or, if significant findings were reported, they were limited only to a few studies.

(e.g., France, Spain, and the United States) affirms the stability and generalizability of CHC constructs, reinforcing the model's utility as a shared framework for cognitive assessment and test development (Wilson et al., 2023). Taken together, these findings underscore the value of a comprehensive, CHC-informed approach to understanding learning difficulties and disabilities.

## Diagnostic Cross-Battery Assessment

Research on cognitive-achievement relations provides a defensible basis to inform diagnostic evaluations. Here, our focus shifts from comprehensive assessments, which adequately represent a broad range of cognitive abilities, to a greater emphasis on identifying the specific, narrow abilities that are theoretically and empirically linked to reading, math, and writing. Rather than broadly sampling abilities, diagnostic XBA targets the abilities most likely to explain the student's academic difficulties and most essential for determining whether a domain-specific cognitive weakness exists.

**DON'T FORGET**

Diagnostic cross-battery assessment integrates three components:

1. **CHC theories**, which specify the cognitive processes underlying academic skills
2. **Empirical research**, which identifies the narrow abilities most predictive of reading, math, and writing outcomes
3. **Clinical reasoning**, which guides the selection of tests or subtests that best measure those abilities for a given student

A well-defined referral is the foundation of an effective diagnostic evaluation because it transforms a vague concern—such as "difficulties in reading"—into a precise question about which academic processes are breaking down and why. Broad referral statements obscure the fact that reading is not a single skill but a constellation of interdependent components, including word reading accuracy, decoding efficiency, reading fluency, and comprehension. Each of these skills is supported by different cognitive processes, and each points to a different set of CHC abilities that must be examined. When the referral question is specific, the assessment can be equally specific: the practitioner can target the narrow abilities most theoretically and empirically linked to the identified academic weakness, select the most appropriate measures across batteries, and construct a diagnostic profile that meaningfully explains the student's learning difficulties. This level of precision is essential for diagnostic cross-battery assessment. Chapter 3 demonstrates how to align the referral concern with the most relevant cognitive processes and illustrates how a targeted, diagnostic approach guides assessment planning for reading, mathematics, and written expression.

## SUMMARY AND CONCLUSIONS

This chapter outlined how to organize, analyze, and interpret cross-battery data within the XBA framework using X-BASS. The central message is that effective assessment requires intentional planning, informed test selection, and disciplined interpretation guided by CHC theory. Rather than relying on a single battery or default test sequence, practitioners must integrate referral information, examinee characteristics, and practical constraints to construct an assessment that is both comprehensive and efficient.

A major focus of the chapter was the importance of understanding task demands and score cohesion when interpreting subtests within a CHC domain. Cohesive scores support the calculation of a composite that meaningfully represents the underlying construct. Non-cohesive patterns, however, signal that the subtests may not be measuring a unified ability for that individual. In these cases, the *pattern itself* becomes diagnostically informative. Examining the direction of a substantial difference between scores helps identify the cognitive, linguistic, or executive processes that differentiate the tasks, guiding hypothesis generation and selection of follow-up measures. X-BASS operationalizes this logic by marking divergent scores, calculating composites only when justified, and providing alternative score configurations when clinically appropriate.

Ultimately, the goal of XBA is not to generate more scores but to yield better information to clarify the nature of an individual's learning strengths and weaknesses and to inform intervention planning directly. By applying the principles and procedures described in this chapter, practitioners can use X-BASS to integrate data across batteries, interpret patterns of performance with precision, and arrive at conclusions that are psychometrically sound and clinically meaningful.

**TEST YOURSELF**

1. **Cross-battery assessment is intended to supplement the limitations of a single test battery by measuring abilities and processes not adequately represented on the core battery. True or False?**
2. **When selecting a core battery within the XBA framework, which factor should be considered first?**
   (a) The battery that yields the highest global ability score
   (b) Referral concerns and examinee characteristics
   (c) The shortest battery available
   (d) The battery most commonly used in the district
3. **Which situation most clearly signals construct underrepresentation?**
   (a) A working memory score is affected by fine-motor demands
   (b) A reasoning task requires complex language beyond the intended construct
   (c) Only one facet of a broad ability is measured
   (d) Scores differ across related subtests
4. **X-BASS will always calculate a composite whenever two or more subtests are entered into a CHC domain. True or False?**

5. **A score marked divergent in X-BASS indicates:**
   (a) The score is invalid and should be discarded
   (b) The score differs meaningfully from cohesive scores and may be clinically informative
   (c) The student refused items during testing
   (d) The test norms are outdated
6. **When two subtests measuring the same broad ability produce substantially different scores, what is the most appropriate next step?**
   (a) Average the scores and move on
   (b) Ignore the lower score
   (c) Examine task demands and generate hypotheses about the difference
   (d) Replace both scores with a different battery
7. **Which CHC broad ability is most directly assessed through phonological awareness tasks such as blending and deletion?**
   (a) *Gwm*
   (b) *Ga*
   (c) *Gv*
   (d) *Gr*
8. **Adding additional subtests to a composite can sometimes make scores appear more cohesive because statistical aggregation reduces visible variability. True or False?**
9. **When scores within a CHC domain do not form a cohesive pattern, the discrepancy itself may provide clinically meaningful information and guide follow-up testing. True or False?**
10. **Diagnostic cross-battery assessment differs from a comprehensive assessment because it:**
    (a) Focuses on global IQ estimates only
    (b) Samples all abilities equally
    (c) Targets narrow abilities most related to the referral concern
    (d) Eliminates the need for cognitive testing

*Answers:* 1. True; 2. b; 3. c; 4. False; 5. b; 6. c; 7. b; 8. True; 9. True; 10. c

## REFERENCES


Barbey, A. K. (2018). Network neuroscience theory of human intelligence. *Trends in Cognitive Sciences, 22*(1), 8–20.

Benson, N. F., Floyd, R. G., Kranzler, J. H., Eckert, T. L., Fefer, S. A., & Morgan, G. B. (2019). Test use and assessment practices of school psychologists in the United States: Findings from the 2017 national survey. *Journal of School Psychology, 72*, 29–48.

Bernacchio, C., & Mullen, M. (2007). Universal design for learning. *Psychiatric Rehabilitation Journal, 31*(2), 167–169. https://doi.org/10.2975/31.2.2007.167.169.

Caemmerer, J. M., Maddocks, D. L. S., Keith, T. Z., & Reynolds, M. R. (2018). Effects of cognitive abilities on child and youth academic achievement: Evidence from the WISC-V and WIAT-III. *Intelligence, 68*, 6–20. https://doi.org/10.1016/j.intell.2018.02.005.

Caemmerer, J. M., Reynolds, M. R., & Keith, T. Z. (2023). Beyond individual tests: Youth's cognitive abilities on their math and writing skills. *Learning and Individual Differences, 102*, 1–11. https://doi.org/10.1016/j.lindif.2023.102271.

Carroll, J. B. (2009). *Human cognitive abilities: A survey of factor-analytic studies*. Cambridge University Press.

Chu, F. W., Van Marle, K., & Geary, D. C. (2016). Predicting children's reading and mathematics achievement from early quantitative knowledge and domain-general cognitive abilities. *Frontiers in Psychology, 7*, 775 https://doi.org/10.3389/fpsyg.2016.00775.

Cormier, D. C., Bulut, O., McGrew, K. S., & Frison, J. (2016). The role of Cattell–Horn–Carroll (CHC) cognitive abilities in predicting writing achievement during the school-age year. *Psychology in the Schools, 53*(8), 787–803. https://doi.org/10.1002/pits.21945.

Cormier, D. C., McGrew, K. S., Bulut, O., & Funamoto, A. (2017). Revisiting the relations between the WJ-IV measures of Cattell-Horn-Carroll (CHC) cognitive abilities and reading achievement during the school-age years. *Journal of Psychoeducational Assessment, 35*(8), 731–754. https://doi.org/10.1177/0734282916659208.

Feifer, S. G., & DeFina, P. A. (2005). *The neuropsychology of mathematics: Diagnosis and intervention*. School Neuropsych Press.

Feifer, S. G., & Della Toffalo, D. A. (2007). *Integrating RTI with cognitive neuropsychology: A scientific approach to reading*. School Neuropsych Press.

Flanagan, D. P., Ortiz, S. O., Alfonso, V. C., & Mascolo, J. T. (2006). *The achievement test desk reference (ADTR): A guide to learning disability identification*. Allyn & Bacon.

Flanagan, D. P., Alfonso, V. C., Mascolo, J. T., & Hale, J. B. (2011). The Wechsler intelligence scale for children–fourth edition in neuropsychological practice. In A. S. Davis (Ed.), *Handbook of pediatric neuropsychology* (pp. 397–414). Springer.

Flanagan, D. P. (2025). The Woodcock-Johnson V: Fifty years of excellence in ability assessment. *Journal of Psychoeducational Assessment, 43*(8), 799–801.

Fletcher, J. M., Lyon, G. R., Fuchs, L. R., & Barnes, M. A. (2007). *Learning disabilities: From identification to intervention*, Guilford.

Fletcher, J. M., Shaywitz, S. E., Shankweiler, D. P., Katz, L., Liberman, I. Y., Stuebing, K. K., Francis, D. J., Fowler, A. E., & Shaywitz, B. A. (1994). Cognitive profiles of reading disability: Comparisons of discrepancy and low achievement definitions. *Journal of Educational Psychology, 86*(1), 6–23. https://doi.org/10.1037/0022-0663.86.1.6.

Fletcher-Janzen, E., & Reynolds, C. R. (Eds.) (2008). *Neuropsychological perspectives on learning disabilities in the era of RTI: Recommendations for diagnosis and intervention*. Wiley.

Floyd, R. G., McGrew, K. S., & Evans, J. J. (2008). The relative contributions of the Cattell-Horn-Carroll cognitive abilities in explaining writing achievement during childhood and adolescence. *Psychology in the Schools, 45*(2), 132–144. https://doi.org/10.1002/pits.20284.

Hajovsky, D. B., Villeneuve, E. F., Schneider, W. J., & Caemmerer, J. M. (2020). An alternative approach to cognitive and achievement relations research: An introduction to quantile regression. *Journal of Pediatric Neuropsychology, 6*(2), 83–95. https://doi.org/10.1037/h0101951.

Hajovsky, D. B., Niileksela, C. R., Flanagan, D. P., Alfonso, V. C., Schneider, J., & Zinkiewicz, C. J.. (2022, August 4-7). *A consensus model of cognitive-achievement relations using meta-SEM* [Poster Presentation]. American Psychological Association Annual Convention, Minneapolis, MN, United States.

Hajovsky, D. B., Niileksela, C. R., Olsen, S. C., & Sekula, M. K. (2023). Do cognitive–achievement relations vary by general ability level? *Journal of Intelligence, 11*(9), 177.

Hajovsky, D. B., Niileksela, C. R., Flanagan, D. P., Alfonso, V. C., Schneider, W. J., & Robbins, J. (2025). Toward a consensus model of cognitive–reading achievement relations using meta-structural equation modeling. *Journal of Intelligence, 13*(8), 104.

Hale, J. B., & Fiorello, C. A. (2004). *School neuropsychology: A practitioner's handbook*. Guilford Press.

Holden, L. R., & Hart, S. A. (2021). Intelligence can be used to make a more equitable society, but only when properly defined and applied. *Journal of Intelligence, 9*(4), 57 https://doi.org/10.3390/jintelligence9040057.

Individuals with Disabilities Education Improvement Act, 20 U.S.C. § 1400 2004.

Juarez, B.M. (2012). *Effects of general and specific cognitive abilities on reading achievement in a referred sample* [Doctoral Dissertation, St. John's University]. ProQuest Dissertations and Theses Global.

Kaufman, A. S., & Kaufman, N. L. (2018). *Kaufman assessment battery for children* (2) Normative Update ed). Pearson.

Keith, T. Z., Fine, J. G., Taub, G. E., Reynolds, M. R., & Kranzler, J. H. (2006). Higher order, multisample, confirmatory factor analysis of the Wechsler Intelligence Scale for Children--Fourth Edition: What does it measure? *School Psychology Review, 35*(1), 108–127.

Lezak, M. D. (1995). *Neuropsychological assessment* (3rd ed). Oxford University Press.

Mather, N., McGrew, K. S., LaForte, E. M., & Wendling, B. J. (2025a). *Woodcock-Johnson V virtual test library*. Riverside Assessments, LLC.

McDonough, E. M., Flanagan, D. P., Sy, M., & Alfonso, V. C. (2017). Specific learning disorder. In S. Goldstein & M. DeVries (Eds.), *Handbook of DSM-5 disorders in children and adolescents* (pp. 77–104). Springer, Cham.

McGrew, K. S. (1997). Analysis of the major intelligence batteries according to a proposed comprehensive CHC framework. In D. P. Flanagan, J. L. Genshaft, & P. L. Harrison (Eds.), *Contemporary intellectual assessment: Theories, tests, and issues* (pp. 151–180). Guilford Press.

McGrew, K. S., & Flanagan, D. P. (1998). *The intelligence test desk reference (ITDR): Gf-Gc cross-battery assessment*. Allyn & Bacon.

McGrew, K. S. (2005). The Cattell-Horn-Carroll theory of cognitive abilities: Past, present, and future. In D. P. Flanagan, J. L. Genshaft, & P. L. Harrison (Eds.), *Contemporary intellectual assessment: Theories, tests, and issues* (pp. 136–182). Guilford Press.

McGrew, K. S. (2009). CHC theory and the human cognitive abilities project: Standing on the shoulders of the giants of psychometric intelligence research. *Intelligence, 37*(1), 1–10.

McGrew, K., & Wendling, B. (2010). CHC cognitive-achievement relations: what we have learned from the past 20 years of research. *Psychology in the Schools, 47*(7), 651–675.

McGrew, K. S., Schneider, W. J., Decker, S. L., & Bulut, O. (2023). A psychometric network analysis of CHC intelligence measures: Implications for research, theory, and interpretation of broad CHC scores "Beyond g.". *Journal of Intelligence, 11*(1), 19 https://doi.org/10.3390/jintelligence11010019.

McGrew, K. S., Mather, N., LaForte, E. M., & Wendling, B. J. (2025). Woodcock-Johnson V. Riverside Assessments, LLC.

McGrew, K. S., Mather, N., & LaForte, E. M. (2025). Woodcock-Johnson V tests of cognitive abilities. Riverside Assessments, LLC.

Messick, S. (1995). Validity of psychological assessment: Validation of inferences from persons' responses and performances as scientific inquiry into score meaning. *American Psychologist, 50*(9), 741–749.

Meyer, E. M., & Reynolds, M. R. (2022). Multidimensional scaling of cognitive ability and academic achievement scores. *Journal of Intelligence, 10*(4), 117 https://doi.org/10.3390/jintelligence10040117.

Miller, D. C. (2010). School neuropsychological assessment and intervention. In D. C. Miller (Ed.), *Best practices in school neuropsychology: Guidelines for effective practice, assessment, and evidence-based intervention* (pp. 81–100). John Wiley & Sons, Inc.

Rohde, T. E., & Thompson, L. A. (2007). Predicting academic achievement with cognitive ability. *Intelligence, 35*(1), 83–92.

Schneider, W. J. (2016). Strengths and weaknesses of the Woodcock–Johnson IV Tests of Cognitive Abilities: Best practice from a scientist–practitioner perspective. In D. P. Flanagan & V. C. Alfonso (Eds.), *WJ IV clinical use and interpretation: Scientist–practitioner perspectives* (pp. 191–210). Academic Press.

Schneider, W. J., & McGrew, K. S. (2018). The Cattell-Horn-Carroll theory of cognitive abilities. In D. P. Flanagan & E. M. McDonough (Eds.), *Contemporary intellectual assessment: Theories, tests, and issues* (4th ed, pp. 73–163). Guilford Press.

Schneider, W. J., & Roman, Z. (2018). Fine-tuning cross-battery assessment procedures: After follow-up testing, use all valid scores, cohesive or not. *Journal of Psychoeducational Assessment, 36*(1), 34–54. https://doi.org/10.1177/0734282917722861.

Tikhomirova, T., Malykh, A., & Malykh, S. (2020). Predicting academic achievement with cognitive abilities: Cross-sectional study across school education. *Behavioral Science, 10*(10), 158.

Van Doren, J., Arns, M., Heinrich, H., Vollebregt, M. A., Strehl, U., & Loo, S. K. (2019). Sustained effects of neurofeedback in ADHD: A systematic review and meta-analysis. *European Child & Adolescent Psychiatry, 28*(3), 293–305.

Vanderwood, M. L., McGrew, K. S., Flanagan, D. P., & Keith, T. Z. (2002). The contribution of general and specific cognitive abilities to reading achievement. *Learning and Individual Differences, 13,* 159–188. https://doi.org/10.1016/S1041-6080(02)00077-8.

Wechsler, D. (2014). *Wechsler intelligence scale for children-fifth edition.* Pearson.

Wilson, C. J., Bowden, S. C., Vannier, L.-C., Byrne, L. K., & Weiss, L. G. (2023). Measurement invariance of the Wechsler Intelligence Scale for Children, Fifth Edition, in Australian and New Zealand and U.S. standardization samples. *Psychological Assessment, 35*(6), 510–521. https://doi.org/10.1037/pas0001221.

Woodcock, R. W. (2002). New looks in the assessment of cognitive ability. *Peabody Journal of Education, 77*(2), 6–22.

Three

# DD/C AS THE CORE OF SLD IDENTIFICATION: HISTORY, DEFINITIONS, AND CONTEMPORARY PRACTICE

The identification of specific learning disability (SLD) has been shaped by more than a century of neurological observation, cognitive theory, and educational policy. Early clinicians documented specific language and reading impairments that could not be explained by general intelligence, while later psychologists and educators refined these observations into theories of psychological processing and "unexpected underachievement." Federal legislation eventually formalized SLD as an educational category, yet the field continues to struggle with inconsistent criteria, competing identification models, and persistent misunderstandings about how SLD should be defined and operationalized (see Kirby and Snowling, 2022).

This chapter brings coherence to that landscape by tracing the historical foundations of SLD, reviewing the evolution of definitions and identification criteria, and clarifying the conceptual logic underlying contemporary approaches. Although three methods—ability–achievement discrepancy (AAD), response to intervention (RtI), and patterns of strengths and weaknesses (PSW)—are permitted under federal law, only PSW directly evaluates the cognitive–academic relationships that define SLD. Within PSW, the Dual Discrepancy/Consistency (DD/C) method provides the most explicit, theory-driven operationalization of these relationships.

DD/C is not simply one PSW option among many; it is the method that most fully embodies the defining features of SLD: specific cognitive processing weaknesses, specific academic weaknesses, and an empirically supported relationship between them. This chapter therefore places DD/C at the center of the conceptual narrative. It clarifies what DD/C is, how it works, and why it has been repeatedly mischaracterized in the scholarly literature. It also explains how each DD/C component is calculated within X-BASS, which automates the psychometric analyses and decision rules that make the method rigorous and accessible.

Building on this foundation, the chapter introduces a contemporary operational definition of SLD that integrates DD/C with a structured, five-step debiasing framework. The operational definition specifies the content and sequence of data required to determine whether a student's academic difficulties reflect a domain-specific, cognitively mediated learning disability. The debiasing framework provides cognitive safeguards that reduce common reasoning errors and strengthen diagnostic accuracy. Together, these systems form a unified, transparent, and defensible approach to SLD identification—one that aligns with historical assumptions, contemporary research, and the practical realities of school-based evaluation.

## HISTORICAL CONTRIBUTIONS

The conceptualization of SLD did not emerge all at once but developed gradually through more than a century of clinical observation, neurological research, and educational innovation. Early physicians and neurologists laid the groundwork by documenting specific language and reading impairments that could not be explained by general intelligence, while later educators and psychologists refined these ideas into coherent theories of cognitive processing and academic learning. By the mid-20th century, the field had begun to coalesce around the notion of "unexpected underachievement," culminating in the formal naming of "learning disabilities" and the eventual adoption of federal definitions and identification procedures. Rapid Reference 3.1 highlights the key contributors and milestones that shaped this evolution, illustrating how foundational insights from medicine, psychology, and education converged to form the modern understanding of SLD (e.g., Alfonso & Flanagan, 2018; Kaufman, 2008; Fletcher-Janzen & Reynolds, 2008).

## DEFINITIONS OF SLD

As the field's understanding of learning disabilities matured, the formal definitions of SLD evolved concurrently, shifting from early clinical descriptions of congenital reading disorders to increasingly precise educational and medical criteria. Each era introduced new assumptions about the nature of learning difficulties, the role of cognitive processes, and the meaning of "unexpected underachievement." These definitional shifts shaped not only how practitioners conceptualized SLD, but also how schools identified and served students. Rapid Reference 3.2 traces this evolution across key historical milestones, highlighting how foundational ideas from Kirk and Bateman ultimately informed federal regulations, contemporary identification models, and the educational and clinical frameworks used today.

Although definitions of SLD have evolved across clinical, educational, and policy contexts, the definition that carries the greatest practical weight for practitioners in educational settings is the one embedded in the Individuals with Disabilities Education Act (IDEA). Unlike the

## Rapid Reference 3.1

### Key Historical Contributions to the Conceptualization and Identification of SLD

| Period | Key Contributor(s) | Contribution | Significance |
|---|---|---|---|
| 1800–1920 | Paul Broca, Adolph Kussmaul, Rudolf Berlin | Identified neurological roots of language impairments; Kussmaul described "word blindness"; Berlin coined "dyslexia" | Established a neurological basis for reading difficulties and differentiated them from general intelligence |
| Late 1800s–Early 1900s | James Hinshelwood, William Pringle Morgan | Extended Berlin's work to children; emphasized the congenital and developmental nature of dyslexia | Shifted focus to developmental reading disorders and early case-study documentation |
| 1920s–1940s | Samuel T. Orton | Linked dyslexia to cerebral organization and hemispheric dominance; foundational work for Orton–Gillingham | Promoted structured, multisensory instruction and comprehensive assessment practices |
| 1940s–1960s | Kurt Goldstein, Alfred Strauss | Explored perceptual, attentional, and neurological deficits; contributed to early concepts of minimal brain dysfunction (MBD) | Influenced early cognitive and neuropsychological models of learning difficulties |
| 1960s | Samuel A. Kirk | Coined "learning disabilities"; articulated psychological processing and neurological components | Shaped early assessment practices and provided the conceptual foundation for federal definitions |
| 1963 | Samuel A. Kirk/U.S. Government | Kirk's Chicago conference presentation; service on President Kennedy's Panel on Mental Retardation | Catalyzed national attention and laid groundwork for federal policy development |
| 1975 | U.S. Congress/National Advisory Committee | Passage of P.L. 94–142 (Education for All Handicapped Children Act) | Institutionalized SLD as a federal category; definition rooted in NAC and Kirk's work |
| 2004–2022 | IDEA (2004), DSM-5 (2013), DSM-5-TR (2022) | Provided educational and medical definitions of SLD; DSM consolidated reading, writing, and math disorders | Clarified dual educational–medical pathways and reinforced definitional distinctions |

Diagnostic and Statistical Manual (DSM), which guides clinical diagnosis, IDEA governs how SLD is identified, documented, and supported in educational settings. For this reason, the statutory definition—and the federal regulations that guide the identification—serves as the primary framework for educational decision-making. The following section presents the IDEA definition of SLD.

According to IDEA, SLD is defined as follows:

> The term "specific learning disability" means a disorder in one or more of the basic psychological processes involved in understanding or using language, spoken or written, which may manifest in the imperfect ability to listen, think, speak, read, spell, or do mathematical calculations. Such a term includes such conditions as perceptual disabilities, brain injury, minimal brain dysfunction, dyslexia, and developmental aphasia. Such a term does not include a learning problem that is primarily the result of visual, hearing, or motor disabilities; of mental retardation; of emotional disturbance; or of environmental, cultural, or economic disadvantage.
>
> (IDEA 2004, §602.30, Definitions)

For over three decades, the SLD definition within IDEA has remained unchanged. Statutory language, particularly phrases such as "a disorder in one or more of the basic psychological processes" and "imperfect ability," has created significant ambiguity regarding how to implement the definition and establish the presence or absence of SLD. In response to this vague terminology, the United States Department of Education (USDOE) issued Federal Regulations (34 CFR, Part 300; 2006) designed to clarify the statute and guide State Educational Agencies in developing their regulatory frameworks. These regulations offered more precise specifications for SLD identification procedures.

## METHODS OF SLD IDENTIFICATION

The 2006 Federal Regulations (34 CFR § 300.307–309) mandate that states establish SLD determination criteria that: (1) cannot mandate a severe discrepancy model between intellectual ability and achievement; (2) must allow for response-to-intervention processes using scientific,

## Rapid Reference 3.2

### Evolution of Definitions and Identification Criteria for SLD

| Period | Source/Policy Document | Core Definition or Criteria | Significance for Identification |
|---|---|---|---|
| Early 1900s | Clinical case studies (Hinshelwood, Morgan) | Reading difficulties are framed as congenital, specific, and unexpected relative to general intelligence | Established the idea of *specific* learning disorders distinct from global impairment |
| 1920s–1940s | Orton's neuropsychological model | Reading disorders linked to cerebral organization and hemispheric dominance; emphasis on perceptual and language processing | Introduced processing-based explanations and multisensory instructional implications |
| 1950s–1960s | Minimal Brain Dysfunction (MBD) era | Learning and behavioral difficulties are attributed to subtle neurological dysfunction | Provided a precursor to LD but was overly broad; helped shift attention to cognitive processes |
| 1963 | Samuel A. Kirk | Coined the term "learning disabilities"; defined LD as disorders in psychological processes affecting language, reading, and writing | First formal definition; emphasized processing deficits and unexpected underachievement |
| 1965 | Barbara Bateman | Defined LD as a significant discrepancy between ability and achievement; emphasized unexpected underachievement and exclusion of other causes | First operational definition of LD; provided the conceptual and methodological foundation for the federal discrepancy model |
| 1968 | National Advisory Committee on Handicapped Children (NACHC) | Adopted a definition centered on disorders in basic psychological processes; included exclusionary criteria | Became the template for federal definitions; directly influenced P.L. 94-142 |
| 1975 | P.L. 94-142 (Education for All Handicapped Children Act) | Adopted the NACHC definition; required evidence of a disorder in psychological processes and unexpected underachievement | Institutionalized SLD as a federal category; formalized eligibility procedures |
| 1977 | US Office of Education Regulations | Introduced the ability–achievement discrepancy as the required identification method | Operationalized Bateman's model; discrepancy became the dominant identification approach for nearly 30 years |
| 1997 | IDEA Amendments | Maintained discrepancy model; encouraged attention to instructional quality and environmental factors | Began shifting focus toward response to instruction and contextual variables |
| 2004 | IDEA 2004 | Allowed RtI as an alternative to discrepancy as part of a comprehensive evaluation; permitted alternative research-based approaches, such as the patterns of strengths and weaknesses (PSW) method | Opened multiple pathways for identification; reduced reliance on IQ–achievement discrepancy |
| 2013 | DSM-5 | Introduced Specific Learning Disorder as a single diagnosis with specifiers; required academic impairment and developmental history | Unified clinical definition; removed IQ discrepancy; emphasized persistent difficulties |
| 2022 | DSM-5-TR | Clarified wording and diagnostic guidance; maintained DSM-5 structure | Reinforced clinical criteria and alignment with educational documentation |

research-based interventions within comprehensive evaluations; and (3) may incorporate additional alternative research-based approaches for SLD determination. This third alternative is commonly associated with the PSW method. As research and methodological advances continue, our understanding of psychological processes and their manifestations in reading, writing, and mathematics difficulties has steadily improved, thereby informing research-based identification of SLD.

Understanding the logic, strengths, and limitations of these methods is essential, as the classification category of SLD cannot be separated from the methods used to identify it (see Alfonso & Flanagan, 2018, for detailed descriptions of SLD identification methods). Tables 3.1–3.3 summarize the three approaches allowable by federal law and highlight the conceptual differences that shape their practical application.

Although all three methods, AAD, RtI, and PSW, are permitted under federal law and each has conceptual, psychometric, and practical limitations, PSW warrants deeper examination in this chapter. It is the most widely debated of the three methods, the most frequently mischaracterized in the research literature, and the method for which misunderstandings have had the greatest impact on practice. Moreover, PSW is the only method whose core logic has been repeatedly distorted in published critiques, leading to widespread misconceptions about what it requires, how it operates, and the empirical safeguards it incorporates. Furthermore, the authors of this book developed one of the most widely used PSW methods, the DD/C method, which is included in the latest edition of X-BASS—a major focus of this book. For these reasons, this chapter focuses on the PSW method of SLD identification (Lockwood & Farmer, 2019).

**Table 3.1 Key Conceptual Features of the Ability–Achievement Discrepancy (AAD) Method**

| Category | Description |
|---|---|
| Core Logic | SLD is inferred when a student shows a significant discrepancy between cognitive ability and academic achievement. |
| Definition of Unexpected Underachievement | Performance is below what would be predicted from overall cognitive ability (e.g., FSIQ). |
| Clarifies the Reason for Academic Difficulty? | No. Does not explain *why* the difficulty exists, even after exclusionary factors have been ruled out. |
| Primary Locus of Difficulty | Within the individual. |
| Link to Intervention | Weak. Does not directly connect cognitive and academic weaknesses to intervention planning. |
| Diagnostic Error Considerations | High risk of false positives/negatives due to the use of strict cut points, regression artifacts, and measurement error. |

**Table 3.2 Key Conceptual Features of the Response to Intervention (RtI) Method**

| Category | Description |
|---|---|
| Core Logic | SLD is inferred when a student shows insufficient response to high-quality, evidence-based instruction. |
| Definition of Unexpected Underachievement | Defined by inadequate response to intervention (i.e., discrepancies in rate and level of learning). |
| Clarifies the Reason for Academic Difficulty? | No. Identifies an instructional response but does not identify plausible underlying cognitive correlates for a lack of response. |
| Primary Locus of Difficulty | Primarily environmental, especially instructional quality and opportunity to learn. |
| Link to Intervention | Moderate. Interventions are associated with deficits in academic skills but not with cognitive processes. |
| Diagnostic Error Considerations | Errors are likely due to the use of cut points for rate and level of learning, variable implementation, and measurement error. |

**Table 3.3 Key Conceptual Features of the Patterns of Strengths and Weaknesses (PSW) Method**

| Category | Description |
|---|---|
| Core Logic | SLD is characterized by a pattern of cognitive and academic strengths and weaknesses in which specific cognitive weaknesses empirically align with specific academic weaknesses. |
| Definition of Unexpected Underachievement | Defined relative to the individual's cognitive strengths, not necessarily global IQ. |
| Clarifies the Reason for Academic Difficulty? | Yes. Assists in identifying *why* the difficulty exists by evaluating cognitive processing weaknesses and other factors, when appropriate, as potential reasons for academic weaknesses. |
| Primary Locus of Difficulty | Within the individual and the environment; environmental (and other exclusionary) factors may be contributory. |
| Link to Intervention | Some PSW models include interventions that address both academic and cognitive weaknesses. |
| Diagnostic Error Considerations | Errors are likely when strict cut points are used. Errors may be reduced by following psychometric guidelines (e.g., Schneider et al., 2024). |

## THE PSW METHOD

The PSW method is built on four core concepts, illustrated in Figure 3.1. First, individuals with SLD demonstrate cognitive strengths that support learning in some academic areas (as indicated by the top oval in the figure). Second, they exhibit at least one specific academic weakness (bottom-right oval). Third, they exhibit at least one specific cognitive processing weakness (bottom-left oval). Fourth, the cognitive weakness must be empirically related to the academic weakness. This cognitive–academic linkage, represented by the double-headed arrows between the two lower ovals, is central to the PSW method.

The arrows connecting the top oval to the two lower ovals in Figure 3.1 represent statistically significant discrepancies between cognitive strengths and the identified cognitive and academic weaknesses. These differences reflect reliable, nonchance variation in performance. Embedded within this pattern is unexpected underachievement, widely regarded as a defining feature of SLD (e.g., Kaufman, 2008; Kavale, 2005; Kavale & Forness, 2000; Lockwood et al., 2021). Equally important, the PSW method requires that the specific cognitive weakness or weaknesses provide the primary or most plausible explanation for the academic deficit (even when other factors are contributory), an element missing from traditional AAD and RtI methods. This emphasis on identifying the underlying processing weaknesses has contributed to the intuitive appeal and growing use of PSW (e.g., Benson et al., 2020; Hale et al., 2010).

To date, PSW has been operationalized in at least five related but distinct ways: the Discrepancy/Consistency method (D/C; Naglieri, 1999), the DD/C method (Flanagan et al., 2002, 2006, 2013), the Concordance-Discordance Model (CDM; Hale & Fiorello, 2004), the Core-Selective Evaluation Process (C-SEP; Schultz & Stephens, 2015), and the Psychological Processing Analyzer (PPA; Dehn & Szasz, 2016). Each uses different criteria to determine whether a student's pattern of strengths and weaknesses aligns with the SLD construct.

## PREVALENCE OF PSW

Survey research indicates that PSW is one of the most widely used SLD identification methods among school psychologists. Maki and Adams (2019) found that 30.4% of practitioners primarily use AAD, while 34.5% and 35.1% primarily use RtI and PSW, respectively. Among PSW users, DD/C was the most frequently applied method. Benson et al. (2020) reported similar findings in a larger sample ($N$ = 1,317): 37% used AAD, while 51% and 53% used RtI and PSW, respectively. Again, DD/C was the most used PSW method. Because many practitioners use multiple methods, percentages exceed 100%.

One factor contributing to PSW's growth is its growing presence in graduate training. Lockwood and Farmer (2019) surveyed faculty teaching cognitive assessment and found that CHC theory (92.9%) and PSW (68.5%) were the most commonly taught interpretive frameworks. Likewise, many widely assigned cognitive assessment textbooks include dedicated chapters on PSW (Miller et al., 2022). As a result, new school psychologists entering the field are more familiar with CHC and PSW frameworks, increasing the likelihood that PSW will be used in practice.

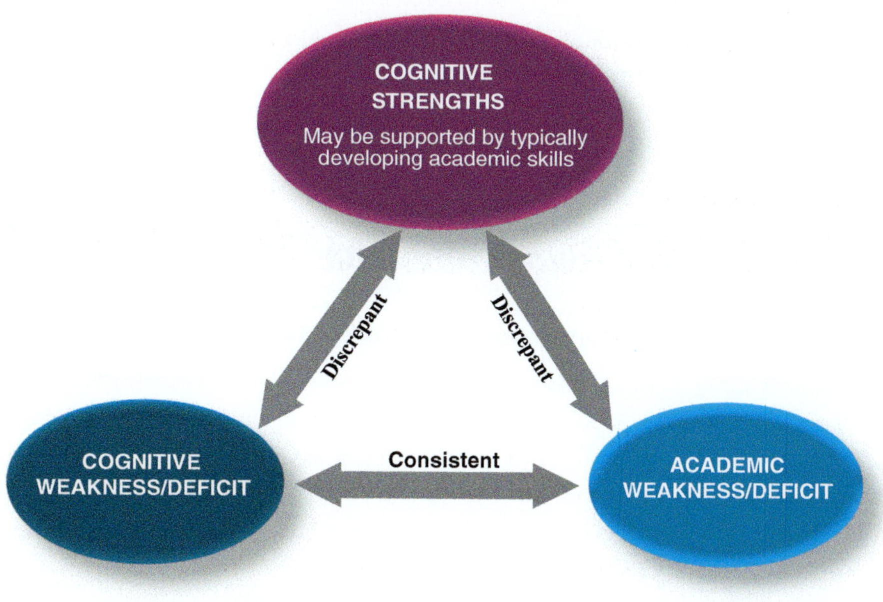


**FIGURE 3.1 Conceptual Understanding of the PSW Method**

## STATE OF THE FIELD: PSW IN 2026

As of 2026, the PSW method remains one of the most widely used and most debated methods for identifying SLD. Although the most recent national prevalence data come from Benson et al. (2020) and Maki and Adams (2019), subsequent research continues to show that PSW is firmly embedded in school psychology practice, driven in part by its strong presence in graduate training programs and its alignment with CHC theory. Recent publications have focused less on documenting prevalence and more on evaluating the psychometric, conceptual, and practical foundations of PSW, including critiques of its reliability, its decision rules, and its consistency across operational criteria. Despite these debates and critiques, PSW persists because it offers something neither traditional discrepancy nor RtI methods do: an explicit attempt to explore the relationships between cognitive and academic weaknesses in a way that reflects the theoretical construct of SLD. As a result, PSW occupies a unique position in the field. It is not only widely taught, widely used, and continually scrutinized, but it is also among the most actively evolving identification frameworks in contemporary practice.

> **DON'T FORGET**
>
> The DD/C method is fully automated by X-BASS. This method is embedded in an extended PSW module in X-BASS that guides the practitioner through the decision-making process from data entry to an SLD/not SLD decision.

Although PSW methods appear more conceptually and psychometrically complex than either AAD or RtI, they are most closely aligned with the construct of SLD, one rooted in specific cognitive and linguistic processing weaknesses that give rise to unexpected academic underachievement (Kaufman, 2008; Mather et al., 2025). Among PSW methods, DD/C offers the most explicit operationalization of this logic. The level of analysis required by the DD/C method is complex, but X-BASS fully automates it, effectively addressing that concern. Specifically, X-BASS organizes the data, performs the psychometric calculations, and guides the practitioner through decision points, ensuring that the DD/C method is applied accurately, transparently, and efficiently. In this way, X-BASS preserves the conceptual rigor of PSW while making the process accessible and defensible for practitioners.

The DD/C method is part of a broader operational definition of SLD, originally proposed nearly 25 years ago (Flanagan et al., 2002; see also Kavale & Flanagan, 2007; Kavale et al., 2006), and each component of this definition, including DD/C, has since been strengthened by advances in CHC theories (McGrew, 2023; Schneider & McGrew, 2018; see Appendix A), cognitive-achievement relations research (Hajovsky et al., 2025; see Appendix C), and psychometric methodology (see Appendices D, F, M, and O). Consistent with psychometric theories and research on SLDs from the early 1900s to the present, the applied practice of SLD identification and diagnosis, as reflected in IDEA, DSM-5-TR, and NASP (2022), rests on several widely agreed-upon assumptions about the nature of SLD, which are summarized in Rapid Reference 3.3.

These assumptions anchor contemporary understandings of SLD and align closely with the operational definition advanced by Flanagan and colleagues, particularly the logic embodied in the DD/C method. With this conceptual foundation established, it becomes essential, before turning to the operational definition itself, to examine how the DD/C method has been represented, evaluated, and, in several cases, misrepresented in the scholarly literature.

## MISCHARACTERIZED, MISMODELED, AND IGNORED: CORRECTING THE NARRATIVE ON DD/C AND THE EVIDENCE THAT REFUTES ITS CRITICS

For more than a decade, the scientific conversation surrounding PSW methods, particularly DD/C, has been shaped by critiques that often misstate the method's assumptions, procedures, and psychometric safeguards. This section examines how these mischaracterizations emerged, why they have persisted, and what the empirical record shows about DD/C's validity and diagnostic utility.

### *Rapid Reference 3.3*

**Commonly Agreed-Upon Assumptions Underlying the SLD Construct**

- Internal causes, most significantly neurologically based weaknesses in cognitive processing, are a distinguishing feature of SLDs.
- These weaknesses in cognitive processing are specific to SLD and hinder the acquisition and development of academic skills.
- SLDs are made up of a diverse range of deficits; there is no singular academic or cognitive deficit that applies to all SLD types.
- While SLDs can coexist with other conditions, these conditions are not a primary cause of SLDs.
- Some exclusionary factors can play a role in learning and academic difficulties, but they are not considered the primary reason.
- The severity of SLDs can vary (e.g., mild, moderate, severe).
- Unexpected underachievement is a distinguishing characteristic of SLDs and is defined as specific weaknesses in cognitive and linguistic processing that differ from one's thinking and reasoning abilities (i.e., cognitive strengths).

## Why Accurate Critique Matters: The Stakes of SLD Identification

Before turning to the specific critiques of DD/C, it is important to acknowledge the broader context in which SLD identification methods operate. The stakes of accurate identification are high. When educational systems function well, they expand opportunity and reduce preventable hardship; when they fail, the consequences reverberate across a student's life. Because resources are finite, every diagnostic error represents a misallocation of support that could have been directed to a student in genuine need. For this reason, all SLD identification procedures, including those advanced by Flanagan and colleagues, should be subject to rigorous, ongoing scrutiny. Critical examination is not only appropriate but also essential for scientific progress; widely used methods must be carefully evaluated, refined when necessary, and revised in response to valid concerns (Flanagan & Schneider, 2016; Schneider et al., 2024).

## Critiquing the Actual Method, Not a Fictional One: The Case of Kranzler et al. (2016a,b, 2019)

As Flanagan and Schneider (2016) emphasized, scientific critique is most productive when it evaluates the strongest and most accurate version of a method, not a distorted, incomplete, or misrepresented one. Yet several published analyses have done precisely the opposite. They have evaluated procedures that bear little resemblance to the DD/C method, drawn conclusions about a version of the method that no one endorses, and then presented those conclusions as evidence against DD/C. This is not scientific scrutiny; it is a case of *mistaken identity* (Flanagan & Schneider, 2016). Here we briefly examine why the studies of Kranzler et al. cannot be taken as an evaluation of DD/C at all, but rather as an analysis of a mischaracterized version of the method that no one has ever endorsed.

A central example is Kranzler et al. (2016a,b), who openly acknowledged that they did not know what Flanagan and colleagues meant by the term *causal*. Rather than seeking clarification or applying the principle of charitable interpretation, which would have led them to the correct, widely accepted meaning of *contributory* or *probabilistic* causation, they assumed that Flanagan et al. (2013) used the term *causal* to mean *deterministic* (Kranzler et al., 2016b). They then built their analysis on that incorrect assumption. As Flanagan and Schneider noted, this misunderstanding was not a trivial semantic issue; it was foundational to the design of Kranzler et al.'s study and to their interpretation of the results.

Kranzler et al. (2016b) argued that it "did not matter" that they did not know what Flanagan et al. meant by *causal*, claiming the distinction was "irrelevant in the interpretation of our results" (p. 152). But this is demonstrably false. Their evaluation of DD/C rested incorrectly on *deterministic logic*: if the causal inputs are known, the outcomes can be predicted *perfectly*. This is an assumption that no one in the social sciences endorses. There are no perfect predictions in school psychology or related disciplines, and the authors of DD/C have never claimed otherwise. By treating probabilistic relations as if they were deterministic, Kranzler et al. set up a straw man, one that DD/C never asserted and that no responsible scholar would defend.

This deterministic misinterpretation led directly to two false assumptions that underpinned their classification of "diagnostic errors" (cited in Flanagan & Schneider, 2016, p. 141):

1. **False assumption #1:** Among children of at least average intelligence, everyone with certain specific cognitive deficits should have corresponding academic deficits. If not, DD/C has "failed," and the child is counted as a false positive.
2. **False assumption #2:** Among children of at least average intelligence, everyone with specific academic deficits should have corresponding cognitive deficits. If not, DD/C has "failed," and the child is counted as a false negative.

As Flanagan and Schneider (2016) explained, these assumptions are extreme, untenable, and have never been endorsed or advocated by the authors of DD/C. These assumptions reflect a deterministic model of human learning that DD/C explicitly rejects. Cognitive deficits increase the *probability* of academic deficits; they do not guarantee them. To treat probabilistic relations as deterministic is to fundamentally misunderstand the nature of the constructs being studied.

Because their premises were false, the conclusions that followed were equally unsound. As Flanagan and Schneider wrote, Kranzler et al.'s critique was "in truth. . . a critique of a set of procedures that are endorsed by no one," and "the differences between what Kranzler et al. call [DD/C] and what Flanagan and colleagues advocate are stark and in many important ways are diametrically opposed" (p. 137). A critique grounded in misapplied terminology, misinterpreted assumptions, and mismodeled procedures cannot meaningfully address whether DD/C supports accurate SLD identification.

Kranzler et al. (2016b) later issued a counter-rebuttal, but they did not address any of the false assumptions, unforced errors, or fatal flaws identified by Flanagan and Schneider. Instead, they resorted to labeling Flanagan and Schneider "pseudoscientists"—a rhetorical move widely recognized in the academic ethics literature as an ad hominem attack that falls outside the norms of professional scientific discourse (see Powell, 2025). Even more concerning, despite the detailed explanation of the term *causal* provided in Flanagan and Schneider's rebuttal, Kranzler and colleagues replicated their 2016a study (i.e., Kranzler et al., 2019) using the same flawed logic and the same mischaracterized version of DD/C.

Needless to say, arguments for revising or abandoning the DD/C method must be grounded in valid evidence. The evidence presented by Kranzler and colleagues does not meet that standard. As Flanagan and Schneider noted, rhetorical attacks and critiques of fictional versions of DD/C do not advance the field. Only an accurate representation and methodologically sound analysis can do that.

## How Mischaracterizations Became the Dominant Narrative

Against this backdrop, the subsequent critiques of DD/C must be understood. Mischaracterizations in Beaujean et al. (2018), along with simulation studies that modeled a simplified and nonrepresentative version of the method (e.g., Miciak et al., 2018; Stuebing et al., 2012; Taylor et al., 2017), have contributed to a distorted view of DD/C. A recent systematic review of the diagnostic accuracy of PSW methods (Dombrowski et al., 2025) that repeated earlier conclusions without critical analysis and that overlooked key corrective evidence has further reinforced a narrative that diverges sharply from DD/C's actual design, intent, and ongoing revisions in response to valid criticisms.

For more than a decade, the scholarly conversation surrounding PSW methods has been shaped by critiques that fundamentally mischaracterize them, particularly DD/C. As noted earlier, Flanagan and Schneider (2016) documented the conceptual and methodological flaws in Kranzler et al.'s (2016a) analysis, specifically their reliance on *deterministic assumptions* about cognitive–academic relationships—assumptions rejected by DD/C. These issues foreshadow the broader pattern of misrepresentation seen in later critiques and reviews.

## Mischaracterizations by Beaujean et al. (2018)

One of the most conceptually flawed critiques (Beaujean et al., 2018) deserves mention. The Beaujean et al. critique of DD/C is often cited as evidence that DD/C is psychometrically unsound, *misuses IQ scores*, and lacks diagnostic utility. Yet their critique rests on fundamental misunderstandings and mischaracterizations of the method (see Appendix 3.A at the end of this chapter). These are not minor interpretive disagreements; they distort DD/C's core logic, procedures, and psychometric safeguards. In effect, the article criticizes a version of DD/C *that does not exist in practice.*

A central error in Beaujean and colleagues' critique is the claim that DD/C relies on strict cut scores to classify cognitive and academic weaknesses. DD/C has never required rigid thresholds, such as <85 for a "weakness." In fact, weaknesses may fall above 85 when supported by converging evidence (see Table 3.4 for details). In general, scores in the 80–89 range are treated cautiously because their confidence intervals often cross traditional cut points. The portrayal of DD/C as a threshold-driven method is therefore wholly inaccurate.

Their critique also asserts that DD/C requires test scores to have properties they "fundamentally lack," such as exact equivalence across metrics. This reflects a misunderstanding of DD/C and the psychometrics of the XBA method. DD/C relies on composite scores rather than subtest scores to ensure adequate reliability. It does not require converting subtest scores across metrics or assuming perfect precision. Beaujean and colleagues conflate DD/C with XBA and then mischaracterize XBA procedures. DD/C can be implemented entirely without XBA using standardized cognitive and achievement batteries, including a standalone set of co-normed tests, such as those included on the Woodcock-Johnson IV (WJ IV) and WJ V. DD/C can also be implemented using data generated by the XBA method. Research shows that the difference between XBA composites and norm-based composites is negligible (and attributable to measurement error). See Appendix E for a description of this research.

Beaujean and colleagues further misrepresent the role of IQ in DD/C by describing the *g*-Value as a "composite general ability score" (p. 7). It is not. The *g*-Value was a metric used in X-BASS 2.0 to assess whether overall cognitive ability (an aggregate of cognitive strengths, called a *Facilitating Cognitive Composite* [FCC]; Flanagan et al., 2017) is likely to be at least average despite specific cognitive

**Table 3.4 How Weakness Is Defined in the DD/C Method**

| Term | Meaning Within the DD/C Method | Comments |
|---|---|---|
| Weakness | Performance on standardized, norm-referenced tests that falls *below average* (when average is defined as standard scores between 90 and 110 [inclusive], based on a scale having a mean of 100 and an SD of 15). Thus, a weakness is associated with standard scores of 85–89 (inclusive). | Interpreting scores in the very narrow range of 85–89 requires a consideration of other data sources, because abilities associated with these scores may or may not pose significant difficulties for the individual. Interpretation of any cognitive construct as a weakness for the individual should include ecological validity (i.e., evidence of how the weakness manifests in real-world performances, such as classroom activities). |
| Normative Weakness or Deficit | Performance on standardized, norm-referenced tests that falls more than one SD below the mean (i.e., standard scores <85). This type of weakness is often referred to as "population relative" or "inter-individual." The terms *normative weakness* and *deficit* are used interchangeably. | The range of 85–115, inclusive, is often referred to as the normal (or typical) range because it encompasses nearly 70% of the population on standardized, norm-referenced tests. Therefore, scores within this range are sometimes classified as *within normal limits* (WNL) or *within typical limits* (WTL). As such, any score that falls outside and below this range is considered a normative weakness *as compared to most people.* Notwithstanding, the meaning of any cognitive construct that emerges as a normative weakness is enhanced by ecological validity, especially at threshold scores (e.g., scores within 1 SEM of the cut point of 85). X-BASS 3.0 addresses this more directly than previous versions by providing decision accuracy data (see Appendix F). |

weaknesses. The *g*-Value is neither a composite nor is it used to classify students. Mislabeling the *g*-Value leads to a cascade of incorrect conclusions about how DD/C uses standardized test scores.

Perhaps the most consequential misrepresentation is the claim that DD/C lacks evidence of diagnostic utility. The studies cited by Beaujean et al. modeled a simplified, rigid threshold-based PSW procedure, not DD/C. They did not model DD/C's predicted–actual discrepancy logic, base-rate analysis, domain-specificity requirements, or ecological validation procedures. Put simply, Beaujean and colleagues' critique, like Kranzler and colleagues' critique, evaluates a method that the DD/C authors neither endorse nor have proposed.

Finally, Beaujean and colleagues portray DD/C as a rebranded form of cognitive profile analysis based on subtest scatter. This is simply not true. DD/C is a CHC theory-driven, psychometrically constrained method requiring composite-level decisions, regression-based predicted scores, and empirically supported cognitive–achievement relationships. By design, DD/C circumvents the pitfalls of subtest scatter analysis (see Flanagan et al., 2007). Taken together, the critiques by Beaujean et al. and Kranzler et al. misstate DD/C's foundational criteria, mischaracterize its procedures, conflate it with unrelated practices, and ignore its psychometric safeguards and rigor.

## How the Simulation Literature Mismodeled DD/C

This pattern of misrepresentation is compounded by widely cited simulation studies purporting to demonstrate that PSW methods are unreliable (e.g., Miciak et al., 2014, 2018; Stuebing et al., 2012; Taylor et al., 2017). These studies modeled a simplified, threshold-based PSW procedure that DD/C has never used. They imposed strict cutoffs on continuous variables and concluded that PSW methods yield unacceptable rates of false positives and false negatives. In reality, DD/C was explicitly designed to avoid rigid thresholds and incorporates multiple safeguards (e.g., requiring ecological validity or other converging data to support the interpretation of scores close to cut points, predicted–actual discrepancy logic that corrects for false negatives [stating no domain-specific cognitive weakness when there is one], and cohesive composite-level decisions), none of which were modeled (or even mentioned) in the simulation studies. As a result, the simulation literature critiques a fictional version of DD/C (one that uses strict cut points) rather than the actual method (which does not).

Importantly, however, Flanagan and Schneider (2016) drew a clear distinction between the methodological flaws in Kranzler et al.'s work and the methodological rigor of the PSW simulation studies. They argued that Kranzler et al.'s analyses were so conceptually and statistically flawed that they could not meaningfully inform any discussion about DD/C. In contrast, the simulation studies, although they misspecified DD/C, were conducted with sound statistical methods and raised legitimate questions about the impact of measurement error and the instability of classifications near diagnostic thresholds. As Flanagan and Schneider noted, these studies did not evaluate DD/C, but they did highlight psychometric challenges that any SLD identification method must address.

Those challenges ultimately sparked the line of inquiry that led to Schneider et al.'s (2024) research, and to refinements in DD/C (as discussed in subsequent sections of this chapter). The irony is that the simulation authors themselves have long acknowledged that the solution to measurement-error-driven misclassification is to avoid strict cut points. For example:

> *Limit the use of strict cut points. Instead, decisions should be based on considerations of a range of plausible scores.* (p. 140)
>
> Miciak et al. (2016)

> *We must recognize the presence of measurement error in the decision-making process and develop procedures that are more immune to its presence.* (p. 31)
>
> Fletcher et al. (2005)

What is rarely acknowledged is that the authors of DD/C implemented "measurement error" safeguards decades ago and have continued to refine them. As early as 2001, the first edition of *Essentials of Cross-Battery Assessment* (Flanagan & Ortiz) instructed practitioners to place a 68% confidence interval (1 SEM) around a composite score and require the entire band to fall below normal limits before classifying a weakness, an approach that parallels the recommendations later made by the authors of the PSW simulation studies (e.g., Francis et al., 2005; Miciak et al., 2016). X-BASS 2.0 continued this practice by requiring practitioners to identify strengths and weaknesses using guidelines rather than strict cut points and by flagging scores near thresholds to signal the need for converging evidence.

In short, although the simulation studies mismodeled DD/C, they raised legitimate psychometric concerns that DD/C had already anticipated and that later work, especially Schneider et al. (2024), addressed with even greater precision. This stands in stark contrast to the work of Kranzler et al., whose methodological errors were so fundamental that their conclusions cannot justify changes to DD/C.

## Reframing Diagnostic Accuracy: The Contributions of Schneider et al. (2024)

The Schneider et al. (2024) buffer-zone study is the first large-scale empirical demonstration, using a 10-million-case simulation, that the appearance of widespread PSW "inaccuracy" is largely an artifact of treating arbitrary diagnostic thresholds as if they were meaningful boundaries (see Appendix F). Their analysis shows that the vast majority of so-called diagnostic "errors" reported in earlier simulation studies occur when observed and true scores fall on opposite sides of a strict cut point but remain within a buffer zone *no larger than typical measurement error* (i.e., <5 points). In these cases, the observed and true scores do not represent functionally different levels of ability because the differences are trivial. When buffer zones are applied (accounting for measurement error), the *illusion of inaccuracy* largely disappears. Schneider et al. also demonstrate that diagnostic decisions become increasingly stable as observed scores move farther from the threshold, underscoring that the real risk lies only in cases near arbitrary cut points, *not in PSW logic itself.* Schneider et al. noted, "We ought to regard with suspicion any analysis that fails to distinguish between trivial and substantive errors" (p. 103).

Schneider and colleagues also showed that the simulation studies conducted by Steubing et al., Miciak et al., and others provided correct answers to a question that is not useful to those who use PSW: *When I randomly select people from the general population, what is the probability that PSW methods correctly identify who is and who is not SLD using strict cut points?* The answer is: When people are randomly selected from the population, PSW methods are excellent at identifying individuals without SLD but poor at identifying those with SLD. The problems associated with using general population base rates rather than referral sample base rates, as well as issues with how diagnostic accuracy statistics are used and interpreted, were addressed elsewhere (e.g., Akobeng, 2007; Roman, 2016; see also Appendix F).

The question that is far more useful to those who use PSW is: *When a student is referred for an evaluation of suspected SLD, what is the probability that the practitioner will correctly arrive at an accurate case conceptualization of the student's academic difficulties when using PSW?* Because the diagnostic accuracy statistics reported in the PSW simulation studies (e.g., overall *unconditional* positive predictive values [PPVs]) cannot be used to estimate the probability of SLD *in an individual,* Schneider et al. introduced a *conditional,* case-level approach to diagnostic accuracy. "The conditional PPV accounts for the distance that the observed scores are from diagnostic thresholds" (p. 14). (See Appendix F for a complete explanation.) Schneider et al. demonstrated how to calculate the probability that the practitioner's classification of an observed score (e.g., "weakness") matches the classification that would be made if the true score were known. The higher the probability, the greater confidence one has in the accuracy of their classification of an observed score. The lower the probability, the less confidence one has. When probabilities are low or equivocal, a review of nontest data or additional testing (or both) should occur to determine if it is consistent with the classification of the score (e.g., do additional data support or fail to support the classification of a score as a weakness?).

In summary, Schneider et al.'s method allows practitioners to determine whether a decision is stable (when the observed score is comfortably distant from the threshold) or inherently uncertain (when the observed score falls within a buffer zone the size of typical measurement error). Schneider et al. showed that most of the "errors" reported in earlier simulations occur in this buffer zone, *cases where the observed and true scores differ only by typical measurement error and do not represent meaningful diagnostic differences.* When conditional PPVs and buffer zones are applied, the illusion of widespread PSW inaccuracy disappears, and the method's actual diagnostic performance becomes clear. The probability of making accurate classification decisions is built into the DD/C method in X-BASS 3.0.

> **CAUTION**
>
> Although Dombrowski et al. (2025) was designated *Article of the Year,* readers should note that a coauthor of the review also coauthored two of the five primary studies summarized in the article (i.e., the *Kranzler et al.* papers). The review does not disclose or critically evaluate this authorship overlap, nor does it adequately engage major corrective analyses (e.g., Flanagan & Schneider, 2016). Equally notable is how the review treats Schneider et al. (2024): it only briefly references the study and fails to engage with its findings, implications, or relevance, despite Schneider et al. *directly addressing* the central issue the review purports to evaluate—the diagnostic accuracy of PSW methods when measurement error is present. Because *independent methodological appraisal and transparent disclosure of potential conflicts of interest* are core elements of rigorous systematic review practice, the absence of such appraisal and disclosure weakens the review's claim to be an impartial synthesis. For these reasons, along with omissions and limited critical analysis, *readers and policymakers should interpret Dombrowski et al.'s conclusions with healthy skepticism.*

### Dombrowski et al. (2025): A Systematic Review that Repeats, Rather than Evaluates

The most recent systematic review of PSW diagnostic accuracy (Dombrowski et al., 2025) exemplifies how repetition, rather than critical analysis, can shape the scientific narrative. Although the review claims to provide a comprehensive synthesis of the diagnostic-accuracy literature, it largely reiterates conclusions drawn from earlier studies, many of which mischaracterized DD/C or evaluated simplified PSW procedures that bear little resemblance to the method as actually implemented. Surprisingly, the review cites both of Kranzler et al.'s papers (Kranzler et al., 2016a, 2019) without acknowledging the extensive conceptual and methodological flaws identified in Flanagan and Schneider's (2016) rebuttal, most notably the deterministic misinterpretation of causality, and the evaluation of a version of DD/C "endorsed by no one" (p. 496).

Equally striking is the review's treatment of Schneider et al. (2024). The article mentions the study only in passing and offers no discussion of its findings, implications, or relevance, even though Schneider et al. directly address the central criticism the review claims to evaluate: the diagnostic accuracy of PSW methods in the presence of measurement error. Instead, Dombrowski et al. (2025) reduce Schneider et al.'s research to another acknowledgement that dichotomizing continuous variables is a limitation of diagnostic accuracy methodology (p. 14). They then dismiss Schneider et al.'s research by stating, ". . .dichotomization of continuous variables is not solely specific to diagnostic accuracy methods..[it] is inherent to special education identification more broadly". . . (p. 14). Dombrowski et al. then conclude that a method less sensitive to dichotomization (i.e., receiver operating curve analysis; McGill et al., 2018) "has been consistent with the conclusions of the diagnostic accuracy studies" and thus, conclude

". . .it appears that the diagnostic accuracy methodology is not. . .wrong. Rather, it seems that PSW tends not to identify SLD at a level greater than chance" (p. 14).

By eschewing the only large-scale, empirically grounded analysis that models diagnostic accuracy at the level of individual cases, the review reinforces the false narrative that PSW methods, and DD/C in particular, rely on rigid cut points and are inherently vulnerable to measurement error, obscuring the fact that DD/C has long incorporated measurement error safeguards critics have called for. In this way, the Dombrowski et al. review does not function as a critical synthesis of the evidence; it functions as a citation amplifier, repeating earlier claims without examining whether those claims were accurate in the first place.

### When Repetition Becomes "Truth": How Mischaracterizations Take Hold

A substantial body of research demonstrates that repetition increases perceived truth, even when the repeated claim is false. This phenomenon, the illusory truth effect, has been replicated for nearly five decades. Classic studies show that statements repeated over time are judged as more accurate simply because they become familiar (Begg et al., 1992; Hasher et al., 1977). More recent work confirms that repetition can make false claims seem true even when individuals possess the correct knowledge (Fazio, 2020; Fazio et al., 2015; Pennycook & Rand, 2021; Pennycook et al., 2018).

This dynamic is not limited to everyday reasoning. Meta-scientific analyses show that repeated citation of an incorrect claim can create the appearance of consensus (as exemplified by Dombrowski et al., 2025), a process sometimes described as a citation cascade (Greenberg, 2009). Over time, the claim becomes entrenched, not because it is empirically supported, but because it is familiar, widely repeated, and rarely reexamined. Ioannidis (2005) and others warn that such cascades can distort entire research areas, allowing unsupported assertions to become "common knowledge."

By repeating conclusions from earlier studies without engaging with the corrective evidence—particularly Schneider et al. (2024) and Flanagan and Schneider's (2016) rebuttal to Kranzler et al. (2016a)—Dombrowski et al.'s review perpetuates a narrative that diverges sharply from the actual design, intent, and evolution of DD/C. Worse, the review treats the findings of a small set of prior studies as if they were settled fact and amplifies unexamined assumptions rather than examining them critically. By failing to weigh study quality, disclose overlapping authorship, or consider large-scale corrective analyses, the review reinforces the very misconceptions that have distorted the PSW literature for more than a decade.

### The Consequences of Repetition Without Evaluation

Taken together, the misrepresentation of DD/C in Beaujean et al. (2018), Kranzler et al. (2016a), and other critiques (e.g., McGill et al., 2016; Miciak & Fletcher, 2020), the flawed assumptions embedded in the simulation literature (e.g., Stuebing et al., 2012), and the uncritical repetition of these claims in a recent systematic review (Dombrowski et al., 2025) have collectively distorted the scientific record. These critiques have led practitioners, researchers, and policymakers to believe that DD/C is rigid, psychometrically naïve, and diagnostically unreliable—when in fact it is the only PSW method that systematically incorporates procedures to mitigate measurement error.

Decker (2026) addressed the broader consequences of these research flaws for students with dyslexia, highlighting two policy arguments that threaten the role of cognitive assessment. The first is the claim that only estimates of *g* from cognitive batteries are interpretable, rendering lower-order composites (e.g., *Gf, Gc, Gv, Gwm*) psychometrically meaningless and devoid of incremental validity—a body of research produced by one research team (see Decker 2020; Decker et al., 2020; and the teams' rebuttal by Dombrowski et al., 2020). The second is the claim that diagnostic information—particularly cognitive strengths and weaknesses—does not inform intervention, making cognitive assessment irrelevant for educational planning. These arguments have produced two erroneous conclusions: (1) cognitive ability is only *g*, and therefore PSW methods are invalid; and (2) even if PSW were valid, it would have no relevance for intervention selection.

Decker and colleagues directly evaluated whether these arguments rest on sound science or flawed statistics. Decker et al. (2020) demonstrated that the "*g*-only" position espoused by Dombrowski, Canivez, and colleagues is an artifact of biased statistical methods, not an accurate reflection of cognitive theory or empirical evidence. Decker and Luedke (2021) further showed that studies claiming cognitive test results are irrelevant for intervention selection were methodologically weak and, critically, did not actually use the test data they purported to evaluate. In other words, the evidence cited against cognitive assessment is overwhelmingly based on research in which cognitive assessment was never meaningfully incorporated for the purpose of intervention selection.

Despite these findings, Decker and colleagues noted that biased tools and questionable validity continue to shape policy. For example, current policies favoring RtI-only approaches to SLD identification rest on this flawed methodological foundation. To address these issues, Decker (2026) outlined a path forward with three essential components: (1) research used to inform policy must be critically evaluated for methodological bias; (2) studies examining the utility of cognitive test scores for intervention planning must be high-quality and must actually use assessment data to drive intervention; and (3) practice must move beyond general remediation strategies toward targeted, domain-specific intervention and treatment.

## No Gold Standard SLD Definition or Identification Method

A critical reality that muddies the SLD literature is that there is no gold-standard definition of SLD and no gold-standard identification method. SLD is a latent construct—an inference drawn from patterns of academic performance, response to instruction and intervention, and underlying cognitive and linguistic processes. It is not a directly observable condition with a definitive diagnostic marker. As a result, no identification method, whether PSW, RtI, or AAD, can be validated against a criterion standard that unequivocally distinguishes "true" cases from "false" ones. This absence of a gold standard raises a fundamental question that should be addressed more prominently, rather than casually mentioned in research papers: *How can we meaningfully test the diagnostic accuracy of a construct for which no universally accepted criterion exists?* Simulation studies, including Schneider et al., helped move this conversation in the right direction.

In the absence of a criterion standard, the most defensible approach is to rely on the core assumptions of the SLD construct, which have remained stable across nearly a century of theory, research, and practice. These include the understanding that SLD is (1) domain-specific, (2) unexpected relative to other abilities and opportunities to learn, and (3) cognitively mediated. When evaluated through this lens, the question shifts from *Which model is empirically superior?* to *Which model most faithfully operationalizes the agreed-upon assumptions of the construct?*

This is precisely where the DD/C method has been misunderstood. DD/C is not a statistical trick, a rigid algorithm, or a narrow PSW variant. It is a structured operationalization of the widely shared assumptions of the SLD construct: that academic weaknesses must be specific (not global) and unexpected (inconsistent with the individual's cognitive strengths). When DD/C is evaluated on this conceptual basis—rather than against a nonexistent gold standard—it aligns more closely with the historical and theoretical foundations of SLD than alternative methods.

This context also clarifies why simulation studies cannot "invalidate" DD/C. Simulations require a criterion variable that defines who "has" and "does not have" SLD. But because no such criterion exists in reality, simulations inevitably embed the authors' assumptions about what SLD *is*, and then test whether DD/C reproduces those assumptions. In other words, simulations test agreement with the modeler's definition, not diagnostic accuracy against an objective standard. This circularity is rarely acknowledged, yet it fundamentally limits what simulation studies can tell us about the validity of any SLD identification method.

Decker's recent analyses further underscore the consequences of relying on flawed or biased methodological assumptions in the absence of a gold standard. His work demonstrates that widely cited arguments—such as the claim that only *g* is interpretable or that cognitive assessment is irrelevant for intervention—are themselves products of statistical bias, low-quality research, or studies that did not actually use cognitive data. These findings reinforce the broader point: when the field lacks a criterion standard, methodological rigor and conceptual alignment become even more essential. Misapplied methods or misinterpreted findings can quickly harden into policy, distorting practice and public understanding of SLD.

Recognizing the absence of a gold standard does not weaken the case for DD/C; it strengthens the rationale for a transparent, theory-driven operational definition and a structured debiasing framework. Without a criterion standard, the integrity of SLD identification depends on the clarity of the definition, the coherence of the operationalization method, and the safeguards in place to account for measurement error and reduce cognitive bias during interpretation. DD/C, when embedded within a well-specified operational definition and supported by debiasing strategies, provides a defensible, conceptually aligned approach to identifying SLD in practice.

Nevertheless, it is essential to acknowledge that all SLD identification methods—whether PSW, RtI, or AAD—have limitations and are error-prone because they rely on imperfectly reliable tools (e.g., Miciak et al., 2016; Nunnally & Bernstein, 1994). No approach is immune to measurement error, thresholds, or conceptual constraints. One could argue that simulation studies are less about PSW diagnostic accuracy and more about the psychometric limitations of the measurement instruments used in diagnostic evaluations.

The bottom line is that progress in the field depends on critiques that accurately represent the methods under evaluation, identify genuine weaknesses, and offer empirically grounded alternatives or refinements. When criticisms are based on mischaracterizations or mismodeled procedures, they cannot meaningfully inform revisions to PSW methods or contribute to the development of stronger approaches that might one day replace them. To correct the record and support constructive scientific advancement, the next section presents the DD/C method as defined by its authors, operationalizes it, and explains how its components work together to guide reliable, research-based identification of SLD.

## An Operational Definition of SLD

Flanagan and colleagues' operational definition of SLD has been described in numerous sources since 2002 (e.g., Flanagan & McDonough, 2018; Flanagan et al., 2006, 2011, 2013; Kavale & Flanagan, 2007). Modeled after Kavale and Forness's (2000) definition, it was adapted in several important ways. First, the definition is anchored in the well-validated CHC taxonomy. Second, it emphasizes specific patterns of cognitive and academic abilities rather than reliance on a traditional aptitude–achievement discrepancy. Third, it prioritizes early consideration of exclusionary factors to prevent unnecessary or misdirected testing. Fourth, it conceptualizes the evaluation process as iterative rather than linear. The operational definition includes five essential elements (or levels) of data gathering and analysis, listed in Rapid Reference 3.4, each of which is described in the sections that follow. X-BASS automates the analyses associated with Levels I through IV.

## Rapid Reference 3.4

### Essential Elements of SLD Identification

Level I. Academic skills analysis

Level II. Evaluation of mitigating and exclusionary factors

Level III. Cognitive ability and processing analysis

Level IV. Data integration—the DD/C pattern

Level V. Evaluation of interference with learning for special education eligibility

### Level I: Academic Skills Analysis

SLD is characterized by underlying cognitive and linguistic processing weaknesses that disrupt the typical acquisition and development of basic academic skills. The federal definition identifies eight academic areas relevant to SLD: basic reading skills, reading fluency, reading comprehension, mathematical calculation, mathematical problem solving, written expression, listening comprehension, and oral expression. These domains represent stores of knowledge acquired through formal instruction and other educational experiences. Although comprehensive school evaluations typically assess all eight domains, reevaluations and diagnostic assessments often focus on the specific areas of concern identified in the referral.

Level I begins by documenting the presence of an academic deficit through standardized assessment in the relevant achievement area(s), reading, writing, mathematics, or oral language, supported by converging evidence from clinical observations, work samples, teacher and parent reports, and other data sources (see Rapid Reference 3.5). When standardized achievement tests do not reveal weaknesses, SLD is unlikely. However, very bright students may mask underlying weaknesses through compensation strategies, necessitating more targeted diagnostic assessment to uncover subtle weaknesses that may be masked by broad achievement composites.

### Level II: Evaluation of Mitigating and Exclusionary Factors

IDEA requires that, before a student can be identified with SLD, certain exclusionary factors must be ruled out. These factors ensure that academic difficulties are not mistakenly attributed to a disability when they are better explained by external, non-disability-related conditions. Appendix G provides an overview of these factors and includes an ***Exclusionary Factors Form*** that practitioners can use as a guide to ensure they have sufficiently evaluated them.

Exclusionary factors serve as safeguards for accurate and equitable identification of SLDs. They help prevent misdiagnosis and ensure that students receive interventions aligned with their actual needs. This is especially important for culturally and linguistically diverse learners, who are at heightened risk for misidentification when contextual variables are overlooked (see Chapter 8; National Center for Learning Disabilities, n.d.; Ortiz, 2014; Zirkel, 2017).

Level II evaluates whether the student's documented academic weaknesses are primarily attributable to factors such as cultural or linguistic differences, emotional or behavioral conditions, sensory impairments, medical issues, or other noncognitive influences, rather than intrinsic cognitive processing weaknesses. Practitioners must gather sufficient data to answer the questions listed in Rapid Reference 3.6.

Because SLD determination is not strictly linear, Levels I and II often occur concurrently. Practitioners must evaluate the extent to which factors other than cognitive processing weaknesses could serve as the *primary* or most plausible reason for academic difficulties. When such factors contribute to, but do not fully explain, the student's performance, SLD should not be ruled out. After reviewing the data necessary to answer the questions in Rapid Reference 3.6, one of three outcomes is possible:

## Rapid Reference 3.5

### Data Sources that May Reveal Academic Difficulties

- Response to quality instruction and intervention via progress monitoring
- Performance on norm-referenced, standardized achievement tests
- Evaluation of work samples
- Observations of academic performance (e.g., listening to a student read)
- Teacher/parent/student interviews
- History of academic performance, including previous evaluations
- Data from other multidisciplinary team members (e.g., speech language pathologists, interventionists, reading specialists)

## Rapid Reference 3.6

### Questions that Must Be Answered to Satisfy the Exclusionary Factors Component in SLD Identification

- **Visual Impairment:** *Is (or was) the student unable to perceive visual stimuli, including letters and numbers, such that this is primarily responsible for academic skill deficits?*
- **Hearing Impairment:** *Is (or was) the student unable to hear sounds well enough to acquire academic skills despite adequate instruction?*
- **Motor Impairment:** *Do motor difficulties prevent the student from developing or demonstrating academic skills?*
- **Cognitive and Adaptive Impairment:** *Does the student meet criteria for intellectual disability (ID), including deficits in both cognitive and adaptive functioning?*
- **Emotional or Behavioral Disorders:** *Are emotional or behavioral problems severe enough to have prevented the development or demonstration of academic skills?*
- **Environmental or Economic Deprivation:** *Has deprivation been so significant that it prevented the development of academic skills?*
- **Cultural or Linguistic Differences:** *Is limited English proficiency the most likely primary explanation for academic skill deficits?*
- **Physical Health Problems.** *Have medical conditions or treatments interfered with the development or demonstration of academic skills?*

## Rapid Reference 3.7

### Decision-Making Protocol for Multidisciplinary Teams

1. Gather comprehensive data from multiple sources.
2. Ensure interventions were evidence-based and implemented with fidelity.
3. Evaluate each exclusionary factor systematically (see Appendix G for guidance).
4. Document findings and the rationale for ruling out each factor.
5. Collaborate with specialists (e.g., mental health specialist, occupational therapist, physical therapist, speech language pathologist).
6. Make a consensus decision based on the full body of evidence.
7. Clearly document the exclusionary factor analysis in the eligibility report.

1. No exclusionary factor primarily explains the student's learning difficulties.
2. One or more factors contribute to the learning difficulties but do not primarily explain them.
3. One or more factors appear to primarily explain the student's learning difficulties, and SLD should not be identified.

The questions in Rapid Reference 3.6, along with the outcome of the exclusionary factor review, are integrated into the X-BASS workflow and can be documented directly within the system. Rapid Reference 3.7 provides a decision-making protocol that multidisciplinary teams may follow to document a sufficient evaluation of exclusionary factors.

### Level III: Cognitive Ability and Processing Analysis

Level III criteria mirror Level I criteria but focus on cognitive abilities and processes, as measured by standardized tests and other relevant data-collection methods and sources. A particularly salient aspect is that cognitive weaknesses or deficits typically underlie academic performance difficulties in students with SLDs. Research demonstrates that this relationship is causal (i.e., contributory or *probabilistic*, not deterministic) and requires data analysis to determine whether the identified cognitive weaknesses are empirically related to previously identified achievement weaknesses (Flanagan & Schneider, 2016; Hajovsky & Niileksela, 2024; Hajovsky et al., 2024, 2025). Theory and research not only specify relevant constructs for measurement at Levels I and III but also predict their relationships, providing a substantive empirical foundation for interpretations and conclusions. Chapter 2 summarized these relationships, and Appendix C presents the data used by X-BASS to determine below-average cognitive aptitude-achievement "consistency" as part of the PSW pattern described at Level IV.

***Levels I and III: A Closer Look.*** In response to DD/C being mischaracterized in the literature as a method that relies on strict cut points, X-BASS has incorporated additional safeguards to address measurement error in test scores. In its current version, when practitioners designate cognitive or academic achievement scores as a weakness, they receive information on the likelihood (expressed as a percentage) that their decision was correct. A correct decision indicates a high likelihood that the observed score and its corresponding true score are on the same side of an arbitrary cut point (e.g., that both scores are below 85). In the DD/C method, cut points are used as *thresholds of convenience*, meaning when scores hover around a cut point of 85, for example, we do not know if the score represents a true weakness without additional information, regardless of what side of the cut point the score falls (i.e., above or below 85). Because we never know the true score, providing likelihood estimates helps us make better decisions about the student we evaluated (Schneider et al., 2024; Appendix F).

- When the likelihood of a true weakness is low or equivocal based on the standard score, converging data sources strengthen the "weakness" classification; a lack of converging data or conflicting evidence means that a true weakness is unlikely.
- When the likelihood of a true weakness is high, the standard score can stand on its own; however, converging data always strengthens interpretation and improves confidence in test findings.
- When exploring the veracity of an academic or cognitive area that has a low probability of being a true weakness, it is important to examine other data sources for converging/diverging evidence. X-BASS provides guidance on this in the SLD Evidence tab, in the form of common manifestations of weaknesses, such as those reported in Appendices H and Q.
- Recent research demonstrated that structured support (like that offered in X-BASS) significantly improved classification accuracy regarding scores near cut points (i.e., 80–89) and confidence in making strengths and weaknesses decisions (see Appendix P).

## Level IV: Data Integration—The DD/C Pattern

Level IV involves PSW analysis through theory- and research-guided examination of academic skills, cognitive abilities, and neuropsychological processes to determine whether the student's PSW is consistent with the SLD construct, as specified by DD/C criteria. When these criteria are met, the following key features are identified: at least average ability to think and reason (despite cognitive weaknesses), unexpected underachievement, domain-specific cognitive weakness, and below-average cognitive-aptitude-achievement consistency. Each component is defined below and is identified using statistical analyses and methods (conducted by X-BASS) that practitioners do not need to know for routine interpretation. Nevertheless, several appendices detail the psychometric rigor underlying the DD/C method. For easy reference, Figure 3.2 shows the appendices associated with each DD/C criterion.

## At Least Average Ability to Think and Reason

SLD is specific, not global. Below-average cognitive aptitude–achievement consistency should be circumscribed and represent a significantly different level of functioning compared to the individual's other cognitive capabilities. Historically, individuals with SLD have been described as having average or better overall cognitive ability or intelligence despite marked difficulty acquiring certain academic skills (see Rapid Reference 3.8).

Contemporary definitions maintain this view. For example, in Lachmann et al.'s (2022) five-level diagnostic framework for dyslexia and dyscalculia, the Specificity Level requires that the impairment be confirmed as *specific* by demonstrating unimpaired general cognitive development through standardized testing. The IDEA definition of SLD does not explicitly reference overall cognitive level; instead, federal regulations refer to a "pattern of strengths and weaknesses in performance, achievement, or both, relative to age, State-approved grade-level standards, or intellectual development." DD/C operationalizes IDEA's terminology of "relative to. . .intellectual development" by requiring evidence that the student's general cognitive ability is unimpaired; that is, it is at least average and therefore is expected to support learning, despite specific cognitive weaknesses.

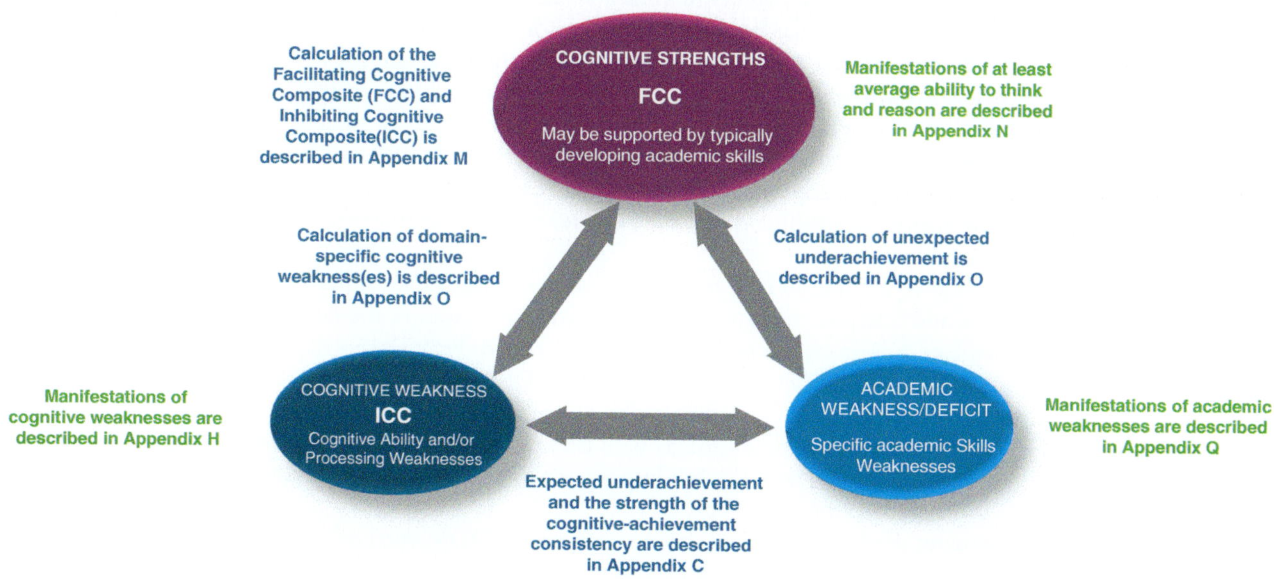


**FIGURE 3.2 Appendices Describing DD/C Calculations and Related Supports.** ***Note:*** **All calculations described in the appendices referenced in this figure are automated in X-BASS**

## *Rapid Reference 3.8*

### Individuals with SLD Have at Least Average Cognitive Capabilities: A Century of Consistent Clinical and Theoretical Observation

**For more than a century, clinical descriptions and theoretical accounts of SLD have consistently emphasized that specific academic weaknesses occur in the context of at least average general cognitive ability. Selected examples include:**

- *The children often have average or above intelligence and good memory in other respects*—Hinshelwood (1902, p. 70)
- *It seems probable that psychometric tests as ordinarily employed give an entirely erroneous and unfair estimate of the intellectual capacity of these children*—Orton (1925, p. 582)
- *Remedial training must continue until reading is in harmony with the child's other capacities and achievements. Some children of superior intelligence struggle to learn to read*—Monroe (1932, p. 197)
- *The clearest expression of a special disability is consistently low scores on a series of tests in a given subject, conjoined with average or superior scores on tests in other subjects*—Travis (1935, p. 37)
- *There is a deficit in learning in the presence of basic integrity*—Johnson and Myklebust (1967, p. 25)
- *The addition of the adjective specific in describing LD was meant to imply that the poor academic performance experienced by students with LD emanated from a limited number of underlying deficits*—Kavale and Forness (2000, p. 239).
- *Weaknesses in word reading and spelling surrounded by a sea of strengths*—Shaywitz and Shaywitz (2003, p. 1301)
- *All historical approaches to SLD emphasize the spared or intact abilities that stand in stark contrast to the deficient abilities*—Kaufman and Kaufman (2008, pp. 7–8)
- *Learning Disabilities refer to a number of disorders which may affect the acquisition, organization, retention, understanding, or use of verbal or nonverbal information. These disorders affect learning in individuals who otherwise demonstrate at least average abilities essential for thinking and/or reasoning (2015)*—Official Definition of Learning Disabilities | LDAC | The Learning Disability Association of Canada
- *. . .the demonstration of unimpaired general cognitive development. . .*—Lachmann et al. (2022, p. 387)

Unimpaired cognitive development in the DD/C method is evaluated through the FCC. The FCC is an aggregate of the student's intact cognitive abilities (in the CHC domains not identified as weaknesses) and therefore represents the level of cognitive functioning most capable of supporting learning. By isolating strengths rather than blending them with weaknesses, the FCC provides an estimate of general ability that is less attenuated by the very deficits that may be contributing to the academic difficulty. This approach ensures that DD/C's requirement of at least average ability to think and reason is grounded in a theoretically aligned and empirically modeled estimate of *g* (see Appendix M).

Note that X-BASS includes a likelihood estimate for the FCC. At least average ability is defined as a standard score of 90 or higher. As such, 90 is a threshold of convenience for "Average" in the same way as 85 is a threshold of convenience for "weakness." An FCC that hovers around 90 (above or below) may or may not reflect at least average ability to think and reason. In such cases, evaluating other data sources is important for arriving at an accurate interpretation of the FCC. For example, students with at least average ability to think and reason typically show age-appropriate problem solving, pattern recognition, concept formation, flexible thinking, and the ability to explain their reasoning. They learn new concepts with typical exposure, make logical connections, and use strategies effectively, even if they struggle with specific academic skills such as decoding, spelling, or math fact retrieval. See Rapid Reference 3.9 for examples of what at least average cognitive ability looks like. For more specific manifestations of at least average ability to think and reason, by grade level, see Appendix N. When the likelihood that the FCC represents at least average ability is equivocal, practitioners should use Appendix N to clarify whether this criterion is met. The more manifestations the student exhibits, the greater the likelihood that the FCC represents at least average ability. If the ecological validity for at least average ability is weak, this criterion is not met.

Users of X-BASS may conduct a PSW analysis using an FCC that falls below the average range. If the PSW pattern is met under those conditions, the practitioner may still describe and interpret the pattern. However, the interpretation should not state that the student met DD/C criteria, because DD/C requires evidence of at least average ability to think and reason. Practitioners may discuss the pattern in any way they find clinically or diagnostically meaningful, as long as they clearly note that the DD/C average cognitive-ability criterion was not met.

A detailed explanation of how the FCC is constructed, including the meta-analytic *g*-weights, the structural modeling procedures, and the evidence showing that different FCC combinations correlate strongly with latent *g*, is provided in Appendix M. Again, practitioners will not need this level of statistical detail for routine interpretation, but it is important to know the appendix exists and can be used to address questions about the validity of the FCC as an estimate of general ability.

**Users of X-BASS 2.0** should be aware of the following information regarding the DD/C method in **X-BASS 3.0** as it applies to the FCC.

- The FCC does not require the evaluator to assess seven or eight CHC domains. With a new method for evaluating whether the FCC is an adequate estimate of *g*, practitioners can streamline their assessments, potentially resulting in briefer, more targeted evaluations (see cases at the end of this chapter for an example).

## Rapid Reference 3.9

### What Stands Out in a Student with at Least Average Ability to Think and Reason (Despite Academic Struggles)

*Students with at least average ability to think and reason do not need to display all of the manifestations listed here. In practice, students may show some of these behaviors more strongly than others, and variation across domains is entirely typical. What matters for DD/C is the overall pattern: the student demonstrates generally adequate reasoning abilities, even if specific academic skills are weak.*

**1. They learn concepts with typical exposure.**

Even if decoding, spelling, math facts, or written output is weak, they:

- grasp new ideas at a typical pace
- understand explanations
- make sense of lessons without excessive repetition

**2. They show age-appropriate reasoning and problem solving.**

They:

- recognize patterns
- make logical connections
- explain their thinking
- adjust strategies when something isn't working

*This is the hallmark of intact Gf/Gc.*

**3. They understand and use language in a typical way.**

Even if reading or writing is hard, they:

- understand discussions
- follow multi-step directions
- use vocabulary appropriately
- express ideas clearly

*This is why many students with SLD "sound smart" even when their academic output lags.*

**4. They can think flexibly.**

They:

- shift strategies
- adapt to new information
- consider multiple solutions
- revise their thinking

*This is not what globally low ability looks like.*

**5. They use visual and conceptual supports effectively.**

They:

- interpret diagrams, charts, and models
- understand relationships among ideas
- use visual information to solve problems

**6. They organize ideas even if they struggle to execute skills.**

For example:

- they can outline a story even if their spelling is weak
- they can explain a math concept even if they can't compute fluently
- they can summarize a text even if reading it was slow

**7. They show curiosity, insight, and "sense-making."**

They ask good questions, make connections, and show interest in understanding how things work.

**8. Their academic struggles are specific, not global.**

They may have:

- weak decoding but strong comprehension
- weak math facts but strong reasoning
- weak written output but strong oral expression

*The pattern is uneven, not uniformly low.*

- The DD/C method no longer calculates a *g*-Value for determining whether the FCC is an adequate estimate of *g*. Appendix M explains how *g*-weights were used in evaluating the FCC, without the need for a *g*-Value.
- At times, the FCC will be slightly above or below the cut point of 90. In those instances, the probability of making a correct decision regarding whether the FCC represents at least average cognitive ability may be low or equivocal. When this occurs, there are three possibilities moving forward:
  - The practitioner clicks on the SLD Evidence tab to add supporting data. The supporting data tab lists any academic areas that were identified as relative strengths. Additional data, such as the manifestations of at least average cognitive ability listed in Rapid Reference 3.9 (and Appendix N) may also be added. If the practitioner judges these additional data sources to provide moderate to strong evidence of ecological validity for the FCC, then the criterion will be indicated as "met."
  - Practitioners may select another estimate from the drop-down menu in the top oval on the PSW Results tab. For example, if the WJ V is administered and scores for the General Intellectual Ability cluster and the *Gf-Gc* cluster are entered, they will be listed in the drop-down menu. If there is no other score to select, the practitioner may use another score for this purpose and opt to "change ability score" on the SLD Evidence tab.
  - If no alternative scores exist and ecological validity for the FCC is weak, then the criterion of at least average overall ability to think and reason is "not met."

**DON'T FORGET**

DD/C's requirement of unimpaired cognitive development is evaluated through the FCC, a strengths-based estimate of general ability that avoids the downward pull of cognitive weaknesses.

## Unexpected Underachievement: The First Discrepancy

Traditional AAD methods attempted to identify "unexpected" underachievement using global IQ scores, which blend strengths and weaknesses and often obscure patterns consistent with SLD. DD/C improves on this approach by comparing academic performance to the FCC—an estimate of general ability based solely on intact cognitive domains. When a student demonstrates at least average ability to think and reason, yet shows an unusually large gap between their obtained and FCC-predicted scores in an academic area, the pattern reflects unexpected underachievement.

In X-BASS, this determination begins by testing whether the difference between the FCC and the academic weakness is statistically significant. Significance is necessary but not sufficient, because real differences may still fall within typical variation, meaning they are common in the general population. Therefore, X-BASS uses a regression-based model to predict expected performance from the FCC and evaluates whether the actual–predicted difference is statistically rare or uncommon (at base rates of 5%, 10%, and 15%). If the difference is uncommon for students with similar predicted scores, the academic weakness is considered unexpected. Appendix O provides the full psychometric explanation of this DD/C criterion, including a correction for false negatives. That is, the correction guards against incorrectly stating that achievement is *not* unexpected when it is unexpected.

## Domain-Specific Cognitive Weaknesses: The Second Discrepancy

SLD is characterized by specific cognitive processing weaknesses rather than global cognitive impairment. DD/C evaluates this by determining whether a student's performance in the identified areas of cognitive weakness is lower than would be expected based on their own cognitive strengths, as represented by the FCC. A cognitive weakness is considered domain-specific when it is statistically significantly lower than the FCC ($p < .05$) and the difference between the student's actual (obtained score) and the FCC-predicted score is statistically rare for same-age peers with similar predicted performance. This protects against misidentifying students with generally low ability and ensures that the cognitive weaknesses are circumscribed. Appendix O provides the full psychometric explanation of this DD/C criterion, including a correction for false negatives. That is, the correction guards against incorrectly stating that the specific cognitive weakness is *not* domain-specific when it is domain-specific.

## Consistency Between Cognitive and Academic Weaknesses

Students with SLD show specific cognitive and academic weaknesses that are both empirically and ecologically related. Decades of research on CHC abilities and academic skills demonstrate that certain cognitive processes reliably predict performance in specific academic domains. When a student shows academic and cognitive weaknesses in an academic skill (e.g., Reading Fluency, Reading Comprehension) and one or more related cognitive abilities (*Gf, Gwm, Gs*) that are supported by research, this reflects below-average cognitive aptitude–achievement consistency in the DD/C method. In this context, "cognitive aptitude" refers to the specific CHC abilities or neuropsychological processes that predict the academic skill in question.

DD/C interprets this pattern as meaningful evidence of SLD, provided it occurs in the context of at least average ability to think and reason and after exclusionary factors have been ruled out. X-BASS summarizes this cognitive-academic weakness relationship as **High**, **Moderate**, or **Low** consistency based on the most current meta-analytic research on cognitive–achievement relations. The full set of effect sizes, methodological details, and interpretive foundations for these consistency ratings is provided in Appendix C.

### Level V: Educational Performance Impact

When SLD diagnostic criteria are met at Levels I–IV, Level V evaluates whether the condition impairs academic functioning to a degree that warrants special education services. This level serves as a quality-control check, ensuring that an SLD diagnosis is not applied when real-world functioning is not substantially limited relative to same-age peers.

Level V requires practitioners to broadly review all collected data and consider how any presumed disability manifests in everyday academic performance. In most cases, when criteria at Levels I–IV are clearly met, Level V will confirm meaningful educational impact. In more equivocal cases, however, Level V helps ensure that patterns suggested by test data correspond to observable, functionally significant classroom difficulties. Appendices H, L, and Q can assist the multidisciplinary team in making these determinations.

> **DON'T FORGET**
>
> Consistency matters in SLD identification. DD/C requires consistency between cognitive and academic weaknesses. DD/C evaluates whether a student's cognitive area of weakness is one that research shows is linked to the academic skill in question. High or Moderate consistency strengthens the case for SLD; Low consistency suggests the pattern likely does not support the cognitive weaknesses as a plausible explanation for the academic weakness.

### Research Supports the Core Principles of DD/C

Decades of CHC-based structural research, neurocognitive studies, and incremental validity studies support the logic underlying DD/C. Intelligence is now understood as a constellation of distinct abilities, not a single monolithic construct, and specific cognitive abilities show differential relations with specific academic outcomes. Narrow abilities often account for variance in reading, writing, and mathematics beyond general intelligence, and predictable cognitive–academic patterns (e.g., phonological processing with decoding, working memory with written expression, quantitative reasoning with mathematics) have been repeatedly documented. Importantly, multiple studies demonstrate that these domain-specific abilities contribute incremental variance beyond *g*, meaning that academic weaknesses cannot be fully explained by general intelligence alone.

The DD/C method leverages this evidence by requiring that identified cognitive weaknesses (1) are domain-specific, (2) occur in the context of cognitive strengths, and (3) align with the student's academic weaknesses in ways that match established research. Table 3.5 presents research supporting the core principles of DD/C.

**Table 3.5 Core Principles of DD/C Are Supported by Research**

| Research Findings Supporting DD/C Principles | Description | Key References |
|---|---|---|
| Intelligence is complex, comprised of many distinct abilities | There are multiple dimensions to intelligence, with ample research supporting the various content and structural validities of differing cognitive abilities and processes measured in typical SLD evaluations | Caemmerer et al. (2020), Carroll (1993), Decker et al. (2020), Flanagan and McGrew (1998), Geary (2026), Horn and Blankson (1997), Kovacs and Conway 2016, Laforte et al. (2025), McGrew (2023), McGrew et al. (2023), Reynolds et al. (2013), Schneider and McGrew (2018) |
| Cognitive abilities have distinct relations with many life outcomes | Specific cognitive abilities and processes have distinct relations to and differentially predict academic achievement | Barnes et al. (2022), Berkowitz et al. (2022), Caemmerer et al. (2018, 2023), Gerst et al. (2021), Hajovsky et al. (2025, see Appendix C), Peng et al. (2022), Spencer et al. (2022) |
| Specific cognitive abilities explain variance in outcomes above and beyond general intelligence (*g*) | The incremental validity of specific cognitive abilities over general ability ranges from modest to substantial, depending on domain and age, particulary when predicting achievement | Breit and Preckel (2020), Fletcher and Wagner (2022), Fuchs et al. (2021), Hajovsky et al. (2025, see Appendix C), McGrew et al. (1997), Nye et al. (2022), Schneider and Newman (2015), Taub et al. (2008) |
| General *and* specific cognitive abilities are important | The strength of the relationships between specific cognitive abilities and academic achievements is dependent on the overall level of general ability and patterns of cognitive and academic strengths and weaknesses | Breit and Preckel (2020), Child et al. (2018), Floyd et al. (2003), Hajovsky et al. (2020, 2023, 2025), Villeneuve et al. (2019) |
| Cognitive abilities provide information related to the response to the intervention | There are predictably different cognitive ability profiles for individuals who do and do not respond as expected to high-quality intervention | Al Otaiba and Fuchs (2002, 2006), Catts et al. (2024), Cho et al. (2015), Cirino et al. (2023), Decker et al. (2020), Fuchs et al. (2021), Peng and Fuchs (2016), Seethaler et al. (2020), Swanson et al. (2022), Torgesen and Davis (1996) |
| Predictable Cognitive-Academic Patterns | An individual's pattern of cognitive difficulties can be predicted from their pattern of academic difficulties | Carmichael et al. (2014), Compton et al. (2012), Feifer et al. (2014), Fenwick et al. (2016), Fuchs et al. (2021), Geary et al. (2012), Huang et al. (2010), Lervåg and Aukrust (2020), Nation (2019), Wagner et al. (2020) |

*Note:* Some individual studies report findings that diverge from those summarized here. However, because the evidence base includes a broad range of study designs, samples, and analytic approaches, we judge the overall pattern of results to be sufficiently robust to support the principles listed in this table.

In conclusion, although Flanagan and colleagues' operational definition of SLD, including criteria for determining the presence of the DD/C pattern, provides a comprehensive, theory- and research-driven framework for data collection and interpretation, the accuracy of any diagnostic system ultimately depends on the reasoning processes used by the practitioner when applying it (Andrews & Saklofske, 2024). Because even a rigorous operational definition can be undermined by intuitive shortcuts and cognitive biases, the following section outlines a debiasing framework designed to help practitioners approach each evaluation step deliberately, systematically, and accurately.

### Debiasing Strategies that Reduce Errors in Classification and Diagnostic Decision-Making

Across medicine and psychology, systematic, step-by-step diagnostic approaches, such as checklists, structured interviews, and evidence-based frameworks, consistently improve reliability and reduce diagnostic errors by mitigating bias and ensuring thoroughness (Croskerry, 2003; Ely et al., 2011). Diagnostic decision-making is vulnerable to cognitive shortcuts, intuitive impressions, and common biases that can distort interpretation at any level of the evaluation.

A debiasing framework that aligns with the operational definition, illustrated in Rapid Reference 3.10, supports more deliberate, analytical reasoning. The five evidence-based steps in this rapid reference are designed to reduce cognitive errors in reasoning and strengthen the accuracy of diagnostic conclusions. A summary of each step follows this rapid reference.

## Rapid Reference 3.10

**Five Steps to Reduce Errors in Making Diagnostic Decisions**

**1. Initial Impression (System 1 Thinking)**

↓

**2. Bias Check**

↓

**3. Structured Review**

↓

**4. Reflection**

↓

**5. Final Decision (System 2 Analytic Reasoning)**

*Note:* Red = Bias risk; Yellow = Caution; Green = Analytic/evidence-based.

### Step 1. Initial Impression (System 1 Thinking)

The first step is to recognize that initial impressions are not always accurate. Most practitioners form first impressions based on a skim of test results. An initial impression is rapid, intuitive reasoning based on pattern recognition (e.g., this pattern of scores resembles an SLD in reading). While efficient, it is prone to cognitive errors. A cognitive error is a mistake in thinking that occurs when practitioners rely on shortcuts (e.g., using a single subtest to represent a cognitive ability), biases (e.g., all children from low-resource environments have learning disabilities), or faulty logic (e.g., concluding that because all PSW criteria were met, SLD is the best classification) without following up with an analytic review. Deliberate, systematic analysis of all data sources is necessary (e.g., Da Silva, 2023; Evans & Stanovich, 2013; Kahneman, 2011).

### Step 2. Bias Check

The second step requires recognizing common cognitive errors and biases, such as *anchoring* (fixating on initial impressions and failing to adjust when new evidence emerges), *availability bias* (relying on recent or memorable cases), *premature closure* (ending the diagnostic process too early, assuming the initial plausible answer is correct), and *confirmation bias* (looking for evidence to support an initial hypothesis, while ignoring contradictory data). Recognizing these biases is necessary to prevent diagnostic mistakes (e.g., Doherty & Carroll, 2020; Croskerry, 2003; Cunningham et al., 2021).

### Step 3. Structured Review

The structured review is central to debiasing because it deliberately slows the diagnostic process and requires a systematic check for bias. Its purposes are to counteract intuitive shortcuts (heuristics or rules of thumb) through deliberate, analytic reasoning, ensure breadth and thoroughness in considering diagnostic possibilities, and reduce the risk of premature closure. Research shows that debiasing strategies reduce cognitive errors in diagnostic decision-making (e.g., Ely et al., 2011; Graber et al., 2012). Some of these strategies include using diagnostic checklists, considering alternative diagnoses, and applying *cognitive forcing* strategies (e.g., asking, "What else could this be?" to force consideration of alternative explanations or diagnoses). Also, consider applying evidence-based protocols, such as structured interviews, to reduce reliance on intuition alone (First et al., 2015; Straus et al., 2011). Finally, compare findings across multiple data sources and look for inconsistencies that could lead to bias-driven misinterpretation. These tools promote thoroughness and help counteract bias by ensuring a systematic evaluation of possibilities.

### Step 4. Reflection

This step requires that you pause and reassess your working diagnosis, which is why it is sometimes called the *two-steps-back* method. Its purpose is to help you critically reassess your reasoning process, following the Structured Review. In this step, to avoid premature closure and ensure critical reflection, you can ask yourself questions such as, *Have I missed something? What assumptions am I making? Am I anchoring too firmly?* A more concrete example is, after completing a PSW analysis, you can deliberately step back and ask, *Do these results truly support SLD, or am I overrelying on standardized test scores?* This question forces a reexamination or a more thorough examination of other data sources.

### Step 5. Final Decision (System 2 Analytic Reasoning)

This final step is a commitment point that requires you to use analytic reasoning to integrate all data sources into a defensible decision. Deliberate, analytical reasoning is referred to as System 2 reasoning. The final decision is based on evidence, clinical data, and structured judgment rather than intuition alone (e.g., Da Silva, 2023).

Steps 3–5 may appear to overlap substantially, but they are distinct. Table 3.6 highlights the distinctions between Structured Review, Reflection, and Final Decision in diagnostic decision-making. This table helps practitioners differentiate between procedural safeguards (Structured Review), metacognitive reflection (Reflection Step), and analytic synthesis (Final Decision), thereby supporting more accurate, bias-aware clinical reasoning.

Together, the operational definition and the debiasing framework form a unified system: the operational definition specifies the content and structure of SLD identification, while the debiasing steps provide cognitive safeguards that ensure each level is interpreted accurately and free of undue influence from intuitive but error-prone reasoning. The integration of these two components reflects a contemporary understanding of diagnostic practice. That is, valid classification depends not only on high-quality data and theory, but also on deliberate,

**Table 3.6 Reducing Errors in Making Diagnostic Decisions: A Comparison of Steps 3–5**

| Step | Core Nature | Goal | Tools/Methods | Mindset |
|---|---|---|---|---|
| Step 3: Structured Review | Procedural, systematic | Ensure breadth and thoroughness; counteract bias with external aids | Diagnostic checklists, guidelines, algorithms, and cognitive forcing strategies | "Slow down and apply structured tools to broaden the lens." |
| Step 4: Reflection Step | Metacognitive, self-monitoring | Critically reassess reasoning after structured review; identify assumptions and biases | Self-questioning prompts ("What else could this be?", "Am I anchoring?"), two-steps-back pause | "Step outside my own thinking and challenge my reasoning process." |
| Step 5: Final Decision | Deliberate, evidence-based | Commit to a diagnostic decision using analytic reasoning grounded in data | Integration of findings, weighing evidence, and structured judgment | "Now synthesize everything systematically and make a reasoned, evidence-based conclusion." |

bias-aware reasoning processes that guide practitioners from initial impressions to defensible decisions. What follows is a description of how these two systems intersect.

## Integrating the Operational Definition of SLD and the Debiasing Framework

Each level of the operational definition is strengthened by specific debiasing steps, and each debiasing step gains clarity and purpose when applied to the structured logic of Levels I–V. This integrated approach, summarized in Table 3.7 and described below, supports practitioners in making empirically grounded, ecologically valid, and bias-aware decisions.

**Initial Impressions** naturally occur as practitioners begin Level I and Level II work. As they review early achievement data, referral concerns, and contextual information, an intuitive hypothesis often forms (e.g., "This looks like a reading disability"). Recognizing this initial impression as *tentative* is essential because Levels I and II require broad data gathering (i.e., standardized achievement results, work samples, observations, and evaluation of exclusionary factors). The Initial Impression step reminds practitioners that early patterns are not conclusions and that premature closure at this stage can distort the entire evaluation.

**A Bias Check** aligns closely with Level II, where practitioners must determine whether factors other than cognitive impairment explain academic difficulties. Anchoring, availability bias, and confirmation bias are particularly likely here—for example, assuming that low achievement must reflect environmental disadvantage, or conversely, assuming that a familiar pattern of scores must indicate SLD. The Bias Check step prompts practitioners to question these assumptions, ensuring that exclusionary factors are evaluated objectively and that neither over- nor under-attribution occurs. This protects the integrity of the determination that academic weaknesses are not primarily due to external factors.

**A Structured Review** is the debiasing step most deeply embedded in Levels III and IV. Level III requires careful analysis of cognitive abilities and processes, and Level IV requires systematic PSW analysis using the DD/C pattern. Both levels demand deliberate, analytic reasoning—precisely the purpose of the Structured Review step. Here, practitioners slow down, examine all cognitive and academic data, consider alternative explanations, and verify that cognitive weaknesses are empirically related to academic weaknesses. Structured Review ensures that the DD/C pattern is not accepted simply because it "looks right," but because it meets the four essential conditions: below-average cognitive-academic consistency, at least average reasoning ability, domain-specific cognitive weakness, and unexpected underachievement. This step counteracts the intuitive pull to rely on familiar score patterns or heuristics and instead promotes a disciplined, evidence-based analysis.

**Reflection** functions as a metacognitive checkpoint between Levels IV and V. After completing PSW analysis, and before determining educational impact, practitioners step back and ask whether their reasoning has been thorough, balanced, and free from bias. Questions such as "Am I overrelying on standardized scores?" or "Have I fully considered contradictory data?" help ensure that the PSW pattern is not accepted uncritically. Reflection also supports the transition to Level V by prompting practitioners to consider whether the identified pattern truly manifests in real-world functioning, rather than assuming that statistical findings automatically translate into educational need.

**Table 3.7 Alignment of the Operational Definition of SLD (Levels I–V) with the Five Debiasing Steps**

| Operational Definition Level | Purpose in SLD Identification | Corresponding Debiasing Step | How the Debiasing Step Strengthens the Level |
|---|---|---|---|
| Level I: Academic Achievement Weaknesses | Document academic deficits using standardized tests and multiple data sources. | Step 1: Initial Impression | Encourages practitioners to treat early hypotheses as tentative and avoid premature closure when reviewing initial achievement data. |
| Level II: Exclusionary Factors | Determine whether external factors (e.g., cultural, linguistic, emotional, medical) are primary causes of academic difficulties. | Step 2: Bias Check | Counters anchoring, availability bias, and confirmation bias when evaluating alternative explanations for low achievement. |
| Level III: Cognitive Abilities and Processes | Identify cognitive weaknesses empirically related to academic weaknesses. | Step 3: Structured Review | Promotes systematic, analytic evaluation of cognitive data and alternative explanations; prevents reliance on heuristics or familiar score patterns. |
| Level IV: PSW Analysis (DD/C Pattern) | Determine whether the student demonstrates a coherent pattern of strengths and weaknesses consistent with SLD. | Step 3: Structured Review and Step 4: Reflection | Structured Review ensures the DD/C pattern meets all four essential conditions; Reflection prompts metacognitive evaluation of whether the pattern is truly meaningful and not overinterpreted. |
| Level V: Educational Performance Impact | Evaluate whether the identified pattern results in real-world functional impairment requiring specialized instruction. | Step 5: Final Decision | Supports analytic synthesis of all data sources into a defensible diagnostic conclusion grounded in evidence rather than intuition. |

**The Final Decision** aligns with Level V, where practitioners synthesize all data—achievement, cognition, exclusionary factors, PSW findings, and functional impact—into a defensible diagnostic conclusion. This step requires System 2 analytic reasoning to integrate multiple data sources into a coherent explanation of the student's learning profile. The Final Decision step ensures that the determination of SLD is not based on isolated findings or intuitive impressions but on a comprehensive, bias-aware evaluation consistent with the operational definition.

Taken together, the operational definition provides the *structure* of SLD identification, while the debiasing framework provides the *discipline* needed to apply that structure accurately. Each level of the operational definition is strengthened by a corresponding debiasing step, and each debiasing step gains clarity and purpose when anchored to the logic of Levels I–V. This integrated model ensures that practitioners do not simply follow a procedural sequence but engage in reflective, evidence-based reasoning that guards against cognitive errors. The result is a unified, contemporary approach to SLD identification—one that is theoretically grounded, empirically supported, and cognitively safeguarded to promote accurate, transparent, and defensible diagnostic decisions.

## CONCLUSION

This chapter establishes a coherent, research-aligned foundation for understanding and identifying SLD and positions the DD/C method as the central analytic framework for doing so. The historical review demonstrates that SLD has always been conceptualized as a domain-specific, cognitively mediated disorder characterized by unexpected underachievement. The definitional and methods review shows that, among the three federally permissible identification methods, only PSW—and most explicitly DD/C—directly evaluate the cognitive–academic relationships that define the construct.

Furthermore, this chapter corrects longstanding mischaracterizations of DD/C by distinguishing the actual method from the fictional versions evaluated in several critiques. When DD/C is understood accurately, its conceptual alignment with the SLD construct, its psychometric safeguards, and its diagnostic value become clear. The chapter also detailed how X-BASS operationalizes each DD/C component, ensuring that the method is applied consistently, transparently, and with full psychometric integrity.

The operational definition of SLD presented here integrates DD/C with a structured debiasing framework, acknowledging that accurate identification requires both high-quality data and disciplined reasoning. Together, these components form a theoretically coherent, empirically grounded, and practically defensible method for SLD identification. This foundation prepares the reader for subsequent chapters, which apply the framework from this chapter to diagnostic XBA in reading, writing, and math, demonstrating how DD/C logic and debiasing steps function in real evaluations.

### TEST YOURSELF

**1. The Dual Discrepancy/Consistency (DD/C) method is designed to identify patterns of cognitive strengths and weaknesses that explain academic difficulties. True or False?**

**2. Which of the following is not one of the five essential levels in the operational definition of SLD?**

(a) Academic skills analysis
(b) Evaluation of exclusionary factors
(c) Cognitive ability and processing analysis
(d) Socioeconomic status analysis

**3. According to the operational definition, SLD is characterized primarily by:**

(a) A discrepancy between IQ and achievement
(b) A pattern of cognitive and academic strengths and weaknesses
(c) Low academic performance alone
(d) Behavioral difficulties in the classroom

**4. Level I of the operational definition focuses primarily on:**

(a) Identifying cognitive processing weaknesses
(b) Documenting academic achievement deficits
(c) Evaluating environmental factors
(d) Determining special education eligibility

**5. The federal definition of SLD identifies how many academic areas that may be considered during evaluation?**

(a) Four
(b) Six
(c) Eight
(d) Ten

**6. In the DD/C method, the pattern of strengths and weaknesses analysis occurs at which level of the operational definition?**

(a) Level II

(b) Level III

(c) Level IV

(d) Level V

**7. When evaluating evidence for a pattern of strengths and weaknesses (PSW), practitioners should determine, using X-BASS, whether the identified cognitive weaknesses are empirically related to the student's academic difficulties.**

True or False?

**8. Which of the following cognitive biases involves fixating on an initial impression and failing to adjust when new evidence emerges?**

(a) Confirmation bias

(b) Anchoring bias

(c) Availability bias

(d) Premature closure

**9. The Structured Review step in the debiasing framework is designed to:**

(a) Replace standardized testing with interviews

(b) Slow the diagnostic process and systematically examine all evidence

(c) Confirm the practitioner's initial hypothesis

(d) Eliminate the need for clinical judgment

**10. The final step in the debiasing framework requires practitioners to:**

(a) Review only cognitive test scores

(b) Integrate all data sources using analytic reasoning to reach a defensible decision

(c) Rely on their first clinical impression

(d) Focus solely on the PSW analysis

*Answers:* 1. True; 2. d; 3. b; 4. b; 5. c; 6. c; 7. True; 8. b; 9. b; 10. b

## REFERENCES


Akobeng, A. K. (2007). Understanding diagnostic tests 1: Sensitivity, specificity and predictive values. *Acta Paediatrica*, *96*(3), 338–341.

Al Otaiba, S., & Fuchs, D. (2002). Characteristics of children who are unresponsive to early literacy intervention: A review of the literature. *Remedial and Special Education*, *23*(5), 300–316.

Al Otaiba, S., & Fuchs, D. (2006). Who are the young children for whom best practices in reading are ineffective? An experimental and longitudinal study. *Journal of Learning Disabilities*, *39*(5), 414–431.

Alfonso, V. C., & Flanagan, D. P. (2018). *Essentials of specific learning disability identification, Second Edition*. John Wiley & Sons.

American Psychiatric Association (2013). *Diagnostic and statistical manual of mental disorders* (5th ed). American Psychiatric Association https://doi.org/10.1176/appi.books.9780890425596.

American Psychiatric Association (2022). *Diagnostic and statistical manual of mental disorders* (5th ed) https://doi.org/10.1176/appi.books.9780890425787.

Andrews, J. J., & Saklofske, D. (Eds.) (2024). *Clinical reasoning and decision-making process: Child and adolescent assessment and intervention*. Elsevier.

Barnes, M. A., Clemens, N. H., & Hale, J. B. (2022). Cognitive predictors of academic achievement: A contemporary review. *Journal of Psychoeducational Assessment*, *40*(3), 267–286.

Beaujean, A. A., Benson, N. F., McGill, R. J., & Dombrowski, S. C. (2018). A misuse of IQ scores: Using the dual discrepancy/consistency model for identifying specific learning disabilities. *Journal of Intelligence*, *6*(3), 36.

Begg, I. M., Anas, A., & Farinacci, S. (1992). Dissociation of processes in belief: Source recollection, statement familiarity, and the illusion of truth. *Journal of Experimental Psychology: General*, *121*(4), 446–458.

Benson, N. F., Maki, K. E., Floyd, R. G., Eckert, T. L., Kranzler, J. H., & Fefer, S. A. (2020). A national survey of school psychologists' practices in identifying specific learning disabilities. *School Psychology*, *35*(2), 146–157.

Berkowitz, T., Schaeffer, M. W., & Hasson, R. (2022). Cognitive processes underlying academic performance: A multidimensional analysis. *Learning and Individual Differences*, *95*, 102–159.

Breit, M., & Preckel, F. (2020). Incremental validity of specific cognitive abilities beyond general intelligence for the explanation of students' school achievement. *Gifted and Talented International, 35*(2), 73–85.

Caemmerer, J. M., Keith, T. Z., & Reynolds, M. R. (2018). Beyond *g*: Broad and narrow cognitive abilities and their prediction of academic achievement. *Journal of School Psychology, 68*, 28–44.

Caemmerer, J. M., Keith, T. Z., & Reynolds, M. R. (2020). Cognitive abilities and academic achievement: A meta-analytic update. *School Psychology Review, 49*(2), 203–217.

Caemmerer, J. M., Reynolds, M. R., & Keith, T. Z. (2023). The structure of cognitive abilities and their relations to achievement: A contemporary synthesis. *Intelligence, 96*, 101708.

Carmichael, C. L., MacDonald, S. W. S., & Dixon, R. A. (2014). Cognitive predictors of academic skills: A longitudinal analysis. *Developmental Psychology, 50*(6), 1492–1503.

Carroll, J. B. (1993). *Human cognitive abilities: A survey of factor-analytic studies*. Cambridge University Press.

Child, A. E., Cirino, P. T., Fletcher, J. M., Willcutt, E. G., & Fuchs, L. S. (2018). A cognitive dimensional approach to understanding shared and unique contributions to reading, math, and attention skills. *Journal of Learning Disabilities, 52*(1), 15–30. https://doi.org/10.1177/0022219418775115.

Cho, E., Roberts, G. J., Capin, P., Roberts, G., Miciak, J., & Vaughn, S. (2015). Cognitive attributes, attention, and self–efficacy of adequate and inadequate responders in a fourth grade reading intervention. *Learning Disabilities Research & Practice, 30*(4), 159–170.

Cirino, P. T., Fuchs, L. S., Powell, S. R., & Fletcher, J. M. (2023). Cognitive predictors of math intervention response: A multi-site longitudinal analysis. *Journal of Educational Psychology, 115*(4), 650–667. https://doi.org/10.1037/edu0000789.

Compton, D. L., Fuchs, L. S., Fuchs, D., Lambert, W., & Hamlett, C. (2012). The cognitive and academic profiles of reading and mathematics learning disabilities. *Journal of Learning Disabilities, 45*(1), 79–95.

Croskerry, P. (2003). The importance of cognitive errors in diagnosis and strategies to minimize them. *Academic Medicine, 78*(8), 775–780. https://doi.org/10.1097/00001888-200308000-00003.

Cunningham, N., Cook, H., Leach, D., Klein, J., & Harrison, J. (2021). Demystifying cognitive bias in the diagnostic process for frontline clinicians and educators: New words for old ideas. *Diagnosis, 8*(3), 322–332. De Gruyter Brill.

Da Silva, S. (2023). System 1 vs. system 2 thinking. *The Psychiatrist, 5*(4), 1057–1076. https://doi.org/10.3390/psych5040071.

Decker, S. L. (2020). *Don't use a bifactor model unless you believe the true structure is bifactor. Journal of Psychoeducational Assessment, 38*(7), 1–11.

Decker, S. L. (2026, February 23). *Learning disabilities and cognitive assessment: Why current research flaws endanger dyslexic students.* Presentation at the Learning Disabilities of America CE Event.

Decker, S. L., Bridges, R. M., Luedke, J. C., & Eason, M. J. (2020). Dimensional evaluation of cognitive measures: Methodological confounds and theoretical concerns. *Journal of Psychoeducational Assessment, 39*(1), 3–27. https://doi.org/10.1177/0734282920940879.

Decker, S. L., & Luedke, J. C. (2021). Evidence-based use of cognitive testing for academic interventions: A critical appraisal of meta-analytic methodologies. *Frontiers in Education, 6*, 637676.

Dehn, M. J., & Szasz, C. (2016). *Psychological processing analyzer 5.6*. Schoolhouse Educational Services.

Doherty, T. S., & Carroll, A. E. (2020). Believing in overcoming cognitive biases. *AMA Journal of Ethics, 22*(9), 773–778.

Dombrowski, S. C., Benson, N. F., & Maki, K. E. (2025). A systematic review of the PSW diagnostic accuracy evidence for SLD identification: Is it time to abandon PSW? *School Psychology Review, 54*(3), 363–381.

Dombrowski, S. C., McGill, R. J., & Canivez, G. L. (2020). Psychometric concerns regarding the use of CHC-based cognitive ability tests in SLD identification. *School Psychology Review, 49*(2), 197–210.

Dombrowski, S. C., McGill, R. J., Canivez, G. L., Watkins, M. W., & Beaujean, A. A. (2021). Factor analysis and variance partitioning in intelligence test research: Clarifying misconceptions. *Journal of Psychoeducational Assessment, 39*(1), 28–38.

Education for All Handicapped Children Act of 1975 (1975). Pub. L. No. 94-142, 89 Stat. 773.

Ely, J. W., Graber, M. L., & Croskerry, P. (2011). Checklists to reduce diagnostic errors. *Academic Medicine, 86*(3), 307–313. https://doi.org/10.1097/ACM.0b013e31820824cd.

Evans, J. S. B. T., & Stanovich, K. E. (2013). *Dual-process theories of higher cognition: Advancing the debate. Perspectives on Psychological Science, 8*(3), 223–241.

Fazio, L. K. (2020). Repetition increases perceived truth even for known falsehoods. *Collabra: Psychology, 6*(1), Article 32.

Fazio, L. K., Brashier, N. M., Payne, B. K., & Marsh, E. J. (2015). Knowledge does not protect against illusory truth. *Journal of Experimental Psychology: General, 144*(5), 993–1002. https://doi.org/10.1037/xge0000098.

Feifer, S. G., De Fina, P. A., & Young, C. (2014). Neuropsychological profiles of learning disabilities: Implications for assessment and intervention. *Applied Neuropsychology: Child, 3*(1), 1–12.

Fenwick, L., Endicott, J., & Humphrey, N. (2016). Cognitive correlates of academic difficulties: A systematic review. *Educational Psychology Review, 28*(1), 1–23.

First, M. B., Williams, J. B. W., Benjamin, L. S., & Spitzer, R. L. (2015). *Structured Clinical Interview for DSM-5 Personality Disorders (SCID-5-PD)*. American Psychiatric Association.

Flanagan, D. P., Alfonso, V. C., Mascolo, J. T., & Hale, J. B. (2011). The Wechsler intelligence scale for children–fourth edition in neuropsychological practice. In A. S. Davis (Ed.), *Handbook of pediatric neuropsychology* (pp. 397–414). Springer.

Flanagan, D. P., & McDonough, E. M. (Eds.) (2018). *Contemporary intellectual assessment: Theories, tests, and issues* (4th ed). Guilford Press.

Fletcher, J. M., Stuebing, K. K., Morris, R. D., & Lyon, G. R. (2014). Classification and definition of learning disabilities: A hybrid model. In H. L. Swanson, K. R. Harris, & S. Graham (Eds.), *Handbook of learning disabilities* (2nd ed, pp. 33–50). The Guilford Press.

Flanagan, D. P., & McGrew, K. S. (1998). Interpreting intelligence tests from contemporary *Gf-Gc* theory: Joint confirmatory factor analysis of the WJ-R and KAIT in a non-white sample. *Journal of School Psychology, 36*(2), 151–182.

Flanagan, D. P., & Ortiz, S. O. (2001). *Essentials of cross-battery assessment.* Wiley.
Flanagan, D. P., Ortiz, S. O., & Alfonso, V. C. (2007). *Essentials of cross-battery assessment* (2nd ed). Wiley.
Flanagan, D. P., Ortiz, S. O., & Alfonso, V. C. (2013). *Essentials of cross-battery assessment* (3rd ed). Wiley.
Flanagan, D. P., Ortiz, S. O., & Alfonso, V. C. (2017). *Cross-battery assessment software system 2.0 (X-BASS 2.0).* Wiley.
Flanagan, D. P., Ortiz, S. O., Alfonso, V. C., & Mascolo, J. T. (2002). *The achievement test desk reference (ADTR): Comprehensive assessment and learning disabilities.* Allyn & Bacon.
Flanagan, D. P., Ortiz, S. O., Alfonso, V. C., & Mascolo, J. T. (2006). *The achievement test desk reference (ADTR): A guide to learning disability identification.* Allyn & Bacon.
Flanagan, D. P., & Schneider, W. J. (2016). Cross-battery assessment? XBA PSW? A case of mistaken identity: A commentary on Kranzler and colleagues' "classification agreement analysis of cross-battery assessment in the identification of specific learning disorders in children and youth". *International Journal of School & Educational Psychology, 4*(3), 137–145. https://doi.org/10.1080/21683603.2016.1192852.
Fletcher-Janzen, E., & Reynolds, C. R. (Eds.). (2008). *Neuropsychological perspectives on learning disabilities in the era of RTI: Recommendations for diagnosis and intervention.* John Wiley & Sons.
Fletcher, J. M., & Wagner, R. K. (2022). Cognitive factors in learning disabilities: A review of evidence for identification and intervention. *Annual Review of Psychology, 73*, 271–298. https://doi.org/10.1146/annurev-psych-021221-011003.
Fletcher, J. M., Francis, D. J., Morris, R. D., & Lyon, G. R. (2005). Evidence-based assessment of learning disabilities in children and adolescents. *Journal of Clinical Child and Adolescent Psychology, 34*(3), 506–522.
Floyd, R. G., Evans, J. J., & McGrew, K. S. (2003). Relations between measures of Cattell–Horn–Carroll (CHC) cognitive abilities and mathematics achievement across the school-age years. *Psychology in the Schools, 40*(2), 155–171.
Francis, D. J., Fletcher, J. M., Stuebing, K. K., Lyon, G. R., Shaywitz, B. A., & Shaywitz, S. E. (2005). Psychometric approaches to the identification of LD: IQ and achievement scores are not sufficient. *Journal of Learning Disabilities, 38*, 98–108.
Fuchs, L. S., Fuchs, D., Compton, D. L., & Davis, G. C. (2021). Cognitive predictors of responsiveness to reading intervention: A meta-analytic update. *Exceptional Children, 87*(4), 389–407. https://doi.org/10.1177/0014402921993423.
Geary, D. C. (2025). *Cognitive foundations of mathematics learning.* Cambridge University Press.
Geary, D. C. (2026). Mathematical cognition: Development, individual differences, and learning difficulties. *Annual Review of Psychology, 77*, (in press).
Geary, D. C., Hoard, M. K., Nugent, L., & Bailey, D. H. (2012). Mathematical cognition and learning disabilities. *Developmental Disabilities Research Reviews, 18*(1), 5–17.
Gerst, E. H., Cirino, P. T., Macdonald, K. T., Miciak, J., Yoshida, H., Woods, S. P., & Gibbs, M. C. (2021). The structure of processing speed in children and its impact on reading. *Journal of Cognition and Development, 22*(1), 84–107.
Graber, M. L., Kissam, S., Payne, V. L., Meyer, A. N. D., Sorensen, A., Lenfestey, N., Tant, E., Henriksen, K., LaBresh, K., & Singh, H. (2012). Cognitive interventions to reduce diagnostic error: A narrative review. *BMJ Quality and Safety, 21*(7), 535–557. https://doi.org/10.1136/bmjqs-2011-000149.
Greenberg, S. A. (2009). How citation distortions create unfounded authority: Analysis of a citation network. *BMJ, 339*, b2680.
Hajovsky, D. B., & Niileksela, C. R. (2025). Cognitive predictors of academic achievement: A CHC-aligned meta-analytic structural equation modeling study. *Journal of Intelligence, 13*(2), Article 22.
Hajovsky, D. B., Niileksela, C. R., Flanagan, D. P., Alfonso, V. C., Schneider, W. J., & Robbins, J. (2025). Toward a consensus model of cognitive–reading achievement relations using meta-structural equation modeling. *Journal of Intelligence, 13*(8), 104 https://doi.org/10.3390/jintelligence13080104.
Hajovsky, D. B., Caemmerer, J. M., & Keith, T. Z. (2020). Cognitive predictors of reading, math, and writing achievement: A meta-analytic structural model. *Journal of School Psychology, 78*, 1–27.
Hajovsky, D. B., Caemmerer, J. M., & Keith, T. Z. (2023). The relations between cognitive abilities and academic achievement: A CHC-based analysis. *Intelligence, 96*, 101708.
Hale, J., Alfonso, V., Berninger, V., Bracken, B., Christo, C., Clark, E., Cohen, M., Davis, A., Decker, S., Denckla, M., Dumont, R., Elliott, C., Feifer, S., Fiorello, C., Flanagan, D., Fletcher-Janzen, E., Geary, D., Gerber, M., Gerner, M., . . . Yalof, J. (2010). Critical issues in response-to-intervention, comprehensive evaluation, and specific learning disabilities identification and intervention: An expert white paper consensus. *Learning Disability Quarterly, 33*(3), 223–236. https://doi.org/10.1177/073194871003300310.
Hale, J. B., & Fiorello, C. A. (2004). *School neuropsychology: A practitioner's handbook.* Guilford Press.
Hasher, L., Goldstein, D., & Toppino, T. (1977). Frequency and the conference of referential validity. *Journal of Verbal Learning and Verbal Behavior, 16*(1), 107–112.
Hinshelwood, J. (1902). Four cases of word-blindness. *The Lancet, 159*(4093), 358–363.
Horn, J. L., & Blankson, N. (1997). Foundations for a better understanding of cognitive abilities. In D. P. Flanagan & P. L. Harrison (Eds.), *Contemporary intellectual assessment* (pp. 41–68). Guilford Press.
Huang, C., O'Connor, R. E., & Keenan, J. M. (2010). Predictors of reading comprehension difficulties. *Scientific Studies of Reading, 14*(6), 498–521.
Individuals with Disabilities Education Improvement Act (2004). 20 U.S.C. § 1400.
Ioannidis, J. P. (2005). Why most published research findings are false. *PLoS Medicine, 2*(8), e124.
Johnson, D. J., & Myklebust, H. R. (1967). *Learning disabilities: Educational principles and practices.* Grune & Stratton.
Kahneman, D. (2011). *Thinking, fast and slow.* Farrar, Straus and Giroux.
Kaufman, A. S. (2008). Specific learning disabilities and the Kaufman tests. In E. Fletcher-Janzen & C. R. Reynolds (Eds.), *Handbook of school neuropsychology* (pp. 485–508). Wiley.
Kaufman, A. S., Johnson, C. K., & Liu, X. (2008). A CHC theory-based analysis of age differences on cognitive abilities and academic skills at ages 22 to 90 years. *Journal of Psychoeducational Assessment, 26*(4), 350–381.
Kavale, K. A. (2005). Identifying specific learning disability: Is responsiveness to intervention the answer? *Journal of Learning Disabilities, 38*(6), 553–562.

Kavale, K. A., & Flanagan, D. P. (2007). Ability—achievement discrepancy, response to intervention, and assessment of cognitive abilities/processes in specific learning disability identification: Toward a contemporary operational definition. In *Handbook of response to intervention* (pp. 130–147). Springer.

Kavale, K. A., & Forness, S. R. (2000). What definitions of learning disability say and don't say: A critical analysis. *Journal of Learning Disabilities, 33*(3), 239–256.

Kavale, K. A., Holdnack, J. A., & Mostert, M. P. (2006). Responsiveness to intervention and the identification of specific learning disability: A critique and alternative proposal. *Learning Disability Quarterly, 29*(2), 113–127.

Kirby, P., & Snowling, M. J. (2022). Dyslexia goes global: Psychology, childhood, and trans-Atlanticism (1925–48). In P. Kirby & M. J. Snowling (Eds.), *Dyslexia: A history* (pp. 36–60). Heracli.

Kovacs, K., & Conway, A. R. (2016). Process overlap theory: A unified account of the general factor of intelligence. *Psychological Inquiry, 27*(3), 151–177.

Kranzler, J. H., Benson, N. F., & Floyd, R. G. (2016). Using confirmatory factor analysis to evaluate the structure of the WISC-V in clinical samples. *Psychological Assessment, 28*(10), 140–153.

Kranzler, J. H., Floyd, R. G., Benson, N., Zaboski, B., & Thibodaux, L. (2016a). Classification agreement analysis of cross-battery assessment in the identification of specific learning disorders in children and youth. *International Journal of School & Educational Psychology, 4*(3), 124–136.

Kranzler, J. H., Floyd, R. G., Benson, N., Zaboski, B., & Thibodaux, L. (2016b). Cross-battery assessment pattern of strengths and weaknesses approach to the identification of specific learning disorders: Evidence-based practice or pseudoscience? *International Journal of School & Educational Psychology, 4*(3), 146–157.

Kranzler, J. H., Gilbert, K., Robert, C. R., Floyd, R. G., & Benson, N. F. (2019). Further examination of a critical assumption underlying the dual-discrepancy/consistency approach to specific learning disability identification. *School Psychology Review, 48*(3), 207–221.

Lachmann, T., Bergström, K., & van Leeuwen, C. (2022). Diagnosis of dyslexia and dyscalculia: Challenges and controversies. In D. C. Geary, D. B. Berch, R. Ochsendorf, & K. M. Koepke (Eds.), *The Cambridge handbook of dyslexia and dyscalculia* (pp. 383–409). Cambridge University Press.

LaForte, E. M., Dailey, D., & McGrew, K. S. (2025). *Technical manual. Woodcock-Johnson V.* Riverside Assessments.

Learning Disabilities Association of Canada (2015). *Official definition of learning disabilities.* https://www.ldac-acta.ca/official-definition-of-learning-disabilities/.

Lervåg, A., & Aukrust, V. G. (2010). Vocabulary knowledge is a critical determinant of the difference in reading comprehension growth between first and second language learners. *Journal of Child Psychology and Psychiatry, 51*(5), 612–620.

Lervåg, A., & Aukrust, V. G. (2020). Vocabulary knowledge is a critical determinant of reading comprehension across grades 1–10. *Developmental Science, 23*(5), e12961 https://doi.org/10.1111/desc.12961.

Lockwood, A. B., & Farmer, R. L. (2019). The cognitive assessment course: Two decades later. *Psychology in the Schools, 57*(2), 265–283.

Lockwood, A. B., Farmer, R. L., Bohan, K. J., Winans, S., & Sealander, K. (2021). Academic achievement test use and assessment practices: A national survey of special education administrators. *Journal of Psychoeducational Assessment, 39*(4), 436–451.

Maki, K. E., & Adams, S. R. (2019). A current landscape of specific learning disability identification: Training, practices, and implications. *Psychology in the Schools, 56*(1), 18–31.

Mather, N., McGrew, K. S., LaForte, E. M., & Wendling, B. J. (2025). *Woodcock-Johnson V virtual test library.* Riverside Assessments, LLC.

McGill, R. J., Dombrowski, S. C., & Canivez, G. L. (2018). Cognitive profile analysis in school psychology: History, issues, and continued concerns. *Journal of School Psychology, 71*, 108–121.

McGrew, K. S. (2023). Carroll's three-stratum (3S) cognitive ability theory at 30 years: Impact, 3S-CHC theory clarification, structural replication, and cognitive–achievement psychometric network analysis extension. *Journal of Intelligence, 11*(2), 32 https://doi.org/10.3390/jintelligence11020032.

McGrew, K. S., Flanagan, D. P., Keith, T. Z., & Vanderwood, M. (1997). Beyond *g:* The impact of *Gf-Gc* specific cognitive abilities research on the future use and interpretation of intelligence tests in the schools. *School Psychology Review, 26*(2), 189–210. https://doi.org/10.1080/02796015.1997.12085858.

McGrew, K. S., Schneider, W. J., Decker, S. L., & Bulut, O. (2023). A psychometric network analysis of CHC intelligence measures: Implications for research, theory, and interpretation of broad CHC scores "Beyond *g*". *Journal of Intelligence, 11*(1), 19 https://doi.org/10.3390/jintelligence11010019.

Miciak, J., & Fletcher, J. M. (2020). The critical role of instructional response for identifying dyslexia and other learning disabilities. *Journal of Learning Disabilities, 53*(5), 343–353.

Miciak, J., Fletcher, J. M., & Stuebing, K. K. (2016). Accuracy and validity of methods for identifying learning disabilities in a RTI delivery framework. In S. Jimerson, M. K. Burns, & A. M. VanDerHeyden (Eds.), *The handbook of response to intervention: The science and practice of assessment and intervention* (2nd ed). Springer.

Miciak, J., Fletcher, J. M., Stuebing, K. K., Vaughn, S., & Tolar, T. D. (2014). Patterns of cognitive strengths and weaknesses: Identification rates, agreement, and validity for learning disabilities identification. *School Psychology Quarterly, 29*(1), 21–37.

Miciak, J., Roberts, G., Taylor, W. P., Solis, M., Ahmed, Y., Vaughn, S., & Fletcher, J. M. (2018). The effects of one versus two years of intensive reading intervention implemented with late elementary struggling readers. *Learning Disabilities Research & Practice, 33*(1), 24–36.

McGill, R. J., Dombrowski, S. C., & Canivez, G. L. (2016). Cognitive profile analysis in school psychology: History, issues, and continued concerns. *Journal of School Psychology, 56*, 7–27.

Miller, D. C., Maricle, D. E., Gettman, J. A., & Bedford, C. L. (Eds.) (2022). *Best practices in school neuropsychology: Guidelines for effective practice, assessment, and evidence-based intervention* (2nd ed). Wiley.

Monroe, M. (1932). *Children who cannot read.* University of Chicago Press.

Naglieri, J. A. (1999). *Essentials of CAS assessment.* John Wiley & Sons.

Nation, K. (2019). Children's reading comprehension difficulties. *Lang & Ling Compass, 13*(1), e12312.

National Association of School Psychologists (2022). *Identification of students with specific learning disabilities (position statement).* https://www.nasponline.org/x59975.xml.

National Center for Learning Disabilities. (n.d.). *What a specific learning disability is not: Examining exclusionary factors.* National Center for Learning Disabilities.

Nunnally, J. C., & Bernstein, I. H. (1994). *Psychometric theory* (3rd ed.). McGraw-Hill.

Nye, C. D., Su, R., Rounds, J., & Drasgow, F. (2022). The incremental validity of specific abilities over general intelligence. *Journal of Applied Psychology, 107*(4), 657–676.

Ortiz, S. O. (2014). CHC theory of intelligence. In *Handbook of intelligence: Evolutionary theory, historical perspective, and current concepts* (pp. 209–227). Springer.

Orton, S. T. (1925). "Word-blindness" in school children. *Archives of Neurology and Psychiatry, 14*(5), 581–615.

Peng, P., & Fuchs, D. (2016). A meta-analysis of working memory deficits in children with learning difficulties: Is there a difference between verbal and visual-spatial domains? *Journal of Learning Disabilities, 49*(1), 3–20. https://doi.org/10.1177/0022219414521667.

Peng, P., Zhang, Z., Wang, W., Lee, K., Wang, T., Wang, C., Luo, J., & Lin, J. (2022). A meta-analytic review of cognition and reading difficulties: Individual differences, moderation, and language mediation mechanisms. *Psychological Bulletin, 148*(3–4), 227–272. https://doi.org/10.1037/bul0000361.

Pennycook, G., Cannon, T. D., & Rand, D. G. (2018). Prior exposure increases perceived accuracy of fake news. *Journal of Experimental Psychology: General, 147*(12), 1865–1880.

Pennycook, G., & Rand, D. G. (2021). The psychology of fake news. *Trends in Cognitive Sciences, 25*(5), 388–402.

Powell, J. L. (2025). Data vs. derision: The ethics of language in scientific publication. The younger dryas impact hypothesis as a case study. *Journal of Academic Ethics, 23*, 807–814.

Reynolds, M. R., Keith, T. Z., Flanagan, D. P., & Alfonso, V. C. (2013). A cross-battery, reference variable, confirmatory factor analytic investigation of the CHC taxonomy. *Journal of School Psychology, 51*(4), 535–555.

Roman, Z. J. (2016). *Optimizing cross-battery assessment procedures for reading-based specific learning disorder diagnosis: A Monte Carlo study.* Illinois State University, MS https://doi.org/10.30707/ETD2016.Roman.Z.

Schneider, W. J., Flanagan, D. P., Niileksela, C. R., & Engler, J. R. (2024). The effect of measurement error on the positive predictive value of PSW methods for SLD identification: How buffer zones dispel the illusion of inaccuracy. *Journal of School Psychology, 103*, 101280.

Schneider, W. J., & McGrew, K. S. (2018). The Cattell–Horn–Carroll theory of cognitive abilities. In D. P. Flanagan & E. M. McDonough (Eds.), *Contemporary intellectual assessment* (pp. 73–163). Guilford Press.

Schneider, W. J., & Newman, D. A. (2015). Intelligence is multidimensional: Evidence from CHC theory. *Intelligence, 50*, 120–135.

Schultz, E. K., & Stephens, T. L. (2015). Core-selective evaluation process: An efficient and comprehensive approach to identify students with SLD using the WJ IV. *DIALOG: Journal of the Texas Educational Diagnosticians Association, 44*(2), 4–13.Seethaler, P. M., Fuchs, L. S., Star, J. R., & Bryant, J. (2020). The role of executive function in math problem-solving intervention response. *Journal of Educational Psychology, 112*(7), 1301–1316. https://doi.org/10.1037/edu0000424.

Shaywitz, S. E., & Shaywitz, B. A. (2003). Dyslexia (specific reading disability). *Pediatrics in Review, 24*(5), 147–153.

Spencer, M., Fuchs, L. S., Geary, D. C., & Fuchs, D. (2022). Connections between mathematics and reading development: Numerical cognition mediates relations between foundational competencies and later academic outcomes. *Journal of Educational Psychology, 114*(2), 273–288.

Straus, S. E., Glasziou, P., Richardson, W. S., & Haynes, R. B. (2011). *Evidence-based medicine: How to practice and teach it* (4th ed). Churchill Livingstone.

Stuebing, K. K., Fletcher, J. M., Branum-Martin, L., Francis, D. J., & VanDerHeyden, A. (2012). Evaluation of the technical adequacy of three methods for identifying specific learning disabilities based on cognitive discrepancies. *School Psychology Review, 41*(1), 3–22.

Swanson, H. L., Lussier, C. M., & Orosco, M. J. (2022). Executive function and reading intervention outcomes in upper elementary students. *Reading and Writing, 35*(5), 1123–1150. https://doi.org/10.1007/s11145-021-10210-3.

Taub, G. E., Keith, T. Z., Floyd, R. G., & Mcgrew, K. S. (2008). Effects of general and broad cognitive abilities on mathematics achievement. *School Psychology Quarterly, 23*(2), 187–198. https://doi.org/10.1037/1045-3830.23.2.187.

Taylor, W. P., Miciak, J., Fletcher, J. M., & Francis, D. J. (2017). Cognitive discrepancy models for specific learning disabilities identification: Simulations of psychometric limitations. *Psychological Assessment, 29*, 446–457.

Torgesen, J. K., & Davis, C. (1996). Individual difference variables that predict response to training in phonological awareness. *Journal of Experimental Child Psychology, 63*(1), 1–21. https://doi.org/10.1006/jecp.1996.0040.

Travis, L. E. (1935). Intellectual factors. In G. M. Whipple (Ed.), *The thirty-fourth yearbook of the National Society for the Study of Education: Educational diagnosis* (pp. 37–47). Public School Publishing Company.

U.S. Department of Education (2006). *Assistance to states for the education of children with disabilities and preschool grants for children with disabilities; final rule (34 C.F.R. pt. 300).* https://www.ecfr.gov/current/title-34/subtitle-B/chapter-III/part-300.

Villeneuve, E. F., Hajovsky, D. B., Mason, B. A., & Lewno, B. M. (2019). Cognitive ability and math computation developmental relations with math problem solving: An integrated, multigroup approach. *School Psychology, 34*(1), 96–108. https://doi.org/10.1037/spq0000267.

Wagner, L., Holenstein, M., Wepf, H., & Ruch, W. (2020). Character strengths are related to students' achievement, flow experiences, and enjoyment in teacher-centered learning, individual, and group work beyond cognitive ability. *Frontiers in Psychology, 11*, 1324.

Zirkel, P. A. (2017). RTI and other approaches to SLD identification under the IDEA: A legal update. *Learning Disability Quarterly, 40*(3), 165–173.

## APPENDIX

**Salient Misconceptions in Beaujean et al. (2018) and Why They Are Egregious**

| Misconception in Beaujean et al. (2018) | Accurate Description of DD/C | Why the Misconception Is Egregious |
|---|---|---|
| 1. DD/C uses strict cut scores (e.g., < 85 = weakness). | DD/C *does not* use rigid cut scores. Weaknesses may fall above 85 when supported by converging data. Examiner judgment, confidence intervals (e.g., Flanagan & Ortiz, 2001), and ecological validity are necessary. | Misrepresents the core logic of DD/C and critiques a method that does not exist in practice. DD/C was explicitly designed to avoid the use of strict cut scores. |
| 2. DD/C requires test scores to have properties they "fundamentally lack." | DD/C relies on cognitive composite scores, achievement composites, and subtest scores (that have ecological validity), rather than exact score equivalence across metrics. | Reflects a misunderstanding of the XBA method, confuses DD/C with XBA score conversions for which their criticisms do not hold (see Appendix E). |
| 3. DD/C misuses IQ scores and relies on a "composite general ability score" that is called the *g*-Value. | The *g*-Value is not a composite score; it is an estimate derived from *g*-weights used to assess whether overall ability is likely to be an adequate estimate of *g*. The FCC—not the *g*-Value—it is the estimate of overall cognitive ability. The FCC should be within normal limits or higher (i.e., >84); however, X-BASS 2.0 conducted PSW analysis regardless of the FCC value. It simply indicated when the DD/C criterion (FCC >84) was not met. X-BASS 3.0 incorporates a more sophisticated calculation of the FCC as an estimate of psychometric *g* (see Appendix M). | Demonstrates a fundamental misunderstanding of DD/C terminology and criteria. Mislabeling the *g*-Value leads to incorrect conclusions about DD/C's use of "IQ." DD/C does not require the use of "IQ" scores, such as FSIQ, VIQ, PIQ, etc. |
| 4. DD/C requires multiple broad ability weaknesses. | DD/C requires at least *one* domain-specific cognitive weakness, as evidenced by a predicted–actual difference that falls <10% (default) or <15% of the population, and is supported by converging data. | Inflates the restrictiveness of DD/C and misrepresents its criteria. |
| 5. DD/C requires specific subtests or batteries (i.e., DD/C = XBA). | DD/C can be implemented with any standardized cognitive and achievement tests. XBA is an assessment method, and DD/C is a score analysis based on specific criteria. | Conflates two distinct systems. Critiques aimed at XBA are incorrectly attributed to DD/C. |
| 6. DD/C lacks evidence of diagnostic utility. | The studies cited by Beaujean et al. modeled a simplified, *incorrect*, and strict threshold-based PSW procedure rather than DD/C. Beaujean and colleagues argued that these studies provide *de facto* evidence that DD/C is unsound because there is evidence "supporting the inability of the method to identify SLD accurately." | Beaujean et al. over rely on Kranzler et al. (2016, 2019), treating simplified, threshold-based simulations as if they represented DD/C in practice while failing to engage Flanagan and Schneider's (2016) rebuttal that identified major conceptual and methodological errors, faulty assumptions, and fatal flaws. Kranzler et al. (2016b), in a rebuttal to Flanagan and Schneider, did not address these errors and flaws of their study. Two coauthors of Beaujean et al.—Dombrowski and Benson—repeated the conclusions of Kranzler and colleagues and the authors of simulation studies (e.g., Steubing et al., 2012) despite corrective analyses (e.g., Schneider et al., 2024). Accepting a small set of studies as definitive without assessing study quality, independence, alternative analyses, and contrary findings amplifies a one-sided narrative rather than providing an impartial, evidence-based synthesis. |
| 7. DD/C is simply cognitive profile analysis rebranded. | DD/C is a theory-driven, CHC-based, psychometrically constrained method requiring composite-level decisions, domain-specificity, and unusual predicted–actual performance differences. | Conflates DD/C with outdated subtest-scatter practices that DD/C was designed to circumvent. |

Four

# HOW TO USE THE PSW AND SLD EVIDENCE TABS IN X-BASS

In Collaboration with Shereen Allison, Ph.D.

California State University, Northridge

The preceding chapter established the DD/C method as the core analytic component of contemporary SLD identification and described how X-BASS automates each component of the method within a unified operational definition and debiasing framework. Before turning to more nuanced diagnostic evaluations, it is useful to see how the SLD module of X-BASS functions in its simplest form. This chapter provides a deliberately straightforward, fictitious case example designed to illustrate the mechanics of the X-BASS workflow once the decision is made to conduct a PSW analysis. This chapter shows how DD/C analyses are conducted and how the structured decision-making process in the SLD Evidence tab leads to an SLD or not-SLD determination. By stripping away real-world complexity, this example allows readers to focus on the logic, sequence, and interpretive checkpoints that form the SLD module and prepare them for more nuanced diagnostic applications in subsequent chapters.

The case that follows, although fictitious, reflects a common pattern in school-based practice: a standard, broadly administered battery used in many districts to evaluate students referred for reading difficulties. Although familiar and widely used, this type of battery does not fully capture the cognitive domains to be assessed in a comprehensive reading referral. Its structure mirrors a persistent gap in practice; namely, the tendency to rely on limited or traditional test combinations that do not reflect the extensive literature on cognitive–achievement relations in reading.

*Referral Form for an Initial Evaluation*

| | |
|---|---|
| **Student Name:** Sian L. | **Chronological Age:** 7 years |
| **Grade:** 2 | **Primary Language**: English |
| **Teacher Name:** Ms. Banes | **Parent's Names:** Rhonda and John L. |

## REASON FOR REFERRAL

Sian was referred for an evaluation due to concerns regarding the development of her basic reading skills. Ms. Banes reported that Sian is having difficulty learning to read grade-level words and demonstrates slow, effortful reading when asked to read aloud. Although Sian participates in phonics instruction and appears motivated to learn, she struggles to read unfamiliar words accurately and to read familiar words automatically. The purpose of this evaluation is to determine the factors contributing to Sian's difficulties with word reading and reading fluency and to assess whether her learning profile is consistent with an SLD in reading.

## BACKGROUND INFORMATION

Sian was born full-term with no reported complications and met early developmental milestones within expected timeframes. Medical history is unremarkable, with no history of significant illness, injury, or hearing or vision concerns. Sian does not take prescription medication. Sian lives with her parents, two younger sisters, and an older brother. Some evidence suggests a family history of reading difficulties, with Sian's father reporting he struggled to learn to read during elementary school, though no formal diagnosis was reported.

## CLASSROOM OBSERVATION

During a small-group reading activity, Sian followed instructions and participated appropriately. When asked to read aloud, she read slowly and relied heavily on sounding out words letter by letter. She often hesitated and needed teacher support to read unfamiliar words. When reading familiar text, Sian showed limited reading fluency and required considerable effort to maintain accuracy.

## INTERVENTION

Sian has participated in a small-group reading intervention focused on letter-sound correspondence and blending. Progress-monitoring data indicate slow, uneven growth, and she remains behind her peers.

## CURRENT ACADEMIC PERFORMANCE

Sian continues to have difficulty with her basic reading skills, especially word reading and reading fluency. In her writing, she struggles to spell simple words. Math skills seem to be developing as expected for her grade level. Sian has expressed frustration during reading activities and has told her teacher that reading is harder for her than for other students in her class.

## SOCIAL/BEHAVIORAL FUNCTIONING

Sian is described as a friendly student who is well-liked by peers. She enjoys school and willingly participates in class activities. She attends an art class on Saturdays with friends in her neighborhood. Aside from her frustration during reading tasks, Sian's teacher reported no behavioral concerns.

## TESTS ADMINISTERED

- Wechsler Intelligence Scale for Children—Fifth Edition (WISC-V)
- Wechsler Individual Achievement Test—Fourth Edition (WIAT-4)
- Comprehensive Test of Phonological Processing—Second Edition (CTOPP-2)

The specific subtests administered from these batteries, along with their corresponding scores and composites, are listed in Tables 4.1 to 4.3. Recall that Chapter 1 demonstrated how to "get started" using X-BASS. That demonstration included a review of the Dashboard and the Data Entry tab. Chapter 2 demonstrated how to use the XBA tab. Specifically, it demonstrated examining scores for cohesion, determining the need for follow-up assessment, and using the Alternative Score Configuration button when testing hypotheses based on initial test findings. Regarding Sian's data, X-BASS determined that all composites were cohesive and that no follow-up assessment was needed in the measured domains. Therefore, from the Data Entry tab, a PSW analysis may be performed by clicking on the "PSW ANALYSIS" button located on the top right of the tab. Clicking this button sends all data entered on the Data Entry tab (WISC-V, WIAT-4, and CTOPP-2) to the PSW Data tab.

## PSW DATA TAB

The purpose of the PSW Data tab is to display all data that will be used in the PSW analysis. A few key points are important when reviewing this information. X-BASS classifies scores into three categories: **strengths** (standard scores of 90 or higher), **weaknesses** (standard scores below 80), and **indeterminant** (standard scores between 80 and 89). Scores of 90 or higher appear in green and are automatically marked as

**Table 4.1 Wechsler Intelligence Scale for Children—Fifth Edition (WISC-V)**

| Subtest/Composite | Scaled Score/Standard Score |
|---|---|
| Similarities | 10 |
| Vocabulary | 9 |
| **Verbal Comprehension Index** | **98** |
| Block Design | 11 |
| Visual Puzzles | 10 |
| **Visual Spatial Index** | **102** |
| Matrix Reasoning | 10 |
| Figure Weight | 10 |
| **Fluid Reasoning Index** | **100** |
| Digit Span | 8 |
| Picture Span | 9 |
| **Working Memory Index** | **92** |
| Coding | 7 |
| Symbol Search | 7 |
| **Processing Speed Index** | **83** |
| **FSIQ** | **96** |

**Table 4.2 Wechsler Individual Achievement Test—Fourth Edition (WIAT-4)**

| Subtest/Composite | Standard Score |
|---|---|
| Word Reading | 80 |
| Reading Comprehension | 75 |
| **Reading Composite** | **77** |
| Spelling | 78 |
| Sentence Composition | 90 |
| **Written Expression Composite** | **84** |
| Numerical Operations | 99 |
| Math Problem Solving | 94 |
| **Mathematics** | **96** |
| *Supplemental Subtests* | |
| Oral Reading Fluency | 74 |
| Pseudoword Decoding | 79 |
| Phonemic Proficiency | 82 |
| Alphabet Writing Fluency | 90 |
| Sentence Writing Fluency | 83 |

**Table 4.3 Comprehensive Test of Phonological Processing—Second Edition (CTOPP-2)**

| Subtest/Composite | Scaled Score/Standard Score |
|---|---|
| Elision | 7 |
| Blending Words | 7 |
| Phoneme Isolation | 8 |
| **Phonological Awareness Composite** | **83** |
| Rapid Letter Naming | 5 |
| Rapid Digit Naming | 7 |
| **Rapid Symbolic Naming Composite** | **76** |

strengths. Scores below 80 appear in red and are automatically marked as weaknesses. Scores between 80 and 89 are highlighted in yellow and require the practitioner to determine whether they function as strengths or weaknesses for the student. Figure 4.1 illustrates the top portion of the PSW Data tab, showing Sian's cognitive scores by CHC domain.

## DON'T FORGET

In the DD/C method, cut points are used as *thresholds of convenience*, meaning when scores hover around a cut point of 85, for example, we do not know if the score represents a true weakness without additional information, regardless of what side of the cut point the score falls (i.e., above or below 85). Errors are most likely to occur when scores are near cut points (e.g., 80–89). Because the true score is unknown, the closer the observed score is to the cut point, the greater the probability that its corresponding true score is on the opposite side of it. Therefore, observed scores slightly above 85 may have corresponding true scores that are slightly below 85, and observed scores slightly below 85 may have true scores that are slightly above 85. This is why X-BASS has always required practitioners to make decisions about strengths and weaknesses, especially near cut points.

X-BASS 3.0, unlike previous versions, provides likelihood estimates that the observed and true scores are below an arbitrary threshold to aid in making decisions about strengths and weaknesses. When the likelihood that the observed and true scores are on the same side of a threshold is low, X-BASS assists the practitioner by providing a list of common manifestations of weakness in the area in question or by suggesting an alternative when scores lack ecological validity. These likelihood estimates are provided in accordance with the recommendations of Schneider et al. (2024), as articulated in Appendix F.

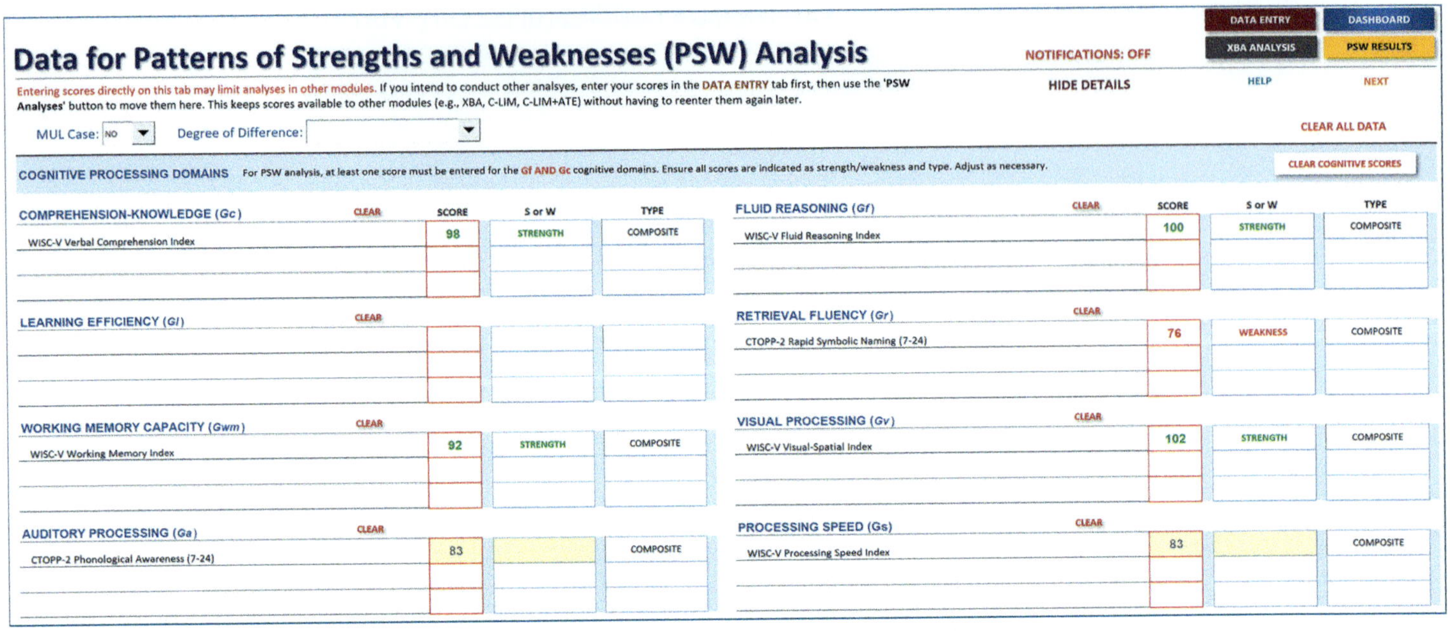


**FIGURE 4.1 Sian's Cognitive Scores on the PSW Data Tab**

The figure shows that Sian's scores for *Gc, Gf, Gwm,* and *Gv* have been marked as strengths, indicating that these domains are likely facilitating her learning. Her *Gr* score has been marked as a weakness, suggesting that this domain is likely inhibiting learning or the acquisition and development of specific academic skills. Sian's *Ga* and *Gs* scores (both 83) are highlighted in yellow, meaning practitioner input is required. The practitioner must determine whether *Ga* and *Gs* facilitate or inhibit learning and academic performance. This judgment is not straightforward; it requires knowledge that practitioners may not always have readily available—specifically, the empirical relationships between these domains and the reason for referral (in Sian's case, weaknesses in decoding and reading fluency).

The relationships between CHC broad and narrow abilities and specific reading skills were presented in Chapter 2 and are summarized in Appendix C. Table 4.4 reviews the most consistent relationships between CHC abilities and reading achievement. This table shows that *Ga* and *Gs* are meaningfully related to reading development in the early elementary years and therefore may be inhibiting Sian's development of basic reading skills. Based on this information, it is appropriate to mark *Ga* and *Gs* as weaknesses.

**Table 4.4 Empirically Established Relationships Between CHC Abilities and Reading**

| CHC Ability | Reading |
|---|---|
| *Gf* | Inductive reasoning (I) and general sequential reasoning (RG), particularly verbal reasoning, show small but meaningful effects on reading comprehension. |
| *Gc* | Language development (LD), lexical knowledge (VL), and listening ability (LS) are important at all ages and become increasingly influential with age. |
| *Gwm* | Auditory short-term storage (Wa) supports basic reading skills (moderate effect), and working memory capacity (Wc) supports reading comprehension. |
| *Gv* | Visualization (Vz) shows small but meaningful relations to early reading (e.g., letter orientation, symbol discrimination) and contributes modestly to comprehension in later years. |
| *Ga* | Phonetic coding (PC) and phonological awareness/processing are essential during the elementary years for developing basic reading skills; phonological memory (UM) also contributes. |
| *Gr* | Naming Facility (NA; rapid automatic naming) and Word Fluency (FW) are important during the elementary years for developing basic reading skills (small–moderate effects). |
| *Gl* | Associative Memory (MA) and Meaningful Memory (MM) contribute at select ages, particularly when learning new vocabulary or story structures. |
| *Gs* | Perceptual speed (P) is important across all school years, especially in elementary grades (e.g., decoding speed). |

*Note:* Information in this table is summarized from Appendix C and Hajovsky et al. (2025).

Marking *Ga* and *Gs* as weaknesses does not mean that they are the *primary* or most plausible reason for Sian's reading difficulties, nor that they are domain-specific weaknesses relative to her cognitive strengths. Rather, it reflects that these domains are empirically linked to the academic skills of concern and may be contributing to her difficulties. It is also helpful to consider how weaknesses in these domains manifest for Sian. For example, given her CTOPP-2 Phonological Awareness score of 83, what observable behaviors might reflect this *Ga* weakness in the classroom? In other words, what real-world manifestations should the practitioner expect to see?

Rapid Reference 4.1 illustrates several common ways a weakness in phonological awareness may manifest in classroom settings. When any of these behaviors has been observed in Sian's day-to-day performance, it provides ecological validity for her *Ga* score and increases the likelihood that *Ga* represents a true cognitive weakness. Likewise, Rapid Reference 4.2 shows how a weakness in *Gs* may manifest during everyday reading tasks. Because many practitioners do not have ready access to behavioral indicators for all cognitive domains that may emerge as weaknesses in an evaluation, X-BASS includes this information to support accurate interpretation and defensible decision-making.

**DON'T FORGET**

When scores are close to cut points, X-BASS provides information about how strengths and weaknesses manifest in the real world to help make informed decisions.

Figure 4.2 shows that the practitioner marked *Ga* and *Gs* as weaknesses on the PSW Data tab using the drop-down menu. The drop-down menu includes three options—**Strength**, **Weakness**, and **Expected**—as shown in the bottom-right portion of the figure. The term *Expected* is used for cases designated as multilingual (MUL). Because MUL learners' performance on standardized cognitive batteries is often attenuated by language demands that do not match their level of English exposure, their scores are marked as either *Expected* or *Weakness*, consistent with the nondiscriminatory assessment guidelines outlined in Chapter 8. The upper-left portion of Figure 4.2 shows that the current case is not an MUL case and therefore the *Gs* score of 83 is marked as a weakness.

Figure 4.3 shows the bottom portion of the PSW Data tab. It includes the eight SLD areas in IDEA, as well as a section on neuropsychological and other processing domains (the latter will be described in subsequent chapters). Two of Sian's achievement

## Rapid Reference 4.1

### How Phonological Awareness Weaknesses Manifest in the Classroom

*Phonological awareness weaknesses often reveal themselves long before formal testing, and they tend to appear in predictable, instructionally meaningful ways during everyday classroom activities. The examples below illustrate the kinds of observable behaviors teachers frequently report when students struggle with core phonological skills that support early reading development.*

- **Phoneme isolation:** Difficulty identifying individual sounds in words
- **Sound blending:** Difficulty blending phonemes to form words
- **Sound segmentation:** Difficulty segmenting words into phonemes accurately
- **Phoneme manipulation:** Difficulty adding, deleting, and substituting sounds
- **Rhyme recognition:** Difficulty identifying and generating rhyming words
- **Syllable awareness:** Difficulty counting and segmenting syllables accurately
- **Decoding:** Slow to learn sound-symbol correspondences

## Rapid Reference 4.2

### How a Processing Speed Weakness Manifests in the Classroom

*Processing speed weaknesses tend to show up most clearly during real reading tasks, where the pace of cognitive work directly affects accuracy, comprehension, and productivity. In classroom settings, these students often appear capable but chronically slow, and their difficulty keeping up becomes especially visible during timed or fluency-dependent activities. The examples below illustrate common ways in which processing-speed weaknesses manifest in everyday reading demands.*

- **Slow decoding:** Takes significantly longer than same grade peers to sound out unfamiliar words
- **Reading fluency:** Word-by-word reading even with familiar text, affecting comprehension
- **Oral reading pace:** Slow reading aloud, often losing listener attention
- **Silent reading:** Slow independent reading that limits the amount of text covered
- **Reading assignments:** Unable to complete grade-level reading tasks within typical time frames

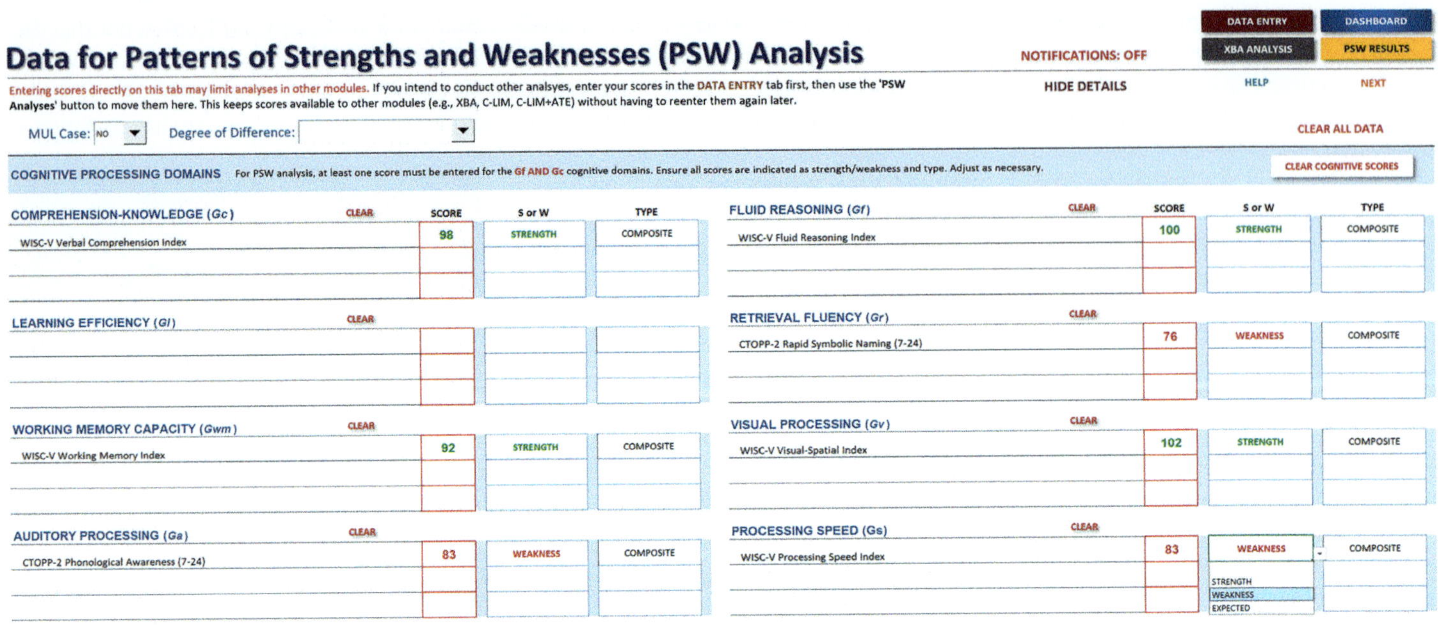


**FIGURE 4.2 Scores in the 80-89 Range Marked as Weaknesses by the User**

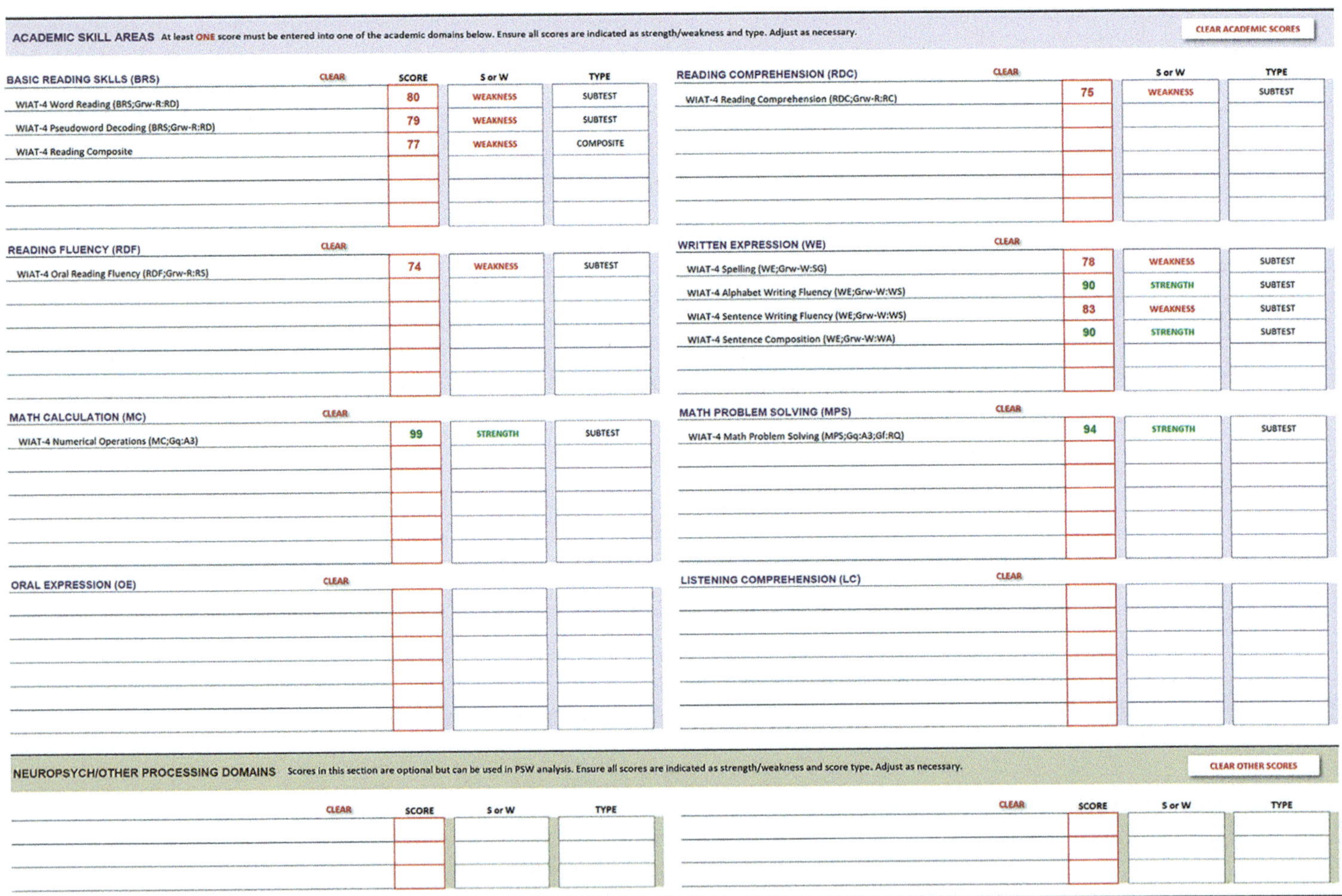


**FIGURE 4.3 Sian's Achievement Scores on the PSW Data Tab**

scores, 80 on WIAT-4 Word Reading and 83 on Sentence Writing Fluency, *initially shaded in yellow—indicating indeterminant range*, were marked as weaknesses by the evaluator.

Figures 4.2 and 4.3 show that each score is associated with a score *type*—either "subtest" or "composite." These distinctions matter because they ensure that X-BASS applies the correct reliability coefficients during analysis. In general, subtests have lower reliability than composites. When the practitioner clicks the "PSW Analysis" button from either the Data Entry tab or the XBA Analysis tab, only *cognitive composites* are transferred to the PSW Data tab, not individual subtest scores. This reflects a core psychometric principle: composites are better estimates of latent constructs than subtests. In contrast, achievement subtests measure *manifest* skills and therefore serve as strong indicators of performance in the specific academic areas they assess.

There are times, however, when a single subtest score is the only available indicator of a cognitive domain. In such cases, it may be used to represent a strength when it reflects at least average ability (i.e., ss = 9 or higher; SS = 95 or higher) and has moderate-to-strong ecological validity. This is because average performance on a cognitive subtest is unlikely to occur without the underlying ability; strong performance is generally a valid indicator of intact ability. The reverse, however, is not true. Low performance on a single subtest cannot be taken as evidence of a cognitive weakness, because subtests are vulnerable to performance factors—attention, motivation, fatigue, anxiety, or misunderstanding directions—that can depress scores without reflecting true ability. For this reason, a subtest score that falls below average, regardless of how low it is, cannot be used to indicate a cognitive weakness.

When a single subtest score is used to represent a cognitive strength, it must be entered manually on the PSW Data tab. Once entered, X-BASS will automatically mark it as a strength if it meets the minimum threshold (a standard score of at least 90, preferably 95). The practitioner must also select "subtest" from the score-type drop-down menu. Note that if the subtest score is associated with a metric other than standard scores, with a mean of 100 and an SD of 15, it must be converted to this metric when entered manually on the PSW Data tab. Although X-BASS will not prevent practitioners from manually entering a single subtest score as a cognitive weakness, it is the practitioner's responsibility to recognize that subtests alone do not provide adequate measurement for identifying weaknesses in latent cognitive domains. Once all scores on the PSW Data tab have been appropriately marked as strengths or weaknesses, the practitioner should click the "PSW Results" button at the top right of the tab to view the PSW analysis results.

## DON'T FORGET

Composites that appear in the "Academic Skills Areas" of the PSW Data tab should be evaluated carefully before accepting or determining a designation of strength or weakness: a composite can mask meaningful variation among its component subtests. For example, a three-test composite of **79** (component scores **78, 82, 90**) would be marked as a weakness automatically on the PSW Data tab, yet the data show a clear weakness (78) and a relative strength (90). When a composite spans very weak to average performance, use the **individual subtest scores** rather than the composite when identifying specific strengths and weaknesses. Note that this applies only to academic skill areas on the PSW Data tab. Variation in cognitive composites was discussed thoroughly in Chapter 2.

## CAUTION

Single subtests should never be used to represent a cognitive weakness. Subtests provide limited and often unstable measurement of latent abilities, and low scores can reflect performance factors—fatigue, attention lapses, anxiety, low motivation, or misunderstanding directions—rather than true processing deficits. In contrast, an average subtest score can *sometimes* support the identification of a cognitive strength because it is unlikely that a student would perform at or above average on a task without the underlying ability. This asymmetry means that *single cognitive subtests* may occasionally support evidence of intact processing, but they can never be used to infer a cognitive weakness.

## PSW RESULTS TAB

Figure 4.4 shows the results of Sian's initial PSW analysis. These results show that overall ability is at least average, represented by a Facilitating Cognitive Composite (FCC) of 97. Sian's cognitive weaknesses are domain-specific, represented by an Inhibiting Cognitive Composite (ICC) of 75, and her academic weakness of 80 in Word Reading is considered unexpected. Finally, there is a moderate relationship between Sian's cognitive and academic weaknesses, which indicates that this consistency is supported by research. Together, these results support a PSW pattern following DD/C criteria.

Note that some of the text in Figure 4.4 is printed in green and some in gold. Green means that the criterion was met; red means the criterion was not met; and gold means more information may strengthen the finding, but the criterion has nevertheless been met. At this point, there are a few options. One option is to click the "SLD Evidence" button in the top-right of the PSW Results tab to provide additional information, when requested, and follow the steps that lead to a final SLD/not SLD decision. Another option is to scroll below the three ovals shown in Figure 4.4 for a summary of the DD/C criteria and additional details on the initial results (e.g., the probability that a score reflects a true weakness). This summary for Sian's initial PSW results is shown in Figure 4.5. If you choose to review the summary, you may then click the yellow "SLD Evidence" button at the bottom-right of the summary, as shown in the figure.

Before advancing to the SLD Evidence tab, it is important to explore the PSW Analysis tab in more detail to understand its functions and features. Each oval includes a drop-down menu. The top oval defaults to the FCC, but if other overall ability scores are available based on the information entered on the Data Entry tab, they will appear in the drop-down. In Sian's case, her WISC-V FSIQ of 96 appears as an alternative. The difference between Sian's FCC and FSIQ is negligible. In many cases, the FCC is higher than other global ability estimates because it is an aggregate of strengths, whereas global scores such as the FSIQ combine strengths and weaknesses. Sian's cognitive weaknesses are in *Ga*, *Gr*, and *Gs*. The FSIQ does not include *Ga* or *Gr*, and it includes only a single subtest of *Gs*. As a result, the FCC and FSIQ are similar for Sian because both composites are based primarily on the same set of intact abilities: *Gc*, *Gf*, *Gwm*, and *Gv*.

The bottom-left "Cognitive Weakness" oval defaults to the ICC. Rapid Reference 4.3 provides key information about the ICC and its role in PSW analysis. Figure 4.6 shows the drop-down menu in the bottom left oval. It lists Sian's cognitive domains (*Gr*, *Ga*, and *Gs*) that were

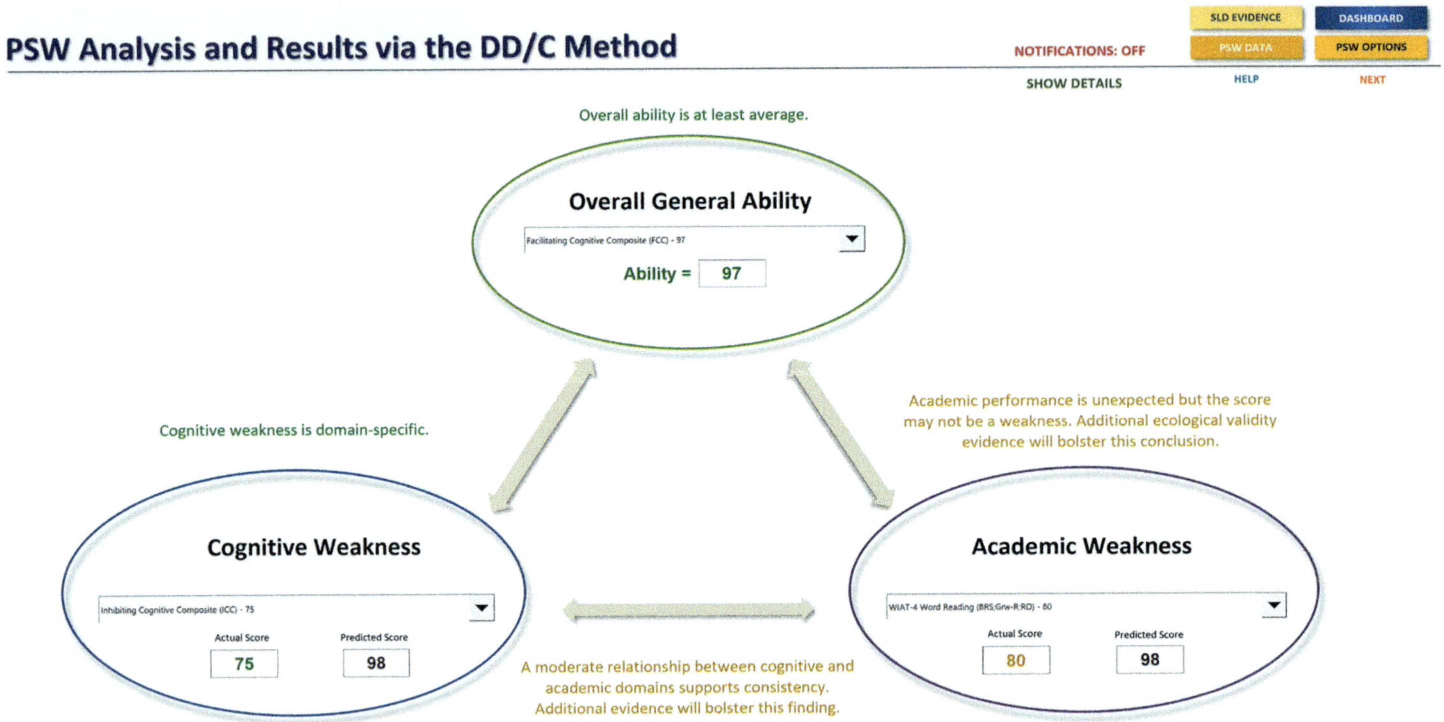


**FIGURE 4.4 Sian's Initial PSW Results**

**FIGURE 4.5 Summary of Initial PSW Results**

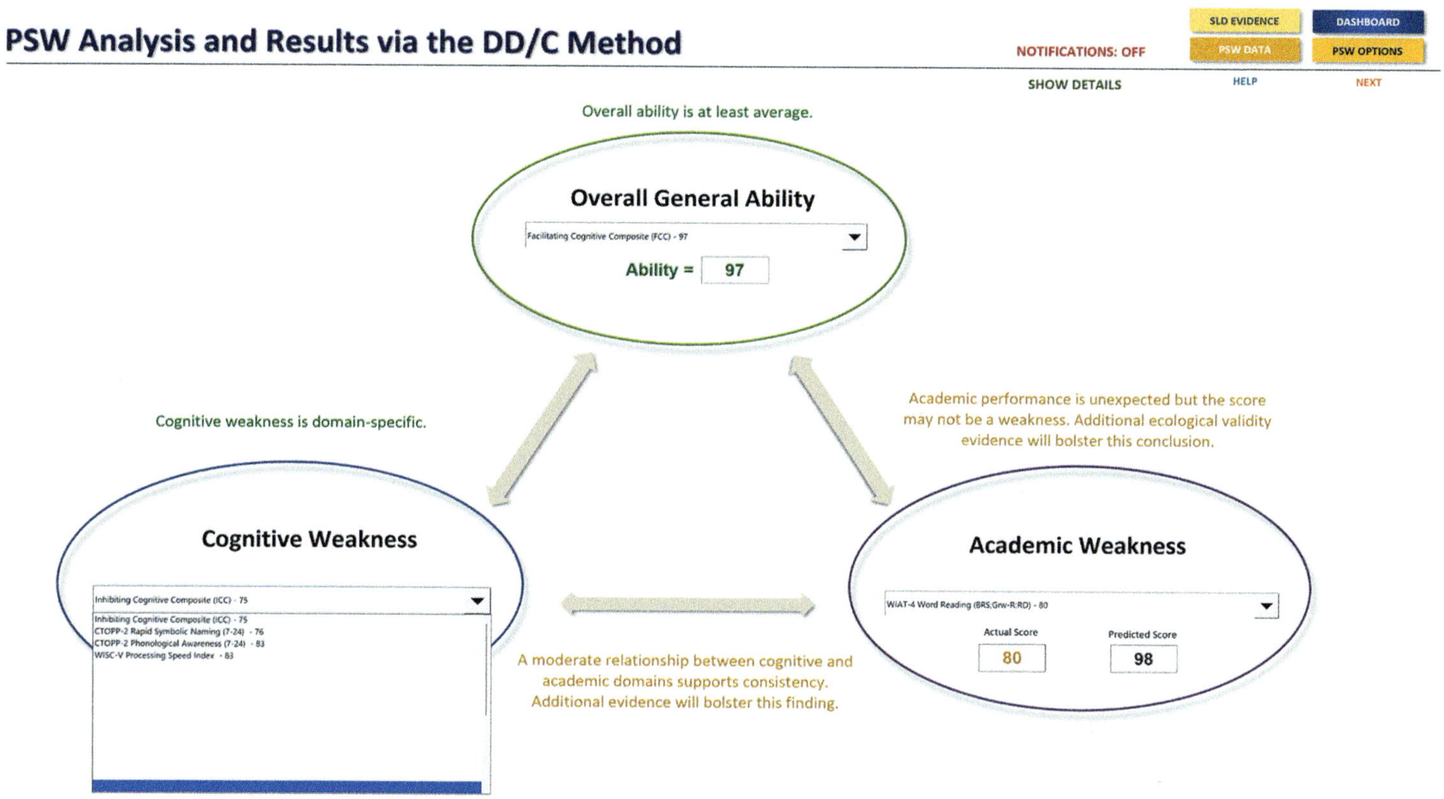


**FIGURE 4.6 Drop-down Menu Showing Areas Marked as Cognitive Weaknesses for Sian**

## Rapid Reference 4.3

### Important Information about the Inhibiting Cognitive Composite (ICC)

- **The ICC is an aggregate of the cognitive areas that were identified as weaknesses.**
  It represents the combined influence of the cognitive processes most likely to inhibit learning and academic skill development.
- **The ICC is restricted to eight CHC domains: *Gf, Gc, Gv, Ga, Gwm, Gl, Gr,* and *Gs*.**
  When at least two of these domains are marked as weaknesses, the ICC is calculated using the scores from those domains.
- **If only one cognitive domain is marked as a weakness, the bottom-left oval defaults to that domain.**
  In this situation, an ICC cannot be formed because aggregation requires at least two domains.
- **Weaknesses outside the eight CHC domains are not included in the ICC.**
  These areas (e.g., executive functions, attention, or other neuropsychological processes) should be examined separately *after* evaluating the ICC in the PSW analysis.
- **If the ICC shows a low relationship with the academic weakness, examine the contributing domains individually.**
  A low ICC–academic relationship may indicate that one of the domains included in the ICC is not theoretically or empirically related to the academic skill in question.
- **The PSW Options tab allows you to refine the ICC by removing unrelated domains.**
  Note that this is a more advanced option available to practitioners. It is helpful to review the information in Appendix C to guide your decisions when recalculating the ICC.
- If one of the domains contributing to the ICC shows a low relationship when examined individually, it can be deselected on the PSW Options tab. [The button for PSW Options is located at the top right of the PSW Results tab.] X-BASS will then recalculate the ICC using only the domains that are relevant to the academic skill. This recalculated composite is labeled the Academic-Specific ICC (AICC) and will automatically appear in the bottom-left oval for use in the PSW analysis.

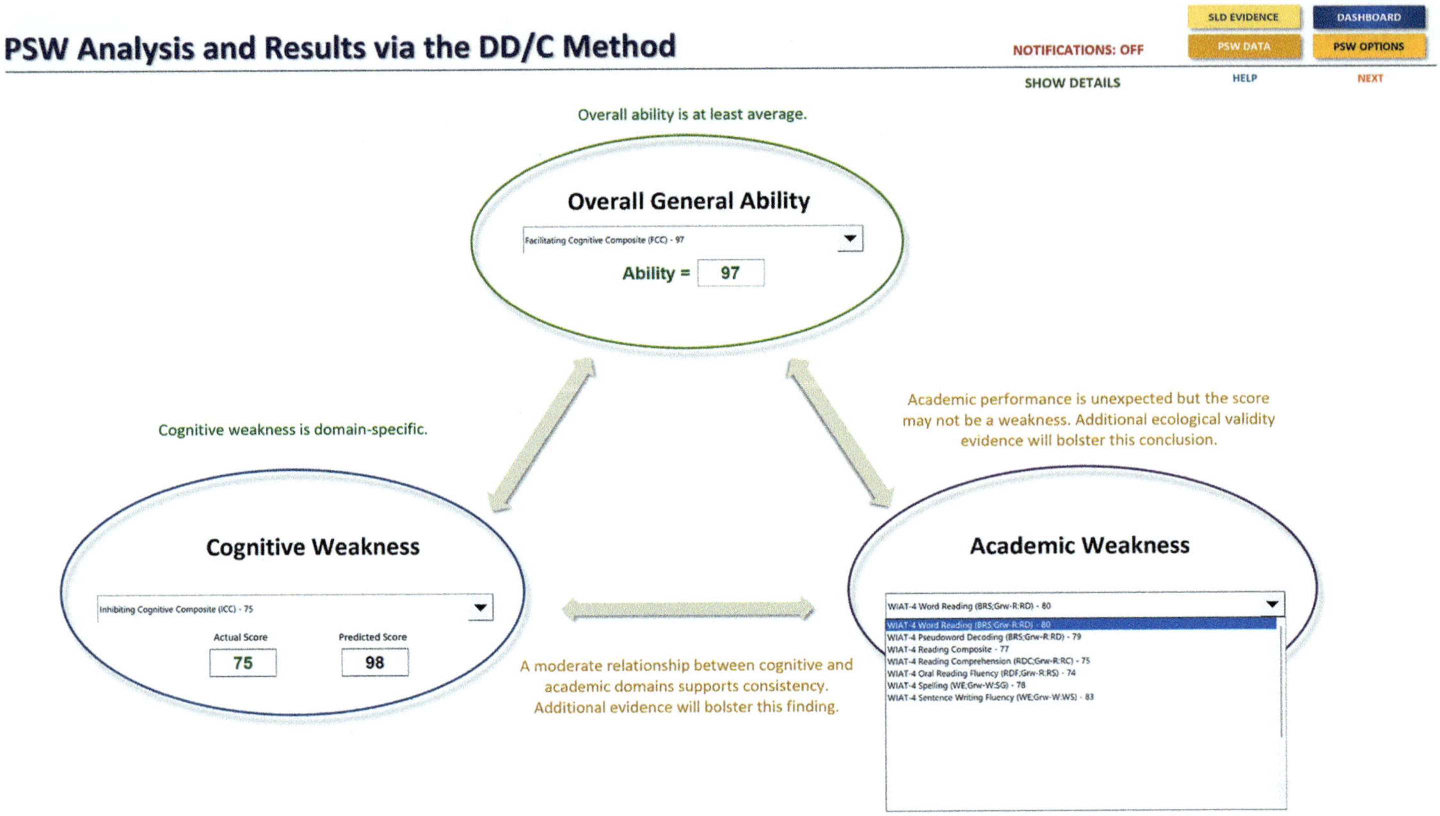


**FIGURE 4.7 Drop-down Menu Showing Areas Marked as Academic Weaknesses for Sian**

marked as weaknesses. Any one of these domains may be selected instead of the ICC for the PSW analysis. X-BASS defaults to the ICC because it is the most parsimonious representation of below-average cognitive aptitude—the aggregate of cognitive processes most likely to interfere with learning and with the acquisition and development of specific academic skills. By starting with the ICC, the program ensures that the initial analysis reflects the broadest and most stable estimate of cognitive functioning before the practitioner considers whether a more specific cognitive weakness provides a better explanatory fit.

The bottom-right "Academic Weakness" oval defaults to the first academic subtest listed in the first academic domain on the PSW Data tab. Figure 4.3 shows that WIAT-4 Word Reading is the first subtest listed under Basic Reading Skills (BRS), and this same subtest appears in the bottom-right oval of Figures 4.4 and 4.6. Figure 4.7 displays the drop-down menu for the Academic Weakness oval, which lists all reading and writing subtests and composites that were marked as weaknesses for Sian. There are seven academic scores marked as weaknesses. How do practitioners make decisions about which scores to use in the PSW analysis?

## Selecting Academic Scores When Multiple Weaknesses Are Present

When several academic scores are marked as weaknesses—as is the case for Sian—practitioners often struggle to determine which scores to select for the PSW analysis and how to justify those choices. A few general guidelines can help ensure that the selection is defensible and aligned with the referral concerns.

The first step is to begin with the most pressing academic concerns. For Sian, the primary concerns are reading decoding and reading fluency. Because decoding is foundational and directly related to her referral question, it is appropriate to start with the decoding measures. For decoding, two WIAT-4 subtests are available: Word Reading and Pseudoword Decoding. Understanding what each subtest measures—and how they differ—is essential for selecting the most appropriate score for the PSW analysis. These subtests are described in Rapid Reference 4.4.

In Sian's case, there is no meaningful difference between her Word Reading and Pseudoword Decoding scores. When two subtests measure closely related constructs and yield comparable results, it is often preferable to use the aggregate of the subtests—in this case, the WIAT-4 Reading Composite. The composite provides a more reliable estimate of decoding skill than either subtest alone, reducing the influence of measurement error. Selecting the Reading Composite is therefore psychometrically defensible and aligned with Sian's referral concerns. It also provides a stable starting point for the PSW analysis before moving on to additional areas of academic weakness, such as reading fluency or written expression. Figure 4.8 shows a comparison of the bottom right oval with the default score for Word Reading and the selected score for the Reading Composite.

## Rapid Reference 4.4

### Differences Between the WIAT-4 Word Reading and Pseudoword Decoding Subtests

- ***Word Reading measures real-word reading.*** It reflects sight-word recognition, phonics application to familiar words, orthographic mapping, and vocabulary support. Performance may be boosted by prior exposure or memorization.
- ***Pseudoword Decoding measures pure phonological decoding.*** It is the ability to map print to sound using grapheme–phoneme correspondences and to blend phonemes into a spoken form. Because the stimuli are nonwords, the task minimizes lexical and semantic support and therefore isolates decoding processes rather than vocabulary or orthographic memory*.
- ***Word Reading reflects consolidated reading skills.*** It shows how well decoding skills have been internalized and stored in long-term orthographic memory.
- ***Pseudoword Decoding is the most sensitive indicator of decoding weakness.*** It removes semantic and memory cues, making it especially useful for identifying dyslexia and other phonological processing deficits.
- ***Discrepancies between the two subtests reveal important diagnostic patterns.*** Higher Word Reading with lower Pseudoword Decoding suggests compensation through memorization; low scores on both indicate broader reading impairment.

**FIGURE 4.8 Comparison of Two Results, One for Word Reading and One for Reading Composite**

Figure 4.8 shows that the score of 80 falls within the indeterminate range and is therefore printed in gold. The score of 77 falls within the weakness range and is printed in green. Although the score of 80 is considered unexpected when the actual–predicted score difference is examined, the score itself should be supported by converging evidence to be interpreted as a true weakness. In contrast, the likelihood that the WIAT-4 Reading Composite score of 77 represents a true weakness is high and does not require additional evidence. Its actual–predicted score difference is also unexpected, but this finding simply reinforces the interpretation. Figure 4.9 shows the final PSW analysis results after selecting the WIAT-4 Reading Composite as the area of academic weakness. These findings meet DD/C criteria, meaning that the pattern aligns with SLD in Basic Reading Skills. However, other information is necessary before making an SLD/not SLD decision (e.g., review of exclusionary factors), which will be addressed on the SLD Evidence tab.

### Selecting the Next Academic Weakness After Decoding

Once the most pressing academic concern has been addressed—in Sian's case, reading decoding—the next step is to determine which additional academic weakness should be included in the PSW analysis. When several academic scores fall in the weak range, this decision can feel overwhelming. A defensible approach is to prioritize weaknesses that are (1) directly related to the referral concerns, (2) empirically linked to the identified cognitive weaknesses, and (3) essential for understanding the student's current instructional needs.

* Orthographic memory is used by many authors informally to refer to the stored representations that result from orthographic mapping. Orthographic mapping describes how readers form durable memory representations of word spellings by linking grapheme–phoneme correspondences to pronunciations and meanings (Ehri, 2014), a process driven by phonological recoding that functions as a self-teaching mechanism (Share, 1995).

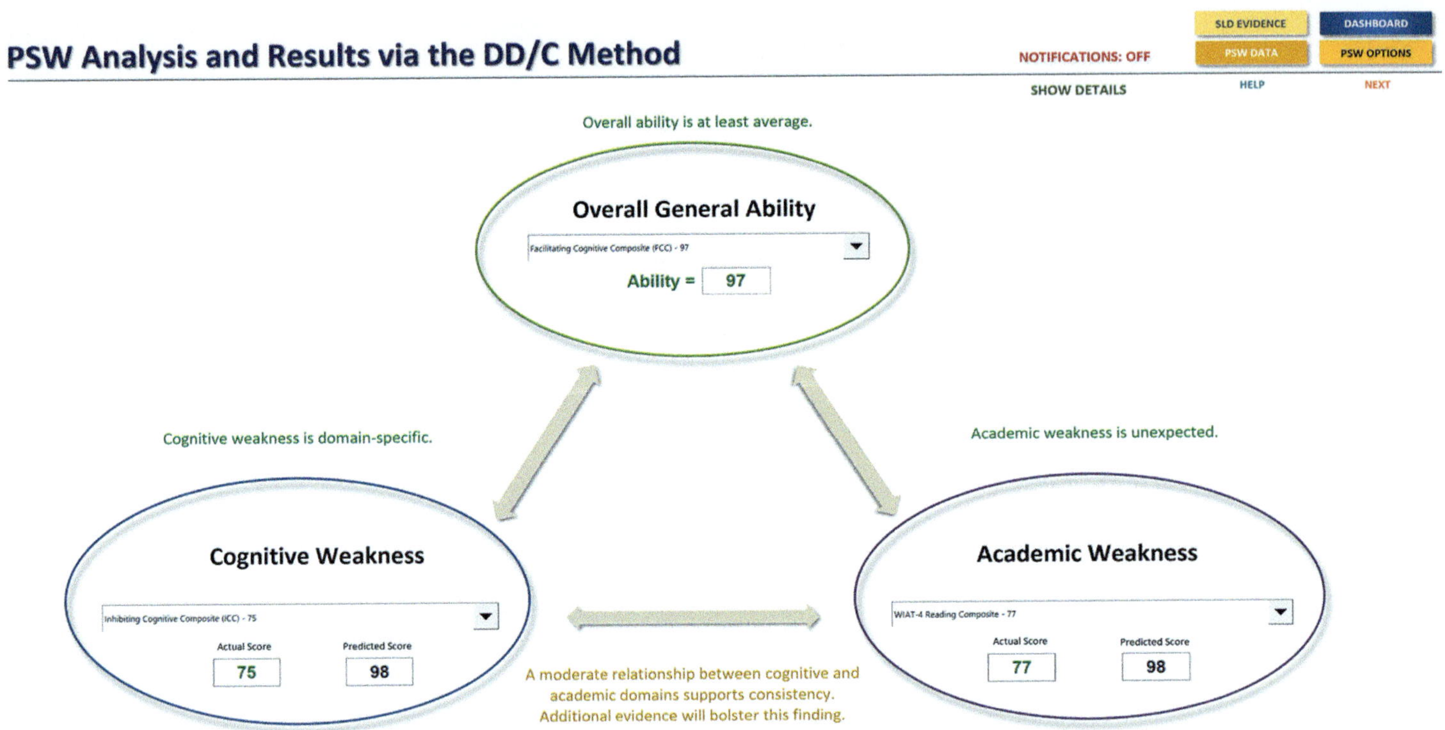


**Note:** The FCC is an aggregate of Gc, Gf, Gwm, and Gv. The ICC is an aggregate of Ga, Gr, and Gs. The Reading Composite is comprised of the Word Reading and Pseudoword Decoding subtests.

**FIGURE 4.9 Final PSW Analysis Results Using Sian's FCC, ICC, and WIAT-4 Reading Composite**

For Sian, the next most relevant area is reading fluency. Fluency is a natural extension of decoding: students must first decode accurately before they can decode efficiently, although reading fluency does not always follow decoding accuracy (this is demonstrated in cases appearing in Chapters 5 and 6). Weaknesses in *Ga* (phonological processing), *Gr* (naming facility/rapid automatic naming), and *Gs* (processing speed) have all been established as related to reading fluency, making fluency an appropriate and theoretically aligned choice for the second academic weakness.

Sian's WIAT-4 Oral Reading Fluency score is marked as a weakness and reflects the automaticity and efficiency with which she applies her decoding skills during connected-text reading. Because fluency is a referral concern and a skill closely tied to her cognitive pattern, it is a defensible and instructionally meaningful choice for the PSW analysis. Like the Reading Composite, Oral Reading Fluency also reflects unexpected underachievement, and there is a moderate relationship between Sian's ICC and Oral Reading Fluency.

After decoding and fluency have been selected, the practitioner can consider whether additional academic weaknesses—such as those in written expression—should be explored. These decisions should be guided by the same principles: relevance to the referral question, theoretical and empirical linkage to cognitive weaknesses, and usefulness for instructional planning.

To this point, the details underlying the PSW analysis have remained hidden. The SHOW DETAILS function allows the practitioner to see precisely which criteria have been met and the basis for each decision in the analysis. This feature is located just below "NOTIFICATIONS: OFF" in Figure 4.9. Once selected, the same location allows the practitioner to toggle back to HIDE DETAILS at any time. Returning to Sian's initial PSW results in Figure 4.4 and activating the SHOW DETAILS function reveals the information displayed in Figure 4.10. Each of these details is explained in the following section.

### Show/Hide Details Function on PSW Results Tab

The details shown in Figure 4.10 may seem overwhelming at first, but once understood, practitioners typically toggle between SHOW DETAILS and HIDE DETAILS to access the specific information they need. Chapter 3 described the DD/C method in depth and included Figure 3.2, which identified the appendices that explain the calculations and analyses X-BASS performs when applying DD/C criteria. That foundational material will not be repeated here. Instead, this section focuses on how to use and interpret the information displayed when the SHOW DETAILS function is activated.

***Probability of making a correct strength/weakness decision.*** The first set of information shown in Figure 4.10 concerns decision accuracy, which is a probability estimate reported as a percentage. These probabilities help the practitioner understand how confident they can be that each classification—overall general ability, cognitive weakness, and academic weakness—reflects the student's true performance rather than measurement error or score fluctuation.

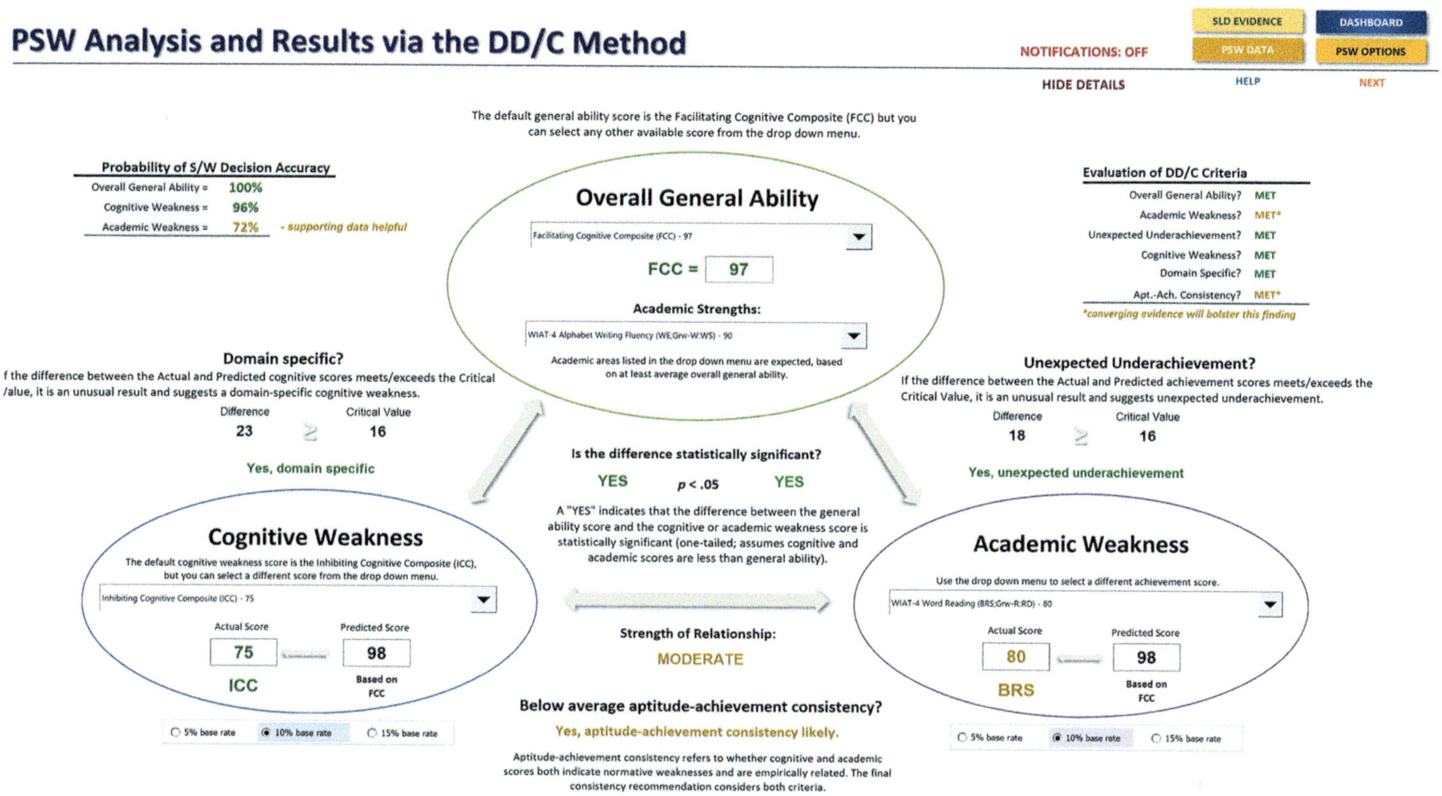


**FIGURE 4.10 PSW Analysis Details Displayed Using the "Show Details" Function**

Three probabilities are shown in the top left side of Figure 4.10:

- **Overall General Ability**
  This value reflects the likelihood that the global ability estimate (typically the FCC) accurately represents at least average ability to think and reason. High probabilities indicate strong confidence that the score is stable and can be interpreted as intended.
- **Cognitive Weakness**
  This probability reflects the likelihood that the identified cognitive weakness (e.g., the ICC) is a *true* weakness rather than a borderline score or a measurement error artifact. Higher values indicate greater confidence that the weakness is real and meaningful. According to the decision accuracy output in Figure 4.10, there is a 96% chance that the true ICC score is below a standard score of 85, indicating a high level of confidence that the weakness is real.
- **Academic Weakness**
  This value reflects the likelihood that the selected academic weakness (e.g., the WIAT-4 Reading Composite) represents a true area of difficulty. Lower probabilities do not invalidate the weakness but signal that additional converging evidence—such as classroom performance, error patterns, or instructional history—may be needed to support the interpretation.

These probabilities do not determine eligibility on their own. Instead, they help the practitioner assess confidence in classification decisions and whether to consider additional data. According to the decision accuracy output in Figure 4.10, there is a 72% chance that the true WIAT-4 Word Reading score is below a standard score of 85, indicating a moderate degree of confidence that the weakness is real. In these cases (i.e., when percentiles are reported in gold), supporting data help to improve confidence in the interpretation of a true weakness.

***Evaluation of DD/C criteria.*** The next block of information in Figure 4.10 summarizes whether each DD/C criterion has been met for the current case. This section, located in the top right of the figure, provides a concise, at-a-glance evaluation of the core components of the DD/C method and is one of the most useful parts of the SHOW DETAILS view. Each criterion is listed separately, along with an indication of whether it is **MET**, **MET***, or **NOT MET**. When MET appears in gold with an asterisk, it indicates that converging evidence will strengthen the interpretation. Together, these indicators provide a structured summary of how the student's data align with the DD/C method. They help the practitioner determine where the evidence is strong, where additional data may be needed, and how defensible the overall pattern is. For a review of domain specificity, unexpected underachievement, and aptitude-achievement consistency, see Rapid Reference 4.5.

## Rapid Reference 4.5

### A Review of the Meaning of Domain Specificity, Unexpected Underachievement, and Aptitude-Achievement Consistency in the DD/C Method

Domain specificity and unexpected underachievement rely on the same underlying logic: each evaluates whether the student's actual score is substantially lower than their predicted score by evaluating the statistical rarity of that difference in the general population of peers with the same predicted score. Both criteria display two key values:

- *Difference*—the numerical gap between the actual score and the predicted score.
- *Critical Value*—the minimum difference required for the observed gap to be considered unusual, based on the default 10% base-rate criterion.

If the Difference between the actual and predicted scores meets or exceeds the Critical Value, the weakness is considered *unusual* (occurring in 10% or fewer same-age peers), and the criterion is marked **MET**. The 10% base rate default criterion can be changed to 5% or 15%. The program defaults to a 10% base rate criterion because it appears to be the percentage most typically associated with statistical rarity in the assessment literature (Urbina, 2014).

***Domain Specificity** asks whether the student's cognitive performance is substantially lower than what would be predicted from their overall cognitive ability. When the actual ICC is substantially lower than the predicted ICC—and the Difference exceeds the Critical Value—the weakness is considered domain-specific rather than part of a more general low-ability pattern. This supports the interpretation that the cognitive weakness is unusual, circumscribed, and theoretically capable of inhibiting learning.*

***Unexpected Underachievement** asks whether the student's academic performance is substantially lower than what would be predicted from their overall cognitive ability. When the actual academic score is substantially lower than the predicted score—and the Difference exceeds the Critical Value—the academic weakness is considered unexpected because it is unusual and cannot be explained by the student's overall general ability.*

The ***below average* Aptitude-Achievement Consistency** criterion is essential in the DD/C method because it links the cognitive processing weakness(es) to the academic weakness(es). When the alignment of the pattern of cognitive and academic weaknesses is supported empirically, the practitioner can more confidently conclude that the cognitive weakness(es) is theoretically capable of producing the observed academic underachievement. Moreover, the practitioner can more confidently assert that the student's academic weakness is not only unexpected but also explained *in part* by the *strength* of the relationship with areas of cognitive weaknesses.

***Base rate information.*** Base rate information helps determine whether a cognitive or academic weakness is uncommon in the general population, which is essential for establishing both domain specificity and unexpected underachievement. While statistical significance indicates that a difference is unlikely to be due to chance, base rates indicate whether differences are unusual or rare in the general population.

Figure 4.10 displays the base rate associated with the student's actual–predicted difference. X-BASS uses a default threshold of 10%, meaning the weakness must occur in 10% or fewer same-age peers to be considered unusual. If the base rate is 10% or lower, the criterion is marked **MET**. If the base rate is above 10%, the program will report either "No, not domain-specific" or "No, not unexpected underachievement." At this point the practitioner may move to the 15% threshold, which is less stringent but still considered unusual (e.g., Kiselica et al., 2024). This option is appropriate when the overall pattern is consistent with the referral concerns and the cognitive–academic alignment is moderate to strong. A base rate of 15% or lower still indicates that the weakness is uncommon and meets the DD/C criterion.

> **DON'T FORGET**
>
> A key advantage of the X-BASS base-rate system is its flexibility that mirrors real-world clinical judgment. When a discrepancy *does not meet* the default 10% threshold, the practitioner may move to the 15% level, which is less stringent but still considered unusual. This flexibility acknowledges that meaningful patterns do not always fall neatly at a single cutoff and that strict adherence to one threshold can obscure clinically important findings. Likewise, when a discrepancy *meets* the 10% threshold, the practitioner may examine the 5% level. A base rate of 5% or below indicates that the finding is rare under a more stringent criterion, strengthening the interpretation that the weakness is highly unusual in the general population.

In addition, X BASS allows the practitioner to examine the 5% base rate level. If the weakness meets the 10% criterion, the practitioner may check the 5% threshold to determine whether the finding is even more unusual. When the base rate falls at or below 5%, it highlights that the weakness is rare at a very stringent level, further strengthening the interpretation that the discrepancy is highly unusual in the general population.

In Sian's case, the base rates for her cognitive and academic discrepancies are in the unusual range, supporting the conclusion that her cognitive weakness is domain-specific (at 5% base rate) and that her academic weakness indicates unexpected underachievement (at 10% base rate). When base-rate information aligns with statistical significance and the overall pattern of strengths and weaknesses, it strongly supports the defensibility of the PSW interpretation.

***Academic strengths.*** A comparison of Figure 4.4 (details hidden) with Figure 4.10 (details shown) reveals that activating SHOW DETAILS adds a second drop-down menu in the top oval of the PSW Results tab (as shown in Figure 4.11). This additional menu lists any academic composites or subtests the practitioner identified as the student's academic strengths on the PSW Data tab. For Sian, these strengths include her WIAT-4 Numerical Operations and Math Problem Solving subtests.

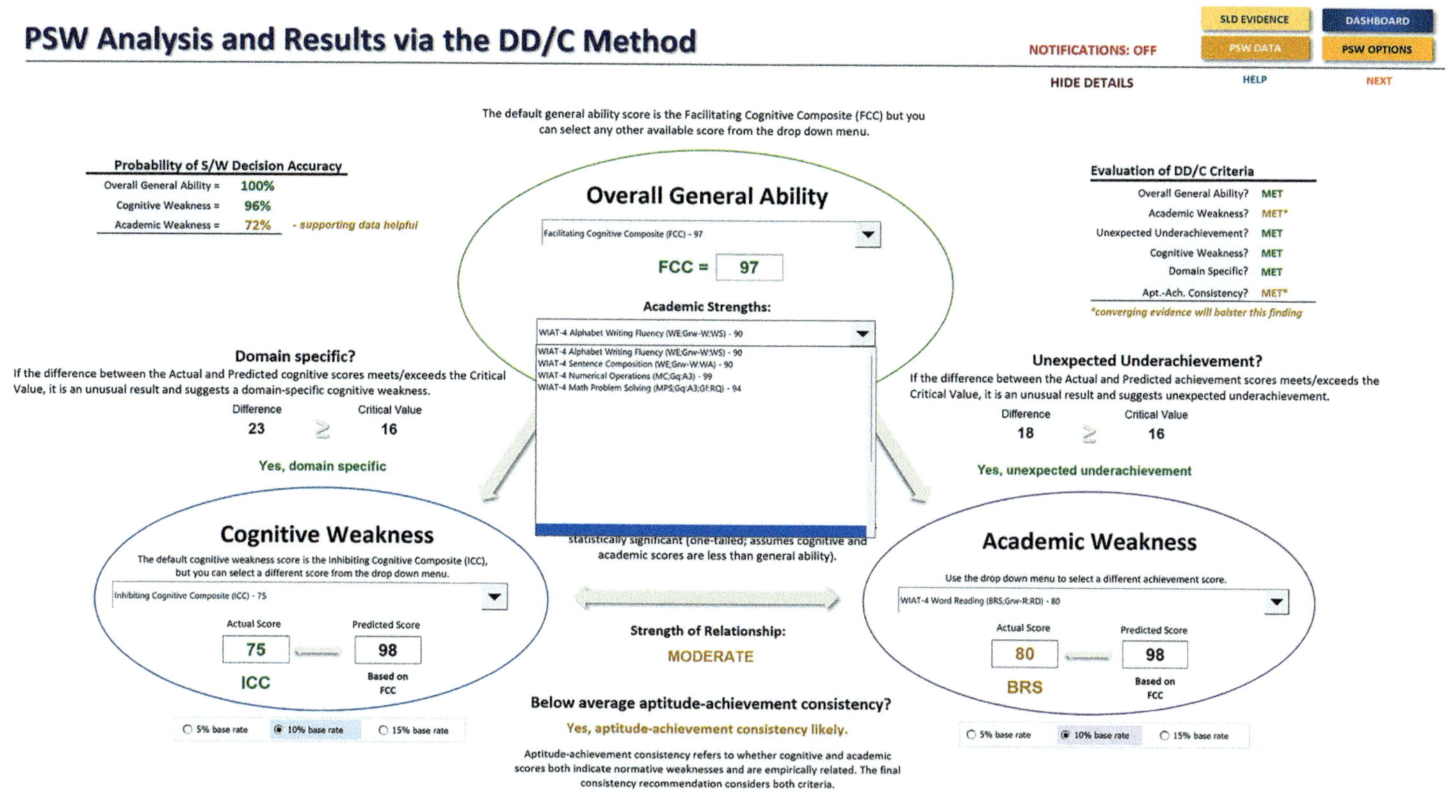


**FIGURE 4.11 PSW Results in "Show Details" Mode Displays Academic Strengths**

When overall general ability is at least average, it is expected that the student will show relative strengths in academic areas that align more closely with their overall ability than with their domain-specific weaknesses. These academic strengths help confirm that the student's learning profile is not uniformly weak and that their difficulties are circumscribed rather than global. When the FCC appears in gold—indicating that the probability of at least average overall ability is equivocal—the presence of clear academic strengths becomes especially important. These strengths bolster confidence in the FCC as a valid estimate of overall ability and support the interpretation that the student's difficulties are domain-specific.

With the PSW Results tab fully explored, including the detailed criteria, probabilities, and base-rate information, the practitioner has a clear statistical and structural picture of the student's pattern of strengths and weaknesses. The next step is to integrate these findings with contextual, qualitative, and exclusionary information on the SLD Evidence tab. This tab becomes especially important when scores identified as weaknesses carry low or equivocal probabilities, because it allows practitioners to document manifestations of the difficulty, consider exclusionary factors, and rate their degree of confidence in the available data. The SLD Evidence tab also provides a summary of all information entered, options for printing a report, and access to graphs of the scores used in the PSW analysis. Together, these features support practitioners in moving from statistical evidence to a defensible, comprehensive determination of whether the student meets criteria for SLD.

## SLD EVIDENCE TAB

To get to the SLD Evidence tab from the PSW Results tab, click on the "SLD Evidence" button on the top right of the screen. There are five sections on the SLD Evidence tab; they are listed in Rapid Reference 4.6. Each section is described briefly below. Note that if the PSW Results tab shows either scores or text in red or gold, the first thing to do on the SLD Evidence tab is "SHOW DETAILS." By doing so, additional necessary functions are available to assist in exploring equivocal PSW results.

### 1. Test Score Evidence and PSW Analysis Summary

This section, illustrated in Figure 4.12, provides a concise summary of the PSW analysis and highlights areas that require additional attention. When the practitioner clicks SHOW DETAILS, the tab expands to display guidance messages that help interpret equivocal, low-probability, or in need of converging evidence scores. For example, if a selected cognitive or academic weakness appears in gold, the system alerts the practitioner that the probability of a correct strength/weakness decision is equivocal and that behavioral manifestations or contextual data may

## Rapid Reference 4.6

### Five Sections of the SLD Evidence Tab in X-BASS

I. Test Score Evidence and PSW Analysis Summary
II. Evaluation of Exclusionary Factors
III. Degree of Confidence in Data for SLD Identification
IV. Summary of Data for SLD Identification
V. Summary Graph of PSW Results

be needed. If a score appears in red, the system indicates that the weakness is unlikely to meet DD/C criteria without strong supporting evidence. This section ensures that the practitioner begins the SLD Evidence process with a clear understanding of which findings are solid and which require further exploration.

Figure 4.12 shows that Sian's BRS score of 80 carries a 72% probability of being a true weakness, which is considered equivocal. When a score falls into this range, X-BASS provides an interpretive prompt recommending that the practitioner click ADD SUPPORTING DATA, located directly below the score. Selecting this option opens the screen shown in Figure 4.13.

The ADD SUPPORTING DATA screen lists ways in which a weakness in basic reading skills may manifest in everyday academic performance. These manifestations are organized by grade level—Elementary School (K–5), Middle School (6–8), and High School (9–12)—so the practitioner can select indicators (manifestations) that are aligned with the curriculum. A complete list of manifestations for all eight SLD areas included in X-BASS is provided in Appendix Q. The practitioner is instructed to check all manifestations that apply based on classroom observations, teacher reports, parent input, work samples, or other relevant sources.

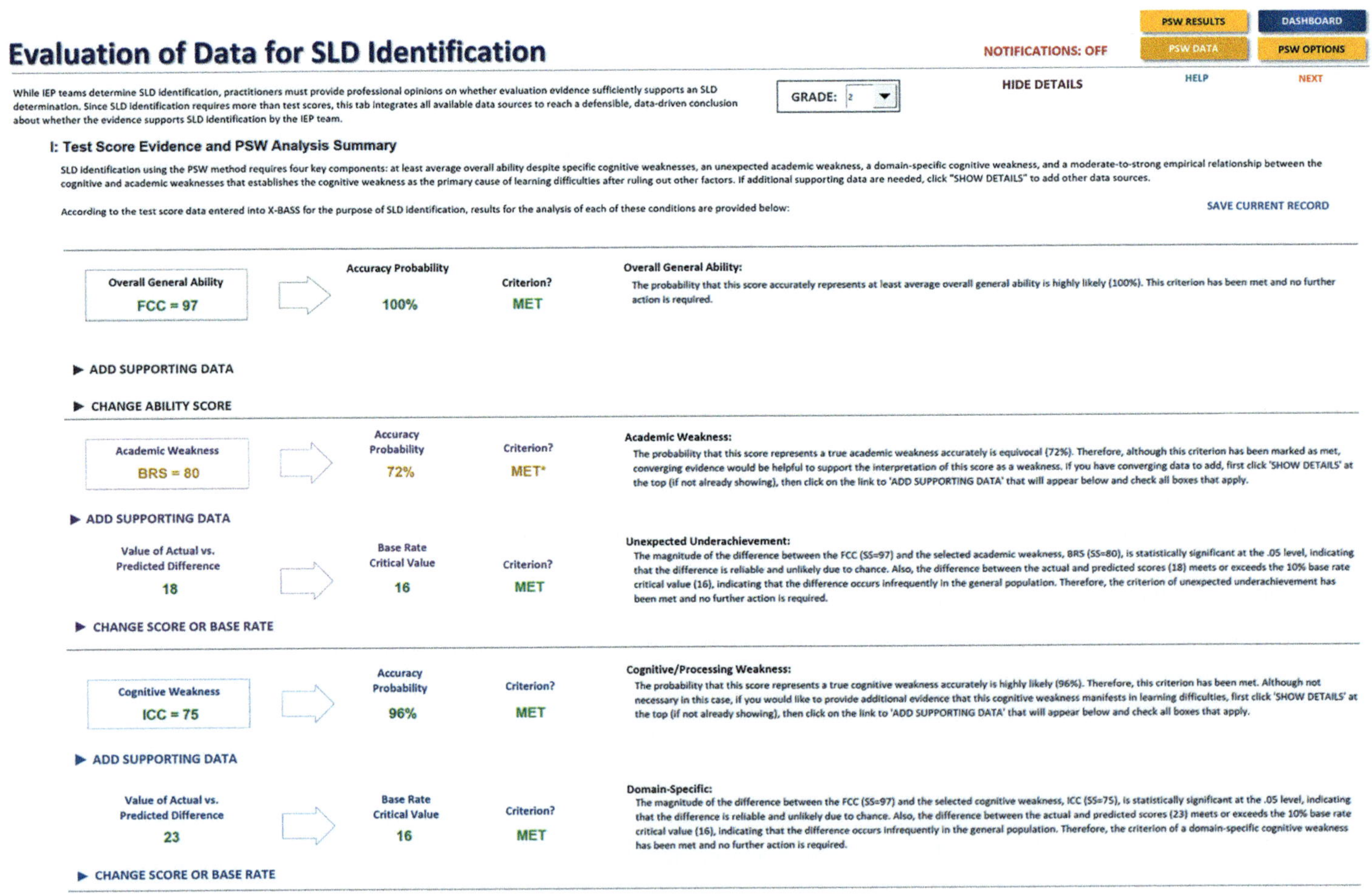


**FIGURE 4.12 Top Portion of the SLD Evidence Tab**

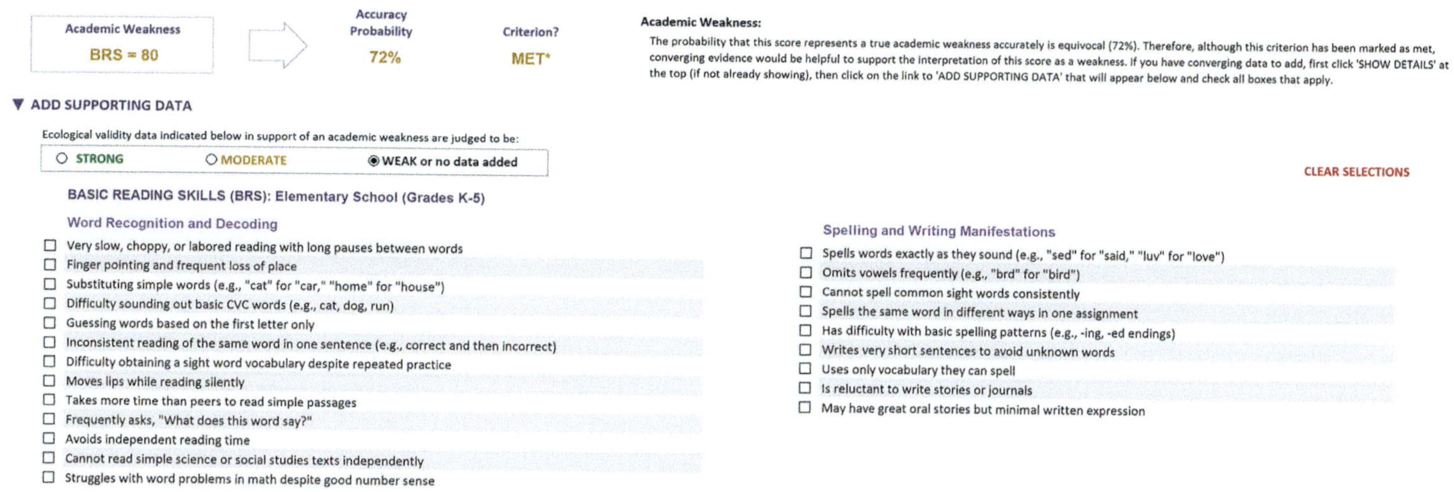


**FIGURE 4.13 Screen Displayed After Clicking "Add Supporting Data"**

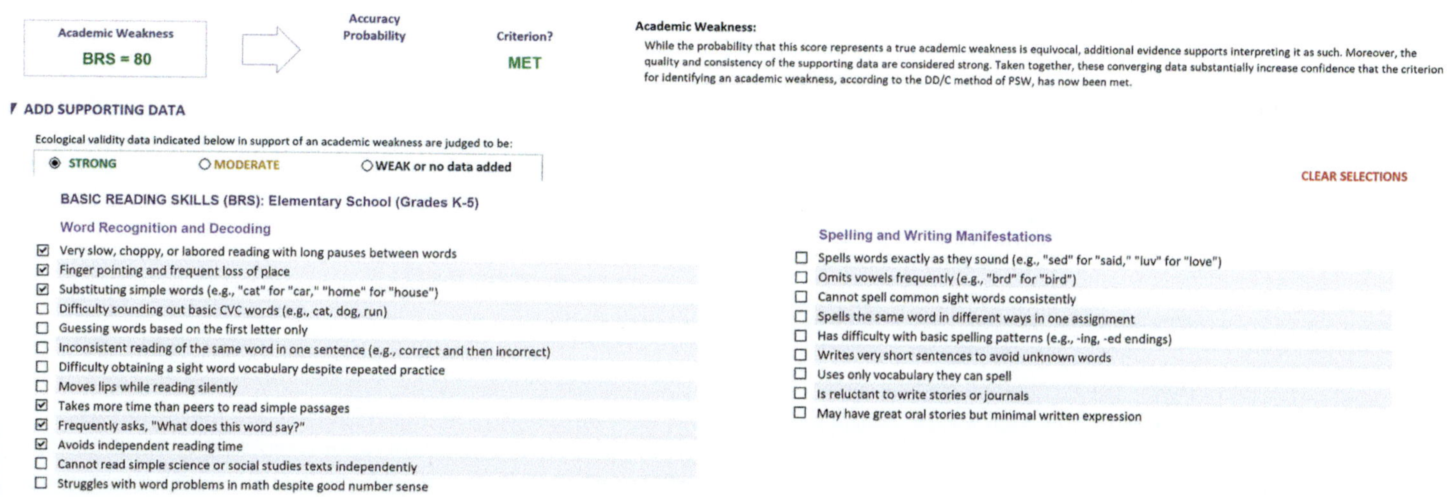


**FIGURE 4.14 Screen After Selecting Manifestations and Judging this Ecological Validity as "Strong"**

After selecting the applicable manifestations, the practitioner must judge whether the checked items provide **strong**, **moderate**, or **weak** support for the ecological validity of the BRS score of 80. In other words, *do the real-world behaviors and difficulties observed for the student converge with what would be expected for a weakness in reading decoding?* For Sian, this judgment reflects whether the manifestations align with her reported difficulties in basic reading skills.

If the practitioner determines that ecological validity is **strong** or **moderate**, X-BASS updates the results and interpretation accordingly. The score appearing in gold changes to green, the probability value is removed, the criterion of MET printed in gold with an asterisk changes to green, and the interpretive statement is revised, as shown in Figure 4.14. Note that the probability disappears because once strong converging evidence is added, the likelihood of a true weakness is clearly elevated—but the exact numerical increase cannot be determined. Thus, the system shifts from a probabilistic estimate to a qualitative confirmation supported by ecological data.

## II. Evaluation of Exclusionary Factors

The second section of the SLD Evidence tab, shown in Figure 4.15, provides a structured place to document the exclusionary factors required by federal and state regulations. These include limited English proficiency, sensory impairments, environmental or economic disadvantage, inadequate instruction, and other conditions that may account for the student's academic difficulties. Each factor is presented as a question. For example, *is the student unable to perceive stimuli including letters and numbers such that this is the primary reason for not developing or displaying academic skills?*

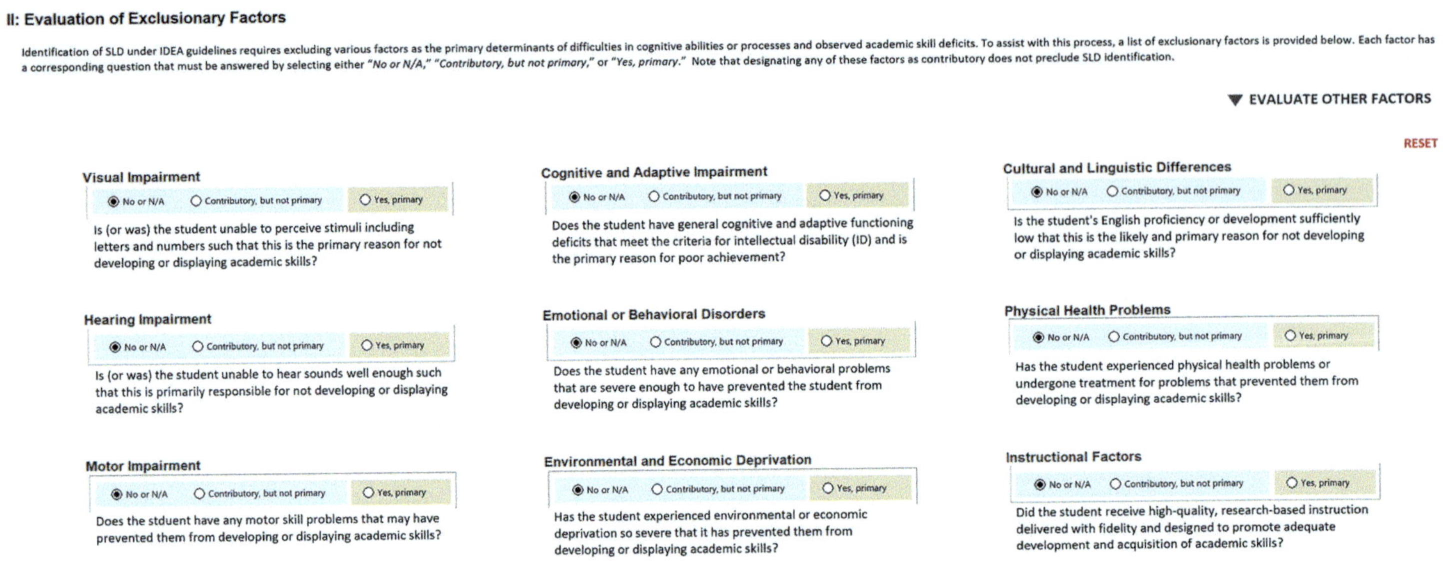
**II: Evaluation of Exclusionary Factors**

Identification of SLD under IDEA guidelines requires excluding various factors as the primary determinants of difficulties in cognitive abilities or processes and observed academic skill deficits. To assist with this process, a list of exclusionary factors is provided below. Each factor has a corresponding question that must be answered by selecting either *"No or N/A," "Contributory, but not primary,"* or *"Yes, primary."* Note that designating any of these factors as contributory does not preclude SLD identification.

▼ EVALUATE OTHER FACTORS

RESET

**Visual Impairment**
◉ No or N/A ○ Contributory, but not primary ○ Yes, primary
Is (or was) the student unable to perceive stimuli including letters and numbers such that this is the primary reason for not developing or displaying academic skills?

**Cognitive and Adaptive Impairment**
◉ No or N/A ○ Contributory, but not primary ○ Yes, primary
Does the student have general cognitive and adaptive functioning deficits that meet the criteria for intellectual disability (ID) and is the primary reason for poor achievement?

**Cultural and Linguistic Differences**
◉ No or N/A ○ Contributory, but not primary ○ Yes, primary
Is the student's English proficiency or development sufficiently low that this is the likely and primary reason for not developing or displaying academic skills?

**Hearing Impairment**
◉ No or N/A ○ Contributory, but not primary ○ Yes, primary
Is (or was) the student unable to hear sounds well enough such that this is primarily responsible for not developing or displaying academic skills?

**Emotional or Behavioral Disorders**
◉ No or N/A ○ Contributory, but not primary ○ Yes, primary
Does the student have any emotional or behavioral problems that are severe enough to have prevented the student from developing or displaying academic skills?

**Physical Health Problems**
◉ No or N/A ○ Contributory, but not primary ○ Yes, primary
Has the student experienced physical health problems or undergone treatment for problems that prevented them from developing or displaying academic skills?

**Motor Impairment**
◉ No or N/A ○ Contributory, but not primary ○ Yes, primary
Does the stduent have any motor skill problems that may have prevented them from developing or displaying academic skills?

**Environmental and Economic Deprivation**
◉ No or N/A ○ Contributory, but not primary ○ Yes, primary
Has the student experienced environmental or economic deprivation so severe that it has prevented them from developing or displaying academic skills?

**Instructional Factors**
◉ No or N/A ○ Contributory, but not primary ○ Yes, primary
Did the student receive high-quality, research-based instruction delivered with fidelity and designed to promote adequate development and acquisition of academic skills?

**FIGURE 4.15 The Exclusionary Factors Section of the SLD Evidence Tab**

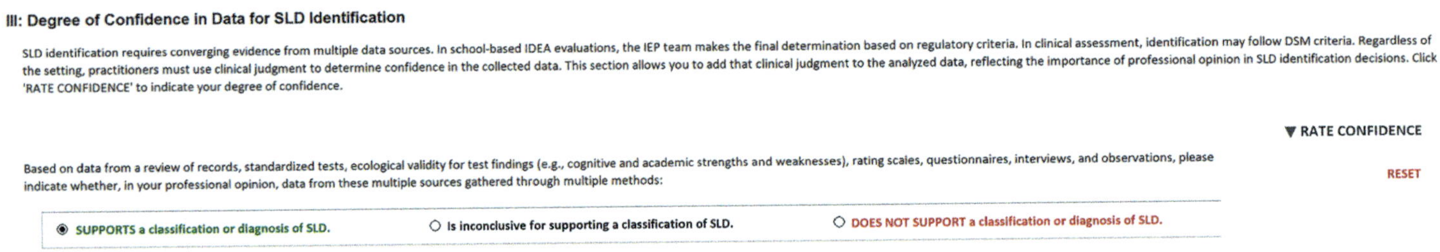
**III: Degree of Confidence in Data for SLD Identification**

SLD identification requires converging evidence from multiple data sources. In school-based IDEA evaluations, the IEP team makes the final determination based on regulatory criteria. In clinical assessment, identification may follow DSM criteria. Regardless of the setting, practitioners must use clinical judgment to determine confidence in the collected data. This section allows you to add that clinical judgment to the analyzed data, reflecting the importance of professional opinion in SLD identification decisions. Click 'RATE CONFIDENCE' to indicate your degree of confidence.

▼ RATE CONFIDENCE

Based on data from a review of records, standardized tests, ecological validity for test findings (e.g., cognitive and academic strengths and weaknesses), rating scales, questionnaires, interviews, and observations, please indicate whether, in your professional opinion, data from these multiple sources gathered through multiple methods:

RESET

◉ SUPPORTS a classification or diagnosis of SLD. ○ Is inconclusive for supporting a classification of SLD. ○ DOES NOT SUPPORT a classification or diagnosis of SLD.

**FIGURE 4.16 Degree of Confidence Section of the SLD Evidence Tab**

For each exclusionary factor, X-BASS defaults to "No or N/A." The practitioner may change this to "Yes, primary" when the factor is considered the most plausible and primary reason for the student's difficulties, or to "Contributory, but not primary" when the factor plays a role but does not adequately explain the academic weakness. Additional information about each exclusionary factor is provided in Appendix G.

This section ensures that the PSW analysis is interpreted within the broader educational, behavioral, psychological, and environmental contexts and that the student's difficulties are not better explained by one or more of these exclusionary factors.

## III. Degree of Confidence in Data for SLD Identification

This section, shown in Figure 4.16, allows the practitioner to rate their confidence in the data used to determine whether the student meets criteria for SLD. The confidence rating applies to the totality of the evidence, including cognitive data, academic data, instructional history, classroom performance, educational records, interviews, behavior rating scales, and any additional sources of converging or diverging information. The practitioner is asked whether data from multiple sources and methods supports, **is inconclusive**, or **does not support** a classification or diagnosis of SLD.

This structured reflection is also a key debiasing strategy. By pausing to evaluate the quality, completeness, and consistency of the evidence, the practitioner deliberately counters common cognitive biases—such as anchoring on a single score, over-interpreting weak data, or prematurely closing on a hypothesis. Rating confidence in the data forces the practitioner to consider whether the evidence truly converges across sources or whether gaps, inconsistencies, or contextual factors require attention.

In this way, the confidence rating helps ensure that the final determination is grounded in a defensible combination of quantitative and qualitative evidence, rather than intuitive impressions or isolated data points. It reinforces the principle that SLD identification requires not only statistical analysis but also careful, bias-aware professional judgment.

## IV. Summary of Data for SLD Identification

This section of the SLD Evidence tab, shown in Figures 4.17 and 4.18, consolidates all relevant information into a single, coherent summary. It includes the practitioner's conclusions regarding each DD/C criterion, the presence or absence of exclusionary factors, and the degree of

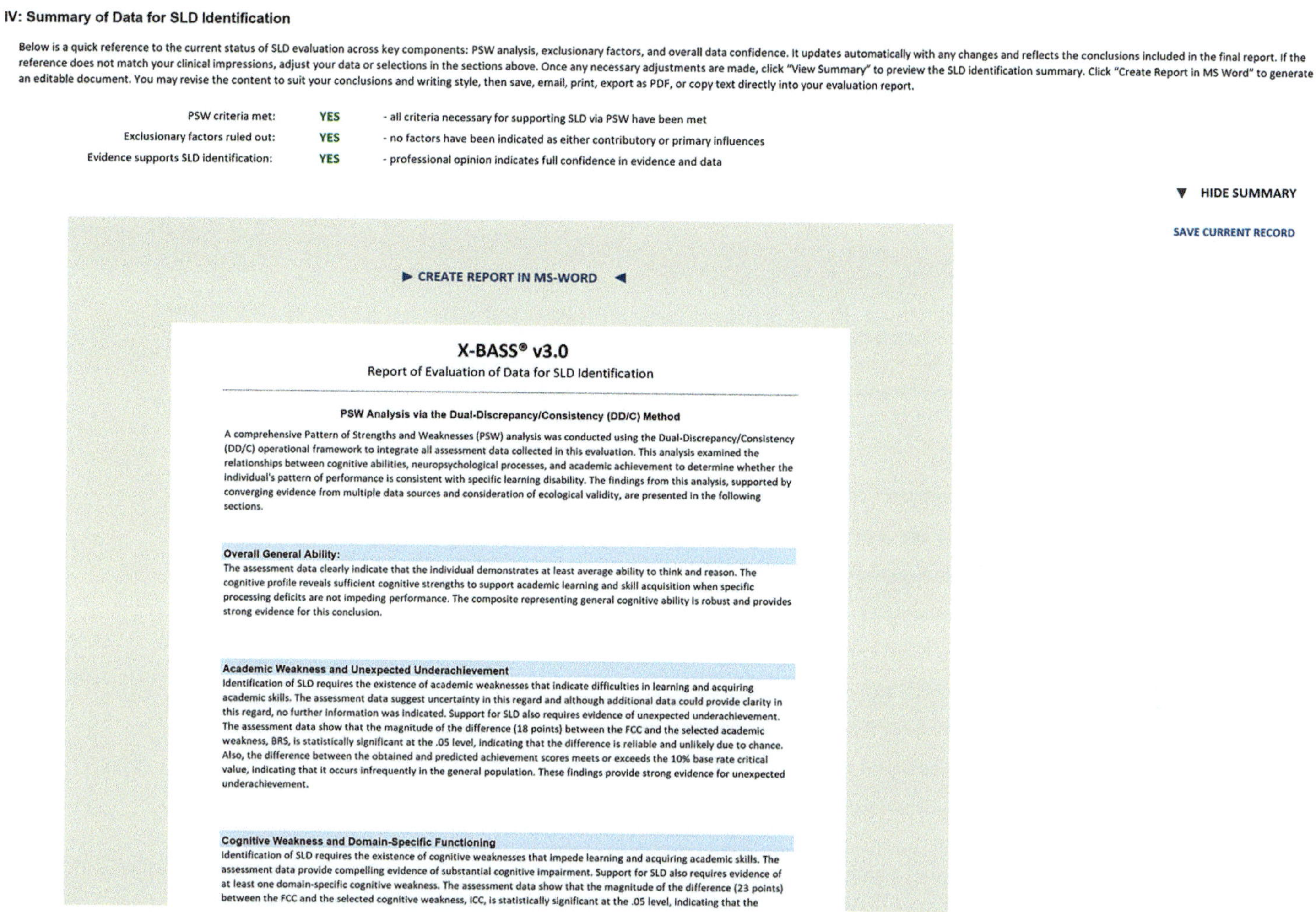


**FIGURE 4.17 Section IV of the SLD Evidence Tab**

confidence in the data. The summary provides a clear, integrated statement of whether the student meets criteria for SLD and the rationale supporting that conclusion. Because it brings together statistical evidence from the PSW analysis and contextual evidence documented on the SLD Evidence tab, this section serves as the bridge between the analytic process and the final eligibility decision. It also forms the basis for the written report generated by X-BASS.

In this section, the practitioner can click **Create Report in MS-Word** (see Figure 4.17), which opens a full report in a Word document on the practitioner's desktop. From there, the report may be edited and personalized to include the student's name. Portions of the report may also be copied and pasted into an existing evaluation report. Finally, graphs that appear in the last section of the SLD Evidence tab, described next, may be copied and pasted into the report as needed.

> **CAUTION**
>
> The report generated by X-BASS includes a note reminding practitioners that they are responsible for the **accuracy, completeness, and integrity** of all information contained in the final document, including any edits or additions they make. The content is not to be used for commercial purposes. The authors of X-BASS have no vested interest in any conclusions or decisions derived from the report. Practitioners should therefore review the generated report carefully to ensure that all interpretations, decisions, and statements accurately reflect the student's data and the team's final impressions.

## V. Summary Graph of PSW Results

The final section of the SLD Evidence tab provides a visual summary of all scores considered in the PSW analysis and SLD decision-making process. Sample graphs for Sian are provided in Figures 4.19 to 4.21. The scores are graphed with a 68% confidence interval, which is the default setting in X-BASS. However, you can change the confidence interval

**Ability-Achievement Consistency:**

Support for SLD requires evidence of an aptitude-achievement consistency. Research indicates that the strength of the relationship between the individual's cognitive weakness (ICC) and academic weakness (BRS) is moderate. Although cognitive weaknesses alone are rarely the only plausible explanation for learning difficulties, these data provide a reasonable explanation for the observed academic area of weakness.

**Evaluation of Exclusionary Factors:**

A diagnosis or classification of SLD requires the exclusion of other primary causes for the documented learning difficulties. When academic struggles can be primarily attributed to factors beyond specific, inherent cognitive weaknesses, SLD is generally not warranted. The exclusionary factors listed below were assessed and determined to be either a primary cause of the learning difficulties, a contributing factor, or neither primary nor contributory:

NONE - **Perceptual factors (vision difficulties)**

NONE - **Below average cognitive or adaptive functioning**

NONE - **Cultural and linguistic factors**

NONE - **Perceptual factors (hearing difficulties)**

NONE - **Social-emotional and psychological factors**

NONE - **Environmental and economic factors**

NONE - **Factors involving fine and gross motor functioning**

NONE - **Physical and health factors**

NONE - **Instructional factors**

Following the assessment of exclusionary factors, no alternative conditions or variables have been identified that could serve as the primary cause of the individual's learning difficulties. Therefore, assuming all other diagnostic criteria for SLD have been satisfied, it can be reasonably concluded that the documented learning problems are not primarily attributable to any of the specified exclusionary factors, and a diagnosis or classification of SLD is warranted.

**Final Clinical Impressions:**

Based on a comprehensive evaluation, analysis of multiple data sources, and professional judgment, it has been determined that the evidence strongly supports a classification or diagnosis of Specific Learning Disability for this individual. All Patterns of Strengths and Weaknesses (PSW) analysis criteria within the parameters of the DD/C method have been satisfied, all exclusionary factors have been ruled out as primary reasons for the academic difficulties, and confidence that the data justify such a classification is high. These findings should be carefully considered when deciding on the individual's eligibility for special education services, educational programming needs, and instructional interventions, supports, and accommodations.

---

**Note: The text and conclusions reported herein were derived using the Cross-Battery Assessment Software System (X-BASS v3.0). All users remain responsible for the accuracy, completeness, and veracity of the information contained in this report, as well as any alterations made to the original content.* ***Commercial use of this report's content is strictly prohibited***. *The authors of X-BASS have no vested interest or financial stake in any conclusions or decisions made based on this information.*



**FIGURE 4.18 A Continuation of Section IV of the SLD Evidence Tab**

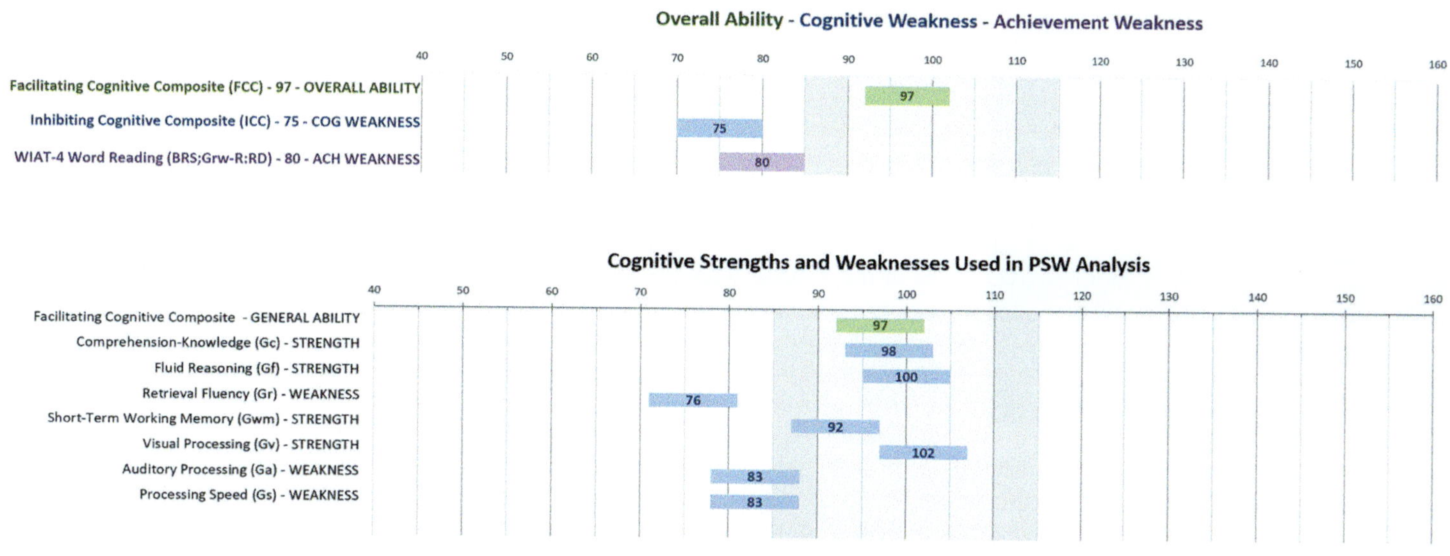


**FIGURE 4.19 PSW and Cognitive Ability Graphs of Sian's Scores in Section V of the SLD Evidence Tab**

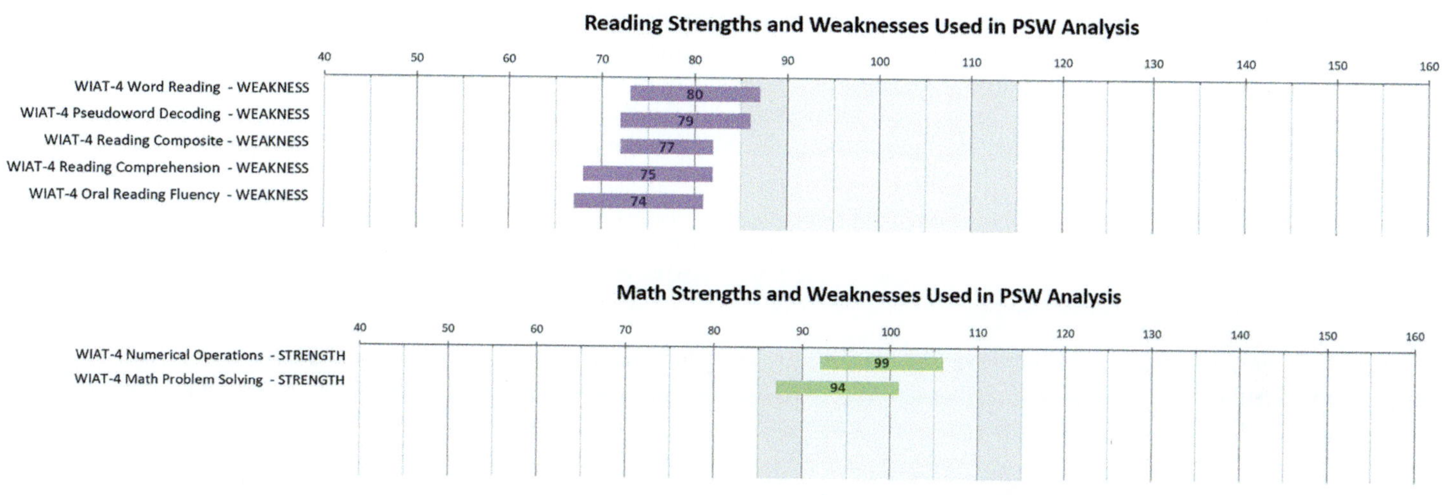


**FIGURE 4.20 Reading and Math Graphs of Sian's Scores in Section V of the SLD Evidence Tab**

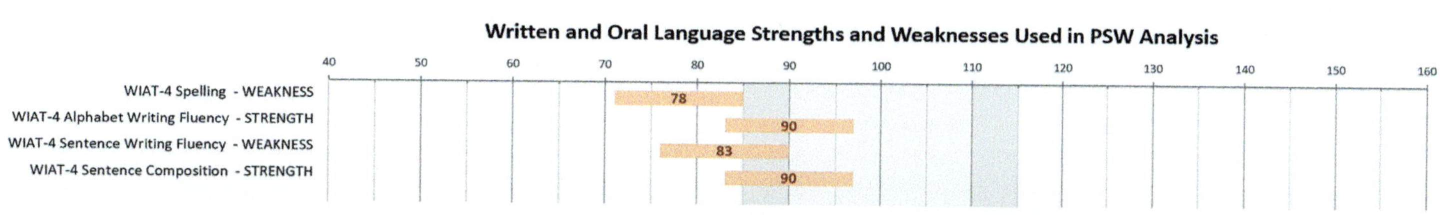


**FIGURE 4.21 Written and Oral Language Graph of Sian's Scores in Section V of the SLD Evidence Tab**

to 90% or 95% directly in this section of the SLD Evidence tab. These graphs may be included in the practitioner's independent reports or in the report generated in the previous section. The best way to integrate these graphs into an existing Word document is to use the "Snipping Tool."

**DON'T FORGET**

To copy graphs from X-BASS into a Word document, practitioners may find it easiest to use the Snipping Tool, which is built into Windows. To access it, click the Start button, then type Snipping Tool in the search bar. Once open, select "New," drag the cursor to capture the graph, and then paste the image directly into the Word report. This method preserves the graph's visual quality and allows the practitioner to position it anywhere within the document.

## SUMMARY AND CONCLUSIONS

This chapter intentionally used a simple, familiar battery to help readers focus on the mechanics of the X-BASS workflow—how DD/C analyses are conducted, how probabilities and base rates are interpreted, how ecological data are integrated, and how the SLD Evidence tab supports a final SLD/not SLD determination. By stripping away real-world complexity, the chapter emphasized the logic, sequence, and interpretive checkpoints of the SLD module.

Sian's case illustrates how the SLD module of X-BASS (i.e., the PSW Data, Analysis, and Results tabs, the SLD Evidence tab, and the PSW Options tab) guides practitioners through an explicit, structured, and defensible decision-making process. Based on the PSW analysis, review of supporting data, the evaluation of exclusionary factors, and the degree of confidence in the data, Sian's profile meets criteria for SLD in Basic Reading Skills and Reading Fluency using the DD/C method. Each component of the method—at least average ability to think and reason, domain specific cognitive weakness, unexpected underachievement, and aptitude–achievement consistency—was satisfied, and the ecological data reported on the SLD Evidence tab strengthened the interpretation where probabilities were equivocal.

At the same time, Sian's case highlights an important limitation of the battery used. Although her scores support an SLD determination, the assessment does not provide the depth of information needed to identify *which type* of reading disability she has, which is needed for targeted intervention. This is a reflection of the constraints of the test battery itself. A limited or traditional battery can confirm the presence of a reading disability, but it cannot fully illuminate the underlying linguistic, orthographic, or cognitive processes that differentiate one type of reading difficulty from another. As a result, the intervention implications drawn from this case are limited.

The next chapter builds directly on this foundation. Using a few case examples, we shift from a basic PSW demonstration to diagnostic XBAs in reading, math, and writing, intentionally designed to capture the most salient cognitive and linguistic processes underlying specific academic skills. These cases illustrate how diagnostic XBA batteries clarify the *type* of disability, strengthen diagnostic precision, and lead to more targeted, evidence-aligned intervention recommendations. In this way, the reader moves from understanding *how* the SLD module works to understanding *why* diagnostic XBA matters.

### TEST YOURSELF

1. **The PSW Data tab displays all cognitive and academic scores that will be used in the PSW analysis. True or False?**
2. **In X-BASS, which score range is automatically classified as a strength on the PSW Data tab?**
   (a) Standard scores of 85 or higher
   (b) Standard scores of 90 or higher
   (c) Standard scores of 95 or higher
   (d) Standard scores of 100 or higher
3. **Scores that fall between 80 and 89 on the PSW Data tab require the evaluator to determine whether they function as strengths or weaknesses. True or False?**
4. **Which of the following best explains why composite scores are generally preferred over subtest scores for representing cognitive abilities in PSW analyses?**
   (a) Composites are easier to interpret
   (b) Composites have higher reliability than individual subtests
   (c) Composites reduce testing time
   (d) Composites eliminate measurement error
5. **A single cognitive subtest score may be used to represent a cognitive weakness if the score is sufficiently low. True or False?**
6. **The Inhibiting Cognitive Composite (ICC) represents:**
   (a) The student's overall intellectual ability
   (b) The combined influence of cognitive processes most likely to interfere with learning
   (c) The average of all cognitive scores
   (d) The relationship between cognitive and academic abilities

**7. Which DD/C criterion evaluates whether an academic weakness is substantially lower than predicted based on the student's overall cognitive ability?**

(a) Domain specificity

(b) Aptitude–achievement consistency

(c) Unexpected underachievement

(d) Ecological validity

**8. Base-rate information in X-BASS helps evaluators determine whether a discrepancy is:**

(a) Statistically significant

(b) Rare in the general population

(c) Psychometrically reliable

(d) Clinically meaningful

**9. The SLD Evidence tab includes sections for documenting exclusionary factors, rating confidence in the data, and summarizing the PSW analysis. True or False?**

**10. The ADD SUPPORTING DATA feature in the SLD Evidence tab allows evaluators to document classroom manifestations that provide ecological validity for an identified cognitive or academic weakness. True or False?**

*Answers:* 1. True; 2. b; 3. True; 4. b; 5. False; 6. b; 7. c; 8. b; 9. True; 10. True

## REFERENCES

Ehri, L. C. (2014). Orthographic mapping in the acquisition of sight word reading, spelling memory, and vocabulary learning. *Scientific Studies of Reading, 18*(1), 5–21.

Hajovsky, D. B., Niileksela, C. R., Flanagan, D. P., Alfonso, V. C., Schneider, W. J., & Robbins, J. (2025). Toward a consensus model of cognitive–reading achievement relations using meta-structural equation modeling. *Journal of Intelligence, 13*(8), 104.

Kiselica, A. M., Karr, J. E., Mikula, C. M. et al. (2024). Recent advances in neuropsychological test interpretation for clinical practice. *Neuropsychol Rev*, ***34***, 637–667. https://doi.org/10.1007/s11065-023-09596-1.

Schneider, W. J., Flanagan, D. P., Niileksela, C. R., & Engler, J. R. (2024). The effect of measurement error on the positive predictive value of PSW methods for SLD identification: How buffer zones dispel the illusion of inaccuracy. *Journal of School Psychology, 103*, 101280.

Share, D. L. (1995). Phonological recoding and self-teaching: Sine qua non of reading acquisition. *Cognition, 55*(2), 151–218.

Urbina, S. (2014). *Essentials of psychological testing* ((2nd ed.). ed). John Wiley & Sons.

Five

# DIAGNOSTIC CROSS-BATTERY ASSESSMENTS FOR READING, WRITING, AND MATH REFERRALS

## INTRODUCTION

Learning disabilities in reading, writing, and mathematics are complex, heterogeneous, and multifactorial. Although decades of research have identified patterns of weakness that tend to cluster together, no single cluster of cognitive and linguistic processes or subtype taxonomy has achieved consensus. Across all three academic domains, students rarely present with a "pure" profile. Instead, most exhibit overlapping features across cognitive, linguistic, attentional, and motor systems—a pattern consistent with contemporary multiple-deficit models of learning disorders (Pennington, 2006; Pennington et al., 2012; van Bergen et al., 2014).

In reading, for example, phonological deficits explain many—but not all—cases of developmental dyslexia (Bradley & Bryant, 1983; Snowling, 1995, 2001). Other students show weaknesses in orthographic processing, naming speed, visual attention, temporal processing, motor coordination, or combinations of these (Heim et al., 2008; Nicolson & Fawcett, 1990; Tallal, 1980; Valdois et al., 2003; Wolf & Bowers, 1999). Neuroscientific and genetic research further demonstrates that dyslexia arises from diverse neurobiological pathways, with different children showing different patterns of brain organization and cognitive risk factors (Gialluisi et al., 2021; Kim, 2021; van Bergen et al., 2014). Similar heterogeneity is observed in mathematics and writing, where difficulties may stem from weaknesses in number sense, working memory, processing speed, language, executive functions, graphomotor skills, or transcription processes (Berninger & Amtmann, 2003; Geary, 2011; McCloskey & Rapp, 2017).

Because of this complexity, subtypes should be understood as functional heuristics, not fixed biological categories. They help us organize information, identify underlying mechanisms, and design interventions that are more precise than global labels such as "SLD-Reading" or "SLD-Math." This position aligns with critiques of traditional behavioral subtyping (e.g., "surface" vs "phonological" dyslexia), which often fails to capture the underlying neurocognitive mechanisms that drive reading impairment or guide intervention (Griffiths & Snowling, 2002). Contemporary perspectives argue that categorizing learning disabilities based on neurocognitive mechanisms, rather than error patterns alone, provides a clearer picture of the difficulties students face and supports more individualized intervention (Zoubrinetzky et al., 2014).

Cross-linguistic research adds another layer of complexity. Orthographic transparency influences how reading difficulties manifest: in transparent orthographies such as Greek or Italian, decoding is relatively easier, and deficits may appear more strongly in processing speed or attention; in opaque orthographies such as English, phonological and orthographic weaknesses are more pronounced (Diamanti et al., 2018; Menghini et al., 2010; White et al., 2006). These differences underscore the importance of interpreting subtypes within a linguistic context and caution against assuming that any single subtype model generalizes across languages.

Given these realities, the purpose of this chapter is not to propose a definitive set of subtypes or to claim that the mechanisms or cognitive processes described here represent fixed biological entities. Rather, our goal is practical: to show how a systematic, component-level analysis of cognitive and academic skills can reveal mechanisms often missed by standard assessment protocols, and how identifying these mechanisms can lead to more targeted, effective interventions. This approach is consistent with calls in the literature to broaden diagnostic assessment beyond intelligence and reading measures to include attention, memory, visual processing, motor skills, and other domains relevant to learning (Heim et al., 2008; Menghini et al., 2010; Pacheco et al., 2014).

To support this goal, each domain—reading, writing, and mathematics—begins with a "Caveats and Context" section. These sections summarize the current state of the research, highlight the limitations of existing subtype models, and clarify how our framework fits within the broader scientific landscape. They are intentionally transparent, acknowledging that:

- subtype research is ongoing and evolving,
- most students show features of more than one subtype,
- comorbidity across domains (and with ADHD, developmental coordination disorders, and language disorders) is common (Nisiotou & Vlachos, 2014; van Bergen et al., 2014), and
- the goal of subtyping is to guide intervention, not to categorize individuals.

The diagnostic pathways presented in Rapid Reference 5.1 show how clusters of underlying mechanisms form coherent routes of academic breakdown across reading, writing, and mathematics, providing a structured way to organize assessment findings before moving into domain-specific analysis.

## Rapid Reference 5.1

### Understanding Diagnostic Pathways Across Reading, Math, and Writing

**What Is a Pathway?**

A diagnostic pathway is the *route of breakdown* through which an academic difficulty develops. Each pathway is defined by a cluster of underlying mechanisms, along with:

- a coherent set of skills
- hallmark error patterns
- targeted process measures
- a corresponding SLD subtype

**In practice, a pathway answers the question:**

*Which mechanism—or cluster of mechanisms—is driving this student's academic weakness?*

**Reading Pathways and Their Defining Mechanisms**

***Phonological Pathway***

Defined by mechanisms such as phonological awareness, decoding, and phonological access.

***Orthographic Pathway***

Defined by mechanisms such as orthographic learning and pattern recognition.

***Language Comprehension Pathway***

Defined by mechanisms such as vocabulary, syntax, and discourse comprehension.

***Efficiency/Automaticity Pathway***

Defined by mechanisms such as rapid naming and reading fluency.

**Math Pathways and Their Defining Mechanisms**

***Procedural Pathway***

Defined by mechanisms such as multistep algorithm execution, executive functioning and working memory demands, and symbolic manipulation.

***Fact Retrieval/Fluency Pathway***

Defined by mechanisms such as automaticity, rapid automatic naming-quantity, and processing speed.

***Conceptual/Reasoning Pathway***

Defined by mechanisms such as number sense, magnitude understanding, and quantitative reasoning.

**Writing Pathways and Their Defining Mechanisms**

***Graphomotor/Transcription Pathway***

Defined by mechanisms such as handwriting fluency and motor planning.

***Spelling/Encoding Pathway***

Defined by mechanisms such as phonological, orthographic, and morphological encoding.

***Sentence Formulation Pathway***

Defined by mechanisms such as syntax, grammar, and linguistic formulation.

***Composition/Executive Pathway***

Defined by mechanisms such as planning, organization, and revision processes.

**Why Pathways Matter**

- Prevent overreliance on achievement scores
- Anchor subtype decisions in mechanisms, not symptoms
- Support defensible, research-aligned diagnostic conclusions
- Guide targeted assessment and interpretation

### Caveats and Context: Reading

Research on developmental dyslexia (DD) has produced a wide range of theoretical models, and no single framework fully explains the diversity of reading difficulties observed in practice. Although phonological deficits are common, they are not universal, and many children with dyslexia exhibit additional weaknesses in naming speed, orthographic processing, visual attention, temporal processing, motor coordination, or executive functions (Heim et al., 2008; Nicolson & Fawcett, 1990; Tallal, 1980; Valdois et al., 2003; Wolf & Bowers, 1999). Contemporary research increasingly supports multiple-deficit models, which propose that dyslexia arises from the interaction of several cognitive and neurobiological risk factors rather than a single underlying cause (Pennington, 2006; Pennington et al., 2012; van Bergen et al., 2014).

Studies attempting to identify discrete subtypes of dyslexia have produced mixed results. Some have found clusters characterized by phonological deficits, processing-speed weaknesses, attention-based difficulties, or motor impairments (Heim et al., 2008; Lewandowska et al., 2014; Menghini et al., 2010). Others have identified subgroups with combined deficits across multiple domains, with the majority of children showing multiple co-occurring weaknesses rather than a single isolated deficit (Menghini et al., 2010; Soriano-Ferrer et al., 2014). Importantly, cognitive clusters do not always map cleanly onto reading performance (accuracy, fluency, comprehension), and behavioral subtypes based solely on error patterns provide limited insight into underlying mechanisms (Griffiths & Snowling, 2002).

Subtyping is further complicated by differences in orthographic transparency. In transparent languages such as Greek, decoding is relatively easier, and deficits may appear more strongly in processing speed or attention; in opaque languages such as English, phonological and orthographic weaknesses are more pronounced (Diamanti et al., 2018; White et al., 2006). These cross-linguistic differences limit the generalizability of any single subtype model.

Given these limitations, the subtypes described in this chapter should be understood as practical heuristics designed to support mechanism-aligned assessment and intervention. They are not intended to represent fixed neurobiological categories. The goal is to help practitioners identify the specific components—phonological, orthographic, naming speed, or automaticity-related—that contribute to a student's reading difficulty, and to use that information to design or select more targeted and effective interventions.

## DIAGNOSTIC XBA FOR READING REFERRALS

This section applies the pathway framework to reading, beginning with teacher interview questions (Rapid Reference 5.2) that clarify the nature of the concern. It then maps commonly used achievement and cognitive batteries onto the four core components of reading. By examining the strengths and limitations of each instrument, practitioners can determine when a single battery is sufficient and when cross-battery supplementation is required. The section concludes with an integrated diagnostic battery that combines the Wechsler Individual Achievement Test, Fourth Edition (WIAT-4; Wechsler, 2020), Tests of Dyslexia-Comprehensive (TOD-C; Mather et al., 2024), and Fiefer Assessment of Reading (FAR; Feifer & Nader, 2015) to support reading disability subtype classification, explain the underlying mechanisms of reading difficulty, and guide intervention planning.

Together, these tools move practitioners beyond simply identifying that a student struggles with reading. They support precise, component-level diagnosis and provide the conceptual and empirical foundation needed to answer the most important question in any reading evaluation: *What exactly is breaking down, and why?*

## *Rapid Reference 5.2*

### Teacher Interview Questions to Identify the Type of Reading Problem

**1. Word Reading Accuracy (untimed accuracy of real words)**

- When the student reads aloud, do they **misread real words**, especially unfamiliar or multisyllabic ones?
- Do they make **phonetic errors** (e.g., saying *lat* for *late*) or **visual errors** (e.g., *house* for *horse*)?
- Do they rely heavily on **context or pictures** to guess words?
- Do they struggle to read **irregular words** (e.g., *said, does, again*)?

**If yes → likely a word reading accuracy problem.**

**2. Decoding Efficiency (speed + accuracy with unfamiliar words)**

- Does the student read **nonsense words** or unfamiliar words **slowly or inaccurately**?
- Do they have difficulty **applying phonics patterns** they have been taught?
- Do they appear to **sound out the same word repeatedly**, as if it never becomes automatic?
- Does decoding break down when the student encounters **longer or more complex words**?

**If yes → likely a decoding efficiency problem.**

**3. Reading Fluency (rate, automaticity, prosody)**

- Does the student read **accurately** but **very slowly**?
- Does their reading sound **choppy, labored, or monotone**, even when they know the words?
- Do they lose their place, skip lines, or struggle to track text smoothly?
- Does slow reading interfere with their **ability to understand** what they read?

**If yes → likely a reading fluency problem.**

**4. Reading Comprehension (understanding text)**

- Can the student read the words correctly but **cannot explain what they read**?
- Do they struggle with **inferential questions**, summarizing, or identifying main ideas?
- Do they have difficulty understanding **grade-level vocabulary** or complex sentences?
- Does comprehension improve when the text is **read aloud to them**?

**If yes → likely a reading comprehension problem.**

**Optional: Reading "Short Cut" Question**

This question often reveals the primary issue:

**"When the student struggles with reading, is it more about *getting the words off the page* or *understanding what the words mean*?"**

- If the teacher says **getting the words off the page** → accuracy, decoding, or fluency
- If the teacher says **understanding the meaning** → comprehension

To support this process, commonly used batteries are organized according to the specific reading components they measure. Across decades of research, four components have consistently emerged as the foundation of skilled reading: accurate word reading, efficient decoding, fluent text reading, and language-based comprehension. Decoding and word-reading accuracy are supported by work on phonological processing, orthographic learning, and lexical quality (e.g., Gough & Tunmer, 1986; Perfetti, 1992, 2007; Share, 1995). Efficiency and automaticity draw on models of automatic processing and rapid access to phonological and orthographic representations (e.g., LaBerge & Samuels, 1974; Wolf & Bowers, 1999). Reading fluency is understood as the integration of accuracy, rate, and prosody (e.g., Fuchs et al., 2001; Kuhn et al., 2010). Finally, comprehension reflects the interaction of decoding and linguistic comprehension, supported by vocabulary, syntax, inferencing, and broader language skills (e.g., Catts et al., 2005; Hoover & Gough, 1990; Nation, 2019).

By mapping each subtest to the four core reading domains, practitioners can quickly identify which tools provide strong coverage, where gaps exist within a given battery, and when cross-battery supplementation is necessary (Gough & Tunmer, 1986; Perfetti, 2007). This structure promotes more intentional test selection and ensures that the assessment battery aligns directly with the referral question and the suspected reading difficulty identified during the teacher interview.

Tables 5.1–5.3 present battery-specific coverage for the WIAT-4, Woodcock-Johnson V Tests of Achievement (WJ V ACH; Mather et al., 2025), and Kaufman Test of Educational Achievement-Third Edition (KTEA-3). The WIAT-4 is often the first battery practitioners reach for when evaluating reading concerns, and for good reason: it provides comprehensive coverage of word-reading accuracy, decoding, and comprehension. However, like any single battery, it offers only a partial view of the reading system. Table 5.1 organizes WIAT-4 subtests by the four core reading components, allowing practitioners to identify where the instrument provides strong measurement and where supplemental assessment may be needed.

The WJ V ACH battery provides unusually broad reading-fluency sampling—Word Reading Fluency, Sentence Reading Fluency, and Oral Reading (Paragraph) Fluency—making it especially useful when the referral question concerns rate, automaticity, and efficiency. The WJ V ACH battery also includes core accuracy and decoding subtests (e.g., Letter-Word Identification, Word Attack) and passage comprehension and recall measures that support both cloze-style and narrative comprehension analyses. Several foundational oral-language and cognitive measures that help explain decoding-based difficulties are distributed across WJ V test sets and clusters (including the WJ V COG and VTL). Practitioners should therefore consult the WJ V test list/clusters and VTL for targeted oral-language, phonological, or working-memory measures when diagnosing underlying mechanisms.

**Table 5.1 WIAT-4: Coverage Across Four Reading Components**

| Reading Component | WIAT-4 Subtests | Coverage Notes |
|---|---|---|
| Word Reading Accuracy | Word Reading; Pseudoword Decoding; Orthographic Choice | Strong coverage of real-word and pseudoword accuracy; Orthographic Choice supplies pattern-level and word-specific orthographic information. |
| Decoding Efficiency | Decoding Fluency | Captures automaticity and speeded phonics application. |
| Reading Fluency | Oral Reading Fluency; Decoding Fluency | Strong connected-text fluency. Decoding Fluency supports single-word automaticity, though single-word fluency coverage is limited. |
| Reading Comprehension | Reading Comprehension; Oral Reading Fluency (prosody) | Solid comprehension measure; no cloze-type task. Oral Reading Fluency contributes diagnostically through prosody and accuracy. |

*Note:* Oral Reading Fluency is included because accuracy, rate, and prosody are among the strongest predictors of reading comprehension. This test helps determine whether comprehension difficulties arise from inefficient decoding or from true language-based comprehension weaknesses.

**Table 5.2 WJ V ACH: Coverage Across Four Reading Components**

| Reading Component | WJ V ACH Subtests | Coverage Notes |
|---|---|---|
| Word Reading Accuracy | Letter-Word Identification; Word Attack | Excellent isolated-word accuracy and phonics/structural decoding coverage. |
| Decoding Efficiency | Word Reading Fluency; Word Attack (untimed support) | Includes a timed single-word fluency measure that indexes speeded decoding; timed decoding sampling is good but not exhaustive. |
| Reading Fluency | Oral Reading (Paragraph) Fluency; Sentence Reading Fluency; Word Reading Fluency | Broadest fluency sampling among major achievement batteries; supports rate, automaticity, and prosodic inference. |
| Reading Comprehension | Passage Comprehension; Reading Recall | Strong passage-based and narrative recall measures; cloze-style items are present in passage tasks. |

**Table 5.3 KTEA-3: Coverage Across Four Reading Components**

| Reading Component | KTEA-3 Subtests | Coverage Notes |
|---|---|---|
| Word Reading Accuracy | Letter & Word Recognition; Nonsense Word Decoding | Strong accuracy coverage. |
| Decoding Efficiency | Nonsense Word Decoding Fluency | Only one timed decoding measure. |
| Reading Fluency | Word Recognition Fluency; Silent Reading Fluency | Good single-word and silent fluency; no oral reading fluency. |
| Reading Comprehension | Reading Comprehension | Solid comprehension; no cloze or recall. |

The KTEA-3 provides a balanced set of academic reading measures, with strong coverage of word-reading accuracy, timed decoding fluency, single-word and silent-reading fluency, and an untimed reading comprehension task. These subtests allow examiners to evaluate accuracy, rate, and text-level understanding within a cohesive framework.

The WIAT-4, WJ V ACH, and KTEA-3 are all achievement batteries—not process-level diagnostic reading batteries: they reliably measure core academic outcomes (word reading and pseudoword decoding accuracy, passage comprehension, and multiple forms of fluency to varying degrees) and are excellent for understanding what a student can read and how quickly. However, none was designed to fully sample the underlying cognitive linguistic mechanisms that explain *why* reading breaks down. Measures of rapid automatized naming, phonological memory and phonological awareness, oral reading prosody, orthographic processing, morphology/syntax, and working-memory/executive functions are either limited or not measured and require supplementing via XBA or for the WJ V ACH, access to the WJ V COG and VTL tests. By supplementing these achievement batteries with targeted process measures, practitioners can gain diagnostic clarity regarding the underlying processes that assist in explaining reading performance.

Table 5.4 summarizes selected subtests from each of the three achievement batteries that best represent the four components of reading. This table should be used to determine which aspects of reading are most important based on the referral and to identify how practitioners may need to supplement their core achievement battery to ensure adequate evaluation of each area of interest.

**Table 5.4 The Best Subtests from the Achievement Batteries for the Four Components of Reading**

| Reading Component | Best Subtests (Across WIAT-4, WJ V/VTL ACH, KTEA-3) | Why They Are the Best |
|---|---|---|
| WORD READING ACCURACY | • WIAT-4 Word Reading<br>• WIAT-4 Pseudoword Decoding<br>• WIAT-4 Orthographic Choice<br>• WJ V ACH Letter-Word Identification<br>• WJ V ACH Word Attack<br>• KTEA-3 Letter & Word Recognition<br>• KTEA-3 Nonsense Word Decoding<br>• WJ V VTL Phonological Awareness | Covers real-word and pseudoword accuracy, phonological foundations, and orthographic pattern knowledge. |
| DECODING EFFICIENCY | • WIAT-4 Decoding Fluency<br>• WJ V ACH Word Reading Fluency<br>• WJ V VTL Rapid Automatized Naming<br>• KTEA-3 Nonsense Word Decoding Fluency | Combines timed decoding, RAN, and processing speed, which are the three pillars of decoding efficiency. |
| READING FLUENCY | • WIAT-4 Oral Reading Fluency<br>• WIAT-4 Decoding Fluency<br>• WJ V ACH Oral Reading Fluency<br>• WJ V ACH Sentence Reading Fluency<br>• WJ V ACH Word Reading Fluency<br>• KTEA-3 Word Recognition Fluency<br>• KTEA-3 Silent Reading Fluency<br>• WJ V VTL Rapid Picture Naming | Provides connected-text fluency, sentence-level fluency, single-word fluency, and automaticity. |
| READING COMPREHENSION | • WIAT-4 Reading Comprehension<br>• WJ V ACH Passage Comprehension<br>• WJ V ACH Reading Recall<br>• KTEA-3 Reading Comprehension<br>• WJ V VTL Oral Vocabulary | Covers cloze, narrative recall, text-based comprehension, vocabulary, inferencing, and reasoning. |

While the cross-battery table demonstrates how practitioners can assemble a comprehensive reading battery from the major achievement tests, it also reveals the limits of those instruments. Achievement tests tell us what a student can do, but they do not always explain why reading breaks down. For that level of diagnostic precision, particularly when dyslexia is suspected, specialized tools are needed. The FAR and TOD-C were designed for exactly this purpose. The next section compares these two instruments and clarifies how each contributes to reading subtype identification and diagnostic decision-making.

## A Comparison of the FAR and TOD-C

The FAR and TOD-C together provide the most comprehensive diagnostic coverage of the linguistic, cognitive, and academic processes involved in reading. Table 5.5 shows that the FAR offers a deep assessment of the underlying mechanisms that support reading development, including phonological processing, orthographic learning, rapid naming, vocabulary, and language-based comprehension, making it uniquely valuable for understanding *why* a student is struggling. Table 5.6 shows that the TOD-C complements this by integrating these linguistic foundations with direct measures of academic reading performance, including real-word and pseudoword accuracy, decoding efficiency, fluency, and comprehension. Because neither instrument was designed to function as a complete reading battery on its own, Tables 5.5 and 5.6 illustrate how FAR and TOD-C subtests align with the four reading components and where additional achievement measures may be needed to complete the diagnostic picture.

## Unique Contributions of the FAR and TOD-C to Comprehensive Dyslexia Assessment

The FAR and TOD-C serve complementary roles in the diagnostic evaluation of dyslexia and reading disorders. Although both assess reading skills, they address different conceptual foundations and answer different diagnostic questions. The FAR is optimized for *explanation*, offering a deep analysis of the cognitive-linguistic processes that underlie reading performance. In contrast, the TOD-C is optimized for *classification*, providing clear, research-aligned indicators of phonological, surface/orthographic, mixed, and comprehension-based profiles. When used together, the two instruments create a diagnostic system that is precise and comprehensive.

**Table 5.5 FAR: Coverage Across Four Reading Components**

| Reading Component | FAR Subtests | Coverage Notes* |
|---|---|---|
| Word Reading Accuracy | Phonemic Awareness; Decoding; Encoding; Orthographic Processing | Strong linguistic foundations; limited real-word accuracy test. |
| Decoding Efficiency | Rapid Automatic Naming; Phonemic Awareness; Decoding | Strong efficiency predictors; limited timed decoding task. |
| Reading Fluency | Rapid Automatic Naming; Fluency Index | Fluency is indirect; limited connected-text fluency. |
| Reading Comprehension | Reading Comprehension; Semantic Concepts | Good linguistic comprehension; limited cloze or narrative recall. |

* The purpose of indicating what the battery does not measure is to ensure a comprehensive understanding of all aspects of reading and their underlying cognitive processes. A lack of certain tasks is not necessarily a limitation of the battery, because its intended purpose is to identify the cognitive-linguistic processes underlying different types of reading difficulties and to understand why a problem occurs.

**Table 5.6 TOD-C: Coverage Across Four Reading Components**

| Reading Component | TOD-C Subtests | Coverage Notes* |
|---|---|---|
| Word Reading Accuracy | Letter & Word Recognition; Sight Word Acquisition; Decoding—Real Words; Decoding—Nonsense Words; Phonics Knowledge; Orthographic Processing | Broad coverage of real-word and pseudoword accuracy, with added depth in orthographic learning and phonics knowledge. Sight Word Acquisition uniquely measures learning rate for new orthographic forms. No separate connected-text accuracy measure. |
| Decoding Efficiency | Reading Efficiency; Rapid Automatized Naming; Timed Real-Word Decoding; Timed Nonsense-Word Decoding; Visual–Verbal Paired-Associate Learning | Strong efficiency coverage combining accuracy, rate, and automaticity. Includes unique paired-associate learning and dynamic decoding tasks not found in other achievement batteries. No standardized measure of growth rate or repeated-reading efficiency. |
| Reading Fluency | Reading Fluency; Reading Efficiency; Rapid Automatized Naming; Timed Letter/Word Recognition | Comprehensive fluency coverage across connected text, single words, and integrated efficiency. RAN adds processing-speed information relevant to fluency development. No formal prosody rating scale. |
| Reading Comprehension | Reading Comprehension; Listening Comprehension; Vocabulary Knowledge; Reasoning; Auditory Working Memory | Deep comprehension coverage, including literal, inferential, and language-based components. Listening comprehension and reasoning help differentiate decoding-based versus language-based comprehension weaknesses. No standardized cloze task; limited multiparagraph comprehension. |

* The purpose of indicating what the battery does not measure is to ensure a comprehensive understanding of all aspects of reading and their underlying cognitive processes. A lack of certain tasks is not necessarily a limitation of the battery because its intended purpose is to classify or diagnose dyslexia.

The FAR offers deep coverage of phonological processing, morphological awareness, orthographic processing, and executive-function-related reading tasks. These measures illuminate the cognitive-linguistic mechanisms that contribute to reading difficulties, helping practitioners understand why a student struggles. FAR's strength lies in its ability to identify the underlying processes—phonological memory, phonological automaticity, morphological problem solving, visual attention, and linguistic comprehension—that shape reading development.

The TOD-C offers measures not commonly found in other achievement batteries, including Sight Word Acquisition, Visual–Verbal Paired Associate Learning, and Integrated Reading Efficiency. These tasks directly assess orthographic learning rate, decoding efficiency, and the mechanisms that support automatic word recognition. TOD-C's inclusion of reading-embedded cognitive tasks, such as Listening Comprehension and Reasoning, provides the contrasts needed to distinguish decoding-based comprehension problems from language-based ones. As a result, the TOD-C is one of the strongest available tool for subtype classification, aligning cleanly with the Simple View of Reading and contemporary dyslexia research.

Although the FAR does not classify dyslexia subtypes as directly as the TOD-C, it provides the most detailed mechanism-level information for intervention planning and for explaining the origins of a student's reading profile. The TOD-C includes an intervention guide as well, but its recommendations are tied to subtest performance rather than to the deeper cognitive-linguistic mechanisms that the FAR more directly assesses.

## A WIAT-4 + TOD-C + FAR Diagnostic Reading Cross-Battery

While the TOD-C and FAR each offer distinct advantages, one excelling in subtype classification and the other in explaining the cognitive-linguistic mechanisms underlying reading difficulties, neither instrument alone provides a complete diagnostic picture. The TOD-C is designed to support classification of which dyslexia subtype best fits the student's pattern of strengths and weaknesses, whereas the FAR clarifies why that pattern emerged by examining phonological processing, morphological skills, and language-based reasoning.

To interpret TOD-C and FAR findings meaningfully, they must be anchored to a clear understanding of the student's academic performance. An achievement battery such as the WIAT-4 can provide this anchor. When WIAT-4 (or another comprehensive achievement battery) subtests representing the four core reading domains are included, the examiner gains a comprehensive picture of the student's strengths and weaknesses in word reading accuracy, decoding efficiency, reading fluency, and reading comprehension. These achievement anchors are essential for determining whether the student's academic weaknesses align with domain-specific cognitive weaknesses in ways that are theoretically and empirically defensible.

Before integrating the WIAT-4, TOD-C, and FAR into a unified diagnostic system, it is important to understand the diagnostic contributions of each proposed subtest. Each measure plays a distinct role: some clarify decoding accuracy and fluency, and others illuminate orthographic learning, phonological processing, efficiency, or language comprehension. Table 5.7 shows that selected subtests from these batteries provide the range of information needed to identify the student's dyslexia subtype and the underlying mechanisms driving their reading profile. Not all 17 subtests in Table 5.7 must be administered in every case. For example, the TOD-C includes a six-subtest Dyslexia Diagnostic Index (DDI) that samples phonological processing, orthographic learning, and reading efficiency. The DDI is designed as a diagnostic index intended to support subtype classification when used within a comprehensive assessment (Mather et al., 2025).

The 17-subtest battery is justified because each subtest contributes unique diagnostic information that the TOD-C DDI alone cannot provide. The DDI samples only the core mechanisms of dyslexia—phonological processing, orthographic learning, and reading efficiency—whereas a comprehensive evaluation also documents unexpected underachievement, rules out alternative explanations (language, morphology, reasoning), and confirms consistency between cognitive and academic domains. The WIAT-4 subtests establish the academic weakness and,

**Table 5.7 A Hypothetical 17-Subtest Diagnostic Reading Cross-Battery Assessment Example with Emphasis on Each Subtest's Contribution to Diagnosis**

| Subtest | Contribution to Diagnosis |
|---|---|
| WIAT-4 Word Reading | Achievement anchor; real-word reading accuracy; foundational indicator of decoding-based weaknesses. |
| WIAT-4 Pseudoword Decoding | Achievement anchor; pure phonological decoding; differentiates phonological versus orthographic weaknesses. |
| WIAT-4 Decoding Fluency | Achievement anchor; timed decoding automaticity; identifies slow, effortful phonological processing and efficiency deficits. |
| WIAT-4 Oral Reading Fluency | Achievement anchor; integrated rate, accuracy, and prosody; captures real-time reading efficiency and fluency-based dyslexia profiles. |
| WIAT-4 Reading Comprehension | Achievement anchor; measures literal and inferential understanding; distinguishes decoding-based versus language-based comprehension weaknesses. |
| TOD-C Rapid Pseudoword Reading | Decoding efficiency; integrates accuracy + rate + automaticity; identifies slow, effortful phonological processing. |
| TOD-C Rapid Irregular Word Reading | Real-word efficiency; sensitive to orthographic learning and automatic word recognition; differentiates surface/orthographic dyslexia. |
| TOD-C Irregular Word Spelling | Stored irregular word knowledge; sensitive to orthographic learning; helps identify surface/orthographic dyslexia by revealing difficulty acquiring and retaining irregular word forms. |
| TOD-C Symbol-to-Sound Learning | Orthographic mapping mechanism; assesses ability to bind visual forms to phonological labels; predicts long-term word learning. |
| TOD-C Letter and Word Choice | Orthographic processing; stored orthographic knowledge; recognition of legal versus illegal letter patterns. |
| TOD-C Silent Reading Efficiency | Silent reading rate + comprehension; identifies efficiency-based comprehension limitations. |
| TOD-C Picture Vocabulary | Higher-order verbal knowledge; supports comprehension and interpretation. |
| TOD-C Geometric Analogies | Nonverbal reasoning; supports comprehension and problem solving. |
| FAR Phonemic Awareness | Depth of phonological skill: manipulation, segmentation, and blending; core indicator of phonological dyslexia. |
| FAR Rapid Automatic Naming | Speed of phonological access; contributes to fluency and efficiency; differentiates slow access from weak awareness. |
| FAR Morphological Processing | Meaning-based decoding supports vocabulary and comprehension and helps rule out morphology-based weaknesses. |
| FAR Semantic Concepts | Measures receptive vocabulary, conceptual knowledge, and semantic reasoning, allowing you to determine whether a student has the language foundation necessary for comprehension. |

together with other data, its unexpectedness; the TOD-C subtests provide subtype-specific evidence across phonological, orthographic, and efficiency domains; and the FAR subtests help rule out alternative explanations by assessing phonemic awareness, rapid naming, morphology, and receptive language. Together, these subtests can form a nonredundant, multidimensional battery that can support diagnostic decision-making for an SLD in reading within a PSW DD/C framework and support precise subtype classification.

The flowchart in Figure 5.1 demonstrates how these subtests can be used flexibly and efficiently in practice. Because the diagnostic pathway depends on the student's performance at each step, the flowchart shows that not all 17 subtests are necessary in every case; instead, the evaluation can be streamlined by selecting only the measures needed to answer the referral question and resolve diagnostic uncertainty.

After the decision pathway in Figure 5.1 is followed and the evaluation is tailored based on the student's performance on the achievement anchors, the next step is to interpret the pattern of results that emerges from the selected subtests. These interpretive patterns, illustrated in Table 5.8, allow the examiner to translate score combinations into clear diagnostic conclusions, linking specific constellations of strengths and

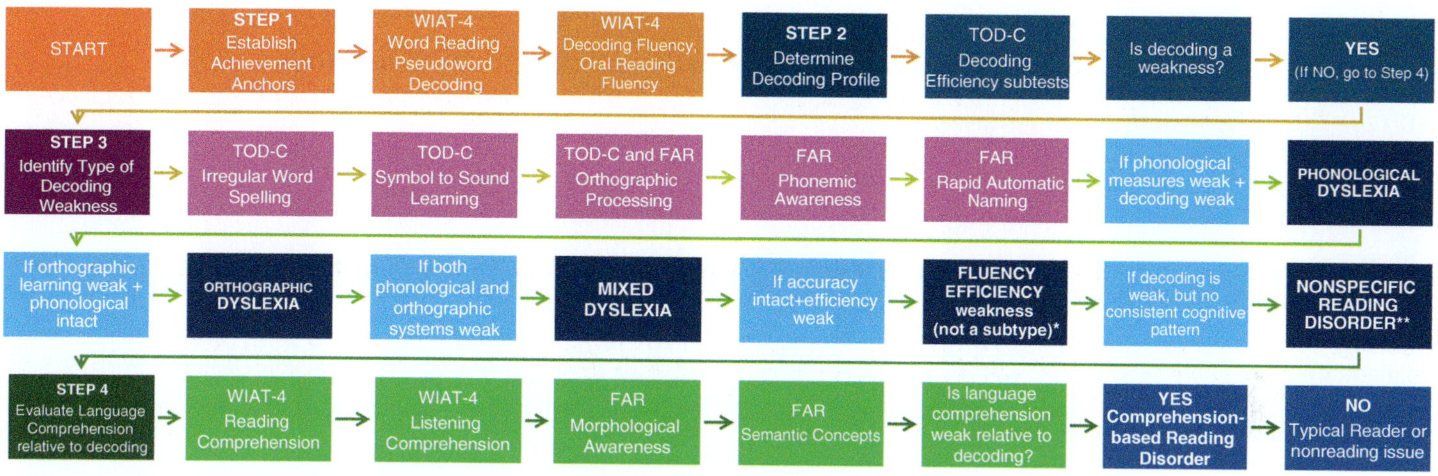


*May reflect RAN-based efficiency deficits without phonological or orthographic impairment.
**Use when decoding is weak but no coherent mechanism cluster emerges.
**Note:** For Step 2, Accuracy = WIAT-4 Word Reading and Pseudoword Decoding; Efficiency = WIAT-4 Oral Reading Fluency and TOD-C Decoding Efficiency. RAN supports subtype differentiation but does not define it. Regarding Mixed Dyslexia, if both systems are weak, this means inconsistent, mixed, or unstable decoding patterns.

**FIGURE 5.1 Flowchart for Identifying Reading Disability Subtype**

**Table 5.8 Decision-Rule Matrix for Interpreting Patterns in a Diagnostic Reading XBA**

| Pattern of Scores | Interpretation | Subtype |
|---|---|---|
| Weak phonological awareness + possible weak phonological memory + weak phonological automaticity + weak pseudoword decoding | Core phonological deficit; impaired phonological decoding | Phonological Dyslexia |
| Weak sight-word acquisition + possible weak paired-associate learning + weak orthographic processing + intact phonological measures | Orthographic learning deficit; inefficient orthographic mapping | Surface/ Orthographic Dyslexia |
| Weak phonological measures + weak orthographic learning + weak decoding across real words and pseudowords | Dual-system impairment; broad decoding weakness | Mixed Dyslexia |
| Strong decoding accuracy + weak listening comprehension + weak reasoning + weak morphological awareness | Language-based comprehension deficit; decoding intact | Comprehension-Based Reading Disorder |
| Weak reading efficiency + intact accuracy + weak phonological automaticity | Efficiency-based reading weakness; may reflect RAN/processing speed or attentional factors and may co-occur with dyslexia or ADHD | Fluency/Efficiency Weakness (not a primary dyslexia subtype) |
| Weak achievement anchors + mixed cognitive profile | General reading delay; not subtype-specific | Nonspecific Reading Disorder |
| All systems intact | No reading disorder identified | Typical Reader |

weaknesses to the four major dyslexia subtypes (phonological, orthographic, mixed, and comprehension-based) and related reading profiles. While the flowchart guides selection of which subtests to administer, the table clarifies what the resulting patterns mean, ensuring that practitioners can move from data collection to accurate, defensible diagnostic decisions with confidence and consistency.

The flowchart and pattern-interpretation matrix are grounded in well-established principles of reading science, including the Simple View of Reading, the dual-component model of word reading, subtype-specific cognitive profiles, and the distinction between accuracy and efficiency. To support practitioners in defending their diagnostic decisions with research, Rapid Reference 5.3 summarizes the key empirical findings underlying each decision rule and subtype pattern. This rapid reference links the assessment framework directly to the scientific literature, providing the evidentiary foundation for interpreting test data and communicating diagnostic conclusions.

## Rapid Reference 5.3

### Research Foundations for the Reading Subtype Decision Rules

**1. Core Principles Underlying the Framework**

**Simple View of Reading**
Reading comprehension reflects the interaction of decoding and language comprehension.
**Foundational:** Gough and Tunmer (1986), Hoover and Gough (1990)

**Recent:**

- Nation (2019)—updated evidence on poor comprehenders
- Castles et al. (2018)—modern synthesis of reading acquisition
- Assessment caveat: instructional history, response to intervention, oral language profile, and comorbid conditions should be considered when applying the Simple View to individual cases.

**Dual-Component Model of Word Reading**
Word reading depends on phonological decoding and orthographic learning.
**Foundational:** Castles and Coltheart (1993), Share (1995)

**Recent:**

- Castles et al. (2018)—large-scale review of decoding + orthography
- Treiman (2018)—updated evidence on spelling, orthotactics, and word learning
- Ouellette and Sénéchal (2021)—orthographic learning mechanisms in children

**Subtype-Specific Cognitive Profiles**
Distinct dyslexia subtypes arise from specific cognitive weaknesses.
**Foundational:** Pennington (2006), Snowling (2001)

**Recent:**

- Peterson et al. (2014)—updated multiple-deficit model
- Elliott and Grigorenko (2014)—subtype validity and cognitive markers
- van Bergen et al. (2020)—genetic and cognitive heterogeneity in dyslexia

**Accuracy Versus Efficiency**
Accuracy and fluency/automaticity are separable dimensions.
**Foundational:** Wolf and Bowers (1999), Wolf and Katzir-Cohen (2001)

**Recent:**

- Norton and Wolf (2012)—updated RAN/fluency evidence
- Kim (2020)—componential model of reading fluency
- Torgesen (2020)—fluency as a distinct intervention target

**2. Decision Rules for Dyslexia Subtypes**

**Phonological Dyslexia**
Hallmark indicators: weak phonemic awareness and phonological processing, weak phonological memory, weak automaticity, and weak pseudoword decoding.
**Foundational:** Hulme and Snowling (2016), Melby-Lervåg et al. (2012), Wagner and Torgesen (1987)

**Recent:**

- Snowling and Hulme (2020)—updated phonological deficit evidence
- van der Kleij et al. (2019)—phonological decoding as core marker
- Elliott and Grigorenko (2014)—phonological subtype validity

**Surface/Orthographic Dyslexia**
Hallmark indicators: weak orthographic learning, weak paired associative learning, weak orthographic processing, intact phonology.
**Foundational:** Castles and Coltheart (1993), Hulme et al. (2007), Share (1995), Treiman and Kessler (2014)

**Recent:**

- Ouellette and Sénéchal (2021)—orthographic learning mechanisms
- Wang et al. (2021)—irregular word reading and orthographic deficits
- Treiman (2018)—updated orthotactic and spelling research

**Mixed Dyslexia**
Hallmark indicators: dual phonological + orthographic weakness.
**Foundational:** Pennington (2006), Vellutino et al. (2004), Ziegler and Goswami (2005)

**Recent:**

- van Bergen et al. (2020)—heterogeneity and dual-deficit profiles
- Peterson et al. (2014)—multiple-deficit model
- Elliott and Grigorenko (2014)—mixed profiles in practice

**3. Decision Rules for Nondyslexia Reading Profiles**

**Comprehension-Based Reading Disorder**
Hallmark indicators: strong decoding + weak listening comprehension.
**Foundational:** Cain and Oakhill (2022); Catts et al. (2006)

**Recent:**

- Nation (2019)—updated review of poor comprehenders
- Kim (2020)—language comprehension as a distinct reading component
- Language and Reading Research Consortium (2015)—comprehension pathways

**Fluency/Efficiency Weakness (Not a Subtype)**
Hallmark indicators: intact accuracy + weak efficiency + weak automaticity.
**Foundational:** Fuchs et al. (2001), Norton and Wolf (2012), Wolf and Bowers (1999)

**Recent:**

- Kim (2020)—fluency as a multicomponent construct
- Torgesen (2020)—fluency intervention and efficiency deficits
- Fuchs et al. (2018)—fluency as a predictor of comprehension
- Requires assessment of RAN and processing speed/attention to distinguish true efficiency deficits from phonological or orthographic weaknesses.

**Nonspecific Reading Disorder**
Hallmark indicators: decoding weakness + inconsistent cognitive pattern.
**Foundational:** Fletcher et al. (2019), Pennington (2006)
**Recent:**

- van Bergen et al. (2020)—heterogeneity in reading disorders
- Elliott and Grigorenko (2014)—diagnostic ambiguity and mixed profiles
- Peterson et al. (2014)—multiple-deficit model

**Minimum Data Checklist for Reading Subtype Diagnosis**

☐ **Minimum data required: Achievement anchors** (word reading, pseudoword decoding, decoding/decoding fluency, oral/silent reading fluency, reading comprehension) + **at least two converging cognitive processing indicators** relevant to the suspected subtype.

☐ **Timed processing measures: RAN (letters/digits/objects), a timed decoding measure, and a phonological memory test** whenever efficiency or phonological mechanisms are in question.

☐ **Instructional history and RTI:** Document quality, duration, and intensity of instruction and prior intervention response; use this to judge unexpectedness of underachievement.

☐ **Rule-outs and comorbidity screen:** Document hearing/vision, primary language status, ADHD/language disorder screening, and working memory/processing speed measures.

☐ **Decision threshold:** Require **converging evidence** (e.g., achievement anchor + two or more cognitive processing indicators) and corroborating classroom/RTI data before assigning a subtype.

## READING CASE STUDIES

With this foundation in place, the following two case studies illustrate how the same integrated assessment system can reveal very different underlying reading profiles. The first case (Aiden) demonstrates a classic pattern of phonological dyslexia, in which weaknesses in phonological awareness, phonological memory, and decoding accuracy drive the student's reading difficulties. The second case (Maya) highlights orthographic dyslexia, in which phonological skills are relatively intact but orthographic learning, sight-word acquisition, and spelling-pattern consolidation break down. Together, these cases show that the XBA and DD/C methods not only help identify that a student is struggling but also clarify why, thereby supporting subtype classification and targeted intervention planning.

### Initial Screening for Intact Overall Ability to Think and Reason

Before applying the DD/C method to determine whether a student's academic weaknesses are unexpected or whether a domain-specific cognitive weakness is present, it is important to evaluate whether the student demonstrates at least average ability to think and reason. In both cases presented here, parents and teachers consistently described the students as *bright*, *intellectually curious*, and *capable learners* who performed well in most academic areas, except reading. These reports, combined with strong classroom engagement and age-appropriate reasoning behaviors, suggested that a full cognitive battery was unnecessary. Instead, a brief, targeted screening was used to evaluate alignment with teacher and parent reports and observations.

To meet this requirement efficiently and with strong ecological validity, each case study begins with two TOD-C subtests—Picture Vocabulary (*Gc*) and Picture Analogies (*Gf*). Together, these subtests provide a Vocabulary and Reasoning Composite. Results are included in Tables 5.9 (for Aiden) and 5.10 (for Maya; see Appendix 5.A at the end of this chapter for Maya's full case) along with their CogAT (Lohman & Latkin, 2021) standard age score (SAS) from the educational school records. Ecological manifestations are also included. These manifestations are observable classroom behaviors that reflect age-appropriate reasoning, problem solving, concept formation, and flexible thinking. When psychometric indicators and ecological manifestations converge, they provide clear and defensible confirmation that the student meets the DD/C criterion of at least average ability to think and reason.

**Table 5.9 Cognitive Screening for at Least Average Cognitive Ability (Aiden)**

| Measure | Standard Score | Interpretation | Ecological Manifestations of At Least Average Ability to Think and Reason |
|---|---|---|---|
| CogAT Verbal SAS | 108 | Age-appropriate verbal reasoning | Uses precise language; grasps new concepts with typical exposure; explains ideas clearly; follows multistep directions; strong oral comprehension despite reading struggles |
| CogAT Quantitative SAS | 110 | Age-appropriate quantitative reasoning | Recognizes numerical patterns; reasons through multistep math tasks; selects efficient strategies; adjusts approach when needed |
| CogAT Nonverbal SAS | 112 | Age-appropriate figural/spatial reasoning | Understands diagrams and visual models; identifies patterns in puzzles; organizes visual information effectively |
| CogAT Composite SAS | 112 | At least average ability to think and reason | Demonstrates balanced reasoning across modalities; engages effectively in classroom problem solving |
| TOD-C Picture Vocabulary (*Gc*) | 104 | Age-appropriate word knowledge and concept formation | Uses grade-level vocabulary; expresses ideas clearly; connects new concepts to prior knowledge |
| TOD-C Picture Analogies (*Gf*) | 109 | Age-appropriate nonverbal reasoning and pattern recognition | Approaches tasks with a plan; shifts strategies when needed; makes logical connections during class discussions |
| **TOD-C Vocabulary and Reasoning Composite** | **107** | At least average ability to think and reason | |

*Note:* The results in this table show that Aiden demonstrates at least average ability to think and reason, supported by CogAT composites, TOD-C subtests, and behavioral manifestations that provide ecological validity for the test scores. This satisfies the DD/C criterion for intact reasoning ability.

**Table 5.10 Cognitive Screening for at Least Average Cognitive Ability (Maya)**

| Measure | Standard Score | Interpretation | Ecological Manifestations of At Least Average Ability to Think and Reason |
|---|---|---|---|
| CogAT Verbal SAS | 117 | Strong verbal reasoning | Uses sophisticated vocabulary; understands abstract ideas; summarizes information accurately; follows complex oral directions |
| CogAT Quantitative SAS | 116 | Strong quantitative reasoning | Identifies numerical relationships; reasons flexibly in math; evaluates multiple solution paths |
| CogAT Nonverbal SAS | 104 | Age-appropriate figural/spatial reasoning | Interprets charts and diagrams accurately; identifies relationships among ideas; organizes visual information efficiently |
| **CogAT Composite SAS** | **114** | At least average ability to think and reason | Demonstrates balanced reasoning across modalities; engages deeply in classroom learning |
| TOD-C Picture Vocabulary (*Gc*) | 115 | Strong verbal knowledge and conceptual understanding | Connects new content to prior knowledge; articulates ideas clearly; grasps nuanced language |
| TOD-C Picture Analogies (*Gf*) | 110 | Age-appropriate nonverbal reasoning and visual-spatial problem solving | Approaches multistep tasks logically; demonstrates flexible thinking; evaluates multiple strategies |
| **TOD-C Vocabulary and Reasoning Composite** | **114** | At least average ability to think and reason | |

*Note:* The results in this table show that Maya demonstrates at least average ability to think and reason, supported by CogAT composites, the TOD-C composite, and behavioral manifestations that provide ecological validity for the test scores. This satisfies the DD/C criterion for intact reasoning ability.

## CASE STUDY: APPLYING A 15-SUBTEST DIAGNOSTIC READING BATTERY TO AIDEN

**Student:** Aiden, age 9 (Grade 3)
**Teacher Report:** Aiden has difficulty *getting the words off the page*, suggesting possible accuracy, decoding, or fluency problems.
**Referral Question:** Why is Aiden struggling with reading, and does he meet the criteria for dyslexia?
**Background:** Average classroom performance in math and writing; persistent difficulty with reading accuracy and fluency; strong oral vocabulary.

### Step 1: Achievement Anchors (WIAT-4)

These establish the baseline and determine whether a reading weakness is present.

| Subtest | Standard Score | Interpretation |
|---|---|---|
| Word Reading | 82 | Weak real-word accuracy |
| Pseudoword Decoding | 78 | Weak phonological decoding |
| Decoding Fluency | 75 | Slow, effortful decoding; reduced automaticity |
| Oral Reading Fluency | 78 | Weak rate + accuracy; fluency vulnerability |
| Reading Comprehension | 80 | Likely depressed by decoding weakness |

**Conclusion:** Aiden demonstrates a decoding weakness with secondary impairment in fluency.
**Debiasing Note:** At this stage, it is important to avoid assuming a phonological subtype simply because decoding is weak.
**Next Step:** Determine *why* decoding is weak.

### Step 2: TOD-C Decoding Efficiency

These subtests clarify the nature of the decoding weakness.

| Subtest | Standard Score | Interpretation |
|---|---|---|
| Rapid Pseudoword Reading | 67 | Slow, effortful phonological decoding; reduced automaticity |
| Rapid Irregular Word Reading | 83 | Real-word accuracy weakness; inefficient access to stored word forms |

**Conclusion:** Aiden appears to have a decoding-based reading disorder driven by weak phonological decoding and reduced decoding fluency.
**Debiasing Note:** Although the pattern suggests a phonological weakness, the evaluator should resist premature closure. Orthographic learning must still be examined to rule out a mixed or orthographic profile.
**Next Step:** Determine whether the weakness is phonological, orthographic, or mixed.

### Step 3: TOD-C Orthographic Learning Indicators

| Subtest | Standard Score | Interpretation |
|---|---|---|
| Irregular Word Spelling | 95 | Stored irregular word knowledge intact |
| Letter and Word Choice | 98 | Orthographic pattern recognition intact |

**Conclusion:** The orthographic system is intact.
**Debiasing Note:** The intact orthographic indicators help guard against confirmation bias. Even though the initial hypothesis leaned toward a phonological explanation, the data must be allowed to contradict or refine it.
**Next Step:** Evaluate the phonological system to determine the subtype.

### Step 4: FAR Phonological Processing and Automaticity

| Subtest | Standard Score | Interpretation |
|---|---|---|
| Phonemic Awareness | 77 | Weak manipulation and segmentation |
| Rapid Automatic Naming | 74 | Slow access to phonological codes |

**Conclusion:** Clear phonological system weakness.
**Debiasing Note:** The phonological weakness is now supported by converging evidence across multiple measures. DD/C emphasizes using multiple indicators, when necessary, to reduce the risk of overinterpreting any single score.
**Subtype Emerging:** Phonological Dyslexia.
**Next Step:** Evaluate language comprehension relative to decoding.

### Step 5: FAR Morphology + Language

| Subtest | Standard Score | Interpretation |
|---|---|---|
| Morphological Processing | 99 | Meaning-based decoding intact |
| Semantic Concepts | 104 | Language comprehension intact |

**Conclusion:** No evidence of a comprehension-based disorder.
**Subtype Supported:** Phonological Dyslexia.

### Step 6: WIAT-4 Comprehension Pair (to Determine Simple View Alignment)

| Subtest | Standard Score | Interpretation |
|---|---|---|
| Reading Comprehension | 80 | Weak comprehension |
| Listening Comprehension | 106 | Language comprehension intact |

**Interpretation:** Reading comprehension is low because decoding is weak, not because language comprehension is impaired. This aligns with Phonological Dyslexia.
**Debiasing Note:** The Simple View alignment prevents misattributing comprehension weaknesses to language deficits when decoding is the limiting factor. This step protects against the common bias of misclassifying a decoding-based comprehension weakness as a language-based one.

### Final Diagnostic Picture

**Subtype: Phonological Dyslexia**

**Why:**

- Weak phonological awareness
- Weak phonological automaticity
- Weak pseudoword decoding
- Weak decoding efficiency
- Intact orthographic learning
- Intact language comprehension

**Debiasing Note:** The subtype conclusion is based on a structured, stepwise evaluation rather than intuitive pattern recognition. Each decision point was anchored in objective data, reducing the influence of expectancy bias.

### X-BASS PSW Analysis Supports a Specific Learning Disability in Basic Reading Skills (Phonological Dyslexia)

Aiden's test findings align closely with the DD/C results generated in X-BASS, as illustrated in Figure 5.2. His overall cognitive profile reflects at least average general ability, as indicated by an FCC of 107 (an aggregate of *Gf* and *Gc*). Within this context of average overall ability, Aiden shows weaknesses in pseudoword decoding and decoding fluency, as well as cognitive weaknesses in phonological processing (*Ga*) and rapid automatic naming (*Gr*). The differences between Aiden's specific academic and cognitive weaknesses and the predicted score of 104 (based on his FCC) are unusual, occurring in only about 5% of the population, indicating unexpected underachievement and domain-specific cognitive weaknesses, respectively. The empirical relationship between his cognitive (*Ga*) and academic (Pseudoword Decoding) weaknesses (shown in Figure 5.2) is strong and demonstrates a below-average aptitude-achievement consistency, meaning that the cognitive weakness is a plausible explanation for the academic weakness. There is also an empirically strong relationship between Aiden's *Gr* and decoding fluency. Together, these findings meet the DD/C criteria and provide strong support for a pattern of strengths and weaknesses that aligns with the SLD construct.

### What This Means for Aiden

Aiden struggles because he cannot efficiently access, store, and manipulate phonological information. His orthographic system is ready to learn, but phonological weaknesses prevent him from building a stable sight-word lexicon and developing fluent, automatic reading.

### Intervention Implications Based on the Identified Pathway

**Subtype Identified:** *Phonological Dyslexia*

**What This Means Mechanistically**

Aiden's reading difficulty is not caused by weak comprehension, vocabulary, or orthographic learning. His profile shows intact language comprehension and intact orthographic learning. The breakdown occurs in a very specific place:

**Mechanism:** Weak phonological processing disrupts Aiden's ability to decode unfamiliar words.

This mechanism affects:

- **Phoneme awareness** (manipulating sounds)
- **Phonological access** (rapid retrieval of phonological codes)
- **Phonological decoding** (mapping graphemes to phonemes)
- **Decoding efficiency** (accuracy + automaticity)

This is why Aiden struggles with

- nonsense words or pseudowords
- unfamiliar real words
- multisyllabic decoding
- decoding accuracy and fluency

but can read irregular words, sight words, and orthographically familiar words better than expected.

### Why This Mechanism Produces Aiden's Pattern

When phonological processing is weak:

- decoding becomes slow and error-prone
- orthographic learning is limited because accurate decoding is needed to store word forms
- fluency cannot develop because decoding is effortful
- comprehension suffers only when decoding breaks down

This is the classic profile of phonological dyslexia.

**CAUTION**

The FCC for Aiden is based on two TOD-C subtests—Picture Vocabulary (*Gc*) and Picture Analogies (*Gf*)—as shown in Table 5.9. These are the only two CHC broad abilities that can generate an FCC from just two indicators. In all other cases (i.e., any other CHC combination), at least three—and sometimes four—strengths are required. The FCC calculation depends on *which* CHC domains are marked as strengths and *how many*, as described in Appendix M.

As discussed in Chapter 4, a single subtest should not be used to represent a CHC cognitive ability. A subtest score in the *weakness range* should *never* be used alone for this purpose. A single average-or-higher subtest score may be used, but *only when supported by ample converging data*. In Aiden's case, the two TOD-C subtests did not stand alone. His FCC of 107 is supported by multiple indicators showing at least average ability to think and reason relative to peers. On the SLD Evidence tab in X-BASS, all of Aiden's academic strengths were automatically populated as *supporting data*, demonstrating expected academic performance (in certain areas) given his FCC. Additional evidence, including his CogAT scores, was entered directly into the supporting-data section (Figure 5.3), providing strong support for his FCC. Appendix N, *Manifestations of at Least Average Ability to Think and Reason*, may also be used to assist in determining the ecological validity of the FCC. To explore the ecological validity for Aiden's scores in *Gc* and *Gf*, see Appendix L, *Manifestations of Cognitive Strengths*.

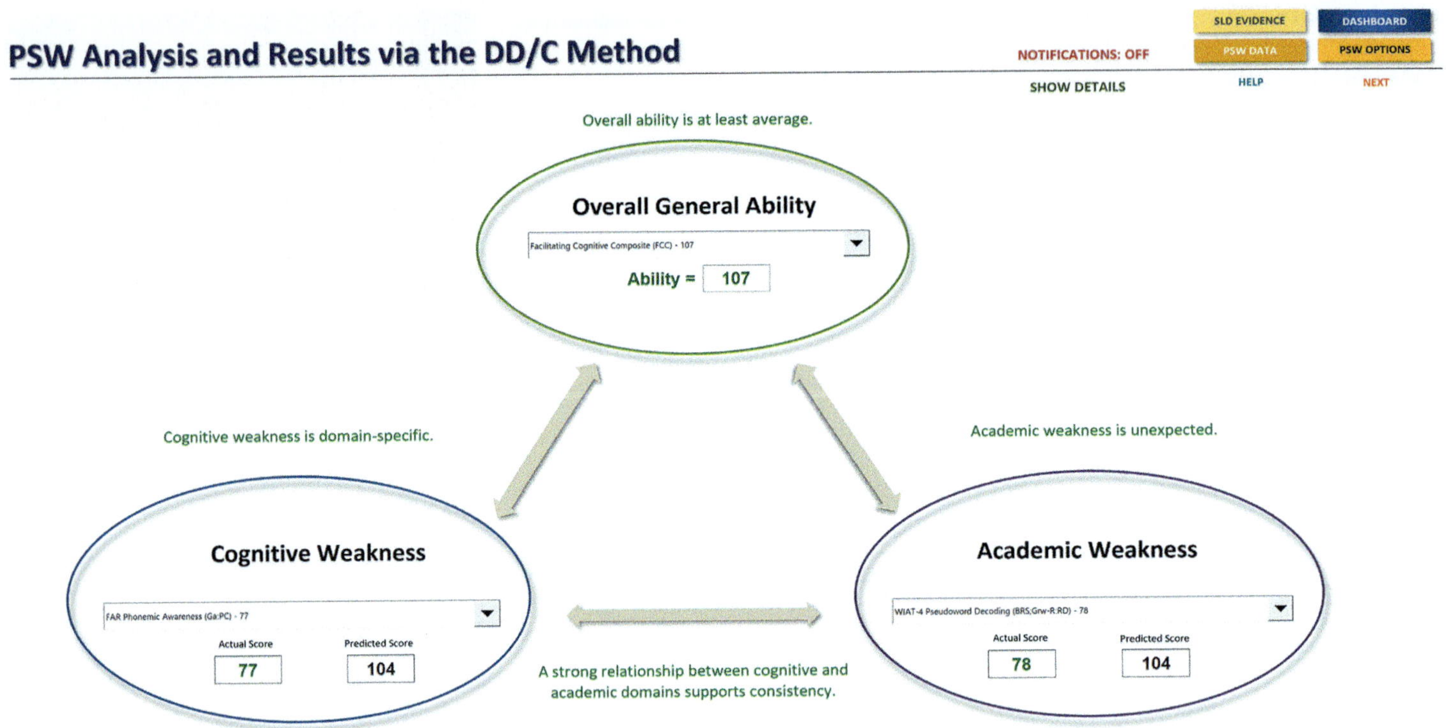


**FIGURE 5.2 PSW Analysis Meeting DD/C Criteria**

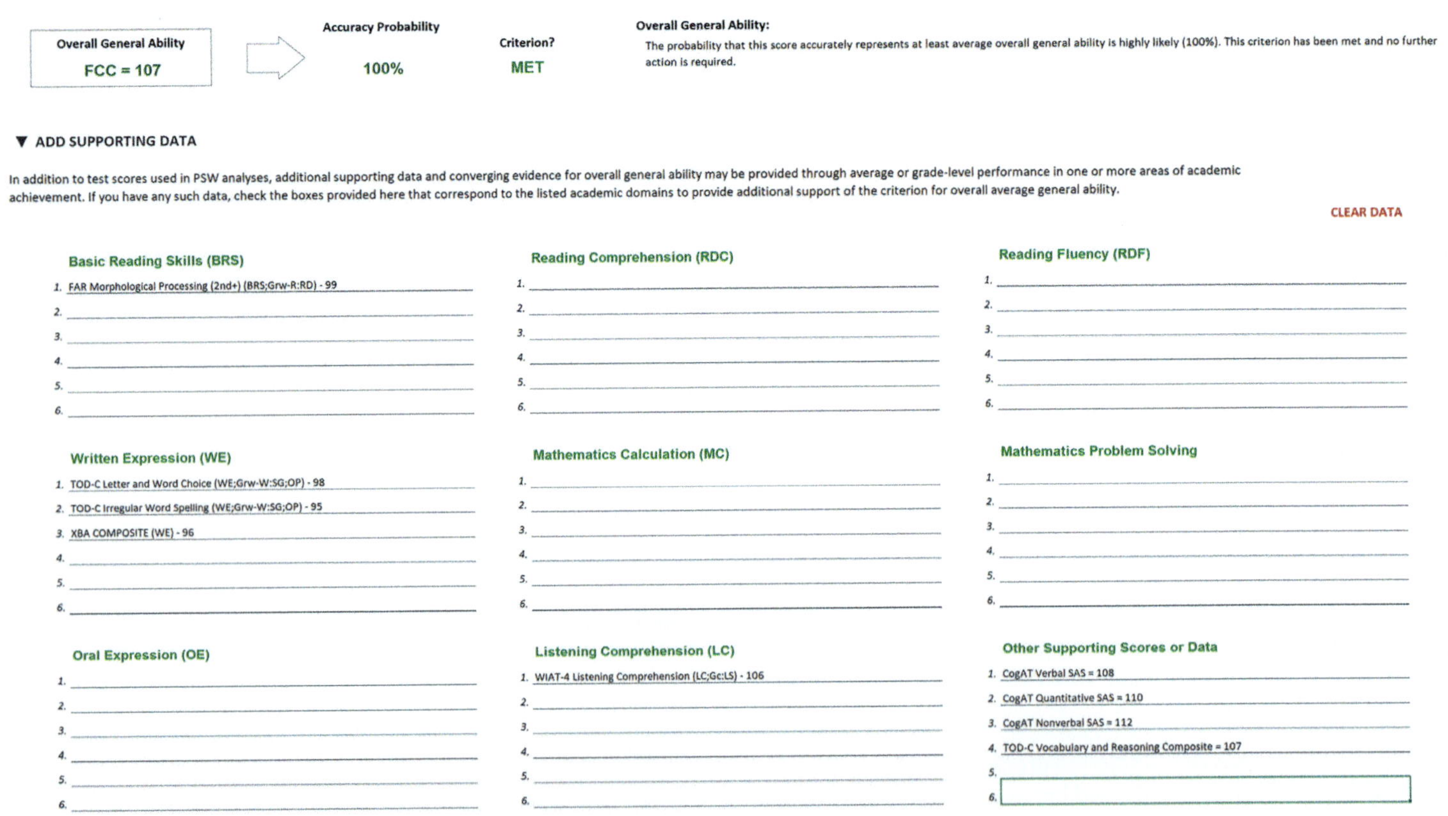


**FIGURE 5.3 Adding Supporting Data on the SLD Evidence Tab**

### What Aiden Needs Instructionally

Aiden needs interventions that:

- strengthen phoneme awareness
- strengthen phoneme–grapheme mapping
- build decoding accuracy
- support orthographic mapping through accurate decoding
- build fluency through controlled text

These are the **high-leverage practices** for the phonological pathway.

> **DON'T FORGET**
>
> High-leverage practices are instructional actions that produce the greatest learning gains because they directly target the underlying mechanism of difficulty. They are efficient, evidence-supported practices that offer a disproportionately large impact relative to the time and effort required to implement them.

### High-Leverage Practices for Phonological Dyslexia

#### A. Explicit, Systematic Phonics Instruction

Direct teaching of:

- phoneme–grapheme correspondences
- blending and segmenting
- decoding routines
- multisyllabic strategies

This is the single most effective intervention for phonological dyslexia.

#### B. Phoneme Manipulation Tasks

Activities such as:

- deleting phonemes
- substituting phonemes
- reversing phonemes
- segmenting and blending

These strengthen the underlying phonological representations needed for decoding.

#### C. Decodable Text Practice

Aiden needs controlled texts that:

- match the phonics patterns he is learning
- allow repeated practice
- support orthographic mapping

This builds accuracy and automaticity.

#### D. Repeated Reading for Fluency

Once decoding accuracy improves, fluency practice:

- increases automaticity
- reduces cognitive load
- supports comprehension

#### E. Immediate, Corrective Feedback

Feedback should be:

- specific
- brief
- tied to the decoding routine

This helps Aiden internalize the correct patterns.

### What Aiden Does *Not* Need

- comprehension interventions
- vocabulary instruction as the primary focus
- fluency drills without decoding support
- guessing strategies
- leveled readers that do not align with phonics patterns

These do not address the mechanism.

**Evidence Base**

- Phonological processing is the core deficit in phonological dyslexia (Castles, et al., 2018; Snowling & Hulme, 2020).
- Phoneme awareness + phonics instruction improves decoding (Melby-Lervåg et al., 2012).
- Orthographic learning depends on accurate decoding (Share, 1995).
- Decodable text supports orthographic mapping (Ehri, 2020).
- Fluency improves only after decoding accuracy is established (Torgesen, 2020).

Remember to go to Appendix 5.A at the end of the chapter for Maya's reading case study emphasizing the orthographic pathway. Although space limitations prevent the inclusion of additional full reading case studies, the remaining reading subtypes are equally important for practitioners to recognize and support. To maintain completeness and parallel structure across domains, Rapid References 5.4 and 5.5 summarize the core mechanisms and high-leverage instructional practices for the two reading pathways that are not illustrated in full cases. These concise guides allow practitioners to connect the diagnostic logic in the flowchart and decision rules to the instructional actions most strongly supported by research.

## *Rapid Reference 5.4*

### Mixed Dyslexia (Phonological + Orthographic Pathways)

**Mechanism**

A combined breakdown in **phonological decoding** *and* **orthographic learning** disrupts the student's ability to read both unfamiliar and familiar words.

This is the most severe and instructionally complex reading subtype.

**Common Indicators**

- Weak decoding of unfamiliar words
- Weak recognition of irregular and high-frequency words
- Slow, effortful reading
- Limited orthographic mapping
- Poor spelling (phonetic + pattern errors)
- Fluency far below expectations
- Comprehension breakdown due to decoding load

**High-Leverage Practices**

- **Explicit, systematic phonics instruction** (phoneme–grapheme mapping, blending, decoding routines)
- **Phoneme manipulation tasks** (segmenting, deleting, substituting)
- **Orthographic pattern instruction** (rimes, syllable types, spelling rules)
- **Integrated reading–spelling instruction** (read → spell → write → analyze)
- **Decodable text practice** aligned with phonics scope and sequence
- **Repeated reading** *after* decoding accuracy improves
- **Morphological instruction** to support multisyllabic decoding and spelling

**What Not to Do**

- Fluency drills before decoding accuracy is established
- Leveled readers that do not align with phonics patterns
- Comprehension-only interventions
- Memorization-only sight-word lists

**Evidence Base**

Mixed dyslexia reflects combined phonological and orthographic deficits (Castles et al., 2018).
Orthographic learning depends on accurate decoding (Share, 1995).
Integrated phonics + spelling instruction improves both decoding and encoding (Ehri, 2020).

## Rapid Reference 5.5

### Language-Comprehension/Reading Comprehension LD (Language Pathway)

**Mechanism**

A breakdown in **oral language comprehension** disrupts the student's ability to construct meaning from text, even when decoding is adequate.

This subtype reflects weaknesses in **vocabulary, syntax, inferencing, background knowledge, and discourse comprehension**.

**Common Indicators**

- Adequate decoding and word reading
- Weak listening comprehension
- Difficulty answering inferential questions
- Limited vocabulary
- Difficulty integrating information across sentences or paragraphs
- Trouble summarizing or identifying main ideas
- Comprehension collapses as text becomes more complex

**High-Leverage Practices**

- **Explicit vocabulary instruction** (morphology, multiple meanings, academic vocabulary)
- **Oral language intervention** (narrative retell, sentence expansion, syntax instruction)
- **Inferencing instruction** (predicting, explaining, connecting ideas)
- **Text-structure instruction** (narrative, informational, argument structures)
- **Background knowledge activation** (preteaching concepts, schema building)
- **Reciprocal teaching** (summarizing, questioning, clarifying, predicting)
- **Graphic organizers** to support comprehension monitoring

**What Not to Do**

- Phonics-only interventions
- Fluency drills as the primary approach
- Isolated comprehension questions without strategy instruction
- Assuming comprehension will improve once decoding improves

**Evidence Base**

Reading comprehension depends on both decoding and language comprehension (Gough & Tunmer, 1986).
Language-based interventions improve comprehension outcomes (Catts et al., 2015; Snow, 2010).
Vocabulary, syntax, and inferencing instruction are high-leverage practices for comprehension LD (Nation, 2019).

The TOD-C identifies which subtype best fits the student's pattern of strengths and weaknesses, while the FAR clarifies why that subtype emerged and which cognitive-linguistic processes require intervention. This integrated approach supports accurate classification or diagnosis, reduces interpretive ambiguity, and ensures that instructional recommendations are both targeted and defensible. For practitioners seeking a comprehensive, evidence-based evaluation of reading disorders, selected subtests from the TOD-C, FAR, and one of the achievement batteries listed in Table 5.7 provide a complete and coherent diagnostic reading battery.

Taken together, the cross-battery analysis and the comparison of specialized dyslexia tools underscore a central theme of this book: no single assessment provides all the information needed to fully understand a student's reading profile. The major achievement batteries offer strong coverage of the four core reading components, but they vary in depth and leave important diagnostic gaps, particularly in orthographic learning, decoding efficiency, and the cognitive-linguistic processes that support comprehension. Instruments such as the TOD-C and FAR extend beyond traditional achievement testing by clarifying the underlying mechanisms of reading breakdown and, when needed, distinguishing among phonological, orthographic, mixed, and comprehension-based reading disorders. By integrating data across these tools, practitioners can move beyond surface-level performance and develop a precise, evidence-based understanding of both what a student can do and why they struggle, ensuring that instructional decisions are targeted, defensible, and aligned with the science of reading.

The reading case presented in this chapter also serves an additional purpose: to demonstrate how students with significant reading difficulties can still show at least average ability to think and reason. The accompanying reasoning tables were included intentionally to help practitioners avoid a common interpretive error—mistaking decoding or language-based weaknesses for global cognitive impairment. Because this point is now clearly established through the reading examples, the subsequent math and writing cases focus more narrowly on identifying subtypes and linking them to intervention, without repeating the reasoning-ability tables. This keeps the chapter streamlined while preserving the diagnostic logic practitioners need. With this foundation in place, we now turn to mathematics, where three distinct pathways—procedural, retrieval, and conceptual—mirror the same mechanism-driven approach used in reading.

### Caveats and Context: Math

Research on mathematical learning difficulties (MLD) spans multiple disciplines, including mathematics education, cognitive psychology, developmental psychology, and neuroscience. Each field brings its own terminology, theoretical assumptions, and classification systems, resulting in a fragmented and often inconsistent literature. As Fletcher et al. (2007) and others have noted, there is still no consensus on the definition, operational criteria, or prevalence of MLD (Lanfranchi et al., 2008; Mazzocco, 2008). This lack of agreement reflects the inherent complexity of mathematics itself, which encompasses diverse domains—arithmetic, problem solving, geometry, algebra, probability, statistics, and calculus—each drawing on different cognitive abilities.

Although foundational number systems such as the object tracking system (OTS) and approximate number system (ANS) play important roles in early numerical cognition (Brannon & Roitman, 2003; Halberda & Feigenson, 2008; Piazza, 2010; Xu, 2003), deficits in these systems alone cannot account for the full range of mathematical difficulties observed in practice. Competing hypotheses emphasize defective ANS, defective OTS, numerosity-coding deficits, access deficits, or multiple interacting deficits (Andersson & Östergren, 2012). These domain-specific explanations are complemented by substantial evidence that domain-general cognitive processes, such as working memory, long-term memory, executive functions, inhibition, and processing speed, play central roles in mathematical performance (Andersson, 2007; Fuchs & Fuchs, 2005; Geary, 2004; Swanson et al., 2008).

Classic subtype models, such as Geary's procedural, semantic memory, and spatial subtypes (Geary, 1994; Geary & Hoard, 2005), have been influential but are limited in their ability to capture the heterogeneity of real students. Many children do not fit neatly into a single subtype; instead, they exhibit mixed profiles that reflect combinations of domain-specific and domain-general weaknesses (Desoete, 2007). More recent multidimensional models attempt to integrate these perspectives by identifying broader cognitive domains, such as core number processing, memory, reasoning/executive functions, and visual-spatial processing, within which specific deficits may reside. However, these models remain in early stages of development, rely partly on clinical observation, and require further empirical validation.

Given these limitations, the subtypes described in this chapter should be understood as practical heuristics designed to support mechanism-aligned assessment and intervention. They are not intended to represent fixed neurobiological categories or definitive diagnostic classifications. The goal is to help practitioners identify the specific components, such as numerical, memory-related, executive, or visual-spatial, that contribute to a student's math difficulty, and to use that information to design or select targeted, strengths-based interventions that support both competence and motivation.

## DIAGNOSTIC XBA FOR MATH REFERRALS

Just as with reading, diagnostic assessment in mathematics begins with clarifying which component of math is breaking down. Rapid Reference 5.6 parallels the structure of the reading interview (Rapid Reference 5.2) by providing targeted questions practitioners can use to understand the nature of a student's math difficulty. The questions are organized into four core components of mathematical performance: math calculation, math fluency, math problem solving, and number sense/early numeracy. Identifying the component most affected helps practitioners select diagnostic subtests that are focused, efficient, and aligned with the referral concern.

### *Rapid Reference 5.6*

### Teacher Interview Questions to Identify the Type of Math Problem

**1. Math Calculation (procedures, algorithms, accuracy)**

- Does the student make **frequent errors** when performing written calculations?
- Do they struggle to remember or correctly apply **basic procedures** (e.g., regrouping, borrowing, long division)?
- Do they confuse **operation signs** or use the wrong operation?
- Do they have difficulty completing **multistep calculations** accurately?

**If yes → likely a math calculation problem.**

**2. Math Fluency (speed + accuracy with basic facts)**

- Does the student know basic math facts but retrieve them **very slowly**?
- Do they rely heavily on **counting strategies** (fingers, tally marks) instead of automatic recall?
- Does slow fact retrieval interfere with **more complex math tasks**?
- Do they struggle on **timed math tasks**, even when untimed accuracy is acceptable?

**If yes → likely a math fluency problem.**

**3. Math Problem Solving (reasoning, language, conceptual understanding)**

- Can the student compute accurately but **cannot solve word problems**?
- Do they struggle to **identify what the problem is asking**?
- Do they have difficulty **translating language into math operations**?
- Do they misunderstand **math vocabulary** (e.g., difference, quotient, fewer than)?
- Do they struggle with **multistep reasoning**?

**If yes → likely a math problem-solving weakness.**

**4. Number Sense/Early Numeracy (conceptual foundations)**

- Does the student struggle with **quantity concepts** (more/less, bigger/smaller)?
- Do they have difficulty **comparing numbers**, understanding place value, or estimating?
- Do they struggle to understand **how numbers relate to each other**?
- Do they have trouble with **mental math** or flexible thinking about numbers?

**If yes → likely a number sense weakness.**

**Optional Math "Short Cut" Question**
**"Does the student struggle more with doing the math, thinking about the math, or explaining the math?"**

- **Doing** → calculation or fluency
- **Thinking** → problem solving or number sense
- **Explaining** → conceptual understanding or language-based math issues

Once the presenting math concern has been clarified through teacher input, the next step—just as in reading—is to verify and refine these hypotheses using standardized assessment data. To support this process, the following tables organize commonly used achievement batteries according to the specific math components they measure. This structure helps practitioners determine when a single battery is sufficient and when cross-battery supplementation is required to fully understand the student's math profile.

The WIAT-4 provides strong coverage of core academic math skills, particularly in calculation, basic fact fluency, and applied problem solving (see Table 5.11). Its combination of Numerical Operations, the three Math Fluency subtests, and Math Problem Solving allows examiners to evaluate procedural accuracy, speeded fact retrieval, and conceptual reasoning within a curriculum-aligned framework. These subtests help determine whether a student's math difficulties stem from weaknesses in procedural knowledge, inefficient fact retrieval, or challenges with quantitative reasoning and language-based problem solving.

The WJ V ACH offers broad and well-balanced coverage of academic math performance, with excellent measures of procedural calculation (Calculation), strong applied reasoning and quantitative analysis (Applied Problems), and one of the most sensitive basic-fact fluency measures available (Math Facts Fluency) (see Table 5.12). Its combination of untimed calculation, timed fact retrieval, and conceptual problem solving

**Table 5.11 WIAT-4 Aligned to Four Math Components**

| Math Component | WIAT-4 Subtests | Notes |
|---|---|---|
| Math Calculation | Numerical Operations | Strong procedural calculation measure. |
| Math Fluency | Math Fluency—Addition; Math Fluency—Subtraction; Math Fluency—Multiplication | Covers all three basic operations; timed. |
| Math Problem Solving | Math Problem Solving | Strong applied reasoning and conceptual understanding. |
| Number Sense/ Early Numeracy | Early Number Concepts (if using Pre-K/Primary forms) | Limited number sense coverage in school-age forms. |

**Table 5.12 WJ V ACH Aligned to Four Math Components**

| Math Component | WJ V ACH Subtests | Notes |
|---|---|---|
| Math Calculation | Calculation | Strong procedural calculation measure. |
| Math Fluency | Math Facts Fluency | Timed basic facts across operations. |
| Math Problem Solving | Applied Problems; Math Problem Identification | Excellent applied quantitative reasoning in real-world contexts (*Gq*). Math Problem Identification measures error detection and meta-mathematical reasoning. Together, these two subtests provide both applied problem-solving and analytical reasoning about problem structure. |
| Number Sense/ Early Numeracy | **Number Sense** (Extended); **Magnitude Comparison** (Extended) | Magnitude Comparison is a speeded, noncomputational number sense screener; Number Sense covers foundational numerical knowledge. Strong dedicated coverage—a significant improvement over WJ IV. |

**Table 5.13 KTEA-3 Aligned to Four Math Components**

| Math Component | KTEA-3 Subtests | Notes |
|---|---|---|
| Math Calculation | Math Computation | Strong procedural calculation measure. |
| Math Fluency | Math Fluency | Single timed subtest covering addition, subtraction, multiplication, and division across items; yields one score. Contrast with WIAT-4, which yields three separate fluency subtest scores. |
| Math Problem Solving | Math Concepts & Applications | Excellent applied reasoning and conceptual math. |
| Number Sense/Early Numeracy | Math Concepts & Applications (partial) | No dedicated early numeracy subtest. |

allows examiners to evaluate both precision and efficiency, and to determine whether a student's math difficulties are rooted in procedural errors, slow retrieval, or weaknesses in quantitative reasoning.

The KTEA-3 offers a balanced set of academic math measures, with strong coverage of procedural calculation (Math Computation), a useful timed basic-facts composite (Math Fluency), and an excellent applied reasoning task (Math Concepts & Applications) (see Table 5.13). Together, these subtests allow examiners to evaluate accuracy, fact retrieval, and conceptual problem solving within a cohesive framework. The KTEA-3 is particularly strong in applied reasoning, where Math Concepts & Applications provides rich information about how students interpret quantitative relationships and apply math knowledge in real-world contexts.

The WIAT-4, WJ V ACH, and KTEA-3 are all strong academic math batteries for measuring curriculum-level performance, but none was designed for a comprehensive diagnostic math evaluation. Each lacks a dedicated number-sense/early-numeracy measure, has limited or no visual–spatial math tasks, has limited or no quantitative-language measures, and provides minimal coverage of working memory/executive processes that underlie multistep calculation and problem solving. Fluency sampling is restricted (basic-facts or a single composite) with little or no multioperation or integrated fluency and limited error analysis to clarify procedural versus conceptual breakdowns; some batteries also have limited cognitive-fluency measures (e.g., RAN-Quantity) and extended multistep quantitative reasoning. Therefore, while each of these batteries provide excellent anchor subtests for math, they need to be supplemented with targeted numeracy, orthogonal (nonoverlapping) cognitive-linguistic, visual-spatial, and processing speed/working memory measures to diagnose why math breaks down and to guide intervention.

The FAM provides comprehensive diagnostic coverage of the cognitive and linguistic processes that underlie math performance. Its subtests assess number sense, magnitude comparison, counting principles, quantitative language, visual–spatial reasoning, working memory, and fact retrieval—skills that are essential for understanding *why* a student struggles with calculation, fluency, or problem solving (see Table 5.14). The FAM is uniquely valuable for identifying the mechanisms that support math development, including conceptual number knowledge, procedural understanding, and the cognitive processes that contribute to efficient fact retrieval and multistep reasoning.

At the same time, the FAM was not designed to function as an academic math battery, and its structure reflects that purpose. It provides no curriculum-aligned calculation tasks, no timed math-fluency measures, and no applied problem-solving tasks that yield academic scores. The FAM does not assess multistep procedural skills such as long division or multidigit multiplication, nor does it include grade-level reasoning items in geometry, measurement, or data analysis. These omissions are not limitations of the instrument but rather reflect its intended purpose: to identify the cognitive and linguistic foundations of math performance and to explain why a student's math profile looks the way

**Table 5.14 FAM Aligned to Four Math Components**

| Math Component | FAM Subtests | FAM Index |
|---|---|---|
| Math Calculation | Sequences; Numeric Capacity; Addition Fluency; Subtraction Fluency; Multiplication Fluency; Division Fluency | Procedural; Verbal |
| Math Fluency | Rapid Number Naming; Addition Fluency; Subtraction Fluency; Multiplication Fluency; Division Fluency | Verbal |
| Math Problem Solving | Linguistic Math Concepts; Spatial Memory; Numeric Capacity; Perceptual Estimation | Verbal; Semantic; Procedural |
| Number Sense/Early Numeracy | Forward Number Count; Backward Number Count; Object Counting; Number Comparison; Addition Knowledge; Subtraction Knowledge | Procedural; Semantic |

**Table 5.15 The Best Subtests from the Achievement Batteries for the Four Components of Math**

| Math Component | Best Subtests (Across WIAT-4, WJ V ACH, KTEA-3) | Why They Are the Best |
|---|---|---|
| Math Calculation | WIAT-4 Numerical Operations; WJ V ACH Calculation; KTEA-3 Math Computation; FAM Written Computation subtests (Addition, Subtraction, Multiplication, Division) | Covers procedural accuracy and the cognitive processes that support calculation. |
| Math Fluency | WIAT-4 Math Fluency (Addition, Subtraction, Multiplication); WJ V ACH Math Facts Fluency; KTEA-3 Math Fluency; FAM Addition Fluency, Subtraction Fluency, Multiplication Fluency, Division Fluency; FAM Rapid Number Naming | Combines timed fact retrieval, automaticity, and processing-speed contributors. |
| Math Problem Solving | WIAT-4 Math Problem Solving; WJ V ACH Applied Problems; WJ V ACH Math Problem Identification; KTEA-3 Math Concepts & Applications; FAM Linguistic Math Concepts; FAM Spatial Memory; FAM Perceptual Estimation | Covers applied problem solving, conceptual reasoning, quantitative language, visuospatial reasoning, and meta-mathematical error detection—together capturing the full range of why problem solving breaks down. |
| Number Sense/ Early Numeracy | WIAT-4 early number concepts (younger forms); FAM Number Knowledge; Forward Number Count; Backward Number Count; Object Counting; Number Comparison; WJ V ACH Number Sense (Extended); WJ V ACH Magnitude Comparison (Extended) | Provides the most comprehensive coverage of foundational numeracy across counting, magnitude comparison, number knowledge, and perceptual estimation. Note: WJ V Number Sense and Magnitude Comparison are Extended-set subtests requiring deliberate selection; Standard-set WJ V ACH administration does not include them. |

it does. As a result, while the FAM is outstanding for understanding the underlying mechanisms of math difficulty, it must be paired with achievement measures to form a complete diagnostic picture.

When viewed individually, each battery provides valuable, but incomplete, information about a student's mathematical abilities. The WIAT-4 and WJ V ACH offer strong academic measures of calculation, fluency, and applied problem solving; the KTEA-3 adds additional depth in conceptual and real-world math reasoning; and the FAM provides essential insight into the cognitive and linguistic foundations of math performance. Because no single instrument captures all four math components comprehensively, practitioners often need to integrate subtests across batteries to construct a complete diagnostic profile. Table 5.15 provides a broad view of how the WIAT-4, WJ V ACH, KTEA-3, and FAM each contribute to the assessment of mathematical skills, highlighting how these instruments capture calculation, fact retrieval, number sense, problem solving, and the cognitive processes that support them.

While this overview clarifies the strengths of each battery, practitioners also need a streamlined, integrated framework that shows how these measures work together to identify math SLD subtypes. The 16-subtest cross-battery math battery presented in Table 5.16 distills the most diagnostically powerful subtests from each instrument into a single, coherent system. Immediately after the table, the flowchart (Figure 5.4) illustrates how these subtests can be used flexibly, allowing the evaluation to narrow based on the student's performance rather than requiring all 16 measures in every case. Finally, the decision-rule matrix (see Table 5.17) translates the resulting score patterns into clear subtype classifications, enabling practitioners to move from data collection to accurate, defensible diagnostic conclusions with consistency and precision.

**Table 5.16 A Hypothetical 16-Subtest Diagnostic Math Cross-Battery Assessment Example with Emphasis on Each Subtest's Contribution to Diagnosis**

| Domain | Subtest (With Options Where Applicable) | Primary Contribution |
|---|---|---|
| Achievement—Calculation Anchor | WIAT-4 Numerical Operations | Core procedural accuracy; algorithm execution |
| Achievement—Problem Solving Anchor | WIAT-4 Math Problem Solving | Word-problem reasoning; conceptual understanding |
| Achievement—Cross-Battery Anchor | **ONE of:** WJ V ACH Calculation *or* WJ V ACH Math Problem Identification *or* WJ V ACH Applied Problems *or* KTEA-3 Math Concepts & Applications | Cross-battery confirmation of procedural or conceptual weakness |
| Cognitive (*Gs*/*Gr*/*Gq*)—Retrieval of Math Facts | **ONE or two of:** FAM Addition Fluency, Subtraction Fluency, Multiplication Fluency, Division Fluency | Automaticity; fact retrieval subtype |
| Achievement (*Gq*)—Procedural Math Knowledge | **ONE of:** FAM Written Computation—Addition; Subtraction; Multiplication; Division | Algorithm knowledge; multistep procedures; procedural subtype |
| Achievement (*Gq*)—Number Sense | FAM Number Comparison; Perceptual Estimation | Magnitude, estimation, and conceptual reasoning |
| Cognitive/Achievement (*Gf*/*Gq*)—Verbal Reasoning with Numbers | FAM Linguistic Math Concepts | Language-based quantitative reasoning |
| Cognitive (*Gv*/*Gf*/*Gq*)—Visual-Spatial Representation and Reasoning | FAM Spatial Memory | Spatial representation of quantity; *Gv*-linked reasoning |
| Cognitive (*Gwm*)—Working Memory | FAM Number Capacity | Online storage; supports all math processes |
| Cognitive—Executive Functions | FAM Math Sequences | Sequential rule application; procedural planning; pattern completion; note: executive function constructs (inhibition, cognitive flexibility, error monitoring) are not directly measured by any FAM subtest; supplemental EF measures should be added when EF involvement is hypothesized |
| Cognitive—*Gf* | WJ V COG Concept Formation *or* WISC-V Matrix Reasoning *or* KABC-II NU Story Completion | Abstract reasoning; supports conceptual math |
| Cognitive—*Gv* | WJ V COG Spatial Relations *or* WISC-V Visual Puzzles *or* KABC-II NU Triangles | Visual-spatial processing; supports conceptual math |
| Cognitive—*Gwm* | WJ V COG Numbers Reversed *or* WISC-V Digit Span *or* KABC-II NU Number Recall | Sequential processing; supports procedures and word problems |
| Cognitive—*Gs* | WJ V COG Pair Cancellation *or* WISC-V Coding *or* Symbol Search | Processing speed; supports fact retrieval and procedural fluency |
| When needed: Additional FAM Process | Choose one additional FAM subtest appropriate to hypothesis (e.g., Rapid Number Naming for naming-speed contributions to fluency; Number Line Estimation for spatial magnitude mapping; Word Problems for multistep linguistic reasoning) | Allows subtype refinement |
| When needed: Additional Cognitive Context | Choose one additional cognitive subtest (*Gf*, *Gv*, *Gwm*, or *Gs*) | Assists in clarifying the expected versus unexpected nature of math difficulties |

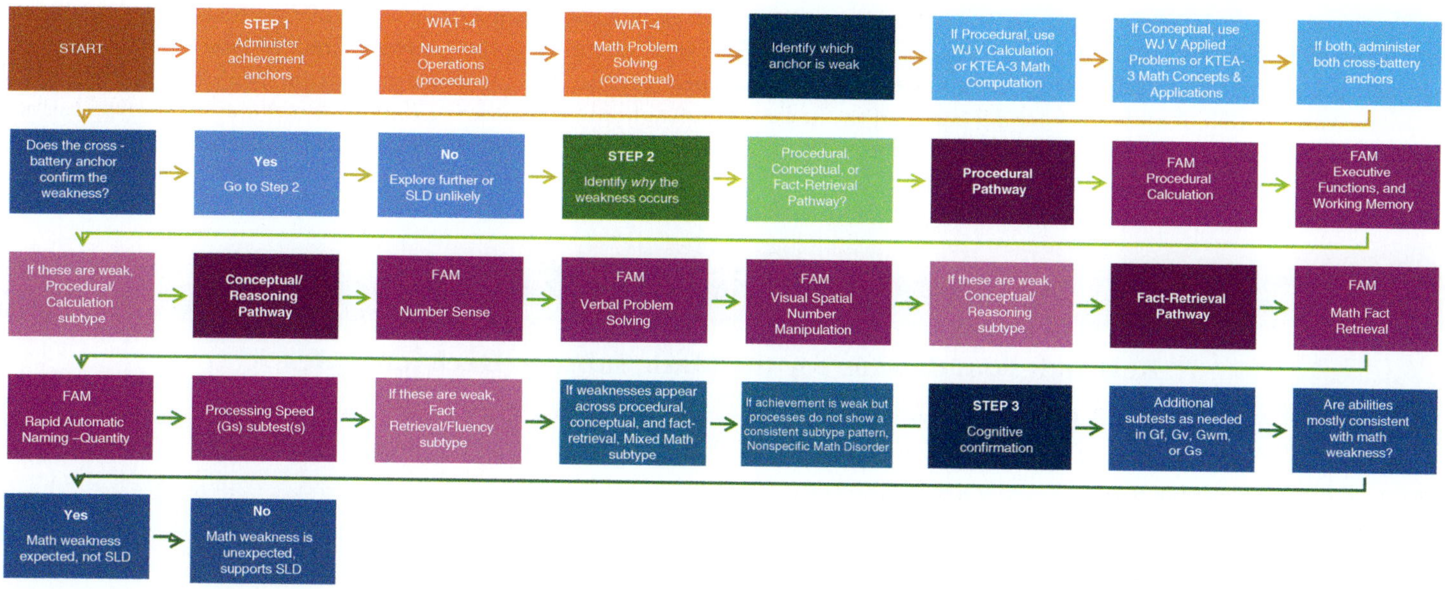


**FIGURE 5.4 Flowchart for Identifying Math Disability Subtype**

**Table 5.17 Decision-Rule Matrix for Interpreting Patterns in a Diagnostic Math XBA**

| Pattern of Scores | Interpretation | Subtype |
|---|---|---|
| Weak calculation + weak FAM Procedural + weak EF/WM (from cognitive battery) + intact number sense + intact reasoning (*Gf*/ *Gv*) | Algorithmic/procedural breakdown; difficulty executing multistep operations despite adequate conceptual understanding; Weakness is specific to sequential execution of procedures and working memory support of those procedures—not a conceptual or reasoning deficit | Procedural/ Calculation LD |
| Weak fact retrieval (math fluency measures from an achievement battery) + slow *Gs* (from cognitive battery) + weak FAM Fact Retrieval + intact concepts (FAM Linguistic Math Concepts) + intact procedures (FAM Written Computation)* | Automaticity deficit; math facts are known but not retrieved efficiently; weakness is speed- and retrieval-based, not knowledge-based. FAM Rapid Number Naming implicates the naming-speed pathway. Slow *Gs* on cognitive battery confirms the processing-speed contribution. | Fact Retrieval/ Fluency LD |
| Weak number sense (FAM Number Comparison; FAM Perceptual Estimation) + weak verbal problem solving (FAM Linguistic Math Concepts) + weak visual-spatial number manipulation (FAM Spatial Memory; FAM Perceptual Estimation) + weak *Gf*/ *Gv* (from cognitive battery) | Conceptual reasoning weakness; difficulty with magnitude representation, numerical relationships, and problem-solving schemas. Deficits span the FAM Semantic Index (spatial/magnitude pathway) and Verbal Index (linguistic math pathway), and are corroborated by low fluid and/or visuospatial reasoning on cognitive battery. | Conceptual/ Reasoning LD |
| Weakness across fact retrieval + procedures + concepts + multiple cognitive weaknesses | Broad impairment across systems; no isolated subtype | Mixed Math LD |
| Low math scores are consistent with low cognitive abilities—*Gf*/ *Gv*/ *Gwm*/ Gs | Weakness is expected given global cognitive profile; not specific | Not SLD according to the DD/C method (Low Ability) |
| All systems intact | No evidence of math disability | Typical Math Learner |

* The difference between math fluency on achievement batteries versus FAM: The Achievement Battery Fluency Measures Answer: "Does the student have a fluency deficit?" WIAT-4 Math Fluency, WJ V Math Facts Fluency, and KTEA-3 Math Fluency are norm-referenced achievement outcome measures. They establish, relative to same-age peers, that the student cannot produce math facts quickly enough to meet academic demands, thus providing an anchor for identifying a fluency-based math LD.

FAM Fluency Subtests Answer: "Which neuropsychological pathway is causing it?" FAM Addition Fluency, Subtraction Fluency, Multiplication Fluency, and Division Fluency are embedded in the FAM Verbal Index—the index that maps the verbal/phonological route to number retrieval. When these are weak, interpreted alongside Rapid Number Naming, the interpretation shifts from "the student is slow" to "the phonological retrieval pathway to math facts is specifically impaired"—which is the neuropsychological signature of verbal dyscalculia. This is what allows the practitioner to assign a subtype, not just document a deficit.

The flowchart and decision-rule matrix for math are grounded in well-established principles of mathematics learning, including the distinction among procedural, fact-retrieval, and conceptual reasoning pathways; the role of working memory and executive functions in multistep calculation; and the separation of accuracy and efficiency in math performance. To support practitioners in defending their diagnostic decisions with research, Rapid Reference 5.7 summarizes the key empirical findings underlying each decision rule and subtype pattern. This rapid reference links the assessment framework directly to the scientific literature, providing the evidentiary foundation for interpreting test data and communicating diagnostic conclusions.

## Rapid Reference 5.7

### Research Foundations for the Math Subtype Decision Rules

#### 1. Core Principles Underlying the Framework

**Componential Nature of Math**

Math performance reflects interacting but separable components:

- procedural accuracy
- fact retrieval
- conceptual reasoning
- executive-function and working-memory support

**Foundational:** Geary (1993, 2004), Jordan and Hanich (2000)

**Recent:**

- Fuchs et al. (2016)—multicomponent model of math learning
- Bailey et al. (2020)—distinct pathways for procedural, conceptual, and retrieval skills
- Peng and Fuchs (2016)—EF and WM as separable contributors to math performance

**Procedural Versus Conceptual Knowledge**

Procedural skill and conceptual understanding develop along partially independent trajectories.

**Foundational:** Rittle-Johnson and Siegler (1998)

**Recent:**

- Rittle-Johnson et al. (2015)—bidirectional but distinct development
- Fyfe et al. (2019)—conceptual knowledge predicts later flexibility
- Schneider et al. (2017)—meta-analysis of conceptual versus procedural knowledge

**Fact Retrieval and Automaticity**

Math fact retrieval depends on efficient access to long-term memory and rapid quantity processing.

**Foundational:** Ashcraft (1982); Geary (1993)

**Recent:**

- De Smedt et al. (2011)—RAN and retrieval deficits
- Bartelet et al. (2014)—retrieval versus procedural distinction
- Fuchs et al. (2018)—fluency as a predictor of later math outcomes

**Executive Functions and Working Memory**

EF and WM support multistep procedures, error monitoring, and problem solving.

**Foundational:** Bull and Scerif (2001)

**Recent:**

- Peng and Fuchs (2016)—WM as a core mechanism in math LD
- Friso-van den Bos et al. (2013)—WM–math meta-analysis
- Cragg and Gilmore (2014)—EF contributions to arithmetic

#### 2. Decision Rules for Math LD Subtypes

**Procedural/Calculation LD**

**Hallmark indicators (when other domains are relatively intact):**

- weak procedural accuracy
- algorithm errors
- weak EF and WM
- intact number sense and fact retrieval

**Foundational:** Geary (1993), Jordan and Hanich (2000)
**Recent:**

- Fuchs et al. (2016)—procedural deficits tied to EF/WM
- Peng and Fuchs (2016)—WM as core mechanism
- Bailey et al. (2020)—procedural pathway evidence

**Fact Retrieval/Fluency LD**
**Hallmark indicators (when other indicators are relatively intact):**

- slow or inaccurate math fact retrieval
- weak RAN-Quantity
- weak processing speed
- intact procedures and concepts

**Foundational:** Ashcraft (1982), Geary (1993)
**Recent:**

- De Smedt et al. (2011)—retrieval deficits
- Fuchs et al. (2018)—fluency as distinct construct
- Bartelet et al. (2014)—retrieval versus procedural dissociation

**Conceptual/Reasoning LD**
**Hallmark indicators (when other indicators are relatively intact):**

- weak number sense
- difficulty with magnitude, estimation, and flexible reasoning
- intact procedures and fact retrieval

**Foundational:** Jordan and Hanich (2000), Rittle-Johnson and Siegler (1998)
**Recent:**

- Schneider et al. (2017)—conceptual knowledge meta-analysis
- Bailey et al. (2020)—conceptual pathway
- Fuchs et al. (2016)—conceptual reasoning as distinct domain

**3. Decision Rules for Non-LD Math Profiles**

**Fluency/Efficiency Weakness (Not a Subtype)**
**Hallmark indicators (when other areas are relatively intact):**

- intact accuracy
- weak efficiency or automaticity
- weak RAN or processing speed

**Foundational:** Ashcraft (1982)
**Recent:**

- Fuchs et al. (2018)—fluency as multicomponent
- Peng and Fuchs (2016)—speed versus accuracy dissociation
- Bailey et al. (2020)—efficiency pathway

**Nonspecific Math Weakness**
**Hallmark indicators (when other areas are relatively intact):**

- broad math weakness
- inconsistent cognitive pattern
- no clear subtype mechanism

**Foundational:** Geary (1993), Pennington (2006)
**Recent:**

- Fuchs et al. (2016)—heterogeneity in math LD
- Elliott and Grigorenko (2014)—diagnostic ambiguity
- Bailey et al. (2020)—mixed profiles

The preceding tables and flowchart outline how the integrated 16-subtest math battery can be used to identify specific patterns of strengths and weaknesses across calculation, fact retrieval, and conceptual reasoning. While these tools provide a structured framework for test selection and interpretation, practitioners often benefit from seeing how the process unfolds with real students. The following case studies illustrate how the revised math flowchart guides subtype identification using a structured, defensible sequence of decisions. Each case begins with achievement anchors, proceeds to FAM process measures to determine the subtype mechanism, and ends with optional cognitive confirmation to evaluate whether the weakness is expected or unexpected. Debiasing checkpoints are embedded at key decision points to help practitioners avoid common interpretive errors such as anchoring, premature closure, and confirmation bias.

## Case Study: Procedural/Calculation Math LD

**Student**: Evan, age 9 (Grade 3)

**Referral Question**: Why does Evan make frequent calculation errors despite strong effort and adequate instruction, and why do these errors persist even though his teacher reports that he understands math concepts during class discussion?

Background:

**Teacher questionnaire responses indicate that Evan**:

- participates actively in math discussions and explains his reasoning clearly,
- grasps new concepts quickly when material is presented verbally or with manipulatives,
- becomes disorganized when completing multistep written work,
- frequently loses track of steps, misaligns place value, or forgets regrouping,
- performs better when allowed to talk through problems than when required to write them independently.

These observations suggest a procedural execution problem, not a conceptual deficit—an important hypothesis to test systematically.

### STEP 1—Achievement Anchors

| Subtest | Standard Score | Interpretation |
|---|---|---|
| **WIAT-4 Numerical Operations** | 78 | Weak procedural accuracy; frequent algorithm errors |
| **WIAT-4 Math Problem Solving** | 94 | Conceptual reasoning intact |
| **WJ V ACH Calculation** | 80 | Confirms procedural weakness across batteries |

### Interpretation (Step 1)

- Procedural weakness is present and confirmed across batteries.
- Conceptual reasoning is intact.
- Weakness is domain-specific, not global.

### Debiasing Checkpoint (Step 1)

To avoid anchoring on the referral concern ("calculation errors"), the examiner briefly considers alternative explanations using only the limited information available from the achievement anchors:

- *Could this be conceptual?*

**Possibly**. Math Problem Solving is in the average range, which makes a conceptual weakness less likely, but a single subtest cannot rule it out.

- *Could this be fact retrieval?*

**Unknown**. No fact-retrieval measures have been administered yet, so this remains an open possibility.

- *Could this be fluency?*

**Unknown**. No fluency measures have been administered, so this cannot be evaluated at Step 1.

Because Step 1 can only suggest a likely procedural weakness—but cannot rule out conceptual, fact-retrieval, or fluency pathways—the examiner proceeds to Step 2 to gather targeted process-level data from the FAM. These measures clarify the underlying mechanism of the weakness and determine which subtype pathway is supported.

### STEP 2—FAM Process Profile (Subtype Mechanism)

| Subtest | Standard Score | Interpretation |
|---|---|---|
| **FAM Procedural Calculation** | 77 | Difficulty executing multistep procedures |
| **FAM Executive Functions/Planning** | 82 | Weak planning, sequencing, and error monitoring |
| **FAM Working Memory** | 80 | Difficulty holding steps in mind |

### Interpretation (Step 2)

- Clear procedural breakdown driven by EF + WM weaknesses.
- Pattern aligns with Procedural/Calculation Math LD subtype.

### Debiasing Checkpoint (Step 2)

To avoid confirmation bias as the examiner begins to see a procedural pattern, explicitly test whether the FAM data could instead or also support a Conceptual/Reasoning subtype or a Retrieval/Fluency subtype. Administer subtests related to these two subtypes.

| Subtest | Standard Score | Interpretation |
|---|---|---|
| **FAM Number Sense** | 99 | Magnitude and conceptual understanding intact |
| **FAM Verbal Problem Solving** | 104 | Strong language-based quantitative reasoning |
| **FAM Visual Spatial Number Manipulation** | 96 | Spatial representation of quantity intact |
| **FAM Math Fact Retrieval** | 97 | Basic math facts are adequately stored and accessible; errors are unlikely to result from a retrieval weakness. |
| **FAM Rapid Automatic Naming-Quantity** | 99 | Quantity access automaticity intact |

1. *Can a Conceptual/Reasoning subtype be ruled out?*

**Yes.**

- FAM Number Sense is average.
- FAM Verbal Problem Solving and Visual-Spatial Number Manipulation are average.
- Conceptual reasoning errors are not evident in the achievement anchors or the process data.

**Interpretation:**
There is no evidence of a conceptual pathway; conceptual reasoning is intact.

2. *Can a Retrieval/Fluency subtype be ruled out?*

**Yes.**

- FAM Math Fact Retrieval is average.
- FAM Rapid Automatic Naming-Quantity is average.
- Given performance on above two measures, it was not considered necessary to administer *Gs* subtests.
- Evan does not show the hallmark pattern of slow or inaccurate fact retrieval.

**Interpretation:**
There is no evidence of a retrieval or fluency-based pathway.

### Conclusion of Step 2 Debiasing

After actively searching for disconfirming evidence, the examiner finds that:

- Conceptual/Reasoning subtype is not supported, and
- Retrieval/Fluency subtype is not supported.

The remaining explanation—consistent with both the achievement anchors and the FAM process data—is a Procedural subtype, driven by weaknesses in procedural calculation, working memory, and EF/planning.

### STEP 3—Cognitive Confirmation (Optional)

| CHC Domain | Subtest | Scaled Score | Interpretation |
|---|---|---|---|
| ***Gf*—Fluid Reasoning** | WISC-V Matrix Reasoning | 10 | Abstract reasoning is average; supports conceptual math |
| ***Gv*—Visual Processing** | WISC-V Visual Puzzles | 9 | Visual-spatial processing is average |
| ***Gwm*—Working Memory** | WISC-V Digit Span | 7 | Weak sequential processing; aligns with procedural difficulty |
| ***Gs*—Processing Speed** | WISC-V Coding | 9 | Processing speed adequate; not a fluency issue |

**Interpretation (Step 3)**
Math weakness is unexpected relative to cognitive profile → supports SLD.
**Debiasing Checkpoint (Step 3)**
Avoid overattribution:

- *Gwm* alone does not fully explain the severity of procedural errors.
- EF weaknesses also contribute.

**Final Diagnostic Picture**
**Subtype**: Procedural/Calculation Math LD
Why:

- Weak procedural calculation
- Weak EF and WM
- Frequent algorithm errors
- Intact number sense and reasoning
- Weakness confirmed across batteries
- Weakness unexpected relative to cognitive profile
- Teacher reports consistent with procedural execution difficulties

**Intervention Implications Based on the Identified Pathway**
**Subtype Identified**: Procedural Math Learning Disability (Procedural Pathway)
**Mechanism**: Weak executive function and working memory disrupt Evan's ability to carry out multistep procedures. This mechanism affects:

- *Sequencing*: losing track of steps
- *Working memory*: forgetting regrouping decisions
- *Attention to detail*: skipping or repeating steps
- *Place-value coordination*: misregrouping or misaligning digits
- *Procedure selection*: choosing the wrong algorithm or switching mid-problem
- *Self-monitoring*: not catching errors as they occur

This is why Evan's errors are inconsistent, step-related, and procedural rather than conceptual.

**Why This Mechanism Leads to the Observed Errors**
When a student must hold steps in mind, remember regrouping decisions, track place value, and monitor accuracy simultaneously, the working memory load becomes overwhelming.
**For Evan, this means**:

- He may know *what* subtraction is but cannot reliably execute the algorithm.
- He may understand *why* regrouping works but cannot manage the steps.
- He may understand *place value* but cannot coordinate it while solving.

This is the hallmark of the Procedural Pathway.

**What Evan Needs Instructionally**
Because the mechanism is executive function and working memory-based, Evan needs interventions that:

- reduce cognitive load,
- make steps explicit,
- provide stable visual structure,
- support sequencing, and
- allow him to internalize the algorithm before performing it independently.

These are the high-leverage practices for the Procedural Pathway.

## High-Leverage Practices for Procedural LD

### A. Traditional Worked Examples

Worked examples are fully solved problems that show each step of the algorithm.
Students study the example rather than solving it independently. This reduces working memory demands and allows Evan to focus on:

- the order of steps
- how regrouping works
- how place value is coordinated
- what the algorithm *looks like* when done correctly

**Traditional Worked Example (Subtraction with Regrouping)**
Solve: 47–19

1. Write the problem vertically.
2. Notice you cannot subtract 9 from 7.
3. Borrow 1 ten → 4 tens becomes 3 tens.
4. Add 10 ones → 7 ones becomes 17 ones.
5. Subtract ones: 17 – 9 = 8.
6. Subtract tens: 3 – 1 = 2.
7. Answer: 28

Evan studies the steps, explains them aloud, and compares multiple worked examples before attempting his own.

### Why this Works

Worked examples reduce cognitive load and improve procedural accuracy for students with executive function and working memory weaknesses (Bailey et al., 2020; Rittle-Johnson & Star, 2007; Sweller et al., 2011).

### B. Faded Worked Examples

After Evan becomes familiar with the structure, some steps are removed.
Example:

- Step 3 is blank → Evan fills in the regrouping
- Step 5 is blank → Evan completes the subtraction

This gradually increases independence without overwhelming working memory.

### C. Explicit Modeling of Each Step

The teacher verbalizes:

- what step is being done
- why it is being done
- what to check before moving on

This externalizes the sequencing Evan cannot yet manage internally.

### D. Sequencing and Self-Monitoring Supports

Examples:

- "First–Then–Next–Last" checklists
- Step cards
- Visual cues for regrouping
- Highlighting or color-coding place value

These supports reduce the executive function load and help Evan stay oriented.

### E. Guided Practice with Gradual Release

Evan should not be asked to solve multistep problems independently until:

- he has studied multiple worked examples,
- practiced faded examples, and
- demonstrated step-by-step accuracy with support.

### What Evan Does *Not* Need

Because Evan's difficulty is procedural, rather than conceptual or retrieval-based, he does not need:

- fact-fluency drills
- speeded practice
- conceptual number-sense interventions
- enrichment or acceleration
- "more practice" without structure

These would not address the mechanism and may increase frustration.

### Evidence Base

- Procedural accuracy depends heavily on EF and working memory (Fuchs et al., 2016; Peng & Fuchs, 2016).
- Worked examples reduce cognitive load and improve procedural learning (Sweller et al., 2011).
- Faded worked examples support transfer to independent performance (Rittle-Johnson & Star, 2007).
- Sequencing supports improve accuracy for students with procedural vulnerabilities (Bailey et al., 2020).

Two additional math cases are included in Appendix 5.B at the end of this chapter. The integrated math assessment framework presented in this chapter demonstrates that Math LD is not a single construct but a set of distinct, identifiable profiles. By combining targeted achievement measures with FAM process data and CHC-aligned cognitive indicators, practitioners can differentiate among procedural, fact-retrieval, and conceptual subtypes with precision. This approach ensures that weaknesses are interpreted within the broader context of the student's cognitive-linguitic abilities, allowing evaluators to determine whether a math difficulty is specific and unexpected—consistent with SLD—or better explained by global cognitive limitations.

The 16-subtest cross-battery math battery provides a streamlined yet comprehensive structure that mirrors the logic of the reading framework. Although practitioners rarely administer all 16 subtests, the full set defines the available pathways and ensures that test selection is driven by the referral question. The flowchart guides efficient decision-making, ensuring that only the measures needed to resolve diagnostic questions are administered, while the decision-rule matrix translates score patterns into clear subtype classifications. The case study illustrates how these tools work together in practice, showing how subtype-specific patterns emerge and how they inform intervention planning.

Taken together, this system offers a coherent, evidence-aligned method for evaluating math difficulties that is diagnostically rigorous and practical for school-based assessment. It supports consistent decision-making, reduces interpretive ambiguity, and ensures that students receive interventions matched to the specific processes underlying their math challenges.

## Caveats and Context: Writing

Research on developmental dysgraphia is far less extensive than the literature on developmental dyslexia. Whereas dyslexia has well-established cognitive profiles and decades of empirical work, dysgraphia research remains comparatively limited, with fewer studies, smaller samples, and less consensus about underlying mechanisms or subtype structure (Döhla & Heim, 2016). As a result, many hypotheses about dysgraphia have been extrapolated from dyslexia research rather than derived from a robust, independent evidence base.

Despite these limitations, several cognitive mechanisms have been consistently implicated in spelling difficulties. Phonological processing—particularly phonological awareness and phonological working memory—reliably distinguishes dysgraphic from typically developing writers (Moll et al., 2009; Steinbrink & Klatte, 2008; Winkes, 2014). However, phonological deficits do not differentiate subtypes within dysgraphia, suggesting that phonological weakness is a general characteristic of the disorder rather than a subtype-defining feature. This stands in contrast to dyslexia, where phonological deficits often play a central role in subtype differentiation (Pennington et al., 2012; Snowling, 2001).

Beyond phonology, both auditory processing and visual magnocellular processing contribute meaningfully to spelling performance. In the largest study to date, dysgraphic children could be subdivided into two preliminary profiles: one characterized by auditory and phonological processing deficits, and another characterized by visual magnocellular deficits alongside phonological working memory weaknesses (Döhla et al., 2020). These profiles appear to be independent of reading ability in the available studies, indicating that dysgraphia is not simply "dyslexia expressed in writing." Auditory-based profiles were more common than visual-magnocellular profiles, but both require further validation (Ramus, 2003; Stein, 2001).

Visual attention contributes to spelling performance as well, though it does not reliably distinguish dysgraphic children from typical writers or differentiate dysgraphia subtypes (Banfi et al., 2017; Bosse et al., 2007). Crossmodal integration, particularly the ability to combine visual and auditory information during grapheme–phoneme and phoneme–grapheme mapping, may contribute to spelling difficulty, though evidence remains limited (Schaadt et al., 2018). Comorbidity with ADHD is common and further complicates the interpretation of cognitive profiles (Adi-Japha et al., 2007; Capodieci et al., 2018).

Taken together, these findings indicate that developmental dysgraphia is a heterogeneous condition influenced by multiple cognitive systems. The disorder shares many underlying mechanisms with dyslexia, such as phonological, auditory, and visual-magnocellular processing, but differs in how these mechanisms combine and cluster (Döhla & Heim, 2016; Heim et al., 2008). Dyslexia and dysgraphia are therefore similar but not homologous: they share a common basis, but differ in individual characteristics, subtype structures, and patterns of cognitive association.

Given the early stage of dysgraphia subtype research, the profiles described here should be understood as descriptive heuristics rather than definitive neurobiological categories. Current models are constrained by narrow assessment batteries, small samples, and the selective inclusion or exclusion of cognitive variables (Ramus, 2004; Stein, 2001). Broader diagnostic approaches, including more comprehensive cognitive assessment and longitudinal or neurobiological studies, are needed to clarify the mechanisms underlying spelling difficulties and to determine whether additional dysgraphia profiles exist.

For practitioners, the key implication is that behavioral spelling errors alone are insufficient for diagnosis. A mechanism-aligned assessment that evaluates phonological processing, auditory discrimination, and other cognitive skills is essential for identifying the specific sources of breakdown. Such information supports more precise, individualized intervention planning that leverages a student's strengths while addressing the mechanisms most relevant to their spelling difficulty.

## DIAGNOSTIC XBA FOR WRITING REFERRALS

Having established parallel, defensible diagnostic systems for reading and math, we now turn to the third major academic domain: writing. As with reading and math, written expression is not a single skill but a constellation of interrelated processes. Effective diagnosis requires clarity about *which* component of writing is breaking down and *why*, because writing difficulties often arise from different combinations of linguistic, motor, and executive-function demands.

To support this analysis, Rapid Reference 5.8 parallels the earlier reading and math interview guides (Rapid References 5.2 and 5.6), providing targeted questions practitioners can use to gather high-quality information from teachers. These questions are organized into four categories that reflect the major components of written expression:

1. Handwriting/Graphomotor
2. Spelling/Encoding
3. Sentence-Level Writing
4. Composition/Organization

These teacher interview questions help evaluators identify the most likely area of breakdown before testing begins, ensuring that the assessment is focused, efficient, and aligned with the student's presenting concerns.

### Rapid Reference 5.8

#### Teacher Interview Questions to Identify the Type of Writing Problem

**1. Handwriting/Graphomotor (legibility, speed, motor control)**

- Is the student's handwriting **slow, labored, or difficult to read**?
- Do they fatigue quickly during writing tasks?
- Do they struggle with **letter formation**, spacing, or alignment?
- Does handwriting interfere with their ability to **express ideas**?

**If yes → likely a graphomotor/handwriting issue.**

**2. Spelling/Encoding (phonological, orthographic, morphological)**

- Does the student make **frequent spelling errors**, even in familiar words?
- Do they spell phonetically but incorrectly (e.g., *sed for said*)?
- Do they struggle with **morphological endings** (-ed, -ing, -s)?
- Do spelling difficulties interfere with **written expression**?

**If yes → likely a spelling/encoding weakness.**

**3. Sentence-Level Writing (syntax, grammar, mechanics)**

- Does the student struggle to write **complete, grammatically correct sentences**?
- Do they omit words, use run-ons, or produce fragmented sentences?
- Do they have difficulty using **punctuation and capitalization** correctly?
- Does their writing lack **variety in sentence structure**?

**If yes → likely a sentence-level writing weakness.**

**4. Composition/Organization (planning, structure, coherence)**

- Does the student have difficulty **generating ideas** for writing?
- Do they struggle to **organize thoughts** into paragraphs or logical sequences?
- Is their writing **brief, vague, or lacking detail**?
- Do they have difficulty revising or expanding their work?

**If yes → likely a composition/organization weakness.**
**Optional Writing "Short Cut" Question**
**"Is the student's biggest challenge getting words on the page, spelling the words, writing correct sentences, or organizing ideas?"**

- Getting words on the page → graphomotor
- Spelling → encoding
- Correct sentences → syntax/grammar
- Organizing ideas → composition

Once the presenting writing problem has been narrowed through teacher input, the next step—just as in reading and math—is to verify and refine these hypotheses using standardized assessment data. To support this process, the following tables organize commonly used achievement batteries according to the specific writing skills they measure.

The **WIAT-4** provides broad academic coverage of written expression, including spelling, sentence writing, and extended composition. It is often the first tool practitioners use when evaluating writing concerns because it aligns closely with classroom expectations. However, like all single batteries, the WIAT-4 captures only part of the writing construct. Table 5.18 organizes WIAT-4 subtests by the four core writing components, highlighting areas of strong measurement and those that may require additional assessment.

Although the WIAT-4 offers a solid foundation for evaluating written expression, it leaves several important areas unmeasured. It does not include a fine-motor or graphomotor precision task, nor does it assess orthographic processing or handwriting legibility. Beyond Alphabet Writing Fluency, it provides no measure of rapid automatic writing or written fluency. The WIAT-4 also lacks error-analysis tools for spelling or writing and does not include executive-function–based writing tasks such as planning, revising, or working-memory–supported composition. These gaps often require supplementation from other batteries.

The WJ V ACH offers a wide range of writing subtests, including spelling, writing fluency, and extended writing tasks (see Table 5.19). Its structure allows practitioners to examine foundational and higher-order writing skills. At the same time, the battery lacks several linguistic and graphomotor components essential for diagnosing handwriting or encoding-based difficulties. It does not include a handwriting legibility or fine-motor measure, and its coverage of orthographic processing is limited to spelling. The WJ V ACH also omits revision, editing, and planning tasks, provides no executive-function–based writing measures, and does not offer error analysis for spelling or writing. Rapid automatic writing is limited to a single fluency task, leaving several aspects of written fluency unmeasured.

**Table 5.18 WIAT-4 Aligned to Four Writing Components**

| Writing Component | WIAT-4 Subtests | Notes |
|---|---|---|
| Handwriting/Graphomotor | Alphabet Writing Fluency | Timed handwriting; letter formation and speed. |
| Spelling/Encoding | Spelling | Strong phonological and orthographic encoding measure. |
| Sentence-Level Writing | Sentence Composition (Sentence Combining; Sentence Building) | Measures grammar, syntax, and sentence construction. |
| Composition/Organization | Essay Composition | Measures planning, organization, development, and conventions. |

**Table 5.19 WJ V ACH Aligned to Four Writing Components**

| Writing Component | WJ V ACH Subtests | Notes |
|---|---|---|
| Handwriting/Graphomotor | Writing Fluency | Timed writing; speed and automaticity. Does not measure handwriting legibility. |
| Spelling/Encoding | Spelling of Sounds; Spelling | Strong phonological and orthographic encoding. |
| Sentence-Level Writing | Writing Samples (sentence-level prompts) | Measures grammar, syntax, and clarity. |
| Composition/Organization | Writing Samples (extended prompts) | Measures organization, elaboration, and conventions. |

**Table 5.20 KTEA-3 Aligned to Four Writing Components**

| Writing Component | KTEA-3 Subtests | Notes |
|---|---|---|
| Handwriting/Graphomotor | Writing Fluency | Timed writing; speed and automaticity. |
| Spelling/Encoding | Spelling | Strong academic spelling measure. |
| Sentence-Level Writing | Written Expression (sentence-level tasks) | Measures grammar and clarity. |
| Composition/Organization | Written Expression (extended tasks) | Measures organization, elaboration, and conventions. |

**Table 5.21 FAW Aligned to Four Writing Components**

| Writing Component | FAW Subtests | Notes |
|---|---|---|
| Handwriting/Graphomotor | Graphomotor Output; Copying; Motor Planning | Strong graphomotor and handwriting foundations. |
| Spelling/Encoding | Phonological Decoding; Orthographic Coding; Encoding | Deep linguistic foundations of spelling. |
| Sentence-Level Writing | Sentence Writing; Working Memory tasks | Cognitive-linguistic processes for sentence construction. |
| Composition/Organization | Planning; Executive Functions; Written Expression | Measures planning, organization, and EF-based writing. |

The KTEA-3 offers a balanced set of writing subtests that assess spelling, written expression, and fluency, with particular strengths in applied writing tasks (see Table 5.20). However, it does not provide deep coverage of graphomotor or linguistic foundations. It lacks measures of graphomotor precision and handwriting legibility, and it does not assess orthographic processing or phonological encoding beyond spelling. The KTEA-3 also does not include executive-function–based writing tasks, nor does it assess planning, revising, or editing. Like the other achievement batteries, it does not provide error analysis for spelling or writing, which limits its usefulness for identifying the specific linguistic sources of encoding or composition difficulties.

The FAW is designed to assess the cognitive, linguistic, and motor processes that underlie writing performance, making it uniquely valuable for understanding why a student struggles with handwriting, spelling, or written expression. It provides insight into graphomotor skills, orthographic processing, working memory, and language formulation—skills that are not directly measured by achievement tests. At the same time, the FAW does not include an academic spelling score, curriculum-aligned writing samples, or timed writing fluency. It does not offer extended composition tasks with academic scoring, nor does it provide conventions scoring for punctuation or capitalization. Finally, it lacks an essay-level organization measure comparable to the WIAT-4 or KTEA-3, making cross-battery integration essential for a complete diagnostic picture (Table 5.21).

The cross-battery writing table outlines how the WIAT-4, WJ V ACH, KTEA-3, and FAW each contributes to different components of written expression, from handwriting and spelling to sentence construction and composition (see Table 5.22). While this overview clarifies the strengths of each measure and highlights the multidimensional nature of writing.

The cross-battery writing battery brings together the strongest subtests from the WIAT-4, WJ V ACH/VTL, KTEA-3, and FAW to create a comprehensive, 16-subtest system that mirrors the structure used for reading and math. Each subtest contributes uniquely to the diagnostic picture, and together they provide full coverage of the four major components of written expression: handwriting/graphomotor skills, spelling/encoding, sentence-level writing, and composition/organization.

**Table 5.22 Cross-Battery Writing Subtests and Their Diagnostic Contributions**

| Writing Component | Subtest | Source | Primary Contribution |
|---|---|---|---|
| Handwriting/ Graphomotor | Graphomotor Output | FAW | Motor planning; handwriting legibility |
| | Copying | FAW | Visual–motor integration; graphomotor precision |
| | Alphabet Writing Fluency | WIAT-4 | Handwriting speed; automaticity |
| | Writing Fluency | KTEA-3 | Speed and accuracy in handwriting |
| Spelling/ Encoding | Spelling | WIAT-4 | Academic spelling accuracy; strong phonological and orthographic encoding measure but not an orthographic processing task |
| | Spelling of Sounds | WJ V ACH | Phoneme–grapheme correspondence |
| | Orthographic Coding | FAW | Orthographic pattern recognition |
| | Encoding | FAW | Linguistic foundations of spelling |
| Sentence-Level Writing | Sentence Composition | WIAT-4 | Syntax, grammar, sentence combining |
| | Writing Samples | WJ V ACH | Sentence construction; conventions |
| | Sentence Writing | FAW | Cognitive-linguistic processes in sentence generation |
| Composition/Organization | Essay Composition | WIAT-4 | Organization, elaboration, conventions |
| | Writing Samples | WJ V ACH | Idea development; structure |
| | Written Expression | KTEA-3 | Organization, clarity, elaboration |
| | Planning/ Executive Functions | FAW | Planning, sequencing, revision processes |
| Cognitive Context | ONE of: *Gwm*, *Gs*, *Gf*, *Gc*-expressive | WJ V COG/WISC-V/ KABC-II | Used to evaluate the plausibility of unexpected underachievement |

The handwriting/graphomotor subtests capture the motor and visual–motor foundations of writing. FAW Graphomotor Output and Copying assess motor planning, legibility, and graphomotor precision, while WIAT-4 Alphabet Writing Fluency and KTEA-3 Writing Fluency measure handwriting speed and automaticity. The spelling/encoding subtests combine academic spelling accuracy with deep linguistic foundations. WIAT-4 Spelling provides curriculum-aligned spelling performance, WJ V ACH Spelling of Sounds assesses phoneme–grapheme correspondence, and FAW Orthographic Coding and Encoding measure orthographic pattern recognition and linguistic encoding processes.

The sentence-level writing subtests assess grammar, syntax, and the cognitive-linguistic processes that support sentence construction. WIAT-4 Sentence Composition and WJ V ACH Writing Samples provide academic measures of sentence combining and conventions, while FAW Sentence Writing captures the linguistic formulation demands that underlie sentence generation. The composition/organization subtests evaluate planning, organization, elaboration, and conventions. WIAT-4 Essay Composition and WJ V ACH Writing Samples assess idea development and structure, KTEA-3 Written Expression provides clarity and elaboration, and FAW Planning/Executive Functions measures the executive-function processes required for planning, sequencing, and revision. Finally, assessment in cognitive domains (*Gwm*, *Gs*, *Gf*, or *Gc*-expressive) provides the cognitive context needed to determine whether the writing weakness is specific and unexpected—consistent with SLD—or better explained by broader cognitive limitations.

Figure 5.5 shows that the writing identification process follows a structured sequence that moves from initial concern to a defensible, mechanism-based understanding of a student's writing difficulty. Each step serves a distinct purpose, and together they ensure that subtype decisions are grounded in observable behavior, validated by achievement data, and supported by process-level evidence.

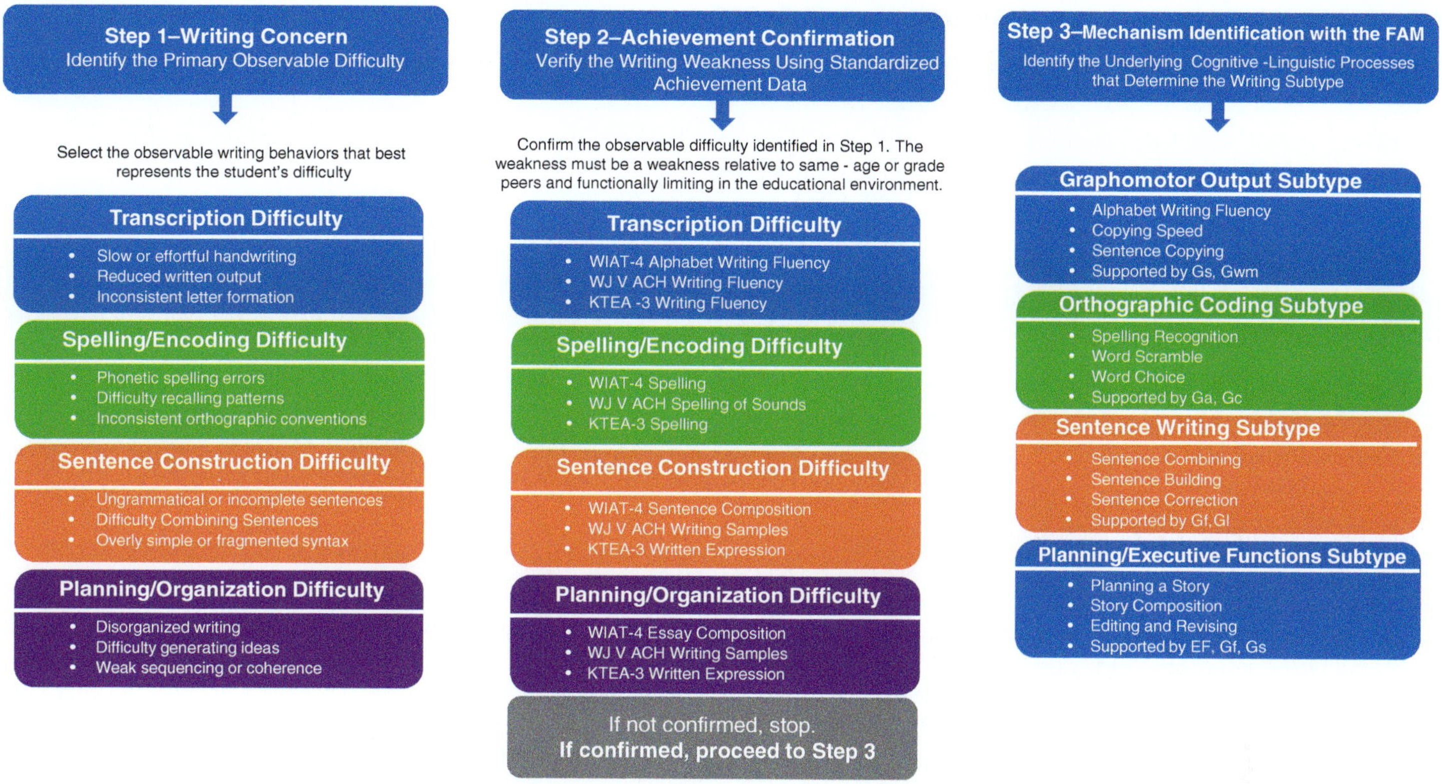


**FIGURE 5.5 Identification of Writing Difficulties and Subtypes**

**Step 1 involves identifying observable indicators of a writing difficulty.** The process begins with the practitioner's direct observations of the student's writing performance in authentic contexts. These indicators may include slow or effortful handwriting, frequent or inconsistent spelling errors, difficulty generating or combining sentences, or written work that lacks coherence, organization, or elaboration. The purpose of this step is to determine whether a meaningful concern exists based on what the student actually does during writing tasks. This step is descriptive in nature; it establishes the presence of a plausible writing difficulty that warrants further examination.

**Step 2 requires confirmation of the concern using standardized achievement data.** Once an observable difficulty has been identified, the practitioner verifies that the concern is supported by formal assessment results. Standardized writing measures provide the statistical and clinical evidence needed to determine whether the student's performance represents a significant weakness rather than a mild, situational, or developmentally typical variation. This step ensures that the identification process proceeds only when the writing difficulty is both educationally meaningful and empirically validated. If the concern is not confirmed through achievement data, the process concludes at this point.

**Step 3 focuses on determining the underlying mechanism responsible for the writing difficulty.** After the weakness has been confirmed, the practitioner examines performance on FAW process-level subtests and considers relevant cognitive correlates to identify the mechanism that best explains the student's difficulty. This analysis leads to one of the writing subtypes, each representing a distinct process: Graphomotor Output, Orthographic Coding, Sentence Writing, or Planning/Executive. The subtype reflects the underlying reason for the student's difficulty and provides a defensible, mechanism-aligned explanation that can guide subsequent interpretation and instructional planning.

The Decision-Rule Matrix for Writing LD Subtypes translates score patterns into clear subtype classifications. It shows how combinations of academic weaknesses and process-level breakdowns map onto specific writing profiles. The matrix also clarifies how to distinguish specific learning disabilities from broader cognitive or instructional explanations.

## DECISION-RULE MATRIX FOR WRITING LD SUBTYPES

| Pattern of Scores | Interpretation | Subtype |
|---|---|---|
| Weak graphomotor output + slow handwriting fluency + intact spelling and composition | Motor-based handwriting weakness | Graphomotor Output/ Handwriting LD |
| Weak spelling + weak orthographic coding + weak encoding + intact handwriting | Linguistic/orthographic weakness | Spelling/Encoding LD |
| Weak sentence composition + weak FAW sentence writing + intact spelling | Syntax/grammar formulation weakness | Sentence-Level Writing LD |
| Weak essay composition + weak planning/ EF + weak organization | Planning/organization weakness | Composition/Organization LD |
| Weakness across handwriting + spelling + sentence + composition | Broad writing impairment | Mixed Writing LD |
| Writing weakness matches global cognitive profile | Expected weakness | Not SLD |

The steps in Figure 5.5 and decision-rule matrix for writing are grounded in well-established principles of writing science, including the multicomponent nature of written expression, the foundational role of transcription skills, the linguistic underpinnings of spelling and sentence formulation, and the executive-function processes that support planning, organization, and revision. To support practitioners in defending their diagnostic decisions with research, Rapid Reference 5.9 summarizes the key empirical findings underlying each decision rule and subtype pattern. This rapid reference links the assessment framework directly to the scientific literature, providing the evidentiary foundation for interpreting test data and communicating diagnostic conclusions.

## *Rapid Reference 5.9*

### Research Foundations for the Writing Subtype Decision Rules

#### 1. Core Principles Underlying the Framework

**Writing as a Multicomponent Construct**

Writing requires integrating graphomotor skills, spelling/encoding, sentence formulation, and composition processes.

**Foundational:** Berninger and Swanson (1994); Graham and Harris (2000)

**Recent:**

- Berninger and Winn (2006)—multicomponent writing model
- Graham (2018)—updated evidence on writing development
- Kim (2020)—componential model of writing

**Graphomotor and Transcription Foundations**

Handwriting fluency and legibility free cognitive resources for higher-order writing.

**Foundational:** Berninger et al. (1992)

**Recent:**

- Abbott and Berninger (1993)—transcription → composition pathway
- Graham et al. (2018)—handwriting as foundational
- Puranik and Al Otaiba (2012)—early graphomotor predictors

**Orthographic and Linguistic Encoding**

Spelling depends on phonological, orthographic, and morphological knowledge.

**Foundational:** Ehri (2000), Treiman (1997)

**Recent:**

- Treiman (2018)—updated orthographic and spelling research
- Ouellette and Sénéchal (2021)—orthographic learning mechanisms
- Kim (2020)—linguistic foundations of writing

**Executive Functions in Writing**
Planning, organizing, and revising depend on EF and working memory.
**Foundational:** Hayes and Flower (1980)
**Recent:**

- Berninger and Winn (2006)—EF in writing
- Graham (2018)—planning and revision processes
- Kim (2020)—EF as core writing mechanism

**2. Decision Rules for Writing LD Subtypes**

**Graphomotor/Handwriting LD**
**Hallmark indicators:**

- weak graphomotor precision
- poor legibility
- slow handwriting fluency
- intact spelling and composition

**Foundational:** Berninger et al. (1992)
**Recent:**

- Puranik and Al Otaiba (2012)—handwriting predictors
- Graham et al. (2018)—transcription bottlenecks
- Kim (2020)—motor → linguistic load interactions

**Spelling/Encoding LD**
**Hallmark indicators:**

- weak phonological, orthographic, or morphological encoding
- inaccurate spelling
- intact graphomotor skills
- intact sentence-level writing

**Foundational:** Ehri (2000), Treiman (1997)
**Recent:**

- Treiman (2018)—orthographic and morphological errors
- Ouellette and Sénéchal (2021)—encoding mechanisms
- Kim (2020)—linguistic encoding pathways

**Sentence-Level Writing LD**
**Hallmark indicators:**

- weak syntax, grammar, or sentence combining
- difficulty generating well-formed sentences
- intact spelling and graphomotor skills

**Foundational: Scott and Windsor (2000)**
**Recent:**

- Graham (2018)—sentence-level instruction
- Kim (2020)—linguistic formulation processes
- Berninger and Winn (2006)—sentence generation mechanisms

**Composition/Organization LD**
**Hallmark indicators:**

- weak planning, organization, elaboration, or cohesion
- difficulty generating multisentence or multiparagraph text
- intact transcription and encoding

**Foundational:** Hayes and Flower (1980)
**Recent:**

- Graham and Harris (2018)—planning and revision
- Kim (2020)—discourse-level writing
- Berninger and Winn (2006)—EF-based composition

**3. Decision Rules for Non-LD Writing Profiles**

**Fluency/Efficiency Weakness (Not a Subtype)**
**Hallmark indicators:**

- intact accuracy
- slow handwriting or slow sentence generation
- weak automaticity

**Foundational:** Berninger et al. (1992)
**Recent:**

- Graham et al. (2018)—transcription bottlenecks
- Kim (2020)—fluency as distinct from accuracy
- Puranik and Al Otaiba (2012)—handwriting fluency

**Nonspecific Writing Weakness**
**Hallmark indicators:**

- broad writing weakness
- inconsistent cognitive pattern
- no clear subtype mechanism

**Foundational:** Berninger and Winn (2006), Pennington (2006)
**Recent:**

- Graham (2018)—heterogeneity in writing difficulties
- Kim (2020)—multicomponent writing model
- Ouellette and Sénéchal (2021)—mixed linguistic profiles

Together, the flowchart and decision-rule matrix provide a coherent, evidence-aligned framework for moving from test selection to subtype identification. They set the stage for the writing case that follows, which illustrates how these tools operate in real evaluations and how subtype-specific patterns inform intervention planning.

## Case Study: Composition/Organization LD (Composition Pathway)

### Background

Sofia is a 10-year-old fourth-grade student referred for evaluation due to persistent difficulty with written expression. Her teacher reports that Sofia:

- has strong verbal ideas and participates actively in class discussions,
- reads at grade level,
- spells adequately for her age,
- writes slowly and produces very little,
- struggles to organize her thoughts on paper,
- becomes overwhelmed by multiparagraph assignments, and
- avoids writing tasks whenever possible.

Her parents report similar concerns at home: Sofia can explain stories in detail but "freezes" when asked to write them. These observations suggest a planning/organization problem, not a transcription or spelling deficit—an important hypothesis to test systematically.

### STEP 1—Achievement Anchors (Writing)

| Subtest | Standard Score | Interpretation |
|---|---|---|
| WIAT-4 Alphabet Writing Fluency | 98 | Average; transcription automaticity intact |
| WIAT-4 Spelling | 100 | Average; encoding intact |
| WIAT-4 Sentence Composition | 85 | Low average; mild sentence-level vulnerability |
| WIAT-4 Essay Composition | 78 | Below average; weakest score; planning/organization difficulty |

| Subtest | Standard Score | Interpretation |
|---|---|---|
| WJ V ACH Spelling of Sounds | 102 | Average; phonological encoding intact |
| WJ V ACH Writing Samples | 80 | Below average; weak organization, elaboration, planning |
| KTEA-3 Writing Fluency | 96 | Average; transcription speed adequate |
| KTEA-3 Written Expression | 78 | Below average; weak planning, limited elaboration, poor organization |

### Interpretation (Step 1)

- Transcription and encoding are intact (Alphabet Fluency, Spelling, Spelling of Sounds, and Writing Fluency all average).
- Weaknesses emerge only when tasks require planning, organizing, and producing extended text (Essay Composition, Writing Samples, and Written Expression).
- Sentence-level writing is mildly weak, but not severe enough to explain the broader pattern.
- The profile suggests a higher-level writing weakness, not a motor or spelling deficit.

### Debiasing Checkpoint (Step 1)

To avoid prematurely concluding a composition weakness, the examiner considers alternative explanations using only Step 1 data:

- *Could this be a graphomotor/transcription weakness?*
- **No**. Alphabet Writing Fluency and Writing Fluency are average.
- *Could this be a spelling/encoding weakness?*
- **No**. WIAT-4 Spelling and WJ Spelling of Sounds are average.
- *Could this be a sentence-level weakness?*
- **Possibly**. Sentence Composition is low-average, but the severity of extended-writing deficits exceeds what sentence-level issues typically produce.
- *Could this be a composition/organization weakness?*
- **Yes**. All extended-writing tasks show below-average performance.

Why Step 1 Requires Step 2
Because Step 1 shows intact transcription and encoding but weak extended writing, Step 2 is needed to determine whether the mechanism is:

- graphomotor,
- encoding,
- sentence-level, or
- planning/organization (composition pathway).

### STEP 2—FAW Process Profile (Subtype Mechanism)

| Subtest | Standard Score | Interpretation |
|---|---|---|
| FAW Graphomotor Output | 98 | Average; motor output intact |
| FAW Copying | 101 | Average; transcription intact |
| FAW Orthographic Coding | 100 | Average; orthographic memory intact |
| FAW Encoding | 102 | Average; spelling/encoding intact |
| FAW Sentence Writing | 86 | Low average; mild sentence-level vulnerability |
| FAW Planning/Executive Functions | 76 | Below average; weak planning, organization, and EF |

### Interpretation (Step 2)

- Graphomotor/transcription pathway ruled out (Graphomotor Output, Copying average).
- Spelling/encoding pathway ruled out (Orthographic Coding, Encoding average).
- Sentence-level pathway mildly weak, but not severe enough to explain the extended-writing deficits.
- Primary weakness is in Planning/Executive Functions, which directly aligns with the Composition Pathway.

### Debiasing Checkpoint (Step 2)

To avoid confirmation bias, the examiner explicitly tests whether the data could support alternative pathways.

*Can a Graphomotor/Transcription subtype be ruled out?*

**Yes**.

- Graphomotor Output = 98
- Copying = 101
- Writing Fluency = 96
- No evidence of motor or transcription difficulty.

*Can a Spelling/Encoding subtype be ruled out?*

**Yes**.

- WIAT-4 Spelling = 100
- WJ Spelling of Sounds = 102
- FAW Orthographic Coding = 100
- Encoding is intact.

*Can a Sentence-Level subtype be ruled out?*

**Yes** (as primary).

- Sentence Writing = 86 (mildly weak)
- But extended-writing deficits are much more severe than sentence-level weaknesses alone would produce.

### Conclusion of Step 2 Debiasing

After actively searching for disconfirming evidence:

- Graphomotor/transcription → not supported
- Spelling/encoding → not supported
- Sentence-level → secondary, not primary

The remaining explanation—consistent with achievement anchors and FAW data—is a Composition/Organization subtype, driven by planning and EF weaknesses.

### STEP 3—Cognitive Context (Optional)

| CHC Domain | Subtest | Standard Score | Interpretation |
|---|---|---|---|
| *Gwm*—Working Memory | WISC-V Digit Span | 85 | Low average; contributes to difficulty holding ideas in mind |
| Gs—Processing Speed | WISC-V Coding | 98 | Average; slow writing not due to motor speed |
| *Gc*—Expressive Language | WJ V Oral Expression | 102 | Average; verbal formulation intact |
| *Gf*—Fluid Reasoning | WISC-V Matrix Reasoning | 100 | Average; reasoning not the source of difficulty |

### Interpretation (Step 3)

- Weak *Gwm* contributes to difficulty juggling ideas during writing.
- *Gs* is average → slow writing is not due to motor speed.
- *Gc* is average → verbal formulation is intact.
- *Gf* is average → reasoning is not the source of difficulty.

### Debiasing Checkpoint (Step 3)

Avoid overattribution:

- *Gwm* weakness alone does not fully explain the writing profile.
- The FAW Planning/EF weakness remains the primary mechanism.

## Final Diagnostic picture—Sofia

**Diagnosis:** Specific Learning Disability—Written Expression, Composition/Organization subtype (Composition Pathway)
Why:

- Weak planning and organization
- Weak EF processes during writing
- Intact transcription, spelling, and language formulation
- Extended-writing tasks consistently below average
- Sentence-level weaknesses mild and secondary
- Cognitive profile supports EF-based mechanism
- Teacher and parent reports align with composition difficulty

## Mechanism Explanation

A breakdown in planning, organization, and executive functions disrupts Sofia's ability to:

- generate ideas,
- structure them logically,
- maintain coherence across paragraphs,
- elaborate meaningfully, and
- revise effectively.

## This mechanism explains:

- why she has strong verbal ideas but cannot translate them into writing,
- why her writing is brief and underdeveloped,
- why she becomes overwhelmed by multiparagraph tasks, and
- why transcription and spelling are intact.

This is the classic profile of Composition LD.

## High-Leverage Practices for Composition LD

**A. SRSD (Self-Regulated Strategy Development)**
Most evidence-supported intervention for composition LD.
Teaches planning, organization, self-monitoring, goal setting, and revision.

**B. Planning Templates & Graphic Organizers**
Externalize the planning process Sofia cannot manage internally.
Examples: story maps, paragraph frames, outline templates, and "boxes and bullets."

**C. Explicit Instruction in Text Structure**
Teach narrative, informational, and opinion structures; transitions; paragraph logic.

**D. Sentence-to-Paragraph Routines**
Support elaboration and coherence by building paragraphs from structured prompts.

**E. Revision Routines with Checklists**
Teach revision as a step-by-step process rather than an open-ended task.

**F. Gradual Release with Modeling**
Teachers model planning, organizing, revising, and self-monitoring before fading supports.

## What Sofia Does NOT Need

Because her difficulty is EF-based—not motor, spelling, or language formulation—she does not need:

- handwriting interventions
- spelling instruction
- phonics or encoding work
- grammar worksheets
- speeded writing tasks
- "write more" without structure

These do not address the mechanism.

## DON'T FORGET

**Pathway = WHAT system is breaking down.**

The pathway is the **diagnostic category** that classifies the student's **academic performance pattern**.

It answers: **"Where is the breakdown occurring?"**

**Identified from:**

- Achievement patterns (Step 1)
- Error analysis
- Cross-battery confirmation
- Teacher report

**Examples:**

- **Reading:** phonological, orthographic, mixed, comprehension
- **Math:** procedural, retrieval, conceptual
- **Writing:** graphomotor, encoding, sentence-level, composition

The pathway tells you **which academic system** is affected.

**Mechanism = WHY that pathway is weak.**

The mechanism is the **underlying cognitive-linguistic process** that produces the student's pattern of errors.

It answers: **"What process is driving the difficulty?"**

**Identified from:**

- Process-level tasks (Step 2)
- FAW, FAM, or reading process measures
- Cognitive-linguistic indicators
- Error patterns tied to specific processes

**Pathways come from academic performance (Step 1). Mechanisms come from process-level data (Step 2).**

**Examples:**

- Unstable phoneme representations → *phonological pathway*
- Inefficient orthographic learning → *orthographic pathway*
- EF/WM overload during multistep algorithms → *procedural math*
- Slow access to quantity representations → *retrieval math*
- Weak planning and organization → *composition writing*

The mechanism tells you **what to target in intervention**.

### Evidence Base

- Writing depends on planning, organization, and EF processes (Berninger & Winn, 2006; Hayes & Flower, 1980).
- SRSD is the most effective intervention for composition difficulties (Graham & Harris, 2018).
- Planning templates and text structure instruction improve organization and elaboration (Graham et al., 2018).
- Revision routines improve writing quality and self-regulation (Harris et al., 2012).
- EF-based writing interventions improve both quality and quantity of written text (Berninger et al., 2008).

As page limitations preclude the inclusion of additional full case studies for the remaining subtypes, interventions corresponding to other writing subtypes are included in Appendix 5.C at the end of this chapter. The writing assessment framework presented in this chapter demonstrates that writing is a multidimensional skill that requires coordinated contributions from motor, linguistic, syntactic, and executive function systems. By integrating achievement measures with FAW process data and CHC-aligned cognitive indicators, practitioners can differentiate among handwriting/graphomotor, spelling/encoding, sentence-level, and composition/organization subtypes with clarity and precision. The 16-subtest cross-battery writing battery provides a coherent structure that mirrors the reading and math frameworks, ensuring consistency across domains. The flowchart guides efficient test selection, while the decision-rule matrix translates score patterns into defensible diagnostic conclusions. The case studies illustrate how these tools work together in practice, showing how subtype-specific patterns emerge and how they inform targeted intervention planning. Together, these components offer a comprehensive, evidence-aligned approach to evaluating writing difficulties that is both diagnostically rigorous and practical for school-based assessment.

## SUMMARY AND CONCLUSIONS

This chapter demonstrated how a mechanism-driven, diagnostic XBA allows practitioners to move beyond surface-level academic performance and toward a precise understanding of *why* a student struggles in reading, math, or writing. Across all three domains, the diagnostic process begins with identifying the presenting concern, selecting achievement anchors that measure the relevant academic components, and then using targeted process measures to clarify the underlying pathway or subtype. The resulting profile is not a list of scores but a coherent explanation of the student's strengths, weaknesses, and instructional needs.

A central theme of this chapter is that no single test is required. What matters is not the specific instrument but whether the selected measures adequately assess the constructs of interest. Any combination of tools can be used—achievement batteries, specialized diagnostic instruments, or cross-battery composites—as long as they collectively capture the academic skills and cognitive-linguistic processes relevant to the suspected subtype. The reading cases illustrated this principle explicitly by showing how students with significant decoding or orthographic weaknesses can still demonstrate at least average reasoning ability. Having established this point, the math and writing cases focused more narrowly on subtype identification and intervention, without repeating the reasoning-ability tables.

Across domains, the same logic applies:

- Identify the pathway (phonological, orthographic, mixed, comprehension; procedural, retrieval, conceptual; graphomotor, encoding, sentence-level, composition).
- Clarify the mechanism driving the difficulty.
- Select assessments that measure the skills and processes aligned with that mechanism.
- Link the findings to high-leverage instructional practices that directly target the source of breakdown.

This approach ensures that classification is accurate, interpretations are defensible, and recommendations are instructionally meaningful. It also reduces the ambiguity that often arises when practitioners rely on isolated scores or assume that a single battery can fully characterize a student's learning profile.

The next chapter extends this logic by examining a student who was evaluated twice—once through a neuropsychological lens and once through a school-based multidisciplinary team. Connor's case illustrates how different assessment frameworks can converge or diverge depending on the constructs measured, the tools selected, and the interpretive assumptions applied. By analyzing both evaluations side-by-side, the chapter highlights how a mechanism-driven lens can reconcile seemingly conflicting data and lead to a more coherent, evidence-based understanding of the student's needs.

## TEST YOURSELF

**1. It is not sufficient to document low academic achievement when diagnosing a learning disability; the evaluation must also identify the underlying mechanism that produces the academic difficulty. True or False?**

**2. What is meant by a diagnostic pathway in cross-battery assessment?**

(a) A sequence of test administrations used to determine IQ
(b) The route of breakdown defined by mechanisms, skills, and error patterns that explain why a student struggles academically
(c) The order in which achievement tests are administered
(d) The statistical relationship between cognitive and achievement scores

**3. Which of the following is not one of the four core reading components described in the chapter?**

(a) Word reading accuracy
(b) Decoding efficiency
(c) Reading fluency
(d) Orthographic memory

**4. Teacher interviews are used early in the diagnostic process to help clarify the nature of the student's academic difficulty and guide test selection. True or False?**

**5. Which of the following best describes the relationship between decoding and language comprehension according to the Simple View of Reading?**

(a) Reading comprehension depends primarily on vocabulary knowledge
(b) Reading comprehension is determined by decoding alone
(c) Reading comprehension reflects the interaction between decoding and language comprehension
(d) Reading comprehension depends primarily on orthographic learning

**6. Achievement batteries such as the WIAT-4, WJ V ACH, and KTEA-3 are designed primarily to measure academic performance rather than to identify the cognitive-linguistic mechanisms underlying academic difficulties. True or False?**

**7. Which of the following reading profiles is characterized by weak phonological awareness, weak phonological automaticity, and weak pseudoword decoding?**

(a) Surface/orthographic dyslexia
(b) Phonological dyslexia
(c) Comprehension-based reading disorder
(d) Fluency/efficiency weakness

**8. A student who demonstrates strong decoding but weak listening comprehension is most likely to show which type of reading difficulty?**

(a) Phonological dyslexia
(b) Surface/orthographic dyslexia
(c) Language-based comprehension weakness
(d) Mixed dyslexia

**9. Accuracy and efficiency represent two separable dimensions of reading performance. True or False?**

**10. In diagnostic assessment, achievement measures help determine what a student can do, whereas cognitive-linguistic measures help explain why the difficulty occurs. True or False?**

*Answers:* 1. True; 2. b; 3. d; 4. True; 5. c; 6. True; 7. b; 8. c; 9. True; 10. True

## REFERENCES


Abbott, R. D., & Berninger, V. W. (1993). Structural equation modeling of relationships among developmental skills and writing skills in primary- and intermediate-grade writers. *Journal of Educational Psychology, 85*(3), 478–508.

Adi-Japha, E., Landau, Y. E., Frenkel, L., Teicher, M., Gross-Tsur, V., & Shalev, R. S. (2007). ADHD and spelling difficulties: A developmental perspective. *Developmental Neuropsychology, 31*(2), 193–209.

Andersson, U. (2007). The contribution of working memory to children's mathematical word problem solving. *Applied Cognitive Psychology, 21*(9), 1201–1216.

Andersson, U., & Östergren, R. (2012). Number magnitude processing and basic cognitive functions in children with mathematical learning disabilities. *Learning and Individual Differences, 22*(6), 701–714.

Ashcraft, M. H. (1982). The development of mental arithmetic: A chronometric approach. *Developmental Review, 2*(3), 213–236.

Bailey, D. H., Oh, Y., Farkas, G., Morgan, P., & Hillemeier, M. (2020). Reciprocal effects of reading and mathematics? Beyond the cross-lagged panel model. *Developmental Psychology, 56*(5), 912.

Banfi, C., Kemény, F., Gangl, M., Schulte-Körne, G., Moll, K., & Landerl, K. (2017). Visuo-spatial attention in dyslexia and dysgraphia. *Scientific Studies of Reading, 21*(6), 457–469.

Bartelet, D., Ansari, D., Vaessen, A., & Blomert, L. (2014). Cognitive subtypes of mathematics learning difficulties. *Journal of Learning Disabilities, 47*(2), 115–125.

Berninger, V. W., & Amtmann, D. (2003). Preventing written expression disabilities through early and continuing assessment and intervention. In H. L. Swanson, K. R. Harris, & S. Graham (Eds.), *Handbook of learning disabilities* (pp. 323–344). Guilford Press.

Berninger, V. W., Nielsen, K. H., Abbott, R. D., Wijsman, E., & Raskind, W. (2008). Writing problems in developmental dyslexia: Under-recognized and under-treated. *Journal of School Psychology, 46*(1), 1–21.

Berninger, V. W., & Swanson, H. L. (1994). Modifying Hayes and Flower's model of skilled writing to explain beginning and developing writing. In E. Butterfield (Ed.), *Children's writing: Toward a process theory of development* (pp. 57–81). JAI Press.

Berninger, V. W., & Winn, W. (2006). Implications of advancements in brain research and technology for writing development, writing instruction, and educational evolution. In C. MacArthur, S. Graham, & J. Fitzgerald (Eds.), *Handbook of writing research* (pp. 96–114). Guilford Press.

Berninger, V. W., Yates, C., Cartwright, A., Rutberg, J., Remy, E., & Abbott, R. (1992). Lower-level developmental skills in beginning writing. *Reading and Writing, 4*(3), 257–280.

Bosse, M. L., Tainturier, M. J., & Valdois, S. (2007). Developmental dyslexia: The visual attention span deficit hypothesis. *Cognition, 104*(2), 198–230.

Bradley, L., & Bryant, P. E. (1983). Categorizing sounds and learning to read—a causal connection. *Nature, 301*(5899), 419–421.

Brannon, E. M., & Roitman, J. (2003). Nonverbal representation of numerical quantity. *Trends in Cognitive Sciences, 7*(8), 289–295.

Bull, R., & Scerif, G. (2001). Executive functioning as a predictor of children's mathematics ability. *Developmental Neuropsychology, 19*(3), 273–293.

Burns, M. K., Ysseldyke, J., Nelson, P. M., & Kanive, R. (2015). Number of repetitions required to retain single-digit multiplication math facts for elementary students. *School Psychology Quarterly, 30*(3), 398.

Cain, K., & Oakhill, J. (2022). Reading comprehension and its development in children. *Annual Review of Psychology, 73*, 271–295.

Capodieci, A., Cornoldi, C., & Re, A. M. (2018). ADHD and spelling: The role of working memory. *Journal of Learning Disabilities, 51*(6), 581–589.

Castles, A., & Coltheart, M. (1993). Varieties of developmental dyslexia. *Cognition, 47*(2), 149–180.

Castles, A., Rastle, K., & Nation, K. (2018). Ending the reading wars: Reading acquisition from novice to expert. *Psychological Science in the Public Interest, 19*(1), 5–51.

Catts, H. W., Herrera, S., Nielsen, D. C., & Bridges, M. S. (2015). Early prediction of reading comprehension within the simple view framework. *Reading and Writing, 28*(9), 1407–1425.

Catts, H. W., Hogan, T. P., & Adlof, S. M. (2005). Developmental changes in reading and reading disabilities. In H. W. Catts & A. G. Kamhi (Eds.), *The connections between language and reading disabilities* (pp. 25–40). Lawrence Erlbaum Associates Publishers.

Catts, H. W., Hogan, T. P., & Adlof, S. M. (2006). Developmental changes in reading and reading disabilities. In D. K. Dickinson & S. B. Neuman (Eds.), *Handbook of early literacy research* (Vol. 2, pp. 25–38). Guilford Press.

Cragg, L., & Gilmore, C. (2014). Skills underlying mathematics: The role of executive function in the development of mathematics proficiency. *Trends in Neuroscience and Education, 3*(2), 63–68.

De Smedt, B., Taylor, J., Archibald, L., & Ansari, D. (2011). How is phonological processing related to individual differences in children's arithmetic skills? *Developmental Science, 13*(3), 508–520.

Desoete, A. (2007). Evaluating and improving mathematics learning. *Learning and Instruction, 17*(6), 645–656.

Diamanti, V., Goulandris, N., Campbell, R., & Protopapas, A. (2018). Dyslexia profiles across orthographies differing in transparency: An evaluation of theoretical predictions contrasting English and Greek. *Scientific Studies of Reading, 22*(1), 55–69.

Döhla, D., & Heim, S. (2016). Developmental dyslexia and dysgraphia: Cognitive profiles and overlaps. *Frontiers in Psychology, 7*, 1–15.

Döhla, D., Heim, S., & Grande, M. (2020). Cognitive profiles of children with dyscalculia and mathematical difficulties: A systematic review. *Frontiers in Psychology, 11*, 1125.

Ehri, L. C. (2000). Learning to read and learning to spell: Two sides of a coin. *Topics in Language Disorders, 20*(3), 19–36.

Ehri, L. C. (2020). The science of learning to read words: A case for systematic phonics instruction. *Reading Research Quarterly, 55*, S45–S60.

Elliott, J. G., & Grigorenko, E. L. (2014). *The dyslexia debate.* Cambridge University Press.

Feifer, S. G. (2016). *Feifer Assessment of Mathematics (FAM).* PAR.

Feifer, S. G. (2020). *Feifer Assessment of Writing (FAW).* PAR.

Feifer, S. G., & Nader, M. (2015). *Feifer Assessment of Reading (FAR).* PAR.

Fletcher, J. M., Lyon, G. R., Fuchs, L. S., & Barnes, M. A. (2007). *Learning disabilities: From identification to intervention.* Guilford Press.

Fletcher, J. M., Lyon, G. R., Fuchs, L. S., & Barnes, M. A. (2019). *Learning disabilities: From identification to intervention* (2nd ed). The Guilford Press.

Friso-van den Bos, I., van der Ven, S. H., Kroesbergen, E. H., & van Luit, J. E. (2013). Working memory and mathematics in primary school children: A meta-analysis. *Educational Research Review, 10*, 29–44.

Fuchs, L. S., & Fuchs, D. (2005). Mathematical problem solving in children with learning disabilities. *Learning Disabilities Research & Practice, 20*(1), 2–10.

Fuchs, L. S., Fuchs, D., Compton, D. L. et al. (2016). The cognitive foundations of children's mathematics learning. *Current Directions in Psychological Science, 25*(3), 187–193.

Fuchs, L. S., Fuchs, D., Hosp, M. K., & Jenkins, J. R. (2001). *Oral reading fluency as an indicator of reading competence. Scientific Studies of Reading, 5*(3), 239–256.

Fuchs, L. S., Fuchs, D., Seethaler, P. M. et al. (2018). Fluency as a predictor of mathematics development. *Journal of Educational Psychology, 110*(7), 1001–1019.

Fyfe, E. R., DeCaro, M. S., & Rittle-Johnson, B. (2019). The role of feedback during learning: A meta-analysis. *Educational Psychology Review, 31*(2), 419–438.

Geary, D. C. (1993). Mathematical disabilities: Cognitive, neuropsychological, and genetic components. *Psychological Bulletin, 114*, 345–362.

Geary, D. C. (1994). *Children's mathematical development: Research and practical applications.* American Psychological Association.

Geary, D. C. (2004). Mathematics and learning disabilities. *Journal of Learning Disabilities, 37*(1), 4–15.

Geary, D. C. (2011). Cognitive predictors of achievement growth in mathematics: A five-year longitudinal study. *Developmental Psychology, 47*(6), 1539–1552.

Geary, D. C., & Hoard, M. K. (2005). Learning disabilities in arithmetic. *Handbook of Mathematical Cognition*, 253–267.

Gialluisi, A., Andlauer, T. F. M., Mirza-Schreiber, N., Moll, K., Becker, J., Hoffmann, P., Ludwig, K. U., Czamara, D., Pourcain, B. S., Honbolygó, F., Tóth, D., Csépe, V., Schulte-Körne, G., & Nöthen, M. M. (2021). Genome-wide association study reveals new insights into the heritability and genetic correlates of developmental dyslexia. *Molecular Psychiatry, 26*(7), 3004–3017.

Gough, P. B., & Tunmer, W. E. (1986). Decoding, reading, and reading disability. *Remedial and Special Education, 7*(1), 6–10.

Graham, S. (2018). A revised writer(s)-within-community model of writing. *Educational Psychologist, 53*(4), 258–279.

Graham, S., & Harris, K. R. (2018). Evidence-based writing practices. In S. Graham, C. MacArthur, & M. Hebert (Eds.), *Best practices in writing instruction* (3rd ed, pp. 3–28). Guilford Press.

Graham, S., & Harris, K. R. (2000). The role of self-regulation and transcription skills in writing and writing development. *Educational Psychologist, 35*(1), 3–12.

Graham, S., Harris, K. R., & Adkins, M. (2018). The impact of supplemental handwriting and spelling instruction with first-grade students who are poor writers. *Reading and Writing, 31*, 1273–1294.

Graham, S., & Perin, D. (2007). *Writing next: Effective strategies to improve writing of adolescents.* Alliance for Excellent Education.

Griffiths, Y. M., & Snowling, M. J. (2002). Predictors of exception word and nonword reading in dyslexic children: The severity hypothesis. *Journal of Educational Psychology, 94*(1), 34.

Halberda, J., & Feigenson, L. (2008). Developmental change in the acuity of the ANS. *Nature, 455*(7213), 665–668.

Harris, K. R., Lane, K. L., Graham, S., Driscoll, S. A., Sandmel, K., Brindle, M., & Schatschneider, C. (2012). Practice-based professional development for self-regulated strategies development in writing: A randomized controlled study. *Journal of Teacher Education, 63*(2), 103–119.

Hayes, J. R., & Flower, L. S. (1980). Writing as problem solving. *Visible language, 14*(4).

Heikkilä, R., Torppa, M., Aro, M., Närhi, V., & Ahonen, T. (2020). Cognitive correlates of math difficulties in adolescents: Evidence for multiple deficit pathways. *Journal of Learning Disabilities, 53*(5), 366–379.

Heim, S., Grande, M., Pape-Neumann, J., van Ermingen-Marbach, M., & Willmes, K. (2008). Cognitive subtypes of dyslexia. *Frontiers in Human Neuroscience, 2*, 1–15.

Hoover, W. A., & Gough, P. B. (1990). The simple view of reading. *Reading and Writing, 2*(2), 127–160.

Hulme, C., Goetz, K., Gooch, D., Adams, J., & Snowling, M. J. (2007). Paired-associate learning, phoneme awareness, and learning to read. *Journal of Experimental Child Psychology, 96*(2), 150–166.

Hulme, C., & Snowling, M. J. (2016). Reading disorders and dyslexia. *Current Opinion in Pediatrics, 28*(6), 731–735.

Jordan, N. C., Glutting, J., & Ramineni, C. (2010). The importance of number sense to mathematics achievement in first and third grades. *Learning and Individual Differences, 20*(2), 82–88.

Jordan, N. C., & Hanich, L. B. (2000). Mathematical thinking in second grade children with different forms of LD. *Journal of Learning Disabilities, 33*(6), 567–578.

Katzir, T., Kim, Y., Wolf, M., O'Brien, B., Kennedy, B., Lovett, M., & Morris, R. (2006). Reading fluency: The whole is more than the parts. *Annals of dyslexia, 56*(1), 51–82.

Kim, S. K. (2021). Recent update on reading disability (dyslexia) focused on neurobiology. *Clinical and Experimental Pediatrics, 64*(10), 497.

Kim, Y. S. G. (2020). Toward an integrated model of reading and writing. *Educational Psychology Review, 32*(1), 1–31.

Koponen, T., Georgiou, G., Salmi, P., Leskinen, M., & Aro, M. (2017). A meta-analysis of the relation between RAN and mathematics. *Journal of Educational Psychology, 109*(7), 977.

Kuhn, M. R., Schwanenflugel, P. J., & Meisinger, E. B. (2010). Aligning theory and assessment of reading fluency: Automaticity, prosody, and definitions of fluency. *Reading Research Quarterly, 45*(2), 230–251.

LaBerge, D., & Samuels, S. J. (1974). Toward a theory of automatic information processing in reading. *Cognitive Psychology, 6*, 293–323.

Lanfranchi, S., Cornoldi, C., & Vianello, R. (2008). Working memory deficits in children with learning disabilities. *Journal of Learning Disabilities, 41*(2), 138–149.

Language and Reading Research Consortium (2015). The dimensionality of language ability in young children. *Journal of Speech, Language, and Hearing Research, 58*(3), 840–852.

Lewandowska, M., Milner, R., Ganc, M., Włodarczyk, E., & Skarżyński, H. (2014). Attention dysfunction subtypes of developmental dyslexia. *Medical Science Monitor: International Medical Journal of Experimental and Clinical Research, 20*, 2256.

Lohman, D. F., & Lakin, J. M. (2021). *Cognitive abilities test™ (CogAT®), forms 7/8: A guide for teachers*. Riverside Insights.

Mather, N., McCallum, S. R., Bell, S. M., & Wendling, B. J. (2024). *Tests of dyslexia (TOD)*. Western Psychological Services.

Mather, N., McGrew, K. S., LaForte, E. M., & Wendling, B. J. (2025). *Woodcock-Johnson V virtual test library*. Riverside Assessments, LLC.

Mazzocco, M. M. (2008). Defining and differentiating mathematical learning disabilities. *Journal of Learning Disabilities*, *41*(4), 284–297.

McCloskey, M., & Rapp, B. (2017). Developmental dysgraphia: An overview and framework for research. *Cognitive Neuropsychology*, *34*(3–4), 65–82.

Melby-Lervåg, M., Lyster, S.-A. H., & Hulme, C. (2012). Phonological skills and their role in learning to read. *Psychological Bulletin*, *138*(2), 322–352.

Menghini, D., Finzi, A., Benassi, M., Bolzani, R., Facoetti, A., Giovagnoli, S., Ruffino, M., & Vicari, S. (2010). Different underlying neurocognitive deficits in developmental dyslexia: A comparative study. *Neuropsychologia*, *48*(4), 863–872.

Moll, K., Kunze, S., Neuhoff, N., Bruder, J., & Schulte-Körne, G. (2009). Specific learning disorder in spelling. *Journal of Learning Disabilities*, *42*(6), 493–503.

Nation, K. (2019). Children's reading difficulties, language, and reflections on the simple view of reading. *Australian Journal of Learning Difficulties*, *24*(1), 47–73.

Nicolson, R. I., & Fawcett, A. J. (1990). Automaticity: A new framework for dyslexia research? *Cognition*, *35*(2), 159–182.

Nisiotou, I., & Vlachos, F. (2014). Neurodevelopmental disorders: Is there a common biological basis. *Child & Adolescent Psychiatry*, *2*, 31–41.

Norton, E. S., & Wolf, M. (2012). Rapid automatized naming and reading fluency. *Child Development Perspectives*, *6*(4), 296–303.

Ouellette, G., & Sénéchal, M. (2021). Orthographic learning revisited. *Journal of Experimental Child Psychology*, *204*, 105066.

Pacheco, A., Reis, A., Araújo, S., Inácio, F., Petersson, K. M., & Faísca, L. (2014). Dyslexia heterogeneity: Cognitive profiling of Portuguese children with dyslexia. *Reading and Writing*, *27*(9), 1529–1545.

Peng, P., & Fuchs, D. (2016). A meta-analysis of working memory deficits in children with math difficulties. *Journal of Learning Disabilities*, *49*(1), 3–20.

Pennington, B. F. (2006). From single to multiple deficit models of developmental disorders. *Cognition*, *101*(2), 385–413.

Pennington, B. F., SanterreLemmon, L., Rosenberg, J., MacDonald, B., Boada, R., Friend, A., & Olson, R. K. (2012). Individual prediction of dyslexia by single vs. multiple deficit models. *Journal of Abnormal Psychology*, *121*(1), 212–224.

Perfetti, C. A. (1992). The representation problem in reading acquisition. In P. B. Gough, L. C. Ehri, & R. Treiman (Eds.), *Reading acquisition* (pp. 145–174). Lawrence Erlbaum Associates, Inc.

Perfetti, C. A. (2007). Reading ability: Lexical quality to comprehension. *Scientific Studies of Reading*, *11*(4), 357–383.

Peterson, R. L., Pennington, B. F., & Olson, R. K. (2014). Subtypes of developmental dyslexia. *Developmental Psychology*, *50*(6), 1520–1533.

Piazza, M. (2010). Neurocognitive origins of number sense. *Trends in Cognitive Sciences*, *14*(7), 314–322.

Puranik, C. S., & Al Otaiba, S. (2012). Examining the contribution of handwriting and spelling to written expression. *Reading and Writing*, *25*(7), 1523–1546.

Purpura, D. J., Baroody, A. J., & Lonigan, C. J. (2013). The transition from informal to formal mathematical knowledge: Mediation by numeral knowledge. *Journal of Educational Psychology*, *105*(2), 453.

Ramus, F. (2003). Developmental dyslexia: A specific auditory processing deficit? *Trends in Cognitive Sciences*, *7*(4), 147–152.

Ramus, F. (2004). Neurobiology of dyslexia: A reinterpretation of the data. *Trends in Neurosciences*, *27*(12), 720–726.

Rittle-Johnson, B., Schneider, M., & Star, J. R. (2015). Not a one-way street. *Educational Psychology Review*, *27*(4), 587–597.

Rittle-Johnson, B., & Siegler, R. S. (1998). The relation between conceptual and procedural knowledge. *Cognitive Psychology*, *36*(3), 203–243.

Rittle-Johnson, B., & Star, J. R. (2007). Does comparing solution methods facilitate conceptual and procedural knowledge? An experimental study on learning to solve equations. *Journal of Educational Psychology*, *99*(3), 561–574.

Saddler, B., & Graham, S. (2005). Peer-assisted sentence combining. *Journal of Educational Psychology*, *97*(1), 43–54.

Schaadt, G., Männel, C., van der Meer, E., & Friederici, A. D. (2018). Crossmodal integration in spelling difficulties. *Developmental Science*, *21*(3), e12572.

Schneider, M., Rittle-Johnson, B., & Star, J. R. (2017). Relations between conceptual and procedural knowledge. *Educational Psychology Review*, *29*(4), 599–621.

Scott, C. M., & Windsor, J. (2000). General language performance measures in spoken and written narrative and expository discourse of school-age children with language learning disabilities. *Journal of Speech, Language, and Hearing Research*, *43*(2), 324–339.

Share, D. L. (1995). Phonological recoding and self-teaching. *Cognition*, *55*(2), 151–218.

Siegler, R. S., & Ramani, G. B. (2009). Playing linear number board games—but not circular ones—improves low-income preschoolers' numerical understanding. *Journal of Educational Psychology*, *101*(3), 545.

Skinner, C. H., McLaughlin, T. F., & Logan, P. (1997). Cover, copy, and compare: A self-managed academic intervention effective across skills, students, and settings. *Journal of Behavioral Education*, *7*(3), 295–306.

Snow, C. E. (2010). Academic language and the challenge of reading for learning about science. *Science*, *328*(5977), 450–452.

Snowling, M. J. (1995). Phonological processing and developmental dyslexia. *Journal of Research in Reading*.

Snowling, M. J. (2001). From language to reading and dyslexia 1. *Dyslexia*, *7*(1), 37–46.

Snowling, M. J., & Hulme, C. (2020). Annual research review: Reading disorders revisited. *Journal of Child Psychology and Psychiatry*, *61*(6), 684–701.

Soriano-Ferrer, M., Nievas-Cazorla, F., Sánchez-López, P., Félix-Mateo, V., & González-Torre, J. A. (2014). Reading-related cognitive deficits in Spanish developmental dyslexia. *Procedia-Social and Behavioral Sciences*, *132*, 3–9.

Stein, J. (2001). The magnocellular theory of dyslexia. *Trends in Neurosciences*, *24*(9), 508–514.

Steinbrink, C., & Klatte, M. (2008). Phonological working memory in dysgraphia. *Journal of Child Psychology and Psychiatry*, *49*(4), 404–412.

Swanson, H. L., Jerman, O., & Zheng, X. (2008). Working memory, math, and reading disabilities. *Journal of Learning Disabilities*, *41*(6), 567–582.

Sweller, J., Ayres, P., & Kalyuga, S. (2011). *Cognitive load theory*. Springer.

Tallal, P. (1980). Auditory temporal perception, phonics, and reading disabilities in children. *Brain and language*, *9*(2), 182–198.

Torgesen, J. K. (2020). The role of fluency in reading development. *Perspectives on Language and Literacy*, *46*(1), 9–15.

Treiman, R. (1997). Spelling in children. *Topics in Language Disorders*, *17*(3), 1–18.

Treiman, R. (2018). Learning to spell. *Child Development Perspectives*, *12*(4), 235–239.

Treiman, R., & Kessler, B. (2014). *How children learn to write words*. Oxford University Press.

Valdois, S., Bosse, M. L., Ans, B., Carbonnel, S., Zorman, M., David, D., & Pellat, J. (2003). Phonological and visual processing deficits can dissociate in developmental dyslexia: Evidence from two case studies. *Reading and Writing, 16*(6), 541–572.
van Bergen, E., van der Leij, A., & de Jong, P. F. (2014). The intergenerational multiple deficit model and the case of dyslexia. *Frontiers in human neuroscience, 8*, 346.
van Bergen, E., van der Leij, A., & de Jong, P. F. (2020). The intergenerational multiple deficit model. *Developmental Review, 55*, 100885.
van der Kleij, S. W., Segers, E., & Verhoeven, L. (2019). Predicting dyslexia in bilingual children. *Scientific Studies of Reading, 23*(6), 507–521.
Vellutino, F. R., Fletcher, J. M., Snowling, M. J., & Scanlon, D. M. (2004). Specific reading disability (dyslexia): What have we learned in the past four decades? *Journal of Child Psychology and Psychiatry, 45*(1), 2–40.
Wagner, R. K., & Torgesen, J. K. (1987). The nature of phonological processing and its causal role in the acquisition of reading skills. *Psychological Bulletin, 101*(2), 192–212.
Wang, H.-C., Castles, A., & Nickels, L. (2021). Orthographic learning in children. *Journal of Experimental Child Psychology, 204*, 105064.
Wechsler, D. (2020). *Wechsler individual achievement test* (4th ed), Pearson.
White, S., Milne, E., Rosen, S., Hansen, P., Swettenham, J., Frith, U., & Ramus, F. (2006). The role of sensorimotor impairments in dyslexia: A multiple case study of dyslexic children. *Developmental Science, 9*(3), 237–255.
Winkes, J. (2014). Phonological working memory and spelling. *Journal of Learning Disabilities, 47*(3), 219–230.
Witzel, B. S., Mercer, C. D., & Miller, M. D. (2003). Teaching algebra to students with learning difficulties: An investigation of an explicit instruction model. *Learning Disabilities Research & Practice, 18*(2), 121–131.
Wolf, M., & Bowers, P. G. (1999). The double-deficit hypothesis for the developmental dyslexias. *Journal of Educational Psychology, 91*(3), 415.
Wolf, M., & Katzir-Cohen, T. (2001). Reading fluency and its intervention. *Scientific Studies of Reading, 5*(3), 211–239.
Xu, F. (2003). Numerosity discrimination in infants. *Cognitive Psychology, 47*(2), 150–178.
Ziegler, J. C., & Goswami, U. (2005). Reading acquisition, developmental dyslexia, and skilled reading. *Psychological Bulletin, 131*(1), 3–29.
Zoubrinetzky, R., Bielle, F., & Valdois, S. (2014). New insights on developmental dyslexia subtypes: Heterogeneity of mixed reading profiles. *PloS one, 9*(6), e99337.

## APPENDIX 5.A

### Reading Case Study: Applying a Diagnostic Reading Battery to Maya

**Student:** Maya, age 10 (Grade 4)

**Teacher Report:** Maya has difficulty decoding long, more complex or irregular words. She has difficulty acquiring sight-word vocabulary for science and other technical terminology. Her reading is slow and choppy. She is embarrassed to read out loud and never volunteers to read. These observations suggest possible word-level accuracy and fluency problems.

**Referral Question:** Why is Maya's reading slow, and why is she having difficulty with irregular words despite adequate instruction?

**Background:** Strong oral language, strong phonological awareness in classroom tasks, persistent difficulty with sight-word recognition, slow reading rate, and heavy reliance on sounding out words.

#### Step 1: Achievement Anchors (WIAT-4)

| Subtest | Standard Score | Interpretation |
|---|---|---|
| Word Reading | 83 | Weak real-world accuracy, especially for irregular words |
| Pseudoword Decoding | 98 | Phonological decoding intact |
| Decoding Fluency | 75 | Slow, effortful decoding despite intact phonics |
| Oral Reading Fluency | 79 | Weak rate + accuracy; fluency vulnerability |

**Conclusion:** A reading disorder appears to be present, but phonological decoding appears intact.

**Debiasing Note:** Even though Maya's phonics instruction has been strong, DD/C requires avoiding the assumption that intact pseudoword decoding automatically rules out dyslexia. The subtype must be determined empirically.

**Next Step:** Examine decoding and efficiency to clarify the nature of the weakness.

#### Step 2: TOD-C Decoding Efficiency

| Subtest | Standard Score | Interpretation |
|---|---|---|
| Rapid Pseudoword Reading | 80 | Slow decoding efficiency despite intact phonics |
| Rapid Irregular Word Reading | 70 | Weak real-world accuracy and efficiency, especially for irregular words |

**Conclusion:** Weakness is not phonological. Real-word decoding and efficiency are weak, suggesting an orthographic learning issue.

**Debiasing Note:** The evaluator should avoid anchoring on the intact phonological decoding score. Orthographic learning must be examined before concluding that the weakness is orthographic in nature.

**Next Step:** Evaluate orthographic learning directly.

### Step 3: TOD-C Orthographic Learning Indicators

| Subtest | Standard Score | Interpretation |
|---|---|---|
| Irregular Word Spelling | 70 | Slow orthographic learning rate |
| Sound-to-Symbol Learning | 80 | Weak orthographic mapping mechanism |
| Word Pattern Choice | 77 | Weak stored orthographic knowledge and pattern sensitivity |
| Letter and Word Choice | 76 | Weak orthographic decision-making and reduced sensitivity to English spelling conventions |

**Conclusion:** Clear orthographic learning deficit. This pattern suggests Orthographic Dyslexia.

**Debiasing Note:** The clear orthographic deficits provide strong evidence, but the evaluator must first verify that the phonological system is intact to avoid misclassification. This step counters confirmation bias.

**Next Step:** Test the hypothesis that phonological processes are intact.

### Step 4: FAR Phonological Processing Cluster

| Subtest | Standard Score | Interpretation |
|---|---|---|
| Phonemic Awareness | 101 | Average manipulation and segmentation |
| Rapid Automatic Naming | 99 | Efficient access to phonological codes |

**Conclusion:** The phonological system is intact. This rules out phonological dyslexia. The orthographic subtype of dyslexia remains viable.

**Debiasing Note:** The intact phonological system supports the orthographic subtype and prevents the evaluator from overinterpreting fluency weaknesses as phonological in origin.

### Step 5: FAR Morphology + Language

| Subtest | Standard Score | Interpretation |
|---|---|---|
| Morphological Processing | 99 | Meaning-based decoding intact |
| Semantic Concepts | 107 | Language comprehension intact |

**Conclusion:** No evidence of a comprehension-based disorder.

**Subtype Supported:** Surface/Orthographic Dyslexia.

### Step 6: WIAT-4 Comprehension Pair (to Determine Simple View Alignment)

| Subtest | Standard Score | Interpretation |
|---|---|---|
| Reading Comprehension | 78 | Weak comprehension |
| Listening Comprehension | 103 | Language comprehension intact |

**Interpretation:** Comprehension is weak because reading is slow and inaccurate, not because language comprehension is impaired. This aligns with surface/orthographic dyslexia, where inefficient word recognition limits comprehension.

**Debiasing Note:** This step guards against the bias of attributing comprehension weaknesses to language deficits when inefficient word recognition is the most plausible source of difficulty.

**Final Diagnostic Picture**

**Subtype: Surface/Orthographic Dyslexia**

**Why:**

- Weak orthographic learning rate
- Weak paired-associate learning
- Weak orthographic processing
- Weak real-word decoding
- Weak reading efficiency
- Intact phonological awareness
- Intact phonological memory
- Intact phonological automaticity
- Intact language comprehension

**Debiasing Note:** The subtype conclusion reflects a systematic evaluation of all relevant components, reducing the risk of premature closure or overreliance on a single indicator.

**X-BASS PSW Analysis Supports a Specific Learning Disability in Basic Reading Skills and Reading Fluency (Orthographic Dyslexia)**

Maya's test findings align closely with the DD/C results generated in X-BASS, as illustrated in Figure 5.6. Her overall cognitive profile reflects at least average general ability, as indicated by an FCC of 114 (an aggregate of *Gc*, *Gf*, *Ga*, and *Gr*). Within this context of average overall ability, Maya shows weaknesses in real-word decoding and efficiency and irregular word spelling, as well as a cognitive weakness in orthographic processing as reflected by her TOD-C Orthographic Processing Composite of 76 and Sight Word Acquisition Composite of 68. The differences between Maya's specific academic and cognitive weaknesses and the predicted scores of 109 and 108 (based on her FCC) are unusual, occurring in only about 5% of the population, indicating unexpected underachievement and domain-specific cognitive weaknesses, respectively. The empirical relationship between her cognitive and academic weaknesses is strong (or high) and demonstrates a below-average aptitude-achievement consistency, meaning that the cognitive weaknesses are a plausible explanation for the academic weaknesses. Together, these findings meet the DD/C criteria and provide strong support for a pattern of strengths and weaknesses that aligns with the SLD construct.

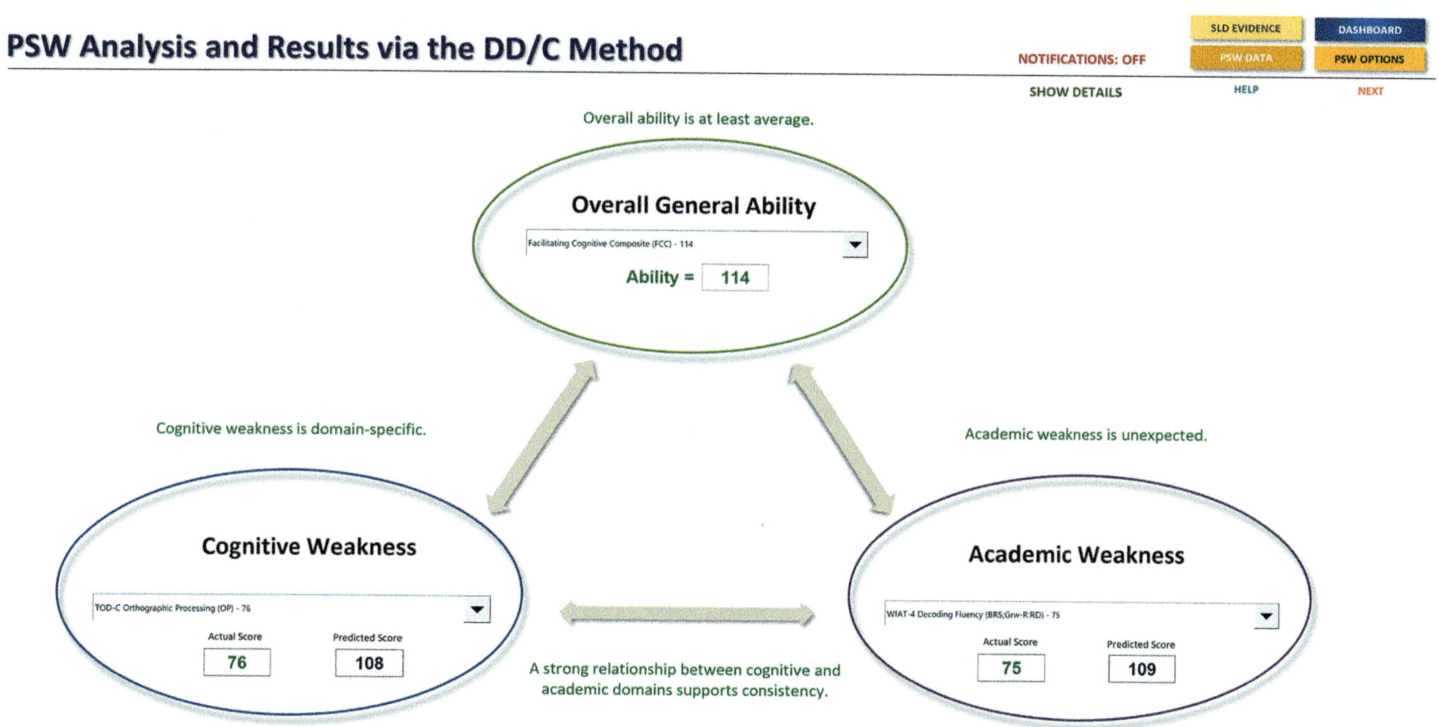


**FIGURE 5.6 PSW Analysis for Maya**

### What This Means for Maya

Maya struggles because she cannot efficiently store, retrieve, or recognize orthographic patterns. She relies heavily on phonological decoding, which slows reading and disrupts comprehension. Her phonological system is strong, but her orthographic mapping system does not support automatic word recognition.

### Intervention Implications Based on the Identified Pathway

**Subtype Identified:** *Orthographic Dyslexia (Orthographic Pathway)*

### What This Means Mechanistically

Maya's difficulty is not caused by weak phonological processing or weak language comprehension. Her profile shows intact phonological decoding and intact comprehension. The breakdown occurs in a different place:

**Mechanism:** Weak orthographic learning disrupts Maya's ability to store and retrieve written word forms.

This mechanism affects:

- orthographic mapping
- pattern recognition
- spelling accuracy
- irregular word reading
- rapid recognition of familiar words

This is why Maya:

- decodes nonsense words well
- decodes unfamiliar words or pseudoword words accurately
- struggles with irregular words
- spells phonetically but inaccurately
- reads accurately but not automatically

This is the hallmark of orthographic dyslexia.

### Why This Mechanism Produces Maya's Pattern

When orthographic learning is weak:

- the student can decode but cannot store the word efficiently
- irregular words remain difficult
- spelling is phonetic rather than pattern-based
- fluency remains low despite accurate decoding

This is the classic "accurate but slow" profile.

### What Maya Needs Instructionally

Maya needs interventions that:

- strengthen orthographic mapping
- build pattern recognition
- integrate spelling and reading
- support morphological awareness
- increase automaticity

These are the high-leverage practices for the orthographic pathway.

### High-Leverage Practices for Orthographic Dyslexia

#### A. Word Study Focused on Orthographic Patterns

Instruction should emphasize:

- spelling patterns
- rime units
- syllable types
- orthographic conventions

This builds the pattern knowledge Maya lacks.

### B. Integrated Spelling–Reading Instruction

Maya should:

- read the word
- spell the word
- write the word
- analyze the pattern

This strengthens orthographic mapping.

### C. Morphological Instruction

Teaching:

- roots
- prefixes
- suffixes
- meaning units

This supports spelling and reading of multisyllabic words.

### D. Irregular Word Instruction

Explicit teaching of:

- tricky parts
- unexpected spellings
- visual analysis of word structure

This is essential for orthographic storage.

### E. Fluency Practice After Orthographic Mapping Improves

Fluency should be:

- accuracy-first
- pattern-aligned
- supported by repeated reading

### What Maya Does *Not* Need

- phonological awareness training
- phonics instruction as the primary focus
- comprehension interventions
- speed drills without orthographic support

These do not address the mechanism.

### Evidence Base

- Orthographic learning depends on repeated, accurate decoding and pattern recognition (Ouellette & Sénéchal, 2021; Share, 1995).
- Morphological instruction improves spelling and word reading (Treiman, 2018).
- Integrated spelling–reading instruction strengthens orthographic mapping (Ehri, 2020).
- Irregular word instruction improves orthographic storage (Wang et al., 2021).
- Fluency improves when orthographic representations become automatic (Katzir et al., 2006).

## APPENDIX 5.B

## Additional Math Case Studies

### Case Study: Fact Retrieval/Fluency Math LD

**Student:** Maria, age 10 (Grade 4)

**Referral Question:** Why does Maria struggle to recall basic math facts quickly, even though she understands concepts, uses strategies effectively, and performs well on untimed reasoning tasks?

**Background**

Teacher questionnaire responses indicate that Maria:

- grasps new concepts quickly,
- uses effective strategies when allowed time,
- is significantly slower than peers during timed tasks,
- often reconstructs facts she "knows,"
- becomes anxious during speeded activities, and
- performs well on reasoning tasks when facts are provided.

These observations suggest a fluency-based difficulty, not a conceptual or procedural deficit.

### STEP 1—Achievement Anchors

| Subtest | Standard Score | Interpretation |
|---|---|---|
| WIAT-4 Numerical Operations | 94 | Procedural accuracy intact; no algorithmic weakness |
| WIAT-4 Math Problem Solving | 96 | Conceptual reasoning intact |
| WJ V ACH Calculation | 92 | Confirms procedural adequacy across batteries |

### Interpretation (Step 1)

- **No evidence of a procedural weakness.**
- Numerical Operations and Calculation are average with no algorithmic error patterns.
- **No evidence of a conceptual weakness.**
- Math Problem Solving is average and consistent with the teacher's report.
- **Weakness is not visible in untimed achievement tasks.**
- This is typical of retrieval/fluency LD.
- **A fluency or retrieval weakness remains the leading hypothesis.**

### Debiasing Checkpoint (Step 1)

To avoid anchoring on the referral concern ("slow facts"), the examiner considers alternative explanations using only Step 1 data:

- *Could this be procedural?*
- **No**. Procedural accuracy is average across two batteries.
- *Could this be conceptual?*
- **No**. Math Problem Solving is average.
- ***Could this be fact retrieval?***
- **Yes**. Slow, effortful performance is consistent with retrieval inefficiency.
- **Could this be fluency?**
- **Yes**. Step 1 does not include fluency measures.

### Why Step 1 Requires Step 2

Because Step 1 shows **intact procedural and conceptual skills**, the examiner must use Step 2 to determine whether:

- the weakness is **retrieval-based**,
- **fluency-based**, or
- **speed-based**.

### STEP 2—FAM Process Profile (Subtype Mechanism)

| Subtest | Standard Score | Interpretation |
|---|---|---|
| FAM Math Fact Retrieval | 74 | Weak automatic retrieval; high effort |
| FAM Rapid Automatic Naming-Quantity | 70 | Slow access to quantity representations |
| FAM Associative Learning | 78 | Reduced efficiency forming stable fact associations |
| FAM Working Memory | 87 | Relative weakness; increases retrieval load |
| FAM Processing Speed | 86 | Slow symbol processing; secondary contributor |

### Interpretation (Step 2)

- Clear cluster: **slow RAN-Quantity + weak fact retrieval + weak associative learning**.
- Processing speed is low but **not sufficient** to explain the pattern alone.
- Mechanism is **fact retrieval/automaticity**, not procedural or conceptual.

### Debiasing Checkpoint (Step 2)

To avoid confirmation bias, the examiner explicitly tests whether the data could support Procedural or Conceptual/Number Sense pathways.

**Additional Subtests Administered**

| Subtest | Standard Score | Interpretation |
|---|---|---|
| FAM Procedural Calculation | 96 | Procedures intact; no algorithmic weakness |
| FAM Executive Functions/Planning | 98 | Planning and sequencing intact |
| FAM Number Sense | 101 | Magnitude and conceptual understanding intact |
| FAM Verbal Problem Solving | 104 | Strong language-based quantitative reasoning |
| FAM Visual Spatial Number Manipulation | 99 | Spatial representation of quantity intact |

#### *Can a Procedural subtype be ruled out?*

**Yes.**

- Procedural Calculation is average.
- EF/Planning is average.
- No algorithmic errors appear in Step 1 or Step 2.

**Interpretation:**

No evidence of a procedural pathway.

#### *Can a Conceptual/Number Sense subtype be ruled out?*

**Yes.**

- Number Sense is average.
- Verbal and visual quantitative reasoning are average.
- No conceptual errors appear in Step 1 or Step 2.

**Interpretation:**

No evidence of a conceptual pathway.

### Conclusion of Step 2 Debiasing

After actively searching for disconfirming evidence:

- Procedural subtype → not supported
- Conceptual subtype → not supported

The remaining explanation—consistent with both achievement anchors and FAM process data—is a **Fact Retrieval/Fluency subtype**, driven by weaknesses in automaticity, RAN-Quantity, and associative learning.

### STEP 3—Cognitive Confirmation (Optional)

| CHC Domain | Subtest | Standard Score | Interpretation |
|---|---|---|---|
| *Gf*—Fluid Reasoning | WISC-V Matrix Reasoning | 98 | Abstract reasoning intact |
| *Gv*—Visual Processing | WISC-V Visual Puzzles | 102 | Visual-spatial processing intact |
| *Gwm*—Working Memory | WISC-V Digit Span | 85 | Borderline; increases retrieval load |
| Gs—Processing Speed | WISC-V Coding | 83 | Slow; secondary contributor to fluency weakness |

### Interpretation (Step 3)

- Weakness is unexpected relative to reasoning and conceptual skills.
- *Gs* is low but does not fully explain fact-specific retrieval weakness.
- Supports SLD with a fact retrieval/fluency mechanism.

### Debiasing Checkpoint (Step 3)

Avoid overattribution:

- Low *Gs* alone does **not** explain slow RAN-Quantity or weak associative learning.
- Retrieval-specific weaknesses remain primary.

### Final Diagnostic Picture—Maria

**Subtype:** Fact Retrieval/Fluency Math SLD

**Why:**

- Weak math fact retrieval
- Slow RAN-Quantity
- Weak associative learning
- Intact procedures and number sense
- Weakness unexpected relative to cognitive profile
- Teacher reports consistent with fluency-based difficulties

### Intervention Implications Based on the Identified Pathway

**Subtype Identified:** Fact Retrieval/Fluency Math SLD

**Mechanism:** Weak automaticity + slow quantity access + inefficient associative learning.

**Why This Mechanism Leads to Maria's Errors**

- She reconstructs facts instead of retrieving them.
- She is slow on any task requiring rapid access to quantity.
- She uses correct strategies but cannot execute them quickly.
- She performs well on untimed tasks because conceptual reasoning is intact.

This is the hallmark of the **Fact Retrieval/Fluency Pathway**.

### High-Leverage Practices for Fact Retrieval/Fluency SLD

**A. Incremental Rehearsal**

Most effective method for building automaticity.

**B. Cover–Copy–Compare**

Supports accuracy and fluency with immediate feedback.

**C. Timed → Untimed → Timed Cycles**

Builds automaticity without anxiety.

**D. Strategic Fact Family Instruction**

Reduces memory load by teaching relationships.

**E. RAN-Based Fluency Practice**

Dot patterns, quick quantity naming, subitizing.

### What Maria Does NOT Need

- Procedural instruction
- Conceptual number sense interventions
- Speeded drills without strategy
- "More practice" without automaticity supports

### Evidence Base

- Automaticity depends on RAN and associative learning (Koponen et al., 2017).
- Incremental rehearsal improves fact retrieval (Burns et al., 2015).
- Cover–copy–compare improves fluency (Skinner et al., 1997).
- RAN predicts math fact fluency (Heikkilä et al., 2020).

## Case Study: Conceptual/Number Sense Math SLD

**Student:** Lila, age 9 (Grade 3)

**Referral Question:** Why does Lila struggle with estimation, magnitude comparison, and understanding place value, even though her teacher reports that she can memorize procedures and complete basic calculations when steps are modeled?

### Background

Teacher questionnaire responses indicate that Lila:

- participates actively in class and enjoys math discussions,
- can memorize procedures but often applies them incorrectly,
- struggles to explain why an answer makes sense,
- has difficulty comparing quantities, estimating, and using benchmark numbers,
- becomes confused when numbers get larger or when problems require flexible reasoning, and
- performs better on rote tasks than on conceptual ones.

These observations suggest a **conceptual/number sense difficulty**, not a procedural or retrieval deficit—an important hypothesis to test systematically.

### STEP 1—Achievement Anchors

| Subtest | Standard Score | Interpretation |
|---|---|---|
| WIAT-4 Numerical Operations | 82 | Procedures partially learned; accuracy inconsistent |
| WIAT-4 Math Problem Solving | 75 | Weak conceptual reasoning; difficulty applying quantitative relationships |
| WJ V ACH Applied Problems | 78 | Confirms conceptual weakness across batteries |

### Interpretation (Step 1)

- **Conceptual reasoning is weak**, as shown by Math Problem Solving and Applied Problems.
- **Procedural accuracy is inconsistent**, but errors appear conceptual rather than algorithmic.
- **Weakness is domain-specific**, not global.

### Debiasing Checkpoint (Step 1)

To avoid anchoring on the referral concern ("number sense"), the examiner considers alternative explanations using only Step 1 data:

- **Could this be procedural?**
  Possibly. Numerical Operations is below average, but error patterns appear conceptual (misunderstanding magnitude, misinterpreting quantities).
- **Could this be retrieval?**
  Unlikely. No evidence of slow or inaccurate fact retrieval in teacher report or Step 1.
- **Could this be conceptual?**
  Yes. Math Problem Solving and Applied Problems are both below average.

### Why Step 1 Requires Step 2

Because Step 1 shows **weak conceptual reasoning but ambiguous procedural performance**, Step 2 is required to determine whether the weakness is:

- conceptual/number sense,
- procedural, or
- retrieval-based.

## STEP 2—FAM Process Profile (Subtype Mechanism)

| Subtest | Standard Score | Interpretation |
|---|---|---|
| FAM Number Sense | 72 | Weak magnitude understanding; difficulty with quantity relationships |
| FAM Relational Concepts | 74 | Weak understanding of more/less, equal, half |
| FAM Number Line Estimation | 70 | Poor mental representation of magnitude |
| FAM Visual Spatial Number Manipulation | 78 | Weak spatial representation of quantity |
| FAM Verbal Problem Solving | 80 | Weak language-based quantitative reasoning |

### Interpretation (Step 2)

- Clear pattern of weak magnitude representation, weak relational concepts, and weak number line estimation.
- Both verbal and visual quantitative reasoning are weak.
- This pattern aligns with a Conceptual/Number Sense subtype, not procedural or retrieval.

### Debiasing Checkpoint (Step 2)

To avoid confirmation bias, the examiner explicitly tests whether the data could support Procedural or Retrieval/Fluency pathways.

**Additional Subtests Administered**

| Subtest | Standard Score | Interpretation |
|---|---|---|
| FAM Procedural Calculation | 88 | Procedures partially learned; errors conceptual rather than algorithmic |
| FAM Executive Functions/Planning | 92 | Planning and sequencing adequate |
| FAM Math Fact Retrieval | 95 | Basic facts adequately stored and accessible |
| FAM Rapid Automatic Naming-Quantity | 97 | Quantity access automaticity intact |

### Can a Procedural subtype be ruled out?

**Yes.**

- Procedural Calculation is low-average, but errors reflect **misunderstanding of quantity**, not algorithmic breakdown.
- EF/Planning is adequate.
- No evidence of procedural execution difficulty.

### Interpretation:

No evidence of a procedural pathway.

### Can a Retrieval/Fluency subtype be ruled out?

**Yes.**

- Math Fact Retrieval is average.
- RAN-Quantity is average.
- No hallmark retrieval weaknesses.

### Interpretation:

No evidence of a retrieval/fluency pathway.

### Conclusion of Step 2 Debiasing

After actively searching for disconfirming evidence:

- Procedural subtype → not supported
- Retrieval/Fluency subtype → not supported

The remaining explanation—consistent with both achievement anchors and FAM process data—is a **Conceptual/Number Sense subtype**, driven by weaknesses in magnitude representation, relational concepts, and number line estimation.

### STEP 3—Cognitive Confirmation (Optional)

| CHC Domain | Subtest | Standard Score | Interpretation |
|---|---|---|---|
| *Gf*—Fluid Reasoning | WISC-V Matrix Reasoning | 80 | Weak abstract reasoning; aligns with conceptual difficulty |
| *Gv*—Visual Processing | WISC-V Visual Puzzles | 88 | Mildly weak visual-spatial processing; contributes to number line difficulty |
| *Gwm*—Working Memory | WISC-V Digit Span | 88 | Mildly reduced; secondary contributor |
| *Gs*—Processing Speed | WISC-V Coding | 95 | Processing speed adequate; not a fluency issue |

### Interpretation (Step 3)

- Weak *Gf* aligns with conceptual reasoning weaknesses.
- Weak *Gv* contributes to difficulty representing magnitude spatially.
- Weakness is **partially expected** but still functionally significant.

### Debiasing Checkpoint (Step 3)

Avoid overattribution:

- *Gf*/*Gv* weaknesses do not fully explain the **math-specific** conceptual deficits.
- The pattern remains consistent with a **Conceptual/Number Sense** pathway.

### Final Diagnostic Picture—Lila

**Subtype:** Conceptual/Number Sense Math SLD

**Why:**

- Weak number sense
- Weak relational concepts
- Poor number line estimation
- Weak verbal and visual quantitative reasoning
- Fact retrieval intact
- Procedures partially learned but errors conceptual
- Weakness consistent across batteries
- Teacher reports align with conceptual difficulty

### Intervention Implications Based on the Identified Pathway

**Subtype Identified:** Conceptual/Number Sense Math SLD

**Mechanism:** Weak magnitude representation + weak relational concepts + weak spatial/quantitative reasoning.

### Why This Mechanism Leads to Lila's Errors

- She cannot reliably judge which quantity is larger.
- She struggles to estimate or use benchmark numbers.
- She applies procedures without understanding why they work.
- She becomes confused when numbers increase in size or complexity.
- She cannot visualize quantities on a number line.

This is the hallmark of the **Conceptual/Number Sense Pathway**.

### High-Leverage Practices for Conceptual/Number Sense SLD

**A. Number Line Interventions**

0–20 → 0–100 → 0–1000; emphasize magnitude and spacing.

**B. Magnitude Comparison Activities**

Quick "which is larger?" tasks; dot arrays; benchmark numbers.

**C. CRA Instruction for Quantity Concepts**

Concrete → representational → abstract progression.

**D. Relational Language Instruction**

Explicit teaching of more, less, equal, half, double, near.

**E. Estimation and Benchmarking Practice**

Use 5, 10, 50, and 100 as anchors for reasoning.

### What Lila Does NOT Need

- Fact fluency drills
- Speeded practice
- Procedural algorithm instruction without conceptual grounding
- Enrichment or acceleration
- "More practice" without conceptual scaffolds

### Evidence Base

- Number sense predicts long-term math outcomes (Jordan et al., 2010).
- Number line interventions improve magnitude understanding (Siegler & Ramani, 2009).
- CRA instruction improves conceptual learning (Witzel et al., 2003).
- Relational language supports quantitative reasoning (Purpura et al., 2013).

## APPENDIX 5.C

### Core Mechanisms & High-Leverage Practices for Additional Writing Pathways

Rapid References 5.10–5.12 summarize the core mechanisms and high-leverage instructional practices for three additional writing pathways. These brief guides allow readers to connect the diagnostic logic in the flowchart and decision rules presented in Chapter 5 to the instructional actions most strongly supported by research.

## Rapid Reference 5.10

### Handwriting/Graphomotor Pathway

**Mechanism**

A breakdown in **motor planning, fine-motor coordination, and transcription fluency** disrupts the student's ability to produce written text efficiently. The difficulty is mechanical, not linguistic.

**Common Indicators**

- Slow, effortful handwriting
- Illegible or inconsistent letter formation
- Difficulty copying
- Fatigue during writing
- Adequate spelling and ideas, but limited output

**High-Leverage Practices**

- **Explicit handwriting instruction** (letter formation, spacing, alignment)
- **Multisensory motor routines** (tracing, sky-writing, tactile input)
- **Handwriting fluency practice** (timed but *not* speed-pressured)
- **Copying with gradual fading** (model → dotted → blank)
- **Keyboarding instruction** as an accommodation, not a replacement
- **Reduced transcription load** during composition tasks

**What Not to Do**

- Grammar worksheets
- Spelling interventions
- Demanding long written output without supports

**Evidence Base**

Handwriting fluency supports composition quality and reduces cognitive load (Berninger & Amtmann, 2003; Graham et al., 2018).

## *Rapid Reference 5.11*

### Spelling/Encoding Pathway

**Mechanism**

A breakdown in **phonological, orthographic, and morphological encoding** disrupts the student's ability to spell accurately and store written word forms.

**Common Indicators**

- Phonetic but inaccurate spelling
- Difficulty with vowel patterns, digraphs, and affixes
- Trouble applying spelling rules
- Accurate decoding but weak encoding
- Writing that is readable only with effort

**High-Leverage Practices**

- **Integrated spelling–reading instruction** (read → spell → write → analyze)
- **Explicit phoneme–grapheme mapping**
- **Orthographic pattern instruction** (rimes, syllable types, spelling rules)
- **Morphological instruction** (roots, prefixes, suffixes)
- **Word study routines** (sorts, pattern analysis, word building)
- **Dictation with immediate corrective feedback**

**What Not to Do**

- Memorization-only spelling lists
- Fluency drills
- Composition-only interventions

**Evidence Base**

Encoding improves through explicit instruction in phonology, orthography, and morphology (Ehri, 2020; Treiman, 2018).

## Rapid Reference 5.12

### Sentence-Level Formulation Pathway

**Mechanism**

A breakdown in **syntax, grammar, and linguistic formulation** disrupts the student's ability to construct well-formed sentences.

**Common Indicators**

- Fragments, run-ons, and incomplete sentences
- Limited use of complex syntax
- Difficulty combining or expanding sentences
- Weak grammar and punctuation
- Adequate ideas but poor sentence structure

**High-Leverage Practices**

- **Sentence combining** (merge two simple sentences into one complex sentence)
- **Sentence expansion** (add who/what/where/when/why details)
- **Explicit grammar instruction** embedded in writing
- **Modeling and imitation of well-formed sentences**
- **Sentence frames and starters**
- **Practice generating multiple sentence types** (simple, compound, complex)

**What Not to Do**

- Open-ended writing tasks without scaffolds
- Grammar worksheets disconnected from writing
- Focusing on composition before sentence-level control

**Evidence Base**

Sentence combining and explicit syntax instruction improve writing quality and complexity (Graham & Perin, 2007; Saddler & Graham, 2005).

Six

# WHEN EVALUATIONS DISAGREE BUT THE DATA DO NOT: HOW INTERPRETATION SHAPED A CHILD'S READING SUPPORT

## CASE INTRODUCTION AND REFERRAL CONTEXT[1]

Connor was eight years old when his parents reached out, exhausted and bewildered after months of trying to understand why their bright, curious son struggled so profoundly with reading. He was a second-grade student who loved math, asked sophisticated questions, and approached the world with an intellectual enthusiasm that made him a favorite among teachers. Yet when reading demands increased, something in him shut down. His parents described a child who was "capable in every way except reading," a child who tried desperately to keep up but whose effort never translated into fluency.

Their first email to me captured the emotional weight of the experience and the methodological confusion they were left to untangle. They wrote:

> We're reaching out as parents who have spent the last several months immersed in your work, trying to understand what happened to our 8-year-old son. He was recently evaluated for a Specific Learning Disability in reading fluency under [the state's] Pattern of Strengths and Weaknesses model. He has a clinical diagnosis of dyslexia from a licensed neuropsychologist, and his standardized reading fluency scores are in the 2nd–4th percentile range. The school district found him ineligible for services.
>
> We are not special education professionals, but we spent significant time trying to understand CHC theory and the cross-battery approach in order to advocate for our son. After the evaluation, we were left with questions about the methodology that the school team either could not or would not answer.
>
> We feel strongly that they cited your work, but then didn't actually apply it to our child's case, and the injustice of this burns a bit. However, if we are wrong, we will admit it to all relevant parties and apologize.

Their message was not accusatory. It was earnest, thoughtful, and deeply respectful. They were not asking for an eligibility reversal. They were asking for clarity—for someone to help them understand whether the evaluation methods used with their son were sound, whether the conclusions drawn were defensible, and whether the school's decision not to provide services was consistent with the evidence.

Connor's parents had already pursued a private neuropsychological evaluation months earlier. That evaluation identified dyslexia, with a profile marked by weak orthographic processing, slow naming speed, and severe reading fluency impairment. When the school conducted its own evaluation later, the team acknowledged the fluency weakness but concluded that Connor did not require specialized instruction. The school's reasoning rested heavily on his improvement in accuracy on curriculum-based measures and on a belief that "fluency will follow accuracy."

During the eligibility meeting, a team member stated:

> I believe Connor doesn't require specialized instruction because he has improved to 96% accuracy. Now that he has accuracy, his fluency will follow.

This statement became a turning point for the family. They knew Connor's accuracy had improved, but they also knew his fluency remained profoundly impaired. They had read enough research to suspect that accuracy and fluency do not always develop in tandem—especially in dyslexia profiles involving orthographic mapping and rapid naming. But they lacked the technical vocabulary to explain why.

Their questions were precise, sophisticated, and grounded in a genuine desire to understand. They asked:

- For a reading fluency referral, is it methodologically appropriate to construct a *Glr* composite using Naming Speed Quantity (counting dots) and Immediate Symbol Translation from the WISC V, while excluding a CTOPP 2 Rapid Symbolic Naming score (82/12th percentile) that was available from an outside evaluation?
- The school psychologist used CTOPP 2 data from the outside evaluation for Auditory Processing (*Ga*) but chose not to use the CTOPP 2 Rapid Symbolic Naming score for Long Term Retrieval (*Glr*). Is there a methodological basis for using outside data selectively in this way?
- The school psychologist stated she chose Naming Speed Quantity over Naming Speed Literacy because she wanted to assess 'overall retrieval' rather than 'literacy specific' retrieval. Is this rationale consistent with the XBA approach for a reading fluency referral?

[1] Connor's parents provided informed consent for the inclusion of his de-identified assessment data and case details in this chapter; all personally identifying information has been removed to protect confidentiality.

- The Auditory Processing composite (88) was derived from subtests with a 30-point spread. Should this have been flagged as non-cohesive?
- Our understanding is that narrow ability analysis is critical, particularly for identifying cognitive weaknesses related to the specific academic deficit. Our son's Rapid Symbolic Naming was 82 (12th percentile), and his Phoneme Isolation score was at the 5th percentile—both narrow abilities with strong research links to reading fluency. Should narrow abilities with direct relevance to the referral concern be analyzed individually rather than only within broad composites?

These were not the questions of confused parents. These were the questions of parents who had done their homework; parents who were trying to reconcile two evaluations that purported to use the same framework but arrived at different conclusions. The final lines of their communication were the most striking:

> We simply want to understand whether our concerns have merit or whether we are misunderstanding something fundamental. We believe this will bring us closure after losing the fight for his services.

Connor's case is not just a diagnostic puzzle. It illustrates how systems can misinterpret data, how methodological shortcuts can obscure a child's true profile, and how the operational framework outlined in Chapter 3, grounded in component-level analysis, DD/C, and debiasing, can bring clarity when interpretations diverge. It is also a reminder of the emotional cost of not identifying a child who clearly meets criteria and needs timely, targeted intervention. Connor's parents were not fighting for a label; they were fighting for understanding. They wanted an explanation that made sense of their son's daily struggles—his slow, effortful reading, his phonetic spelling, his frustration, and his growing belief that something was wrong with him. Their email was not a request for advocacy. It was a request for sense-making. They had two evaluations that did not agree, a child who was clearly struggling, and a growing fear that the system had missed something important.

*This chapter exists because of that email.*

What follows is an analysis of how a mechanism-aligned interpretation of existing data can transform confusion into clarity. It illustrates how to interpret data in ways that honor the complexity of reading development, how to recognize when cognitive and academic patterns do not align, and how to avoid the interpretive traps that so often lead teams astray. Most importantly, it is an account of a child whose difficulties are specific, identifiable, and remediable when viewed through a research-based operational framework (hereafter referred to as the DD/C method for brevity).

## ACHIEVEMENT PROFILE: WHAT THE ACADEMIC DATA REVEAL

The DD/C method begins with achievement rather than cognition. For Connor, the academic data reveal a pattern that is internally consistent, subtype-specific, and not visible through composites alone. Although his broad reading scores appear unremarkable, the subtest scores tell a different story. When examined at the component level, Connor shows intact phonological decoding, significant orthographic weaknesses, and severe fluency impairment. This profile aligns with orthographic dyslexia. The tables that follow integrate data from both evaluations, allowing the academic pattern to emerge as a single, coherent profile rather than two competing narratives. Each domain is examined in turn.

### Decoding and Word Level Accuracy

Connor's decoding skills are stronger than one might expect, given his overall reading struggles. His WIAT-4 pseudoword decoding and phonemic proficiency fall squarely in the average range, and his curriculum-based nonsense-word fluency scores meet benchmark expectations. As shown in Table 6.1, Connor applies phonics rules accurately and efficiently.

Connor can segment, blend, and manipulate phonemes at a level consistent with age expectations. This pattern rules out phonological dyslexia as the primary mechanism of difficulty. If his reading disorder were phonological in nature, we would expect weak pseudoword

**Table 6.1 Connor's Decoding and Word-Level Accuracy**

| Measure | Score/Interpretation |
|---|---|
| WIAT-4 Pseudoword Decoding | 95 (average) |
| WIAT-4 Phonemic Proficiency | 96 (average) |
| WIAT-4 Phonological Processing Composite | 93 (average) |
| CBM NWF CLS/WWR | At benchmark |

*Note:* CBM = Curriculum-Based Measurement (CBM); NWF CLS = Nonsense Word Fluency—Correct Letter Sounds; NWF WWR = Nonsense Word Fluency—Whole Words Read.

decoding, weak phonemic awareness, and below-benchmark performance on Nonsense Word Fluency (NWF). None of these appear. Connor's difficulty does not originate in the phonological system.

## Orthographic Processing, Irregular Word Reading, and Writing Sample Analysis

Connor begins to struggle with orthographic processing, the system responsible for forming, storing, and retrieving written word forms. Across both evaluations, his orthographic scores cluster in the below-average range. These weaknesses are consistent, converging deficits that reflect difficulty forming stable orthographic representations, the hallmark of orthographic dyslexia (Ehri, 2014; Perfetti, 2007). Table 6.2 summarizes these findings.

To understand how these weaknesses appear in authentic writing, Figure 6.1 presents a sample Connor produced independently, and Table 6.3 provides a translation. The content of his writing is important. He describes a Minecraft adventure sequence, a genre common among writers his age. Minecraft is a sandbox exploration game in which players navigate strongholds, search libraries for treasure chests, battle skeletons and spiders, and attempt to reach the End Portal room, all of which Connor references accurately.

What this sample demonstrates immediately is that Connor's ideas, language formulation, and narrative structure are intact. He generates a coherent sequence of events, uses appropriate vocabulary for his age and interests, and maintains perspective throughout the story. There is no evidence of a language formulation disorder, conceptual weakness, or graphomotor impairment. His difficulties lie not in what he wants to say, but in how his orthographic system represents the words he intends to write.

**Table 6.2 Orthographic and Irregular Word Measures**

| Measure | Standard Score/Interpretation |
|---|---|
| Orthographic Processing | 77 (6th percentile) |
| Orthographic Fluency | 76 (5th percentile) |
| Irregular Word Fluency | 79 (8th percentile) |
| Spelling | 82 (12th percentile) |
| Writing Sample | Phonetic spellings; unstable orthographic patterns |

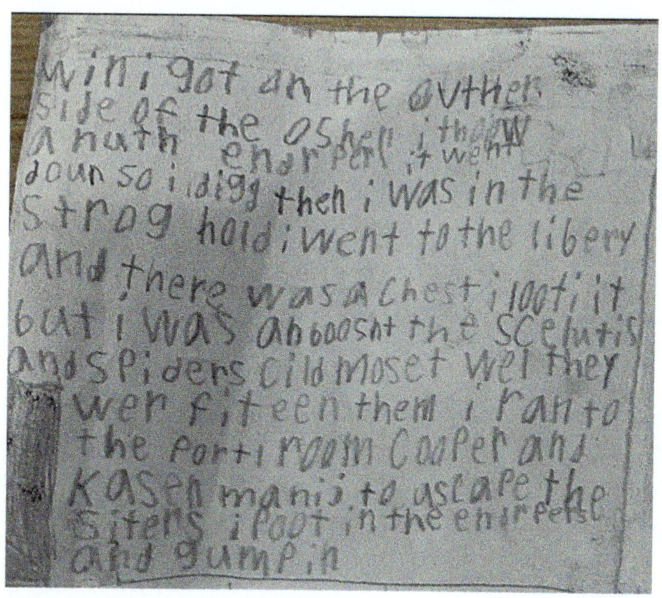


**FIGURE 6.1 Connor's Writing Sample (Minecraft Adventure Narrative)**

**Table 6.3 Original Text and Translation**

| Original | Best-Effort Translation (Meaning-Based) |
|---|---|
| win i got on the outher side of the oshen i thoow a nuth endr perl it went doun so i digg then i was in the strog hold | When I got to the other side of the ocean, I threw another Ender Pearl. It went down, so I dug, and then I was in the stronghold. |
| i went to the libery And there was a chest i looti it but i was amboosht | I went to the library and there was a chest. I looted it, but I was ambushed. |
| the scelutis and spiders cild moset wel they were fiteen them i ran to the portl room Cooper and Kassen manij to uscape the siters | The skeletons and spiders killed most. Well, they were fighting. Then I ran to the portal room. Cooper and Kassen managed to escape up the stairs. |
| i poot in the endr perls and gump in" | I put in the Ender Pearls and jumped in. |

*Note:* "Best-Effort Translation" prioritizes the child's intended meaning rather than literal wording. Phonetic spellings, compressed forms, and Minecraft-specific vocabulary require interpretation to ensure the narrative is understandable to readers.

## Spelling Error Analysis: Orthographic Instability in Action

Connor's writing reflects the same weaknesses seen in his orthographic scores. He produces numerous phonologically plausible but orthographically inaccurate spellings, demonstrating that he can perceive and represent phonemes accurately but cannot retrieve or store the correct orthographic forms. Students with dyslexia often rely on phonological decoding because their orthographic lexical memory is weak (Cidrim & Madeiro, 2017; Cidrim et al., 2024). Nearly every invented spelling is phonetic, indicating heavy reliance on "sound-it-out" strategies due to limited access to stored word forms. Table 6.4 provides examples.

**Table 6.4 Examples of Connor's Spelling Errors**

| Phonetic Spelling | Target Word |
|---|---|
| *libery* | **library** |
| *lootid* | **looted** |
| *sartid* | **started** |
| *fite* | **fight** |
| *sum* | **some** |
| *resors's* | **resources** |
| *abilt* | **able** |
| *abandin* | **abandon** |
| *perls* | **pearls** |
| *floar* | **floor** |
| *atack* | **attack** |

Morphological spellings are also missing in Connor's writing, though they appear in subtler forms embedded within his phonetic approximations. Examples include *loot* (omitted **-ed**), *fiteen* (omitted **-ing**), and *digg* (irregular past-tense confusion or omitted **-ed**). These errors reflect omitted inflectional endings, reduced awareness of morphemes, and reliance on oral speech patterns. Research consistently shows that students with dyslexia often omit or alter morphological markers because they have difficulty storing and retrieving the orthographic forms of morphemes, even when phonology is intact (Carlisle, 2010; Tsesmeli & Seymour, 2006). Because orthographic mapping integrates phonological, orthographic, and morphological information, these morphological errors further indicate that Connor's orthographic representations are not yet stable or fully specified (Ehri, 2014).

## Interpretation: What the Writing Sample Confirms

Connor's writing sample provides ecological validation of his academic profile. His spelling reflects phonetic over-reliance, missing morphological endings, and inconsistent orthographic patterns—indicators of weak orthographic mapping. These patterns align with research showing that students with dyslexia often rely on phonological decoding because their orthographic lexical memory is weak and their stored word forms are unstable (Cidrim et al., 2024; Cidrim & Madeiro, 2017; Ehri, 2014). Morphological omissions such as *manig* (managed) and *amboosht* (ambushed) further indicate difficulty storing the orthographic forms of morphemes, a pattern well documented in dyslexia (Carlisle, 2010; Tsesmeli & Seymour, 2006).

At the same time, the sample does not align with dysgraphia and demonstrates no evidence of a language-based writing disorder. Connor's handwriting is legible, spacing is adequate, and motor execution is smooth, ruling out graphomotor dysgraphia. His sentence-level ideas are coherent and sequential, ruling out a language formulation impairment. The text's density and limited punctuation may reflect ADHD-related executive-function load, such as reduced self-monitoring, working-memory strain, and difficulty sustaining attention during writing (Barkley, 2015; Graham et al., 2016). These ADHD-related features affect organization and mechanics but do not affect spelling accuracy or orthographic storage.

The writing sample illustrates a bright, imaginative second-grade writer whose ideas exceed his orthographic skills. It reinforces the orthographic subtype of dyslexia, aligns with his testing profile, and helps rule out dysgraphia (see Rapid Reference 6.1), language impairment, and motor-based writing disorders.

## Rapid Reference 6.1

### Why Connor's Profile Does Not Meet Criteria for Dysgraphia

**1. *Dysgraphia requires evidence of motor-execution impairment.***
Graphomotor dysgraphia is characterized by motor-based handwriting weaknesses, including malformed letters, inconsistent letter size, poor pencil control, excessive pressure, or motor fatigue (Berninger & Amtmann, 2003; Feder & Majnemer, 2007). Connor's handwriting sample does not show these features.

**2. *Legibility is reduced, but not due to motor dysfunction.***
Connor's handwriting is legible but difficult to read, with variable spacing and a somewhat "sloppy" appearance. These features reflect reduced self-monitoring and attention, not impaired motor planning or execution. We did not directly observe him writing, so conclusions are based solely on the written product.

**3. *Poor spacing is an executive-function issue, not a graphomotor one.***
Spacing between words relies on attention, inhibition, and visual monitoring, all of which are commonly affected in ADHD (Barkley, 2015; Graham et al., 2016). Spacing problems are not diagnostic of dysgraphia and do not indicate motor impairment.

**4. *His spelling errors are linguistic, not motoric.***
Connor's errors are:

- phonologically plausible,
- orthographically unstable, and
- morphologically reduced.

These patterns are consistent with orthographic dyslexia rather than dysgraphia. Dysgraphia does not cause phonetic spellings (Cidrim et al., 2024; Ehri, 2014).

**5. *He was unable to read back what he wrote.***
This difficulty is consistent with unstable orthographic representations and weak access to stored word forms—not with dysgraphia, which does not impair reading of one's own writing (Perfetti, 2007).

## FLUENCY: THE CENTRAL ACADEMIC WEAKNESS

If orthographic processing is the root, fluency is the symptom—and in Connor's case, the symptom is severe. Across both evaluations, his fluency scores fall in the impaired range despite adequate accuracy, a pattern well documented in students whose phonological decoding is intact but whose orthographic mapping and retrieval processes are inefficient (Ehri, 2014; Perfetti, 2007). Table 6.5 illustrates the severity of this discrepancy.

This is the pattern that misled the school team. They saw accuracy improve to 96% and assumed fluency would naturally follow. But fluency is not simply "fast accuracy." Reading fluency reflects the efficiency of orthographic mapping, automatic retrieval of word forms, rapid naming, and the integration of visual and phonological information—processes that operate beyond basic decoding accuracy (Hudson et al., 2009; Wolf & Katzir-Cohen, 2001). Connor's accuracy improved because his phonics skills are intact. His fluency did not improve because his orthographic mapping and naming speed remain weak. Accuracy does not equal fluency—and for Connor, accuracy will not lead to fluency without targeted intervention that strengthens orthographic learning and retrieval efficiency.

**Table 6.5 Connor's Reading Fluency Measures**

| Measure | Score/Interpretation |
|---|---|
| Oral Reading Fluency | 69 (2nd percentile) |
| Isolated Word Reading Fluency | 74 (4th percentile) |
| Irregular Word Fluency | 79 (8th percentile) |
| Reading Fluency Composite | 69 (2nd percentile) |
| CBM ORF | Well below benchmark |
| Accuracy | At benchmark |
| Rate | Persistently impaired |

## Reading Comprehension in Context

Connor's comprehension profile is exactly what we expect in orthographic dyslexia: adequate listening comprehension, reduced reading comprehension, and strong retell when the decoding burden is removed. Table 6.6 compares these domains. This pattern is well documented in students whose phonological decoding is intact, but whose orthographic mapping and reading fluency are weak—a combination that limits comprehension during independent reading but not during listening (Catts & Kamhi, 2017; Hudson et al., 2009).

**Table 6.6 Listening and Reading Comprehension**

| Measure | Score/Interpretation |
|---|---|
| Listening Comprehension | 91 (27th percentile) |
| Reading Comprehension | 86 (18th percentile) |
| Retell | Above benchmark |

His comprehension weakness is secondary to fluency, not a primary language deficit. When text is read aloud, he understands it. When he must decode it himself, slow, effortful reading reduces comprehension efficiency, leaving fewer cognitive resources available for meaning construction (Perfetti & Stafura, 2014). In other words, Connor's comprehension difficulties emerge only when decoding demands overwhelm his processing system, not because he lacks the language skills needed to understand the text.

## Synthesis of Academic Findings

Connor's academic profile is coherent, internally consistent, and subtype-specific. Across both evaluations, the same pattern emerges: intact phonological skills, weak orthographic skills, and secondary fluency-based effects on comprehension and writing. Table 6.7 summarizes the distribution of strengths, weaknesses, and downstream impacts.

Connor demonstrates strong phonological awareness, accurate decoding, and adequate listening comprehension, which rule out phonological dyslexia and language-based comprehension disorders. His weaknesses cluster tightly in the orthographic domain—orthographic processing, orthographic fluency, irregular word reading, and spelling—supported by consistent evidence from both standardized measures

**Table 6.7 Summary of Academic Strengths and Weaknesses**

| Intact Skills | Weak Skills | Secondary Effects |
|---|---|---|
| Phonological Awareness | Orthographic processing | Reading comprehension (fluency-limited) |
| Phonemic Decoding | Irregular word reading | Writing (orthographic + ADHD organization) |
| Nonsense Word Reading | Spelling (orthographic) | |
| Listening Comprehension | Reading fluency | |
| Math Reasoning | Naming speed | |

and his writing sample. These weaknesses directly explain his severe reading fluency impairment, as fluency depends on the automatic retrieval of stored word forms, not on phonics alone (Ehri, 2014; Perfetti, 2007; Wolf & Katzir-Cohen, 2001).

The secondary effects in Table 6.7 follow naturally from this mechanism. Connor's reading comprehension is reduced only when he must decode text himself, not when he listens to text read aloud—a pattern characteristic of fluency-limited comprehension rather than a primary language deficit (Catts & Kamhi, 2017; Perfetti & Stafura, 2014). His writing shows the same dissociation: age-appropriate ideas and narrative structure, but orthographically unstable spellings and ADHD-related organizational density. These downstream effects reinforce the subtype rather than complicate it. Taken together, the profile reflects the classic signature of orthographic (surface) dyslexia with a secondary naming-speed–based fluency impairment. Before finalizing that conclusion, however, we must apply the debiasing framework to ensure that interpretation is grounded in mechanism-level evidence rather than assumptions or heuristics.

## INTERPRETING THE DATA WITHOUT BIAS: APPLYING THE DEBIASING FRAMEWORK

Even when academic data are clear, interpretation can be distorted by cognitive shortcuts, institutional habits, and well-intentioned but inaccurate assumptions. Connor's case illustrates how easily this can happen. The school team had access to much of the same information, yet their conclusions diverged sharply from the mechanism-aligned interpretation presented here. The difference was not the data—it was the lens.

The debiasing framework helps ensure that interpretation remains anchored in evidence rather than assumptions. In Connor's case, five biases were especially influential: anchoring, confirmation bias, the accuracy-equals-fluency heuristic, the composite fallacy, and the overgeneralization of MTSS gains. Each shaped the school team's conclusions in predictable ways. Table 6.8 summarizes these biases and their effects.

**Table 6.8 Debiasing Framework: How Biases Shaped Connor's Initial Interpretation**

| Bias | How It Appeared in Connor's Case | Corrective Lens |
|---|---|---|
| Anchoring | Early improvement in accuracy became the anchor for all subsequent judgments. | Reexamine rate and automaticity separately from accuracy. |
| Confirmation Bias | Team selectively attended to data that supported "he's catching up." | Look for disconfirming evidence (e.g., persistent fluency impairment). |
| Accuracy = Fluency Heuristic | Assumed that 96% accuracy meant fluency would follow. | Treat fluency as a separate construct requiring separate data. |
| Composite Fallacy | Broad reading composites were interpreted as "average." | Examine subtests over composites to reveal mechanism-level patterns. |
| Overgeneralization of MTSS Gains | Growth in decoding was generalized to all reading domains. | Distinguish between phonics gains and orthographic/naming speed deficits. |

*Note:* MTSS = Multi-Tiered System of Supports.

### Anchoring: Expecting Fluency to Follow Accuracy

The school team did not overlook Connor's fluency weakness; they saw it clearly. The difficulty was not in noticing the data, but in how they understood what fluency represents. Once Connor's decoding accuracy improved, the team assumed fluency would naturally follow because, in typical readers, accuracy gains often lead to rapid increases in rate. This assumption reflects a linear, stage-based model of reading development in which accuracy → fluency → comprehension are treated as sequential steps in a single pathway.

What this model fails to capture is that each component is driven by a different underlying mechanism. Accuracy depends on phonological decoding; fluency depends on orthographic mapping and naming speed; comprehension depends on language and efficient lexical retrieval (Ehri, 2014; Perfetti & Stafura, 2014; Wolf & Katzir-Cohen, 2001). Improvement in one mechanism does not guarantee improvement in the others.

Because the team expected fluency to improve as a natural consequence of better accuracy, the persistent fluency impairment was minimized rather than integrated into the diagnostic picture. This is anchoring: the initial improvement in accuracy became the reference point against which all subsequent data were judged.

In MTSS contexts, anchoring is especially potent because growth is often treated as evidence of adequate response, even when the underlying deficit remains unresolved (Burns et al., 2005; Fuchs & Fuchs, 2006; VanDerHeyden, 2013). This systemic tendency to equate upward progress-monitoring trends with intervention success can obscure persistent, mechanism-specific weaknesses.

Once the team anchored on the belief that accuracy gains would naturally lead to fluency gains, a second bias emerged: they began to see only the data that supported that narrative.

## Confirmation Bias: Seeing What We Expect to See

Once the team adopted the narrative that Connor was improving, confirmation bias took hold. Data that supported this narrative—such as benchmark-level accuracy—received disproportionate attention. Data that contradicted it—such as his 2nd-percentile fluency performance—were minimized or explained away. Table 6.9 illustrates how confirmation bias shaped the interpretation of Connor's reading profile. This bias did not arise from negligence; it reflects a natural human tendency to seek coherence.

**Table 6.9 Confirmation Bias in Connor's Case**

| Data Point | School Team Interpretation | Mechanism-Aligned Interpretation |
| --- | --- | --- |
| 96% accuracy | "He's decoding well now." | Accuracy is intact; fluency remains impaired. |
| ORF rate well below benchmark | "He's still developing." | Rate impairment is severe and persistent. |
| Irregular word fluency = 79 | "Not a major concern." | Indicates weak orthographic mapping. |
| Spelling = 82 | "Within functional limits." | Orthographic instability consistent with subtype. |

The team's interpretation felt simple because the developmental model they were using was simple. Once they assumed that accuracy naturally leads to fluency, the entire narrative became self-reinforcing: *he improved, therefore he is fine*. But reading development is not linear; gains in one component do not automatically produce gains in another because accuracy, fluency, and comprehension rely on distinct underlying mechanisms (Ehri, 2014; Perfetti & Stafura, 2014). This assumption—that accuracy and fluency are interchangeable—is inconsistent with decades of research showing that fluency depends on automatic retrieval, naming speed, and orthographic mapping rather than phonological decoding alone (Hudson et al., 2005; Wolf & Katzir-Cohen, 2001).

## The Accuracy-Equals-Fluency Heuristic

Perhaps the most consequential bias in Connor's case was the assumption that accuracy and fluency are interchangeable. This heuristic is common in school settings, where accuracy is easier to measure and often emphasized in instruction.

- Accuracy reflects phonological decoding.
- Fluency reflects orthographic mapping, automatic retrieval, and naming speed.

Connor's accuracy improved because his phonics skills are intact. His fluency did not improve because his orthographic and naming-speed systems remain weak. Fluency is not "fast accuracy"; it is a separate skill with separate neurological underpinnings and separate instructional needs. Table 6.10 highlights this distinction.

**Table 6.10 Why Accuracy Does Not Equal Fluency**

| Construct | What It Measures | Connor's Pattern |
| --- | --- | --- |
| Accuracy | Phonological decoding; ability to apply phonics rules | Average; improved with instruction |
| Fluency | Automaticity; retrieval speed; orthographic mapping | Severely impaired across all measures |
| Implication | Accuracy gains ≠ fluency gains | Fluency requires targeted intervention |

## Composites Can Mask Specific Deficits and Give the Illusion of Age-Appropriate Cognitive and Academic Development

Broad scores, whether formal composites or broad percentile summaries, can create a misleading sense of "average" performance. This happens because composites often blend strengths and weaknesses, producing a single number that obscures the mechanism of difficulty. When the composite falls in the low-average or average range, it can give the impression that development is broadly intact (or within typical limits) even when one or more component subtest scores are below average or well below average. This masking effect is illustrated using data from Connor's neuropsychological evaluation.

In the neuropsychological evaluation, several WIAT-4 composites fell in the low-average to average range. On the surface, these scores appear reassuring. But the subtests that contribute to those composites tell a different story: severe fluency impairment and persistent orthographic weakness, even in the presence of intact phonological decoding. Table 6.11 illustrates how these broad WIAT-4 composites obscure the mechanism of difficulty (see also Chapter 2). Importantly, the neuropsychologist did not rely on composites or overlook subtest-level

**Table 6.11 How WIAT-4 Composites Can Mask Mechanism-Specific Weaknesses: Results from Connors Neuropsychological Evaluation**

| Composite (WIAT-4) | Composite Score | Typical Interpretation | Subtest Pattern | Mechanism-Aligned Interpretation |
|---|---|---|---|---|
| Basic Reading | 89 (23rd %ile) | "Reading is in the average range." | Word Reading = 81; Pseudoword Decoding = 95 | Composite blends a strength (decoding) with a weakness (sight-word reading), masking orthographic weakness. |
| Orthographic Processing | 77 (6th %ile) | "Well below average but improving." | Orthographic Fluency = 76; Spelling = 82 | Core mechanism of difficulty: orthographic mapping weakness. |
| Dyslexia Index | 88 (21st %ile) | "Within typical limits." | Word Reading = 81; Pseudoword Reading = 95; Orthographic Choice = 93 | Underestimates a severe orthographic-retrieval and fluency impairment because intact phonological decoding and orthographic recognition elevate the index*. |

*Orthographic Choice measures Connor's ability to visually recognize which spelling pattern looks correct, a task that does not require a fully mapped or easily retrievable word representation. His impairment lies in orthographic mapping—the ability to form stable, instantly retrievable word representations—which is why his reading fluency breaks down even though his pattern-recognition score is average. The Dyslexia Index is not sensitive to the process of orthographic mapping, so it underestimates Connor's impairment in forming and rapidly retrieving stable word representations.

information. The purpose of Table 6.11 is to highlight the masking effect of composites because this pattern occurs frequently in practice and can easily mislead interpretation when present.

Although the school's multidisciplinary team did not use formal composites, their interpretive statements reflected composite-like reasoning. By blending disparate scores—benchmark categories, percentiles, and subtests from different batteries—the team drew broad conclusions about Connor's reading development that obscured the severity and specificity of his fluency and orthographic weaknesses (see Table 6.12).

**Table 6.12 How the School's Interpretation of Subtest-Level Data Reflected Composite-Like Interpretations**

| Area/Subtests Used by School | School Interpretation | Actual Subtest Pattern | Mechanism-Aligned Interpretation |
|---|---|---|---|
| Oral Reading Fluency (KTEA-3) | "Percentiles indicate skills generally within the average range… not severely delayed." | ORF = 74 (4th %ile) | Severe fluency impairment is a hallmark of orthographic dyslexia. |
| Isolated Word Reading Fluency (KTEA-3) | Not highlighted as a major concern. | IWRF = 74 (4th %ile) | Fluency impairment extends to isolated words; retrieval-speed and orthographic mapping weakness. |
| Irregular Word Reading Fluency (KTEA-3) | "Some growth… continued needs." | Irregular Word Fluency = 79 (8th %ile) | Weak orthographic lexicon; consistent with orthographic dyslexia. |
| Orthographic Choice (WIAT-4) | "Within the average range." | Orthographic Choice = 93 (32nd %ile) | Recognition task only; does not contradict orthographic mapping weakness. |
| Acadience ORF | "Slightly below average… not severely delayed." | ORF percentiles = 16th–23rd | Reflects weak orthographic mapping and slow retrieval of word representations, limiting automaticity. |
| Spelling | "Below benchmark… main area of concern." | Spelling = 88 (21st %ile) | Orthographic instability consistent with orthographic dyslexia; not motor-based. |

For example, after noting intact foundational decoding skills alongside multiple fluency scores in the 2nd–8th percentiles, the MDT concluded that his skills were "generally within the average range, rather than severely delayed." This is not a literal composite, but it functions like one: a global conclusion is drawn from data showing severely limited to average skill development.

The school's written interpretation blends intact decoding with impaired fluency to produce a global conclusion of adequate development, despite multiple fluency scores in the 2nd–8th percentiles. In their summary, the team acknowledged that Connor's Oral Reading Fluency met the district's definition of an academic weakness. However, they attributed this weakness to pacing and automaticity rather than a reading disorder, emphasizing his "positive response to intervention" and describing his overall academic development as progressing toward his "strong cognitive potential" within the general education setting.

The pattern that emerges from the academic data—intact phonological skills alongside significant orthographic and fluency weaknesses—sets the stage for the next step in the DD/C method. Once the academic profile is clear, the focus shifts to cognitive abilities and processes to understand *why* the academic pattern looks the way it does. In Connor's case, the cognitive findings deepen and clarify the nature of his academic weaknesses, revealing the same mechanism already visible in his reading and writing performance.

What follows is a synthesis of cognitive data from both evaluations, organized to illuminate the underlying processes that drive Connor's academic strengths and weaknesses.

## Phonological Processing: Intact and Efficient

In Connor's case, the cognitive data do not introduce new questions or contradictions. Instead, they reinforce the pattern already visible in the achievement data: intact phonological processing, weak orthographic and naming-speed systems, and executive-function variability consistent with ADHD. Contemporary reading science recognizes this constellation as a well-documented pathway to fluency impairment, particularly when phonology is intact but orthographic learning is inefficient (Castles et al., 2018; Hulme & Snowling, 2020). The following sections integrate data across both evaluations to yield a unified cognitive profile (see Tables 6.13–6.16).

**Table 6.13 Phonological Processing Measures from the Neuropsychological Evaluation**

| Measure | Score | Percentile |
|---|---|---|
| CTOPP-2 Elision | 8 | 25th |
| CTOPP-2 Blending Words | 11 | 63rd |
| CTOPP-2 Phoneme Isolation | 5 | 5th |
| CTOPP-2 Phonological Awareness Composite | 88 | 21st |
| CTOPP-2 Phonological Memory Composite | 92 | 30th |
| WIAT-4 Phonemic Proficiency | 96 | 39th |
| WIAT-4 Pseudoword Decoding | 95 | 37th |

*Note:* CTOPP-2 subtests have a mean of 10 and a standard deviation of 3. CTOPP-2 composites and WIAT-4 subtests and composites have a mean of 100 and a standard deviation of 15.

**Interpretation:**
Connor's phonological system is intact. His isolated weakness in Phoneme Isolation reflects task-specific segmentation difficulty rather than a core phonological deficit, and phonological accuracy is not the mechanism underlying his reading impairment. His solid average performances on the Blending Words, Phonemic Proficiency, and Pseudoword Decoding subtests support intact phonological accuracy.

## Orthographic Processing: Weak and Inefficient

In contrast to his phonological strengths, Connor shows consistent weaknesses in orthographic and visual processing. These tasks require rapid visual discrimination, symbol recognition, and the formation of stable orthographic representations—processes that support fluent word reading and accurate spelling. Across both evaluations, Connor's performance on these measures falls well below age expectations, mirroring the irregular-word difficulties, slow retrieval of familiar word forms, and spelling inconsistencies seen in his academic work.

**Table 6.14 Orthographic and Visual Processing Measures**

| Measure | Score | Percentile | Source |
|---|---|---|---|
| WIAT-4 Orthographic Fluency | 76 | 5th | Neuropsych |
| WIAT-4 Orthographic Processing Composite | 77 | 6th | Neuropsych |
| KTEA-3 Orthographic Choice | 93 | 32nd | School MDT |
| Irregular Word Reading Fluency | 79 | 8th | School MDT |
| Isolated Word Reading Fluency | 74 | 4th | School MDT |

*Note:* MDT = Multidisciplinary Team.

Recent research underscores the centrality of orthographic learning in reading fluency and identifies orthographic-processing deficits as a primary mechanism in many struggling readers (O'Brien et al., 2020; van der Kleij et al., 2019; Wang et al., 2021). Computational models similarly demonstrate how weak orthographic representations impair fluency even when phonology is intact (Ziegler & Perry, 2020). Connor's profile aligns closely with this evidence.

**Interpretation:**
Orthographic processing is the primary mechanism of difficulty. These weaknesses are consistent, convergent, and subtype-specific.

## Naming Speed: A Secondary but Significant Contributor

Connor's naming-speed performance reflects slow retrieval of phonological labels for visual stimuli. Naming speed does not affect accuracy, but it has a substantial impact on rate—particularly in connected text. This pattern helps explain why Connor reads accurately yet slowly and effortfully.

Recent meta-analytic and longitudinal research confirms that naming-speed deficits are a distinct contributor to fluency impairment, independent of phonological skill (Araújo & Faísca, 2019; Georgiou et al., 2021; Norton & Wolf, 2012). Connor's naming-speed profile fits this pattern: it does not cause his orthographic weakness, but it meaningfully amplifies his fluency impairment.

**Table 6.15 Naming Speed Measures**

| Measure | Score | Percentile | Source |
|---|---|---|---|
| CTOPP-2 Rapid Digit Naming | 7 | 16th | Neuropsych |
| CTOPP-2 Rapid Letter Naming | 7 | 16th | Neuropsych |
| CTOPP-2 Rapid Symbolic Naming Composite | 82 | 12th | Neuropsych |
| WIAT-4 Oral Reading Fluency | 69 | 2nd | Neuropsych |

**Interpretation:**
Naming-speed weakness amplifies the fluency impairment but does not explain the orthographic deficits.

## Working Memory and Executive Function: ADHD-Consistent Variability

Connor's working-memory and executive-function profile shows the variability commonly seen in ADHD. He demonstrates strong verbal working memory but reduced efficiency in tasks requiring sustained attention, inhibition, and rapid shifting. These patterns were evident in formal testing and behavioral observations.

Recent research highlights the heterogeneity of ADHD and the central role of variability in executive function in academic performance (Kofler et al., 2019). Importantly, EF weaknesses affect efficiency, organization, and task persistence but do not explain dyslexia profiles (Willcutt, 2020). Connor's pattern aligns with this evidence: his EF variability influences his academic stamina and consistency but does not account for his reading impairment.

**Table 6.16 Working Memory and Executive Function Measures**

| Measure | Score | Percentile | Source |
|---|---|---|---|
| WISC-V Short-Term Memory | 118 | 88th | School MDT |
| WISC-V Processing Speed | 96 | 40th | School MDT |
| WISC-V Fluid Reasoning | 83 | 13th | School MDT |
| CTOPP-2 Memory for Digits | 7 | 16th | Neuropsych |
| Behavioral Indicators | — | — | MDT Observations |

**Interpretation:**
Executive-function variability is consistent with ADHD and affects academic efficiency, but it is not the mechanism of Connor's reading disability.

### Cognitive Summary

Connor's cognitive profile is coherent and highly consistent with his academic presentation. His phonological system is intact, supporting accurate decoding and confirming that his reading difficulty is not phonologically based (Castles et al., 2018; Hulme & Snowling, 2020). In contrast, his orthographic processing is weak and inefficient, producing unstable word forms, slow retrieval, and the irregular-word and fluency difficulties seen throughout his achievement testing (O'Brien et al., 2020; van der Kleij et al., 2019). Naming-speed weaknesses further depress his reading rate, amplifying—but not causing—his fluency impairment (Araújo & Faísca, 2019; Georgiou et al., 2021). Executive-function variability contributes to inconsistent performance and reduced academic efficiency but does not account for his reading profile (Kofler et al., 2019; Willcutt, 2020).

Together, these findings reinforce a single, mechanism-driven conclusion: Connor's reading difficulties arise from orthographic processing weaknesses, secondarily compounded by slow naming speed, within the broader context of ADHD-related executive-function variability. The cognitive data do not compete with the academic findings—they explain them. With this alignment established, we can now turn to the diagnostic synthesis and identify the subtype.

## DETERMINING THE SUBTYPE: CONVERGING EVIDENCE

Subtype determination is not a matter of matching a student to a label. It is the process of identifying the mechanism that explains the student's academic, cognitive, and lived experience. When the DD/C method is applied, the subtype emerges not from a single score but from the convergence of evidence from multiple data sources and data-gathering methods. For Connor, that convergence is striking, as illustrated in Table 6.17. When viewed through the subtype framework introduced in Chapter 5, the pattern aligns with Orthographic Dyslexia: intact phonology, weak orthographic processing, and reading fluency, with a secondary weakness in naming speed or RAN. No competing subtype fits the data. The mechanism is consistent across academic performance, cognitive processes, and real-world writing.

## CONCLUSION: CLASSIFICATION, DIAGNOSIS, AND SUBTYPE

When academic and cognitive data converge, the DD/C method moves from analysis to classification and diagnosis. Although classification and diagnosis identify the difficulty, they do so within different systems, for different purposes, and with different implications for services and documentation. Subtype determination adds a third layer—one that is not required by law or billing systems but is essential for mechanism-aligned intervention.

**Table 6.17 Converging Evidence Consistent with Orthographic Dyslexia**

| Domain | Evidence | Interpretation |
|---|---|---|
| Decoding | Average pseudoword decoding; benchmark NWF | Phonological system intact |
| Orthographic Processing | 76–82 range across tasks | Weak orthographic mapping |
| Fluency | ORF = 69; rate impairment persistent | Automaticity deficit |
| Naming Speed | Below average RAN | Secondary fluency contributor |
| Writing | Phonetic spellings; unstable patterns | Orthographic instability |
| Cognition | Weak visual orthographic efficiency | Confirms orthographic mechanism |
| Comprehension | Listening > reading | Fluency-limited comprehension |
| History | Slow, effortful reading; phonetic spelling | Ecological validation |

### IDEA: Educational Classification

In school settings, eligibility is determined under the Individuals with Disabilities Education Act (IDEA). IDEA provides **broad disability categories** that identify the area of academic difficulty and determine access to special education services.

Based on Connor's persistent rate-based impairment, his school-based classification is:

**Specific Learning Disability in Reading Fluency**
*(IDEA, 34 C.F.R. § 300)*

Classification tells us **what area of learning is impaired** for the purpose of educational planning and legal protections. It does not specify the underlying cognitive mechanism.

## DSM-5-TR and ICD-10-CM: Clinical Diagnosis

In private clinical settings, diagnosis follows the **DSM-5-TR**, which provides diagnostic criteria and its own coding system. However, insurance companies typically require **ICD-10-CM** codes for reimbursement. As a result, clinicians assign a DSM-5-TR diagnosis and then pair it with the corresponding ICD-10-CM code for documentation and billing.

Based on Connor's profile, the appropriate DSM-5-TR diagnosis is:

**Specific Learning Disorder with Impairment in Reading, Severe**
*(American Psychiatric Association, 2022)*

For insurance and medical documentation, this diagnosis is paired with:

**ICD-10-CM Code: F81.0—Specific Reading Disorder**
In some medical settings, including pediatrics, clinicians may use ICD-10-CM directly and refer to the condition as "dyslexia" while coding it as F81.0.

Diagnosis, like classification, identifies **what** the difficulty is—but within a clinical framework rather than an educational one.

## Subtype: Mechanism

Subtype determination is different from both classification and diagnosis.

It is not a legal category (IDEA) and not a billing code (ICD-10-CM).

Subtype identifies the **mechanism** that explains *why* the difficulty occurs.

Subtype integrates:

- academic performance
- cognitive processes
- developmental history
- ecological observations

Subtypes, as introduced in Chapter 5, describe how the learner processes print and why the observed pattern emerges. Subtypes provide the level of specificity needed for targeted, mechanism-aligned intervention. When viewed through this mechanism-driven lens, Connor's cross-system pattern clearly aligns with:

**Orthographic Dyslexia (Surface Dyslexia)**

- **with a Secondary Naming-Speed Impairment**
- **in the Context of ADHD-Related Executive-Function Variability**

Each evaluation provided a piece of the pattern. The DD/C method integrates these pieces into a mechanism-aligned explanation that guides intervention. The next section translates this mechanism into a targeted intervention plan aligned with the DD/C method.

# INTERVENTION ROADMAP: TRANSLATING MECHANISM INTO ACTION

A mechanism-aligned diagnosis is only meaningful if it leads to a mechanism-aligned intervention. For Connor, the academic and cognitive data converge on a clear profile: Orthographic Dyslexia with a secondary naming-speed impairment, occurring in the context of ADHD-related executive-function variability. This profile points directly to the instructional components most likely to produce meaningful, measurable change.

The DD/C method emphasizes precision: target the mechanism, not the symptom. For Connor, this means shifting the instructional focus:

- from phonics to orthographic mapping,
- from accuracy to automaticity,
- from decoding to retrieval, and
- from viewing executive-function weaknesses as causal to understanding them as barriers to efficient learning.

The following roadmap outlines the core components of an intervention plan aligned with Connor's subtype. Each section includes a narrative explanation, a table of instructional components, and expected outcomes grounded in contemporary research.

## Orthographic Mapping Intervention

Connor's primary mechanism of difficulty is weak orthographic processing. Orthographic mapping—the process by which written words become stored for instant retrieval—requires efficient integration of phonology, orthography, and meaning. When this system is inefficient, students rely on phonetic strategies long after their peers have transitioned to automatic word recognition (O'Brien, et al., 2020; van der Kleij et al., 2019; Wang et al., 2021). Intervention must therefore strengthen the formation, storage, and retrieval of written word forms (see Table 6.18).

**Table 6.18 Orthographic Mapping Intervention Components**

| Key Components | Instructional Approaches | Expected Outcomes |
|---|---|---|
| High-frequency irregular word instruction | Structured word-study routines | More stable word representations |
| Orthographic pattern study | Explicit instruction in spelling patterns | Reduced reliance on phonetic strategies |
| Morphological instruction (roots, affixes) | Morphology-integrated word study | Improved spelling accuracy |
| Repeated exposure to target words | Distributed practice across contexts | Increased automaticity with familiar words |
| Visual word-form practice with feedback | Orthographic mapping routines | Faster retrieval of known words |

## Fluency Intervention (Rate-Based)

Connor's fluency impairment is severe and persistent. Because his accuracy is intact, fluency intervention must focus on rate, automaticity, and retrieval rather than decoding (see Table 6.19). Contemporary fluency research emphasizes repeated reading, modeling, and controlled text as the most effective approaches for students with intact accuracy but slow rate (Georgiou et al., 2021; Norton & Wolf, 2012).

**Table 6.19 Fluency Intervention Components**

| Key Components | Instructional Approaches | Expected Outcomes |
|---|---|---|
| Repeated reading with modeling | Assisted reading (teacher or audio) | Increased reading rate |
| Timed phrase-cued reading | Repeated reading protocols | Reduced cognitive load |
| Controlled text with predictable patterns | Gradual release to less controlled text | Improved comprehension efficiency |
| Integration of RAN-supportive tasks | Timed retrieval practice | Greater stamina and confidence |

## Naming-Speed Support

Naming speed weaknesses do not cause dyslexia, but they significantly reduce reading fluency by slowing the retrieval of phonological labels for visual stimuli (Araújo & Faísca, 2019; Norton & Wolf, 2012). While RAN cannot be "fixed," retrieval efficiency can be strengthened through targeted practice (see Table 6.20).

**Table 6.20 Naming-Speed Support Components**

| Key Components | Instructional Approaches | Expected Outcomes |
|---|---|---|
| Rapid retrieval of familiar words | Incremental rehearsal | Faster retrieval of phonological labels |
| Timed naming of letters, numbers, symbols | Timed flashcard routines | Improved fluency in connected text |
| Alternating naming tasks | Rapid alternating naming grids | Reduced hesitations and pauses |
| Speeded word-recognition drills | Speed-accuracy tradeoff training | More efficient word retrieval |

## Comprehension Support (Fluency-Limited)

Connor's comprehension weakness is secondary to fluency. When decoding demands are removed, his comprehension is average. Therefore, comprehension intervention should focus on access rather than language (see Table 6.21). Research on fluency-limited comprehension emphasizes scaffolding, vocabulary, and strategic supports that reduce cognitive load (Castles et al., 2018; Hulme & Snowling, 2020).

**Table 6.21 Comprehension Support Components**

| Key Components | Instructional Approaches | Expected Outcomes |
|---|---|---|
| Prereading supports | Previewing key concepts | Improved comprehension when fluency is supported |
| Vocabulary instruction | Read-alouds with discussion | Stronger vocabulary and background knowledge |
| Listening comprehension practice | Graphic organizers | Reduced frustration during independent reading |
| Scaffolded text access | Chunking text | More efficient comprehension processing |

### Writing Support (Orthographic+ADHD)

Connor's writing difficulties stem from orthographic instability and ADHD-related organization challenges. Effective writing intervention must therefore integrate spelling, morphology, sentence-level practice, and executive-function supports (Kofler et al., 2019; See Table 6.22).

**Table 6.22 Writing Support Components**

| Key Components | Instructional Approaches | Expected Outcomes |
|---|---|---|
| Explicit spelling instruction | Word study integrated with writing | More accurate spelling |
| Morphological awareness | Morphology-based spelling routines | Improved word formation |
| Sentence-level practice | Sentence frames and templates | Increased writing fluency |
| Structured writing templates | Graphic organizers | Improved organization |
| Executive-function supports | Checklists for planning and revision | Reduced frustration and avoidance |

### ADHD-Related Executive-Function Supports

These supports do not treat the reading disorder, but they remove barriers to learning. ADHD-related EF variability affects task initiation, persistence, and organization (Kofler et al., 2019; Willcutt, 2020). When these barriers are reduced, academic intervention becomes more efficient (see Table 6.23).

**Table 6.23 Executive-Function Support Components**

| Key Components | Expected Outcomes |
|---|---|
| Environmental structure | Improved task persistence |
| Task chunking | Reduced variability in performance |
| Visual schedules | Greater independence |
| Movement breaks | Increased regulation |
| Externalized organization systems | More consistent academic engagement |

## CLOSING THE LOOP: MECHANISM → INSTRUCTION → CHANGE

Connor's intervention roadmap is not generic. It is mechanism-specific, research-aligned, and responsive to his lived experience. Orthographic mapping is the primary target. Naming speed, efficiency, and fluency rate are secondary but essential. Executive-function supports ensure that the intervention can take hold.

The roadmap clarifies what Connor needs and why those instructional components matter. But effective intervention is never only about mechanisms, rate gains, or instructional precision. It is also about the child who must live inside this plan—day after day, session after session—bringing his effort, his emotions, and his sense of self to the work (Guthrie & Wigfield, 2000; Kim & Schatschneider, 2021). Mechanism tells us where to intervene; identity tells us how to sustain that intervention over time (Haimovitz & Dweck, 2017).

For Connor, this means holding his strengths in full view as we address the areas where he struggles. The *How I Am Smart* reflection recenters the child in the story of his own learning, ensuring that the work ahead is grounded not only in data, but in dignity.

## *HOW I AM SMART*: RECENTERING THE CHILD

Connor's profile is rich with strengths—strengths that matter, strengths that shape how he learns, and strengths that must remain visible even as we address the areas where he struggles. The "How I Am Smart" reflection (see Rapid Reference 6.2 for an example) reframes the narrative from a deficit to an identity. It reminds adults and the child that a reading disorder is not a reflection of intelligence, potential, or character. It is a specific, identifiable difference in how the brain processes written language (Lyon et al., 2003; Shaywitz & Shaywitz, 2020).

### Rapid Reference 6.2

**A "How I am Smart" Reflection Example**

**For Connor: How am I Smart?**

**My Brain Works in Cool Ways**

I learn in a way that is different from some kids—and that difference ***gives me strengths that not everyone has***.

I am smart in **how I think**, not in how fast I read.

**The Ways *I* Am Smart**

**I Am Smart With IDEAS**

I come up with creative solutions.
I notice things other people miss.
I make connections that help me understand big ideas.

**I Am Smart With PEOPLE**

I care about others.
I understand feelings.
I'm a good friend and a good teammate.

**I Am Smart With PROBLEM SOLVING**

I figure things out.
I can think through tricky situations.
I don't give up when something is hard.

**I Am Smart With STORIES**

When someone reads to me, I understand the story really well.
I can picture what's happening in my mind.
I can explain ideas clearly.

**I Am Smart With MY HANDS**

I build, create, design, and make things.
I learn by doing.
I like to explore and try new things.

**What Makes Reading Hard for Me**

Reading is hard for me, **not because I'm not smart**, but because my brain learns words in a different way.

This is called **dyslexia**.

It means:

- I need more time to learn how words look
- My brain works harder to read quickly
- I learn best with special tools and strategies

***And that's okay—lots of amazing people have dyslexia!***

**What Helps Me Learn**

- Using audiobooks
- Practicing words in fun ways
- Getting extra time
- Having teachers who understand me
- Knowing that reading is only ONE kind of smart

**My Kind of Smart**

My brain is strong.
My brain is creative.
My brain is brave.
My brain is capable.
My brain is smart—**my kind of smart!**

And I can learn anything with the right tools.

When I shared the reflection (from Rapid Reference 6.2) with Connor's mother, it was because she had told me something important: that Connor's self-esteem was low, that he felt embarrassed by his reading, and that he had begun to believe he was "dumb." She wanted a way to help him see himself more fully. A few days later, she wrote back:

> Thank you so much for this! I printed it out and I've been slowly introducing this to him because he's very perceptive. If I do too much too quick, he wouldn't think it was genuine. In the car, we started talking about all of the things he can do, and I added just the word 'I' below each section so that he and I could create some together. We've added 'I can see the whole court and make good plays on the court,' 'I am determined when I want to accomplish something,' 'I am good at math,' and 'I am a problem-solver.'

When Connor's mother described his reaction to the reflection, she wasn't describing a sudden transformation. She was describing the beginning of a shift—a moment when the story he had been living ("reading is hard for me, so something must be wrong with me") began to inch toward the story he was being offered ("your difficulty has a name, a mechanism, and it does not diminish who you are"). He is not standing in the middle yet, but he is moving toward it—toward a version of himself that can hold both truths at once. His mother sensed this, which is why she introduced the reflection slowly, adding just the word I beneath each section so they could build it together. These were not affirmations handed to him; they were strengths he recognized in himself. That is the work—helping him gradually assemble a story of himself that feels coherent, capable, and whole.

Practitioners should strive to see the whole child—not just the mechanism of difficulty, but the constellation of strengths that surround it. "How I Am Smart" is not an add-on or a softening gesture; it is a necessary counterbalance to the weight of the data. It recenters the child in the story of his own learning, ensuring that as we implement a mechanism-aligned intervention plan, we do so with a clear understanding of the learner behind the scores.

This chapter exists because one parent reached out asking for clarity. It concludes with the reminder that *assessment is, at its core, an act of clarity, guidance, and care.*

## TEST YOURSELF

**1. Connor demonstrates accurate phonological decoding but severe reading-rate impairment. Which interpretation best explains this pattern?**

(a) Phonological dyslexia
(b) Orthographic dyslexia
(c) Language comprehension disorder
(d) Graphomotor dysgraphia

2. **Which academic pattern most strongly supports an orthographic dyslexia profile?**
   (a) Weak phonological awareness with strong spelling
   (b) Weak listening comprehension and strong reading comprehension
   (c) Accurate decoding with weak irregular word reading and spelling
   (d) Weak handwriting and poor fine-motor control
3. **In Connor's case, the assumption that "accuracy will lead to fluency" represents which cognitive bias?**
   (a) Anchoring
   (b) Composite fallacy
   (c) Accuracy-equals-fluency heuristic
   (d) Confirmation bias
4. **Which of the following best explains why Connor's reading comprehension appears lower during independent reading?**
   (a) Limited vocabulary knowledge
   (b) Weak language comprehension
   (c) Reduced fluency that increases cognitive load
   (d) Poor working memory capacity
5. **Connor's spelling errors are primarily phonologically plausible but orthographically incorrect. This pattern indicates difficulty with:**
   (a) Motor planning
   (b) Orthographic mapping
   (c) Phonological segmentation
   (d) Listening comprehension
6. **Connor's phonological system is likely the primary cause of his reading impairment. True or False?**
7. **Which cognitive factor contributes secondarily to Connor's fluency impairment but does not explain the orthographic deficit?**
   (a) Fluid reasoning
   (b) Naming speed
   (c) Verbal working memory
   (d) Listening comprehension
8. **Which interpretive principle is emphasized in the DD/C method when evaluating academic and cognitive data?**
   (a) Begin with cognitive testing before reviewing achievement
   (b) Interpret composite scores as the primary source of evidence
   (c) Start with academic performance and identify the underlying mechanism
   (d) Focus primarily on IQ–achievement discrepancies
9. **Connor's writing sample demonstrates coherent ideas but unstable spelling patterns. This pattern helps rule out which disorder?**
   (a) Orthographic dyslexia
   (b) Dysgraphia
   (c) Dyslexia with naming-speed impairment
   (d) Fluency-based reading disorder
10. **According to the mechanism-aligned framework described in this chapter, subtype identification primarily helps practitioners:**
    (a) Determine eligibility under IDEA
    (b) Assign ICD diagnostic codes
    (c) Select targeted, mechanism-aligned interventions
    (d) Calculate composite scores for eligibility decisions

*Answers:* 1. b; 2. c; 3. c; 4. c; 5. b; 6. False; 7. b; 8. c; 9. b; 10. c

## REFERENCES


Araújo, S., & Faísca, L. (2019). A meta-analytic review of naming-speed deficits in developmental dyslexia. *Scientific Studies of Reading, 23*(5), 349–368.

Barkley, R. A. (2015). *Attention-deficit hyperactivity disorder: A handbook for diagnosis and treatment* (4th ed). Guilford Press.

Berninger, V. W., & Amtmann, D. (2003). Preventing written expression disabilities through early and continuing assessment and intervention for handwriting and/or spelling problems: Research into practice. In H. L. Swanson, K. R. Harris, & S. Graham (Eds.), *Handbook of learning disabilities* (pp. 345–363). The Guilford Press.

Burns, M. K., Appleton, J. J., & Stehouwer, J. D. (2005). Meta-analytic review of responsiveness-to-intervention research. *School Psychology Review, 34*(3), 308–326.

Carlisle, J. F. (2010). Effects of instruction in morphological awareness on literacy achievement. *Reading Research Quarterly, 45*(4), 464–487.

Catts, H. W., & Kamhi, A. G. (2017). Prologue: Reading comprehension is not a single ability. *Language, Speech, and Hearing Services in Schools, 48*(2), 73–77.

Castles, A., Rastle, K., & Nation, K. (2018). Ending the reading wars: Reading acquisition from novice to expert. *Psychological Science in the Public Interest, 19*(1), 5–51.

Cidrim, L., & Madeiro, F. (2017). Spelling performance in children with dyslexia. *Frontiers in Psychology, 8*, 1–10.

Cidrim, L., Batista, A. O., Madeiro, F., & Capellini, S. A. (2024). Analysis of spelling errors from the 'dyslexic sight words' list. *Frontiers in Psychology, 15*, 1160247.

Ehri, L. C. (2014). Orthographic mapping in the acquisition of sight word reading, spelling memory, and vocabulary learning. *Scientific Studies of Reading, 18*(1), 5–21.

Feder, K. P., & Majnemer, A. (2007). Handwriting development, competency, and intervention. *Developmental Medicine and Child Neurology, 49*(4), 312–317.

Fuchs, D., & Fuchs, L. S. (2006). Introduction to response to intervention. *Reading Research Quarterly, 41*(1), 93–99.

Georgiou, G. K., Martinez, D., Vieira, A. P. A., & Guo, K. (2021). Is orthographic knowledge a strength or a weakness in individuals with dyslexia? Evidence from a meta-analysis. *Annals of Dyslexia, 71*(1), 5–27.

Graham, S., Fishman, E. J., Reid, R., & Hebert, M. (2016). Writing characteristics of students with attention deficit hyperactive disorder: A meta–analysis. *Learning Disabilities Research & Practice, 31*(2), 75–89.

Guthrie, J. T., & Wigfield, A. (2000). Engagement and motivation in reading. In M. L. Kamil, P. B. Mosenthal, P. D. Pearson, & R. Barr (Eds.), *Handbook of reading research* (Vol. 3, pp. 403–422). Lawrence Erlbaum Associates.

Haimovitz, K., & Dweck, C. S. (2017). The origins of children's growth and fixed mindsets. *Child Development, 88*(6), 1849–1859.

Hudson, R. F., Pullen, P. C., Lane, H. B., & Torgesen, J. K. (2005). The complex nature of reading fluency: A multidimensional view. *Reading & Writing Quarterly, 21*(4), 319–338.

Hudson, R. F., Lane, H. B., & Pullen, P. C. (2009). Reading fluency assessment and instruction. *The Reading Teacher, 62*(6), 526–538.

Hulme, C., & Snowling, M. J. (2020). Reading disorders and dyslexia: A developmental perspective. *Child Development Perspectives, 14*(1), 50–55.

Kim, Y.-S. G., & Schatschneider, C. (2021). Expanding developmental models of reading: The role of motivation and socioemotional factors. *Reading Research Quarterly, 56*(S1), S99–S118.

Kofler, M. J., Irwin, L. N., Soto, E. F., Groves, N. B., Harmon, S. L., & Sarver, D. E. (2019). Executive functioning heterogeneity in pediatric ADHD. *Journal of Abnormal Child Psychology, 47*(2), 273–286.

Lyon, G. R., Shaywitz, S. E., & Shaywitz, B. A. (2003). A definition of dyslexia. *Annals of Dyslexia, 53*, 1–14.

Norton, E. S., & Wolf, M. (2012). Rapid automatized naming (RAN) and reading fluency: Implications for understanding and treatment of reading disabilities. *Annual Review of Psychology, 63*, 427–452.

O'Brien, B. A., Wolf, M., & Lovett, M. W. (2020). Orthographic learning and reading fluency in dyslexia. *Developmental Science, 23*(1), e12810.

Perfetti, C. (2007). Reading ability: Lexical quality to comprehension. *Scientific Studies of Reading, 11*(4), 357–383.

Perfetti, C., & Stafura, J. (2014). Word knowledge in a theory of reading comprehension. *Scientific Studies of Reading, 18*(1), 22–37.

Shaywitz, S. E., & Shaywitz, B. A. (2020). *Overcoming dyslexia* (2nd ed). Knopf.

Tsesmeli, S. N., & Seymour, P. H. (2006). Derivational morphology and spelling in dyslexia. *Reading and Writing, 19*(6), 587–625.

VanDerHeyden, A. M. (2013). RTI and decision making. *School Psychology Review, 42*(3), 306–319.

van der Kleij, S. W., Groen, M. A., Segers, E., & Verhoeven, L. (2019). Sequential implicit learning ability predicts growth in reading skills in typical readers and children with dyslexia. *Scientific Studies of Reading, 23*(1), 77–88.

Wang, H., Castles, A., & Nickels, L. (2021). Surface dyslexia revisited. *Cognitive Neuropsychology, 38*(3), 145–170.

Willcutt, E. G. (2020). Assessment of attention-deficit/hyperactivity disorder and comorbid reading disorder with consideration of executive functioning. In M. M. Martel (Ed.), *The clinical guide to assessment and treatment of childhood learning and attention problems* (pp. 55–73). Elsevier Academic Press.

Wolf, M., & Katzir-Cohen, T. (2001). Reading fluency and its intervention. *Scientific Studies of Reading, 5*(3), 211–239.

Ziegler, J. C., & Perry, C. (2020). *Beyond the simplicity of dual-route models: The CDP+ model as a computational framework for understanding reading aloud and its development. Developmental Cognitive Neuroscience, 42*, 100751 https://doi.org/10.1016/j.dcn.2020.100751.

Seven

# A CASE OF CONCEPTUAL/REASONING DYSCALCULIA


Gail M. Cheramie, Ph.D.

Educational Consultant

Mertie M. Gomez, Ph.D.

Educational Consultant


Jeremy Tyler (JT)'s case illustrates one of the most frequently misunderstood and most commonly overlooked profiles of math learning disability: the *Conceptual/Reasoning subtype of dyscalculia.* Unlike students whose math difficulties stem from weak fact retrieval or procedural inefficiency, JT demonstrates solid foundational skills. He can compute accurately, read fluently, write well, and participate meaningfully in classroom instruction. His teachers describe him as attentive, motivated, and well-liked. Yet despite these strengths, JT has struggled with mathematics since 2nd grade, particularly when tasks require reasoning with quantities, interpreting relationships, or solving word problems.

This pattern, adequate calculation paired with significant difficulty applying mathematical concepts, is a hallmark of the conceptual subtype. Students with this profile often have intact phonological and linguistic skills, average visuospatial reasoning, and strong associative memory, but show weaknesses in fluid reasoning, auditory working memory for numbers, and retrieval fluency for numerical information. These cognitive processes form the backbone of quantitative reasoning, and when they are weak, students may understand individual steps of a procedure but fail to grasp the underlying structure of a problem.

JT's evaluation provides a clear example of how this subtype emerges in practice. His reading and writing skills are solidly average. His calculation skills fall within the low-average to average range. But when asked to interpret a word problem, identify relevant information, select an operation, or reason through a multistep task, his performance decreases sharply. Teachers report that he "understands the basic skills" but "cannot apply them," and that he becomes increasingly frustrated as the conceptual demands of 3rd-grade math intensify.

This chapter uses JT's case to illustrate how the operational definition of specific learning disability (SLD), the pattern of strengths and weaknesses/dual discrepancy-consistency (PSW/DD/C) method, and a Cattell-Horn-Carroll (CHC)-aligned math-subtype framework converge to support accurate diagnosis. His profile demonstrates why a student can appear to "know the math" yet still struggle profoundly with mathematical thinking, and why identifying the correct subtype is essential for designing effective interventions.

## COMPREHENSIVE PSYCHOEDUCATIONAL EVALUATION

| | |
|---|---|
| **Name:** Jeremy Tyler (JT) Gates | **Grade:** 3rd |
| **Date of Birth:** 3/1/2017 | **Dates of Assessment:** 12/4, 9, 11, 17/2025; 1/8/2026 |
| **Age:** 8 years, 10 months | **Date of Report:** 1/20/2026 |

## REASON FOR REFERRAL

JT was referred for a comprehensive psychoeducational evaluation by the school intervention team in accordance with the Individuals with Disabilities Education Improvement Act (IDEA) procedures. JT is making academic progress in reading and written expression, but he has not met grade-level expectations in mathematics. He has been involved in academic intervention in mathematics, and an analysis of his limited progress led the intervention team to recommend an evaluation due to suspected learning disability in this area. The purpose of this evaluation is to identify JT's ability strengths and weaknesses, determine if he meets the criteria for a learning disability, and provide recommendations for educational programming and progress.

## EVALUATION PROCEDURES/TESTS ADMINISTERED

Review of Educational Records
Interviews:
Parent
Teachers
Student
Classroom Observations
Wechsler Intelligence Scale for Children-Fifth Edition (WISC-V)
Woodcock-Johnson V Tests of Achievement (WJ V ACH)
Selected tests/subtests of the
Woodcock-Johnson V Tests of Cognitive Abilities (WJ V COG)
Comprehensive Test of Phonological Processing-2nd ed. (CTOPP-2)

## BACKGROUND INFORMATION

JT is an 8-year-old male student in the 3rd grade at Timberwood Elementary. He lives with his mother, father, and a younger sister (age 6 years). His parents are employed in the healthcare industry at the local hospital; Mrs. Gates is a nurse, and Mr. Gates is a radiologic technologist. JT participates in many activities with his family (e.g., watching movies, taking trips, attending sports events).

JT met developmental milestones within normal limits. There were no complications during pregnancy, birth, or delivery. His medical history is unremarkable. Overall, JT is described as in "very good" health and taking no prescribed medications. At school, he has passed vision and hearing screenings, and there are no suspected concerns in these sensory areas.

JT was enrolled in a church preschool at the ages of 3 and 4 years. He performed well there, and his parents reported no academic or behavioral concerns at these ages. JT enrolled in the local public elementary school in kindergarten and has remained enrolled there since. There are no concerns regarding school attendance. During the second half of 2nd grade, JT began experiencing difficulties with mathematics and also exhibited attentional challenges. Nevertheless, no major behavioral concerns were noted.

A work colleague of Mrs. Gates recommended that they have JT evaluated for possible attention deficit hyperactivity disorder (ADHD), and JT was evaluated at a "clinic that specializes in this" during the summer, upon completion of 2nd grade. The evaluation consisted of an interview with JT's parents, completion of the Conners-4 rating scale, and the Conners Continuous Performance Test (a direct computer-based measure of inattention, impulsivity, and vigilance). Based on the evaluation, "JT does not exhibit a pattern consistent with ADHD as direct measures of attention and rating scales were not significant for the condition." JT's parents had stated that JT was having difficulty in math, and the evaluator did recommend that he "receive a school-based evaluation for a learning disability."

At the beginning of this academic year (3rd grade), JT did not perform adequately on the NWEA Measures of Academic Progress (MAP) in math, obtaining a score at the 10th percentile. He was placed in an intervention based on beginning-of-year (BOY) MAP results and poor classroom performance. The intervention consisted of small-group instruction (30 min/3x per week) and focused on reviewing and practicing computational skills. The intervention teacher indicated that he was progressing "well" in this area and understands the basic skills of addition, subtraction, and multiplication; however, "JT's difficulty is in applying this knowledge in word problems." The general classroom and intervention teachers began working more on word problems at the end of October. On the classroom benchmark assessment at the end of November, JT did not meet the expected standard and was therefore referred for evaluation. Results of the middle-of-year (MOY) MAP were available in the second week of January, and JT's score was at the 12th percentile, remaining well below expectations for mid-third-grade level.

Socially, JT gets along well with his peers at school and also in the community. His parents did not report any behavioral or emotional difficulties. JT enjoys sports and is a member of a community Little League team. He is considered a "very good" player (left outfielder), has a "strong throwing arm," and is also "good at batting and showing improvement" in this skill. JT is described by his parents as kindhearted and respectful toward others, and they explained that they strive to instill these qualities in him and his sister, given their medical professions. JT gets along with his sister, and their relationship is "typical." The only concern that the parents have is JT's reluctance to do homework ("getting him to do it is a challenge…he wants to be outside playing with friends"). The parents indicated that JT requires "more help" in math but is otherwise doing well in school. They hope that JT attends college and enters the medical field, but for now, they want him to "pass 3rd grade."

## ASSESSMENT OBSERVATIONS

JT was assessed across several sessions. Rapport was easily established, and JT commented that he knew he was "doing these tests because I am not good at math." JT was attentive and cooperative throughout all procedures, attempted all tasks, and demonstrated effort even when tasks became difficult. At times, he commented, "these are easy for me" (e.g., reading words) and "I like this kind of stuff" (e.g., blocks). He also commented when items were "hard" (e.g., math word problems). Overall, the results obtained in this evaluation are considered reliable and valid estimates of his level of functioning in the areas assessed.

## EVALUATION RESULTS

### Intellectual/Cognitive Functioning

To assess the various domains of intellectual/cognitive functioning, the WISC-V served as the core battery, supplemented by selected subtests from the WJ V COG and the CTOPP-2. The Cross-Battery Assessment (XBA) approach and the Cross-Battery Assessment Software System (X-BASS) were used to analyze and synthesize the data obtained. This approach provides guidelines for assessments to use multiple batteries to measure a broader range of abilities than a single instrument can provide. XBA is based on current research evidence regarding the structure of cognitive abilities and their relationships to various academic abilities. JT's results are presented in the following tables. Where applicable, the scaled score for each subtest has been converted to a standard score to facilitate comparisons across instruments. Where applicable, the X-BASS was used to generate composite scores. The first table presents JT's cognitive strengths/intact abilities. The second table presents cognitive weaknesses and processing domains that reflect mixed abilities.

### Cognitive Strengths

| Instrument Composite/Index and Subtests | Scaled/Standard Score | Percentile Rank | Subtest/Test Description |
|---|---|---|---|
| WISC-V Verbal Comprehension Index (VCI; *Gc*) | 98 | 45 | |
| Similarities (SI) | 9/95 | | Explaining the similarity of common objects or concepts represented by pairs of words presented orally |
| Vocabulary (VO) | 10/100 | | Naming a pictured item and defining orally presented words |
| WISC-V Visual Spatial Index (VSI; *Gv*) | 92 | 30 | |
| Block Design (BD) | 9/95 | | Viewing a model and/or picture and using blocks to reproduce the design within a specified time limit |
| Visual Puzzles (VP) | 8/90 | | Viewing a completed puzzle and selecting three response options that, when combined, reconstruct the puzzle |
| Processing Speed XBA Composite (*Gs*) | 94 | 34 | |
| Coding (CD) | (5)* | | Drawing symbols that are paired with a series of numbers according to a key within a time limit |
| Symbol Search (SS) | 8/90 | | Scanning a search group of symbols and determining whether one of the symbols in the target group matches within a time limit |
| Cancellation (CA) | 10/100 | | Scanning two arrangements of objects (structured and random) and marking target objects within a time limit |
| Learning Efficiency XBA Composite (*Gl*) | 101 | 53 | |
| WISC-V Immediate Symbol Translation (IST) | 95 | | Learning visual–verbal pairs and translating symbol strings into phrases or sentences |
| WJ V COG Story Recall (SR) | 106 | | Listening to stories from an audio recording and retelling the stories with as many details as can be recalled |
| CTOPP-2 Phonological Awareness (*Ga*) | 96 | 39 | |
| Elision (EL) | 8/90 | | Saying a word after dropping designated sounds/phonemes |
| Blending Words (BW) | 10/100 | | Combining sounds/phonemes to form words |
| Phoneme Isolation (PI) | 10/100 | | Identifying target sounds (e.g., 3rd sound) in words |

* Not used in the calculation of the *Gs* cluster.

JT performed in the average range in several cognitive areas. Verbal, language-related (VCI = 98, 45th percentile) and visuo-spatial (VSI = 92, 30th percentile) skills are adequately developed for his age. These scores represent the cognitive processing domains of *Gc* (language development and acquired knowledge) and *Gv* (perceiving, analyzing, synthesizing, manipulating, and thinking with visual patterns and stimuli). Phonological Awareness (*Ga*) is average (SS = 96, 39th percentile) and consistent with his performance in basic reading and school-based assessments. JT has acquired phonetic coding skills in blending, deletion, and phoneme manipulation, consistent with age expectations. JT's performance in *Gl*, Learning Efficiency (SS = 101, 53rd percentile), indicates that he can adequately encode information and retrieve it. Within this cognitive process, associative and meaningful memory are average, indicating that JT learns and retains information through associative or contextual cues. Within the *Gs* domain (Processing Speed), JT performed lower on a subtest (Coding) that involved associating symbols with numbers. He appears more cautious when numbers are involved in the task. He made no errors but approached the task more slowly. When *Gs* subtests did not involve numerical stimuli, he performed in the average range (*Gs* = 94, 34th percentile). Visual scanning and visual discrimination fall within the average range.

## Cognitive Weaknesses and Mixed Abilities

| Instrument Composite/Index and Subtests | Scaled/ Standard Score | Percentile Rank | Test Description |
|---|---|---|---|
| WISC-V Fluid Reasoning Index (FRI; *Gf*) | 76 | 5 | |
| Matrix Reasoning (MR) | 7/85 | | Viewing an incomplete matrix or series and selecting the response option that completes the matrix or series |
| Figure Weights (FW) | 5/75 | | Viewing a scale balanced by weights and a scale with missing weights, and then selecting the response option that keeps the scale balanced |
| XBA Composite Retrieval Fluency (*Gr*): Stimuli involving numbers | 74 | 4 | |
| WISC-V Naming Speed Quantity (NSQ) | 76 | | Naming the quantity of squares inside a series of boxes as quickly as possible |
| CTOPP-2 Rapid Digit Naming (RDN) | 6/80 | | Naming a set of numbers presented on a page as quickly as possible |
| CTOPP-2 *Gr* Rapid Letter Naming (RLN) | (9/95)* | | Naming a set of letters presented on a page as quickly as possible |
| WISC-V Auditory Working Memory Index (*Gwm*: Wa) | 73 | 4 | |
| Digit Span (DS) | 6/80 | | Repeating a series of numbers verbatim (Forward), in reverse order (Backward), and in ascending order (Sequencing) |
| Letter-Number Sequencing (LNS) | 4/70 | | Recalling numbers in ascending order and letters in alphabetical order when orally presented with a sequence of numbers and letters |
| WJ V COG Memory for Words (MW) | (104)** | | Repeating a list of unrelated words (presented via audio recording) in the same order |
| XBA Composite Visual Working Memory (*Gwm*: Wv) | 101 | 53 | |
| WISC-V Picture Span (PS) | 10/100 | | Viewing one or more pictures for a limited time, then identifying the pictures in sequence from options on a response page |
| WJ V COG Visual Working Memory (VWM) | 102 | | Recalling the location of a pattern of dots inside randomly placed squares after completing a simple distractor task |

* Not used in the calculation of *Gr*.
** Not used in the calculation of AWMI.

JT displayed a weakness in Fluid Reasoning (*Gf*), which involves inductive and deductive reasoning to solve problems (FRI = 76, 5th percentile). On the MR and FW tasks, JT had to identify underlying concepts or rules and apply them to solve a novel problem. In MR, a measure of inductive reasoning, JT had to discern the rule governing presented relationships to solve for the missing element. In FW, a measure of general sequential/deductive reasoning, a model was presented depicting the rule governing the relationships among items, and JT had to apply that rule to solve for the missing element. In FW, the quantitative concept of equality is applied, rendering the task a quantitative fluid-reasoning task. JT had noticeable difficulty on FW, as reflected in the score, but also in his comments. During this subtest, he often said, "I can't really figure this out." During the MR and FW subtests, he tried each item, paying attention to the stimulus presented, but did comment on several items, saying, "These are hard." Although fluid reasoning is very low, other tasks involving verbal and visuo-spatial reasoning are average (VCI > FRI, VSI > FRI).

Retrieval Fluency (*Gr*) reflects the rate and fluency of selectively and strategically retrieving information stored in long-term memory. Within the Retrieval Fluency processing cluster, JT demonstrated weakness in the efficient processing of numerical stimuli (*Gr* = 74; 4th percentile). JT had difficulty rapidly naming numbers (SS = 80), not because he did not know them, but because he slowed his naming. This contrasts with letter naming, which is average (SS = 95). He also scored low on Naming Speed Quantity (SS = 76), which is a measure of subitizing (i.e., quantifying sets without counting). Within *Gr*, JT evidenced greater difficulty with numerical versus alphabetic input and did not demonstrate automaticity in processing numerical stimuli.

JT's initial Working Memory cluster on the WISC-V was not cohesive. That is, he obtained a significantly different scaled score on Digit Span (6) than on Picture Span (10). Additional subtests were administered to determine the reason for the differential performance between auditory and visual working memory. JT displayed a weakness in auditory working memory (AWMI = 73, 4th percentile), but his visual working memory is average (*Gwm*: Wv = 101, 53rd percentile). An additional test of *Gwm* was administered (Memory for Words) from the WJ V COG to determine whether this was an auditory versus visual matter or an item content matter. On Memory for Words, JT earned a standard score in the average range (SS = 104). Therefore, JT's difficulty is not a general weakness in short-term storage and working memory (*Gwm*), but rather a specific difficulty in manipulating numerical stimuli in working memory. Working memory capacity for numbers is more than two standard deviations lower than that for visual information and words.

JT's performance pattern on the cognitive assessment shows significant difficulty in number processing abilities. He has difficulty holding and manipulating numbers in short-term and working memory, retrieving numerical information efficiently, and applying quantitative concepts during problem-solving. Together, this information suggests a deficit in Number Sense, which involves the basic processing of numerical information. This pattern is associated with math disabilities/dyscalculia, and JT's cognitive profile is consistent with referral information and documented difficulties in math.

It should be noted that JT's Full Scale Intelligence Quotient (FSIQ) on the WISC-V is 80 (9th percentile). The subtests which comprise the FSIQ are as follows: Similarities (ss = 9), Vocabulary (ss = 10), Block Design (ss = 9), Matrix Reasoning (ss = 7), Figure Weights (ss = 5), Digit Span (ss = 6), and Coding (ss = 5). The FSIQ is at the 9th percentile due to performance on subtests associated with numerical processing. When JT's cognitive strengths are aggregated, the Facilitating Cognitive Composite (FCC) calculated through X-BASS reflects average intellectual/cognitive functioning (FCC = 96, 39th percentile). The FCC standard score indicates that JT possesses sufficient cognitive strengths to support academic learning and skill acquisition, provided that specific processing deficits do not impede performance.

The table below presents a graphic depiction of the pattern of cognitive strengths and weaknesses used in the analysis.

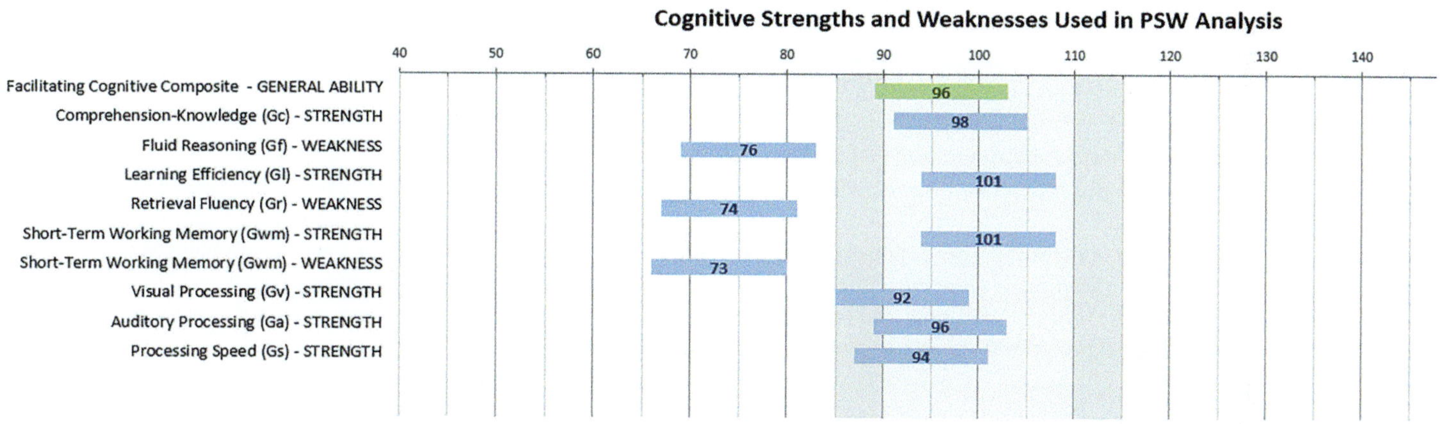


## Classroom Observations and Teacher Interviews

In accordance with IDEA-mandated procedures (34 CFR § 300.310), JT was observed in his math classroom to document academic performance and behavior in the area of difficulty. In addition to the math observation, a reading observation was conducted to assess the consistency of behavior and performance across settings.

In reading, students read a grade-level passage and answered five questions about the story. The lesson length was 20 minutes. JT was on-task 91%; the class on-task percentage was 89%. JT completed his work and answered all five questions correctly. He did not require assistance with the task.

In math, students were instructed as a group on a number sentence (equation) to reflect a word problem and the order of operations. The class solved two equations with teacher guidance and then completed a worksheet with 10 problems. JT was 83% on-task; the class's on-task percentage was 87%. JT required assistance with this task and appropriately requested help (by raising a hand). He completed 8 of the 10 problems within the time limit established by the teacher. Of the eight completed, four were correct.

JT's performance in reading (100% correct) versus math (40% correct) was noticeably different, but he remained on task and put forth effort on the assignments. He displayed some off-task behaviors during these observations, including looking around the room, drumming on his desk, and making comments to his peers seated nearby. These behaviors were consistent with those of his classmates, occurred to a limited extent, and did not interfere with his academic work.

A brief interview with his teachers after these observations revealed that his behavior during the observation was consistent with his typical daily classroom behavior. He is attentive and participates in all tasks. The reading teacher has no concerns with JT and considers him a "good reader, both in basic skills and comprehension." She noted that JT has acquired basic skills and that, in 3rd grade, greater emphasis is placed on comprehension. The math teacher has no concerns regarding JT's behavior, effort, or attention. She indicated that his math skills are below the 3rd-grade level. Sometimes JT becomes frustrated, but he has developed a plan to raise his hand to receive assistance when he encounters difficulty. This has worked well in "giving him the help he needs on an assignment, but he really needs remediation and more than what can be provided in my class. . .he is getting farther behind because he can't do word problems."

Additional interviews with the reading and math teachers yielded information consistent with checklists completed by these teachers in the referral process. Academically, JT is a good reader, motivated to perform well, and has no behavioral challenges. He shows an even disposition and is described as a "typical third-grade boy." He has many friends and gets along well with his peers. JT can be "immature at times" but responds well to redirection and is compliant. He is highly interested in sports and discusses his baseball games. His teachers noted that he is insightful about his baseball games, explaining at times why his team did not win.

## STUDENT INTERVIEW

JT was asked interview questions throughout the assessment sessions. He provided information regarding his family and noted that he gets along with his sister, although at times she can be "annoying." He reported a good relationship with his parents and stated that they do many things together. He particularly likes that his parents are present at his baseball games. His parents work "at the hospital," and he likes that they "help people." JT has many friends. He explained that several of the boys on his baseball team also attend the same school; some are in the same grade as he is, but only one is in his class. JT likes his teachers and his school ("we are the Lions"). JT acknowledged that he is better at reading than at math. His favorite subject is social studies because his teacher is "awesome" and they are learning about important people in history and also use maps to learn about the environment in different places. JT wants to go to college (University of Texas) and be a baseball player when he grows up.

## ACADEMIC ACHIEVEMENT

### Reading

Multiple data sources indicate that JT's basic reading, reading comprehension, and reading fluency skills are within age/grade-level expectations. His reading grades from K-3rd grade either met expectations or were above expectations. His district kindergarten reading universal screener results indicated that he exhibited phonological awareness (rhyme, sound matching, and sound manipulation) and phonics and word recognition (letter identification, matching sounds to letters, and word recognition) within the "Meets Grade Level Expectations" range. JT's 2nd and 3rd-grade NWEA MAP results consistently indicated adequate progress toward grade-level expectations.

The above data are consistent with his WJ V ACH Basic Reading Skills (SS = 106) and Reading Comprehension Skills (SS = 103). He exhibits well-developed, average-range abilities to read real and nonsense words in isolation. Whether reading connected text or unconnected words, he read aloud in an even and controlled manner, without repetition or having to reread words. When reading a passage format (connected text), he consistently demonstrated the proper recognition and application of phrases, clauses, and sentences by chunking words into meaningful units, at 560L (at grade-level NWEA Lexile expectations). Since BOY 2nd grade, his reading Lexile levels have consistently met expectations. JT adjusted to the meaning of an emotion being conveyed by the passage by reading at a conversational and appropriate pace. According to the NWEA MAP (3rd-grade fall) and the reading teacher's running records (on grade-level passages), his words correct per minute (wcpm) met grade-level expectations, varying between 101 and 109, respectively.

### WJ V ACH—Reading

| CLUSTER/Test Name | Standard Score | Percentile Rank | Test Description |
|---|---|---|---|
| BASIC READING SKILLS | 106 | 66 | |
| Letter-Word Identification | 108 | 70 | Reading a list of individual words aloud |
| Word Attack | 103 | 58 | Reading a list of nonsense words aloud |
| READING COMPREHENSION | 103 | 57 | |
| Passage Comprehension | 104 | 62 | After reading a short passage, provide a missing word that makes sense in the context of the passage |
| Paragraph Reading Comprehension | 101 | 53 | After silently reading a passage, answering story-specific questions presented orally by examiner |

When asked about his reading skills, JT reported that he "enjoys reading" and has read three books in *The Bad Guys* series. His parents take him to the library twice a month to check out "as many books" as he wants.

### Writing

Overall, multiple data sources indicate that JT's written expression skills are at age/grade-level expectations. He was observed to be right-hand dominant with an efficient tripod pencil grip. His pencil rested in the center of the thumb webspace. His paper placement (tilted slightly to the left) and posture were appropriate (upright with feet on the floor). JT used his helper hand to stabilize the Student Response Booklet. He formed his letters with standard sequences and with appropriate spacing between letters and words. The letters and words adhered to the baseline and were well-sized. He worked carefully, erasing appropriately and editing as needed. Consistent with his 3rd-grade work samples, JT wrote complete compound and complex sentences with subject-verb agreement, including past and present verb tenses, on the Written Language Samples (SS = 113) and Sentence Writing Fluency (SS = 108) tests. His 3rd-grade teacher reported that he uses commas and quotation marks in dialogue, capitalizes story titles, and provides facts, definitions, and details to develop a topic. Per the 3rd-grade Fall District Level Assessment (DLA) for Writing, he is projected to "Meet Expectations" on the state-mandated writing test administered at the end of the school year.

### WJ V ACH—Written Expression

| CLUSTER/Test Name | Standard Score | Percentile Rank | Test Description |
|---|---|---|---|
| WRITTEN EXPRESSION | 113 | 80 | |
| Written Language Samples | 113 | 81 | Writing responses to prompts presented orally by the examiner, which are evaluated for their quality of expression |
| Sentence Writing Fluency | 108 | 69 | Writing simple sentences about pictures using a given set of words provided for each picture within a five-minute time limit. |

### Math

Multiple data sources indicate that JT's math calculation skills are intact, at grade-level expectations, and math problem-solving skills are well below age/grade-level expectations. His math grades from K-3rd grade have indicated struggles with grade-level math content. His final math grades in 1st and 2nd grade were "S" and 75, respectively. His current grade is 68. Based on his 3rd-grade Fall NWEA MAP results, he was placed in Tier 2 Intervention and received 30-minutes small-group instruction (3x per week) focused on reviewing and practicing computational skills. His 3rd-grade math intervention teacher reported that "he is progressing well in this area and understands basic skills of addition, subtraction, and multiplication; he has difficulty applying this knowledge in word problems."

JT's performance on the Math Calculation Cluster (SS = 88) falls within the upper limits of the low-average range. WJ V Calculation (SS = 93) and Math Facts Fluency (SS = 81) tests were average to low average. Noted on his Student Response Booklet were the tally marks he utilized to obtain answers to the untimed Calculation items. He did not exhibit automaticity in recalling math facts, as he was observed using his fingers to count on several items. His 2nd and 3rd-grade math teachers reported his consistent use of classroom support, including counting manipulatives and graph paper. These teachers explained that JT is accurate but not fluent in his computational skills. JT can add two-digit numbers without regrouping. When regrouping is required, he uses graph paper (to align his place-value columns) and relies on tally marks. His 2nd-grade math DLA (Q1, Q2, and Q3) results were mixed. His place value, addition, and subtraction skills "Approached" expectations, but his problem-solving and understanding relationships between operations skills "Did Not Meet" expectations. JT "Did Not Meet" the grade level standard on his EOY 2nd-grade MAP. He is receiving intervention; however, on the most recent MOY 3rd-grade MAP, he did not meet grade-level expectations (12th percentile).

JT's performance on Applied Problems (SS = 77) and Math Problem Identification (SS = 79) was in the low range. After the examiner read the problems to JT, he struggled to identify relevant data and choose the right operation to complete the item. He would frequently record the data in his Student Response Booklet, verbally solve problems, and finally select a procedure. Often, this process was inefficient and resulted in an incorrect response. His 3rd-grade math (Q1 and Q2) DLA results are "Below Expectations" in multiplication, problem-solving strategies, and fractions.

### WJ V ACH—Math

| CLUSTER/Test Name | Standard Score | Percentile Rank | Test Description |
|---|---|---|---|
| MATH CALCULATION SKILLS | 88 | 21 | |
| Calculation | 93 | 31 | Solving math problems in a Response Booklet that includes addition, subtraction, multiplication, division, and more complex mathematical operations |
| Math Facts Fluency | 81 | 11 | Solving simple math problems within a three-minute time limit |
| MATH PROBLEM SOLVING | 78 | 7 | |
| Applied Problems | 77 | 6 | Solving various types of problems presented by the examiner that involve the application of math operations |
| Math Problem Identification | 79 | 8 | After hearing an unsolvable math problem presented by the examiner, describing what is missing or what is wrong with the problem that makes it unsolvable |

JT reported that he enjoys working with bar graphs and pictographs. He can solve one-step problems using categorical data (e.g., "Which food item do most students prefer?"). He acknowledged that he does not do well in math but does better when his teacher helps him.

## CONCLUSIONS

JT is a 3rd-grade student who performs well in reading, science, and social studies. He displays academic difficulties in math. He is friendly, well-liked by peers and teachers, and has no discipline problems. JT's athletic abilities are well-developed, and he is considered a very good player on his community baseball team. There are no physical/health, motor, perceptual, emotional/behavioral, or environmental factors that are impacting his performance. Quite the contrary, his parents have provided an environment conducive to learning and development, and his educational history shows continued enrollment with regular attendance. Multiple sources of data were used in this evaluation to describe JT's educational performance, strengths, and weaknesses. These data sources were used to draw conclusions about the presence of a disability and to inform recommendations for educational programming.

### SLD Math

According to the IDEA [34 CFR 300.8(c)], an SLD is a disorder in processing that impairs the ability to learn an academic skill. To analyze the data and determine whether JT exhibits a PSW, the DD/C operational framework and its associated statistical analyses were applied. SLD identification using the PSW method requires four key components: average overall ability despite specific cognitive weaknesses, an unexpected academic weakness, a domain-specific cognitive weakness, and a moderate-to-strong empirical relationship between the cognitive and academic weaknesses. The following components were used to guide the process of investigating a PSW consistent with SLD.

***Overall General Ability***

JT has many cognitive assets/intact abilities (*Gc, Gv, Ga, Gl, Gs, Gwm*:Wv), and when these are aggregated, his FCC = 96 in the average range. There are additional supporting indicators of average learning ability within the academic profile (average standard scores in reading and written language, a passing MAP assessment in reading, classroom grades, and teacher reports).

***Academic Weakness and Unexpected Underachievement***

JT displayed a significant academic deficit in Math Problem Solving. This is supported by multiple data sources. JT's teacher indicated poor math skills, and he is currently failing in math. His grades have declined each year. His teacher estimates that his academic skill level is approximately 1.5 grade levels below his current placement. He did not meet the grade-level standard on the benchmark assessments in Mathematics. JT has been involved in a math intervention. The intervention initially focused on calculation, and he made progress in this area. His intervention teacher indicated that he remains unable to apply foundational math skills to solve problems requiring reasoning. This is true for word problems, although JT is considered a good reader with average comprehension skills. MOY MAP data indicated functioning at the 12th percentile, and an analysis of the MAP showed that he did better in areas involving operations and geometry versus analyzing patterns and relationships to solve problems. Standardized testing revealed a low standard score in Math Problem Solving (SS = 78). Thus, all data converge to indicate an academic deficit in this academic area. JT's deficit in Math Problem Solving is below what would be expected based on his overall cognitive functioning. This academic deficit is also unexpected given his other academic skills (e.g., reading, written expression).

***Domain-Specific Cognitive Ability/Processing Deficit***

JT has specific weaknesses in three cognitive abilities/processes: *Gf* (fluid reasoning), *Gwm*:Wa (auditory working memory), and *Gr* (retrieval fluency). Collectively, these weaknesses reflect difficulty with processing numerical information; within X-BASS, their aggregate is termed the *Academic-Specific Inhibiting Cognitive Composite* (AICC). JT's fluid reasoning is well below his ability to reason with linguistic and visuospatial input. Within the *Gwm* domain, JT does well on visual working memory and on memory for words. This contrasts with his ability to recall and manipulate number-based items (DS, LNS). Within the *Gr* domain, JT is not efficient at retrieving numbers or numerical representations, but his letter naming is average. JT's weaknesses are significantly below what would be expected based on his overall cognitive functioning and are not attributable to low general ability.

***Relationship Between Cognitive Ability/Processing and Academic Deficits***

As noted earlier, JT has three areas of cognitive weakness, but the most relevant weaknesses associated with his difficulty in MPS are *Gf* and *Gwm*. These processing domains were combined to create the AICC = 71, which collectively has a strong relationship with MPS. This indicates that these (*Gf* and *Gwm*) are the primary cognitive processes that interfere with JT's academic performance in MPS. *Gf* leads to difficulties in reasoning with quantitative information, internalizing procedures and processes for solving problems, and apprehending relationships among numbers. Deficits in *Gwm* affect automaticity in and recall of math facts and procedures, effective completion of multistep problems, and extraction of information for use in word problems.

***Diagnostic Impressions***

The figure below presents the PSW analysis, indicating that all criteria for the DD/C method are met. JT displays the core characteristics of a specific learning disability based on a PSW: he has an unexpected weakness in academic achievement (MPS = 78), a domain-specific deficit in cognitive processing (AICC = 71), and these cognitive and academic deficits are strongly empirically related. This pattern occurs within

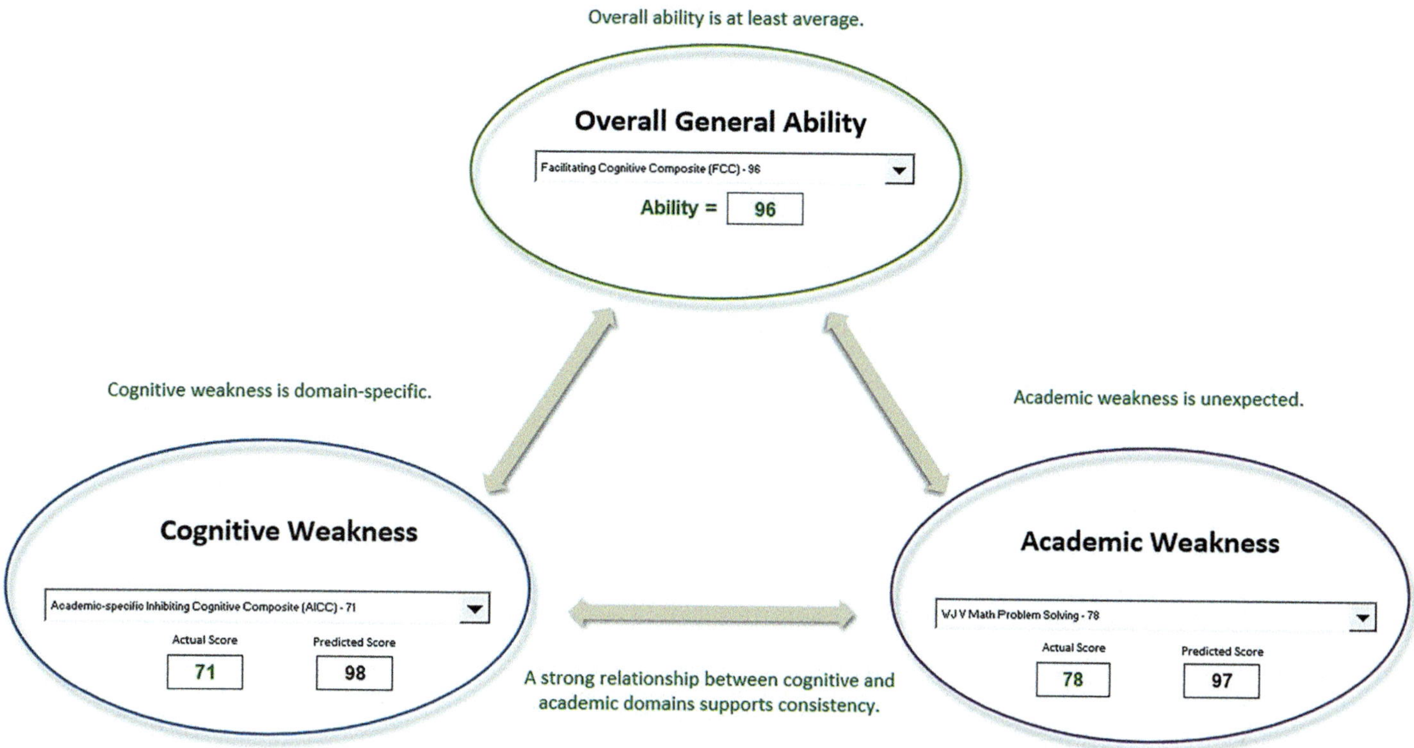


**FIGURE 7.1 PSW Output from X-BASS 3.0**

a cognitive profile indicating average learning ability (FCC = 96). As such, JT displays a pattern of performance consistent with SLD and meets the criteria for the educational disability classification of SLD in Math Problem Solving. This classification is also referred to as Dyscalculia (Figure 7.1).

It should be noted that the presence of a disability classification is not synonymous with eligibility for special education. JT's evaluation will need to be reviewed by the Individual Education Plan team, and eligibility for special education services is decided by this team.

## RECOMMENDATIONS

Since JT struggled to identify what is missing or what is wrong with the problem that makes it unsolvable, teach JT using these activities:

- Working in a small group, several students create a mathematical story problem with missing information. The groups swap their story problems and determine that information is missing. The groups are then tasked with editing the story problem to include all necessary information for completing the item.
- After working within a small group, give JT unsolvable word problems (with missing information). Have JT identify the missing information, create the information, and then solve the problem.
- Highlight important information in a word problem

Given his deficits in *Gf*, the classroom teacher should provide guided practice to help JT internalize the procedures and processes necessary for solving mathematical problems. For example:

- Identify procedural vocabulary (e.g., more than, less than, total, left-over, quotient, sum) to determine the function necessary for problem completion (e.g., addition, subtraction, multiplication, and/or division)
- Use demonstrations to externalize the reasoning process (think-alouds)
- Visually organize the data (e.g., table, chart, graph)
- Use guided lists for implementing procedures and formulae. For example:
  - PEMDAS (parentheses, exponents, multiplication, division, addition, subtraction)
  - Algorithms (rules for math procedures)
    - Steps taken for subtraction involving regrouping
    - Steps taken for long division
    - Steps to find the least common denominator

Given his deficits in *Gwm*, JT's classroom teacher should review newly presented information and math procedures. At the same time, JT should be provided with procedural study guides and checklists to use during direct instruction and independent practice. Procedural and problem-solving charts will be required.

The math teacher should provide JT with a variety of graphic organizers specifically aligned with the math procedure being taught. For example, Divide, Multiply, Subtract, and Bring Down (DMSB) would be in the first column of a two-column table. The second column would contain four (4) cells, one for each step of the long division problem.

It will be important to use meaningful stimuli in JT's intervention program. Use of word problems and math operations that involve baseball would be appropriate.

Provide JT with access to an individualized computer-administered evidence-based math intervention program. Such programs include DreamBox, IXL Math, and iReady. These programs address both math facts fluency and math problem solving. This would enable a personalized instructional plan aligned with classroom instruction. This additional support should scaffold his math abilities, promoting growth.

## TEST YOURSELF

**1. JT's case illustrates a subtype of dyscalculia in which students demonstrate adequate calculation skills but significant difficulty applying mathematical concepts and reasoning through word problems. True or False?**

**2. Which of the following best describes the conceptual/reasoning subtype of dyscalculia?**

(a) Weak math fact retrieval with otherwise intact reasoning

(b) Accurate computation but difficulty interpreting quantitative relationships and solving word problems

(c) Difficulty remembering multiplication tables only

(d) Weak reading comprehension that interferes with math learning

**3. Which of the following academic areas represented a strength for JT?**

(a) Reading and written expression

(b) Math problem solving

(c) Mathematical reasoning

(d) Quantitative pattern recognition

**4. JT's teachers reported that he understood basic math procedures but struggled to apply them in word problems. This pattern is characteristic of conceptual dyscalculia. True or False?**

**5. Which cognitive ability was identified as a primary weakness contributing to JT's math difficulties?**

(a) Comprehension knowledge (*Gc*)

(b) Visual processing (*Gv*)

(c) Fluid reasoning (*Gf*)

(d) Phonological processing (*Ga*)

**6. JT demonstrated a weakness in auditory working memory for numbers but average performance in visual working memory. This pattern suggests that his working memory difficulties are specific to numerical information rather than general memory capacity. True or False?**

**7. Which CHC-related processing weakness was associated with JT's difficulty efficiently retrieving numerical information?**

(a) Processing speed (*Gs*)

(b) Retrieval fluency (*Gr*)

(c) Comprehension knowledge (*Gc*)

(d) Visual processing (*Gv*)

**8. Within the DD/C framework, which of the following must be demonstrated to support identification of a specific learning disability?**

(a) Unexpected academic underachievement

(b) A domain-specific cognitive weakness

(c) Evidence that the cognitive and academic weaknesses are empirically related

(d) All of the above

**9. JT's FCC indicated that his overall ability to learn was within the average range despite specific processing weaknesses. True or False?**

**10. In students with conceptual/reasoning dyscalculia, the primary difficulty typically involves:**

(a) Basic number recognition
(b) Phonological decoding of numbers
(c) Understanding quantitative relationships and selecting appropriate operations in word problems
(d) Copying numbers accurately

*Answers:* 1. True; 2. b; 3. a; 4. True; 5. c; 6. True; 7. b; 8. d; 9. True; 10. c

Eight

# CROSS-BATTERY ASSESSMENT AND EVALUATION OF CULTURALLY AND LINGUISTICALLY DIVERSE POPULATIONS

## INTRODUCTION

As of the publication of this fourth edition of Essentials of Cross-Battery Assessment and X-BASS, approximately two and half decades will have passed since the initial volume of Essentials of Cross-Battery Assessment (Flanagan & Ortiz, 2001) was released and as we have constantly asserted, Cross-Battery Assessment (XBA) is a dynamic framework designed to keep up with advancements in modern cognitive theory and psychometrics. Accordingly, much has changed with respect to how XBA was originally, and how it is presently, conducted.

Those familiar with XBA in the past will notice that the pillars that served as the foundations of XBA have been updated, revised, and rethought in response to concerns, criticisms, as well as the research and CHC theoretical developments that have occurred over the past decade alone (Flanagan & McDonough, 2018; Schneider & McGrew, 2018). However, with respect to evaluation of individuals who come from linguistically and acculturatively diverse backgrounds, it is difficult to say that progress has been equally progressive. There remains a conspicuous absence of evidence-based methods for enacting the vast majority of aspirations that emanate from professional organizations regarding the provision of psychological services to diverse populations (APA, 2017; NASP, 2015; Ortiz, 2019). One would think that by this point in time, the Culture-Language Interpretive Matrix (C-LIM; Ortiz, 2001; Ortiz et al., 1998) might have long since been replaced by better, advanced methods for conducting evaluations on diverse individuals and with more sophisticated frameworks for establishing test score validity but this has not happened. At the very least, the fact that the field of testing has existed for more than a century now should mean that test authors and publishers have had more than enough opportunity to address development of new and fully valid tests designed expressly for this very purpose. Yet there have been only two such tests published capable of providing valid test scores for multilingual populations: (1) the Ortiz Picture Vocabulary Acquisition Test (Ortiz PVAT; Ortiz, 2018); and (2) the Bilingual English-Spanish Assessment (BESA; Pena et al., 2018). That nearly a decade has now passed since publication of these two tests combined with the fact that they still remain the only tests that can claim validity with all multilinguals (and monolinguals), is a commentary in itself regarding the glacial pace at which evidence-based methods and tools for working with diverse individuals appears to proceed.

For these and other reasons, it would appear that the often maligned C-LIM remains the sole option for test score validity and is anything but obsolete. Perhaps tragically, the need for it and its utility both remain as valuable now as when it was first developed (Ortiz, 2001; Ortiz et al., 1998). Recent investigations of the impact of acculturative knowledge and language acquisition on test performance have reinforced use of the principles underlying the C-LIM in clinical practice (Cormier et al., 2014, Cormier et al., 2022; Ortiz, 2019; Wong, 2023). Yet, from some of the studies that managed to get past peer review and into the literature, one might think that the basic premise underlying the C-LIM, that multilinguals perform differently than monolinguals on some tests, is an erroneous proposition! If this were not true, there would be no need for a discussion such as this and all current tests designed for use with monolingual English speakers would be considered fully valid for use with any individual regardless of their level of development and proficiency in English. The absurdity of this premise is strongly rejected by both the literature on multilingual test performance as well as the anecdotal experiences of clinicians working daily with diverse populations (Ortiz, 2019, 2023).

Despite what should be obvious and evident regarding the test performance of multilinguals, there continues to be significant misunderstanding of what the basic principles are such that they become convoluted in many investigations to the point that no one seems to actually comprehend the findings, including the authors. For example, the Styck and Watkins (2013) study has been promoted with great fanfare as an example of why the C-LIM "doesn't work" when in reality, it provides immense support for the C-LIM. Mention the C-LIM on any psychology listserv and immediately a host of presumed experts will jump in and point to this study as "evidence" that supposedly undermines the utility or validity of the approach as operationalized in the C-LIM. But one only need conduct a cursory review of the study (and the subsequent one in 2014) to see that they mistakenly believed that the typical pattern of performance (described as indicative of "likely invalid" results) is applicable to all multilinguals. This is wrong. Rather, according to research, a pattern of performance that declines relative to a test's language or acculturative demands is seen only for multilinguals who are of average ability and who are not disabled. Styck and Watkins (2013) dutifully describe their sample as one where "roughly 97% of (n = 83) of participants were identified as meeting criteria for an educational disability (86% as SLD)" (p. 371). Then without regard to this principle, Styck and Watkins

(2013) set out to find the "likely invalid" (average, nondisabled) pattern in a sample that they themselves describe as being almost totally comprised of children who have a disability. Instead, given their sample, they should have looked for the "likely valid" which their findings revealed in spectacular fashion. They reported that 89.5% of the sample (N=77) showed the "likely valid" pattern which indicates that proper interpretation of the C-LIM did indeed support the presence of a disability as had been assigned in nearly all cases. Moreover, the C-LIM correctly identified three children in the sample (3.5%) who displayed a "likely invalid" pattern, meaning they were unlikely to have a disability which is also consistent with the clinical decision not to identify one. In total, the C-LIM was consistent with 93% of the decisions that had been made across the entire sample, and these results are remarkable in their support for the C-LIM. That the erroneous conclusions and mistaken interpretations offered in the Styck and Watkins (2013, 2014) studies continue to be held up as the paragon of evidence that undermines the C-LIM only serves as an example regarding the extent to which many in the field fail to apprehend these issues well and offer what are very ill informed opinions.

Of course, there are other examples of research that highlights more the lack of understanding of its authors than it does problems in the C-LIM. Notably, a study by Calderon-Tena and colleagues (including Styck) (2022) stands out as another investigative effort that is sunk by mistaken notions of what it means to be multilingual as well as the research principles and foundations of the C-LIM. The reason the C-LIM exists at all is that research has constantly shown a pattern of decline in performance for multilinguals as compared to monolinguals relative to the increased measurement focus on language skills and acculturative knowledge. This is not a debatable point. The performance of normal, average-ability multilinguals tends to decline as a function of linguistic and acculturative knowledge variables, whereas no such decrease occurs for normal, average-ability monolinguals. The decline is absent in monolinguals (when a speech-language impairment is also absent) because age effectively controls for language development in monolinguals. It does not do so, however, for multilinguals as they have begun learning an additional language in their life at different points after birth. The authors in this second study believed, for unknown reasons, that the C-LIM is intended to be or can be used as some sort of EL identification tool. This is patently false, of course, but that did not stop Calderon-Tena and colleagues from thinking that ELs who were included in the WJ-III norm sample should show a "typical" declining pattern of performance. That expectation reveals that the authors did not understand the many differences in development that may exist among multilinguals and failed to recognize two major problems with their rationale. First, multilinguals are often treated as if they were a homogenous and monolithic group despite the fact that multilinguals vary greatly in their levels of exposure to and development in English and their acquisition of acculturative knowledge. This is why, for the C-LIM to be effective, a determination must be made regarding the degree of difference relative to monolinguals for the purpose of true peer comparison. Not only did the authors fail to discern or create such categories, but they might well have been unable to do so had they wanted because there isn't enough information available about ELs in the WJ-III normative sample to determine how much they might differ. Even had they done it, it would not likely have helped their cause given the second problem they ignored regarding the narrow stratification within their sample. According to the WJ-III technical manual, and for obvious reasons, for any non-monolingual English speaker to have been included in the norm sample, they would have had to show a high level of English proficiency. Thus, the "ELs" that Calderon-Tena pulled out of the WJ-III norm sample represent an intentionally homogenized group characterized by high levels of English development—something that might be described as "slightly different" by C-LIM standards. To what extent these "ELs" should have shown a clear and identifiable pattern of declining performance and to what extent it should have been evident cannot be discerned via this sample or through their methods given that the participants were deliberately screened for inclusion in the WJ-III norm sample based on having sufficiently developed English language ability. One could hardly expect to find differences in C-LIM patterns when the main variable that creates the difference in performance between multilinguals and monolinguals has been carefully and systematically controlled by the sampling process. Essentially, the entire sample is "likely valid," meaning that there is no particular pattern of performance discernible with the C-LIM, which is exactly what they concluded. But in no way does this "conclusion" undermine the utility or validity of the C-LIM or the principles that underlie it. The C-LIM was never created to assist in identifying ELs or distinguishing them from monolinguals once again, it offered precisely what it should have, no differences, which apparently confused the researchers. Being proficient enough to be included in a monolingual, English-speaking norm sample likely creates a degree of difference that is negligible and attempting to identify an EL via the use of C-LIM is not only misguided but also represents a lack of understanding of its foundations and use as well as potential ignorance of what it actually means to be a multilingual and how it affects test performance.

The conceptual and methodological errors noted in these and other studies aside, it is perhaps important to remind users that the C-LIM is not a diagnostic tool or a test or scale of any kind. The C-LIM cannot be relied upon to directly or definitively point to whether any set of test scores do or do not support the presence or absence of any type of disorder or other condition. Rather, the C-LIM is intended only to assist practitioners in being able to make a decision regarding the validity of their test results with multilingual learners, because, if the results are unlikely to be valid, they should not be interpreted in the first place. There is no argument that test performance of multilinguals is not equal or commensurate to monolingual English speakers on all tests, and all the C-LIM does is use research on actual test performance of multilinguals, as categorized by degree of difference to enhance true peer comparison, to provide a systematic framework for assessing the impact of linguistic and acculturative knowledge factors on test performance that helps ascertain validity. Furthermore, the empirical structure and rationale that underlies the C-LIM has been used quite successfully as the basis for both the Ortiz PVAT (Ortiz, 2018) and the BESA (Pena et al., 2018) and demonstrates both the reliability and validity of the concept of controlling for differences in performance relative to differences in language development. Research that fails to properly grasp this conceptualization speaks more to the inadequacies of the investigators than it does the C-LIM and serves only to confuse and potentially oppress efforts necessary to support social justice and promote equity in testing by practitioners. This is particularly important, given that, to date, not a single researcher claiming problems with the C-LIM has provided an alternative method or procedure for engaging in this critical activity leaving practitioners to resort to gut instinct, experience, and nothing more than guessing when it comes to deciding whether their results are valid or not. The C-LIM makes this process systematic, research-based, and given a proper read of the Styck and Watkins (2013) study, impressively accurate and consistent with clinical decision-making—something that was reinforced by Cormier et al. (2022) who used the same norm sample from the WJ-III and came to a vastly different conclusion, to wit:

> One such challenge is assessing the cognitive abilities of the growing number of students who are considered ELs; limited English proficiency can lead to linguistically biased test results, which would lead to a misrepresentation of the examinee's true cognitive abilities. To eliminate this potential source of bias, psychologists testing EL students could consider examinee characteristics before administering a standardized measure of cognitive ability. This idea is not new. More than a decade ago, Flanagan et al. (2007) noted the critical need for psychologists to collect information regarding students' level of English proficiency, and the level of English required for the student to be able to comprehend test directions, formulate and communicate responses, or otherwise use their English language abilities within the testing process. Nonetheless, the results of our study provide an empirical basis in support of this broad recommendation.
>
> (p. 9)

**DON'T FORGET**

The fundamental issue in testing of diverse individuals rests with establishing score validity. X-BASS provides a range of modules and programming that assists practitioners in being able to evaluate the extent to which score validity may have been compromised by the presence of factors related to differences in language and acculturative knowledge.

Previous versions of X-BASS contained various forms of assistance for practitioners working with diverse populations, most notably the C-LIM. This support continues in X-BASS v3.X, but has been further expanded and integrated throughout all modules so that working with multilingual cases is facilitated in much the same and automated manner as when working with monolingual English speakers. This chapter will outline several new instruments, graphs, features, and operations within X-BASS that are particularly useful to practitioners in conducting nondiscriminatory evaluations and which align better with the manner in which clinical decision-making and interpretation take place. Use of X-BASS can help practitioners feel more confident in the conclusions they make, particularly with respect to establishing test score validity and ruling out exclusionary factors in identification of disabilities related to acculturative and linguistic differences, experiences, and development.

The descriptions and process described throughout this chapter are based on how X-BASS provides support for engaging in the process of evaluation. This chapter is not intended to be a stand-alone treatise on how to conduct evaluations on children that are acculturatively and linguistically different in general, and the reader is referred to other comprehensive sources for such a discussion (e.g., Ortiz, 2023; Ortiz & Cehelyk, 2023; Ortiz & Oganes, 2022; see also Rapid Reference 8.1). The primary purpose of this chapter is to provide instruction and guidance in how to properly and effectively use X-BASS in service of making defensible decisions and drawing nondiscriminatory conclusions when evaluating children from diverse acculturative and linguistic backgrounds.

*Rapid Reference 8.1*

**Additional Sources on the Assessment of Diverse Individuals**

For information on comprehensive evaluation of acculturatively and linguistically diverse individuals, the following sources are recommended: Ortiz (2023), Ortiz & Cehelyk (2023), Ortiz & Oganes (2022), and Ortiz, S. O., & Wong, J.Y.T. (2020a).

## WHAT'S NEW AND DIFFERENT ABOUT EVALUATING MULTILINGUALS IN X-BASS V3.0

It is probably most helpful to begin with a brief review and comparison of some of the major changes between the previous functions, features, and operations of the older version of X-BASS (v2.X) and the current version (3.X). Users of the old version of X-BASS will likely remember that the major component was inclusion of an advanced C-LIM which remains the central tool in the current version, albeit with some significant changes and updates. In general, the current version of X-BASS has a lighter, more intuitive, and accessible feel as well as streamlined data entry and fine-tuned analysis. The standard 3 × 3 matrix that has historically been the classification structure of the C-LIM is retained and is still the primary way in which the data are organized and can be entered. However, additional avenues for interpretation break away significantly from the matrix to focus also on the graphs and the ability to evaluate results at both the subtest and composite level.

In the previous version of X-BASS, users were required to enter their data into the C-LIM first and evaluate the impact of cultural and linguistic factors. After doing so, the results could be transferred over to the core data tabs or to the XBA Analyzer if the test or subtest came from a battery that did not have a dedicated core test tab. Although it is still possible to follow this procedure, in the current version it is recommended that users first enter their data on the dedicated Data Entry tab which allows the scores to be moved from module to module as desired rather than going straight to the C-LIM. This slight change in procedure is not intended to suggest a different approach to evaluation of diverse individuals. Evaluation of test scores in the C-LIM remains the first step in the process as will be described. The change in how and where scores are entered is designed to facilitate use of X-BASS by allowing scores to be entered once, in one location, and then have the data moved around to the modules automatically as needed and to permit transfer to the appropriate tab for achievement tests into the new Culture-Language Interpretive Matrix + Achievement Test Extensions (C-LIM+ATE). That said, it is still possible to enter information and scores directly into the C-LIM by navigating to it from the Dashboard. Once on the C-LIM, a drop down menu is provided from which a user can select the test/battery of interest to have all the constituent subtests loaded in the matrix automatically. Entering scores would then allow generation of the graphs and subsequent analysis. However, this approach is no longer recommended as there is no way to move the entered scores back to the Data Entry tab for use in other analyses (e.g., XBA, PSW) and does not automatically load data from academic testing either. Entering scores on the Data Entry tab also ensures that any changes to your data on that tab will be properly updated to other modules keeping all data current.

Users of the C-LIM in older versions of X-BASS (i.e., v2.X) will recall that it provided four graphs that permitted analyses of the impact of culture and language on test performance. The first graph was a tiered or leveled graph which combined the levels of impact, five in total, from the upper left to the lower right in the matrix. It was thought that this arrangement might better retain the hierarchical nature of the classifications and analysis, however, it tended to hide some important information regarding highly divergent performance within a given cell. For example, if there was significant variability between someone's performance on two or more of the subtests in the same cell, it was very difficult to see that without looking back at the matrix. Consequently, this graph has been dropped in the current version as newer features make it unnecessary.

The main Culture-Language (C-L) graph in previous versions of the C-LIM contained in X-BASS provided the primary analysis for examining the impact of acculturative and linguistic factors on test performance within each of the cells in the matrix. They are displayed as bars in the C-L graph with each one corresponding to one of the nine cells in the matrix. This level of analysis permitted a better examination of the overall pattern of decline as well as possibly some score variation among the cells that might be important. Nevertheless, it too could mask variability between scores that were in the same cell. For this reason, additional buttons were provided to offer guidance in automatically identifying relevant score variability within cells. The main elements of the C-L graph have been retained in the current version of X-BASS but additional features now include a display of the actual value for each bar and the addition of error bands/confidence intervals for each bar to assist in determining whether it is in the selected expected range, among other minor updates.

The two remaining graphs from prior versions of the C-LIM in X-BASS v2.X included the Culture-Only and Language-Only graphs and both have also been retained and updated with many of the same features as the main C-L graph. Although not often used or necessary, feedback in previous years from users has been that there is some value to these, so they were not eliminated entirely. However, they remain, as before, secondary and are not used as the primary means for evaluating the impact of acculturative knowledge and language acquisition on test performance.

Last, the C-LIM Summary is no longer included as it became unnecessary based on the manner in which the new version of X-BASS handles the input of new data or modifications to existing data. The C-LIM Summary was primarily used to update the main C-LIM pattern itself based on any new scores entered into X-BASS in locations apart from the C-LIM itself. Because the current version allows transfer of scores directly from the XBA and Data Entry tab, any updates made on either one will carry over automatically to the C-LIM as long as the buttons provided for this purpose are used. For this reason, the tab names that usually appear at the bottom of X-BASS have been hidden as their use would not conduct this type of automatic updating. Although the tab names can be toggled back on, it is not recommended and instead use of the navigation buttons should always be the method by which a user moves throughout X-BASS.

> **CAUTION**
>
> The tab names that usually appear at the bottom of the window in X-BASS have been hidden intentionally to prevent bypassing various functions. Using the navigation buttons provided ensures that all data and scores are transferred and updated properly and that all functions of X-BASS are carried out as necessary.

## X-BASS v3.X New Features for Evaluating Multilinguals

In general, the new version of X-BASS handles evaluation of children that are acculturatively and linguistically diverse in a much more integrated manner. Previously, for example, users were initially routed to a C-LIM-specific index page where they were told to select the degree of difference, given a little bit of guidance, and after making a selection, would be taken to the main C-LIM tab for data entry. The degree of difference could also be changed directly from the C-LIM tab. The index tab no longer exists and instead the True Peer Estimator (TPE) is now included and has been developed as a guided way of estimating "degree of difference." Users can navigate to the TPE directly from the Dashboard, C-LIM, C-LIM+ATE and PSW Data tab using the lavender button provided in each module. The TPE contains eight items which relate to linguistic and acculturative learning experiences for an individual that may be rated via a Likert-type scale to assess the degree to which the individual or their family matches the stated characteristics or conditions (Ortiz, 2019; Ortiz & Wong, 2022). These items provide a more systematic and formal way of looking specifically at the issues most important and relevant to the factors that can affect test performance. By making the respective ratings, the TPE will automatically sum them and provide an indication regarding what category the value represents. In short, the process of determining the degree of difference has now been made easier while at the same time offering more rigor and systematicity to prevent important factors from being overlooked.

Perhaps the most significant updates to the C-LIM involve the generation of two new graphs that allow for evaluation of the impact of cultural and linguistic factors at the broad ability and test composite level (refer to Rapid Reference 8.2). The first graph is one in which the subtests are organized according to the broad ability categories they measure according to their classifications under CHC Theory (see Appendix A). This information is built into X-BASS and allows it identify all subtests measuring the same broad ability then combine them mathematically to create both an overall average on the "actual" scores, as well as an overall average regarding the "expected" score for performance in each domain.

This expected score is determined on the basis of the Culture-Language Test Classifications contained within X-BASS and where the relative average impact of acculturative and linguistic factors has been drawn from the literature on multilingual performance. X-BASS draws on the classification of each individual subtest to establish its expected value and aggregates them together as an average for comparison to the actual values entered by the user in X-BASS. For example, if the primary ability measured by three subtests entered by the user is say, *Gc*, then those subtests are likely to be classified as having a high impact relative to acculturative and linguistic variables and which are found in cell number nine in the matrix. Whatever the domain being measured, and no matter in which cell they are classified, X-BASS can take the average value for each subtest that would be expected based also on the selected degree of difference for the examinee and calculate an average or aggregate mean. A graph is then provided where the actual and expected values are mapped side by side as confidence bands (using 1SEM, 68% CI). By organizing the analysis according to CHC broad ability domain, users can now compare directly whether performance in a particular cognitive area is likely to have been affected primarily by acculturative and linguistic factors (typical performance, hence likely invalid scores) or whether they were insufficient to account for the performance that was observed (atypical performance, hence potentially valid scores). Being able to examine performance at the broad ability level is more consistent with the way that practitioners typically interpret data and with the principles of XBA. Another benefit is that it also provides a direct way of identifying areas that may require subsequent follow-up evaluation in the heritage language. By knowing which areas are those that likely indicate possible deficits in ability, and for which the primary influence of acculturative and linguistic factors has been excluded, practitioners have a much clearer path for follow-up evaluation in the heritage language (Ortiz, 2019, 2023).

Before the development of this graph, guidance in using X-BASS recommended that users return to the test protocol to find the indexes/composites/clusters that were normatively low and consider follow-up in the heritage language in those domains. This recommendation could be, at times, admittedly ambiguous and is no longer necessary as guidance now basically dictates that if the actual and expected bands do not overlap (or the actual band is above the expected band), then there is likely to be no statistically significant difference between the scores and performance can be interpreted as being typical, normal, or even "average" in the colloquial sense such that follow-up in the heritage language is unnecessary and would be uninformative (Ortiz, 2023). This approach enhances the efficiency by which evaluations on multilinguals can be conducted while aligning well with the manner in which evaluations are typically carried out by practitioners working with diverse populations.

Another notable enhancement to the C-LIM is the Test Composite graph based on principles first developed as part of the Diverse Student Normal Ability Profile (D-SNAP; Ortiz & Pristo, 2023; Pristo (in press); Pristo & Ortiz, 2022; Pristo & Ortiz, 2023). The Test Composite graph displays the scores from test composites contained in the data that have been entered on the Data Entry tab and which are not mixed regarding the domains being measured. These actual values are also graphed alongside what the expected values are as determined by X-BASS using D-SNAP principles. Calculation of the expected value for the Test Composite graph, however, is not based on average or mean performance but rather determination of a composite value. This is a more appropriate method as the number of subtests within the composite is a fixed or known value, the names of the subtests and their classifications are also known values, and the actual score was originally calculated as a composite by the test publisher, not as a mean. Therefore, X-BASS replicates this process with the expected values using median reliabilities and intercorrelations for each subtest and based on its classification within the C-LIM in terms of impact due to acculturative and linguistic influences as well as selected degree of difference. As with the CHC Domain graph, the Test Composite graph displays the actual value for a composite, as entered by the user, next to the expected value for the composite as calculated by X-BASS for visual comparison. The same interpretive rules apply here as well in that when the 1SEM error bands/confidence intervals overlap it likely means that the scores are not statistically significantly different and therefore actual performance is typical or what would be expected for that composite and whatever domain it may measure. If the error bands do not overlap and the actual score is lower than the designated expected value, then performance is atypical and below what would ordinarily be expected if it were affected primarily by acculturative and linguistic factors. In this way, it is possible to evaluate performance of the examinee at the composite or index/cluster level within the structure and organization provided by the test's publisher in cases where this may be preferred in lieu of examination according to CHC Theory, while still addressing the issue of test score validity. And as with the CHC Domain graph, examining test score validity at this level assists in directing follow-up evaluation in the heritage language for providing cross-linguistic confirmation of the validity of the results obtained originally in English and without the need to re-evaluate areas that have already been determined to be intact or within the expected range when compared to other multilinguals with similar levels of acculturative and linguistic development.

## Rapid Reference 8.2

### Using the C-LIM Graphs to Evaluate Examinee Performance

The C-LIM includes two new graphs, the CHC Domain graph and the Test Composite graph. Both are used to evaluate the impact of acculturative knowledge and language differences on test performance at the broad ability level in the same way that practitioners typically evaluate test results.

Other notable features of the new version of X-BASS includes the addition of the Culture-Language Interpretive Matrix plus Achievement Test Extensions (C-LIM+ATE). The C-LIM+ATE was developed recently as a way of trying to account for the impact of differences in acculturative knowledge and language acquisition on achievement test performance. The C-LIM cannot evaluate academic skills tasks as performance on tests that measure reading, writing, or arithmetic is not based simply on age, development, or normal maturational processes. Rather, performance is heavily influenced by the grade the individual is currently in, how long and consistently they have been attending school, and for multilinguals, the type of educational program they have been receiving. The C-LIM+ATE is based on large-scale studies examining the academic achievement and benchmark performance of multilinguals from kindergarten through 12th grade (e.g., Thomas and Collier, 1997, 2002). For this reason, the C-LIM+ATE requires specific information including: (1) current grade; (2) the primary type of educational program that a student is in or was given previously; and (3) the degree of difference which can be determined via the TPE.

The C-LIM+ATE will then generate on demand a graph for reading, writing, or math that permits evaluation as to whether current levels of performance might be explainable primarily by acculturative and linguistic differences. Like the C-LIM, the C-LIM+ATE is not intended to be a diagnostic tool in any way. Rather, the C-LIM+ATE is simply indicating whether or not the scores might or might not be subject to the influence of acculturative knowledge and language acquisition factors. It does not mean, however, that even if the scores are within the expected range, that the child does not have a problem or a deficit of some kind. Questions regarding whether a child has a disability cannot be answered using the C-LIM+ATE by itself as it cannot establish the presence of intrinsic deficits merely because performance is low. Nevertheless, when used in conjunction with information derived from cognitive evaluation, use of the C-LIM, and follow-up evaluation in the heritage language, it can provide valuable information for establishing test score validity and supporting diagnostic conclusions.

### DON'T FORGET

The impact of acculturative knowledge and language differences on cognitive tests is handled by the C-LIM just as before. The new C-LIM+ATE is used for the same purpose but is specifically developed for academic skills tests (whether or not the test appears on an academic or cognitive battery).

It was noted previously that X-BASS handles evaluation of children who are acculturatively and linguistically diverse in a more integrated manner. Apart from the new additions and features described in this section, this integration may not be apparent on the surface. The level of support provided by X-BASS in support of multilingual evaluations will, however, become evident throughout the program in the form of popup messages with specific guidance and recommendations regarding how scores and results should be handled in terms of fairness. For example, if a user is interested in PSW analysis, it is now permissible to mark any score on the PSW Data tab as "EXPECTED" rather than having to choose between "STRENGTH" or "WEAKNESS" only. Previously, users may have been unsure or hesitant to mark a score with low magnitude, for example a *Gc* score of 76, as a strength even when so indicated by C-LIM analysis. Using it in this manner, although entirely appropriate and recommended (but only when indicated), in a PSW process meant having to convince others that the magnitude was not indicative of deficient performance. This may have been exacerbated via use of the label "strength" and the change "expected" helps to alleviate this possible conflict by allowing a better explanation regarding the reason why the score is being treated as an intact ability, not one that is problematic. Users may now state that any score marked as "expected" means that the performance is considered typical for the examinee, that is, it is within the range of the degree of difference that was selected and thus reflects the average performance when compared to other multilinguals with similar levels of acculturative and linguistic development. Therefore, measured performance is likely due primarily to acculturative and linguistic factors and does not provide evidence that it is an area of deficit.

Previously, the only ability in X-BASS that was handled in this fashion, although with less sophistication, was *Gc*. The new version of X-BASS now conducts automatic analyses in the background for multilingual cases and permits as well as provides guidance in marking any score as expected so that it too is handled in an appropriate, nondiscriminatory manner when conducting PSW analysis or interpreting meaning. When a score is below the expected range for a multilingual case, X-BASS does not alter the indication of "weakness" so that again, the score is used and characterized properly and fairly in subsequent PSW analysis. Likewise, for any score that is 90 or above, X-BASS will use the "strength" designation just as it would for a monolingual case as the magnitude is now consistent with the meaning of the label. These procedures provide both protection and fairness regarding efforts to identify SLD in a nondiscriminatory fashion as well as consistency with the manner in which the process is carried out with monolinguals.

New users are advised to keep "NOTIFICATIONS ON" as a way of ensuring that they receive full guidance regarding management of scores in multilingual cases. Experienced users can toggle notifications off after becoming confident in the handling and use of scores within X-BASS. An attempt has been made to balance messaging in X-BASS so that even when notifications are not toggled on, users may still see some pop-ups with directions and recommendations for various actions that are critical. Again, for new users, it is highly recommended that any such pop-ups be read carefully and that the guidance provided be followed. X-BASS will permit users to over-ride any recommendation and work with the data as they see fit, however, unless the user is very experienced in the process, ignoring the recommendations is likely to lead to discriminatory results.

**CAUTION**

When X-BASS determines that a score from a case involving a multilingual should be indicated as "EXPECTED," it will either indicate it as such automatically or provide a pop-up message indicating that it should be manually marked as such. Unless there is strong rationale for not doing so, following X-BASS guidance is recommend to prevent discriminatory interpretation and analyses.

Another new tab in X-BASS devoted to SLD identification is referred to as the SLD Evidence tab. This tab serves as both a summary of PSW results as well as a collection point for all data and evidence that may be generated in support of efforts regarding SLD identification. Not only are scores from PSW analysis carried over automatically, but additional score evidence, validity evidence, qualitative information, and more can be documented and used to support of SLD identification. One component of that evidence is evaluation of exclusionary factors for which the SLD Evidence tab provides radio buttons corresponding to nine exclusionary variables that must be considered in all cases where SLD is suspected. Users can directly indicate to what extent any one or more particular exclusionary factor is or is not primary. By making such indications, the information is then included and integrated into a final overall summary report for SLD identification that is created in Microsoft Word and which can be either printed out, sent electronically via email, or used to copy and paste information into a practitioner's own report. How any particular variable is indicated may well depend on the analyses conducted via the C-LIM and C-LIM+ATE as assisted by the TPE and based on results from PSW analysis where scores have been treated properly to prevent discriminatory outcomes. X-BASS can now document this process when working with multilinguals.

## A Guided Case Study Evaluation of a Multilingual: Maria

Perhaps the best way to understand how to evaluate multilinguals via the use of X-BASS and its attendant modules for working with acculturatively and linguistically diverse populations is to provide a sample case study. This section will permit the reader to follow along as a complete case is conducted for the purpose of illustrating how the various features and modules within X-BASS operate in an integrated manner and can be used throughout the process of SLD identification performing the functions required for engaging in nondiscriminatory assessment and interpretation of test score results. This section is not intended, however, to serve as a comprehensive framework for evaluation of individuals from diverse backgrounds. The procedures to be used for the purpose of illustrating the case study are aligned with the recommendations for testing as outlined in Best Practice in Nondiscriminatory Assessment (Ortiz, 2024). This framework offers a systematic method for evaluation and establishing test score validity that is accessible by all practitioners, not merely those who are bilingual. Of particular interest are the processes described by Ortiz (2024) that pertain to "Step 3. Evaluate Impact of Differences" as this represents the most important and difficult hurdle to overcome in evaluation of multilinguals and where testing runs directly up against the issue of score validity.

The previous section described the manner in which X-BASS has been expressly designed to wrestle specifically with the issue of test score validity as well as other issues encountered when conducting evaluations on multilinguals. Accordingly, the following case study example will describe the process for evaluation, how X-BASS assists in the process, and will provide illustrations along the way that may assist practitioners in learning and understanding the overall methodology and process.

## Evaluation of Multilinguals with X-BASS: Maria Case Study

According to Ortiz (2024), the initial phase of testing and true peer assessment involves evaluation in English first as this represents the only avenue for examining test score validity from an evidence-based perspective via the C-LIM while also providing accessibility for non-bilingual practitioners. Apart from the noted exceptions (e.g., BESA), tests in the heritage language cannot yield valid scores for multilinguals as none of them contain norm samples that control for differences in development in the heritage language. Mere inclusion of multilinguals in any norm sample does not constitute adequate representation any more than would including "children" in a norm sample without regard to their age. In addition, testing in English first provides a way of ensuring that it is conducted without any violation or variation to a test's standardized protocol, including all aspects of administration and scoring. Alterations to a publisher's standardization procedures effectively undermines the psychometric properties of the test and render scores invalid which precludes interpretation. Once the initial phase of testing is complete, the results can be entered into X-BASS for further analyses regarding establishing test score validity and guiding subsequent interpretation and follow up evaluation in the heritage language when or as necessary.

Figure 8.1 provides an illustration of the Dashboard tab within X-BASS which is where the program opens upon first use. The initial step is to create a new case by entering the required information denoted by an asterisk next to the descriptions for each box (i.e., examinee's name, grade, and age). Other information such as the evaluator's name can also be entered, however, it is optional. Because this is a multilingual case,

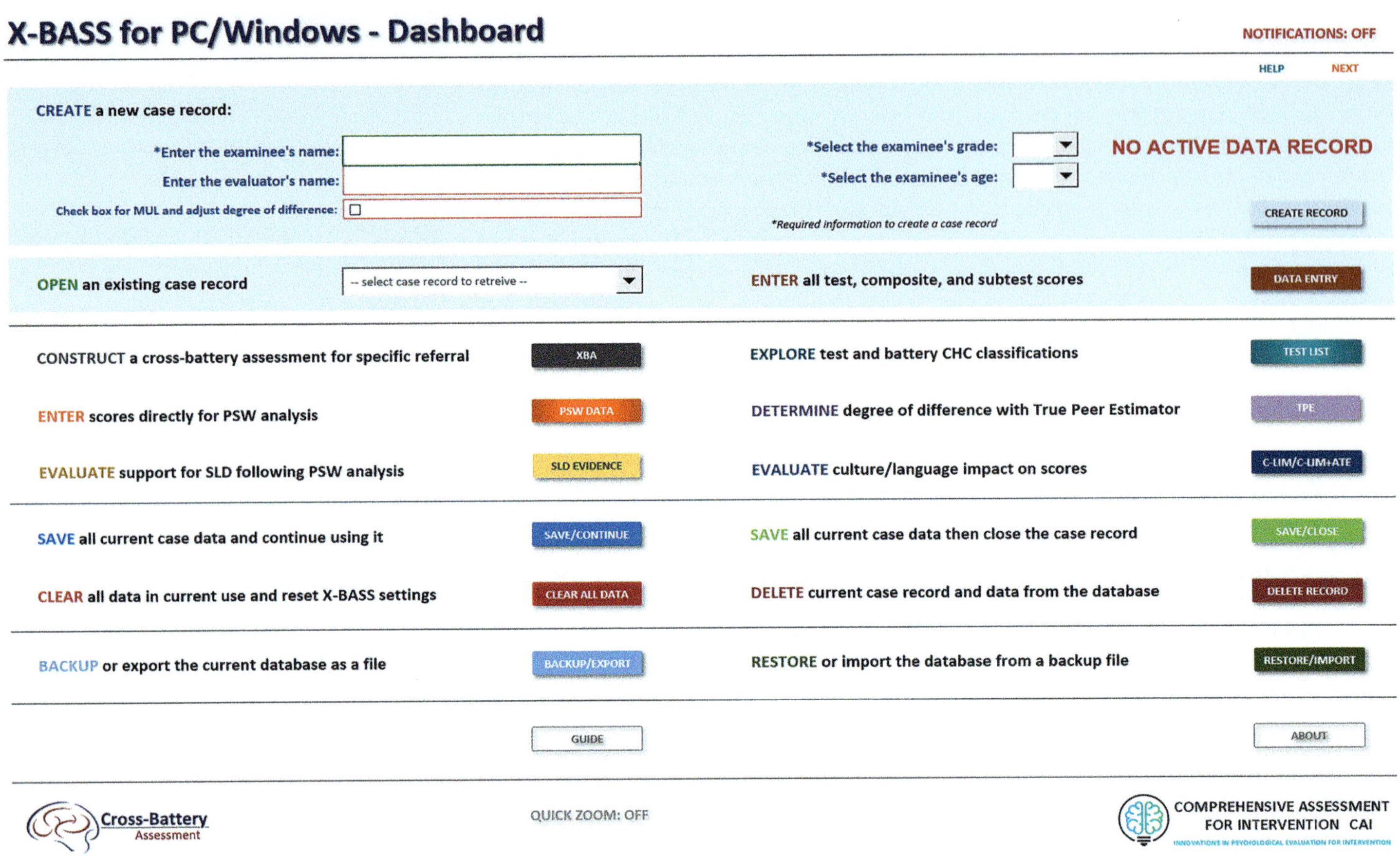


**FIGURE 8.1 X-BASS 3.0 Dashboard**

> **DON'T FORGET**
>
> It is highly recommended that a new Case Record be created for any case data that are to be entered into X-BASS. Doing so permits saving all information, scores, and settings, and later retrieval on demand.

the box indicating so (below the space for the evaluator's name) should be checked and which will automatically set the "degree of difference" to the default "MODERATELY DIFFERENT" which will be adjusted later, if necessary. The importance of this setting is summarized in Rapid Reference 8.3.

Figure 8.2 shows the required information that has been entered for Maria's case as well as the checked box to inform X-BASS that this is a multilingual, not monolingual, case. Checking this box is extremely important because it automatically sets X-BASS up to handle data and scores in a manner that is nondiscriminatory throughout the process of evaluation, interpretation, and use of other modules. The box can be checked at any time to indicate a multilingual case even if not so indicated here on the Dashboard. It is best, however, to do so now to ensure that the entire process from beginning to end is handled in this manner. In addition, whenever the box is checked, or when the degree of difference is indicated on the Dashboard during creation of a new case record, X-BASS will automatically assign a degree of difference corresponding to "MODERATELY DIFFERENT." This is necessary to ensure that results are being evaluated under the assumption that the examinee is multilingual where some designation of degree of difference is required. The degree of difference, however, can be easily changed at any time including via the TPE, C-LIM, C-LIM+ATE or

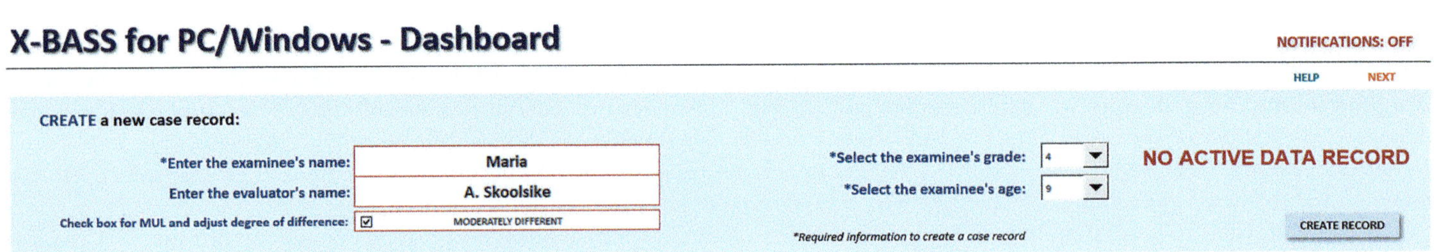


**FIGURE 8.2 Creating a Case Record**

## Rapid Reference 8.3

### Indicating Cases as Multilingual in X-BASS

Checking the box to indicate that a case involves a multilingual is critical to ensuring that X-BASS handles scores in a nondiscriminatory manner and provides guidance on how scores are to be interpreted, particularly for PSW analysis. Indicating a case as multilingual can be done at any time on the Dashboard, PSW Data tab, C-LIM, and C-LIM+ATE.

PSW Data tabs to set the level of expected performance in accordance with what is actually known about the examinee's accculturative and linguistic development and experiences.

After entering the required information and indicating that the case involves a multilingual, the next step is to actually create the case record by using the blue button labelled "CREATE RECORD" located on the far right-hand side, as shown in Figure 8.2. Doing this creates the new case record for Maria and changes the look of X-BASS slightly by removing the blue shading. In addition, the words "NO ACTIVE DATA RECORD" in red color font will disappear and become "DATA RECORD IS ACTIVE" in green color font. This is done so that the user will know that an active case record has been created for which data can now be entered into X-BASS and later saved/archived for retrieval in the future. For each case record, the name should be unique and identify a single person, thus, "Maria" may not be unique enough and use of the surname or some other code would be helpful to ensure that if there are multiple case records with the same name, or for the same individual, that they can still be distinguished. In Maria's case, Figure 8.3 illustrates how the Dashboard tab looks after all information has been entered and a new case record using her name has been created.

Users of the older version of X-BASS may recall that recommendations for the next step involved going directly to the C-LIM or C-LIM Index tab to begin entering data there for evaluation of the impact of acculturative and linguistic factors. While it remains important that evaluation with the C-LIM continues to be the first step, it is no longer necessary to go there directly to enter data. The new version of X-BASS provides a Data Entry tab where scores may be entered only once and then transferred as needed to any other module. X-BASS no longer has any core test tabs and instead uses the Data Entry tab to provide the structure, composite names, and subtest names for all 124 batteries currently classified within it (refer to Rapid Reference 8.4 for additional guidance in test selection). The Data Entry tab can hold up to 40 different composites, indexes, or clusters, and up to 240 different subtests and serves as the repository and central location for all data, which can then be transferred automatically to and from any other modules within X-BASS for further analysis. Thus, after a case record has been created, the current recommendation is to use the brown Data Entry button to navigate there for the purposes of data entry. Figure 8.4 provides an illustration of the Data Entry tab.

One of the goals of the current version of X-BASS was to reduce the amount of visual load that users would see when coming to a particular tab and this is the reason why there may seem to be a lot of white space to the right of where scores are entered. On the more

**CAUTION**

Unlike with the older version of X-BASS, scores for multilingual cases should not be entered directly into the C-LIM or C-LIM+ATE. Instead, scores should be entered into the Data Entry tab and then transferred to the C-LIM and C-LIM+ATE for analysis. Entering data directly in the modules will require re-entry of the same data into the Data Entry tab.

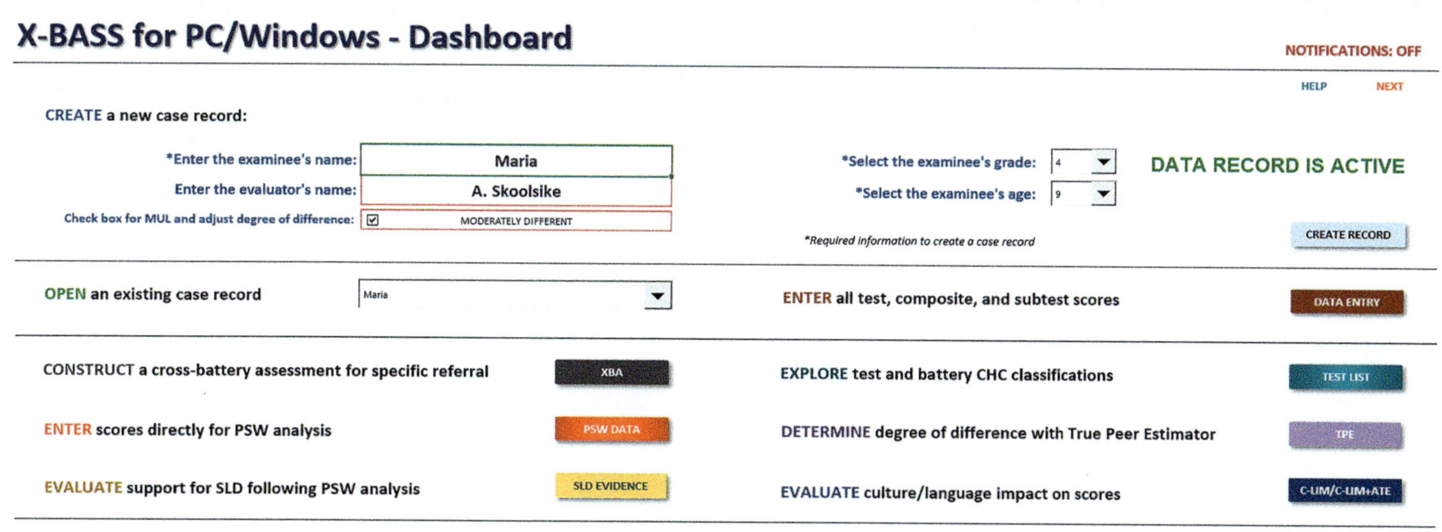


**FIGURE 8.3 Completed Case Record**

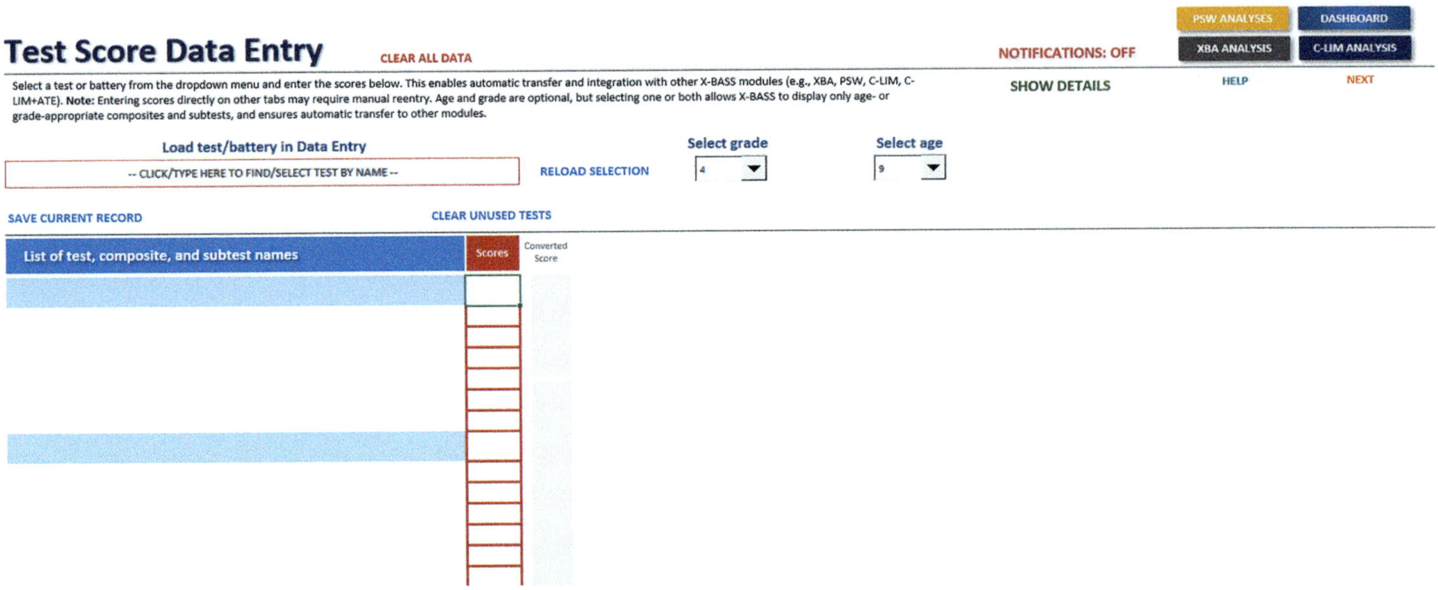


**FIGURE 8.4 Data Entry Tab**

extensive ones, there is now a feature that allows the toggling of details to be either hidden or unhidden on demand and as desired. The default is for details to be hidden and is likely the best setting for new users. More advanced users can reveal the details by using the button labeled "SHOW DETAILS" that appears underneath the "SHOW/HIDE NOTIFICATIONS" button. This action toggles the details on and off at will. On the Data Entry tab, the details are primarily related to the automatic graphs of the scores entered. At this point, no data have been entered for Maria, so there is no reason to show any details. In addition, unlike the previous versions of X-BASS where scores were entered on dedicated "core" test tabs, the new version allows users to enter scores for any test by selecting it from the drop-down menu at the top left. When a test is selected, X-BASS will automatically populate the spaces with the composite names and subtest names that comprise them and which are appropriate to the age or grade for the case record, along with any supplemental tests that may appear on the battery. In cases where an age or grade is missing, X-BASS will ask the user if they want to have all age-level composites, and if not, to then select the age or grade for which to enter the appropriate composite names and subtests. In this manner, data entry is faster, more efficient, and follows the test publisher's protocol to facilitate the process.

Table 8.1 provides a list of the tests administered to Maria for the purposes of conducting her evaluation. These include the Wechsler Intelligence Scale for Children-V (WISC-V), the Wechsler Individual Achievement Test-IV (WIAT-IV), and the Test of Dyslexia-Comprehensive (TOD-C), all of which were administered in English, although only selected subtests and composites from the TOD-C were used to supplement areas of ability not measured easily or at all by the WISC-V. The Ortiz Picture Vocabulary Test (Ortiz PVAT) was also administered and its inclusion and utility in evaluation of monolinguals will be discussed later in this section.

Having arrived at the Data Entry tab, and in possession of the scores generated from testing of Maria, the data entry process begins by selecting the main battery that was used, which in this case, was the WISC-V. By clicking on the space designated for selecting a test or battery in X-BASS, a drop-down menu will appear. However, to reduce the need for scrolling, users can type in the first letter or combination of letters of the name of the test as shown in Figure 8.5. The letter "W" was entered and X-BASS filtered the results automatically making it quick and easy to find and select the WISC-V from the list as show in Figure 8.5.

## Rapid Reference 8.4

### Using the Dropdown Menu to Quickly Find Tests in X-BASS

There are 124 batteries currently classified within X-BASS. Selecting one from any drop down menu can be expedited by simply typing in the first letter of the test, its abbreviation, or some word contained in the title. This helps eliminate having to scroll the entire list.

With the WISC-V selected (or any other test), X-BASS automatically lists the composites, indexes, clusters and their constituent subtests in the spaces on the right side of the Data Entry tab, including providing shading for the subtests that contribute to the index. For the most part, the indexes are listed in the same order as they appear on the protocols to enhance the speed of score entry. Moreover, X-BASS will know

**Table 8.1 Test Scores from Cognitive and Academic Evaluation of Maria**

| WECHSLER INTELLIEGENCE SCALE FOR CHILDREN-V (WISC-V) | | | | | |
|---|---|---|---|---|---|
| **Verbal Comprehension Index** | **76** | **Fluid Reasoning Index** | **82** | **Visual-Spatial Index** | **92** |
| Similarities | 5 | Matrix Reasoning | 7 | Block Design | 9 |
| Vocabulary | 4 | Figure Weights | 7 | Visual Puzzles | 8 |
| **Working Memory Index** | **71** | **Processing Speed Index** | **94** | **Ortiz PVAT (EL Norms)** | **93** |
| Digit Span | 5 | Coding | 9 | | |
| Picture Span | 4 | Symbol Search | 8 | | |

| WECHSLER INDIVIDUAL ACHIEVEMENT TEST-IV (WIAT-IV) | | | | | | | |
|---|---|---|---|---|---|---|---|
| **Basic Reading** | **89** | **Reading** | **72** | **Written Expression** | **83** | **Reading Fluency** | **75** |
| Pseudoword Decoding | 91 | Reading Comprehension | 67 | Spelling | 83 | Oral Reading Fluency | 72 |
| Phonemic Proficiency | 87 | Word Reading | 89 | Sentence Composition | 81 | Orthographic Fluency | 79 |
| Word Reading | 89 | Essay Composition | 89 | Alphabet Writing Fluency | 83 | | |

| TEST OF DYSLEXIA—COMPREHENSIVE (TOD-C) | | | |
|---|---|---|---|
| **Phonological Awareness** | **91** | **Rapid Automatized Naming** | 66 |
| Phonological Manipulation | 99 | Rapid Letter Naming | 69 |
| Blending | 84 | Rapid Number and Letter Naming | 67 |
| Segmenting | 89 | | |

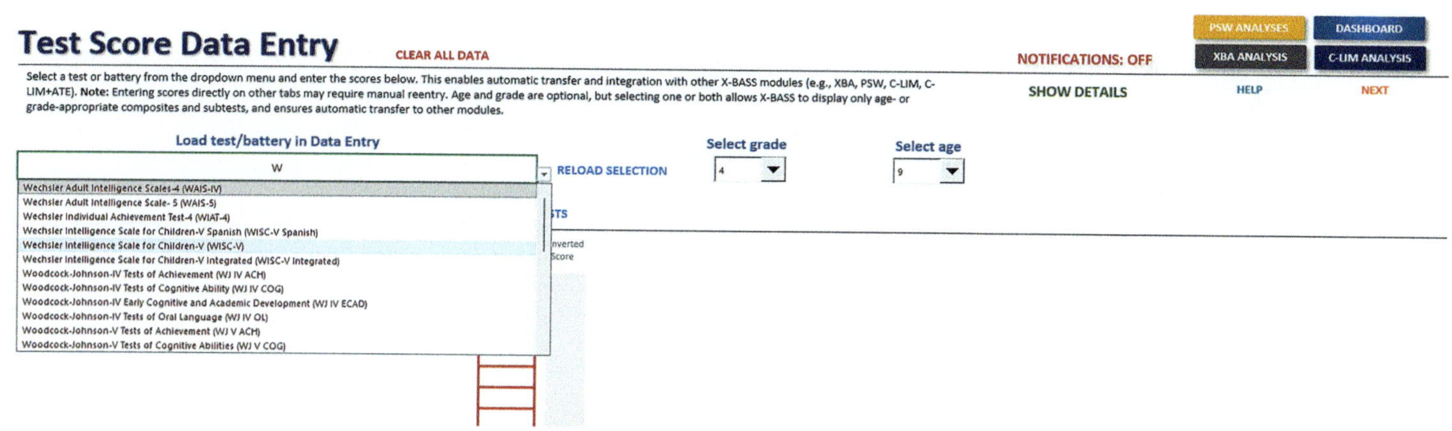


**FIGURE 8.5 Data Entry Dropdown List**

what type of score (e.g., Scaled Score, Standard Score, T-Score) is to be entered and notify the user if a different type of score is used. Note also that some tests provide a single score (e.g., Ortiz PVAT) rather than composites and subtests. Such scores typically have established validity and should not be thought of as being similar to subtests. Their reliability is generally as good, sometimes better, than the reliability of most composites/indexes/clusters and may be interpreted as reliable measures of the domain they are intended to represent. An example of some of the data for Maria entered into the Data Entry tab is shown in Figure 8.6.

Because Maria was evaluated with more than one test/battery, all of the scores from each of them should be entered. For example, once the scores for the WISC-V have been entered, the next step is to select the name of the next test, say the WIAT-IV, from the same drop-down menu as before. X-BASS will now clear out any unused subtests and composites (those for which a score was not entered) and repopulate

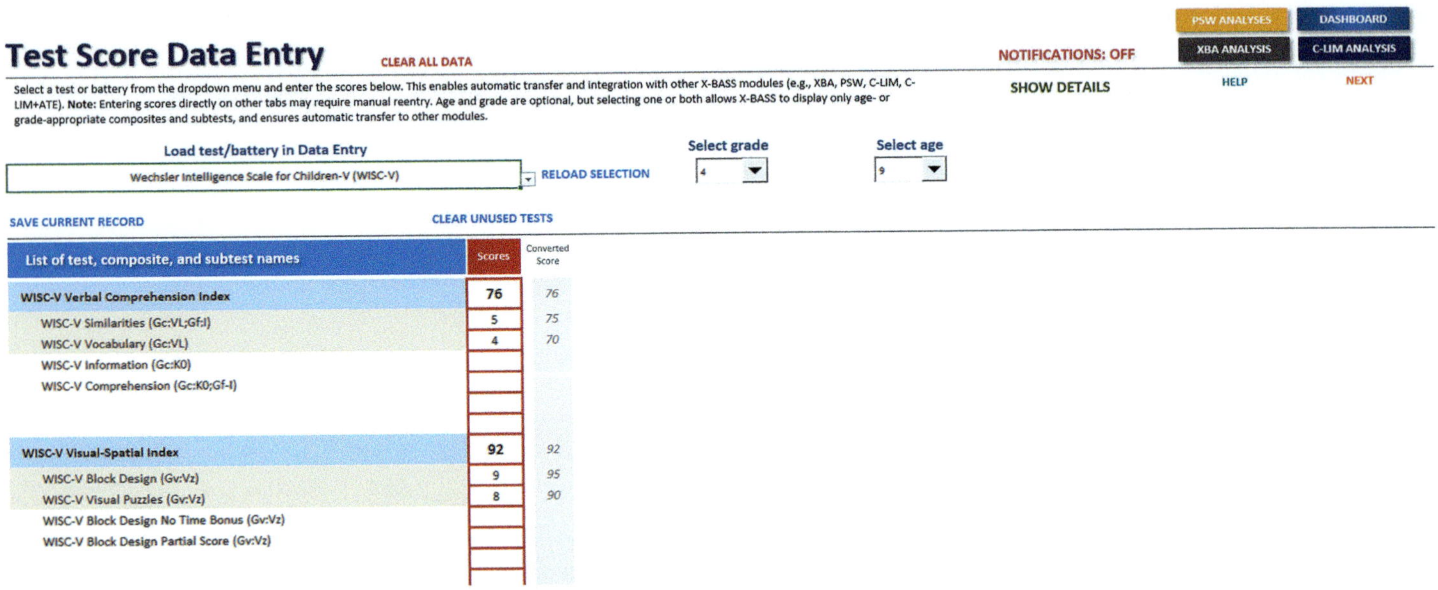


**FIGURE 8.6 Example Complete Data Entry Tab**

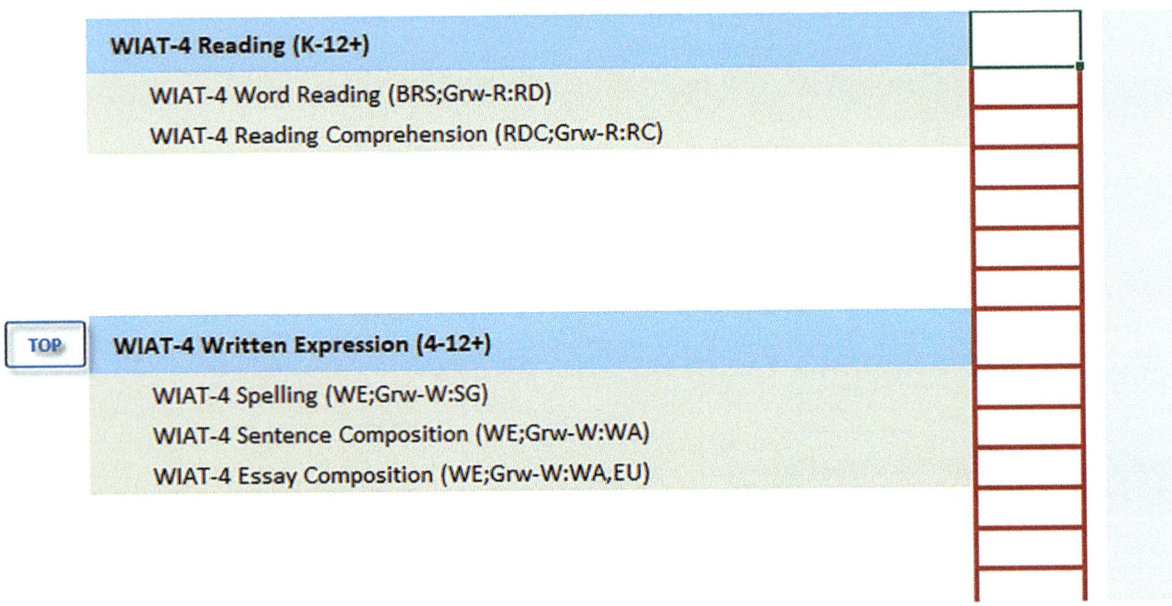


**FIGURE 8.7 WIAT-4 Composites**

the available spaces with the new subtests and composites (or single scores) from the new test/battery. In Maria's case, the WIAT-IV was selected as the next test for data entry and the initial list of composites and subtests are shown in Figure 8.7 prior to scores being entered.

> **DON'T FORGET**
>
> Make sure to enter all scores from all tests administered into the Data Entry tab. Having all scores there can facilitate later follow-up and analyses so it's best to ensure that all data from testing have been included.

Another helpful feature in X-BASS related to entering scores on the Data Entry tab is the automatic scrolling of the tab to the first listed composite of any new test selected via the drop-down menu. As with the WISC-V, the composite and subtest names are listed and arranged in the manner in which they correspond to the scoring protocol to further streamline data entry. Figure 8.8 shows an example of the first two composite and subtest scores entered for the WIAT-4.

After all scores for the WIAT-4 have been entered, the process is repeated by selecting the Test of Dyslexia (TOD-C) from the drop-down menu and entering the scores for the corresponding subtests and composites as well, followed by selection of the Ortiz

| | | |
|---|---|---|
| **WIAT-4 Reading (K-12+)** | **72** | 72 |
| WIAT-4 Word Reading (BRS;Grw-R:RD) | 89 | 89 |
| WIAT-4 Reading Comprehension (RDC;Grw-R:RC) | 67 | 67 |
| TOP **WIAT-4 Written Expression (4-12+)** | **83** | 83 |
| WIAT-4 Spelling (WE;Grw-W:SG) | 83 | 83 |
| WIAT-4 Sentence Composition (WE;Grw-W:WA) | 81 | 81 |
| WIAT-4 Essay Composition (WE;Grw-W:WA,EU) | 89 | 89 |

**FIGURE 8.8 WIAT-4 with Scores Entered**

PVAT and entering its single score. The resulting tab now contains a complete set of scores representing the full data drawn from evaluation of Maria.

Before moving on, users may want to review some of the graphs that have already been generated by X-BASS. Clicking the "SHOW DETAILS" link at the top of the tab will toggle details from being hidden to being revealed, including two additional links labeled "SHOW SCORE GRAPH" and "SHOW DOMAIN SUMMARY." Clicking on each of these links also toggles the display of the graphs (controllable individually) and reveals a visual display corresponding to different aspects of the data that have been entered in Maria's case and as depicted in Figure 8.9.

Together, the score graphs on the right side and in the middle of the tab provide a complete summary of the entire data set and scores entered on the left side of X-BASS to this point. On the far right-hand side, the graphs provide a summary of CHC broad ability domains as measured in the current data in columnar format. At the top of the column, a graph of Overall General Ability scores (e.g., FSIQ, GIA, FCI, GCA, etc.) is displayed first and provides a representation of scores measuring general ability and which may be selected later in lieu of the Facilitating Cognitive Composite (FCC) calculated by X-BASS and used for PSW analysis and SLD identification. The general ability graph is followed downward in the column by the various CHC broad ability domains beginning with *Gc*, then *Gf*, and so forth. Last, any composites or indexes that are "mixed" due to being comprised of two different broad abilities, are also graphed in the domain summary and listed at the bottom of the column, although it is easily accessed via the "MIXED DOMAINS" link provided at the top. Mixed domains are those in which the composite or index measures two different broad abilities and therefore may not represent a single domain well by itself. Not only can this make interpretation ambiguous, but it also makes it difficult to classify where that test should go in relation to other tests since there is no way of knowing which ability may have influenced performance more or less than the other.

**CAUTION**

If you think that some composite scores are not being graphed, scroll to the bottom of the Data Entry tab and look at the graph for "Mixed Domains." There are still many mixed composites on numerous batteries which represent measures of two or more broad abilities. Such composites have limited utility in XBA and X-BASS will identify and manage them accordingly.

Review of the graphs on the Data Entry tab is optional and after all scores from testing conducted on Maria have been entered into X-BASS, and because she is multilingual, the next step is to evaluate the impact of acculturative and linguistic factors on her performance. This is accomplished by transferring the scores automatically to the C-LIM and the C-LIM+ATE via the dark blue button labeled "C-LIM ANALYSIS" at the top right corner of the tab. Scores that are classified as measuring cognitive, linguistic, and neuropsychological abilities will be sent directly to the C-LIM for further analysis according to their respective Culture-Language Test Classifications (C-LTC). Tests that measure academic skills or knowledge will instead be sent to the C-LIM+ATE for analysis there as they cannot be evaluated in the same way or with the same research as with the cognitive tests. In this way, X-BASS automatically distributes scores to the module that is most appropriate for evaluating the impact of linguistic and acculturative factors on test performance whether the scores come from cognitive or academic testing.

Some batteries and scales have a mixture of both cognitive and academic skills tasks. If this is the case, X-BASS will send each individual test or subtest to their respective tabs so that the classifications are correct and interpretation can proceed normally. X-BASS will then take you

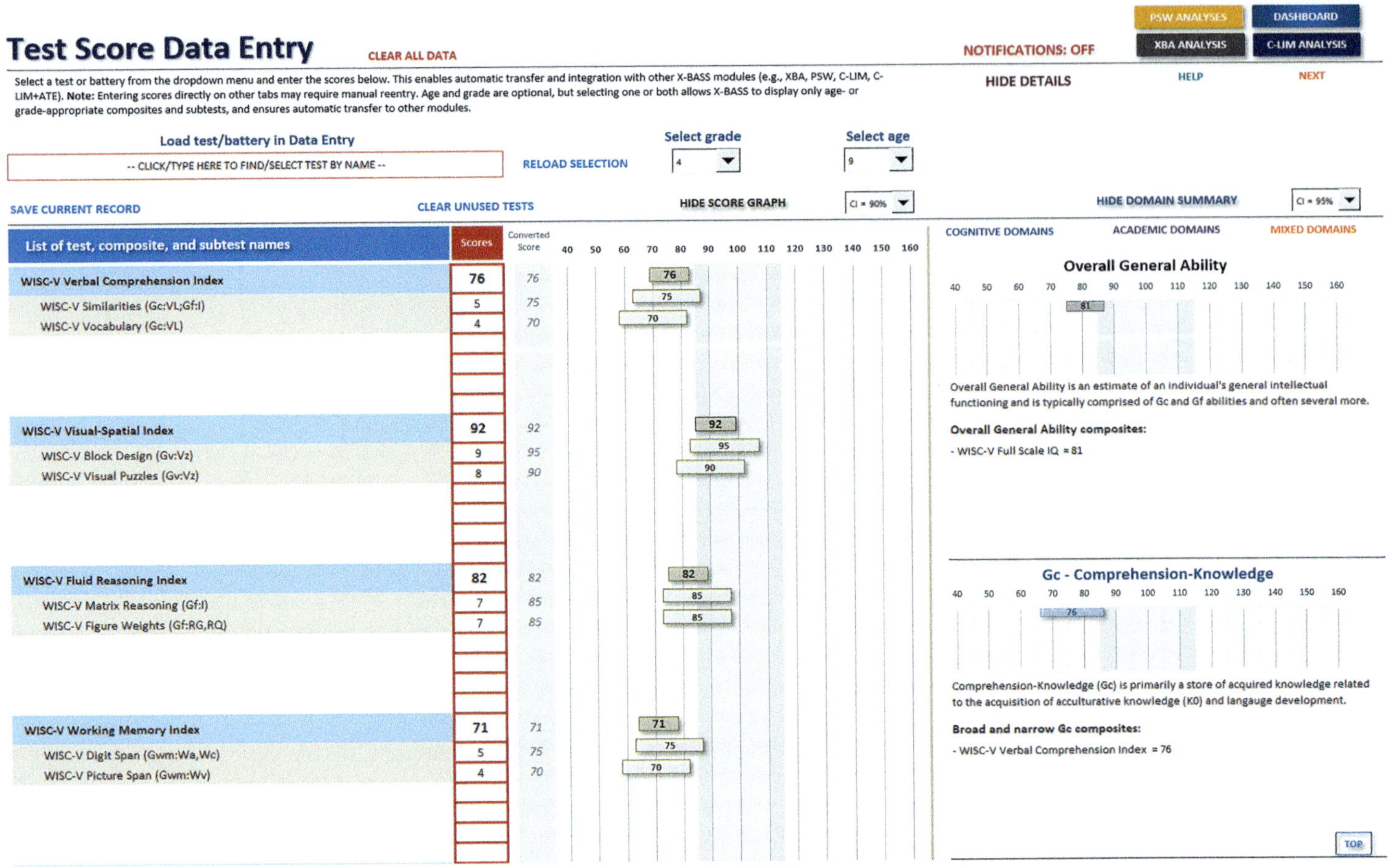


**FIGURE 8.9 Visual Displays of Data**

to the C-LIM when the selected test is primarily a cognitive battery or to the C-LIM+ATE when the selected test is primarily an academic battery. Note that if X-BASS takes you to the C-LIM tab, it does not mean that there are no tests that might have ended up in the C-LIM+ATE and vice versa. For this reason, when notifications are on, X-BASS will provide a pop-up message informing the user that this has occurred, reminding them not to forget to check the other module. Likewise, some achievement tests and batteries may have one or more subtests that are classified primarily as cognitive measures. If so, X-BASS may take you first to the C-LIM+ATE tab and once again provide a notice that some tests may have been entered into the C-LIM as well.

## Establishing Degree of Difference

Norm-referenced testing is predicated on comparison of individual performance to a normative standard. If the examinee's performance is consistent with others who have been given the same tests in the same way and who represent a level of average ability, then it stands to reason that the examinee is likewise of average ability. The C-LIM operates in the same manner except that the "average" range must be based on what research indicates is typical performance for multilinguals of varying levels of development in language, not merely age (Cormier et al., 2022; Ortiz & Cehelyk, 2024; Ortiz & Wong, 2022a; Ortiz & Wong, 2022b; Wong, 2023). Within a monolingual sample, age is a very good proxy for language development, assuming normal developmental experiences. This is not the case with multilinguals, however, given that their experiences in two or more languages are not only different in comparison to monolinguals but also in comparison to each other (Ortiz, 2019). For this reason, nondiscriminatory evaluation of multilinguals must engage in true peer comparison by ensuring that individuals are only evaluated against the performance of others with the same level of development and acquisition experiences in language, not merely because they are of the same age or grade (see Rapid Reference 8.5). Therefore, prior to attempting any interpretation of the results within the C-LIM or the C-LIM+ATE, it is necessary to determine whether the degree of difference, which was automatically set to "MODERATELY DIFFERENT" by default when the case was created, is appropriate or not. This is done by using the True Peer Estimator (TPE) which can be accessed via the Dashboard, C-LIM, or C-LIM+ATE using the lavender button labelled "TPE." The full TPE is shown in Figure 8.10.

## Rapid Reference 8.5

### The Need for the True Peer Estimator (TPE) When Assessing Diverse Individuals

Nondiscriminatory evaluation of individuals from diverse backgrounds is not based on race or ethnicity. It is based on the extent to which the individual's acculturative and linguistic development differs from those who comprise the norm sample of a test. Thus, establishing the degree of difference with the TPE is crucial to ensuring fairness in evaluation and interpretation of test scores.

**True Peer Estimator (TPE)** CLEAR RATINGS NOTIFICATIONS: OFF C-LIM DASHBOARD C-LIM+ATE DATA ENTRY

**Currently Selected Degree of Difference:** [ ▾ ]

This worksheet helps practitioners systematically collect data about examinees to identify developmental differences in experiences relative to typical age or grade expectations. Considering these differences is essential for fair, nondiscriminatory test score interpretation. While a student's degree of cultural or linguistic difference can change over time, documenting them helps estimate their impact on academic, cognitive, and linguistic test scores. The degree of difference categories are:

A) **Slightly Different.** This category is characterized by minor differences in culture, language, and experiences that although not fully representative of the U.S. mainstream, have still been supported by high family SES, well-educated parents, formal elementary education in the heritage language, bilingual parents, etc.) and where opportunity for developing English language proficiency constitutes at least ½ or more of a student's life.

B) **Moderately Different.** This category is characterized by moderate to large differences in culture, language, and experiences that are not representative of the U.S. mainstream and where few supporting factors are present (e.g., low family SES, parental lack of education, no formal education in the heritage language, parents with limited English proficiency, etc.) or where opportunity for developing English proficiency constitutes less than ½ of a student's life.

C) **Markedly Different.** This category is characterized by major differences in culture, language, and experiences where the opportunity for developing English proficiency constitutes a small percentage of a student's life, for example being a newcomer and having extremely limited English language development. It may also include other atypical factors that adversely influence development (e.g., exposure to war, trauma, violence, abuse, neglect, immigrant or migrant worker experience, refugee status, etc.).

| *To what extent does the examinee's or the examinee's family...?* (1 Very Much — 2 — 3 Some — 4 — 5 Very Little) | ENTER RATING HERE |
|---|---|
| 1. ... ***heritage or home culture match*** *middle-class, mainstream U.S. values, traditions, and beliefs in supporting acquisition of school-based acculturative knowledge?* | |
| 2. ... ***socio-economic status match*** *middle-class, mainstream families in the U.S. in supporting development of school-based learning and academic skills?* | |
| 3. ... ***heritage or home language match*** *middle-class, mainstream, monolingual English-speakers in supporting the acquisition of school-based English?* | |
| 4. ... ***school attendance*** *indicate consistent and sufficient engagement for age- or grade-expected academic instruction and opportunity for learning?* | |
| 5. ... ***formal schooling include heritage language instruction*** *either while attending school in the U.S. or prior to coming to the U.S.?* | |
| 6. ... ***experiences include exposure to high level language models in English*** *over their lifetime as compared to middle-class, monolingual English-speakers of the same age?* | |
| 7. ... ***English language development match*** *same-age/grade, middle-Class, monolingual, English-speaking peers (including, reading/writing, vocabulary, and speech)?* | |
| 8. ... ***residential neighborhood use English as the daily language,*** *as well as exhibit cultural practices and attitudes that primarily reflect middle-class, mainstream U.S. values?* | |
| PRINT TPE — TOTAL = | |

Note: The calculated degree of difference will automatically apply to subsequent C-LIM or C-LIM-ATE score analyses. However, practitioners can later select a different category from the "degree of difference" drop-down menu without recalculating. They may adjust categories based on additional relevant information, especially for scores near cutoff values.

8 - 16 = **SLIGHTLY DIFFERENT** 17 - 31 = **MODERATELY DIFFERENT** 32 - 40 = **MARKEDLY DIFFERENT**

**FIGURE 8.10 True Peer Estimator**

The TPE acts as a semi-structured interview/rating scale that focuses on eight of the most important factors that might be present in Maria's life and which may have affected her linguistic and acculturative knowledge acquisition to the extent that it creates a measurable difference between her development and experiences as compared to those of the monolingual normative samples from the tests that she was administered. The TPE requires that evaluators look at a wide range of factors that are related to developmental differences that are created by various familial, environmental, and socio-economic circumstances present within an individual's childhood. Many of these relate to language experience, obviously, but also acculturative knowledge acquisition and opportunities for engaging in different types of language development experiences. In Maria's case, the following developmental history was gathered in the course of the evaluation:

Family Experiences:

- Maria was born in the U.S. about a year after parents immigrated from a rural area outside of Oaxaca, Mexico
- Father had minimal education, maybe around a 2nd grade equivalency, and her mother had no formal education at all--neither parent has elementary-level literacy

- She has a brother who is three years older but despite some language concerns, he was never reported to have had any difficulties and has never been evaluated
- Upon arrival in the U.S., the parents were migrant farm workers and traveled with the harvest moving quite often
- When Maria turned five, her parents settled in the present community and have not moved since
- At that time, her father took a job with a landscape company and mother began cleaning homes now that both kids were in school
- The overall parental SES is low, but Maria has had a relatively normal upbringing without any circumstances of note

Language Experiences:

- Parents originally spoke Mixtec (indigenous language) and learned Spanish as well since it was the language used in broader society and when arriving in the U.S.
- Upon arrival in the U.S., parents report that they only spoke Spanish to their children and not Mixtec at all as there was no need
- Maria was identified as a limited English proficient student in kindergarten and placed in a traditional ESL pullout program
- Maria passed the State Title III Proficiency exam at the end of 3rd grade but was not given any transitional support in 4th grade
- Maria speaks English with her brother primarily, but mostly Spanish with her parents at home

Educational Experiences:

- Maria had no preschool experience prior to kindergarten but displays variable academic performance with most problems in reading
- Although her basic reading skills are relatively good, she has always been observed to have trouble with reading comprehension
- She has difficulty retelling or paraphrasing a sentence she just read and often cannot explain it in her own words
- Despite having a basic command of writing, Maria's written expression suffers from a lack of cohesion, organization, and inclusion of important features and elements of longer passages and chapters
- Maria is able to read in a manner that seems appropriate for grade level although her rate is a little slow
- Maria's math skills are generally good, although multi-step procedures have been difficult for her to learn and have taken more time
- Once Maria has learned a mathematical procedure, she is able to apply it consistently, however, she makes mistakes in some cases where she forgets to make an annotation when borrowing or carrying over in double-digit multiplication or division
- Maria's teacher believes that Maria is struggling more than usual and that her difficulties are making it hard to keep up with instruction given the absence of additional support services that she was previously getting while in ESL
- The pre-referral team feels Maria's overall performance can no longer be ascribed to language differences and that a comprehensive evaluation for SLD is warranted

**CAUTION**

When asking about the factors listed in the TPE, care and sensitivity should be used with parents to ensure that they do not feel that the questions are intended judgmentally. Obtaining the information is crucial to assisting their child and it should be made clear that this is the only purpose for it and the only reason the questions are being asked.

**DON'T FORGET**

The degree of difference may be changed or modified at any time when using X-BASS. Selecting a new level of difference can be done on the Dashboard, C-LIM, C-LIM+ATE, and PSW Data tab and doing so, updates the degree of difference on these same tabs and updates any PSW analyses and indications that may have already been made to ensure they are correct and nondiscriminatory.

Based on the referral information available in Maria's case, as well as a review of Maria's cumulative education folder, conversations with her, her parents, and her teacher, the evaluator considered and then entered the best rating for each of the eight items within the TPE, as shown in Figure 8.11. The result of these ratings indicated that Maria's experiences and development place her within the moderately different group and indicates the extent to which she differs in her development and acquisition regarding language and acculturative knowledge in comparison to monolingual English speakers raised in the U.S. cultural mainstream. Accordingly, Maria should be evaluated against expectations regarding how children with "MODERATELY DIFFERENT" developmental backgrounds perform on tests given to them in English, not against the monolingual standard which will invariably lead to potentially significant underestimates of her actual ability.

In this case, the default setting of "MODERATELY DIFFERENT," which was automatically selected by X-BASS as the default level when the case record for Maria was first established, is correct and can remain as is. However, had the total sum in the TPE indicated that she was not accurately reflected by this level of difference, for example due to having the good fortune of many opportunities for advanced English learning, or highly educated or multilingual parents, and other such advantages, then the degree of difference can be easily changed to "SLIGHTLY DIFFERENT" simply by returning to the TPE and selecting the appropriate degree of difference there or more easily, by selecting it directly from the C-LIM, C-LIM+ATE, Dashboard, or PSW Data Entry tabs. Likewise, if Maria's developmental experiences included other substantially inhibiting factors (e.g., exposure to trauma/violence, poverty, interrupted formal education, etc.), she might have been found to be "MARKEDLY DIFFERENT," instead and again, that adjustment could be made here or elsewhere in X-BASS.

Making a change to the degree of difference on the TPE or on any other tab is carried throughout X-BASS to all the other relevant tabs. For example, any change made on the TPE will be reflected when returning to Dashboard. Similarly, any change made on the

**True Peer Estimator (TPE)** CLEAR RATINGS

NOTIFICATIONS: ON

C-LIM | DASHBOARD | C-LIM+ATE | DATA ENTRY

Currently Selected Degree of Difference: MODERATELY DIFFERENT

This worksheet helps practitioners systematically collect data about examinees to identify developmental differences in experiences relative to typical age or grade expectations. Considering these differences is essential for fair, nondiscriminatory test score interpretation. While a student's degree of cultural or linguistic difference can change over time, documenting them helps estimate their impact on academic, cognitive, and linguistic test scores. The degree of difference categories are:

A) Slightly Different. This category is characterized by minor differences in culture, language, and experiences that although not fully representative of the U.S. mainstream, have still been supported by high family SES, well-educated parents, formal elementary education in the heritage language, bilingual parents, etc.) and where opportunity for developing English language proficiency constitutes at least ½ or more of a student's life.

B) Moderately Different. This category is characterized by moderate to large differences in culture, language, and experiences that are not representative of the U.S. mainstream and where few supporting factors are present (e.g., low family SES, parental lack of education, no formal education in the heritage language, parents with limited English proficiency, etc.) or where opportunity for developing English proficiency constitutes less than ½ of a student's life.

C) Markedly Different. This category is characterized by major differences in culture, language, and experiences where the opportunity for developing English proficiency constitutes a small percentage of a student's life, for example being a newcomer and having extremely limited English language development. It may also include other atypical factors that adversely influence development (e.g., exposure to war, trauma, violence, abuse, neglect, immigrant or migrant worker experience, refugee status, etc.).

| *To what extent does the examinee's or the examinee's family...?* (1 Very Much — 2 — 3 Some — 4 — 5 Very Little) | ENTER RATING HERE |
|---|---|
| 1. ... ***heritage or home culture match*** *middle-class, mainstream U.S. values, traditions, and beliefs in supporting acquisition of school-based acculturative knowledge?* | 5 |
| 2. ... ***socio-economic status match*** *middle-class, mainstream families in the U.S. in supporting development of school-based learning and academic skills?* | 4 |
| 3. ... ***heritage or home language match*** *middle-class, mainstream, monolingual English-speakers in supporting the acquisition of school-based English?* | 4 |
| 4. ... ***school attendance*** *indicate consistent and sufficient engagement for age- or grade-expected academic instruction and opportunity for learning?* | 1 |
| 5. ... ***formal schooling include heritage language instruction*** *either while attending school in the U.S. or prior to coming to the U.S.?* | 5 |
| 6. ... ***experiences include exposure to high level language models in English*** *over their lifetime as compared to middle-class, monolingual English-speakers of the same age?* | 2 |
| 7. ... ***English language development match*** *same-age/grade, middle-Class, monolingual, English-speaking peers (including, reading/writing, vocabulary, and speech)?* | 3 |
| 8. ... ***residential neighborhood use English as the daily language,*** *as well as exhibit cultural practices and attitudes that primarily reflect middle-class, mainstream U.S. values?* | 4 |
| PRINT TPE — TRUE PEER GROUP: Moderately Different — TOTAL = | 28 |

Note: The calculated degree of difference will automatically apply to subsequent C-LIM or C-LIM-ATE score analyses. However, practitioners can later select a different category from the "degree of difference" drop-down menu without recalculating. They may adjust categories based on additional relevant information, especially for scores near cutoff values.

8 - 16 = SLIGHTLY DIFFERENT    17 - 31 = MODERATELY DIFFERENT    32 - 40 = MARKEDLY DIFFERENT

**FIGURE 8.11 Completed True Peer Estimator**

C-LIM will be reflected on the TPE, Dashboard, C-LIM+ATE, and PSW Data tabs as well. In this manner, changes to the degree of difference in one location can be instantly applied to any other location where it is used to maintain the correct level of expectation and fairness in all analyses.

## Academic Testing and Analysis with C-LIM+ATE

After a determination regarding degree of difference has been made, Step 3 of nondiscriminatory assessment framework (Ortiz, 2024) moves on to examine academic test results. Maria's performance on the tests classified as a primary measure of academic skill or knowledge have already been transferred automatically to the C-LIM+ATE from the Data Entry tab when the "C-LIM ANALYSIS" button was clicked. Navigating over to the C-LIM+ATE via the buttons at the upper left corner of the TPE or C-LIM tab reveals that the necessary demographic information from the Case Record has also been transferred, including the degree of difference, whether drawn from the default when creating the case or from actual use of the TPE. Figure 8.12 shows the results of this transfer on the C-LIM+ATE tab.

Because the C-LIM+ATE involves abilities that are specifically taught in school, as opposed to cognitive abilities that are acquired primarily through maturation, there is an entirely different research base necessary to establish true peer comparison standards. Grade becomes significant, of course, but also the type of "Primary Educational Program" is equally important, along with degree of difference. In Maria's case we already have the grade and degree of difference entered and all that remains is to indicate the educational program she is currently in, or in which she was previously, by selecting it from the drop down menu as shown in Figure 8.13. Without indication of primary educational program, or grade and degree of difference, the C-LIM+ATE will not generate the desired graphs. It is also important to understand that achievement scores are not inherently diagnostic and do not speak strongly to possible intrinsic causes of difficulty, such as a learning disorder. Rather, they can sometimes be manifestations or the measurable effect of such intrinsic difficulties, and they are always "valid" in the sense

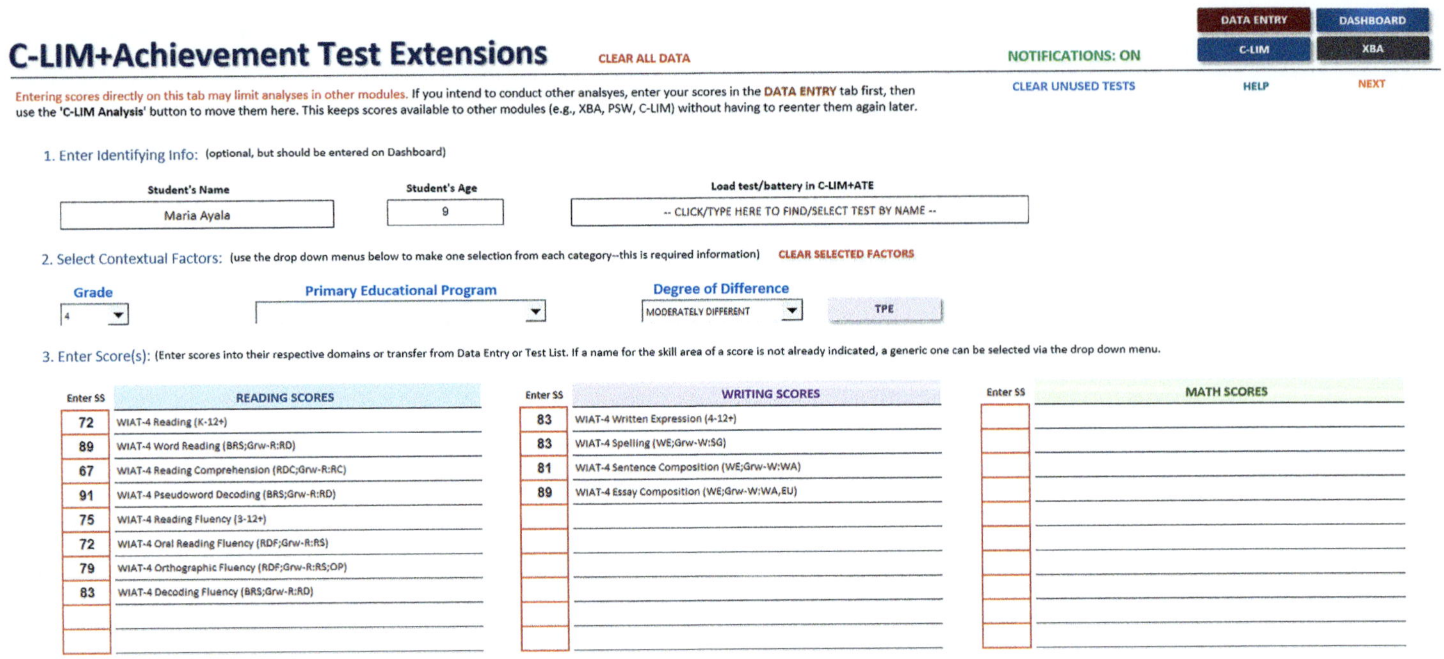


**FIGURE 8.12 C-LIM+ATE with Transferred Data**

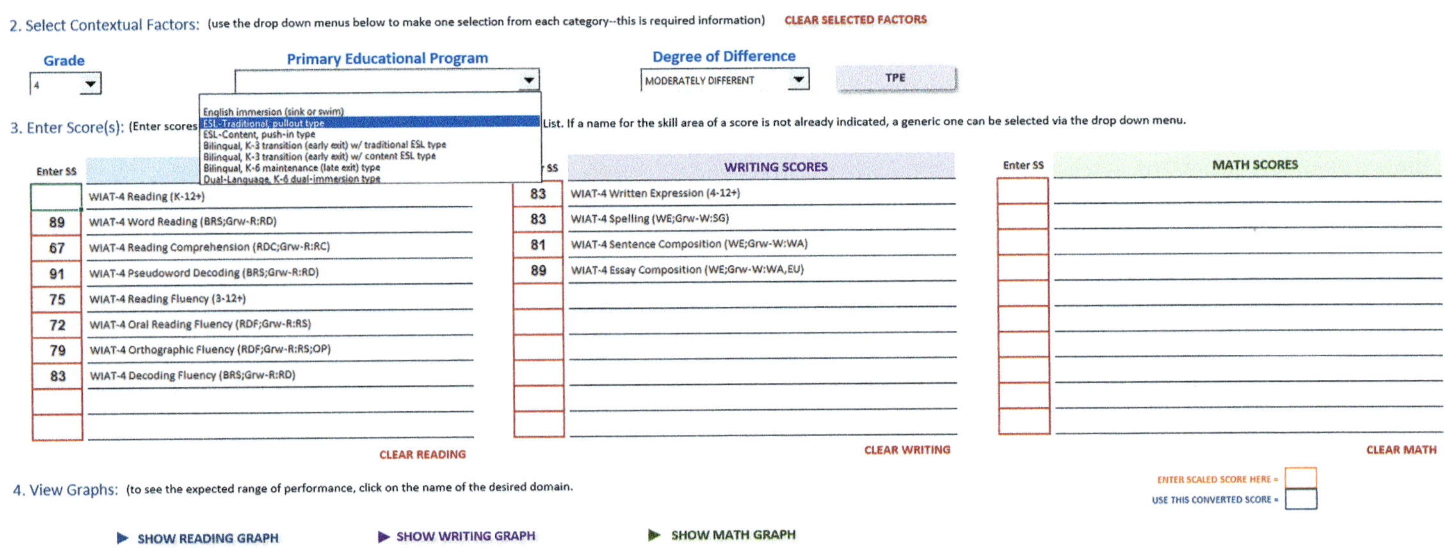


**FIGURE 8.13 C-LIM+ATE Selecting Educational Program**

that they do indicate current level of skill or knowledge development relative to grade level norms. The C-LIM+ATE assists practitioners in examining whether performance may or may not be due to acculturative or linguistic factors, but cannot be used to directly address test score validity in the absence of additional data.

According to the educational experience information contained in the referral information, it is known that Maria was in a traditional, ESL pullout type program and this program has been selected from the menu. After all required information has been entered, the next step is to generate the graphs (in this case reading and writing, as math was not evaluated) by clicking on the links shown below the table of scores and labeled as "SHOW READING GRAPH" and "SHOW WRITING GRAPH." The graph for each of these is shown respectively in Figures 8.14 and 8.15.

Unlike with cognitive ability testing, academic testing should not be viewed as diagnostic evidence, per se. Rather, academic testing serves as a valid indicator of current skill and performance level relative to grade-level standards. That is, the scores do in fact point to difficulties in Maria's current level of performance relative to other children in the same grade in reading and writing. As such, it is not incorrect to state that

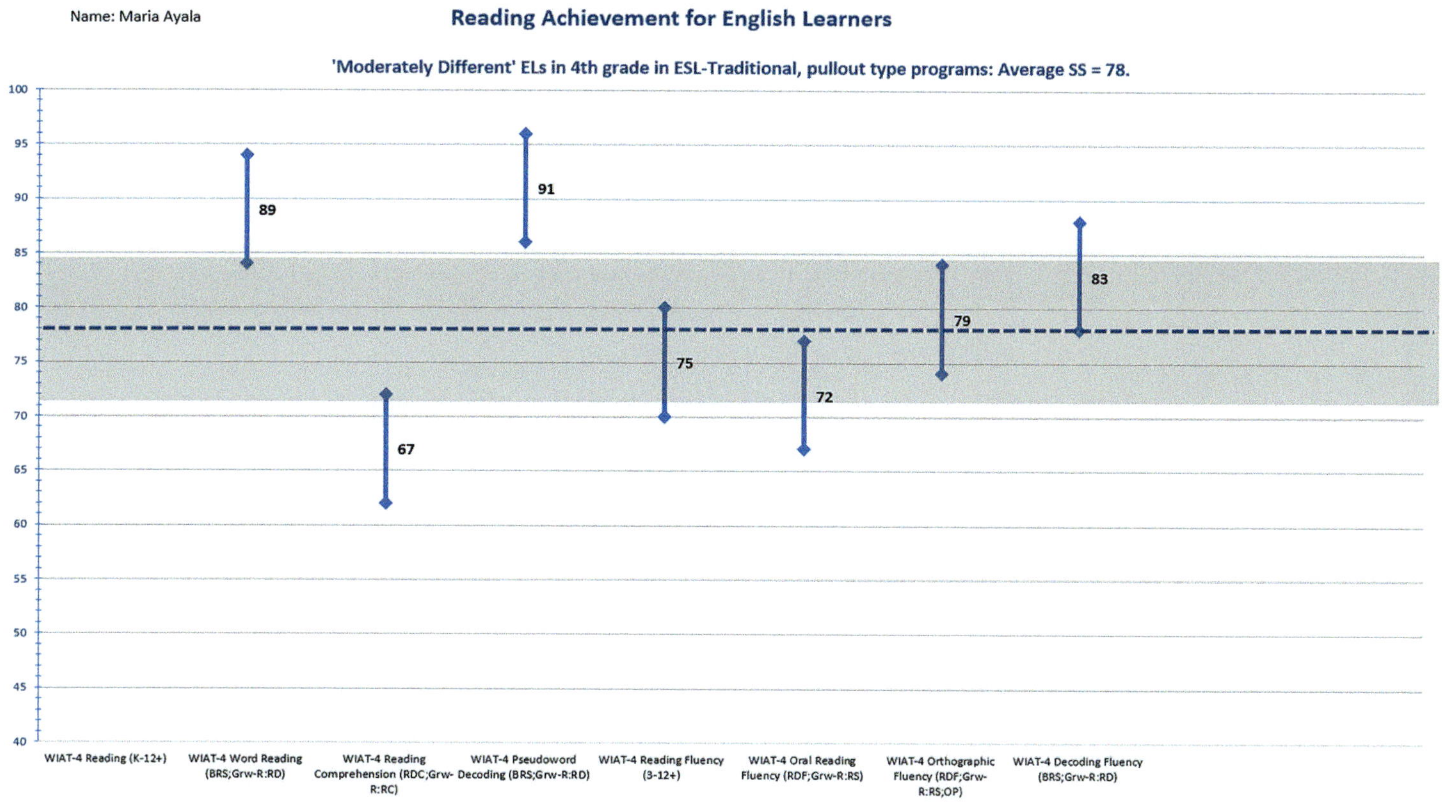


**FIGURE 8.14 C-LIM+ATE Reading Graph**

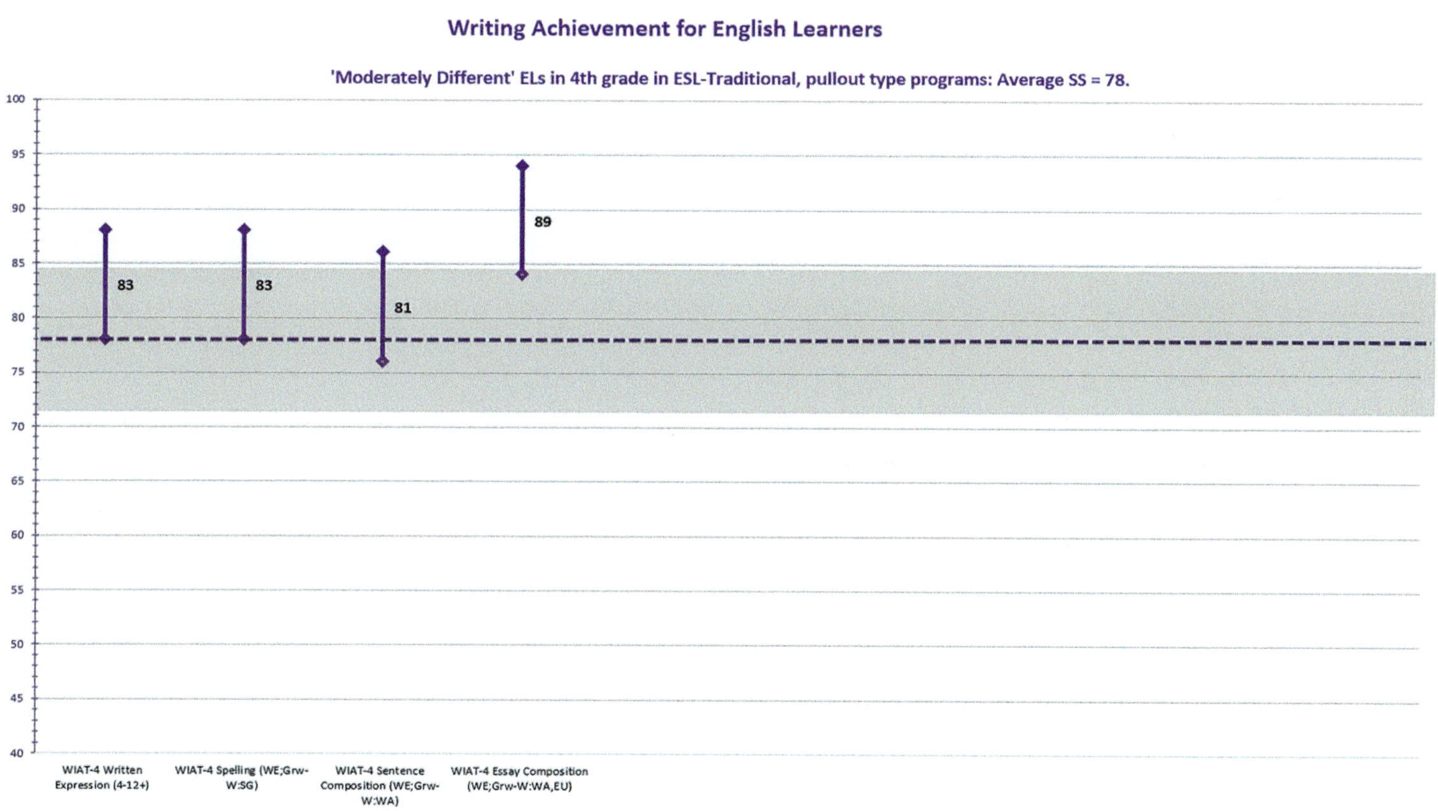


**FIGURE 8.15 C-LIM+ATE Writing Graph**

**CAUTION**

Even when scores are below the expected level of performance on the C-LIM+ATE, the results should not be construed as suggestive of a deficit or disability. Achievement tests provide information regarding what an individual can do, but they do not directly address the question regarding why they may be at that level. Additional evidence from cognitive testing is required to answer diagnostic questions.

her reading ability, in some areas, and possibly some areas of her writing, are below grade level given that the scores fall outside and below normal limits. However, whether this performance supports the presence of a disability cannot be ascertained by this comparison. Much like with the C-LIM, Maria's performance must be examined in comparison to true peers, that is, to other individuals who have similar educational, acculturative, and linguistic developmental experiences. In the graphs, the dotted line represents the expected level of performance for children like Maria drawn from large scale academic studies of multilingual performers (Thomas & Collier, 1997, 2002) who are in the same grade, the same program, and with the same degree of difference. When conducting this type of true peer comparison, it is clear that nearly all of her performances could be attributed primarily to the impact of language and acculturative knowledge differences, with the exception of her score on the WIAT-4 Reading Comprehension (SS = 67) which is well below the expected range to be considered typical. Nevertheless, these scores do not automatically rule out or imply the presence of any particular deficit and measured performance may well be explainable in other ways. To gain clinical significance requires that there be some causal explanation that can be made on the basis of the presence of a latent cognitive deficit with an empirically established relationship to this manifest skill. As that has not yet been established in the process of evaluating Maria, the only interpretation that may be offered from the C-LIM+ATE graphs is that she has difficulty in reading comprehension that cannot yet be fully explained by linguistic or acculturative knowledge factors, but which are not necessarily attributable to a disability either.

## Initial Cognitive Testing and Analysis with the C-LIM

Using the navigation buttons, the evaluation now returns to the C-LIM module. Figure 8.16 below shows the initial Culture-Language Interpretive Matrix tab with all of the cognitive tests that were entered on the Data Entry tab and which were subsequently transferred along with their respective scores. In previous versions of X-BASS, the matrix itself was used primarily for initial scanning of the data as well as manual examination of intra-cell score variability. Whereas the C-LIM can still support these functions and continues to provide a visual index of the locations of the subtests relative to each other with respect to their impact on culture and language, score variability is now automatically evaluated and additional graphs have been created to further assist with interpretation as will be described, diminishing the need to conduct any direct analysis on the matrix itself.

Scores are placed into the C-LIM as a function of the respective culture-language classifications for each test or subtest and its value carried over from the Data Entry tab. An aggregate or mean average score is calculated automatically for each of the nine cells in the matrix corresponding to the classifications relative to being high or low in terms of language demands and acculturative knowledge content. The classifications are drawn from research on multilinguals that provides guidance regarding expected levels of performance and impact that is from linguistic and acculturative knowledge differences (Cormier, 2014, 2022; Dynda, 2008, Sotelo-Dynega et al., 2013; Ortiz, 2019). Note that the score from the Ortiz Picture Vocabulary Acquisition Test (Ortiz PVAT; Ortiz, 2018) has been deliberately removed from the C-LIM for this case study. This is because its inclusion would alter the expected values for the "Low/Low" cell and cause confusion. Furthermore, the Ortiz PVAT score is the only *Gc* test which can be interpreted validly as is and therefore there is no need to include it in the C-LIM. Later on in the case study, use of the Ortiz PVAT and its ability to obviate the need for generation of other types of *Gc* scores will be highlighted. In short, one of the major advantages in using the Ortiz PVAT is that it provides an efficient way of deriving a *Gc* score that is not subject to the same potentially discriminatory interpretations as other measures of *Gc* that lack language exposure norms.

Returning to the C-LIM, Maria's performance on the cognitive tests that were administered to her can now be examined properly. The process beings by scrolling down and using the toggle links for the various graphs, which are located just underneath the matrix and labeled individually as "SHOW CULTURE-LANGUAGE GRAPH," "SHOW CHC DOMAIN GRAPH," "SHOW TEST COMPOSITE GRAPH," and so forth. It is generally best to begin with the main Culture-Language (C-L) graph which is accessed via the link indicated by the arrow in Figure 8.17.

The main culture language graph is quite similar to the one contained in previous versions of X-BASS with one of the obvious changes being the use of color, but another includes display of the calculated aggregate mean for the cell corresponding to each bar and the addition of error bars/confidence bands, which may assist in interpreting whether or not a particular bar is within the selected expected range or not. Interpretation of the main C-L graph is the same as before and requires investigation of the presence of three particular conditions representing criteria that must be met to support the primary impact of acculturative and linguistic factors on test performance:

1. Existence of an overall pattern of decline from left to right. Although that is somewhat evident in Maria's case, there are some disruptions of that.
2. All scores are within the expected range or above. Clearly, in a couple of bars in the low culture high language and the high culture low language cells, the scores are not actually rising up to the expected level of performance here.

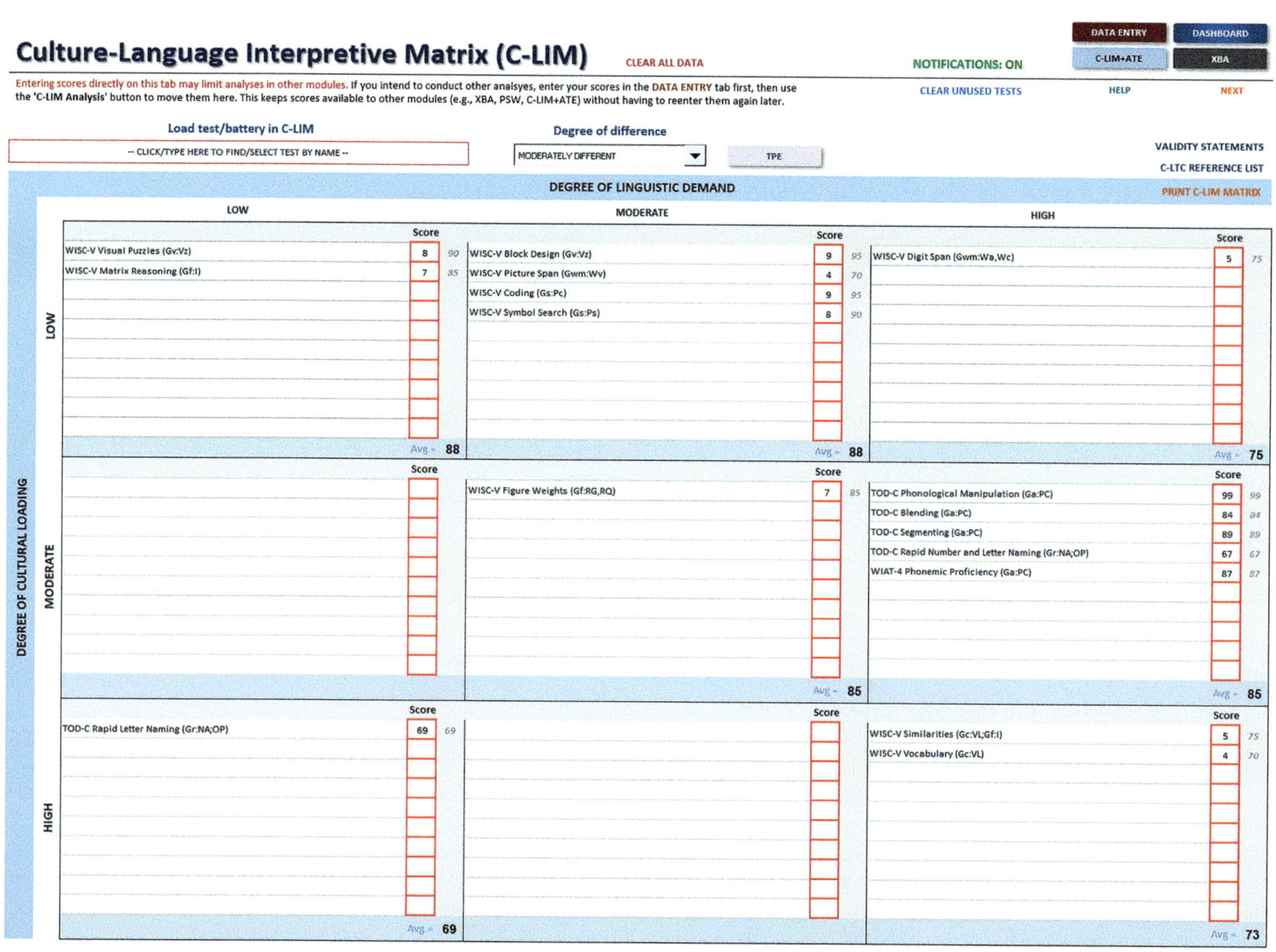


**FIGURE 8.16 C-LIM Module**

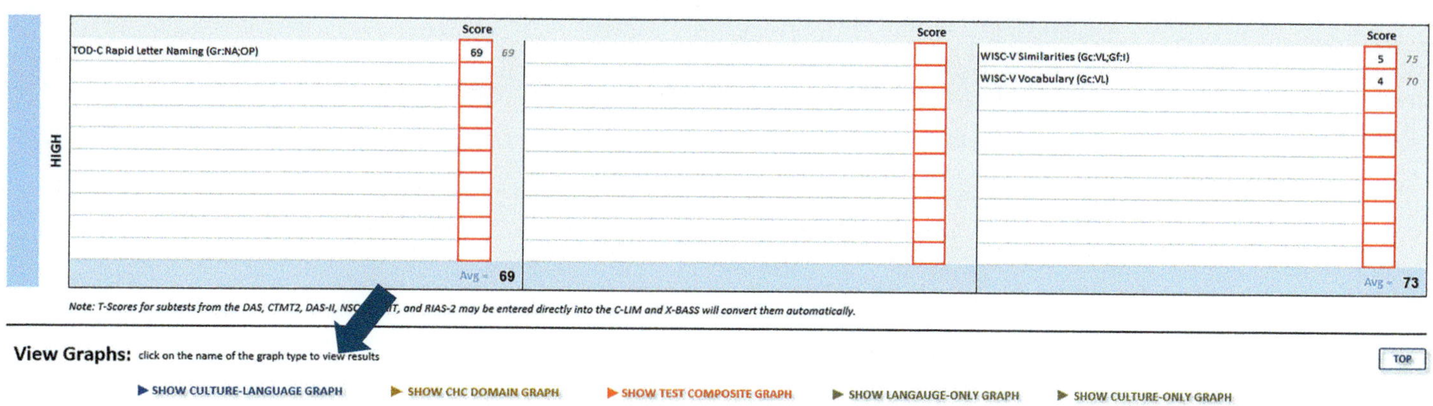


**FIGURE 8.17 Selecting the Culture-Language (CL) Graph**

3. Absence of any type of score variability. If criterion one and two have been met, then the third criterion involves examination of score variability where a high score in a cell might be masking the presence of a low score in the same cell thereby potentially hiding a true area of deficit. In Maria's case, this criterion is rendered moot given that both preceding criteria were not met. Were this analysis necessary, however, simply clicking on the link labeled "SUBTEST VARIABILITY" would provide the requisite analysis.

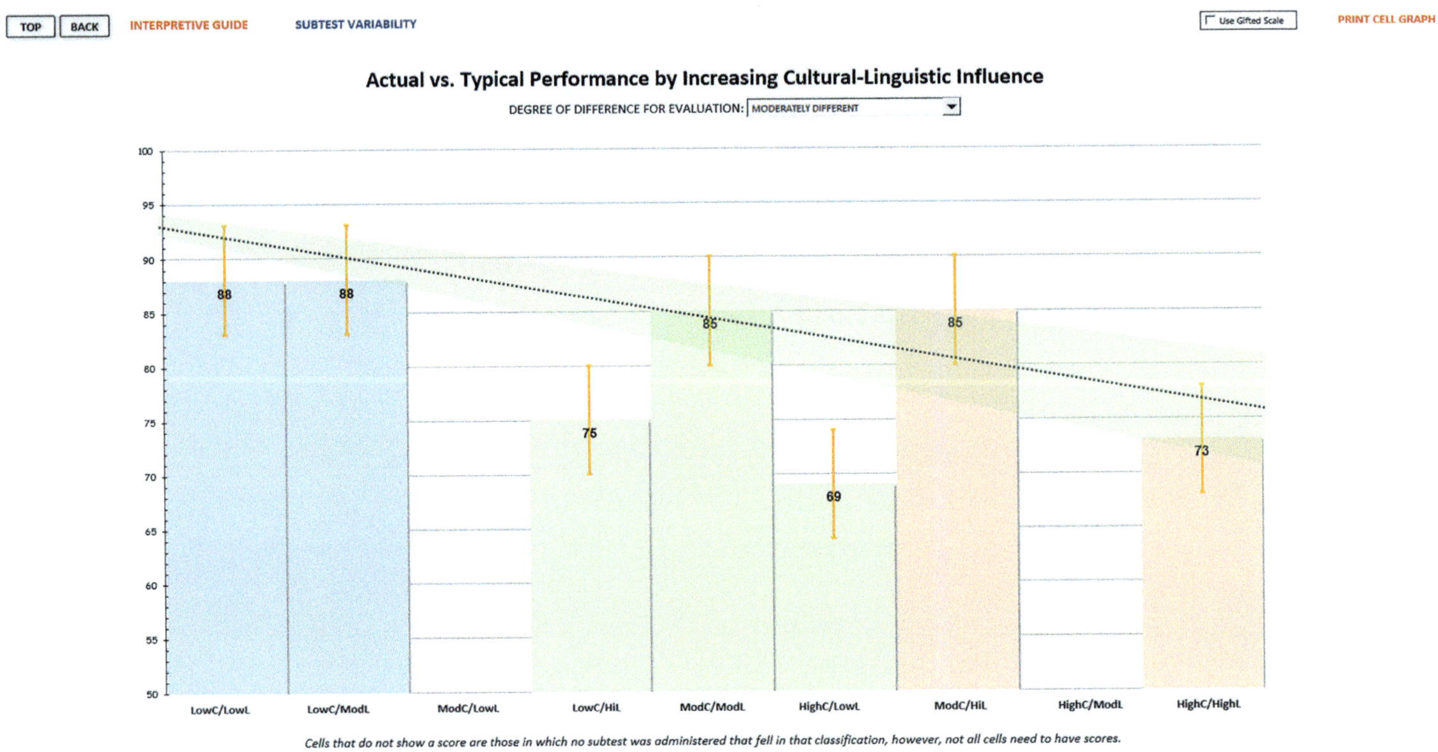


**FIGURE 8.18 Main Culture Language Graph for Maria**

Again, subtest variability would only be important if the first two criteria were in fact met. That is, if Maria's performance was following an overall pattern of decline and if all of the scores were within or above the expected range. Since that is not the case here, we need not go any further, and we can establish via the Culture-Language graph that her performance is not typical of what we would expect for an English learner or a multilingual who is of average ability and who has no deficits whatsoever. Rather, her performance is atypical, that is, not what we would expect if she were of average ability across all domains, and therefore the results may well suggest the presence of one or more deficits in terms of her performance on the tests that were administered. Figure 8.18 provides an illustration of the main Culture-Language graph for Maria and Rapid Reference 8.6 summarizes the criteria for interpretation of the Main Culture-Language graph.

## *Rapid Reference 8.6*

### Determining "Typical" Performance on the Culture-Language Graph

For performance to be considered "typical" (and scores likely to be invalid), all three criteria (i.e., declining pattern, within expected range, lack of score variability) must be met. If so, this suggests that performance was due primarily to acculturative and linguistic factors, likely means the individual is of average ability, and thus it may preclude identification of a disability or eligibility for special education services.

Earlier it was stated that previous versions of X-BASS contained a tiered graph which had five bars, which is no longer necessary and has been replaced not only by the more advanced cultural language graph here and the automatic subtest variability, but also by the addition of two new graphs that assist in evaluating the scores at the broad ability level. The first of these is the CHC Domain graph shown next in Figure 8.19.

The CHC Domain graph is the second link under the "View Graphs" heading on the C-LIM tab just below the matrix. This graph allows comparison of performance at the broad ability level and as organized by CHC broad ability domains. X-BASS takes all subtests that measure the same domain, excluding mixed-loaded subtests or subtests that have mixed classifications, and brings them together to create an aggregate (in this case, an average) and plots this actual value next to the expected values. The expected values are calculated on the basis of the known classifications for all of the subtests measuring the same domain as well as the selected degree of difference. X-BASS uses the classification and difference information to compute the expected mean value for each individual subtest within each broad ability domain and combines them

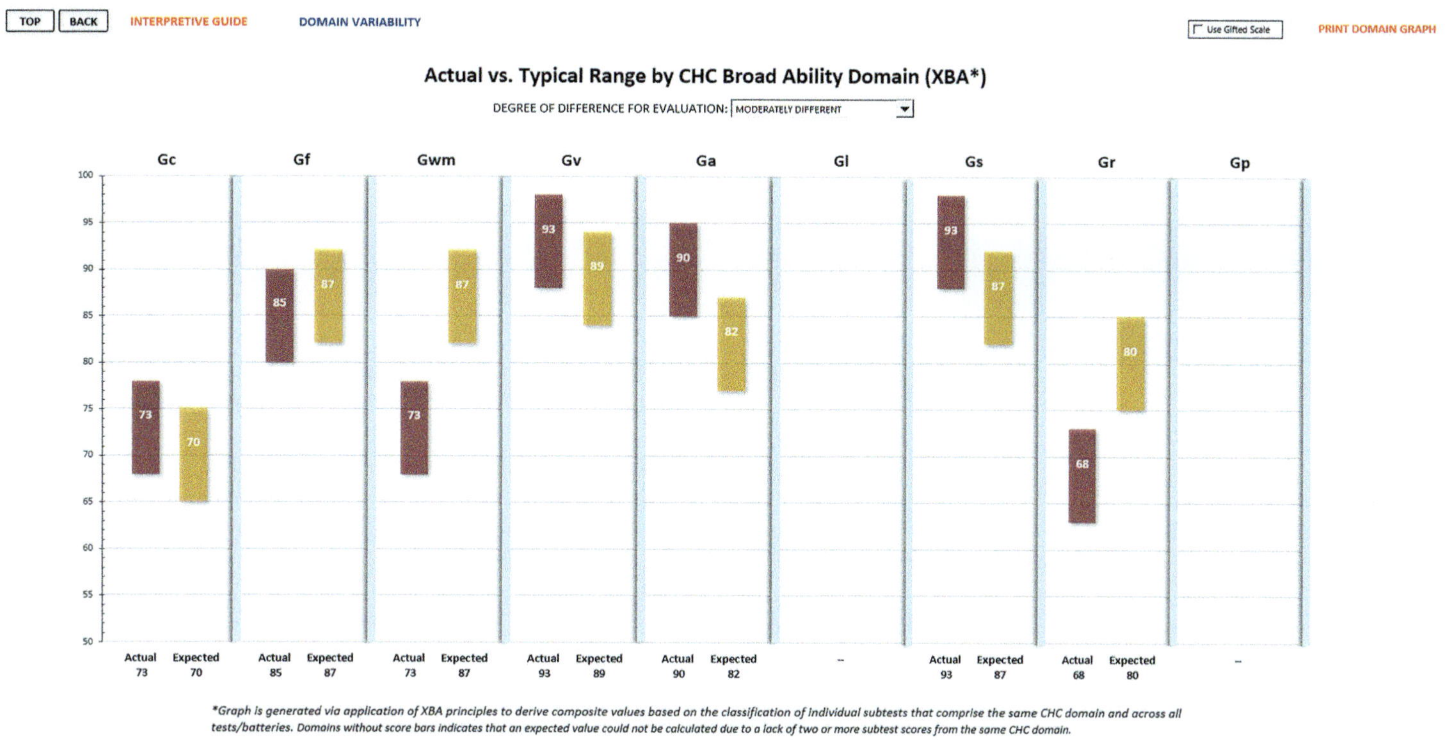


**FIGURE 8.19 C-LIM CHC Domain Graph**

with the other expected mean values from the same domain to produce the expected mean score. Both the actual and the expected scores are plotted as bars alongside each other, with 1SEM confidence bands, to allow visual inspection and direct comparison regarding whether Maria's performance in each broad ability domain is or is not within the expected range as a function of the impact of acculturative and linguistic factors. Interpretation proceeds under the assumption that if the bars overlap or touch, it likely means that the two scores are relatively similar, if not the same, and therefore performance is as expected or typical (and the score is likely invalid). If the actual performance is lower than the expected performance (that is, the bars do not touch or overlap), it can be interpreted as indicating that performance is atypical (and the score is likely valid) and that the low performance must be due to factors other than just the presence or impact of acculturative knowledge or language difference.

In Maria's case, it is clear that there are two areas in which her performance appears to be atypical. Those would be Short-term Working Memory (*Gwm*) and Retrieval Fluency (*Gr*). In those areas, her actual performance, denoted by the reddish bars, is much lower than her expected performance, denoted by the gold bars. This means that her performance in these two areas is not typical or consistent with what would be expected of other children of her age who are moderately different multilinguals with average ability in these domains. Given her experience, her performance in these areas is lower than what can be confidently or primarily attributed to acculturative or linguistic factors. In this way, the evaluator can systematically rule out the influence of acculturative and linguistic variables on test performance as part of the process and regulations governing SLD identification. The graph provides direct evidence to suggest that acculturative knowledge and language development differences are not likely to be the primary influences in this case and in these domains. At best, these factors might exert only a contributory influence according to the research, and because Maria's performance is less than what can be reasonably accounted for by their presence, it implies that there must be some other factor which is attenuating her performance further and which is unrelated to such differences. This finding does not automatically suggest the presence of a disability; however, it does provide evidence to support such a notion should there be additional evidence with which to bolster the conclusion. At this point in the process of evaluation, there is insufficient evidence for the claim, but further evaluation and follow-up may yet provide the necessary supplementary data to corroborate it.

Maria's performance in the area of language, or *Gc*, was measured as a 73 (standard score = 73). Ordinarily, this might be a cause for concern because it suggests that her functioning is extremely low in this area, much like it is with *Gwm*. However, the expected range for *Gc* for others who are moderately different, like Maria, is only a SS = 70, indicating that her performance is actually slightly above the expected value and is therefore typical. Because it is typical, it does not suggest that that is an area of weakness for her, despite the fact that the magnitude of the score, the standard score of 73, is quite low. A potential issue, however, in using this score is that its magnitude does not correspond to the interpretation of expected, typical, or normal performance that will be assigned to it. For this reason, it was discussed previously that use of a valid *Gc* score, such as the one from the Ortiz PVAT, is recommended as an alternative to other measures of Gc in that it facilitates and simplifies measurement of the domain while also providing a valid score that can be used for later analysis without worry regarding possible

> **DON'T FORGET**
>
> X-BASS now allows all broad cognitive ability domain scores to be marked as "expected" to indicate that performance, even if normatively low, is commensurate with other individuals with similar developmental backgrounds. Marking scores in this way ensures they are handled properly in PSW analysis and that they are interpreted in a fair manner.

discriminatory outcomes. Alternatively, X-BASS has built-in protections for multilinguals that can assist in handling the meaning of such "low" *Gc* scores even in PSW analysis but it will not change the magnitude of the score or alter the fact that users may encounter fierce arguments about the propriety (or sanity) of calling a SS = 73 "average" or expected.

In general, results from the CHC Domain graph would suggest that follow-up in her heritage language would be necessary for Maria in the areas of *Gwm* and *Gr*. The graph also highlights that there is no need to repeat all of the same testing on Maria in the heritage language, a practice which is commonly used but which can actually waste time and precious resources. Since her functioning is seen to be typical and expected across the board, except for the two areas noted, there is no reason to have to re-evaluate the others as doing so will not provide any information that isn't already known. That is, Maria likely has no true deficit in any of the areas in which her performance was typical when compared to true peers and in some cases even when compared to monolinguals. This is not to say that additional evaluation couldn't be conducted; it certainly can. However, it would seem to be rather unnecessary and redundant in this particular case. For users who are new to XBA or who may not be very familiar with CHC Theory, the CHC Domain graph in Maria's case may serve as a soft introduction into why the use of modern cognitive theory is so helpful. It provides an illustration regarding why organizing all scores and data via alignment with the CHC Theory framework is preferable to other approaches, in that doing so eliminates possible confusion and ambiguity that may result from trying to interpret mixed clusters or composites.

For users not yet well versed in CHC Theory or for those who may want to examine results strictly from the perspective regarding how the test/battery publisher views measurement of various ability, the C-LIM provides another graph illustrated in Figure 8.20 called the Test Composite graph. Much like the CHC Domain graph, it too provides a visual comparison of the actual or obtained composite, index, or cluster scores contained in the data alongside the expected values based on the collective impact of linguistic and acculturative knowledge acquisition on the respective subtests that comprise them. However, only indexes, clusters, or composites that adequately measure a broad ability are shown. This graph does not include any such scores that are classified as being mixed-loaded, meaning that they measure two or more different broad ability levels, to ensure that interpretation remains unambiguous. For this reason, X-BASS intentionally excludes them from appearing in the Test Composite graph.

Much like the analysis with the CHC Domain Graph, there are two scores that stand out as being potential areas of weakness for Maria. They include the WISC-V Working Memory Index and the TOD-C Rapid Automatized Naming Composite. Both are lower than expected

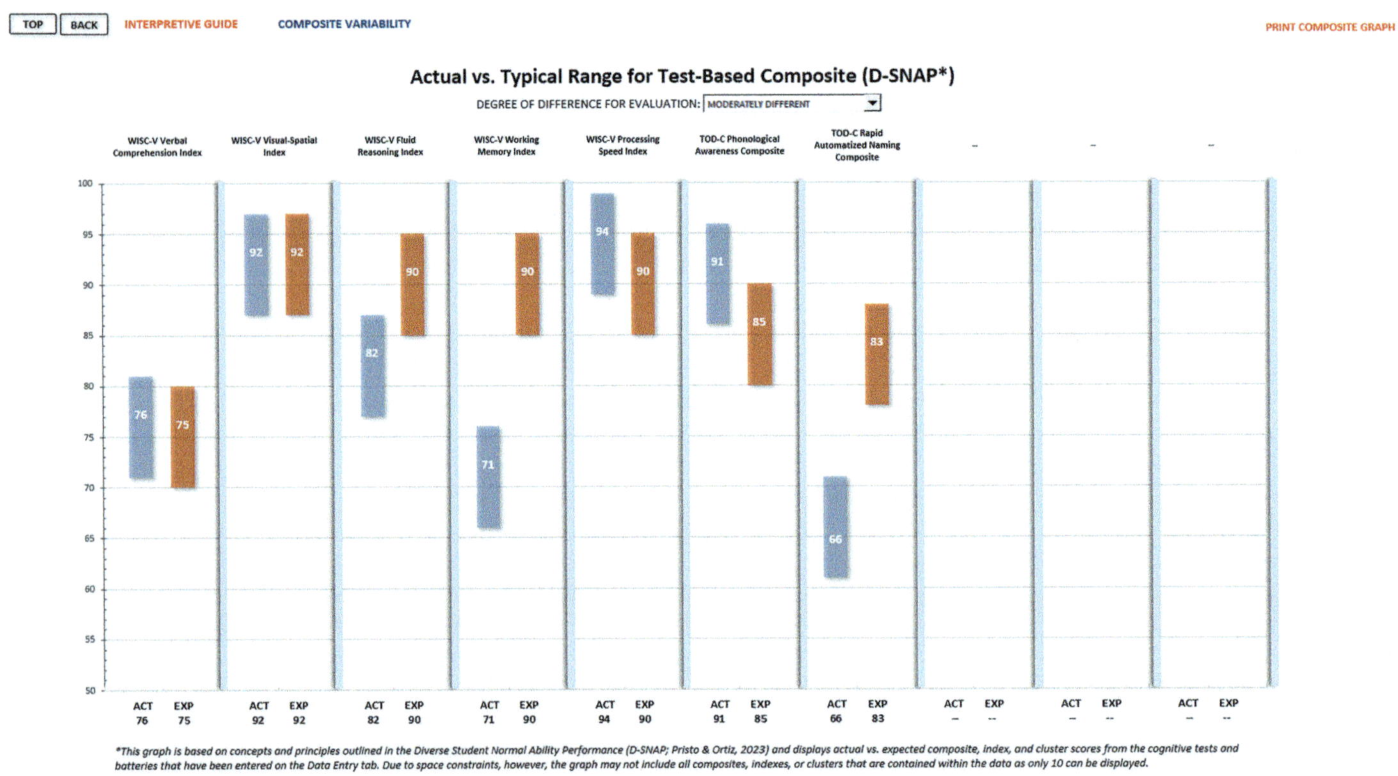


**FIGURE 8.20 C-LIM Test Composite Graph**

and suggest that performance is atypical and cannot be attributed primarily to acculturative or linguistic factors and that the scores may well be valid. Not surprisingly, the WISC-V Working Memory Index is a measure of Short-term Working Memory (*Gwm*), and the TOD-C Rapid Automatized Naming Composite is a measure of Retrieval Fluency (*Gr*). Generally speaking, when clusters and indexes are consistent with the CHC domains that they are named after and which they are intended to measure, you will see this kind of consistency along the way.

One minor variation in performance that is not as evident in the CHC Domain graph comes from the WISC-V Fluid Reasoning Index, which shows a SS = 82 for the actual obtained score (the light blue bar) and a SS = 90 for the expected score (the copper-colored bar). In some cases, it may well be determined that this score is low enough to suggest that it should also be re-evaluated, despite the fact that the bands are overlapping. This is the type of clinical decision that is best left up to the evaluator. For example, an evaluator could argue that Fluid Reasoning on the CHC Domain graph (which utilizes all measures of *Gf*) was not outside the expected range and, in fact, was a little bit higher. This means that overall performance, not from the WISC-V alone, was within normal limits and ordinarily would not be an area that needs to be revisited in the heritage language. On the other hand, *Gf* may play a role in the types of reading comprehension difficulties reported as part of the referral information on Maria and further investigation could be helpful in illuminating her academic troubles. Such decisions are, of course, made on a case by case basis and subject to clinical judgment that goes beyond what test scores can alone provide and may necessitate different and unique choices and in this case, the evaluated made the decision to go ahead and re-evaluate *Gf* due to its importance and relevance to reading comprehension.

**CAUTION**

Decisions regarding whether to follow-up with testing in the heritage language depend on whether the score is interpreted as a "weakness" or not. For scores at or near the cutoff for classification ranges suggesting below average functioning, it will be necessary for the clinician to use clinical judgment in deciding how any given score should be interpreted, particularly those that range from SS = 80–89.

### Follow-up Cognitive Testing and Analysis with the C-LIM

There is a tendency to think that testing multilinguals always and absolutely requires testing in the heritage language in all cases. Part of the reason for this mistaken assumption is the requirement in IDEA (34 CFR § 300.304(c)(1)(ii)) that specifies tests are "provided and administered in the child's native language or other mode of communication and in the form most likely to yield accurate information. . ." which contrasts somewhat with the attending statutory regulations that require tests to be "provided and administered in the language and form most likely to yield accurate information. . ." (IDEA § 1414 (a)(3)(A)(ii)). Few practitioners, however, stop to consider the logic and intent of both of these regulations, which is in essence a procedural safeguard (see Rapid Reference 8.7 for further clarification). Testing in the heritage language is necessary to ensure that the individual displays difficulties in both languages, not merely one them, otherwise the very definition of disability cannot be applied. By the same token, testing in one language that results in across-the-board average performance is sufficient by itself to rule out the presence of a disability as results from testing in the other language cannot then alter what is already a failure to meet criteria necessary for identifying a disability, regardless of the language. Furthermore, without any current method available to systematically and empirically evaluate heritage language test results for validity vis-à-vis the impact of language and acculturative knowledge differences, beginning an evaluation in the heritage language may well force the clinician into a corner from which it is difficult, if not impossible, to be extricated.

These additional considerations make it clear why Ortiz (2024) recommends that, whenever feasible and possible, testing begin in English and that follow-up testing in the heritage language be conducted when potentially valid deficits are identified (via the C-LIM) and then only in those areas so identified as possible weaknesses. This method provides significantly greater efficiency in the evaluation process for monolinguals by avoiding needless and redundant testing of areas already found to be intact or average in English while remaining fully compliant with IDEA regulations given that some part of the evaluation was indeed conducted in the heritage language as required.

There is also a tendency in evaluation to avoid administration of the same tests during an evaluation that likely stems from concerns regarding practice effects. However, when the evaluation is focused on determining a learning disability, or indeed many other types of disabilities, practice effects become diagnostic tools. When an examinee is somehow able to move their performance from the deficient to the average range simply on the basis of incidental exposure to some materials and without benefit of any teaching or explicit instruction, it would seem to offer significant clinical information regarding the fact that the examinee is quite the capable learner. For this and other reasons, Ortiz

## *Rapid Reference 8.7*

**Legal Basis for Selecting the Language for Test Administration**

IDEA specifications found in 34 CFR § 300.304(c)(1)(ii) and § 1414 (a)(3)(A)(ii) do not indicate that testing should be in one language only, or which language should be used first in evaluation, or that heritage language evaluation must be conducted in every case for every individual and without respect for any other findings. However, IDEA specifications do emphasize that evaluation of multilinguals should be carried out in the manner most likely to yield accurate, reliable, and valid information.

(2024) recommends using precisely the same tests given in English that indicated likely valid scores suggesting possible areas of deficit and re-administering them in the heritage language. Any change or improvement that subsequently rises into the average range would then serve to disconfirm the validity of the original score in English and establishes the domain as intact or within normal limits and not something that can support an area of cognitive dysfunction.

Because there are important differences in the competencies of professionals who may be conducting an evaluation on multilinguals, it is impossible for the process to look exactly the same for each. There are practitioners who are bilingual and many who are not. There are some who are bilingual but not in the language spoken by the examinee. There are heritage language tests available in Spanish, but not in any other language. This means that completing an evaluation when moving to testing in the heritage language cannot and will not follow one particular path; rather, there will be divergence based on all of the factors so noted. In Maria's case, the evaluator was proficient in Spanish. Moreover, there was a Spanish version of the WISC available (WISC-V Spanish) which could be administered by the evaluator. However, there was not a Spanish version of the TOD-C which meant the evaluator had to translate the tests themself. It is not difficult to apprehend the many permutations that can arise in such situations and generally, the process will follow one of four directions: (1) administration of Spanish language tests by a Spanish-speaking examiner; (2) administration of a Spanish language test via assistance from a interpreter; (3) administration of an English language test translated by an examiner who speaks the examinee's language; or (4) administration of an English language tests translated via assistance from an interpreter who speaks the examinee's language. Sometimes more than one option may be used as in Maria's case where in addition to administering the WISC-V Spanish tests, the need to translate the TOD-C tests of *Gr* required the evaluator to do it since no interpreter was required.

The sequence in which the evaluation has been conducted means that at this point, follow-up testing is not being conducted strictly for the purpose of generating new scores. Rather, it is being conducted to provide cross-linguistic confirmatory evidence for the original scores obtained from testing in English. For this reason, the need to translate the TOD-C tests do not undermine the process or render the data automatically invalid. It is not the production of test scores that is valuable but the opportunity to observe the examinee's approach to tasks (which they have seen before) and ascertain (directly or with the aid of the interpreter) whether the examinee continues to display difficulties similar to those first observed when tested in English, or whether those difficulties appear to be lessened or entirely absent. Should they be absent, then the original score in English may be discarded as invalid and the domain being measured interpreted as intact. Whether it can be called "average" or higher depends on clinical judgement but it cannot be denied that if performance is within the average range, then it did not rise to that level by accident and whatever the reason it improved (even if solely by practice effect, albeit unlikely), the original performance is not confirmed as a valid indicator of an area of deficit. Only when performance in the heritage language is comparable to performance in English (whether it may be slightly higher or markedly lower) can the original score obtained in English be considered cross-validated. Of course, a third layer of validity evidence is required to further substantiate this finding. The results of the follow-up testing in the heritage language are presented in Table 8.2.

A cursory review of Table 8.2 indicates that in Maria's case, her performance on the WISC-V WMI went from SS = 71 in English to SS = 67 in Spanish. A small drop to be sure, but still indicative of relatively comparable performance that likely confirms the validity of the English language score and suggests a true deficit in the short-term working memory (*Gwm*) domain. Similarly, her performance on the TOD-C Rapid Automatized Naming cluster went from SS = 66 in English to a SS = 74 in Spanish. This increase, however, does not alter the fact that her performance, while slightly better in Spanish than in English, remains problematic and also continues to suggest that the initial score in English is a valid indicator of a true deficit in retrieval fluency (*Gr*). A different result occurred in her performance

**Table 8.2 Follow-Up Test Scores from Cognitive Evaluation of Maria in the Heritage Language**

| WISC-V (INITIAL ENGLISH ADMINISTRATION) | | WISC-V SPANISH (FOLLOW-UP ADMINISTRATION) | |
|---|---|---|---|
| **WISC-V Fluid Reasoning Index** | **82** | **WISC-V Spanish Fluid Reasoning Index** | **91** |
| Matrix Reasoning | 7 | Matrix Reasoning | 8 |
| Figure Weights | 7 | Figure Weights | 9 |
| **WISC-V Working Memory Index** | **71** | **WISC-V Spanish Working Memory Index** | 67 |
| Digit Span | 5 | Digit Span | 4 |
| Picture Span | 4 | Picture Span | 3 |
| **TOD-C (INITIAL ENGLISH ADMINISTRATION)** | | **TOD-C (ADMINISTERED VIA INTERPRETER IN SPANISH)** | |
| **Rapid Automatized Naming** | **66** | **Rapid Automatized Naming** | **74** |
| Rapid Letter Naming | 69 | Rapid Letter Naming | 75 |
| Rapid Number and Letter Naming | 67 | Rapid Number and Letter Naming | 71 |

on the WISC-V FRI where in English she initially had a SS = 82, her Spanish performance improved to SS = 92 and well into the average range. It is highly unlikely that Maria's score of 92 is invalid given that guessing, chance, or practice effects play almost no role in obtaining an average or higher score on the types of tests she was administered. Whereas her ability may even be higher, it clearly cannot be lower and therefore, the validity of the original score of 82 in English is disconfirmed, and her *Gf* abilities must be viewed as intact or even average, whether or not the new score in Spanish is used in lieu of the invalid score in English.

In summary, Maria's performance reveals only two likely areas of true weakness, *Gwm* and *Gr*. Had the results not been analyzed via the C-LIM, it is likely that she may have been viewed as having at least 3 areas of deficit (*Gc* included) and possibly even four if *Gf* were so interpreted. Such a pattern would have likely led to hypotheses along the lines of intellectual disability or failed attempts to identify specific learning disability due to inadequate overall general ability. Nevertheless, there remains an additional layer of validity evidence necessary to support a learning disability in particular that comes from examination of overall ecological validity and the relationship between established cognitive deficits and measured academic difficulties.

**DON'T FORGET**

The purpose of follow-up testing in the heritage language is not so much to generate new scores as it is to provide cross-linguistic confirmatory evidence that the original scores in English are likely valid. For this reason, differences in how follow-up evaluation occurs (e.g., bilingual evaluator, use of an interpreter, etc.) and strict adherence to standardize protocol are less important than when testing in English.

### Issues in PSW Analysis for SLD with Multilinguals

There are various procedures that are commonly used for identification of SLD and other disabilities. In all cases, however, academic performance must be viewed as the likely manifestations of underlying or latent cognitive weaknesses or else no causal explanation can be given. X-BASS approaches SLD identification in particular via an approach rooted in patterns of strengths and weaknesses, called the "Dual-Discrepancy/Consistency" model. One major component of the model is "consistency" which is the term that captures the relationship between cognitive and academic abilities. How X-BASS operationalizes this concept and the manner in which it assists with SLD identification has been described in detail in other chapters of this edition (e.g., Chapters 3–5) and will not be repeated here. However, it is important to highlight how X-BASS continues to support evaluation of multilinguals with respect to SLD identification in ways that serve to enhance as well as protect them from what can be discriminatory practices.

In X-BASS, the PSW Data tab where scores are brought together for the purposes of conducting PSW and other SLD identification procedures. It is automatically populated with the appropriate results when the transfer is initiated from the Data Enty tab via the "PSW ANALYSES" button. Additional data and scores can also be transferred from the XBA tab so that any XBA or alternative composites that may have been formed can also be utilized in PSW analyses. Although not discussed previously, follow-up testing in the heritage language of an area of weakness found in English should not occur until the composite has been satisfactorily found to be cohesive. In the event that the composite is not cohesive, the principles of XBA should be utilized first, as described in Chapter 1, to establish that the construct is a good measure of what it is intended to measure prior to engaging in re-testing in the heritage language. As before, whatever the constellation of tests used to establish the composite in English the same ones should also be re-administered in the necessary manner when conducting follow-up evaluation in the heritage language. This step was not necessary in Maria's case but should not be overlooked in situations where it is necessary. All composites should then be transferred to the PSW Data tab for examination prior to running PSW Analyses. Results from the aggregation of the composite and academic subtests generated in Maria's case (with the "SHOW DETAILS" option toggled) are shown below in Figure 8.21.

The results shown in Figure 8.21 have been modified temporarily by indicating in the MUL Case selection box that Maria is NOT a multilingual, when, of course, she is. This was done deliberately to highlight the manner in which X-BASS automates handling of data obtained from testing of multilinguals. When a case is not indicated as involving a multilingual, as above, designations for composites can only be either "weakness" or "strength" for the purpose of PSW analysis. Scores that are over 90 are automatically indicated as strengths and scores lower than 80 are automatically indicated as weaknesses. Score between 80 and 89 inclusive are highlighted in yellow (e.g., WISC-V Fluid Reasoning, SS = 82) as it is not appropriate for X-BASS to make what is essentially a clinical determination that can only be accomplished by the examiner. When a case does involve a multilingual, like Maria, this would have already been indicated when the case record was created and the degree of difference would be reflected here or as updated via the TPE. Even if it had not been done prior, it can actually be so indicated on this tab and either way, X-BASS will implement the protections for multilinguals and the results of the same data for Maria would instead look slightly different as showing in Figure 8.22.

Previously, the WISC-V VCI was indicated as a weakness, which would be true if Maria were a monolingual English speaker. She is not, and when so indicated the degree of difference indicator is now visible along with the lavender TPE navigation button as a multilingual, and more importantly, her performance on the WISC-V VCI and the WISC-V FRI are correctly identified as being "EXPECTED." This designation is now used in X-BASS to denote a score or value from testing in which the magnitude is below the normative average range but which falls within the "expected" range of performance for multilinguals with backgrounds corresponding to the selected or indicated degree of difference. Contrast this designation with the one for the Ortiz PVAT score and the

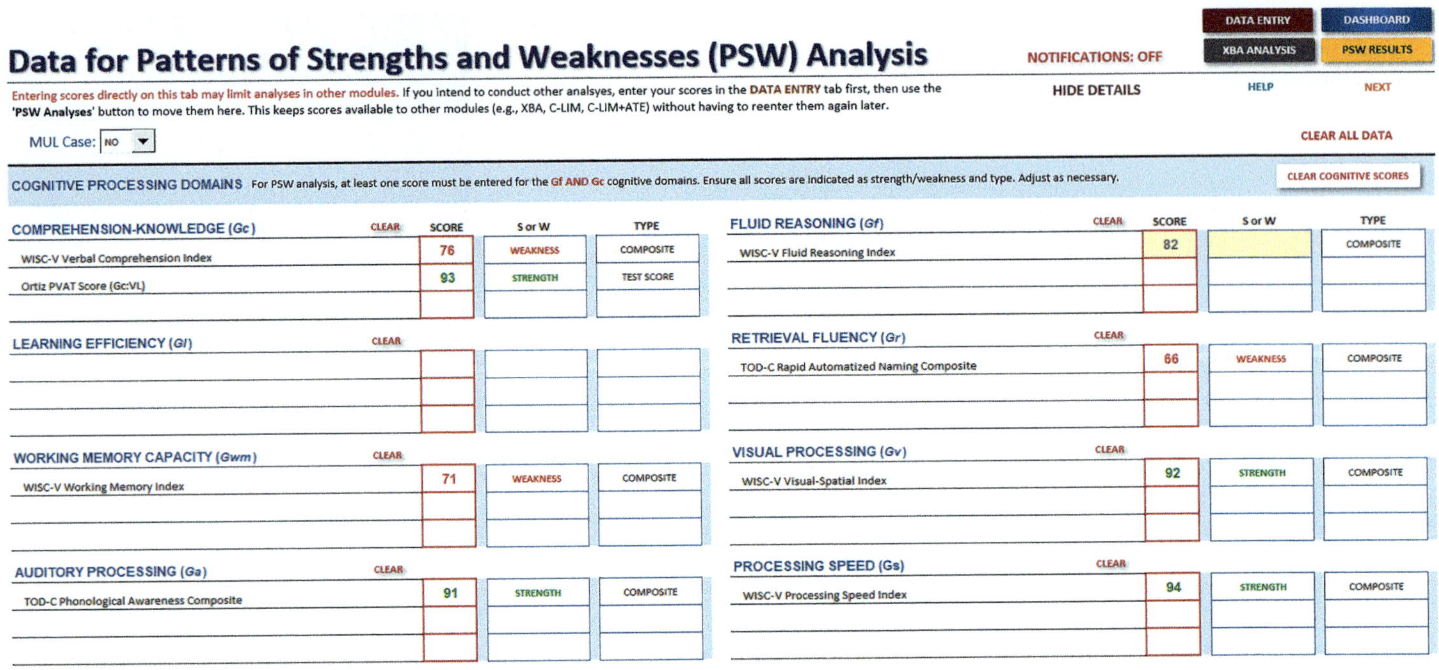


**FIGURE 8.21 PSW Data Tab Results Indicating Non-Multilingual Status**

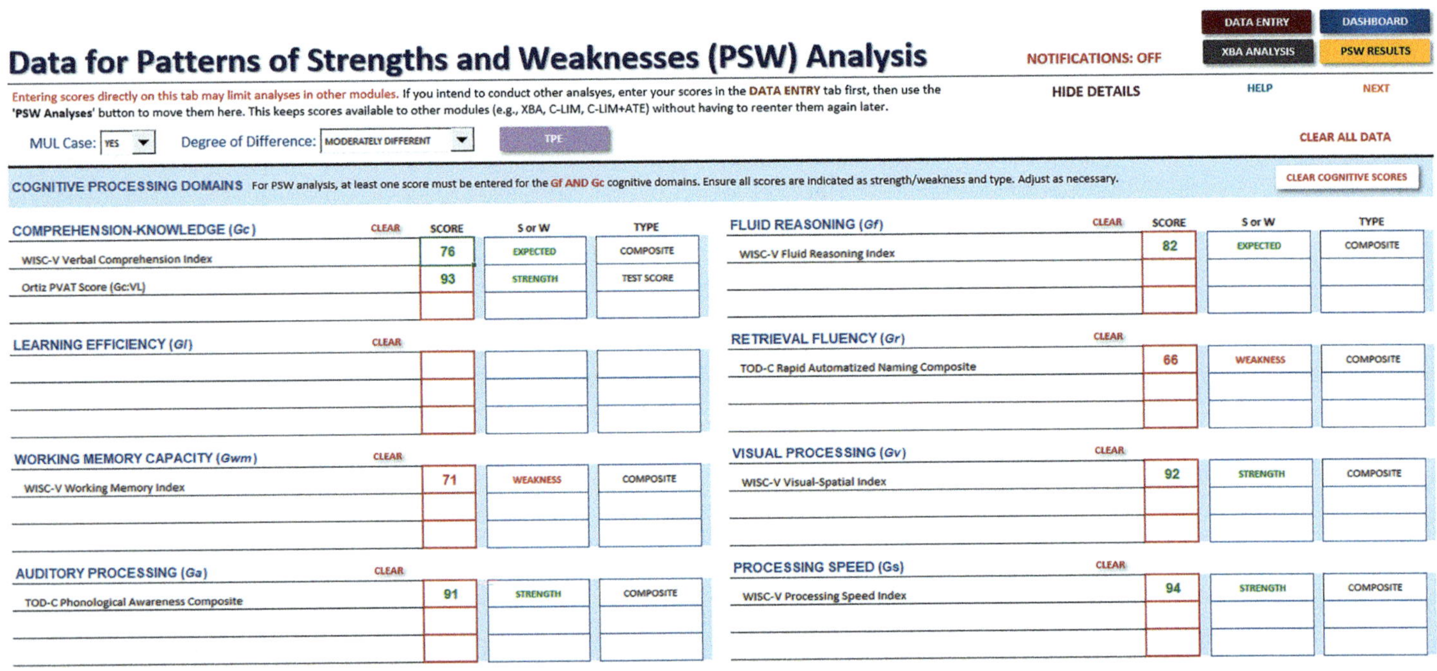


**FIGURE 8.22 PSW Data Tab Results Indicating Multilingual Status**

distinction between how scores are labeled and treated is further refined. Because the Ortiz PVAT may be interpreted as is, it can and should only be designated as a strength or weakness based on the same criteria used for any other score. There is no need for it to be marked as expected since it validly indicates strength or weakness (or as may also be determined by the evaluator in cases where it the score is between SS = 80 and 89). This highlights the ease and simplicity with which scores that are controlled on the basis of language exposure provide outright validity and obviate the need to be careful and deliberate when interpreting meaning or conducting additional analyses such as PSW.

In this case, X-BASS has determined that the VCI is within the expected range and marked it so that subsequent PSW analysis handles the score in a proper manner that prevents problems such as attenuation of the FCC, lack of sufficiency regarding overall ability, identification as a weakness when it is not a weakness, and so forth. In earlier versions of X-BASS, this feature was only partially implemented and did not apply to all of the domains. Now, X-BASS can automatically handle and assign the correct designation for the purpose of PSW to any score within any cognitive domain. This is evident in the WISC-V Fluid Reasoning score as well. When viewed as a monolingual case in Figure 8.21, the score was questionable and needed input from the evaluator to establish it as a strength or weakness. When indicated to be a multilingual case, X-BASS automatically identifies and marks the score as expected so that it is handled properly and to prevent possible discriminatory actions.

**DON'T FORGET**

Marking scores as "EXPECTED" is crucial to nondiscriminatory evaluation. When scores in a multilingual case are marked as "EXPECTED," X-BASS takes steps to prevent them from adversely and unfairly affecting PSW analysis. This also avoids the problem with older versions of X-BASS where practitioners have had to engage in arguments regarding why a low score (e.g., SS = 76) has been marked as a "strength."

From this point forward, any PSW analyses that are performed with X-BASS will proceed in the same manner using the same rules, principles, and calculations as are used when working with monolinguals. Therefore, there is no need to repeat that process since it has already been outlined and discussed at length in Chapter 2. On the SLD tab, X-BASS also provides a section for indicating whether any of the exclusionary factors applicable in SLD identification are primary, contributory, or not applicable (Whittaker & Ortiz, 2019). In the case of Maria, language and acculturative knowledge differences were ruled out as being the primary determinants of her performance and were insufficient to account for the difficulties she is displaying in school. Her reading and writing difficulties (although to be fair, more likely her reading comprehension difficulties) appear to be attributable much more to deficits in *Gwm* and *Gr* than to these differences. Therefore, all other factors are either not present or "N/A" or "contributory" at best, none of which prevents or undermines identification of SLD that seems to be appropriate in Maria's case. Conversely, any time any factor is indicated on the SLD tab to be the primary reason why an individual is displaying the academic problems that led to the referral for evaluation, it will result in a report summary that strongly suggests identification of SLD may be precluded (Ortiz & Walsh, 2024).

This conclusion is supported by the PSW Analyzer where the results shown in Figure 8.23 that there is a "moderate" relationship between the WISC-V Working Memory Index (WMI; SS = 71) as the cognitive weakness and WIAT-4 Reading Comprehension (RDC; SS = 67) as the academic weakness.

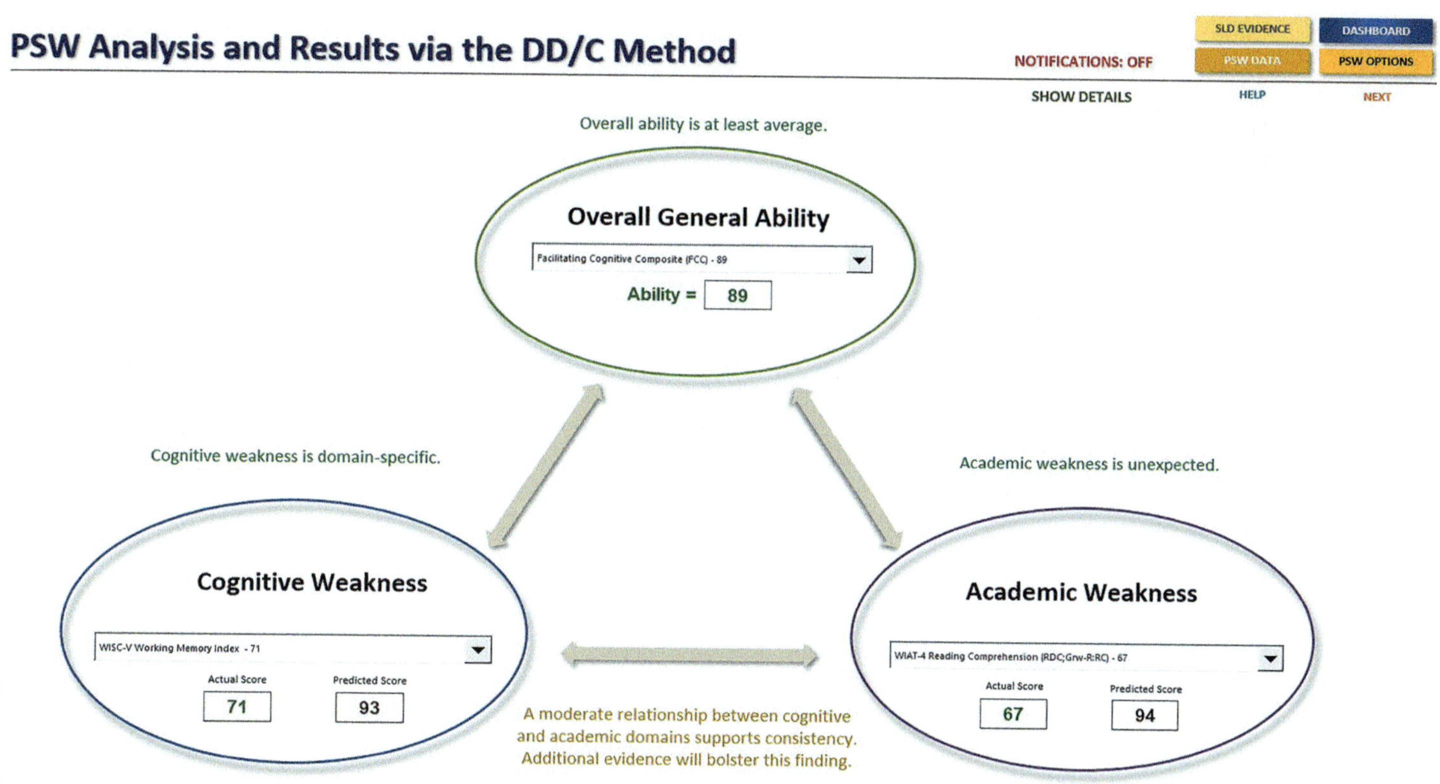


**FIGURE 8.23 PSW Analyzer with Moderate Relationship**

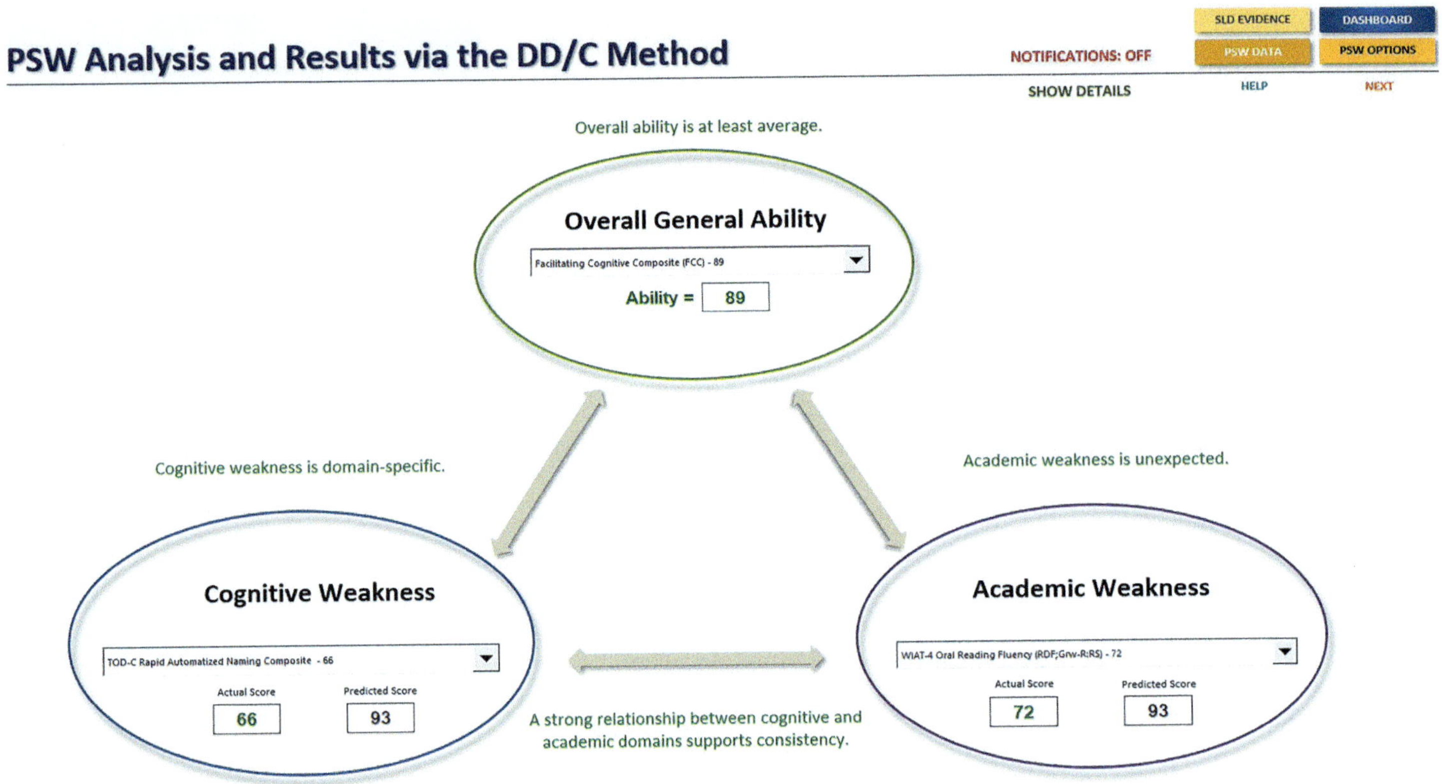


**FIGURE 8.24 PSW Analyzer with High Relationship**

In similar fashion, when the selected cognitive weakness is changed to the TOD-C Rapid Automatized Naming Composite (*Gr*; SS = 66) and the academic weakness is selected to be WIAT-4 Oral Reading Fluency (RDF; SS = 72), the relationship increases and becomes "high" demonstrating the type of ecological validity that supports SLD identification (see Figure 8.24).

> **CAUTION**
>
> The new SLD evidence tab permits users to indicate whether one or more exclusionary factors are "primary," "contributory," or "not applicable." In cases where the C-LIM analysis suggests that the results are "typical," the selection for cultural/linguistic factors should be marked as "primary." Such indications will be summarized in the Evaluation of SLD Evidence report that can be generated on the tab.

## SUMMARY

It was stated at the outset that X-BASS and its constituent modules (i.e., C-LIM, C-LIM+ATE, TPE) are not designed to be and do not constitute a comprehensive framework for full nondiscriminatory assessment. Taken together, they do, however, assist greatly in engaging in the process of true peer comparison and addressing the most central problem in evaluation of multilinguals—test score validity. Previous versions of X-BASS have always attempted to support evaluation of multilinguals to the maximum extent possible. The current version of X-BASS not only continues this support but integrates fully throughout all of the modules and analyses and incorporates protections designed to prevent inadvertent decisions and mistakes in the way that scores are handled and interpreted. In addition, development and inclusion of the CHC Domain graph and the Test Composite graph elevate the utility of X-BASS and C-LIM in ways that are consonant with how psychologists practice and interpret their data also facilitating the process and making it simpler and easier overall. Practitioners who follow best practice in nondiscriminatory assessment can now engage in a framework that is easily replicable, systematic, and founded on evidence-based procedures that assist in creating defensible evaluations and the validity of any conclusions and opinions that may be rendered.

## TEST YOURSELF

1. **The primary goal of evaluating culturally and linguistically diverse examinees is to determine whether test scores are valid indicators of ability. True or False?**
2. **What is the primary purpose of the Culture-Language Interpretive Matrix (C-LIM)?**
   (a) To diagnose learning disabilities
   (b) To estimate intelligence in multilingual students
   (c) To evaluate the potential impact of linguistic and acculturative factors on test performance
   (d) To determine eligibility for special education
3. **Which of the following must be established before interpreting test performance for multilingual individuals?**
   (a) Degree of difference from the normative sample
   (b) Opportunities for linguistic and acculturative knowledge acquisition
   (c) Language exposure history
   (d) All of the above
4. **The True Peer Estimator (TPE) was developed to:**
   (a) Replace the C-LIM
   (b) Estimate the examinee's degree of linguistic and acculturative difference
   (c) Measure academic achievement
   (d) Determine IQ
5. **When using the C-LIM, performance is considered typical when:**
   (a) Scores follow a declining pattern across the matrix
   (b) Scores fall within the expected range
   (c) There is no significant score variability within cells
   (d) All of the above
6. **The C-LIM+ATE was developed primarily to evaluate:**
   (a) Cognitive test scores
   (b) Academic achievement scores
   (c) Behavioral ratings
   (d) Language proficiency
7. **In X-BASS, scores that are below the normative average range but which fall within the typical range for multilingual examinees may be marked as:**
   (a) Strength
   (b) Weakness
   (c) Expected
   (d) Average
8. **Which of the following graphs allows practitioners to examine performance organized according to CHC broad ability while considering the impact of linguistic and acculturative variables**
   (a) Culture-Language graph
   (b) CHC Domain graph
   (c) Test Composite graph
   (d) C-LIM Summary graph
9. **When the obtained score and expected score bands overlap on the CHC Domain graph, performance is considered:**
   (a) Atypical
   (b) Deficient
   (c) Typical for the examinee's degree of difference
   (d) Evidence of a disability
10. **Academic test results alone cannot determine the presence of a disability because they indicate what a student can do, but not why the difficulty occurs. True or False?**

*Answers:* 1. True; 2. c; 3. d; 4. b; 5. d; 6. b; 7. c; 8. b; 9. c; 10. True

## REFERENCES


Calderón-Tena, C. O., Styck, K. M., Vega, D., & Kranzler, J. H. (2022). Evaluating cultural and linguisticload of IQ scores for English language learners. *International Journal of School and Educational Psychology, 10*(1), 46–62. https://doi.org/10.1080/21683603.2020.1803164.

Cormier, D. C., McGrew, K. S., & Ysseldyke, J. E. (2014). The influences of linguistic demand and cultural loading on cognitive test scores. *Journal of Psychoeducational Assessment, 32*(7), 610–623.

Cormier, D. C., Bulut, O., McGrew, K. S., & Kennedy, K. (2022). Linguistic influences on cognitive test performance: Examinee characteristics are more important than test characteristics. *Journal of Intelligence, 10*(1), Advance online copy: https://www.mdpi.com/2079-3200/10/1/8.

Dynda, A. M. (2008). *The relation between language proficiency and IQ test performance.* Unpublished manuscript. St. John's University.

Figueroa, R., & A., & Newsome, P. (2006). The diagnosis of LD in English learners: Is it nondiscriminatory? *Journal of Learning Disabilities, 39*, 206–214.

Flanagan, D. P., & Ortiz, S. O. (2001). *Essentials of cross-battery assessment* (1st ed). Wiley Press.

Flanagan, D. P., Ortiz, S. O., & Alfonso, V. C. (2007). *Essentials of cross-battery assessment* (2nd ed). Wiley Press.

Flanagan, D. P., Ortiz, S. O., & Alfonso, V. C. (2013). *Essentials of cross-battery assessment* (3rd ed). Wiley Press.

Individuals with Disabilities Education Act. (2007), 20 U.S.C. § 1400

Ortiz, S. O. (2001). Assessment of cognitive abilities in Hispanic children. *Seminars in Speech and Language, 22*(1), 17–37.

Ortiz, S. O. (2017). Evaluation of English learners: Issues in measurement, interpretation and reporting. *The Score, APA Division 5 (Quantitative and Qualitative Methods) Newsletter*, January 2017. Available at. https://www.apadivisions.org/division-5/publications/score/2017/01/english-learners.aspx.

Ortiz, S. O. (2018). *Ortiz picture vocabulary acquisition test (Ortiz PVAT).* Multi-Health Systems, Toronto, Canada.

Ortiz, S. O. (2019). On the measurement of cognitive abilities in English learners. *Contemporary School Psychology, 23*(1), 68–86. https://doi.org/10.1007/s40688-018-0208-8.

Ortiz, S. O. (2022). Diverse Student True Peer Group Estimator (D-STPGE). An automated, Excel-based program for determining degree of difference. Available freely at:. https://facpub.stjohns.edu/~ortizs/CLIM/

Ortiz, S. O. (2023). Best practices in nondiscriminatory assessment. In A. Thomas & P. Harrison (Eds.), *Best practices in school psychology VII.* National Association of School Psychologists.

Ortiz, S. O., & Cehelyk, S. K. (2024). The bilingual is not two monolinguals of same age: Normative testing implications for multilinguals. *Journal of Intelligence, 12*(1), 3 https://doi.org/10.3390/jintelligence12010003.

Ortiz, S. O., & Oganes, M. (2022). Multicultural issues in school neuropsychology. In D. Miller (Ed.), *Nondiscriminatory, cross-cultural school neuropsychological assessment* (pp. 41–64). Wiley & Sons, Inc., New Jersey.

Ortiz, S. O., McGrew, K. S., & Flanagan, D. P. (1998). Gf-Gc cross-battery interpretation and selective cross-battery assessment: Referral concerns and the needs of culturally and linguistically diverse populations. In K. S. McGrew & D. P. Flanagan (Eds.), *The Intelligence Test Desk Reference (ITDR): Gf-Gc Cross-Battery Assessment* (pp. 401–444). Allyn & Bacon, Boston.

Ortiz, S. O., & Pristo, L. J. (2023, February). *Evaluation of SLD in English learners: Visualizing normal ability via Cattell-Horn-Carroll domain-level analysis.* In *Learning disabilities association of America 60th International Conference, Las Vegas, NV.*

Ortiz, S. O., & Walsh, O. A. (2024). effective writing about multicultural individuals: False caution vs. true discretion. In R. Flanagan (Ed.), *Clinical guide to effective psychological assessment and report writing* (pp. 95–114). Springer. https://doi.org/10.1007/978-3-031-67184-5_6.

Ortiz, S. O., & Wong, J. Y. T. (2020a). Psychoeducational assessment of culturally and linguistically diverse preschool children. In V. C. Alfonso, B. A. Bracken, & R. J. Nagle (Eds.), *Psychoeducational assessment of preschool children* (pp. 346–364). Routledge.

Ortiz, S. O., & Wong, J. Y. T. (2020b, October). *Fairness in tests and test score interpretation with English learners.* The Score Retrieved from https://www.apadivisions.org/division-5/publications/score/2020/10/assessing-english-learners.

Ortiz, S. O., & Wong, J. Y. T. (2022). Addressing theoretical, empirical, and practical deficiencies when testing English learners. In K. Geisinger & J. Jonson (Eds.), *Fairness in educational and psychological testing: Examining theoretical, research, practice, and policy implications of 2014 Standards.* American Educational Research Association.

Pristo, L. J., & Ortiz, S. O. (2023, February). *Assessing domain level performance impact for diverse students: Evaluation of cultural-linguistic factors on score validity at the level of broad CHC ability constructs.* National Association of School Psychologists, Denver, CO.

Pristo, L., & Ortiz, S. O. (2022). *Learning disability identification with English learners: An evidence-based approach for evaluating measurement validity and examining exclusionary factors in the identification of SLD.* In *Learning disabilities association of America, Science 2 Practice Conference, New Orleans, LA.*

Pristo. L. (in press). *The objective measurement of cultural-linguistic impact on cognitive ability scores.* In L. Suzuki, S. Ortiz, & V. Alfonso (Eds.), Special Issue on Culture and Testing, Journal of Intelligence.

Rhodes, R., Ochoa, S. H., & Ortiz, S. O. (2005). *Assessing culturally and linguistically diverse students: A practical guide.* The Guilford Press.

Schneider, W. J., & McGrew, K. S. (2018). The Cattell–Horn–Carroll theory of cognitive abilities. In D. P. Flanagan & E. M. McDonough (Eds.), *Contemporary intellectual assessment: Theories, tests, and issues* (pp. 73–163). The Guilford Press.

Sotelo-Dynega, M., Ortiz, S. O., Flanagan, D. P., & Chaplin, W. (2013). *English language proficiency and test performance: evaluation of bilinguals with the Woodcock-Johnson III tests of cognitive ability. Psychology in the Schools, 50*(8), 781–797.

Styck, K. M., & Watkins, M. W. (2013). Diagnostic utility of the culture-language interpretive matrix for the Wechsler intelligence scales for children—Fourth Edition among Referred Students. *School Psychology Review, 42*(4), 367–382.

Styck, K. M., & Watkins, M. W. (2014). Discriminant validity of the WISC-IV culture-language interpretive matrix. *Contemporary School Psychology, 18*, 168–177.

Thomas, W.P., & Collier, V.P.1997*)*. School effectiveness for language minority students. National Clearinghouse for English Language Acquisition (NCELA) Resource Collection Series, No. 9, December 1997 .

Thomas, W. P., & Collier, V. P. (2002). *A national study of school effectiveness for language minority students' long-term academic achievement.* Center for Research on Education, Diversity and Excellence, University of California-Santa Cruz, Santa Cruz, CA.

Valdés, G., & Figueroa, R. A. (1994). *Bilingualism and testing: A special case of bias.* Ablex.

Whittaker, M., & Ortiz, S. O. (2019). *Exclusionary factors—what a specific learning disability is not: Examining exclusionary factors.* National Center for Learning Disabilities Available at https://www.ncld.org/wp-content/uploads/2019/09/What-a-Specific-Learning-Disability-Is-Not-Examining-Exclusionary-Factors.pdf.

Wong, J. Y. T. (2023). On the Importance of True Peer Norms in the Assessment of English Learners: A validation study of the Ortiz Picture Vocabulary Acquisition Test. Unpublished manuscript. St. John's University

Nine

# THE COGNITIVE PROFILES OF STUDENTS WITH READING AND MATH LEARNING DIFFICULTIES AND CORRESPONDING EVIDENCE-BASED INTERVENTIONS

Peng Peng, Ph.D.

The University of Texas at Austin

## THE COGNITIVE PROFILES AND INTERVENTIONS FOR STUDENTS WITH LEARNING DIFFICULTIES

Learning difficulties in reading (RD) and mathematics (MD), along with comorbid challenges in both areas (RDMD), are among the most common and impactful obstacles faced by students in educational settings. These difficulties often stem from complex cognitive profiles. Understanding the cognitive challenges is crucial for accurate diagnosis, tailored intervention, and effective instructional design. This appendix synthesizes recent findings on the cognitive profiles of students with RD, MD, and RDMD, identifies instructional approaches tailored to these profiles, and explores innovative strategies that integrate cognitive training into academic instruction.

## COGNITIVE PROFILES OF LEARNING DISABILITIES

The research studies collectively underscore the significance of cognitive abilities and processes in identifying students with reading or math difficulties. For RD, Peng et al. (2022) conducted a meta-analysis of 378 studies. Results suggested that compared to typically developing (TD) peers, individuals with RD exhibited deficits in processing speed, short-term memory, attention, working memory, inhibition, switching, visuospatial skills, and updating. RD profiles also showed greater individual differences in inhibition, processing speed, switching, attention, visuospatial skills, and short-term memory compared to TD peers, while minimal individual variability was observed for working memory and updating. Cognitive deficits in RD were more severe with age, verbal task materials, and lower IQ or reading scores used during identification. Furthermore, the use of comprehensive/nonverbal IQ measures and reading comprehension measures for identification increased individual variability. Mediation analysis revealed that cognition, executive function, and visuospatial skills uniquely contributed to the differences between RD and TD even after controlling for phonological processing and language comprehension. However, phonological processing and language comprehension accounted for over 70% of the variance in cognitive differences between RD and TD across all cognitive skills.

Peng et al. (2018) conducted a meta-analysis of 75 cognitive profiling studies on students with MD. Results showed that MD are associated with deficits across cognitive domains, with the most severe deficits observed in phonological processing, processing speed, and working memory; MD identified through word problem-solving difficulties showed less severe deficits in phonological processing, working memory, and executive functions compared to those identified with calculation difficulties or comprehensive MD. The domain of tasks influenced processing speed and working memory deficits, which were most severe in the numerical domain among individuals with MD. The severity of MD was significantly linked only to the severity of processing speed deficits. Age affected deficits in phonological processing and attention, with younger individuals with MD exhibiting more severe deficits in these areas than older individuals.

Viesel-Nordmeyer et al. (2023) conducted a meta-analysis of 74 studies to investigate the cognitive profiles with a focus on students with RDMD. Results suggested that the cognitive profiles of RDMD presented an additive pattern for domain-specific deficits (reading and math skills) but an under-additive pattern for domain-general deficits like executive functions. This highlights how comorbid conditions interact to create unique cognitive challenges, differing from isolated learning disabilities. The findings also revealed specific areas of difficulty, such as phonological processing for reading and symbolic tasks for math, which can inform the diagnostic processes for RDMD.

Taken together, the cognitive profiles of students with RD, MD, or RDMD share similarities but also exhibit distinct patterns. All three groups demonstrate deficits in processing speed, working memory, attention, short-term memory, executive functions, and visuospatial skills compared to TD peers. For RD, cognitive deficits seem more severe with age and verbal tasks. There is also greater individual variability with age and with nonverbal task materials. Language explains a significant portion of cognitive differences between RD and TD, but executive functions and visuospatial skills also uniquely contribute to RD even after controlling for language skills. For MD, deficits of processing speed and working memory seem the core deficits. Phonological processing and attention deficits are more severe in younger individuals, while processing speed and working memory deficits are most pronounced in numerical tasks. MD profiles also vary by screening type, with more severe deficits in calculation-based or comprehensive MD compared to word problem-solving MD. RDMD presents a unique cognitive profile characterized by additive deficits in domain-specific skills (reading and math) and under-additive deficits in domain-general skills like executive functions. Phonological processing for reading and symbolic reasoning for math emerge as distinct challenges in RDMD. These findings emphasize the importance of tailored diagnostic approaches and interventions that address shared and specific cognitive challenges across RD, MD, and RDMD profiles.

## INSTRUCTION

### Compensation Approach

The most common and popular instruction designed based on the cognitive profile of students with learning difficulties is the compensation approach, where explicit instruction is adopted to reduce the cognitive load of learning. Based on What Works Clearinghouse practice guide for students with MD by Fuchs et al. (2021), instruction should be systematic, structured, and scaffolded. Specifically, instruction should start teaching concepts in a logical, step-by-step progression, building on prior knowledge and ensuring clear connections between previously learned and new material. Regularly review and reinforce past lessons alongside introducing new content to solidify retention and understanding. Employ concrete-to-abstract progression, starting with accessible numbers and visual aids like manipulatives to establish a strong foundational understanding before transitioning to abstract representations such as equations. Use multiple representations—concrete, semiconcrete, and abstract—and explicitly link visual tools like number lines or fraction tiles to mathematical symbols to bridge comprehension gaps. Teach precise mathematical language with accessible definitions and consistently reinforce its use to support clear communication and deeper understanding. For word problems, break them into manageable parts and provide explicit strategies for identifying relevant information and solving problems, ensuring students grasp the mathematical relationships involved. Incorporate short, focused fluency activities to develop automaticity in basic arithmetic, reducing cognitive load and enabling students to focus on more complex problem-solving tasks. Immediate feedback throughout the process helps correct misconceptions and refine understanding, ensuring a supportive learning environment.

Based on What Works Clearinghouse practice guide for students with RD by Gersten et al. (2009), reading instruction should also be explicit, systematic, and closely aligned with students' needs. Specifically, instruction should begin with universal screening to identify students at risk for reading challenges. Use the results to group students for differentiated instruction that targets their specific skill levels. Instruction should prioritize foundational reading skills such as phonemic awareness, phonics, fluency, vocabulary, and comprehension, and these should be taught incrementally, starting with the basics and building toward more complex skills. Small-group settings are ideal, with regular sessions (20–40 minutes, 3–5 times a week) to ensure focused, personalized teaching. Teachers should provide clear, step-by-step demonstrations, frequent opportunities for guided practice, and immediate, specific feedback. Emphasizing active teacher–student interactions and using systematic curricula help reduce cognitive load, enabling students to master individual skills before integrating them. For students showing minimal progress in these settings, daily intensive instruction with individualized support and extended practice opportunities can further reinforce learning and help overcome persistent challenges.

Taken together, the compensation instruction approach for RD and MD shares similarities in emphasizing explicit, systematic, and scaffolded teaching to address the cognitive challenges. Instruction aims to reduce cognitive load by breaking complex tasks into manageable components, ensuring a logical progression of skills, and providing ample opportunities for guided practice and immediate feedback. For RD, instruction that focuses on foundational reading skills, including phonemic awareness, phonics, fluency, vocabulary, and reading comprehension, taught incrementally to build toward reading comprehension. Small-group settings and differentiated instruction tailored to students' specific needs are central, with more intensive, individualized support recommended for students who demonstrate minimal progress. In contrast, for MD, the use of visual aids and multiple representations in instruction is more pronounced than in RD instruction, reflecting the need to bridge abstract mathematical concepts with tangible understanding. Regular review, reinforcement, and precise mathematical language also play crucial roles, alongside strategies for tackling word problems and developing arithmetic fluency to reduce cognitive demands.

### Integrated Approach

In addition to the compensation instruction approach, recent studies advocate for integrating cognitive skills directly into academic instruction for students with learning difficulties. This approach is grounded in the domain-specific hypothesis of cognition, which posits that cognition is not solely a domain-general construct but also functions in domain-specific ways. According to this perspective, the effectiveness of cognitive skills in learning is influenced by their connection to domain-specific knowledge (Doebel, 2020; Peng & Swanson, 2022; Peng et al., 2022). The closer the bond between cognition and domain-specific knowledge, the more significant the role of cognition in facilitating learning.

Several studies explore how domain-specific cognition may be uniquely contributing to academic learning. For example, Cartwright et al. (2010) investigated the development of graphophonological-semantic cognitive flexibility, an executive function critical for processing phonological and semantic aspects of print, and its unique contribution to reading comprehension in beginning readers. The study compared this reading-specific cognitive flexibility to general cognitive flexibility assessed through color-shape sorting tasks among 1st and 2nd graders. Results showed that 2nd graders outperformed 1st graders on both tasks, reflecting developmental progression. However, performance on graphophonological-semantic tasks was significantly lower than on color-shape tasks, indicating the greater challenge posed by domain-specific cognitive flexibility. Additionally, reading experience, as measured by print exposure, uniquely predicted graphophonological-semantic flexibility beyond age and general cognitive flexibility. Hierarchical regression analyses revealed that graphophonological-semantic flexibility contributed unique variance to reading comprehension after controlling for phonological and semantic processing, age, and general cognitive flexibility. This highlights the specificity of graphophonological-semantic flexibility to reading tasks. Importantly, print exposure did not mediate this relationship, emphasizing the independent role of this executive function in reading development. These findings suggest that interventions targeting graphophonological-semantic flexibility could enhance reading comprehension, particularly for beginning and struggling readers, by improving their ability to flexibly integrate phonological and semantic features of print.

More recently, Peng et al. (2024) investigated the distinct contributions of domain-general, behavioral, and reading-specific executive functions to reading comprehension in 4th and 5th graders and explored whether foundational literacy skills (reading fluency and vocabulary) mediate and moderate relationships between executive functions with reading comprehension. Guided by the context-specific theory of executive function, the authors hypothesized that reading-specific executive function, which integrates domain-general executive function and reading-specific processes, would be particularly crucial for reading comprehension. Results showed that while all types of executive function explained variance in reading comprehension independently, only behavioral executive function and reading-specific executive function uniquely contributed when controlling for foundational literacy skills. Reading fluency and vocabulary partially mediated the relationship between reading-specific executive function and reading comprehension. Moderation analyses indicated that reading-specific executive function was more critical for students with lower vocabulary levels. These findings support the context-specific hypothesis, suggesting that executive function tailored to reading processes is more important for reading comprehension than domain-general executive function. The study emphasizes the importance of integrating executive function skills with reading instruction, particularly for students with foundational literacy deficits, offering implications for developing targeted interventions that combine executive function training with literacy skill-building.

Peng and Swanson (2022) reviewed studies that tried to integrate working memory into academic instruction. Specifically, the authors proposed and examined a domain-specific approach to working memory training, emphasizing the integration of working memory training with academic content to enhance educational outcomes. It is suggested that the traditional domain-general working memory training, which focuses on general working memory tasks training and isolated from academic instruction, has shown limited far-transfer effects on academic skills. In contrast, the domain-specific approach incorporates two key components to link working memory training to academic skills: working memory-academic tasks and task-linking strategies. Working memory-academic tasks embed working memory training into meaningful academic activities, such as reading comprehension and mathematical problem-solving.

For example, García-Madruga et al. (2013) embedded working memory tasks within instructional activities. In their study, students participated in tasks such as solving anaphora and analogy problems, requiring them to actively recall and sequence word solutions while also keeping track of dynamically changing information within stories (e.g., tracking race standings or scoreboard scores). This approach produced significant improvements in standardized reading comprehension measures compared to control groups (Cohen's $d$ = .79). Similarly, Fuchs et al. (2018) applied working memory-intensive tasks within reading instruction for struggling 3rd and 5th graders. Examples included a "What If?" task, where students retold stories and adjusted endings, requiring an updating in the working memory; a cloze span task, combining cloze exercises with word recall; and a working memory-main idea task, summarizing and recalling main ideas across paragraphs. These tasks aimed to directly exercise working memory processes relevant to reading. Although effects on standardized measures were not statistically significant, the embedded working memory-training group showed meaningful gains on researcher-developed vocabulary and reading comprehension measures compared to controls, with effect sizes ranging from .31 to 1.46 (Hedges' $g$).

Task-linking strategies complement working memory-academic tasks by teaching students transferable cognitive strategies to manage working memory demands. These include rehearsal (repeating information), chunking (organizing data into manageable units), and retrieval practice (actively recalling information). Studies reviewed in the paper illustrate the effectiveness of these strategies in enhancing both working memory and academic outcomes. Goodrich et al. (2023) demonstrated that preschoolers trained in rehearsal strategies within early literacy tasks showed significant gains in syntax and vocabulary (Hedges' $g$ = .67–1.30). Similarly, Peng and Fuchs (2017) trained first graders in rehearsal strategies using adaptive working memory span tasks, resulting in improved listening comprehension and retell abilities (Hedges' $g$ = .43–.65). These examples underscore the promise of the domain-specific approach in producing meaningful gains in both working memory and academic performance, particularly when tailored to the specific needs and capacities of learners. However, the authors emphasized the need for further randomized controlled trials to validate these findings and refine the approach.

In summary, the integrated approach is rooted in the domain-specific hypothesis of cognition, which suggests that cognitive skills are most effective when closely linked to domain-specific knowledge. Research highlights that reading-specific executive functions play a unique and critical role in reading, surpassing the contributions of foundational literacy and domain-general executive functions among elementary students (Cartwright et al., 2010; Peng et al., 2024). Additionally, intervention studies that integrate working memory and executive function training into academic activities, such as reading comprehension and problem solving, show promising outcomes. These interventions emphasize the importance of designing tasks that simultaneously and explicitly engage both cognitive and academic processes (e.g., working memory-main tasks). Furthermore, incorporating task-linking strategies, such as rehearsal, chunking, and retrieval practice, complements cognitive-academic tasks and enhances their effectiveness.

Before closing this chapter, the authors of this book asked me to make readers aware of a resource they developed, the Intervention Library (IL®), a multidisciplinary digital tool designed to support evidence-based instructional planning across cognitive and academic domains. Although I have not yet had the opportunity to explore the IL® personally, I want to highlight its availability for practitioners seeking structured, searchable intervention options aligned with students' profiles. Rapid Reference 9.1 provides a brief overview of the IL® system, and Appendices R, S, and T offer sample IL®-generated reports to illustrate the type of intervention suggestions the program produces. These examples are intended to help readers understand how the IL® can be used to translate assessment findings into targeted, actionable instructional supports.

## *Rapid Reference 9.1*

### Overview of the Intervention Library (IL®)

**What the Intervention Library (IL®) Is**

A multidisciplinary digital resource containing 1,000+ strategies, instructional supports, and evidence-based interventions across cognitive, academic, and language domains.

Designed for use by school psychologists, educational diagnosticians, LDTCs, SLPs, special educators, general educators, and private practitioners.

Generates customized intervention reports tailored to a student's profile.

**IL® allows users to search interventions by:**

**1. *Cognitive Domain***

Includes:

- *Gf* (Fluid Reasoning)
- *Gc* (Comprehension Knowledge)
- *Gwm* (Working Memory)
- *Gs* (Processing Speed)
- *Gr* (Retrieval Fluency)
- *Ga* (Auditory Processing; PA/phonemic awareness)
- *Gv* (Visual Processing)
- OP (Orthographic Processing)

**2. *Academic Skills by IDEA SLD Area***

- Basic Reading Skills
- Reading Fluency
- Reading Comprehension
- Math Calculation
- Math Problem Solving
- Written Expression
- Oral Expression
- Listening Comprehension

**3. *Intervention Type***

- Instructional (teaching procedures and techniques)
- Environmental (supports in the learning setting)
- Curricular (materials and resources)
- Remedial Programs (targeted skill remediation)
- Skill-Building Techniques (practice and development)
- Compensatory Strategies (supports to minimize the impact of weaknesses)

**4. *Grade Level and Delivery Method***

- Early Elementary, Middle School, High School
- Individual, Small Group, or Whole Class

**Key Features**

- Provides practical, evidence-based prereferral recommendations.
- Includes links to tools, templates, organizers, games, and instructional supports.
- Helps teams differentiate instruction, design IEPs/504s, and support RTI/MTSS implementation.
- All content areas reviewed by leading experts.
- Includes interventions reviewed by the Institute of Education Sciences (IES).

**Why IL® Matters for Practitioners**

- Connects assessment results to actionable instructional planning.
- Supports cognitive-aligned intervention selection, consistent with the DD/C method.
- Helps practitioners move from classification or diagnosis to targeted intervention with precision and efficiency.

## TEST YOURSELF

**1. Research indicates that students with RD, MD, and RDMD often demonstrate weaknesses across multiple cognitive domains. True or False?**

**2. According to meta-analytic research, which cognitive processes account for the largest proportion of variance in differences between students with reading difficulties and typically developing peers?**

(a) Visual processing and processing speed
(b) Phonological processing and language comprehension
(c) Working memory and attention
(d) Fluid reasoning and retrieval fluency

**3. Research on MD suggests that the most pronounced cognitive deficits are typically observed in which areas?**

(a) Processing speed and working memory
(b) Crystallized knowledge and vocabulary
(c) Visual processing and reasoning
(d) Auditory processing and phonological awareness

**4. Students with RDMD often show additive deficits in domain-specific skills but under-additive patterns in domain-general executive functions. True or False?**

**5. The compensation approach to instruction primarily emphasizes:**

(a) Increasing task difficulty to build resilience
(b) Explicit, systematic, and scaffolded instruction designed to reduce cognitive load
(c) Eliminating the use of visual supports
(d) Teaching cognitive skills separately from academic content

**6. According to What Works Clearinghouse practice guides, effective reading instruction should prioritize which foundational skills?**

(a) Phonemic awareness, phonics, fluency, vocabulary, and comprehension
(b) Reasoning, vocabulary, and general intelligence
(c) Grammar, spelling, and handwriting
(d) Visual processing and working memory

**7. Instruction for students with mathematics difficulties often emphasizes the use of multiple representations (e.g., manipulatives, visual models, and equations) to help students connect concrete and abstract concepts. True or False?**

**8. The domain-specific hypothesis of cognition proposes that:**

(a) Cognitive abilities operate independently of academic knowledge

(b) Cognitive skills are most effective when closely linked to domain-specific knowledge and learning tasks

(c) General intelligence explains all academic outcomes

(d) Cognitive training should occur separately from academic instruction

**9. Research on integrated interventions suggests that embedding working memory and executive function tasks directly into academic activities can improve learning outcomes. True or False?**

**10. Examples of task-linking strategies used to support working memory during instruction include:**

(a) Rehearsal, chunking, and retrieval practice

(b) Memorization drills only

(c) Repeating entire lessons verbatim

(d) Eliminating academic tasks that require memory

*Answers:* 1. True; 2. b; 3. a; 4. True; 5. b; 6. a; 7. True; 8. b; 9. True; 10. a

## ACKNOWLEDGMENTS

This research was supported by grants from the Institute of Education Sciences [R324A220268] and the National Science Foundation [2405797].

## REFERENCES

Cartwright, K. B., Marshall, T. R., Dandy, K. L., & Isaac, M. C. (2010). The development of graphophonological-semantic cognitive flexibility and its contribution to reading comprehension in beginning readers. *Journal of Cognition and Development, 11*(1), 61–85. https://doi.org/10.1080/15248370903453584.

Doebel, S. (2020). Rethinking executive function and its development. *Perspectives on Psychological Science, 15*(4), 942–956. https://doi.org/10.1177/1745691620904771.

Fuchs, D., Hendricks, E., Walsh, M. E., Fuchs, L. S., Gilbert, J. K., Patton, S., Zhang-Tracy, W., Davis, N., Elleman, A., & Peng, P. (2018). Evaluating a multi-dimensional reading comprehension program and reconsidering the lowly reputation of tests of near transfer. *Learning Disabilities Research and Practice, 33*, 11–23.

Fuchs, L. S., Fuchs, D., & Compton, D. L. (2021). *Assisting students struggling with mathematics: Intervention in the elementary grades*. In *What works clearinghouse practice guide*. National Center for Education Evaluation and Regional Assistance.

García-Madruga, J. A., Elosúa, M. R., Gil, L., Gómez-Veiga, I., Vila, J. Ó., Orjales, I., . . . Duque, G. (2013). Reading comprehension and working memory's executive processes: An intervention study in primary school students. *Reading Research Quarterly, 48*(2), 155–174. https://doi.org/10.1002/rrq.44.

Gersten, R., Compton, D., Connor, C. M., Dimino, J., Santoro, L., Linan-Thompson, S., & Tilly, W. D. (2009). *Assisting students struggling with reading: Response to intervention and multi-tier intervention for reading in the primary grades*. In *What works clearinghouse practice guide*. National Center for Education Evaluation and Regional Assistance.

Goodrich, J. M., Peng, P., Bohaty, J., Leiva, S., & Thayer, L. (2023). Embedding executive function training into early literacy instruction for dual language learners: A pilot study. *Journal of Speech, Language, and Hearing Research, 66*(2), 573–588. https://doi.org/10.1044/2022_JSLHR-22-00253.

Peng, P., & Fuchs, D. (2017). A randomized control trial of working memory training with and without strategy instruction: Effects on young children's working memory and comprehension. *Journal of Learning Disabilities, 50*(1), 62–80. https://doi.org/10.1177/0022219415594609.

Peng, P., Liu, Y., Cartwright, K., Goodrich, M., Koziol, N., Ma, C., & Whitmarsh, C. (2024). The role of domain-general, behavioral, and reading-specific executive function in reading comprehension: Does context-specific executive function matter? *Scientific Studies of Reading, 28*(6), 713–736. https://doi.org/10.1080/10888438.2024.2409635.

Peng, P., & Swanson, H. L. (2022). The domain-specific approach of working memory training. *Developmental Review, 65*, 101035 https://doi.org/10.1016/j.dr.2022.101035.

Peng, P., Wang, C., & Namkung, J. (2018). Understanding the cognition related to mathematics difficulties: A meta-analysis on the cognitive deficit profiles and the bottleneck theory. *Review of Educational Research, 88*(3), 434–476. https://doi.org/10.3102/0034654317753350.

Peng, P., Zhang, Z., Wang, W., Lee, K., Wang, T., Wang, C., Luo, J., & Lin, J. (2022). A meta-analytic review of cognition and reading difficulties: Individual differences, moderation, and language mediation mechanisms. *Psychological Bulletin, 148*(3–4), 227–272. https://doi.org/10.1037/bul0000361.

Viesel-Nordmeyer, N., Reuber, J., Kuhn, J. T., Moll, K., Holling, H., & Dobel, C. (2023). Cognitive profiles of children with isolated and comorbid learning difficulties in reading and math: A meta-analysis. *Educational Psychology Review, 35*(1), 34 https://doi.org/10.1007/s10648-023-09735-3.

Appendix A

# THE CONTEMPORARY CATTELL-HORN-CARROLL TAXONOMY: BROAD AND NARROW ABILITY DEFINITIONS AND TASK EXAMPLES

The contemporary Cattell-Horn-Carroll taxonomy has evolved over nearly a century of research across scientific disciplines. By the mid-1980s, there was considerable evidence for 8–10 broad cognitive abilities (e.g., Horn & Noll, 1997), including the synthesis of the world's literature on cognitive abilities, presented in the three-stratum theory by Carroll (1993). In the late 1990s, Kevin McGrew conducted analyses to resolve discrepancies between the Cattell-Horn and Carroll models of cognitive ability structure. Based on this research, McGrew (1997) proposed an "integrated" Horn-Cattell *Gf-Gc* and Carroll model that had immediate applicability to test development (e.g., Woodcock-Johnson III; Woodcock, McGrew, & Mather, 2001), test interpretation (e.g., Flanagan & McGrew, 1998; Flanagan & Ortiz, 2001; Flanagan et al., 2000), and research (e.g., Flanagan, 2000; Keith & Reynolds, 2010; see Bryan & Mayer, 2020; Wilhelm & Kyllonen, 2021). This integrated model became known as the Cattell-Horn-Carroll (CHC) (in order of author contribution) theory of cognitive abilities or "CHC theory" shortly after that (McGrew, 2005). The term "taxonomy" refers to the totality of broad and narrow CHC abilities and their corresponding classification codes. Joel Schneider and Kevin McGrew made two substantial revisions and refinements to the CHC taxonomy more recently (2012, 2018). The current CHC taxonomy is comprised of 17 broad abilities and over 80 narrow abilities. Table A.1 provides definitions of broad and narrow abilities, based on Schneider and McGrew (2018), along with examples of tasks that measure each narrow ability.

**Table A.1 CHC Broad and Narrow Ability Definitions and Task Examples**

| Narrow Ability Name (*Code*) | Narrow Ability Definition | Narrow Ability Task Example |
|---|---|---|
| **Fluid Reasoning (*Gf*):** The use of deliberate and controlled procedures (often requiring focused attention) to solve novel, "on-the-spot" problems that cannot be solved by using previously learned habits, schemas, and scripts. | | |
| Induction (*I*) | The ability to observe a phenomenon and discover the underlying principles or rules that determine its behavior (also known as rule inference). | An examinee is presented with a certain pattern of related stimuli and is required to select one of several stimuli that completes or continues the pattern. |
| General Sequential Reasoning (*RG*) | The ability to reason logically using known premises and principles (also known as deductive reasoning or rule application). | An examinee is presented with an incomplete logic puzzle and is required to deduce the missing components by carefully analyzing the stimuli. |
| Quantitative Reasoning (*RQ*) | The ability to reason with quantities, mathematical relations, and operators. | An examinee is presented with an incomplete series of related numbers and is required to select the number(s) that best completes the series. |
| **Comprehension-Knowledge (*Gc*):** The ability to comprehend and communicate culturally valued knowledge (includes the depth and breadth of both declarative and procedural knowledge, and skills such as language, words, and general knowledge developed through experience, learning, and acculturation). | | |
| Lexical Knowledge (*VL*) | Knowledge of the definitions of words and the concepts that underlie them; vocabulary knowledge. | An examinee is required to provide oral definitions for words of increasing difficulty. |
| General Knowledge (*K0*) | The breadth and depth of knowledge considered essential, practical, or worthwhile for everyone in a culture to know. | An examinee is required to provide specific responses to questions of general factual information (e.g., In what direction does the sun set?). |
| Listening Ability (*LS*) | The ability to understand speech (begins with comprehending single words and increases to long complex verbal statements). | An examinee is required to point to pictures or manipulate objects as per the direction of the examiner. |
| Communication Ability (*CM*) | The ability to use speech to communicate effectively (similar to listening ability but is expressive rather than receptive). | An examinee is required to generate stories from visual and verbal cues. |
| Grammatical Sensitivity (*MY*) | Awareness of the formal rules of grammar and morphology of words in speech. | An examinee is required to correctly label the parts of speech contained in a sentence and/or correct those parts of speech that are utilized incorrectly. |
| Language Development (*LD*) | The ability to comprehend language and use it to communicate; the general understanding of spoken language at the level of words, idioms, and sentences. | Language development is an ***intermediate category*** between *Gc* and more specific-related abilities (e.g., vocabulary knowledge). It is a label for all language abilities. ***This classification should be reserved for Gc measures that do not meet the definition of any narrow Gc ability.*** |
| **Domain-Specific Knowledge (*Gkn*):** The depth, breadth, and mastery of specialized declarative and procedural knowledge (knowledge not all members of a society are expected to have). | | |
| General Science Information (*K1*) | Range of scientific knowledge. | An examinee is required to correctly respond to questions demonstrating general knowledge of basic scientific ideas or facts (e.g., What is the largest planet in our solar system? What is the ozone layer?) |
| Knowledge of Culture (*K2*) | Range of knowledge about the humanities. | An examinee is required to correctly respond to questions demonstrating general knowledge about the humanities (e.g., art, literature, history, politics, etc.). |

**Table A.1 (Continued)**

| Narrow Ability Name (*Code*) | Narrow Ability Definition | Narrow Ability Task Example |
|---|---|---|
| Mechanical Knowledge (*MK*) | Knowledge about the function, terminology, and operation of ordinary tools, machines, and equipment. | An examinee is required to demonstrate mechanical knowledge and reasoning used for personnel selection. |
| Foreign-Language Proficiency (*KL*) | Similar to language development, but in another language besides one's native language. | This narrow ability is not measured by any current cognitive or neuropsychological battery; therefore, no task example is provided. |
| Knowledge of Signing (*KF*) | Knowledge of finger spelling and signing (e.g., American Sign Language). | This narrow ability is not measured by any current cognitive or neuropsychological battery; therefore, no task example is provided. |
| Skill in Lip Reading (*LP*) | Competence in the ability to understand communication from others by watching the movements of their mouths and expressions. | This narrow ability is not measured by any current cognitive or neuropsychological battery; therefore, no task example is provided. |
| **Quantitative Knowledge (*Gq*):** The depth and breadth of declarative and procedural knowledge related to mathematics. | | |
| Number Sense (*NS*) | The basic processing of numerical information, including number representation (quantifying sets without counting) and number comparison (estimating the relative magnitude of sets). | An examinee is required to point to the greater of two values presented in a response booklet (e.g., groups of two to four shapes and single-digit numbers) as quickly as possible within a 1-min time limit. |
| Mathematical Knowledge (*KM*) | Range of general knowledge about mathematics, not the performance of mathematical operations or the solving of math problems. | An examinee is required to define words, such as *diameter*. |
| Mathematical Achievement (*A3*) | Measured (tested) mathematics achievement. | An examinee is required to solve problems (e.g., $72 \times 65$) using paper and pencil. |
| Math Speed (Fluency) (*MS*) | The speed and fluency of completing basic arithmetic operations. | An examinee is required to solve simple addition and subtraction problems as quickly as possible within a 3-min time limit. |
| **Reading and Writing (*Grw*):** The depth and breadth of declarative and procedural knowledge and skills related to written language. | | |
| Reading Decoding (*RD*) | The ability to identify words from text. | An examinee is required to pronounce a list of real or nonsense words accurately (words are typically arranged in ascending order of difficulty). |
| Reading Speed (Fluency) (*RS*) | The rate at which a person can read connected discourse with full comprehension. | An examinee is required to read a list of short statements silently and as quickly as possible and indicate whether each statement is true or false. |
| Reading Comprehension (*RC*) | The ability to understand written discourse. | An examinee is required to read a short passage and respond to questions about the passage. |
| Writing Speed (*WS*) | The ability to copy or generate text quickly. | An examinee is required to write simple sentences corresponding to cues (e.g., words, pictures) as quickly as possible. |
| English Usage Knowledge (*EU*) | Knowledge of the mechanics of writing (e.g., capitalization, punctuation, and word usage). | An examinee is required to correct sentences for capitalization, punctuation, spelling, and word usage errors. |
| Spelling Ability (*SG*) | The ability to spell words. | An examinee is required to spell a series of increasingly difficult words that are orally presented. |
| Writing Speed (Fluency) (*WS*) | The ability to use text to communicate ideas clearly. | An examinee is given a stimulus and is required to write a well-organized story that adheres to the structural rules of writing (e.g., examinee begins a new paragraph when presenting a new idea). |

(*continued*)

**Table A.1 (Continued)**

| Narrow Ability Name (*Code*) | Narrow Ability Definition | Narrow Ability Task Example |
|---|---|---|
| **Working Memory Capacity (*Gwm*):** The ability to maintain and manipulate information in active attention. | | |
| Auditory Short-Term Storage (*Wa*) | The ability to encode and maintain verbal information in primary memory. | An examinee is required to repeat sentences of increasing length verbatim after they are spoken by the examiner. |
| Visual-Spatial Short-Term Storage (*Wv*) | The ability to encode and maintain visual information in primary memory. | An examinee is shown a pattern of block tapping and is required to copy it in the same order. |
| Attentional Control (*AC*) | The ability to manipulate the spotlight of attention flexibly to focus on task-relevant stimuli and ignore task-irrelevant stimuli (sometimes referred to as spotlight or focal attention, focus, control of attention, executive controlled attention, or executive attention). | An examinee is required to name the ink color of a color word (e.g., the word "blue" is printed in red ink) as quickly as possible. |
| Working Memory Capacity (*Wc*) | The ability to manipulate information in primary memory. | An examinee is presented with a series of numbers and words in a mixed-up order and is required to say the complete list of numbers in order, followed by the words in order. |
| **Learning Efficiency (*Gl*):** The ability to learn, store, and consolidate new information over periods measured in minutes, hours, days, and years. | | |
| Associative Memory (*MA*) | The ability to form a link between two previously unrelated stimuli, such that the subsequent presentation of one of the stimuli serves to activate the recall of the other stimuli. | An examinee is presented with a set of visual stimuli paired with nonsense words and is required to correctly identify the nonsense word that was presented with a certain visual stimulus. |
| Meaningful Memory (*MM*) | The ability to remember narratives and other forms of semantically related information. | An examinee is presented with a short story and is required to retell it as accurately as possible immediately after a single presentation. |
| Free-Recall Memory (*M6*) | The ability to recall lists in any order. | An examinee is required to recall lists of 10–20 words across a series of trials. |
| **Retrieval Fluency (*Gr*):** The rate and fluency at which individuals can produce and selectively and strategically retrieve verbal and nonverbal information or ideas stored in long-term memory. | | |
| Ideational Fluency (*FI*) | The ability to rapidly produce a series of ideas, words, or phrases related to a specific condition or object. | An examinee is required to name as quickly as possible as many uses of a pencil as possible in 1 min. |
| Speed of Lexical Access (LA) *Intermediate ability which subsumes NA and FW* | The ability to rapidly and fluently retrieve words from an individual's lexicon (also described as verbal efficiency or automaticity of lexical access). | Refer to the examples provided for NA and FW. |
| Naming Facility (NA) | The ability to rapidly call common objects by their names (also known as continuous naming speed or rapid automatic naming [*RAN*]). | An examinee is required to name pictures of common objects as quickly as possible. |
| Word Fluency (*FW*) | The ability to rapidly produce words that share a phonological (e.g., fluency of retrieval of words via a phonological cue) or semantic (e.g., fluency of retrieval of words via a meaning-based representation) feature. | An examinee is required to name as many words as they can that start with the "sh" sound within a specified time limit. |
| Associational Fluency (*FA*) | The ability to rapidly produce a series of original or useful ideas related to a particular concept. | An examinee is required to name as many uses of a pencil as possible in 1 min (as with *FI*), but credit is given for creative and high-quality answers. |

**Table A.1 (Continued)**

| Narrow Ability Name (*Code*) | Narrow Ability Definition | Narrow Ability Task Example |
|---|---|---|
| Expressional Fluency (*FE*) | The ability to rapidly think of different ways of expressing an idea. | An examinee is required to identify how many ways to say a person is intoxicated. |
| Sensitivity to Problems/Alternative Solution Fluency (*SP*) | The ability to rapidly think of several alternative solutions to a practical problem. | An examinee is required to state as many ways as possible they can think of to influence a reluctant child to go to school. |
| Originality/Creativity (*FO*) | The ability to rapidly produce original, clever, and insightful responses (expressions, interpretations) to a given topic, situation, or task. | This narrow ability is not measured by any current cognitive or neuropsychological battery; therefore, no task example is provided. |
| Figural Fluency (*FF*) | The ability to rapidly draw or sketch as many things (or elaborations) as possible when presented with a nonmeaningful visual stimulus (e.g., a set of unique visual elements). | An examinee is required to draw as many unique things as they can when presented with a nonmeaningful starting visual stimulus. |
| Figural Flexibility (*FX*) | The ability to rapidly draw different solutions to figural problems. | An examinee is required to draw as many ways as possible to fit several small shapes into a larger one. |
| **Visual Processing (*Gv*):** The ability to make use of simulated mental imagery to solve problems—perceiving, discriminating, manipulating, and recalling nonlinguistic images in the "mind's eye." | | |
| Visualization (*Vz*) | The ability to perceive complex patterns and mentally simulate how they might look when transformed (e.g., rotated, twisted, inverted, changed in size, partially obscured). | An examinee is required to assemble blocks to match a picture or a standing model. |
| Speeded Rotation (*SR*) | The ability to solve problems quickly by using mental rotation of simple images. | An examinee is shown an array of letters in various degrees of rotation and direction and is required to identify all backward-facing letters as quickly as possible. |
| Imagery (*IM*) | The ability to voluntarily mentally produce vivid images of objects, people, or events that are not present. | This narrow ability is not measured by any current cognitive or neuropsychological battery; therefore, no task example is provided. |
| Flexibility of Closure (*CF*) | The ability to identify a visual figure or pattern embedded in a complex distracted or disguised visual pattern or array, when one knows in advance what the pattern is. | An examinee is required to identify 10 animals embedded in a complex visual scene. |
| Closure Speed (*CS*) | The ability to quickly identify and access a familiar, meaningful visual object stored in long-term memory from incomplete or obscured (e.g., vague, partially obscured, disguised, disconnected) visual cues of the object, without knowing in advance what the object is (sometimes called gestalt perception) (in this context, "speed" refers to the mental ease/fluency of completing these tasks). | An examinee is required to identify an object from a line drawing that has portions of the lines missing, such as a computer keyboard. |
| Visual Memory (*MV*) | The ability to remember complex images over short periods (less than 30 s). | An examinee is shown a visual stimulus briefly and is required to reproduce or recognize it after it has been removed. |
| Spatial Scanning (*SS*) | The ability to quickly and accurately survey (visually explore) a wide or complicated spatial field or pattern with multiple obstacles and identify a target configuration or identify a path through the field to a target endpoint. | An examinee is required to complete a series of increasingly difficult mazes within 3 min. |

(*continued*)

**Table A.1 (Continued)**

| Narrow Ability Name (*Code*) | Narrow Ability Definition | Narrow Ability Task Example |
|---|---|---|
| Serial Perceptual Integration (*PI*) | The ability to recognize an object after only parts of it are shown in rapid succession. | An examinee is required to identify or name a stimulus correctly when portions of the stimulus are presented serially (e.g., portions of a line drawing of a cat are passed through a small "window"). |
| Length Estimation (*LE*) | The ability to visually estimate the length of objects (without using measuring instruments). | This narrow ability is not measured by any current cognitive or neuropsychological battery; therefore, no task example is provided. |
| Perceptual Illusions (*IL*) | The ability not to be fooled by visual illusions. | This narrow ability is not measured by any current cognitive or neuropsychological battery; therefore, no task example is provided. |
| Perceptual Alternations (*PN*) | Consistency in the rate of alternating between different visual perceptions. | This narrow ability is not measured by any current cognitive or neuropsychological battery; therefore, no task example is provided. |
| **Auditory Processing (*Ga*):** The ability to discriminate, remember, reason, and work creatively with auditory stimuli, which may consist of tones, environmental sounds, and speech units. | | |
| Phonetic Coding (*PC*) | The ability to distinctly hear phonemes, blend sounds into words, and segment words into parts, sounds, or phonemes (also known as phonological processing, phonological awareness, and phonemic awareness). | An examinee is required to blend sounds fluently to form words or identify specific, isolated sounds within words. |
| Speech Sound Discrimination (*US*) | The ability to detect and discriminate differences in speech sounds (other than phonemes) under conditions of little or no distraction or distortion. | An examinee is presented with a series of tape-recorded nonphonemic sounds and is required to indicate whether each pair is the same or different. |
| Resistance to Auditory Stimulus Distortion (*UR*) | The ability to hear words or extended speech passages correctly under conditions of distortion or background noise. | An examinee is required to identify mono- and multisyllabic words while listening to increasing levels of noise through earphones. |
| Maintaining and Judging Rhythm (*U8*) | The ability to recognize and maintain a musical beat. | This narrow ability is not measured by any current cognitive or neuropsychological battery; therefore, no task example is provided. |
| Memory for Sound Patterns (*UM*) | The ability to retain (on a short-term basis) auditory events such as tones, tonal patterns, voices, or speech sounds. | The examinee is required to hold in mind a musical phrase they hear so they can reproduce it later. |
| Musical Discrimination and Judgement (*U1*, *U9*) | The ability to discriminate and judge tonal patterns in music for melodic, harmonic, and expressive aspects (phrasing, tempo, harmonic complexity, intensity variations). | The examinee is required to decide if sounds from two instruments are the same or different. |
| Sound Localization (*UL*) | The ability to localize heard sounds in space. | The examinee is required to listen to two sentences presented at the same time: one in the right ear and one in the left ear. The examinee then must repeat the sentence spoken in the left ear first and the sentence spoken in the right ear second. |
| **Olfactory Abilities (*Go*):** The abilities to detect and process meaningful information in odors. | | |
| Olfactory Memory (*OM*) | The ability to recognize previously encountered distinctive odors. | This narrow ability is not measured by any current cognitive or neuropsychological battery; therefore, no task example is provided. |
| **Tactile Abilities (*Gh*):** The abilities to detect and process meaningful information in haptic (touch) sensations. This domain includes perceiving, discriminating, and manipulating touch stimuli. | | |
| **Psychomotor Abilities (*Gp*):** The ability to perform physical body motor movements (e.g., movement of fingers, hands, legs) with precision, coordination, or strength. | | |

**Table A.1 (Continued)**

| Narrow Ability Name (*Code*) | Narrow Ability Definition | Narrow Ability Task Example |
|---|---|---|
| Manual Dexterity (*P*1) | The ability to make precisely coordinated movements of a hand or a hand and the attached arm. | The examinee is required to perform alternating hand movements. |
| Finger Dexterity (*P*2) | The ability to make precisely coordinated movements of the fingers (with or without the manipulation of objects). | The examinee is required to draw, cut, or fold within a specified boundary. |
| Static Strength (*P*3) | The ability to exert muscular force to move (push, lift, pull) a relatively heavy or immobile object. | This narrow ability is not measured by any current cognitive or neuropsychological battery; therefore, no task example is provided. |
| Gross Body Equilibrium (*P*4) | The ability to maintain the body in an upright position in space or regain balance after it has been disturbed. | The examinee is required to walk using various gaits. |
| Multilimb Coordination (*P*6) | The ability to make quick, specific, or discrete motor movements of the arms or legs. | The examinee is required to demonstrate coordination of the upper and lower limbs, such as the ability to coordinate the arms and legs when doing jumping jacks. |
| Arm-Hand Steadiness (*P*7) | The ability to precisely and skillfully coordinate arm-hand positioning in space. | This narrow ability is not measured by any current cognitive or neuropsychological battery; therefore, no task example is provided. |
| Control Precision (*P*8) | The ability to exert precise control over muscle movements, typically in response to environmental feedback (e.g., changes in speed or position of object being manipulated). | This narrow ability is not measured by any current cognitive or neuropsychological battery; therefore, no task example is provided. |
| Aiming (*AI*) | The ability to precisely and fluently execute a sequence of eye-hand coordination movements for positioning purposes. | An examinee is required to aim at a circle (i.e., target) and toss a bean bag at the target to try to land the bean bag on or close to it. |
| **Kinesthetic Abilities (*Gk*):** The ability to detect and process meaningful information in proprioceptive sensations. | | |
| Kinesthetic Sensitivity (*KS*)<br>*A sensory ability, not a cognitive ability* | The ability to make fine discriminations in proprioceptive sensations (e.g., whether and how much a limb has been moved). | The examinee is required to identify which of their fingers the examiner is touching without looking. |
| **Processing Speed (*Gs*):** The average speed at which a series of simple items is completed in succession, with sustained concentration over all items over a sustained period (e.g., 2–3 min). | | |
| Perceptual Speed-Search (*Ps*) | The speed and fluency of searching or scanning an extended visual field to locate one or more simple visual patterns. | An examinee is required to scan a page visually and cross out all occurrences of a specific symbol as quickly as possible. |
| Perceptual Speed-Compare (*Pc*) | The speed and fluency of looking up and comparing visual stimuli that are side by side or more widely separated in an extended visual field. | An examinee is given a stimulus and required to find an identical stimulus in rows of various stimuli as quickly as possible. |
| Math Speed (Fluency) (*MS*) | The speed and fluency of completing basic arithmetic operations (also listed under *Gq*). | An examinee is required to complete simple arithmetic problems as quickly as possible. |
| Reading Speed (Fluency) (*RS*) | The speed and fluency of reading text with full comprehension (also listed under *Grw*). | The examinee is required to read simple sentences displayed on the tablet screen and indicate if the sentence is true or false by tapping "yes" or "no" as quickly as possible within 3 min. |
| Writing Speed (Fluency) (*WS*) | The speed and fluency of generating or copying words or sentences (also listed under *Grw* and *Gps*). | An examinee is required to write simple sentences corresponding to cues (e.g., words, pictures) as quickly as possible. |

(*continued*)

**Table A.1 (Continued)**

| Narrow Ability Name (*Code*) | Narrow Ability Definition | Narrow Ability Task Example |
|---|---|---|
| **Reaction and Decision Speed (*Gt*):** The speed at which a single item can be performed (tasks require making very simple decisions or judgments when items are presented one at a time). | | |
| Simple Reaction Time (*R1*) | Reaction time to the onset of a single visual or auditory stimulus. | An examinee is timed from the moment they decide to make a response until they remove their finger from a button. |
| Choice Reaction Time (*R2*) | Reaction time when a very simple choice must be made. | An examinee is timed from looking at two buttons to hitting the one that lights up. |
| Inspection Time (*IT*) | The speed at which differences in visual stimuli can be perceived. | An examinee is shown a picture of two lines for a brief period and, after the picture is covered, is required to determine which was longer. |
| Semantic Processing Speed (*R4*) | Reaction time when a decision requires very simple encoding and mental manipulation of the stimulus content. | This narrow ability is not measured by any current cognitive or neuropsychological battery; therefore, no task example is provided. |
| Mental Comparison Speed (*R7*) | Reaction time is the time it takes to compare stimuli for a particular characteristic or attribute. | This narrow ability is not measured by any current cognitive or neuropsychological battery; therefore, no task example is provided. |
| **Psychomotor Speed (*Gps*):** The ability to perform skilled physical body motor movements (e.g., movement of fingers, hands, legs) with precision, coordination, fluidity, or strength. | | |
| Speed of Limb Movement (*R3*) | The speed of arm and leg movements (accuracy is not important). | This narrow ability is not measured by any current cognitive or neuropsychological battery; therefore, no task example is provided. |
| Writing Speed (Fluency) (*WS*) | The speed at which written words can be copied (also listed under *Grw* and *Gs*). | An examinee is required to write simple sentences corresponding to cues (e.g., words, pictures) as quickly as possible. |
| Speed of Articulation (*PT*) | The ability to rapidly perform successive articulations with the speech musculature. | This narrow ability is not measured by any current cognitive or neuropsychological battery; therefore, no task example is provided. |
| Movement Time (*MT*) | The time taken to physically move a body part (e.g., a finger) to make the required response after a decision or choice has been made in an elementary cognitive task. | This narrow ability is not measured by any current cognitive or neuropsychological battery; therefore, no task example is provided. |
| **Emotional Intelligence (*Gei*):** The ability to perceive the expression of emotions, understand emotional behavior, and solve problems using emotions. | | |
| Emotion Perception (*Ep*) | The ability to accurately recognize emotions in the face, voice, and behavior. | This narrow ability is not measured by any current cognitive or neuropsychological battery; therefore, no task example is provided. |
| Emotion Knowledge (*Ek*) | Knowledge of the antecedents of emotions and the consequences of emotional expression. | This narrow ability is not measured by any current cognitive or neuropsychological battery; therefore, no task example is provided. |
| Emotion Management (*Em*) | The ability to regulate one's emotions deliberately and adaptively. | This narrow ability is not measured by any current cognitive or neuropsychological battery; therefore, no task example is provided. |
| Emotion Utilization (*Eu*) | The ability to make adaptive use of emotion, primarily to facilitate reasoning. | This narrow ability is not measured by any current cognitive or neuropsychological battery; therefore, no task example is provided. |

*Note:* Broad ability names and definitions are in darker shaded areas.

## REFERENCES

Bryan, V. M., & Mayer, J. D. (2020). A meta-analysis of the correlations among broad intelligences: Understanding their relations. *Intelligence, 81*, 101469.

Carroll, J. B. (1993). *Human cognitive abilities: A survey of factor-analytic studies.* Cambridge University Press.

Flanagan, D. P., & McGrew, K. S. (1998). Interpreting intelligence tests from modern Gf-Gc theory: Joint confirmatory factor analysis of the WJ-R and Kaufman Adolescent and Adult Intelligence Test (KAIT). *Journal of School Psychology, 36*(151), 182.

Flanagan, D. P. (2000). Wechsler-based CHC cross-battery assessment and reading achievement: Strengthening the validity of interpretations drawn from Wechsler test scores. *School Psychology Quarterly, 15*(3), 295.

Flanagan, D. P., McGrew, K. S., & Ortiz, S. O. (2000). *The Wechsler intelligence scales and Gf-Gc theory: A contemporary approach to interpretation.* Allyn & Bacon.

Flanagan, D. P., & Ortiz, S. O. (2001). *Essentials of cross-battery assessment.* Wiley.

Horn, J. L., & Noll, J. (1997). Human cognitive capabilities: *Gf-Gc* theory. In D. P. Flanagan, J. L. Genshaft, & P. L. Harrison (Eds.), *Contemporary intellectual assessment: Theories, tests and issues* (pp. 53–91). Guilford Press.

Keith, T. Z., & Reynolds, M. R. (2010). CHC and cognitive abilities: What we've learned from 20 years of research. *Psychology in the Schools, 47*, 635–650.

McGrew, K. S., Flanagan, D. P., Keith, T. Z., & Vanderwood, M. (1997). Beyond *g*: The impact of CHC specific cognitive abilities research on the future use and interpretation of intelligence tests in the schools. *School Psychology Review, 26*, 189–210.

McGrew, K. S. (2005). The Cattell-Horn-Carroll theory of cognitive abilities: Past, present, and future. In D. P. Flanagan, J. L. Genshaft, & P. L. Harrison (Eds.), *Contemporary intellectual assessment: Theories, tests, and issues* (pp. 136–182). Guilford Press.

Schneider, W. J., & McGrew, K. (2012). The Cattell-Horn-Carroll model of intelligence. In D. Flanagan & P. Harrison (Eds.), *Contemporary intellectual assessment: Theories, tests, and issues* ((3rd ed, pp. 99–144). Guilford Press.

Schneider, W. J., & McGrew, K. S. (2018). The Cattell-Horn-Carroll theory of cognitive abilities. In D. P. Flanagan & E. M. McDonough (Eds.), *Contemporary intellectual assessment: Theories, tests, and issues* ((4th ed, pp. 73–163). Guilford Press.

Wilhelm, O., & Kyllonen, P. (2021). To predict the future, consider the past: Revisiting Carroll (1993) as a guide to the future of intelligence research. *Intelligence, 89*, 101585.

Woodcock, R. W., McGrew, K. S., & Mather, N. (2001). *Woodcock-Johnson III.* Riverside.

Appendix B

# EXPERT-CONSENSUS STUDY FOR NEW TESTS/SUBTESTS INCLUDED IN X-BASS 3.0


## In Collaboration with Ridge Bynum, Psy.D.

Gonzaga University


## STUDY SCOPE AND PURPOSE

An expert-consensus study of 46 batteries and 283 subtests was conducted to provide content-validity evidence for recently published measures and to update Cross-Battery Assessment Software System (X-BASS) 3.0 classifications. The study used a two-phase design. Phase I (pilot) produced neutral subtest descriptions, a Cattell-Horn-Carroll (CHC) codebook, and an initial set of broad and narrow ability classifications produced by two expert dyads. Phase I classifications are included in X-BASS 3.0. Phase II (a larger, independent expert panel) is underway to replicate and extend Phase I and to confirm or revise classifications (Bynum et al., 2026).

## CONTENT VALIDITY

Content validity assesses whether subtest content actually samples the CHC constructs claimed and is the foundational strand of a broader validity argument required by contemporary testing standards (AERA et al., 2014). Bynum (2026) frames validity as a unified argument assembled from multiple sources of evidence and treats content validity as a necessary foundation for interpreting ability measures within CHC theories (Schneider & McGrew, 2018). Consistent with this perspective, Bynum used a multimethod framework consisting of the following: (1) structured expert consensus, (2) systematic review of test manuals and prior classifications, and (3) secondary-data analyses (correlations and CFA/loadings). He then integrated these methods in a cross-method synthesis matrix to identify where CHC classifications were robust or ambiguous.

The *Standards for Educational and Psychological Testing* require that validity claims be tied to specific score interpretations and supported by multiple strands of evidence (AERA et al., 2014); this view is consistent with longstanding conceptualizations of validity as an argument about score interpretation rather than an intrinsic property of an instrument (Kane, 2009; Messick, 1989; Sireci & Rodriguez, 2022; Urbina, 2014). Although some scholars have argued for alternative framings (e.g., Borsboom et al., 2004), the consensus in the measurement literature is that users must evaluate whether the available evidence supports the intended interpretation and use of scores in their specific context (Sireci & Benítez, 2022). Accordingly, Phase II mirrors Bynum's multimethod approach and documents the cross-method synthesis and any residual uncertainty for each subtest so that final CHC labels rest on a defensible, transparent validity argument (AERA et al., 2014; Bynum, 2026; Schneider & McGrew, 2018).

To operationalize this multimethod validity argument in Phase II, the study will also:

- supply empirical evidence (correlations, factor loadings) to test whether score relations comport with the labeled constructs; and
- produce a cross-method synthesis that yields defensible final classifications and transparent uncertainty flags.

To operationalize the multimethod validity argument above, Phase I produced the neutral subtest descriptions, rater codebook, and initial dyad classifications. Phase II (Bynum et al., 2026) will (1) re-evaluate with a larger expert panel, (2) triangulate against manuals and structural evidence, and (3) adjudicate where uncertainty remains.

## GOALS OF PHASE I (PILOT)

- **Generate clear, neutral subtest descriptions** that convey task demands without presuming the CHC construct being measured.
- **Produce a standard set of CHC classifications** (broad and narrow) for the 283 subtests to serve as the Phase II reference and the X-BASS 3.0 baseline.

## MATERIALS AND PROCEDURES (PILOT)

- **Subtest corpus:** 283 neutral subtest descriptions entered into Excel, edited for clarity, and randomized into two identical files to control order effects.
- **CHC manual:** A codebook of broad and narrow CHC definitions and task exemplars based on Schneider & McGrew (2018), similar to Appendix A of this book.
- **Raters:** Four experts formed two dyads: **Dyad A** (Dawn Flanagan and Vincent Alfonso) and **Dyad B** (Andrew Shanock and Craig Zinkiewicz). Each dyad produced one collaborative set of classifications.
- **Questionnaire:** For each subtest, dyads answered a fixed set of classification questions (see Question Set in Rapid Reference B.1).

### Rapid Reference B.1

**Question Set (Applied to Every Subtest)**

**Broad 1:** Which broad CHC ability best describes the subtest? (drop-down of broad abilities)
**Narrow 1:** Which narrow ability within Broad 1 is primary? (filtered drop-down)
**Narrow 2:** Is another narrow ability within Broad 1 also likely measured? If yes, select it.
**Broad 2:** Is another broad ability measured to about the same degree as Broad 1? If yes, select it.
**Narrow 3:** If Broad 2 was selected, which narrow ability within Broad 2 is likely measured?

- **Comparison and adjudication:** Dyad classifications were compared using prespecified agreement rules. Disagreements were reviewed jointly by all four experts; subtest descriptions and codebook exemplars were revised as needed to resolve ambiguity and produce final Phase I classifications.

## AGREEMENT RULES

Agreement is resolved hierarchically: first at the broad level, then at the narrow level (narrow comparisons are meaningful only when broad domains overlap). Levels map to interpretive confidence: Level 1 = high confidence, Level 4 = low confidence/disagreement.

### Broad Ability Agreement (Apply First)

- **Level 1—Exact/Perfect**
  - Both dyads selected the same single **Broad 1, OR** both selected the same two broad abilities in the same order.
  - *Interpretation:* Highest confidence in the primary construct.
- **Level 2—Strong/High**
  - Both dyads selected the same two broad abilities but in different order; **OR** one dyad selected one broad ability and the other selected two, and the **primary** broad ability (Broad 1) is the same.
  - *Interpretation:* Strong confidence; mixed measure possible.
- **Level 3—Partial/Moderate**
  - One dyad selected one broad ability and the other selected two, and the single broad ability matches the **secondary** broad ability of the other dyad; **OR** both dyads selected two broad abilities but matched on only one (not consistently primary).
  - *Interpretation:* Moderate confidence; interpret with caution.
- **Level 4—Minimal/Low/Disagreement**
  - Dyads share no common broad ability selection, or matches are only on secondary selections that conflict with primary choices.
  - *Interpretation:* Low confidence; requires adjudication.

### Narrow Ability Agreement (Apply After Broad Comparison)

- **Case A—Both dyads agreed on the same single Broad 1 (no Broad 2):**
  - *Level 1 (Exact):* Same single narrow (Narrow 1), or same two narrows in same order.
  - *Level 2 (Strong):* Same two narrows in different order; or one dyad chose one narrow and the other chose two where the primary narrow matches.
  - *Level 3 (Partial):* One dyad chose one narrow and the other chose two where the single narrow matches the secondary narrow of the other.
  - *Level 4 (Low):* No meaningful overlap.

- **Case B—Both dyads agreed on the same two broad abilities in the same order:**
  - *Level 1 (Exact):* Match on Narrow 1 (primary for Broad 1) and Narrow 3 (narrow for Broad 2), or match on Narrow 1, Narrow 2 (in order), and Narrow 3.
  - *Level 2 (Strong):* Match on Narrow 1 and Narrow 3 but differ on Narrow 2 order/selection in a way that preserves interpretive confidence.
  - *Level 3 (Partial):* Match on only one narrow across the two broad domains.
  - *Level 4 (Low):* Little or no overlap across narrow selections.
- **Case C—Same two broad abilities but different order:**
- Treat as a broad Level 2 match; evaluate narrow agreement relative to each dyad's primary/secondary mapping. Exact corresponding narrow matches (primary→primary, secondary→secondary) = Level 1; partial matches = Level 2–3.
- **Case D—One dyad chose one broad and the other chose two, with matching primary broad:**
- Evaluate narrow agreement within the shared primary broad using Case A rules. Matches where the single narrow aligns with the other dyad's secondary narrow are Level 3.

**DON'T FORGET**

**Practical scoring note:** these rules are intentionally parsimonious to support automated scoring and consistent adjudication while preserving the nuanced distinctions needed for mixed measures.

## PILOT RESULTS (PHASE I)

- **Broad-level agreement:** Approximately **95%** of subtests met at least Level 3 broad-level agreement. **77%** met Level 1 (exact) criteria; **9%** met Level 2; **10%** met Level 3.
- **Narrow-level agreement:** Nearly **90%** total agreement across narrow classifications using the multilevel rules. Narrow agreement was predictably lower than broad agreement because narrow abilities require finer distinctions.
- **Primary sources of disagreement:**
  1. **Missing procedural details** in subtest descriptions (e.g., time limits, response mode).
  2. **Ambiguous modality information** (e.g., whether stimuli are auditory or visual).
  3. **Close distinctions between narrow abilities** (e.g., *Gc*:LS vs. *Gl*:MM), requiring clearer definitions and exemplars.

## RESOLUTION AND PHASE I OUTPUTS

- The dyads reconciled differences in joint meetings, updated subtest descriptions to include missing procedural metadata, clarified narrow ability definitions and exemplars, and produced the final Phase I classification set now implemented in X-BASS 3.0. Phase II will confirm and, if necessary, revise these classifications.

## RELATIONSHIP TO PRIOR CHC CONSENSUS WORK

Early CHC consensus studies (e.g., Flanagan et al., 2002, 2006, 2013; McGrew, 1997) established the methodological conventions used here: anchoring broad labels in structural evidence, operationalizing narrow labels via expert panels, using multilevel agreement rules, reporting multiple reliability indices, and documenting adjudication. Those studies consistently found very high broad ability agreement and lower but acceptable narrow ability agreement—patterns that were replicated in this pilot. Bynum (2026) extended this approach by integrating consensus with systematic review and secondary data analysis. Phase II adopts a similar multimethod synthesis to strengthen claims of content validity.

## CROSS-SOURCE CONVERGENT VALIDATION

Evidence that independent content-based classifications converge with test-author classifications and empirical structural results increases confidence that subtest content and score behavior reflect the same CHC constructs. We compared the Phase I pilot CHC classifications for Woodcock-Johnson V (WJ V; McGrew et al., 2025) tests with the WJ V authors' CHC classifications and structural analyses to obtain cross-source convergent evidence. The WJ V Technical Manual (LaForte et al., 2025) reports very high concordance after adjustments: broad ability agreement approached 98% (complete + partial agreement) and narrow ability agreement approached 93% for the 60 WJ V tests examined. These high concordance rates provide supportive evidence for the validity of the Phase I pilot classifications. Where disagreements occurred, we documented methodological differences (e.g., coding conventions, access to structural results, narrow ability definitions) and flagged those subtests for Phase II adjudication and empirical review. (See Table B.1 for the comparison summary.)

**Table B.1 Broad and Narrow CHC Classifications of WJ V Tests by the Authors and Independent Experts**

| Test Number: Name | WJ V Authors' Classifications | Independent Experts' Classifications | Agreement? |
|---|---|---|---|
| Test 1: Oral Vocabulary | *Gc*—VL | *Gc*—VL | **Yes** |
| Test 2: Matrices | *Gf*—I | *Gf*—I | **Yes** |
| Test 3: Spatial Relations | *Gv*—Vz | *Gv*—Vz | **Yes** |
| Test 4: Story Recall | *Gl*—MM | *Gl*—MM | **Yes** |
| Test 5: Semantic Word Retrieval | *Gr*—FI | *Gr*—FI | **Yes** |
| Test 6: Verbal Attention | *Gwm*—Wc, Wa | *Gwm*—Wa, Wc | **Yes**. Note that the authors primarily use Wa to refer to the modality (i.e., auditory). |
| Test 7: Number-Pattern Matching | *Gs*—Ps-*Gq* | *Gs*—P | **Yes**. Note that *Gq* in the authors' classification reflects the nature of the stimuli (numbers). Also, the independent experts did not separate Ps and Pc because many *Gs* tests appear to require searching *and* comparing. Instead, they used the code "P," which is an intermediate factor, for all *Gs* tests that align with the cognitive facet of *Gs* (see Flanagan et al., 2025). |
| Test 8: Verbal Analogies | *Gc*/*Gf*—VL/I | *Gc*/*Gf*—VL/I | **Yes** |
| Test 9: Analysis-Synthesis | *Gf*—RG | *Gf*—RG | **Yes** |
| Test 10: Block Rotation | *Gv*—Vz | *Gv*—Vz | **Yes** |
| Test 11: Story Comprehension | *Gl*—MM | *Gl*—MM | **Yes** |
| Test 12: Phonemic Word Retrieval | *Gr*—FW | *Gr*—FW | **Yes** |
| Test 13: Numbers Reversed | *Gwm*—Wc, Wa | *Gwm*—Wc | **Yes** |
| Test 14: Letter-Pattern Matching | *Gs*—Ps-*Grw* | *Gs*—P, OP | **Yes**, for broad ability and similar classifications for narrow ability. Note that *Grw* in the authors' classification reflects the nature of the stimuli (letters). The independent experts use OP to represent orthographic processing. Individuals with OP weakness will likely perform worse on this task as compared to *Gs* tests with abstract stimuli. |
| Test 15: General Information | *Gc*—K0 | *Gc*—K0 | **Yes** |
| Test 16: Concept Formation | *Gf*—I | *Gf*—I | **Yes** |
| Test 17: Number Series | *Gq*/*Gf*—A3/RQ | *Gf*—RQ | Agreement on *Gf*—RQ. The independent experts did not provide a classification of *Gq*—A3 because they assumed that A3 is inherent in RQ. In other words, basic math skills (A3) are crucial for performing higher-level math tasks that require critical thinking and reasoning (RQ). |
| Test 18: Visual-Auditory Learning | *Gv*/*Gf*—MV/RG | *Gl*—MA | **No**. The independent experts continued to use the same classification as was used in previous editions of the WJ III. However, they were not aware of the validity studies reported in the WJ V Technical Manual at the time of their classifications. The WJ V authors' classifications align with the results of new analyses conducted using the WJ V tests, as reported in the technical manual (LaForte et al., 2025). |
| Test 19: Visual Working Memory | *Gwm*/*Gv*—Wc, Wv/MV | *Gwm*—Wc | Agreement on *Gwm*—Wc. The authors' secondary classification of *Gv*—MV is supported by the studies reported in the WJ V Technical Manual. |

**Table B.1 (Continued)**

| Test Number: Name | WJ V Authors' Classifications | Independent Experts' Classifications | Agreement? |
|---|---|---|---|
| Test 20: Symbol Inhibition | *Gs*—Pc-*Gv* | *Gs*—P | **Yes**. See explanation for Letter-Pattern Matching above. |
| **Nonsense Word Repetition** | *Ga*/*Gwm*—UM/Wa | *Gwm*/*Ga*—Wa, UM | **Yes** |
| **Rapid Picture Naming** | *Gs*/*Gr*—NA | *Gr*—NA | **Yes** |
| **Animal-Number Sequencing** | *Gwm*—Wc, Wa | *Gwm*—Wc | **Yes** |
| **Sound Reversal** | *Ga*—UM | *Gwm*/*Ga*—Wc/PC | **No** |
| **Rapid Letter Naming** | *Gs*/*Gr*—NA | *Gr*—NA | **Partial agreement**. New research reported by LaForte et al. (2025) shows that RAN tests are *Gr* and *Gs*, a finding not evident in previous CHC structural research due to the underrepresentation of RAN tests in analyses. |
| **Understanding Directions** | *Gwm*/*Gf*—Wc, Wa/RQ | *Gc*/*Gwm*—LS/Wc | **No** |
| **Sound Blending** | *Ga*—PC | *Ga*—PC | **Yes** |
| **Rapid Phoneme Naming** | *Gs*/*Gr*/*Ga*—NA/PC | *Gr*—NA | **Agreement on *Gr*–NA** |
| **Memory for Words** | *Gwm*—Wa | *Gwm*—Wa | **Yes** |
| **Segmentation** | *Ga*—PC | *Ga*—PC | **Yes** |
| **Rapid Number Naming** | *Gs*/*Gr*—N/NA | *Gr*—NA | **Agreement on *Gr*–NA** |
| **Sentence Repetition** | *Gwm*—Wa | *Gwm*—Wa | **Yes** |
| **Sound Deletion** | *Ga*—PC | *Ga*—PC | **Yes** |
| **Rapid Quantity Naming** | *Gs*/*Gr*/*Gv*—N/NA/Vz | *Gq*/*Gr*—NS/NA | **Agreement on *Gr*–NA** |
| **Sound Substitution** | *Ga*—PC | *Ga*—PC | **Yes** |

*Note:* Test names in bold are from the Virtual Test Library (VTL; Mather et al., 2025b). For more information on the Cattell-Horn-Carroll (CHC) classification expert consensus process, see LaForte et al. (2025, pp. 213–218). See Appendix A in this volume for CHC broad and narrow ability codes, definitions, and task examples.

### Comparison

The comparison juxtaposes three sources for each WJ V test:

1. **Phase I pilot classification** (independent expert dyads using neutral test descriptions and the CHC manual),
2. **WJ V author classification** (test authors' CHC labels informed by item knowledge and the WJ V structural validity analyses), and
3. **Structural evidence** reported in the WJ V Technical Manual (CFA/network results and other psychometric analyses).

Convergence across these sources strengthens content validity claims because it shows that (1) task demands (what the item requires) and (2) score behavior (how the item relates to other measures) point to the same CHC construct. Where sources diverge, the discrepancy identifies subtests that require adjudication, additional documentation, or targeted empirical study.

## EMPIRICAL OUTCOMES FOR WJ V VERSUS EXPERT CHC CLASSIFICATIONS

- **Broad ability agreement:** After reconciling coding conventions and implied codes, total agreement ≈98% (complete + partial). Complete agreement alone was 77% in the WJ V example.
- **Narrow ability agreement:** Total agreement ≈93% (complete + partial); baseline complete agreement was lower (≈63%), reflecting the greater granularity and ambiguity at the narrow level.

- **Primary sources of disagreement:** Differences in narrow ability taxonomies (e.g., WJ authors' use of Ps/Pc vs. experts' P), RAN classification (*Gr* vs mixed *Gs*/*Gr*), working memory coding conventions (Wc vs Wa/Wv/AC), and access to structural analysis results that informed WJ V authors' labels. Table B.1 provides greater detail about WJ V authors' and experts' classifications.

## PHASE I SUMMARY AND CONCLUSION

We compared Phase I pilot CHC classifications with the WJ V authors' CHC labels and the WJ V structural analyses to obtain convergent, cross-method evidence. High concordance at the broad level and substantial concordance at the narrow level support the content validity of the pilot classifications. Discrepancies were documented with explicit reasons (e.g., coding conventions, access to structural results, narrow ability definitions) and flagged for Phase II adjudication and empirical review (LaForte et al., 2025).

## PHASE II: CURRENT STATUS AND NEXT STEPS

1. **Panel composition and sampling**
   - Recruit **15–25 independent experts**; each subtest should be independently rated by **~12–15 experts** to balance workload and ensure robust interrater statistics. Collect CVs and declare conflicts of interest.
2. **Materials and metadata standardization**
   - Use finalized neutral subtest descriptions from Phase I and ensure each includes modality, timing, response format, and exemplar items.
3. **Rater training and calibration**
   - Conduct a synchronous calibration session (90–120 min) with practice items and require a calibration threshold (e.g., ≥80% agreement with pilot "gold standard") before independent rating.
4. **Rating instrument and workflow**
   - Deploy an online survey with drop-downs and mandatory metadata checks. Force a primary classification and allow optional secondary classifications.
5. **Automated scoring and thresholds**
   - Implement the streamlined hierarchical rules in an automated script to compute Level 1–4 agreement and flag items for adjudication. Predefine adjudication thresholds (e.g., <Level 2 broad agreement or <70% narrow agreement).
6. **Triangulation**
   - **Systematic review:** extract manual descriptions, technical manual CHC labels, and published factor/correlation evidence for each subtest.
   - **Secondary data analysis:** compile correlation matrices, CFA loadings, or cross-battery evidence where available.
   - **Cross-method synthesis matrix:** display expert consensus, manual classification, and empirical evidence for each subtest to guide final decisions.
7. **Reliability indices and reporting**
   - Report percent agreement and Gwet's AC1 as primary indices; include Cohen's kappa and Scott's pi for comparability. Provide per-subtest and per-domain statistics and contingency analyses.
8. **Adjudication and documentation**
   - Convene an adjudication panel (three to five experts not involved in initial dyads) to review flagged items with full documentation. Maintain a decision log recording final labels, rationale, and any codebook or description changes.

## APPENDIX MATERIALS TO BE INCLUDED FOR TRANSPARENCY

- **CHC codebook excerpt** (broad and narrow definitions with exemplars; see Appendix A)
- **Finalized neutral subtest descriptions** used in Phase I (omitted due to page limitations, but available upon request following the completion of Phase II)
- **Consensus instrument** (survey) and the exact question set
- **Agreement rule algorithm** and example cases illustrating each agreement level
- **Cross-method synthesis matrix template** (for Phase II)
- **Summary reliability statistics** and a log of adjudicated disagreements with rationale

## CONCLUSION

This appendix documents the design, procedures, and initial outcomes of the expert consensus study that underlies the X-BASS 3.0 CHC classifications for subtests new to this version. Phase I demonstrated that structured expert consensus, anchored in neutral subtest descriptions and a standardized CHC codebook, can produce reliable broad- and narrow ability classifications across 283 subtests from 46 batteries.

Cross-source comparison with the WJ V author classifications and structural analyses yielded high concordance at the broad level (≈98%) and substantial concordance at the narrow level (≈93%), providing convergent content-validity evidence for the pilot labels. Where discrepancies were identified, they were documented with explicit rationale and flagged for Phase II adjudication. Phase II, now underway, will extend these findings with a larger independent panel, triangulate against manual descriptions and empirical evidence, and apply a formal cross-method synthesis to produce final, defensible CHC classifications for all subtests in X-BASS 3.0. The materials, decision rules, and transparency documentation provided in this appendix are intended to support replication, peer review, and ongoing refinement of CHC-based test classification.

## LIMITATIONS

Several limitations should be noted. First, Phase I relied on two expert dyads; while inter-dyad agreement was high, the small number of raters limits generalizability of reliability estimates. Phase II addresses this by recruiting 15–25 independent experts. Second, pilot classifications were based on neutral subtest descriptions without access to actual test materials or structural data. This design choice supports independence but may reduce sensitivity to task features not captured in descriptions. Third, narrow ability classifications are inherently more ambiguous than broad ability classifications, and some residual disagreements reflect genuine taxonomic uncertainty within CHC theory rather than rater error. Fourth, the cross-source comparison was conducted only for the WJ V tests; convergent evidence for other batteries awaits completion of Phase II. Finally, the CHC taxonomy itself continues to evolve (e.g., the *Glr*-to-*Gl* relabeling), and classifications should be understood as reflecting the best available evidence at the time of the study.

## REFERENCES

American Educational Research Association, American Psychological Association, & National Council on Measurement in Education (2014). *Standards for educational and psychological testing.* American Educational Research Association.

Borsboom, D., Mellenbergh, G. J., & van Heerden, J. (2004). The concept of validity. *Psychological Review, 111*(4), 1061–1071. https://doi.org/10.1037/0033-295X.111.4.1061.

Bynum, R. (2026). What do preschool tests measure? A multi-method content validity study. Dissertation Abstracts.

Bynum, R., Flanagan, D. P., & Alfonso, V. C. (2026). Structured expert consensus and cross-method synthesis of CHC test classifications across 46 batteries: Content validity evidence for applied practice. Manuscript in preparation.

Flanagan, D. P., Ortiz, S. O., & Alfonso, V. C. (2025). *Cross-Battery Assessment Software System, Version 3.0.* Wiley.

Flanagan, D. P., Ortiz, S. O., & Alfonso, V. C. (2013). *Essentials of cross-battery assessment* (3rd ed). Wiley.

Flanagan, D. P., Ortiz, S. O., Alfonso, V. C., & Mascolo, J. T. (2002). *The achievement test desk reference: Comprehensive assessment and learning disabilities.* Wiley.

Flanagan, D. P., Ortiz, S. O., Alfonso, V. C., & Mascolo, J. T. (2006). *The achievement test desk reference 2e: A guide to learning disability identification.* Wiley.

Kane, M. T. (2009). Validating the interpretations and uses of test scores. In R. W. Lissitz (Ed.), *The concept of validity: Revisions, new directions, and applications* (pp. 39–64). Information Age Publishing.

LaForte, E. M., Dailey, D., & McGrew, K. S. (2025). Technical manual. In *Woodcock-Johnson V.* Riverside Assessments, LLC.

Mather, N., McGrew, K. S., LaForte, E. M., & Wendling, B. J. (2025b). *Woodcock-Johnson V Virtual Test Library.* Riverside Assessments, LLC.

McGrew, K. S. (1997). Analysis of the major intelligence batteries according to a proposed comprehensive CHC framework. In D. P. Flanagan, J. L. Genshaft, & P. L. Harrison (Eds.), *Contemporary intellectual assessment: Theories, tests, and issues* (pp. 151–180). Guilford Press.

McGrew, K. S., Mather, N., LaForte, E. M., & Wendling, B. J. (2025). *Woodcock-Johnson V.* Riverside Assessments, LLC.

Messick, S. (1989). Validity. In R. L. Linn (Ed.), *Educational measurement* (3rd ed, pp. 13–104). American Council on Education & Macmillan.

Schneider, W. J., & McGrew, K. S. (2018). The Cattell–Horn–Carroll theory of cognitive abilities. In D. P. Flanagan & E. M. McDonough (Eds.), *Contemporary intellectual assessment: Theories, tests, and issues* (4th ed, pp. 73–163). Guilford Press.

Sireci, S. G., & Benítez, I. (2022). Evidence for test validation: A guide for practitioners. *Psicothema, 35*(3), 217–226.

Sireci, S. G., & Rodriguez, G. (2022). *Validity in educational testing.* Routledge. https://doi.org/10.4324/9781138609877-REE180-1.

Urbina, S. (2014). *Essentials of psychological testing* (2nd ed). Wiley.

Appendix C

# THE EVOLUTION OF COGNITIVE-ACHIEVEMENT RELATIONS RESEARCH: PAST, PRESENT, AND FUTURE

Daniel B. Hajovsky, Ph.D.

Texas A&M University

Christopher R. Niileksela, Ph.D.

University of Kansas

## THE EVOLUTION OF COGNITIVE-ACHIEVEMENT RELATIONS RESEARCH: PAST, PRESENT, AND FUTURE

The scientific study of individual differences has captured the attention of researchers and practitioners since the 19th century, including differences in cognitive abilities and cognitive processes (hereafter collectively referred to as *cognitive abilities* for brevity). Researchers have shown that cognitive abilities are influenced by a complex interaction of genetic and environmental factors (Deary et al., 2022; Jensen, 1998; Plomin & Deary, 2015). Numerous studies indicate that cognitive ability tests provide robust (but far from perfect!) predictions of many relevant educational outcomes, like school grades, achievement test scores, and levels of educational attainment. The influence of cognitive abilities and processes on learning outcomes has shaped our understanding of the development of academic skills and led to deeper insights into their role in facilitating or inhibiting academic skill development.

Over the past several decades, studies have explicitly examined how cognitive abilities predict or influence academic achievement. This research is often referred to as *cognitive-achievement relations* in the literature. Cognitive-achievement relations research has influenced specific learning disability (SLD) identification practices, and the development of SLD identification models, often referred to as *patterns of strengths and weaknesses* (PSW). Although previous work has found that specific cognitive abilities influence the development of academic skills (e.g., phonological processing and reading), continuing this investigation in other domains and using novel approaches can better equip researchers and practitioners with the tools needed to understand and identify difficulties that give rise to SLDs. Cognitive-achievement relations research sets the foundation for an essential component of the PSW methods based on the definition of SLD in the Individuals with Disabilities Education Act (IDEA, U.S. Department of Education, 2004). That is, if difficulties in academic skills are due to one or more weaknesses in underlying cognitive abilities or processes (and other potential causes are ruled out), then the cognitive abilities related to academic skills may be contributing to those difficulties. All PSW methods use this cognitive-achievement relations component (called *consistency* in PSW methods) as one of the bases for identifying SLDs.

When practitioners understand cognitive-achievement relations, they can infer the nature of learning difficulties and identify SLDs. The accumulation of empirical knowledge on these relationships has brought the field into a new scientific era, in which researchers ask more finely tuned questions, often requiring new methods. In this appendix, we explore the past, present, and future of cognitive-achievement relations research.

## PAST COGNITIVE-ACHIEVEMENT RELATIONS RESEARCH (1990–2010)

One of the most prevalent lines of research in this era was centered on how both general intelligence and specific cognitive abilities predicted achievement. In an early comprehensive study using the Woodcock-Johnson Psycho-Educational Battery-Revised (WJ-R; Woodcock & Johnson, 1989) standardization sample data, Keith (1999) analyzed the unique influence of general intelligence and specific cognitive abilities on academic skills across ethnic groups (Hispanic, Caucasian, and African American) and grade levels (grades 1–4, 5–8, and 9–12). Using multigroup structural equation modeling (SEM), Keith found the following: (1) specific cognitive abilities explained substantial variance in math and reading above and beyond the variance explained by general intelligence; (2) the same subset of specific cognitive abilities demonstrated the same magnitude of effects across ethnic groups; and (3) the specific cognitive abilities that were important for reading and math achievement differed across grade levels. In another contemporaneous study, Youngstrom et al. (1999) conducted hierarchical regression analyses to examine the incremental validity of the cognitive factor scores from the Differential Ability Scales (DAS; Elliott, 1990) in predicting the DAS achievement scores (Word Reading, Basic Number Skills, and Spelling). Unlike Keith's findings, Youngstrom and colleagues' findings suggested that specific cognitive abilities (Verbal, Nonverbal, and Spatial Abilities) explained little variance in achievement scores beyond that explained by the overall general ability score of the DAS. Similarly, Canivez (2013) used hierarchical regression with the Wechsler Individual Achievement Test-Second Edition (WIAT-II, Psychological Corporation, 2002), Wechsler Individual Achievement Test-Third Edition (WIAT-III, Wechsler, 2009), and Wechsler Adult Intelligence Scale-Fourth Edition (WAIS-IV, Wechsler, 2008) scores and found that the overall general ability score or Full-Scale IQ (FSIQ) explained 8% (Oral Reading Accuracy) to 63.5% (Math Reasoning) of the variance in WIAT-II/III scores while the WAIS-IV factor index scores (e.g., Working Memory Index) explained an additional 0–5.6% of variance. Canivez concluded that because specific cognitive abilities provided only small unique contributions to WIAT-II/III achievement scores, the FSIQ should be the primary index interpreted when using the WAIS-IV to predict WIAT-II/III scores. The results of these three research studies varied primarily because of differences in tests, methods, statistical analyses, and degree of emphasis on psychometric theories.

In two notable syntheses of cognitive-achievement relations research (Flanagan et al., 2006; McGrew & Wendling, 2010), scholars summarized evidence of statistically significant differential relationships between specific cognitive abilities and reading and math achievement across developmental age groups, based on studies published since the early 1990s. These two syntheses used earlier versions of the Cattell-Horn-Carroll (CHC) taxonomy (Schneider & McGrew, 2018) as a general framework for categorizing cognitive and academic abilities. A consistent finding across these studies was that comprehension knowledge (often colloquially referred to as background knowledge and verbal ability), a broad cognitive ability, had statistically significant relations with multiple areas of reading and math achievement, and the strength of these relations increased with age. This finding has been replicated multiple times in subsequent studies with different samples and cognitive and achievement batteries. Although much of the research on cognitive-achievement relations used the Woodcock-Johnson family of test batteries, these syntheses depicted a clearer picture of the relations between cognitive abilities and academic achievement. These two research syntheses were instrumental in developing PSW methods of SLD identification, most notably the Dual Discrepancy/Consistency (DD/C) method proposed by Flanagan and colleagues (2013, 2018).

## CURRENT COGNITIVE-ACHIEVEMENT RELATIONS RESEARCH (2011–2024)

CHC theory has been increasingly used for intelligence research, test development, and assessment interpretation (Schneider & McGrew, 2018). CHC theory is a taxonomy of human cognitive abilities that integrates the Horn-Cattell fluid and crystallized (*Gf-Gc*) theory (Horn & Noll, 1997) and Carroll's (1993) three-stratum theory.[1] Within this multidimensional and hierarchical framework, the general factor (*g* or psychometric *g*) is at the apex at Stratum III. All measures of mental performance reflect *g* to some extent with individual differences in *g* related to important behaviors and outcomes such as academic achievement, job complexity, occupational performance, health, income, and years of education attained (Jensen, 1998; Neisser et al., 1996). Stratum II comprises 17 broad cognitive abilities (e.g., auditory processing, comprehension knowledge; see Appendix A for a complete list) that coalesce due to shared cognitive processes. Broad cognitive abilities (also called group factors) also reflect *g* to some extent and are typically represented as composite scores on cognitive ability tests. Stratum I includes over 80 narrow abilities that reflect a wide range of more specific cognitive capacities (e.g., lexical knowledge, phonetic coding, working memory, general sequential reasoning), each measured by a subtest. Most modern cognitive ability tests and the constructs they are purported to measure are developed, classified, and interpreted according to CHC theory, which is supported by ample structural validity evidence across multiple test batteries (e.g., Caemmerer et al., 2020; Reynolds et al., 2013).

An extensive literature base of empirical research on cognitive-achievement relations has documented how cognitive abilities predict reading, writing, and mathematics achievement across the lifespan (e.g., Caemmerer et al., 2018; Decker & Roberts, 2015; Hajovsky et al., 2014, 2018; Niileksela et al., 2016, 2025a; Villeneuve et al., 2019). There is substantial extant literature on some of the most salient findings regarding cognitive-achievement relations across reading, mathematics, and writing. In the following section, the effects of general intelligence (Stratum III) on academic skills are discussed first, followed by the effects of broad cognitive abilities (Stratum II) on academic skills. We distinguish the effects of general and broad cognitive abilities on specific areas of academic skills (e.g., basic reading and reading comprehension) reported in empirical studies. In general, the effects of *g* on academic skills are large, whereas the effects of broad abilities on academic skills are typically in the small-to-moderate range.

### General Intelligence

The *g* factor tends to be one of the strongest predictors across all academic skills and overall educational achievement (e.g., Caemmerer et al., 2018; Gottfredson, 1997; Jensen, 1998; Kaufman et al., 2012). Within latent variable higher-order CHC models in which *g* and broad abilities are specified, *g* effects on reading, mathematics, and writing skills are typically fully mediated by the broad abilities (Hajovsky et al., 2014, 2018; Niileksela et al., 2016, 2025a), though some studies have found direct effects of *g* on academic skill (Parkin & Beaujean, 2012; Villeneuve et al., 2019). In other words, *g* effects on achievement are indirect via their effects on different broad abilities (e.g., auditory processing, comprehension knowledge), which, in turn, influence academic skills (e.g., Floyd et al., 2012; Hajovsky et al., 2014). Researchers

[1] In a recent article on theories of cognitive abilities spanning 30 years, McGrew (1993) recommended that the Cattell, Horn, and Carroll theories be referred to as "CHC theories" rather than one theory.

have also employed bifactor models to examine cognitive-achievement relations. In these models, *g* and broad abilities are modeled as independent factors. First, variance attributable to *g* is partialled from the subtests. Then, broad cognitive abilities are modeled using the residualized variance not attributable to *g*. Cognitive-achievement relations are examined by estimating the direct effects of *g* and the residualized broad abilities on academic skills. The direct effects of *g* on academic skills are large and stronger than the residualized effects of the broad abilities (Caemmerer et al., 2018; Hajovsky et al., 2018; Villeneuve et al., 2019), but the total indirect effects of *g* in the higher-order model and the direct effects of *g* from the bifactor model tend to have similarly sized effects (Hajovsky et al., 2018).

The status of *g* as a distinct cognitive ability has not been without controversy, despite its long history. Some researchers have considered *g* to be a statistical artifact (e.g., Horn & Blankson, 2005), and others have suggested that the *g* factor arises because there are similar cognitive processes invoked across all ability tests, rather than *g* being a separate, distinct ability (e.g., process overlap theory; Kovacs & Conway, 2016, 2020). The positive manifold, or positive correlations among mental tests, has been posited to exist because of a reciprocal causation or mutualism (van der Maas et al., 2006). According to this theory of mutualism, there are beneficial positive interactions between cognitive processes during development that explain the positive manifold. The theory of mutualism has been offered as a worthy contender to explain *g* (though *g* is not usually represented in these models) but also how the development of cognitive-achievement relations may, in fact, be bidirectional with implications for specific abilities (e.g., Peng & Kievit, 2020; Zhang & Peng, 2023). Whatever the true nature or origin of *g*, the theoretical developments and empirical research on this front aim to further enhance our understanding of this construct and how it may trickle down to inform cognitive-achievement relations research.

## Reading Achievement

In reading, cognitive-achievement relations research focuses on basic reading skills, reading fluency, and reading comprehension. Basic reading skills, including decoding and word recognition, are likely affected by multiple broad cognitive abilities (Floyd et al., 2012; Hajovsky et al., 2014; Niileksela et al., 2016, 2025a). For example, comprehension knowledge, short-term memory, and processing speed are related to basic reading skills mainly across school-age children, but the magnitude of effects has differed across test batteries and ages (cf. Caemmerer et al., 2018; Cormier et al., 2017; Evans et al., 2002; Floyd et al., 2007; Hajovsky et al., 2014; Niileksela et al., 2016; Vanderwood et al., 2002). Less research has examined broad cognitive ability influences on reading fluency, which involves the speed and accuracy at which an individual can read a passage with clear understanding. Comprehension knowledge and processing speed are related to reading fluency (Caemmerer et al., 2018; Cormier et al., 2017; Niileksela et al., 2016), and Cormier et al. (2017) also suggest that fluid reasoning may be related to reading fluency at younger ages. One of the most robust broad cognitive ability effects on reading comprehension is comprehension knowledge (Caemmerer et al., 2018; Floyd et al., 2012; Hajovsky et al., 2014; Keith, 1999; McGrew et al., 1997; Niileksela et al., 2016, 2025a). These effects tend to increase with age as reading comprehension requires increased use of linguistic comprehension skills, background knowledge, and vocabulary. In addition, short-term memory, processing speed, and fluid reasoning are related to reading comprehension (Cain et al., 2004; Cormier et al., 2017; Floyd et al., 2012; Hajovsky et al., 2014; Niileksela et al., 2016). Hajovsky et al. (2014) found visual processing is related to reading comprehension with the KABC-II for younger children, but this finding is atypical. Importantly, basic reading skills are also considered a precursor to, and essential skill for, reading comprehension, and research suggests that the effects of cognitive abilities on reading comprehension may be mediated through basic reading skills (e.g., Floyd et al., 2012).

## Mathematics Achievement

In mathematics, findings have mostly been reported on math calculation and problem solving, and math fluency is often included with math calculation rather than considered a separate academic skill. Math calculation involves basic math skills like computation, whereas math problem solving involves more word problems and the application of math concepts to real-world scenarios. While mathematical calculation involves knowledge of procedural rules, mathematical problem solving involves more appropriate selection and application of those rules to problems with varying linguistic demands. Thus, math computation has been found to be related to math problem solving (Villeneuve et al., 2019). There is consistent evidence that comprehension knowledge, fluid reasoning, and processing speed are related to both math calculation and math problem solving (Floyd et al., 2003; Keith, 1999; Niileksela et al., 2016, 2025a; Villeneuve et al., 2019). Findings suggest that short-term memory is also related to math calculation and math problem solving (Floyd et al., 2003; Villeneuve et al., 2019), with some studies finding effects of visual processing on math problem solving (McGrew & Hessler, 1995; Niileksela et al., 2016; Villeneuve et al., 2019). In one study that examined a component of mathematics achievement referred to as math fluency, or how quickly an individual completes simple math operations (timed tests of simple math operations), processing speed was related to (after controlling for basic math) performance (Niileksela et al., 2016), whereas Caemmerer et al. (2018) found both processing speed and short-term memory were related to math fluency.

## Writing Achievement

Writing achievement has received the least attention in research on cognitive-achievement relations, and writing presents several difficulties in this type of research. Writing is closely related to reading, and in CHC theory reading and writing tend to be categorized under a single broad ability. Writing is complex and requires the coordination of multiple cognitive, executive, and motor skills. In the cognitive-achievement relations research on writing, researchers typically distinguish between basic writing skills and written expression. The former includes skills like spelling and editing, while the latter includes skill in expressing ideas in a written format. Comprehension knowledge, processing speed, and short-term memory are related to basic writing skills (Cormier et al., 2016; Floyd et al., 2008; Niileksela et al., 2016, 2025a), while others have found fluid reasoning may be related to basic writing skills at different ages (Cormier et al., 2016; Floyd et al., 2008; McGrew & Knopik, 1993). Conversely, processing speed is related to written expression across different editions of the WJ (Cormier et al., 2016; Floyd et al., 2008; Hajovsky et al., 2019; McGrew & Knopik, 1993; Niileksela et al., 2016). Comprehension knowledge has been consistently related to written expression (Floyd et al., 2008; Hajovsky et al., 2018; McGrew & Knopik, 1993), except in the WJ IV (Cormier et al., 2016; Niileksela et al., 2016) and WJ V (Niileksela et al., 2025a). There are inconsistent findings with fluid reasoning and short-term memory relations with written expression (Cormier et al., 2016; Floyd et al., 2008; McGrew & Knopik, 1993; Niileksela et al., 2016, 2025a). Visual processing relations on written expression have been reported in two separate batteries (Hajovsky et al., 2018; Niileksela et al., 2016).

While substantial research has examined cognitive-achievement relations using a variety of test batteries and samples, inconsistencies across studies remain. The synthesis of this research to bring together the most consistent findings is essential to develop a strong underlying foundation to how cognitive-achievement relations can be applied to the identification of SLDs.

### Empirical and Methodological Shortcomings

A noted limitation of previous syntheses of cognitive-achievement relations is that the reviews by Flanagan et al. (2006) and McGrew and Wendling (2010) did not quantify the size of the relations between cognitive abilities and academic achievement, only indicating whether the relations were statistically significant. Statistical significance is highly dependent on sample size and does not provide information on the magnitude of the relationships among variables. Quantifying the strength of relations is important because it can provide a more nuanced understanding of how strongly variables are related, rather than only whether they are related. Zaboski et al. (2018) conducted a comprehensive meta-analysis to investigate the magnitude of effects between general and broad cognitive abilities and reading and mathematics achievement. They reported psychometric *g* (the first factor extracted from a variance–covariance matrix of cognitive tests that tends to account for the most shared variance among test scores) explained the lion's share of variance in all measured achievement skills ($r^2 = .54$) with comprehension knowledge accounting for the most variance in all measured achievement skills relative to other broad abilities. However, the meta-analytic correlations among broad abilities and achievement in the Zaboski et al. study appear very low compared to other evidence (e.g., examining correlations between cognitive abilities and academic skills in single-test batteries). Zaboski et al. may have significantly underestimated the size of the correlations between cognitive abilities and academic achievement. This is one notable study that examined whether cognitive abilities matter (statistical significance) and, if so, how they matter (effect sizes). It should be noted, however, that methodologies like those used by Zaboski and colleagues have been criticized for being ill-equipped to determine the direct, causal effect of neurocognitive tests on academic outcomes (Decker & Luedke, 2021). Another meta-analysis by Kudo et al. (2015) investigated the extent to which IQ, specific cognitive abilities, and academic skills moderated differences between children with and without reading disabilities. Their results indicated that, across studies comparing these two groups, intelligence (*g*) and domain-general cognitive abilities (i.e., short-term memory) yielded moderate effect sizes. On the other hand, verbal IQ and domain-specific cognitive abilities (i.e., phonological awareness) demonstrated large effect sizes. Similarly, Compton et al. (2012) and Swanson (2012) reported cognitive profile differences between those with reading and mathematics disabilities, suggesting meaningful differences in specific cognitive abilities between the groups.

The effect size component of cognitive-achievement relations research became increasingly important during this era. There was an increased emphasis on *which* abilities matter and *how much* they matter for different academic domains, and whether these effect sizes differed across ages and grade levels. Rather than focusing only on which cognitive abilities were statistically significant predictors of academic skills, the focus shifted to which cognitive abilities were more or less strongly related to academic skills. Thus, there was more emphasis on effect sizes and different moderators (e.g., age/grade, sex/gender). During this period, there was also increased focus on integrated models of reading development (e.g., Floyd et al., 2012; Hajovsky et al., 2014) and math development (e.g., Villeneuve et al., 2019), where the relations among academic skills were also considered in these models (e.g., cognitive abilities predict basic reading skills, which in turn predict reading comprehension). We predict that integrated models of cognitive abilities and academic skill development will become more important as we examine the interplay of these constructs within a more interconnected, mutually developing framework (Hajovsky et al., 2022).

## THE FUTURE OF COGNITIVE-ACHIEVEMENT RELATIONS RESEARCH (2025 AND BEYOND)

Despite previous studies that synthesize research on cognitive-achievement relations, there are several gaps that need to be addressed. Much of the work on cognitive-achievement relations has been conducted using single test batteries and samples. There is a need for multibattery, multisample studies to support stronger inferences about construct-specific relations that generalize across batteries. For example, cross-battery confirmatory factor analysis (CB-CFA) has been used to analyze scores from multiple batteries simultaneously (Caemmerer et al., 2020; Reynolds et al., 2013). The CB-CFA method has been applied within the context of intelligence research to examine the underlying structure of intelligence tests and the constructs measured across different test batteries (e.g., Flanagan & McGrew, 1998; Johnson et al., 2004; Keith et al., 2001; Phelps et al., 2005; Sanders et al., 2007; Woodcock, 1990).

This multibattery, multisample framework can be applied to examining cognitive-achievement relations by analyzing correlation matrices from multiple batteries and samples simultaneously using meta-analytic structural equation modeling (meta-SEM). Emerging meta-analyses of cognitive-achievement relations have documented moderate relations between working memory and mathematics ($r = .35$; Peng et al., 2016), working memory and reading ($r = .29$; Peng et al., 2018), fluid reasoning and reading and mathematics ($r = .38$ and .41, respectively; Peng et al., 2019), language and mathematics ($r = .42$; Peng et al., 2020), and spatial skills and mathematics ($r = .36$; Atit et al., 2022). Importantly, meta-SEM not only provides an estimate of the average correlation among cognitive abilities and academic skills, but also the distribution of correlations among cognitive abilities and academic skills. For example, the average correlation between tests of phonological awareness and tests of word reading may be .50. However, the standard deviation of correlations may be .13, so the average range of correlations may span from .37 to .63. This is important information because it can help provide a more nuanced understanding of how the correlations among tests vary. It can help researchers examine reasons why there may be differences among the correlations across tests. Practically speaking, findings from a meta-SEM approach to studying cognitive-achievement relations may better inform SLD identification than previous research. As those with SLD tend to have lower scores on cognitive abilities correlated with academic skills (e.g., Johnson et al., 2010; Swanson, 2015), more comprehensive examinations of cognitive-achievement relations will enhance our understanding of how cognitive processes contribute to learning difficulties that may manifest as SLD.

Overall, the research on cognitive-achievement relations has continued to evolve and has been an important component of models for SLD identification. We hope to see this research develop further and help researchers and practitioners better understand how cognitive abilities and academic skills relate to one another, especially how cognitive abilities influence the development of those academic skills.

## New Cognitive-Achievement Relations Research

One important consideration with cognitive-achievement relations research is whether these relations can be generalized across populations. Research has found that the relations change for some populations, with the most notable research showing differences across ages. For example, the relationship between comprehension knowledge and reading comprehension increases with age, and the relationship between phonological awareness and reading comprehension decreases with age (e.g., Floyd et al., 2012). These differences make theoretical sense, and they are important to consider to understand reading development. As people age, their decoding skills become automatic, and phonological awareness no longer differentiates between those who have good reading comprehension or poor reading comprehension. Rather, a person's background knowledge and verbal skills differentiate between those who have good reading comprehension or poor reading comprehension.

A more complex question that has only begun to be addressed in research is whether cognitive-achievement relations are the same across the distributions of cognitive abilities and academic skills. For instance, is the relationship between comprehension knowledge and reading comprehension the same for individuals with low reading comprehension compared with those with high reading comprehension? A few studies have specifically examined this question and found that some cognitive abilities may have stronger influences on reading comprehension among individuals with lower reading comprehension (e.g., Hajovsky et al., 2020; Language and Reading Research Consortium & Logan, 2017). These findings suggest that cognitive-achievement relations may differ across the distribution of academic skill levels, with some cognitive abilities becoming increasingly important for those with lower academic skills. Conversely, some cognitive abilities may become increasingly important for those with higher academic skills for specific academic domains. Similarly, some studies have examined whether cognitive-achievement relations differ across the distribution of general intelligence (e.g., Caemmerer et al., 2024; Hajovsky et al., 2023, 2025a; Niileksela et al., 2025b). Findings from these studies using different test batteries show that general intelligence and some broad abilities may have differential influences on reading and mathematics achievement depending on their level of general intelligence. Although preliminary, these studies help highlight that the interpretive weight given to understanding which cognitive abilities contribute to learning difficulties may need to consider the overall level of ability or academic skill. This research could potentially influence how cognitive-achievement relations are incorporated into PSW methods, by considering general ability level when using correlations among test scores to determine whether score differences are statistically significant.

## Developing Consensus Models of Cognitive-Achievement Relations

Recent cognitive-achievement relations research using meta-SEM that is in progress has the potential to yield the most robust findings to date. This type of work is a significant advancement in cognitive-achievement relations research because the scope of the meta-analysis is unprecedented, encompassing over 600 correlation matrices and over 80,000 correlations. While meta-analysis has been common in intervention research, it has been underutilized in correlational research, and especially with cognitive-achievement relations research. Meta-analyses consolidate the results of studies to estimate an overall effect size across studies and can account for differences in samples, sample sizes, sites, methods, measures, etc. Although prior work in this area (e.g., Atit et al., 2022; Peng et al., 2018, 2019) has examined cognitive-achievement relations, our ongoing work extends previous meta-analyses by examining a much larger set of correlation matrices across published test batteries. We are working to combine subtests that measure the same broad and narrow CHC abilities to examine the average correlations between broad and narrow cognitive abilities and academic skills. To demonstrate the utility of this research, we include some preliminary results of this work here. While these analyses are preliminary, they include a large number of correlations. The addition of further correlation matrices will ultimately be included in the dataset, but at this point the addition of further data is not expected to substantially alter the results.

A full description of all methods and analyses is beyond the scope of this appendix, but they will be forthcoming in future work and were described in a recent presentation, and part of this work is currently under review for publication (Hajovsky et al., 2025b). These analyses included subtests that were classified as measures of 1 of 8 CHC broad cognitive abilities (i.e., *Gc*, *Gf*, *Gv*, *Ga*, *Gl*, *Gr*, *Gwm*, and *Gs*), and 1 of 11 academic skills (i.e., Reading Decoding-Phonological, Reading Decoding-Lexical, Reading Decoding-Speed, Reading Speed, Reading Comprehension, Math Speed, Math Calculation, Math Knowledge, Math Problem Solving, Spelling, English Usage, Writing Speed, and Writing Ability). Basic reading skills were divided into two separate decoding skills—decoding real words (Reading Decoding-Lexical) and decoding nonsense words (Reading Decoding-Phonological). Skilled readers identify words automatically because they have been stored in their orthographic memory. Therefore, Reading Decoding-Lexical provides information about the size of an individual's sight word vocabulary. When reading nonsense words, or words that have not been seen before and are not stored in orthographic memory, phonetic skills (e.g., knowledge of letter-sound relationships) are used to decode the words. Reading Decoding-Phonological provides information about the individual's ability to use phonetic skills. In addition, Reading Speed was divided into two narrow skills, Reading Decoding-Speed (identifying individual words on timed tests) and Reading Speed (rate of reading connected text).

The following results were estimated through five steps that are similar to the two-stage meta-SEM (Cheung & Chan, 2005): (1) sample sizes and correlations among subtests from 568 correlation matrices obtained from published test manuals were compiled, (2) meta-analytic correlations among the subtests that measure the same broad cognitive abilities and narrow academic abilities were estimated using the metafor package in R (Viechtbauer, 2010), (3) the meta-analytic correlations among broad cognitive abilities and narrow academic skills were pooled into a single correlation matrix, (4) the meta-analytic correlations among subtests were used to estimate a correlation matrix of cognitive abilities and academic skills for two-test composites of cognitive abilities and academic skills, and (5) the correlation matrix of estimated two-test composites was used to carry out cognitive-achievement relations analyses. When estimating meta-analytic correlations, a three-level random effects model was used. This model estimates the average correlation between the cognitive and academic skills, and also estimates: (1) the variance among correlations between the same cognitive abilities and academic skills (e.g., how much variability is present across all of the correlations between Reading Comprehension and *Gc* for all correlations included in the database) and (2) the variance of correlations between the same cognitive abilities and academic skills within the same correlation matrix (e.g., how much variability is present in the correlations between Reading Comprehension and *Gc* with correlation matrices that have multiple correlations between measures of Reading Comprehension and *Gc*).

Two types of models were estimated in these analyses. First, a model regressing narrow academic skills on all the broad CHC abilities was estimated. In this model, all broad cognitive abilities loaded on a single latent *g* factor so the indirect effects of *g* on academic skills could be estimated. There was a residual correlation between *Gf* and *Gv* (likely due to *Gf* tests commonly using visual stimuli) and between *Gr* and *Gs* (likely due to timed tests for these two abilities). Second, integrated achievement models were estimated, in which cognitive abilities were predictors of all academic skills, and basic academic skills were predictors of advanced academic skills. We wanted to include integrated models in this analysis to examine how narrow academic skills relate to more advanced academic skills. These integrated achievement models were separately estimated for reading, writing, and mathematics. For example, cognitive abilities predicted Reading Decoding-Lexical and Reading Decoding-Phonological, and those two reading decoding skills, in turn, predicted Reading Decoding-Speed, Reading Speed, and Reading Comprehension.

The final dataset used in this analysis included 67,212 correlations using data from 151 different test batteries, 857 subtests, with a total of 213,605 individuals. Due to the nature of these analyses, the statistical significance of regression coefficients was not a focus because the estimated correlation matrix from the meta-analytic correlations included a large number of observations, so very small regression coefficients would be statistically significant. Rather, we focus on the size of standardized regression coefficients, following recommendations from Keith (2019): coefficients $\geq .25$ are considered large, between .10 and .24 moderate, between .05 and .09 small, and $<.05$ negligible. The correlation matrix used for all analyses is included in Table C.1. The results of the nonintegrated models are included in Tables C.2 and C.3, and results of the integrated models are included in Tables C.4 and C.5. Tables C.2 and C.4 include the coefficients from the meta-SEM models, and Tables C.3 and C.5 include descriptors of the size of the coefficients for the meta-SEM models.

### *Reading: Nonintegrated Achievement Models*

First, we describe the results of nonintegrated achievement models. The path from *Gv* to all reading skills was negative and sometimes moderate in size, suggesting a suppressor effect. The models were estimated without paths from *Gv* to help ensure that the large negative relationships from *Gv* to reading skills were not artificially inflating the size of the other relationships in the models.

For Reading Decoding-Phonological, there was a large effect from *Ga*, moderate effects from *Gc* and *Gwm*, and small effects from *Gf*, *Gl*, and *Gr*. For Reading Decoding-Lexical, there were large effects from *Gc* and *Ga*, and small effects from *Gf*, *Gr*, *Gwm*, and *Gs*. For Reading Decoding-Speed, there were large effects from *Ga* and *Gs*, moderate effects from *Gc* and *Gr*, and a small effect from *Gf*. For Reading Speed, there was a large effect from *Gs*, moderate effects from *Gc*, *Ga*, and *Gr*, and small effects from *Gf* and *Gwm*. For Reading Comprehension, there was a large effect from *Gc*, moderate effects from *Gf* and *Ga*, and small effects from *Gl*, *Gr*, *Gwm*, and *Gs*. For all reading skills, the indirect effects of *g* were large. This model is shown in Figure C.1.

**Table C.1 Meta-Analytic Correlation Matrix Used in Meta-Analysis**

| | *Gc* | *Gf* | *Gv* | *Ga* | *Gl* | *Gr* | *Gwm* | *Gs* | RDL | RDP | RDS | RS | RC | MPS | MC | MS | KM | SG | EU | WS | WA |
|---|---|---|---|---|---|---|---|---|---|---|---|---|---|---|---|---|---|---|---|---|---|
| ***Gc*** | 1.00 | | | | | | | | | | | | | | | | | | | | |
| ***Gf*** | .59 | 1.00 | | | | | | | | | | | | | | | | | | | |
| ***Gv*** | .51 | .60 | 1.00 | | | | | | | | | | | | | | | | | | |
| ***Ga*** | .53 | .49 | .42 | 1.00 | | | | | | | | | | | | | | | | | |
| ***Gl*** | .51 | .47 | .42 | .45 | 1.00 | | | | | | | | | | | | | | | | |
| ***Gr*** | .37 | .33 | .33 | .35 | .35 | 1.00 | | | | | | | | | | | | | | | |
| ***Gwm*** | .52 | .51 | .44 | .51 | .41 | .40 | 1.00 | | | | | | | | | | | | | | |
| ***Gs*** | .39 | .41 | .43 | .36 | .30 | .44 | .40 | 1.00 | | | | | | | | | | | | | |
| **RDL** | .62 | .50 | .38 | .58 | .42 | .40 | .50 | .41 | 1.00 | | | | | | | | | | | | |
| **RDP** | .50 | .46 | .35 | .61 | .42 | .37 | .49 | .33 | .84 | 1.00 | | | | | | | | | | | |
| **RDS** | .45 | .42 | .27 | .50 | .34 | .46 | .40 | .53 | .79 | .75 | 1.00 | | | | | | | | | | |
| **RS** | .51 | .45 | .28 | .45 | .37 | .46 | .46 | .53 | .72 | .61 | .76 | 1.00 | | | | | | | | | |
| **RC** | .69 | .56 | .42 | .60 | .49 | .40 | .51 | .41 | .79 | .66 | .63 | .66 | 1.00 | | | | | | | | |
| **MPS** | .63 | .66 | .49 | .53 | .47 | .39 | .52 | .45 | .65 | .57 | .53 | .53 | .70 | 1.00 | | | | | | | |
| **MC** | .55 | .61 | .44 | .45 | .40 | .36 | .47 | .47 | .63 | .52 | .48 | .51 | .65 | .80 | 1.00 | | | | | | |
| **MS** | .37 | .45 | .27 | .36 | .29 | .42 | .39 | .55 | .50 | .45 | .56 | .60 | .46 | .62 | .71 | 1.00 | | | | | |
| **KM** | .73 | .75 | .45 | .50 | .50 | .39 | .56 | .49 | .58 | .54 | .42 | .49 | .68 | .83 | .76 | .62 | 1.00 | | | | |
| **SG** | .56 | .49 | .35 | .56 | .40 | .40 | .51 | .44 | .86 | .81 | .73 | .69 | .71 | .64 | .65 | .57 | .54 | 1.00 | | | |
| **EU** | .59 | .54 | .37 | .51 | .45 | .39 | .50 | .50 | .77 | .71 | .61 | .73 | .73 | .64 | .64 | .59 | — | .83 | 1.00 | | |
| **WS** | .38 | .47 | .32 | .42 | .36 | .44 | .43 | .61 | .53 | .48 | .55 | .67 | .51 | .48 | .51 | .60 | .57 | .58 | .75 | 1.00 | |
| **WA** | .57 | .53 | .39 | .57 | .45 | .40 | .48 | .43 | .70 | .64 | .57 | .56 | .70 | .63 | .64 | .51 | .65 | .72 | .66 | .58 | 1.00 |

*Note:* Correlations represent estimates of two-test composite scores for each correlation pair. There were no studies to combine to estimate a correlation between Math Knowledge (KM) and Grammatical Sensitivity (EU).

*Gc* = Comprehension Knowledge; *Gf* = Fluid Reasoning; *Gv* = Visual Spatial Processing; *Ga* = Auditory Processing; *Gl* = Learning Efficiency; *Gr* = Retrieval Fluency; *Gwm* = Short-Term Working Memory; *Gs* = Processing Speed; RDL = Reading Decoding-Lexical; RDP = Reading Decoding-Phonological; RDS = Reading Decoding-Speed; RS = Reading Speed; RC = Reading Comprehension; MPS = Path Problem Solving; MC = Math Calculation; MS = Math Speed; KM = Math Knowledge; SG = Spelling; EU = English Usage; WS = Writing Speed; WA = Writing Ability.

**Table C.2 Meta-Analysis Results for Nonintegrated Models of Achievement**

| | *Gc* | *Gf* | *Gv* | *Ga* | *Gl* | *Gr* | *Gwm* | *Gs* | *g* |
|---|---|---|---|---|---|---|---|---|---|
| **Reading** | | | | | | | | | |
| *Reading Decoding-Phonological* | .12 | *.07* | — | .38 | *.07* | *.09* | .14 | .00 | .59 |
| *Reading Decoding-Lexical* | .32 | *.06* | — | .26 | .01 | *.09* | .10 | *.08* | .64 |
| *Reading Decoding-Speed* | .11 | *.05* | — | .25 | −.01 | .19 | .00 | .29 | .54 |
| *Reading Speed* | .19 | *.06* | — | .11 | .02 | .16 | *.09* | .27 | .57 |
| *Reading Comprehension* | .40 | .10 | — | .24 | *.07* | *.06* | *.06* | *.06* | .69 |
| **Mathematics** | | | | | | | | | |
| *Math Speed* | .00 | .21 | — | *.06* | −.01 | .16 | *.05* | .35 | .49 |
| *Math Calculation* | .16 | .30 | .11 | *.06* | .02 | .03 | *.07* | .16 | .62 |
| *Math Knowledge* | .37 | .41 | — | −.01 | **0.05** | .01 | *.09* | .12 | .75 |
| *Math Problem Solving* | .23 | .27 | .14 | .11 | .04 | *.05* | *.07* | *.09* | .69 |
| **Writing** | | | | | | | | | |
| *Spelling* | .23 | *.08* | — | .26 | .02 | *.08* | .14 | .13 | .62 |
| *English Usage* | .24 | .14 | — | .14 | *.08* | *.05* | *.09* | .22 | .64 |
| *Writing Speed* | −.05 | .16 | — | .11 | *.07* | .13 | *.07* | .41 | .54 |
| *Writing Ability* | .21 | .15 | — | .25 | *.08* | *.08* | *.06* | .11 | .63 |

*Note:* Cells with the dark gray shading and bold text indicate large effects ≥.25, cells with medium gray shading and bold text indicate moderate effects (.10–.24), cells with light gray shading and bold italicized text indicate small effects (.05–.09), and cells with no shading and italicized text indicate negligible effects (<.05).

*Gc* = Comprehension Knowledge; *Gf* = Fluid Reasoning; *Gv* = Visual Spatial Processing; *Ga* = Auditory Processing; *Gl* = Learning Efficiency; *Gr* = Retrieval Fluency; *Gwm* = Short-Term Working Memory; *Gs* = Processing Speed.

**Table C.3 Descriptions for Effect Sizes of Nonintegrated Models of Achievement**

| | *Gc* | *Gf* | *Gv* | *Ga* | *Gl* | *Gr* | *Gwm* | *Gs* | *g* |
|---|---|---|---|---|---|---|---|---|---|
| **Reading** | | | | | | | | | |
| *Reading Decoding-Phonological* | **Moderate** | ***Small*** | — | **Large** | ***Small*** | ***Small*** | **Moderate** | *Negligible* | **Large** |
| *Reading Decoding-Lexical* | **Large** | ***Small*** | — | **Large** | *Negligible* | ***Small*** | **Moderate** | ***Small*** | **Large** |
| *Reading Decoding-Speed* | **Moderate** | ***Small*** | — | **Large** | *Negligible* | **Moderate** | *Negligible* | **Large** | **Large** |
| *Reading Speed* | **Moderate** | ***Small*** | — | **Moderate** | *Negligible* | **Moderate** | ***Small*** | **Large** | **Large** |
| *Reading Comprehension* | **Large** | **Moderate** | — | **Moderate** | ***Small*** | ***Small*** | ***Small*** | ***Small*** | **Large** |
| **Mathematics** | | | | | | | | | |
| *Math Speed* | *Negligible* | **Moderate** | — | ***Small*** | *Negligible* | **Moderate** | ***Small*** | **Large** | **Large** |
| *Math Calculation* | **Moderate** | **Large** | **Moderate** | ***Small*** | *Negligible* | *Negligible* | ***Small*** | **Moderate** | **Large** |
| *Math Knowledge* | **Large** | **Large** | — | *Negligible* | ***Small*** | *Negligible* | ***Small*** | **Moderate** | **Large** |
| *Math Problem Solving* | **Moderate** | **Large** | **Moderate** | **Moderate** | *Negligible* | ***Small*** | ***Small*** | ***Small*** | **Large** |
| **Writing** | | | | | | | | | |
| *Spelling* | **Moderate** | ***Small*** | — | **Large** | *Negligible* | ***Small*** | **Moderate** | **Moderate** | **Large** |
| *English Usage* | **Moderate** | **Moderate** | — | **Moderate** | ***Small*** | ***Small*** | ***Small*** | **Moderate** | **Large** |
| *Writing Speed* | *Negligible* | **Moderate** | — | **Moderate** | ***Small*** | **Moderate** | ***Small*** | **Large** | **Large** |
| *Writing Ability* | **Moderate** | **Moderate** | — | **Large** | ***Small*** | ***Small*** | ***Small*** | **Moderate** | **Large** |

*Note: Gc* = Comprehension Knowledge; *Gf* = Fluid Reasoning; *Gv* = Visual Spatial Processing; *Ga* = Auditory Processing; *Gl* = Learning Efficiency; *Gr* = Retrieval Fluency; *Gwm* = Short-Term Working Memory; *Gs* = Processing Speed.

**Table C.4 Meta-Analysis Results for Integrated Models of Achievement**

| Reading | *Gc* | *Gf* | *Gv* | *Ga* | *Gl* | *Gr* | *Gwm* | *Gs* | RDP | RDL | RDS | RS | RC | *g* |
|---|---|---|---|---|---|---|---|---|---|---|---|---|---|---|
| *Reading Decoding-Phonological* | .12 | .07 | — | .38 | .07 | .09 | .14 | .00 | — | — | — | — | — | .64 |
| *Reading Decoding-Lexical* | .32 | .06 | — | .26 | .01 | .09 | .10 | .08 | — | — | — | — | — | .59 |
| *Reading Decoding-Speed* | −.08 | .00 | — | .01 | −.04 | .12 | −.09 | .25 | .33 | .46 | — | — | — | .54 |
| *Reading Speed* | .02 | .02 | — | −.04 | .01 | .11 | .03 | .23 | .03 | .53 | — | — | — | .57 |
| *Reading Comprehension* | .22 | .07 | | .12 | .06 | .01 | .00 | −.01 | −.06 | .52 | −.04 | .13 | — | .69 |
| **Mathematics** | *Gc* | *Gf* | *Gv* | *Ga* | *Gl* | *Gr* | *Gwm* | *Gs* | MS | MC | MPS | KM | | |
| *Math Speed* | .00 | .21 | — | .06 | −.01 | .16 | .05 | .35 | — | — | — | — | — | .49 |
| *Math Calculation* | .17 | .21 | .06 | .03 | .03 | −.05 | .05 | −.01 | .52 | — | — | — | — | .62 |
| *Math Knowledge* | .32 | .29 | — | −.04 | .05 | −.02 | .06 | .02 | .16 | .27 | — | — | — | .75 |
| *Math Problem Solving* | .16 | .10 | .10 | .07 | .03 | .02 | .03 | −.04 | .11 | .48 | — | — | — | .69 |
| **Writing** | *Gc* | *Gf* | *Gv* | *Ga* | *Gl* | *Gr* | *Gwm* | *Gs* | SG | EU | WS | WA | | |
| *Spelling* | .23 | .08 | — | .26 | .02 | .08 | .14 | .13 | — | — | — | — | — | .62 |
| *English Usage* | .24 | .14 | — | .14 | .08 | .05 | .09 | .22 | — | — | — | — | — | .64 |
| *Writing Speed* | — | .02 | — | .00 | −.01 | .09 | −.02 | .27 | — | .58 | — | — | — | .56 |
| *Writing Ability* | .13 | .09 | — | .13 | .06 | .03 | −.01 | −.02 | .41 | — | .18 | — | — | .64 |

*Note:* Cells with the dark gray shading and bold text indicate large effects ≥.25, cells with medium gray shading and bold text indicate moderate effects (.10–.24), cells with light gray shading and bold italicized text indicate small effects (.05–.09), and cells with no shading and italicized text indicate negligible effects (<.05).

*Gc* = Comprehension Knowledge; *Gf* = Fluid Reasoning; *Gv* = Visual Spatial Processing; *Ga* = Auditory Processing; *Gl* = Learning Efficiency; *Gr* = Retrieval Fluency; *Gwm* = Short-Term Working Memory; *Gs* = Processing Speed; RDP = Reading Decoding-Phonological; RDL = Reading Decoding-Lexical; RDS = Reading Decoding-Speed; RS = Reading Speed; RC = Reading Comprehension; MPS = Path Problem Solving; MC = Math Calculation; MS = Math Speed; KM = Math Knowledge; SG = Spelling; EU = English Usage; WS = Writing Speed; WA = Writing Ability.

**Table C.5 Descriptions for Effect Sizes of Integrated Models of Achievement**

| Reading | *Gc* | *Gf* | *Gv* | *Ga* | *Gl* | *Gr* | *Gwm* | *Gs* | RDP | RDL | RDS | RS | *g* |
|---|---|---|---|---|---|---|---|---|---|---|---|---|---|
| *Reading Decoding-Phonological* | **Mod.** | ***Small*** | — | **Large** | ***Small*** | ***Small*** | **Mod.** | *Neg.* | — | — | — | — | **Large** |
| *Reading Decoding-Lexical* | **Large** | ***Small*** | — | **Large** | *Neg.* | ***Small*** | **Mod.** | ***Small*** | — | — | — | — | **Large** |
| *Reading Decoding-Speed* | *Neg.* | *Neg.* | — | *Neg.* | *Neg.* | **Mod.** | *Neg.* | **Large** | **Large** | **Large** | — | — | **Large** |
| *Reading Speed* | *Neg.* | *Neg.* | — | *Neg.* | *Neg.* | **Mod.** | *Neg.* | **Large** | *Neg.* | **Large** | — | — | **Large** |
| *Reading Comprehension* | **Large** | ***Small*** | — | **Mod.** | ***Small*** | *Neg.* | *Neg.* | *Neg.* | *Neg.* | **Large** | *Neg.* | **Mod.** | **Large** |
| **Mathematics** | ***Gc*** | ***Gf*** | ***Gv*** | ***Ga*** | ***Gl*** | ***Gr*** | ***Gwm*** | ***Gs*** | **MS** | **MC** | **MPS** | **KM** | |
| *Math Speed* | *Neg.* | **Mod.** | — | ***Small*** | *Neg.* | **Mod.** | ***Small*** | **Large** | — | — | — | — | **Large** |
| *Math Calculation* | **Mod.** | **Mod.** | ***Small*** | *Neg.* | *Neg.* | *Neg.* | ***Small*** | *Neg.* | **Large** | — | — | — | **Large** |
| *Math Knowledge* | **Large** | **Large** | — | *Neg.* | ***Small*** | *Neg.* | ***Small*** | *Neg.* | **Mod.** | **Large** | — | — | **Large** |
| *Math Problem Solving* | **Mod.** | **Mod.** | **Mod.** | ***Small*** | *Neg.* | *Neg.* | *Neg.* | *Neg.* | **Mod.** | **Large** | — | — | **Large** |
| **Writing** | ***Gc*** | ***Gf*** | ***Gv*** | ***Ga*** | ***Gl*** | ***Gr*** | ***Gwm*** | ***Gs*** | **SG** | **EU** | **WS** | **WA** | |
| *Spelling* | **Mod.** | ***Small*** | — | **Large** | *Neg.* | ***Small*** | .14 | .13 | — | — | — | — | **Large** |
| *English Usage* | **Mod.** | **Mod.** | — | **Mod.** | ***Small*** | ***Small*** | ***Small*** | .22 | — | — | — | — | **Large** |
| *Writing Speed* | — | *Neg.* | — | *Neg.* | *Neg.* | ***Small*** | *Neg.* | **Large** | **Large** | — | — | — | **Large** |
| *Writing Ability* | **Mod.** | ***Small*** | — | **Mod.** | ***Small*** | *Neg.* | *Neg.* | *Neg.* | **Large** | — | **Mod.** | — | **Large** |

*Note:* Mod. = Moderate; Neg. = Negligible; *Gc* = Comprehension Knowledge; *Gf* = Fluid Reasoning; *Gv* = Visual Spatial Processing; *Ga* = Auditory Processing; *Gl* = Learning Efficiency; *Gr* = Retrieval Fluency; *Gwm* = Short-term Working Memory; *Gs* = Processing Speed; RDP = Reading Decoding-Phonological; RDL = Reading Decoding-Lexical; RDS = Reading Decoding-Speed; RS = Reading Speed; RC = Reading Comprehension; MPS = Path Problem Solving; MC = Math Calculation; MS = Math Speed; KM = Math Knowledge; SG = Spelling; EU = English Usage; WS = Writing Speed; WA = Writing Ability.

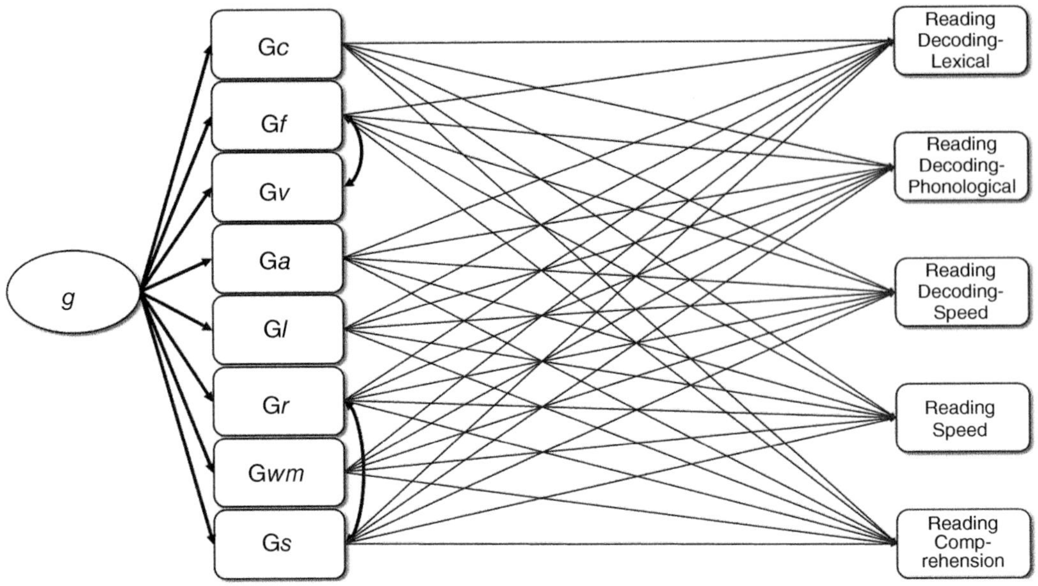


**FIGURE C.1 Nonintegrated Model of Cognitive-Reading Relations**

### *Reading: Integrated Achievement Models*

In the integrated reading achievement models, the effects of cognitive abilities on Reading Decoding-Lexical and Reading Decoding-Phonological were the same as those reported in the nonintegrated achievement model. However, in these models Reading Decoding-Lexical and Reading Decoding-Phonological predicted Reading Decoding-Speed and Reading Speed, and then Reading Decoding-Lexical, Reading Decoding-Phonological, Reading Decoding-Speed, and Reading Speed predicted Reading Comprehension. For Reading Decoding-Speed, there were large effects from *Gs*, Reading Decoding-Lexical, and Reading Decoding-Phonological, and a moderate effect from *Gr*. For Reading Speed, there was a large effect from Reading Decoding-Lexical, and moderate effects from *Gs* and *Gr*. For Reading Comprehension, there was a large effect from Reading Decoding-Lexical, a moderate effect from *Gc* and *Ga*, and a small effect from Reading Speed, *Gf*, and *Gl*. Importantly, in the integrated model the direct effects of the cognitive abilities on advanced reading skills (e.g., Reading Comprehension) appear smaller, but these effects were mediated through basic reading skills. For instance, when examining the total effects of the broad CHC abilities on Reading Comprehension (i.e., adding together the direct effects and indirect effects), they are nearly the same as those in the nonintegrated model that only had the broad abilities predicting Reading Comprehension. The effects of cognitive abilities on Reading Comprehension were partially mediated through Reading Decoding-Lexical, Reading Decoding-Phonological, and Reading Speed, but the total effects of cognitive abilities on the more advanced skills still suggested important relationships. This model is shown in Figure C.2.

### *Mathematics: Nonintegrated Achievement Model*

First, the results describe models where cognitive abilities predicted each mathematics skill separately. For Math Speed and Math Knowledge, *Gv* had a moderate negative effect, suggesting a suppressor effect. This path was removed from the model for these two math skills. Otherwise for Math Speed, there was a large effect from *Gs*, moderate effects from *Gf* and *Gr*, and a small effect from *Ga* and *Gwm*. For Math Calculation, there was a large effect from *Gf*, moderate effects from *Gc*, *Gv*, and *Gs*, and a small effect from *Ga* and *Gwm*. For Math Knowledge, there were large effects from *Gc* and *Gf*, a moderate effect from *Gs*, and small effects from *Gl* and *Gwm*. For Math Problem Solving, there was a large effect from *Gf*, moderate effects from *Gc*, *Gv*, and *Ga*, and small effects from *Gr*, *Gs*, and *Gwm*. For all mathematics skills, the indirect effects of *g* were large. This model is shown in Figure C.3.

### *Mathematics: Integrated Achievement Model*

In the integrated model, the effects for Math Speed were the same as those reported in the nonintegrated achievement model. For Math Calculation, there were large effects from Math Speed, moderate effects from *Gc* and *Gf*, and small effects from *Gv* and *Gwm*. For Math Knowledge, there were large effects from Math calculation, *Gc*, and *Gf*, a moderate effect from Math Speed, and small effects from *Gl* and *Gwm*. For Math Problem Solving, there was a large effect from Math Calculation, moderate effects from *Gc*, *Gf*, *Gv*, and Math Speed, and a small effect from *Ga*. This model is shown in Figure C.4.

### *Writing: Nonintegrated Achievement Model*

First, the results describe models where cognitive abilities predicted each writing skill separately. In the writing models, the path from *Gc* to Writing Speed was moderate in size and negative. It was not included in these models.

For Spelling, there was a large effect from *Ga*, moderate effects from *Gc*, *Gwm*, and *Gs*, and small effects from *Gf* and *Gr*. For English Usage, there were moderate effects from *Gc*, *Gf*, *Ga*, and *Gs*, and small effects from *Gl*, *Gr*, and *Gwm*. For Writing Speed, there was a large

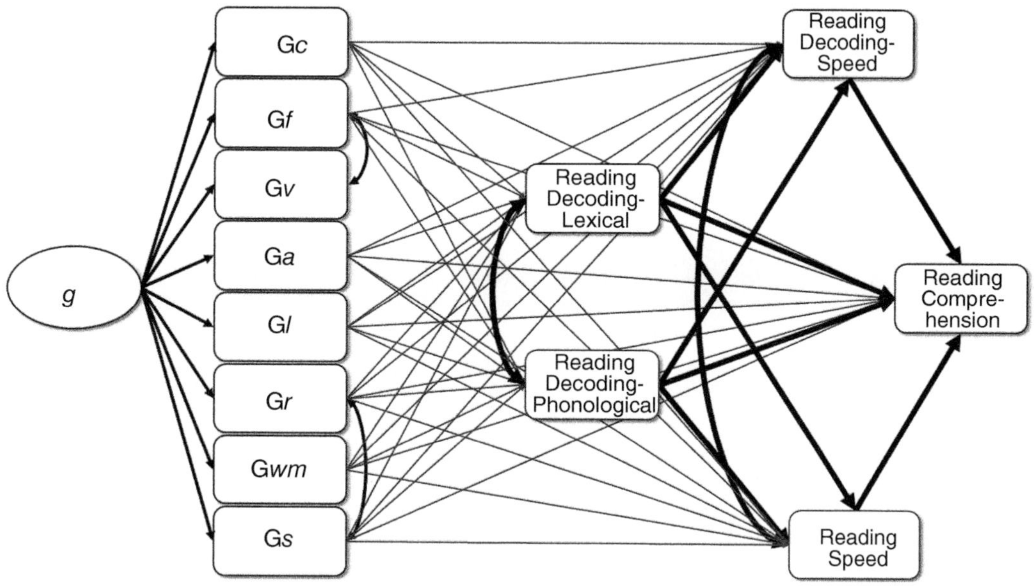


**FIGURE C.2 Integrated Model of Cognitive-Reading Relations**

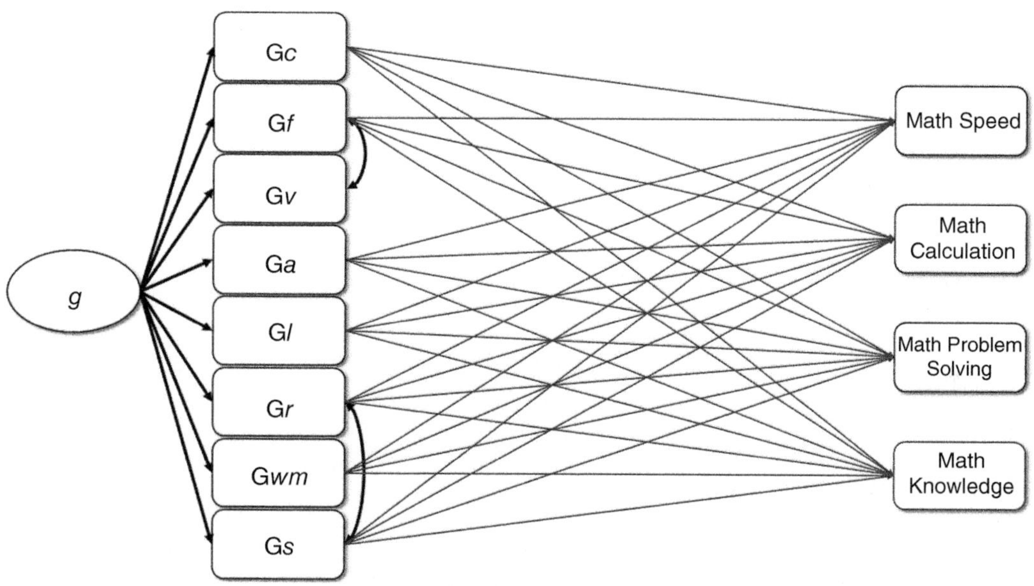


**FIGURE C.3 Nonintegrated Model of Cognitive-Mathematics Relations**

effect from *Gs*, moderate effects from *Gf*, *Ga*, and *Gr*, and small effects from *Gl* and *Gwm*. For Writing Ability, there was a large effect from *Ga*, moderate effects from *Gc*, *Gf*, and *Gs*, and small effects from *Gr*, *Gl*, and *Gwm*. For all writing skills, the indirect effects of *g* were large. This model is shown in Figure C.5.

***Writing: Integrated Achievement Model***

In the integrated model, the effects of cognitive abilities on Spelling and English Usage were the same as those reported in the nonintegrated achievement model. For Writing Speed, the effect from Spelling was negative and moderate in size, so it was removed from the model. Otherwise, for Writing Speed there were large effects from English Usage and *Gs*, and a small effect from *Gr*. For Writing Ability, the effect from English Usage was negative and moderate in size, so it was removed from the model. Otherwise, for Writing Ability there was a large effect from Spelling, moderate effects from Writing Speed, *Gc*, and *Ga*, and small effects from *Gf* and *Gl*. Again, in these models the total effects of several cognitive abilities on Writing Ability and Writing Speed were moderate but were mediated through Spelling and English Usage. An interesting observation with these results is that there were not many large effects of cognitive abilities on writing skills, but there tended to be small and moderate effects from a broad-range cognitive abilities, supporting the notion that writing is a complex skill that relies on the simultaneous influence of multiple cognitive abilities. This model is shown in Figure C.6.

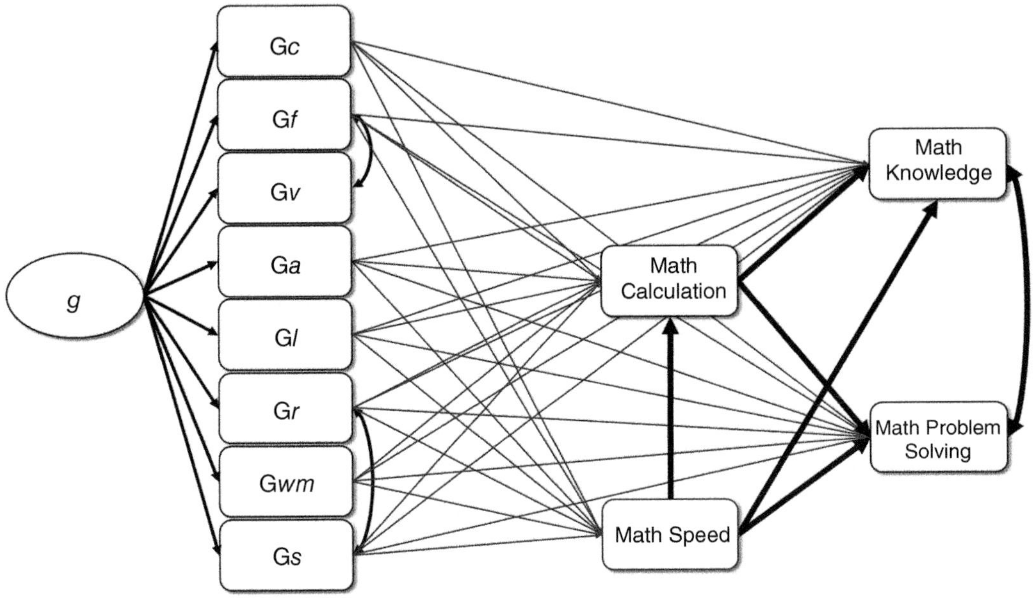


**FIGURE C.4 Integrated Model of Cognitive-Mathematics Relations**

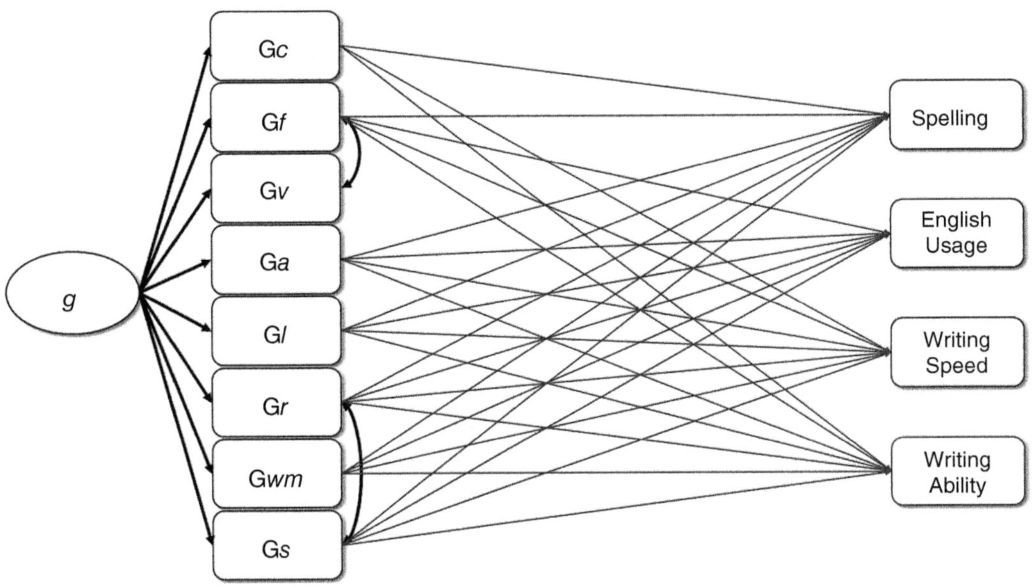


**FIGURE C.5 Nonintegrated Model of Cognitive-Writing Relations**

***Summary***

The analyses presented here provide several important, although preliminary insights. First, many of these results were consistent with previous research. For instance, *Gc* tended to have moderate to strong effects across multiple academic skills, supporting research that shows language development and background knowledge are important aspects of academic skill development across all domains. *Gf* had stronger effects on mathematics when compared to reading or writing, consistent with research indicating that fluid reasoning abilities are important for math achievement. *Ga* had stronger effects on reading and writing than on mathematics, consistent with research suggesting that phonological and phonics skills are important cognitive abilities related to reading and writing.

Second, *Gv* was not meaningfully related to reading or writing in these models, and it tended to be negatively related to these academic skills. It is likely that *Gv* acted as a suppressor variable because of its high correlation with *Gf*, which is likely due to many *Gf* tests relying on visual stimuli. However, both *Gv* and *Gf* had moderate to large effects on Math Calculation and Math Problem Solving, suggesting they each explain unique variance in those mathematics skills. Third, *Gl*, *Gr*, and *Gwm* did not have large effects on any academic skills. Instead, these effects were small to moderate in size. The effects from *Gs* on most academic skills were moderate, with a few small and large effects. The large effects of *Gs* were primarily on academic fluency tests, which makes sense given the timed nature of *Gs* tests and academic fluency tests.

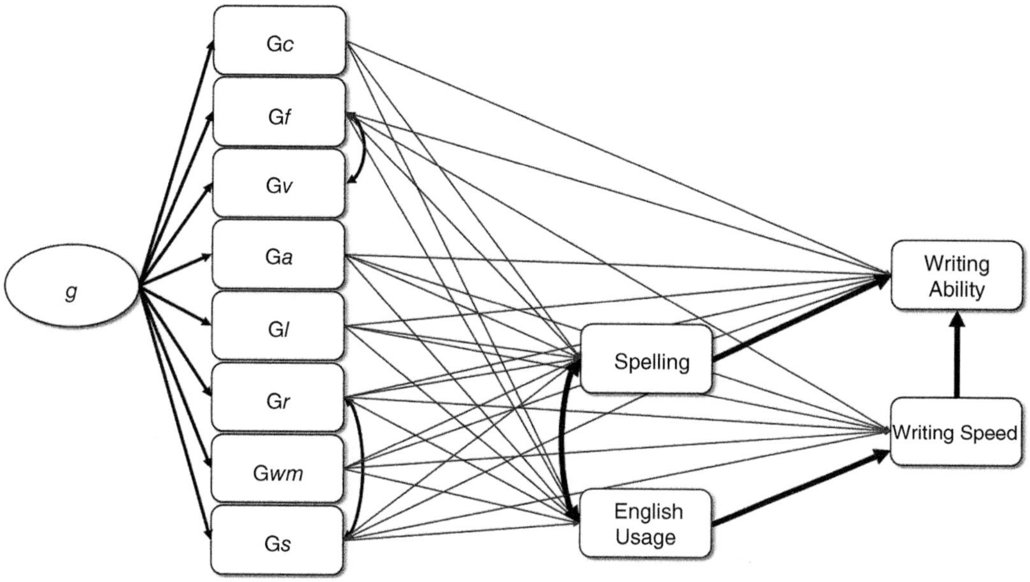


**FIGURE C.6 Integrated Model of Cognitive-Writing Relations**

Fourth, the integrated models that were estimated here included direct effects of basic academic skills on advanced academic skills, examining the assumption that mastery of the foundational skills (such as decoding words) is an important precursor and predictor of the ability to engage in advanced academic skills (such as understanding what is read). The results of this study support the importance of decoding, calculation, and basic spelling/grammar skills as important predictors of more advanced academic skills across reading, mathematics, and writing, respectively. Fifth, in this analysis we separated basic reading skills into Reading Decoding-Lexical and Reading Decoding-Phonological. This was done to help determine if the ability to read real words and nonsense words had differential relations with cognitive abilities. We found some initial evidence that this is the case, especially when examining the size of the relationships between *Gc* and *Ga* on Reading Decoding-Lexical and Reading Decoding-Phonological. As expected, *Gc* had a stronger relationship with Reading Decoding-Lexical than with Reading Decoding-Phonological, and *Ga* had a stronger relationship with Reading Decoding-Phonological than with Reading Decoding-Lexical. Additionally, Reading Decoding-Lexical was more strongly related to Reading Comprehension, Reading Decoding-Speed, and Reading Speed than Reading Decoding-Phonological, suggesting that the ability to read real words was a stronger predictor of more advanced reading skills than the ability to decode nonsense words. Finally, the indirect effects of *g* on all academic skills were large. This is consistent with previous research, where general intelligence strongly predicts academic skills.

As stated previously, these results are preliminary, and further analyses will be conducted as data are added to the database. Several limitations should be mentioned. First, there was substantial heterogeneity in the correlations among the broad cognitive abilities and narrow academic skills. This indicates that the size correlations across tests measuring the same cognitive abilities and academic skills can differ substantially across batteries and samples. The reasons for this heterogeneity were not explored here, but could include differences in age, test batteries (e.g., Wechsler vs Kaufman), or psychometric properties of the tests (e.g., subtest reliability). These are avenues for future research that will be explored with these data. Despite these limitations, we think the results of this meta-SEM will ultimately provide more robust and confident estimates of cognitive-achievement relations, and it will also help show the general range of relationships among broad cognitive abilities and narrow academic skills across the universe of tests that measure those constructs. Ultimately, this information can be useful in selecting tests and measuring cognitive abilities and academic skills when working with individuals with learning difficulties.

Meta-SEM will be applied to further extend cognitive-achievement relations research in innovative ways. Current research is also being conducted using a network analysis framework to examine the sequence and cascade of developmental effects of cognitive abilities and academic skills (Hajovsky et al., 2022; Figure C.7). In the research, multidimensional scaling and exploratory network analysis are used to build models of cognitive-achievement relations. Guided by theory and patterns based on the correlations, the rationale of this more advanced cognitive-achievement relations model is that relationships among cognitive and academic skills are consistent with the idea that more foundational and basic abilities precede and underlie more advanced and acquired abilities. For example, in this model, processing speed is likely to influence the development of other cognitive abilities such as working memory, fluid reasoning, and comprehension knowledge, which in turn influences written expression. However, processing speed also influences other academic skills like reading speed which then influences reading comprehension and ultimately written expression. Thus, in this model, processing speed may function as a "bottleneck" and facilitate or hinder the development of other cognitive abilities and academic skills, directly or indirectly, ultimately influencing the development of written expression. What this model shows is that cognitive-achievement relations should not be thought of as a single, static correlation but rather as an array of simultaneous correlational patterns that give rise to different outcomes. The development of such a model to illustrate

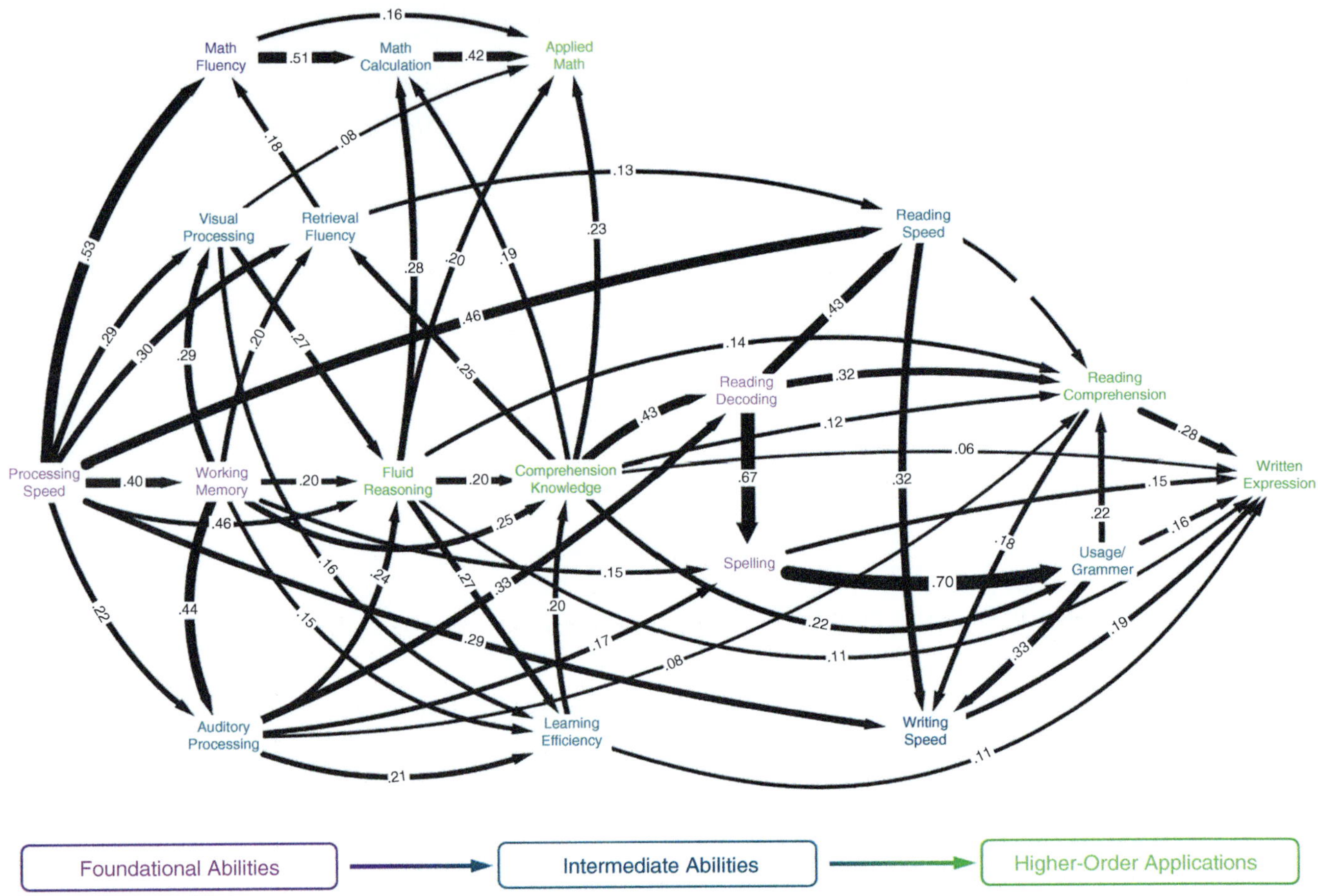


**FIGURE C.7 Meta-SEM and Exploratory Path Analysis of Cognitive and Achievement Tests.** ***Note:*** **Results from a meta-SEM and exploratory path analysis of multiple standardized cognitive and achievement tests (e.g., KABC-II, WISC-IV, WISC-V, WAIS-IV, WJ III, WJ IV, DAS-II, WIAT-II, WIAT-III, WIAT-4, KTEA-II, KTEA-3) guided by the Developmental Cascade Hypothesis, Investment Theory, Expanded Simple View of Reading, and Simple View of Writing theories**

cognitive-achievement relations using a combination of innovative methodologies demonstrates the forward-thinking ways this work is now being conducted. It also shows that cognitive-achievement relations may differ across individuals and may require new approaches to advance this line of work.

## ACKNOWLEDGMENTS

A note of gratitude to Jacob Robbins, doctoral student at Texas A&M University, for assistance with revisions on subsequent drafts. We also want to thank Joel Schneider and Craig Zinkiewicz for their work compiling and organizing the data used in the preliminary results of the meta-analysis reported in this chapter. The authors do not have any financial conflicts of interest to declare. This research did not receive any specific grant from funding agencies in the public, commercial, or not-for-profit sector.

## REFERENCES

Atit, K., Power, J. R., Pigott, T., Lee, J., Geer, E. A., Uttal, D. H., Ganley, C. M., & Sorby, S. A. (2022). Examining the relations between spatial skills and mathematical performance: A meta-analysis. *Psychonomic Bulletin & Review*, *29*, 699–720. https://doi.org/10.3758/s13423-021-02012-w.

Caemmerer, J. M., Keith, T. Z., & Reynolds, M. R. (2020). Beyond individual intelligence tests: Application of Cattell-Horn-Carroll Theory. *Intelligence*, *79*, 101433 https://doi.org/10.1016/j.intell.2020.101433.

Caemmerer, J. M., Maddocks, D. L. S., Keith, T. Z., & Reynolds, M. R. (2018). Effects of cognitive abilities on child and youth academic achievement: Evidence from the WISC-V and WIAT-III. *Intelligence*, *68*, 6–20. https://doi.org/10.1016/j.intell.2018.02.005.

Caemmerer, J. M., Young, S. R., Maddocks, D., Charamut, N. R., & Blemahdoo, E. (2024). Predicting achievement from WISC-V composites: Do cognitive-achievement relations vary based on general intelligence? *Journal of Psychoeducational Assessment*, *42*(4), 390–408. https://doi.org/10.1177/07342829241240346.

Cain, K., Oakhill, J., & Bryant, P. (2004). Children's reading comprehension ability: Concurrent prediction by working memory, verbal ability, and component skills. *Journal of Educational Psychology, 96*(1), 31–42. https://psycnet.apa.org/buy/2004-11358-003.

Canivez, G. L. (2013). Incremental criterion validity of WAIS–IV factor index scores: Relationships with WIAT–II and WIAT–III subtest and composite scores. *Psychological Assessment, 25*(2), 484–495.

Carroll, J. B. (1993). *Human cognitive abilities: A survey of factor-analytic studies.* Cambridge University Press, New York, NY.

Cheung, M. W.-L., & Chan, W. (2005). Meta-analytic structural equation modeling: A two-stage approach. *Psychological Methods, 10*(1), 40–64. https://doi.org/10.1037/1082-989X.10.1.40.

Compton, D. L., Fuchs, L. S., Fuchs, D., Lambert, W., & Hamlett, C. (2012). The cognitive and academic profiles of reading and mathematics learning disabilities. *Journal of Learning Disabilities, 45*(1), 79–95. https://doi.org/10.1177/0022219410393012.

Cormier, D. C., Bulut, O., McGrew, K. S., & Frison, J. (2016). The role of Cattell–Horn–Carroll (CHC) cognitive abilities in predicting writing achievement during the school-age year. *Psychology in the Schools, 53*(8), 787–803. https://doi.org/10.1002/pits.21945.

Cormier, D. C., McGrew, K. S., Bulut, O., & Funamoto, A. (2017). Revisiting the relations between the WJ-IV measures of Cattell-Horn-Carroll (CHC) cognitive abilities and reading achievement during the school-age years. *Journal of Psychoeducational Assessment, 35*(8), 731–754. https://doi.org/10.1177/0734282916659208.

Deary, I. J., Cox, S. R., & Hill, W. D. (2022). Genetic variation, brain, and intelligence differences. *Molecular Psychiatry, 27*, 335–353. https://doi.org/10.1038/s41380-021-01027-y.

Decker, S. L., & Luedke, J. C. (2021). Evidence-based use of cognitive testing for academic interventions: A critical appraisal of meta-analytic methodologies. *Frontiers in Education, 6*, 637676, Frontiers Media SA.

Decker, S. L., & Roberts, A. M. (2015). Specific cognitive predictors of early math problem solving. *Psychology in the Schools, 52*(5), 477–488. https://doi.org/10.1002/pits.21837.

Elliott, C. D. (1990). *Differential Ability Scales.* Psychological Corporation, San Antonio, TX.

Evans, J. J., Floyd, R. G., McGrew, K. S., & Leforgee, M. H. (2002). The relations between measures of Cattell–Horn–Carroll (CHC) cognitive abilities and reading achievement during childhood and adolescence. *School Psychology Review, 31*, 246–262. https://doi.org/10.1080/02796015.2002.12086154.

Flanagan, D. P., Alfonso, V. C., Sy, M. C., Mascolo, J. T., McDonough, E. M., & Ortiz, S. O. (2018). Dual discrepancy/consistency operational definition of SLD: Integrating multiple data sources and multiple data gathering methods. In V. C. Alfonso & D. P. Flanagan (Eds.), *Essentials of specific learning disability identification* (2nd ed). Wiley.

Flanagan, D. P., & McGrew, K. S. (1998). Interpreting intelligence tests from contemporary *Gf-Gc* theory. *Journal of School Psychology, 36*(2), 151–182. https://doi.org/10.1016/S0022-4405(98)00003-X.

Flanagan, D. P., Ortiz, S. O., & Alfonso, V. C. (2013). *Essentials of cross-battery assessment* (3rd ed). John Wiley & Sons, Hoboken, NJ.

Flanagan, D. P., Ortiz, S. O., Alfonso, V. C., & Mascolo, J. T. (2006). *The achievement test desk reference, 2nd ed. (ATDR-2).* Wiley, New York.

Floyd, R., Meisinger, E., Gregg, N., & Keith, T. Z. (2012). An explanation of reading comprehension across development using models from Cattell–Horn–Carroll theory: Support for integrative models of reading. *Psychology in the Schools, 49*, 725–743. https://doi.org/10.1002/pits.21633.

Floyd, R. G., Evans, J. J., & McGrew, K. S. (2003). Relations between measures of CattellHorn-Carroll (CHC) cognitive abilities and mathematics achievement across the school-age years. *Psychology in the Schools, 40*(2), 155–171. https://doi.org/10.1002/pits.10083.

Floyd, R. G., Keith, T. Z., Taub, G. E., & McGrew, K. S. (2007). Cattell-Horn-Carroll cognitive abilities and their effects on reading decoding skills: *g* has indirect effects, more specific abilities have direct effects. *School Psychology Quarterly, 22*(2), 200–233. https://doi.org/10.1037/1045-3830.22.2.200.

Floyd, R. G., McGrew, K. S., & Evans, J. J. (2008). The relative contributions of the Cattell-Horn-Carroll cognitive abilities in explaining writing achievement during childhood and adolescence. *Psychology in the Schools, 45*(2), 132–144. https://doi.org/10.1002/pits.20284.

Gottfredson, L. S. (1997). Why *g* matters: The complexity of everyday life. *Intelligence, 24*(1), 79–132. https://doi.org/10.1016/S0160-2896(97)90014-3.

Hajovsky, D. B., Niileksela, C. R., Flanagan, D. P., Alfonso, V. C., Schneider, J., & Zinkiewicz, C. J. (2022). *A consensus model of cognitive-achievement relations using meta-SEM* [Poster Presentation]. American Psychological Association Annual Convention, Minneapolis, MN, United States.

Hajovsky, D. B., Niileksela, C. R., Olsen, S. C., & Sekula, M. K. (2023). Do cognitive-achievement relations vary by general ability level? *Journal of Intelligence, 11*(9), 177 https://doi.org/10.3390/jintelligence11090177.

Hajovsky, D. B., Niileksela, C. R., Robbins, J., & Sun, Y. (2025a). Understanding contextual specificity in cognitive-reading relations: Moderation by age and IQ. *Journal of Psychoeducational Assessment, 43*. https://doi.org/10.1177/07342829251352605, 897–917.

Hajovsky, D. B., Niileksela, C. R., Flanagan, D. P., Alfonso, V. C., Schneider, W. J., & Robbins, J. (2025b). Toward a consensus model of cognitive-reading achievement relations using meta-structural equation modeling. *Journal of Intelligence, 13*(8), 104 https://doi.org/10.3390/jintelligence13080104 (IF = 3.4; 5-yr IF: 3.5).

Hajovsky, D. B., Niileksela, C. R., Villeneuve, E. F., & Reynolds, M. R. (2019). Gender matters in neuropsychological assessment of child and adolescent writing skill. *Journal of Pediatric Neuropsychology, 5*(3), 103–118. https://doi.org/10.1007/s40817-019-00071-5 (IF unavailable).

Hajovsky, D. B., Reynolds, M. R., Floyd, R. F., Turek, J. J., & Keith, T. Z. (2014). A multi-group investigation of latent cognitive abilities and reading achievement relations. *School Psychology Review, 43*, 385–406.

Hajovsky, D. B., Villeneuve, E. F., Reynolds, M. R., Niileksela, C. R., Mason, B. A., & Shudak, N. J. (2018). Cognitive ability influences on written expression: Evidence for developmental and sex-based differences in school-age children. *Journal of School Psychology, 67*, 104–118. https://doi.org/10.1016/j.jsp.2017.09.001.

Hajovsky, D. B., Villeneuve, E. F., Schneider, W. J., & Caemmerer, J. M. (2020). An alternative approach to cognitive and achievement relations research: An introduction to quantile regression. *Journal of Pediatric Neuropsychology, 6*, 83–95. https://doi.org/10.1007/s40817-020-00086-3.

Horn, J. L., & Blankson, N. (2005). Foundations for better understanding of cognitive abilities. In D. P. Flanagan & P. L. Harrison (Eds.), *Contemporary intellectual assessment: Theories, tests, and issues* (pp. 41–68). The Guilford Press.

Horn, J. L., & Noll, J. (1997). Human cognitive capabilities: *Gf-Gc* theory. In D. P. Flanagan, J. L. Genshaft, & P. L. Harrison (Eds.), *Contemporary intellectual assessment: Theories, tests, and issues* (pp. 53–91). The Guilford Press.

Jensen, A. R. (1998). *The g factor*. Prager, Westport, CT.

Johnson, E. S., Humphrey, M., Mellard, D. F., Woods, K., & Swanson, H. L. (2010). Cognitive processing deficits and students with specific learning disabilities: A selective meta-analysis of the literature. *Learning Disability Quarterly, 33*, 3–18. https://doi.org/10.1177/073194871003300101.

Johnson, W., Bouchard, T. J., Krueger, R. F., McGue, M., & Gottesman, I. I. (2004). Just one *g*: Consistent results from three test batteries. *Intelligence, 32*, 95–107. https://doi.org/10.1016/S0160-2896(03)00062-X.

Kaufman, S. B., Reynolds, M. R., Liu, X., Kaufman, A. S., & McGrew, K. S. (2012). Are cognitive *g* and academic achievement g one and the same *g*? An exploration on the Woodcock–Johnson and Kaufman tests. *Intelligence, 40*(2), 123–138. https://doi.org/10.1016/j.intell.2012.01.009.

Keith, T., Kranzler, J., & Flanagan, D. (2001). What does the cognitive assessment system (CAS) measure? Joint confirmatory factor analysis of the CAS and the Woodcock Johnson tests of cognitive ability. 3 School Psychology Review, 30(1), 89–119. https://doi.org/10.1080/02796015.2001.12086102

Keith, T. Z. (1999). Effects of general and specific abilities on student achievement: Similarities and differences across ethnic groups. *School Psychology Quarterly, 14*(3), 239–262. https://doi.org/10.1037/h0089008.

Keith, T. Z. (2019). *Multiple regression and beyond: An introduction to multiple regression and structural equation modeling* (3rd ed). Routledge, New York, NY.

Kovacs, K., & Conway, A. R. A. (2016). Process overlap theory: A unified account of the general factor of intelligence. *Psychological Inquiry, 27*(3), 151–177. https://doi.org/10.1080/1047840X.2016.1153946.

Kovacs, K., & Conway, A. R. A. (2020). Process overlap theory, executive functions, and the interpretation of cognitive test scores: Reply to commentaries. *Journal of Applied Research in Memory and Cognition, 9*(3), 419–424. https://doi.org/10.1016/j.jarmac.2020.04.005.

Kudo, M. F., Lussier, C. M., & Swanson, H. L. (2015). Reading disabilities in children: A selective meta-analysis of the cognitive literature. *Research in Developmental Disabilities, 40*, 51–62.

Language and Reading Research Consortium, & Logan, J. (2017). Pressure points in reading comprehension: A quantile multiple regression analysis. *Journal of Educational Psychology, 109*(4), 451–464. https://doi.org/10.1037/edu0000150.

McGrew, K. (1993). The relationship between the Woodcock-Johnson Psycho-Educational Battery-Revised Gf-Gc cognitive clusters and reading achievement across the life-span. *Journal of Psychoeducational Assessment Monograph Series*. WJ-R Monograph, 39–53.

McGrew, K. S., Flanagan, D. P., Keith, T. Z., & Vanderwood, M. (1997). Beyond *g*: The impact of *Gf-Gc* specific cognitive abilities research on the future use and interpretation of intelligence tests in the schools. *School Psychology Review, 26*(2), 189–210. https://doi.org/10.1080/02796015.1997.12085858.

McGrew, K. S., & Hessler, G. L. (1995). The relationship between the WJ-R *Gf-Gc* cognitive clusters and mathematics achievement across the life-span. *Journal of Psychoeducational Assessment, 13*, 21–38. https://doi.org/10.1177/073428299501300102.

McGrew, K. S., & Knopik, S. N. (1993). The relationship between the WJ-R *Gf-Gc* cognitive clusters and writing achievement across the life-span. *School Psychology Review, 22*(4), 687–695. https://doi.org/10.1080/02796015.1993.12085684.

McGrew, K. S., & Wendling, B. J. (2010). Cattell-Horn-Carroll cognitive-achievement relations: What we have learned from the past 20 years of research. *Psychology in the Schools, 47*, 651–675. https://doi.org/10.1002/pits.20497.

Neisser, U., Boodoo, G., Bouchard, T. J., Boykin, A. W., Ceci, S. J., Loehlin, J. C., & Sternberg, R. J. (1996). Intelligence: Knowns and unknowns. *American Psychologist, 51*(2), 77–101. https://doi.org/10.1037/0003-066X.51.2.77.

Niileksela, C. R., Hajovsky, D. B., He, Z., & Villeneuve, E. F. (2025a). Cognitive-achievement relations with the Woodcock–Johnson V. *Journal of Psychoeducational Assessment, 43*. https://doi.org/10.1177/07342829251353032, 880–896.

Niileksela, C. R., Reynolds, M. R., Keith, T. Z., & McGrew, K. S. (2016). A special validity study of the Woodcock–Johnson IV: Acting on evidence for specific abilities. In D. P. Flanagan & V. C. Alfonso (Eds.), *WJ IV clinical use and interpretation: Scientist-practitioner perspectives* (pp. 65–106). Elsevier.

Niileksela, C. R., Robbins, J., & Hajovsky, D. B. (2025b). General ability level moderates cognitive–achievement relations for mathematics. *Journal of Intelligence, 13*(6), 65 https://doi.org/10.3390/jintelligence13060065.

Parkin, J. R., & Beaujean, A. A. (2012). The effects of Wechsler intelligence scale for children-fourth edition cognitive abilities on math achievement. *Journal of School Psychology, 50*(1), 113–128. https://doi.org/10.1016/j.jsp.2011.08.003.

Peng, P., Barnes, M., Wang, C., Wang, W., Li, S., Swanson, H. L., & Tao, S. (2018). A meta-analysis on the relation between reading and working memory. *Psychological Bulletin, 144*(1), 48–76, https://psycnet.apa.org/buy/2017-48448-001.

Peng, P., & Kievit, R. A. (2020). The development of academic achievement and cognitive abilities: A bidirectional perspective. *Child Development Perspectives, 14*(1), 15–20. https://doi.org/10.1111/cdep.12352.

Peng, P., Lin, X., Ünal, Z. E., Lee, K., Namkung, J., Chow, J., & Sales, A. (2020). Examining the mutual relations between language and mathematics: A meta-analysis. *Psychological Bulletin, 146*(7), 595–634. https://doi.org/10.1037/bul0000231.

Peng, P., Namkung, J., Barnes, M., & Sun, C. (2016). A meta-analysis of mathematics and working memory: Moderating effects of working memory domain, type of mathematics skill, and sample characteristics. *Journal of Educational Psychology, 108*(4), 455–473. https://doi.org/10.1037/edu0000079.

Peng, P., Wang, T., Wang, C., & Lin, X. (2019). A meta-analysis on the relation between fluid intelligence and reading/mathematics: Effects of tasks, age, and social economic status. *Psychological Bulletin, 145*(2), 189–236, https://psycnet.apa.org/buy/2019-01878-003.

Phelps, L., McGrew, K. S., Knopik, S. N., & Ford, L. (2005). The general (g), broad, and narrow CHC stratum characteristics of the WJ III and WISC-III tests: A confirmatory cross-battery investigation. *School Psychology Quarterly, 20*(1), 66–88. https://doi.org/10.1521/scpq.20.1.66.64191.

Plomin, R., & Deary, I. J. (2015). Genetics and intelligence differences: Five special findings. *Molecular Psychiatry, 20*, 98–108. https://doi.org/10.1038/mp.2014.105.

Psychological Corporation (2002). *Wechsler individual achievement test* (2nd ed). Author, San Antonio, TX.

Reynolds, M. R., Keith, T. Z., Flanagan, D. P., & Alfonso, V. C. (2013). A cross-battery, reference variable, confirmatory factor analytic investigation of the CHC taxonomy. *Journal of School Psychology, 51*(4), 535–555. https://doi.org/10.1016/j.jsp.2013.02.003.

Sanders, S., Mcintosh, D. E., Dunham, M., Rothlisberg, B. A., & Finch, H. (2007). Joint confirmatory factor analysis of the differential abilities scales and the Woodcock Johnson tests of cognitive abilities—third edition. *Psychology in the Schools, 44*(2), 119–138. https://doi.org/10.1002/pits.20211.

Schneider, W. J., & McGrew, K. S. (2018). The Cattell–Horn–Carroll theory of intelligence. In D. P. Flanagan & E. M. McDonough (Eds.), *Contemporary intellectual assessment* (4th ed, pp. 73–163). Guilford Press, New York, NY.

Swanson, H. L. (2012). Cognitive profile of adolescents with math disabilities: Are the profiles different from those with reading disabilities? *Child Neuropsychology, 18*(2), 125–143. https://doi.org/10.1080/09297049.2011.589377.
Swanson, H. L. (2015). Intelligence, working memory, and learning disabilities. In *Cognition, Intelligence, and Achievement* (pp. 175–196. https://doi.org/10.1016/B978-0-12-410388-7.00010-5). Elsevier.
U.S. Department of Education (2004). Individuals with disabilities education act. Public Law 108–446. https://www.congress.gov/bill/108th-congress/house-bill/1350/text.
van der Maas, H. L. J., Dolan, C. V., Grasman, R. P. P. P., Wicherts, J. M., Huizenga, H. M., & Raijmakers, M. E. J. (2006). A dynamical model of general intelligence: The positive manifold of intelligence by mutualism. *Psychological Review, 113,* 842–861. https://doi.org/10.1037/0033295X.113.4.842.
Vanderwood, M. L., McGrew, K. S., Flanagan, D. P., & Keith, T. Z. (2002). The contribution of general and specific cognitive abilities to reading achievement. *Learning and Individual Differences, 13,* 159–188. https://doi.org/10.1016/S1041-6080(02)00077-8.
Viechtbauer, W. (2010). Conducting meta-analyses in R with the metafor package. *Journal of Statistical Software, 36,* 1–48. https://doi.org/10.18637/jss.v036.i03.
Villeneuve, E. F., Hajovsky, D. B., Mason, B. A., & Lewno, B. M. (2019). Cognitive ability and math computation developmental relations with math problem solving: An integrated, multigroup approach. *School Psychology, 34*(1), 96–108, https://psycnet.apa.org/buy/2018-32191-001.
Wechsler, D. (2008). *Wechsler adult intelligence scale–fourth edition.* Pearson, San Antonio, TX.
Wechsler, D. (2009). *Wechsler adult intelligence scale–fourth edition.* Pearson, San Antonio, TX.
Woodcock, R. W. (1990). Theoretical foundations of the WJ-R measures of cognitive ability. *Journal of Psychoeducational Assessment, 8,* 231–258. https://doi.org/10.1177/073428299000800303.
Woodcock, R. W., & Johnson, M. B. (1989). *Woodcock-Johnson psycho-educational battery-revised.* DLM Teaching Resources, Allen, TX.
Youngstrom, E. A., Kogos, J. L., & Glutting, J. J. (1999). Incremental efficacy of differential ability scales factor scores in predicting individual achievement criteria. *School Psychology Quarterly, 14*(1), 26–39.
Zaboski, B. A., Kranzler, J. H., & Gage, N. A. (2018). Meta-analysis of the relationship between academic achievement and broad abilities of the Cattell-horn-Carroll, theory. *Journal of School Psychology, 71,* 42–56. https://doi.org/10.1016/j.jsp.2018.10.001.
Zhang, Z., & Peng, P. (2023). Co-development among reading, math, science, and verbal working memory in the elementary stage. *Child Development, 94*(6), e328–e343. https://doi.org/10.1111/cdev.13962.

Appendix D

# INTERCORRELATIONS AND RELIABILITY COEFFICIENTS USED TO CALCULATE XBA COMPOSITES IN X-BASS

The calculation of Cross-Battery Assessment (XBA) composites in the Cross-Battery Assessment Software System (X-BASS) 3.0 is grounded in a rigorous psychometric framework that balances accuracy, practicality, and consistency across batteries. Although the standard formula for composite reliability requires subtest-level reliability coefficients and intercorrelations, locating these values for every subtest at every age range—and for every possible subtest pairing—is prohibitively cumbersome for practitioners. X-BASS resolves this challenge by using meta-analytic average reliabilities and intercorrelations derived from an exceptionally large dataset of contemporary cognitive and achievement batteries and tests. These aggregated values allow X-BASS to generate stable, defensible composite estimates that reflect the best available evidence.

Meta-analytic average reliabilities and intercorrelations provide a more stable and defensible foundation for XBA composite calculations than age-specific coefficients drawn from individual test manuals. Age-specific values fluctuate across editions, norming samples, and technical supplements, and they are often based on relatively small subsamples. These fluctuations introduce noise rather than meaningful psychometric precision. In contrast, the meta-analytic values used in X-BASS are derived from tens of thousands of examinees across hundreds of correlation matrices and over a thousand subtests. This breadth dramatically reduces sampling error and idiosyncratic test-manual variability.

Because X-BASS composites are intended to generalize across batteries, ages, and subtest combinations, meta-analytic estimates offer the most reliable representation of the *true* relationships among Cattell-Horn-Carroll (CHC) abilities. They smooth out anomalies, minimize instability, and ensure that composite calculations are not distorted by the quirks of a single test's technical manual. The result is a set of composite estimates that are more robust, more replicable, and more appropriate for cross-battery interpretation than any age-specific coefficient could provide.

## SUMMARY OF THE DATA AND METHODOLOGY

The X-BASS composite engine draws on a uniquely comprehensive psychometric database (Hajovsky et al., 2022; Hajovsky et al., 2025; Niileksela & Hajovsky, 2024). The meta-analytic correlation matrix used to estimate cross-battery composites is based on:

- 568 correlation matrices
- 148 batteries or tests
- 1,160 subtests (counting revisions separately)
- 52,092 individual correlations
- 202,267 examinees across all matrices

Each matrix contributed, on average, 92 correlations and 356 participants, providing a robust foundation for estimating relationships among CHC broad abilities (for more information on the database see Hajovsky et al., 2025). In Table D.1, the diagonal of the matrix represents correlations among subtests measuring the same broad ability (e.g., *Gc* with *Gc*), while off-diagonal cells represent cross-ability relationships. In Table D.2, the diagonal of the matrix represents correlations between cognitive and academic abilities when two subtests are used to form a composite.

To support composite calculations, X-BASS also incorporates a large-scale database of reliability coefficients drawn from the large database, but only from tests currently in use. This dataset includes:

- 89 unique batteries or tests
- 789 unique subtests
- 170,595 individuals contributing to reliability estimates

Tables D.1 through D.6 include data used by X-BASS to calculate XBA composites. Together, these tables provide a transparent, empirically grounded foundation for the composite scores generated in X-BASS 3.0.

**Table D.1 Subtest-Level Meta-Analytic Correlation Matrix**

| | *Gc* | *Gf* | *Gv* | *Ga* | *Gl* | *Gr* | *Gs* | *Gwm* | LC | OE | BRS | RS | RC | MC | MPS | WA |
|---|---|---|---|---|---|---|---|---|---|---|---|---|---|---|---|---|
| *Gc* | .658 | | | | | | | | | | | | | | | |
| *Gf* | .473 | .517 | | | | | | | | | | | | | | |
| *Gv* | .393 | .440 | .436 | | | | | | | | | | | | | |
| *Ga* | .409 | .364 | .305 | .472 | | | | | | | | | | | | |
| *Gl* | .411 | .363 | .311 | .339 | .541 | | | | | | | | | | | |
| *Gr* | .302 | .241 | .232 | .255 | .257 | .419 | | | | | | | | | | |
| *Gs* | .313 | .311 | .315 | .269 | .226 | .324 | .505 | | | | | | | | | |
| *Gwm* | .399 | .377 | .314 | .370 | .304 | .289 | .294 | .453 | | | | | | | | |
| LC | .574 | .429 | .335 | .412 | .408 | .267 | .281 | .394 | .514 | | | | | | | |
| OE | .613 | .324 | .246 | .390 | .287 | .245 | .159 | .378 | .564 | .626 | | | | | | |
| BRS | .508 | .384 | .292 | .468 | .325 | .299 | .297 | .389 | .415 | .386 | .725 | | | | | |
| RS | .466 | .353 | .219 | .394 | .288 | .365 | .408 | .350 | .371 | .341 | .632 | .679 | | | | |
| RC | .571 | .434 | .323 | .460 | .383 | .301 | .320 | .390 | .542 | .454 | .623 | .546 | .611 | | | |
| MC | .482 | .490 | .340 | .355 | .325 | .274 | .373 | .369 | .395 | .336 | .505 | .424 | .532 | .681 | | |
| MPS | .554 | .530 | .389 | .419 | .381 | .307 | .365 | .412 | .502 | .414 | .530 | .456 | .588 | .685 | .727 | |
| WA | .448 | .398 | .286 | .419 | .341 | .286 | .317 | .350 | .422 | .488 | .537 | .451 | .543 | .506 | .504 | .473 |

*Note:* This table presents the meta-analytic correlations among CHC broad cognitive abilities and academic areas at the subtest level, aggregated across 568 correlation matrices, and more than 52,000 individual correlations. Diagonal values represent average correlations among subtests measuring the same broad ability or academic area. Off-diagonal values represent cross-ability relationships used in other X-BASS analyses.

*Gc* = Comprehension Knowledge; *Gf* = Fluid Reasoning; *Gv* = Visual Processing; *Ga* = Auditory Processing; *Gl* = Learning Efficiency; *Gr* = Retrieval Fluency; *Gs* = Processing Speed; *Gwm* = Short-Term Storage and Working Memory; LC = Listening Comprehension; OE = Oral Expression; BRS = Basic Reading Skills; RS = Reading Speed; RC = Reading Comprehension; MC = Math Calculation; MPS = Math Problem Solving; WA = Writing Ability.

**Table D.2 Estimated Two-Test Composite Meta-Analytic Correlation Matrix**

| | *Gc* | *Gf* | *Gv* | *Ga* | *Gl* | *Gr* | *Gs* | *Gwm* | LC | OE | BRS | RS | RC | MC | MPS | WA |
|---|---|---|---|---|---|---|---|---|---|---|---|---|---|---|---|---|
| *Gc* | .732 | | | | | | | | | | | | | | | |
| *Gf* | .578 | .644 | | | | | | | | | | | | | | |
| *Gv* | .502 | .574 | .582 | | | | | | | | | | | | | |
| *Ga* | .514 | .479 | .415 | .611 | | | | | | | | | | | | |
| *Gl* | .507 | .468 | .415 | .445 | .661 | | | | | | | | | | | |
| *Gr* | .395 | .329 | .326 | .352 | .348 | .568 | | | | | | | | | | |
| *Gs* | .398 | .410 | .424 | .362 | .300 | .437 | .636 | | | | | | | | | |
| *Gwm* | .506 | .497 | .430 | .495 | .405 | .399 | .396 | .596 | | | | | | | | |
| LC | .681 | .549 | .448 | .536 | .522 | .363 | .372 | .517 | .642 | | | | | | | |
| OE | .698 | .413 | .326 | .497 | .367 | .326 | .208 | .486 | .675 | .714 | | | | | | |
| BRS | .586 | .474 | .376 | .571 | .403 | .386 | .374 | .487 | .509 | .464 | .765 | | | | | |
| RS | .549 | .443 | .288 | .496 | .363 | .469 | .507 | .447 | .464 | .417 | .697 | .743 | | | | |
| RC | .661 | .542 | .423 | .577 | .481 | .398 | .411 | .501 | .656 | .548 | .700 | .634 | .705 | | | |
| MC | .565 | .592 | .438 | .450 | .407 | .359 | .466 | .469 | .491 | .412 | .580 | .503 | .621 | .744 | | |
| MPS | .630 | .628 | .490 | .519 | .467 | .395 | .454 | .513 | .600 | .494 | .599 | .531 | .668 | .741 | .766 | |
| WA | .557 | .519 | .391 | .550 | .448 | .392 | .422 | .470 | .548 | .605 | .642 | .559 | .664 | .616 | .609 | .612 |

*Note:* This table displays the estimated correlations among CHC broad cognitive abilities and academic areas when two subtests are combined to form a composite. These values are derived from the meta-analytic subtest correlations and reflect the expected relationships among two-indicator composites across batteries.

*Gc* = Comprehension Knowledge; *Gf* = Fluid Reasoning; *Gv* = Visual Processing; *Ga* = Auditory Processing; *Gl* = Learning Efficiency; *Gr* = Retrieval Fluency; *Gs* = Processing Speed; *Gwm* = Short-Term Storage and Working Memory; LC = Listening Comprehension; OE = Oral Expression; BRS = Basic Reading Skills; RS = Reading Speed; RC = Reading Comprehension; MC = Math Calculation; MPS = Math Problem Solving; WA = Writing Ability.

**Table D.3 Number of Individual Correlations Used to Estimate the Meta-Analytic Correlation Matrix**

| | *Gc* | *Gf* | *Gv* | *Ga* | *Gl* | *Gr* | *Gs* | *Gwm* | LC | OE | BRS | RS | RC | MC | MPS | WA |
|---|---|---|---|---|---|---|---|---|---|---|---|---|---|---|---|---|
| *Gc* | 1916 | | | | | | | | | | | | | | | |
| *Gf* | 1471 | 400 | | | | | | | | | | | | | | |
| *Gv* | 2818 | 1219 | 1125 | | | | | | | | | | | | | |
| *Ga* | 568 | 386 | 400 | 190 | | | | | | | | | | | | |
| *Gl* | 1004 | 679 | 1791 | 384 | 495 | | | | | | | | | | | |
| *Gr* | 646 | 519 | 541 | 381 | 496 | 331 | | | | | | | | | | |
| *Gs* | 1942 | 824 | 1427 | 342 | 556 | 503 | 501 | | | | | | | | | |
| *Gwm* | 3294 | 1582 | 2756 | 566 | 1350 | 817 | 1929 | 1619 | | | | | | | | |
| LC | 661 | 270 | 252 | 247 | 225 | 314 | 226 | 391 | 117 | | | | | | | |
| OE | 201 | 22 | 22 | 26 | 16 | 77 | 21 | 31 | 154 | 26 | | | | | | |
| BRS | 652 | 321 | 334 | 351 | 284 | 389 | 282 | 503 | 221 | 61 | 226 | | | | | |
| RS | 265 | 169 | 143 | 228 | 128 | 369 | 147 | 261 | 160 | 74 | 350 | 142 | | | | |
| RC | 336 | 153 | 160 | 159 | 135 | 213 | 145 | 236 | 127 | 44 | 353 | 199 | 25 | | | |
| MC | 297 | 138 | 168 | 130 | 132 | 166 | 122 | 204 | 100 | 37 | 244 | 136 | 147 | 111 | | |
| MPS | 270 | 132 | 152 | 139 | 128 | 162 | 122 | 205 | 100 | 32 | 204 | 123 | 105 | 185 | 13 | |
| WA | 285 | 142 | 138 | 145 | 112 | 206 | 145 | 218 | 135 | 51 | 237 | 173 | 134 | 112 | 109 | 57 |

*Note.* This table shows the number of individual correlations underlying each cell in the meta-analytic correlation matrix. Larger Ns indicate greater stability and precision in the estimated relationships among CHC abilities.

*Gc* = Comprehension Knowledge; *Gf* = Fluid Reasoning; *Gv* = Visual Processing; *Ga* = Auditory Processing; *Gl* = Learning Efficiency; *Gr* = Retrieval Fluency; *Gs* = Processing Speed; *Gwm* = Short-Term Storage and Working Memory; LC = Listening Comprehension; OE = Oral Expression; BRS = Basic Reading Skills; RS = Reading Speed; RC = Reading Comprehension; MC = Math Calculation; MPS = Math Problem Solving; WA = Writing Ability.

**Table D.4 Number of Correlation Matrices Used to Estimate the Meta-Analytic Correlation Matrix**

| | *Gc* | *Gf* | *Gv* | *Ga* | *Gl* | *Gr* | *Gs* | *Gwm* | LS | CM | BRS | RS | RC | MC | MPS | WA |
|---|---|---|---|---|---|---|---|---|---|---|---|---|---|---|---|---|
| *Gc* | 277 | | | | | | | | | | | | | | | |
| *Gf* | 207 | 150 | | | | | | | | | | | | | | |
| *Gv* | 266 | 222 | 263 | | | | | | | | | | | | | |
| *Ga* | 62 | 49 | 55 | 34 | | | | | | | | | | | | |
| *Gl* | 117 | 111 | 160 | 48 | 126 | | | | | | | | | | | |
| *Gr* | 87 | 89 | 107 | 65 | 70 | 76 | | | | | | | | | | |
| *Gs* | 171 | 154 | 198 | 44 | 70 | 85 | 133 | | | | | | | | | |
| *Gwm* | 246 | 199 | 278 | 63 | 142 | 106 | 182 | 220 | | | | | | | | |
| LS | 95 | 61 | 61 | 56 | 53 | 59 | 42 | 53 | 41 | | | | | | | |
| CM | 34 | 10 | 8 | 21 | 6 | 27 | 8 | 10 | 55 | 14 | | | | | | |
| BRS | 128 | 61 | 70 | 72 | 57 | 72 | 51 | 76 | 65 | 27 | 112 | | | | | |
| RS | 52 | 28 | 27 | 47 | 22 | 64 | 27 | 34 | 46 | 25 | 83 | 61 | | | | |
| RC | 114 | 52 | 52 | 62 | 45 | 65 | 47 | 58 | 61 | 29 | 140 | 78 | 21 | | | |
| MC | 111 | 53 | 56 | 57 | 43 | 57 | 46 | 59 | 59 | 26 | 118 | 60 | 111 | 14 | | |
| MPS | 85 | 51 | 55 | 62 | 46 | 59 | 47 | 57 | 60 | 25 | 97 | 58 | 86 | 95 | 10 | |
| WA | 75 | 42 | 41 | 50 | 32 | 58 | 39 | 47 | 70 | 39 | 83 | 58 | 84 | 80 | 78 | 33 |

*Note:* This table reports how many separate correlation matrices contributed to each cell in the meta-analytic matrix. Higher counts reflect broader representation across batteries or tests, age groups, and samples.

*Gc* = Comprehension Knowledge; *Gf* = Fluid Reasoning; *Gv* = Visual Processing; *Ga* = Auditory Processing; *Gl* = Learning Efficiency; *Gr* = Retrieval Fluency; *Gs* = Processing Speed; *Gwm* = Short-Term Storage and Working Memory; LS = Listening Ability; CM = Communication Ability; BRS = Basic Reading Skills; RS = Reading Speed; RC = Reading Comprehension; MC = Math Calculation; MPS = Math Problem Solving; WA = Writing Ability.

**Table D.5 Reliability Dataset Summary**

| Broad/Narrow | *N* Reliabilities | *N* People |
|---|---|---|
| ***Ga*** | **508** | **103,343** |
| **PC** | 486 | 100,313 |
| **UR** | 17 | 2,023 |
| **US** | 5 | 1,007 |
| | | |
| ***Gc*** | **1,361** | **257,119** |
| **K0** | 216 | 51,563 |
| **K1** | 37 | 8,599 |
| **K2** | 85 | 18,330 |
| **LD** | 23 | 3,795 |
| **MY** | 87 | 13,127 |
| **VL** | 913 | 161,705 |
| | | |
| ***Gf*** | **958** | **170,206** |
| **I** | 512 | 87,974 |
| **RG** | 272 | 45,729 |
| **RQ** | 174 | 36,503 |
| | | |
| ***Gl*** | **365** | **75,003** |
| **M6** | 114 | 19,324 |
| **MA** | 136 | 30,490 |
| **MM** | 115 | 25,189 |
| | | |
| ***Gr*** | **535** | **85,156** |
| **FF** | 17 | 6,050 |
| **FI** | 174 | 26,362 |
| **FW** | 44 | 9,336 |
| **RAN** | 300 | 43,408 |
| | | |
| ***Gs*** | **372** | **75,382** |
| **Pc** | 170 | 40,296 |
| **Ps** | 202 | 35,086 |
| | | |
| ***Gv*** | **1,066** | **160,353** |
| **CF** | 91 | 11,985 |
| **CS** | 23 | 3,899 |
| **MV** | 342 | 46,519 |
| **SS** | 11 | 1,189 |
| **Vz** | 599 | 96,761 |

**Table D.5 (Continued)**

| Broad/Narrow | *N* Reliabilities | *N* People |
|---|---|---|
| ***Gwm*** | **967** | **196,496** |
| Wa | 425 | 84,227 |
| Wc | 429 | 93,581 |
| Wv | 113 | 18,688 |
| | | |
| ***Gq*** | **422** | **67,895** |
| MC | 171 | 24,900 |
| MPS | 135 | 28,083 |
| MS | 116 | 14,912 |
| | | |
| ***Grw*** | **1,272** | **256,944** |
| BRS | 345 | 76,983 |
| RC | 218 | 50,332 |
| RS | 278 | 43,540 |
| SG | 242 | 46,206 |
| WA | 189 | 39,883 |
| | | |
| ***Gc* (SLD Categories)** | **699** | **125,136** |
| CM | 185 | 24,364 |
| LS | 514 | 100,772 |

*Note:* This table summarizes the number of reliability coefficients and examinees contributing to the average reliability estimates for each CHC broad ability. Only batteries or tests currently in use were included, ensuring contemporary and relevant reliability values.

*Ga* = Auditory Processing; PC = Phonetic Coding; UR = Resistance to Auditory Stimulus Distortion; US = Speech Sound Discrimination; *Gc* = Comprehension Knowledge; K0 = General Knowledge; K1 = General Science Information; K2 = Knowledge of Culture; LD = Language Development; MY = Grammatical Sensitivity; VL = Lexical Knowledge; *Gf* = Fluid Reasoning; I = Induction; RG = General Sequential Reasoning; RQ = Quantitative Reasoning; *Gl* = Learning Efficiency; M6 = Free-Recall Memory; MA = Associative Memory; MM = Meaningful Memory; *Gr* = Retrieval Fluency; FF = Figural Fluency; FI = Ideational Fluency; FW = Word Fluency; RAN = Rapid Automatic Naming; *Gs* = Processing Speed; Pc = Perceptual Speed-Compare; Ps = Perceptual Speed-Search; *Gv* = Visual Processing; CF = Flexibility of Closure; CS = Closure Speed; MV = Visual Memory; SS = Spatial Scanning; Vz = Visualization; *Gwm* = Short-Term Storage and Working Memory; WA = Auditory Short-Term Storage; Wc = Working Memory Capacity; Wv = Visual Spatial Short-Term Storage; *Gq* = Quantitative Knowledge; MC = Math Calculation; MPS = Math Problem Solving; MS = Math Speed; *Grw* = Reading and Writing; BRS = Basic Reading Skills; RC = Reading Comprehension; RS = Reading Speed; SG = Spelling Ability; WA = Writing Ability; CM = Communication Ability; LS = Listening Ability.

**Table D.6 Broad Ability Average Reliabilities and Estimated Composite Reliabilities**

| CHC Ability Area | *K* Reliabilities Included in Averages | Meta-Analytic Average Subtest Reliability | Estimated 2-Test Composite Reliability | Estimated 3-Test Composite Reliability |
|---|---|---|---|---|
| *Gc* | 1361 | .893 | .944 | .962 |
| *Gf* | 958 | .874 | .933 | .954 |
| *Gv* | 1066 | .821 | .902 | .932 |
| *Ga* | 508 | .886 | .940 | .959 |
| *Gl* | 365 | .865 | .928 | .951 |
| *Gr* | 535 | .830 | .907 | .936 |
| *Gwm* | 967 | .854 | .921 | .946 |
| *Gs* | 372 | .853 | .921 | .946 |
| OE | 185 | .894 | .944 | .962 |
| LC | 514 | .876 | .934 | .955 |
| BRS | 345 | .931 | .964 | .976 |
| RC | 218 | .909 | .952 | .968 |
| RS | 278 | .923 | .960 | .973 |
| MC | 171 | .922 | .960 | .973 |
| MPS | 135 | .920 | .958 | .972 |
| MS | 116 | .917 | .957 | .971 |
| WA | 189 | .857 | .923 | .947 |
| SG | 242 | .920 | .958 | .972 |

*Note:* OE refers to Oral Expression, which comprises subtests classified under *Gc*:CM (Communication Ability). LC refers to Listening Comprehension, which comprises subtests classified under *Gc*:LS (Listening Ability). This table includes the number of reliabilities used in the calculation of averages, along with estimated two-test and three-test composite reliabilities. These values are used by X-BASS to calculate XBA composites.

*Gc* = Comprehension Knowledge; *Gf* = Fluid Reasoning; *Gv* = Visual Processing; *Ga* = Auditory Processing; *Gl* = Learning Efficiency; *Gr* = Retrieval Fluency; *Gs* = Processing Speed; *Gwm* = Short-Term Storage and Working Memory; OE = Oral Expression; LC = Listening Comprehension; BRS = Basic Reading Skills; RC = Reading Comprehension; RS = Reading Speed; MC = Math Calculation; MPS = Math Problem Solving; MS = Math Speed; WA = Writing Ability; SG = Spelling Ability.

## CONCLUSION

This appendix provides the psychometric foundation for how X-BASS 3.0 calculates XBA composites. The approach used by Flanagan and colleagues integrates methodological rigor with practical usability. By leveraging meta-analytic average reliabilities and intercorrelations derived from tens of thousands of data points, X-BASS ensures that composites are defensible and accessible, without requiring practitioners to locate and cross-reference dozens of technical manuals. XBA composites align with the complexities of CHC theory and current battery design while streamlining the analytic process for real-world assessment. These composite estimates allow examiners to make informed, research-based interpretations that are consistent across batteries, age ranges, and subtest combinations, strengthening the validity and utility of the XBA method.

## ACKNOWLEDGMENTS

We are grateful to Drs. Chris Nilleksela and Joel Schneider for their assistance in compiling and managing the meta-analytic database. Chris Nilleksela conducted the analyses included in this appendix.

## REFERENCES

Hajovsky, D. B., Niileksela, C. R., Flanagan, D. P., Alfonso, V. C., Schneider, W. J., & Robbins, J. (2025). Toward a consensus model of cognitive–reading achievement relations using meta-structural equation modeling. *Journal of Intelligence*, *13*(8), 104 https://doi.org/10.3390/jintelligence13080104.

Hajovsky, D. B., Niileksela, C. R., Flanagan, D. P., Alfonso, V. C., Schneider, J., & Zinkiewicz, C. J. (2022, 4–7 August). *A consensus model of cognitive-achievement relations using meta-SEM* [Poster Presentation]. American Psychological Association, Minneapolis, MN.

Niileksela, C. R., & Hajovsky, D. B. (2024, 25–24 January). *Consolidating evidence of cognitive-achievement relations: A preliminary meta-analysis of 496 data-sets* [Conference Presentation]. State of the Art of Specific Learning Disabilities Identification: Innovations in Theory, Research, and Practice, Virtual.

Appendix E

# CONVERGENT VALIDITY OF X-BASS CHC COMPOSITES: A LARGE-SCALE COMPARISON WITH NORM-REFERENCED COMPOSITES

In Collaboration with Craig Zinkiewicz, Psy.D.

Scottsdale Unified School District

## INTRODUCTION

The Cross-Battery Assessment (XBA) method and the Cattell-Horn-Carroll (CHC) composites generated by Cross-Battery Assessment Software System (X-BASS) are widely used in psychoeducational evaluations, yet their validity has been questioned because they combine subtests from different batteries rather than relying solely on publisher-generated composites. According to the *Standards for Educational and Psychological Testing* (Standards: AERA et al., 2014), validity refers to the degree to which evidence and theory support the interpretations of test scores for their intended uses. When a new scoring procedure or interpretive method is introduced, the Standards emphasize the need for evidence based on relations to other variables, particularly convergent validity, to demonstrate that the resulting scores behave as expected in relation to established measures of the same construct.

This requirement is especially relevant for the XBA method. X-BASS generates CHC composites by combining subtests from within and across batteries using a psychometric engine grounded in meta-analytic average reliabilities and intercorrelations. As described in Appendix D, "the meta-analytic correlation matrix used to estimate cross-battery composites is based on 568 correlation matrices, 148 test batteries, 1,160 subtests, 52,092 individual correlations, and 202,267 examinees across all matrices." These aggregated values provide a stable, defensible foundation for estimating relationships among CHC abilities and academic areas across instruments. Because "XBA composites are intended to generalize across batteries, ages, and subtest combinations, meta-analytic estimates offer the most reliable representation of the true relationships among CHC abilities."

However, the Standards make clear that such theoretical and methodological rationale must be supported by empirical evidence. In the absence of a cross-battery norm group, the most direct way to evaluate the precision of XBA composites is to compare them to publisher-generated norm-based composites using the exact same subtests within a single battery. If X-BASS can reproduce those composites with high precision across thousands of score combinations, this provides strong convergent validity evidence for the composite engine itself. Given that all batteries in X-BASS contributed to the meta-analytic database, it is reasonable to infer that similar precision will hold when subtests are combined across batteries.

The present study, therefore, examined the degree of correspondence between X-BASS-generated composites and norm-based composites from major cognitive and achievement batteries, using identical subtest combinations. This provides a rigorous test of the **convergent validity and precision** of XBA composites and, by extension, supports the defensibility of XBA-based interpretations.

## METHOD

### Meta-Analytic Foundation for XBA Composite Calculations

The X-BASS composite engine is built on a uniquely comprehensive psychometric database (See Appendix D). The meta-analytic correlation matrix used to estimate relationships among CHC broad abilities and academic areas is based on:

- **568 correlation matrices**
- **148 batteries**
- **1,160 subtests** (counting revisions separately)
- **52,092 individual correlations**
- **202,267 examinees** across all matrices

Each matrix contributed, on average, 92 correlations and 356 participants, providing a robust foundation for estimating relationships among CHC broad abilities. Diagonal cells in the matrix represent average correlations among subtests measuring the same broad ability (e.g., *Gc* with *Gc*), whereas off-diagonal cells represent cross-ability relationships. These values are summarized in Table D.1 (subtest-level meta-analytic correlation matrix) and Table D.2 (estimated two-test composite correlation matrix).

To support composite reliability estimation, X-BASS also incorporates a large-scale database of reliability coefficients drawn from batteries and tests currently in use and included in X-BASS. This dataset includes:

- **89 unique batteries**
- **789 unique subtests**
- **170,595 individuals** contributing to reliability estimates

Table D.5 summarizes the number of reliability coefficients and the total number of examinees contributing to the average reliability estimates for each CHC ability. Table D.6 reports the meta-analytic average subtest reliabilities and the corresponding estimated reliabilities for two- and three-subtest composites (e.g., *Gc* subtest reliability = .893; estimated two-subtest composite reliability = .944; three-subtest composite reliability = .962). These values are used by X-BASS to calculate XBA composites in a way that is psychometrically rigorous and practically feasible.

### Design of the Convergent Validity Study

Because there is no cross-battery norm group, the empirical evaluation focused on within-battery comparisons using identical subtests. The goal was to determine how closely XBA composites generated by X-BASS match the publisher's norm-based composite when both are based on the same set of subtests from a single battery.

Ten widely used cognitive, achievement, and special-purpose batteries were included: WISC-V, WAIS-V, DAS-II NU, KABC-II NU, SB5, WRAML-3, CELF-5, CTOPP-2, WIAT-4, and KTEA-3. A total of 84 two- and three-subtest composites were identified across these instruments. Only composites measuring a single construct (e.g., basic reading skills, reading comprehension, math calculation) were included; composites that intentionally blend constructs (e.g., a reading composite combining word reading and reading comprehension) were excluded. Composites designed exclusively for very young children (e.g., WIAT-4 K–1 Written Expression, DAS-II Early Years composites, KABC-II NU four to six year composites) were also excluded to focus on school-age examinees.

For each composite, all possible combinations of scaled scores, T-scores, or standard scores were generated across the full range of publisher norms (e.g., scaled scores 2–19; standard scores 40–160). For each score combination:

1. The **publisher's norm-based composite** was obtained using the manual's tables.
2. The **XBA composite** was generated by entering the same subtest scores into X-BASS.
3. The **difference** between the XBA composite and the norm-based composite was calculated.

Frequencies were then computed for the proportion of XBA composites falling within the **68%, 90%, and 95% confidence intervals** (CIs) of the norm-based composite. Analyses were conducted for:

- the **full score range** (SS 40–160)
- a **restricted range** of ±2 SD (SS 70–130)
- a **restricted range** of ±3 SD (SS 55–145)
- **achievement-only** composites (WIAT-4, KTEA-3)
- **cognitive-only** composites (all other batteries)

Composites involving WIAT-4 Writing Fluency were excluded due to poor reliability, consistent with publisher guidance that such scores should not be used for quantitative comparisons.

## RESULTS

### Overall Precision of X-BASS Composites

Across 3,962 comparisons in the full score range (SS 40–160), X-BASS composites demonstrated a high degree of precision relative to publisher norm-based composites. Notably, 91.92% of all X-BASS composites fell within the 68% CI (±1 SEM) of the norm-based composite. Because the 68% CI is the narrowest band around the true score, this represents the strictest possible criterion for evaluating composite agreement.

### Precision in Clinically Relevant Score Ranges

Precision increased substantially when analyses were restricted to the score ranges most relevant to diagnostic interpretation.

- **±2 SD (SS 70–130):**
  - **98.43%** of X-BASS composites fell within the **68% CI** of the norm-based composite.
  - **99.09%** of X-BASS composites fell within the **95% CI** of the norm-based composite.
  - The average difference was **.77 standard score points.**
- **±3 SD (SS 55–145):**
- **95.61%** of X-BASS composites fell within the **68% CI** of the norm-based composite.
- **98.15%** of X-BASS composites fell within the **95% CI** of the norm-based composite.
  - The average difference was **1.19 standard score points.**

The 68% CI findings are especially important. They show that, in the score range where nearly all diagnostic decisions occur, XBA composites were virtually indistinguishable from publisher composites. Falling within ±1 SEM means the XBA composite is as close to the norm-based composite as two independent administrations of the same test would be expected to be.

### Achievement and Cognitive Composites

Both domains showed similarly strong precision.

- **Achievement composites (±2 SD):**
  - **96.43%** of X-BASS composites fell within the **68% CI** of the norm-based composite.
  - **98.90%** of X-BASS composites fell within the **95% CI** of the norm-based composite.
  - The average difference was **.93 standard score points.**
- **Cognitive composites (±2 SD):**
  - **99.16%** of X-BASS composites fell within the **68% CI** of the norm-based composite.
  - **99.16%** of X-BASS composites fell within the **95% CI** of the norm-based composite.
  - The average difference was **.71 standard score points.**

**DON'T FORGET**

X-BASS composites match publisher composites so closely that they differ by less than one SEM in nearly every case.

These results indicate that XBA composite precision is consistent across cognitive and academic domains.

### Extreme Score Differences

The largest discrepancies occurred only at extreme score combinations, particularly in several KABC-II NU composites at the upper end of the scaled-score range. These differences reflect ceiling limitations in the publisher's subtests rather than error in X-BASS. Because such extreme combinations fall outside the range typically used for diagnostic decision-making, they do not meaningfully affect clinical interpretation. Table E.1 summarizes accuracy across score ranges; Table E.2 summarizes accuracy by domain within ±2 SD.

**Table E.1 Accuracy of X-BASS Composites Across Score Ranges**

| Score Range | *N* Comparisons | % Within 68% CI (%) | % Within 90% CI (%) | % Within 95% CI (%) | Avg Difference | Largest Difference |
|---|---|---|---|---|---|---|
| Full Range (SS 40–160) | 3,962 | 91.92 | 96.70 | 97.49 | 1.33 | 13.32 |
| ±3 SD (SS 55–145) | 2,895 | 95.61 | 97.82 | 98.15 | 1.19 | 12.47 |
| ±2 SD (SS 70–130) | 1,994 | 98.43 | 99.00 | 99.09 | .77 | 6.80 |

**Table E.2 Accuracy by Domain (±2 SD Range)**

| Domain | *N* Comparisons | % Within 90% CI (%) | % Within 95% CI (%) | Avg Difference | Largest Difference |
|---|---|---|---|---|---|
| Achievement Only | 655 | 98.58 | 98.90 | .93 | 6.80 |
| Cognitive Only | 1,339 | 99.16 | 99.16 | .71 | 2.82 |

## CONCLUSION

The findings provide strong evidence of convergent validity for XBA composites generated by X-BASS. When the same subtests are used, X-BASS reproduces publisher-norm-based composites with remarkable precision, regardless of subtest variability (i.e., whether cohesive or not). The most compelling evidence comes from the 68% CI, where 98.43% of XBA composites in the clinically relevant score range (SS 70–130) fell within ±1 SEM of the norm-based composite. This level of agreement exceeds what would typically be expected from two independent administrations of the same test.

Because the X-BASS composite engine is built on a massive meta-analytic database and all batteries included in X-BASS contributed to that database, it is reasonable to infer that similar precision will hold when subtests are combined across batteries. Together, these results support the use of XBA composites as a defensible, efficient, and theoretically grounded method for interpreting CHC abilities and academic skills within a cross-battery framework.

## IMPLICATIONS FOR PRACTITIONERS

These findings provide clear and practical guidance for clinicians using X-BASS in cross-battery assessment. The most compelling evidence comes from the 68% CI, where 98.43% of XBA composites in the clinically relevant score range (SS 70–130) fell within ±1 SEM of the publisher composite. Because the 68% CI is the narrowest band around the true score, this level of agreement reflects exceptional precision, the kind of precision typically expected only from two administrations of the same test. For practitioners, this means that XBA composites are as reliable and precise as the publisher composites when the same subtests are used. The following analogy provides clarity when explaining the accuracy of XBA composites to others:

**Imagine throwing darts:**

- The 68% CI is like hitting the inner ring around the bullseye.
- The 95% CI is like hitting the larger outer ring.

If 98% of your darts land in the inner ring, that's far more impressive than 98% landing somewhere in the outer ring. *XBA composites land in the inner ring.*

The meta-analytic foundation of X-BASS further strengthens its interpretive utility. As described in Appendix D, the composite engine is built on "568 correlation matrices. . .1,160 subtests. . .52,092 individual correlations" and a reliability dataset including "789 unique subtests" and "170,595 individuals." These values represent the most stable and representative estimates available for CHC ability relationships. Because all major batteries included in X-BASS contributed to this database, practitioners can reasonably expect similar precision when combining subtests across batteries, even though no cross-battery norm group exists.

Finally, X-BASS helps practitioners avoid the interpretive pitfalls of comparing isolated subtest scores across batteries. By generating composites grounded in a unified psychometric framework, X-BASS supports clearer, more consistent, and more defensible interpretations of cognitive and academic profiles. This reduces interpretive noise, improves communication with stakeholders, and enhances the overall quality of diagnostic decision-making.

## REFERENCE

American Educational Research Association, American Psychological Association, & National Council on Measurement in Education (2014). *Standards for educational and psychological testing.* American Educational Research Association.

Appendix F

# CONTINUOUS VARIABLES AND CATEGORICAL DECISIONS ABOUT SLD

W. Joel Schneider, Ph.D.

Temple University

In any assessment, we would like to know whether our measurements are accurate enough to support valid inferences and subsequent decisions based on the scores. To understand diagnostic accuracy, we need to be clear about what type of variables we are considering. Categorical variables differ in kind, and continuous variables differ in degree. Some measures are designed to detect conditions or things that are either present or absent. By contrast, many measures, including ability tests, are not intended to detect the presence or absence of a condition but instead to quantify a value on a continuous dimension. Typically, confusion arises when a continuous dimensional variable is unknowingly and carelessly evaluated with statistics designed to assess the accuracy of categorical decisions (Schneider et al., 2024).

Specific learning disabilities (SLDs) might seem like they are categorical—one either has an SLD diagnosis or one does not. It may not be immediately apparent that this categorical distinction necessitates making decisions about inherently continuous variables using thresholds established for practical rather than inherent reasons (Peters & Ansari, 2019). The *Diagnostic and Statistical Manual-Fifth Edition, Text Revision* (DSM-5-TR; American Psychiatric Association, 2022) acknowledges this problem candidly:

> Academic skills are distributed along a continuum, so there is no natural cutpoint that can be used to differentiate individuals with and without specific learning disorder. Thus, any threshold used to specify what constitutes significantly low academic achievement (e.g., academic skills well below age expectations) is, to a large extent, arbitrary. (p. 79)

Thus, SLD differs from a disorder such as Huntington's disease, which is caused by a mutation in a single gene (Roos, 2010). The diverse visible manifestations of Huntington's disease (e.g., random involuntary movements, rigid posturing, and cognitive decline) differ in degree, but there is an underlying binary distinction at the core of the diagnostic decision—the presence or absence of a gene variant that causes Huntington's Disease.

At the time of writing, no SLD variants are known to have a single cause, similar to Huntington's disease. Instead, SLDs are identified by particular patterns of continuous variables. These patterns are not "things" that are present or absent. In the space spanned by these continuous variables, what we call SLD consists of multidimensional regions with unclear boundaries. If that sounds strange, think again. We encounter multivariate entities with unclear boundaries all the time. What constitutes a good friend, an important play, an effective legal code, or a satisfying career is a pattern of many variables, most of which lack clear and definitive boundaries. We can disagree about cases that are on the edge of those boundaries. However, cases at the extremes generate limited to no controversy—Shakespeare's *Romeo and Juliet* has greater historic importance than a forgotten flop of yesteryear. Likewise, SLDs are easily distinguishable at the extremes. It is not difficult to identify SLD in a bright student with a severe cognitive processing deficit that led to extreme reading difficulties that multiple rounds of well-chosen, well-implemented, and empirically supported interventions have failed to remediate. Similarly, a student who has always performed all academic tasks with ease does not have SLD. Cases at the margins, however, require careful consideration of whether SLD exists.

With categorical diagnoses—conditions that are present or absent—there are two ways to be incorrect or inaccurate: not detecting what is truly present (false negatives) or detecting what is truly absent (false positives). For example, bulimia might be missed if a person does not disclose their purging behavior; bulimia might be falsely diagnosed after a single act of purging, never to be repeated.

Some categorical conditions are easily detectable and reliable. The outward manifestations of categorical diagnoses are often continuous instead of categorical. For example, Down syndrome is a categorical condition caused by having an extra copy of the 21st chromosome. The visible features of Down syndrome (e.g., a large tongue, a short neck, and extra space between the first and second toes) can be quite pronounced but are often not visibly distinct from those of the general population. If we had to rely on such features instead of genetic testing to identify Down syndrome, we would still diagnose most cases correctly, but there would be far more misdiagnoses than there are now.

Many assessment targets cannot be said to be present or absent. They are quantitative entities with a specific value. For example, height is not something you either have or do not have; it is a continuous variable. Everyone has a height, but some are taller (or shorter) than others. However, there is no sharp threshold at which we all agree that a person changes classifications from *not tall* to *tall* or *not short to short.*

For convenience, we might decide that, for a particular population, a certain height is a reasonable threshold for classifying a person as tall or short. However, few people think of such thresholds as having inherent meaning or that there is any qualitative difference between people whose height is barely above the threshold and those whose height is barely below it.

Some thresholds in continuous variables *do* have inherent meaning. Heat is a continuous variable, but there are known thresholds at which solids melt, and liquids become gases. For example, a thermometer can indicate whether a block of ice will stay frozen, melt, or eventually boil. Knowing whether water will be solid, liquid, or gas has many valuable applications, and in some situations, is a matter of life and death. Melting and boiling points can vary depending on factors such as pressure and water purity; however, their underlying physical processes do not depend on arbitrary human choices.

There is a long-standing and much-discussed mismatch between largely categorical diagnostic systems and the continuous nature of mental health phenomena (e.g., Brown & Barlow, 2005; Helzer, 2008; Milinkovic & Tiliopoulos, 2020). Unlike melting points, diagnostic thresholds are primarily determined by practical considerations. There are few thresholds at which a dimension of mental health abruptly transitions from normal to abnormal or disordered. Instead, there is a smooth gradient by which symptom severity predicts distress, dysfunction, and important life outcomes. By tradition and experience, we determine that scores above or below a threshold indicate a concern.

Symptom severity is a continuous variable, but diagnoses are categorical. All-or-nothing diagnoses can create challenges, ethical dilemmas, and even critical misdiagnoses. People whose symptoms barely miss the diagnostic threshold might be denied help that would benefit them. Lowering the threshold does not solve this problem; it intensifies it by creating an even larger group of people who barely miss the new threshold for diagnosis. A common solution to this problem is to establish multiple thresholds at which individuals can receive progressively higher levels of support. In such systems, errors will still occur—someone with mild symptoms might be deemed eligible for more services than are needed, and someone with severe symptoms might only receive a moderate amount of support—but the consequences of these errors are far better than what happens in an all-or-nothing classification system. For this reason, the Appropriate Academic Supports to Meet the Needs of All Students (2009) recommends Multitiered System of Supports (MTSS) to provide increasing levels of support to students with more intense or severe needs.

## TRUE SCORES AND THE RELIABILITY OF CONTINUOUS VARIABLES

All measurements have measurement error. Some measurement error is due to carelessness or outright mistakes. However, even when the assessment procedure is performed flawlessly, the inherent imprecision in every measure causes scores to fluctuate each time measurements are taken. If we could eliminate random fluctuations due to measurement error, we would be left with a *true score*. The more reliable the measure, the closer the observed score is likely to be to the person's true score on that measure.

To be precise, a *true score* is the long-term average a person would receive on a measurement if the measure were given repeatedly without carryover effects (e.g., practice or fatigue effects). True scores cannot be observed directly, but we can estimate their approximate values. To do so, we note that observed scores $X$ are the sum of true scores $T$ and error scores $e$:

$$X = T + e$$

Because true scores and error scores are uncorrelated, the variance of an observed score $\sigma_X^2$ is the sum of its true score variance $\sigma_T^2$ and error variance $\sigma_e^2$:

$$\sigma_X^2 = \sigma_T^2 + \sigma_e^2$$

The classical reliability coefficient $\rho_{XX}$ is defined as the ratio of true score variance to observed score variance $\sigma_T^2$:

$$\rho_{XX} = \frac{\sigma_T^2}{\sigma_T^2 + \sigma_e^2} = \frac{\sigma_T^2}{\sigma_X^2}$$

In Figure F.1, the observed score is depicted as a square with an area of 1. The true score is a black circle with an area of .90, and error is a gray circle with an area of .10. The black portion of the observed score represents the variance of $X$ that comes from the true score $T$, and the gray portion of the observed score represents the variance of $X$ that comes from measurement error $e$. The ratio of true score variance to total variance in $X$ is the reliability coefficient $\rho_{XX} = .90$.

The square root of the reliability coefficient is equal to the correlation of observed and true scores $r_{XT}$, also known as the *reliability index*.

$$\rho_{XT} = \sqrt{\rho_{XX}} = \sqrt{\frac{\sigma_T^2}{\sigma_X^2}} = \frac{\sigma_T}{\sigma_X}$$

The mean of the true scores $\mu_T$ is equal to the mean of the observed scores $\mu_X$.

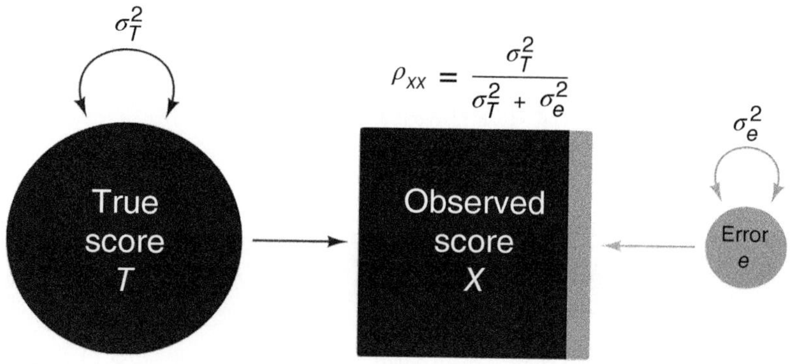


**FIGURE F.1 The Reliability Coefficient Is the Proportion of Observed Score Variance that Is Attributable to the True Score**

$$\mu_T = \mu_X$$

With this information, we can create a regression equation to predict the location of the true score. A regression formula may be difficult to remember, but it is easily reconstructed from two simple, easily remembered formulas. When $X$ predicts $Y$:

$$\hat{z}_Y = \rho_{XY} z_X$$

Recall that a z-score for any variable $X$ has this formula:

$$\hat{z} = \frac{X - \mu_X}{\sigma_X}$$

In this case, instead of predicting some outside variable $Y$, we are using $X$ to predict the true score for $X$. After some simplification, the estimated true score $\widehat{T}$ can be expressed in terms of observable statistics only:

$$\begin{aligned}\frac{\widehat{T} - \mu_T}{\sigma_T} &= \rho_{XT} \frac{X - \mu_X}{\sigma_X} \\ \widehat{T} - \mu_T &= \rho_{XT} \frac{\sigma_T}{\sigma_X}(X - \mu_X) \\ \widehat{T} &= \rho_{XT}^2 (X - \mu_X) + \mu_T \\ \widehat{T} &= \rho_{XX} (X - \mu_X) + \mu_X\end{aligned}$$

The standard error of the estimate $\sigma_{T-\widehat{T}}$ can be viewed as the typical distance between the true score $T$ and the estimated true score $\widehat{T}$. Because $\sigma_T^2 = \sigma_X^2 \rho_{XX}$, we can simplify the standard error of the estimate so that it is expressed using observable statistics only:

$$\begin{aligned}\sigma_{T-\widehat{T}} &= \sigma_T \sqrt{1 - \rho_{XT}^2} \\ &= \sqrt{\sigma_T^2 (1 - \rho_{XX})} \\ &= \sqrt{\sigma_X^2 \rho_{XX} (1 - \rho_{XX})} \\ &= \sigma_X \sqrt{\rho_{XX} - \rho_{XX}^2}\end{aligned}$$

Once we know the estimated true score and the standard error of the estimate, we can use the cumulative distribution function of the standard normal curve $\Phi()$ to estimate the probability that the true score is below a given threshold score $\tau$:

$$P(T \le \tau) = \Phi\left(\frac{\tau - \hat{T}}{\sigma_{T-\hat{T}}}\right)$$

Where

$$\begin{aligned}
X &= \text{Observed Score}\\
\tau &= \text{Criterion Threshold}\\
T &= \text{True Score for } X\\
\hat{T} &= \text{Estimated True Score}\\
&= \rho_{XX}(X - \mu_X) + \mu_X\\
\sigma_{T-\hat{T}} &= \text{Standard Error of the Estimate}\\
&= \sigma_X\sqrt{\rho_{XX} - \rho_{XX}^2}\\
\Phi(\ ) &= \text{Standard Normal Cumulative Distribution Function}
\end{aligned}$$

The $\Phi$ function does not have a closed algebraic formula. However, it is easily accessed in various applications (e.g., *=NORM.S.DIST* in Excel, *pnorm* in R, or *norm.cdf* in Python's scipy library).

If we identify low academic scores, we need to be specific about which scores are considered low. For example, we might say that scores of 90 or lower are considered low. We aim to minimize two types of errors: *false positives*, where the observed score is below the threshold but the true score is above it, and *false negatives*, where the observed score is above the threshold but the true score is below it.

Suppose our primary concern is to minimize false positives. In that case, we can create a "buffer zone" with a separate, more stringent threshold for decision-making about observed scores (Schneider et al., 2024), so that the true scores are more likely to be below the original threshold. Changing the decision threshold for observed scores will alter the numbers of false positives and false negatives. For example, setting the decision threshold very low (e.g., 70) will all but ensure that all observed scores identified as low have true scores below 90. However, doing so will greatly increase the number of false negatives—many true scores below 90 will have observed scores above 70. Selecting a decision threshold that strikes the right balance between the two types of errors primarily depends on the practical and ethical implications of each. If minimizing false positives to a sufficient level results in too many false negatives, the decision rule should include an additional step (e.g., follow-up testing when scores fall within the buffer zone).

Suppose that we want the true score to be $\tau_2 = 90$ or lower about 95% of the time on a measure with a reliability coefficient of 0.97. In this case, the observed score threshold $\tau_1$ should be:

$$\begin{aligned}
\tau_1 &= \frac{\tau_2 - \mu_X - \Phi^{-1}(.95)\sigma_{\hat{T}-T}}{r_{XX}} + \mu_X\\
&\approx \frac{90 - 100 - 1.6449 \times 15\sqrt{.97 - .97^2}}{.97} + 100\\
&\approx 85.4
\end{aligned}$$

Under these assumptions, if the observed score is 85, the accompanying true score will be $\tau_2 = 90$ or lower in more than 95% of cases. Observed scores right at the threshold (85) will have the lowest probability that their accompanying true scores will be below that threshold. The lower the observed score, the greater the probability that the true score will be 90 or lower.

For example, if the observed score is 80, what is the probability that the true score will be 90 or lower? The large normal distribution in Figure F.2 is the population distribution, and the smaller normal distribution is the true-score distribution for all people with an observed score of $X = 80$. The proportion of the true-score distribution below $\tau_1 = 85$ is .96. The probability the true score is greater than $\tau_2 = 90$ is .00012. Thus, when $X = 80$, there is a low probability that the true score would not also be classified as *low*. Stated differently, when $X = 80$, there is a high probability that the true score will be below 90.

It is good to know that for scores at 85 or lower, there is at least 95% confidence that the true score is 90 or lower, and the confidence increases quickly to nearly 1 for scores well below 85. What about scores between 85 and 90? For these scores, we are not as confident. To increase our confidence, we can administer follow-up tests. These additional test scores might resolve the ambiguity in one or two ways.

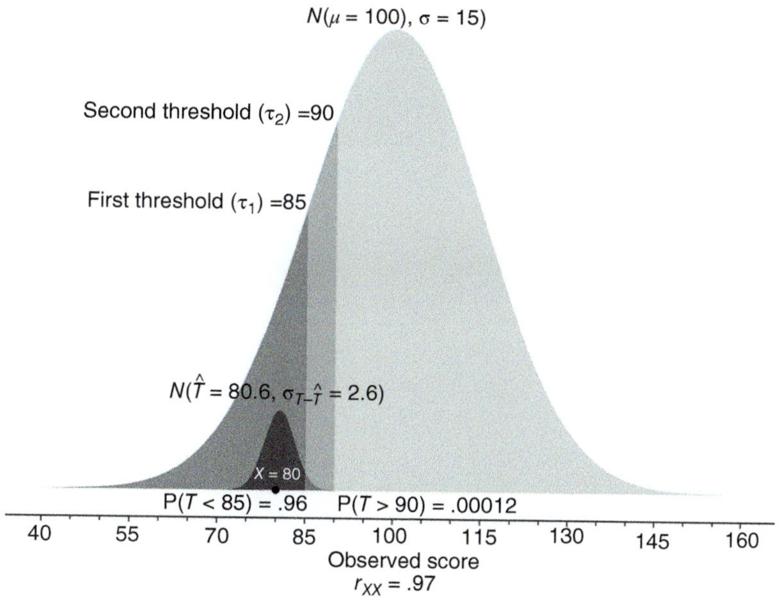


**FIGURE F.2 Given an Observed Standard Score of 80 with a Reliability Coefficient of .97, What Is the Probability that the True Score Is Below 85 or Above 90?**

One possibility is that the follow-up tests might result in revised score estimates that are well above or well below the threshold of 90. If so, the decision is easy. Another possibility is that the follow-up tests might not change the initial score estimate, but the revised confidence interval has narrowed sufficiently to be confident that the true score is indeed low.

If ambiguity persists and additional testing is not feasible, a systematic evaluation of evidence outside of testing will be necessary to inform the decision one way or the other. Discomfort arising from such cases can be mitigated if there is the option to increase support as scores decline. This often means setting multiple thresholds for varying levels of diagnostic certainty and intervention intensity. Statistical calculations can inform decisions about where and how many thresholds to set, but practical and ethical considerations are the primary drivers of any decision framework.

## MULTIPLE THRESHOLDS AND MULTIDIMENSIONAL CONFIDENCE REGIONS

A 95% confidence interval contains the true score in 95% of cases having the same observed score. Univariate confidence intervals are ideal for interpreting one score at a time. For constructs such as SLD, which are inherently multidimensional, it is possible to create a univariate confidence interval for each score. However, for the same reasons that an ANOVA is better than a series of t-tests, it is better to base a multivariate decision on multivariate statistics. The idea of univariate confidence intervals can be extended to multidimensional *confidence regions*—shapes that contain the true scores of more than one variable.

An interesting feature of multidimensional confidence regions is that all the scores jointly predict the region's size and location. By contrast, a univariate confidence interval is based on a single score. Thus, if the scores are correlated, multidimensional confidence regions use all the available information to locate true scores more precisely than their univariate counterparts.

## TWO-DIMENSIONAL CONFIDENCE REGIONS

When there are two variables with normally distributed measurement errors, a 95% confidence region is often represented as an ellipse that contains the two true scores 95% of the time when measurements are repeatedly taken. For illustrative purposes, we can consider a simplified ability-achievement discrepancy model of SLD. We do so not because this is our preferred SLD model, but because what can be learned from a simple model with two scores can be generalized to a more complex model with many scores. The problems of decision instability apply equally to all types of SLD identification, including response-to-intervention models, patterns of strengths and weaknesses models, and ability-achievement discrepancy models.

Decisions made using one of the many ability-achievement discrepancy models of SLD involve two variables, general intellectual ability *G* and academic achievement *A*. All ability-achievement discrepancy models require that general intellectual ability must exceed an area of academic achievement by a specified amount. Some discrepancy models also require that general ability be at least average and that academic achievement be lower than average. There are more sophisticated ways of specifying SLD criteria, but to keep things simple in this illustration,

**Table F.1 Criteria for Simplified Ability-Achievement Discrepancy Model**

| | Observed Score | True Score |
|---|---|---|
| Criteria | Criteria $\tau_1$ | Criteria $\tau_2$ |
| General ability is not low. | $G \geq 90$ | $g \geq 85$ |
| Academic achievement is low. | $A \leq 85$ | $a \leq 90$ |
| Achievement lags predicted achievement | $A - \hat{A} \leq -15$ | $a - \hat{a} \leq -10$ |

*Note:* $G$ = Observed General Ability, $g$ = General Ability true score, $A$ = Observed Achievement, $a$ = Achievement true score, $\hat{A}$ = Predicted Achievement Observed Score, $\hat{a}$ = Predicted Achievement True Score.

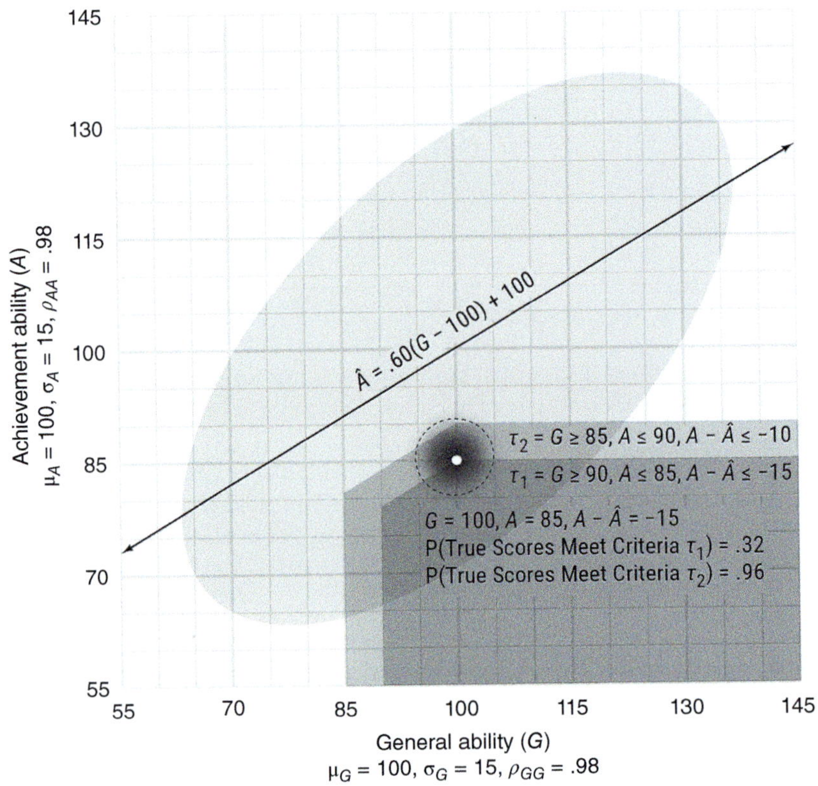


**FIGURE F.3 Given Observed Scores G = 100 and A = 85, What Is the Probability that Their True Scores Meet SLD Criteria $\tau_1$ and $\tau_2$?**

let us say our ability-achievement discrepancy model of SLD has the observed and true score criteria in Table F.1. These criteria can be visualized in Figure F.3. Scores meeting criteria $\tau_1$ are in the dark gray region. Scores meeting criteria $\tau_2$ are in the light gray region adjacent to $\tau_1$. The gray ellipse in the middle of the figure is the region where 95% of the population's scores will fall.

The width of the buffer zone between the two criterion sets is currently 5 points, which is a conveniently round number analogous to the 5-point buffer zone of 70–75 in the threshold for intellectual disability diagnosis. The observed-score difference criterion is set at 15 points to ensure that at least 95% of the confidence region is contained by criteria set $\tau_2$ (when the correlation between the score is .60 and the reliability coefficient of both scores is .98).

If we have reason to set the widths of the buffer zone to other values, we could do so in accordance with our goals and priorities. For example, if the reliability coefficient of either score is lower than .98, we can widen the buffer zone. That is, we would make criterion set $\tau_1$ more stringent to ensure at least 95% confidence that the true scores will meet criterion set $\tau_2$.

If general ability is $G$ = 100, and the achievement score is $A$ = 85, the pair of scores (the white dot in Figure F.3) is barely within the region defined by criteria $\tau_1$. The shaded ellipse with the dashed lines is the 95% confidence region for this pair of observed scores. If we imagine the set of all the people who have this pair of observed scores, what proportion of them will have true scores also meeting criteria $\tau_1$?

The answer to this question requires that we understand the variables in question. We need to know their population means, standard deviations, correlations, and reliability coefficients. In addition, if we assume the scores are multivariate normal (or nearly so), we can use the properties of the multivariate normal distribution to make approximate probability estimates. Suppose that the scores are multivariate normal standard scores with mean = 100 and standard deviation of 15. The reliability of the general score $G$ is $r_{GG} = .98$, and the reliability coefficient of the achievement score $A$ is $r_{AA} = .98$. The correlation between the scores is $r_{GA} = .60$.

With a univariate confidence interval, we created a regression equation in which the observed score predicts the true score. With a multivariate confidence region, we create a multivariate regression equation in which the observed scores simultaneously predict the true scores and any true score differences that are needed. More precisely, we can use the observed scores to create a conditional distribution of true scores and true score differences (Schneider & Ji, 2023; Schneider et al., 2024).

In the current example, the covariance matrix of observed scores $\mathbf{\Sigma}_X$ has the variances of the observed scores ($\sigma_G^2$ and $\sigma_A^2$) on the diagonal and the covariance between them $\sigma_{GA}$ on the off-diagonal:

$$\Sigma_X = \begin{bmatrix} \sigma_G^2 & \sigma_{GA} \\ \sigma_{GA} & \sigma_A^2 \end{bmatrix} = \begin{bmatrix} 15^2 & .60 \cdot 15 \cdot 15 \\ .60 \cdot 15 \cdot 15 & 15^2 \end{bmatrix} = \begin{bmatrix} 225 & 135 \\ 135 & 225 \end{bmatrix}$$

Note that the symbol $\mathbf{\Sigma}$ is being used as a variable here, not as the summation operator $\sum$. The covariance matrix of the true scores $\mathbf{\Sigma}_T$ is the same as $\mathbf{\Sigma}_X$ except that the diagonal elements are multiplied by the reliability coefficients $\rho_{GG}$ and $\rho_{AA}$.

$$\Sigma_T = \begin{bmatrix} \rho_{GG}\sigma_G^2 & \sigma_{GA} \\ \sigma_{GA} & \rho_{AA}\sigma_A^2 \end{bmatrix} = \begin{bmatrix} .98 \cdot 15^2 & .60 \cdot 15 \cdot 15 \\ .60 \cdot 15 \cdot 15 & .98 \cdot 15^2 \end{bmatrix} = \begin{bmatrix} 220.5 & 135 \\ 135 & 220.5 \end{bmatrix}$$

The covariance matrix of observed and true scores $\mathbf{\Sigma}_{XT}$ is constructed like so:

$$\Sigma_{XT} = \begin{bmatrix} \Sigma_X & \Sigma_T \\ \Sigma_T & \Sigma_T \end{bmatrix}$$

Most Ability-Achievement Discrepancy models require a difference score of some kind. Regression-based difference scores are generally preferred to simple difference scores because they properly frame the expected academic performance and thus do not over-identify SLD among students with high cognitive ability and do not under-identify SLD among students with low cognitive ability (Braden & Weiss, 1988; Evans, 1992; Reynolds & Willson, 1984).

There are two observed scores $G$ and $A$, with their respective true scores, $g$ and $a$. We can use $G$ and $g$ to predict $A$ and $a$, respectively.

$$\frac{\hat{A} - \mu_A}{\sigma_A} = \rho_{GA}\frac{G - \mu_G}{\sigma_G}$$

$$\hat{A} - \mu_A = \rho_{GA}\frac{\sigma_A}{\sigma_G}(G - \mu_G)$$

$$\hat{A} = \rho_{GA}\frac{\sigma_A}{\sigma_G}(G - \mu_G) + \mu_A$$

$$\hat{A} = \rho_{GA}\frac{\sigma_A}{\sigma_G}(G - \mu_G) + \mu_A$$

$$\hat{a} = \rho_{ga}\frac{\sigma_a}{\sigma_g}(g - \mu_g) + \mu_a$$

$$\hat{a} = \frac{\rho_{GA}}{\sqrt{\rho_{GG}\rho_{AA}}}\frac{\sigma_A\sqrt{\rho_{AA}}}{\sigma_G\sqrt{\rho_{GG}}}(g - \mu_G) + \mu_A$$

$$\hat{a} = \frac{\rho_{GA}}{\rho_{GG}}\frac{\sigma_A}{\sigma_G}(g - \mu_G) + \mu_A$$

To calculate the covariances among these scores and the difference between $a$ and $\hat{a}$, we construct a weight matrix $\mathbf{W}$ that is a $4 \times 4$ identity matrix with a column added that represents the predicted true-score difference $a - \hat{a}$.

$$\mathrm{W} = \begin{bmatrix} 1 & 0 & 0 & 0 & 0 \\ 0 & 1 & 0 & 0 & 0 \\ 0 & 0 & 1 & 0 & \frac{\rho_{GA}}{\rho_{GG}} \\ 0 & 0 & 0 & 1 & -1 \end{bmatrix}$$

The weight matrix can be used to compute the covariances among observed, true, and difference scores $\mathbf{\Sigma}_{XTD}$ like so:

$$\Sigma_{XTD} = \mathbf{W}'\,\Sigma_{XT}\,\mathbf{W}$$

If $\mathbf{\Sigma}_{TD}$ is the portion of $\mathbf{\Sigma}_{XTD}$ that concerns the true scores $g$ and $a$ and the predicted true score difference $a - \hat{a}$, then their conditional means $\mu_{TD|X}$ and conditional covariance matrix $\mathbf{\Sigma}_{TD|X}$ of these scores, given the observed scores $X$ (i.e., $G$ and $A$) are calculated using the standard formulas for conditional distributions (Eaton, 2007, pp. 116–119):

$$\mu_{TD|X} = \mu_{TD} + \Sigma_{TD}\Sigma_X^{-1}(X - \mu_X)$$
$$\Sigma_{TD|X} = \Sigma_{TD} - \Sigma_{TD}\Sigma_X^{-1}\Sigma_{TD}'$$

If the unconditional true scores $T$ and observed scores $X$ are multivariate normal $(\{X,T\} \sim \mathcal{N}(\mu_{XT}, \Sigma_{XT}))$, then the conditional true scores and predicted true score difference $\{T, D\}\,|\,X$ will also be multivariate normal (Eaton, 2007, p. 117):

$$\{T,D\}\,|\,X \sim \mathcal{N}(\mu_{TD|X}, \Sigma_{TD|X})$$

In the same way that we can use the cumulative distribution function of the univariate normal distribution to find the probability that a true score is below a threshold, we can use the cumulative distribution function of the multivariate normal distribution to find the probability that the true scores meet criteria $\tau_1$ and $\tau_2$.

Given the observed scores $G$ = 100 and $A$ = 85, the probability that the true scores will all meet criteria $\tau_1$ is not high ($p$ = .32). However, the probability that the true scores are within the buffer zone defined by criteria $\tau_2$ is much higher ($p$ = .96).

When reliably measured observed scores are far from the diagnostic threshold, the probability that the true scores will be on the same side of the diagnostic thresholds will be high (Schneider et al., 2024). For example, if $G$ = 110 and $A$ = 70, the probability that the true scores meet criteria $\tau_1$ is nearly 1.

Among people with $G$ = 100 and $A$ = 85, the proportion of individuals with true scores meeting criteria $\tau_1$ is .32. Why is this probability so low? As scores approach the diagnostic thresholds, the decisions become unstable. Because observed scores and true scores are imperfectly correlated, true scores regress to the population mean. Consequently, if the scores are right on one of the thresholds, more than half of the confidence region will be on the side of the diagnostic threshold that contains the population mean. This truth is as unavoidable as it is uncomfortable. Decision instability near the thresholds will occur no matter where we set the threshold, and it will happen even when the reliability of the score is extremely high. When a condition is rare, most of the cases that meet criteria will be near the thresholds because scores far from the thresholds are much less frequent than scores near the thresholds.

Our discomfort with scores that barely meet criteria is mitigated by the fact that most of the confidence region is within a narrow buffer zone adjacent to the observed score criteria and that reliable scores within a narrow confidence region are not associated with dramatically different outcomes. When the construct we are measuring is inherently continuous and the decision threshold is set for practical reasons rather than logically or scientifically necessary reasons, then we are not talking about a condition that is present or absent. In the case of Ability-Achievement Discrepancy definitions of SLD, we are talking about degrees of underachievement. Again, if the help we can offer to students who are evidencing academic difficulties is either offered or withheld, then the injustice resulting from score instability is not in the scores but in our decision framework. If the help offered is allowed to be commensurate with the academic difficulty, injustice resulting from score instability is substantially reduced. Even so, we would like our decisions to be as reliable as is practically possible.

If the observed scores meet criteria for SLD, but the probability that the true scores also meet criteria is not sufficiently high, then there are a number of additional steps that can be taken to increase the reliability of the decision (Schneider et al., 2024). In the example with $G = 100$ and $A = 85$, the proportion of true scores meeting criteria $\tau_2$ is .59. In this case, the general ability score is well above the threshold of 90, but the academic achievement score is right on the achievement threshold (as is the difference score). One or more follow-up achievement tests could be administered to obtain a more reliable composite score. The additional scores could resolve the ambiguity in the academic achievement score by either revising the estimate to be well above 85 or well below it. In such cases, we no longer need to consider decision instability because the score is more reliable than before, and most of the confidence region lies on one side of the threshold.

Often enough, however, follow-up testing reveals that the initial estimate was about right. In these situations, the estimate remains unchanged, but the confidence interval of the score narrows. Note that in this case, our interpretation of the academic achievement score's level has not changed. What has changed is that we are more confident that its true score is not in the average range of 90 or higher.

If follow-up testing does not sufficiently increase our confidence in the decision and additional testing is either impractical or impossible, then our decision will depend on non-test evidence. If evidence from interviews, questionnaires, direct observations, and official records strongly indicates academic difficulty, one might be willing to accept that the true scores are likely to meet criteria. Absent this assurance, there is reason to be conservative about assigning the SLD label.

## SETTING BUFFER ZONE WIDTHS

The width of a buffer zone depends on which type of error you wish to minimize. When identifying something rare, not having a buffer zone (i.e., a width of 0) will result in many false positives—observed scores that meet the criteria but have true scores that do not. A wide buffer zone will decrease false positives but will increase false negatives—true scores that meet criteria but with observed scores that do not. We have recommended a buffer zone wide enough to reduce false positives and seeking additional information to resolve scores within the buffer zone (Schneider et al., 2024).

In Figure F.3, the priority was to be at least 95% confident in all decisions. The score displayed ($G = 100$, $A = 85$) has the highest achievement score and the smallest ability-achievement difference and yet still has a 95% probability of meeting criteria $tau_2$. All other score pairs have a higher probability.

## CONFIDENCE REGIONS IN PSW MODELS OF SLD IDENTIFICATION

Patterns of Strengths and Weaknesses Models (PSW) of SLD identification are diverse (Flanagan et al., 2022; Miller et al., 2016) but have considerable overlap with Ability-Achievement Discrepancy models in that they usually require that cognitive abilities in general exceed academic achievement. They are more stringent and specific than Ability-Achievement Discrepancy models in that they also require that the ability-achievement discrepancy be given an explanation. That is, PSW models identify a specific cognitive processing deficit that partially or fully explains why a student's academic achievement lags behind what would have been predicted from the student's overall cognitive abilities.

We will take the Dual Discrepancy/Consistency Model (Flanagan et al., 2013; DD/C; 2018) as an example of a PSW model. Some of the criteria for SLD identification refer to test scores:

- Overall cognitive ability indicates at least average ability to think and reason (Standard Score = $90 \pm 5$). The overall cognitive ability is indicated by the Facilitating Cognitive Composite (FCC), which summarizes cognitive abilities that are not identified as cognitive weaknesses.
- A major area of academic achievement is
  - *Low*: Standard score $\leq 85$, but sometimes up to SS = 90 if non-test data strongly indicate difficulty.
  - *Specific*: The academic achievement is substantially lower than what would be predicted from the FCC.
- One or more specific cognitive processing abilities, as summarized by the Inhibiting Cognitive Composite (ICC) are
  - *Low*: ICC $\leq 85$, but sometimes higher when non-test data strongly indicate difficulty (e.g., ecological validity).
  - *Specific*: The cognitive weaknesses summarized by the ICC are substantially lower than what would be predicted by the cognitive strengths summarized by the FCC.
  - *Relevant*: The cognitive processing deficits must be plausible explanations of a substantial portion of the academic deficit. Usually, this means that the abilities summarized by the ICC are known to interfere with academic skill learning and performance. Because academic difficulties are often compounded by factors beyond cognitive processing deficits, it is not necessary that cognitive deficits be the only reasons for academic difficulty.

There are many criteria that are based on information that does not come from test data. The test data must be plausibly consistent with other assessment data from interviews, questionnaires, direct observations, official records, and previous assessments. In addition, the cognitive and academic deficits cannot be primarily due to a host of exclusionary factors such as sensory/motor deficits, physical or mental health problems, inadequate instruction, or barriers to learning arising from cultural/linguistic differences and/or systemic injustices. The X-BASS software includes a checklist to systematically consider exclusionary criteria.

Assuming that non-test information is consistent with the DD/C definition of SLD, we can estimate the probability that the true scores will also meet the DD/C criteria. This probability will not be substantially high for any scores near criterion thresholds—and among people with scores meeting criteria for SLD, having scores near the thresholds is quite common. Indeed, if we evaluate the accuracy of PSW methods using the same thresholds for observed and true scores, they will appear to have unacceptably high false-positive rates (Miciak et al., 2018; Stuebing et al., 2012). However, there is no requirement that we use the same thresholds. To reduce false-positive identifications, we need to set the observed-score criteria more stringently than the true-score criteria (Schneider et al., 2024).

In the DD/C model, the observed score criteria are already set, but there is an implicit buffer zone of 5 points for academic and cognitive criteria. Given any set of observed scores, we can estimate the probability that the true scores will at least fall within DD/C's buffer zones. More generally—and more importantly—we can distinguish between cases that we can confidently interpret as having SLD and cases that prompt additional action before a decision can be made.

The same multivariate procedures from the simplified ability-achievement model example can be applied to the FCC, ICC, and academic score. As before, we need the means, standard deviations, correlations, and reliability coefficients for all our observed scores. From these statistics, we can calculate the means and covariances of the conditional true scores and true score residuals. Then we use the multivariate normal

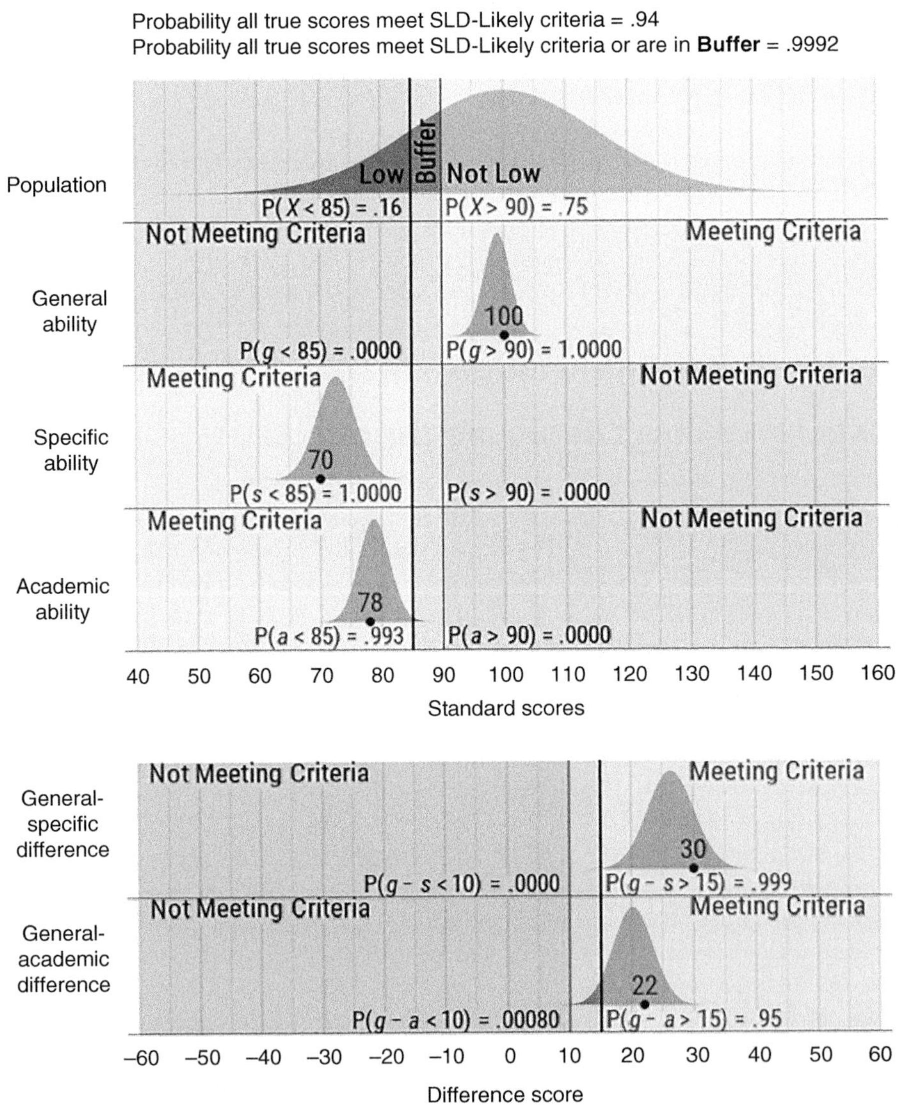


**FIGURE F.4 Probability True Scores Will Meet Simplified SLD Criteria When Observed Scores Meet Criteria by a Wide Margin**

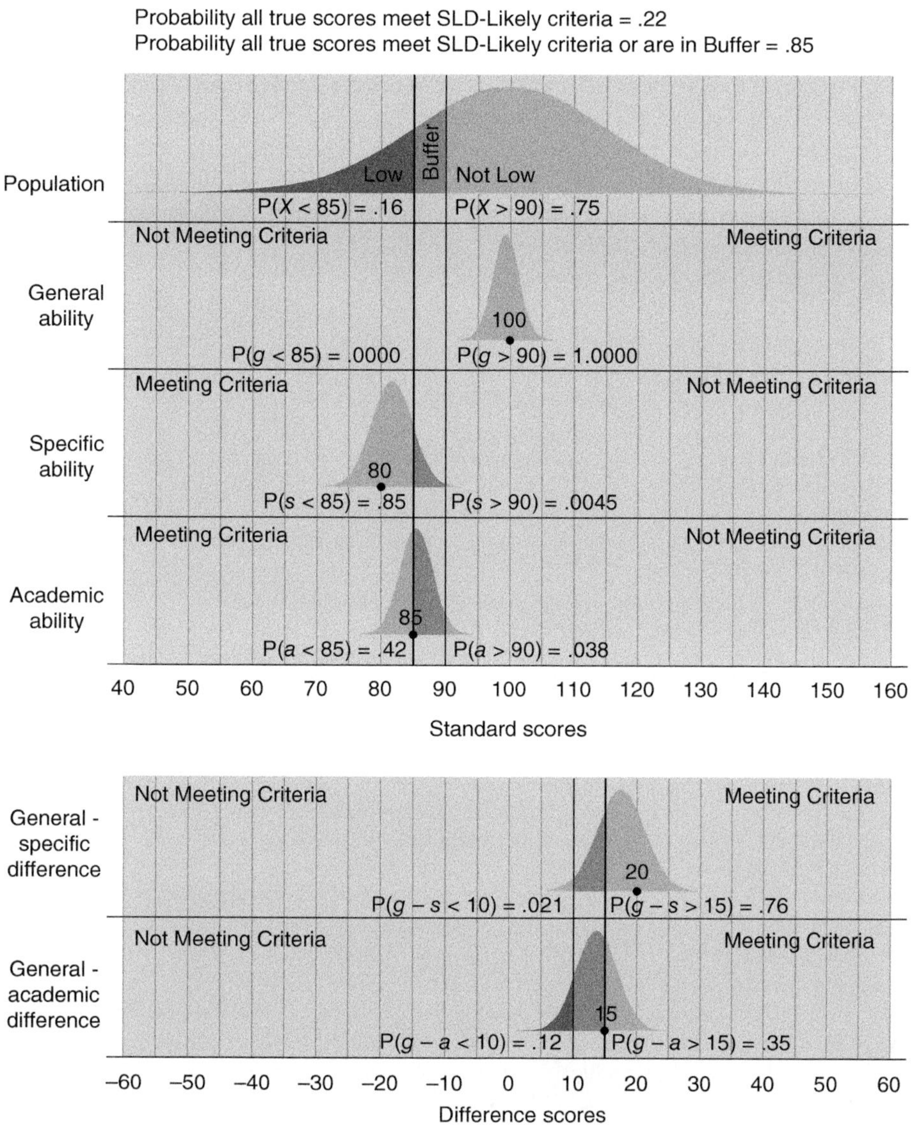


**FIGURE F.5 Probability True Scores Will Meet Simplified SLD Criteria When Observed Scores Narrowly Meet Criteria**

cumulative distribution function to estimate the probability that the true scores and true residuals meet the DD/C criteria or are at least within its implicit buffer zone.

X-BASS 3.0 conducts these calculations automatically. Joel Schneider has also made a web app available at https://w-joel-schneider.shinyapps.io/conditionalppv/ that can be used to develop insights about how measurement error affects the stability of decisions based on a simplified SLD model. It was made to illustrate the key points of Schneider et al. (2024) and thus uses simple differences rather than the preferred regression-based differences used by DD/C. Thus, it was not designed for routine use in SLD identification decisions.

The app requires the user to specify the general ability score, the specific processing score, and the academic achievement score, along with their respective reliability coefficients and intercorrelations. By default, the threshold for a low score is set at SS = 85, with a buffer width of 5. We can set the threshold for a meaningful difference at 15 to mirror the previous examples.

Suppose the general (*G*), specific (*S*), and academic ability (*A*) scores have reliability coefficients of .98, .95, and .97, respectively. Let us say the correlation between the general score and the specific processing ability is .70, the correlation between the general and academic scores is .65, and the correlation between the specific and academic scores is .60.

Suppose the observed scores easily meet criteria: $G = 100$, $S = 70$, and $A = 78$, the app calculates the probability that the respective true scores and true score differences will meet criteria or at least are within the 5-point buffer. As seen in Figure F.4, the probability that the true scores meet criteria is high ($p = .94$), and the probability that the true scores are at least within the buffer zone is very high ($p = .9992$).

Cases that easily meet criteria exist but are far less common than cases with scores near the diagnostic thresholds. For example, suppose that the scores had been much closer to the score thresholds: $G = 100$, $S = 80$, and $A = 85$ (see Figure F.5). As expected, the probability that the true scores will meet criteria is low ($p = .22$). The probability that the true scores will at least be in the 5-point buffer zone is higher ($p = .85$), but not to the traditional 95% level of confidence one hopes to be present. In this case, the academic score is close to the threshold, and its true score has a non-trivial probability of being outside the buffer zone ($p = .038$). Furthermore, the probability that the difference from the general ability true score is outside the buffer zone is $p = .12$. Follow-up testing might resolve the ambiguity in this case. Otherwise, additional evidence of academic difficulty would need to be particularly strong. X-BASS provides ample guidance on the type of additional evidence needed to resolve ambiguities (see SLD Evidence tab in X-BASS).

## REFERENCES


American Psychiatric Association. (2022). *Diagnostic and statistical manual of mental disorders* (DSM-5-TR). https://dx.doi.org/10.1176/appi.books.9780890425787

Braden, J. P., & Weiss, L. (1988). Effects of simple difference versus regression discrepancy methods: An empirical study. *Journal of School Psychology, 26*(2), 133–142. https://doi.org/10.1016/0022-4405(88)90015-5.

Brown, T. A., & Barlow, D. H. (2005). Dimensional versus categorical classification of mental disorders in the fifth edition of the diagnostic and statistical manual of mental disorders and beyond: Comment on the special section. *Journal of Abnormal Psychology, 114*(4), 551–556. https://doi.org/10.1037/0021-843X.114.4.551.

Eaton, M. L. (2007). *Multivariate statistics: A vector space approach.* Institute of Mathematical Statistics.

Evans, L. D. (1992). A comparison of the impact of regression and simple difference discrepancy models on identification rates. *Journal of School Psychology, 30*(1), 17–29. https://doi.org/10.1016/0022-4405(92)90017-Y.

Flanagan, D. P., Alfonso, V. C., Mascolo, J. T., McDonough, E. M., & Ortiz, S. O. (2018). The dual discrepancy/consistency method of SLD identification: Integrating multiple data sources and multiple data gathering methods. In V. C. Alfonso & D. P. Flanagan (Eds.), *Essentials of specific learning disability identification* (2nd ed, pp. 329–430). Wiley.

Flanagan, D. P., Alfonso, V. C., Zinkiewicz, C. J., Ortiz, S. O., Dynda, & M., A. (2022). An integrative theoretical framework for cognitive test interpretation in school neuropsychological evaluations. In D. C. Miller, D. E. Maricle, C. Bedford, & J. A. Gettman (Eds.), *Best practices in school neuropsychology: Guidelines for effective practice, assessment, and evidence-based intervention* (2nd ed, pp. 87–119). John Wiley & Sons, Inc. https://awspntest.apa.org/record/2023-08304-006.

Flanagan, D. P., Ortiz, S. O., & Alfonso, V. C. (2013). *Essentials of cross-battery assessment* (3rd ed.). John Wiley & Sons.

Helzer, J. E. (2008). *Dimensional approaches in diagnostic classification: Refining the research agenda for DSM-V.* American Psychiatric Publishing.

Miciak, J., Taylor, W. P., Stuebing, K. K., & Fletcher, J. M. (2018). Simulation of LD identification accuracy using a pattern of Processing Strengths and Weaknesses method with multiple measures. *Journal of Psychoeducational Assessment, 36*(1), 21–33. https://doi.org/10.1177/0734282916683287.

Milinkovic, M. S., & Tiliopoulos, N. (2020). A systematic review of the clinical utility of the DSM–5 section III alternative model of personality disorder. *Personality Disorders, Theory, Research, and Treatment, 11*(6), 377–397. https://doi.org/10.1037/per0000408.

Miller, D. C., Maricle, D. E., & Jones, A. M. (2016). Comparing three patterns of strengths and weaknesses models for the identification of specific learning disabilities. *Learning Disabilities: A Multidisciplinary Journal, 21(2,* 2) http://dx.doi.org/10.18666/LDMJ-2016-V21-I2-7349.

Appropriate academic supports to meet the needs of all students. (2009).

Peters, L., & Ansari, D. (2019). Are specific learning disorders truly specific, and are they disorders? *Trends in Neuroscience and Education, 17*(100), 115 https://doi.org/10.1016/j.tine.2019.100115.

Reynolds, C. R., & Willson, V. L. (1984). Critical measurement issues in learning disabilities. *The Journal of Special Education, 18*(4), 451–476. https://doi.org/10.1177/002246698401800403.

Roos, R. A. (2010). Huntington's disease: A clinical review. *Orphanet Journal of Rare Diseases, 5*(1), 40 https://doi.org/10.1186/1750-1172-5-40.

Schneider, W. J., Flanagan, D. P., Niileksela, C. R., & Engler, J. R. (2024). The effect of measurement error on the positive predictive value of PSW methods for SLD identification: How buffer zones dispel the illusion of inaccuracy. *Journal of School Psychology, 103*, https://doi.org/10.1016/j.jsp.2023.101280.

Schneider, W. J., & Ji, F. (2023). Detecting unusual score patterns in the context of relevant predictors. *Journal of Pediatric Neuropsychology, 9*, 1–17. https://doi.org/10.1007/s40817-022-00137-x.

Stuebing, K. K., Fletcher, J. M., Branum-Martin, L., & Francis, D. J. (2012). Evaluation of the technical adequacy of three methods for identifying specific learning disabilities based on cognitive discrepancies. *School Psychology Review, 41*(1), 3–22. https://doi.org/10.1080/02796015.2012.12087373.

Appendix G

# EXCLUSIONARY CRITERIA IN THE DIAGNOSIS OF SLD

Benjamin J. Lovett, Ph.D.

Teacher's College – Columbia University

Despite the many debates over how to properly identify SLD, virtually all diagnostic models agree on the necessity of exclusionary criteria, and, indeed, the exclusionary criteria date back at least to the original regulations implementing IDEA (see U.S. Office of Education, 1977). The federal definition of SLD requires that academic skill deficits be caused by a disorder in a basic psychological process. Still, different diagnostic models disagree on whether and how to assess psychological processes directly (see contributions to Alfonso & Flanagan, 2018). Even so, all diagnostic models agree that it would be inappropriate to diagnose SLD in a student whose academic deficits are better explained by a lack of exposure to the English language or by being Deaf.

Using the exclusionary criteria is sometimes relatively simple, particularly in obvious or extreme cases. Consider, for instance, Student A, who comes to the United States at age 10 with virtually no prior exposure to English but a history of high academic performance in their country of birth. The student is placed in a typical fourth-grade classroom where the instruction is entirely in English, and the student performs poorly. This would be a clear case where exclusionary criteria would apply, and SLD would be an inappropriate classification for Student A.

In other gray-area cases, the criteria are more difficult to apply. For instance, consider Student B, a first-grade student who is referred for difficulties in learning mathematics. The child is given a vision screening as part of a comprehensive evaluation and is discovered to have mild hyperopia (farsightedness). It's *possible* that Student B is having difficulty perceiving instructional materials at some distance (e.g., a classroom smartboard), which *could be* the primary cause of the problems. Still, the situation is far less clear than it was for Student A.

## SPECIFIC EXCLUSION DOMAINS

Below, we consider each condition or situation that should be excluded as the primary cause of academic deficits. Table G.1 lists the data to be collected as part of the exclusion process. Below, we list the key questions to ask and provide guidance for reviewing that data.

1. Visual impairment. Key question: ***Is (or was) the student unable to perceive stimuli, including letters and numbers, such that this is primarily responsible for any academic skills deficits?*** Here, the optimal data would come from a recent vision test, health records, and a history of academic performance to date. If a student has an active, uncorrected vision problem that is likely present during the period where academic deficits are evident, SLD should generally not be identified. If, however, there is a history of a corrected vision problem (such as one caught early and corrected with eyeglasses), it is unlikely to be primarily responsible for any academic deficits. Finally, a vision test is the appropriate next step if there is a suspected vision problem but no prior diagnosis.
2. Hearing impairment. Key question: ***Is (or was) the student unable to hear sounds well enough to have developed academic skills despite adequate exposure to instruction?*** Again, the optional data would come from a recent hearing test, health records, and academic history. The decision process is very similar to that for vision. If there is a hearing problem that is significant enough to have a significant effect on the ability to understand aural instruction (i.e., bilateral hearing loss and in at least some sound frequencies associated with speech) and that has been present during the period of academic impairment, SLD should generally not be identified. In contrast, a history of corrected hearing problems (such as a cochlear implant installed very early in life) would meet the exclusionary criteria if the student has passed hearing tests using speech stimuli. And finally, suspected hearing problems that are not yet documented should prompt a hearing test.
3. Motor impairment. Key question: ***Does the student have motor skill problems that prevent them from developing or demonstrating academic skills?*** School staff generally do not formally screen students for motor problems, and some fine-motor problems may not even be apparent in physical education classes. If the student has a diagnosed motor disorder or delay that prevents typical handwriting, academic skills should be assessed using alternate means. Depending on the specific motor problems, this may mean using a keyboard to permit dictation of answers or using more advanced technology. If, with these alternate means, there are no academic skills deficits, SLD should generally not be identified. If the student has suspected motor problems based on observations by parents, teachers, or evaluators, an evaluation of motor skills is appropriate, and this might involve an occupational therapist, since fine motor difficulties are most likely to prevent a student from demonstrating academic skills.

**Table G.1 Exclusionary Factors Form**

***Evaluation and Consideration of Exclusionary Factors for SLD Identification***

An evaluation of specific learning disability (SLD) requires an assessment of factors that may be the primary cause of an individual's academic skill weaknesses and learning difficulties. These factors include (but are not limited to) vision, hearing, or motor disabilities, intellectual disability (ID), social/emotional or psychological disturbance, environmental or economic disadvantage, cultural and linguistic factors (e.g., limited English proficiency), insufficient instruction or opportunity to learn, and physical/health factors. These factors may be evaluated via behavior rating scales, parent and teacher interviews, classroom observations, attendance records, social/developmental history, family history, vision/hearing exams, medical records, prior evaluations, and interviews with current or past counselors, psychiatrists, and paraprofessionals who have worked with the individual. Individuals with (and without) SLD often have one or more factors (listed below) contributing to academic and learning difficulties. However, these factors must be ruled out as the ***primary*** reason for the individual's educational and learning challenges to maintain SLD as a viable classification/diagnosis.

**Vision (Check All that Apply):**

☐ Vision test recent (within 1 year)
☐ Vision test outdated (> 1 year)
☐ Passed
☐ Failed
☐ Wears Glasses

☐ History of visual disorder/disturbance
☐ Diagnosed visual disorder/disturbance
Name of disorder: ________________
☐ Vision difficulties suspected or observed
(e.g., difficulty with far or near point copying, misaligned numbers in written math work, squinting or rubbing eyes during visual tasks such as reading, computers)

**NOTES:** ____________________________________________
____________________________________________
____________________________________________

**Hearing (Check All that Apply):**

☐ Hearing test recent (within 1 year)
☐ Hearing test outdated (> 1 year)
☐ Passed
☐ Failed
☐ Uses hearing aides/devices

☐ History of auditory disorder/disturbance
☐ Diagnosed auditory disorder/disturbance
☐ Name of disorder: ________________
☐ Hearing difficulties suggested in the referral
(e.g., frequent requests for repetition of auditory information, misarticulates words, attempts to self-accommodate by moving closer to the sound source, obvious attempts to speech read)
☐ Chronic ear infections

**NOTES:** ____________________________________________
____________________________________________
____________________________________________

**Motor Functioning (Check All that Apply):**

☐ Fine Motor Delay/Difficulty
☐ Gross Motor Delay/Difficulty
☐ Improper pencil grip (Specify type: ____________)
☐ Assistive devices/aides used
(e.g., weighted pens, pencil grip, slant board)

☐ History of motor disorder
☐ Diagnosed motor disorder
Name of disorder: ________________
☐ Motor difficulties suggested in the referral
(e.g., illegible writing; issues with letter or number formation, size, spacing; difficulty with fine motor tasks such as using scissors, folding paper)
☐ Received OT or PT services
Explain: ________________

**NOTES:** ____________________________________________
____________________________________________
____________________________________________

**Table G.1 (Continued)**

**Cognitive and Adaptive Functioning (Check All that Apply):**

☐ Substantially below average intellectual ability (e.g., IQ or overall cognitive ability score of 75 or below)

☐ Pervasive cognitive deficits (e.g., weaknesses or deficits in many cognitive areas, including *Gf* ***and*** *Gc*)

☐ Deficits in adaptive functioning (e.g., social, communication, self-care)

Areas of significant adaptive skill weaknesses (check all that apply):

| | | |
|---|---|---|
| ☐ Motor Skill | ☐ Communication | ☐ Socialization |
| ☐ Daily Living Skills | ☐ Behavior/Emotional Skills | ☐ Other |

**NOTES:**________________________________________

**Social-Emotional/Psychological Factors (Check All that Apply):**

☐ Diagnosed psychological disorder (Specify: ____________________)

Date of Diagnosis____________________)

☐ Family history significant for psychological difficulties

☐ Disorder presently treated - specify treatment modality (e.g., counseling, medication): _______________

☐ Reported difficulties with social/emotional functioning (e.g., social phobia, anxiety, depression)

☐ Social-emotional/psychological issues suspected or suggested by referral

☐ Home-school adjustment difficulties

☐ Lack of motivation/effort

☐ Emotional stress or trauma (e.g., loss of a parent, violence in the home/neighborhood, foster care placement)

☐ Autism

☐ Present Medications (type, dosage, frequency, duration) ____________________

☐ Prior Medication Use (type, dosage, frequency, duration) ____________________

☐ Hospitalization for psychological difficulties (date(s): ____________________)

☐ Deficits in social, emotional, or behavioral [SEB] functioning (e.g., as assessed by standardized rating scales)

Significant scores from SEB measures: ______________________________

**NOTES:**________________________________________

**Environmental/Economic Factors (Check All that Apply):**

☐ Limited access to educational materials in the home

☐ Caregivers unable to provide instructional support

☐ Economic status precludes treatment of identified issues (e.g., filling a prescription replacing broken glasses, tutoring)

☐ Temporary crisis (e.g., homelessness)

☐ Student attended two or more schools in one year

☐ History of educational neglect (e.g., truancy)

☐ Frequent transitions (e.g., shared custody)

☐ Environmental space issues (e.g., no space for studying, sleep disruptions due to shared sleeping space)

☐ Poverty

**NOTES:**________________________________________

(*continued*)

**Table G.1 (Continued)**

**Cultural/Linguistic Factors (Check All that Apply)*:**

☐ Limited number of years in U.S. ( ___ )
☐ Language(s) other than English spoken at home
☐ History of early or developmental problems in the native language (# of years _____ )
☐ Lack of or limited instruction in the native language
☐ Native language proficiency: (Dates: __________ Scores: ______________ )
☐ English language proficiency: (Date: ____________ Scores: ________________ )
☐ Knowledge of mainstream U.S. culture (Circle one: High – Moderate – Low)
☐ Parent level of education ____________________
☐ Parent income or SES ____________________
☐ Home-school correspondence is difficult due to cultural or language differences
☐ Student has been exposed to instruction in English for ____ years
☐ Student has basic interpersonal communication skills (BICS)
☐ Student has cognitive and academic language proficiency (CALP)
☐ Student has received nontraditional instruction (e.g., home-schooled, remote instruction)

**NOTES:**________________________________________________________________
________________________________________________________________
________________________________________________________________

**Physical/Health Factors (Check All that Apply):**

☐ Limited access to healthcare
☐ Minimal documentation of health history/status
☐ Chronic health condition (Specify: ________________)
☐ Migraines
☐ ADHD/Executive Dysfunction
☐ Temporary health condition (Date/Duration: __________________)
☐ Hospitalization (Dates: ________)
☐ History of Medical Condition (Date Diagnosed ___________)
☐ Medical Treatments (Specify: ________________)
☐ Repeated visits to the school nurse
☐ Repeated visits to a doctor
☐ Medication (type, dosage, frequency, duration: ______________________________________)

**NOTES:**________________________________________________________________
________________________________________________________________
________________________________________________________________

**Instructional Factors (Check All that Apply):**

☐ Interrupted schooling (e.g., pandemic, changed schools) Specify why: ________________________
☐ New teacher (past 6 months)
☐ Retained or advanced a grade(s)
☐ Nontraditional curriculum (e.g., homeschooled)
☐ Accelerated curriculum (e.g., AP classes)
☐ Nontraditional Instruction (e.g., remote)
☐ Days Absent ______
☐ Student taught by noncertified teacher(s)
☐ School suspension
☐ Student not progressing academically at a rate consistent with peers of similar culture and language background

**NOTES:**________________________________________________________________
________________________________________________________________
________________________________________________________________

**Table G.1 (Continued)**

**Determination of Primary and Contributory Causes of Academic Weaknesses and Learning Difficulties (Check One):**

☐ Based on the available data, it is reasonable to conclude that one or more factors are ***primarily*** responsible for the student's observed learning difficulties. Specify: ______________________________

☐ Based on the available data, it is reasonable to conclude that one or more factors ***contribute*** to the student's observed learning difficulties. Specify: ______________________________

☐ ***No* factors** listed here appear to be the primary cause of the student's observed learning difficulties.

* When evaluating the impact of language and cultural factors on an individual's functioning, consider whether and to what extent other individuals with similar linguistic and cultural backgrounds are progressing and responding to instruction in the curriculum (e.g., if an English learner is not progressing at a rate similar to peers who possess a similar level of English proficiency and acculturative knowledge, it is likely that cultural and linguistic differences are not the sole or primary factors contributing to the learning difficulties). Note that as the number of cultural and linguistic differences in a student's background increases, the likelihood that poor academic performance is attributable primarily to such differences rather than a disability increases. For guidance on making these determinations, use the *True Peer Estimator* and the *Culture-Language Interpretive Matrix* in X-BASS 3.0.

**Note:** This form was developed by Dawn P. Flanagan, Ph.D. and Jennifer T. Mascolo, Psy.D. and revised and updated for this Appendix.

4. Cognitive and adaptive impairment. Key question: ***Does the student have both general cognitive and adaptive functioning deficits that meet the criteria for intellectual disability (ID)?*** A detailed discussion of assessing ID is beyond the scope of this chapter, and the precise criteria for identification differ across jurisdictions (McNicholas et al., 2018). However, generally speaking, the criteria for ID involve an IQ score below approximately 70 (considering measurement error) and deficits in at least one major domain of adaptive functioning (often listed as communication, socialization, and daily living skills). If a student meets both criteria, ID would be a more appropriate identification than SLD, and any academic deficits are presumed to be due to a more general learning impairment.
5. Emotional or behavioral disorders. Key question: ***Does the student have any emotional or behavioral problems that are severe enough to have prevented the student from developing or displaying academic skills?*** Here, typical evidence will include a diagnosis of a psychological disorder. Many such disorders (anxiety, depression, ADHD, oppositional defiant disorder) will lead to difficulties paying attention to instruction or completing classwork or homework that is important for developing academic skills. Because SLD can certainly co-exist with these disorders, two considerations are especially helpful. First, compare the onset of the emotional/behavioral problems with that of the academic difficulties. Suppose the academic difficulties were only present after the emotional/behavioral problems. In that case, SLD is unlikely to be an appropriate identification, whereas SLD is more likely to be present if the academic difficulties came first. Second, look for a logical connection between the symptoms of the psychological disorder and the academic impairment; how are this particular student's symptoms preventing engagement with academic instruction? (This often requires a teacher interview.) SLD is more likely to be present if no logical connection can be found.
6. Environmental or economic deprivation. Key question: ***Has the student experienced environmental or economic deprivation so severe that this has prevented the development of academic skills?*** Unfortunately, environmental and economic deprivation are common and constitute psychosocial stressors; they are important to document in any evaluation. However, in the United States, deprivation is rarely so severe as to be the *primary* cause of academic skill deficits. When it is, the deprivation often prevents consistent school attendance, an issue we treat separately (see exclusion domain #9 below). At times, young children from deprived environments do come to school with such significant deficits in exposure to basic concepts that they cannot benefit substantially from instruction. In such cases, the special education eligibility category of Developmental Delay (rather than SLD) is often appropriate, as the student is far behind typical peers across multiple skill domains.
7. Cultural or linguistic differences. Key question: ***Is the student's English proficiency sufficiently low that this is the likely primary reason for academic skill deficits?*** For students referred for academic concerns and whose native language is not English, three strategies are particularly valuable. First, a detailed history is essential information. Where has the student lived, and what language exposure (in academic instruction and daily life) have they had? How did they perform in school in their native language if they attended school elsewhere prior to coming to the United States? If the student performed well academically in school in their native language, SLD is unlikely to be present. Second, what is the student's *oral* proficiency in English like? Poor oral proficiency in English generally prevents SLD from being the most appropriate classification (as opposed to the Speech/Language Impairment classification), and learning about the student's oral proficiency in a different, first language helps to differentiate between lack of exposure to English and a developmental language disorder. Finally, elsewhere (in Chapter 8), we cover procedures for looking for trends in performance across different diagnostic tasks to help determine if greater cultural and linguistic loading is associated with worse performance. If so, SLD is less likely to be an appropriate classification.
8. Physical health problems. Key question: ***Has the student experienced any physical health problems or undergone treatments for such problems that prevented the student from developing or displaying academic skills appropriately?*** Here, a general health history

from records and interviews with the family (and student, if appropriate) is most helpful. This history information should focus on the onset and course of problems because if a student has a significant physical health problem but showed academic deficits earlier, SLD is more likely to be present. As with other exclusionary domains, the logic underlying the relationship between the physical health problem and academic deficits is important to identify. Typically, when the physical health problem is the primary cause of academic deficits, the health problem—or its treatments—will induce fatigue, changes in consciousness, or other states that make engaging with instruction too difficult. This is precisely what the Other Health Impairment (OHI) category in special education law was developed for—that is, for conditions that limit a student's "alertness, strength, or vitality" (Briesch et al., 2023). In that case, OHI is a far more appropriate classification than SLD.

9. Insufficient instructional exposure. Key question: ***Has the student experienced either such interruptions to instruction or such an atypical curriculum that these factors are the likely primary cause of academic skill deficits?*** For this final exclusionary domain, the primary high-quality evidence is historical in nature. For students with a clear history of attending typical public schools of reasonable quality, good attendance records, and no exposure to unusually poor-quality teaching, instructional factors can be excluded. However, if a student has a poor attendance record, try to correlate the onset of academic problems with when that started. (For instance, consider a fifth grader whose parents just separated and who has shown good achievement levels until now. The child lives with a parent in an apartment far from the school most of the time and begins to miss about 2 days of school per week. If the child's achievement levels begin to fall now, this is likely primarily due to interrupted instruction. Atypical curriculum exposure is rare but possible in the case of homeschooling or, occasionally, in nonpublic schools with a very narrow curriculum. In the former case, ask the parent for more information about the curriculum materials; in the latter, ask for report cards (which list class subjects) and copies of teacher-made assessments. Suppose the curriculum does not include substantial grade-level information. In that case, this is likely the primary cause of academic skill deficits, and it would be premature to identify SLD.

## GENERAL ADVICE ON EXCLUSIONARY CRITERIA

We conclude with two pieces of general advice regarding excluding other primary causes of academic skill deficits. First, exclusionary criteria are perhaps the most fundamental reason why suspected SLD requires a *comprehensive* evaluation. Admittedly, high academic skills generally rule out a diagnosis of SLD. However, low academic skills can be caused by factors other than SLD, and only a comprehensive evaluation can rule out those factors. Therefore, if academic deficits are the sole referral concern, an achievement battery might be considered a screener, but any deficits therein would necessitate a comprehensive evaluation. Similarly, response-to-intervention analyses with curriculum-based measures, implemented as part of a multi-tiered system of supports (e.g., Shapiro & Clemens, 2023), can be a first step. However, insufficient response to intervention would not necessarily indicate SLD.

The second piece of general advice: although exclusion of other causes of academic deficits is a core part of SLD identification, the exclusion process does not lend itself to simple formulas or algorithms. We have presented a guide to all of the relevant data to be collected (again, see Table G.1), and we have discussed the key questions for each exclusionary domain and how to think through each one, but the exclusion process requires thoughtful judgment, particularly regarding the logic of how these other factors could have affected a student's academic skills. The end goal is to find a classification that best fits each student's situation. This is precisely the reason why thoughtful, trained professionals are needed to make SLD determinations.

## REFERENCES

Alfonso, V. C., & Flanagan, D. P. (Eds.) (2018). *Essentials of specific learning disability identification* (2nd ed). Wiley.

Briesch, A. M., Waldron, F. M., & Beneville, M. A. (2023). State variation regarding other health impairment eligibility criteria for attention deficit hyperactivity disorder. *School Mental Health*, *15*(3), 765–776.

McNicholas, P. J., Floyd, R. G., Woods, I. L.Jr., Singh, L. J., Manguno, M. S., & Maki, K. E. (2018). State special education criteria for identifying intellectual disability: a review following revised diagnostic criteria and Rosa's Law. *School Psychology Quarterly*, *33*(1), 75–82.

Shapiro, E. S., & Clemens, N. H. (2023). *Academic skills problems* (5th ed). Guilford.United States Office of Education (1977). Procedures for evaluating specific learning disabilities. *Federal Register*, *42*(250), 65082–65085.

Appendix H

# MANIFESTATIONS OF COGNITIVE WEAKNESSES

As with academic weaknesses, when the probability of making a correct decision is low or equivocal, ecological validity, in the form of manifestations, or other corroborating data, must be present to support a weakness. This appendix is organized by CHC domain. There are three grade levels in each domain: Elementary School (K-5), Middle School (6–8), and High School (9–12). Each CHC domain lists manifestations in reading, writing, and math. Note that this information is built into X-BASS on the SLD Evaluation tab.

## Fluid Reasoning (*Gf*)

### Manifestations by Grade Level and Academic Area: Reading, Writing, and Math

### Elementary School (K-5)

#### Reading

- **Phonological pattern recognition:** Difficulty identifying sound patterns and applying phonics rules to new words
- **Reading comprehension:** Difficulty making inferences beyond explicitly stated information
- **Story structure:** Difficulty predicting what might happen next or understanding cause-and-effect relationships
- **Vocabulary acquisition:** Slower development of new vocabulary through context clues

#### Writing

- **Sentence construction:** Difficulty organizing ideas into coherent sentences
- **Story planning:** Difficulty developing logical story sequences or organizing narrative elements
- **Creative writing:** Limited ability to generate novel ideas or elaborate on basic concepts
- **Editing skills:** Difficulty identifying and correcting errors in their own work

#### Math

- **Pattern recognition:** Difficulty identifying number patterns, skip counting, or geometric sequences
- **Problem-solving strategies:** Difficulty selecting appropriate strategies for word problems
- **Mental math:** Challenges with flexible thinking about numbers and operations
- **Mathematical reasoning:** Difficulty understanding "why" math procedures work

### Middle School (6–8)

#### Reading

- **Abstract thinking:** Difficulty understanding metaphors, symbolism, and figurative language
- **Complex text structure:** Difficulty following multilayered plots or argument structures
- **Critical analysis:** Challenges comparing and contrasting ideas across texts
- **Inference complexity:** Difficulty making sophisticated inferences requiring multiple logical steps

#### Writing

- **Essay organization:** Difficulty structuring multiparagraph essays with logical flow
- **Argument development:** Difficulty generating supporting evidence and counterarguments
- **Revision strategies:** Challenges reorganizing content for clarity and coherence
- **Genre adaptation:** Difficulty adjusting writing style for different purposes and audiences

#### Math

- **Algebraic thinking:** Difficulty understanding variables and abstract mathematical relationships
- **Multistep problem solving:** Difficulty breaking complex problems into manageable components

- **Mathematical reasoning:** Challenges with proof-based thinking and logical justification
- **Pattern generalization:** Difficulty extending patterns to create rules or formulas

### High School (9–12)

#### Reading

- **Complex analysis:** Difficulty analyzing multiple themes, perspectives, or layers of meaning
- **Synthesis across texts:** Difficulty integrating ideas from multiple sources
- **Theoretical concepts:** Challenges understanding abstract philosophical or literary theories
- **Critical evaluation:** Difficulty evaluating author bias, argument validity, or source credibility

#### Writing

- **Sophisticated argumentation:** Difficulty developing nuanced thesis statements and complex arguments
- **Research integration:** Difficulty synthesizing multiple sources into coherent analysis
- **Rhetorical awareness:** Challenges adapting writing for sophisticated audiences and purposes
- **Abstract concept development:** Difficulty articulating complex or theoretical ideas clearly

#### Math

- **Advanced problem solving:** Difficulty with multistep, nonroutine problems requiring novel approaches
- **Abstract mathematical concepts:** Challenges with calculus, advanced algebra, and theoretical mathematics
- **Mathematical modeling:** Difficulty translating real-world situations into mathematical representations
- **Proof construction:** Difficulty with formal mathematical reasoning and logical proof development

## Comprehension Knowledge (*Gc*)

### Manifestations by Grade Level and Academic Area: Reading, Writing, and Math

### Elementary School (K-5)

#### Reading

- **Limited vocabulary:** Difficulty understanding age-appropriate texts due to unknown words
- **Background knowledge gaps:** Difficulty comprehending texts about unfamiliar topics (e.g., animals, geography, history)
- **Context clue struggles:** Inability to use surrounding text to determine word meanings
- **Literal comprehension:** Difficulty understanding basic story elements due to vocabulary limitations
- **Cultural references:** Missing meaning in texts with cultural or historical references

#### Writing

- **Limited word choice:** Repetitive use of basic vocabulary in written expression
- **Topic development:** Difficulty elaborating on ideas due to insufficient background knowledge
- **Sentence complexity:** Uses simple sentence structures due to limited vocabulary repertoire
- **Creative expression:** Constrained storytelling due to limited knowledge of story elements and themes

#### Math

- **Math vocabulary:** Confusion with terms like "sum," "difference," "altogether," and "fewer than"
- **Word problems:** Difficulty understanding problem contexts (e.g., money, time, measurement scenarios)
- **Conceptual understanding:** Difficulty grasping mathematical concepts without sufficient verbal labels
- **Real-world connections:** Limited ability to connect math to everyday experiences

### Middle School (6–8)

#### Reading

- **Academic vocabulary:** Difficulty with discipline-specific terms across subjects
- **Complex text comprehension:** Difficulty with informational texts requiring background knowledge
- **Literary analysis:** Difficulty understanding themes, motifs, and literary devices
- **Cross-curricular reading:** Challenges in science and social studies texts due to knowledge gaps
- **Inferential comprehension:** Difficulty making connections between text and prior knowledge

### Writing

- **Academic writing:** Limited ability to write informative or persuasive essays due to knowledge gaps
- **Source integration:** Difficulty incorporating and citing information from multiple sources
- **Audience awareness:** Difficulty adjusting writing for different readers due to limited cultural knowledge
- **Content development:** Shallow treatment of topics due to insufficient background information
- **Research skills:** Challenges evaluating and synthesizing information from various sources

### Math

- **Applied mathematics:** Difficulty with real-world math applications (e.g., percentages, ratios, proportions)
- **Mathematical reasoning:** Difficulty understanding mathematical concepts embedded in verbal contexts
- **Problem-solving contexts:** Challenges with word problems involving unfamiliar scenarios
- **Cross-curricular math:** Difficulty applying math in science contexts (e.g., measurement, data analysis)
- **Mathematical communication:** Difficulty explaining mathematical thinking using appropriate vocabulary

## High School (9–12)

### Reading

- **Advanced academic texts:** Difficulty with college-level reading in literature, science, and social studies
- **Specialized vocabulary:** Difficulty with technical terms across disciplines
- **Cultural literacy:** Missing references to historical events, literary works, and cultural knowledge
- **Critical thinking:** Difficulty analyzing complex arguments due to insufficient background knowledge
- **Independent learning:** Challenges with self-directed reading and research projects

### Writing

- **Research papers:** Difficulty producing sophisticated analysis due to limited knowledge base
- **Argumentative writing:** Difficulty developing complex arguments without sufficient evidence and examples
- **Discipline-specific writing:** Challenges with scientific reports, historical analysis, literary criticism
- **College preparation:** Inadequate preparation for college-level writing expectations
- **Professional communication:** Limited ability to write for workplace or academic audiences

### Math

- **Advanced applications:** Difficulty with calculus, statistics, and advanced problem-solving requiring broad knowledge
- **Mathematical modeling:** Difficulty creating mathematical representations of real-world phenomena
- **Cross-disciplinary integration:** Challenges applying math in physics, chemistry, economics, and other subjects
- **College preparation:** Insufficient preparation for math courses requiring extensive vocabulary and conceptual knowledge
- **Standardized testing:** Lower performance on math sections requiring reading comprehension and cultural knowledge

# Learning Efficiency (*Gl*)

## Manifestations by Grade Level and Academic Area: Reading, Writing, and Math

## Elementary School (K-5)

### Reading

- **Slow phonics acquisition:** Takes much longer to learn letter-sound correspondences than peers
- **Sight word development:** Requires many more exposures to recognize high-frequency words automatically
- **Reading fluency:** Slow progress from decoding to automatic word recognition
- **Retention difficulties:** Frequently "forgets" previously learned reading skills and needs re-teaching
- **Practice requirements:** Needs significantly more repetition to master basic reading concepts

### Writing

- **Letter formation:** Slow to automate handwriting despite repeated practice
- **Spelling patterns:** Takes longer to internalize spelling rules and common patterns
- **Writing stamina:** Fatigues quickly during writing tasks due to effortful processing
- **Skill integration:** Difficulty combining multiple writing skills (e.g., spelling, grammar, ideas) simultaneously
- **Revision skills:** Slow to develop self-editing and proofreading abilities

### Math

- **Math facts:** Requires extensive practice to automate basic addition/subtraction facts
- **Procedural learning:** Slow to master computational algorithms despite repeated instruction
- **Conceptual retention:** Needs frequent review to maintain understanding of mathematical concepts
- **Transfer difficulties:** Difficulty applying learned math skills to new but similar problems
- **Multistep procedures:** Takes longer to learn and automate complex math processes

## Middle School (6–8)

### Reading

- **Complex decoding:** Slow progress with multisyllabic word reading despite adequate phonics knowledge
- **Reading comprehension strategies:** Takes longer to learn and apply comprehension techniques
- **Vocabulary acquisition:** Slower rate of learning new academic vocabulary from context
- **Genre familiarity:** Needs more exposure to master different text structures and formats
- **Reading independence:** Requires more scaffolding to become an independent reader

### Writing

- **Essay structure:** Slow to internalize paragraph and essay organization patterns
- **Grammar application:** Takes longer to apply grammar rules consistently in writing
- **Research skills:** Slower development of note-taking, summarizing, and citation skills
- **Drafting process:** Needs more time and support to develop effective writing processes
- **Genre conventions:** Requires additional instruction to master different writing formats

### Math

- **Algebraic thinking:** Slow to develop understanding of variables and abstract mathematical relationships
- **Problem-solving strategies:** Takes longer than same grade peers to learn and apply systematic approaches to word problems
- **Fraction concepts:** Requires extended instruction to understand fraction operations and relationships
- **Mathematical reasoning:** Slower development of logical thinking and proof-based reasoning
- **Calculator efficiency:** Takes longer to become proficient with technological tools

## High School (9–12)

### Reading

- **Advanced comprehension:** Slow to develop sophisticated analysis and critical thinking skills
- **Research proficiency:** Takes longer than same grade peers to master advanced research and synthesis skills
- **Literary analysis:** Requires extended instruction to analyze complex themes and literary devices
- **Academic reading:** Slower adaptation to discipline-specific reading demands
- **Independent learning:** Needs more structure and support for self-directed learning

### Writing

- **Sophisticated argumentation:** Slow development of complex analytical and persuasive writing
- **Research integration:** Takes longer to learn effective source integration and citation
- **Voice and style:** Slower development of mature writing voice and audience awareness
- **College preparation:** Requires additional time and support to meet college writing standards
- **Professional writing:** Slow adaptation to workplace and technical writing demands

### Math

- **Advanced mathematics:** Slower mastery than same grade peers of calculus, statistics, and advanced mathematical concepts
- **Mathematical modeling:** Takes longer than same grade peers to learn real-world application of mathematical principles
- **Abstract reasoning:** Requires extended instruction for theoretical mathematical concepts
- **Technology integration:** Slower adoption than same grade peers of advanced mathematical software and graphing tools
- **College readiness:** Needs additional preparation time for college-level mathematics

## Retrieval Fluency (*Gr*)

### Manifestations by Grade Level and Academic Area: Reading, Writing, and Math

### Elementary School (K-5)

#### Reading

- **Word retrieval hesitations:** Frequent pauses and "tip-of-the-tongue" moments when reading familiar words aloud
- **Slow reading pace:** Adequate decoding skills but labored, effortful reading that affects comprehension
- **Oral reading difficulties:** Frequent word substitutions or circumlocutions during read-alouds
- **Sight word recognition:** Inconsistent automatic recognition of high-frequency words previously learned
- **Reading fluency:** Choppy, labored word-by-word reading despite adequate phonics knowledge

#### Writing

- **Word-finding during composition:** Long pauses while searching for specific words to express ideas
- **Limited vocabulary use:** Reliance on simple, easily retrieved words despite a larger receptive vocabulary
- **Spelling retrieval:** Difficulty accessing known spelling patterns under time pressure
- **Slow writing pace:** Extended time needed to generate written responses
- **Circumlocution:** Uses many words to describe something when unable to retrieve the precise term

#### Math

- **Math fact retrieval:** Slow, effortful recall of basic addition, subtraction facts despite knowing them
- **Counting strategies:** Reliance on finger counting or other strategies when facts should be automatic
- **Number word retrieval:** Hesitations when naming numbers, especially larger or less common ones
- **Math vocabulary:** Difficulty quickly accessing mathematical terms during problem-solving
- **Timed assessments:** Poor performance on math fluency measures despite conceptual understanding

### Middle School (6–8)

#### Reading

- **Academic vocabulary retrieval:** Slow access to content-specific terminology across subjects
- **Reading comprehension impact:** Reduced comprehension due to cognitive resources spent on word retrieval
- **Oral participation:** Reluctance to participate in class discussions due to word-finding difficulties
- **Text-to-speech benefits:** Improved comprehension when listening vs. reading due to retrieval demands
- **Reading stamina:** Quick fatigue during sustained reading tasks

#### Writing

- **Essay composition delays:** Extended planning time needed to retrieve appropriate vocabulary and ideas
- **Revision difficulties:** Difficulty accessing alternative word choices during editing process
- **Academic writing challenges:** Difficulty retrieving discipline-specific terminology for content area writing
- **Timed writing struggles:** Significantly reduced performance on standardized writing assessments with time limits
- **Writer's block:** Frequent inability to access words or ideas, leading to production difficulties

#### Math

- **Multistep problem solving:** Slow retrieval of procedures interferes with complex problem completion
- **Mental math difficulties:** Poor performance on activities requiring quick number fact access
- **Formula retrieval:** Inconsistent access to mathematical formulas and procedures under pressure
- **Mathematical reasoning:** Slower mathematical discourse due to difficulty retrieving mathematical language
- **Standardized test performance:** Poor performance on timed math sections despite adequate knowledge

### High School (9–12)

#### Reading

- **Advanced text processing:** Slow reading of complex academic texts affects comprehension and analysis
- **Literature analysis:** Difficulty retrieving literary terms and concepts during class discussions
- **Research efficiency:** Slower information processing when reading multiple sources
- **Standardized test reading:** Poor performance on timed reading comprehension sections
- **Content area reading:** Difficulty with rapid access to technical vocabulary in science and social studies

#### Writing

- **Advanced composition:** Difficulty accessing sophisticated vocabulary and complex sentence structures
- **Research paper writing:** Slow integration of sources due to retrieval difficulties with academic language
- **Rhetorical skills:** Difficulty accessing appropriate writing techniques for different audiences and purposes
- **College application essays:** Extended time needed for thoughtful, articulate personal writing
- **Professional writing preparation:** Challenges with workplace writing requiring quick, precise communication

#### Math

- **Advanced mathematics:** Slow retrieval of algebraic procedures affects calculus and higher-level math
- **Mathematical problem-solving:** Difficulty accessing multiple solution strategies quickly
- **Math-science integration:** Struggles with retrieving mathematical procedures needed for physics and chemistry
- **Standardized assessments:** Poor performance on SAT/ACT math sections due to time constraints
- **Mathematical communication:** Difficulty explaining mathematical reasoning using precise terminology

## Short-term Storage and Working Memory (*Gwm*)

### Manifestations by Grade Level and Academic Area: Reading, Writing, and Math

### Elementary School (K-5)

#### Reading

- **Phonemic blending difficulties:** Difficulty holding individual sounds in memory while blending them into words
- **Sentence comprehension:** Forgetting the beginning of a sentence by the time they reach the end
- **Following directions:** Difficulty remembering multistep reading instructions (e.g., "Read the passage, then answer questions 1-3")
- **Story comprehension:** Difficulty keeping track of characters, plot elements, and the sequence of events
- **Phonics application:** Difficulty holding phonetic rules in mind while attempting to decode unfamiliar words

#### Writing

- **Sentence construction:** Forgetting the beginning of their thought while writing longer sentences
- **Spelling during composition:** Losing track of spelling patterns while focusing on idea generation
- **Multistep writing process:** Difficulty remembering and following writing steps (e.g., plan, draft, revise, edit)
- **Handwriting interference:** Working memory consumed by letter formation, leaving little capacity for content
- **Story writing:** Difficulty maintaining story elements and sequence throughout composition

#### Math

- **Multistep problems:** Forgetting earlier steps while working through word problems
- **Mental math:** Difficulty holding numbers in mind during computation (e.g., $23+47$)
- **Place value:** Difficulty keeping track of different place value columns during computation
- **Word problem solving:** Forgetting key information from the problem while performing calculations
- **Following math procedures:** Difficulty remembering and executing multistep algorithms

### Middle School (6–8)

#### Reading

- **Complex sentence processing:** Difficulty holding multiple clauses and ideas in mind simultaneously
- **Reading comprehension:** Difficulty integrating information across paragraphs and chapters
- **Note-taking while reading:** Challenges maintaining comprehension while simultaneously taking notes

- **Inference making:** Difficulty holding background knowledge and text information together to make inferences
- **Literature analysis:** Difficulty tracking multiple themes, characters, and literary devices simultaneously

### Writing

- **Essay organization:** Difficulty maintaining thesis and supporting points throughout longer compositions
- **Research integration:** Difficulty holding multiple source ideas in mind while synthesizing information
- **Grammar application:** Losing track of sentence structure while focusing on content and ideas
- **Revision process:** Difficulty holding original ideas in mind while making editorial changes
- **Paragraph development:** Difficulty maintaining topic focus throughout extended paragraphs

### Math

- **Algebraic manipulation:** Difficulty tracking multiple variables and operations in complex equations
- **Multistep word problems:** Forgetting problem constraints while working through solution steps
- **Geometric proofs:** Difficulty holding theorem information and proof steps in working memory
- **Fraction operations:** Difficulty maintaining multiple fraction components during computation
- **Data analysis:** Difficulty holding dataset information while performing calculations and drawing conclusions

## High School (9–12)

### Reading

- **Advanced text analysis:** Difficulty simultaneously considering multiple interpretations and evidence
- **Research synthesis:** Difficulty holding information from multiple sources while creating unified analysis
- **Critical thinking:** Challenges maintaining competing arguments and evidence in working memory
- **Standardized test reading:** Difficulty holding passage information while answering complex questions
- **Content area integration:** Difficulty connecting information across different subject areas

### Writing

- **Complex argumentation:** Difficulty maintaining thesis, evidence, and counterarguments simultaneously
- **Research paper composition:** Difficulty integrating multiple sources while maintaining original analysis
- **College application essays:** Challenges holding personal reflection and audience awareness together
- **Rhetorical analysis:** Difficulty tracking author's purpose, audience, and rhetorical strategies simultaneously
- **Peer editing:** Difficulty holding multiple editing criteria in mind while reviewing others' work

### Math

- **Advanced problem solving:** Difficulty maintaining multiple solution strategies and constraints
- **Calculus procedures:** Difficulty holding derivative rules and integration techniques in working memory
- **Mathematical modeling:** Challenges maintaining real-world context while manipulating mathematical representations
- **Proof construction:** Difficulty holding logical sequence and mathematical justifications simultaneously
- **Statistics analysis:** Difficulty maintaining dataset characteristics while applying statistical procedures

# Visual Processing (*Gv*)

## Manifestations by Grade Level and Academic Area: Reading, Writing, and Math

## Elementary School (K-5)

### Reading

- **Letter discrimination:** Confusion between similar letters (e.g., b/d, p/q, m/w) even after typical age for reversals
- **Word recognition:** Difficulty recognizing common sight words due to problems processing visual word forms
- **Line tracking:** Loses place while reading, skipping lines, or re-reading the same line
- **Visual scanning:** Difficulty efficiently scanning left-to-right across text or finding specific words on a page
- **Letter spacing:** Difficulty distinguishing where one word ends and another begins

### Writing

- **Letter formation:** Inconsistent letter size, spacing, and alignment on lined paper
- **Spatial organization:** Poor use of margins, uneven spacing between words and letters
- **Copying difficulties:** Errors when copying from the board or from books due to visual-motor integration problems

- **Handwriting legibility:** Generally poor handwriting that does not improve with practice
- **Visual memory for spelling:** Difficulty remembering what words "look like" for spelling accuracy

### Math

- **Number discrimination:** Confusion between similar-looking numbers (e.g., 6/9, 2/5, 17/71)
- **Column alignment:** Difficulty lining up numbers in math problems, leading to computation errors
- **Visual–spatial math:** Difficulty with geometry concepts involving shapes, patterns, and spatial relationships
- **Math symbol recognition:** Confusion between operation signs (e.g., +, ×, ÷) or directional symbols (e.g., < >)
- **Place value understanding:** Difficulty understanding number position and its relationship to value

## Middle School (6–8)

### Reading

- **Complex text navigation:** Difficulty tracking information across multiple columns, charts, or text boxes
- **Graphic interpretation:** Difficulty reading and interpreting charts, graphs, diagrams, and maps
- **Visual text features:** Missing important information in sidebars, captions, or highlighted text
- **Reading stamina:** Visual fatigue leading to decreased comprehension during sustained reading
- **Digital text challenges:** Difficulty navigating online texts, hyperlinks, and multimedia presentations

### Writing

- **Essay organization:** Poor visual organization of paragraphs and sections on the page
- **Note-taking:** Difficulty creating organized, visually coherent notes from lectures or readings
- **Research formatting:** Difficulty with proper formatting of citations, bibliographies, and research papers
- **Editing challenges:** Missing visual cues for editing (e.g., capitalization, punctuation, paragraph breaks)
- **Technology integration:** Difficulty with word processing, formatting, and document organization

### Math

- **Algebraic notation:** Confusion with complex mathematical expressions and equation formatting
- **Geometric reasoning:** Difficulty with shape recognition, angle measurement, and spatial transformations
- **Graph interpretation:** Difficulty reading coordinate planes, interpreting data displays, and creating graphs
- **Multistep organization:** Poor visual organization of work, making it hard to follow solution steps
- **Formula application:** Difficulty visually organizing and applying mathematical formulas

## High School (9–12)

### Reading

- **Advanced text analysis:** Difficulty processing complex visual layouts in textbooks and academic materials
- **Research skills:** Difficulty with navigating complex databases, websites, and digital research tools
- **Scientific diagrams:** Difficulty interpreting complex scientific charts, molecular structures, and technical diagrams
- **Literature analysis:** Missing visual literary devices, formatting cues, and textual organization
- **Standardized test navigation:** Difficulty with bubble sheets, complex test formats, and visual answer choices

### Writing

- **Advanced composition:** Poor visual presentation of complex essays, research papers, and presentations
- **Technical writing:** Difficulty with formatting requirements for lab reports, technical documents, and research papers
- **College application materials:** Difficulty with visual presentation of portfolios, resumes, and application essays
- **Digital literacy:** Challenges with creating visually appealing and well-organized digital presentations
- **Professional communication:** Poor visual organization of business correspondence and professional documents

### Math

- **Advanced mathematics:** Difficulty with complex calculus notation, advanced geometric proofs, and statistical displays
- **Mathematical modeling:** Difficulty with creating and interpreting visual representations of mathematical concepts
- **Technology integration:** Difficulty using graphing calculators, mathematical software, and data visualization tools
- **Applied mathematics:** Challenges interpreting real-world visual data in engineering, science, and economics contexts
- **Standardized assessments:** Poor performance on visually complex math problems and data interpretation sections

## Auditory Processing (*Ga*—General)

### Manifestations by Grade Level and Academic Area: Reading, Writing, and Math

### Elementary School (K-5)

#### Reading

- **Phonemic awareness difficulties:** Difficulty identifying, blending, and manipulating individual sounds in words
- **Phonics confusion:** Difficulty distinguishing between similar sounds (e.g., b/p, d/t, m/n) affecting decoding
- **Rhyming challenges:** Difficulty recognizing and producing rhyming words despite adequate vocabulary
- **Sound blending:** Difficulty combining individual phonemes to form complete words
- **Auditory discrimination:** Confusion with words that sound similar (e.g., cat/cap, pen/pin)

#### Writing

- **Sound-symbol correspondence:** Difficulty connecting heard sounds to appropriate letters during spelling
- **Phonetic spelling errors:** Inconsistent spelling of words based on misperceived sounds
- **Dictation challenges:** Poor performance when writing words or sentences from verbal dictation
- **Self-monitoring difficulties:** Difficulty "hearing" errors when reading their own writing aloud
- **Sound sequencing:** Difficulty maintaining correct order of sounds in multisyllabic words

#### Math

- **Verbal math instruction:** Difficulty following oral directions for math procedures and problem-solving
- **Number word confusion:** Difficulty distinguishing between similar-sounding numbers (e.g., thirteen/thirty, fifteen/fifty)
- **Word problem comprehension:** Challenges understanding math problems presented orally
- **Skip counting:** Difficulty with auditory patterns in counting by 2 seconds, 5 seconds, 10 seconds
- **Math fact recall:** Difficulty with auditory rehearsal strategies for memorizing math facts

### Middle School (6–8)

#### Reading

- **Phonological processing:** Continued difficulty with complex phonological patterns in multisyllabic words
- **Reading comprehension:** Difficulty processing complex sentences when reading aloud or listening to text
- **Vocabulary development:** Slower acquisition of new vocabulary due to unclear auditory input
- **Fluency challenges:** Choppy oral reading due to uncertainty about pronunciation
- **Listening comprehension:** Poor understanding of content delivered through lectures or audio materials

#### Writing

- **Complex spelling patterns:** Difficulty with advanced spelling rules involving similar-sounding letter combinations
- **Proofreading challenges:** Difficulty detecting errors when reading work aloud for revision
- **Note-taking from lectures:** Difficulty processing and writing down orally presented information
- **Grammar application:** Difficulty "hearing" grammatical errors in their own writing
- **Dictated writing tasks:** Poor performance on writing assignments given through oral instruction

#### Math

- **Multistep verbal problems:** Difficulty processing and retaining complex oral math instructions
- **Mathematical discourse:** Challenges participating in math discussions and explaining reasoning orally
- **Algebraic language:** Difficulty distinguishing between similar-sounding mathematical terms
- **Formula recall:** Difficulty using auditory rehearsal to memorize mathematical formulas
- **Collaborative problem-solving:** Difficulty following peer explanations and group math discussions

### High School (9–12)

#### Reading

- **Advanced phonological processing:** Difficulty with pronunciation of technical and academic vocabulary
- **Literature analysis:** Challenges appreciating literary devices that rely on sound patterns (e.g., alliteration, rhythm)
- **Foreign language learning:** Significant difficulty with pronunciation and auditory discrimination in new languages

- **Lecture-based learning:** Poor comprehension of content delivered primarily through teacher lectures
- **Audio-visual integration:** Difficulty coordinating information from both visual texts and audio presentations

### Writing

- **Advanced composition:** Difficulty with rhythm, flow, and "sound" of sophisticated writing
- **Research integration:** Difficulty processing and incorporating information from interviews or audio sources
- **Peer review activities:** Challenges providing and receiving feedback through oral discussion
- **Presentation skills:** Difficulty monitoring their own speech patterns and vocal delivery
- **Technical writing:** Difficulty with precise language where similar-sounding terms have different meanings

### Math

- **Advanced mathematical reasoning:** Difficulty following complex oral explanations of mathematical concepts
- **STEM integration:** Challenges in science classes where mathematical concepts are explained verbally
- **Collaborative problem-solving:** Difficulty in group projects requiring verbal mathematical communication
- **Test-taking strategies:** Difficulty with oral portions of assessments or verbal reasoning problems
- **College preparation:** Challenges with math courses that rely heavily on lecture-based instruction

## Auditory Processing (*Ga*—Phonological Processing/Phonemic Awareness)

## Manifestations by Grade Level and Academic Area: Reading, Writing, and Math

### Elementary School (K-5)

### Reading

- **Phoneme isolation:** Cannot identify individual sounds in words (e.g., first sound in "cat" is /k/)
- **Sound blending:** Difficulty combining separate sounds to form words (e.g., /c/ /a/ /t/ = cat)
- **Sound segmentation:** Cannot break words into individual phonemes (e.g., cat = /c/ /a/ /t/)
- **Phoneme manipulation:** Difficulty with tasks like "say cat without the /c/" or "change /c/ in cat to /b/"
- **Rhyme recognition:** Difficulty identifying words that rhyme or generating rhyming words
- **Syllable awareness:** Cannot count syllables or break words into syllable units
- **Decoding struggles:** Extreme difficulty learning sound-symbol correspondences for reading

### Writing

- **Invented spelling:** Severe phonetic spelling errors showing poor sound awareness (e.g., KT for cat, JRAGIN for dragon)
- **Sound-symbol mapping:** Difficulty connecting heard sounds to appropriate letters
- **Spelling development:** Very slow progress through typical spelling stages
- **Letter-sound confusion:** Inconsistent use of letter sounds in spelling attempts
- **Word writing:** Difficulty spelling even simple, phonetically regular words

### Math

- **Number word confusion:** Difficulty with similar-sounding number words (e.g., fourteen/forty, thirteen/thirty)
- **Rhyming patterns:** Difficulty with counting songs and number rhymes that aid math learning
- **Verbal math instructions:** Challenges following oral directions containing similar-sounding math terms
- **Word problem comprehension:** Misunderstanding math problems due to phonological confusion
- **Math vocabulary:** Difficulty distinguishing between similar-sounding mathematical terms

### Middle School (6–8)

### Reading

- **Advanced phonological patterns:** Continued struggles with complex syllable structures and morphophonemic patterns
- **Multisyllabic word reading:** Difficulty breaking down and pronouncing longer academic vocabulary
- **Reading fluency:** Persistently slow, labored reading affecting comprehension across content areas
- **Phonological recoding:** Difficulty using sound-based strategies to read unfamiliar words
- **Vocabulary development:** Slower acquisition of new words due to unclear phonological representations

### Writing

- **Complex spelling patterns:** Continued difficulty with advanced spelling involving multiple syllables
- **Morphological spelling:** Difficulty with spelling changes when adding prefixes and suffixes
- **Homophones:** Confusion with words that sound the same but are spelled differently (e.g., their/there/they're)
- **Proofreading difficulties:** Cannot "hear" errors when reading their writing aloud
- **Academic vocabulary spelling:** Struggles with discipline-specific terminology

### Math

- **Mathematical discourse:** Difficulty with oral math discussions and explanations
- **Complex word problems:** Challenges processing mathematical language with similar-sounding terms
- **Algebraic language:** Confusion with mathematical terms that sound similar (coefficient/quotient)
- **Mathematical reasoning:** Difficulty following complex verbal explanations of mathematical concepts
- **Formula verbalization:** Difficulty with oral recitation and explanation of mathematical procedures

## High School (9–12)

### Reading

- **Academic vocabulary:** Severe difficulty with pronunciation and recognition of advanced academic terms
- **Foreign language learning:** Extreme difficulty with phonological systems in second languages
- **Literature analysis:** Challenges with phonological literary devices (alliteration, assonance, rhythm)
- **Technical reading:** Difficulty with pronunciation of scientific and technical terminology
- **Reading efficiency:** Continued slow reading pace affecting academic performance across subjects

### Writing

- **Advanced composition:** Persistent spelling difficulties limiting sophisticated vocabulary use
- **Technical writing:** Difficulty with accurate spelling of specialized terminology
- **Editing skills:** Continued difficulty detecting and correcting phonological errors
- **Professional preparation:** Inadequate spelling skills for college and workplace writing
- **Creative expression:** Limited vocabulary use in writing due to phonological uncertainty

### Math

- **Advanced mathematical language:** Difficulty with complex mathematical terminology and notation
- **STEM integration:** Challenges with mathematical language in science courses
- **Mathematical communication:** Difficulty explaining mathematical reasoning clearly
- **Collaborative problem-solving:** Difficulty in group work requiring verbal mathematical discussion
- **College preparation:** Inadequate phonological skills for university-level mathematics discourse

# Orthographic Processing (OP)

## Manifestations by Grade Level and Academic Area: Reading, Writing, and Math

## Elementary School (K-5)

### Reading

- **Sight word recognition:** Extreme difficulty learning high-frequency words that don't follow phonetic patterns (e.g., said, would, through)
- **Irregular word reading:** Difficulty with words that can't be sounded out phonetically (e.g., yacht, colonel, island)
- **Reading fluency:** Slow, labored reading due to inability to recognize whole words automatically
- **Word pattern recognition:** Difficulty recognizing common letter chunks and morphemes (e.g., –ing, –tion, pre-, un-)
- **Visual word memory:** Difficulty storing and retrieving visual representations of familiar words

### Writing

- **Spelling difficulties:** Severe and persistent inaccurate spelling, especially with irregular words
- **Phonetic over-reliance:** Writing words exactly as they sound (e.g., sed for said, wuz for was, thru for through)
- **Inconsistent spelling:** Same word spelled differently within the same sentence, paragraph, etc.

- **Visual spelling strategies:** Inability to use "looks right" strategy for spelling correction
- **Letter pattern errors:** Difficulty with common spelling patterns and word endings

### Math

- **Math vocabulary:** Difficulty recognizing mathematical terms in written form (e.g., difference, quotient, equation)
- **Number word recognition:** Difficulty reading number words (e.g., forty vs. fourteen, hundred vs. thousand)
- **Symbol recognition:** Inconsistent recognition of mathematical symbols and notation
- **Word problem reading:** Difficulty with reading mathematical word problems fluently
- **Mathematical notation:** Difficulty with conventional mathematical writing patterns

## Middle School (6–8)

### Reading

- **Academic vocabulary:** Severe difficulty with content-specific terms across all subject areas
- **Morphological awareness:** Difficulty recognizing root words, prefixes, and suffixes in complex words
- **Reading comprehension impact:** Reading comprehension is affected negatively due to cognitive resources devoted to word recognition
- **Content area reading:** Difficulty with science and social studies texts containing technical vocabulary
- **Reading rate:** Significantly slower reading speed than same grade peers affecting academic performance across subjects

### Writing

- **Advanced spelling patterns:** Continued difficulty with complex spelling rules and exceptions
- **Vocabulary limitation:** Tendency to use simple words to avoid spelling errors, limiting expression
- **Proofreading difficulties:** Inability to detect spelling errors in their own writing
- **Academic writing:** Difficulty with discipline-specific terminology and conventional writing formats
- **Technology dependence:** Heavy reliance on spell-check and predictive text features

### Math

- **Algebraic notation:** Difficulty with complex mathematical expressions and variable recognition
- **Mathematical terms:** Difficulty reading and writing advanced mathematical vocabulary
- **Formula recognition:** Difficulty with visual recognition and reproduction of mathematical formulas
- **Geometric terminology:** Difficulty with specialized vocabulary in geometry and measurement
- **Problem-solving notation:** Challenges with conventional mathematical problem-solving formats

## High School (9–12)

### Reading

- **Advanced academic texts:** Severe difficulty with college-level vocabulary and technical terminology
- **Specialized content:** Difficulty with subject-specific terms in AP courses and advanced classes
- **Standardized test reading:** Poor performance on vocabulary sections of SAT/ACT assessments
- **Independent reading:** Avoidance of recreational reading due to word recognition difficulties
- **Foreign language learning:** Extreme challenges with orthographic systems in second languages

### Writing

- **College preparation:** Inadequate spelling skills for college-level writing expectations
- **Professional writing:** Difficulty with workplace writing requiring accurate spelling and formatting
- **Research documentation:** Difficulty with proper citation formats and academic writing conventions
- **Creative expression:** Limited vocabulary use in creative writing due to spelling concerns
- **Digital literacy:** Continued heavy dependence on technological spelling and grammar supports

### Math

- **Advanced mathematics:** Difficulty with complex notation in calculus, statistics, and advanced algebra
- **STEM writing:** Difficulty with technical writing in science and engineering contexts
- **Mathematical communication:** Challenges writing mathematical explanations and proofs
- **College mathematics:** Inadequate preparation for university-level mathematical notation and terminology
- **Standardized assessments:** Poor performance on math sections requiring reading of complex problems

## Processing Speed (*Gs*)

## Manifestations by Grade Level and Academic Area: Reading, Writing, and Math

### Elementary School (K-5)

#### Reading

- **Slow decoding:** Takes significantly longer than same grade peers to sound out unfamiliar words
- **Reading fluency:** Word-by-word reading even with familiar text, affecting comprehension
- **Oral reading pace:** Extremely slow reading aloud, often losing listener attention
- **Silent reading:** Very slow independent reading that limits the amount of text covered
- **Reading assignments:** Unable to complete grade-level reading tasks within typical time frames

#### Writing

- **Letter formation:** Extremely slow handwriting, often incomplete assignments due to time constraints
- **Copying tasks:** Takes much longer to copy from board or books, often incomplete
- **Spelling retrieval:** Long pauses while searching memory for correct spelling of known words
- **Composition pace:** Very slow idea generation and written expression
- **Assignment completion:** Consistently needs more time than provided for writing tasks

#### Math

- **Math fact retrieval:** Slow recall of basic addition, subtraction, multiplication facts
- **Computation speed:** Takes much longer to complete math calculations than peers
- **Timed assessments:** Poor performance on math fluency measures despite knowing the facts
- **Problem-solving pace:** Slow processing of word problems, often not finishing assessments
- **Mental math:** Difficulty with rapid mental calculations and number manipulations

### Middle School (6–8)

#### Reading

- **Complex text processing:** Extremely slow reading of longer, more complex academic texts
- **Content area reading:** Difficulty completing reading assignments across all subjects within time limits
- **Reading comprehension:** Reduced understanding due to cognitive fatigue from slow processing
- **Note-taking while reading:** Cannot simultaneously read and take notes at typical pace
- **Research tasks:** Takes much longer than same grade peers to locate and process information from multiple sources

#### Writing

- **Essay composition:** Extremely slow planning, drafting, and revision processes
- **In-class writing:** Poor performance on timed writing assessments and journal prompts
- **Note-taking:** Cannot keep up with teacher lectures, missing important information
- **Research writing:** Takes significantly longer than same grade peers to integrate sources and develop ideas
- **Editing and revision:** Slow proofreading and editing processes

#### Math

- **Multistep problems:** Slow processing of complex word problems and algebraic procedures
- **Mathematical reasoning:** Takes longer than same grade peers to work through logical problem-solving steps
- **Geometric constructions:** Slow completion of drawings, measurements, and spatial tasks
- **Data analysis:** Difficulty processing and interpreting charts, graphs, and statistical information quickly
- **Standardized testing:** Poor performance on timed math sections despite adequate knowledge

### High School (9–12)

#### Reading

- **Advanced academic texts:** Extremely slow processing of college-level reading materials
- **Standardized test reading:** Significant challenges with timed reading comprehension sections
- **Research efficiency:** Takes much longer than same grade peers to review and synthesize multiple sources

- **Literature analysis:** Slow processing of complex literary works and analytical tasks
- **Content integration:** Difficulty keeping up with reading demands across multiple AP or honors courses

### Writing

- **College preparation:** Inadequate writing fluency for college-level timed writing expectations
- **Research papers:** Takes significantly longer than same grade peers to complete complex writing projects
- **Standardized essay writing:** Poor performance on SAT/ACT writing sections due to time constraints
- **In-class assessments:** Difficulty completing written exams within standard time limits
- **Professional writing preparation:** Slow development of workplace writing efficiency

### Math

- **Advanced mathematics:** Slow processing of complex calculus, statistics, and advanced algebra
- **STEM applications:** Difficulty keeping up with math-intensive science and engineering coursework
- **Standardized assessments:** Poor performance on SAT/ACT math sections despite knowledge
- **Mathematical modeling:** Takes longer than same grade peers to set up and solve real-world mathematical problems
- **College preparation:** Inadequate processing speed for university-level mathematics courses

Appendix I

# BATTERIES AND TESTS INCLUDED IN X-BASS 3.0

| Battery or Test | Abbreviation | Publication Date | Publisher | Author(s) |
|---|---|---|---|---|
| Academic Achievement Battery | AAB | 2014 | Psychological Assessment Resources | Melissa A. Messer |
| Auditory Phoneme Sequencing Test | APST | 2014 | Academic Therapy Publications | Deborah Ross-Swain, James Aten |
| Bankson Expressive Language Test, Third Edition | BELT-3 | 2018 | Western Psychological Services | Nicholas W. Bankson, Michelle Mentis, Jennifer R. Jagielko |
| Bateria IV Woodcock-Munoz: Pruebas de Aprovechamiento | Bateria IV APROV | 2019 | Riverside Insights | Richard Woodcock, Criselda G. Alvarado, Frederick A. Shrank, Nancy Mather, Kevin S. McGrew, Ana F. Munoz-Sandoval |
| Bateria IV Woodcock-Munoz: Pruebas de Habilidades Cognitivas | Bateria IV COG | 2019 | Riverside Insights | Richard Woodcock, Criselda G. Alvarado, Frederick A. Shrank, Kevin S. McGrew, Nancy Mather, Ana F. Munoz-Sandoval |
| Beery-Buktenica Developmental Test of Visual-Motor Integration, Sixth Edition | Beery VMI | 2010 | Pearson | Keith E. Beery, Norman A. Buktenica, Natasha A. Beery |
| Beta-4 | Beta-4 | 2016 | Pearson | C. E. Kellog, N. W. Morton |
| Bracken Basic Concept Scale, Fourth Edition: Receptive | BBCS-4:R | 2022 | Pearson | Bruce A. Bracken |
| Bracken School Readiness Assessment, Fourth Edition | BSRA-4 | 2022 | Pearson | Bruce A. Bracken |
| Bruininks-Oseretsky Test of Motor Proficiency, Third Edition | BOT-3 | 2024 | Pearson | Brett D. Bruininks, Robert H. Bruininks |
| California Verbal Learning Test, Third Edition | CVLT3 | 2017 | Pearson | Dean C. Delis, Joel H. Kramer, Edith Kaplan, Beth A. Ober |
| Child and Adolescent Memory Profile | ChAMP | 2015 | Psychological Assessment Resources | Elisabeth M.S. Sherman, Brian L. Brooks |
| Clinical Assessment of Articulation and Phonology, Second Edition | CAAP-2 | 2014 | pro-ed | Wayne Secord, JoAnn S. Donohue |
| Clinical Evaluation of Language Fundamentals Preschool-3 | CELF Preschool-3 | 2020 | Pearson | Elisabeth H. Wiig, Wayne A. Secord, Eleanor Semel |
| Clinical Evaluation of Language Fundamentals, Fifth Edition | CELF-5 | 2013 | Pearson | Elisabeth H. Wiig, Eleanor Semel, Wayne A. Secord |

| Battery or Test | Abbreviation | Publication Date | Publisher | Author(s) |
|---|---|---|---|---|
| Clinical Evaluation of Language Fundamentals-5 Metalinguistics | CELF-5 Metalinguistics | 2014 | Pearson | Elisabeth H. Wiig, Wayne A. Secord |
| Cognitive Assessment System, Second Edition | CAS2 | 2014 | Psychological Assessment Resources | Jack A. Naglieri, J.P. Das, Sam Goldstein |
| Comprehensive Assessment of Spoken Language, Second Edition | CASL-2 | 2017 | Western Psychological Services | Elizabeth Carrow-Woolfolk |
| Comprehensive Mathematical Abilities Test, Second Edition | CMAT-2 | 2022 | pro-ed | Wayne P. Hresko, Shelley R. Herron, Rita J. Sherrbenou |
| Comprehensive Receptive and Expressive Vocabulary Test, Third Edition | CREVT-3 | 2013 | pro-ed | George Wallace, Donald D. Hammill |
| Comprehensive Test of Nonverbal Intelligence, Second Edition | CTONI-2 | 2009 | pro-ed | Donald D. Hammill, Nils A. Pearson, J. Lee Wiederholt |
| Comprehensive Test of Phonological Processing, Second Edition | CTOPP-2 | 2013 | pro-ed | Richard K. Wagner, Joseph K. Torgesen, Carol A. Rashotte, Nils A. Pearson |
| Comprehensive Trail-Making Test, Second Edition | CTMT-2 | 2020 | pro-ed | Cecil R. Reynolds |
| Delis-Kaplan Executive Function System | D-KEFS | 2001 | Pearson | Dean C. Delis, Joel H. Kramer, Edith Kaplan |
| Detailed Assessment of the Speed of Handwriting, Second Edition | DASH-2 | 2024 | Pearson | Anna Barnett, Sheila E. Henderson, Beverly Scheib |
| Detroit Tests of Learning Abilities, Fifth Edition | DTLA-5 | 2018 | pro-ed | Donald D. Hammill, Ronnie L. McGhee, David J. Ehrler |
| Developmental Test of Visual Perception-Adolescent and Adult, Second Edition | DTVP-A:2 | 2021 | pro-ed | Cecil Reynolds, Nils Pearson, Judy Voress |
| Developmental Test of Visual Perception, third edition | DTVP-3 | 2013 | pro-ed | Donald D. Hammill, Nils A. Pearson, Judith K. Voress |
| Diagnostic Achievement Battery, Fourth Edition | DAB-4 | 2014 | pro-ed | Phyllis L. Newcomer, Herbert P. Ginsburg |
| Diagnostic Achievement Battery-Intermediate | DAB-I | 2013 | pro-ed | Phyllis L. Newcomer |
| Differential Ability Scales, Second Edition Normative Update | DAS-II NU | 2023 | Pearson | Colin D. Elliot |
| Early Reading Assessment | ERA | 2012 | pro-ed | Donald D. Hammill, Nils A. Pearson, Wayne P. Hresko, John J. Hoover |
| Executive Functions Test-Elementary: Normative Update | EFT-E:NU | 2017 | pro-ed | Linda Bowers, Rosemary Huisingh |
| Expressive Language Test, Second Edition: Normative Update | ELT-2: NU | 2018 | pro-ed | Linda Bowers, Rosemary Huisingh, Carolyn LoGiudice, Jane Oman |
| Expressive One-Word Picture Vocabulary Test, 4th Edition: Spanish Bilingual Edition | EOWPVT-4: SBE | 2012 | Academic Therapy Publications | Nancy A. Martin |
| Expressive One-Word Picture Vocabulary Test-4 | EOWPVT-4 | 2010 | Academic Therapy Publications | Nancy A. Martin, Rick Brownell |

| Battery or Test | Abbreviation | Publication Date | Publisher | Author(s) |
|---|---|---|---|---|
| Expressive Vocabulary Test, Third Edition | EVT-3 | 2018 | Pearson | Kathleen T. Williams |
| Feifer Assessment of Math | FAM | 2016 | Psychological Assessment Resources | Steven G. Feifer |
| Feifer Assessment of Reading | FAR | 2015 | Psychological Assessment Resources | Steven G. Feifer |
| Feifer Assessment of Writing | FAW | 2020 | Psychological Assessment Resources | Steven G. Feifer |
| Gray Oral Reading Tests, Fifth Edition | GORT-5 | 2012 | pro-ed | J. Lee Wiederholt, Brian R. Bryant |
| Kaplan Baycrest Neurocognitive Assessment | KBNA | 2000 | Pearson | Larry Leach, Edith Kaplan, Dmytro Rewilak, Brian Richards, Guy B. Proulx |
| Kaufman Assessment Battery for Children, Second Edition Normative Update | KABC-II NU | 2018 | Pearson | Alan S. Kaufman, Nadeen L. Kaufman |
| Kaufman Brief Intelligence Test, Second Edition Revised | KBIT-2 Revised | 2022 | Pearson | Alan S. Kaufman, Nadeen L. Kaufman |
| Kaufman Test of Educational Achievement, Third Edition | KTEA-3 | 2014 | Pearson | Alan S. Kaufman, Nadeen L. Kaufman |
| Leiter International Performance Scale, Third Edition | Leiter-3 | 2013 | Stoelting | Gale H. Roid, Lucy J. Miller, Mark Pomplun, Chris Koch |
| Listening Comprehension Test-Adolescent: Normative Update | LCT-A:NU | 2018 | pro-ed | Linda Bowers, Rosemary Huisingh, Carolyn LoGiudice |
| Mathematics Fluency and Calculation Tests, Complete Elementary Kit | MFaCTs: Elementary | 2014 | pro-ed | Cecil R. Reynolds, Judith K. Voress, Randy W. Kamphaus |
| Mathematics Fluency and Calculation Tests, Complete Secondary Kit | MFaCTs: Secondary | 2014 | pro-ed | Cecil R. Reynolds, Judith K. Voress, Randy W. Kamphaus |
| Motor-Free Visual Perception Test, Fourth Edition | MVPT-4 | 2015 | pro-ed | Ronald P Colarusso; Donald D. Hammill |
| Movement Assessment Battery for Children, Third Edition | MABC-3 | 2023 | Pearson | Sheila E. Henderson, Anna Barnett |
| Multiple Auditory Processing Assessment, Second Edition | MAPA-2 | 2018 | Academic Therapy Publications | Ronald L. Schow, J. Anthony Seikel, Jeff E. Brockett, Mary M. Whitaker |
| Naglieri Nonverbal Ability Test, Third Edition | NNAT3 | 2015 | Pearson | Jack A. Naglieri |
| Nelson-Denny Reading Test Forms I and J | NDRT | 2019 | pro-ed | Vivian Vick Fishco |
| NEPSY-II | NEPSY-II | 2007 | Pearson | Marit Korkman, Ursula Kirk, Sally Kemp |
| Nonverbal Stroop Card Sorting Test | NSCST | 2012 | Stoelting | Chris Koch, Gale Roid |
| Oral Passage Understanding Scale | OPUS | 2016 | Western Psychological Services | Elizabeth Carrow-Woolfolk, Amber M. Klein |
| Ortiz Picture Vocabulary Acquisition Test | Ortiz PVAT | 2018 | Mental Health Systems | Samuel O. Ortiz |

| Battery or Test | Abbreviation | Publication Date | Publisher | Author(s) |
|---|---|---|---|---|
| Peabody Picture Vocabulary Test, Fifth Edition | PPVT-5 | 2018 | Pearson | Douglas M. Dunn |
| Phonological and Print Awareness Scale | PPA Scale | 2014 | Western Psychological Services | Kathleen T. Williams |
| Phonological Awareness Test, Second Edition: Normative Update | PAT-2: NU | 2018 | pro-ed | Carolyn Robertson, Wanda Salter |
| Preschool Early Numeracy Screener | PENS | 2021 | pro-ed | David J. Purpura |
| Preschool Language Scales, Fifth Edition | PLS-5 | 2011 | Pearson | Irla Lee Zimmerman, Violette G. Steiner, Roberta Evatt Pond |
| Preschool Language Scales, Fifth Edition Spanish | PLS-5 Spanish | 2012 | Pearson | Irla Lee Zimmerman, Violette G. Steiner, Roberta Evatt Pond |
| Ravens Progressive Matrices, Second Edition | Ravens-2 | 2018 | Pearson | John C. Raven |
| Receptive One-Word Picture Vocabulary Test, 4th Edition: Spanish Bilingual Edition | ROWPVT-4: SBE | 2012 | Academic Therapy Publications | Nancy A. Martin |
| Receptive One-Word Picture Vocabulary Test-4 | ROWPVT-4 | 2010 | Academic Therapy Publications | Rick Brownell |
| Receptive, Expressive & Social Communication Assessment-Elementary | RESCA-E | 2015 | Academic Therapy Publications | Patricia Hamaguchi, Deborah Ross-Swain |
| Reynolds Adaptable Intelligence Test | RAIT | 2014 | Psychological Assessment Resources | Cecil R. Reynolds |
| Reynolds Intellectual Assessment Scales, Second Edition | RIAS-2 | 2015 | Psychological Assessment Resources | Cecil R. Reynolds; Randy W. Kamphaus |
| Social Language Development Test-Adolescent: Normative Update | SLDT-A:NU | 2017 | pro-ed | Linda Bowers, Rosemary Huisingh, Carolyn M. LoGiudice |
| Social Language Development Test-Elementary: Normative Update | SLDT-E:NU | 2017 | pro-ed | Linda Bowers, Rosemary Huisingh, Carolyn M. LoGiudice |
| Stanford-Binet Intelligence Scales-Fifth Edition | SB5 | 2003 | pro-ed | Gale H. Roid |
| Test of Adolescent and Adult Word Finding, Second Edition | TAWF-2 | 2016 | pro-ed | Diane J. German |
| Test of Auditory Comprehension of Language, Fourth Edition | TACL-4 | 2014 | pro-ed | Elizabeth Carrow-Woolfolk |
| Test of Auditory Processing Skills, Fourth Edition | TAPS-4 | 2018 | Academic Therapy Publications | Nancy A. Martin; Rick Brownell; Patricia Hamaguchi |
| Test of Dyslexia | TOD | 2024 | Western Psychological Services | Nancy Mather, Steve McCallum, Sherry Mee Bell, Barbara J. Wendling |
| Test of Early Language Development, Fourth Edition | TELD-4 | 2018 | pro-ed | Wayne P. Hresko, D. Kim Reid, Donald D. Hammill |

| Battery or Test | Abbreviation | Publication Date | Publisher | Author(s) |
|---|---|---|---|---|
| Test of Early Reading Ability, Fourth Edition | TERA-4 | 2018 | pro-ed | D. Kim Reid, Wayne P. Hresko, Donald D. Hammill |
| Test of Early Written Language, Third Edition | TEWL-3 | 2012 | pro-ed | Wayne Hresko, Shelley Herron, Pamela Peak, Deanna L. Hicks |
| Test of Expressive Language | TEXL | 2014 | pro-ed | Elizabeth Carrow-Woolfolk, Elizabeth A. Allen |
| Test of General Reasoning Ability | TOGRA | 2014 | Psychological Assessment Resources | Cecil R. Reynolds |
| Test of Integrated Language and Literacy Skills | TILLS | 2016 | Brookes Publishing | Nickola Nelson, Elena Plante, Nancy Helm-Estabrooks, Gillian Hotz |
| Test of Language Development, Intermediate: Fifth Edition | TOLD-I:5 | 2020 | pro-ed | Donald D. Hammill, Phyllis L. Newcomer |
| Test of Language Development-Primary: Fifth Edition | TOLD-P:5 | 2019 | pro-ed | Phyllis L. Newcomer, Donald D. Hammill |
| Test of Mathematical Abilities for Gifted Students, Second Edition | TOMAGS-2 | 2020 | pro-ed | Gail R. Ryser, Susan K. Johnson |
| Test of Mathematical Abilities, Third Edition | TOMA-3 | 2012 | pro-ed | Virginia Brown, Mary E. Cronin, Diane P. Bryant |
| Test of Narrative Language, Second Edition | TNL-2 | 2017 | pro-ed | Robert B. Gillam, Nils A. Pearson |
| Test of Nonverbal Intelligence, Fourth Edition | TONI-4 | 2010 | pro-ed | Linda Brown, Rita J. Sherbenou, Susan K. Johnsen |
| Test of Orthographic Competence | TOC | 2008 | pro-ed | Nancy Mather, Rhia Robers, Donald D. Hammill, Elizabeth A. Allen |
| Test of Orthographic Competence, Second Edition | TOC-2 | 2023 | pro-ed | Nancy Mather, Rhia Roberts, Donald D. Hammill, Elizabeth A. Allen |
| Test of Preschool Vocabulary | TOPV | 2015 | pro-ed | Steven C. Matthews, Lynda Miller |
| Test of Problem Solving-Third Edition Elementary: Normative Update | TOPS-3E: NU | 2018 | pro-ed | Linda Bowers, Rosemary Huisingh, Carolyn LoGuidice |
| Test of Semantic Reasoning | TOSR | 2016 | Academic Therapy Publications | Beth Lawrence, Deena Seifert |
| Test of Semantic Skills-Intermediate: Normative Update | TOSS-I: NU | 2018 | pro-ed | Rosemary Huisingh, Linda Bowers, Carolyn LoGiudice, Jane Orman |
| Test of Silent Contextual Reading Fluency, Second Edition | TOSCRF-2 | 2014 | pro-ed | Donald D. Hammill, J. Lee Wiederholt, Elizabeth A. Allen |
| Test of Silent Word Reading Fluency, Second Edition | TOSWRF-2 | 2014 | pro-ed | Nancy Mather, Donald D. Hammill, Elizabeth A. Allen, Rhia Roberts |
| Test of Visual Perceptual Skills, Fourth Edition | TVPS-4 | 2017 | Academic Therapy Publications | Nancy A. Martin |
| Test of Word Finding, Third Edition: Computer Administered | TWF-3: Computer Administered | 2015 | pro-ed | Diane J. German |
| Test of Word Reading Efficiency, Second Edition | TOWRE-2 | 2012 | pro-ed | Joseph K. Torgesen, Richard K. Wagner, Carol A. Rashotte |

| Battery or Test | Abbreviation | Publication Date | Publisher | Author(s) |
|---|---|---|---|---|
| Test of Written Language, Fourth Edition | TOWL-4 | 2009 | pro-ed | Donald D. Hammill, Stephen C. Larsen |
| Test of Written Spelling, Fifth Edition | TWS-5 | 2013 | pro-ed | Stephen C. Larsen, Donald Hammill, Louisa Moats |
| The WORD Test 3-Elementary | WORD-3: Elementary | 2014 | pro-ed | Linda Bowers, Rosemary Huisingh, Carolyn LoGuidice, Jane Orman |
| Universal Nonverbal Intelligence Test, Second Edition | UNIT-2 | 2016 | pro-ed | Bruce A. Bracken, R. Steve McCallum |
| Visual Skills Appraisal, Second Edition | VSA-2 | 2019 | Academic Therapy Publications | Regina G. Richards |
| Vocabulary Assessment Scales | VAS | 2013 | Psychological Assessment Resources | Rebecca Gerhardstein Nader |
| Wechsler Adult Intelligence Scale, Fifth Edition | WAIS-5 | 2024 | Pearson | David Wechsler |
| Wechsler Adult Intelligence Scale, Fourth Edition | WAIS-IV | 2008 | Pearson | David Wechsler |
| Wechsler Individual Achievement Test, Fourth Edition | WIAT-4 | 2020 | Pearson | David Wechsler |
| Wechsler Preschool and Primary Scale Of Intelligence, Fourth Edition | WPPSI-IV | 2012 | Pearson | David Wechsler |
| Wechsler Intelligence Scale For Children, Fifth Edition | WISC-V | 2014 | Pearson | David Wechsler |
| Wechsler Intelligence Scale for Children, Fifth Edition, Integrated | WISC-V Integrated | 2015 | Pearson | David Wechsler |
| Wechsler Intelligence Scale for Children, Fifth Edition, Spanish | WISC-V Spanish | 2017 | Pearson | David Wechsler |
| Wide Range Achievement Test, Fifth Edition | WRAT-5 | 2017 | Pearson | Gary S. Wilkinson, Gary J. Robertson |
| Wide Range Assessment of Memory and Learning, Third Edition | WRAML-3 | 2021 | Pearson | Wayne Adams, David Sheslow |
| Woodcock-Johnson IV Early Cognitive and Academic Development | WJ IV ECAD | 2015 | Riverside Insights | Frederick A. Schrank, Kevin S. McGrew, Nancy Mather |
| Woodcock-Johnson IV Tests of Achievement | WJ IV ACH | 2014 | Riverside Insights | Frederick A. Schrank, Nancy Mather, Kevin S. McGrew |
| Woodcock-Johnson IV Tests of Cognitive Abilities | WJ IV COG | 2014 | Riverside Insights | Frederick A. Schrank, Kevin S. McGrew, Nancy Mather |
| Woodcock-Johnson IV Tests of Oral Language | WJ IV OL | 2014 | Riverside Insights | Frederick A. Schrank, Nancy Mather, Kevin S. McGrew |
| Woodcock-Johnson V Tests of Achievement | WJ V ACH | 2025 | Riverside Insights | Nancy Mather, Kevin McGrew, Erica LaForte,<br>Barbara Wendling |

| Battery or Test | Abbreviation | Publication Date | Publisher | Author(s) |
|---|---|---|---|---|
| Woodcock-Johnson V Tests of Cognitive Abilities | WJ V COG | 2025 | Riverside Insights | Kevin McGrew, Nancy Mather, Erica LaForte, Barbara Wendling |
| Woodcock-Johnson V Virtual Test Library | WJ V VTL | 2025 | Riverside Insights | Nancy Mather, Kevin McGrew, Erica LaForte, Barbara Wendling |
| Woodcock-Munoz Language Survey III | WMLS III | 2017 | Riverside Insights | Richard W. Woodcock, Criselda Alvardo, Mary L. Ruef, Frederick A. Schrank |
| Young Children's Achievement Test, Second Edition | YCAT-2 | 2018 | pro-ed | Wayne P. Hresko, Pamela K. Peak, Shelly R. Herron, Deanna L. Hicks |

*Note:* Most tests and batteries included in X-BASS have a publication date of 2012-present to ensure recency in norms for cross-battery assessment. Exceptions include batteries that are used frequently in neuropsychological evaluations but have yet to be revised (e.g., NEPSY-II), and special requests from practitioners who use a specific test statewide, despite the age of its norms (e.g., the use of the Beery in CA). If you are looking for a test or battery that is not included in this list, it may have been omitted because it was published before 2012, it was not normed in the United States, or the quality of the standardization procedure, representativeness of the U.S. population, or number of individuals in the normative sample or at specific age levels was considered inadequate. The darkest shaded batteries and tests indicate those newly added in X-BASS 3.0 that were not included in earlier versions (e.g., X-BASS 2.4).

Appendix J

# PHONOLOGICAL AND ORTHOGRAPHIC READING ERRORS: A DIAGNOSTIC GUIDE AND RELATED INTERVENTIONS

Accurate interpretation of reading errors is essential for understanding the underlying processes that support or hinder skilled reading. When students misread words, the nature of those errors provides direct evidence about the integrity of their phonological system, the efficiency of their orthographic learning, and the stability of their sound–symbol connections. Because reading requires integrating phonological decoding, orthographic pattern recognition, and morphological knowledge, analyzing reading errors allows psychologists to determine which components of the reading system are functioning as expected and which are breaking down.

This appendix offers a structured diagnostic framework for interpreting reading errors within the context of Specific Learning Disability (SLD) identification. Table J.1 outlines the observable features of reading errors and links them to likely phonological, orthographic, or dual-deficit processing weaknesses. Table J.2 extends this analysis by describing the cognitive mechanisms that underlie these patterns and clarifying how sound-based and pattern-based systems contribute to decoding, sight-word development, and reading fluency. Together, these tools support practitioners in distinguishing between phonological decoding deficits, orthographic processing weaknesses, and combined profiles. These distinctions are central to accurate SLD identification in Basic Reading Skills and Reading Fluency.

By grounding interpretation in linguistic science and cognitive research, this appendix helps practitioners move beyond surface-level error descriptions toward a deeper understanding of the reading system. The goal is to support precise, equitable diagnostic decisions and ensure that assessment findings translate directly into targeted, evidence-based intervention planning.

## Intervention Recommendations Based on Reading Error Patterns*

**1. If the pattern of reading errors suggests a phonological processing weakness, the goal is to strengthen the student's ability to perceive, segment, blend, and manipulate sounds *during decoding.***

### Core Instructional Priorities

**Explicit phonemic awareness instruction (linked directly to print)**

- Segmenting, blending, isolating, deleting, and substituting phonemes
- Move from oral → letters → connected text
- Emphasize phoneme–grapheme mapping, not oral-only tasks

**Systematic phonics instruction**

- Direct teaching of sound–symbol correspondences
- Multi-letter graphemes (sh, ch, th, igh, tion)
- Explicit blending routines (continuous and stop-sound blending*)

* Stop-sound blending is a decoding strategy used when a word contains stop consonants, which are sounds that are produced with a quick burst of air and cannot be elongated. These include:

**/p/, /b/, /t/, /d/, /k/, /g/**

Because these sounds are so brief, students cannot "stretch" them the way they can stretch continuous sounds like **/m/, /s/, /f/, /n/, /l/**. If a student tries to stretch a stop sound, it distorts the word and makes blending harder. Stop-sound blending is a small technique, but it can be impactful for students with phonological processing weaknesses.

**Decodable text practice**

- Reinforces newly learned phonics patterns
- Builds accuracy and automaticity in controlled contexts

**Table J.1 Phonological and Orthographic Reading Errors**

| Feature Observed in Reading | Phonological Weakness | Orthographic Weakness | Both Processes Weak (Dual Deficit) |
|---|---|---|---|
| Misreading due to sound confusion | Difficulty perceiving or distinguishing phonemes (e.g., b/p) | | If misreadings are also visually implausible or inconsistent |
| Confusion of similar consonants | b/p, d/t, m/n substitutions | | If pattern-based errors also occur (e.g., misreading -ck, -due) |
| Vowel misreadings | Short vowel–to–short vowel substitutions (bit/bet); short/long vowel confusion (hop/hope) | | If vowel errors vary across attempts or combine with pattern errors |
| Missing sounds | Omits phonemes when decoding (fog/frog) | | If omissions co-occur with letter-pattern or grapheme errors |
| Adding sounds | Inserts phonemes not present (filum/film) | | If additions also distort visual patterns or irregular words |
| Reversing sound order | flim/film | gril/girl, form/from | |
| Highly phonetic reading | | Over-reliance on letter-by-letter decoding; compensatory sounding out due to weak orthographic lexicon | If irregular words AND phoneme-level decoding are both weak |
| Same word read differently | Unstable phonological representations | Weak visual memory for word forms | Both sound and visual representations unstable |
| Difficulty with irregular words | | Misreads exception words (said, thought) | If misreadings are also phonologically inaccurate |
| Phonetically plausible substitutions | | rite/right, thru/through | |
| Difficulty with patterns | | Struggles with -tion, -ough, -dge, -ight | If phoneme-level errors also appear |
| Difficulty with morphology | Misreads due to sound-based confusion (jumped → jump) | Misreads due to pattern-based confusion (tion, sion) | Both types appear across words |
| Letter order errors | | gril/girl, form/from | If also omits or confuses phonemes |
| Difficulty with multi-letter graphemes | | sh, th, ch, igh, ough misread | If grapheme errors co-occur with sound confusions |
| Over-reliance on sounding out | Decoding is primary weakness | Sight word recognition is weak | Both decoding and sight word reading significantly weak |
| Errors don't match phonics rules | Sound-based confusion | | |
| Errors don't match visual patterns | | Errors violate expected letter patterns | If also phonologically inaccurate |
| Difficulty decoding AND sight words | Decoding is primary issue | Sight words are primary issue | Both systems weak |
| Mixed, inconsistent errors | | | Strong indicator of dual weakness |

*Note:* Information in this table is based primarily on the following sources: Adams (1990), Castles and Nation (2006), Nation (2005), Rastle and Coltheart (2006), Stanovich (1988), Vellutino et al. (2004), and Wang et al. (2019).

**Elkonin boxes/sound boxes for decoding**

- Map each phoneme to a grapheme before reading
- Strengthens phoneme–grapheme alignment

**Table J.2 Underlying Mechanisms of Processing Weaknesses Related to Reading**

| Underlying Mechanism Category | Phonological Processing Weakness | Orthographic Processing Weakness | Both Processes Weak (Dual Deficit) |
|---|---|---|---|
| **Core cognitive breakdown** | Difficulty perceiving, segmenting, blending, or manipulating phonemes during reading | Difficulty storing, retrieving, and consolidating visual word forms and letter-pattern sequences | Breakdown in both phonological decoding and orthographic pattern retrieval |
| **Nature of the representation** | Unstable or fuzzy phonological representations of words; difficulty anchoring sounds to print | Weak or inefficient orthographic lexicon; difficulty forming stable visual word memories | Both sound representations and orthographic representations are unstable or weak |
| **Primary system affected** | Phonological decoding system (sound-symbol processing) | Orthographic reading system (pattern recognition, visual word memory) | Both systems required for efficient word reading |
| **What the brain struggles to do** | Map graphemes to phonemes accurately and consistently; hold sound sequences in working memory | Recognize familiar letter patterns, retrieve stored word forms, and use visual memory to support reading | Build stable sound–letter bonds AND stable visual word forms |
| **Impact on word learning** | Difficulty decoding unfamiliar words; slow or inaccurate phoneme-grapheme mapping | Difficulty developing a robust sight-word bank; slow consolidation of orthographic patterns | Difficulty with both decoding new words and building a sight-word vocabulary |
| **Impact on reading accuracy** | Errors reflect misheard or misprocessed sounds (e.g., b/p, d/t, vowel confusions) | Errors reflect misread patterns or visually similar words (e.g., -tion, -ough, irregular words) | Errors are mixed, inconsistent, and unpredictable across attempts |
| **Typical error patterns** | Missing sounds, added sounds, sound reversals, vowel substitutions, and inaccurate blending | Pattern-based misreadings, irregular-word errors, letter-order confusions, and visually plausible substitutions | Errors that violate both phonics rules AND visual pattern expectations |
| **Fluency impact** | Slow because decoding is effortful and non-automatic | Slow because the visual retrieval of word forms is inefficient | Very slow because both decoding and retrieval require conscious effort |
| **Morphology impact** | Difficulty decoding morphemes accurately (e.g., misreading plural or tense endings) | Difficulty recognizing morphological spelling shifts (e.g., magic → magician) | Difficulty with both sound-based and pattern-based morphological reading |
| **Sight-word development** | Slow because mapping requires stable phonological representations | Slow because mapping requires stable orthographic patterns | Very slow because both systems required for orthographic mapping are weak |
| **Reading profile** | Weak decoder; struggles with unfamiliar words; may compensate with context | Good basic decoder but poor sight-word reader; struggles with irregular words and patterns | Common in more severe dyslexia profiles |
| **Error consistency** | Errors are phonologically predictable | Errors are visually predictable | Errors are inconsistent and unpredictable |
| **Instructional priority** | Strengthen phonemic awareness, decoding, and phoneme-grapheme mapping | Strengthen orthographic pattern learning, visual word recognition, and morphological reading | Structured literacy integrating phonological, orthographic, and morphological instruction |

*Note:* Information in this table is based primarily on the following sources: Castles et al. (2022), Deacon and Francis (2023), Hulme and Snowling (2020), Perfetti (2007), Pugh et al. (2000), and Seidenberg and Hoard (2023).

**Articulation cues**

- Teach how sounds are produced (lips, tongue, airflow)
- Supports discrimination of similar phonemes (b/p, d/t, short vowels)

**High-frequency irregular words taught through phonemic anchoring**

- Identify the predictable phonetic parts
- Mark the "heart part" that breaks the rule
- Anchor the word to its phonemes before storing it as a sight word

**Cumulative review and spiraling**

- Revisit previously taught patterns to strengthen retention
- Supports orthographic mapping and decoding fluency

**Helpful Instructional Materials**

- Sound boxes
- Phoneme manipulation tasks
- Decodable readers
- Structured literacy programs

**What NOT to rely on**

- Visual-only memorization
- Predictable text that encourages guessing
- Picture cues
- Whole-word flashcards without phoneme mapping

**2. If the pattern suggests an orthographic processing weakness, strengthen the student's ability to store, retrieve, and apply visual word forms and letter-pattern sequences during reading.**

### Core Instructional Priorities

**Explicit teaching of orthographic patterns**

- -tion, -sion, -ture, -dge, -ck, vowel teams, r-controlled vowels
- Teach what the pattern says in reading and how it behaves in words

**Morphological instruction**

- Prefixes, suffixes, roots
- Why spelling and pronunciation shift (magic → magician; sign → signal)
- Build morphological decoding and meaning-based pattern recognition

**Word study focused on visual patterns**

- Pattern sorts (not sound sorts)
- Highlighting letter sequences
- Comparing visually similar words

**Orthographic mapping routines for reading**

- Say the word
- Tap the sounds
- Identify the tricky part
- Read the word in context
- Re-read for automaticity

**Repeated exposure to irregular words**

- Visual memory + pattern explanation
- Contrast irregular versus regular patterns

**Visual word recognition activities**

- "Does it look right?" comparisons
- Flash recognition of high-frequency words
- Rapid retrieval practice

**Helpful Instructional Materials**

- Pattern-based word lists
- Word study notebooks

- Morphology charts
- Visual scaffolds (color-coding, chunking)

**What NOT to rely on**

- Phonics alone (they need pattern instruction)
- Asking students to "sound it out" for irregular words
- Oral phonemic tasks without visual pattern work

**3. If the pattern suggests both phonological and orthographic weaknesses, strengthen the sound system and the visual pattern system and integrate them.**

### Core Instructional Priorities

**Integrated structured literacy**

- Phonemic awareness + phonics + orthographic mapping + morphology
- Teach → practice → review → spiral

**Intensive, explicit, cumulative instruction**

- Skills are built in a sequence
- Previously taught skills are revisited for consolidation

**High-frequency practice with immediate feedback**

- Corrective modeling
- Guided decoding practice

**Word building (sound + pattern changes)**

- Change one phoneme or grapheme at a time
- Strengthens both decoding and pattern recognition

**Integrated decoding routines**

- Say the word → tap the sounds → map the graphemes → read the word → check the pattern

**Irregular words are taught through both systems**

- Identify the phonetic part
- Identify the "heart part" (see Appendix X for explanation)
- Practice retrieval in connected text

**Instructional Materials That Help**

- Multisensory structured literacy programs
- Word ladders (sound + pattern changes)
- Cumulative review lists
- Decodable + pattern-rich text

**What NOT to rely on**

- Visual memorization alone
- Phonics alone
- Worksheets without explicit instruction

** Instructional recommendations are based primarily on the following sources: Bowers and Bowers (2017), Brady (2020), Ehri (2020, 2022), Goodwin and Ahn (2013), Kilpatrick (2015), Share (1995), and Snow (2020).*

Table J.3 highlights how the same underlying weaknesses in phonological and orthographic processing can surface differently (or similarly) across reading and spelling. Because the spelling appendix preceded this reading appendix, Table J.3 serves as a bridge between the two, showing how parallel error patterns reflect shared cognitive mechanisms. By placing reading and spelling manifestations side-by-side, practitioners

**Table J.3 A Comparison of Reading and Spelling Errors**

| Feature | Reading Error Pattern | Spelling Error Pattern | Likely Weakness |
|---|---|---|---|
| Misheard or misread sounds | Phoneme confusions | Misheard sounds | Phonological |
| Missing or added sounds | Omissions or additions | Omissions or additions | Phonological |
| Reversals of sound order | Reversing phoneme order | Reversing phoneme order | Phonological or Dual |
| Highly phonetic attempts | Phonetic but inaccurate | Phonetic but inaccurate | Phonological |
| Difficulty with irregular words | Phonetically plausible errors | Heart-part errors | Orthographic |
| Pattern errors | Misreading patterns | Misspelling patterns | Orthographic |
| Letter-order errors | Letter sequence errors | Letter sequence errors | Orthographic or Dual |
| Inconsistent attempts | Same word read differently | Same word spelled differently | Dual |
| Difficulty with morphology | Misreading morphemes | Misspelling morphemes | Phonological, Orthographic, or Dual |
| Slow, effortful reading | Slow decoding | Slow spelling production | Phonological or Dual |
| Weak sight-word reading | Slow retrieval | Slow retrieval | Orthographic or Dual |

Ehri (1998, 2022), Ouellette and Sénéchal (2022), Shaywitz and Shaywitz (2005), Snowling (2000), and Torgesen (2000).

can more easily identify whether a student's profile reflects phonological, orthographic, or dual-deficit processing, and can interpret reading errors with the same diagnostic precision applied to spelling.

## CONCLUSION

Reading errors provide one of the clearest windows into the cognitive and linguistic processes that support skilled reading. When psychologists analyze these errors through a structured framework, they can determine whether a student's difficulties stem from weaknesses in phonological decoding, orthographic pattern learning, or both. These distinctions are essential for valid SLD identification, as they clarify the specific processes that are impaired and guide the selection of interventions that address the root cause of the difficulty rather than its surface symptoms.

The tables and explanations in this appendix are designed to support psychologists in making these determinations with clarity and confidence. By linking observable reading behaviors to underlying mechanisms and then to instructional priorities, the framework ensures that assessment leads directly to meaningful, targeted support. Ultimately, effective intervention depends on understanding how a student processes print and where the breakdown occurs. When interpreted through the lens of linguistic and cognitive science, reading errors provide powerful diagnostic information that strengthens both eligibility decisions and instructional recommendations.

## REFERENCES


Adams, M. J. (1990). *Beginning to read: Thinking and learning about print*. MIT Press.

Bowers, P. N., & Bowers, J. S. (2017). Beyond phonics: The case for teaching children the logic of the English spelling system. *Educational Psychologist, 52*(2), 124–141. https://doi.org/10.1080/00461520.2017.1288571.

Brady, S. (2020). A 2020 perspective on phonemic awareness: Why, when, and how to teach it. *The Reading League Journal, 1*(2), 55–63.

Castles, A., Coltheart, M., Larsen, L., Jones, P., Saunders, S., & McArthur, G. (2022). What is the evidence for phonics instruction in teaching reading? *Educational Psychology Review, 34*(3), 1771–1799.

Castles, A., & Nation, K. (2006). How does orthographic learning happen? *Journal of Research in Reading, 29*(1), 1–9.

Deacon, S. H., & Francis, K. (2023). Morphological instruction and literacy: A contemporary review. *Journal of Learning Disabilities, 56*(2), 83–98.

Ehri, L. C. (2022). What teachers need to know and do to teach letter–sounds, phonemic awareness, word reading, and phonics. *The Reading Teacher, 76*(1), 53–61.

Ehri, L. C. (2020). The science of learning to read words. *The Reading League Journal, 1*(3), 5–12.

Ehri, L. C. (1998). Research on learning to read and spell: A personal-historical perspective. *Scientific Studies of Reading, 2*(2), 97–114.

Goodwin, A. P., & Ahn, S. (2013). A meta-analysis of morphological interventions in English: Effects on literacy outcomes for school-age children. *Scientific Studies of Reading, 17*(4), 257–285.

Hulme, C., & Snowling, M. J. (2016). Reading disorders and dyslexia. *Current Opinion in Pediatrics, 28*(6), 731–735.

Kilpatrick, D. A. (2015). *Essentials of assessing, preventing, and overcoming reading difficulties*. Wiley.

Nation, I. S. P. (2005). Teaching and learning vocabulary. In E. Hinkel (Ed.), *Handbook of research in second language teaching and learning* (pp. 581–595). Routledge.

Ouellette, G., & Sénéchal, M. (2022). Orthographic learning revisited: The role of decoding, vocabulary, and memory. *Scientific Studies of Reading, 26*(2), 97–113.
Perfetti, C. (2007). Reading ability: Lexical quality to comprehension. *Scientific Studies of Reading, 11*(4), 357–383.
Pugh, K. R., Mencl, W. E., & Shaywitz, B. A. (2000). The anatomy of reading disability: Converging evidence for a phonological deficit. *Biological Psychiatry, 47*(4), 332–339.
Rastle, K., & Coltheart, M. (2006). Is there a dual-route to reading? *Trends in Cognitive Sciences, 10*(12), 540–548.
Seidenberg, M. S., & Hoard, M. K. (2023). The reading brain in the digital age. *Annual Review of Linguistics, 9*, 1–22.
Share, D. L. (1995). Phonological recoding and self-teaching: Sine qua non of reading acquisition. *Cognition, 55*(2), 151–218.
Shaywitz, S. E., & Shaywitz, B. A. (2005). Dyslexia (specific reading disability). *Biological Psychiatry, 57*(11), 1301–1309.
Snow, C. E. (2020). The science of reading and the need for a comprehensive approach. *The Reading League Journal, 1*(3), 20–29.
Snowling, M. J. (2000). *Dyslexia* (2nd ed). Blackwell Publishing.
Stanovich, K. E. (1988). Explaining the differences between the dyslexic and the garden-variety poor reader. *Journal of Learning Disabilities, 21*(10), 590–604.
Torgesen, J. K. (2000). Individual differences in response to early interventions in reading. *Learning and Individual Differences, 12*(1), 49–68.
Vellutino, F. R., Fletcher, J. M., Snowling, M. J., & Scanlon, D. M. (2004). Specific reading disability (dyslexia): What have we learned in the past four decades? *Journal of Child Psychology and Psychiatry, 45*(1), 2–40.
Wang, H., Castles, A., & Nation, K. (2019). Vocabulary growth and orthographic learning in children learning to read English. *Scientific Studies of Reading, 23*(1), 8–23.

Appendix K

# PHONOLOGICAL AND ORTHOGRAPHIC SPELLING ERRORS: A DIAGNOSTIC GUIDE AND RELATED INTERVENTIONS

Accurate identification of a Specific Learning Disability (SLD) requires more than documenting low achievement or inconsistent response to intervention. Psychologists must determine why a student struggles. This means that they need to identify which underlying cognitive processes are impaired, how those weaknesses manifest in academic tasks, and whether the pattern is consistent with an SLD. Spelling errors provide one of the most direct and interpretable windows into these underlying processes. Because spelling requires the integration of phonological, orthographic, and morphological knowledge, the nature of a student's errors can reveal which linguistic systems are intact, which are inefficient, and which are significantly impaired (e.g., Castles et al., 2018; Ehri, 2014; Melby-Lervåg et al., 2012).

This appendix provides a structured diagnostic framework for analyzing spelling errors within the context of SLD identification. Table K.1 links observable spelling features to likely phonological, orthographic, or dual-deficit processing weaknesses. Table K.2 extends this analysis by describing the cognitive mechanisms underlying these patterns and clarifying how sound-based and pattern-based systems contribute to reading and spelling development. Together, the information in these tables helps psychologists differentiate between phonological processing deficits, orthographic processing deficits, and mixed profiles. These distinctions are essential when evaluating SLD in Basic Reading Skills, Reading Fluency, or Written Expression.

By grounding interpretation in linguistic science and orthographic learning research, this appendix helps psychologists move beyond surface-level error descriptions toward a deeper understanding of the cognitive architecture of skilled and unskilled spelling. The goal is to support accurate SLD identification and ensure that assessment findings translate directly into targeted, evidence-based intervention recommendations.

Orthographic mapping is the brain's process of *bonding the sounds in spoken words to the letters that represent those sounds.* It requires phonemic awareness, phoneme–grapheme connections, repeated successful decoding, and stable sound representations (Ehri, 2014). Orthographic mapping is *not* a visual memory task. It is a *phonological anchoring process.* A student orthographically maps a word when they can segment its sounds, match each sound to its spelling, and retrieve the word instantly. This is why orthographic mapping breaks down when phonological processing is weak.

**Table K.1 Phonological and Orthographic Spelling Errors**

| Feature Observed in Spelling | Phonological Weakness | Orthographic Weakness | Both Processes Weak (Dual Deficit) |
|---|---|---|---|
| Errors reflect misperceived or inaccurately represented sounds | ✔ Difficulty perceiving sounds | | ✔ If also visually implausible |
| Confusion of similar-sounding consonants | ✔ b/p, d/t, m/n, f/th, ch/sh | | ✔ If pattern errors are also present |
| Vowel confusion | ✔ sed/sid, flut/flute | | ✔ If inconsistent across attempts |
| Missing phonemes | ✔ bak/black, fog/frog | | ✔ If also letter-pattern errors |
| Added phonemes | ✔ filum/film | | ✔ If also irregular word errors |
| Reversed sound order | ✔ gril/girl, flim/film | | ✔ If also visual-sequencing errors |
| Highly phonetic spellings | ✔ wuz, sed, frend | | ✔ If also irregular word errors |
| Same word spelled differently | ✔ If due to unstable sound map* | ✔ If due to weak visual memory** | ✔ If both sound + visual unstable |
| Difficulty with irregular words | | ✔ sed/said, thot/thought | ✔ If also phonologically inaccurate |
| Phonetically plausible but wrong | | ✔ rite/right, thru/through | |
| Difficulty with spelling patterns | | ✔ -tion, -ough, -dge, -ck | ✔ If phoneme errors are also present |
| Difficulty with morphological units | ✔ If sound-based | ✔ If pattern-based | ✔ If both types appear |
| Letter order errors | | ✔ gril/girl, frmo/from | ✔ If also phoneme omissions |
| Difficulty with multi-letter graphemes | | ✔ shugar/sugar, cherch/church | ✔ If also sound confusions |
| Over-reliance on phonetic spelling | ✔ Due to sound weakness | ✔ Due to weak visual memory | ✔ If both systems are weak |
| Errors don't match phonics rules | ✔ If sound-based confusion | | |
| Errors don't match visual patterns | | ✔ If pattern-based confusion | ✔ If also phonologically inaccurate |
| Difficulty decoding AND sight words | ✔ If decoding is the primary issue | ✔ If sight words are primary | ✔ If both are significantly weak |
| Errors are inconsistent and mixed | | | ✔ Strong possible indicator of dual weakness |

*Note:* Information in this table is based primarily on the following sources: Apel (2011), Bear et al. (2016), Cunningham (2006), Moats (2020), and Treiman (1993).

* An unstable sound map means the student does not store or retrieve the sounds in words consistently, so their spelling varies because the underlying phonological representation is weak or fuzzy.

** It is important to distinguish visual memory and orthographic mapping as they are often conflated. Visual memory is *one small piece* of what orthographic mapping requires, but orthographic mapping is primarily a *phonological anchoring process*, rather than a visual memorization task. Visual memory is the ability to remember what something *looks like* (e.g., remembering the visual appearance of a word, recalling letter sequences based on sight, recognizing a word because it "looks right"). This is *not* how skilled readers store most words.

**Table K.2 Underlying Mechanisms of Processing Weaknesses Related to Spelling**

| Underlying Mechanism Category | Phonological Processing Weakness | Orthographic Processing Weakness | Both Processes Weak (Dual Deficit) |
|---|---|---|---|
| Core Cognitive Breakdown | Difficulty perceiving, storing, and manipulating speech sounds | Difficulty storing, retrieving, and consolidating written word patterns | Breakdown in both sound representations and pattern storage |
| Nature of the Representation | Unstable or fuzzy sound map of words | Weak or inefficient orthographic lexicon (letter-pattern memory) | Both sound maps and orthographic representations are unstable |
| Primary System Affected | Phonological system (speech-sound processing) | Orthographic system (pattern learning, letter-sequence memory) | Both phonological and orthographic systems |
| What the Brain Struggles to Do | Accurately hear, segment, blend, or manipulate phonemes | Retain and retrieve spelling patterns, letter sequences, and morphological structures | Build stable sound–letter bonds AND stable spelling patterns |
| Impact on Word Learning | Difficulty decoding unfamiliar words; slow orthographic mapping | Difficulty building a sight-word bank; slow pattern consolidation | Difficulty with both decoding and sight-word growth |
| Impact on Spelling | Errors reflect misheard or misrepresented sounds | Errors reflect poor pattern storage (phonetically plausible but visually wrong) | Errors are inconsistent, mixed, and unpredictable |
| Typical Error Patterns | Missing sounds, added sounds, sound reversals, vowel confusion | Pattern errors (-tion, -ough), irregular word errors, letter-order errors | Errors that don't match phonics OR orthographic rules |
| Fluency Impact | Slow because decoding is effortful | Slow because pattern retrieval is inefficient | Slow because both decoding and retrieval are effortful |
| Morphology Impact | Difficulty hearing morphological changes (plural /s/, tense endings) | Difficulty storing morphological spelling shifts (magic → magician) | Difficulty with both sound-based and pattern-based morphology |
| Sight-Word Development | Slow because mapping requires stable phonemes | Slow because mapping requires stable patterns | Very slow because both systems needed for mapping are weak |
| Reading Profile | Weak decoder, weak speller | Relatively efficient decoder, poor speller (decoding adequate; spelling disproportionately weak) | Weak decoder, poor speller |
| Spelling Profile | Phonetically inaccurate errors | Phonetically accurate but visually incorrect errors | Mixed, inconsistent, unpredictable errors |
| Instructional Priority | Strengthen phonemic awareness + phonics | Strengthen pattern storage + morphology + orthographic mapping | Structured literacy integrating both systems |

*Note:* When phonological processing is intact, but a student still shows an orthographic processing weakness, the underlying issue is typically rooted in inefficient storage, retrieval, or consolidation of written word patterns—not in sound-based skills. Information in this table is based primarily on the following sources: Apel (2011), Decker et al. (2016), Goswami (2015), Hulme et al. (2005), and Treiman and Kessler (2014).

## Intervention Recommendations Based on Spelling Error Patterns*

**1. If the pattern of spelling errors suggests a phonological processing weakness, the goal is to strengthen *the student's ability to perceive, segment, blend, and manipulate sounds.***

### Core Instructional Priorities

- **Explicit phonemic awareness instruction**
  - Segmenting, blending, isolating, deleting, and substituting phonemes
  - Move from oral → letters → connected text
- **Systematic phonics instruction**
  - Direct teaching of sound–symbol correspondences
  - Multi-letter graphemes (sh, ch, th, igh, tion)
- **Decodable text practice**
  - Reinforces newly learned phonics patterns
- **Elkonin boxes/sound boxes**
  - Map each phoneme to a box before writing
- **Articulation cues**
  - Teach how sounds are produced (lips, tongue, airflow)
- **High-frequency irregular words taught through phonemic anchoring**
  - Identify the "heart part" that breaks the rule

*Phonemic anchoring:*

- **Map** each sound to its expected spelling.
- **Anchor** the predictable parts to phonemes.
- **Mark** the heart part (often with a heart symbol) to show the irregularity.

Phonemic anchoring supports orthographic mapping by making the word as decodable as possible and isolating the exception.

**Helpful Instructional Materials**

- Phoneme manipulation tasks
- Sound chips, counters, or tiles
- Decodable readers
- Structured literacy programs (phonics-forward)

**What NOT to rely on**

- Visual-only memorization
- Word walls without phoneme–grapheme mapping
- Worksheets without explicit sound instruction

**2. If the pattern suggests an orthographic processing weakness, *strengthen the student's ability to store, retrieve, and apply visual word forms and spelling patterns.***

### Core Instructional Priorities

- **Explicit teaching of spelling patterns**
  - -tion, -sion, -ture, -dge, -ck, -ough, vowel teams
- **Morphological instruction**
  - Prefixes, suffixes, roots
  - Why spelling changes (hop → hopping; magic → magician)
- **Word study focused on visual patterns**
  - Word sorts (pattern sorts, not sound sorts)
  - Highlighting letter patterns

- **Orthographic mapping practice**
  - Identify the "tricky part"
  - Say the word → tap the sounds → write → check
- **Repeated exposure to irregular words**
  - Visual memory + pattern explanation
- **Visual word recognition activities**
  - "Does it look right?" comparisons
  - Flash recognition of high-frequency words

**Helpful Instructional Materials**

- Word study notebooks
- Pattern-based word lists
- Morphology charts
- Visual scaffolds (color-coding, chunking)

**What NOT to rely on**

- Pure phonics alone (they need pattern instruction)
- Asking them to "sound it out" for irregular words
- Overemphasis on oral phonemic tasks

**3. If the pattern suggests phonological and orthographic weaknesses, *strengthen the sound system and the visual pattern system—and integrate them.***

**Core Instructional Priorities**

- Structured literacy with both components
  - Phonemic awareness + phonics + orthographic mapping + morphology
- Intensive, explicit, cumulative instruction
  - Teach → practice → review → spiral

"Spiral" in this context means to revisit the skill later, after other instruction, to strengthen retention, deepen mastery, and integrate it with new learning. Spiraling supports long-term consolidation, orthographic mapping, skill generalization to new contexts, and retrieval strength (faster and more automatic). Spiraling supports key instructional principles, such as cumulative instruction, distributed practice, orthographic mapping, and pattern consolidation.

- **High-frequency practice with immediate feedback**
  - Dictation with corrective modeling
  - Word building (change one sound or pattern at a time)
- **Integrated sound–symbol–pattern routines**
  - Say the word
  - Tap the sounds
  - Map the graphemes
  - Write the word
  - Check the pattern
- **Teach irregular words using both systems**
  - Identify the phonetic part
  - Identify the "heart part" (see Rapid Reference K.1 for explanation)
  - Practice retrieval

**Instructional Materials That Help**

- Multisensory structured literacy programs
- Word ladders (sound + pattern changes)

- Cumulative review lists
- Decodable + pattern-rich text

**What NOT to rely on**

- Visual memorization alone
- Phonics alone
- Worksheets without explicit instruction

** Instructional recommendations are based primarily on the following sources: Bowers and Bowers (2017), Bowers et al. (2010), Ehri (2014), Hulme et al. (2005), Kilpatrick (2015), Melby-Lervåg et al. (2012), Moats (2020), Share (1995), and Wagner et al. (1994).*

## Rapid Reference K.1

### What "Heart Part" Means in Structured Literacy

In structured literacy, especially in approaches like phonemic anchoring and heart words, the *heart part* refers to the portion of a high-frequency word that cannot be decoded using regular phonics rules and therefore must be learned "by heart." It is the unexpected, nonphonetic, or rule-breaking element of the word—the part that *doesn't map cleanly* from phoneme to grapheme.

Because even irregular words are mostly decodable, the instructional goal is to anchor as much of the word as possible to phonemes, and then isolate the *one small part* that needs extra attention. This prevents students from treating the whole word as a visual blob and instead supports orthographic mapping.

### Examples of Identifying the Heart Part

| Word | Regular Parts | Heart Part | Why It's the Heart Part |
|---|---|---|---|
| said | /s/ = s | ai | "ai" usually spells /ā/, not /ĕ/ |
| does | /d/ = d | oe | "oe" usually spells /ō/, not /ŭ/ |
| give | /g/ = g, /v/ = v | e | Final "e" is not marking a long vowel |
| come | /c/ = c, /m/ = m | o-e | "o-e" usually spells /ō/, not /ŭ/ |
| they | /th/ = th | ey | "ey" usually spells /ē/ |

*Note:* In each case, most of the word is decodable. Only a small piece needs special attention.

## DON'T FORGET

| Pattern | What It Means | What to Do |
|---|---|---|
| **Phonological** | The sound system is weak | Phonemic awareness, phonics, decodable text, sound mapping |
| **Orthographic** | The visual word memory/pattern system is weak | Pattern instruction, morphology, orthographic mapping, word study |
| **Both** | Sound + visual systems are weak | Structured literacy integrating both systems; intensive, explicit, cumulative |

## CONCLUSION

Spelling analysis is a powerful diagnostic tool because it exposes the specific linguistic and cognitive processes a student relies on when attempting to represent spoken language in print. For psychologists engaged in SLD identification, these patterns provide critical evidence about the integrity of the phonological system, the efficiency of orthographic learning, and the degree to which both systems interact to support reading and writing. When interpreted through a structured framework, spelling errors help clarify whether a student's difficulties stem from a phonological processing deficit, an orthographic processing deficit, or a dual weakness. These distinctions directly inform eligibility decisions and intervention planning.

The tables and guidance in this appendix are designed to support psychologists in making these determinations with precision. By linking observable errors to underlying mechanisms and then to instructional priorities, the framework ensures that assessment does not end with classification but leads to meaningful, targeted support. Ultimately, accurate SLD identification depends on understanding *how* a student learns and *where* the breakdown occurs. Spelling analysis, when interpreted through the lens of linguistic and cognitive science, provides one of the clearest pathways to that understanding and strengthens the validity of both diagnostic conclusions and instructional recommendations.

## REFERENCES

Apel, K. (2011). What is orthographic knowledge? *Language, Speech, and Hearing Services in Schools, 42*(4), 592–603. https://doi.org/10.1044/0161-1461(2011/10-0085).

Bear, D. R., Invernizzi, M., Templeton, S., & Johnston, F. (2016). *Words their way: Word study for phonics, vocabulary, and spelling instruction* (6th ed). Pearson.

Bowers, P. N., & Bowers, J. S. (2017). Beyond phonics: The case for teaching children the logic of the English spelling system. *Educational Psychologist, 52*(2), 124–141. https://doi.org/10.1080/00461520.2017.1288571.

Bowers, P. N., Kirby, J. R., & Deacon, S. H. (2010). The effects of morphological instruction on literacy skills: A systematic review. *Review of Educational Research, 80*(2), 144–179. https://doi.org/10.3102/0034654310366689.

Castles, A., Rastle, K., & Nation, K. (2018). Ending the reading wars: Reading acquisition from novice to expert. *Psychological Science in the Public Interest, 19*(1), 5–51. https://doi.org/10.1177/1529100618772271.

Cunningham, A. E. (2006). Accounting for children's orthographic learning while reading text: Do children self-teach? *Journal of Experimental Child Psychology, 95*(1), 56–77. https://doi.org/10.1016/j.jecp.2006.03.008.

Decker, S. L., Roberts, A. M., & Roberts, G. (2016). Cognitive processes underlying reading disabilities: A selective meta-analysis. *Learning and Individual Differences, 49*, 270–277. https://doi.org/10.1016/j.lindif.2016.05.015.

Ehri, L. C. (2014). Orthographic mapping in the acquisition of sight word reading, spelling memory, and vocabulary learning. *Scientific Studies of Reading, 18*(1), 5–21.

Goswami, U. (2015). Sensitivity to sound structure in language: The role of phonology in reading development and dyslexia. *Developmental Science, 18*(4), 979–993. https://doi.org/10.1111/desc.12272.

Hulme, C., Snowling, M. J., Caravolas, M., & Carroll, J. (2005). Phonological skills are (still) key to learning to read words in English. *Journal of Experimental Child Psychology, 92*(4), 239–263.

Kilpatrick, D. A. (2015). *Essentials of assessing, preventing, and overcoming reading difficulties*. Wiley.

Melby-Lervåg, M., Lyster, S. A. H., & Hulme, C. (2012). Phonological skills and their role in learning to read: A meta-analytic review. *Psychological Bulletin, 138*(2), 322–352. https://doi.org/10.1037/a0026744.

Moats, L. C. (2020). *Speech to print: Language essentials for teachers* (3rd ed). Brookes.

Share, D. L. (1995). Phonological recoding and self-teaching: Sine qua non of reading acquisition. *Cognition, 55*(2), 151–218.

Treiman, R. (1993). *Beginning to spell: A study of first-grade children*. Oxford University Press.

Treiman, R., & Kessler, B. (2014). How children learn to write words. In A. Pollatsek & R. Treiman (Eds.), *The Oxford handbook of reading* (pp. 435–452). Oxford University Press.

Wagner, R. K., Torgesen, J. K., & Rashotte, C. A. (1994). Development of reading-related phonological processing abilities: New evidence of bidirectional causality from a latent variable longitudinal study. *Developmental Psychology, 30*(1), 73–87. https://doi.org/10.1037/0012-1649.30.1.73.

Appendix L

# MANIFESTATIONS OF COGNITIVE STRENGTHS

At times, you may have a constellation of scores within a cognitive domain, such as *Gf*, that shows one score is at least average, and all others are below average. Alternatively, you may have a relative strength in a broad CHC ability within a larger profile of weaknesses. In either case, supporting evidence is important to ensure your findings of relative strengths have ecological validity. This appendix is organized by CHC domain. There are three grade levels in each domain: Elementary School (K-5), Middle School (6–8), and High School (9–12). Each CHC domain lists manifestations in reading, writing, and math.

## Fluid Reasoning (*Gf*)

### Manifestations by Grade Level and Academic Area: Reading, Writing, and Math

#### Elementary School (K-5)

##### Reading

- **Phonological pattern recognition:** Quickly identifies sound patterns and applies phonics rules to new words
- **Reading comprehension:** Easily makes inferences beyond explicitly stated information
- **Story structure:** Predicts upcoming events and understands cause-and-effect relationships
- **Vocabulary acquisition:** Rapidly learns new vocabulary from context clues

##### Writing

- **Sentence construction:** Organizes ideas into coherent, well-structured sentences
- **Story planning:** Creates logical story sequences and organizes narrative elements effectively
- **Creative writing:** Generates novel ideas and elaborates on concepts with ease
- **Editing skills:** Identifies and corrects errors independently

##### Math

- **Pattern recognition:** Quickly identifies number patterns, skip-counting sequences, and geometric relationships
- **Problem-solving strategies:** Selects appropriate strategies for word problems with flexibility
- **Mental math:** Demonstrates flexible thinking about numbers and operations
- **Mathematical reasoning:** Understands and explains why math procedures work

#### Middle School (6–8)

##### Reading

- **Abstract thinking:** Understands metaphors, symbolism, and figurative language
- **Complex text structure:** Follows multilayered plots and argument structures with ease
- **Critical analysis:** Compares and contrasts ideas across texts effectively
- **Inference complexity:** Makes sophisticated inferences requiring multiple logical steps

##### Writing

- **Essay organization:** Structures multiparagraph essays with clear, logical flow
- **Argument development:** Generates strong supporting evidence and anticipates counterarguments
- **Revision strategies:** Reorganizes content for clarity and coherence
- **Genre adaptation:** Adjusts writing style for different purposes and audiences

### Math

- **Algebraic thinking:** Understands variables and abstract mathematical relationships
- **Multistep problem solving:** Breaks complex problems into manageable components
- **Mathematical reasoning:** Demonstrates proof-based thinking and logical justification
- **Pattern generalization:** Extends patterns to create rules or formulas

### High School (9–12)

### Reading

- **Complex analysis:** Analyzes multiple themes, perspectives, and layers of meaning
- **Synthesis across texts:** Integrates ideas from multiple sources
- **Theoretical concepts:** Understands abstract philosophical or literary theories
- **Critical evaluation:** Evaluates author bias, argument validity, and source credibility

### Writing

- **Sophisticated argumentation:** Develops nuanced thesis statements and complex arguments
- **Research integration:** Synthesizes multiple sources into coherent analysis
- **Rhetorical awareness:** Adapts writing for sophisticated audiences and purposes
- **Abstract concept development:** Articulates complex or theoretical ideas clearly

### Math

- **Advanced problem solving:** Excels with multistep, nonroutine problems requiring novel approaches
- **Abstract mathematical concepts:** Understands calculus, advanced algebra, and theoretical mathematics
- **Mathematical modeling:** Translates real-world situations into mathematical representations
- **Proof construction:** Demonstrates strong formal mathematical reasoning and logical proof development

## Comprehension Knowledge (*Gc*)

### Manifestations by Grade Level and Academic Area: Reading, Writing, and Math

### Elementary School (K-5)

### Reading

- **Strong vocabulary:** Understands age-appropriate and advanced words
- **Background knowledge:** Easily comprehends texts across a wide range of topics
- **Context clues:** Uses surrounding text to determine word meanings
- **Literal comprehension:** Understands story elements with ease
- **Cultural references:** Recognizes and understands cultural and historical references

### Writing

- **Rich word choice:** Uses varied and precise vocabulary
- **Topic development:** Elaborates on ideas with depth
- **Sentence complexity:** Uses increasingly complex sentence structures
- **Creative expression:** Produces detailed, imaginative stories

### Math

- **Math vocabulary:** Understands and uses terms like "sum," "difference," and "quotient"
- **Word problems:** Easily understands problem contexts
- **Conceptual understanding:** Grasps mathematical concepts with verbal labels
- **Real-world connections**: Connects math to everyday experiences

### Middle School (6–8)

### Reading

- **Academic vocabulary:** Understands discipline-specific terms
- **Complex text comprehension:** Reads informational texts requiring background knowledge

- **Literary analysis:** Understands themes, motifs, and literary devices
- **Cross-curricular reading:** Excels in science and social studies texts
- **Inferential comprehension:** Makes connections between text and prior knowledge

#### Writing

- **Academic writing:** Produces strong informative and persuasive essays
- **Source integration:** Incorporates and cites information from multiple sources
- **Audience awareness:** Adjusts writing for different readers
- **Content development:** Provides depth and detail
- **Research skills:** Evaluates and synthesizes information effectively

#### Math

- **Applied mathematics:** Understands real-world math applications
- **Mathematical reasoning:** Understands concepts embedded in verbal contexts
- **Problem-solving contexts:** Handles unfamiliar scenarios with ease
- **Cross-curricular math:** Applies math in science contexts
- **Mathematical communication:** Explains mathematical thinking clearly

### High School (9–12)

#### Reading

- **Advanced academic texts:** Reads college-level material across disciplines
- **Specialized vocabulary:** Understands technical terms
- **Cultural literacy:** Recognizes historical, literary, and cultural references
- **Critical thinking:** Analyzes complex arguments
- **Independent learning:** Excels in self-directed reading and research

#### Writing

- **Research papers:** Produces sophisticated analysis
- **Argumentative writing:** Develops complex arguments with strong evidence
- **Discipline-specific writing:** Excels in scientific reports, historical analysis, and literary criticism
- **College preparation:** Meets or exceeds college-level writing expectations
- **Professional communication:** Writes effectively for academic and workplace audiences

#### Math

- **Advanced applications:** Excels in calculus, statistics, and advanced problem solving
- **Mathematical modeling:** Creates strong mathematical representations
- **Cross-disciplinary integration:** Applies math in physics, chemistry, and economics
- **College preparation:** Ready for advanced math courses
- **Standardized testing:** Performs well on math sections requiring reading comprehension

## Learning Efficiency (*Gl*)

## Manifestations by Grade Level and Academic Area: Reading, Writing, and Math

### Elementary School (K-5)

#### Reading

- **Rapid phonics acquisition:** Quickly learns letter-sound correspondences
- **Sight word development:** Recognizes high-frequency words with few exposures
- **Reading fluency:** Moves quickly from decoding to automatic recognition
- **Retention:** Retains previously learned reading skills
- **Practice efficiency:** Learns new reading concepts with minimal repetition

#### Writing

- **Letter formation:** Automates handwriting quickly
- **Spelling patterns:** Internalizes spelling rules efficiently

- **Writing stamina:** Sustains writing tasks with ease
- **Skill integration:** Combines spelling, grammar, and ideas smoothly
- **Revision skills:** Develops self-editing skills early

### Math

- **Math facts:** Quickly automates basic facts
- **Procedural learning:** Masters computational algorithms efficiently
- **Conceptual retention:** Retains mathematical concepts over time
- **Transfer:** Applies learned skills to new problems
- **Multistep procedures:** Learns complex processes quickly

## Middle School (6–8)

### Reading

- **Complex decoding:** Reads multisyllabic words with ease
- **Comprehension strategies:** Quickly learns and applies strategies
- **Vocabulary acquisition:** Rapidly learns new academic vocabulary
- **Genre familiarity:** Adapts to different text structures
- **Reading independence:** Becomes an independent reader early

### Writing

- **Essay structure:** Internalizes paragraph and essay patterns
- **Grammar application:** Applies grammar rules consistently
- **Research skills:** Develops strong note-taking and summarizing skills
- **Drafting process:** Writes efficiently with minimal scaffolding
- **Genre conventions:** Masters multiple writing formats

### Math

- **Algebraic thinking:** Quickly understands variables and relationships
- **Problem-solving strategies:** Learns systematic approaches efficiently
- **Fraction concepts:** Understands fraction operations with ease
- **Mathematical reasoning:** Develops logical thinking quickly
- **Calculator efficiency:** Uses tools effectively

## High School (9–12)

### Reading

- **Advanced comprehension:** Develops sophisticated analysis and critical thinking
- **Research proficiency:** Masters advanced research and synthesis skills
- **Literary analysis:** Analyzes complex themes and devices
- **Academic reading:** Adapts quickly to discipline-specific demands
- **Independent learning:** Excels in self-directed learning

### Writing

- **Sophisticated argumentation:** Writes complex analytical and persuasive pieces
- **Research integration:** Integrates sources effectively
- **Voice and style:** Develops a mature writing voice
- **College preparation:** Meets college writing standards
- **Professional writing:** Adapts to workplace and technical writing

### Math

- **Advanced mathematics:** Masters calculus, statistics, and advanced concepts
- **Mathematical modeling:** Applies math to real-world problems
- **Abstract reasoning:** Understands theoretical concepts
- **Technology integration:** Uses advanced mathematical software
- **College readiness:** Prepared for university-level mathematics

## Retrieval Fluency (*Gr*)

### Manifestations by Grade Level and Academic Area: Reading, Writing, and Math

### Elementary School (K-5)

#### Reading

- **Word retrieval:** Quickly retrieves familiar words
- **Reading pace:** Reads smoothly and efficiently
- **Oral reading:** Reads aloud with accuracy and expression
- **Sight word recognition:** Automatically recognizes high-frequency words
- **Reading fluency:** Demonstrates smooth, connected reading

#### Writing

- **Word-finding:** Retrieves vocabulary quickly during composition
- **Vocabulary use:** Uses varied and precise words
- **Spelling retrieval:** Accesses known spelling patterns easily
- **Writing pace:** Writes efficiently
- **Concise expression:** Uses precise terms without circumlocution

#### Math

- **Math fact retrieval:** Quickly recalls basic facts
- **Counting strategies:** Uses efficient mental strategies
- **Number word retrieval:** Names numbers quickly
- **Math vocabulary:** Accesses mathematical terms easily
- **Timed assessments:** Performs well on fluency measures

### Middle School (6–8)

#### Reading

- **Academic vocabulary retrieval:** Quickly accesses content-specific terms
- **Reading comprehension:** Maintains comprehension due to efficient retrieval
- **Oral participation:** Contributes readily to discussions
- **Reading stamina:** Sustains reading without fatigue
- **Text processing:** Processes academic texts efficiently

#### Writing

- **Essay composition:** Retrieves vocabulary and ideas quickly
- **Revision:** Accesses alternative word choices easily
- **Academic writing:** Uses discipline-specific terminology effectively
- **Timed writing:** Performs well under time constraints
- **Idea generation:** Produces ideas readily

#### Math

- **Multistep problem solving:** Retrieves procedures efficiently
- **Mental math:** Performs quick mental calculations
- **Formula retrieval:** Accesses formulas easily
- **Mathematical reasoning:** Communicates mathematical ideas fluently
- **Standardized tests:** Performs well on timed math sections

### High School (9–12)

#### Reading

- **Advanced text processing:** Reads complex texts efficiently
- **Literature analysis:** Retrieves literary terms and concepts quickly
- **Research efficiency:** Processes multiple sources effectively

- **Standardized test reading:** Performs well on timed sections
- **Content area reading:** Accesses technical vocabulary quickly

### Writing

- **Advanced composition:** Uses sophisticated vocabulary and structures
- **Research writing:** Integrates sources efficiently
- **Rhetorical skills:** Accesses appropriate techniques for audience and purpose
- **College essays:** Writes articulate, thoughtful pieces efficiently
- **Professional writing:** Communicates clearly and precisely

### Math

- **Advanced mathematics:** Retrieves algebraic procedures quickly
- **Problem solving:** Accesses multiple strategies efficiently
- **Math-science integration:** Retrieves procedures needed for physics and chemistry
- **Standardized assessments:** Performs well on timed math sections
- **Mathematical communication:** Explains reasoning clearly

## Short-Term Storage and Working Memory (*Gwm*)

## Manifestations by Grade Level and Academic Area: Reading, Writing, and Math

### Elementary School (K-5)

### Reading

- **Phonemic blending:** Holds sounds in mind and blends them accurately
- **Sentence comprehension:** Remembers sentence beginnings and integrates meaning
- **Following directions:** Remembers multistep reading instructions
- **Story comprehension:** Tracks characters, plot, and sequence
- **Phonics application:** Holds phonetic rules in mind while decoding

### Writing

- **Sentence construction:** Maintains ideas while writing longer sentences
- **Spelling during composition:** Holds spelling patterns in mind
- **Multistep writing:** Follows writing steps independently
- **Handwriting:** Automates letter formation, freeing cognitive resources
- **Story writing:** Maintains story elements and sequence

### Math

- **Multistep problems:** Remembers earlier steps while solving
- **Mental math:** Holds numbers in mind during computation
- **Place value:** Tracks place value columns accurately
- **Word problems:** Retains key information while calculating
- **Math procedures:** Remembers and executes multistep algorithms

### Middle School (6–8)

### Reading

- **Complex sentence processing:** Holds multiple clauses in mind
- **Reading comprehension:** Integrates information across paragraphs
- **Note-taking:** Maintains comprehension while taking notes
- **Inference making:** Holds background knowledge and text information together
- **Literature analysis:** Tracks multiple themes and devices

### Writing

- **Essay organization:** Maintains thesis and supporting points
- **Research integration:** Holds multiple source ideas while synthesizing

- **Grammar application:** Maintains sentence structure while writing
- **Revision:** Holds original ideas while editing
- **Paragraph development:** Maintains topic focus

#### Math

- **Algebraic manipulation:** Tracks variables and operations
- **Multistep word problems:** Remembers constraints while solving
- **Geometric proofs:** Holds theorem information and proof steps
- **Fraction operations:** Tracks multiple components
- **Data analysis:** Holds dataset information while calculating

### High School (9–12)

#### Reading

- **Advanced text analysis:** Considers multiple interpretations simultaneously
- **Research synthesis:** Holds information from multiple sources
- **Critical thinking:** Maintains competing arguments and evidence
- **Standardized test reading:** Holds passage information while answering
- **Content integration:** Connects information across subjects

#### Writing

- **Complex argumentation:** Maintains thesis, evidence, and counterarguments
- **Research papers:** Integrates multiple sources while maintaining analysis
- **College essays:** Balances reflection and audience awareness
- **Rhetorical analysis:** Tracks purpose, audience, and strategies
- **Peer editing:** Holds multiple criteria while reviewing

#### Math

- **Advanced problem solving:** Maintains multiple strategies and constraints
- **Calculus procedures:** Holds derivative and integration rules
- **Mathematical modeling:** Maintains real-world context
- **Proof construction:** Holds logical sequence and justifications
- **Statistics:** Maintains dataset characteristics while applying procedures

## Visual Processing (*Gv*)

### Manifestations by Grade Level and Academic Area: Reading, Writing, and Math

### Elementary School (K-5)

#### Reading

- **Letter discrimination:** Easily distinguishes similar letters
- **Word recognition:** Recognizes sight words quickly
- **Line tracking:** Tracks lines accurately
- **Visual scanning:** Efficiently scans text
- **Letter spacing:** Easily identifies word boundaries

#### Writing

- **Letter formation:** Produces consistent letter size and spacing
- **Spatial organization:** Uses margins and spacing effectively
- **Copying:** Copies accurately from board or book
- **Handwriting legibility:** Produces neat, readable handwriting
- **Visual memory for spelling:** Remembers what words look like

#### Math

- **Number discrimination:** Easily distinguishes similar-looking numbers
- **Column alignment:** Aligns numbers accurately

- **Visual-spatial math:** Understands shapes, patterns, and spatial relationships
- **Symbol recognition:** Recognizes math symbols quickly
- **Place value:** Understands number position visually

### Middle School (6–8)

#### Reading

- **Complex text navigation:** Tracks information across columns and charts
- **Graphic interpretation:** Reads and interprets charts, graphs, and diagrams
- **Visual text features:** Notices sidebars, captions, and highlights
- **Reading stamina:** Sustains visual attention
- **Digital text:** Navigates online texts effectively

#### Writing

- **Essay organization:** Organizes paragraphs visually
- **Note-taking:** Creates visually coherent notes
- **Research formatting:** Formats citations and papers correctly
- **Editing:** Notices visual cues for editing
- **Technology integration:** Uses word processing tools effectively

#### Math

- **Algebraic notation:** Reads and writes complex expressions
- **Geometric reasoning:** Understands shapes, angles, and transformations
- **Graph interpretation:** Reads coordinate planes and data displays
- **Multistep organization:** Organizes work clearly
- **Formula application:** Applies formulas accurately

### High School (9–12)

#### Reading

- **Advanced text analysis:** Processes complex visual layouts
- **Research skills:** Navigates databases and digital tools
- **Scientific diagrams:** Interprets complex charts and diagrams
- **Literature analysis:** Notices visual literary devices
- **Standardized test navigation:** Handles complex test formats

#### Writing

- **Advanced composition:** Produces visually organized essays and papers
- **Technical writing:** Meets formatting requirements
- **College materials:** Creates visually strong portfolios and resumes
- **Digital literacy:** Creates well-organized digital presentations
- **Professional communication:** Produces visually clear documents

#### Math

- **Advanced mathematics:** Reads complex notation
- **Mathematical modeling:** Creates visual representations
- **Technology integration:** Uses graphing calculators and software
- **Applied mathematics:** Interprets real-world visual data
- **Standardized assessments:** Performs well on visually complex items

## Auditory Processing (*Ga*—General)

### Manifestations by Grade Level and Academic Area: Reading, Writing, and Math

### Elementary School (K-5)

#### Reading

- **Phonemic awareness:** Identifies, blends, and manipulates sounds easily
- **Phonics:** Distinguishes similar sounds accurately

- **Rhyming:** Recognizes and produces rhymes
- **Sound blending:** Combines phonemes smoothly
- **Auditory discrimination:** Distinguishes similar-sounding words

### Writing

- **Sound-symbol correspondence:** Maps sounds to letters accurately
- **Phonetic spelling:** Uses phonetic knowledge effectively
- **Dictation:** Performs well on dictated tasks
- **Self-monitoring:** Hears errors when reading aloud
- **Sound sequencing:** Maintains correct sound order

### Math

- **Verbal math instruction:** Follows oral directions easily
- **Number word discrimination:** Distinguishes similar-sounding numbers
- **Word problem comprehension:** Understands orally presented problems
- **Skip counting:** Recognizes auditory patterns
- **Math fact recall:** Uses auditory rehearsal effectively

## Middle School (6–8)

### Reading

- **Phonological processing:** Handles complex phonological patterns in multisyllabic academic vocabulary
- **Oral reading:** Reads aloud with accurate pronunciation and smooth phrasing
- **Vocabulary development:** Learns new words efficiently through auditory exposure
- **Fluency:** Demonstrates strong prosody and rhythm in oral reading
- **Listening comprehension:** Understands lectures and audio materials with ease

### Writing

- **Complex spelling patterns:** Applies advanced spelling rules involving similar-sounding letter combinations
- **Proofreading:** Detects errors effectively when reading and writing aloud
- **Note-taking:** Processes oral information quickly and records key ideas accurately
- **Grammar awareness:** "Hears" grammatical correctness and uses it to guide writing
- **Dictated tasks:** Performs well on writing assignments delivered orally

### Math

- **Multistep verbal problems:** Follows complex oral math instructions accurately
- **Mathematical discourse:** Participates actively in math discussions and explains reasoning clearly
- **Algebraic language:** Distinguishes and uses similar-sounding mathematical terms correctly
- **Formula recall:** Uses auditory rehearsal effectively to remember formulas
- **Collaborative problem solving:** Follows peer explanations and contributes meaningfully

## High School (9–12)

### Reading

- **Advanced phonological processing:** Pronounces technical and academic vocabulary accurately
- **Literature analysis:** Appreciates sound-based literary devices (alliteration, rhythm, and assonance)
- **Foreign language learning:** Learns pronunciation and auditory distinctions efficiently
- **Lecture processing:** Extracts key ideas from fast-paced lectures
- **Audio-visual integration:** Integrates information from text and audio presentations

### Writing

- **Advanced composition:** Uses rhythm, flow, and sound awareness to strengthen writing
- **Research integration:** Incorporates information from interviews and audio sources effectively
- **Peer review:** Gives and receives oral feedback with clarity
- **Presentation skills:** Monitors speech patterns and vocal delivery effectively
- **Technical writing:** Uses precise language where similar-sounding terms differ in meaning

### Math

- **Advanced mathematical reasoning:** Follows complex oral explanations of mathematical concepts
- **STEM integration:** Understands verbally delivered mathematical explanations in science courses
- **Collaborative problem solving:** Communicates mathematical reasoning clearly in group settings
- **Test-taking:** Performs well on oral or verbally supported math tasks
- **College preparation:** Succeeds in lecture-heavy math courses

## Auditory Processing (*Ga*—Phonological Processing/Phonemic Awareness)

## Manifestations by Grade Level and Academic Area: Reading, Writing, and Math

### Elementary School (K-5)

### Reading

- **Phoneme isolation:** Easily identifies individual sounds in words
- **Sound blending:** Quickly blends phonemes to form words
- **Sound segmentation:** Breaks words into phonemes accurately
- **Phoneme manipulation:** Easily adds, deletes, or substitutes sounds
- **Rhyme recognition:** Identifies and generates rhyming words
- **Syllable awareness:** Counts and segments syllables accurately
- **Decoding:** Learns sound-symbol correspondences rapidly

### Writing

- **Invented spelling:** Produces phonologically accurate early spellings
- **Sound–symbol mapping:** Connects sounds to letters with ease
- **Spelling development:** Progresses quickly through spelling stages
- **Letter-sound consistency:** Applies phonics knowledge consistently
- **Word writing:** Spells simple, phonetically regular words accurately

### Math

- **Number word discrimination:** Distinguishes similar-sounding number words
- **Rhyming patterns:** Uses counting songs and rhymes effectively
- **Verbal math instructions:** Follows oral directions accurately
- **Word problem comprehension:** Understands math problems presented orally
- **Math vocabulary:** Distinguishes similar-sounding math terms

### Middle School (6–8)

### Reading

- **Advanced phonological patterns:** Handles complex syllable structures and morphophonemic patterns
- **Multisyllabic word reading:** Breaks down and pronounces long academic vocabulary accurately
- **Reading fluency:** Reads smoothly with strong decoding efficiency
- **Phonological recoding:** Uses sound-based strategies to read unfamiliar words
- **Vocabulary development:** Learns new words quickly due to clear phonological representations

### Writing

- **Complex spelling patterns:** Applies advanced spelling rules accurately
- **Morphological spelling:** Uses prefixes, suffixes, and roots effectively
- **Homophones:** Distinguishes and uses homophones correctly
- **Proofreading:** Detects phonological errors when reading aloud
- **Academic vocabulary spelling:** Spells discipline-specific terms accurately

### Math

- **Mathematical discourse:** Participates effectively in oral math discussions
- **Complex word problems:** Processes mathematical language efficiently

- **Algebraic language:** Distinguishes similar-sounding math terms (coefficient/quotient)
- **Mathematical reasoning:** Follows complex verbal explanations
- **Formula verbalization:** Recites and explains procedures accurately

### High School (9–12)

#### Reading

- **Academic vocabulary:** Pronounces and recognizes advanced academic terms accurately
- **Foreign language learning:** Learns phonological systems efficiently
- **Literature analysis:** Appreciates phonological literary devices
- **Technical reading:** Pronounces scientific and technical terminology accurately
- **Reading efficiency:** Reads quickly and accurately across subjects

#### Writing

- **Advanced composition:** Uses sophisticated vocabulary confidently
- **Technical writing:** Spells specialized terminology accurately
- **Editing skills:** Detects and corrects phonological errors
- **Professional preparation:** Produces spelling-accurate writing for college/workplace
- **Creative expression:** Uses rich vocabulary due to strong phonological foundations

#### Math

- **Mathematical language:** Uses complex terminology accurately
- **STEM integration:** Understands mathematical language in science courses
- **Mathematical communication:** Explains reasoning clearly
- **Collaborative problem solving:** Communicates effectively in group work
- **College preparation:** Ready for university-level mathematical discourse

## Orthographic Processing (*OP*)

## Manifestations by Grade Level and Academic Area: Reading, Writing, and Math

### Elementary School (K-5)

#### Reading

- **Sight word recognition:** Quickly learns high-frequency irregular words
- **Irregular word reading:** Reads nonphonetic words accurately
- **Reading fluency:** Reads smoothly due to strong whole-word recognition
- **Word pattern recognition:** Recognizes common letter chunks and morphemes
- **Visual word memory:** Stores and retrieves visual word forms efficiently

#### Writing

- **Spelling accuracy:** Spells irregular words correctly
- **Orthographic awareness:** Uses conventional spelling patterns
- **Consistent spelling:** Spells the same word consistently
- **Visual spelling strategies:** Uses "looks right" judgment effectively
- **Letter pattern mastery:** Applies common spelling patterns accurately

#### Math

- **Math vocabulary:** Recognizes mathematical terms in written form
- **Number word recognition:** Reads number words accurately
- **Symbol recognition:** Recognizes mathematical symbols and notation
- **Word problem reading:** Reads math word problems fluently
- **Mathematical notation:** Uses conventional notation accurately

### Middle School (6–8)

#### Reading

- **Academic vocabulary:** Reads content-specific terms accurately
- **Morphological awareness:** Recognizes roots, prefixes, and suffixes
- **Reading comprehension:** Frees cognitive resources for comprehension due to automatic word recognition
- **Content area reading:** Handles technical vocabulary in science/social studies
- **Reading rate:** Reads at or above grade-level speed

#### Writing

- **Advanced spelling:** Applies complex spelling rules accurately
- **Vocabulary expansion:** Uses sophisticated words confidently
- **Proofreading:** Detects spelling errors effectively
- **Academic writing:** Uses discipline-specific terminology accurately
- **Technology use:** Uses spell-check as a support, not a crutch

#### Math

- **Algebraic notation:** Reads and writes complex expressions accurately
- **Mathematical terms:** Reads and writes advanced vocabulary
- **Formula recognition:** Recognizes and reproduces formulas accurately
- **Geometric terminology:** Uses specialized vocabulary correctly
- **Problem-solving notation:** Organizes mathematical work conventionally

### High School (9–12)

#### Reading

- **Advanced academic texts:** Reads college-level vocabulary accurately
- **Specialized content:** Handles subject-specific terms in AP/advanced courses
- **Standardized tests:** Performs well on vocabulary-heavy sections
- **Independent reading:** Reads widely due to ease with word recognition
- **Foreign language learning:** Learns orthographic systems efficiently

#### Writing

- **College preparation:** Meets college-level spelling expectations
- **Professional writing:** Produces accurate workplace writing
- **Research documentation:** Uses correct citation formats
- **Creative expression:** Uses rich vocabulary without spelling hesitation
- **Digital literacy:** Uses technology to enhance, not compensate for, spelling

#### Math

- **Advanced mathematics:** Reads complex notation accurately
- **STEM writing:** Writes technical explanations clearly
- **Mathematical communication:** Writes clear mathematical proofs
- **College mathematics:** Ready for university-level notation
- **Standardized assessments:** Performs well on visually complex math items

## Processing Speed (*Gs*)

### Manifestations by Grade Level and Academic Area: Reading, Writing, and Math

### Elementary School (K-5)

#### Reading

- **Rapid decoding:** Sounds out unfamiliar words quickly
- **Reading fluency:** Reads smoothly and efficiently
- **Oral reading pace:** Reads aloud at an appropriate, engaging pace

- **Silent reading:** Reads independently at grade-level speed
- **Reading assignments:** Completes reading tasks within typical time frames

### Writing

- **Letter formation:** Writes letters quickly and legibly
- **Copying tasks:** Copies from the board or book efficiently
- **Spelling retrieval:** Retrieves known spellings quickly
- **Composition pace:** Generates and writes ideas efficiently
- **Assignment completion:** Completes writing tasks within allotted time

### Math

- **Math fact retrieval:** Recalls basic facts quickly
- **Computation speed:** Completes calculations efficiently
- **Timed assessments:** Performs well on math fluency measures
- **Problem-solving pace:** Processes word problems efficiently
- **Mental math:** Performs rapid mental calculations

## Middle School (6–8)

### Reading

- **Complex text processing:** Reads longer academic texts efficiently
- **Content area reading:** Completes reading assignments on time
- **Reading comprehension:** Maintains comprehension due to efficient processing
- **Note-taking while reading:** Reads and takes notes simultaneously
- **Research tasks:** Locates and processes information quickly

### Writing

- **Essay composition:** Plans, drafts, and revises efficiently
- **In-class writing:** Performs well on timed writing tasks
- **Note-taking:** Keeps up with the teacher's lectures
- **Research writing:** Integrates sources efficiently
- **Editing and revision:** Proofreads quickly and accurately

### Math

- **Multistep problems:** Processes complex word problems efficiently
- **Mathematical reasoning:** Works through logical steps quickly
- **Geometric constructions:** Completes drawings and measurements efficiently
- **Data analysis:** Processes charts and graphs quickly
- **Standardized testing:** Performs well on timed math sections

## High School (9–12)

### Reading

- **Advanced academic texts:** Processes college-level reading efficiently
- **Standardized test reading:** Performs well on timed reading sections
- **Research efficiency:** Synthesizes multiple sources quickly
- **Literature analysis:** Processes complex literary works efficiently
- **Content integration:** Keeps up with reading demands across AP/honors courses

### Writing

- **College preparation:** Meets college-level timed writing expectations
- **Research papers:** Completes complex writing projects efficiently
- **Standardized essay writing:** Performs well on timed writing assessments
- **In-class assessments:** Completes written exams within time limits
- **Professional writing:** Demonstrates workplace-ready writing fluency

### Math

- **Advanced mathematics:** Processes calculus, statistics, and algebra efficiently
- **STEM applications:** Keeps up with math-intensive science coursework
- **Standardized assessments:** Performs well on timed math sections
- **Mathematical modeling:** Sets up and solves real-world problems efficiently
- **College preparation:** Ready for university-level math processing demands

Appendix M

# CALCULATION OF THE FACILITATING COGNITIVE COMPOSITE IN THE DUAL DISCREPANCY/CONSISTENCY PATTERN OF STRENGTHS AND WEAKNESSES METHOD

In Collaboration with Christopher R. Niileksela, Ph.D.

University of Kansas

The Facilitating Cognitive Composite (FCC) within the Dual Discrepancy/Consistency (DD/C) Pattern of Strengths and Weaknesses (PSW) method serves as a unique and essential estimate of general cognitive ability or *g*. Unlike global scores from individual cognitive and intelligence tests, which include strengths and weaknesses, the FCC includes intact cognitive abilities to approximate a student's cognitive potential for academic skill acquisition and development that rely less or not at all on cognitive weaknesses. For example, if an evaluation includes *Gf, Gc, Gv, Ga, Gr,* and *Gwm*, but *Gr* and *Gwm* are identified as cognitive weaknesses, the FCC is calculated from the remaining intact abilities (i.e., *Gf, Gc, Gv, Ga*). The result is an estimate of *g* that is likely more aligned with the student's relative academic strengths and avoids the "downward pull" of cognitive weaknesses (aggregated into an Inhibiting Cognitive Composite [ICC]) that may be highly related to academic deficits in students with specific learning disabilities (SLDs). The FCC comprises the abilities that, separately or in combination, are likely to *facilitate* learning and academic performance. The ICC comprises abilities that are likely to *inhibit* learning and academic performance. The FCC satisfies the DD/C criterion of *at least average ability to think and reason.*

One question that may arise about using the FCC as an estimate of general ability is whether different combinations of broad Cattell-Horn-Carroll (CHC) abilities reliably estimate *g*. Previous research indicates that IQ scores from commonly used intelligence tests are not perfect indicators of *g*, but they are very highly correlated with *g* (*r*s between IQ scores and latent *g* = .88–.95; Farmer et al., 2014). Importantly, IQ scores that use as few as four subtests that have high *g* loadings can provide estimates of *g* that are as reliable as IQ scores that use more than four subtests (Farmer et al., 2014). To evaluate whether the minimum requirements for FCCs using different combinations of CHC abilities are adequate estimates of *g*, the correlation between each minimum combination and *g* was estimated using the meta-analytic correlations among broad CHC abilities that have been estimated in previous research (e.g., Hajovsky et al., 2025) and are used in the analyses included in Appendix C of this book (Hajovsky & Niileksela).

## METHODOLOGY

To determine which combinations of intact cognitive abilities can serve as adequate FCCs, we first derived *g*-weights for each broad CHC ability. These weights, shown in Table M.1, were calculated from the meta-analytic two-test composite correlation estimates and reflect the relative contribution of each broad ability to general intelligence. Next, the broad abilities were ordered from highest to lowest *g*-loading and grouped into three levels with similar cumulative *g*-weights. These levels serve as the basis for determining which combinations of intact cognitive abilities meet the minimum criteria for an adequate FCC.

Figure M.1 illustrates the model specified in M*plus* used to estimate the implied correlation between latent *g* and an FCC constructed from a specific combination of intact CHC broad cognitive abilities (in this example: *Gc, Ga,* and *Gwm*). All broad cognitive abilities load on a single latent *g* factor, and the FCC composite is modeled as a weighted combination of its constituent abilities using the *g*-weights reported in Table M.1. The dotted line represents the implied correlation between the FCC and *g*, which is not directly estimated but is provided in the M*plus* output. This model structure was used to generate the FCC–*g* correlations reported in Table M.2.

The correlations between each minimum combination[1] of broad CHC cognitive abilities used to estimate the FCC and *g* ranged from .83 to .88. These correlations, shown in Table M.2, are slightly lower than those reported in Farmer et al. (2014), but it is important to note that these FCCs were based on fewer CHC indicators than those included in Farmer et al. (2014). For example, an FCC based on *Gc* and *Gf* correlated .85 with the latent *g* factor. Squaring the correlations between the FCCs and latent *g* yields the variance shared between the FCCs and *g*. This can be interpreted similarly to a reliability coefficient, where *g* represents the "true score" for general intelligence and the FCC

[1] Minimum combinations meet the DD/C criteria for calculation of the FCC but include the fewest intact abilities possible.

**Table M.1 Meta-Analytic *g*-Weights for Broad CHC Abilities Used in FCC Construction**

| | Broad Ability | *g*-Weight Based on Two-Test Composite Correlation Estimates |
|---|---|---|
| Level 1 | *Gc* | .153 |
| | *Gf* | .148 |
| Level 2 | *Gwm* | .132 |
| | *Gv* | .130 |
| | *Ga* | .127 |
| Level 3 | *Gl* | .116 |
| | *Gs* | .102 |
| | *Gr* | .093 |

*Note:* This table presents the *g*-weights derived from the meta-analytic two-test composite correlation estimates. These weights quantify the relative contribution of each Cattell-Horn-Carroll (CHC) broad ability to general intelligence (*g*) and are used to determine which combinations of intact cognitive abilities can serve as adequate facilitating cognitive composites (FCCs) within the Dual Discrepancy/Consistency/Pattern of Strengths and Weaknesses method. The abilities are grouped into three levels based on their cumulative *g*-weights, reflecting their relative importance in estimating *g*. *Gc* = Comprehension Knowledge; *Gf* = Fluid Reasoning; *Gwm* = Working Memory Capacity; *Gv* = Visual Processing; *Ga* = Auditory Processing; *Gl* = Learning Efficiency; *Gs* = Processing Speed; *Gr* = Retrieval Fluency.

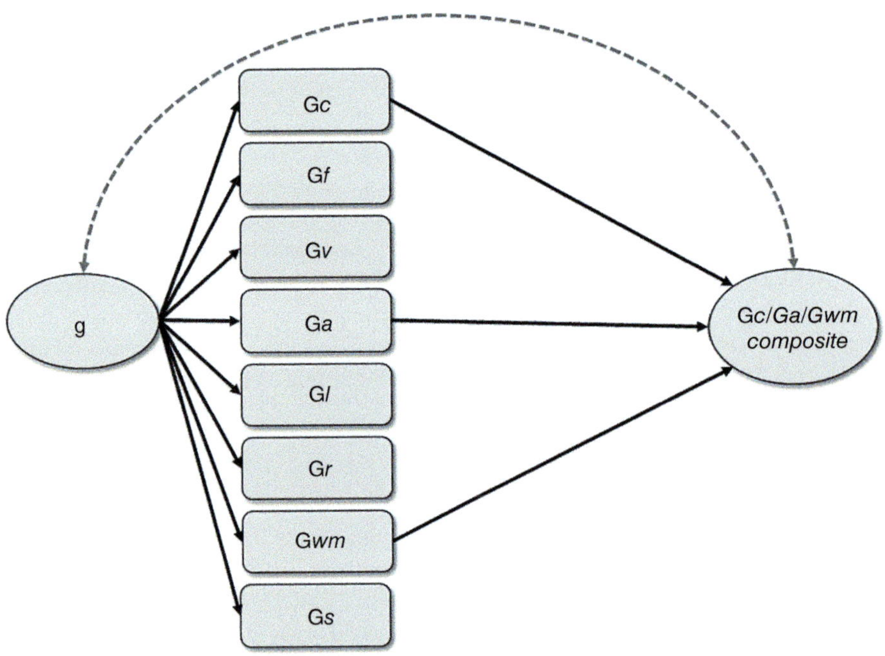


**FIGURE M.1 Structural Model Used to Estimate the Correlation Between Latent g and an FCC**

represents the observed score. For all FCCs estimated in the model, the squared correlations ranged from .68 to .77, suggesting that these combinations are adequate estimates of *g*. These findings align with prior research (e.g., Farmer et al., 2014, 2020) showing that IQ scores based on as few as four high-*g*-loading subtests can approximate *g* as well as composites based on larger batteries. These findings also align with more recent research showing that reliable *g*-estimates require broad, balanced batteries covering at least three broad abilities (Breit et al., 2025), which is precisely the nature of the FCC estimates calculated in the DD/C component of Cross-Battery Assessment Software System (X-BASS).[2]

[2] One exception to Breit et al.'s (2025) recommendation of at least three broad abilities is Level 1 in Table M.1. We allow the FCC to be calculated if only *Gf* and *Gc* are indicated as intact abilities because they have the highest *g*-weights, showing the strongest loadings on general intelligence across decades of factor-analytic research (Carroll, 1993).

**Table M.2 Meta-Analytic Correlations Between FCC Minimum Combinations and Latent *g*, Cognitive Abilities, and Academic Domains**

| Different Types of FCCs | *g* | *Gc* | *Gf* | *Gv* | *Ga* | *Gl* | *Gr* | *Gs* | *Gwm* | LC | OE | BRS | RS | RC | MC | MPS | WA |
|---|---|---|---|---|---|---|---|---|---|---|---|---|---|---|---|---|---|
| 2 Level 1 | | | | | | | | | | | | | | | | | |
| *Gc, Gf* | **.857** | .889 | .887 | .600 | .588 | .539 | .445 | .470 | .581 | .620 | .556 | .637 | .582 | .691 | .617 | .663 | .640 |
| 1 Level 1, 2 Level 2 | | | | | | | | | | | | | | | | | |
| *Gc, Gv, Ga* | **.868** | .855 | .674 | .791 | .796 | .547 | .451 | .476 | .589 | .628 | .564 | .645 | .590 | .700 | .626 | .672 | .649 |
| *Gc, Gv, Gwm* | **.867** | .857 | .674 | .795 | .595 | .546 | .450 | .476 | .783 | .628 | .563 | .644 | .589 | .699 | .625 | .671 | .648 |
| *Gc, Ga, Gwm* | **.877** | .866 | .641 | .558 | .808 | .552 | .455 | .481 | .791 | .635 | .570 | .652 | .596 | .708 | .632 | .679 | .656 |
| *Gf, Gv, Ga* | **.838** | .663 | .859 | .815 | .775 | .528 | .435 | .460 | .569 | .607 | .544 | .623 | .570 | .676 | .604 | .649 | .626 |
| *Gf, Gv, Gwm* | **.836** | .661 | .863 | .819 | .573 | .526 | .434 | .458 | .761 | .605 | .542 | .621 | .568 | .674 | .602 | .647 | .624 |
| *Gf, Ga, Gwm* | **.862** | .682 | .847 | .594 | .800 | .543 | .447 | .473 | .784 | .624 | .560 | .640 | .586 | .695 | .621 | .667 | .644 |
| 1 Level 1, 1 Level 2, 2 Level 3 | | | | | | | | | | | | | | | | | |
| *Gc, Gv, Gl, Gr* | **.870** | .833 | .670 | .759 | .597 | .758 | .628 | .514 | .590 | .630 | .565 | .647 | .592 | .702 | .627 | .674 | .650 |
| *Gc, Gv, Gl, Gs* | **.872** | .832 | .671 | .756 | .598 | .755 | .492 | .660 | .592 | .631 | .566 | .648 | .593 | .703 | .628 | .675 | .652 |
| *Gc, Gv, Gr, Gs* | **.853** | .829 | .659 | .762 | .585 | .537 | .675 | .706 | .578 | .617 | .553 | .633 | .580 | .688 | .614 | .660 | .637 |
| *Gc, Ga, Gl, Gr* | **.878** | .840 | .641 | .558 | .775 | .763 | .633 | .518 | .595 | .635 | .570 | .652 | .597 | .708 | .632 | .679 | .656 |
| *Gc, Ga, Gl, Gs* | **.879** | .838 | .643 | .559 | .773 | .760 | .496 | .665 | .597 | .636 | .571 | .653 | .598 | .709 | .634 | .681 | .657 |
| *Gc, Ga, Gr, Gs* | **.861** | .837 | .629 | .548 | .776 | .542 | .680 | .711 | .584 | .623 | .559 | .640 | .585 | .694 | .620 | .667 | .643 |
| *Gc, Gwm, Gl, Gr* | **.876** | .841 | .640 | .557 | .601 | .766 | .635 | .519 | .763 | .634 | .569 | .651 | .596 | .707 | .632 | .678 | .655 |
| *Gc, Gwm, Gl, Gs* | **.878** | .840 | .642 | .559 | .603 | .763 | .496 | .667 | .760 | .636 | .570 | .653 | .597 | .708 | .633 | .680 | .656 |
| *Gc, Gwm, Gr, Gs* | **.859** | .839 | .628 | .547 | .590 | .541 | .684 | .715 | .763 | .622 | .558 | .638 | .584 | .693 | .619 | .665 | .642 |
| *Gf, Gv, Gl, Gr* | **.847** | .670 | .832 | .783 | .581 | .743 | .616 | .501 | .574 | .613 | .550 | .629 | .576 | .683 | .610 | .656 | .633 |
| *Gf, Gv, Gl, Gs* | **.850** | .672 | .830 | .780 | .583 | .741 | .481 | .648 | .576 | .615 | .552 | .631 | .578 | .685 | .612 | .658 | .635 |
| *Gf, Gv, Gr, Gs* | **.826** | .653 | .832 | .786 | .567 | .520 | .661 | .691 | .560 | .598 | .536 | .614 | .561 | .666 | .595 | .639 | .617 |
| *Gf, Ga, Gl, Gr* | **.866** | .685 | .815 | .589 | .770 | .759 | .629 | .513 | .587 | .627 | .562 | .643 | .589 | .698 | .624 | .670 | .647 |
| *Gf, Ga, Gl, Gs* | **.868** | .687 | .813 | .590 | .768 | .756 | .491 | .661 | .589 | .628 | .563 | .645 | .590 | .700 | .625 | .672 | .649 |
| *Gf, Ga, Gr, Gs* | **.847** | .670 | .815 | .580 | .770 | .533 | .677 | .708 | .575 | .613 | .550 | .629 | .576 | .683 | .610 | .656 | .633 |
| *Gf, Gwm, Gl, Gr* | **.864** | .684 | .818 | .589 | .593 | .762 | .632 | .512 | .757 | .625 | .561 | .642 | .587 | .697 | .623 | .669 | .646 |
| *Gf, Gwm, Gl, Gs* | **.866** | .685 | .815 | .590 | .594 | .759 | .491 | .664 | .755 | .627 | .562 | .644 | .589 | .699 | .624 | .671 | .647 |
| *Gf, Gwm, Gr, Gs* | **.845** | .668 | .817 | .580 | .580 | .532 | .680 | .711 | .756 | .612 | .549 | .628 | .574 | .682 | .609 | .654 | .631 |

*Note:* This table displays the correlations between each minimum facilitating cognitive composite (FCC) combination and the latent *g* factor, estimated using M*plus* 7.4 and the meta-analytic Cattell-Horn-Carroll broad-ability correlation matrix. Each FCC composite was modeled by weighting its constituent broad abilities using the *g*-weights shown in Table M.1. The resulting correlations (ranging from .83 to .88) indicate the degree to which each combination approximates general intelligence and demonstrate that the minimum FCC configurations permitted by the Dual Discrepancy/Consistency Pattern of Strengths and Weaknesses method provide psychometrically adequate estimates of *g*. *g* = general intelligence; *Gc* = Comprehension Knowledge; *Gf* = Fluid Reasoning; *Gv* = Visual Processing; *Ga* = Auditory Processing; *Gl* = Learning Efficiency; *Gr* = Retrieval Fluency; *Gs* = Processing Speed; *Gwm* = Working Memory Capacity; LC = Listening Comprehension; OE = Oral Expression; BRS = Basic Reading Skills; RS = Reading Speed; RC = Reading Comprehension; MC = Math Calculation; MPS = Math Problem Solving; WA = Writing Ability.

It is important to reiterate that the FCCs included in this analysis are the *minimum* requirements for FCCs based on CHC abilities that are considered strengths. For a person with strengths in *Gf, Gc, Gwm*, and *Gv* (i.e., two level 1 and two level 2 abilities), the correlation between this combination and *g* will be higher than *Gc* and *Gf* alone.

## CONCLUSION

The FCC is a central innovation of the DD/C PSW method used in X-BASS. By constructing an estimate of *g* based solely on intact cognitive abilities, the FCC avoids the attenuating influence of cognitive weaknesses and provides a clearer picture of the student's cognitive potential for acquiring and developing specific academic skills. This is particularly important when evaluating patterns of strengths and weaknesses in suspected SLD evaluations. For example, if a cognitive weakness predicts an academic weakness (the consistency component of PSW), the discrepancy between the FCC-predicted academic score and the academic deficit score, if unusual, provides evidence of unexpected underachievement. If cognitive strengths and weaknesses were aggregated (as with total test scores on cognitive batteries), the resultant composite is often not discrepant from the academic weakness, leading to false negatives (i.e., not identifying SLD when it is present).

The meta-analytic *g*-weights (Table M.1), the M*plus* modeling results (Table M.2), and the structural model (Figure M.1) collectively demonstrate that the FCC is a psychometrically sound estimate of general ability. The combinations of intact CHC cognitive abilities permitted by X-BASS consistently correlate strongly with latent *g*, even when based on the minimum number of abilities required by the DD/C method. As a result, the FCC provides a more accurate, defensible, and theoretically aligned estimate of *g*, for the purpose of SLD identification, than traditional IQ scores and overall ability scores from current batteries.

## REFERENCES

Breit, M., Conway, A. R., & Kovacs, K. (2025). 99 ways to obtain a general factor of intelligence-and they are not all created equal. *Journal of Psychoeducational Assessment, 43*(8), 918–932. https://doi.org/10.1177/07342829251380405.

Carroll, J. B. (1993). *Human cognitive abilities: A survey of factor-analytic studiess.* Cambridge University Press https://doi.org/10.1017/CBO9780511571312.

Farmer, R. L., Floyd, R. G., Reynolds, M. R., & Berlin, K. S. (2020). How can general intelligence composites most accurately index psychometric *g* and what might be good enough? *Contemporary School Psychology, 24*(1), 52–67. https://doi.org/10.1007/s40688-019-00244-1.

Farmer, R. L., Floyd, R. G., Reynolds, M. R., & Kranzler, J. H. (2014). IQs are very strong but imperfect indicators of psychometric *g*: Results from joint confirmatory factor analysis. *Psychology in the Schools, 51*(8), 801–813. https://doi.org/10.1002/pits.21785.

Hajovsky, D. B., Niileksela, C. R., Flanagan, D. P., Alfonso, V. C., Schneider, W. J., & Robbins, J. (2025). Toward a consensus model of cognitive–reading achievement relations using meta-structural equation modeling. *Journal of Intelligence, 13*(8), 104.

Appendix N

# MANIFESTATIONS OF AT LEAST AVERAGE ABILITY TO THINK AND REASON ACROSS GRADE LEVELS

This appendix provides a consolidated set of observable manifestations of at least average ability to think and reason across upper elementary, middle school, and high school grade levels. The manifestations listed in the table below are derived from CHC theory (McGrew, 2009; Schneider & McGrew, 2018), developmental research on reasoning (Kuhn, 2009; Zelazo & Carlson, 2012), and grade-band expectations from Common Core State Standards (CCSS) and National Assessment of Educational Progress (NAEP) frameworks. These sources collectively describe how cognitive abilities (*Gf, Gc, Gv, Gwm*, executive functions) typically appear in classroom behavior across grade levels.

In the Dual Discrepancy/Consistency (DD/C) method, the Facilitating Cognitive Composite (FCC) serves as a psychometric estimate of overall ability to think and reason, providing a strengths-based indicator of general cognitive ability (*g*). The examples in this appendix are not intended as a checklist or diagnostic tool; rather, they illustrate what average thinking and reasoning commonly look like in real classrooms. Students may show some manifestations more strongly than others, and variation (sometimes substantial) across domains is typical. Viewed together, however, these examples help clarify the student's overall cognitive competence.

| Domain | Upper Elementary (Grades 3–5) | Middle School (Grades 6–8) | High School (Grades 9–12) |
|---|---|---|---|
| **Problem Solving and Reasoning** | Uses simple strategies to solve problems; identifies patterns; explains thinking; adjusts approach when stuck. | Plans multistep solutions; evaluates strategies; draws logical conclusions from data or text. | Analyzes complex problems; evaluates evidence; justifies conclusions; identifies underlying principles or flaws in reasoning. |
| **Verbal Reasoning and Concept Formation** | Understands grade-level vocabulary; grasps main ideas; groups information meaningfully; follows multistep directions. | Understands abstract academic vocabulary; summarizes complex information; makes inferences; connects new learning to prior knowledge. | Synthesizes information from multiple sources; interprets abstract concepts; makes nuanced inferences; uses advanced academic vocabulary. |
| **Visual-Spatial and Nonverbal Reasoning** | Interprets diagrams, charts, and simple maps; solves visual patterns; mentally manipulates shapes. | Understands models, graphs, and multistep visual representations; recognizes patterns in data. | Interprets complex graphs, models, and technical diagrams; visualizes transformations and relationships in math and science. |
| **Working Memory and Mental Organization** | Holds information long enough to complete tasks; keeps track of steps; organizes ideas in basic writing. | Manages multistep tasks; holds multiple pieces of information in mind; organizes writing and explanations logically. | Integrates information from lectures, readings, and discussions; manages extended, multicomponent tasks; organizes complex arguments or projects. |
| **Flexible Thinking** | Shifts strategies; understands multiple ways to solve problems; adapts when given feedback. | Switches between tasks or perspectives; adapts strategies to new situations; revises thinking when needed. | Evaluates multiple perspectives; adapts reasoning based on new evidence; applies concepts to unfamiliar or real-world contexts. |
| **Academic Indicators of Reasoning** | Understands cause-and-effect; uses context clues; makes predictions; grasps relationships in math. | Analyzes characters, arguments, and data; understands proportional reasoning; interprets scientific relationships. | Analyzes complex texts and arguments; understands relationships among variables and systems; uses logic in advanced math and science. |

## REFERENCES

Kuhn, D. (2009). The development of higher-order reasoning. In M. S. Khine & I. M. Saleh (Eds.), *New science of learning: Cognition, computers and collaboration in education* (pp. 57–78). Springer. https://doi.org/10.1007/978-1-4419-0278-6_4, (doi.org in Bing).

McGrew, K. S. (2009). CHC theory and the human cognitive abilities project: Standing on the shoulders of giants. *Intelligence, 37*(1), 1–10. https://doi.org/10.1016/j.intell.2008.08.004, (doi.org in Bing).

Schneider, W. J., & McGrew, K. S. (2018). The Cattell–Horn–Carroll theory of cognitive abilities. In D. P. Flanagan & E. M. McDonough (Eds.), *Contemporary intellectual assessment: Theories, tests, and issues* (4th ed, pp. 73–163). Guilford Press.

Zelazo, P. D., & Carlson, S. M. (2012). Hot and cool executive function in childhood and adolescence: Development and plasticity. *Child Development Perspectives, 6*(4), 354–360. https://doi.org/10.1111/j.1750-8606.2012.00246.x, (doi.org in Bing).

Appendix O

# CALCULATION OF DOMAIN-SPECIFIC COGNITIVE WEAKNESS AND UNEXPECTED UNDERACHIEVEMENT IN THE DUAL DISCREPANCY/CONSISTENCY PATTERN OF STRENGTHS AND WEAKNESSES METHOD IN X-BASS

The Dual Discrepancy/Consistency (DD/C) Pattern of Strengths and Weaknesses (PSW) method requires evidence of two distinct conditions: a *domain-specific cognitive weakness* and *unexpected underachievement*. These criteria ensure that the student demonstrates (a) a meaningful cognitive processing deficit and (b) an academic skill deficit that is weaker than would be expected based on their cognitive strengths. X-BASS evaluates these criteria using a two-step analytic process that is grounded in psychometric principles and supported by meta-analytic CHC data.

This appendix describes the two-step process. The first step determines whether the difference between the student's FCC and a cognitive or academic weakness is statistically significant, indicating the difference is real and not attributable to measurement error or shared variance. The second step evaluates whether that real difference is statistically rare, using a regression-based prediction model to determine whether the student performed substantially below what would be expected given their FCC. Together, these steps provide a defensible method for identifying domain-specific weaknesses and unexpected underachievement within the DD/C PSW framework.

## Step 1: Determine Whether the Obtained Difference Is Statistically Significant

The first step asks:

***Is the observed difference between the FCC and the cognitive (or academic) weakness large enough to be considered real and not a chance occurrence?***

This step uses:

- the **actual FCC score**
- the **actual cognitive (or academic) weakness score**
- the **reliability** of both scores in the comparison
- the **correlation** between the FCC and the cognitive (or academic) domain

X-BASS applies a **fixed 95% confidence level** (1.65 SD, one-tailed). This threshold is not user-adjustable.

This analysis does **not** involve regression, predicted scores, base rates, or distributions of difference scores. It is simply a test of whether the magnitude of the observed difference exceeds what would be expected from measurement error and shared variance.

If the difference does **not** reach statistical significance:

- the two scores must be treated as **psychometrically equal**
- no meaningful discrepancy exists
- a base-rate analysis would be inappropriate, because one cannot evaluate the rarity of a difference that does not actually exist

Only when a **true, reliable difference** is established does X-BASS proceed to Step 2.

***Summary of Step 1***: X-BASS first tests whether the observed difference between the FCC and a cognitive or academic weakness score is statistically significant. This step uses the actual obtained scores, their reliabilities, and the correlation between them. If the difference does not exceed the 95% confidence threshold, the scores are treated as psychometrically equal, and no further analysis is conducted.

### Step 2: If the Difference Is Significant, Evaluate Whether It Is Statistically Rare (Base-Rate Analysis)

Once a real difference exists, X-BASS determines whether the cognitive or academic weakness is **unexpectedly low** by using a **regression-based prediction model**.

This step answers:

***Given the student's FCC, how far below expectation did they actually perform (in the cognitive or academic area), and is that difference rare or uncommon?***

This process works as follows:

#### 2a. Predict the expected score in the weak cognitive or academic domain

Use:

- **the student's FCC score, and**
- **the correlation between the FCC and the cognitive domain (e.g., Gr) or academic domain (e.g., BRS)**

X-BASS computes a **predicted score** using regression principles.

This predicted score represents w**here students with this FCC typically perform in this cognitive (or academic) domain.**

#### 2b. Compare the predicted score to the student's actual score

X-BASS then determines h**ow far below the predicted score the student actually performed.**

This difference reflects the **unexpected portion** of the weakness.

#### 2c. Generate the distribution of predicted difference scores

To evaluate how rare the difference is, X-BASS mathematically generates a **distribution of difference scores** using the normal probability function.

This distribution represents h**ow much same-age peers with the same predicted score typically vary around that prediction.**

It is based on:

- **the correlation between the FCC and the cognitive (or academic) domain**
- **the standard error of estimate**
- **the assumption of normality**

This is a **hypothetical distribution**, not a sample-based one.

#### 2d. Determine whether the difference is rare

The user selects a base-rate cutoff (e.g., 5%, 10%, or 15%).These correspond to:

- **5% ≈ 1.65 SD**
- **10% ≈ 1.28 SD**
- **15% ≈ 1.00 SD**

X-BASS checks whether the student's observed difference is **equal to or greater than** the SD value associated with the selected base rate. If it does, the weakness is considered **statistically rare** (or unusual).

- **Domain-Specific Cognitive Weakness is identified when the difference between the actual and predicted cognitive scores is rare or uncommon.**
- **Unexpected Underachievement is identified when the difference between the actual and predicted achievement scores is rare or uncommon.**

#### 2e. Apply a small upward adjustment to protect against false negatives

To avoid excluding students who fall just below the cutoff due to measurement error, X-BASS makes a **small upward adjustment** to the observed difference.

This ensures that:

- **students near the cutoff are not penalized**
- **the system errs on the side of identifying meaningful weaknesses**
- **borderline cases are not misclassified as "not rare" or common**

***Summary of Step 2***: When a significant difference exists, X-BASS uses regression to predict the student's expected performance in the weak domain based on their FCC. The gap between the predicted and actual scores is then evaluated against the mathematically generated distribution of difference scores for same-age peers with the same predicted score. This determines whether the weakness is statistically rare at the selected base-rate cutoff.

Together, these features ensure that X-BASS provides a psychometrically defensible method for determining domain-specific cognitive weakness and unexpected underachievement. By requiring a statistically significant and statistically rare or uncommon discrepancy, the DD/C PSW method supports accurate, evidence-based identification of SLD.

Appendix P

# ADDRESSING MEASUREMENT ERROR TO IMPROVE SPECIFIC LEARNING DISABILITY IDENTIFICATION ACCURACY AND SCHOOL PSYCHOLOGISTS' CONFIDENCE

Olivia Rogers, Psy.D.

St. John's University

## INTRODUCTION

Specific Learning Disability (SLD) is the most common special education classification in the United States, with more students identified under this category than the second- and third-most prevalent classifications combined (Fletcher & Miciak, 2019; Maki & Adams, 2022; National Center for Education Statistics [NCES], 2021). Given its prevalence and impact on students' learning and their emotional well-being, accurate and consistent identification of SLD is critical. Yet, despite decades of research and practice, significant debate remains regarding the most reliable and valid methods of SLD identification. Flexibility in operationalizing these methods has resulted in considerable state-to-state variability (e.g., Maki et al., 2015) and mixed findings regarding school psychologists' accuracy in making SLD eligibility decisions (Maki et al., 2017, 2022).

Studies consistently demonstrate that when assessment data are ambiguous, particularly when standardized scores fall near the thresholds considered indicative of a normative weakness, school psychologists' diagnostic accuracy and confidence decrease (Maki et al., 2017, 2018, 2021, 2022; Psyridou et al., 2020; Sullivan et al., 2019). These difficulties appear across identification methods, underscoring the need for additional tools to assist decision-making in borderline cases. That is, cases where assessment data are not definitive.

This appendix provides an overview of a 2025 study (conducted by Olivia Rogers of St. John's University) that was the first to examine whether providing probability-based information increases school psychologists' diagnostic accuracy and confidence in classifying SLD when presented with ambiguous assessment data (score) profiles. Given the high-stakes nature of special education eligibility decisions, improving diagnostic decision-making can increase consistency, accuracy, and equity in identifying students with SLD.

### Challenges Associated with SLD Identification

Identifying SLD remains a complex task because of a lack of consensus on the most effective diagnostic methods and the coexistence of multiple, often conflicting, approaches (Maki et al., 2017; Schroeder et al., 2017). This methodological variability contributes to inconsistent classification practices across states, school districts, and schools, limiting equitable access to services for students with academic challenges (Al Dahhan et al., 2021).

A core conceptual challenge stems from the dimensional nature of SLD. Unlike categorical disorders, which are defined by clear boundaries, dimensional conditions exist along a continuum without natural cut-points (Zachar & Kendler, 2017). SLD falls within this latter category, yet school psychologists are tasked with making yes or no eligibility decisions. This requires the use of artificial thresholds, or "cut points" typically based on empirical associations with academic outcomes and introduces inherent ambiguity into diagnostic decisions as this is in direct opposition to the nature of the disability (Zachar & Kendler, 2017).

SLD is also a latent construct—it cannot be directly observed or measured. All assessment tools, whether standardized tests, observations, or rating scales, are imperfect measures that include error and uncertainty (Fletcher & Miciak, 2019). There is no definitive "litmus test" for SLD; its identification depends entirely on the interpretation of indirect evidence.

### Diagnostic Thresholds and Decision-Making

Due to the dimensional characteristics of SLD, the application of fixed diagnostic cut points introduces inherent limitations. Cognitive and achievement measures used in SLD evaluations exist on a continuum, yet school psychologists must make dichotomous eligibility decisions (Psyridou et al., 2020; Schneider et al., 2024; Zachar & Kendler, 2017). In the absence of a natural threshold that distinguishes students with SLD from those without, any decision boundary, cut-off point, or value is necessarily arbitrary and will produce false negatives and false positives (Miciak et al., 2016; Schneider et al., 2024; Streiner & Cairney, 2007). This issue, measurement error, affects all SLD identification methods—including Aptitude-Achievement Discrepancy, Response to Intervention, and Pattern of Strengths and Weaknesses—which rely on thresholds in some form

(Miciak et al., 2016). Even when cut-points are informed by statistics and based on normative data, identification accuracy remains sensitive to the placement of thresholds, the reliability of measures, and the base rate of SLD in the population (Schneider et al., 2024). As a result, students with marginally different scores may fall on opposite sides of a decision boundary (Schneider & Kaufman, 2017).

While techniques such as receiver operating characteristic analysis have improved classification accuracy in psychiatry by minimizing Type I and Type II errors, they are less applicable to SLD, where a definitive gold standard for classification does not exist (Schneider et al., 2024; Streiner & Cairney, 2007). In the absence of a definitive gold standard for classification, best practice emphasizes integrating multiple data sources, using confidence intervals, and avoiding rigid cut-offs to support more reliable decision-making (Fletcher & Miciak, 2019). Nonetheless, the field continues to lack formalized methods for increasing diagnostic consistency across practitioners and settings.

## The Role of Measurement Error in SLD Identification

Another major concern is the role of measurement error in standardized assessments commonly used in SLD identification. Measurement error refers to the difference between a student's observed score and their true score. It arises from factors such as test design, environmental influences, examiner variability, and the inherent variability in the areas being assessed (Schneider et al., 2024). When measurement error is minimal, classification decisions based on observed scores are likely to approximate those made using true scores if they were obtainable. However, increased error raises the risk of misclassification—particularly for students whose scores fall near diagnostic cut-offs (Psyridou et al., 2020). This concern is amplified in pattern of strengths and weaknesses (PSW) approaches, which rely heavily on interpreting standardized cognitive test scores. Findings from a longitudinal study demonstrated that measurement error and reliance on single cut-off scores significantly compromise the accuracy of identifying reading difficulties, often resulting in misclassification (Psyridou et al., 2020). The authors showed that simulation-based buffer zones can help mitigate the impact of measurement error and the largely arbitrary use of rigid cut-points, leading to more accurate classifications—particularly for students whose scores fall near the threshold. This approach is advantageous because observed scores near the cut-off are at high risk of misrepresenting the student's true score, which may lie on the opposite side of the decision boundary (Schneider et al., 2024). Despite these concerns, few formal safeguards exist to ensure consistent interpretation of assessment data, underscoring the need to continue refining methodology and practice in SLD identification (e.g., Flanagan et al., 2025).

## Confidence and Decision-Making Accuracy

Given the consistent and often heated debate surrounding SLD identification, it is not surprising that school psychologists often report difficulty and uncertainty in making these decisions. In a national survey of 176 school psychologists, confidence ratings in identifying reading disabilities ranged widely from 1 (least confident) to 10 (most confident), with school psychologists reporting significantly lower confidence than those in clinical settings (Al Dahhan et al., 2021). Notably, higher confidence levels were positively correlated with more training in SLD identification during graduate education, highlighting the importance of thorough professional preparation.

Particular confusion arises in the face of ambiguous test score data, namely scores near cut points between normative strengths and weaknesses (e.g., standard scores 85–89). Maki et al. (2017) found that, while overall accuracy in identifying SLD was 73.7%, it decreased to near-chance levels (51.2%) when school psychologists were presented with ambiguous scores near common cut points. These findings underscore the diagnostic uncertainty introduced by scores near cut-points and the need for more robust procedures to support decision-making in such cases. In a follow-up study, Maki et al. (2018) further demonstrated that school psychologists' confidence also significantly declined in these scenarios.

Maki et al. (2022) conducted a vignette-based study evaluating school psychologists' classification accuracy using the Dual-Discrepancy/Consistency (DD/C) method when supported by the Cross-Battery Assessment Software System (X-BASS's) *PSW Analyzer*. The authors concluded that while school psychologists made accurate decisions in clear-cut cases, overall classification accuracy remained low (65%) when qualitative and quantitative data were considered—particularly in ambiguous score profiles. Notably, the authors also found that confidence levels did not significantly differ between accurate and inaccurate decisions, raising concerns that school psychologists may not always recognize when their decisions are incorrect. It also highlights a key gap in the literature; that is how best to support school psychologists in improving classification decisions and calibration between decision accuracy and confidence, especially when evaluating diagnostically ambiguous profiles.

Further supporting these findings, Psyridou et al. (2020) examined the impact of measurement error on the longitudinal stability of reading disability classifications. They concluded that errors around diagnostic thresholds contribute to instability over time and advocated for the use of simulation-based buffer zones to improve classification accuracy—particularly for students earning scores near cut-points.

Despite increasing recognition of these challenges (Al Dahhan et al., 2021; Maki et al., 2017, 2018; Psyridou et al., 2020; Sullivan et al., 2019), the field still lacks standardized, empirically validated procedures to mitigate decision-making variability beyond general recommendations to use multiple data sources and avoid rigid cut-points.

## Probability Interpretation of Ambiguous Scores

Schneider (2022) introduced a conditional positive predictive value (condPPV) model to address the impact of measurement error on score interpretation in SLD identification. The tool applies a probability framework to estimate the likelihood that a student's true score falls on the same side of a diagnostic threshold as their observed score. This approach reframes classification as a probability-based decision rather than a rigid cut-point judgment, making it especially useful for interpreting scores near common or standard thresholds (e.g., SS < 85). Although this application provides a valuable theoretical demonstration of the concepts discussed in Schneider et al. (2024), it was explicitly developed for educational purposes and is not intended for clinical use. Consequently, a gap remains in the field, as no instrument has yet been systematically evaluated or validated to support such applied diagnostic decision-making. The summarized study represents the first empirical effort to bridge the gap by incorporating structured decision support—such as probability estimates and confidence interval cues—to guide school psychologists' real-time interpretations of diagnostically ambiguous scores.

## Current Study

The recently conducted study responded to concerns raised by Maki et al. (2022), who questioned the reliability of PSW-based decisions, even when paired with supporting qualitative information, due to poor classification accuracy in ambiguous cases. In contrast, the study examined whether receiving specific, supplemental information can increase accuracy and confidence in decision-making when using a PSW framework. Grounded in Schneider's (2022) condPPV model, the study incorporated two additional key sources of supplemental information: (1) brief qualitative context (i.e., academic manifestations) linked to each cognitive domain and (2) probability estimates representing the likelihood that an observed score had a corresponding true score that was below the diagnostic threshold (e.g., <85), indicating a true normative weakness. Participants in one group received probability values and a brief psychoeducation module on measurement error, confidence intervals, and the probability of making a correct decision (weakness or not a weakness). This design allowed for a practical test of whether adding probability and manifestation information enhances classification decisions—particularly for diagnostically ambiguous scores.

### Research Questions

Three research questions guided the investigation:

1. To what extent does the provision of contextual and/or probability information influence the accuracy of strength/weakness classifications for ambiguous standard scores (i.e., SS = 85–89)?
2. To what extent does the inclusion of qualitative and/or probability information affect participants' confidence in their classification decisions?
3. How do participants perceive the utility of probability and measurement error information in supporting classification decisions and score interpretation?

# METHOD

## Design Overview

The study used a between-subjects experimental vignette design to examine whether different forms of supplemental decision information improved school psychologists' classification accuracy, confidence, and calibration when evaluating ambiguous cognitive data (i.e., standardized scores) within a PSW framework. Participants were randomly assigned to one of three conditions: Scores Only, Scores + Contextual Academic Information, or Scores + Contextual Academic Information + Probability Information. All participants evaluated the same student vignette, which was designed to mimic real-world assessment data in which standardized cognitive scores fall near common threshold ranges.

## Participants

Participants were recruited via school psychology–focused Facebook groups and professional email listservs. Additional recruitment emails were sent to 101 NASP-accredited or NASP-approved school psychology program directors, requesting distribution of the survey to current students, alumni, and faculty. To reach practicing professionals, 1405 special education administrators (e.g., Directors of Special Education, Assistant Superintendents of Pupil Personnel Services, Committee on Special Education [CSE] Chairs) across six states (Colorado, Massachusetts, New York, New Jersey, Texas, and Wyoming) were contacted via publicly available contact information on state education department websites. These administrators were asked to forward the survey to any school psychologists employed in their districts.

Three hundred fifty-four individuals consented to participate in the study and began the online survey. Of these, 323 met the inclusion criterion of being certified to work as a school psychologist in their state. Full data were available for 301 participants who completed the entire survey and were included in the analyses.

Most participants identified SLD as a high-frequency area of evaluation in their work and reported substantial familiarity with PSW-based approaches, including XBA and DD/C. Demographically and professionally, the sample was consistent with the national school psychology workforce (Goforth et al., 2021). The sample was predominantly female ($n$ = 263, 87.4%), with smaller proportions identifying as male ($n$ = 35, 11.6%), nonbinary/third gender ($n$ = 1, 0.3%), or preferring not to disclose ($n$ = 2, 0.7%). The majority identified as European Origin/White ($n$ = 246, 81.7%), with additional representation from Latino/a or Hispanic ($n$ = 20, 6.6%), African American/Black/African Origin ($n$ = 10, 3.3%), Asian American/Asian Origin/Pacific Islander ($n$ = 8, 2.7%), Biracial/Multiracial ($n$ = 8, 2.7%), and "Other" ($n$ = 8, 2.7%) ethnicities.

Most participants held a Specialist-level degree (e.g., PsyS, EdS, SSP, CAS, or Master's + 30 credits; $n$ = 165, 54.8%), followed by a Master's degree ($n$ = 69, 22.9%) and a Doctoral degree (e.g., PsyD, PhD, EdD; n = 67, 22.3%). With respect to professional experience, 35.5% of the sample reported working in the field for 0–5 years ($n$ = 107), followed by more than 15 years ($n$ = 92, 30.6%), 6–10 years ($n$ = 58, 19.3%), and 11–15 years ($n$ = 44, 14.6%).

## Design and Procedure

Data were collected through the web-based Qualtrics platform. The study was designed to take approximately 5 to 20 minutes to complete depending on randomized group assignment. Following informed consent, participants answered demographic and background questions related to SLD and PSW experience. One inclusion question ("Are you certified to work as a school psychologist in your state?") was used to screen for eligibility. Participants were then randomly assigned to one of three experimental groups (Control Group A, Experimental Group B, or Experimental Group C).

Participants first completed a baseline classification task in which they were shown eight cognitive composite scores presented as standard scores. Participants were instructed to classify each score as a "strength" or "weakness", as per PSW. For each decision, they rated their confidence using a 3-point Likert scale (1 = Not at all confident, 2 = Somewhat confident, 3 = Very confident).

Following the baseline task, each participant was randomly assigned to a group until each experimental condition included 100 completed responses. All participants completed a second task that varied by experimental condition (described in the Experimental Conditions section). After completing their classification task(s), participants were asked to complete an Exit Survey, which assessed their perceptions of score interpretation, the clarity and consistency of PSW rules, and the value of qualitative and/or probability information.

Participants in Control Group A and Experimental Group B responded to seven Exit Survey items using a 5-point Likert scale (1 = Strongly Disagree to 5 = Strongly Agree). Items addressed confidence in interpreting ambiguous scores, the perceived necessity of qualitative information, variability in PSW classification practices, and interest in decision-making tools.

Participants in Experimental Group C completed the same core Exit Survey items, along with four additional items specific to the psychoeducational module and probability information they received. These items evaluated the extent to which information about confidence intervals, measurement error, and probability of a score being a true weakness improved their understanding of test score interpretation, supported their classification decisions, and influenced their likelihood of considering measurement error in future evaluations.

## Scores

The eight composite scores were deliberately selected to vary classification difficulty while minimizing extraneous influences. Four scores were clustered within the most ambiguous interpretive range (SS = 85–89) and served as the primary analytic focus. Two "easy" scores (SS = 100; SS = 75) were positioned approximately 10–11 points beyond the upper and lower bounds of this interval, whereas two "moderate" scores (SS = 92; SS = 82) were placed three points outside the range (see Figure P.1).

Strength–weakness valence was counterbalanced across scores (four strengths; four weaknesses), including within the "difficult" ambiguous range (two strengths; two weaknesses), permitting examination of decision-making under increasing ambiguity while holding constant overall distributional features. As shown in Figure P.1, scores in this study were deemed a "strength" when they met the following criteria: (1) the score's 90% confidence interval included a standard score of 85, and (2) ecological validity via alternative data sources (i.e., qualitative information of observed academic manifestations) ruled out difficulty in the domain. This is in alignment with

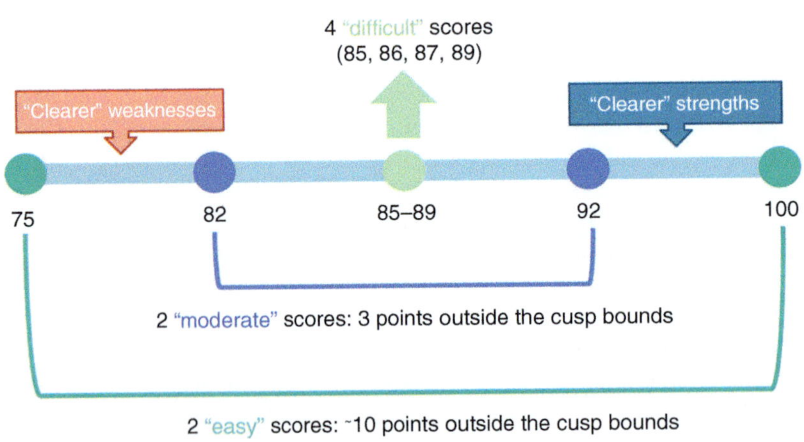


**FIGURE P.1 Strength/Weakness Classification Difficulty for Scores Near and Far from a Threshold of 85**

Flanagan et al. (2018) longstanding assertion that while scores 85–89 are considered *below average* on standardized, norm-referenced tests (where average is defined as standard scores between 90 and 109, inclusive, based on a scale having a mean of 100 and SD of 15), interpreting scores in this very narrow range requires clinical judgement, as abilities with these scores may or may not pose or represent significant problems for the individual.

## Experimental Conditions

**Control Group A—Standard Scores Only.** Participants in Group A completed only the baseline task, followed by the Exit Survey. No additional information was provided.

**Experimental Group B—Standard Scores + Qualitative Context.** After the baseline task, participants in Group B were presented with the same composite standard scores supplemented with brief, observed academic manifestations related to each domain beside each score. These descriptions included brief narrative examples of classroom behavior or academic functioning relevant to each cognitive domain (e.g., easily draws connections between verbal concepts [*Gc*], completes work at an efficient pace [*Gs*], follows multi-step directions well [*Gwm*], etc.). Participants then repeated the PSW designation and confidence-rating task with this additional contextual information.

**Experimental Group C—Standard Scores + Context + Probability Information.** Participants in Group C completed the same baseline task and were then provided with a psychoeducation module covering key psychometric concepts and the application of probability estimates grounded in Schneider's (2022) *condPPV* framework (see examples in Figure P.4). This instructional component aimed to enhance participants' understanding of uncertainty in score interpretation. To ensure comprehension, participants then completed a four-item true/false quiz on these concepts before proceeding. Following the module and quiz, participants were re-presented with the same cognitive standard scores, each accompanied by: (a) qualitative classroom-based manifestations (identical to those used in Group B), (b) the 90% confidence interval for the score, (c) a yes/no statement of whether the confidence interval included scores below the common cut-off (SS = 85), and (d) a probability estimate indicating the likelihood that the individual's true standard score fell below 85 (e.g., "There is a 72% chance this score reflects a true score below 85").

**Examples of Psychoeducation Module.** Participants in Group C received the psychoeducation module in a structured, stepwise format designed to build conceptual understanding through increasing levels of complexity, as outlined in Rapid Reference P.1, and Figures P.2 and P.4. Initial screens introduced foundational psychometric concepts (e.g., measurement error and confidence intervals). Subsequent content addressed the increased likelihood of classification error when rigid cut scores are used. The final segment introduced Schneider's condPPV framework and provided worked examples illustrating how conditional probabilities can be applied to interpret cognitive and academic test results within eligibility decision-making. Participants were also given the module as one comprehensive document available to download and reference as needed throughout the task. See below for examples of presented information.

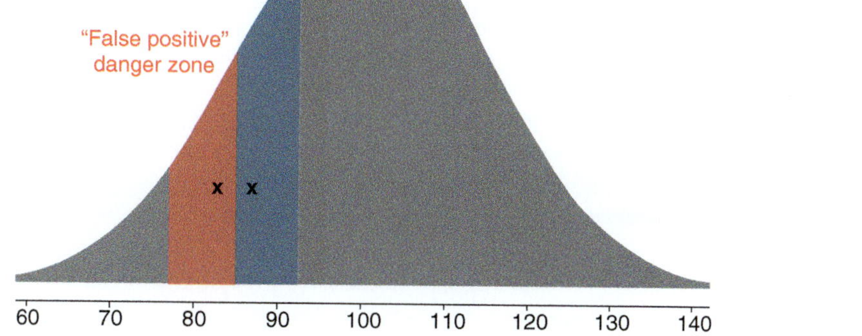


**FIGURE P.2 Making Accurate Strength/Weakness Score Classification Decisions**

## Rapid Reference P.1

*Example of a Psychoeducation Module Used for Group C*

### IMPORTANT TERMS

- Observed score. The actual score a student obtains on a test.
- True score. The theoretical score a student would earn on a test if the test was perfectly reliable.
- Measurement error. The difference between a student's observed score on a test and their true score. All assessments have some degree of error due to factors like fatigue, distraction, test conditions, or the limitations of the test itself.
- Standard Error of Measurement (SEM). An estimate of how much an individual's observed score might vary from their true score. The SEM is used to create confidence intervals around an observed score, providing the range within which a person's true score likely falls.
- Confidence interval. A range of scores in which the true score is expected to fall based on a specified level of confidence (e.g., 68%, 90%, 95%).

### IMPORTANT FACTS

- The cognitive and academic constructs that school psychologists measure (e.g., fluid reasoning, reading decoding) are continuous variables, meaning there is no point along the ability continuum where a cut point can be set that represents a transition from "normal" to "disabled." Regardless of method (e.g., PSW, RTI), all cut points used in SLD identification are *arbitrary*.
- *Nonarbitrary* cut points that distinguish between *meaningful* differences are rare. One example is the freezing point of a liquid. This cut point matters because it is the precise point (32°) at which liquid undergoes a phase transition to a solid state.
- There is no precise cut point where a construct (continuous variable) transitions from *strength to weakness* or from *not SLD* to *SLD*. Instead, cut points used in SLD identification are *thresholds of convenience*, alerting us to possible difficulties that need further exploration (Schneider et al., 2024).

### COMMON CUT POINT USED IN THE PSW METHOD

- A weakness is often defined as a standard score below 85. When a cut point of 85 is used as a natural (nonarbitrary) boundary, *errors are inevitable*, especially when the scores are close to the cut point. These errors occur because continuous variables are used to make dichotomous decisions (strength/weakness), the measures used are imperfectly reliable, and the cut point is arbitrary.

Scores far from the cut point:

- When an observed score is either below or above but ***far from*** the cut point, the observed score and corresponding true score are likely on the *same side* of the cut point, leading to true positives (score is a weakness) and true negatives (score is not a weakness), respectively. The table below illustrates these scenarios.

| | **Observed Score** | **True Score**[a] | **Does *Observed* score meet criteria for Weakness (<85)?** | **Does *True Score* meet criteria for Weakness (<85)?** | **Agreement between True & Observed?** |
|---|---|---|---|---|---|
| Case 1 | 75 | 78 | Yes | Yes | **Yes:** True Positive |
| Case 2 | 91 | 95 | No | No | **Yes:** True Negative |

[a] Scores are for demonstration purposes only. Test correlations and reliabilities are used in the PSW literature to simulate true scores.

Scores close to the cut point:

- When an observed score is either below or above a cut point but *close to* the cut point, the observed score and corresponding true score are likely to be on *opposite sides*, leading to false positives (incorrectly labeling observed score a weakness) and false negatives (incorrectly labeling observed score as not a weakness), respectively. The information below illustrates these scenarios.

| | **Observed Score** | **True Score**[a] | **Does *Observed score* meet criteria for Weakness (<85)?** | **Does *True Score* meet criteria for Weakness (<85)?** | **Agreement between True & Observed?** |
|---|---|---|---|---|---|
| Case 3 | 81 | 86 | Yes | No | **No:** False Positive |
| Case 4 | 87 | 82 | No | Yes | **No:** False Negative |

[a] Scores are for demonstration purposes only. Test correlations and reliabilities are used in the PSW literature to simulate true scores.

## RESULTS

### Classification Accuracy

#### *Within Groups Comparisons*

Participants' classification accuracy improved significantly following the addition of supplemental information in both experimental groups. In the contextual-only condition (Group B), classification accuracy increased from 6.60 (SD = 0.85) to 7.55 (SD = 0.77) out of 8 composite scores, $W = 524.00$, $p < 0.001$, $r = 0.65$. Participants in the contextual-plus-probability condition (Group C) also demonstrated significant improvement, with accuracy increasing from 6.46 (SD = 1.01) to 7.59 (SD = 0.67), $W = 0.00$, $p < 0.001$, $r = 0.82$. These within-group improvements in classification accuracy were statistically significant and reflected large effect sizes, supporting the efficacy of both forms of supplemental information.

#### *Accuracy by Score Type*

When analyzed by score difficulty, classification accuracy for "easy" and "moderate" scores remained high across all groups and time points (97%–100%). In contrast, diagnostically ambiguous ("difficult") scores (standard scores = 85–89) were substantially more challenging at baseline—Group A: 67.6%, Group B Pre: 64.5%, Group C Pre: 65.3%—but improved markedly following the addition of supplemental information (Group B Post: 89.3%; Group C Post: 89.5%). McNemar's tests confirmed significant improvement across all four difficult domains in both experimental groups ($ps < 0.01$), indicating the strongest effects occurred among diagnostically ambiguous scores. Accuracy gains were especially notable for Auditory Processing (Group B: 48% to 83%; Group C: 47% to 84%), Working Memory (Group B: 61% to 90%; Group C: 70% to 89%), and Retrieval Fluency (Group B: 67% to 88%; Group C: 57% to 88%). Following the supplemental information, both groups achieved ≥88% accuracy across all domains, underscoring the effectiveness of the added information, particularly in supporting accurate classification of ambiguous scores (see Tables P.1 and P.2; Figure P.3).

*Note for Figure P.3.* This figure depicts mean classification accuracy (%) in the cognitive domains for the four "difficult" scores—Processing Speed (SS = 89), Auditory Processing (SS = 86), Working Memory (SS = 87), and Retrieval Fluency (SS = 85)—across five group/time-point combinations: Group A (control), Group B pre- and posttest and Group C pre- and posttest. Accuracy improved posttest in both experimental groups (Groups B and C), particularly in domains with lower baseline accuracy. Baseline accuracy was comparable across all three groups.

### Between-Group Comparisons

The results revealed a significant difference in median accuracy scores across the three groups, $H(2) = 397.90$, $p < 0.0001$. Group A, which received no additional information, achieved a mean posttest accuracy of 6.55 (SD = 0.78), comparable to the pretest accuracy of Groups B and C and confirming similar baselines. However, Group A's accuracy was significantly lower than the posttest accuracy of Group B (M = 7.47, SD = 0.93) and Group C (M = 7.22, SD = 1.00), indicating meaningful improvements following the supplemental information.

To examine potential differences in performance between the two experimental conditions, Mann–Whitney U tests were conducted comparing posttest accuracy and net change in accuracy for Group B and Group C. Results indicated no significant difference in posttest classification accuracy between the groups, $U = 4935$, $p = 0.844$, suggesting that participants achieved similarly high levels of accuracy following their respective supplemental information. A separate comparison of net change in accuracy likewise revealed no significant difference, $U = 4948$, $p = 0.895$, indicating that both groups improved by a comparable magnitude. Together, these findings support the conclusion that the two types of supplemental information were similarly effective in enhancing participants' classification performance.

**Table P.1 Classification Accuracy (%) by Group and Score Type**

| Domain (SS) | Score Category | Group A | Group B Pre | Group B Post | Group C Pre | Group C Post |
|---|---|---|---|---|---|---|
| *Gc* (100) | Easy | 100 | 100 | 100 | 100 | 100 |
| *Gf* (75) | Easy | 100 | 98 | 99 | 98 | 95 |
| *Gv* (92) | Moderate | 99 | 100 | 98 | 99 | 98 |
| *Gl* (82) | Moderate | 97 | 94 | 96 | 95 | 98 |
| *Gs* (89) | Difficult | 83 | 82 | 96 | 87 | 97 |
| *Ga* (86) | Difficult | 55 | 48 | 83 | 47 | 84 |
| *Gwm* (87) | Difficult | 68 | 61 | 90 | 70 | 89 |
| *Gr* (85) | Difficult | 63 | 67 | 88 | 57 | 88 |

*Note:* SS = standard score. Percentages reflect the proportion of participants in each group who correctly classified each domain as a strength or weakness. Domains are ordered by difficulty level.

**Table P.2 McNemar's Exact Test (Binomial) Results for Accuracy Improvements**

| | | Group B | | | | Group C | | | |
|---|---|---|---|---|---|---|---|---|---|
| Domain (SS) | Score Type | b | c | p | Significance | b | c | p | Significance |
| *Gc* (100) | Easy | 0 | 0 | – | – | 0 | 0 | – | – |
| *Gf* (75) | Easy | 1 | 2 | >0.9999 | ns | 4 | 1 | 0.375 | ns |
| *Gv* (92) | Moderate | 2 | 0 | 0.5 | ns | 2 | 1 | >0.9999 | ns |
| *Gl* (82) | Moderate | 2 | 4 | 0.6875 | ns | 2 | 4 | 0.6875 | ns |
| *Gs* (89) | Difficult | 3 | 17 | 0.0026 | ** | 1 | 11 | 0.0063 | ** |
| *Ga* (86) | Difficult | 0 | 34 | <0.0001 | **** | 6 | 42 | <0.0001 | **** |
| *Gwm* (87) | Difficult | 2 | 31 | <0.0001 | **** | 7 | 26 | 0.0013 | ** |
| *Gr* (85) | Difficult | 1 | 22 | <0.0001 | **** | 5 | 36 | <0.0001 | **** |

*Note:* b = number of scores reclassified incorrectly post-supplemental information; c = number of scores reclassified correctly post-supplemental information. McNemar's exact binomial test used to evaluate pre–post change in classification accuracy. $^{**}p < 0.01$. $^{****}p < 0.001$. ns = not significant.

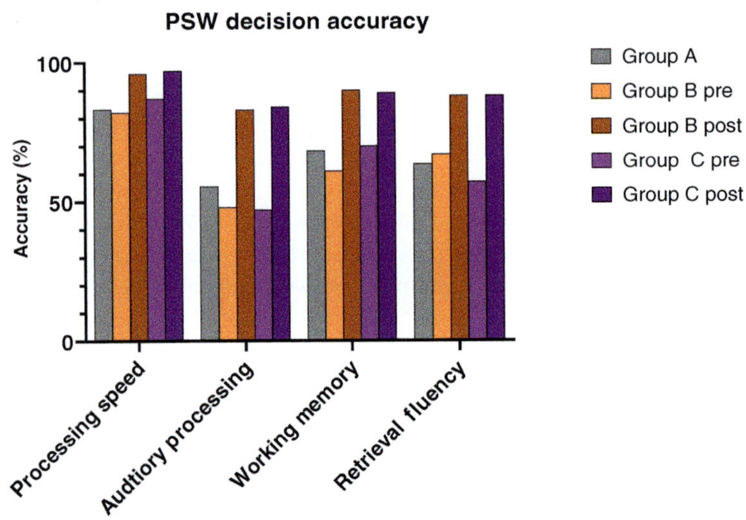


**FIGURE P.3 PSW Decision Accuracy for Ambiguous Scores**

## Confidence Ratings

### *Within Groups Comparisons*

Participants' confidence in their PSW decisions improved significantly following supplemental information in both experimental groups. A Wilcoxon signed-rank test revealed that participants in the contextual-only condition (Group B) demonstrated a significant increase in confidence from pretest to posttest, $W = 2805$, $p < 0.001$, $r = 0.75$, with a median gain of 2 points. Similarly, participants in the contextual-plus-probability condition (Group C) showed a significant increase in confidence ratings, $W = 2937$, $p < 0.001$, $r = 0.58$, with a median gain of 3 points. These within-group improvements were statistically significant and suggest that both sets of supplemental information successfully enhanced participants' certainty in their PSW decisions (i.e., weakness or not a weakness).

### *Confidence by Score Type*

Confidence ratings were also examined for the subset of diagnostically ambiguous "difficult" scores (standard scores = 85–89), which were a primary focus of the study. Median posttest confidence ratings for these four scores were 1.5 in Group B and 1.0 in Group C. A

**Table P.3 Between-Group Comparisons of Classification Confidence**

| Comparison | Test | Test Statistic | P Significance | Interpretation |
|---|---|---|---|---|
| Group A vs. Group B (Posttest) | Dunn's post hoc (Kruskal–Wallis) | $Z = 3.72$ | .0008*** | Group B > A |
| Group A vs. Group C (Posttest) | Dunn's post hoc (Kruskal–Wallis) | $Z = 3.55$ | .0015** | Group C > A |
| Group A vs. Group B (Net Change) | Dunn's post hoc (Kruskal–Wallis) | $Z = 9.79$ | <.0001**** | Group B > A |
| Group A vs. Group C (Net Change) | Dunn's post hoc (Kruskal–Wallis) | $Z = 9.86$ | <.0001**** | Group C > A |
| Group B vs. Group C (Posttest) | Mann–Whitney U test | $U = 4823$ | .663 ns | No difference |
| Group B vs. Group C (Net Change) | Mann–Whitney U test | $U = 4955$ | .912 ns | No difference |

*Note:* Kruskal–Wallis tests with Dunn's post hoc pairwise comparisons were used to evaluate differences across groups. Mann–Whitney U tests were used to compare experimental groups. **$p < .01$. ***$p < .001$. ****$p < .0001$. ns = not significant.

Mann–Whitney U test indicated no significant difference between the groups on these items, $U = 4678$, $p = 0.426$, suggesting that both types of supplemental information led to similarly elevated confidence when interpreting diagnostically ambiguous scores.

***Between Groups Comparisons***

To evaluate differences in confidence ratings across all groups, Kruskal–Wallis tests were conducted comparing posttest confidence and net change in confidence from pre- to posttest. Results revealed significant differences among the three groups on both outcomes. Follow-up pairwise comparisons using Dunn's post hoc tests indicated that both experimental groups reported significantly greater posttest confidence than the control group. Specifically, Group B reported higher confidence than Group A, $Z = 3.72$, $p = 0.0008$, and Group C likewise reported higher confidence than Group A, $Z = 3.55$, $p = 0.0015$ (see Table P.3).

For net change in confidence, Dunn's post hoc tests again showed significant differences between the control group and both experimental groups. Group B demonstrated significantly greater improvement than Group A, $Z = 9.79$, $p < .0001$, as did Group C, $Z = 9.86$, $p < .0001$. These findings confirm that both types of supplemental information produced substantial improvements in participants' confidence from pretest to posttest.

To compare directly the effectiveness of the two types of supplemental information, Mann–Whitney U tests were conducted on posttest confidence and net change scores between experimental groups. No significant difference emerged between Group B and Group C on posttest confidence ratings, $U = 4823$, $p = .663$, or on overall confidence gain, $U = 4955$, $p = .912$. These results suggest that both types of supplemental information yielded comparable improvements in confidence and were similarly effective in enhancing perceived classification (strength/weakness) certainty.

## Calibration Analysis

In the present study, *calibration* refers to the degree of correspondence between participants' reported confidence in their classifications and the objective accuracy of those classifications. A well-calibrated judgment is one in which subjective confidence closely matches the observed probability of being correct (e.g., decisions made with 80% confidence are correct approximately 80% of the time). Overconfidence reflects confidence exceeding observed accuracy, whereas underconfidence reflects confidence lower than observed accuracy. Calibration was evaluated using calibration curves, which plot mean confidence against observed accuracy across levels of reported certainty. Calibration curves were examined to evaluate the alignment between participants' confidence ratings and actual classification accuracy for the four diagnostically ambiguous cognitive scores (Retrieval Fluency: SS = 85, Auditory Processing: SS = 86, Working Memory: SS = 87, and Processing Speed: SS = 89; Figure P.4). In the control condition (Group A), curves indicated overconfidence. Initial curves for the experimental groups (B and C) showed inconsistent calibration across domains, with some evidence of overconfidence. After receiving the supplemental information, the experimental groups demonstrated upward shifts in their curves, reflecting improved accuracy across all confidence levels, with the largest gains observed in moderately and highly confident decisions. Gains were particularly pronounced in Group C, which achieved near-perfect calibration at the highest confidence level in all four domains.

*Note.* This figure demonstrates the relationship between participant confidence levels and classification accuracy for four diagnostically ambiguous scores. Data are shown separately for each group and time point. Calibration improved posttest for Groups B and C, with accuracy increasing alongside confidence for most domains. Control group calibration remained relatively flat or declined at higher confidence levels, particularly in Retrieval Fluency and Auditory Processing.

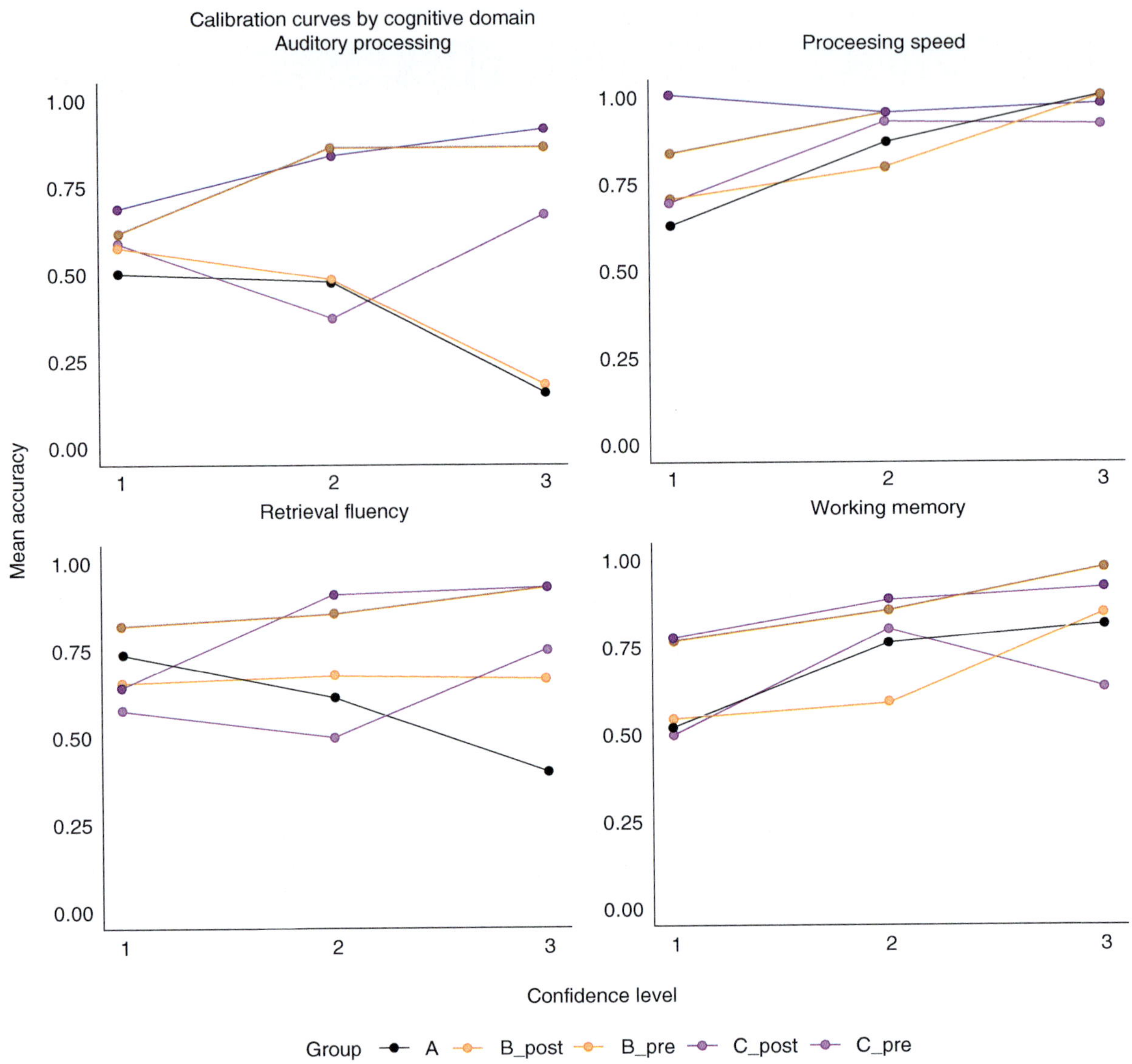


**FIGURE P.4 Calibration Curves for Ambiguous Scores**

## Participant Feedback and Perceived Utility

### *Perceived PSW Competence*

Participants rated their general confidence in making PSW decisions (i.e., classifying scores as a strength or weakness) before and after receiving the supplemental information. A Kruskal–Wallis H test revealed significant differences in change scores across the groups, $H(2) = 16.77$, $p < .001$. Only Group C, which received contextual and probability-based information, demonstrated a significant within-group improvement, $W = 210.5$, $p < .001$ (Wilcoxon signed-rank test). Post hoc comparisons using Mann–Whitney U tests indicated that Group C outperformed the control group ($U = 6392.0$, $p = .0003$, $r = .23$) and Group B ($U = 6323.0$, $p = .0004$, $r = .23$). These findings suggest that the combination of contextual and probability information was uniquely effective in enhancing perceived competence and understanding of score interpretation (see Table P.4).

### *Confidence in Interpreting Ambiguous Scores*

One item on the exit survey assessed participants' confidence in interpreting diagnostically ambiguous scores. A Kruskal–Wallis H test revealed significant differences across groups, H(2) = 12.42, p = .002. Post hoc Mann–Whitney U tests indicated that Experimental Groups B reported significantly greater confidence than the control group (M = 3.42), p = 0.49, as did Experimental Group C (M = 3.90), p = .002.

A chi-square test of independence confirmed significant differences in the distribution of confidence ratings across groups, $\chi^2(8) = 16.57$, p = .035, with control participants more likely to endorse lower confidence levels. These results suggest that both types of supplemental information improved perceived confidence when interpreting diagnostically ambiguous scores.

**Table P.4 Self-Reported Confidence in PSW Decision-Making Ability**

| Comparison | Statistic | P | Significance | Effect Size |
|---|---|---|---|---|
| **Within-Group Comparisons** | | | | |
| Group C (Pre–Post) | $W = 210.5$ | <.001 | *** | – |
| Group B (Pre–Post) | $W = 566.0$ | .1513 | ns | – |
| **Between-Group Comparisons** | | | | |
| Group C vs. Control A | $U = 6392.0$ | .0003 | *** | r = .23 |
| Group B vs. Control A | $U = 4810.5$ | .2444 | ns | r = .09 |
| Group C vs. Group B | $U = 6323.0$ | .0004 | *** | r = .23 |

*Note:* W = Wilcoxon signed-rank test statistic. U = Mann–Whitney U test statistic. Effect size r calculated as $Z / \sqrt{N}$, where N is the total number of observations across groups. ***$p < .001$. ns = not significant.

### *Utility of the Statistical/Probability Information*

Participants in Group C evaluated the perceived utility of confidence intervals and probabilities. Most respondents agreed that the information in the psychoeducation module (e.g., confidence intervals, measurement error reminders, probabilities of true score < 85) improved their understanding (80%), aided decision-making (85%), and would be considered for future use (79%) (see Table P.5). The likelihood of future implementation was rated highest (M = 4.29, SD = 0.91), suggesting that participants viewed the combined contextual-probability supplemental information as effective and feasible for applied settings.

**Table P.5 Participants' Reporting on Utility of Probability Information (Group C, n = 100)**

| Exit Survey Statement | Agreement Rating | | | | |
|---|---|---|---|---|---|
| | Strongly Disagree | Disagree | Neutral | Agree | Strongly Agree |
| The psychoeducation module improved my understanding of PSW score interpretation. | 1% | 4% | 15% | 41% | 39% |
| The probability value was helpful in clarifying ambiguous test scores. | 1% | 3% | 11% | 41% | 44% |
| I would consider using probability values in my own clinical work. | 3% | 3% | 15% | 27% | 52% |
| I am likely to use probability values in future SLD evaluations. | 2% | 3% | 10% | 34% | 51% |

*Note:* Values represent the percentage of participants in Group C who selected each agreement level on a 5-point Likert scale (1 = Strongly Disagree, 5 = Strongly Agree) for each item related to the psychoeducation module and probability information.

## DISCUSSION

### Accuracy

The addition of domain-level accuracy data provides further support for the conclusion that supplemental information meaningfully improves the accuracy of PSW decisions—particularly when decisions are most difficult. Accuracy for "easy" and "moderate" scores (i.e., those well above or below the SS = 85–89 range) was consistently high across all groups, suggesting that such classifications are relatively straightforward even without additional support. In contrast, "difficult" scores within the ambiguous range were far more error-prone at baseline, with accuracy in the control group and pretest phases of the experimental groups averaging just 64%–68%. After the supplemental information, however, accuracy for these same scores rose by over 20 percentage points in each experimental group, aligning with McNemar's test results and confirming that the supplemental information had its greatest impact where it was most needed. These findings suggest that while participants are generally accurate when classifying obvious strengths or weaknesses, structured supplemental information is particularly beneficial when interpreting diagnostically ambiguous cognitive profiles. Importantly, because most psychoeducational evaluations for suspected SLD include at least some scores near cut points, systematically incorporating such interpretive supports should be considered a standard and necessary component of practice to promote more accurate and defensible identification decisions.

The contextual-only and contextual-plus-probability conditions produced similarly large and statistically significant gains in overall classification accuracy. Posttest accuracy was high across both experimental groups, with no significant difference between them in either raw posttest scores or magnitude of improvement. These results indicate that both forms of supplemental information—contextual alone or contextual combined with probability data—were similarly effective in enhancing classification performance. The consistently high accuracy observed post-supplemental information also reinforces the value of providing decision aids that align with clinical reasoning and everyday school psychology practice.

### Confidence

In addition to improving classification accuracy, the supplemental information had a measurable impact on participants' confidence in their decision-making. Participants in the experimental groups demonstrated significant increases in confidence from pre- to posttest, suggesting that access to structured, domain-relevant supplemental information enhances not only performance but also perceived certainty when making PSW decisions. This finding aligns with existing literature on the value of contextual and probability cues in clinical reasoning and reinforces the idea that confidence is not merely a reflection of correctness, but also of interpretive clarity.

Importantly, Group C participants—who received both contextual and probability information—were able to integrate more complex information (e.g., confidence intervals, probability estimates) without experiencing reduced confidence. Their statistically significant gains suggest that the inclusion of confidence interval and probability metrics did not overwhelm decision-making but instead clarified ambiguous situations. This outcome supports the feasibility of embedding probability data tools within PSW frameworks to promote clarity and decision confidence.

Moreover, participants in Group C reported significantly greater gains in perceived competence than those in either the control or contextual-only groups. These findings suggest that the integration of probability information did more than enhance accuracy—it also bolstered school psychologists' sense of efficacy. This echoes previous research showing that professional development tools effectively increase confidence in clinical decision-making (Al Dahhan et al., 2021). The current study thus supports the inclusion of targeted psychoeducation and decision aids in training models for school psychologists, particularly for navigating diagnostically ambiguous cases.

### Calibration

In addition to independent gains in accuracy and confidence, the supplemental information improved the calibration between participants' confidence ratings and actual classification accuracy for diagnostically ambiguous scores. After receiving the supplemental information, both experimental groups demonstrated improved calibration, with the greatest gains occurring at moderate and high confidence levels. These findings underscore that decision quality is not only a matter of being correct, but also of knowing when one is correct. By embedding contextual and probability information directly alongside the relevant test scores, the information appeared to support metacognitive monitoring, helping school psychologists better judge when their certainty was warranted. This capacity for calibrated decision-making is essential in school psychology, where overconfidence in inaccurate classifications and hesitation in accurate ones can have meaningful implications for eligibility determinations and subsequent service provision.

### Relation to Previous Research

The results of this study build on recent calls for more structured and integrative approaches to PSW decision-making (Schneider et al., 2024). By providing contextual information and probability information in applied, clinician-friendly formats, the findings demonstrated that even brief, low-burden PSW decision supports can significantly improve classification accuracy and decision confidence. The outcomes mirrored findings in broader judgment and decision-making research, where contextual scaffolds and uncertainty indicators have been hypothesized to enhance calibration and reduce cognitive bias (Schneider et al., 2024; Streiner & Cairney, 2007).

Contrary to prior assertions that PSW-based SLD identification decisions remain unstable even with supplemental qualitative data, participants in the 2025 study showed substantial improvements in accuracy and perceived competence when provided with structured supports. Notably, gains were most pronounced for diagnostically ambiguous scores, suggesting that decision quality can be meaningfully enhanced when supplemental information is targeted and accessible. The study's findings highlighted the potential of evidence-informed tools to support more consistent and confident classification outcomes.

Notably, prior similar research, such as Maki et al. (2022), provided participants with qualitative information and test scores separately, requiring them to align behavioral information with score profiles during decision-making. In contrast, this 2025 study presented academic manifestations and probability information adjacent to each score, clearly indicating what to consider during interpretation. This structural difference may help explain the divergent outcomes: when connections between domains and real-world functioning are left implicit, school psychologists may struggle to integrate them effectively—especially when scores are ambiguous. Embedding such prompts into the evaluation process appeared to scaffold more accurate, confident, and defensible decisions under diagnostic uncertainty.

### Implications for the Field

The notable gains observed in the contextual-plus-probability group (Group C) highlight the practical utility of integrating conditional probabilities and measurement error considerations into everyday clinical decision-making. Again, given that most evaluations of suspected SLD involve diagnostically ambiguous scores, probability-based information should not be viewed as supplemental, but rather as a core component of defensible, data-informed practice. Incorporating such interpretive scaffolds enables school psychologists to evaluate ambiguous scores with greater accuracy, reducing the likelihood of misclassification. Tools such as the decision tree proposed by Schneider et al. (2024) are a strong start, but embedded supports within assessment platforms (e.g., X-BASS) will play a critical role in translating these concepts into routine practice, offering accessible, evidence-based guidance at the point of interpretation.

This vision is already being realized in the newly released X-BASS 3.0, which features the inclusion of probabilities and ecological validity checkpoints in the PSW tabs. In XBASS 3.0, new decision-support features mirror the structure of the experimental conditions tested here: when users encounter scores with low probabilities of reflecting true deficits, the software flags the data and prompts consideration of relevant academic or behavioral manifestations. These embedded supports encourage school psychologists to pause, reflect, and seek convergence across multiple data points before making classification decisions.

As such, this study and X-BASS 3.0 contribute to a growing shift in school psychology toward evidence-informed, calibrated decision-making under uncertainty. By equipping school psychologists with tools that improve accuracy without constraining professional judgment, the field can reduce diagnostic variability and promote more equitable access to services under IDEA. These findings support the integration of targeted, scalable decision aids into training and practice, advancing the goals of technical rigor and educational fairness in special education eligibility determination.

## SUMMARY

Ambiguity in cognitive test standard score interpretation, particularly for scores near diagnostic thresholds, presents a persistent challenge in the identification of SLD. The study examined whether providing school psychologists with structured supplemental information could improve the accuracy, confidence, and perceived competence of strength/weakness classifications within a PSW framework. Results demonstrated that structured support significantly improved classification accuracy and confidence, particularly for diagnostically ambiguous scores (i.e., standard scores of 85–89). The experimental groups also showed improved calibration between confidence and accuracy. Participants who received probability information reported increased perceived competence and endorsed the statistical data as useful for future practice. Importantly, the inclusion of contextual and probability information enhanced decision-making without constraining professional judgment.

These findings provide empirical support for integrating structured decision aids into SLD evaluation practice and contribute to a growing body of evidence advocating for calibrated, data-informed approaches. By addressing key sources of diagnostic uncertainty, such supports can promote more consistent, confident, and defensible assessments. The results have clear implications for professional training, score interpretation practices, and the development of technology-based tools to assist school psychologists in making accurate and equitable SLD determinations.

## REFERENCES

Al Dahhan, N. Z., Mesite, L., Feller, M. J., & Christodoulou, J. A. (2021). Identifying reading disabilities: A survey of practitioners. *Learning Disability Quarterly*, *44*(4), 235–247. https://doi.org/10.1177/0731948721998707.

Flanagan, D. P., Ortiz, S. O., & Alfonso, V. C. (2025). *Cross-battery assessment software system (version 3.0 [Computer Software])*. Wiley.

Flanagan, D. P., Alfonso, V. C., Sy, M. C., Mascolo, J. T., McDonough, E. M., & Ortiz, S. O. (2018). Dual discrepancy/consistency operational definition of SLD: Integrating multiple data sources and multiple data-gathering methods. In V. C. Alfonso & D. P. Flanagan (Eds.), *Essentials of specific learning disability identification* (pp. 329–430). Wiley.

Fletcher, J. M., & Miciak, J. (2019). The identification of specific learning disabilities: A summary of research on best practices. In *Grantee Submission*. https://eric.ed.gov/?id=ED606380

Goforth, A. N., Farmer, R. L., Kim, S. Y., Naser, S. C., Lockwood, A. B., & Affrunti, N. W. (2021). Status of School Psychology in 2020: Part 1, Demographics of the NASP Membership Survey. *NASP Research Reports*, *5*(2).

Maki, K., Floyd, R., & Roberson, T. (2015). State learning disability eligibility criteria: A comprehensive review. *School Psychology Quarterly*, *30*, https://doi.org/10.1037/spq0000109.

Maki, K. E., & Adams, S. R. (2022). Special education evaluation practices and procedures: Implications for referral and eligibility decision-making. *Contemporary School Psychology*, *26*(3), 350–358. https://doi.org/10.1007/s40688-020-00335-4.

Maki, K. E., Burns, M. K., & Sullivan, A. (2017). Learning disability identification consistency: The impact of methodology and student evaluation data. *School Psychology Quarterly*, *32*(2), 254–267. https://doi.org/10.1037/spq0000165.

Maki, K. E., Burns, M. K., & Sullivan, A. L. (2018). School psychologists' confidence in learning disability identification decisions. *Learning Disability Quarterly, 41*(4), 243–256. https://doi.org/10.1177/0731948718769251.

Maki, K. E., Kranzler, J. H., & Moody, M. E. (2022). Dual discrepancy/consistency pattern of strengths and weaknesses method of specific learning disability identification: Classification accuracy when combining clinical judgment with assessment data. *Journal of School Psychology, 92,* 33–48. https://doi.org/10.1016/j.jsp.2022.02.003.

Maki, K. E., McGill, R. J., Conoyer, S. J., Fefer, S. A., & Ward, T. (2021). Assessing the impact of sequential data presentation on specific learning disabilities identification decisions using patterns of strengths and weaknesses methods. *Journal of Psychoeducational Assessment, 39*(3), 372–380. https://doi.org/10.1177/0734282920983951.

Miciak, J., Williams, J. L., Taylor, W. P., Cirino, P. T., Fletcher, J. M., & Vaughn, S. (2016). Do processing patterns of strengths and weaknesses predict differential treatment response? *Journal of Educational Psychology, 108*(6), 898–909. https://doi.org/10.1037/edu0000096.

National Center for Education Statistics. (2021). https://nces.ed.gov/.

Psyridou, M., Tolvanen, A., Lerkkanen, M.-K., Poikkeus, A.-M., & Torppa, M. (2020). Longitudinal stability of reading difficulties: Examining the effects of measurement error, cut-offs, and buffer zones in identification. *Frontiers in Psychology, 10,* https://www.frontiersin.org/articles/dx.doi.org/10.3389/fpsyg.2019.02841.

Schneider, W. J. (2022). *condppv: Conditional positive predictive value in the accuracy of specific learning disability identification [Software].* AssessingPsyche Retrieved from https://github.com/wjschne/conditionalppv.

Schneider, W. J., & Kaufman, A. S. (2017). Let's not do away with comprehensive cognitive assessments just yet. *Archives of Clinical Neuropsychology, 32*(1), 8–20. https://doi.org/10.1093/arclin/acw104.

Schneider, W. J., Flanagan, D. P., Niileksela, C. R., & Engler, J. R. (2024). The effect of measurement error on the positive predictive value of PSW methods for SLD identification: How buffer zones dispel the illusion of inaccuracy. *Journal of School Psychology, 103,* 101280.

Schroeder, M., Drefs, M. A., & Cormier, D. C. (2017). The messiness of LD identification: Contributions of diagnostic criteria and clinical judgment. *Canadian Psychology/Psychologie Canadienne, 58*(3), 218–227. https://doi.org/10.1037/cap0000115.

Streiner, D. L., & Cairney, J. (2007). What's under the ROC? An introduction to receiver operating characteristics curves. *The Canadian Journal of Psychiatry, 52*(2), 121–128. https://doi.org/10.1177/070674370705200210.

Sullivan, A. L., Sadeh, S., & Houri, A. K. (2019). Are school psychologists' special education eligibility decisions reliable and unbiased?: A multi-study experimental investigation. *Journal of School Psychology, 77,* 90–109. https://doi.org/10.1016/j.jsp.2019.10.006.

Zachar, P., & Kendler, K. S. (2017). The philosophy of nosology. *Annual Review of Clinical Psychology, 13*(1), 49–71. https://doi.org/10.1146/annurev-clinpsy-032816-045020.

Appendix Q

# REAL-WORLD MANIFESTATIONS OF ACADEMIC SKILL WEAKNESSES

This appendix provides a comprehensive set of real-world manifestations associated with weaknesses in each of the eight SLD areas included in X-BASS. These manifestations are organized by grade level—Elementary, Middle, and High School—to help evaluators identify developmentally appropriate indicators of difficulty across academic domains. The lists are intentionally broad and behaviorally specific, reflecting the kinds of challenges teachers, parents, and students commonly report during instruction, homework, and everyday academic tasks.

These manifestations serve two primary purposes within the X-BASS workflow. First, they support the **ADD SUPPORTING DATA** function on the SLD Evidence tab by helping evaluators determine whether observed behaviors converge with the statistical evidence of a weakness. Second, they provide a practical reference for understanding how skill deficits appear in authentic learning environments, thereby strengthening ecological validity and informing intervention planning.

The items included here are not exhaustive, nor are they intended to function as diagnostic checklists. Rather, they offer illustrative examples of how weaknesses in basic reading skills (BRS), reading fluency (RDF), reading comprehension (RDC), math calculation (MC), math problem solving (MPS), written expression (WE), oral expression (OE), and listening comprehension (LC) may manifest across grade levels. Practitioners should use these manifestations in conjunction with test data, instructional history, classroom observations, and professional judgment to form a comprehensive understanding of the student's learning profile.

### BRS + ELEMENTARY + WORD RECOGNITION AND DECODING

- Very slow, choppy, or labored reading with long pauses between words
- Finger pointing and frequent loss of place
- Substituting simple words (e.g., "cat" for "car," "home" for "house")
- Difficulty sounding out basic CVC words (e.g., cat, dog, run)
- Guessing words based on the first letter only
- Inconsistent reading of the same word in one sentence (e.g., correct and then incorrect)
- Difficulty obtaining a sight word vocabulary despite repeated practice
- Moves lips while reading silently
- Takes more time than peers to read simple passages
- Frequently asks, "What does this word say?"
- Avoids independent reading time
- Cannot read simple science or social studies texts independently
- Struggles with word problems in math despite good number sense

### BRS + MIDDLE + WORD RECOGNITION AND DECODING

- Reads slowly but may have learned to mask difficulties
- Stumbles reading multisyllabic words (e.g., reading "hospital" as "hos-pit-al")
- Substitutes simpler words for more complex words that change meaning (e.g., "large" for "enormous")
- Avoids reading aloud by saying, "I didn't bring my book."
- Reads with some fluency but lacks expression and phrasing
- Cannot keep up with assigned reading pace
- Takes hours to complete what peers finish in a shorter period of time (e.g.,30 minutes)
- Frequently re-reads paragraphs without gaining understanding
- Skips difficult words and, as a result, loses meaning
- Falls behind in classes such as history due to heavy reading requirements
- Has difficulty reading science textbooks and lab instructions

- Cannot complete research projects requiring multiple sources
- Math word problems become increasingly challenging
- Foreign language learning is extremely difficult

### BRS + HIGH SCHOOL + WORD RECOGNITION AND DECODING

- Continues to struggle with technical vocabulary in content areas
- Cannot decode unfamiliar words in SAT/ACT preparation materials
- Difficulty with academic vocabulary (e.g., synthesis, phenomenon, hypothesis)
- Reading rate is significantly slower than grade-level peers or expectations
- Lacks prosody and expression, even in familiar texts
- Cannot read aloud effectively in class presentations
- Silent reading rate affects ability to complete timed tests
- Cannot read classic literature independently (e.g., Shakespeare, Dickens)
- Has difficulty reading poetry and figurative language
- Has difficulty understanding themes and symbolism
- Cannot analyze character development or plot structure effectively
- Has difficulty reading scientific journal articles or advanced texts
- Has difficulty reading technical manuals or instructions
- Has challenges reading complex sentence structures and dense paragraphs

### BRS + ELEMENTARY + SPELLING AND WRITING MANIFESTATIONS

- Spells words exactly as they sound (e.g., "sed" for "said," "luv" for "love")
- Omits vowels frequently (e.g., "brd" for "bird")
- Cannot spell common sight words consistently
- Spells the same word in different ways in one assignment
- Has difficulty with basic spelling patterns (e.g., -ing, -ed endings)
- Writes very short sentences to avoid unknown words
- Uses only vocabulary they can spell
- Is reluctant to write stories or journals
- May have great oral stories but minimal written expression

### BRS + MIDDLE + SPELLING AND WRITING MANIFESTATIONS

- Spells complex words phonetically (e.g., "fotograf" for "photograph")
- Cannot spell common words with irregular patterns
- Avoids sophisticated vocabulary in writing due to spelling concerns
- Relies heavily on spell-check, but doesn't recognize when suggestions are wrong
- Uses simpler sentence structures to avoid spelling difficulties
- Has sophisticated ideas, but writing appears elementary
- Takes much longer than peers to complete written assignments
- May have strong ideas but struggles to get them on paper

### BRS + HIGH SCHOOL + SPELLING AND WRITING MANIFESTATIONS

- Cannot spell sophisticated vocabulary needed for academic writing
- Relies heavily on simple words to avoid spelling errors
- Has difficulty expressing technical terms in science and social studies
- Cannot spell words needed for college application essays
- Gap between oral expression and written work becomes more obvious
- Cannot produce college-level writing despite good ideas
- Avoids complex sentence structures due to spelling/grammar concerns
- Takes much longer than peers to complete written assignments
- Cannot keep up with reading demands in AP or honors classes
- Struggles with college preparatory coursework
- Science textbooks and lab manuals are incomprehensible
- Foreign language expression becomes nearly impossible
- Cannot finish timed tests due to slow reading speed
- Misreads test questions despite knowing the content

- Has difficulty writing essay portions of standardized tests
- Cannot effectively use test-taking strategies that require reading

### RDF + ELEMENTARY + RATE AND FLUENCY

- Reading significantly below grade-level pace (i.e., fewer than expected words per minute)
- Choppy or labored word-by-word reading without natural phrasing or rhythm
- Frequent pausing and hesitation, even with familiar words
- Monotone reading lacking expression and appropriate intonation
- Poor attention to punctuation (e.g., reading through periods and commas
- Has difficulty reading sight words resulting in frequent stops
- Frequent self-corrections and repetitions that disrupt the flow of reading
- Avoiding volunteer reading opportunities or appearing anxious during oral reading
- Losing place frequently while reading aloud
- Reading that sounds robotic rather than conversational
- Consistently slow reading pace relative to peers
- Inability to increase speed without losing accuracy

### RDF + MIDDLE + RATE AND FLUENCY

- Reading rate is significantly below grade-level peers or expectations (i.e., typically 100–150 wpm by grade 6)
- Continued word-by-word reading or inappropriate phrasing in longer texts
- Difficulty maintaining fluency when text complexity increases
- Poor prosody—lack of appropriate stress, intonation, and expression
- Frequent regression (i.e., re-reading words or phrases) that interrupts flow
- Has difficulty with multisyllabic words, causing breaks in fluency
- Has difficulty adjusting reading rate based on text purpose (e.g., skimming vs. careful reading)
- Avoids oral reading tasks or participates reluctantly
- Fluency is disrupted when encountering unfamiliar vocabulary or complex sentence structures
- Reading that interferes with comprehension due to cognitive resources focused on word recognition
- Consistently slow reading rate for grade level
- Inability to increase speed without losing accuracy

### RDF + HIGH SCHOOL + RATE AND FLUENCY

- Reading rate below expectations for grade level (i.e., typically 200+ wpm for high school)
- Has difficulty maintaining fluency reading academic texts and content-area materials
- Has difficulty reading h complex sentence structures, causing choppy reading patterns
- Poor prosody when reading literature aloud, missing emotional nuances
- Has difficulty with specialized vocabulary in different subject areas, disrupting flow
- Avoids presentations or oral reading assignments
- Has difficulty with fluency that interfere with timed reading tasks or standardized tests
- Has difficulty adjusting reading rate appropriately for different text types and purposes
- Reading lacks sophistication in phrasing and expression appropriate for mature texts
- Has difficulty with reading complex poetry, speeches, or dramatic works with appropriate expression

### RDC + ELEMENTARY + GENERAL

- Reads words correctly but is unable to answer basic questions about the text
- Can retell simple stories but misses details
- Has difficulty answering "why" and "how" questions
- Cannot make simple predictions about story outcomes
- Loses meaning when focusing hard on sounding out words
- Has difficulty with picture books that have complex text
- Has difficulty identifying main characters, settings, or basic plot elements
- Has difficulty comprehending what they've read aloud, even when decoding is accurate
- Has difficulty with inferential and critical thinking questions
- Cannot identify the author's purpose or point of view
- Has difficulty comparing and contrasting information across texts
- Has difficulty with cause-and-effect relationships in complex texts

### RDC + MIDDLE + GENERAL

- Has difficulty identifying themes, author's purpose, or main ideas in literature
- Has difficulty making inferences or reading between the lines
- Has difficulty analyzing character motivations or understanding complex relationships
- Has difficulty reading across different subjects (e.g., science, social studies)
- Has difficulty understanding figurative language, metaphors, and symbolism
- Has difficulty synthesizing information from multiple sources
- Has difficulty distinguishing between fact and opinion
- Has difficulty with understanding text structure and organization
- Has difficulty connecting reading material to broader concepts or real-world applications

### RDC + HIGH SCHOOL + GENERAL

- Has difficulty with complex literary analysis and critical thinking about texts
- Has difficulty understanding abstract concepts and philosophical ideas in literature
- Has difficulty analyzing multiple perspectives or conflicting viewpoints
- Has difficulty synthesizing information from various sources for research projects
- Has difficulty understanding complex sentence structures and academic vocabulary
- Has difficulty reading comprehension in advanced content areas (AP courses, dual enrollment)
- Has difficulty understanding subtext, irony, and sophisticated literary devices
- Has difficulty making connections between historical contexts and literary works
- Has difficulty with close reading and textual analysis skills
- Has difficulty evaluating credibility and bias in sources
- Has difficulty understanding complex argumentative structures and rhetorical strategies

#### Academic Avoidance

- "Forgets" to bring home reading books
- Chooses books far below reading level
- Rushes through reading assignments without attention to meaning
- Copies answers from classmates during reading activities
- Prefers math or other non-reading subjects
- Asks to go to the nurse during reading time

#### Strategy Development (typically not effective)

- Over-relies on the first letter sounds to guess words
- Makes up stories based on pictures rather than reading text
- Memorizes sight words without understanding the meaning in context
- Uses context clues inappropriately or illogically

### MC + ELEMENTARY + GENERAL

#### Number Sense

- Cannot reliably count beyond 10–20, even in upper elementary
- Has difficulty recognizing numerals consistently (e.g., confuses 6/9, 12/21)
- Cannot understand the concept of "how many" (i.e., counts objects but cannot say total)
- Has difficulty with one-to-one correspondence when counting
- Cannot count backwards from 10
- Has difficulty with skip counting (e.g., 2 seconds, 5 seconds, 10 seconds)
- Cannot identify which number is bigger/smaller

#### Place Value

- Cannot understand that 23 means 2 tens and 3 ones
- Treats multi-digit numbers as separate single digits
- Cannot line up numbers properly in columns
- Has difficulty understanding regrouping in addition/subtraction
- Cannot explain what the zero means in numbers like 105

### Basic Operations

- Counts on fingers well beyond an appropriate age
- Cannot memorize basic math facts despite extensive practice
- Uses immature strategies (e.g., counting all instead of counting on)
- Cannot solve simple word problems (e.g., 5 +? = 8)
- Has difficulty with facts involving zero
- Cannot understand inverse relationship (e.g., if 5 + 3 = 8, then 8–3 = 5)
- Cannot understand multiplication as repeated addition
- Memorizes times tables without understanding patterns
- Cannot solve simple division problems
- Has difficulty with fact families
- Cannot apply multiplication to area concepts

### Time, Money, and Measurement

- Cannot read analog clocks
- Has difficulty understanding elapsed time
- Cannot sequence events chronologically
- Has difficulty with before/after, earlier/later concepts
- Cannot identify coin values consistently
- Has difficulty making change or counting money
- Cannot understand dollar/cent relationships
- Has difficulty with practical money applications
- Cannot use rulers or measuring tools effectively
- Has difficulty comparing lengths, weights, volumes
- Cannot understand standard vs. non-standard units
- Has difficulty with measurement word problems

MC + MIDDLE + GENERAL

### Fractions, Decimals, and Percentages

- Cannot understand fraction concepts (i.e., part-whole relationships)
- Has difficulty comparing fractions (e.g., cannot tell if 1/3 > 1/4)
- Cannot convert between fractions, decimals, and percentages
- Has difficulty with equivalent fractions
- Cannot add/subtract fractions with unlike denominators
- Has difficulty understanding decimal place value

### Integers and Rational Numbers

- Cannot understand negative numbers
- Has difficulty with number line concepts
- Cannot apply integer rules consistently
- Has difficulty with absolute value concepts

### Pre-Algebra Concepts

- Cannot solve simple equations with variables
- Has difficulty understanding that letters represent numbers
- Cannot identify patterns in sequences
- Has difficulty with input/output tables
- Cannot understand function concepts

### Order of Operations

- Cannot follow order of operations consistently
- Has difficulty with multi-step calculations
- Cannot evaluate expressions with multiple operations

## MC + HIGH SCHOOL + GENERAL

### Algebra

- Cannot solve linear equations consistently
- Has difficulty with factoring and polynomial operations
- Cannot understand function concepts deeply
- Has difficulty with graphing linear and quadratic functions
- Cannot solve systems of equations
- Has difficulty with exponential and logarithmic functions

### Geometry

- Cannot understand geometric proofs
- Has difficulty with trigonometric ratios
- Cannot apply formulas to complex problems
- Has difficulty with coordinate geometry
- Cannot understand geometric transformations

### Higher-Level Math

- Cannot access Pre-Calculus or Calculus
- Has difficulty with advanced algebraic concepts
- Cannot understand limits, derivatives, or integrals
- Has difficulty with statistical analysis

## MPS + ELEMENTARY + GENERAL

### GRADES K-1

- Has difficulty transitioning from manipulatives to abstract number symbols
- Inability to identify the "question" being asked in simple word problems
- Random guessing of numbers without attempting to understand the problem
- Focuses on irrelevant details in story problems (e.g., character names, colors) while missing mathematical information
- Has difficulty connecting real-world scenarios to mathematical operations
- Has difficulty recognizing when to count forward vs. backward
- Has difficulty with comparative language (e.g., "more than," "less than," "altogether")

### GRADES 2–3

- Has difficulty breaking down multi-step word problems into component parts
- Has difficulty identifying relevant vs. irrelevant information in word problems
- Does not understand mathematical vocabulary and key terms
- Inability to visualize or represent problems using pictures, diagrams, or manipulatives
- Has difficulty checking answers for reasonableness
- Has difficulty translating word problems into mathematical expressions
- Has difficulty with problems involving multiple operations
- Has difficulty with time, money, and measurement word problems

### GRADES 4–5

- Has difficulty breaking down multi-step word problems into component parts
- Has difficulty identifying relevant vs. irrelevant information in word problems
- Does not understand mathematical vocabulary and key terms
- Inability to visualize or represent problems using pictures, diagrams, or manipulatives
- Has difficulty checking answers for reasonableness
- Has difficulty translating word problems into mathematical expressions
- Has difficulty with problems involving multiple operations
- Has difficulty with time, money, and measurement word problems

## MPS + MIDDLE + GENERAL

- Has severe difficulty translating word problems into algebraic expressions or equations
- Has difficulty understanding variables and their role in mathematical relationships
- Has difficulty with proportional reasoning and rate problems

- Has difficulty interpreting and creating mathematical models from real-world situations
- Has difficulty with geometric applications requiring spatial reasoning and formula application
- Inability to work with systems of equations arising from word problems
- Has difficulty with probability and statistical reasoning in context

MPS + HIGH SCHOOL + GENERAL

- Has extreme difficulty with complex algebraic word problems involving quadratic equations, exponential functions, or logarithmic relationships
- Has difficulty with calculus applications requiring interpretation of rates of change
- Has difficulty with statistical analysis and hypothesis testing in real-world contexts
- Has difficulty with trigonometric applications and geometric modeling
- Has difficulty integrating mathematical concepts from multiple domains
- Inability to model real-world phenomena using mathematical functions
- Has difficulty with optimization problems and constraint-based scenarios

WE + ELEMENTARY + GENERAL

**Fine Motor and Handwriting**

- Cannot hold a pencil with an appropriate grip despite instruction
- Writing is illegible even when the student takes excessive time
- Cannot form letters consistently (same letter looks different each time)
- Confuses upper and lowercase letters randomly
- Cannot write on lines or within appropriate spaces
- Becomes extreme fatigued from writing even short sentences
- Reverses letters well beyond typical developmental age
- Cannot copy from the board accurately

**Basic Writing Mechanics**

- Cannot remember to put spaces between words
- Writes in all capitals or all lowercase
- Cannot remember basic punctuation (periods, question marks)
- Has difficulty with left-to-right progression
- Starts writing in middle of page randomly

**Advanced Spelling Patterns**

- Cannot learn spelling rules (e.g., -ing, -ed endings)
- Has difficulty with consonant blends and digraphs
- Cannot spell words with silent letters
- Has difficulty with prefixes and suffixes

**Basic Sentence Structure**

- Cannot write complete sentences
- Writes run-on sentences without punctuation
- Cannot use capital letters for sentence beginnings
- Has difficulty with subject-verb agreement
- Cannot use basic pronouns correctly

**Word Retrieval**

- Cannot think of words to express ideas
- Uses very simple vocabulary despite rich oral language
- Frequently uses of "thing" or "stuff" instead of specific words
- Has long pauses while trying to think of words

**Content Generation**

- Cannot think of ideas to write about
- Writes only one or two sentences when peers write paragraphs
- Cannot expand on ideas or add details
- Has difficulty staying on topic

### Story Structure

- Cannot organize stories with a beginning, middle, and end
- Does not have an understanding of sequence in narrative writing
- Cannot write stories that make logical sense
- Has difficulty with character and setting development

### Content Area Writing

- Cannot complete simple writing tasks in science or social studies
- Has difficulty writing about math problem-solving processes
- Cannot write basic reports or responses
- Has difficulty with any assignment requiring written output

## WE + MIDDLE + GENERAL

### Complex Sentence Structure

- Cannot write compound or complex sentences
- Overuses simple conjunctions (and, then, so)
- Cannot use transitional phrases effectively
- Has difficulty with dependent and independent clauses
- Cannot vary sentence length or structure

### Advanced Grammar and Usage

- Cannot use commas correctly in complex sentences
- Has difficulty with apostrophes and quotation marks
- Cannot maintain consistent verb tense
- Has difficulty with pronoun-antecedent agreement
- Cannot use advanced punctuation (semicolons, colons)

### Paragraph Development

- Cannot write coherent paragraphs with topic sentences
- Cannot develop supporting details for main ideas
- Has difficulty with paragraph transitions
- Cannot conclude paragraphs effectively
- Writes everything as one long paragraph

### Multi-Paragraph Writing

- Cannot organize ideas into multiple paragraphs
- Does not understand the introduction-body-conclusion structure
- Cannot write thesis statements or main ideas
- Cannot create a logical flow between paragraphs

### Idea Elaboration

- Cannot expand simple ideas into detailed writing
- Has difficulty providing specific examples or evidence
- Cannot explain reasoning or thought processes
- Writes in very general, vague terms
- Cannot develop arguments or persuasive points

### Writing Voice and Style

- Writing sounds very immature compared to oral expression
- Cannot adapt writing style for different purposes
- Does not have a sense of audience awareness
- Cannot create engaging or interesting writing
- Uses a mechanical, robotic writing style

### Research Skills

- Cannot take practical notes from sources
- Has difficulty organizing information from multiple sources

- Cannot synthesize information into coherent writing
- Has difficulty with paraphrasing and summarizing
- Cannot cite sources appropriately

**Informational Writing**

- Cannot write clear explanations or instructions
- Has difficulty with cause-and-effect organization
- Cannot compare and contrast effectively in writing
- Has difficulty with classification and description

**Story Development**

- Cannot develop complex characters or settings
- Has difficulty with plot development and conflict resolution
- Cannot use dialogue effectively
- Has difficulty with point of view consistency
- Cannot create engaging narratives

**Cross-Curricular Impact**

- Cannot write lab reports in science
- Has difficulty with historical essays and document analysis
- Cannot explain mathematical problem-solving in writing
- Has difficulty with creative writing in language arts
- Cannot complete written assignments that demonstrate learning

### WE + HIGH SCHOOL + GENERAL

**Essay Writing**

- Cannot write analytical essays required for English classes
- Has difficulty with literary analysis and interpretation
- Cannot support arguments with textual evidence
- Has difficulty with thesis development and argumentation
- Cannot write comparison/contrast or cause-effect essays

**Research and Documentation**

- Cannot write research papers with proper citations
- Has difficulty synthesizing multiple sources effectively
- Cannot distinguish between reliable and unreliable sources
- Has difficulty with citation formats such as MLA or APA
- Cannot avoid plagiarism while incorporating sources

**Higher-Level Language Use**

- Cannot use advanced vocabulary appropriately in writing
- Has difficulty with complex grammatical structures
- Cannot create sophisticated, varied sentence patterns
- Has difficulty with formal academic writing conventions
- Cannot eliminate informal language from academic writing

**Revising and Editing**

- Cannot revise for content, organization, and style
- Has difficulty identifying and correcting grammatical errors
- Cannot improve clarity and coherence in multiple drafts
- Has difficulty with proofreading and final editing
- Cannot use feedback effectively to improve writing

**Literary Analysis**

- Cannot analyze themes, symbols, or literary devices
- Has difficulty writing about character development

- Cannot support interpretations with textual evidence
- Has difficulty with close reading and textual analysis

**Persuasive and Argumentative Writing**

- Cannot develop logical arguments
- Has difficulty addressing counterarguments
- Cannot use rhetorical strategies effectively
- Has difficulty with evidence selection and presentation

**Creative Writing**

- Cannot develop sophisticated narratives
- Has difficulty with advanced literary techniques
- Cannot experiment with style and voice
- Has difficulty with creative expression through writing

**Science Writing**

- Cannot write lab reports with proper methodology
- Has difficulty explaining scientific processes and conclusions
- Cannot write research proposals or scientific arguments
- Has difficulty with technical writing conventions

**Social Studies Writing**

- Cannot analyze historical documents effectively
- Has difficulty with argumentative essays about social issues
- Cannot write research papers on historical topics
- Has difficulty with evaluating and using primary sources

**College and Career Preparation**

- Cannot complete essay portions of SAT, ACT, or AP exams effectively
- Has difficulty with timed writing under pressure
- Cannot demonstrate knowledge through written responses
- May need significant accommodations for writing assessments

**College Application Writing**

- Cannot write effective personal statements or essays
- Has difficulty communicating strengths and experiences
- Cannot complete scholarship application essays
- Has difficulty with supplemental writing requirements
- Cannot write professional emails or communications
- Has difficulty with resumes and cover letters

## OE + ELEMENTARY + GENERAL

**Articulation and Phonological Issues**

- Has difficulty pronouncing "r" sounds, saying "wabbit" instead of "rabbit"
- Lisps with "s" and "z" sounds, saying "thun" instead of "sun"
- Drops final consonants, saying "ca" instead of "cat"

**Language Structure**

- Uses incomplete sentences: "Me want juice" instead of "I want juice"
- Has difficulty with verb tenses: "Yesterday I go to store"
- Has difficulty with plural forms: "I have two book"

**Vocabulary and Word Retrieval**

- Overuses generic words like "thing" or "stuff" when more specific vocabulary is needed
- Has difficulty explaining what they did over the weekend beyond "It was fun."
- Has difficulty describing objects without pointing or using gestures

## OE + MIDDLE + GENERAL

### Discourse and Organization

- Expresses stories without a clear beginning, middle, or end
- Has difficulty staying on topic during class discussions
- Uses excessive filler words: "like," "um," "you know" throughout speech

### Social Communication

- Interrupts others frequently during group work
- Has difficulty reading social cues about when to speak or listen
- Has difficulty adjusting language formality between talking to peers versus talking to teachers

### Academic Language

- Has trouble explaining math problem-solving steps aloud
- Has difficulty participating in Socratic seminars or literature discussions
- Has difficulty giving clear directions for science lab procedures

## OE + HIGH SCHOOL + GENERAL

### Complex Language Skills

- Has difficulty with abstract reasoning in oral presentations
- Has difficulty synthesizing information from multiple sources during debates
- Has difficulty using sophisticated vocabulary appropriately in formal speaking contexts

### Pragmatic Challenges

- Has difficulty with job interview skills and professional communication
- Has difficulty advocating for themselves with teachers about grades or assignments
- Has difficulty with peer mediation or conflict resolution conversations

### Academic and Preparation Skills

- Freezes up during oral presentations despite knowing the material
- Has difficulty thinking on their feet during class discussions
- Has difficulty asking clarifying questions when instructions are unclear
- Has difficulty explaining their reasoning during math or science problem-solving

## LC + ELEMENTARY + GENERAL

### Following Instructions

- Starts activities before the teacher finishes explaining all the steps
- Completes only the first part of multi-step directions ("Get your math book, turn to page 47, and do problems 1-10" results in only getting the book)
- Asks, "What are we supposed to do?" immediately after instructions are given
- Looks at other students to see what they're doing instead of listening to directions

### Academic Listening

- Misses key information during story time, unable to answer basic comprehension questions
- Has difficulty following along during math lessons, getting lost when the teacher explains problem-solving steps
- Has difficulty with phonics lessons, unable to distinguish between similar sounds like "b" and "d"
- Does not respond appropriately during classroom discussions

### Social Listening

- Interrupts others because they haven't processed that someone is still talking
- Gives inappropriate responses to peers' comments during play
- Misses social cues in conversations, leading to misunderstandings with friends
- Has difficulty following the game rules when they are explained verbally

### Attention-Related Issues

- Appears to daydream or "zone out" during instruction time
- Is easily distracted by background noises like pencil sharpeners or hallway sounds
- Needs frequent repetition of simple requests
- Has difficulty transitioning between activities when verbal cues are given

## LC + MIDDLE + GENERAL

### Academic Challenges

- Takes incomplete or inaccurate notes during lectures because they miss key points
- Has difficulty in foreign language classes due to difficulty processing spoken language
- Misses important details during science experiments or lab instructions
- Has difficulty following verbal math explanations, especially word problems read aloud

### Social and Peer Interactions

- Misunderstands jokes or sarcasm, responding inappropriately to humor
- Misses subtle social cues about group dynamics or peer relationships
- Has difficulty participating in group projects because they miss planning discussions
- Has difficulty with phone conversations with friends or family

### Organizational Issues

- Misses announcements about schedule changes, field trips, or important dates
- Has difficulty processing homework assignments given verbally at the end of class
- Has difficulty following multi-step project instructions given during class
- Misses details about test formats or study requirements

### Processing Information Quickly

- Needs extra time to process questions before responding
- Asks, "What?" frequently, even in quiet environments
- Has difficulty keeping up with fast-paced discussions or debates
- Has difficulty with verbal instructions that include time pressure

## LC + HIGH SCHOOL + GENERAL

### Complex Academic Listening

- Has difficulty following advanced lectures in history, science, or literature classes
- Misses nuanced arguments in class discussions or Socratic seminars
- Has difficulty taking effective notes during college prep or AP courses
- Has difficulty processing verbal feedback on essays or projects

### Critical Thinking and Analysis

- Misses implied meanings or subtext in literature discussions
- Has difficulty following complex debates or philosophical arguments
- Struggles to identify bias or perspective in oral presentations
- Misses connections between concepts during interdisciplinary lessons

### Technology and Media

- Has difficulty following podcasts, audiobooks, or educational videos
- Misses key information in verbal announcements over school intercoms
- Struggles with voice-to-text technology or verbal computer commands
- Has difficulty processing rapid speech in movies or TV shows without captions

Appendix R

# SAMPLE REPORT FROM INTERVENTION LIBRARY—IL® FOR A 3RD-GRADE STUDENT WITH A WEAKNESS IN RETRIEVAL FLUENCY

The practitioner selected **Retrieval Fluency (*Gr*)** as the cognitive domain, **Early Elementary (K–4)** as the intervention grade level, and **All Methods** for delivery (individual, small group, whole class), along with **all intervention types** (Instructional Techniques, Environmental, Curricular, Remedial Programs, Skill-Building Techniques, and Compensatory Strategies and Supports). Based on these selections, the IL generated the full set of interventions that met the specified criteria.

In practice, the practitioner is encouraged to select only those interventions that are most appropriate, given an understanding of the whole individual. The sample report below includes the entire list of matched interventions to illustrate the full range of options available within the IL. Users may edit, refine, or reorganize the report in any way that best fits their professional needs.

**Intervention Library—IL v1.0**

**Resources for Instruction and Intervention**

| | | | |
|---|---|---|---|
| **Name:** | Erika | **School:** | Yantacaw Elementary |
| **Age:** | 8 | **Report generated by:** | Diane Fine |
| **Grade:** | 3 | **Report created on:** | 7 July 2025 |

The interventions and resources provided below are for informational purposes. Although the style and format of the report are copyrighted, users are granted permission to copy, edit, modify, and use the text included in this summary for the purpose of creating their own report.

**_Gr_—Retrieval Fluency**

**INSTRUCTIONAL TECHNIQUES for _Gr_**

- **Use experiential learning to enhance later recall**

Experiential learning involves a student learning by taking initiative to complete a task, making decisions, using problem-solving skills, and reflecting on the process and outcome. Experiential learning builds the development of multiple memory pathways to enhance later recall. For more information and resources, visit the following link(s).

*Suggestions for using experiential learning* https://tinyurl.com/active-experiential-learning
*K-12 experiential education classrooms* https://tinyurl.com/Experiential-Learning-Schools

- **Present material in a manner that increases the likelihood of recall**

Presentation formats that facilitate recall include the following characteristics:

1. organize (e.g., by similarity, related to previously learned information);
2. integrate visual and verbal information (e.g., drawings, graphs, pictures);
3. incorporate sound when possible (e.g., music);
4. evoke emotions (e.g., personal stories, experiential learning);
5. encourage the use of mental imagery; and
6. capitalize on distinctive learning events (e.g., unique, unexpected, atypical, or initially implausible).

For more information and resources, visit the following link(s).

*Facilitate recall with evidence-based strategies* https://tinyurl.com/Recall-Strategies

- **Engage student in active retrieval of previous knowledge to improve recall of information**

Encourage the student to retrieve memories from long-term stores (i.e., previously acquired knowledge) by engaging him or her in active retrieval activities. Active retrieval helps to improve knowledge retention and reduce memory decay. Actively recalling and using information (e.g., answering questions) has been found to be more effective than simply reviewing information (e.g., passively reading a summary). For more information and resources, visit the following link(s).

*How to use retrieval practice* https://tinyurl.com/using-retrieval-practice

- **Use close-ended questions during classroom instruction to reduce retrieval demands**

The use of closed-ended questions, such as those requiring a yes/no or true/false response, reduces word-retrieval demands. Prior to asking a closed-ended question of the student in a classroom setting, prime the student's knowledge by saying, "Now I am going to ask questions about...." In this way, the student may have sufficient time to access the knowledge, answer the question correctly, and remain engaged.

- **Use closed-ended questions and recognition formats for testing to reduce retrieval demands**

Questions and formats that allow for recognition of information enable a student to demonstrate his or her knowledge by minimizing retrieval demands. For example, when assessing student knowledge, ask yes/no and true/false questions and give multiple-choice response options during in-class discussions and on tests.

- **Provide short quizzes at frequent intervals in addition to a full-length examination (repeated testing) to reduce memory load**

For a student with retrieval difficulties, it may be beneficial to give more frequent, shorter quizzes in between learning and the full-length examination to reduce memory load and reinforce learning. Tests should be given when retrieval will be effortful, but mostly successful. Therefore, quizzes should be given at expanding intervals. The best results are likely to be obtained with at least 3 quizzes or tests between initial learning and the full-length examination. For more information and resources, visit the following link(s).

*Repeated testing* https://tinyurl.com/Research-frequent-tests

*More or less testing?* https://tinyurl.com/more-or-less-testing

- **Allow the use of retrieval aids during instructional tasks**

Retrieval aids, such as mind maps, can serve as prompts to help the student access learned information. For more information and resources, visit the following link(s).

*How to use mind maps* https://tinyurl.com/mind-mapping-for-kids

*Mind mapping strategies* https://tinyurl.com/mind-mapping-strategies

- **Use practice tests while teaching**

Practice tests provide multiple opportunities for the student to retrieve information. They also help the student identify areas that have not yet been learned and serve to focus new learning on weak areas. Practice tests provide students with feedback on the areas they have already learned, suggesting that minimal time will be needed to review that information for future tests. Practice tests are most beneficial when they focus on key concepts and are administered after the material is learned. Also, to facilitate learning, feedback should be provided at a slight delay, and the student should be told why specific answers were correct and incorrect. For more information and resources, visit the following link(s).

*To create practice tests* https://tinyurl.com/Quiz-Generator

- **Provide increasingly specific prompts and cues to guide the retrieval of information**

If a student is having difficulty recalling material, provide hints or clues that gradually become more specific until he or she can access the target information. For more information and resources, visit the following link(s).

*Phonics cueing system* https://tinyurl.com/cuesforlearning

- **Increase "wait time" to answer questions**

Built-in extra wait time for the student to answer questions. First, give the student a "heads up" that he or she will be called upon. Be sure to communicate the nature and content of the question to allow the student time to access specific stores of knowledge. Include at least one other student, where possible, so that the target student does not feel different. For example, you might say, "John and Rosina, after I finish writing some instructions on the board, I am going to ask you a couple of questions about the barometer we used for yesterday's weather experiment."

- **Model and provide practice in retelling**

Retelling can be an effective tool for improving and assessing comprehension and for enhancing information retrieval. For more information and resources, visit the following link(s).

| | |
|---|---|
| *Comprehensive guide on teaching retelling* | https://tinyurl.com/resource-retelling |
| *Retelling strategies and content examples* | https://tinyurl.com/retelling-strategies |

- **Teach synonyms to expand vocabulary and aid in word retrieval**

Synonyms provide multiple associations for a single word, thereby facilitating word retrieval. For more information and resources, visit the following link(s).

| | |
|---|---|
| *Synonyms lesson plan* | https://tinyurl.com/lesson-synonyms |
| *Over a dozen synonym worksheets* | https://tinyurl.com/synonym-worksheets |

- **Provide context before asking a question to facilitate recall**

Providing context for a question that is about to be asked will help prime the student's memory by activating relevant, related information (e.g., background knowledge), thereby facilitating retrieval.

- **Promote recognition rather than recall for tests**

For tests, consider requiring students to recognize answers rather than recall them from memory (e.g., word banks, multiple-choice).

- **Build in wait-time after asking questions to facilitate retrieval**

Because it may take the student longer to retrieve the target content from memory, allow more time for a response. For more information and resources, visit the following link(s).

| | |
|---|---|
| *Wait-time techniques* | https://tinyurl.com/how-to-build-in-wait-time |

## ENVIRONMENTAL INTERVENTIONS for *Gr*

- **Provide preferential seating to reduce distractions during learning and retrieval**

Seat the student near the front of the room or close to the teacher, and away from windows, doors, and distracting peers. This will reduce the likelihood of interference during learning and retrieval.

- **Provide access to environmental aids that facilitate retrieval**

Ensure the student has access to environmental aids (e.g., daily schedules, word walls, problem-solving charts) to facilitate retrieval.

- **Display posters and charts to reduce retrieval demands**

Academic posters that contain steps and procedures (e.g., problem-solving charts, parts of an essay) reduce retrieval demands and enable independent learning. For more information and resources, visit the following link(s).

| | |
|---|---|
| *Creating classroom posters to enhance learning* | https://tinyurl.com/Classroom-Poster-Tips |

- **Display written directions for tasks or assignments to reduce memory demands**

Displaying written instructions (e.g., projected on a SMART Board) serves as an external memory aid, reducing retrieval demands.

- **Minimize visual and auditory distractions**

To minimize visual distractions, remove nonessential items from view when the student is completing a task, taking a test, or studying. To minimize auditory distractions, provide a quiet environment for the student to work (e.g., a study carrel, a quiet work zone, closed doors and windows). Minimizing visual and auditory distractions may improve concentration and attentional focus, which are necessary for efficient information retrieval.

- **Display word walls in the classroom to aid word retrieval**

Word walls can help students with word-retrieval difficulties by reducing the need to independently locate words and their meanings in memory. It is important to ensure that the student can access the word wall and is encouraged to use it (e.g., during writing assignments). For more information and resources, visit the following link(s).

| | |
|---|---|
| *Instructions on how to use word walls* | https://tinyurl.com/word-strategies |
| *Create a word wall* | https://tinyurl.com/create-word-wall |

- **Display word walls in the classroom to aid word retrieval**

Word walls can help students with word-retrieval difficulties by reducing the need to independently locate words and their meanings in memory. It is important to ensure that the student can access the word wall and is encouraged to use it (e.g., during writing assignments). For more information and resources, visit the following link(s).

| | |
|---|---|
| *Word wall apps for early elementary school* | https://tinyurl.com/My-World-Wall-Review |
| *World Wall App* | https://tinyurl.com/My-World-Wall-App |

- **Make a dictionary and a thesaurus available to aid word retrieval**

Dictionaries and thesauri allow a student to develop learner autonomy by providing several meanings and examples of everyday words while simultaneously reducing the cognitive load associated with word retrieval and recall. For more information and resources, visit the following link(s).

| | |
|---|---|
| *Dictionary apps for kids* | https://tinyurl.com/dictionary-apps |

- **Provide access to teacher-recommended websites that include activities that facilitate the retrieval of information**

Web-based activities that facilitate retrieval fluency include those that allow for repeated practice with existing academic content (i.e., content built into a program or website) or self-generated content (i.e., content the student or teacher adds to a program or website). For example, Arcademic Skill Builders is a website that combines an arcade with academics to make learning fun. The math and language arts games on this website are free and designed to improve fact fluency in an engaging, fun way. For more information and resources, visit the following link(s).

| | |
|---|---|
| *Arcademics® Skill Builders* | https://www.arcademics.com/ |
| *Retrieval fluency games (Funbrain)* | https://www.funbrain.com/ |
| *Retrieval fluency games (Gamequarium)* | https://www.gamequarium.com/ |

- **Allow access to tools that facilitate retrieval**

Tools such as individual dry-erase boards and flashcards help the student practice retrieving newly learned information and can increase retrieval fluency. For more information and resources, visit the following link(s).

| | |
|---|---|
| *Using dry-erase boards to facilitate learning* | https://tinyurl.com/White-Board-for-Learning |
| *How to learn with flashcards* | https://tinyurl.com/flashcards-how-to-use |
| *Make and study flashcards* | https://quizlet.com/features/flashcards |
| *Free printable flash card maker* | https://tinyurl.com/free-flashcard-maker |
| *Flashcard information for parents/teachers* | https://tinyurl.com/flashcard-maker-for-parents |

- **Provide tangible reminders to aid in retrieval**

Providing the student with tangible reminders (e.g., Post-its, color-coded systems, checklists, timers, calendar with due dates) can reduce memory demands and facilitate timely completion of tasks. For more information and resources, visit the following link(s).

| | |
|---|---|
| *Tips on how to use Post-its as reminders* | https://tinyurl.com/tips-post-it-reminders |
| *Tips on how to color-code notes* | https://tinyurl.com/tips-color-coding |
| *Create checklists* | https://tinyurl.com/checklist-maker |

**CURRICULAR INTERVENTIONS for *Gr***

- **Direct the student to available resources for making checklists (e.g., online checklist makers or checklist templates) to reduce retrieval demands**

Checklists containing operational steps or procedures may be used as a guide when a task has too many components to remember. As tasks become more complex, checklists can help reduce errors and demands on memory. For more information and resources, visit the following link(s).

| | |
|---|---|
| *Checklists and their benefits* | https://tinyurl.com/information-on-checklists |
| *How checklists improve learning* | https://tinyurl.com/checklists-improve-learning |
| *How teachers can create checklists* | https://tinyurl.com/teacher-create-checklist |

- **Direct the student to word banks to assist with vocabulary development**

A word bank is a teacher- or student-created list of words related to the content and academic material the student is learning, and it assists with recalling newly learned words. For more information and resources, visit the following link(s).

| | |
|---|---|
| *Word bank worksheet maker* | https://tinyurl.com/word-bank-maker |

- **Provide practice tests that are similar in format to the actual test to facilitate recall**

When practice tests are similar in format to the actual test, they provide familiarity, allowing the student to focus primarily on retrieving newly learned information. Also, when cues provided on practice tests are similar to those provided on the actual test (e.g., similar sentence stems for multiple-choice questions), recall is enhanced. For more information and resources, visit the following link(s).

| | |
|---|---|
| *Create practice tests online* | https://www.easytestmaker.com/ |

- **Allow access to supports during test taking to reduce memory demands**

To minimize the demands on retrieval, provide supports during test taking, such as word banks, textbooks, and a formula sheet.

- **Direct the student to electronic, audio, or printed glossary of terms**

Direct the student to content-area glossaries, such as math and science, to look up word meanings when they have difficulty retrieving them from memory independently. Book publishers (e.g., Pearson, Houghton Mifflin/Harcourt) provide printed glossaries within textbooks and typically offer online glossaries on their website. Teachers typically have the online code needed to access these glossaries.

- **Direct student to external memory aids (e.g., timers, clocks, lists)**

Direct the student to available memory aids, such as cueing and storage devices. Examples include memory books, alarms and timers, notebooks/daily planners, computer reminders, schedules and assignment calendars, checklists, folders for organizing notes and materials, lists of tasks to complete, and step-by-step strategy instructions. For more information and resources, visit the following link(s).

| | |
|---|---|
| *External memory aids* | https://tinyurl.com/Memory-Aids |

- **Direct the student to semantic maps to create multiple associations to aid in later retrieval**

Direct the student to resources that allow him or her to create a semantic map. In a semantic map, a word to be elaborated is circled and surrounded by lines with connecting boxes where new associations can be placed. Associations can include the item's category, action, function, location, and so forth. Using various associations to learn a new word can enhance background knowledge, providing more opportunities to retrieve it. For more information and resources, visit the following link(s).

| | |
|---|---|
| *Semantic mapping overview* | https://tinyurl.com/connect-word-to-meaning |
| *Create semantic maps* | https://tinyurl.com/concept-map-maker |

## SKILL-BUILDING TECHNIQUES for *Gr*

- **Teach multi-sensory methods to facilitate retrieval**

Teaching a student to use multisensory methods can aid retrieval by providing multiple cues to elicit information. Multi-sensory methods include visual, auditory, tactile, and kinesthetic elements. For more information and resources, visit the following link(s).

| | |
|---|---|
| *Teaching multi-sensory methods* | https://tinyurl.com/multisensory-cues |
| *Creating multi-sensory experiences for reading* | https://tinyurl.com/Multisensory-Learning |

- **Use the Flashcards App for comprehensive studying**

The Flashcards app allows students to create downloadable sets of flashcards on any topic for comprehensive study. Creators can add images and multiple-choice-style response sets to their flashcards and share them with classmates. The app also offers progress-monitoring tools to enable tailored study and fosters quicker, easier recall of information. By offering multiple-choice options, flashcards minimize the effects of retrieval difficulties by providing learning and review through cued, rather than free, recall, and reducing the likelihood of encoding errors. For more information and resources, visit the following link(s).

| | |
|---|---|
| *Access the Flashcards app* | https://tinyurl.com/card-creation |

- **Incorporate games in remedial lessons to practice word retrieval**

Increase quick word retrieval in a fun, interactive way using games such as Scattergories, Taboo, Catchphrase, and UpWords.

- **Use interventions and apps to aid in word retrieval/word finding**

Teach the student to use a variety of interventions and apps that help him or her retrieve words and information more efficiently. Two interventions aimed at facilitating efficient retrieval include retrieval strategy instruction and self-advocacy instruction. For more information and resources, visit the following link(s).

| | |
|---|---|
| *Word retrieval intervention/accommodation* | http://wordfinding.com/intervention.html |
| *Word retrieval app* | https://tinyurl.com/word-retrieval-app |
| *Categories Learning Center Smarty Ears app* | https://tinyurl.com/SmartyEars-app |
| *Multiple Meanings Library app* | https://tinyurl.com/Multiple-Meanings-app |

- **Play board or card games that encourage retrieval**

Certain commercially available games (e.g., The 5-Second Rule, WordBURST, Find the Word, Taboo, Catchphrase) require the student to retrieve information from memory to play successfully. Such games provide multiple opportunities to practice retrieving information from long-term stores in a fun context.

## COMPENSATORY STRATEGIES AND SUPPORTS for *Gr*

- **Request an extended time accommodation on tests to allow enough time to retrieve information**

Extending the duration of a test allows the student additional time to access and apply learned information. Note that the use of this accommodation should consider the extent of the student's retrieval weakness as well as his or her current difficulties with test-taking under typical time parameters. Also, this accommodation should be maintained only when there is a demonstrable benefit, as determined by the student's performance (e.g., completion of additional test items).

- **Use self-testing to practice retrieving information**

Self-testing is one method of practicing information retrieval, which can also strengthen long-term memory. For more information and resources, visit the following link(s).

*How parents can assist with good study habits* https://tinyurl.com/Develop-Study-Skills

- **Use elaborative encoding and rehearsal to increase the likelihood that information will be retrieved at a later time**

Information is remembered better when it is processed fully. Elaborative rehearsal is an active process that involves elaborating on the new information in different ways, such as: (1) making associations between the new information and what is already known; (2) creating a mental image of the new information; and (3) recording information in some way (e.g., taking notes on a chapter while reading it; creating a mnemonic device). When elaborative rehearsal is used, new information is more readily retrieved later, such as on tests. For more information and resources, visit the following link(s).

*Use of elaboration to facilitate learning* https://tinyurl.com/elaboration-for-learning

*Strategies for elaborative rehearsal* https://tinyurl.com/elaborative-rehearsal-guide

- **Use the successive relearning technique**

Successive relearning involves self-testing until the student can correctly recall the target information from memory across practice sessions. Retrieval practice (e.g., practice testing) and restudying are alternated during the initial learning phase until all content is remembered correctly. This process is repeated over successive days to ensure correct recall. This procedure can be done using handmade flashcards or digital flashcards personalized online. For more information and resources, visit the following link(s).

*Make and study flashcards* https://quizlet.com/features/flashcards

*Free printable flash card maker* https://tinyurl.com/free-flashcard-maker

*Create and print flashcards (CANVA)* https://tinyurl.com/Canva-Flashcards

- **Create context clues to facilitate later recall of new information**

Providing context clues when learning new information can cue recall later. For example, when multiple associations are made while learning a new word (e.g., synonyms, visual representations, linking it to known information, drawing a picture), there are several ways to retrieve its meaning, which facilitates recall. For more information and resources, visit the following link(s).

*Types of context clues and implementation* https://tinyurl.com/aid-recall-via-context-clues

*Strategies for using context clues in reading* https://tinyurl.com/context-clues-reading

- **Make text-to-text, text-to-self, and text-to-world connections**

Information is more readily retrieved when multiple and meaningful connections are made during the learning process. For more information and resources, visit the following link(s).

*Handout to assist making connections* https://tinyurl.com/connections-handout

- **Overlearn material to improve retention**

Overlearning involves practicing skills after they have already been mastered. Repeated rehearsal of new material (i.e., several error-free repetitions) is necessary to solidify the information. When overlearning material, it is helpful to engage in active learning strategies, such as self-quizzing. When reading, use the 3R strategy (Read-Recite-Review). Also, spread studying over time (i.e., avoid cramming). For more information and resources, visit the following link(s).

*The importance of overlearning* https://tinyurl.com/What-Is-Overlearning

*Overlearning strategies* https://tinyurl.com/overlearning-strategies

- **Develop and use memory checklists to aid in retrieval**

Memory checklists consist of written procedure steps and boxes to check off each step. This type of checklist reduces the demands on memory to recall every step that needs to be completed and the order of those steps. For more information and resources, visit the following link(s).

| | |
|---|---|
| *Checklist resources* | https://tinyurl.com/learning-checklists |
| *Develop and personalize checklists* | https://www.checkli.com/ |

*Note:* The interventions, programs, techniques, strategies, and resources in this report were derived from the IL. Responsibility for the selection, implementation, and monitoring of any interventions listed herein remains with the individual user, team, committee, or organization. Likewise, users are responsible for any alterations made to the original content from the IL. The authors of the IL have no vested interest or financial stake in any interventions provided, and there is no expressed endorsement of their selection or use, nor any guarantee of their potential effectiveness.

Appendix S

# SAMPLE REPORT FROM INTERVENTION LIBRARY—IL® FOR A 7TH-GRADE STUDENT WITH A WEAKNESS IN WORKING MEMORY CAPACITY

The practitioner selected Working Memory Capacity (***Gwm***) as the cognitive domain, **Middle School (6–8)** as the intervention grade level, and **All Methods** for delivery (individual, small group, whole class), along with **all intervention types** (Instructional Techniques, Environmental, Curricular, Remedial Programs, Skill-Building Techniques, and Compensatory Strategies and Supports). Based on these selections, the IL® generated the full set of interventions that met the specified criteria.

In practice, the practitioner is encouraged to select only those interventions that are most appropriate, given an understanding of the whole individual. The sample report below includes the entire list of matched interventions to illustrate the full range of options available within the IL®. Users may edit, refine, or reorganize the report in any way that best fits their professional needs.

**Intervention Library—IL® v1.0**
**Resources for Instruction and Intervention**

| | | | |
|---|---|---|---|
| **Name:** | Marianna | **School:** | Edison Middle School |
| **Age:** | 13 | **Report generated by:** | Dr. Vuluntino |
| **Grade:** | 7 | **Report created on:** | 1/25/2026 |

The interventions and resources provided below are for informational purposes. Although the style and format of the report are copyrighted, users are granted permission to copy, edit, modify, and use the text included in this summary for the purpose of creating their own report, without the need for any specific attribution.

## *Gwm*—Working Memory Capacity

### INSTRUCTIONAL TECHNIQUES FOR *Gwm*

- **Pair instructional strategies to observable memory difficulties**

Manifestations of a student's working memory difficulties can be observed in the classroom and addressed with specific interventions that improve the student's access to instruction and the curriculum. For more information and resources, visit the following link(s).

*Strategies for working memory weaknesses* https://tinyurl.com/aid-memory

- **Limit the length of oral directions**

Shortening directions may facilitate students' ability to manage and encode information by reducing the time between receiving and executing directives.

- **Check for student's understanding**

Intermittently checking that the student is grasping the information throughout instruction allows the student to receive the repetition and review needed for information missed or not understood. Checking student understanding and repeating information may facilitate encoding and consolidation.

- **Teach strategies to aid memory**

Several strategies may be used to assist the student in remembering information more efficiently, such as employing multisensory instructional approaches and encouraging overlearning of material. For more information and resources, visit the following link(s).

*Strategies that may be used to aid memory* https://tinyurl.com/10-Memory-Strategies

- **Paraphrase and identify key points throughout teaching to reduce cognitive load**

To reduce cognitive load and increase the likelihood of encoding and recall, paraphrase lengthy introductions to new concepts and information, and highlight main ideas and "take-away" points. Following any lesson, provide a concise overview of the most important points. For more information and resources, visit the following link(s).

*Summarizing strategies and materials* https://tinyurl.com/help-to-summarize

*How working memory relates to teaching* https://tinyurl.com/work-mem-teach

- **Teach and encourage the use of rehearsal strategies to facilitate encoding and consolidation**

Teach a variety of rehearsal strategies and encourage their use to repeatedly practice information, facilitating encoding and consolidation. Strategies include rhymes, acronyms, associations, and semantic rehearsal. For more information and resources, visit the following link(s).

*Rehearsal strategies (information, examples)* https://tinyurl.com/ASC-memory

- **Provide written directions and information for tasks, assignments, and lessons to aid memory**

Written instructions and information may be used for reference when information is missed or forgotten. Examples include providing a hard copy of instructions, projecting instructions on a SMART Board®, and writing information on the board throughout instruction.

- **Deliver instructions in manageable parts to reduce memory demands**

Present instructions clearly and succinctly. Break instructions into parts, presenting only one or two parts at a time. Check for understanding prior to moving on to subsequent steps.

- **Provide "repeat and review" opportunities during instruction to aid memory**

Repeat important information at a high rate, emphasizing keywords through inflection. Encourage the student to immediately write or otherwise record key concepts, vocabulary, or information as they are presented during a lesson or when read in the text. Recording information will reduce memory demands by providing a bank of information for the student to refer to and review.

- **Use songs or rhymes to help the student remember rote information**

Consider presenting rote information (particularly sequential information) as a song or rhyme to facilitate encoding. Use rhymes, songs, movements, and patterns, such as the "30 days hath September" rhyme, for remembering the number of days in each calendar month. Musical and physical routines linked to fact learning can help students memorize faster and serve as cues for retrieving specific information. For more information and resources, visit the following link(s).

*How rhymes aid memorization* https://tinyurl.com/remember-through-rhyme

- **Build in extra time during instruction for the student to copy information**

Difficulty copying notes may arise from an inability to hold information in immediate awareness long enough to write on paper. Therefore, provide extra time to copy notes to alleviate working memory demands and ensure that the student receives important information.

- **Provide guided notes when possible to reduce memory demands during note-taking**

Providing guided notes in which the student is only required to fill in keywords, phrases, or concepts reduces working memory demands, thereby allowing the student to encode information, remain engaged in instruction, and have a complete set of notes from which to study for tests. For more information and resources, visit the following link(s).

*Tips on how to create effective guided notes* https://tinyurl.com/guiding-note-taking

- **Review previously learned material at the start of each lesson to aid memory**

Provide a brief review of immediately relevant, previously taught material before introducing new information. This is particularly helpful when a topic or specific content will be taught over several lessons.

- **Summarize at the end of a lesson to aid encoding**

End each lesson with a summary of what was learned, including keywords and concepts, to provide repetition, which allows for identification of missed information and aids encoding. For more information and resources, visit the following link(s).

*Summarizing strategies, free templates* https://tinyurl.com/sum-and-remember

- **Use scaffolding to minimize working memory demands**

Break down tasks into smaller steps and teach each step separately. The scaffolding technique of "guided practice," for example, can reduce the working memory load for multistep assignments and allow the student to focus on individual parts rather than holding multiple parts in mind at once. For more information and resources, visit the following link(s).

*Scaffolding techniques* https://tinyurl.com/scaffolding-strategies

- **Build in instructional time to allow opportunities for independent practice and rehearsal of new information to facilitate retention**

Devote a portion of instructional time to allow the student opportunities to rehearse newly taught content through a variety of activities. It may be most beneficial to have the student practice new skills or information in short sessions throughout the day rather than in one long session. Practicing new skills and rehearsing newly learned content in different ways (e.g., drawing, discussing, making up a game) reinforces learning and aids retention. For additional information on how to design meaningful independent practice, visit the following link(s).

*Creating meaningful independent practice* https://tinyurl.com/Independent-Practice

- **Incorporate the use of color coded materials when teaching**

Color coding may be used when teaching new concepts. For example, when teaching sentence structure, nouns are always red, verbs are always green, etc. When teaching spelling, highlight parts of new words, such as prefixes or suffixes. When teaching vocabulary, group new words into categories or families and color-code them. When the student understands how to use color to aid meaning and support memory, encourage him or her to use colored pens or highlighters. For more information and resources, visit the following link(s).

*Several ways to use color-coding strategies* https://tinyurl.com/coded-classrooms

- **Allow the student to provide answers in close proximity to questions**

Immediately after a question is asked and the student raises his or her hand, call upon the student to prevent forgetting the question and/or answer.

- **Follow consistent instructional routines**

Instructional routines are basic learning procedures that follow consistent steps and provide the structure needed to remember information through repetition and rehearsal. Once learned, more memory space may be allocated to new learning. For more information and resources, visit the following link(s).

*Why use instructional routines?* https://tinyurl.com/Why-Instructional-Routines

*Examples of instructional routines* https://tinyurl.com/teach-routine

- **Increase student engagement during initial learning activities**

Increasing student engagement during learning activities facilitates encoding and consolidation. Ways to engage the student throughout a lesson include using a question-and-answer format, active participation techniques, learning structures, and multisensory activities. Student engagement activities at the end of a lesson, such as Exit Cards, Brain Dumps, Checklists of Mastery, and Fact Storming, allow for closure and self-reflection. For more information and resources, visit the following link(s).

*Student engagement strategies* https://tinyurl.com/engaging-students

- **Teach mnemonic strategies to aid memory**

A student relates new information to what he or she has already learned through visual and verbal cues. The basic types of mnemonic strategies rely on keywords, rhyming words, or acronyms. Discuss the topic to be learned and preselect a mnemonic strategy. Consider using verbal cues, such as "A good way to remember this is. . .," for an introduction to the technique, or have the student create his or her own mnemonics. Alternatively, commonly used mnemonic strategies can be selected, such as Keyword, Pegword, and Letter. For more information and resources, visit the following link(s).

*Information on mnemonic strategies* https://tinyurl.com/Mnemonics-Info

- **Incorporate paraphrasing activities into instruction to support memory**

At the end of a lesson or set of instructions, have the student paraphrase material just presented or have another student paraphrase verbally delivered instructions or information. For more information and resources, visit the following link(s).

*How to teach paraphrasing* https://tinyurl.com/paraphrasing-how-to-teach

## ENVIRONMENTAL INTERVENTIONS FOR G*wm*

- **Assign a peer helper to assist with following classroom instruction**

When a student misses information during instruction, a peer helper can assist by reviewing notes, restating directions, and clarifying assignment details.

- **Provide preferential seating to limit distractions and minimize interference during initial learning, which offers an optimal set of conditions for encoding new information**

Seat the student near the front of the room or in close proximity to the teacher's voice, and away from windows, doors, and distracting peers. This will reduce the likelihood of interference during learning. Creating this set of conditions for the student may facilitate the encoding of new information.

- **Display step-by-step instructions to aid memory**

Step-by-step instructions typically include pictures and words. They are designed to remind the student of the steps that are necessary to carry out a task or solve a problem.

## CURRICULAR INTERVENTIONS FOR G*wm*

- **Direct student to practice materials, such as study guides and supplemental workbooks to facilitate encoding and consolidation**

Direct student to study guides, workbooks, skill-building activities, practice quizzes, and the like, where available, to increase time engaged with newly taught information, thereby facilitating encoding and consolidation.

- **Direct student to rubrics as reminders of the sequence necessary for a project or assignment**

Provide a rubric for the student to reference so that he or she has access to the specific steps or exact sequence of steps needed for a project or assignment, thereby allowing the student to focus on the broader goals and purpose. Providing a sample of what the project or assignment might look like when completed may promote understanding of overall expectations, meaning, and purpose, thereby facilitating the encoding of steps both initially and over time.

- **Direct student to educational technology or aids that reduce working memory demands**

Connect the student with educational technology or aids that can reduce the demands on working memory. Such resources include, but are not limited to, a number line, calculator, formula sheets, math fact lists, spell-checkers, grammar check devices, and audio text readers. For more information and resources, visit the following link(s).

*Memory aids and how to use them* https://tinyurl.com/Memory-aids-External

- **Direct the student to resources for making checklists to reduce working memory demands**

Checklists containing operational steps or procedures may be used as a guide when a task has many components to remember. As tasks become more complex, checklists can help reduce errors and demands on memory. For more information and resources, visit the following link(s).

*Checklists and their benefits* https://tinyurl.com/information-on-checklists

*How checklists improve learning* https://tinyurl.com/checklists-improve-learning

*How teachers can create checklists* https://tinyurl.com/teacher-create-checklist

*Free checklist maker* https://www.checkli.com/

- **Direct student to multisensory materials that can facilitate memory**

To increase engagement with the lesson, use multisensory materials such as paint, coloring, felt, and technology. Effective use of multisensory materials allows information to be encoded in multiple areas of the brain. Learning information in this way facilitates storage through multiple associations, thereby enhancing later recall.

- **Allow for the use of student-made reference sheets to aid memory in task initiation and completion**

Encourage the student to create a reference sheet containing important steps and procedures that may be used while taking a test or for studying. For more information and resources, visit the following link(s).

*How to make a study sheet* https://tinyurl.com/Using-Study-Sheets

- **Allow for the use of student-made reference sheets to aid memory in task initiation and completion**

Encourage the student to create a reference sheet containing key steps and procedures that may be used during a test or while studying. For more information and resources, visit the following link(s).

*Middle school math reference sheets* https://tinyurl.com/MS-Reference-Sheets

- **Direct the student to word banks to aid memory**

A word bank is a teacher- or student-created list of words relating to the content and academic material the student is learning. Word banks help the student manage the amount of information he or she has to consider during certain activities (e.g., writing, homework) and instructional formats (e.g., tests).

- **Direct the student's attention to color-coded materials and make sure the meaning of the color is understood**

Using consistent colors for curricular materials (e.g., folders, textbook covers) across different subject areas provides visual cues that aid memory, thereby allowing students to access materials more readily.

- **Direct the student to online resources associated with textbooks and other curricular materials that allow for repetition and review of content**

Frequent repetition and review of content are necessary for encoding and consolidation of new information. Examples of online resources associated with textbooks that provide ongoing exposure to new content include reviews, practice problems, quick quizzes, and reinforcement activities. Ensure that the student has access to these online resources and monitor their use throughout the learning process.

- **Direct the student to resources that can be used to aid memory**

Resources such as calendars, to-do lists, planners, and apps typically include features like audible alarms, visual reminders, and alerts that aid memory.

## REMEDIAL PROGRAMS FOR *Gwm*

- **Cogmed Working Memory Training**

Working memory plays an important role in learning. Cogmed is a computerized program comprised of cognitive exercises designed to train and improve working memory through increasingly complex and specialized programs that use real-time techniques and offer recreational games as rewards for completing daily training sessions. For more information and resources, visit the following link(s).

*Cogmed overview* https://www.cogmed.com/

- **BrainJogging™**

Consistent with the demands of ongoing education, BrainJogging™ enhances mental endurance and performance in areas such as processing speed, visual recognition, spelling, reading, focus, concentration, and overall understanding of the material by strengthening the student's neural connections. Used twice daily, BrainJogging teaches the student to process information more efficiently by blocking out extraneous stimuli, enhancing learning and memory through multisensory activities tailored to the student. For more information and resources, visit the following link(s).

*BrainJogging overview* http://brainjogging.com/

- **Brain Builder®**

Brain Builder® is a computer program scientifically designed to promote attention, memory, concentration, visual and auditory processing, problem-solving skills, and processing speed through engaging visual and auditory exercises lasting a few minutes daily. For more information and resources, visit the following link(s).

*Brain Builder® overview* https://tinyurl.com/Brainbuilder-Download

- **Captain's Log (Brain Train)**

Captain's Log is a computerized brain-training program that uses over 2,000 customized, flexible training programs to target improvements in 20 cognitive areas, such as memory, attention, perception, planning, and reasoning. For more information and resources, visit the following link(s).

*Captain's Log overview* http://tinyurl.com/training-the-brain

- **Memory Challenge!**

Memory Challenge! is a program designed to help the student develop and test his or her visual memory skills. For more information and resources, visit the following link(s).

*Memory Challenge! overview* https://tinyurl.com/MemoryChallengeK-12

## SKILL-BUILDING TECHNIQUES FOR G*wm*

- **Working memory exercises**

Engaging in working memory exercises may enhance a central component of the brain used for reasoning and problem solving. These exercises may be visual or auditory. For more information and resources, visit the following link(s).

*Online visual memory games* https://www.memozor.com/

*Auditory memory games* https://tinyurl.com/fun-with-auditory-memory

*Visual-spatial working memory activities* https://tinyurl.com/visual-spatial-task

- **Working memory exercises**

Engaging in working memory exercises may enhance a central component of the brain used for reasoning and problem solving. These exercises may be visual or auditory. For more information and resources, visit the following link(s).

*Online visual memory games* https://www.memozor.com/

*Auditory memory activities* https://tinyurl.com/games-with-hearing

*Auditory memory games* https://tinyurl.com/fun-with-auditory-memory

*Visual-spatial working memory activities* https://tinyurl.com/visual-spatial-task

- **Use flashcards to rehearse information**

Flashcards can help the student learn rote information. For example, write the question on one side and the answer on the other side. Review them as often as necessary and keep track of accuracy. For more information and resources, visit the following link(s).

*Make and study flashcards* https://quizlet.com/features/flashcards

*Free printable flashcard maker* https://tinyurl.com/free-flashcard-maker

*Pre-made Scholastic flashcard sets* https://tinyurl.com/Scholastic-Flashcard-Sets

- **Dual-N-Back**

Dual-N-Back is an app for iOS and Android devices that targets working memory skills via ongoing and fast-paced games asking the student to remember and match a series of stimuli before advancing to new levels. For more information and resources, visit the following link(s).

*Dual-N-Back app* https://tinyurl.com/apps-for-memory

- **Teach chunking strategies to facilitate encoding**

Teach the student how to use chunking strategies to break up long strings of information into separate units or "chunks." The resulting chunks are easier to commit to memory than a longer uninterrupted string of information (e.g., phone numbers). For more information and resources, visit the following link(s).

*How to teach chunking* https://tinyurl.com/teach-chunking

## COMPENSATORY STRATEGIES AND SUPPORTS FOR G*wm*

- **Chunk information**

Chunking means grouping individual pieces of information to make them easier to remember. Chunking can help with learning and retrieving information from long-term memory. For more information and resources, visit the following link(s).

*Examples of how to use chunking* https://tinyurl.com/strategy-chunking

*Video explanation of chunking* https://tinyurl.com/youtube-chunking

- **Use chunking strategies to aid memory**

Use chunking strategies to break up long strings of information into separate units or "chunks." The resulting chunks are easier to commit to memory than a longer uninterrupted string of information (e.g., phone numbers). For more information and resources, visit the following link(s).

*How to chunk information* https://tinyurl.com/howtochunk

- **Use graphic organizers to display connections and associations visually to aid memory**

A graphic organizer is a visual display that demonstrates relationships between facts, concepts, or ideas to aid memory. It can be in the form of a concept map, web, or mind map. Concept maps graphically illustrate relationships between two or more concepts and are linked by words that describe the relationship. Webs are often used for brainstorming and show how different categories of information relate to one another. Mind maps are visual representations of hierarchical information that include a central idea or image surrounded by connected branches of associated topics or ideas. For more information and resources, visit the following link(s).

*Webbing tool* https://tinyurl.com/webbing-tool

*How and why to use concept maps* https://tinyurl.com/use-concept-maps

*Information on mind maps* https://tinyurl.com/use-mind-maps

*Free student accounts to create mind maps* http://tinyurl.com/create-maps

- **Use active reading strategies to facilitate memory**

Use active reading strategies during reading tasks to facilitate memory. Such techniques may include underlining, making outlines, rereading, marking important parts, writing in margins, writing summaries, and teaching a peer information the student just read. For more information and resources, visit the following link(s).

*Active reading strategies* https://tinyurl.com/Active-Reading-Strategies

- **Use speech recognition or speech-to-text software**

Thoughts and ideas, or instructions might be forgotten before the student writes them down on paper. Speech recognition or speech-to-text software allows speech to be translated into text and can help the student to keep track of ideas and instructions so that they do not get lost. For more information and resources, visit the following link(s).

*Dictation technology overview* https://tinyurl.com/Dictation-Technology

*Dictation within the classroom* https://tinyurl.com/dictation-reading-rockets

*Speech Recognition for Learning* https://tinyurl.com/Speech-Recognition

- **Use online calendars and planners that contain features, such as alerts, to aid memory**

Resources such as calendars, to-do lists, planners, and apps typically contain features such as audible alarms, visual reminders, and alerts that aid memory.

- **Use notes or outlines provided by a teacher or peer**

Provide the student lecture notes either produced by the teacher or those written by another student. The student may experience difficulty when copying information from a book or the board with speed and facility. This may be the result of difficulty keeping information to be copied in mental awareness (i.e., the student forgets information before getting it copied). As a result, the student may be able to only transfer short bits of information at a time. Therefore, provide extra time to copy information, provide information already in copied form, or reduce the demands of copying on tasks.

- **Use paraphrasing to encode information for later recall**

Paraphrase verbally delivered instructions or information just read to support memory during note-taking, studying, and completing homework. For more information and resources, visit the following link(s).

*Paraphrasing to aid encoding/consolidation* http://tinyurl.com/paraphrase-for-memory

*Note:* The interventions, programs, techniques, strategies, and resources in this report were derived from the IL. Responsibility for the selection, implementation, and monitoring of any interventions listed herein remains with the individual user, team, committee, or organization. Likewise, users are responsible for any alterations made to the original content from the IL. The authors of the IL have no vested interest or financial stake in any interventions provided, and there is no expressed endorsement for their selection or use, or any guarantee regarding their potential effectiveness.

Appendix T

# SAMPLE REPORT FROM INTERVENTION LIBRARY—IL® FOR A 10TH-GRADE STUDENT WITH A WEAKNESS IN READING COMPREHENSION

The practitioner selected **Reading Comprehension (RDC)** as the cognitive domain, **High School (8–12+)** as the intervention grade level, and **Individual** for delivery method, along with **all intervention types** (Instructional Techniques, Environmental, Curricular, Remedial Programs, Skill-Building Techniques, and Compensatory Strategies and Supports). Based on these selections, the IL® generated the full set of interventions that met the specified criteria.

In practice, the practitioner is encouraged to select only those interventions that are most appropriate, given an understanding of the whole individual. The sample report below includes the entire list of matched interventions to illustrate the full range of options available within the IL®. Users may edit, refine, or reorganize the report in any way that best fits their professional needs.

**Intervention Library—IL® v1.0**
**Resources for Instruction and Intervention**

| | | | |
|---|---|---|---|
| **Name:** | Theo | **School:** | Nutley High School |
| **Age:** | 15 | **Report generated by:** | Mr. Palentino |
| **Grade:** | 10 | **Report created on:** | 1/25/2026 |

The interventions and resources provided below are for informational purposes. Although the style and format of the report are copyrighted, users are granted permission to copy, edit, modify, and use the text included in this summary for the purpose of creating their own report, without the need for any specific attribution.

**RDC—Reading Comprehension**

**INSTRUCTIONAL TECHNIQUES FOR RDC**

- **Use elaboration**

Teachers present additional information and explanations about concepts. Text redundancy and repetition reinforce learning, and activities can aid this process.

- **Use story maps to aid reading comprehension**

Story maps aid reading comprehension by providing students with a framework for identifying the essential elements of a story (e.g., plot, setting, characters) to help organize and learn information. Common types of story maps are the Five W's (Who, What, When, Where and Why) and the Somebody-Wanted-But-So map. For more information and resources, visit the following link(s).

| | |
|---|---|
| *More information on using story maps* | https://tinyurl.com/map-stories |
| *Five W's Chart* | https://tinyurl.com/Five-W |
| *Somebody-Wanted-But-So strategy* | https://tinyurl.com/SWBS-Strategy |

- **Model reading comprehension strategies**

Model effective reading comprehension strategies (e.g., previewing texts, checking for understanding, question generating, and making predictions) throughout instruction. For more information and resources, visit the following link(s).

| | |
|---|---|
| *Model reading comprehension strategies* | https://tinyurl.com/Think-Alouds-Comp |

- **Use story maps to aid reading comprehension**

Story maps aid reading comprehension by providing students with a framework for identifying the essential elements of a story (e.g., plot, setting, characters) to help organize and learn information. A common type of story map analyzes the Five W's of summarizing: Who, What, When, Where, and Why. For more information and resources, visit the following link(s).

| | |
|---|---|
| *More information on story maps* | https://tinyurl.com/story-maps |
| *Five W's Chart* | https://tinyurl.com/Five-Ws-Chart |

- **Teach morphology to improve reading comprehension**

Morphology is the study and description of how words are formed in language. A morpheme represents a unit of language that carries meaning and cannot be further divided. For example, the Latin root "spect" in words like "introspection" and "spectacle" signals not only a commonality in spelling but a kinship in meaning (i.e., to see). Teaching morphological awareness skills helps the student understand that words are formed by combining prefixes, suffixes, and roots. These skills enhance vocabulary and improve reading comprehension. For more information and resources, visit the following link(s).

| | |
|---|---|
| *Lesson plans about morphology* | https://tinyurl.com/Morphology-to-Teach-Vocabulary |
| *Prefix, suffix, and root word worksheets* | https://tinyurl.com/Word-Parts-Worksheets |
| *How to teach prefixes, roots, and suffixes* | https://tinyurl.com/Teach-Word-Parts |

- **Remind student to use strategy cues**

Teachers give reminders to use strategies before, during, and after reading. If necessary, teachers explicitly explain the steps of the strategies, use think-aloud modeling, and identify the benefits of using the strategies.

- **Use think-alouds**

Think-aloud processes can be utilized by teachers and students. Teachers can think aloud during explicit strategy instruction and modeling. The student's use of the think-aloud process leads to increased comprehension of the text through effective summarization. For more information and resources, visit the following link(s).

| | |
|---|---|
| *More information on using think-alouds* | https://tinyurl.com/Think-Alouds |

- **Use the Directed Reading-Thinking Activity (DR-TA) strategy**

This involves activating the student's prior knowledge and making predictions before reading, reading a section, stopping to confirm/revise predictions, and continuing to read text. For more information and resources, visit the following link(s).

| | |
|---|---|
| *Directed Reading-Thinking Activity strategy* | https://tinyurl.com/DRTA-Strategy |
| *DRTA for adolescent literacy* | https://tinyurl.com/DRTA-Adolescent |

- **Use the ART (Ask-Read-Tell) Strategy**

This strategy involves 3 steps:

1. ASK: the student previews the title of the passage before reading the text, ask themselves what the topic of the text might be, and generate two questions that they hope to answer,
2. READ: the student stops after each paragraph to determine whether they understand what they just read, and
3. TELL: the student answers the two questions they generated.

For more information and resources, visit the following link(s).

| | |
|---|---|
| *More information on using the ART Strategy* | https://tinyurl.com/Ask-Read-Tell |

- **Use the keyword memorization strategy**

The keyword memorization strategy requires the student to select the main idea of text and summarize it as a keyword, then recode this term as a mental image, recalling the keyword when needed, and retrieving important information related to the text. For more information and resources, visit the following link(s).

| | |
|---|---|
| *Using the keyword memorization strategy* | https://tinyurl.com/kwd-memorization |

- **Teach the Text Lookback strategy**

Prompt the student to look back and review text after they have read. For more information and resources, visit the following link(s).

| | |
|---|---|
| *Teaching the Text Lookback strategy* | https://tinyurl.com/text-lookback |

- **Use directed response/questioning**

Teachers ask the student questions about text, encourage the student to ask the teacher and peers about text, and allow for discussions about literal and inferential content.

- **Teach reading comprehension strategies**

To be successful academically, the student must be able to understand what they read. Explicitly teaching reading comprehension strategies and monitoring their use is likely to improve comprehension. The student should practice reading comprehension strategies daily to increase the likelihood that he or she will eventually use them independently. Examples of reading strategies are:

1. Connecting information from text to prior knowledge
2. Determining main ideas
3. Generating and answering questions based on text
4. Use knowledge of genre to understand text
5. Constructing mental images of text
6. Making inferences based on text

For more information and resources, visit the following link(s).

*Strategies to improve reading comprehension* https://tinyurl.com/RC-strategies

- **Use collaborative strategic reading (CSR)**

CSR employs reciprocal teaching and students working in pairs or groups. Teachers provide direct instruction on four comprehension strategies that the student learns to apply before, during, and after reading in pairs or groups:

1. Preview (before reading)
2. Click and clunk (during reading)
3. Get the gist (during reading)
4. Wrap up (after reading)

The student then works in groups or pairs to complete activities after being assigned roles (e.g., leader, announcer) that rotate among students, and the review is completed with the whole class. During collaborative work, teachers provide "fix-up" strategies for when students experience difficulty, which can be written on index cards. Such cues include rereading sentences without unknown words, using surrounding text to identify potential word meanings, breaking words apart, and looking for clues.
For more information and resources, visit the following link(s).

*Collaborative Strategic Reading information* https://tinyurl.com/CSR-Info

*CSR strategy implementation* https://tinyurl.com/CSR-Implementation

- **Use repeated readings**

Comprehension is improved when the student reads text more than once. The student reads the passage aloud twice with error correction. When the student misreads or hesitates, the teacher points to the word, reads it aloud correctly, and reads the entire sentence with the correct word. The student is prompted to read the sentence with the correct word three times. Repeated reading utilizes the LaBerge and Samuels model that states when "attention is required for accurate decoding, little remains for the purpose of comprehending what is read" (Sindelar et al., 1990, p. 220). In other words, as reading fluency increases, decoding and word identification become more automatic. With gained automaticity, attention is no longer used to decode words. Therefore, increased automaticity and fluency allow the student to utilize the newly available attention to comprehend materials read. For more information and resources, visit the following link(s).

*More information on repeated readings* https://tinyurl.com/Repeated-Reading

*Effectiveness of repeated readings* https://tinyurl.com/Repeated-Reading-Effectiveness

- **Use retelling**

Retelling stories, which includes describing and summarizing what has been read aloud to peers or teachers, improves reading comprehension. For more information and resources, visit the following link(s).

*Retelling* https://tinyurl.com/Retelling-Strategy

*More information on retelling* https://tinyurl.com/strategies-promote-comp

- **Activate prior knowledge**

Teachers ask a series of guided questions to activate prior knowledge of a specific topic relevant to the text, helping build comprehension by linking knowledge together. Teachers explain the benefits of using prior knowledge to help students understand texts. Teachers also demonstrate the prediction strategy through the "think-aloud" process. For more information and resources, visit the following link(s).

*Information on activating prior knowledge* https://tinyurl.com/edutopia-priorknowledge

- **Teach text structures**

Text structure is the way in which the author has organized the information in the text. It's how the text is organized. Having an understanding of text structure helps the student organize readers' thoughts, comprehension, and inferences based on text. Students who use knowledge of text structure have a greater understanding of texts, as they use this information to activate prior knowledge, preview texts, and understand their purpose. For more information and resources, visit the following link(s).

*Teaching text structure in 5 days* https://tinyurl.com/text-structure

*Teaching expository text structures* https://tinyurl.com/Expository-Text

- **Preview vocabulary**

The student is explicitly taught word meanings of target words that are found in texts they will read.

- **Use Reader's Workshop**

Teachers provide mini lessons to provide explicit instruction on specific content areas. The student then reads independently and works collaboratively. Pairs or groups of students complete reading activities (e.g., generating or answering questions, making predictions, summarizing). For more information and resources, visit the following link(s).

*More information on Readers' Workshops* http://www.readersworkshop.org

- **Teach strategies to facilitate comprehension**

Incorporate activities that encourage the use of strategies that good readers use to maximize comprehension (e.g., steps for before, during, and after reading). For more information and resources, visit the following link(s).

*Examples of comprehension strategies* https://tinyurl.com/strategies-promote-comp

- **Teach the student to use a holistic reading approach, such as the GIST procedure**

An example of a holistic approach to reading is the GIST procedure. Generating Interactions between Schemata and Texts (GIST) is a summarization procedure that helps students comprehend complex texts. One way to utilize this procedure is to have the student fill out the "5Ws and H" (who, what, where, when, why, and how) in a GIST organizer worksheet template. Then, the student is asked to use their notes to write a summary using a given amount of words (i.e., 20 words, 15 words, 10 words). Instruction in this strategy begins with reading a passage and completing a GIST organizer worksheet as a group to teach and model correct use of the organizer. Instruction may then progress to reading and completing organizer worksheets in small groups, then pairs, and then individually. For more information and resources, visit the following link(s).

*Summarizing using a GIST holistic approach* https://tinyurl.com/GIST-strategy

## SKILL-BUILDING TECHNIQUES FOR RDC

- **Use reader's workshop**

Teachers provide mini lessons to provide explicit instruction on specific content areas. The student then reads independently and works collaboratively. Pairs or groups of students complete reading activities, such as generating or answering questions, making predictions, summarizing, etc. For more information and resources, visit the following link(s).

*More information on readers' workshops* http://www.readersworkshop.org

- **Reciprocal teaching intervention package**

Teach the student to use comprehension skills independently. The student learns each of these strategies on four separate instructional days: (1) Prediction, (2) Summarization, (3) Question generation, and (4) Clarifying. Teachers use the "think-aloud" procedure as each strategy is introduced. Students work in groups, and one student is designated as the "instructor," who guides the group in implementing these strategies as they read. Once mastery is achieved, the student reads silently and independently. For more information and resources, visit the following link(s).

*More information on reciprocal teaching* https://tinyurl.com/Reciprocal-Teaching-Read

*How to use Reciprocal Teaching* https://tinyurl.com/use-reciprocal-teaching

- **Teach how to use context clues**

Context clues assist a student in accessing unknown words to gain a deeper meaning of the text. The use of context clues needs to be directly taught to the student. For more information and resources, visit the following link(s).

| | |
|---|---|
| *Strategies for teaching and using context clues* | https://tinyurl.com/Reading-Context-Clues |
| *Context clues worksheets by grade level* | https://tinyurl.com/Context-Clues-Worksheets |

## COMPENSATORY STRATEGIES AND SUPPORTS FOR RDC

- **Use clarifying or "fix-up" strategies to facilitate reading comprehension**

Examples of clarifying or fix-up reading comprehension strategies include rereading the text, reading aloud, using context clues, asking questions, reflecting on what was read, and making connections to existing knowledge. For more information and resources, visit the following link(s).

| | |
|---|---|
| *Fix-up strategies for comprehension* | https://tinyurl.com/clarify-comprehension |
| *Fix-up strategies* | https://tinyurl.com/Fix-Up-Strategies |

- **Use the SQ3R strategy (Survey, Question, Read, Recite, Review)**

In the SQ3R strategy, the student is taught to preview a text, generate initial questions, read the selection, set it aside, and recite all content remembered. Next, the student reads the text a second time to strengthen learning and facilitate later recall. For more information and resources, visit the following link(s).

| | |
|---|---|
| *More information on the SQ3R strategy* | https://www.virtualsalt.com/learn8.html |
| *How to use the PQRST method of reading* | https://tinyurl.com/StepsSQ3R |

- **Use the PQRST strategy (Preview, Question, Read, State, and Test) when reading**

PQRST (Preview, Question, Read, State, and Test) is a reading strategy that enhances memory. The student skims the passage, generates questions to be answered (e.g., who, what, where, when), actively reads the passage to answer them, reviews the answers, and then self-tests. For more information and resources, visit the following link(s).

| | |
|---|---|
| *Video explanation of PQRST* | https://tinyurl.com/youtube-PQRST |
| *Listen and sketch visualization strategy* | https://tinyurl.com/PQRST-Method-Reading |

- **Use visual imagery to support reading comprehension**

Use visualization strategies to supplement auditory memory when learning new information. Visual imagery helps readers create mental images while reading, strengthening comprehension. For more information and resources, visit the following link(s).

| | |
|---|---|
| *Resources about visual imagery* | https://tinyurl.com/Visual-Imagery |

- **Use reading comprehension strategies**

Examples of language comprehension strategies include rereading the text, reading aloud, using context clues, asking questions, reflecting on what was read or heard, and making connections to existing knowledge. Students should receive explicit instruction on reading strategies, such as:

1. Connecting information from text to prior knowledge
2. Determining main ideas
3. Generating and answering questions based on text
4. Use knowledge of genre to understand text
5. Constructing mental images of text
6. Making inferences based on text
7. Monitoring understanding
8. Summarizing and paraphrasing
9. Clarifying with teachers when experiencing difficulty understanding text.

- **Use strategies before, during, and after reading**

The student should receive explicit instruction in pre-reading strategies (i.e., previewing text, making predictions, vocabulary building, background knowledge, text purpose), strategies to use while reading (i.e., comprehension monitoring, integrating new information with proper knowledge), and strategies for after reading (i.e., summarizing, evaluating ideas, application of knowledge). For more information and resources, visit the following link(s).

| | |
|---|---|
| *Strategies before, during, and after reading* | https://tinyurl.com/strategies-promote-comp |

- **Make predictions about the text**

The student should receive explicit instruction on how to make predictions:

1. Teacher provides a clear description of the strategy and when and how to use it
2. Teacher models the strategy in action
3. Collaborative use of the strategy
4. Guided practice using the strategy
5. Independent use of the strategy

- **Summarize reading using a holistic approach, such as the GIST procedure**

An example of a holistic approach to reading is the GIST procedure. Generating Interactions between Schemata and Texts (GIST) is a summarization procedure that helps students comprehend complex texts. One way to utilize this procedure is to have the student fill out the "5Ws and H" (who, what, where, when, why, and how) in a GIST organizer worksheet template. Then, the student is asked to use their notes to write a summary in a given number of words (e.g., 20, 15, or 10). For more information and resources, visit the following link(s).

*Summarizing using a GIST holistic approach* https://tinyurl.com/GIST-strategy

- **Apply the question-answer-relationships (QAR) strategy**

Having the student engage in developing questions and answering questions based on text improves comprehension. Questions should be both literal and inferential. The question-answer-relationships (QAR) strategy is a method for helping the student differentiate the types of questions they can generate:

1. Right There (literal questions)
2. Think and Search (inferential questions)
3. On My Own (questions based on prior knowledge)

Similarly, the questioning the author approach is an interactive strategy that encourages the student to identify the message that the author is trying to convey. The process includes initial questions (e.g., "What is the author trying to say?") and follow-up questions (e.g., "Does the author explain this clearly?"). For more information and resources, visit the following link(s).

*More information about question generating* https://tinyurl.com/question-generation

- **Apply the INSERT strategy to self-monitor when reading**

The Interactive Notation to Effective Reading and Thinking (INSERT) strategy was designed to help the student monitor his or her thinking and learning while reading. The student is taught to reflect on his or her reading, connect to prior knowledge, and insert one of four symbols as he or she thinks about it.

INSERT: Confirms what the student already knew: "I knew that." Contradicts what the student thought: "I thought differently." Confuses the student: "I don't understand this." Something new: "I didn't know that!"

- **Read a text more than once to improve comprehension**

Comprehension is improved when the student reads the text more than once. The student reads the passage aloud twice with error correction. When the student misreads or hesitates, the teacher points to the word, reads it aloud correctly, and reads the entire sentence with the correct word. The student is prompted to read the sentence with the correct word three times. For more information and resources, visit the following link(s).

*Information on reading a text more than once* https://tinyurl.com/Repeated-Reading

- **Retell stories to someone else to assist with reading comprehension**

Retelling stories, which includes describing and summarizing what has been read aloud to peers or teachers, improves reading comprehension. The teacher directs the student to recite everything remembered during a three-minute time period. This can be completed orally or in writing. For more information and resources, visit the following link(s).

*More information on retelling stories* https://tinyurl.com/Repeated-Reading-Retell

- **Use of graphic and semantic organizers to connect text to prior knowledge**

Graphic organizers use visual, concrete representations of information to help connect new text to prior knowledge. The student improves his or her comprehension by forming patterns from the text and forming content relationships. This strategy can be used before, during, and after reading.

For example, a story map can help the student identify:

1. Important characters
2. Main problem/significant plot points
3. Characters' attempts to solve the main problem
4. Main idea and conclusion of the text

These story maps can help the student understand how the ideas of a multiparagraph passage fit together. Graphic organizers can also help the student to separate main ideas from conclusions as well as compare and contrast different characters or different texts. For more information and resources, visit the following link(s).

| | |
|---|---|
| *Webbing tool* | https://tinyurl.com/Webbing-Tool-organizer |
| *Generating a graphic organizer of main ideas* | https://tinyurl.com/IC-main-idea-maps |

*Note:* The interventions, programs, techniques, strategies, and resources in this report were derived from the IL. Responsibility for the selection, implementation, and monitoring of any interventions listed herein remains with the individual user, team, committee, or organization. Likewise, users are responsible for any alterations made to the original content from the IL. The authors of the IL have no vested interest or financial stake in any interventions provided, and there is no expressed endorsement of their selection or use, nor any guarantee of their potential effectiveness.



## REFERENCE

Sindelar, P. T., Monda, L. S., & O'Shea, L. J. (1990). Effects of repeated readings on Instructional and Mastery-Level Readers. *Journal of Educational Research*, *83*, 220–226. https://doi.org/10.1080/00220671.1990.10885959.

# AFTERWORD

Scott L. Decker, Ph.D.

University of South Carolina

The Cross-Battery Assessment (XBA) method was introduced nearly three decades ago as an application of the Cattell–Horn Fluid-Crystallized (Gf–Gc) model and was later refined within the broader Cattell–Horn–Carroll (CHC) framework (Flanagan & McGrew, 1997; McGrew & Flanagan, 1998). From its inception, XBA was intended to bridge theory and practice by aligning assessment with contemporary models of cognitive functioning. Grounded in CHC theory and informed by neuropsychological research, XBA reframes assessment as a problem of construct representation rather than test selection, enabling practitioners to integrate measures across instruments to more fully capture the breadth and depth of cognitive abilities relevant to a given referral question (Flanagan et al., 2018; Schneider & McGrew, 2018).

As demonstrated throughout this book, assessment is not a fixed procedure but a design process. Decisions regarding test selection, subtest inclusion, and composite formation must be guided by referral concerns, examinee characteristics, and the goal of achieving adequate construct representation. Subtests that share a common classification may differ substantially in their task demands, and failure to account for these differences introduces threats to validity, including construct underrepresentation and construct-irrelevant variance. Consequently, valid interpretation depends on deliberate, theory-driven decisions at every stage of the assessment process.

These principles are most consequential in the identification of specific learning disabilities (SLD). SLD is not defined by low overall ability, but by specific patterns in which particular cognitive processing weaknesses, in contrast with cognitive strengths, are meaningfully related to particular academic difficulties. The patterns of strengths and weaknesses (PSW) framework—and specifically the Dual Discrepancy/Consistency (DD/C) method—operationalizes this logic by requiring evidence of both cognitive and academic weaknesses, as well as an empirically supported relationship between them. In this sense, SLD identification is inherently multidimensional.

A central issue addressed in this book concerns the role of the general factor of intelligence (*g*) in interpretation. Although there is broad agreement that *g* is robust and consistently observed, the critical question is how to interpret it. Some have argued that the statistical dominance of *g*—particularly in bifactor and related models—justifies focusing primarily, if not exclusively, on global scores such as IQ. This conclusion reflects a conflation of statistical dominance with conceptual sufficiency. Methodological research indicates that certain modeling approaches can preferentially allocate variance to *g*, even when multidimensional structure is present (Decker et al., 2020). A strong general factor does not negate the validity or relevance of specific cognitive processes, nor does it justify restricting interpretation to a single score. The issue is not the validity of these methods, but the assumptions underlying their interpretation. When statistical outcomes are treated as definitive, the result is a narrowing—rather than a clarification—of the construct space.

Approaches such as PSW rely on detecting meaningful variation across cognitive domains and linking it to academic performance. When interpretation is restricted to global ability alone, this variation is lost, and the defining features of SLD—specific cognitive processing weaknesses related to academic deficits—become difficult, if not impossible, to identify. This limitation is particularly consequential for children with learning disabilities, who do not present with uniform impairments. A child with dyslexia, for example, may demonstrate intact reasoning alongside specific weaknesses in phonological processing or naming speed. These distinctions are central to both identification and intervention, yet they are obscured when interpretation is limited to a single global score.

Within this context, XBA provides a framework for implementing PSW as part of a comprehensive evaluation. By enabling the measurement of a broader range of cognitive abilities than any single battery affords, XBA preserves the ability to identify the patterns of strengths and weaknesses that define learning disabilities in contemporary theory and practice.

Recent advances in psychometric network analysis and neuroscience further support a shift toward multidimensional, process-oriented models of cognitive functioning, a direction that is closely aligned with the principles underlying cross-battery assessment. Network models conceptualize cognitive abilities as dynamically interacting systems in which relationships arise from direct connections among processes rather than a single latent factor. Research applying network analysis to CHC-based measures demonstrates that broad abilities form interconnected systems, with processes related to cognitive efficiency and attentional control occupying central roles (McGrew et al., 2023).

Converging evidence from neuroscience similarly indicates that intelligence reflects distributed brain systems rather than a single underlying mechanism. Neuroimaging research has consistently demonstrated that cognitive ability is associated with coordinated activity across frontal and parietal regions, as well as broader large-scale networks involved in cognitive control and information integration (Barbey et al., 2012; Basten et al., 2015; Jung & Haier, 2007). These findings suggest that intelligence emerges from the efficiency and organization of interacting neural systems rather than from a single localized source.

Together, these developments support a view of intelligence as an emergent property of interacting processes and provide a coherent foundation for multidimensional assessment. Looking forward, the integration of network-based approaches with cross-battery assessment represents a promising direction for the field. XBA already facilitates the measurement of diverse cognitive processes across domains; future developments may extend this framework by directly modeling the relationships among these processes. Such an approach would move cognitive assessment beyond static score interpretation toward a more comprehensive understanding that adequately reflects the complexity of cognition at the individual level.

The position advanced in this book is straightforward. Cognitive assessment should not be reduced to what is most statistically dominant. It should be guided by what is necessary to understand learning and performance. Cross-battery assessment represents a critical step toward that goal—not because it adds complexity, but because it preserves the ability to see patterns that would otherwise be lost.

And those patterns matter.

## REFERENCES


Barbey, A. K., Colom, R., & Grafman, J. (2012). An integrative architecture for general intelligence and executive function revealed by lesion mapping. *Brain, 135*(4), 1154–1164. https://doi.org/10.1093/brain/aws021.

Basten, U., Hilger, K., & Fiebach, C. J. (2015). Where smart brains are different: A quantitative meta-analysis of functional and structural brain imaging studies on intelligence. *Intelligence, 51*, 10–27. https://doi.org/10.1016/j.intell.2015.04.009.

Decker, S. L., Bridges, R. M., Luedke, J. C., & Eason, M. J. (2020). Dimensional evaluation of cognitive measures: Methodological confounds and theoretical concerns. *Journal of Psychoeducational Assessment, 39*(1), 3–27. https://doi.org/10.1177/0734282920940879.

Flanagan, D. P., Ortiz, S. O., & Alfonso, V. C. (2018). *Essentials of Cross-Battery Assessment* (3rd ed). Wiley.

Flanagan, D. P., & McGrew, K. S. (1997). Interpreting intelligence tests from contemporary Gf–Gc theory: Joint confirmatory factor analysis of the WJ-R and K-ABC. *Journal of School Psychology, 35*(2), 151–182.

Jung, R. E., & Haier, R. J. (2007). The Parieto-Frontal Integration Theory (P-FIT) of intelligence: Converging neuroimaging evidence. *Behavioral and Brain Sciences, 30*(2), 135–154. https://doi.org/10.1017/S0140525X07001185.

McGrew, K. S., & Flanagan, D. P. (1998). *The Intelligence Test Desk Reference (ITDR): Gf–Gc Cross-Battery Assessment*. Allyn & Bacon.

McGrew, K. S., Schneider, W. J., Decker, S. L., & Bulut, O. (2023). A psychometric network analysis of CHC intelligence measures: Implications for research, theory, and interpretation of broad CHC scores "beyond g". *Journal of Intelligence, 11*(1), 19 https://doi.org/10.3390/jintelligence11010019.

Schneider, W. J., & McGrew, K. S. (2018). The Cattell–Horn–Carroll theory of cognitive abilities. In D. P. Flanagan & E. M. McDonough (Eds.), *Contemporary intellectual assessment: Theories, tests, and issues* (4th ed, pp. 73–163). Guilford Press.

# INDEX